Relationship Section

Rotated Alphabetical Terms Section

Term Clusters Section

Margin Index: To use, bend pages of book backward and follow
margin index to pages with black edge markers.

THESAURUS

OF PSYCHOLOGICAL INDEX TERMS

NINTH EDITION

Library of Congress Cataloging-in-Publication Data

Thesaurus of psychological index terms. — 9th ed.
    p. cm.
    Includes bibliographical references and index.
    ISBN 1-55798-775-0 (alk. paper)
    1. Subject headings—Psychology. I. American Psychological Association.

Z695.1.P7 T48 2001
025.4915—dc21   00-067650

Printed in the United States of America
ISBN 1-55798-775-0

Table of Contents

Preface

The *Thesaurus of Psychological Index Terms* is a reference tool for use with the PsycINFO® and ClinPSYC® databases or *Psychological Abstracts*. The *Thesaurus* has been developed by the PsycINFO Department of the American Psychological Association. The 9th edition is one more effort in PsycINFO's mission to advance scientific and professional knowledge in and about psychology and related disciplines by providing the best access to psychological information, thus ensuring high user satisfaction. As with all previous editions, many changes in this edition are in direct response to our users' needs, and we remain committed to continuing to provide you with a high quality reference product. For a brief history of the development of the *Thesaurus*, including the most recent terminology included in this edition, refer to pages vii-xvii.

We suggest a brief orientation to the *Thesaurus* to help you become acquainted with how to use this new edition. A small investment of time spent familiarizing yourself with the features of this edition can result in better search retrieval.

Review the **USER GUIDE** on pages xxii-xxv to learn how to read an index term entry. The **USER GUIDE** explains the components of term hierarchies, and also provides introductory details about other useful sections of the *Thesaurus*.

In the **RELATIONSHIP SECTION** on pages 1-282 you will find an alphabetical listing of controlled vocabulary (also referred to as "descriptors" or "index terms") complete with hierarchical structures providing information on broader, narrower, and related concepts. This section is useful for information on dates terms entered the vocabulary as well as definitions of term usage.

Consider using the **ROTATED ALPHABETICAL TERMS SECTION** on pages 283-376 when you have a general idea of the terminology you wish to use, but are unsure of the exact wording for the controlled vocabulary. This section serves as an index to terminology found in the **RELATIONSHIP SECTION** and is also useful when you want to see how many terms are embedded with a particular concept or word.

The **TERM CLUSTERS SECTION** on pages 377-400 lists terms grouped according to broad subject categories. Each broad cluster is divided into meaningful subcluster subject areas. Use this section to introduce yourself to a range of terms which may be relevant to your research topic.

In the front matter, the section entitled **Subject Searching in PsycINFO** provides a brief introduction to electronic database searching. This section is followed by **APPENDICES** which you will find helpful as quick reference guides when executing a search.

Best wishes for your research!

Terri Bernhardt
Thesaurus Development Coordinator

History of the *Thesaurus*

Psychology has multiple roots in the older disciplines of philosophy, medicine, education, and physics. As a result, the vocabulary of the psychological literature is characterized by considerable diversity. As the field of psychology has grown, each new generation of psychologists has added to the vocabulary in attempting to describe their studies and perceptions of behavioral processes. This uncontrolled evolution of the psychological vocabulary has contributed to complex literature search and retrieval problems.

In response to these problems, the American Psychological Association developed the first edition of the *Thesaurus of Psychological Index Terms* in 1974. This controlled vocabulary was designed to provide a means of structuring the subject matter of psychology and to serve as an efficient indexing and retrieval tool. Since the publication of the first edition, the PsycINFO indexing staff has charted trends and newly emerging areas of interest reflected in the psychological literature as a way of updating and revising the *Thesaurus*. The present edition of the *Thesaurus* represents a concerted effort to provide a more valuable tool for researchers, practitioners, information science providers, students, and others interested in the field of psychology.

First Edition (1974)

Term selection was the first step in the development of the 1974 edition. The 800 index terms used by *Psychological Abstracts* (PA) prior to 1973 and a list of the frequencies of the occurrence of single words in titles and abstracts in PA over a 5-year period were taken as the starting points. In addition, phrases and terms were obtained from key-word-in-context (KWIC) lists produced from 10,000 titles of journal articles, books, separates, and dissertations. Inclusion/ exclusion rules were developed, with a resulting list of about 3,000 potential terms reviewed by subject matter specialists for final selection. These terms were arranged to express interrelationships, including use, used for, broader, narrower, and related categories.

Second Edition (1977)

The first major revision of the *Thesaurus*, which included 204 new terms, was published in 1977. Some 180 never-used terms from the original *Thesaurus* were deleted, and a rotated alphabetical term section was added to make it faster and easier to find index terms.

Third Edition (1982)

The second major revision of the *Thesaurus*, which included 240 new terms, was published in 1982. The most significant change introduced in the third edition was the development of scope notes or definitions for over 1,300 terms. In addition superscript dates were added to all terms to indicate the date of inclusion in the *Thesaurus* vocabulary.

Fourth Edition (1985)

The third major revision of the *Thesaurus* included 247 new terms and over 162 new and revised scope notes. Posting notes (PN) were added to each index term to indicate the number of times the terms had been used for indexing. Also, each postable index term was given a unique five-digit code that can be used in online searching as an alternative to entering the term text.

Fifth Edition (1988)

An important change occurred during the fourth major revision—the incorporation of all nonpostable terms into the Rotated Alphabetical Terms Section. These terms appeared in nonbold italic print and were marked with a star (★). Over 250 postable terms and 100 nonpostable terms were added to the vocabulary. In addition, over 100 new scope notes were added and over 75 scopes notes were revised. Because the *Thesaurus* had been in use for many years, an extensive hierarchy reconstruction project was begun with the intention of continuing the process for development of future editions.

Sixth Edition (1991)

The fifth major revision of the *Thesaurus* included the addition of 238 new postable terms and 100 new nonpostable terms. Over 50 scope notes were rewritten and 120 new scope notes were added to the vocabulary. In a continuing effort to make the *Thesaurus* more useful, the Relationship Section was enhanced by the addition of down arrows (↓) in each main term's hierarchy next to narrower and related terms that also have narrower terms. Term Clusters were developed to present a collection of index terms based on conceptual similarity to assist users unfamiliar with the *Thesaurus* vocabulary. As in earlier editions, revision of existing hierarchical relationships continued.

Seventh Edition (1994)

The 20 year anniversary edition of the *Thesaurus* was marked with many changes to the Relationship Section of the *Thesaurus*. Approximately 220 new postable terms and 115 new nonpostable terms were added and nearly 110 new scope notes were added to the existing 1,970 scope notes. These included scope notes for terms new to the seventh edition as well as terms from previous editions. Revision of almost 2,000 hierarchies also occurred to increase their accuracy and to ensure consistent relationships. The hierarchies for array terms, conceptually broad terms identified with a slash (/), were reconstructed for the first time since the inception of the *Thesaurus* and the slash was removed. Posting notes were updated to indicate how many times each postable term was used to index a record through June 1993. A new "Neuropsychology and Neurology" cluster was added to the Term Clusters Section complete with 7 subclusters. Finally, the Rotated Alphabetical Terms section was completely revised so that nonpostable terms appeared for the first time with their "Use" reference.

Eighth Edition (1997)

The seventh major revision of the *Thesaurus* included the addition of 254 new postable terms and 191 new nonpostable terms. Over 200 term hierarchies were revised, and 115 new scope notes were added. The 2,026 existing scope notes were reviewed for clarity, and over 225 of these were revised or rewritten. In addition, close to 60 terms changed from a postable to a nonpostable status and were referred to a synonymous term or a term of broader scope. Finally, all index terms that contained the word "handicapped" (e.g., Multiply Handicapped) were reviewed and changed to "disabled" (e.g., Multiply Disabled) to reflect the changing terminology in the literature.

Development of the Ninth Edition (2001)

NEW TERMS

Since the publication of the eighth edition, 100 new postable index terms and 50 nonpostable index terms have been added to the ninth edition. The new terms represent concepts and terminology expressed in the psychological and behavioral literature as well as the literature found in fringe areas of psychology, e.g., social work, education, sociology, and medicine. In addition, new terminology was developed for classic psychological concepts requiring appropriate controlled vocabulary. These additions to the vocabulary bring the total number of postable index terms to 5295, nonpostable terms to 1716, and the total number of terms to 7003.

The criteria for index term inclusion involved: (1) the frequency of the term's occurrence in the psychological literature, (2) the term's potential usefulness in providing access to a concept, (3) the term's relationship to or overlap with existing *Thesaurus* terminology, (4) user feedback and need, and (5) lack of potential application problems by indexing staff. Every term has been researched extensively and integrated into the hierarchies in the Relationship Section. The Rotated Alphabetical Terms Section has been updated with the new terms as well. See Tables 1–6 on pages xi-xxi for a listing of all new postable index terms, nonpostable index terms, and other significant term changes occurring in this edition.

OTHER CHANGES

Term Hierarchies

Extensive revision of hierarchical relationships occurred during the development of this edition. Hierarchies were examined to ensure accuracy, completeness, and consistency. In a continuation of our efforts to examine hierarchical structures with each edition, over 375 hierarchies were revised to minimize any misleading and redundant relationships as well as to maintain a coherent and cohesive vocabulary structure.

Scope Notes

Approximately 13 new scope notes (SNs) have been added to the existing 2141 scope notes in the eighth edition (1997). Scope notes were added to terms with ambiguous meanings, terms that need to be differentiated from existing terms, or terms with restricted indexing usage. Over 115 scope notes were also rewritten or revised to improve clarity, to broaden or restrict the term's range of application, to accommodate new 2001 terms, or to expand dates indicating years of usage from 2 to 4 digits (e.g., "67-81" was changed to "1967-1981"). Scope notes were also added to or revised for the 244 terms that were part of the mapping/stripping project described below.

Nonpostable Terminology

In an effort to provide additional entry points into the *Thesaurus* vocabulary, and to direct users more efficiently to terms "not used" for indexing to preferred terms "used for" indexing, approximately 50 new nonpostable terms were added to this edition. See Table 2 on page xii for a full listing of these terms.

Posting Notes

Primarily as an aid to psychologists, researchers, librarians, and students, each postable index term in the Relationship Section appears with a posting note (PN) reference indicating how many times that index term has been used in the indexing process at the time of this publication. These posting notes are based on cumulations of term usage through September 2000. Index terms with posting notes (PN) = 0 are new 2001 terms that have been added to this edition. These terms have 0 postings because they have not been used in the indexing process prior to January 2001 and have yet to accumulate any postings.

Change in Status Terms

Terms with very low postings, obsolete and out-of-date terms, and terms that have undergone change in usage in the field of psychology were identified for a change in status during this revision. Approximately 10 terms changed from a nonpostable to postable status, and 26 terms changed from a postable to nonpostable status and now refer to a synonymous term or a term of broader scope. See Table 3 on page xiii for a full listing of these changes.

Discontinued and Deleted Terms and the Mapping/Stripping Project

In a continuing effort to increase precision, to decrease overlap and the inconsistent use of terms, and to reflect current terminology, 26 terms were changed from postable to nonpostable status. Although these discontinued terms appear in the *Thesaurus* as nonpostable, and hence are no longer used in indexing, each is accompanied by a scope note designating the period during which it was used. For these 26 terms with a change of status, in addition to the 100 terms that have undergone such a change in the past, records once containing such terms have been mapped to their appropriate postable counterparts; the nonpostable terms were then removed from the records. Table 6 on pages xvii-xxi contains a listing of these discontinued terms and of the postable terms which have replaced them.

In addition, with the 1998 advent of the Population/ Location, Age Group, and Form/Content Type document identifier fields, 213 terms with content areas overlapping those of these fields have been deleted from the *Thesaurus* entirely. The overlapping content areas include those representing countries and specific geographical locations (175 terms; e.g., Switzerland, United States) and document form/content type (19 terms; e.g., Book, Errata). Additionally, the terms which were used in the past as mandatory age group identifiers (19 terms; e.g., Adulthood, Adolescence, and Childhood) have also been deleted from the *Thesaurus*. Records once containing such terms have been mapped to the appropriate document field identifiers; the terms were then removed from the records. All of these concepts can thus now be searched using the appropriate field identifiers. See Table 5 on pages xvi-xvii for a listing of all terms deleted due to the advent of field identifiers.

Lastly, because of insufficient usage or overlap with other terminology, 25 terms were removed from the *Thesaurus* altogether. See Table 5 on page xv for a listing of these changes.

Changes to Spelling or Text of Terms

In an effort to use language that is consistent with that used by the general public, to expand terms that have historically been truncated (due to former system constraints), and to correct spelling errors from previous *Thesaurus* editions, 18 terms received spelling or format modifications. See Table 4 on page xiv for a listing of these changes.

Term Cluster Section

The Term Cluster section of the *Thesaurus* received some revisions to make it more inclusive and logical. A Computer Cluster and its 8 Subclusters were added as subject areas, and the Geographic Cluster and its Subclusters were deleted. Additions to and deletions from existing Subclusters were also made. See Table 7 on page xxv for a listing of the Term Cluster/ Subcluster subject areas.

Table 1: New Postable Terms (100)

Adventitious Disorders
Affective Disorders
Attachment Disorders
Attention Deficit Disorder with Hyperactivity
Barrett Lennard Relationship Inventory
Behavior Analysis
Bipolar Disorder
Body Dysmorphic Disorder
Borderline Personality
Bradykinesia
Circumcision
Clinical Psychology Graduate Training
College Entrance Examination Board Scholastic Aptitude Test
Computer Anxiety
Conversion Disorder
Coprophagia
Cosmetic Techniques
Dementia with Lewy Bodies
Dietary Supplements
Dissociation
Dissociative Disorders
Duty to Warn
Electronic Communication
Epidemics
Evaluation Criteria
Explosive Disorder
Female Delinquency
Frostig Developmental Test of Visual Perception
Functional Analysis
Fundamental Interpersonal Relation Orientation Behavior Ques
Generativity
Guided Imagery
Guilford Zimmerman Temperament Survey
Halstead Reitan Neuropsychological Battery

Harassment
Hawaii Natives
Health Impairments
High School Personality Questionnaire
Histrionic Personality Disorder
Illinois Test of Psycholinguistic Abilities
Indigenous Populations
Ingestion
International Classification of Diseases
Internet
Interview Schedules
Inuit
Kaufman Assessment Battery for Children
Kirton Adaption Innovation Inventory
Kleine Levin Syndrome
Luria Nebraska Neuropsychological Battery
Male Delinquency
Marlowe Crowne Social Desirability Scale
Massage
Medicinal Herbs and Plants
Mental Disorders due to General Medical Conditions
Mental Retardation (Attitudes Toward)
Mild Mental Retardation
Minnesota Multiphasic Personality Inventory
Moderate Mental Retardation
Multiple Disabilities
Needle Exchange Programs
Neonatal Period
Obsessive Compulsive Disorder
Pacific Islanders
Paraphilias
Pervasive Developmental Disorders

Physical Disabilities (Attitudes Toward)
Primipara
Profound Mental Retardation
Psychological Theories
Racial and Ethnic Groups
Regional Differences
Relationship Satisfaction
Research Setting
Risk Factors
Rotter Internal External Locus of Control Scale
Rumination (Cognitive Process)
Rumination (Eating)
Savants
Schizophrenia (Disorganized Type)
Self Managing Work Teams
Sensory Disabilities (Attitudes Toward)
Sensory System Disorders
Severe Mental Retardation
Single Sex Environments
Sixteen Personality Factors Questionnaire
Slosson Intelligence Test
Somatization Disorder
Somatoform Disorders
Somatosensory Disorders
Stalking
Structured Clinical Interview
Taste Disorders
Theory of Mind
Therapeutic Environment
Treatment Guidelines
Wechsler Intelligence Scale for Children
Wepman Auditory Discrimination Test
Woodcock Johnson Psychoeducational Battery
Work Teams

Table 2: New Nonpostable Terms (50)

Aboriginal Populations
    USE Indigenous Populations
ADHD
    USE Attention Deficit Disorder
    with Hyperactivity
Alcohol Addiction
    USE Alcoholism
Assessment Criteria
    USE Evaluation Criteria
Body Art
    USE Cosmetic Techniques
Cecotrophy
    USE Coprophagia
Closed Head Injuries
    USE Head Injuries
Complementary Medicine
    USE Alternative Medicine
Dementia of Alzheimers Type
    USE Alzheimers Disease
Disabilities
    USE Disorders
Disease Outbreaks
    USE Epidemics
Executive Functioning
    USE Cognitive Ability
Experimental Environment
    USE Research Setting
Female Genital Mutilation
    USE Circumcision
Female Only Environments
    USE Single Sex Environments
Functional Status
    USE Ability Level
Geographical Differences
    USE Regional Differences

Handicaps
    USE Disorders
Heterosexism
    USE Homosexuality (Attitudes
    Toward)
Homeopathic Medicine
    USE Alternative Medicine
Hyperalgesia
    USE Somatosensory Disorders
Hyperesthesia
    USE Somatosensory Disorders
Hypesthesia
    USE Somatosensory Disorders
Hypokinesia
    USE Bradykinesia
Interpersonal Relationship
    Satisfaction
    USE Relationship Satisfaction
Kinesics
    USE Body Language
Level of Functioning
    USE Ability Level
Lewy Body Disease
    USE Dementia with Lewy Bodies
Lobectomy
    USE Psychosurgery
Male Only Environments
    USE Single Sex Environments
Maori
    USE Indigenous Populations
Mind Blindness
    USE Theory of Mind
Native Alaskans
    USE Alaska Natives

Native Hawaiians
    USE Hawaii Natives
Natives
    USE Indigenous Populations
Naturalistic Observation
    USE Observational Methods
Nutritional Supplements
    USE Dietary Supplements
Pain Disorder
    USE Somatoform Pain Disorder
Paresthesia
    USE Somatosensory Disorders
Piercings
    USE Cosmetic Techniques
Regurgitation
    USE Vomiting
Same Sex Environments
    USE Single Sex Environments
SCID
    USE Structured Clinical Interview
Selective Mutism
    USE Elective Mutism
Stereotyping
    USE Stereotyped Attitudes
Tattoos
    USE Cosmetic Techniques
Transgendered
    USE Transsexualism
Treatment Environment
    USE Therapeutic Environment
Vulnerability (Disorders)
    USE Susceptibility (Disorders)
World Wide Web (WWW)
    USE Internet

Table 3: Change in Status Terms (26)

The following terms changed from postable to nonpostable status. Consult the Relationship Section for the appropriate "Use" term.

Affective Disturbances
Concurrent Validity
Construct Validity
Conversion Neurosis
Directed Reverie Therapy
Dissociative Patterns
Dysmorphophobia
Eating
Educable Mentally Retarded

Eskimos
Ethnic Groups
Explosive Personality
Factorial Validity
Hebephrenic Schizophrenia
Hysterical Personality
Idiot Savants
Information Exchange
Manic Depression

Neurotic Depressive Reaction
Obsessive Compulsive Neurosis
Organic Therapies
Predictive Validity
Psychosomatic Disorders
Sexual Deviations
Slow Learners
Trainable Mentally Retarded

The following terms changed from nonpostable to postable status. Consult the Relationship Section for the appropriate "Use For" term.

Affective Disorders
Behavior Analysis
Circumcision
Histrionic Personality Disorder

Mild Mental Retardation
Moderate Mental Retardation
Obsessive Compulsive Disorder
Paraphilias

Schizophrenia (Disorganized Type)
Somatization Disorder

Table 4: Changes to Spelling or Text of Terms (18)

The following terms were altered due to changes in spelling, in conceptualization, or to their expansion from their previously truncated forms.

Cattell Culture Fair Intelligence Test
Formerly truncated as
Cattell Culture Fair Intell Test

Clinical Judgment (Medical Diagnosis)
Formerly truncated as
Clinical Judgment (Med Diagnosis)

Computer Programming
Formerly
Computer Programing

Computer Programming Languages
Formerly
Computer Programing Languages

Henmon Nelson Tests of Mental Ability
Formerly truncated as
Henmon Nelson Tests Mental Ability

Instruction (Programmed)
Formerly
Instruction (Programed)

Intermittent Explosive Disorder
Formerly
Intermittent Explosive Personality

Laborers (Construction and Industry)
Formerly truncated as
Laborers (Construct and Indust)

Latinos/Latinas
Formerly
Latinos

Neurolinguistic Programming
Formerly
Neurolinguistic Programing

Pearson Product Moment Correllation Coefficient
Formerly truncated as
Pearson Prod Moment Correl Coeff

Physical Handicaps (Attitudes Toward)
Formerly truncated as
Physical Handicaps (Attit Toward)

Programmed Instruction
Formerly
Programed Instruction

Programmed Textbooks
Formerly
Programed Textbooks

Programming (Computer)
Formerly
Programing (Computer)

Programming Languages (Computer)
Formerly
Programing Languages (Computer)

Resilience (Psychological)
Formerly misspelled as
"Resilence"

Sensory Handicaps (Attitudes Toward)
Formerly truncated as
Sensory Handicaps (Attit Toward)

Table 5: Term Deletions (262)

Adventitiously Disabled
Amputees
Aurally Disabled
Barrett Lennard Relationship Invent
Borderline Mentally Retarded
Brain Damaged
Clinical Psychology Grad Training
Coll Ent Exam Bd Scholastic Apt Test
Congenitally Disabled
Disabled
Female Delinquents
Frostig Development Test Vis Percept
Fund Interper Rela Orientat Beh Ques
Guided Daydreams
Guilford Zimmerman Temperament Serv
Halstead Reitan Neuropsych Battery
Health Impaired
High Sch Personality Questionnaire
Hysterical Anesthesia
Illinois Test Psycholinguist Abil
International Class of Diseases
Juvenile Delinquents
Kaufman Assessment Battery Children
Kirton Adaption Innovation Inven
Luria Nebraska Neuropsych Battery

Male Delinquents
Marlowe Crowne Soc Desirabil Scale
Mental Retardation (Attit Toward)
Mentally Retarded
Mildly Mentally Retarded
Minimally Brain Damaged
Minn Multiphasic Personality Inven
Moderately Mentally Retarded
Multiply Disabled
Physical Disabilities (Attit Toward)
Physically Disabled
Profoundly Mentally Retarded
Retarded (Mentally)
Rotter Intern Extern Locus Cont Scal
Sensorially Disabled
Sensory Disabilities (Attit Toward)
Severely Mentally Retarded
Sixteen Personality Factors Question
Slosson Intelligence Test for Child
Speech Disabled
Visually Disabled
Wechsler Intelligence Scale Children
Wepman Test of Auditory Discrim
Woodcock Johnson Psychoed Battery

Table 5: Term Deletions (262), Cont'd

The following terms were deleted entirely from the *Thesaurus* due to the advent of the document field identifiers.

Population/Location Terms:

Afghanistan
Africa
Alaska
Algeria
American Samoa
Angola
Antarctica
Appalachia
Arctic Regions
Argentina
Asia
Australia
Austria
Bahama Islands
Bangladesh
Barbados
Belgium
Belize
Benin
Bermuda
Bolivia
Botswana
Brazil
Bulgaria
Burma
Cambodia
Cameroon
Canada
Central America
Chile
China
Colombia
Commonwealth of
   Independent States
Congo
Costa Rica
Cuba
Cyprus
Czechoslovakia
Denmark
Dominican Republic
East Africa
East Germany

Eastern Europe
Ecuador
Egypt
El Salvador
England
Ethiopia
Europe
Fiji
Finland
France
Germany
Ghana
Great Britain
Greece
Guatemala
Guinea
Guyana
Haiti
Hawaii
Hispaniola
Honduras
Hong Kong
Hungary
Iceland
India
Indonesia
Iran
Iraq
Ireland
Israel
Italy
Ivory Coast
Jamaica
Japan
Jordan
Kenya
Korea
Kuwait
Laos
Latin America
Lebanon
Liberia
Libya

Liechtenstein
Madagascar
Malawi
Malaysia
Mali
Mauritius
Mexico
Middle East
Morocco
Mozambique
Nepal
Netherlands
Netherlands Antilles
New Guinea
New Zealand
Nicaragua
Niger
Nigeria
North America
North Korea
North Vietnam
Northern Ireland
Norway
Pacific Islands
Pakistan
Panama
Papua New Guinea
Paraguay
Peoples Republic of China
Peru
Philippines
Poland
Portugal
Puerto Rico
Romania
Rwanda
Saint Lucia
Saint Vincent
Saudi Arabia
Scandinavia
Scotland
Senegal
Sierra Leone

Table 5: Term Deletions (262), Cont'd

Singapore
Somalia
South Africa
South America
South Korea
South Pacific
South Vietnam
Southeast Asia
Spain
Sri Lanka
Sudan
Surinam
Swaziland
Sweden
Switzerland
Syria
Taiwan

Tanzania
Thailand
Tibet
Tonga
Trinidad
Trinidad and Tobago
Tunisia
Turkey
Uganda
Union of South Africa
Union of Soviet Socialist
    Republics
United Arab Republic
United Kingdom
United States
Uruguay
Venezuela

Vietnam
Virgin Islands
Wales
West Africa
West German Federal
    Republic
West Germany
West Indies
Western Europe
Western Samoa
Yemen
Yugoslavia
Zaire
Zambia
Zimbabwe

Age Group Terms:

Adolescence
Adolescents
Adulthood
Adults
Aged
Childhood

Children
Infancy
Infants
Middle Aged
Neonates
Old Age

Preadolescents
Preschool Age Children
School Age Children
Very Old
Young Adults

Form/Content Type Terms:

Annual Report
Bibliography
Book
Case Law
Conference Proceedings
Dictionary

Errata
Glossary
Obituary
Professional Criticism
Professional Criticism Reply
Rebuttal

Professional Meetings and
    Symposia
Retraction of Publication
Selected Readings
Symposia

Table 6: Terms Receiving "Mapping and Stripping" (118)

Previous Postable Term	Mapped to New Postable Term
Acculturation	Cultural Assimilation
Acute Psychotic Episode	Acute Psychosis
Adrenolytic Drugs	Adrenergic Drugs
Adventitiously Disabled	Adventitious Disorders
Adventitiously Handicapped	Adventitious Disorders
Aldolases	Enzymes
Allport Vernon Lindzey Study Values	Attitude Measures
Amputees	Amputation
Animal Innate Behavior	Instinctive Behavior
Animal Instinctive Behavior	Instinctive Behavior
Antiepileptic Drugs	Anticonvulsive Drugs
Antipsychotic Drugs	Neuroleptic Drugs
Antischizophrenic Drugs	Neuroleptic Drugs
Anxiety Neurosis	Anxiety Disorders
Appetite Disorders	Eating Disorders
Asian Americans	Asians
Asthenic Personality	Personality Disorders
Aurally Disabled	Hearing Disorders
Aurally Handicapped	Hearing Disorders
Authoritarianism Rebellion Scale	Nonprojective Personality Measures
Barrett Lennard Relationship Invent	Barrett Lennard Relationship Inventory
Blacky Pictures Test	Projective Personality Measures
Brain Damaged	Brain Damage
Butyrylperazine	Phenothiazine Derivatives
Carbonic Anhydrase	Enzymes
Cardiotonic Drugs	Drugs

Previous Postable Term	Mapped to New Postable Term
Caucasians	Whites
Chloralose	Hypnotic Drugs
Chlorisondamine	Amines
Chronic Schizophrenia	Schizophrenia
Clinical Psychology Grad Training	Clinical Psychology Graduate Training
Coll Ent Exam Bd Scholastic Apt Test	College Entrance Examination Board Scholastic Aptitude Test
Color Pyramid Test	Projective Personality Measures
Concept Learning	Concept Formation
Concurrent Validity	Statistical Validity
Congenitally Disabled	Congenital Disorders
Congenitally Handicapped	Congenital Disorders
Construct Validity	Statistical Validity
Deanol	Antidepressant Drugs
Developmental Differences	Age Differences
Dieldrin	Insecticides
Differential Personality Inventory	Nonprojective Personality Measures
Disabled	Disorders
Drug Adverse Reactions	Side Effects (Drug)
Drug Effects	Drugs
Drug Potentiation	Drug Interactions
Drug Synergism	Drug Interactions
Drug Withdrawal Effects	Drug Withdrawal
Dysmorphophobia	Body Dysmorphic Disorder
Eating	Ingestion
Eating Patterns	Feeding Practices

Table 6: Terms Receiving "Mapping and Stripping" (118), Cont'd

Previous Postable Term	Mapped to New Postable Term
Educable Mentally Retarded	Mild Mental Retardation
Eskimos	Inuit
Ethnic Groups	Racial and Ethnic Groups
Factorial Validity	Statistical Validity
Female Delinquents	Female Delinquency
Frostig Development Test Vis Percept	Frostig Developmental Test of Visual Perception
Fund Interper Rela Orientat Beh Ques	Fundamental Interpersonal Relations Orientation Behavior Questionnaire
Guilford Zimmerman Temperament Surv	Guilford Zimmerman Temperament Survey
Halstead Reitan Neuropsych Battery	Halstead Reitan Neuropsychological Battery
Handicapped	Disorders
Handicapped (Attitudes Toward)	Disabled (Attitudes Toward)
Health Impaired	Health Impairments
Hebephrenic Schizophrenia	Schizophrenia (Disorganized Type)
Henmon Nelson Tests Mental Ability	Intelligence Measures
High Sch Personality Questionnaire	High School Personality Questionnaire
Homatropine	Alkaloids
Huntingtons Chorea	Huntingtons Disease
Hysterical Personality	Histrionic Personality Disorder

Previous Postable Term	Mapped to New Postable Term
Illinois Test Psycholinguist Abil	Illinois Test of Psycholinguistic Abilities
Interest Patterns	Interests
International Class of Diseases	International Classification of Diseases
Juvenile Delinquents	Juvenile Delinquency
Kaufman Assessment Battery Children	Kaufman Assessment Battery for Children
Kirton Adaption Innovation Inven	Kirton Adaption Innovation Inventory
Kupfer Detre Self Rating Scale	Nonprojective Personality Measures
Leiter Adult Intelligence Scale	Intelligence Measures
Lithium Bromide	Bromides
Luria Nebraska Neuropsych Battery	Luria Nebraska Neuropsychological Battery
Male Delinquents	Male Delinquency
Man Machine Systems	Human Machine Systems
Man Machine Systems Design	Human Machine Systems Design
Manic Depression	Bipolar Disorder
Manic Depressive Psychosis	Bipolar Disorder
Marlowe Crowne Soc Desirabil Scale	Marlowe Crowne Social Desirability Scale
Medics	Paramedical Personnel
Mental Health Consultation	Professional Consultation

Table 6: Terms Receiving "Mapping and Stripping" (118), Cont'd

Previous Postable Term	Mapped to New Postable Term
Mental Retardation (Attit Toward)	Mental Retardation (Attitudes Toward)
Mentally Retarded	Mental Retardation
Mephenesin	Muscle Relaxing Drugs
Mildly Mentally Retarded	Mild Mental Retardation
Minimally Brain Damaged	Minimal Brain Disorders
Minn Multiphasic Personality Inven	Minnesota Multiphasic Personality Inventory
Minnesota Teacher Attitude Inventory	Attitude Measures
Minority Group Discrimination	Race and Ethnic Discrimination
Moderately Mentally Retarded	Moderate Mental Retardation
Morals	Morality
Multiple Personality	Dissociative Identity Disorder
Multiply Disabled	Multiple Disabilities
Multiply Handicapped	Multiple Disabilities
Narcoanalytic Drugs	Drugs
Negroes	Blacks
Neurotic Depressive Reaction	Major Depression
Nonmetallic Elements	Chemical Elements
Novocaine	Procaine
Obsessive Compulsive Neurosis	Obsessive Compulsive Disorder
Onomatopoeia and Images Test	Projective Personality Measures
Opinion Attitude and Interest Survey	Attitude Measures

Previous Postable Term	Mapped to New Postable Term
Organic Therapies	Physical Treatment Methods
Otosclerosis	Ear Disorders
Paraldehyde	Anticonvulsive Drugs
Phenaglycodol	Sedatives
Phobic Neurosis	Phobias
Physical Disabilities (Attit Toward)	Physical Disabilities (Attitudes Toward)
Physical Handicaps (Attit Toward)	Physical Disabilities (Attitudes Toward)
Physically Disabled	Physical Disorders
Physically Handicapped	Physical Disorders
Practice Effects	Practice
Predictive Validity	Statistical Validity
Problem Drinking	Alcohol Abuse
Profoundly Mentally Retarded	Profound Mental Retardation
Pseudopsychopathic Schizophrenia	Schizophrenia
Psychogenic Pain	Somatoform Pain Disorder
Psychopathy	Antisocial Personality
Psychosocial Resocialization	Psychosocial Readjustment
Psychotic Depressive Reaction	Major Depression
Quinidine	Alkaloids
Race Attitudes	Racial and Ethnic Attitudes
Race Relations	Racial and Ethnic Relations

Table 6: Terms Receiving "Mapping and Stripping" (118), Cont'd

Previous Postable Term	Mapped to New Postable Term
Racial Differences	Racial and Ethnic Differences
Racial Discrimination	Race and Ethnic Discrimination
Racial Integration	Social Integration
Rauwolfia	Alkaloids
Reliability (Statistical)	Statistical Reliability
Review (of Literature)	Literature Review
Rotter Intern Extern Locus Cont Scal	Rotter Internal External Locus of Control Scale
School and College Ability Test	Aptitude Measures
School Integration (Racial)	School Integration
Sensorially Disabled	Sensory System Disorders
Sensorially Handicapped	Sensory System Disorders
Sensory Disabilities (Attit Toward)	Sensory Disabilities (Attitudes Toward)
(Sensory Handicaps (Attit Toward)	Sensory Disabilities (Attitudes Toward)
Severely Mentally Retarded	Severe Mental Retardation
Sexual Deviations	Paraphilias
Shuttle Box Grids	Shuttle Boxes
Shuttle Box Hurdles	Shuttle Boxes
Simple Schizophrenia	Schizophrenia
Sixteen Personality Factors Question	Sixteen Personality Factors Questionnaire

Previous Postable Term	Mapped to New Postable Term
Slosson Intelligence Test for Child	Slosson Intelligence Test
Slow Learners	Borderline Mental Retardation
Somnambulism	Sleepwalking
Spanish Americans	Hispanics
Speech Disabled	Speech Disorders
Speech Handicapped	Speech Disorders
Stammering	Stuttering
Temporal Spatial Concept Scale	Intelligence Measures
Thyroid Extract	Thyroid Hormones
Trainable Mentally Retarded	Moderate Mental Retardation
Transistors (Apparatus)	Apparatus
Triflupromazine	Phenothiazine Derivatives
Vane Kindergarten Test	Intelligence Measures
Visually Disabled	Vision Disorders
Visually Handicapped	Vision Disorders
Volt Meters	Apparatus
Wechsler Intelligence Scale Children	Wechsler Intelligence Scale for Children
Wepman Test of Auditory Discrim	Wepman Auditory Discrimination Test
White Betz A B Scale	Nonprojective Personality Measures
Woodcock Johnson Psychoed Battery	Woodcock Johnson Psychoeducational Battery

User Guide

GENERAL INFORMATION

Word Form Conventions

Conventions dealing with singular and plural word forms, direct and indirect entries, abbreviations, acronyms, homographs, and punctuation have been used to ensure standardization of the *Thesaurus* vocabulary. For example, noun forms are preferred entries, with the plural form used when the term is a noun that can be qualified (e.g., **Computers, College Students,** or **Employment Tests**) and the singular form when the term refers to processes, properties, or conditions (e.g., **Learning, Grief, or Rehabilitation**). Direct entry or natural word order is preferred when a concept is represented by two or more words (e.g., **Mental Health** vs "Health, Mental" or **Artificial Intelligence** vs "Intelligence, Artificial").

In cases where ambiguity may occur and to clarify the meaning of homographs, qualifying expressions are included in parentheses (e.g., **Culture (Anthropological), Conservation (Ecological Behavior), and Reconstruction (Learning).**

Also, a selected number of acronyms are used, such as **DOPA, REM Sleep,** and **ROTC Students.**

Term Relationships

The terms in the Relationship Section are displayed to reflect the following relationships:

USE. Directs the user from a term that cannot be used (nonpostable) to a term that can be used (postable) in indexing and searching. The **Use** reference indicates preferred forms of synonyms, abbreviations, spelling, and word sequence:

> Facilitated Communication
> **Use** Augmentative Communication

UF (Used For). Reciprocal of the **Use** reference. Terms listed as **UF** (used for) references represent some but not all of the most frequently encountered synonyms, abbreviations, alternate spellings, or word sequences:

> **Augmentative Communication** 1994
> **UF** Facilitated Communication

B (Broader Term) and **N (Narrower Term).** Reciprocal designators used to indicate hierarchical relationships:

> **Anxiety Disorders**1997
> **B** Mental Disorders1967

> **Mental Disorders**1967
> **N** Anxiety Disorders1997

R (Related Term). Reciprocal designator used to indicate relationships that are semantic or conceptual, but not hierarchical. Related term references indicate to searchers (or indexers) terms that they may not have considered, but may be related to their topic of interest:

> **Anxiety Management**1997
> **R** Stress Management1985

RELATIONSHIP SECTION

Each *Thesaurus* term is listed alphabetically and, as appropriate, is cross-referenced and displayed with its broader, narrower, and related terms (i.e., subterms). Since the beginning of the database in 1967, PsycINFO's indexing vocabulary has been updated periodically with new terms. The date of the term's inclusion in the *Thesaurus* appears as a four-digit superscript. Each postable subterm in a main term's hierarchy also has its date of inclusion shown as well. Twelve dates can be found: 1967, 1971, 1973, 1978, 1982, 1984, 1985, 1988, 1991, 1994, 1997, and 2001. It is important to note that new terms added to the vocabulary are not "mapped back" to older records to which they are conceptually relevant.

The subject code **(SC)** gives the unique five-digit code associated with the term, and can used to retrieve records instead of entering the term text on some online search systems.

Each postable index term in the Relationship Section appears with a posting note **(PN)** reference indicating how many times that term has been used in the indexing of PsycINFO records. Posting notes are based on cumulations of term usage through September 2000. Terms that have an indicator PN=0 are new 2001 terms that have been added to this edition and have yet to accumulate any postings. These terms will appear in the next edition of the *Thesaurus* with appropriate posting notes.

Many terms that have ambiguous meanings, applications unique to the PsycINFO database, or usage patterns that have changed over time have scope notes **(SN)**. In many cases, a scope note provides a definition and/or information on proper use of the term. The scope note always refers to the one term with which it is associated and does not necessarily have implications for the subterms displayed in the term's hierarchy. The following are examples of some of the scope notes found in the Relationship Section:

Definition and Usage | **Parental Investment**[1997]
SN: Parental provision of resources and/or care to offspring. Used for both human and animal populations.

Change in Usage | **Brain Lesions**[1967]
SN: Not defined prior to 1982. From 1982 limited to experimentally induced lesions and used primarily for animal populations.

Change in Status | **Appetite Disorders**
SN: Term was discontinued in 1997. In 2000, the term was stripped from all records containing it, and replaced with EATING DISORDERS, its postable counterpart.

Nonpostable index terms, those not used in the indexing process, are shown in nonbold print with an appropriate **USE** reference. Nonpostable terms are provided as points of entry into the *Thesaurus* vocabulary.

The following example from the Relationship Section illustrates a nonpostable term entry:

Nonpostable Index Term: Working Memory

Use Term   **USE** Short Term
(Postable Index Term)   Memory[1967]

Finally, the Relationship Section has been enhanced by the use of down arrows (↓) in front of any narrower (**N**) or related (**R**) terms that have narrower terms themselves. This feature alerts the user to consider another more specific hierarchical level. The PsycINFO database is indexed to the level of specificity in a given document. In using the Relationship Section and in choosing index terms, consider following any main term's subterms (**N** and **R** terms only) to its lowest level of specificity by turning to the page in the *Thesaurus* where the narrower (**N**) or related (**R**) subterm appears as a main entry to determine if more specific terminology is available. Below is a sample of an index term entry in the Relationship Section.

The following example from the Relationship Section illustrates the various components that may be included in the hierarchy of a postable index term:

Postable Index Term (With date of entry)	**Chronic Mental Illness** [1997]
Posting Note and Subject Code	**PN** 313 **SC** 09184
Scope Note	**SN** A mental illness that persists for a prolonged period of time. Use a more specific term if possible.
Used for (Nonpostable term)	**UF** Persistent Mental Illness
Broader Term	**B** Chronic Illness [1991] Mental Disorders [1967]
Narrower Terms (Down arrow indicates more specific terms)	**N** Chronic Psychosis [1973]
Related Terms (Down arrow indicates more specific terms)	**R** Chronicity (Disorders) [1982] Prognosis [1973] Severity (Disorders) [1982] ↓Treatment Resistant Disorders [1994]

ROTATED ALPHABETICAL TERMS SECTION

Many terms represent concepts not expressed in a single word; therefore, postable and non-postable *Thesaurus* terms in this section are listed in alphabetical order by each word contained within them. The Rotated Alphabetical Terms Section is useful in finding all *Thesaurus* terms that have a particular word in common. This display groups related terms when they may otherwise be separated in the alphabetical Relationship Section. It is important to note that this section should be used in conjunction with the Relationship Section since hierarchies, scope notes, posting notes, and term dates do not appear in the Rotated Alphabetical Terms Section. A term containing three words will appear in three locations in this section as illustrated below:

	Animal	Courtship	Behavior
	Animal	Courtship	Displays
	Animal	Defensive	Behavior
Animal	**Courtship**	Behavior	
Animal	**Courtship**	Displays	
Human	**Courtship**		
	Displays		
Animal	Courtship	**Displays**	
Auditory	**Displays**		

Nonpostable index terms (terms not used for indexing) are represented in nonbold print followed by the appropriate "**Use**" term in italics. Each word of the term, just like the postable terms above, appear in different locations depending on how many words are contained in the index term as illustrated below:

	Illumination
	Illumination Therapy
	USE Phototherapy
Autokinetic	**Illusion**
Hormone	**Therapy**
Illumination	Therapy
	USE Phototherapy
Implosive	**Therapy**

TERM CLUSTERS SECTION

Clusters are collections of index terms that are related to one another conceptually rather than hierarchically, and are displayed together under broad subject categories. This section is useful for viewing all terms in each cluster collectively.

Clusters provide an entry point into the *Thesaurus* vocabulary by allowing a large group of similar terms to be scanned easily and efficiently, and helping the user translate their search vocabulary into *Thesaurus* vocabulary. In a sense, the clusters present an "index" to the indexing vocabulary found in the Relationship Section.

It is important to note that the Clusters Section should not be used alone, but in conjunction with the Relationship Section. Useful details regarding particular index terms can be found in the Relationship Section such as scope notes, posting notes, hierarchies, dates for term inclusion, and links to additional search terms.

Not every index term will appear in the Term Clusters Section. Terms appear under nine broad cluster subject areas. The nine subject areas are meant to present index terms for selected subject areas that are frequent in psychological research, but do not cover all subject areas in psychology. Terms may appear in more than one broad cluster area, and also in more than one subcluster under any broad subject area, if appropriate. The Term Clusters and Subclusters are listed in Table 7 on page xxv.

Table 7: Term Cluster/Subcluster Subject Areas

Computers Cluster
   Applications
   Automation
   Computers & Communication
   Computers & Media
   Education & Training
   Equipment
   Human Machine Systems and Engineering
   Information

Disorders Cluster
   Antisocial Behavior & Behavior Disorders
   Diagnosis
   Disorder Characteristics
   Learning Disorders & Mental Retardation
   Physical & Psychosomatic Disorders
   Psychological Disorders
   Speech & Language Disorders
   Symptomatology

Educational Cluster
   Academic Learning & Achievement
   Curricula
   Educational Personnel & Administration
   Educational Testing & Counseling
   Schools & Institutions
   Special Education
   Student Characteristics & Academic
        Environment
   Student Populations
   Teaching and Teaching Methods

Legal Cluster
   Adjudication
   Criminal Groups
   Criminal Offenses
   Criminal Rehabilitation
   Laws
   Legal Issues
   Legal Personnel
   Legal Processes

Neuropsychology & Neurology Cluster
   Assessment & Diagnosis
   Electrophysiology
   Neuroanatomy
   Neurological Disorders
   Neurological Intervention
   Neurosciences
   Neurotransmitters & Neuroregulators

Occupational & Employment Cluster
   Career Areas
   Employee, Occupational & Job Characteristics
   Personnel Management & Professional
        Personnel Issues
   Occupational Groups
   Organizations & Organizational Behavior

Statistical Cluster
   Design, Analysis & Interpretation
   Statistical Reliability & Validity
   Statistical Theory & Experimentation

Tests & Testing Cluster
   Academic Achievement & Aptitude Measures
   Attitude & Interest Measures
   Intelligence Measures
   Nonprojective Personality Measures
   Perceptual Measures
   Projective Personality Measures
   Testing
   Testing Methods

Treatment Cluster
   Alternative Therapies
   Behavior Modification
   Counseling
   Hospitalization & Institutionalization
   Medical & Physical Treatment
   Psychotherapy
   Rehabilitation
   Treatment (General)
   Treatment Facilities

SUBJECT SEARCHING IN PsycINFO

INTRODUCTION

Using the *Thesaurus of Psychological Index Terms* to search PsycINFO, ClinPSYC, and *Psychological Abstracts* (PA) can enhance the precision of your retrieved references and guide you to closely related topics that you might otherwise miss. The standardized vocabulary in the *Thesaurus* eliminates the need to worry about phraseology used by authors to describe a concept. For effective searches and development of comprehensive search strategies, follow the steps outlined below:

1. Select a search topic

   Example: "I'm interested in high school students and AIDS."

2. Specifically define the concepts of the topic and develop a list of synonyms that represent the concepts. This can include independent and/or dependent experimental variables and/or a population. A properly defined concept can result in an efficient search with precise retrieval of highly relevant articles, and will also reduce the need to scan and eliminate irrelevant references. The following example shows a more specific and defined topic:

   Example: "I'm interested in AIDS educational and prevention programs for high school students."

3. Look up your concepts in the *Thesaurus of Psychological Index Terms*. Start in any of the three sections, choosing terms on the basis of your topic and familiarity with the *Thesaurus* vocabulary. See the User Guide on page xxii for a description of each section of the *Thesaurus*.

   No matter which section of the *Thesaurus* you look in first, be sure to check the Relationship Section before finalizing your terms. The Relationship Section includes scope notes to describe how terms are used, as well as posting notes, subject codes, term dates, and the critical *used for*, *broader*, *narrower*, and *related* terms.

   The most important things to look for in the Relationship Section are the narrower terms and the dates for main term entry (for articles indexed after that date). It is important to note each descriptor's year of entry in the *Thesaurus* (indicated by a four-digit superscript number appended to each term in the Relationship Section) because some new terminology is not "mapped back" to older records to which they are conceptually relevant.

   To retrieve articles relevant to terms before their inclusion in the *Thesaurus*, consider their broader concepts as index terms or use free text strategies to find records added to the database before the starting date.

   Also, note each entry's posting note, which is a rough guide to the number of articles you can expect to find under that term.

   It is important to remember that all PsycINFO records are indexed to the source document's level of specificity. For example, an author who calls an experimental population "high school students" will find this article indexed under "**High School Students**", not the broader and less specific term "**Students**". Therefore, any applicable narrower terms should be added as synonyms to the list of index terms in your search. Related terms may also closely match a search topic, and should be considered carefully when formulating a strategy.

   Example 1:
   a. AIDS Prevention

   b. Acquired Immune Deficiency Syndrome (This is the term PsycINFO uses for AIDS)

   c. Educational Programs or Health Education or Health Promotion (These terms can be used to describe the concept of educational and prevention programs)

   d. High School Students or High Schools or Secondary Education (These terms form the context of high school education)

Using these terms, your search statement would be:

   aids prevention OR (acquired immune deficiency syndrome AND (educational programs OR health education OR health promotion OR prevention)) AND (high school students OR high schools OR secondary education)

ELECTRONIC SEARCHING

Each vendor system that carries PsycINFO or ClinPSYC operates differently, yet each has the capability to limit a search to the descriptor or index term field. Electronic search systems give you the opportunity to manipulate your search statement to provide precision and recall in retrieval. Formulate your topic and refer to the *Thesaurus* for appropriate terminology, then consult **Appendix D**, a quick reference guide to vendor systems that offer command-line searching, to determine how to enter index terms as descriptors. Also, refer to **Appendix D** for other specific field names and search examples.

Electronic systems allow the use of Boolean logic in a search, which is difficult to do in a manual search of *PA*. Use the Boolean logical operators **AND**, **OR**, and **NOT** to combine terms.

Example of Boolean Logic

(Shaded Areas Indicate Retrieval)

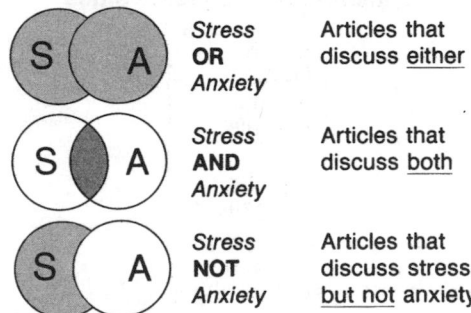

Stress **OR** *Anxiety*	Articles that discuss <u>either</u>
Stress **AND** *Anxiety*	Articles that discuss <u>both</u>
Stress **NOT** *Anxiety*	Articles that discuss stress <u>but not</u> anxiety

Example:

AIDS Prevention

OR Acquired Immune Deficiency Syndrome

AND (Educational Programs **OR** Health Education **OR** AIDS Prevention)

AND (High School Students **OR** High Schools **OR** Secondary Education)

ELECTRONIC THESAURUS: For added convenience in searching, most vendor systems offer an electronic thesaurus that can automatically display terms along with their broader, narrower, and related concepts. This feature can help reduce typing and enhance the speed of a search, especially when several narrower terms need to be entered, by allowing users to move from term to term and find new appropriate search terms with ease.

EXPLODE FEATURE: The Explode feature is available on some search systems. See the Master Quick Reference Guide **Appendix D** for the systems that make this feature available. When a search system's explode command is used, the system will automatically search the index term and the first level of its narrower terms. Some terms listed as narrower to an index term may have narrower terms of their own—"narrowers of narrowers." In the *Thesaurus*, narrower terms that have narrower terms of their own are marked with a down-arrow. To achieve comprehensive retrieval, they must be exploded as well.

MAJOR TERMS: Index terms applied to Psyc-INFO or ClinPSYC records that represent the primary focus of the reference are designated as "major." Many search systems allow for searching of major terms. See the Master Quick Reference Guide **Appendix D** for each system's label for searching major terms, if applicable.

SAVED SEARCHES: Saved Searches are stored sets of index terms in popular subject areas that save valuable search time. See **Table 9** below for a full listing of search topics currently available. When a Saved Search is executed, the index terms are searched automatically, and the resulting sets can be manipulated.

The list of terms searched in each Saved Search is available on our web site at *www.apa.org/psycinfo/training/saved*. Consult the documentation for your search system for details on how to run saved searches.

Table 9—Saved Search Topics

Achievement Measures
APA Journals
Attitude Measures
Communication/Language/Speech Disorders
Developing Countries
Intelligence Measures
Learning Disabilities
Neuropsychological Assessment
Neurotransmitters
Nonprojective Personality Measures
Perceptual Measures
Projective Personality Measures
Rehabilitation
Tomography

ADJUSTING YOUR SEARCH RETRIEVAL

If your search retrieves too many records, try making your search more specific by adding another concept. If nearly all of your records appear relevant, but there are still too many, consider restricting your retrieval to recent publication years or a particular language material.

If you retrieve too few records, consider dropping a concept, adding synonymous terms, or eliminating restrictions to specific fields.

Content Classification Code Searching

PsycINFO uses a content classification system that divides the field of psychology into 22 major or broad categories and 135 subcategories. Content classification codes can be searched in most systems. Use of the content classification system in searching can shorten online time and screen out undesired references. Content classification codes are particularly useful to retrieve records from a broad subject area in which many different index terms may have been used. Classification codes generally limit a search, since only one or two codes are assigned to each record. Keep in mind, however, that a classification code search usually does not retrieve everything in the database that is relevant to a respective topic. A well-constructed search will always include relevant descriptors.

Search classification codes at their broad level. Using the first two digits of a category retrieves the entire category and enables the search to be executed throughout the entire year range of the database. If more specific information is needed, search one or more four-digit subcategories. Four-digit subcategories were added in 1976; therefore, a search on a four-digit subcategory will limit retrieval to records added in 1976 and later.

A list of the content classification codes appears in **Appendix C**.

Age Group Searching

All search systems use identifying tags for the ages of human populations. A record may have more than one age group tag. Search for age groups in the Age Group field. The following table lists the values that are available in the Age Group field. Values that are indented indicate that they are narrower. When the broader value is searched, the narrower values are searched as well.

Age Group Field Values

> Childhood (birth-12 yrs)
>   Neonatal (birth-1 mo)
>   Infancy (1-23 mo)
>   Preschool Age (2-5 yrs)
>   School Age (6-12 yrs)
>
> Adolescence (13-17 yrs)
>
> Adulthood (18 yrs & older)
>   Young Adulthood (18-29 yrs)
>   Thirties (30-39 yrs)
>   Middle Age (40-64 yrs)
>   Aged (65 yrs & older)
>   Very Old (85 yrs & older)

Population Group Searching

Search for population group characteristics other than age in the Population Group field. The following table lists the values that are available in the Population Group field. A record may have more than one population group value.

Population Group Field Values

> Human
> Animal
> Female
> Male
> Inpatient
> Outpatient

Form/Content Type Searching

The Form/Content Type field indicates the form of the source document. It is helpful for distinguishing what a source document IS as opposed to what it is ABOUT. For example, if you want to limit your retrieval to literature reviews, you would search LITERATURE REVIEW/RESEARCH REVIEW in the Form/Content Type field. If you want documents that are about how to do a literature review, you would search Literature Review as a *Thesaurus* term.

The following table lists the values that are available in the Form/Content Type field. A record may have more than one value. Values that are indented indicate that they are narrower. When the broader value is searched, the narrower values are searched as well. Values that are also *Thesaurus* terms are marked with an asterisk (*).

Form/Content Type Field Values

Autobiography/Personal Account
Bibliography
Biography*
Case Law
Comment
      Comment Appended
Conference Proceedings/Symposia
Editorial
Empirical Study
     Case Study
     Clinical Case Report
     Experimental Replication*
     Followup Studies*
     Longitudinal Studies*
         Prospective Studies*
         Retrospective Studies*
     Treatment Outcome Study
         Clinical Trials
Errata/Retractions/Corrections
Fiction/Creative Work
Interview
Letter
Literature Review/Research Review*
Meta Analysis*
	Obituary
	Oral History
	Panel Discussion
	Professional Policies/Standards
	Program Evaluation
	Reprint
	Translation
	Classroom Material
	     Textbook
	         Introductory
	         Undergraduate
	         Graduate
	     Study/Curriculum/Resources
	     Workbook
	Collected Works
	Handbook/Manual/Guide
	     Self Help Guide
	Reference Material
	     Dictionary/Glossary
	     Directory
	     Encyclopedia
	     Taxonomy
	     Thesaurus
	Selected Readings

Searching for Special Features

Special Features, such as the presence of references, an index, or an assessment instrument are indicated in the Special Features field. The following table lists the values that are available in the Special Features field. A record may have more than one value.

Special Features Field Values

Index
Non English Abstracts
Peer Reviewed
References
Assessment Instrument
Auxiliary Materials
Audiocassette
   Computer Software
   Instructors Manual
   Manual
   Study Guide
   Test Bank
   Transparencies
   Videocassette
   Workbook

Searching for Geographic Locations

As discussed on page ix, terms indicating geographical locations were removed from the *Thesaurus*. If you are looking for studies done in a particular country, you should now search for it in the Location field.

Searching in *Psychological Abstracts* (PA)

Look up *Thesaurus* terms in the annual PA Subject Volume Indexes from your years of interest—typically the most recent year first—and work backward. Start with the terms you consider most relevant to your search. If all the terms are of equal relevance, begin with the one with the fewest postings. You will find a short key phrase to describe each article indexed with that term. Select the most relevant phrases, then note the volume, which is printed on the spine of the index, and the abstract number, which is listed after each phrase in the index.

A separate Brief Subject Index appears at the back of each monthly issue of *PA* as a guide to that issue's contents only. No phrases are included in this index. The Brief Subject Index allows access to the current literature otherwise available only in the annual Volume Indexes published at the end of each year.

The final step in the search is to look up the abstracts themselves from the individual monthly issues of *PA*, using the volume and abstract numbers as a guide. Read the abstracts, then copy the citations of the ones of interest in order to locate the complete articles. Abstracts should never be used as substitutes for original articles.

HOW TO CONTACT US

To contact us, call our toll free line at 800-374-2722 in North America, 9:00 a.m. to 5:00 p.m., U.S. Eastern time, Monday through Friday.

For those who do not have toll free access, we can be contacted at 202-336-5650, FAX 202-336-5633, TTY 202-336-6123 or E-mail at *psycinfo@apa.org*.

Information on ordering documents, subscriptions, vendor system documentation, journals covered in PsycINFO, and search aids can also be found on PsycINFO's web site:

www.apa.org/psycinfo

APPENDIX A: Sample Journal Record

FIELD NAME	SAMPLE JOURNAL RECORD
Accession Number :	2000-00078-003
Document Type:	Journal-Article
Title:	Modeling the growth of decoding skills in first-grade children.
Author:	Compton,-Donald-L..
First Author Affiliation:	U Colorado, Dept of Psychology, Boulder, CO, US
Source:	Scientific-Studies-of-Reading. 2000; Vol 4(3): 219-259.
Publication Year:	2000
Language:	English
Abstract:	Demonstrated the usefulness of combining curriculum-based measurement and hierarchical linear modeling procedures to identify the characteristics of 75 1st grade children that predict growth rates in the acquisition of decoding skills (as assessed through measures of isolated word and nonword reading). This study examined the relative importance of both static (initial levels of performance) and dynamic (rate of growth) measures of cognitive-processing abilities (i.e., phonemic awareness and rapid naming speed) and emergent print knowledge (i.e., letter name, letter sound, more advanced graphophoneme knowledge, and orthographic awareness) as predictors of decoding growth. Over the course of an academic year, a set of parallel word and nonword reading tasks, constructed using curriculum-base measurement techniques and administered on a monthly basis, were capable of demonstrating individual change in decoding skill. Furthermore, results indicate that growth in cognitive-processing abilities and general knowledge about print could likewise be measured and adequately modeled. Results suggest that in the very earliest stages of word reading development there may be a strong association between the rate of growth in cognitive processing, print knowledge, and decoding skills. (© 2000 APA/PsycINFO, all rights reserved)
Key Phrase:	cognitive processes and print knowledge, predicting development of decoding skills, 1st grade children
Major Descriptors:	*Cognitive-Development; *Cognitive-Processes; *Human-Information-Storage; *Reading-Ability; *Word-Recognition
Classification Code:	2820-Cognitive-and-Perceptual-Development; 3550-Academic-Learning-and-Achievement; 2820; 3550; 28; 35
Age Group:	Childhood; Preschool-Age; School-Age
Population:	Human; Male; Female
Location:	US
Publication Type:	Empirical-Study; Longitudinal-Study
Special Feature:	References
Update Code:	20000719

APPENDIX B: Sample Book/Chapter Record

FIELD NAME	SAMPLE BOOK RECORD
Accession Number:	2000-07592-000
Document Type:	Edited-Book; Book
Title:	Infant development: The essential readings.
Author:	Muir,-Darwin (Ed); Slater,-Alan (Ed)
Author Affiliation:	Queen's U, Kingston, ON, Canada
Publisher:	Malden, MA, US: Blackwell Publishers, Inc. (2000). xxviii, 369 pp.
Source:	Essential readings in development psychology.
ISBN:	0631217460 (hardcover); 0631217479 (paperback)
Publication Year:	2000
Language:	English
Abstract:	(from the cover) Infant Development: The Essential Readings introduces the reader to the field of infancy research and to some of the current...[abstract continues]
Key Phrase:	theoretical issues and sensation and perception and cognitive and social development and communication in infant development
Major Descriptors:	*Infant-Development
Minor Descriptors:	Cognitive-Development; Communication-; Perceptual-Development; Psycho-social-Development; Theories-
Classification Code:	2800-Developmental-Psychology; 2800; 28
Age Group:	Childhood; Infancy
Population:	Human
Publication Type:	Selected-Readings
Special Feature:	Index; References
Audience Type:	Psychology:-Professional-and-Research
Table of Contents:	(Abbreviated) Preface Acknowledgments Introduction: Infancy Research: History and methods [by] Darwin Muir and Alan Slater Part I: Theoretical issues SEE CHAPTER Shifting the focus from what to why / C. Rovee-Collier SEE CHAPTER Nativism, empiricism, and the origins of knowledge / E. S. Spelke SEE CHAPTER Connectionist modelling and infant development / D. Mareschal...[table of contents continues]
Update Code:	200006

APPENDIX B: Sample Book/Chapter Record (cont'd)

FIELD NAME	SAMPLE CHAPTER RECORD
Accession Number:	2000-07592-003
Document Type:	Chapter
Title:	Connectionist modelling and infant development.
Author:	Mareschal,-Denis
Book:	Muir, Darwin (Ed); Slater, Alan (Ed); et-al. (2000). Infant development: The essential readings. Essential readings in development psychology. (pp. 55-65). Malden, MA, US: Blackwell Publishers, Inc. xxviii, 369 pp.
ISBN:	0631217460 (hardcover); 0631217479 (paperback)
Publication Year:	2000
Language:	English
Abstract:	(from the chapter) The real challenge for developmental psychology is to explain how and why behaviors emerge. The traditional approach...[abstract continues]
Key Phrase:	connectionist computer modelling of infant development
Major Descriptors:	*Computer-Simulation; *Connectionism-; *Infant-Development
Classification Code:	2800-Developmental-Psychology; 2800; 28
Age Group:	Childhood; Infancy
Population:	Human
Special Feature:	References
Audience Type:	Psychology:-Professional-and-Research
Update Code:	200006

APPENDIX C: Content Classification System

NOTE: This Classification code system was designed to describe the content of the PsycINFO database, not the field of psychology.

2100 General Psychology
2140 History & Systems

2200 Psychometrics & Statistics & Methodology
2220 Tests & Testing
  2221 Sensory & Motor Testing
  2222 Developmental Scales & Schedules
  2223 Personality Scales & Inventories
  2224 Clinical Psychological Testing
  2225 Neuropsychological Assessment
  2226 Health Psychology Testing
  2227 Educational Measurement
  2228 Occupational & Employment Testing
  2229 Consumer Opinion & Attitude Testing
2240 Statistics & Mathematics
2260 Research Methods & Experimental Design

2300 Human Experimental Psychology
2320 Sensory Perception
  2323 Visual Perception
  2326 Auditory & Speech Perception
2330 Motor Processes
2340 Cognitive Processes
  2343 Learning & Memory
  2346 Attention
2360 Motivation & Emotion
2380 Consciousness States
2390 Parapsychology

2400 Animal Experimental & Comparative Psychology
2420 Learning & Motivation
2440 Social & Instinctive Behavior

2500 Physiological Psychology & Neuroscience
2510 Genetics
2520 Neuropsychology & Neurology
2530 Electrophysiology
2540 Physiological Processes
2560 Psychophysiology
2580 Psychopharmacology

2600 Psychology & the Humanities
2610 Literature & Fine Arts
2630 Philosophy

2700 Communication Systems
2720 Linguistics & Language & Speech
2750 Mass Media Communications

2800 Developmental Psychology
2820 Cognitive & Perceptual Development
2840 Psychosocial & Personality Development
2860 Gerontology

2900 Social Processes & Social Issues
2910 Social Structure & Organization
2920 Religion
2930 Culture & Ethnology
2950 Marriage & Family
  2953 Divorce & Remarriage
  2956 Childrearing & Child Care
2960 Political Processes & Political Issues
2970 Sex Roles & Womens Issues

2980 Sexual Behavior & Sexual Orientation
2990 Drug & Alcohol Usage (Legal)

3000 Social Psychology
3020 Group & Interpersonal Processes
3040 Social Perception & Cognition

3100 Personality Psychology
3120 Personality Traits & Processes
3140 Personality Theory
  3143 Psychoanalytic Theory

3200 Psychological & Physical Disorders
3210 Psychological Disorders
  3211 Affective Disorders
  3213 Schizophrenia & Psychotic States
  3215 Neuroses & Anxiety Disorders
  3217 Personality Disorders
3230 Behavior Disorders & Antisocial Behavior
  3233 Substance Abuse & Addiction
  3236 Criminal Behavior & Juvenile Delinquency
3250 Developmental Disorders & Autism
  3253 Learning Disorders
  3256 Mental Retardation
3260 Eating Disorders
3270 Speech & Language Disorders
3280 Environmental Toxins & Health
3290 Physical & Somatoform & Psychogenic Disorders
  3291 Immunological Disorders
  3293 Cancer
  3295 Cardiovascular Disorders
  3297 Neurological Disorders & Brain Damage
  3299 Vision & Hearing & Sensory Disorders

3300 Health & Mental Health Treatment & Prevention
3310 Psychotherapy & Psychotherapeutic Counseling
  3311 Cognitive Therapy
  3312 Behavior Therapy & Behavior Modification
  3313 Group & Family Therapy
  3314 Interpersonal & Client Centered & Humanistic Therapy
  3315 Psychoanalytic Therapy
3340 Clinical Psychopharmacology
3350 Specialized Interventions
  3351 Clinical Hypnosis
  3353 Self Help Groups
  3355 Lay & Paraprofessional & Pastoral Counseling
  3357 Art & Music & Movement Therapy
3360 Health Psychology & Medicine
  3361 Behavioral & Psychological Treatment of Physical Illness
  3363 Medical Treatment of Physical Illness
  3365 Promotion & Maintenance of Health & Wellness
3370 Health & Mental Health Services
  3371 Outpatient Services
  3373 Community & Social Services
  3375 Home Care & Hospice

3377 Nursing Homes & Residential Care
3379 Inpatient & Hospital Services
3380 Rehabilitation
  3383 Drug & Alcohol Rehabilitation
  3384 Occupational & Vocational Rehabilitation
  3385 Speech & Language Therapy
  3386 Criminal Rehabilitation & Penology

3400 Professional Psychological & Health Personnel Issues
3410 Professional Education & Training
3430 Professional Personnel Attitudes & Characteristics
3450 Professional Ethics & Standards & Liability
3470 Impaired Professionals

3500 Educational Psychology
3510 Educational Administration & Personnel
3530 Curriculum & Programs & Teaching Methods
3550 Academic Learning & Achievement
3560 Classroom Dynamics & Student Adjustment & Attitudes
3570 Special & Remedial Education
  3575 Gifted & Talented
3580 Educational/Vocational Counseling & Student Services

3600 Industrial & Organizational Psychology
3610 Occupational Interests & Guidance
3620 Personnel Management & Selection & Training
3630 Personnel Evaluation & Job Performance
3640 Management & Management Training
3650 Personnel Attitudes & Job Satisfaction
3660 Organizational Behavior
3670 Working Conditions & Industrial Safety

3700 Sport Psychology & Leisure
3720 Sports
3740 Recreation & Leisure

3800 Military Psychology

3900 Consumer Psychology
3920 Consumer Attitudes & Behavior
3940 Marketing & Advertising

4000 Engineering & Environmental Psychology
4010 Human Factors Engineering
4030 Lifespace & Institutional Design
4050 Community & Environmental Planning
4070 Environmental Issues & Attitudes
4090 Transportation

4100 Intelligent Systems
4120 Artificial Intelligence & Expert Systems
4140 Robotics
4160 Neural Networks

4200 Forensic Psychology & Legal Issues
4210 Civil Rights & Civil Law
4230 Criminal Law & Criminal Adjudication
4250 Mediation & Conflict Resolution
4270 Crime Prevention
4290 Police & Legal Personnel

APPENDIX D: PsycINFO and ClinPSYC Master Quick Reference Guide

The chart on the following pages is a guide to the command syntax required to search Psyc-INFO and ClinPSYC record fields on the vendor systems available at the time of this edition's publication. Vendors not listed in this chart do not offer command syntax for searching.

The far-left column of the chart contains Psyc-INFO and ClinPSYC field names. To find a field's corresponding label and search syntax, read across the field's row to the appropriate vendor column. Blank fields indicate that the field is not searchable in that vendor's interface.

For complete information about searching, users should consult the PsycINFO User Manual or contact PsycINFO to obtain vendor-specific documentation or searching information.

PsycINFO MASTER QUICK REFERENCE GUIDE

FIELD NAME	Cambridge Scientific Abstracts		Datastar		DIALOG	
	LABEL	SEARCH EXAMPLES	LABEL	SEARCH EXAMPLES	LABEL	SEARCH EXAMPLES
Accession Number	AN=	an=1997-38405-001	AN	1997-38405-001.an.	AA	s aa=1997-38405-001
Publication Type	PT=	pt=(journal article)	PT	pt=journal-article	DT	s dt=journal article
Author	AU=	au=vye, nancy	AU	vye-n$.au.	AU	s au=vye, nancy?
Author Affiliation	AF=	af=(vanderbilt u)	IN	vanderbilt adj u.in.	CS	s cs=(technology(w)group)
Title	TI=	ti=(job obsolescence)	TI	job adj obsolesce$4.ti.	TI	s job(w)obsolescence/ti
Source	SO=	so=(cognition & instruction)	SO	cognition-and-instruction.so.	SO	s so=(cognition and instruction)
Journal Name					JN	s jn=cognition
Special Issue Title						[display-only field]
Book Series Title					SE	s se=(behavioral(w)science)
Parent Book Title					SO	s job(w)creation/so
Publisher	PB=	pb=(jossey bass)			PU	s pu=(jossey(w)bass)
ISSN	IS=	is=0737-0008	SO	0737-0008.so.	SN	s sn=0737-0008
ISBN	IB=	ib=0787901253	SO	0-7879-0125-3.so.	BN	s bn=0-7879-0125-3
UMI Dissertation Order Number			UM	aam9835792.um.		[display-only field]
Language	LA=	la=english	LG	lg=english	LA	s la=english
Abstract	AB=	ab=(solution space analysis)	AB	solution adj space adj analysis.so.	AB	s solution(w)space(w)analysis /ab
Key Phrase	ID=	id=(job retraining)	ID	job with retraining.id.	ID	s job(w)retraining/id
Descriptors All		de=career change	DE	career-change.de.	DE	s personnel/de
Exact Term	DE=	de=(program development)			DF	s personnel/df
Word/Phrase	DE=	de=train*			DE	s career(w)change/de
Explode (with narrower terms)		exp teaching methods				s marital relations!
Major			MJ	professional-ethics.mj.	MAJ	s career change/maj
Classification Code	CL=	cl=28*; cl=331*; cl=3620	CC	28#.cc.; 331#.cc.; 3620.cc.	SH	s sh=28; s sh=3620
Age Group	PO=	po=(school age)	AGE	age=school-age-6-12-yrs	AG	s ag=school age
Population Group	PO=	po=human	PO	po=human	PG	s pg=human
Population Location	PO=	po=france	CN	cn=usa	GN	s gn=usa
Form/Content Type	PT=	pt=(empirical study)	AT	at=empirical-study	DT	s dt=literature review?
Special Feature	FE=	fe=(assessment instrument)	SF	sf=assessment-instrument	SF	s sf=assessment instrument
Intended Audience	TA=	ta=professional	TA	psychology.ta.	AI	s ai=psychology?
Conference Information	CF=	cf=(american psychological)	CF	american with psychological.cf.	CT	s ct=(american and psycho-logical)
Notes	NT=	nt=(dubin and lecture)	NT	reprint.nt.		[display-only field]
Table of Contents	TB=	tb=(job creation)	TC	job adj creation.tc.	AB	s employee(w)development/ab
Publication Year	PY=	py=1997	YR	yr=1997	PY	s py=1997
Update Code	UD=	ud=19970101	ED	19970101.ed.	UD	s ud=9999

PsycINFO MASTER QUICK REFERENCE GUIDE

FIELD NAME	DIMDI LABEL	DIMDI SEARCH EXAMPLES	EBSCO LABEL	EBSCO SEARCH EXAMPLES	The Gale Group LABEL	The Gale Group SEARCH EXAMPLES
Accession Number	ND	find nd=1997-38405-001	AN	AN 1997-38405-001		
Publication Type	DTP	find dtp=journal article	PT	PT journal article	DT	dt journal article
Author	AU	find au=vye n?	AU	AU vye, nancy*	AU	au vye nancy
Author Affiliation	CS	find cs=harriman	AA	AA vanderbilt	AF	af vanderbilt u
Title	TI	find job obsolescence /ti	TI	TI job obsolescence	TI	ti job obsolescence
Source			SO	SO cogni*		
Journal Name	JT	find jt=?cognition?	JN	JN cognition & instruction		
Special Issue Title	JT	find jt=?special issue?		[display-only field]		
Book Series Title	SE	find behavioral science/se		[display only field]		
Parent Book Title		[display-only field]		[display only field]		
Publisher	PU	find pu=jossey bass	PB	PB jossey bass	PU	pu jossey bass
ISSN	ISSN	find issn=0737-0008	IS	IS 07370008	IS	is 0737-0008
ISBN	ISBN	find isbn=0-7879-0125-3	IB	IB 0-7879-0125-3	IS	is 0-7879-0125-3
UMI Dissertation Order Number	CN	find cn=aam9835792	DN	DN aam9835792		
Language	LA	find la=english	LA	LA english	LA	la english
Abstract	AB	find solution space analysis/ab	AB	AB solution space analysis	AB	ab solution space analysis
Key Phrase	KP	find retraining/kp	KP	KP job retraining	KP	kp job retraining
Descriptors All	CT	find ct=program development	SU	SU program development	SU	su=program development
Exact Term						
Word/Phrase					SU	su train*
Explode (with narrower terms)		find ct down problem solving				
Major	W1	find ct=problem solving/w1			SU	su career change
Classification Code	SC	find sc=28.2.0; find sc down 28	CC	CC 28*; CC 3620	CL	cl 28*; cl 3620
Age Group	AGE	find school age/age	AG	AG school age	PO	po adulthood
Population Group	POP	find pop=human	PO	PO human	PO	po human
Population Location	POPLOC	find poploc=france	PL	PL france		
Form/Content Type	DT	find dt=empirical study	CT	CT empirical study		
Special Feature	ASI	find asi=assessment instrument	SC	SC assessment instrument		
Intended Audience	AUD	find aud=psychology?	AI	AI psychology*		
Conference Information	CF	find cf=american psych?	CN	CN american psychological		
Notes	NOTE	[display-only field]		[display-only field]		
Table of Contents	TC	find tc=job creation	TC	TC job creation		
Publication Year	PY	find py>1989	YR	YR 1997		
Update Code	EDAT	find edat=19970101		[display-only field]		

PsycINFO MASTER QUICK REFERENCE GUIDE

FIELD NAME	NISC LABEL	NISC SEARCH EXAMPLES	OCLC LABEL	OCLC SEARCH EXAMPLES	Ovid LABEL	Ovid SEARCH EXAMPLES
Accession Number	ID	id=1997-38405-001	NO	no:1997-38405-001	AN	1997-38405-001.an.
Publication Type	PT	pt=journal article	DT	dt=journal article	PT	journal article.pt.
Author	AU	au=vye	AU	au:vye	AU	vye nancy$.au.
Author Affiliation	AF	af=vanderbilt u	AA	aa:vanderbilt u	IN	vanderbilt u.in.
Title	TI	ti=job obsolescence	TI	ti:job obsolescence	TI	job obsolescence.ti.
Source	SO	so=cognition and instruction			SO	instruct$.so.
Journal Name	JR	jr=cognition and instruction	SO	so=cognition & instruction	JN	cognition & instruction.jn.
Special Issue Title	SO	so=special issue			SI	cognition.si.
Book Series Title	SE	se=behavioral science	SE	se:behavioral science	ST	behavioral science.st.
Parent Book Title	BT	bt=job creation	CB	cb:job creation	BT	job creation.bt.
Publisher	PU	pu=jossey bass	PB	pb:jossey-bass	PU	jossey bass.pu.
ISSN	SN	sn=07370008	NS	ns:0737-0008	IS	0737-0008.is.
ISBN	SN	sn=0787901253	SN	sn:0787901253	IB	0787901253.ib.
UMI Dissertation Order Number	SO	so=aam9835792			ON	aam9835792.on.
Language	LA	la=english	LN	ln=english	LG	english.lg.
Abstract		solution near space near analysis	AB	ab:solution space analysis	AB	solution space analysis.ab.
Key Phrase	KP	kp=job retraining	ID	id:job retraining	ID	job retraining.id.
Descriptors All	KT	kt=program development	DE	de=career change	DE	career change.de.
Exact Term			DE	de=program development	SH	program development.sh.
Word/Phrase			DE	de:program	HW	train$.hw.
Explode (with narrower terms)		kt=exp personnel training				exp program development
Major	KM	km=career change	MJ	mj:career development		*career change
Classification Code	CC	cc=28*; cc=222*; cc=3620	CD	cd:3620*	CC	28.cc. ; 222.cc. 3620.cc.
Age Group	AG	ag=adolescence	AG	ag=180*	AG	school age.ag.
Population Group	PO	po=human	PG	pg=10 human	PO	human.po.
Population Location	PL	pl=usa	GC	gc=usa	LO	usa.lo.
Form/Content Type	FC	fc=empirical study	CT	ct=0800*	FC	empirical study.fc.
Special Feature	SF	sf=assessment instrument	SF	sf=300*	SF	assessment instrument.sf.
Intended Audience	TA	ta=psychology*	IA	ia:juvenile	IA	psychology$.ia.
Conference Information	CF	cf=american psychological	CN	cn=american psychological*	CF	american psychological.cf.
Notes	SO	so=dubin		[display-only field]	NT	reprint$.nt.
Table of Contents		job near creation	TC	tc:job w creation	TC	job creation.tc.
Publication Year	PY	py=1997	YR	yr:1997	YR	1997.yr.
Update Code	UP	up=19970401	DA	da:19980401	UP	19970101.up.

PsycINFO MASTER QUICK REFERENCE GUIDE

FIELD NAME	ProQuest LABEL	ProQuest SEARCH EXAMPLES	SilverPlatter LABEL	SilverPlatter SEARCH EXAMPLES
Accession Number	NO	no(1997-38405-001)	AN	1997-38405-001 in an
Publication Type	DT	dt("journal article")	DT	dt=journal-article
Author	AU	au("vye nancy j")	AU	vye-nancy* in au
Author Affiliation	AA	aa("vanderbilt u")	AF	vanderbilt u in af
Title	TI	ti("job obsolescence")	TI	job obsolescence in ti
Source	SO	so(cognition & instruction)	SO	cognition-and-instruction in so
Journal Name			JN	cognition-and-instruction in jn
Special Issue Title			SI	cognition in si
Book Series Title	SE	se(neuropsychology)	SE	behavioral science in se
Parent Book Title			BK	[display-only field]
Publisher	PB	pb(jossey-bass)	PB	jossey-bass in pb
ISSN	SN	sn(0737-0008)	IS	0737-0008 in is
ISBN	SN	sn(0787901253)	IB	0787901253 in ib
UMI Dissertation Order Number			UM	aam9428690 in um
Language	LN	ln(english)	LA	la=english
Abstract	AB	ab("solution space analysis")	AB	solution space analysis in ab
Key Phrase	ID	id(job retraining)	KP	job retraining in kp
Descriptors All	DE	de("program development")	DE	dyads- in de
Exact Term				
Word/Phrase				
Explode (with narrower terms)			DE	exp teaching methods in de
Major	MJ	mj("career development")	MJ	career-change in mj
Classification Code	CD	cd(2820)	CC	cc=28 ; cc=3620
Age Group	AG	ag("300 adulthood 18 yrs & older")	AG	ag=school-age
Population Group	PG	pg("10 human")	PO	po=human
Population Location	GC	gc(usa)	LO	lo=usa
Form/Content Type	CT	ct("0800 empirical study")	PT	pt=empirical-study
Special Feature	SF	sf(references)	SF	sf=assessment-instrument
Intended Audience	IA	ia(psychology*)	AT	at=psychology*
Conference Information	CN	cn("american psychological")	CF	american psychological in cf
Notes			NT	[display-only field]
Table of Contents	TC	tc(job creation)	TC	job creation in tc
Publication Year	PD	py(1997)	PY	py=1997
Update Code			UD	ud=199701-199712

RELATIONSHIP SECTION

Abandonment [1997]
PN 46   SC 00005
SN Loneliness, anxiety, and emotional and psychological loss of support resulting from desertion or neglect. Used for human populations.
UF   Desertion
R   Attachment Behavior [1985]
↓ Child Abuse [1971]
Child Neglect [1988]
Dependency (Personality) [1967]
↓ Emotional States [1973]
Loneliness [1973]
↓ Relationship Termination [1997]
Separation Anxiety [1973]
↓ Separation Reactions [1997]

Abdomen [1973]
PN 183   SC 00010
B   Anatomy [1967]

Abdominal Wall [1973]
PN 9   SC 00020
B   Muscles [1967]

Abducens Nerve [1973]
PN 20   SC 00030
UF   Nerve (Abducens)
B   Cranial Nerves [1973]

Ability [1967]
PN 3291   SC 00070
SN Conceptually broad term referring to the skills, talents or qualities that enable one to perform a task. Use a more specific term if possible.
UF   Aptitude
Skills
Talent
N   Academic Aptitude [1973]
↓ Cognitive Ability [1973]
↓ Communication Skills [1973]
↓ Employee Skills [1973]
Learning Ability [1973]
↓ Nonverbal Ability [1988]
↓ Reading Skills [1973]
Self Care Skills [1978]
Social Skills [1978]
R   Ability Grouping [1973]
Ability Level [1978]
↓ Achievement Potential [1973]
↓ Competence [1982]
Creativity [1967]
Gifted [1967]
Intelligence [1967]
↓ Performance [1967]

Ability Grouping [1973]
PN 347   SC 00040
SN Grouping or selection of individuals for instructional or other purposes based on differences in ability or achievement.
R   ↓ Ability [1967]
Ability Level [1978]
Academic Aptitude [1973]
↓ Education [1967]
Educational Placement [1978]
Grade Level [1994]
Special Education [1967]

Ability Level [1978]
PN 1048   SC 00050
SN Demonstrated level of performance. Used in academic, cognitive, perceptual, or occupational contexts, as well as an indicator of a patient's level of functioning.

Ability Level — (cont'd)
UF   Functional Status
Level of Functioning
R   ↓ Ability [1967]
Ability Grouping [1973]
Activities of Daily Living [1991]
Adaptive Testing [1985]

Ability Tests
Use   Aptitude Measures

Ablation
Use   Lesions

Aboriginal Populations
Use   Indigenous Populations

Abortion (Induced)
Use   Induced Abortion

Abortion (Spontaneous)
Use   Spontaneous Abortion

Abortion Laws [1973]
PN 82   SC 00110
B   Laws [1967]
R   Induced Abortion [1971]

Abreaction
Use   Catharsis

Absenteeism (Employee)
Use   Employee Absenteeism

Absorption (Physiological) [1973]
PN 69   SC 00140
B   Physiology [1967]
R   Bioavailability [1991]
↓ Cells (Biology) [1973]
Intestines [1973]
Skin (Anatomy) [1967]

Abstinence (Drugs)
Use   Drug Abstinence

Abstinence (Sexual)
Use   Sexual Abstinence

Abstraction [1967]
PN 1027   SC 00160
SN Process of selecting or isolating a certain conceptual aspect from a concrete whole.
B   Thinking [1967]
N   ↓ Imagery [1967]
R   Divergent Thinking [1973]

Abuse of Power [1997]
PN 32   SC 00165
B   Power [1967]
R   Authority [1967]
Coercion [1994]
↓ Dominance [1967]
↓ Leadership [1967]

Abuse Potential (Drugs)
Use   Drug Abuse Liability

Abuse Reporting [1997]
PN 89   SC 00180
N   Child Abuse Reporting [1997]
R   Battered Females [1988]

Abuse Reporting — (cont'd)
R   ↓ Child Abuse [1971]
Duty to Warn [2001]
Elder Abuse [1988]
Informants [1988]
↓ Laws [1967]
Partner Abuse [1991]
Physical Abuse [1991]
Privileged Communication [1973]
Professional Ethics [1973]
↓ Sexual Abuse [1988]

Academic Achievement [1967]
PN 18866   SC 00190
UF   Gradepoint Average
Scholastic Achievement
School Achievement
B   Achievement [1967]
N   Academic Overachievement [1967]
Academic Underachievement [1967]
College Academic Achievement [1967]
Mathematics Achievement [1973]
Reading Achievement [1973]
Science Achievement [1997]
R   Academic Achievement Motivation [1973]
Academic Achievement Prediction [1967]
Academic Aptitude [1973]
Academic Failure [1978]
Academic Self Concept [1997]
↓ Education [1967]
Educational Attainment Level [1997]
School Graduation [1991]
School Learning [1967]
School Transition [1997]

Academic Achievement Motivation [1973]
PN 1840   SC 00200
B   Achievement Motivation [1967]
R   ↓ Academic Achievement [1967]
Academic Self Concept [1997]

Academic Achievement Prediction [1967]
PN 2826   SC 00210
SN Prediction of future academic achievement based on results of tests, inventories, or other measures.
B   Prediction [1967]
R   ↓ Academic Achievement [1967]

Academic Aptitude [1973]
PN 1376   SC 00220
SN Potential ability to perform or achieve in scholastic pursuits.
UF   Aptitude (Academic)
Scholastic Aptitude
B   Ability [1967]
Achievement Potential [1973]
R   Ability Grouping [1973]
↓ Academic Achievement [1967]
↓ Education [1967]
↓ Nonverbal Ability [1988]
Reading Ability [1973]
Student Admission Criteria [1973]
Verbal Ability [1967]

Academic Environment [1973]
PN 513   SC 00230
SN Physical setting or emotional climate where formal instruction takes place.
B   Social Environments [1973]
N   Classroom Environment [1973]
↓ School Environment [1973]
R   Single Sex Environments [2001]

3

Academic Failure [1978]
PN 895   SC 00233
B   Failure [1967]
R ↓ Academic Achievement [1967]
      Academic Underachievement [1967]

Academic Grade Level
Use Grade Level

Academic Overachievement [1967]
PN 471   SC 00240
SN Academic achievement greater than that antici-
pated on basis of one's scholastic aptitude score or
individual intelligence.
UF   Overachievement (Academic)
B   Academic Achievement [1967]

Academic Records
Use Student Records

Academic Self Concept [1997]
PN 316   SC 00248
B   Self Concept [1967]
R ↓ Academic Achievement [1967]
      Academic Achievement Motivation [1973]
      Self Confidence [1994]
      Self Efficacy [1985]
      Self Perception [1967]

Academic Specialization [1973]
PN 1818   SC 00250
SN Concentration of effort or interest in a special
area of knowledge or discipline at an institution of
learning.
UF   College Major
      Specialization (Academic)
R   Educational Aspirations [1973]
      Professional Specialization [1991]

Academic Underachievement [1967]
PN 1624   SC 00260
SN Academic achievement less than that expected
based on one's scholastic aptitude score or individual
intelligence.
UF   Underachievement (Academic)
B   Academic Achievement [1967]
R   Academic Failure [1978]
   ↓ Failure [1967]

Acalculia [1973]
PN 112   SC 00270
SN Form of aphasia involving impaired ability to
perform simple arithmetic calculations.
UF   Dyscalculia
B   Aphasia [1967]
R ↓ Learning Disabilities [1973]

Accelerated Speech
Use Speech Rate

Acceleration Effects [1973]
PN 174   SC 00290
SN Behavioral, physiological, or psychological
effects resulting from acceleration onset/offset or the
effects of changes in acceleration rate. Used for both
human and animal populations.
R ↓ Aviation [1967]
      Decompression Effects [1973]
      Flight Simulation [1973]
   ↓ Gravitational Effects [1967]
      Physiological Stress [1967]
      Spaceflight [1967]

Acceptance (Social)
Use Social Acceptance

Accessory Nerve
Use Cranial Nerves

Accident Prevention [1973]
PN 511   SC 00330
B   Prevention [1973]
R ↓ Accidents [1967]
      Risk Management [1997]
   ↓ Safety [1967]
   ↓ Transportation Accidents [1973]
      Warning Labels [1997]
   ↓ Warnings [1997]

Accident Proneness [1973]
PN 165   SC 00340
R ↓ Accidents [1967]
   ↓ Safety [1967]

Accidents [1967]
PN 749   SC 00350
N   Home Accidents [1973]
      Industrial Accidents [1973]
      Pedestrian Accidents [1973]
   ↓ Transportation Accidents [1973]
R   Accident Prevention [1973]
      Accident Proneness [1973]
   ↓ Disasters [1973]
      Driving Under The Influence [1988]
   ↓ Hazardous Materials [1991]
      Hazards [1973]
   ↓ Injuries [1973]
   ↓ Safety [1967]
      Warning Labels [1997]
   ↓ Warnings [1997]

Acclimatization (Thermal)
Use Thermal Acclimatization

Accomplishment
Use Achievement

Accountability [1988]
PN 381   SC 00385
SN Liability and/or responsibility for specified results
or outcomes of an activity over which one has author-
ity.
B   Responsibility [1973]
R   Blame [1994]
   ↓ Competence [1982]
      Consumer Protection [1973]
      Criminal Responsibility [1991]
      Duty to Warn [2001]
   ↓ Management [1967]
      Professional Liability [1985]
   ↓ Professional Standards [1973]
      Quality Control [1988]
      Quality of Care [1988]

Accountants [1973]
PN 291   SC 00390
UF   Certified Public Accountants
B   White Collar Workers [1973]

Accreditation (Education Personnel) [1973]
PN 97   SC 00400
SN Professional licensing or certification of teach-
ers, school psychologists, or other educational per-
sonnel, usually required for employment.
UF   Teacher Accreditation
B   Professional Certification [1973]

Accreditation (Education Personnel) —
(cont'd)
R   Professional Licensing [1973]
   ↓ Education [1967]
      Educational Quality [1997]
      Professional Examinations [1994]

Accreditation (Educational Programs)
Use Educational Program Accreditation

Acculturation
SN Term was discontinued in 1982. In 2000, the
term was stripped from all records containing it, and
replaced with CULTURAL ASSIMILATION, its postable counterpart.
Use Cultural Assimilation

Acetaldehyde [1982]
PN 81   SC 00415
SN First oxidation product of primary alcohol
metabolism. Acetaldehyde has narcotic properties.
UF   Acetic Aldehyde
      Ethanal
      Ethylaldehyde
R ↓ Alcohols [1967]
   ↓ Carbohydrate Metabolism [1973]
   ↓ Dopamine Metabolites [1982]

Acetazolamide [1973]
PN 30   SC 00420
B   Diuretics [1973]
      Enzyme Inhibitors [1985]
R ↓ Anticonvulsive Drugs [1973]

Acetic Aldehyde
Use Acetaldehyde

Acetylcholine [1973]
PN 837   SC 00430
B   Cholinergic Drugs [1973]
      Cholinomimetic Drugs [1973]
      Neurotransmitters [1985]
R   Acetylcholinesterase [1973]
   ↓ Choline [1973]
      Cholinergic Nerves [1973]

Acetylcholinesterase [1973]
PN 287   SC 00440
B   Esterases [1973]
R   Acetylcholine [1973]
      Cholinesterase [1973]

Acetylsalicylic Acid
Use Aspirin

Aches
Use Pain

Achievement [1967]
PN 3316   SC 00470
UF   Accomplishment
      Attainment (Achievement)
UF   Success
N ↓ Academic Achievement [1967]
      Occupational Success [1978]
R ↓ Achievement Measures [1967]
   ↓ Competence [1982]
   ↓ Failure [1967]
   ↓ Performance [1967]

Achievement Measures [1967]
PN 2053   SC 00490

Achievement Measures — (cont'd)
SN Tests designed to measure knowledge and/or skills acquired from learning, experience, or training.
UF Tests (Achievement)
B Measurement [1967]
N Iowa Tests of Basic Skills [1973]
     Stanford Achievement Test [1973]
     Wide Range Achievement Test [1973]
     Woodcock Johnson Psychoeducational Battery [2001]
R ↓ Achievement [1967]
     Criterion Referenced Tests [1982]

Achievement Motivation [1967]
PN 3429   **SC** 00500
SN Need that drives an individual to improve, succeed, or excel.
UF NAch
     Need Achievement
B Motivation [1967]
N Academic Achievement Motivation [1973]
R ↓ Achievement Potential [1973]
     Fear of Success [1978]
     ↓ Needs [1967]

Achievement Potential [1973]
PN 180   **SC** 00510
SN One's general ability to achieve in any area, including academic.
UF Potential (Achievement)
N Academic Aptitude [1973]
R ↓ Ability [1967]
     ↓ Achievement Motivation [1967]

Achilles Tendon Reflex [1973]
PN 14   **SC** 00520
B Reflexes [1971]

Achromatic Color [1973]
PN 143   **SC** 00530
SN Visual quality which lacks hue and saturation, consequently varying only in brilliance. Includes variations from black through gray to white.
B Color [1967]
R ↓ Chromaticity [1997]
     Color Saturation [1997]

Acids [1973]
PN 520   **SC** 00550
N ↓ Amino Acids [1973]
     Ascorbic Acid [1973]
     Aspirin [1973]
     Dihydroxyphenylacetic Acid [1991]
     ↓ Fatty Acids [1973]
     Heparin [1973]
     Homovanillic Acid [1978]
     Hydroxyindoleacetic Acid (5-) [1985]
     Kainic Acid [1988]
     Lactic Acid [1991]
     Lysergic Acid Diethylamide [1967]
     Nicotinic Acid [1973]
     ↓ Nucleic Acids [1973]
N Taurine [1982]
     Uric Acid [1973]
R ↓ Drugs [1967]
     ↓ Solvents [1982]

Acoustic Nerve [1973]
PN 122   **SC** 00570
UF Auditory Nerve
     Nerve (Acoustic)
B Cranial Nerves [1973]

Acoustic Reflex [1973]
PN 450   **SC** 00580
SN Bilateral contraction of stapedius muscles when a loud sound is presented.
UF Intra Aural Muscle Reflex
     Stapedius Reflex
B Reflexes [1971]
R Startle Reflex [1967]

Acoustic Stimuli
Use Auditory Stimulation

Acoustics [1997]
PN 364   **SC** 00591
SN Structural properties of auditorially perceived stimuli or sounds.
UF Sound Waves
R ↓ Auditory Perception [1967]
     ↓ Auditory Stimulation [1967]
     Noise Effects [1973]
     ↓ Speech Characteristics [1973]
     ↓ Stimulus Parameters [1967]

Acquaintance Rape [1991]
PN 248   **SC** 00593
SN Rape perpetrated by a person or persons known to the victim.
UF Date Rape
B Rape [1973]
R ↓ Human Courtship [1973]
     Social Dating [1973]

Acquired Immune Deficiency Syndrome [1988]
PN 5855   **SC** 00595
UF AIDS
B Human Immunodeficiency Virus Syndromes [1991]
R AIDS (Attitudes Toward) [1997]
     AIDS Dementia Complex [1997]
     AIDS Prevention [1994]
     HIV Testing [1997]
     ↓ Venereal Diseases [1973]
     Zidovudine [1994]

Acrophobia [1973]
PN 53   **SC** 00600
SN Fear of heights.
B Phobias [1967]

ACTH (Hormone)
Use Corticotropin

ACTH Releasing Factor
Use Corticotropin Releasing Factor

Acting Out [1967]
PN 525   **SC** 00620
SN Behavioral manifestation of those impulses and desires that are unacceptable or irreconcilable with an individual's conscience. When such behavior becomes maladaptive, socially or personally, it is classified as an acting out disorder.
B Symptoms [1967]
R ↓ Behavior Disorders [1971]
     ↓ Emotionally Disturbed [1973]
     Enactments [1997]

Active Avoidance
Use Avoidance Conditioning

Activism (Student)
Use Student Activism

Activist Movements [1973]
PN 465   **SC** 00650
SN Doctrines or practices emphasizing direct, vigorous action (usually political) in support of or opposition to one side of a controversial issue.
B Social Movements [1967]
N Student Activism
R Black Power Movement [1973]
     Civil Rights Movement [1973]
     Homosexual Liberation Movement [1973]
     School Integration [1982]
     ↓ Social Integration [1982]
     Womens Liberation Movement [1973]

Activities of Daily Living [1991]
PN 1224   **SC** 00655
SN Basic personal care skills such as eating, bathing, dressing, and other personal hygienic skills used to measure functional ability in the elderly and the emotionally and physically disabled. Compare DAILY ACTIVITIES.
R Ability Level [1978]
     Activity Level [1982]
     Daily Activities [1994]
     Geriatric Assessment [1997]
     Habilitation [1991]
     Hygiene [1994]
     Independent Living Programs [1991]
     Physical Mobility [1994]
     ↓ Rehabilitation [1967]
     Self Care Skills [1978]

Activity Level [1982]
PN 5471   **SC** 00660
SN General energetic state of an organism, frequently used as a measure of drug effects but not restricted to this application.
B Motor Processes [1967]
R Activities of Daily Living [1991]
     Daily Activities [1994]
     ↓ Motivation [1967]
     Physical Mobility [1994]
     Rotational Behavior [1994]

Activity Therapy
Use Recreation Therapy

Actualization (Self)
Use Self Actualization

Acupuncture [1973]
PN 341   **SC** 00690
B Alternative Medicine [1997]
     Physical Treatment Methods [1973]

Acute Alcoholic Intoxication [1973]
PN 46   **SC** 00700
SN Temporary mental disturbance marked by muscle incoordination and paresis as the result of excessive alcohol ingestion.
B Alcohol Intoxication [1973]
     Brain Disorders [1967]
     Toxic Disorders [1973]
R Toxic Encephalopathies [1973]

Acute Paranoid Disorder
Use Paranoia (Psychosis)

Acute Psychosis [1973]
PN 365   **SC** 00710
SN In 1988, this term replaced the discontinued term ACUTE PSYCHOTIC EPISODE. In 2000, ACUTE PSYCHOTIC EPISODE was stripped from all records and replaced with ACUTE PSYCHOSIS.

Acute Psychosis — (cont'd)
UF　Acute Psychotic Episode
　　Brief Reactive Psychosis
　　Psychotic Episode (Acute)
B　Psychosis　1967
N　Acute Schizophrenia　1973
R　Postpartum Depression　1973

Acute Psychotic Episode
SN　Term was discontinued in 1988. In 2000, the term was stripped from all records containing it, and replaced with ACUTE PSYCHOSIS, its postable counterpart.
Use　Acute Psychosis

Acute Schizophrenia　1973
PN　600　　　　　　　　　　　　SC　00730
B　Acute Psychosis　1973
　　Schizophrenia　1967
R　Postpartum Depression　1973

Adaptability (Personality)　1973
PN　628　　　　　　　　　　　　SC　00740
SN　Ability to be flexible and to maximize functioning in the face of environmental changes. See ADJUST-MENT for terms relating to the process of adapting.
UF　Flexibility (Personality)
B　Personality Traits　1967
R　↓ Adjustment　1967
　　Agreeableness　1997
　　Coping Behavior　1967
　　Hardiness　1997
　　Openness to Experience　1997

Adaptation　1967
PN　1384　　　　　　　　　　　SC　00750
SN　Physiological or biological modification of an organism or its morphology in response to the physical environment. For psychological, social, or emotional adaptation, use ADJUSTMENT or one of its narrower or related terms.
UF　Readaptation
N　Environmental Adaptation　1973
　　↓ Sensory Adaptation　1967
　　Thermal Acclimatization　1973

Adaptation (Dark)
Use　Dark Adaptation

Adaptation (Environmental)
Use　Environmental Adaptation

Adaptation (Light)
Use　Light Adaptation

Adaptation (Sensory)
Use　Sensory Adaptation

Adaptation (Social)
Use　Social Adjustment

Adaptive Behavior　1991
PN　560　　　　　　　　　　　　SC　00793
SN　Behaviors indicating ability to take care of personal needs, function socially, and control problem behavior. Primarily used for disabled or disordered populations.
B　Behavior　1967
R　↓ Adjustment　1967
　　↓ Mental Disorders　1967
　　↓ Mental Retardation　1967
　　↓ Rehabilitation　1967
　　Self Care Skills　1978

Adaptive Behavior — (cont'd)
R　Social Skills　1978
　　Special Education　1967

Adaptive Testing　1985
PN　213　　　　　　　　　　　　SC　00795
SN　Testing method, usually using a computer, in which test items of varying difficulty levels are selected according to the degree to which the examinee's previous answers were correct.
UF　Tailored Testing
B　Testing Methods　1967
R　Ability Level　1978
　　Computer Assisted Testing　1988
　　Item Analysis (Statistical)　1973
　　↓ Test Construction　1973

Addiction　1973
PN　880　　　　　　　　　　　　SC　00800
B　Behavior Disorders　1971
N　↓ Alcoholism　1967
　　↓ Drug Addiction　1967
　　Sexual Addiction　1997
R　Craving　1997
　　↓ Drug Abuse　1973
　　↓ Drug Usage　1971
　　Pathological Gambling　1988

Addisons Disease　1973
PN　18　　　　　　　　　　　　　SC　00810
B　Adrenal Gland Disorders　1973
　　Syndromes　1973
R　↓ Tuberculosis　1973

Adenosine　1973
PN　424　　　　　　　　　　　　SC　00820
B　Nucleic Acids　1973

ADHD
Use　Attention Deficit Disorder with Hyperactivity

Adjectives　1973
PN　412　　　　　　　　　　　　SC　00830
B　Form Classes (Language)　1973

Adjudication　1967
PN　3722　　　　　　　　　　　SC　00840
SN　Process of judicial decision-making. Use ADJUDICATION to access references to juries from 1967-1984.
UF　Courts
UF　Juvenile Court
　　Sentencing
　　Verdict Determination
B　Law Enforcement　1978
N　Court Referrals　1994
R　Criminal Conviction　1973
　　↓ Criminal Justice　1991
　　Criminal Responsibility　1991
　　Juries　1985
　　Jury Selection　1994
　　Legal Decisions　1991
　　↓ Legal Evidence　1991

Adjunctive Behavior　1982
PN　58　　　　　　　　　　　　　SC　00845
SN　Noncontingent appropriate or inappropriate behavior that is maintained by an event which acquires its reinforcing characteristics as the result of some other ongoing reinforcement contingency.
B　Behavior　1967
N　Polydipsia　1982
R　↓ Operant Conditioning　1967

Adjunctive Behavior — (cont'd)
R　Pica　1973

Adjustment　1967
PN　7961　　　　　　　　　　　SC　00850
SN　Conceptually broad term referring to a state of harmony between internal needs and external demands and the processes used in achieving this condition. Use a more specific term if possible. Differentiate from ADAPTATION, which refers to physiological or biological adaptation.
N　↓ Emotional Adjustment　1973
　　Occupational Adjustment　1973
　　School Adjustment　1967
　　Social Adjustment　1973
R　Adaptability (Personality)　1973
　　Adaptive Behavior　1991
　　Person Environment Fit　1991
　　Well Being　1994
　　Work Adjustment Training　1991

Adjustment Disorders　1994
PN　150　　　　　　　　　　　　SC　00855
SN　Maladaptive reaction to psychosocial stressors which impairs social or occupational functioning. Usually a temporary condition that remits after new levels of adaptation are obtained or stressors have been removed.
B　Mental Disorders　1967
R　Coping Behavior　1967
　　↓ Emotional Adjustment　1973
　　Emotional Trauma　1967
　　Occupational Adjustment　1973
　　Posttraumatic Stress Disorder　1985
　　School Adjustment　1967
　　Social Adjustment　1973
　　↓ Stress　1967
　　Stress Reactions　1973

Adler (Alfred)　1967
PN　372　　　　　　　　　　　　SC　00860
SN　Identifies biographical or autobiographical studies and discussions of Adler's works.
R　Adlerian Psychotherapy　1997
　　Individual Psychology　1973
　　↓ Psychologists　1967

Adlerian Psychotherapy　1997
PN　188　　　　　　　　　　　　SC　00865
UF　Individual Psychotherapy (Adlerian)
B　Psychoanalysis　1967
B　Psychotherapy　1967
R　Adler (Alfred)　1967
　　Individual Psychology　1973

Administration (Test)
Use　Test Administration

Administrators
Use　Management Personnel

Administrators (School)
Use　School Administrators

Admission (Hospital)
Use　Hospital Admission

Admission (Psychiatric Hospital)
Use　Psychiatric Hospital Admission

Admission Criteria (Student)
Use　Student Admission Criteria

Adolescent Attitudes 1988
PN 3146 **SC** 00925
SN Attitudes of, not toward, adolescents.
B Attitudes 1967

Adolescent Development 1973
PN 4872 **SC** 00930
SN Process of physical, cognitive, personality, and psychosocial growth occurring from age 13 through 17. Use a more specific term if possible.
B Human Development 1967
R ↓ Childhood Development 1967
Developmental Age Groups 1973
↓ Developmental Stages 1973
↓ Physical Development 1973
↓ Psychogenesis 1973
Sex Linked Developmental Differences 1973
Sexual Development 1973

Adolescent Fathers 1985
PN 178 **SC** 00932
SN Fathers aged 13-17 years.
UF Teenage Fathers
B Fathers 1967
R Adolescent Pregnancy 1988

Adolescent Mothers 1985
PN 1025 **SC** 00935
SN Mothers aged 13-17 years. Consider also UNWED MOTHERS.
UF Teenage Mothers
B Mothers 1967
R Adolescent Pregnancy 1988

Adolescent Pregnancy 1988
PN 947 **SC** 00936
UF Teenage Pregnancy
B Pregnancy 1967
R Adolescent Fathers 1985
Adolescent Mothers 1985
↓ Social Issues 1991

Adolescent Psychiatry 1985
PN 552 **SC** 00937
B Psychiatry 1967
R Adolescent Psychotherapy 1994

Adolescent Psychology 1973
PN 277 **SC** 00940
SN Branch of developmental psychology devoted to the study and treatment of adolescents. Use a more specific term if possible.
B Developmental Psychology 1973

Adolescent Psychotherapy 1994
PN 470 **SC** 00945
B Psychotherapy 1967
R Adolescent Psychiatry 1985
↓ Child Psychotherapy 1967

Adopted Children 1973
PN 717 **SC** 00960
B Adoptees 1985
Family Members 1973
R ↓ Adoption (Child) 1967
Interracial Adoption 1994

Adoptees 1985
PN 302 **SC** 00965
SN Anyone who has been formally adopted as a dependent. Limited to human populations.
N Adopted Children 1973
R ↓ Adoption (Child) 1967

Adoptees — (cont'd)
R Interracial Adoption 1994

Adoption (Child) 1967
PN 930 **SC** 00970
B Legal Processes 1973
N Interracial Adoption 1994
R Adopted Children 1973
↓ Adoptees 1985
Adoptive Parents 1973
Child Welfare 1988

Adoptive Parents 1973
PN 471 **SC** 00980
B Parents 1967
R ↓ Adoption (Child) 1967
Interracial Adoption 1994

Adrenal Cortex Hormones 1973
PN 189 **SC** 00990
B Hormones 1967
N Aldosterone 1973
Corticosterone 1973
Cortisone 1973
Deoxycorticosterone 1973
↓ Glucocorticoids 1982
Hydrocortisone 1973
Prednisolone 1973
R ↓ Adrenal Glands 1973
↓ Adrenal Medulla Hormones 1973
↓ Corticosteroids 1973
↓ Stress 1967

Adrenal Cortex Steroids
Use Corticosteroids

Adrenal Gland Disorders 1973
PN 61 **SC** 01010
B Endocrine Disorders 1973
N Addisons Disease 1973
Cushings Syndrome 1973
R ↓ Endocrine Sexual Disorders 1973
↓ Pituitary Disorders 1973

Adrenal Gland Secretion 1973
PN 80 **SC** 01020
B Endocrine Gland Secretion 1973

Adrenal Glands 1973
PN 471 **SC** 01030
B Endocrine Glands 1973
N Hypothalamo Pituitary Adrenal System 1997
R ↓ Adrenal Cortex Hormones 1973

Adrenal Medulla Hormones 1973
PN 45 **SC** 01040
B Hormones 1967
N Norepinephrine 1973
R ↓ Adrenal Cortex Hormones 1973

Adrenalectomy 1973
PN 376 **SC** 01050
B Endocrine Gland Surgery 1973

Adrenaline
Use Epinephrine

Adrenergic Blocking Drugs 1973
PN 1071 **SC** 01070
UF Beta Blockers
B Drugs 1967
N Alpha Methylparatyrosine 1978

Adrenergic Blocking Drugs — (cont'd)
N Dihydroergotamine 1973
Hydroxydopamine (6-) 1978
Phenoxybenzamine 1973
Propranolol 1973
Yohimbine 1988
R ↓ Antihypertensive Drugs 1973
↓ Ergot Derivatives 1973
↓ Sympathetic Nervous System 1973
↓ Sympatholytic Drugs 1973
↓ Tricyclic Antidepressant Drugs 1997

Adrenergic Drugs 1973
PN 411 **SC** 01080
SN In 1997, this term replaced the discontinued term ADRENOLYTIC DRUGS. In 2000, ADRE-NOLYTIC DRUGS was stripped from all records and replaced with ADRENERGIC DRUGS.
UF Adrenolytic Drugs
B Drugs 1967
N ↓ Amphetamine 1967
Dextroamphetamine 1973
Ephedrine 1973
Epinephrine 1967
Methoxamine 1973
Tyramine 1973
R ↓ Catecholamines 1973
Serotonin 1973
↓ Sympathetic Nervous System 1973
↓ Sympathomimetic Drugs 1973

Adrenergic Nerves 1973
PN 327 **SC** 01090
UF Nerves (Adrenergic)
B Autonomic Nervous System 1967

Adrenocorticotropin
Use Corticotropin

Adrenolytic Drugs
SN Term was discontinued in 1997. In 2000, the term was stripped from all records containing it, and replaced with ADRENERGIC DRUGS, its postable counterpart.
Use Adrenergic Drugs

Adult Attitudes 1988
PN 6361 **SC** 01122
SN Attitudes of, not toward, adults.
B Attitudes 1967

Adult Children
Use Adult Offspring

Adult Day Care 1997
PN 67 **SC** 01125
SN In home- or center-based care of physically or mentally disabled adults during daytime hours, providing personal, social, and homemaker services.
R Day Care Centers 1973
Elder Care 1994
Home Care 1985
Home Visiting Programs 1973
Long Term Care 1994

Adult Development 1978
PN 3028 **SC** 01127
SN Process of physical, cognitive, personality, and psychosocial growth occurring from age 18. Use a more specific term if possible.
B Human Development 1967
R Adult Learning 1997
Developmental Age Groups 1973

Adult Development — (cont'd)
R　↓ Developmental Stages　1973
　　Generativity　2001
　　Mentor　1985
　　Physiological Aging　1967
　↓ Psychogenesis　1973

Adult Education　1973
PN 1513　　　　　　　　**SC** 01130
SN Formal or informal education for adults, including but not limited to basic education, high school equivalency, vocational education, correspondence courses, continuing education, non-degree coursework, and lifelong learning programs.
UF　High School Equivalency
B　Education　1967
N　↓ Continuing Education　1985
R　Adult Learning　1997
　　Literacy Programs　1997
　　Reentry Students　1985

Adult Learning　1997
PN 146　　　　　　　　**SC** 01133
B　Learning　1967
R　Adult Development　1978
　↓ Adult Education　1973
　↓ Continuing Education　1985
　　Reentry Students　1985

Adult Offspring　1985
PN 2384　　　　　　　　**SC** 01135
SN Ages 18 or older.
UF　Adult Children
　　Grown Children
B　Family Members　1973
　　Offspring　1988
R　Empty Nest　1991

Adultery
Use　Extramarital Intercourse

Advance Directives　1994
PN 170　　　　　　　　**SC** 01163
SN Declaration of personal wishes through legal documents or written instructions pertaining to future medical care if one becomes incapacitated.
UF　Living Wills
R　Assisted Suicide　1997
　↓ Client Rights　1988
　↓ Death and Dying　1967
　　Euthanasia　1973
　↓ Legal Processes　1973
　　Life Sustaining Treatment　1997
　　Palliative Care　1991
　　Terminally Ill Patients　1973
　　Treatment Refusal　1994
　　Treatment Withholding　1988

Advance Organizers　1985
PN 183　　　　　　　　**SC** 01165
SN Structural overview of material to be taught to facilitate incorporation of new material into that previously learned or known.
UF　Structured Overview
B　Instructional Media　1967
　　Teaching Methods　1967
R　↓ Learning Strategies　1991
　　Study Habits　1973

Adventitious Disorders　2001
PN 0　　　　　　　　**SC** 01168

Adventitious Disorders — (cont'd)
SN Disabilities that are accidental or acquired, rather than congenital. The term ADVENTITIOUSLY HANDICAPPED was used to represent the concept from 1973-1996, and ADVENTITIOUSLY DISABLED was used from 1997-2000. In 2000, ADVENTITIOUS DISORDERS was created to replace the discontinued and deleted term ADVENTITIOUSLY DISABLED. ADVENTITIOUSLY DISABLED and ADVENTITIOUSLY HANDICAPPED were stripped from all records and replaced with ADVENTITIOUS DISORDERS.
UF　Adventitiously Handicapped
B　Disorders　1967
R　↓ Congenital Disorders　1973

Adventitiously Handicapped
SN The term was discontinued in 1997, when the term ADVENTITIOUSLY DISABLED was created to capture this concept. In 2000, with the deletion of the term ADVENTITIOUSLY DISABLED, ADVENTITIOUSLY HANDICAPPED was made a nonpostable term for the postable term ADVENTITIOUS DISORDERS. ADVENTITIOUSLY DISABLED and ADVENTITIOUSLY HANDICAPPED were stripped from all records and replaced with ADVENTITIOUS DISORDERS.
Use　Adventitious Disorders

Adverbs　1973
PN 65　　　　　　　　**SC** 01180
B　Form Classes (Language)　1973

Advertising　1967
PN 2567　　　　　　　　**SC** 01190
N　Television Advertising　1973
R　Brand Names　1978
　　Brand Preferences　1994
　↓ Consumer Research　1973
　　Marketing　1973
　↓ Mass Media　1967
　　Product Design　1997
　　Public Relations　1973
　↓ Quality of Services　1997
　　Retailing　1991

Advocacy　1985
PN 790　　　　　　　　**SC** 01195
SN The process of defending or pleading the cause of another individual or group.
UF　Child Advocacy
R　Child Welfare　1988
　↓ Civil Rights　1978
　　Empowerment　1991
　↓ Government Policy Making　1973
　　Legislative Processes　1973
　　Right to Treatment　1997

Aerobic Exercise　1988
PN 429　　　　　　　　**SC** 01197
B　Exercise　1973
R　Health Behavior　1982
　　Physical Fitness　1973
　　Weight Control　1985

Aerospace Personnel　1973
PN 457　　　　　　　　**SC** 01200
UF　Aircraft Crew
　　Aviation Personnel
　　Flight Attendants
　　Navigators (Aircraft)
B　Professional Personnel　1978
N　Aircraft Pilots　1973
　　Astronauts　1973

Aerospace Personnel — (cont'd)
R　↓ Business and Industrial Personnel　1967
　　Engineers　1967
　　Physicists　1973
　　Scientists　1967

Aesthetic Preferences　1973
PN 1233　　　　　　　　**SC** 01210
B　Preferences　1967
R　Aesthetics　1967
　　Interior Design　1982

Aesthetics　1967
PN 1052　　　　　　　　**SC** 01220
SN Scientific or philosophical study of beauty or judgments of beauty. Also, the aesthetic qualities themselves.
R　Aesthetic Preferences　1973
　↓ Arts　1973
　　Interior Design　1982

Aetiology
Use　Etiology

Affairs (Sexual)
Use　Extramarital Intercourse

Affection　1973
PN 486　　　　　　　　**SC** 01250
UF　Liking
B　Emotional States　1973
R　↓ Interpersonal Interaction　1967
　　Intimacy　1973
　　Love　1973
　　Physical Contact　1982
　↓ Psychosexual Behavior　1967
　　Romance　1997
　　Sexuality　1973

Affective Disorders　2001
PN 5532　　　　　　　　**SC** 01255
SN Mental disorder characterized by a disturbance in mood which is abnormally depressed or elated. Compare EMOTIONAL STABILITY or EMOTIONALLY DISTURBED. AFFECTIVE DISTURBANCES was used for this concept from 1967-2000.
UF　Affective Disturbances
　　Mood Disorders
B　Mental Disorders　1967
N　↓ Bipolar Disorder　2001
　↓ Major Depression　1988
　↓ Mania　1967
　　Seasonal Affective Disorder　1991
R　↓ Affective Psychosis　1973
　　Schizoaffective Disorder　1994

Affective Disturbances
SN In 2000, the term was discontinued, and all records containing it were stripped of the term and replaced with AFFECTIVE DISORDERS, its postable counterpart.
Use　Affective Disorders

Affective Education　1982
PN 461　　　　　　　　**SC** 01265
SN Curriculum aimed at changing emotional and social behavior of students and enhancing their understanding of such behavior.
UF　Humanistic Education
B　Curriculum　1967
R　Self Actualization　1973
　↓ Self Concept　1967
　　Social Skills　1978

Affective Psychosis [1973]
PN 350   SC 01270
B   Psychosis [1967]
N   ↓ Involutional Depression [1973]
R   ↓ Affective Disorders [2001]
     ↓ Bipolar Disorder [2001]

Afferent Pathways [1982]
PN 1087   SC 01275
SN   Collections of fibers that carry neural impulses toward neural processing areas from sensory mechanisms or other processing areas.
UF   Sensory Pathways
B   Neural Pathways [1982]
N   ↓ Lemniscal System [1985]
     Spinothalamic Tracts [1973]
R   Dorsal Horns [1985]
     ↓ Efferent Pathways [1982]
     ↓ Receptive Fields [1985]
     ↓ Sensory Neurons [1973]

Afferent Stimulation [1973]
PN 172   SC 01280
SN   Sensory stimulation causing nerve impulses to be carried toward the brain, spinal cord, or sensory relay and processing areas.
UF   Afferentation
B   Stimulation [1967]
R   ↓ Nervous System [1967]
     ↓ Perceptual Stimulation [1973]
     ↓ Stereotaxic Techniques [1973]
     ↓ Surgery [1971]

Afferentation
Use   Afferent Stimulation

Affiliation Motivation [1967]
PN 674   SC 01300
SN   Need for association with others and formation of friendships.
UF   Need for Affiliation
B   Motivation [1967]
R   ↓ Needs [1967]

Affirmative Action [1985]
PN 305   SC 01305
SN   Programs or policies designed to actively recruit females and minority group members for employment or higher education, in an effort to correct underrepresentative distributions of these groups relative to the general population.
R   Age Discrimination [1994]
     ↓ Civil Rights [1978]
     Disability Discrimination [1997]
     Employment Discrimination [1994]
     Minority Groups [1967]
     ↓ Personnel [1967]
     ↓ Personnel Management [1973]
     ↓ Personnel Recruitment [1973]
     ↓ Personnel Selection [1967]
     Race and Ethnic Discrimination [1994]
     Sex Discrimination [1978]
     ↓ Social Discrimination [1982]
     Social Equality [1973]

African Americans
Use   Blacks

Aftercare [1973]
PN 631   SC 01320
SN   Continuing program of rehabilitation designed to reinforce and maintain the effects of treatment and to help clients adjust to their environment after hospital release.

Aftercare — (cont'd)
B   Treatment [1967]
R   Discharge Planning [1994]
     Maintenance Therapy [1997]
     Outpatient Commitment [1991]
     ↓ Outpatient Treatment [1967]
     Partial Hospitalization [1985]
     Posttreatment Followup [1973]
     ↓ Treatment Planning [1997]

Aftereffect (Perceptual)
Use   Perceptual Aftereffect

Afterimage [1967]
PN 258   SC 01340
SN   Persistence of sensory excitation, usually visual, after cessation of stimulation. This temporary illusory sensation is due to physiological changes in the receptor cells.
UF   Successive Contrast
B   Perceptual Aftereffect [1967]

Age Differences [1967]
PN 38350   SC 01360
SN   Age comparisons of behavioral, developmental, and cognitive variations between individuals or groups. Used for human or animal subjects. In 1982, this term replaced the discontinued term DEVELOPMENTAL DIFFERENCES. In 2000, DEVELOPMENTAL DIFFERENCES was stripped from all records and replaced with AGE DIFFERENCES.
UF   Developmental Differences
R   Animal Development [1978]
     Cohort Analysis [1988]
     ↓ Development [1967]
     Developmental Age Groups [1973]
R   Generation Gap [1973]
     Grade Level [1994]
     ↓ Human Development [1967]
     ↓ Physical Development [1973]
     ↓ Psychogenesis [1973]

Age Discrimination [1994]
PN 50   SC 01363
SN   Use SOCIAL DISCRIMINATION to access references from 1982-1993.
B   Social Discrimination [1982]
R   Affirmative Action [1985]
     Aged (Attitudes Toward) [1978]
     Aging (Attitudes Toward) [1985]
     ↓ Civil Rights [1978]
     Employment Discrimination [1994]
     ↓ Prejudice [1967]

Age Regression (Hypnotic) [1988]
PN 69   SC 01365
SN   Technique used to recapture early or past life experiences by guiding clients back through their history, usually year by year.
B   Hypnosis [1967]
     Hypnotherapy [1973]
R   Early Experience [1967]
     Early Memories [1985]
     Enactments [1997]
     False Memory [1997]
     Life Experiences [1973]
     ↓ Psychotherapeutic Techniques [1967]
     Repressed Memory [1997]

Aged (Attitudes Toward) [1978]
PN 1150   SC 01372
B   Attitudes [1967]
R   Age Discrimination [1994]
     ↓ Aging [1991]

Aged (Attitudes Toward) — (cont'd)
R   Aging (Attitudes Toward) [1985]
     Geriatrics [1967]
     Gerontology [1967]
     Physiological Aging [1967]

Agencies (Groups)
Use   Organizations

Aggressive Behavior [1967]
PN 9487   SC 01390
UF   Agonistic Behavior
     Fighting
B   Social Behavior [1967]
N   ↓ Animal Aggressive Behavior [1973]
     Attack Behavior [1973]
     Coercion [1994]
     ↓ Conflict [1967]
R   ↓ Behavior Disorders [1971]
     Conduct Disorder [1991]
     Cruelty [1973]
     Retaliation [1991]
     ↓ Social Interaction [1967]
     Torture [1988]

Aggressiveness [1973]
PN 1591   SC 01400
B   Personality Traits [1967]

Agility (Physical)
Use   Physical Agility

Aging [1991]
PN 3101   SC 01413
N   Physiological Aging [1967]
R   Aged (Attitudes Toward) [1978]
     Aging (Attitudes Toward) [1985]
     Developmental Age Groups [1973]
     ↓ Developmental Stages [1973]
     Generativity [2001]
     Geriatric Psychiatry [1997]
     Geriatric Psychotherapy [1973]
     Geriatrics [1967]
     Gerontology [1967]
     ↓ Human Development [1967]
     Life Expectancy [1982]

Aging (Attitudes Toward) [1985]
PN 566   SC 01415
SN   Attitudes toward the aging process. Includes attitudes toward one's own physical aging and psychological and social maturation.
B   Attitudes [1967]
R   Age Discrimination [1994]
     Aged (Attitudes Toward) [1978]
     ↓ Aging [1991]
     ↓ Physical Development [1973]
     Physiological Aging [1967]
     ↓ Psychosocial Development [1973]
     Self Perception [1967]

Aging (Physiological)
Use   Physiological Aging

Agitated Depression
Use   Major Depression

Agitation [1991]
PN 340   SC 01440
SN   State usually characterized by restlessness, anxiety, and anguish.
R   Akathisia [1991]
     ↓ Anxiety [1967]

Agitation — (cont'd)
R   Distress [1973]
    Restlessness [1973]

Agnosia [1973]
PN   391   SC   01450
SN   Inability to recognize, understand, or interpret sensory stimuli in the absence of sensory defects. Also, the selective loss of knowledge of specific objects due to emotional disturbance, as seen in schizophrenia, hysteria, or depression.
B   Aphasia [1967]
    Perceptual Disturbances [1973]
N   Anosognosia [1994]
    Prosopagnosia [1994]

Agonistic Behavior
   Use   Aggressive Behavior

Agoraphobia [1973]
PN   1843   SC   01480
SN   Excessive fear of being alone, or being in public places or situations (e.g., in crowds or elevators) from which there is no easy escape or where help cannot be obtained in the event of an incapacitating reaction or panic.
B   Phobias [1967]

Agrammatism
   Use   Aphasia

Agraphia [1973]
PN   236   SC   01490
SN   Inability to write (letters, syllables, words, or phrases) due to an injury to a specific cerebral area or occasionally due to emotional factors.
B   Aphasia [1967]
R   ↓ Learning Disabilities [1973]

Agreeableness [1997]
PN   49   SC   01495
SN   Extent to which an individual is altruistic, sympathetic to others and eager to help versus being egocentric and skeptical of others' intentions.
B   Personality Traits [1967]
R   Adaptability (Personality) [1973]
    Cooperation [1967]
    Cynicism [1973]
    Egocentrism [1978]
    Empathy [1967]
    Likability [1988]
    Openmindedness [1978]
    ↓ Tolerance [1973]

Agricultural Extension Workers [1973]
PN   65   SC   01500
SN   Government employees (usually local, county, or state) who assist with agricultural matters, distribute educational materials, and provide services pertaining to agriculture.
UF   County Agricultural Agents
    Extension Workers (Agricultural)
B   Government Personnel [1973]
R   ↓ Agricultural Workers [1973]

Agricultural Workers [1973]
PN   519   SC   01510
UF   Farmers
    Laborers (Farm)
B   Nonprofessional Personnel [1982]
N   Migrant Farm Workers [1973]
R   Agricultural Extension Workers [1973]
    ↓ Business and Industrial Personnel [1967]

AIDS
   Use   Acquired Immune Deficiency Syndrome

AIDS (Attitudes Toward) [1997]
PN   308   SC   01516
B   Physical Illness (Attitudes Toward) [1985]
R   AIDS Prevention [1994]
    Acquired Immune Deficiency Syndrome [1988]
    ↓ Human Immunodeficiency Virus [1991]

AIDS Dementia Complex [1997]
PN   36   SC   01514
SN   Use ACQUIRED IMMUNE DEFICIENCY SYNDROME and DEMENTIA to access references from 1988-1996.
B   Dementia [1985]
R   Acquired Immune Deficiency Syndrome [1988]
    ↓ Human Immunodeficiency Virus [1991]

AIDS Prevention [1994]
PN   1570   SC   01517
SN   Health related programs or services directed toward those at risk for HIV/AIDS. Includes prevention of HIV/AIDS and personal risk through health behavior and lifestyle characteristics.
B   Prevention [1973]
R   AIDS (Attitudes Toward) [1997]
    Acquired Immune Deficiency Syndrome [1988]
    Condoms [1991]
    HIV Testing [1997]
R   Health Behavior [1982]
    ↓ Health Education [1973]
    Health Promotion [1991]
    ↓ Human Immunodeficiency Virus [1991]
    Needle Exchange Programs [2001]
    Sexual Risk Taking [1997]

AIDS Testing
   Use   HIV Testing

Air Encephalography
   Use   Pneumoencephalography

Air Force Personnel [1967]
PN   1137   SC   01530
B   Military Personnel [1967]
R   National Guardsmen [1973]

Air Traffic Accidents [1973]
PN   216   SC   01540
B   Transportation Accidents [1973]
R   Air Traffic Control [1973]
    Air Transportation [1973]
    ↓ Aviation Safety [1973]

Air Traffic Control [1973]
PN   355   SC   01550
B   Aviation Safety [1973]
R   Air Traffic Accidents [1973]
    Air Transportation [1973]
    ↓ Transportation Accidents [1973]

Air Transportation [1973]
PN   199   SC   01560
B   Transportation [1973]
R   Air Traffic Accidents [1973]
    Air Traffic Control [1973]
    ↓ Aircraft [1973]
    Public Transportation [1973]
    Spacecraft [1973]

Aircraft [1973]
PN   236   SC   01570

Aircraft — (cont'd)
UF   Airplanes
N   Helicopters [1973]
R   Air Transportation [1973]
    Aircraft Pilots [1973]

Aircraft Crew
   Use   Aerospace Personnel

Aircraft Pilots [1973]
PN   1573   SC   01580
UF   Aviators
    Pilots (Aircraft)
B   Aerospace Personnel [1973]
R   ↓ Aircraft [1973]
    Astronauts [1973]
    ↓ Aviation Safety [1973]

Airplanes
   Use   Aircraft

Akathisia [1991]
PN   200   SC   01595
SN   The inability to remain in a sitting posture or motor restlessness often resulting from heavy doses of tranquilizing drugs.
R   Agitation [1991]
    Restlessness [1973]
R   ↓ Side Effects (Drug) [1973]
    ↓ Symptoms [1967]

Akinesia
   Use   Apraxia

Alanines [1973]
PN   29   SC   01610
B   Amino Acids [1973]
N   ↓ Phenylalanine [1973]

Alanon
   Use   Alcohol Rehabilitation

Alarm Responses [1973]
PN   344   SC   01620
SN   Behavioral, emotional, or physiological reactions to actual or perceived physical threat. Used primarily for animal populations.
R   ↓ Animal Defensive Behavior [1982]
    Animal Distress Calls [1973]
    Animal Escape Behavior [1973]
    ↓ Animal Ethology [1967]
    ↓ Fear [1967]
    Startle Reflex [1967]
    Tonic Immobility [1978]

Alaska Natives [1997]
PN   60   SC   01635
UF   Native Alaskans
B   Indigenous Populations [2001]
R   American Indians [1967]
    Inuit [2001]
    Minority Groups [1967]
    ↓ Pacific Islanders [2001]
    Tribes [1973]

Alateen
   Use   Alcohol Rehabilitation

Albinism [1973]
PN   64   SC   01640
B   Genetic Disorders [1973]
R   ↓ Eye Disorders [1973]

Albinism — (cont'd)
R ↓ Skin Disorders 1973

Albino Rats
Use Rats

Alcohol (Grain)
Use Ethanol

Alcohol Abstinence
Use Sobriety

Alcohol Abuse 1988
PN 4980   SC 01660
SN In 1988, this term replaced the discontinued term PROBLEM DRINKING. In 2000, PROBLEM DRINKING was stripped from all records and replaced with ALCOHOL ABUSE.
UF Problem Drinking
B Alcohol Drinking Patterns 1967
Drug Abuse 1973
N ↓ Alcoholism 1967
R ↓ Alcohol Intoxication 1973
Alcohol Withdrawal 1994
Blood Alcohol Concentration 1994
Codependency 1991
Drug Abuse Liability 1994
R Polydrug Abuse 1994

Alcohol Addiction
Use Alcoholism

Alcohol Dehydrogenases 1973
PN 79   SC 01670
B Dehydrogenases 1973
R ↓ Alcohols 1967

Alcohol Drinking Attitudes 1973
PN 1275   SC 01680
SN Attitudes toward the use or abuse of alcohol.
UF Drinking Attitudes
B Drug Usage Attitudes 1973
R Sobriety 1988

Alcohol Drinking Patterns 1967
PN 7608   SC 01690
UF Drinking (Alcohol)
B Drinking Behavior 1978
Drug Usage 1971
N ↓ Alcohol Abuse 1988
↓ Alcohol Intoxication 1973
Social Drinking 1973
R ↓ Alcoholism 1967
Blood Alcohol Concentration 1994

Alcohol Education
Use Drug Education

Alcohol Intoxication 1973
PN 1314   SC 01700
UF Drunkenness
Intoxication (Alcohol)
B Alcohol Drinking Patterns 1967
N Acute Alcoholic Intoxication 1973
Chronic Alcoholic Intoxication 1973
R ↓ Alcohol Abuse 1988
↓ Alcoholism 1967
Blood Alcohol Concentration 1994
Driving Under The Influence 1988
↓ Toxic Disorders 1973
Toxic Psychoses 1973

Alcohol Rehabilitation 1982
PN 4306   SC 01705
SN Treatment for alcoholism or alcohol abuse which may include detoxification, psychotherapy, behavior therapy, Alcoholics Anonymous, and medication. Use DRUG REHABILITATION to access references from 1973-1981.
UF Alanon
Alateen
B Drug Rehabilitation 1973
N Alcoholics Anonymous 1973
Detoxification 1973
R Alcohol Withdrawal 1994
Rehabilitation Counseling 1978
Sobriety 1988

Alcohol Withdrawal 1994
PN 290   SC 01707
SN Processes and symptomatic effects resulting from abstinence from alcohol. Used for both human and animal populations. Use DRUG WITHDRAWAL to access references from 1973-1993.
B Drug Withdrawal 1973
R ↓ Alcohol Abuse 1988
↓ Alcohol Rehabilitation 1982
↓ Alcoholic Psychosis 1973
R ↓ Alcoholism 1967
Detoxification 1973
Sobriety 1988

Alcoholic Beverages 1973
PN 670   SC 01710
UF Beverages (Alcoholic)
N Beer 1973
Liquor 1973
Wine 1973
R Beverages (Nonalcoholic) 1978
↓ Drinking Behavior 1978
Prenatal Exposure 1991

Alcoholic Hallucinosis 1973
PN 47   SC 01720
B Alcoholic Psychosis 1973
Hallucinosis 1973
N Delirium Tremens 1973
Korsakoffs Psychosis 1973
Wernickes Syndrome 1973

Alcoholic Psychosis 1973
PN 72   SC 01730
B Alcoholism 1967
Organic Brain Syndromes 1973
Psychosis 1967
N ↓ Alcoholic Hallucinosis 1973
R Alcohol Withdrawal 1994
↓ Nutritional Deficiencies 1973
Toxic Psychoses 1973

Alcoholics Anonymous 1973
PN 540   SC 01740
SN A self-supporting, informal, international fellowship whose primary purpose is to help members achieve sobriety.
B Alcohol Rehabilitation 1982
Twelve Step Programs 1997
R ↓ Community Services 1967

Alcoholism 1967
PN 15032   SC 01750
UF Alcohol Addiction
B Addiction 1973
Alcohol Abuse 1988
N ↓ Alcoholic Psychosis 1973
R ↓ Alcohol Drinking Patterns 1967

Alcoholism — (cont'd)
R ↓ Alcohol Intoxication 1973
Alcohol Withdrawal 1994
Fetal Alcohol Syndrome 1985
↓ Nutritional Deficiencies 1973
Sobriety 1988
↓ Toxic Disorders 1973

Alcohols 1967
PN 1503   SC 01760
B Drugs 1967
N Ephedrine 1973
Ethanol 1973
Isoproterenol 1973
Methanol 1973
Methoxamine 1973
Propranolol 1973
Tetrahydrocannabinol 1973
Trihexyphenidyl 1973
R Acetaldehyde 1982
Alcohol Dehydrogenases 1973
Blood Alcohol Concentration 1994
↓ Solvents 1982

Aldolases
SN Term was discontinued in 1997. In 2000, the term was stripped from all records containing it, and replaced with ENZYMES, its postable counterpart.
Use Enzymes

Aldosterone 1973
PN 85   SC 01780
B Adrenal Cortex Hormones 1973
Corticosteroids 1973

Alexia 1982
PN 209   SC 01785
SN Inability to read which may be the result of neurological impairment. In a less severe form, often referred to as dyslexia.
UF Word Blindness
B Dysphasia 1978
N Dyslexia 1973
R ↓ Reading Disabilities 1967

Alexithymia 1982
PN 737   SC 01788
SN Affective and cognitive disturbances characterized by impaired fantasy life and an inability to verbalize or differentiate emotions. These disturbances overlap diagnostic categories and appear generally in psychosomatic patients.
B Mental Disorders 1967

Algebra
Use Mathematics

Algorithms 1973
PN 1512   SC 01800
SN Set of well-defined rules established for step-by-step solution of problems in a finite number of steps.
B Mathematics (Concepts) 1967
R Computer Programming 2001

Alienation 1971
PN 1379   SC 01810
SN Withdrawal or estrangement from persons, objects, or positions of former attachment; feelings of detachment from self or avoidance of emotional experiences.
B Emotional States 1973
R Anomie 1978
Depersonalization 1973

11

Alienation — (cont'd)
R ↓ Separation Reactions 1997

Alkaloids 1973
PN 285   SC 01820
SN In 1997, this term replaced the discontinued terms HOMATROPINE, QUINIDINE, and RAUWOLFIA. In 2000, these terms were stripped from all records and replaced with ALKALOIDS.
UF   Homatropine
    Opium Alkaloids
    Quinidine
    Rauwolfia
B   Drugs 1967
N   Apomorphine 1973
    Atropine 1973
    Bromocriptine 1988
    Caffeine 1973
    Cocaine 1973
    Codeine 1973
    Ephedrine 1973
    ↓ Gamma Aminobutyric Acid Antagonists 1985
    Heroin 1973
    Mescaline 1973
    Morphine 1973
    Nicotine 1973
    Papaverine 1973
    Peyote 1973
    Physostigmine 1973
    Pilocarpine 1973
    Quinine 1973
    Reserpine 1967
    Scopolamine 1973
    Strychnine 1973
    Theophylline 1973
    Tubocurarine 1973
R   ↓ Anti Inflammatory Drugs 1982
    Curare 1973
    ↓ Ergot Derivatives 1973

Allergens
Use   Antigens

Allergic Disorders 1973
PN 220   SC 01830
B   Immunologic Disorders 1973
N   Allergic Skin Disorders 1973
    Drug Allergies 1973
    Food Allergies 1973
    Hay Fever 1973
R   Anaphylactic Shock 1973

Allergic Skin Disorders 1973
PN 21   SC 01840
B   Allergic Disorders 1973
    Skin Disorders 1973
R   ↓ Dermatitis 1973
    Eczema 1973
    Neurodermatitis 1973

Alligators
Use   Crocodilians

Allocation of Resources
Use   Resource Allocation

Allport Vernon Lindzey Study Values
SN Term was discontinued in 1997. In 2000, the term was stripped from all records containing it, and replaced with ATTITUDE MEASURES, its postable counterpart.
Use   Attitude Measures

Alopecia 1973
PN 81   SC 01880
SN Baldness or the loss of hair.
UF   Baldness
    Hair Loss
B   Skin Disorders 1973
R   ↓ Genetic Disorders 1973
    Hair 1973

Alpha Methylparatyrosine 1978
PN 129   SC 01887
UF   Alpha Methyltyrosine
B   Adrenergic Blocking Drugs 1973
    Antihypertensive Drugs 1973
    Tyrosine 1973

Alpha Methyltyrosine
Use   Alpha Methylparatyrosine

Alpha Rhythm 1973
PN 683   SC 01890
SN Electrically measured impulses or waves of low amplitude and a frequency of 8-13 cycles per second usually observable in the electroencephalogram during wakeful rest.
B   Electrical Activity 1967
    Electroencephalography 1967

Alphabets 1973
PN 144   SC 01900
SN Systems for writing a language.
B   Written Language 1967
N   Initial Teaching Alphabet 1973
    ↓ Letters (Alphabet) 1973
R   Orthography 1973

Alprazolam 1988
PN 534   SC 01903
B   Benzodiazepines 1978
    Minor Tranquilizers 1973
    Sedatives 1973

Alternative Medicine 1997
PN 266   SC 01904
SN Treatments, health care practices, or culturally based healing traditions which are not generally used in conventional medical practice.
UF   Complementary Medicine
    Homeopathic Medicine
B   Treatment 1967
N   Acupuncture 1973
    Faith Healing 1973
    Folk Medicine 1973
R   Biofeedback Training 1978
    Dietary Supplements 2001
    Holistic Health 1985
    ↓ Hypnotherapy 1973
    Massage 2001
    Medical Treatment (General) 1973
    Medicinal Herbs and Plants 2001
    Meditation 1973
    Phototherapy 1991
    ↓ Physical Treatment Methods 1973
    Preventive Medicine 1973
    ↓ Shock Therapy 1973
    Transcultural Psychiatry 1973

Alternative Schools
Use   Nontraditional Education

Altitude Effects 1973
PN 193   SC 01910
B   Environmental Effects 1973

Altitude Effects — (cont'd)
R   ↓ Aviation 1967
    ↓ Gravitational Effects 1967

Altruism 1973
PN 1144   SC 01920
SN Consideration for well-being of others as opposed to self-love or egoism. Used for human or animal populations.
B   Personality Traits 1967
    Prosocial Behavior 1982
R   Assistance (Social Behavior) 1973
    Charitable Behavior 1973
    Sharing (Social Behavior) 1978

Aluminum 1994
PN 34   SC 01930
B   Metallic Elements 1973

Alzheimers Disease 1973
PN 9234   SC 01940
UF   Dementia of Alzheimers Type
B   Organic Brain Syndromes 1973
    Presenile Dementia 1973
R   ↓ Dementia 1985
    Dementia with Lewy Bodies 2001
    Picks Disease 1973
    ↓ Senile Dementia 1973

Amantadine 1978
PN 117   SC 01945
UF   Amatadine
B   Antibiotics 1973
    Antitremor Drugs 1973
R   Parkinsons Disease 1973

Amatadine
Use   Amantadine

Amaurotic Familial Idiocy 1973
PN 22   SC 01950
UF   Familial Idiocy (Amaurotic)
    Idiocy (Amaurotic Familial)
    Tay Sachs Disease
B   Genetic Disorders 1973
    Lipid Metabolism Disorders 1973
    Mental Retardation 1967
    Neonatal Disorders 1973

Ambiguity (Stimulus)
Use   Stimulus Ambiguity

Ambiguity (Tolerance)
Use   Tolerance for Ambiguity

Ambition
Use   Aspirations

Ambivalence 1973
PN 263   SC 01990
B   Emotional States 1973

Amblyopia 1973
PN 209   SC 02000
SN An optically uncorrectable loss of visual acuity without apparent organic change or defect.
B   Eye Disorders 1973
R   ↓ Refraction Errors 1973
    Strabismus 1973

Ambulatory Care
Use   Outpatient Treatment

Amenorrhea [1973]
PN　124　　　　　　　　　　SC　02010
SN　Absence or abnormal cessation of the menses.
　B　　Menstrual Disorders [1973]

Amentia
　Use　Mental Retardation

American Indians [1967]
PN　2773　　　　　　　　　　SC　02030
　UF　Indians (American)
　　　Native Americans
　B　　Indigenous Populations [2001]
　R　　Alaska Natives [1997]
　　　Inuit [2001]
　　　Minority Groups [1967]
　　　↓ Pacific Islanders [2001]
　　　Tribes [1973]

Amine Oxidase Inhibitors [1973]
PN　14　　　　　　　　　　SC　02040
　B　　Enzyme Inhibitors [1985]
　N　　↓ Dopamine Antagonists [1982]
　　　Iproniazid [1973]
　　　Isocarboxazid [1973]
　　　Lysergic Acid Diethylamide [1967]
　　　Nialamide [1973]
　R　　↓ Monoamine Oxidase Inhibitors [1973]

Amines [1973]
PN　518　　　　　　　　　　SC　02060
SN　In 1997, this term replaced the discontinued
term CHLORISONDAMINE. In 2000, CHLORISOND-
AMINE was stripped from all records and replaced
with AMINES.
　UF　Chlorisondamine
　B　　Drugs [1967]
　N　　Amitriptyline [1973]
　　　Atropine [1973]
　　　Bufotenine [1973]
　　　Chlordiazepoxide [1973]
　　　Chlorimipramine [1973]
　　　Chlorpromazine [1967]
　　　Chlorprothixene [1973]
　　　Cocaine [1973]
　　　Diphenhydramine [1973]
　　　Galanthamine [1973]
　　　Guanethidine [1973]
　　　Histamine [1973]
　　　Hydroxylamine [1973]
　　　Imipramine [1973]
　　　Mecamylamine [1973]
　　　Meperidine [1973]
　　　Methylphenidate [1973]
　　　Orphenadrine [1973]
　　　Phenethylamines [1985]
　　　Phenoxybenzamine [1973]
　　　Physostigmine [1973]
　　　Puromycin [1973]
　　　Scopolamine [1973]
　　　Serotonin [1973]
　　　↓ Sympathomimetic Amines [1973]
　　　Thalidomide [1973]
　　　Trihexyphenidyl [1973]
　　　Tryptamine [1973]
　R　　↓ Amino Acids [1973]

Amino Acids [1973]
PN　1012　　　　　　　　　　SC　02070
　B　　Acids [1973]
　N　　↓ Alanines [1973]
　　　↓ Aspartic Acid [1973]
　　　Cysteine [1973]

Amino Acids — (cont'd)
　N　　DOPA [1973]
　　　Folic Acid [1973]
　　　Gamma Aminobutyric Acid [1978]
　　　Glutamic Acid [1973]
　　　Glutamine [1973]
　　　Glycine [1973]
　　　Histidine [1973]
　　　Leucine [1973]
　　　Methionine [1973]
　　　↓ Neurokinins [1997]
　　　Proline [1982]
　　　↓ Tryptophan [1973]
　　　↓ Tyrosine [1973]
　R　　↓ Amines [1973]
　　　Dietary Supplements [2001]
　　　Nerve Growth Factor [1994]
　　　↓ Neurotransmitters [1985]
　　　↓ Proteins [1973]

Aminotransferases
　Use　Transaminases

Amitriptyline [1973]
PN　1018　　　　　　　　　　SC　02090
　UF　Elavil
　B　　Amines [1973]
　　　Tranquilizing Drugs [1967]
　　　Tricyclic Antidepressant Drugs [1997]

Amnesia [1967]
PN　2672　　　　　　　　　　SC　02120
SN　Partial or complete loss of memory caused by
organic or psychological factors. The loss may be
temporary or permanent, and may involve old or
recent memories. Compare FORGETTING and
MEMORY DECAY.
　B　　Memory Disorders [1973]
　N　　Global Amnesia [1997]
　R　　Dissociation [2001]
　　　↓ Dissociative Disorders [2001]
　　　False Memory [1997]
　　　Forgetting [1973]
　　　↓ Memory [1967]
　　　Repressed Memory [1997]

Amniocentesis
　Use　Prenatal Diagnosis

Amniotic Fluid [1973]
PN　42　　　　　　　　　　SC　02130
　B　　Body Fluids [1973]

Amobarbital [1973]
PN　215　　　　　　　　　　SC　02140
　UF　Amobarbital Sodium
　　　Amytal
　B　　Barbiturates [1967]
　　　CNS Depressant Drugs [1973]
　　　Hypnotic Drugs [1973]
　　　Sedatives [1973]

Amobarbital Sodium
　Use　Amobarbital

Amphetamine [1967]
PN　3014　　　　　　　　　　SC　02160
　UF　Amphetamine (dl-)
　　　Amphetamine Sulfate
　　　Benzedrine
　B　　Adrenergic Drugs [1973]
　　　Appetite Depressing Drugs [1973]
　　　CNS Stimulating Drugs [1973]

Amphetamine — (cont'd)
　B　　Dopamine Agonists [1985]
　　　Sympathomimetic Amines [1973]
　　　Vasoconstrictor Drugs [1973]
　N　　Dextroamphetamine [1973]
　　　Methamphetamine [1973]
　R　　Phenethylamines [1985]

Amphetamine (d-)
　Use　Dextroamphetamine

Amphetamine (dl-)
　Use　Amphetamine

Amphetamine Sulfate
　Use　Amphetamine

Amphibia [1973]
PN　89　　　　　　　　　　SC　02200
　B　　Vertebrates [1973]
　N　　Frogs [1967]
　　　Salamanders [1973]
　　　Toads [1973]

Amplifiers (Apparatus) [1973]
PN　41　　　　　　　　　　SC　02210
　B　　Apparatus [1967]

Amplitude (Response)
　Use　Response Amplitude

Amputation [1973]
PN　256　　　　　　　　　　SC　02230
SN　In 2000, this term replaced the discontinued and
deleted term AMPUTEES. AMPUTEES was stripped
from all records and replaced with AMPUTATION.
　B　　Surgery [1971]
　N　　Mastectomy [1973]
　R　　Phantom Limbs [1973]
　　　↓ Prostheses [1973]

Amygdaloid Body [1973]
PN　2000　　　　　　　　　　SC　02250
　B　　Basal Ganglia [1973]
　　　Limbic System [1973]
　R　　Medial Forebrain Bundle [1982]

Amytal
　Use　Amobarbital

Anabolism [1973]
PN　12　　　　　　　　　　SC　02280
SN　Constructive part of metabolism concerned
especially with macromolecular synthesis.
　B　　Metabolism [1967]

Anabolites
　Use　Metabolites

Anaclitic Depression [1973]
PN　39　　　　　　　　　　SC　02290
SN　Syndrome of withdrawal characterizing infants
separated from their mothers for a long period of
time.
　B　　Major Depression [1988]
　R　　Attachment Behavior [1985]
　　　Object Relations [1982]
　　　↓ Parental Absence [1973]
　　　↓ Separation Reactions [1997]

Anagram Problem Solving [1973]
PN　302　　　　　　　　　　SC　02300

Anagram Problem Solving — (cont'd)
B   Problem Solving 1967
R   Anagrams 1973

Anagrams 1973
PN 38   SC 02310
SN Words or phrases made by rearranging letters of other words or phrases (e.g., leader from dealer).
B   Vocabulary 1967
R   Anagram Problem Solving 1973

Analeptic Drugs 1973
PN 75   SC 02320
UF   Antagonists (CNS Depressant Drugs)
      CNS Depressant Drug Antagonists
B   CNS Stimulating Drugs 1973
N   Bemegride 1973
      Bicuculline 1994
      Picrotoxin 1973
      Strychnine 1973
R   Barbiturate Poisoning 1973
      Caffeine 1973
      ↓ Cholinomimetic Drugs 1973
      ↓ Heart Rate Affecting Drugs 1973
      Methylphenidate 1973
      Pentylenetetrazol 1973
      Theophylline 1973

Analgesia 1982
PN 1937   SC 02325
SN Pain insensitivity chemically or electrically induced or occurring as a natural phenomenon (e.g., Kiesow's area on the inner cheek).
B   Pain Perception 1973
R   ↓ Analgesic Drugs 1973
      Anesthesia (Feeling) 1973
      ↓ Endorphins 1982
      Enkephalins 1982
      Pain Management 1994
      Pain Measurement 1997

Analgesic Drugs 1973
PN 1132   SC 02330
UF   Anodynes
      Pain Relieving Drugs
B   Drugs 1967
N   Aspirin 1973
      Atropine 1973
      Carbamazepine 1988
      Codeine 1973
      Dihydroergotamine 1973
      Heroin 1973
      Meperidine 1973
      Methadone 1973
      Morphine 1973
      Papaverine 1973
      Pentazocine 1991
      Phencyclidine 1982
      Procaine 1982
      Quinine 1973
      Scopolamine 1973
R   Analgesia 1982
      ↓ Anesthetic Drugs 1973
      ↓ Anti Inflammatory Drugs 1982
      ↓ CNS Depressant Drugs 1973
      ↓ Hypnotic Drugs 1973
      ↓ Narcotic Drugs 1973
      ↓ Pain 1967
      Pain Management 1994
      ↓ Sedatives 1973

Analog Computers 1973
PN 22   SC 02340

Analog Computers — (cont'd)
SN Electronic, mechanical, or electromechanical machines that measure continuous electrical or physical magnitudes (e.g., automobile speedometer) rather than operating on discrete digits.
B   Computers 1967

Analogy 1991
PN 438   SC 02345
R   Connotations 1973
      ↓ Figurative Language 1985
      Inference 1973
      Logical Thinking 1967
      Metaphor 1982
R   ↓ Reasoning 1967

Analysis 1967
PN 1824   SC 02370
SN Conceptually broad term referring to the process of examination of a complex problem, its elements, and their relations. Use a more specific term if possible.
N   ↓ Behavior Analysis 2001
      Causal Analysis 1994
      Cohort Analysis 1988
      ↓ Content Analysis 1978
      Content Analysis (Test) 1967
      ↓ Costs and Cost Analysis 1973
      Error Analysis 1973
      Item Analysis (Test) 1967
      Job Analysis 1967
      Risk Analysis 1991
      ↓ Statistical Analysis 1967
      Systems Analysis 1973
      Task Analysis 1967
R   Analysis of Covariance 1973
      Analysis of Variance 1967
      Functional Analysis 2001
      Multidimensional Scaling 1982

Analysis of Covariance 1973
PN 465   SC 02350
B   Variability Measurement 1973
R   ↓ Analysis 1967
      Analysis of Variance 1967
      Multiple Regression 1982
      ↓ Multivariate Analysis 1982

Analysis of Variance 1967
PN 1196   SC 02360
UF   ANOVA (Statistics)
B   Variability Measurement 1973
R   ↓ Analysis 1967
      Analysis of Covariance 1973
      Multiple Regression 1982
      ↓ Multivariate Analysis 1982
      ↓ Statistical Regression 1985
      Variance Homogeneity 1985

Analysts
Use   Psychoanalysts

Analytic Psychology
Use   Jungian Psychology

Analytical Psychotherapy 1973
PN 606   SC 02390
SN Form of psychotherapy based on work of C. G. Jung. The unconscious, personal and collective, is disclosed through free association and dream analysis. Therapeutic goals include integration of conscious and unconscious for growth and personality development and a life of fuller awareness.
UF   Jungian Psychotherapy

Analytical Psychotherapy — (cont'd)
B   Psychotherapy 1967
R   Archetypes 1991
      ↓ Collective Unconscious 1997
      Jung (Carl) 1973
      ↓ Jungian Psychology 1973

Anankastic Personality
Use   Obsessive Compulsive Personality

Anaphylactic Shock 1973
PN 17   SC 02400
SN Immunologic or allergic reaction to antigens such as drugs or foreign proteins to which a hypersensitivity has been established by previous contact.
UF   Protein Sensitization
      Sensitization (Protein)
B   Immunologic Disorders 1973
R   ↓ Allergic Disorders 1973
      Shock 1967

Anatomical Systems 1973
PN 36   SC 02410
SN Conceptually broad term referring to anatomically related structures (e.g., vascular system). Use a more specific term if possible.
B   Anatomy 1967
      Systems 1967
N   ↓ Cardiovascular System 1967
      ↓ Digestive System 1967
      ↓ Endocrine System 1973
      ↓ Musculoskeletal System 1973
      ↓ Nervous System 1967
      ↓ Respiratory System 1973
      ↓ Urogenital System 1973

Anatomically Detailed Dolls 1991
PN 62   SC 02415
SN Dolls used in a general play setting or for evaluation and assessment purposes in a therapeutic or legal context.
B   Toys 1973
R   ↓ Child Abuse 1971
      Childhood Play Behavior 1978
      Clinical Judgment (Not Diagnosis) 1973
      Doll Play 1973
      ↓ Sexual Abuse 1988

Anatomy 1967
PN 1239   SC 02420
SN Conceptually broad array term referring both to the science of anatomy and the actual structure or morphology of an organism. Use specific anatomical or neuroanatomical terms if possible.
N   Abdomen 1973
      ↓ Anatomical Systems 1973
      Back (Anatomy) 1973
      ↓ Body Fluids 1973
      Breast 1973
      ↓ Cells (Biology) 1973
      Face (Anatomy) 1973
      Feet (Anatomy) 1973
      Hair 1973
      Hand (Anatomy) 1967
      Head (Anatomy) 1973
      Neck (Anatomy) 1973
      Palm (Anatomy) 1973
      Scalp (Anatomy) 1973
      ↓ Sense Organs 1973
      Thigh 1973
      ↓ Tissues (Body) 1973
R   Morphology 1973
      Neuroanatomy 1967
      ↓ Physiology 1967

Ancestors 1973
PN 24   SC 02430
  UF Great Grandparents
  B Family Members 1973
  N Grandparents 1973
  ↓ Parents 1967

Androgen Antagonists
  Use Antiandrogens

Androgens 1973
PN 568   SC 02440
  B Sex Hormones 1973
  N Testosterone 1973
  R Antiandrogens 1982
     Antiestrogens 1982

Androgyny 1982
PN 729   SC 02445
  SN Combination of masculine and feminine personality characteristics in one individual.
  B Personality Traits 1967
  R Femininity 1967
  ↓ Gender Identity 1985
  ↓ Human Sex Differences 1967
     Masculinity 1967
     Sex Roles 1967

Anemia 1973
PN 154   SC 02450
  B Blood and Lymphatic Disorders 1973
  R ↓ Genetic Disorders 1973
     Sickle Cell Disease 1994

Anencephaly 1973
PN 9   SC 02460
  B Brain Disorders 1967
     Mental Retardation 1967
     Neonatal Disorders 1973

Anesthesia (Feeling) 1973
PN 204   SC 02470
  R Analgesia 1982
  ↓ Physical Disorders 1997
  ↓ Sense Organ Disorders 1973
  ↓ Tactual Perception 1967

Anesthesiology 1973
PN 125   SC 02480
  B Medical Sciences 1967

Anesthetic Drugs 1973
PN 630   SC 02490
  B Drugs 1967
  N ↓ General Anesthetics 1973
     Hexobarbital 1973
     Ketamine 1997
  ↓ Local Anesthetics 1973
     Pentobarbital 1973
     Phencyclidine 1982
     Procaine 1982
  R ↓ Analgesic Drugs 1973
  ↓ Anticonvulsive Drugs 1973
  ↓ Barbiturates 1967
  ↓ CNS Depressant Drugs 1973
  ↓ Hypnotic Drugs 1973
  ↓ Muscle Relaxing Drugs 1973
  ↓ Narcotic Drugs 1973
  ↓ Sedatives 1973

Aneurysms 1973
PN 114   SC 02500

Aneurysms — (cont'd)
  B Cardiovascular Disorders 1967

Anger 1967
PN 2717   SC 02510
  UF Rage
  B Emotional States 1973
  N Hostility 1967
  R Anger Control 1997
     Hate 1973
     Jealousy 1973
     Tantrums 1973

Anger Control 1997
PN 164   SC 02520
  B Emotional Control 1973
  R ↓ Anger 1967
  ↓ Behavior Modification 1973
  ↓ Behavior Therapy 1967
     Explosive Disorder 2001
     Self Control 1973

Angina Pectoris 1973
PN 134   SC 02530
  B Heart Disorders 1973
  R Myocardial Infarctions 1973

Angiography 1973
PN 44   SC 02540
  B Roentgenography 1973

Angiotensin 1973
PN 413   SC 02550
  B Peptides 1973
     Vasoconstrictor Drugs 1973
  R Captopril 1991

Anglos 1988
PN 417   SC 02553
  SN Generally applied to English-speaking White populations of non-Hispanic descent. From 2000, used only to reflect author's terminology.
  B Whites 1982

Angst
  Use Anxiety

Anguish
  Use Distress

Anhedonia 1985
PN 203   SC 02575
  SN Loss or absence of ability to experience pleasure.
  B Symptoms 1967
  R Dysthymic Disorder 1988
  ↓ Neurosis 1967
     Pleasure 1973
  ↓ Schizophrenia 1967

Animal Aggressive Behavior 1973
PN 4896   SC 02580
  B Aggressive Behavior 1967
     Animal Social Behavior 1967
  N Animal Predatory Behavior 1978
     Attack Behavior 1973
     Muricide 1988
     Threat Postures 1973
  R Animal Dominance 1973
     Territoriality 1967

Animal Assisted Therapy 1994
PN 75   SC 02585
  SN A type of therapy based on the human-animal companion bond used in an effort to assist in restoring feelings of hope, self worth, responsibility, and communication.
  UF Pet Therapy
  B Psychotherapeutic Techniques 1967
  R ↓ Animals 1967
     Geriatric Psychotherapy 1973
     Interspecies Interaction 1991
     Pets 1982
  ↓ Rehabilitation 1967

Animal Behavior
  Use Animal Ethology

Animal Biological Rhythms 1973
PN 448   SC 02600
  SN Rhythmic and periodic variations in behavioral or physiological functions of animals. Use BIOLOGICAL RHYTHMS to access references from 1967-1972.
  UF Biological Clocks (Animal)
  B Animal Ethology 1967
     Biological Rhythms 1967
  N Animal Circadian Rhythms 1973
  R Animal Sexual Receptivity 1973
     Estrus 1973
     Hibernation 1973

Animal Breeding 1973
PN 2887   SC 02610
  SN Propagation (or reproduction) of a species in its natural environment or in captive settings. Includes birth rate and breeding success. Compare ANIMAL DOMESTICATION, EUGENICS, and SELECTIVE BREEDING.
  UF Breeding (Animal)
  N Selective Breeding 1973
  R Animal Captivity 1994
     Animal Domestication 1978
  ↓ Animal Mating Behavior 1967
  ↓ Animal Sexual Behavior 1985
     Animal Strain Differences 1982
  ↓ Animals 1967
     Assortative Mating 1991
  ↓ Genetics 1967
     Litter Size 1985
  ↓ Sexual Reproduction 1973

Animal Captivity 1994
PN 437   SC 02615
  UF Captivity (Animal)
     Zoo Environment
  B Animal Environments 1967
  R ↓ Animal Breeding 1973
     Animal Domestication 1978
     Animal Rearing 1991
     Animal Welfare 1985

Animal Circadian Rhythms 1973
PN 2352   SC 02620
  SN Diurnal cyclical variations or patterns of behavioral or physiological functions of animals. Use BIOLOGICAL RHYTHMS to access references from 1967-1972.
  UF Circadian Rhythms (Animal)
     Daily Biological Rhythms (Animal)
  B Animal Biological Rhythms 1973
  R Animal Nocturnal Behavior 1973

Animal Coloration 1985
PN 345   SC 02625

Animal Coloration — (cont'd)
SN Physical aspect of body color.
R   Animal Courtship Displays [1973]
    ↓ Animal Defensive Behavior [1982]
    ↓ Pigments [1973]

Animal Communication [1967]
PN 1547   **SC** 02630
B   Animal Social Behavior [1967]
    Communication [1967]
N   Animal Distress Calls [1973]
R   Animal Scent Marking [1985]
    ↓ Animal Vocalizations [1973]
    ↓ Vocalization [1967]

Animal Courtship Behavior [1973]
PN 987   **SC** 02640
UF   Courtship (Animal)
B   Animal Sexual Behavior [1985]
    Animal Social Behavior [1967]
N   Animal Courtship Displays [1973]
R   Animal Mate Selection [1982]
    ↓ Animal Mating Behavior [1967]

Animal Courtship Displays [1973]
PN 299   **SC** 02650
UF   Courtship Displays (Animal)
B   Animal Courtship Behavior [1973]
    Animal Social Behavior [1967]
R   Animal Coloration [1985]
    ↓ Animal Mating Behavior [1967]
    Territoriality [1967]

Animal Defensive Behavior [1982]
PN 1948   **SC** 02652
SN Innate protective responses that occur in presence of predator or other threatening stimulus.
UF   Defensive Behavior (Animal)
B   Animal Ethology [1967]
N   Animal Escape Behavior [1973]
    Threat Postures [1973]
R   Alarm Responses [1973]
    Animal Coloration [1985]
    Animal Distress Calls [1973]
    Attack Behavior [1973]
    Instinctive Behavior [1982]
    Tonic Immobility [1978]

Animal Development [1978]
PN 2775   **SC** 02655
SN Conceptually broad term. Use a more specific term if possible.
B   Development [1967]
R   Age Differences [1967]
    ↓ Animals [1967]
    ↓ Motor Development [1973]
    Neural Development [1985]
    Perceptual Motor Development [1991]
    ↓ Physical Development [1973]
    ↓ Prenatal Development [1973]

Animal Distress Calls [1973]
PN 316   **SC** 02660
UF   Distress Calls (Animal)
B   Animal Communication [1967]
    Animal Vocalizations [1973]
R   Alarm Responses [1973]
    ↓ Animal Defensive Behavior [1982]
    Instinctive Behavior [1982]

Animal Division of Labor [1973]
PN 214   **SC** 02670
UF   Division of Labor (Animal)

Animal Division of Labor — (cont'd)
B   Animal Social Behavior [1967]
    Division of Labor [1988]
R   Animal Dominance [1973]

Animal Domestication [1978]
PN 157   **SC** 02677
SN Adaptation of wild animals to life and breeding in tame conditions according to the interests of human society. Compare ANIMAL BREEDING, EUGENICS, and SELECTIVE BREEDING.
UF   Domestication (Animal)
R   ↓ Animal Breeding [1973]
    Animal Captivity [1994]
    Pets [1982]
    Selective Breeding [1973]

Animal Dominance [1973]
PN 1930   **SC** 02680
UF   Dominance (Animal)
    Pecking Order
B   Animal Social Behavior [1967]
    Dominance [1967]
R   ↓ Animal Aggressive Behavior [1973]
    Animal Division of Labor [1973]
    Animal Scent Marking [1985]
    Dominance Hierarchy [1973]
    Territoriality [1967]

Animal Drinking Behavior [1973]
PN 1904   **SC** 02690
UF   Drinking Behavior (Animal)
B   Animal Ethology [1967]
    Drinking Behavior [1978]
R   ↓ Ingestion [2001]
    Licking [1988]
    Polydipsia [1982]
    Sucking [1978]
    Thirst [1967]
    Water Intake [1967]

Animal Emotionality [1978]
PN 936   **SC** 02696
UF   Emotionality (Animal)
R   Animal Motivation [1967]
    ↓ Emotional Responses [1967]

Animal Environments [1967]
PN 6059   **SC** 02700
SN Physical and social conditions of an animal's existence or habitat.
UF   Habitats (Animal)
B   Social Environments [1973]
N   Animal Captivity [1994]
R   Animal Rearing [1991]
    ↓ Animals [1967]
    Place Conditioning [1991]
    Single Sex Environments [2001]

Animal Escape Behavior [1973]
PN 784   **SC** 02710
UF   Escape Behavior (Animal)
B   Animal Defensive Behavior [1982]
R   Alarm Responses [1973]

Animal Ethology [1967]
PN 4080   **SC** 02720
SN Study of animal behavior especially in relation to ecology, evolution, neuroanatomy, neurophysiology, and genetics. Used for the discipline or the ethological processes themselves. Use a more specific term if possible.
UF   Animal Behavior
    Ethology (Animal)

Animal Ethology — (cont'd)
B   Behavior [1967]
N   ↓ Animal Biological Rhythms [1973]
    ↓ Animal Defensive Behavior [1982]
    Animal Drinking Behavior [1973]
    Animal Exploratory Behavior [1973]
    Animal Feeding Behavior [1973]
    Animal Foraging Behavior [1985]
    Animal Grooming Behavior [1978]
    Animal Hoarding Behavior [1973]
    Animal Homing [1991]
    Animal Nocturnal Behavior [1973]
    Animal Open Field Behavior [1973]
    ↓ Animal Parental Behavior [1982]
    Animal Play [1973]
    Animal Sex Differences [1967]
    ↓ Animal Sexual Behavior [1985]
    ↓ Animal Social Behavior [1967]
    ↓ Animal Vocalizations [1973]
    Hibernation [1973]
    Imprinting [1967]
    Licking [1988]
    Migratory Behavior (Animal) [1973]
    Nest Building [1973]
    Species Recognition [1985]
    Territoriality [1967]
R   Alarm Responses [1973]
    Animal Motivation [1967]
    ↓ Animals [1967]
    Echolocation [1973]
    Instinctive Behavior [1982]
    Stereotyped Behavior [1973]
    Tool Use [1991]

Animal Exploratory Behavior [1973]
PN 1756   **SC** 02730
SN Use EXPLORATORY BEHAVIOR to access references from 1967-1972.
B   Animal Ethology [1967]
    Exploratory Behavior [1967]
R   Animal Foraging Behavior [1985]
    Instinctive Behavior [1982]
    Neophobia [1985]
    Spontaneous Alternation [1982]

Animal Feeding Behavior [1973]
PN 5231   **SC** 02740
UF   Feeding Behavior (Animal)
B   Animal Ethology [1967]
R   Animal Foraging Behavior [1985]
    Animal Maternal Behavior [1973]
    Animal Paternal Behavior [1991]
    ↓ Feeding Practices [1973]
    Food Intake [1967]
    Hunger [1967]
    ↓ Ingestion [2001]
    Sucking [1978]

Animal Foraging Behavior [1985]
PN 1806   **SC** 02743
UF   Foraging (Animal)
B   Animal Ethology [1967]
R   Animal Exploratory Behavior [1973]
    Animal Feeding Behavior [1973]
    Animal Predatory Behavior [1978]

Animal Grooming Behavior [1978]
PN 741   **SC** 02745
UF   Grooming Behavior (Animal)
B   Animal Ethology [1967]
R   Licking [1988]

Animal Hoarding Behavior [1973]
PN 244   SC 02750
  UF   Hoarding Behavior (Animal)
  B   Animal Ethology [1967]

Animal Homing [1991]
PN 125   SC 02755
  SN Returning accurately to one's home or natal area from a distance.
  UF   Homing (Animal)
  B   Animal Ethology [1967]
  R   Instinctive Behavior [1982]
      Migratory Behavior (Animal) [1973]
      Territoriality [1967]

Animal Human Interaction
  Use Interspecies Interaction

Animal Innate Behavior
  SN Term was discontinued in 1982. In 2000, the term was stripped from all records containing it, and replaced with INSTINCTIVE BEHAVIOR, its postable counterpart.
  Use Instinctive Behavior

Animal Instinctive Behavior
  SN Term was discontinued in 1982. In 2000, the term was stripped from all records containing it, and replaced with INSTINCTIVE BEHAVIOR, its postable counterpart.
  Use Instinctive Behavior

Animal Licking Behavior
  Use Licking

Animal Locomotion [1982]
PN 2598   SC 02775
  SN Any form of motor activity resulting in bodily propulsion.
  B   Motor Processes [1967]

Animal Mate Selection [1982]
PN 1257   SC 02778
  SN Ethological processes surrounding the choice of mate for sexual reproduction.
  UF   Mate Selection
  R   ↓ Animal Courtship Behavior [1973]
      ↓ Animal Mating Behavior [1967]
      ↓ Animal Sexual Behavior [1985]
      Assortative Mating [1991]
      ↓ Genetics [1967]
      ↓ Sexual Reproduction [1973]

Animal Maternal Behavior [1973]
PN 2636   SC 02780
  UF   Maternal Behavior (Animal)
  B   Animal Parental Behavior [1982]
  R   Animal Feeding Behavior [1973]
      Animal Maternal Deprivation [1988]
      Animal Paternal Behavior [1991]
      Animal Rearing [1991]
      Licking [1988]

Animal Maternal Deprivation [1988]
PN 188   SC 02785
  SN Consider using ANIMAL MATERNAL BEHAVIOR prior to 1988.
  R   Animal Maternal Behavior [1973]
      Animal Rearing [1991]
      ↓ Social Isolation [1967]

Animal Mating Behavior [1967]
PN 5088   SC 02790

Animal Mating Behavior — (cont'd)
  UF   Coitus (Animal)
      Copulation (Animal)
      Mating Behavior (Animal)
  B   Animal Sexual Behavior [1985]
      Animal Social Behavior [1967]
  N   Animal Sexual Receptivity [1973]
  R   ↓ Animal Breeding [1973]
      ↓ Animal Courtship Behavior [1973]
      Animal Courtship Displays [1973]
      Animal Mate Selection [1982]
      Assortative Mating [1991]
      Nest Building [1973]
      Pheromones [1973]
      ↓ Sexual Reproduction [1973]

Animal Models [1988]
PN 3890   SC 02797
  SN Experimentally induced simulations of human conditions in animals designed to investigate the etiology and characteristics of diseases, psychological and psychiatric disorders, or learning processes.
  B   Models [1967]
  R   ↓ Animals [1967]
      ↓ Experimental Design [1967]
      ↓ Experimentation [1967]

Animal Motivation [1967]
PN 1464   SC 02800
  B   Motivation [1967]
  R   Animal Emotionality [1978]
      ↓ Animal Ethology [1967]
      ↓ Animals [1967]
      Instinctive Behavior [1982]

Animal Navigation
  Use Migratory Behavior (Animal)

Animal Nocturnal Behavior [1973]
PN 148   SC 02820
  UF   Nocturnal Behavior (Animal)
  B   Animal Ethology [1967]
  R   Animal Circadian Rhythms [1973]

Animal Open Field Behavior [1973]
PN 1851   SC 02825
  SN Spontaneous animal behavior studied in relatively unrestricted laboratory environments. Prior to 1985 also used for spontaneous animal behavior in natural environments.
  UF   Open Field Behavior (Animal)
  B   Animal Ethology [1967]

Animal Parental Behavior [1982]
PN 940   SC 02828
  SN Nurturance and care of offspring performed by male and/or female parents.
  UF   Parental Behavior (Animal)
  B   Animal Ethology [1967]
      Animal Social Behavior [1967]
  N   Animal Maternal Behavior [1973]
      Animal Paternal Behavior [1991]
  R   Animal Rearing [1991]
      Parental Investment [1997]

Animal Paternal Behavior [1991]
PN 226   SC 02829
  B   Animal Parental Behavior [1982]
  R   Animal Feeding Behavior [1973]
      Animal Maternal Behavior [1973]
      Animal Rearing [1991]

Animal Play [1973]
PN 471   SC 02830
  UF   Play (Animal)
  B   Animal Ethology [1967]
  R   ↓ Animal Social Behavior [1967]

Animal Predatory Behavior [1978]
PN 1614   SC 02834
  UF   Predatory Behavior (Animal)
  B   Animal Aggressive Behavior [1973]
  R   Animal Foraging Behavior [1985]
      Attack Behavior [1973]
      Instinctive Behavior [1982]
      Threat Postures [1973]

Animal Rearing [1991]
PN 658   SC 02836
  SN Conditions or environment in which animals are bred, nourished, and raised. Compare ANIMAL PARENTAL BEHAVIOR.
  R   Animal Captivity [1994]
      ↓ Animal Environments [1967]
      Animal Maternal Behavior [1973]
      Animal Maternal Deprivation [1988]
      ↓ Animal Parental Behavior [1982]
      Animal Paternal Behavior [1991]

Animal Scent Marking [1985]
PN 335   SC 02837
  UF   Scent Marking (Animal)
  R   ↓ Animal Communication [1967]
      Animal Dominance [1973]
      Pheromones [1973]
      Territoriality [1967]

Animal Sex Differences [1967]
PN 3576   SC 02840
  SN Animal behavioral, developmental, and physiological/anatomical differences between the sexes.
  UF   Sex Differences (Animal)
  B   Animal Ethology [1967]
  R   Sex [1967]
      Sex Recognition [1997]
      Single Sex Environments [2001]

Animal Sexual Behavior [1985]
PN 1967   SC 02845
  SN Any form of sexual behavior in animals.
  B   Animal Ethology [1967]
  N   ↓ Animal Courtship Behavior [1973]
      ↓ Animal Mating Behavior [1967]
  R   ↓ Animal Breeding [1973]
      Animal Mate Selection [1982]
      Instinctive Behavior [1982]
      Sex [1967]

Animal Sexual Receptivity [1973]
PN 1270   SC 02850
  UF   Lordosis (Animal)
      Sexual Receptivity (Animal)
  B   Animal Mating Behavior [1967]
  R   ↓ Animal Biological Rhythms [1973]
      Estrus [1973]

Animal Social Behavior [1967]
PN 6439   SC 02860
  B   Animal Ethology [1967]
      Social Behavior [1967]
  N   ↓ Animal Aggressive Behavior [1973]
      ↓ Animal Communication [1967]
      ↓ Animal Courtship Behavior [1973]
      Animal Courtship Displays [1973]
      Animal Division of Labor [1973]

Animal Social Behavior — (cont'd)
N   Animal Dominance [1973]
    ↓ Animal Mating Behavior [1967]
    ↓ Animal Parental Behavior [1982]
R   Animal Play [1973]
    Interspecies Interaction [1991]
    Physical Contact [1982]

Animal Strain Differences [1982]
PN 2691   SC 02863
SN Anatomical, physiological, and/or behavioral
variations between members of different subspecies
or strains. Use GENETICS and ANIMAL BREEDING
together to access references from 1973-1981. Compare SPECIES DIFFERENCES.
UF Strain Differences (Animal)
R   ↓ Animal Breeding [1973]
    ↓ Genetics [1967]

Animal Tool Use
Use Tool Use

Animal Vocalizations [1973]
PN 3495   SC 02870
UF Vocalizations (Animal)
B   Animal Ethology [1967]
    Vocalization [1967]
N   Animal Distress Calls [1973]
R   ↓ Animal Communication [1967]
    Echolocation [1973]

Animal Welfare [1985]
PN 455   SC 02875
R   Animal Captivity [1994]
    Experimental Ethics [1978]

Animals [1967]
PN 3746   SC 02880
SN Conceptually broad term. Use a more specific
term if possible (e.g., VERTEBRATES, MAMMALS,
DOGS).
N   Female Animals [1973]
    Infants (Animal) [1978]
    ↓ Invertebrates [1973]
    Male Animals [1973]
    ↓ Vertebrates [1973]
R   Animal Assisted Therapy [1994]
    ↓ Animal Breeding [1973]
    Animal Development [1978]
    ↓ Animal Environments [1967]
    ↓ Animal Ethology [1967]
    Animal Models [1988]
    Animal Motivation [1967]
    Biological Symbiosis [1973]
    Interspecies Interaction [1991]
    Pets [1982]
    Species Differences [1982]

Animism [1973]
PN 84   SC 02890
SN Ascribing life to inanimate objects. Also, the
Piagetian stage of development in which children
ascribe emotional attributes and intentions to inanimate objects.
B   Philosophies [1967]
R   Ethnology [1967]
    Myths [1967]
    Taboos [1973]

Ankle [1973]
PN 31   SC 02900
B   Joints (Anatomy) [1973]

Ankle — (cont'd)
R   Feet (Anatomy) [1973]
    Leg (Anatomy) [1973]

Anniversary Events [1994]
PN 10   SC 02905
SN Annual occurrence of a specific date that marks
a notable event or experience. Includes aspects of
both positive or negative reactions to the event or
experience.
UF Anniversary Reactions
B   Experiences (Events) [1973]
R   Autobiographical Memory [1994]
    Early Experience [1967]
    Early Memories [1985]
    Life Experiences [1973]
    Life Review [1991]
    Reminiscence [1985]

Anniversary Reactions
Use Anniversary Events

Annual Leave
Use Employee Leave Benefits

Anodynes
Use Analgesic Drugs

Anomie [1978]
PN 194   SC 02940
SN Sense of alienation or despair resulting from the
loss or weakening of previously held values. Also, a
state of lawlessness or a lack of normative standards
within groups or societies.
B   Social Processes [1967]
R   Alienation [1971]
    Personal Values [1973]
    Social Values [1973]

Anonymity [1973]
PN 214   SC 02945
SN Unknown, unacknowledged, or concealed personal identity.
R   Privileged Communication [1973]
    Secrecy [1994]
    Self Disclosure [1973]
    ↓ Social Perception [1967]

Anorexia Nervosa [1973]
PN 4120   SC 02950
SN Syndrome in which the primary features include
excessive fear of becoming overweight, body image
disturbance, significant weight loss, refusal to maintain minimal normal weight, and amenorrhea. This
disorder occurs most frequently in adolescent
females.
B   Eating Disorders [1997]
    Underweight [1973]
R   ↓ Body Image Disturbances [1973]
    Bulimia [1985]
    ↓ Nutritional Deficiencies [1973]
    ↓ Somatoform Disorders [2001]

Anorexigenic Drugs
Use Appetite Depressing Drugs

Anosmia [1973]
PN 165   SC 02970
SN Loss of the sense of smell.
UF Olfactory Impairment
B   Sense Organ Disorders [1973]
R   ↓ Olfactory Perception [1967]
    Taste Disorders [2001]

Anosognosia [1994]
PN 73   SC 02975
SN Lack of awareness of, or refusal or failure to
deal with or recognize that one has a mental or physical disorder.
B   Agnosia [1973]
R   Coping Behavior [1967]
    Denial [1973]
    Illness Behavior [1982]

ANOVA (Statistics)
Use Analysis of Variance

Anoxia [1973]
PN 529   SC 02990
SN Absence or reduction of oxygen in body tissue.
UF Asphyxia
    Hypoxia
    Suffocation
B   Symptoms [1967]
R   ↓ Ischemia [1973]
    ↓ Respiratory Distress [1973]

Antabuse
Use Disulfiram

Antagonism
Use Hostility

Antagonists (CNS Depressant Drugs)
Use Analeptic Drugs

Anthropologists [1973]
PN 52   SC 03030
B   Professional Personnel [1978]
R   Scientists [1967]
    Sociologists [1973]

Anthropology [1967]
PN 956   SC 03040
SN Science dealing with the study of the interrelations of biological, cultural, geographical, and historical characteristics of the human species. Use a more
specific term if possible.
B   Social Sciences [1967]
R   Ethnography [1973]
    Ethnology [1967]
    Folk Psychology [1997]

Anti Inflammatory Drugs [1982]
PN 227   SC 03041
SN Agents which reduce inflammation by acting on
body mechanisms, without directly antagonizing the
causative agent.
UF Antipyretic Drugs
B   Drugs [1967]
N   Aspirin [1973]
    ↓ Glucocorticoids [1982]
    ↓ Neurokinins [1997]
R   ↓ Alkaloids [1973]
    ↓ Analgesic Drugs [1973]
    ↓ Enzymes [1973]
    ↓ Hormones [1967]
    Hydrocortisone [1973]
    Prostaglandins [1982]
    ↓ Steroids [1973]

Antiadrenergic Drugs
Use Sympatholytic Drugs

Antiandrogens [1982]
PN 115   SC 03042

Antiandrogens — (cont'd)

SN Substances capable of preventing the normal effects of androgenic hormones on responsive tissues by antagonistic effects on tissue or by inhibiting androgenic effects.

UF Androgen Antagonists
B   Drugs   1967
R ↓ Androgens   1973
   ↓ Estrogens   1973
   ↓ Steroids   1973

Antianxiety Drugs

Use Tranquilizing Drugs

Antibiotics   1973
PN 252   **SC** 03050

B   Drugs   1967
N   Amantadine   1978
   Cycloheximide   1973
   Penicillins   1973
   Puromycin   1973
R   Antineoplastic Drugs   1982

Antibodies   1973
PN 508   **SC** 03060

B   Globulins   1973
R   Antigens   1982
   Blood Serum   1973
   ↓ Drugs   1967
   Gamma Globulin   1973
   Immunization   1973
   ↓ Immunoglobulins   1973
   ↓ Neurotoxins   1982

Anticholinergic Drugs

Use Cholinergic Blocking Drugs

Anticholinesterase Drugs

Use Cholinesterase Inhibitors

Anticipation (Serial Learning)

Use Serial Anticipation (Learning)

Anticoagulant Drugs   1973
PN 41   **SC** 03100

B   Drugs   1967
N   Heparin   1973

Anticonvulsive Drugs   1973
PN 1382   **SC** 03110

SN In 1982, this term replaced the discontinued term ANTIEPILEPTIC DRUGS, and in 1997 it replaced PARALDEHYDE. In 2000, these terms were stripped from all records and replaced with ANTICONVULSIVE DRUGS.

UF Antiepileptic Drugs
   Paraldehyde
B   Drugs   1967
N   Carbamazepine   1988
   Chloral Hydrate   1973
   Clonazepam   1991
   Diphenylhydantoin   1973
   Nitrazepam   1978
   Oxazepam   1978
   Pentobarbital   1973
   Phenobarbital   1973
   Primidone   1973
   Valproic Acid   1991
R   Acetazolamide   1973
   ↓ Anesthetic Drugs   1973
   ↓ Antispasmodic Drugs   1973
   ↓ Barbiturates   1967
   ↓ Benzodiazepines   1978

Anticonvulsive Drugs — (cont'd)
R ↓ CNS Depressant Drugs   1973
   ↓ Convulsions   1967
   ↓ Epilepsy   1967
   ↓ Hypnotic Drugs   1973
   ↓ Muscle Relaxing Drugs   1973
   ↓ Narcotic Drugs   1973
   ↓ Sedatives   1973
   ↓ Spasms   1973
   ↓ Tranquilizing Drugs   1967

Antidepressant Drugs   1971
PN 6676   **SC** 03120

SN In 1997, this term replaced the discontinued term DEANOL. In 2000, DEANOL was stripped from all records and replaced with ANTIDEPRESSANT DRUGS.

UF Deanol
B   Drugs   1967
N   Bupropion   1994
   Citalopram   1997
   Fluoxetine   1991
   Fluvoxamine   1994
   Iproniazid   1973
   Isocarboxazid   1973
   Lithium Carbonate   1973
   Methylphenidate   1973
   Mianserin   1982
   Moclobemide   1997
   Molindone   1982
   Nialamide   1973
   Nomifensine   1982
   Paroxetine   1994
   Phenelzine   1973
   Pheniprazine   1973
   Pipradrol   1973
   Sertraline   1997
   Sulpiride   1973
   Tranylcypromine   1973
   Trazodone   1988
   ↓ Tricyclic Antidepressant Drugs   1997
   Zimeldine   1988
R ↓ CNS Stimulating Drugs   1973
   ↓ Lithium   1973
   ↓ Monoamine Oxidase Inhibitors   1973

Antiemetic Drugs   1973
PN 91   **SC** 03140

UF Antinauseant Drugs
B   Drugs   1967
N   Chlorpromazine   1967
   Chlorprothixene   1973
   Fluphenazine   1973
   Perphenazine   1973
   Piracetam   1982
   Prochlorperazine   1973
   Promethazine   1973
   Sulpiride   1973
R ↓ Cholinergic Blocking Drugs   1973
   ↓ Hypnotic Drugs   1973
   Nausea   1973
   ↓ Sedatives   1973
   ↓ Tranquilizing Drugs   1967
   Vomiting   1973

Antiepileptic Drugs

SN Term was discontinued in 1982. In 2000, the term was stripped from all records containing it, and replaced with ANTICONVULSIVE DRUGS, its postable counterpart.

Use Anticonvulsive Drugs

Antiestrogens   1982
PN 38   **SC** 03155

Antiestrogens — (cont'd)

SN Substances capable of preventing the normal effects of estrogenic hormones on responsive tissues by antagonistic effects on tissue or by inhibiting estrogenic effects.

UF Estrogen Antagonists
B   Drugs   1967
R ↓ Androgens   1973
   Antineoplastic Drugs   1982
   ↓ Estrogens   1973
   ↓ Steroids   1973

Antigens   1982
PN 247   **SC** 03158

SN Substances such as microorganisms or foreign tissues, cells, proteins, toxoids, or exotoxins having the ability to induce antibody formation.

UF Allergens
   Immunogens
R   Antibodies   1973
   Blood Groups   1973
   ↓ Immunoglobulins   1973
   Interleukins   1994

Antihistaminic Drugs   1973
PN 271   **SC** 03160

B   Drugs   1967
N   Chlorprothixene   1973
   Cimetidine   1985
   Diphenhydramine   1973
   Mianserin   1982
   Orphenadrine   1973
   Promethazine   1973
R   Histamine   1973
   Hydroxyzine   1973
   ↓ Hypnotic Drugs   1973
   ↓ Sedatives   1973

Antihypertensive Drugs   1973
PN 264   **SC** 03170

B   Drugs   1967
N   Alpha Methylparatyrosine   1978
   Captopril   1991
   Chlorpromazine   1967
   Clonidine   1973
   Guanethidine   1973
   Hexamethonium   1973
   Hydralazine   1973
   Iproniazid   1973
   Mecamylamine   1973
   Methyldopa   1973
   Pargyline   1973
   Pheniprazine   1973
   Phenoxybenzamine   1973
   Quinpirole   1994
   Reserpine   1967
R ↓ Adrenergic Blocking Drugs   1973
   ↓ Diuretics   1973
   ↓ Ganglion Blocking Drugs   1973
   ↓ Heart Rate Affecting Drugs   1973
   ↓ Hypertension   1973
   ↓ Hypnotic Drugs   1973
   ↓ Muscle Relaxing Drugs   1973
   ↓ Sedatives   1973
   ↓ Tranquilizing Drugs   1967
   ↓ Vasodilator Drugs   1973

Antinauseant Drugs

Use Antiemetic Drugs

Antineoplastic Drugs   1982
PN 99   **SC** 03179

SN Drugs used in the prevention of the development, maturation, or spread of neoplastic cells.

Antineoplastic Drugs — (cont'd)
- **B**   Drugs [1967]
- **R**   ↓ Antibiotics [1973]
  - Antiestrogens [1982]
  - ↓ Hormones [1967]
  - Interferons [1994]
  - ↓ Neoplasms [1967]
  - ↓ Steroids [1973]

Antiparkinsonian Drugs
- **Use**   Antitremor Drugs

Antipathy
- **Use**   Aversion

Antipsychotic Drugs
SN Term was discontinued in 1982. In 2000, the term was stripped from all records containing it, and replaced with NEUROLEPTIC DRUGS, its postable counterpart. From 1982, see the specific tranquilizing drugs, neuroleptic drugs, or other appropriate drug classes.
- **Use**   Neuroleptic Drugs

Antipyretic Drugs
- **Use**   Anti Inflammatory Drugs

Antischizophrenic Drugs
SN Term was discontinued in 1982. In 2000, the term was stripped from all records containing it, and replaced with NEUROLEPTIC DRUGS, its postable counterpart. From 1982, see the specific tranquilizing drugs, neuroleptic drugs, or other appropriate drug classes.
- **Use**   Neuroleptic Drugs

AntiSemitism [1973]
PN 322   **SC** 03220
- **B**   Racial and Ethnic Attitudes [1982]
  - Religious Prejudices [1973]
- **R**   Holocaust [1988]
  - Jews [1997]
  - Judaism [1967]
  - ↓ Prejudice [1967]
  - Racism [1973]

Antisocial Behavior [1971]
PN 3036   **SC** 03230
- **UF**   Deviant Behavior
  - Sociopathology
- **B**   Behavior [1967]
- **N**   Child Neglect [1988]
  - ↓ Crime [1967]
  - Cruelty [1973]
  - Elder Abuse [1988]
  - Emotional Abuse [1991]
  - ↓ Harassment [2001]
  - ↓ Juvenile Delinquency [1967]
  - Partner Abuse [1991]
  - Patient Abuse [1991]
  - Persecution [1973]
  - Physical Abuse [1991]
  - Recidivism [1973]
  - Runaway Behavior [1973]
  - ↓ Sexual Abuse [1988]
  - Terrorism [1982]
  - Torture [1988]
  - ↓ Violence [1973]
- **R**   Antisocial Personality [1973]
  - ↓ Behavior Disorders [1971]
  - Erotomania [1997]
  - Explosive Disorder [2001]
  - ↓ Impulse Control Disorders [1997]

Antisocial Behavior — (cont'd)
- **R**   ↓ Prosocial Behavior [1982]
  - Psychopathology [1967]
  - ↓ Social Behavior [1967]

Antisocial Personality [1973]
PN 1767   **SC** 03240
SN Personality disorder characterized by conflict with others, low frustration tolerance, inadequate conscience development, and rejection of authority and discipline. In 1997, this term replaced the discontinued term PSYCHOPATHY. In 2000, PSYCHOPATHY was stripped from all records and replaced with ANTISOCIAL PERSONALITY.
- **UF**   Psychopath
  - Psychopathy
  - Sociopath
- **B**   Personality Disorders [1967]
- **R**   ↓ Antisocial Behavior [1971]
  - ↓ Autism [1967]
  - ↓ Criminals [1967]
  - ↓ Juvenile Delinquency [1967]
  - Narcissistic Personality [1973]

Antispasmodic Drugs [1973]
PN 7   **SC** 03250
SN Drugs that prevent or reduce spasms usually by relaxation of smooth muscle.
- **B**   Drugs [1967]
- **N**   Atropine [1973]
  - Chlorprothixene [1973]
  - Meperidine [1973]
  - Orphenadrine [1973]
  - Papaverine [1973]
  - Trihexyphenidyl [1973]
- **R**   ↓ Anticonvulsive Drugs [1973]
  - ↓ Cholinergic Blocking Drugs [1973]
  - ↓ Muscle Relaxing Drugs [1973]
  - ↓ Spasms [1973]

Antitremor Drugs [1973]
PN 192   **SC** 03260
SN Drugs that diminish skeletal muscle tone through action on the central nervous system.
- **UF**   Antiparkinsonian Drugs
- **B**   Drugs [1967]
- **N**   Amantadine [1978]
  - Diphenhydramine [1973]
  - Levodopa [1973]
  - Nomifensine [1982]
  - Orphenadrine [1973]
  - Trihexyphenidyl [1973]
- **R**   ↓ Decarboxylase Inhibitors [1982]
  - Parkinsons Disease [1973]
  - Tremor [1973]

Antitubercular Drugs [1973]
PN 11   **SC** 03270
- **B**   Drugs [1967]
- **N**   Iproniazid [1973]
  - Isoniazid [1973]
- **R**   ↓ Tuberculosis [1973]

Antiviral Drugs [1994]
PN 78   **SC** 03280
- **B**   Drugs [1967]
- **N**   Zidovudine [1994]

Antonyms [1973]
PN 55   **SC** 03290
- **B**   Semantics [1967]
  - Vocabulary [1967]
- **R**   Words (Phonetic Units) [1967]

Ants [1973]
PN 503   **SC** 03300
- **B**   Insects [1967]
- **R**   Larvae [1973]

Anxiety [1967]
PN 19596   **SC** 03310
SN Apprehension or fear of impending actual or imagined danger, vulnerability, or uncertainty. Prior to 1988, also used for anxiety disorders.
- **UF**   Angst
  - Anxiousness
  - Apprehension
  - Worry
- **B**   Emotional States [1973]
- **N**   Computer Anxiety [2001]
  - Mathematics Anxiety [1985]
  - Performance Anxiety [1994]
  - Social Anxiety [1985]
  - Speech Anxiety [1985]
  - Test Anxiety [1967]
- **R**   Agitation [1991]
  - ↓ Anxiety Disorders [1997]
  - Anxiety Management [1997]
  - ↓ Fear [1967]
  - Fear of Success [1978]
  - Guilt [1967]
  - Jealousy [1973]
  - ↓ Neurosis [1967]
  - Panic [1973]
  - Panic Disorder [1988]
  - ↓ Phobias [1967]
  - Shame [1994]
  - ↓ Stress [1967]

Anxiety Disorders [1997]
PN 4992   **SC** 03315
SN Disorders characterized by anxiety or dread without apparent object or cause. Symptoms include irritability, anxious expectations, pangs of conscience, anxiety attacks, or phobias. In 1997, this term was created to replace the discontinued term ANXIETY NEUROSIS. In 2000, ANXIETY NEUROSIS was stripped from all records and replaced with ANXIETY DISORDERS.
- **UF**   Anxiety Neurosis
  - Generalized Anxiety Disorder
- **B**   Mental Disorders [1967]
- **N**   Castration Anxiety [1973]
  - Death Anxiety [1978]
  - Obsessive Compulsive Disorder [1985]
  - Panic Disorder [1988]
  - ↓ Phobias [1967]
  - Posttraumatic Stress Disorder [1985]
  - Separation Anxiety [1973]
- **R**   ↓ Anxiety [1967]
  - Anxiety Management [1997]
  - Fear of Success [1978]
  - Guilt [1967]
  - Hypochondriasis [1973]
  - Mathematics Anxiety [1985]
  - Performance Anxiety [1994]
  - Social Anxiety [1985]
  - Speech Anxiety [1985]
  - Test Anxiety [1967]

Anxiety Management [1997]
PN 107   **SC** 03318
- **R**   ↓ Anxiety [1967]
  - ↓ Anxiety Disorders [1997]
  - ↓ Behavior Modification [1973]
  - ↓ Behavior Therapy [1967]
  - ↓ Cognitive Techniques [1985]
  - Cognitive Therapy [1982]
  - ↓ Relaxation Therapy [1978]

Anxiety Management — (cont'd)
R   Stress Management [1985]

Anxiety Neurosis
SN   Term was discontinued in 1997. In 2000, the term was stripped from all records containing it, and replaced with ANXIETY DISORDERS, its postable counterpart.
Use   Anxiety Disorders

Anxiety Reducing Drugs
Use   Tranquilizing Drugs

Anxiolytic Drugs
Use   Tranquilizing Drugs

Anxiousness
Use   Anxiety

Aorta [1973]
PN   24   SC   03360
B   Arteries (Anatomy) [1973]

Apathy [1973]
PN   152   SC   03380
UF   Indifference
B   Emotional States [1973]
R   Hopelessness [1988]
    ↓ Separation Reactions [1997]

Apes
Use   Primates (Nonhuman)

Aphagia [1973]
PN   48   SC   03400
SN   Not eating, the refusal to eat, or an inability to swallow foods or fluids.
B   Pain [1967]
    Symptoms [1967]
R   ↓ Eating Disorders [1997]

Aphasia [1967]
PN   3839   SC   03410
SN   Partial or complete impairment of language comprehension, formulation, or use due to brain damage.
UF   Agrammatism
    Word Deafness
B   Brain Disorders [1967]
    Language Disorders [1982]
N   Acalculia [1973]
    ↓ Agnosia [1973]
    Agraphia [1973]
    ↓ Dysphasia [1978]
R   ↓ Learning Disabilities [1973]
    ↓ Perceptual Disturbances [1973]

Aphrodisiacs [1973]
PN   18   SC   03420
R   ↓ Cannabis [1973]

Aplysia
Use   Snails

Apnea [1973]
PN   181   SC   03430
SN   Temporary absence of breathing or prolonged respiratory failure.
B   Respiratory Distress [1973]
    Respiratory Tract Disorders [1973]
N   Sleep Apnea [1991]
R   ↓ Neonatal Disorders [1973]

Apnea — (cont'd)
R   Sudden Infant Death [1982]

Apomorphine [1973]
PN   1460   SC   03440
UF   Apomorphine Hydrochloride
B   Alkaloids [1973]
    Dopamine Agonists [1985]
    Emetic Drugs [1973]
    Hypnotic Drugs [1973]
    Narcotic Drugs [1973]

Apomorphine Hydrochloride
Use   Apomorphine

Apoplexy
Use   Cerebrovascular Accidents

Apparatus [1967]
PN   3577   SC   03480
SN   Set of materials, instruments, or equipment designed for specific operation in any setting. Use a more specific term if possible. In 1997, this term replaced the discontinued terms TRANSISTORS (APPARATUS) and VOLT METERS. In 2000, these terms were stripped from all records and replaced with APPARATUS.
UF   Devices (Experimental)
    Equipment
    Experimental Apparatus
    Transistors (Apparatus)
    Volt Meters
N   Amplifiers (Apparatus) [1973]
    Audiometers [1973]
    Cage Apparatus [1973]
    Cameras [1973]
    ↓ Computer Peripheral Devices [1985]
    ↓ Computers [1967]
    Electrodes [1967]
    Generators (Apparatus) [1973]
    Incubators (Apparatus) [1973]
    Keyboards [1985]
    ↓ Mazes [1967]
    Metronomes [1973]
    Microscopes [1973]
    Oscilloscopes [1973]
    Polygraphs [1973]
    Shuttle Boxes [1973]
    Skinner Boxes [1973]
    Sonar [1973]
    ↓ Stimulators (Apparatus) [1973]
    Tachistoscopes [1973]
    ↓ Tape Recorders [1973]
    Timers (Apparatus) [1973]
    Transducers [1973]
    Vibrators (Apparatus) [1973]
R   ↓ Augmentative Communication [1994]
    ↓ Television [1967]

Apparent Distance [1973]
PN   108   SC   03490
SN   Subjective perception of distance as opposed to actual distance, based on comparison of retinal and familiar sizes.
B   Distance Perception [1973]

Apparent Movement [1967]
PN   889   SC   03500
SN   Subjective perception of movement in the absence of real physical movement.
UF   Stroboscopic Movement
B   Motion Perception [1967]
N   Autokinetic Illusion [1967]

Apparent Size [1973]
PN   249   SC   03510
SN   Subjective perception of size as opposed to real or actual size.
UF   Size (Apparent)
B   Size Discrimination [1967]

Apperception [1973]
PN   68   SC   03520
SN   Process of assimilating new perceptions and relating them to existing body of knowledge.
R   ↓ Attention [1967]
    ↓ Perception [1967]

Appetite [1973]
PN   660   SC   03530
SN   Indicates an instinctive or acquired motivation, impulse, or desire stemming from internal physiological conditions. Compare HUNGER.
B   Physiology [1967]
N   Hunger [1967]
R   ↓ Appetite Depressing Drugs [1973]
    Craving [1997]
    Dietary Restraint [1994]
    Eating Attitudes [1994]
    ↓ Eating Disorders [1997]
    Satiation [1967]

Appetite Depressing Drugs [1973]
PN   171   SC   03540
UF   Anorexigenic Drugs
B   Drugs [1967]
N   ↓ Amphetamine [1967]
    Dextroamphetamine [1973]
    Fenfluramine [1973]
    Phenmetrazine [1973]
R   ↓ Appetite [1973]

Appetite Disorders
SN   Term was discontinued in 1997. In 2000, the term was stripped from all records containing it, and replaced with EATING DISORDERS, its postable counterpart.
Use   Eating Disorders

Applied Psychology [1973]
PN   634   SC   03560
SN   Broad discipline in which psychological principles and theories are used to solve practical problems.
B   Psychology [1967]
N   ↓ Clinical Psychology [1967]
    Community Psychology [1973]
    Consumer Psychology [1973]
    Counseling Psychology [1973]
    ↓ Educational Psychology [1967]
N   Engineering Psychology [1967]
    Environmental Psychology [1982]
    Industrial Psychology [1967]
    Military Psychology [1967]
    Political Psychology [1967]
    Social Psychology [1967]
    Sport Psychology [1982]

Apprehension
Use   Anxiety

Apprenticeship [1973]
PN   141   SC   03580
B   Personnel Training [1967]
R   ↓ Experiential Learning [1997]
    Mentor [1985]

Approval (Social)
　Use　Social Approval

Apraxia 1973
PN　632　　　　　　　　　　SC　03600
SN　Inability to execute complex coordinated movements resulting from lesions in the motor area of the cortex but involving no sensory impairment or paralysis.
　UF　Akinesia
　B　Movement Disorders 1985
　　　Symptoms 1967
　R　Parkinsonism 1994
　　↓ Speech Disorders 1967

Aptitude
　Use　Ability

Aptitude (Academic)
　Use　Academic Aptitude

Aptitude Measures 1967
PN　2317　　　　　　　　　SC　03630
SN　Tests designed to assess capacities or potential abilities in performing tasks, skills, or other acts which have not yet been learned. In 1997, this term replaced the discontinued term SCHOOL AND COLLEGE ABILITY TEST. In 2000, SCHOOL AND COLLEGE ABILITY TEST was stripped from all records and replaced with APTITUDE MEASURES.
　UF　Ability Tests
　　　School and College Ability Test
　　　Tests (Aptitude)
　B　Measurement 1967
　N　Army General Classification Test 1967
　　　College Entrance Examination Board Scholastic Aptitude Test 2001
　　　Differential Aptitude Tests 1973
　　　General Aptitude Test Battery 1973
　　　Graduate Record Examination 1973
　　　Modern Language Aptitude Test 1973

Arabs 1988
PN　409　　　　　　　　　　SC　03635
　UF　Palestinians
　B　Racial and Ethnic Groups 2001
　R　Minority Groups 1967

Arachnida 1973
PN　326　　　　　　　　　　SC　03640
　UF　Spiders
　B　Arthropoda 1973

Arachnophobia
　Use　Phobias

Archetypes 1991
PN　364　　　　　　　　　　SC　03650
SN　Unconscious representation of inherited collective experience on which the personality is built. Anima, animus, and the shadow are major archetypes. Consider JUNGIAN PSYCHOLOGY to access references from 1973-1990.
　B　Collective Unconscious 1997
　R　Analytical Psychotherapy 1973
　　↓ Imagery 1967
　　　Jung (Carl) 1973
　　↓ Jungian Psychology 1973
　　　Myths 1967
　　　Unconscious (Personality Factor) 1967

Architects 1973
PN　80　　　　　　　　　　　SC　03670

Architects — (cont'd)
　B　Business and Industrial Personnel 1967

Architecture 1973
PN　639　　　　　　　　　　SC　03680
　B　Arts 1973
　N　Interior Design 1982
　R　Computer Assisted Design 1997
　　↓ Environment 1967
　　↓ Environmental Planning 1982
　　　Religious Buildings 1973
　　　Urban Planning 1973

Arecoline 1973
PN　79　　　　　　　　　　　SC　03690
　UF　Arecoline Hydrobromide
　B　Cholinomimetic Drugs 1973
　R　Bromides 1973

Arecoline Hydrobromide
　Use　Arecoline

Arguments 1973
PN　476　　　　　　　　　　SC　03710
　B　Conflict 1967
　　　Interpersonal Communication 1973
　R　Debates 1997

Arithmetic
　Use　Mathematics

Arm (Anatomy) 1973
PN　518　　　　　　　　　　SC　03730
　B　Musculoskeletal System 1973
　R　Elbow (Anatomy) 1973
　　　Hand (Anatomy) 1967
　　　Shoulder (Anatomy) 1973
　　　Wrist 1973

Army General Classification Test 1967
PN　8　　　　　　　　　　　SC　03740
　B　Aptitude Measures 1967

Army Personnel 1967
PN　1182　　　　　　　　　SC　03750
　B　Military Personnel 1967
　R　Draftees 1973
　　　National Guardsmen 1973

Arousal (Physiological)
　Use　Physiological Arousal

Arousal (Sexual)
　Use　Sexual Arousal

Arrest (Law)
　Use　Legal Arrest

Arrhythmias (Heart) 1973
PN　221　　　　　　　　　　SC　03790
　B　Heart Disorders 1973
　N　Bradycardia 1973
　　　Fibrillation (Heart) 1973
　　　Tachycardia 1973

Arson 1985
PN　162　　　　　　　　　　SC　03795
　UF　Firesetting
　B　Crime 1967

Art 1967
PN　1367　　　　　　　　　SC　03800

Art — (cont'd)
SN　Products of aesthetic expression. Not used as a document type identifier.
　UF　Artwork
　B　Arts 1973
　N　Crafts 1973
　　　Drawing 1967
　　　Painting (Art) 1973
　　　Photographic Art 1973
　　　Sculpturing 1973

Art Education 1973
PN　592　　　　　　　　　　SC　03810
　B　Curriculum 1967

Art Therapy 1973
PN　1511　　　　　　　　　SC　03820
SN　Therapy that uses the creative work of clients for emotional expression, sublimation, achievement, and to reveal underlying conflicts.
　B　Creative Arts Therapy 1994
　R　Educational Therapy 1997
　　　Movement Therapy 1997
　　　Recreation Therapy 1973

Arterial Pulse 1973
PN　375　　　　　　　　　　SC　03830
　UF　Pulse (Arterial)
　R　Blood Circulation 1973

Arteries (Anatomy) 1973
PN　180　　　　　　　　　　SC　03840
　UF　Coronary Vessels
　　　Retinal Vessels
　B　Blood Vessels 1973
　N　Aorta 1973
　　　Carotid Arteries 1973

Arteriosclerosis 1973
PN　41　　　　　　　　　　　SC　03850
　B　Cardiovascular Disorders 1967
　N　Atherosclerosis 1973
　　　Cerebral Arteriosclerosis 1973
　R　↓ Blood Pressure Disorders 1973

Arthritis 1973
PN　509　　　　　　　　　　SC　03860
　UF　Rheumatism
　B　Joint Disorders 1973
　N　Rheumatoid Arthritis 1973
　R　↓ Infectious Disorders 1973

Arthropoda 1973
PN　39　　　　　　　　　　　SC　03870
　B　Invertebrates 1973
　N　Arachnida 1973
　　↓ Crustacea 1973
　　↓ Insects 1967

Articulation (Speech) 1967
PN　1483　　　　　　　　　SC　03880
SN　Production of speech sounds resulting from vocal tract movements.
　B　Speech Characteristics 1973
　　　Verbal Communication 1967
　R　Phonetics 1967
　　　Pronunciation 1973

Articulation Disorders 1973
PN　413　　　　　　　　　　SC　03890
SN　Speech disorders involving the substitution, omission, distortion, and addition of phonemes.
　UF　Misarticulation

Articulation Disorders — (cont'd)
B   Speech Disorders [1967]
N   Dysarthria [1973]

Artificial Insemination
Use   Reproductive Technology

Artificial Intelligence [1982]
PN   2075   SC   03895
SN   Study and application of computers to simulate and perform functions of human information processing.
B   Computer Applications [1973]
N   ↓ Expert Systems [1991]
    Neural Networks [1991]
R   Automated Speech Recognition [1994]
    Automation [1967]
    ↓ Cognitive Processes [1967]
    ↓ Computers [1967]
    Cybernetics [1967]
    Decision Support Systems [1997]
    Human Machine Systems [1997]
    Intelligence [1967]
    Robotics [1985]

Artificial Limbs
Use   Prostheses

Artificial Pacemakers [1973]
PN   47   SC   03910
UF   Pacemakers (Artificial)
B   Medical Therapeutic Devices [1973]

Artificial Respiration [1973]
PN   50   SC   03920
UF   Lifesaving
B   Physical Treatment Methods [1973]
R   Respiration [1967]
    ↓ Respiratory System [1973]
    ↓ Respiratory Tract Disorders [1973]

Artistic Ability [1973]
PN   260   SC   03930
B   Nonverbal Ability [1988]
N   Musical Ability [1973]
R   Creativity [1967]

Artists [1973]
PN   1222   SC   03940
B   Personnel [1967]
N   Musicians [1991]
    Writers [1991]

Arts [1973]
PN   405   SC   03950
SN   Conceptually broad term referring to all forms of the arts, including the performing arts. Use a more specific term if possible.
UF   Performing Arts
N   ↓ Architecture [1973]
    ↓ Art [1967]
    Dance [1973]
    ↓ Literature [1967]
    ↓ Music [1967]
    ↓ Theatre [1973]
R   Aesthetics [1967]
    Postmodernism [1997]

Artwork
Use   Art

Asbestos
Use   Hazardous Materials

Asceticism [1973]
PN   30   SC   03970
B   Philosophies [1967]
    Religious Practices [1973]
R   Religion [1967]
    ↓ Religious Beliefs [1973]

Ascorbic Acid [1973]
PN   96   SC   03980
UF   Vitamin C
B   Acids [1973]
    Vitamins [1973]

Asian Americans
SN   Term was discontinued in 1982. In 2000, the term was stripped from all records containing it, and replaced with ASIANS, its postable counterpart.
Use   Asians

Asians [1982]
PN   4018   SC   04007
SN   In 1982, this term was created to replace the discontinued term ASIAN AMERICANS. In 2000, ASIAN AMERICANS was stripped from all records and replaced with ASIANS.
UF   Asian Americans
    Orientals
B   Racial and Ethnic Groups [2001]
N   Chinese Cultural Groups [1997]
    Japanese Cultural Groups [1997]
    Korean Cultural Groups [1997]
    Vietnamese Cultural Groups [1997]
R   Minority Groups [1967]

Aspartic Acid [1973]
PN   451   SC   04010
B   Amino Acids [1973]
    Neurotransmitters [1985]
N   N-Methyl-D-Aspartate [1994]

Aspergers Syndrome [1991]
PN   258   SC   04015
SN   Syndrome or disorder usually first diagnosed in childhood, characterized by severe and sustained impairment in social interactions and restricted, repetitive patterns of behaviors, interests, and activities.
UF   Autistic Psychopathy
B   Pervasive Developmental Disorders [2001]
    Syndromes [1973]
R   ↓ Autism [1967]
    Developmental Disabilities [1982]
    Rett Syndrome [1994]

Asphyxia
Use   Anoxia

Aspiration Level [1973]
PN   286   SC   04030
SN   Level of expectations for future achievement.
R   ↓ Aspirations [1967]

Aspirations [1967]
PN   742   SC   04040
SN   Individual desires to achieve goals and ideals. Use a more specific term if possible.
UF   Ambition
N   Educational Aspirations [1973]
    Occupational Aspirations [1973]
R   Aspiration Level [1973]
    Goal Setting [1997]

Aspirations — (cont'd)
R   ↓ Goals [1967]
    ↓ Motivation [1967]

Aspirin [1973]
PN   107   SC   04050
UF   Acetylsalicylic Acid
B   Acids [1973]
    Analgesic Drugs [1973]
    Anti Inflammatory Drugs [1982]

Assassination (Political)
Use   Political Assassination

Assertiveness [1973]
PN   1823   SC   04070
B   Personality Traits [1967]
R   Assertiveness Training [1978]
    Empowerment [1991]
    Extraversion [1967]
    ↓ Resistance [1997]

Assertiveness Training [1978]
PN   947   SC   04072
SN   Training in the social skills required to be able to refuse requests; to express both positive and negative feelings; to initiate, engage in, and terminate conversation; and to make personal requests without suffering from excessive stress.
B   Human Potential Movement [1982]
R   Assertiveness [1973]
    ↓ Behavior Modification [1973]
    Communication Skills Training [1982]
    Human Relations Training [1978]
    Social Skills Training [1982]

Assessment
Use   Measurement

Assessment (Cognitive)
Use   Cognitive Assessment

Assessment (Psychological)
Use   Psychological Assessment

Assessment Centers [1982]
PN   274   SC   04082
SN   Centers specializing in standardized, systematic behavioral evaluation process used to make selection, promotion, development, counseling, and career planning personnel decisions.
R   Occupational Guidance [1967]
    ↓ Personnel Evaluation [1973]
    Personnel Placement [1973]
    Personnel Promotion [1978]
    ↓ Personnel Selection [1967]

Assessment Criteria
Use   Evaluation Criteria

Assimilation (Cultural)
Use   Cultural Assimilation

Assistance (Social Behavior) [1973]
PN   1907   SC   04100
SN   Act of rendering aid or help. Limited to human populations.
UF   Helping Behavior
B   Interpersonal Interaction [1967]
    Prosocial Behavior [1982]
R   Altruism [1973]
    Charitable Behavior [1973]
    ↓ Help Seeking Behavior [1978]

Assistance (Social Behavior) — (cont'd)
R   Social Support Networks   1982

Assistance Seeking (Professional)
Use   Health Care Utilization

Assisted Suicide   1997
PN   182   SC   04105
SN   Provision of support and/or means that gives a patient the power to take his or her own life.
B   Suicide   1967
R   Advance Directives   1994
   ↓ Death and Dying   1967
    Euthanasia   1973
    Life Sustaining Treatment   1997
    Palliative Care   1991
    Professional Ethics   1973
    Terminally Ill Patients   1973
    Treatment Refusal   1994
    Treatment Withholding   1988

Association (Free)
Use   Free Association

Associationism   1973
PN   68   SC   04120
SN   Theory which holds that learning and mental development consist mainly of combinations and recombinations of irreducible mental elements. Also, the basis for theories that explain learning in terms of stimulus and response.
B   History of Psychology   1967
    Psychological Theories   2001

Associations (Contextual)
Use   Contextual Associations

Associations (Groups)
Use   Organizations

Associations (Word)
Use   Word Associations

Associative Processes   1967
PN   2848   SC   04160
SN   Development or maintenance of learned or cognitive connections (associations) between events, sensations, ideas, memories, or behavior as the result of functional relationships, similarity-contrast, or spatial-temporal contiguity.
B   Cognitive Processes   1967
N   Cognitive Contiguity   1973
    Connotations   1973
    Contextual Associations   1967
    Isolation Effect   1973
R   Cognitive Generalization   1967
    Connectionism   1994
    Cues   1967
    Word Associations   1967
    Word Recognition   1988

Assortative Mating   1991
PN   85   SC   04165
SN   Nonrandom mating between unrelated individuals with similar characteristics. Used for human or animal populations.
UF   Assortive Mating
R   ↓ Animal Breeding   1973
    Animal Mate Selection   1982
   ↓ Animal Mating Behavior   1967
    Family Resemblance   1991
   ↓ Genetics   1967
    Human Mate Selection   1988

Assortative Mating — (cont'd)
R   Phenotypes   1973
    Population Genetics   1973
   ↓ Psychosexual Behavior   1967

Assortive Mating
Use   Assortative Mating

Asthenia   1973
PN   51   SC   04170
SN   Physical weakness, lack of strength and vitality, or a lack of concentration.
B   Symptoms   1967
N   Myasthenia   1973
R   Neurasthenic Neurosis   1973

Asthenic Personality
SN   Term was discontinued in 1997. In 2000, the term was stripped from all records containing it, and replaced with PERSONALITY DISORDERS, its postable counterpart.
Use   Personality Disorders

Asthma   1967
PN   1368   SC   04190
B   Dyspnea   1973
R   ↓ Immunologic Disorders   1973
   ↓ Somatoform Disorders   2001

Astrology   1973
PN   102   SC   04200
R   ↓ Parapsychology   1967
    Superstitions   1973

Astronauts   1973
PN   112   SC   04210
B   Aerospace Personnel   1973
R   Aircraft Pilots   1973
   ↓ Military Personnel   1967
    Spacecraft   1973

Asylums
Use   Psychiatric Hospitals

At Risk Populations   1985
PN   12306   SC   04225
SN   Groups or individuals considered in danger of developing a physical, mental, emotional, behavioral, or other disorder due to adverse internal or external factors.
UF   High Risk Populations
    Risk Populations
R   Coronary Prone Behavior   1982
    Predisposition   1973
    Premorbidity   1978
    Risk Factors   2001
    Susceptibility (Disorders)   1973

Ataractic Drugs
Use   Tranquilizing Drugs

Ataraxic Drugs
Use   Tranquilizing Drugs

Ataxia   1973
PN   321   SC   04250
SN   Loss of coordination of voluntary muscular movement.
UF   Dysmetria
B   Movement Disorders   1985
    Symptoms   1967
R   Hyperkinesis   1973

Atheism   1973
PN   37   SC   04260
B   Religious Beliefs   1973

Atherosclerosis   1973
PN   117   SC   04270
B   Arteriosclerosis   1973

Athetosis   1973
PN   26   SC   04280
SN   Nonprogressive, developmentally-evolving disorder arising from basal ganglia damage in the full term brain characterized by postural reflex impairments, involuntary movements, and dysarthria with preservation of sensation, ocular movement, and frequently, intelligence.
B   Brain Disorders   1967
    Movement Disorders   1985
R   Cerebral Palsy   1967

Athletes   1973
PN   3171   SC   04287
N   College Athletes   1994
R   Athletic Participation   1973
    Athletic Performance   1991
    Athletic Training   1991
   ↓ Sports   1967

Athletic Participation   1973
PN   1154   SC   04290
B   Participation   1973
    Recreation   1967
R   ↓ Athletes   1973
    College Athletes   1994
   ↓ Extracurricular Activities   1973
   ↓ Sports   1967

Athletic Performance   1991
PN   1031   SC   04300
UF   Sport Performance
B   Performance   1967
R   ↓ Athletes   1973
    Athletic Training   1991
    College Athletes   1994
   ↓ Sports   1967
   ↓ Teams   1988

Athletic Training   1991
PN   314   SC   04305
UF   Sport Training
    Training (Athletic)
R   ↓ Athletes   1973
    Athletic Performance   1991
    Coaches   1988
    College Athletes   1994
   ↓ Education   1967
   ↓ Extracurricular Activities   1973
   ↓ Sports   1967
   ↓ Teams   1988

Atmospheric Conditions   1973
PN   416   SC   04310
UF   Barometric Pressure
    Climate (Meteorological)
    Weather
B   Environmental Effects   1973
R   Pollution   1973
   ↓ Temperature Effects   1967
    Thermal Acclimatization   1973

Atomism
Use   Reductionism

Atria (Heart)
Use Heart Auricles

Atrial Fibrillation
Use Fibrillation (Heart)

Atrophy (Cerebral)
Use Cerebral Atrophy

Atrophy (Muscular)
Use Muscular Atrophy

Atropine 1973
PN 495   **SC** 04350
  UF Hyoscyamine (dl-)
      Methylatropine
  B Alkaloids 1973
      Amines 1973
      Analgesic Drugs 1973
      Antispasmodic Drugs 1973
      Cholinergic Blocking Drugs 1973
      Narcotic Drugs 1973
      Sedatives 1973

Attachment Behavior 1985
PN 4790   **SC** 04355
SN Formation of and investment in significant relationships. Usually refers to the emotional and biological attachment of human or animal infants to caretaking figures.
  UF Bonding (Emotional)
  B Behavior 1967
  R Abandonment 1997
      Anaclitic Depression 1973
      Attachment Disorders 2001
      Dependency (Personality) 1967
      Emotional Development 1973
      Erotomania 1997
      Intimacy 1973
      Love 1973
      Object Relations 1982
      ↓ Parent Child Relations 1967
      Postpartum Depression 1973
      Separation Anxiety 1973
      Separation Individuation 1982
      ↓ Separation Reactions 1997
      Stranger Reactions 1988

Attachment Disorders 2001
PN 0   **SC** 04357
  UF Reactive Attachment Disorder
  R Attachment Behavior 1985
      ↓ Child Abuse 1971
      Child Neglect 1988
      Failure to Thrive 1988
      ↓ Parent Child Relations 1967
      ↓ Relationship Termination 1997
      Separation Anxiety 1973
      ↓ Separation Reactions 1997

Attack Behavior 1973
PN 743   **SC** 04360
SN Forceful, assaultive behavior. Used for human or animal populations.
  B Aggressive Behavior 1967
      Animal Aggressive Behavior 1973
  R ↓ Animal Defensive Behavior 1982
      Animal Predatory Behavior 1978
      Instinctive Behavior 1982
      Retaliation 1991

Attainment (Achievement)
Use Achievement

Attainment Level (Education)
Use Educational Attainment Level

Attempted Suicide 1973
PN 3504   **SC** 04380
  UF Parasuicide
      Suicide (Attempted)
  B Behavior Disorders 1971
      Self Destructive Behavior 1985
  R Suicidal Ideation 1991
      ↓ Suicide 1967
      Suicide Prevention 1973

Attendance (School)
Use School Attendance

Attendants (Institutions) 1973
PN 319   **SC** 04400
  UF Hospital Attendants
      Residential Care Attendants
  B Paramedical Personnel 1973
  R Prison Personnel 1973
      ↓ Psychiatric Hospital Staff 1973

Attention 1967
PN 10717   **SC** 04410
SN Condition of perceptual or cognitive awareness of or focusing on some aspect of one's environment. Compare ATTENTION SPAN and VIGILANCE.
  B Awareness 1967
  N Divided Attention 1973
      ↓ Monitoring 1973
      Selective Attention 1973
      ↓ Sustained Attention 1997
      Vigilance 1967
  R Apperception 1973
      Attention Span 1973
      Concentration 1982
      Distraction 1978
      Human Channel Capacity 1973
      Listening (Interpersonal) 1997
      ↓ Perception 1967
      Rotary Pursuit 1967
      Signal Detection (Perception) 1967
      Time On Task 1988
      ↓ Tracking 1967

Attention Deficit Disorder 1985
PN 4283   **SC** 04412
SN A disorder characterized by persistent developmentally inappropriate inattention and impulsivity.
  N Attention Deficit Disorder with Hyperactivity 2001
  R Attention Span 1973
      Distractibility 1973
      Impulsiveness 1973
      ↓ Mental Disorders 1967
      Minimal Brain Disorders 1973
      Oppositional Defiant Disorder 1997

Attention Deficit Disorder with Hyperactivity 2001
PN 0   **SC** 04414
SN A behavior disorder in which the essential features are signs of developmentally inappropriate inattention, impulsivity, and hyperactivity. Use both ATTENTION DEFICIT DISORDER and HYPERKINESIS to access references prior to 2000.
  UF ADHD
  B Attention Deficit Disorder 1985
  R Attention Span 1973
      Distractibility 1973
      Hyperkinesis 1973
      Impulsiveness 1973

Attention Deficit Disorder with Hyperactivity — (cont'd)
  R ↓ Mental Disorders 1967
      Minimal Brain Disorders 1973
      Oppositional Defiant Disorder 1997

Attention Span 1973
PN 350   **SC** 04413
SN Temporal duration of concentration or amount of material grasped during exposure to stimuli or information. Compare ATTENTION.
  B Sustained Attention 1997
  R ↓ Attention 1967
      ↓ Attention Deficit Disorder 1985
      Attention Deficit Disorder with Hyperactivity 2001
      Conceptual Tempo 1985
      Distraction 1978
      Vigilance 1967

Attitude Change 1967
PN 4928   **SC** 04430
SN Significant alteration in individual or group attitudes or opinions.
  UF Opinion Change
  R ↓ Attitudes 1967
      Brainwashing 1982

Attitude Formation 1973
PN 710   **SC** 04440
SN Process of developing an opinion or attitude, especially as influenced by psychological, emotional, social, and experiential factors.
  R ↓ Attitudes 1967

Attitude Measurement 1973
PN 842   **SC** 04460
SN Projective, physiological, self-report, or other approaches to the assessment of attitudes.
  B Measurement 1967
  R ↓ Attitude Measures 1967
      ↓ Attitudes 1967
      Likert Scales 1994

Attitude Measures 1967
PN 3018   **SC** 04470
SN Instruments or devices used in the assessment of attitudes. In 1997, this term replaced the discontinued terms ALLPORT VERNON LINDZEY STUDY VALUES, MINNESOTA TEACHER ATTITUDE INVENTORY, and OPINION ATTITUDE AND INTEREST SURVEY. In 2000, these terms were stripped from all records and replaced with ATTITUDE MEASURES.
  UF Allport Vernon Lindzey Study Values
      Minnesota Teacher Attitude Inventory
      Opinion Attitude and Interest Survey
      Opinion Questionnaires
      Opinion Surveys
  B Measurement 1967
  N Parent Attitude Research Instrument 1973
      Wilson Patterson Conservatism Scale 1973
  R Attitude Measurement 1973
      ↓ Attitudes 1967
      Likert Scales 1994
      ↓ Preference Measures 1973
      Semantic Differential 1967

Attitude Similarity 1973
PN 992   **SC** 04480
  R ↓ Attitudes 1967

Attitudes 1967
PN 10650   **SC** 04500

Attitudes — (cont'd)

SN Conceptually broad term referring to a mental position or feeling toward certain ideas, facts, or persons. Use a more specific term if possible.

UF   Beliefs (Nonreligious)
      Opinions
N   Adolescent Attitudes 1988
      Adult Attitudes 1988
      Aged (Attitudes Toward) 1978
      Aging (Attitudes Toward) 1985
      Child Attitudes 1988
      Childrearing Attitudes 1973
      ↓ Client Attitudes 1982
      Community Attitudes 1973
      Computer Attitudes 1988
      ↓ Consumer Attitudes 1973
      Counselor Attitudes 1973
      Death Attitudes 1973
      ↓ Disabled (Attitudes Toward) 1997
      ↓ Drug Usage Attitudes 1973
      Eating Attitudes 1994
      ↓ Employee Attitudes 1967
      Employer Attitudes 1973
      Environmental Attitudes 1978
      Family Planning Attitudes 1973
      Health Attitudes 1985
      ↓ Health Personnel Attitudes 1985
      Homosexuality (Attitudes Toward) 1982
      Job Applicant Attitudes 1973
      Marriage Attitudes 1973
      Obesity (Attitudes Toward) 1997
      Occupational Attitudes 1973
      ↓ Parental Attitudes 1973
      ↓ Physical Illness (Attitudes Toward) 1985
      ↓ Political Attitudes 1973
      Psychologist Attitudes 1991
      Public Opinion 1973
      ↓ Racial and Ethnic Attitudes 1982
      ↓ Sex Role Attitudes 1978
      Sexual Attitudes 1973
      ↓ Socioeconomic Class Attitudes 1973
      Stereotyped Attitudes 1967
      Student Attitudes 1967
      ↓ Teacher Attitudes 1967
      Work (Attitudes Toward) 1973
R   Attitude Change 1967
      Attitude Formation 1973
      Attitude Measurement 1973
      ↓ Attitude Measures 1967
      Attitude Similarity 1973
      Attribution 1973
      ↓ Cognitions 1985
      Hedonism 1973
      Impression Formation 1978
      Irrational Beliefs 1982
      Labeling 1978
      Planned Behavior 1997
      ↓ Prejudice 1967
      ↓ Religious Beliefs 1973
      Stigma 1991
      Superstitions 1973
      World View 1988

Attorneys 1973

PN 775   **SC** 04510
UF   Lawyers
B   Legal Personnel 1985
R   ↓ Law Enforcement Personnel 1973
      Law Students 1978

Attraction (Interpersonal)

Use Interpersonal Attraction

Attribution 1973

PN 11221   **SC** 04525
SN Perception of causes of behavior or events or of dispositional properties of an individual or group.
B   Social Perception 1967
R   ↓ Attitudes 1967
      Blame 1994
      Causal Analysis 1994
      Impression Formation 1978
      Inference 1973
      Internal External Locus of Control 1967
      Learned Helplessness 1978
      Self Fulfilling Prophecies 1997

Atypical Paranoid Disorder

Use Paranoia (Psychosis)

Atypical Somatoform Disorder

Use Body Dysmorphic Disorder

Audiences 1967

PN 648   **SC** 04530
SN Groups of spectators or listeners.
N   Sports Spectators 1997
R   Observers 1973

Audiogenic Seizures 1978

PN 91   **SC** 04536
B   Convulsions 1967
R   ↓ Auditory Stimulation 1967

Audiology 1973

PN 172   **SC** 04540
SN Scientific study of hearing, including: anatomical and functional properties of the ear; hearing disorders and their assessment and treatment; and the rehabilitation of hearing-impaired persons. Consider also AUDIOMETRY and SPEECH AND HEARING MEASURES.
B   Paramedical Sciences 1973

Audiometers 1973

PN 19   **SC** 04550
B   Apparatus 1967

Audiometry 1967

PN 1051   **SC** 04560
SN Specific procedures or audiometric tests used to measure hearing acuity and range in the diagnosis and evaluation of hearing impairments. Consider also AUDIOLOGY and SPEECH AND HEARING MEASURES.
UF   Bekesy Audiometry
N   Bone Conduction Audiometry 1973
R   Auditory Acuity 1988
      ↓ Auditory Stimulation 1967
      ↓ Perceptual Measures 1973

Audiotapes 1973

PN 391   **SC** 04570
SN Tape recordings of sound used in both educational and noneducational settings. Not used as a document type identifier.
B   Audiovisual Communications Media 1973

Audiovisual Aids (Educational)

Use Educational Audiovisual Aids

Audiovisual Communications Media 1973

PN 265   **SC** 04590
B   Communications Media 1973
N   Audiotapes 1973

Audiovisual Communications Media — (cont'd)

N   ↓ Educational Audiovisual Aids 1973
      Film Strips 1967
      ↓ Motion Pictures 1973
      Photographs 1967
      Radio 1973
      ↓ Television 1967
      Television Advertising 1973
      Videotapes 1973

Audiovisual Instruction 1973

PN 298   **SC** 04600
B   Teaching Methods 1967
N   Televised Instruction 1973
      Videotape Instruction 1973
R   ↓ Educational Audiovisual Aids 1973

Audition

Use Auditory Perception

Auditory Acuity 1988

PN 141   **SC** 04615
SN The ability or capacity of a listener to perceive fine detail. Consider AUDITORY THRESHOLDS or AUDITORY DISCRIMINATION to access references prior to 1988.
UF   Hearing Acuity
B   Auditory Perception 1967
      Perceptual Discrimination 1973
R   ↓ Audiometry 1967
      Auditory Discrimination 1967
R   Auditory Localization 1973
      Auditory Thresholds 1973

Auditory Cortex 1967

PN 611   **SC** 04620
UF   Cortex (Auditory)
B   Temporal Lobe 1973

Auditory Discrimination 1967

PN 3352   **SC** 04630
SN Distinguishing between sounds of different intensity, frequency, pattern, complexity, or other characteristics.
B   Auditory Perception 1967
      Perceptual Discrimination 1973
R   Auditory Acuity 1988

Auditory Displays 1973

PN 81   **SC** 04640
SN Presentations of patterned auditory stimulation.
B   Auditory Stimulation 1967
      Displays 1967

Auditory Evoked Potentials 1973

PN 3154   **SC** 04650
B   Evoked Potentials 1967
R   ↓ Cortical Evoked Potentials 1973

Auditory Feedback 1973

PN 338   **SC** 04660
SN Return of information on specified behavioral functions or parameters by means of auditory stimulation. Such stimulation may serve to regulate or control subsequent behavior, cognition, perception, or performance. Also, the process of hearing one's own vocalizations, especially as pertains to regulating the parameters of one's speech.
B   Auditory Stimulation 1967
B   Sensory Feedback 1973
N   Delayed Auditory Feedback 1973

Auditory Hallucinations 1973
PN 451   SC 04670
  B   Hallucinations 1967

Auditory Localization 1973
PN 812   SC 04680
SN Subjective determination of the specific spatial location of a sound source or relative locations of sound sources.
  UF   Localization (Sound)
        Sound Localization
  B   Auditory Perception 1967
        Perceptual Localization 1967
  R   Auditory Acuity 1988

Auditory Masking 1973
PN 1038   SC 04690
SN Change in perceptual sensitivity to an auditory stimulus due to the presence of a second stimulus in close temporal proximity.
  B   Masking 1967
  R   ↓ Auditory Stimulation 1967

Auditory Nerve
  Use   Acoustic Nerve

Auditory Neurons 1973
PN 247   SC 04710
  B   Sensory Neurons 1973

Auditory Perception 1967
PN 8013   SC 04720
SN Awareness, detection, or identification of sounds.
  UF   Audition
        Listening
  B   Perception 1967
  N   Auditory Acuity 1988
        Auditory Discrimination 1967
        Auditory Localization 1973
        ↓ Loudness Perception 1973
        Music Perception 1997
        ↓ Pitch Perception 1973
        Speech Perception 1967
  R   Acoustics 1997
        Auditory Thresholds 1973
        ↓ Ear Disorders 1973
        Listening (Interpersonal) 1997
        Pattern Discrimination 1967
        ↓ Rhythm 1991

Auditory Stimulation 1967
PN 8457   SC 04730
  UF   Acoustic Stimuli
        Noise (Sound)
        Sound
  B   Perceptual Stimulation 1973
  N   Auditory Displays 1973
        ↓ Auditory Feedback 1973
        Dichotic Stimulation 1982
        Filtered Noise 1973
        ↓ Loudness 1967
        ↓ Pitch (Frequency) 1967
        White Noise 1973
  R   Acoustics 1997
        Audiogenic Seizures 1978
        ↓ Audiometry 1967
        Auditory Masking 1973
        Bone Conduction Audiometry 1973
        ↓ Speech Processing (Mechanical) 1973

Auditory Thresholds 1973
PN 1530   SC 04740
SN The minimal level of auditory stimulation, the minimal difference between any auditory stimuli, or the minimal stimulus change that is perceptually detectable.
  B   Thresholds 1967
  R   Auditory Acuity 1988
        ↓ Auditory Perception 1967
        ↓ Perceptual Measures 1973

Augmentative Communication 1994
PN 407   SC 04750
SN Communication that is supported by keyboards, typewriters, books, gestural systems, or other devices to enable individuals with communication or speech disorders to communicate effectively.
  UF   Facilitated Communication
  B   Communication 1967
  N   ↓ Manual Communication 1978
  R   ↓ Apparatus 1967
        ↓ Communication Disorders 1982
        ↓ Medical Therapeutic Devices 1973
        ↓ Speech Disorders 1967
        Speech Therapy 1967

Aura 1973
PN 70   SC 04760
SN Sensations experienced immediately prior to the onset of a seizure, migraine headache, or other nervous system disorder symptoms. Also, the patient's recognition of the beginning of an epileptic attack. Use PARAPSYCHOLOGY or PARAPSYCHOLOGICAL PHENOMENA to access references on psychic auras and halos.
  B   Symptoms 1967
  R   ↓ Epilepsy 1967

Aurally Handicapped
SN The term was discontinued in 1997, when the term AURALLY DISABLED was created to capture this concept. In 2000, with the deletion of the term AURALLY DISABLED, AURALLY HANDICAPPED was made a nonpostable term for the postable term HEARING DISORDERS. AURALLY DISABLED and AURALLY HANDICAPPED were stripped from all records containing them and replaced with HEARING DISORDERS.
  Use   Hearing Disorders

Auricles (Heart)
  Use   Heart Auricles

Auricular Fibrillation
  Use   Fibrillation (Heart)

Authoritarianism 1967
PN 1947   SC 04820
SN Complex of personality characteristics expressed as antidemocratic social attitudes, rigid attachment to traditional values, uncritical acceptance of authority, and intolerance of opposing views.
  UF   Domination
  B   Personality Traits 1967
  R   Dogmatism 1978
        ↓ Dominance 1967
        Egalitarianism 1985
        Openmindedness 1978

Authoritarianism (Parental)
  Use   Parental Permissiveness

Authoritarianism Rebellion Scale
SN Term was discontinued in 1997. In 2000, the term was stripped from all records containing it, and replaced with NONPROJECTIVE PERSONALITY MEASURES, its postable counterpart.
  Use   Nonprojective Personality Measures

Authority 1967
PN 849   SC 04845
SN Ability or vested power to influence thought, attitudes, and behavior.
  R   Abuse of Power 1997
        Coercion 1994
        ↓ Dominance 1967
        ↓ Leadership 1967
        Omnipotence 1994
        ↓ Power 1967
        ↓ Social Influences 1967
        ↓ Status 1967

Authors
  Use   Writers

Autism 1967
PN 4049   SC 04850
  B   Mental Disorders 1967
        Pervasive Developmental Disorders 2001
  N   Early Infantile Autism 1973
  R   Antisocial Personality 1973
        Aspergers Syndrome 1991
        Autistic Children 1973
        Autistic Thinking 1973
        Developmental Disabilities 1982
        Theory of Mind 2001

Autistic Children 1973
PN 2585   SC 04860
  B   Emotionally Disturbed 1973
  R   ↓ Autism 1967
        ↓ Childhood Psychosis 1967
        Early Infantile Autism 1973

Autistic Psychopathy
  Use   Aspergers Syndrome

Autistic Thinking 1973
PN 30   SC 04870
  B   Thinking 1967
        Thought Disturbances 1973
  R   ↓ Autism 1967

Autobiographical Memory 1994
PN 499   SC 04875
SN Personal memories of past events that have occurred over the course of one's life. Compare REMINISCENCE and LIFE REVIEW.
  B   Memory 1967
  R   Anniversary Events 1994
        Early Experience 1967
        Early Memories 1985
        Life Experiences 1973
        Life Review 1991
        Reminiscence 1985

Autobiography 1973
PN 495   SC 04880
SN Recorded account of one's own life. Not used as a document type identifier.
  B   Biography 1967

Autoeroticism 1997
PN 10   SC 04890

Autoeroticism — (cont'd)
SN Use MASTURBATION to access references from 1973-1996.
R   Eroticism   1973
     Masturbation   1973
     Narcissism   1967
     ↓ Psychosexual Behavior   1967

Autogenic Training   1973
PN 433   **SC** 04900
SN Physiological form of psychotherapy based on studies of sleep and hypnosis and the application of yoga principles.
B   Psychotherapeutic Techniques   1967
     Psychotherapy   1967
R   Biofeedback Training   1978
     ↓ Relaxation Therapy   1978

Autohypnosis   1973
PN 241   **SC** 04910
SN Practice, process, or hypnotic state resulting from self-induced hypnosis.
UF Self Hypnosis
B   Hypnosis   1967
R   Catalepsy   1973

Autoimmune Disorders
Use Immunologic Disorders

Autokinetic Illusion   1967
PN 250   **SC** 04930
SN Apparent movement of a fixated light in a dark field.
UF Illusion (Autokinetic)
B   Apparent Movement   1967
     Visual Perception   1967

Automated Information Coding   1973
PN 68   **SC** 04940
B   Automated Information Processing   1973
R   ↓ Computers   1967

Automated Information Processing   1973
PN 637   **SC** 04950
UF Information Processing (Automated)
N   Automated Information Coding   1973
     ↓ Automated Information Retrieval   1973
     Automated Information Storage   1973
R   ↓ Communication Systems   1973
     ↓ Computers   1967
     ↓ Data Processing   1967
     Electronic Communication   2001
     ↓ Expert Systems   1991
     Information   1967
     ↓ Information Systems   1991
     Internet   2001

Automated Information Retrieval   1973
PN 295   **SC** 04960
UF Information Retrieval (Automated)
B   Automated Information Processing   1973
N   Computer Searching   1991
R   Automated Information Storage   1973
     ↓ Computers   1967
     Databases   1991
     Information Services   1988
     ↓ Information Systems   1991

Automated Information Storage   1973
PN 90   **SC** 04970
B   Automated Information Processing   1973
R   ↓ Automated Information Retrieval   1973

Automated Information Storage — (cont'd)
R   ↓ Computers   1967
     Databases   1991
     ↓ Information Systems   1991

Automated Speech Recognition   1994
PN 148   **SC** 04975
SN Machine or other apparatus used in the automatic recognition and understanding of human speech.
UF Automatic Speaker Recognition
B   Speech Processing (Mechanical)   1973
R   ↓ Artificial Intelligence   1982
     ↓ Computer Applications   1973
     ↓ Expert Systems   1991
     Speech Perception   1967

Automatic Speaker Recognition
Use Automated Speech Recognition

Automation   1967
PN 467   **SC** 04980
SN Use of mechanical and/or electronic devices to automatically control the operation of an apparatus, system, or process.
R   ↓ Artificial Intelligence   1982
R   ↓ Computers   1967

Automatism   1973
PN 174   **SC** 04990
SN An act or movement performed without conscious control.
B   Symptoms   1967

Automobile Accidents
Use Motor Traffic Accidents

Automobile Safety
Use Highway Safety

Automobiles   1973
PN 306   **SC** 05020
B   Motor Vehicles   1982
R   Drivers   1973

Autonomic Ganglia   1973
PN 21   **SC** 05050
UF Celiac Plexus
     Hypogastric Plexus
     Myenteric Plexus
     Postganglionic Autonomic Fibers
     Preganglionic Autonomic Fibers
     Stellate Ganglion
     Submucous Plexus
B   Autonomic Nervous System   1967
     Ganglia   1973
R   ↓ Peripheral Nervous System   1973

Autonomic Nervous System   1967
PN 1188   **SC** 05060
B   Peripheral Nervous System   1973
N   Adrenergic Nerves   1973
     Autonomic Ganglia   1973
     Cholinergic Nerves   1973
     ↓ Parasympathetic Nervous System   1973
     ↓ Sympathetic Nervous System   1973
R   Autonomic Nervous System Disorders   1973

Autonomic Nervous System Disorders   1973
PN 62   **SC** 05070
B   Nervous System Disorders   1967

Autonomic Nervous System Disorders — (cont'd)
R   ↓ Autonomic Nervous System   1967

Autonomy (Government)   1973
PN 39   **SC** 05080
R   Government   1967

Autonomy (Personality)
Use Independence (Personality)

Autopsy   1973
PN 139   **SC** 05090
R   ↓ Diagnosis   1967
     ↓ Medical Diagnosis   1973
     Psychological Autopsy   1988

Autoregulation
Use Homeostasis

Autoshaping   1978
PN 373   **SC** 05106
SN Learned behavior or the experimental paradigm involving a Pavlovian pairing of a reinforcer and a stimulus independent of the subject's behavior until the subject makes a response to the stimulus. At that point the reinforcer is made contingent on the acquired response to the stimulus, thereby bringing the response under operant control.
B   Conditioning   1967
R   Noncontingent Reinforcement   1988
     ↓ Reinforcement   1967

Autosome Disorders   1973
PN 99   **SC** 05110
B   Chromosome Disorders   1973
N   Crying Cat Syndrome   1973
     Downs Syndrome   1967
     Trisomy 21   1973
R   Autosomes   1973

Autosomes   1973
PN 40   **SC** 05120
B   Chromosomes   1973
R   ↓ Autosome Disorders   1973

Autotomy
Use Self Mutilation

Aversion   1967
PN 705   **SC** 05130
UF Antipathy
     Dislike
B   Emotional States   1973
N   Hate   1973
R   Disgust   1994

Aversion Conditioning   1982
PN 1865   **SC** 05135
SN Conditioning paradigm in which aversive effects are paired with external stimuli resulting in an aversion to the stimuli. Also, the learned aversion itself.
UF Odor Aversion Conditioning
     Taste Aversion Conditioning
B   Conditioning   1967
N   Covert Sensitization   1988
R   Aversive Stimulation   1973

Aversion Therapy   1973
PN 492   **SC** 05140

Aversion Therapy — (cont'd)

SN Form of behavior therapy designed to eliminate undesirable behavior patterns through learned associations with unpleasant or painful stimuli. Also known as aversive conditioning therapy.

B   Behavior Therapy [1967]
N   Covert Sensitization [1988]
R   Counterconditioning [1973]
     ↓ Shock Therapy [1973]

Aversive Stimulation [1973]

PN 1663   **SC** 05150

SN Presentation of a noxious stimulus. Also, any noxious stimuli (i.e., stimuli that an organism attempts to avoid or escape from). Compare PUNISHMENT.

B   Stimulation [1967]
R   ↓ Aversion Conditioning [1982]
     Covert Sensitization [1988]

Aviation [1967]

PN 662   **SC** 05160

N   Flight Instrumentation [1973]
     Spaceflight [1967]
R   Acceleration Effects [1973]
     Altitude Effects [1973]
     ↓ Aviation Safety [1973]
     ↓ Gravitational Effects [1967]

Aviation Personnel
Use Aerospace Personnel

Aviation Safety [1973]

PN 170   **SC** 05170

B   Safety [1967]
N   Air Traffic Control [1973]
R   Air Traffic Accidents [1973]
     Aircraft Pilots [1973]
     ↓ Aviation [1967]
     ↓ Transportation Accidents [1973]

Aviators
Use Aircraft Pilots

Avoidance [1967]

PN 2397   **SC** 05190

UF Escape
R   Avoidance Conditioning [1967]
     Neophobia [1985]
     ↓ Resistance [1997]

Avoidance Conditioning [1967]

PN 6714   **SC** 05200

SN Learned behavior or the operant conditioning procedure in which the subject learns a behavior that prevents the occurrence of an aversive stimulus. Compare ESCAPE CONDITIONING.

UF Active Avoidance Conditioning (Avoidance) Passive Avoidance
B   Operant Conditioning [1967]
R   Avoidance [1967]

Avoidant Personality [1994]

PN 68   **SC** 05205

SN Personality disorder characterized by excessive social discomfort, extreme sensitivity to negative perceptions of oneself, pervasive preoccupation with being criticized or rejected in social situations, and low self esteem.

B   Personality Disorders [1967]
R   Social Anxiety [1985]
     Social Phobia [1985]

Awareness [1967]

PN 2576   **SC** 05210

SN Conscious realization, perception, or knowledge.

B   Consciousness States [1971]
N   ↓ Attention [1967]
     Body Awareness [1982]
R   Metacognition [1991]
     Sensory Gating [1991]

Axons [1973]

PN 221   **SC** 05220

B   Neurons [1973]

Azidothymidine
Use Zidovudine

AZT
Use Zidovudine

Babbling
Use Infant Vocalization

Babinski Reflex [1973]

PN 3   **SC** 05250

B   Reflexes [1971]

Baboons [1973]

PN 614   **SC** 05260

B   Primates (Nonhuman) [1973]

Babysitting
Use Child Care

Back (Anatomy) [1973]

PN 145   **SC** 05270

B   Anatomy [1967]

Back Pain [1982]

PN 996   **SC** 05275

B   Pain [1967]
R   Chronic Pain [1985]
     ↓ Physical Disorders [1997]

Background (Family)
Use Family Background

Backward Masking
Use Masking

Baclofen [1991]

PN 122   **SC** 05293

B   Muscle Relaxing Drugs [1973]

Bacteria
Use Microorganisms

Bacterial Disorders [1973]

PN 77   **SC** 05300

B   Infectious Disorders [1973]
N   Bacterial Meningitis [1973]
     Gonorrhea [1973]
     Pulmonary Tuberculosis [1973]
     ↓ Tuberculosis [1973]
R   Pneumonia [1973]
     Rheumatic Fever [1973]

Bacterial Meningitis [1973]

PN 15   **SC** 05310

B   Bacterial Disorders [1973]

Bacterial Meningitis — (cont'd)

B   Meningitis [1973]

Balance (Motor Processes)
Use Equilibrium

Baldness
Use Alopecia

Ballet
Use Dance

Bannister Repertory Grid [1973]

PN 29   **SC** 05360

B   Nonprojective Personality Measures [1973]

Baptists
Use Protestants

Barbital [1973]

PN 61   **SC** 05380

B   Barbiturates [1967]
     CNS Depressant Drugs [1973]
     Hypnotic Drugs [1973]
     Sedatives [1973]

Barbiturate Poisoning [1973]

PN 4   **SC** 05390

B   Toxic Disorders [1973]
R   ↓ Analeptic Drugs [1973]
     ↓ Barbiturates [1967]

Barbiturates [1967]

PN 250   **SC** 05400

B   Drugs [1967]
N   Amobarbital [1973]
     Barbital [1973]
     Hexobarbital [1973]
     Methohexital [1973]
     Pentobarbital [1973]
     Phenobarbital [1973]
     Secobarbital [1973]
     Thiopental [1973]
R   ↓ Anesthetic Drugs [1973]
     ↓ Anticonvulsive Drugs [1973]
     Barbiturate Poisoning [1973]
     ↓ CNS Depressant Drugs [1973]
     ↓ Hypnotic Drugs [1973]
     Primidone [1973]
     ↓ Sedatives [1973]

Bargaining [1973]

PN 638   **SC** 05410

B   Negotiation [1973]

Barium [1973]

PN 9   **SC** 05420

B   Metallic Elements [1973]

Barometric Pressure
Use Atmospheric Conditions

Baroreceptors [1973]

PN 82   **SC** 05440

UF Pressoreceptors
B   Neural Receptors [1973]
     Sensory Neurons [1973]
     Sympathetic Nervous System [1973]

Barrett Lennard Relationship Inventory [2001]

PN 10   **SC** 05455

Barrett Lennard Relationship Inventory — (cont'd)

SN In 2000, the truncated term BARRETT LEN-NARD RELATIONSHIP INVENT (which was used from 1973-2000) was deleted, removed from all records containing it, and mapped to its expanded form BARRETT LENNARD RELATIONSHIP INVENTORY.
  B Nonprojective Personality Measures [1973]

Barron Welsh Art Scale [1973]
PN 6   **SC** 05460
  B Nonprojective Personality Measures [1973]

Basal Ganglia [1973]
PN 2321   **SC** 05470
  UF Corpus Striatum
  B Ganglia [1973]
        Telencephalon [1973]
  N Amygdaloid Body [1973]
        Caudate Nucleus [1973]
        Globus Pallidus [1973]
        Putamen [1985]
  R Extrapyramidal Symptoms [1994]
        Nucleus Basalis Magnocellularis [1994]
        Progressive Supranuclear Palsy [1997]
        Substantia Nigra [1994]

Basal Metabolism [1973]
PN 44   **SC** 05480
SN The amount of heat produced by the body to maintain life processes at the lowest level of cell activity in the waking state.
  B Metabolism [1967]

Basal Readers
  Use Reading Materials

Basal Skin Resistance [1973]
PN 14   **SC** 05500
SN Baseline or minimum electrical current generated or conducted by the body as measured on the skin surface during a resting state.
  B Skin Resistance [1973]

Baseball [1973]
PN 234   **SC** 05510
  B Recreation [1967]
        Sports [1967]

Basic Skills Testing
  Use Minimum Competency Tests

Basketball [1973]
PN 428   **SC** 05520
  B Recreation [1967]
        Sports [1967]

Bass (Fish) [1973]
PN 25   **SC** 05530
  B Fishes [1967]

Bats [1973]
PN 319   **SC** 05550
  UF Chiroptera
  B Mammals [1973]

Battered Child Syndrome [1973]
PN 32   **SC** 05560
SN Behavioral pattern, including inability to relate to others and feelings of rejection, characteristic of infants and children who have been abused.
  B Child Abuse [1971]

Battered Child Syndrome — (cont'd)
  B Syndromes [1973]
  R Physical Abuse [1991]

Battered Females [1988]
PN 1348   **SC** 05561
SN Use FAMILY VIOLENCE to access references from 1985-1987.
  B Human Females [1973]
  R ↓ Abuse Reporting [1997]
        ↓ Family Violence [1982]
        Partner Abuse [1991]
        Physical Abuse [1991]
        Shelters [1991]

Bayes Theorem
  Use Statistical Probability

Bayley Scales of Infant Development [1994]
PN 37   **SC** 05575
  B Developmental Measures [1994]
  R ↓ Intelligence Measures [1967]

Beavers [1973]
PN 15   **SC** 05580
  B Rodents [1973]

Beck Depression Inventory [1988]
PN 298   **SC** 05588
  B Nonprojective Personality Measures [1973]

Bedwetting
  Use Urinary Incontinence

Beer [1973]
PN 119   **SC** 05590
  B Alcoholic Beverages [1973]

Bees [1973]
PN 666   **SC** 05600
  B Insects [1967]
  R Larvae [1973]

Beetles [1973]
PN 210   **SC** 05610
  B Insects [1967]
  R Larvae [1973]

Behavior [1967]
PN 7654   **SC** 05670
SN Conceptually broad term referring to any or all aspects of human or animal behavior. Use a more specific term if possible.
  N Adaptive Behavior [1991]
        ↓ Adjunctive Behavior [1982]
        ↓ Animal Ethology [1967]
        ↓ Antisocial Behavior [1971]
        Attachment Behavior [1985]
        Childhood Play Behavior [1978]
        Choice Behavior [1967]
        Classroom Behavior [1973]
        Conservation (Ecological Behavior) [1978]
        ↓ Consumer Behavior [1967]
        Coping Behavior [1967]
        Coronary Prone Behavior [1982]
        ↓ Drinking Behavior [1978]
        ↓ Driving Behavior [1967]
        ↓ Exploratory Behavior [1967]
        Health Behavior [1982]
        Illness Behavior [1982]
        Instinctive Behavior [1982]
        ↓ Psychosexual Behavior [1967]
        Self Defeating Behavior [1988]

Behavior — (cont'd)
  N ↓ Self Destructive Behavior [1985]
        ↓ Social Behavior [1967]
        Stereotyped Behavior [1973]
        Voting Behavior [1973]
        Wandering Behavior [1991]
  R ↓ Behavior Analysis [2001]
        Behavior Change [1973]
        ↓ Behavior Disorders [1971]
        ↓ Behavior Modification [1973]
        ↓ Behavior Problems [1967]
        ↓ Behavior Therapy [1967]
        ↓ Behavioral Assessment [1982]
        Behavioral Contrast [1978]
        ↓ Behavioral Sciences [1997]
        Behaviorism [1967]
        Human Nature [1997]
        Planned Behavior [1997]

Behavior Analysis [2001]
PN 0   **SC** 05613
SN Field of psychology emphasizing the experimental, conceptual, and applied analysis of behavior in humans and animals.
  B Analysis [1967]
  N ↓ Behavioral Assessment [1982]
  R ↓ Behavior [1967]

Behavior Change [1973]
PN 3609   **SC** 05620
SN Detectable changes in behavior due to psychotherapeutic, behavioral or other intervention, or spontaneous occurrence.
  R ↓ Behavior [1967]
        ↓ Behavior Modification [1973]
        Lifestyle Changes [1997]
        Personality Change [1967]

Behavior Contracting [1978]
PN 265   **SC** 05624
SN Therapeutic technique involving a formal written contract, usually between two parties, which explicitly states the relationship between a particular behavior and its consequences (sanctions). Viewed as a structural means of scheduling reinforcement between the two parties, it is used as a method of controlling contingencies of reinforcement.
  R ↓ Behavior Modification [1973]
        ↓ Behavior Therapy [1967]

Behavior Disorders [1971]
PN 4573   **SC** 05630
SN Disorders characterized by persistent and repetitive patterns of behavior that violate societal norms or rules or that seriously impair a person's functioning. Compare BEHAVIOR PROBLEMS.
  N ↓ Addiction [1973]
        Attempted Suicide [1973]
        ↓ Drug Abuse [1973]
        ↓ Homicide [1967]
        ↓ Juvenile Delinquency [1967]
        Self Mutilation [1973]
  R Acting Out [1967]
        ↓ Aggressive Behavior [1967]
        ↓ Antisocial Behavior [1971]
        ↓ Behavior [1967]
        ↓ Behavior Problems [1967]
        Body Rocking [1973]
        Conduct Disorder [1991]
        ↓ Crime [1967]
        Faking [1973]
        Fecal Incontinence [1973]
        Hair Pulling [1973]
        ↓ Mental Disorders [1967]

Behavior Disorders — (cont'd)
- R   Oppositional Defiant Disorder [1997]
-     Pathological Gambling [1988]
- ↓ Self Destructive Behavior [1985]
- ↓ Symptoms [1967]
-     Thumbsucking [1973]
-     Urinary Incontinence [1973]

Behavior Modification [1973]
PN 7626   **SC** 05640
SN Use of classical conditioning or operant (instrumental) learning techniques to modify behavior.
- B   Treatment [1967]
- N   ↓ Behavior Therapy [1967]
-     Biofeedback Training [1978]
-     Classroom Behavior Modification [1973]
-     ↓ Contingency Management [1973]
-     Fading (Conditioning) [1982]
-     Omission Training [1985]
-     Overcorrection [1985]
-     ↓ Self Management [1985]
-     Time Out [1985]
- R   Anger Control [1997]
-     Anxiety Management [1997]
-     Assertiveness Training [1978]
-     ↓ Behavior [1967]
-     Behavior Change [1973]
-     Behavior Contracting [1978]
-     ↓ Behavioral Assessment [1982]
-     Cognitive Restructuring [1985]
-     Cognitive Therapy [1982]
-     Communication Skills Training [1982]
-     Constant Time Delay [1997]
-     Counterconditioning [1973]
-     Functional Analysis [2001]
-     ↓ Operant Conditioning [1967]
-     ↓ Prompting [1997]
-     ↓ Relaxation Therapy [1978]
-     ↓ Self Help Techniques [1982]
-     Self Monitoring [1982]
-     Social Skills Training [1982]
-     Stress Management [1985]

Behavior Problems [1967]
PN 9877   **SC** 05650
SN Disruptive or improper behaviors that generally fall within societal norms and do not seriously impair a person's functioning. Compare BEHAVIOR DISORDERS.
- UF   Disruptive Behavior
-     Misbehavior
-     Misconduct
- N   Tantrums [1973]
- R   ↓ Behavior [1967]
-     ↓ Behavior Disorders [1971]
-     Conduct Disorder [1991]
-     ↓ Crime [1967]
-     Functional Analysis [2001]

Behavior Therapy [1967]
PN 8332   **SC** 05660
SN Therapeutic approach that may employ classical conditioning, operant learning techniques, or other behavioral techniques, in an attempt to eliminate or modify problem behavior, addressing itself primarily to the client's overt behavior, as opposed to thoughts, feelings, or other cognitive processes.
- B   Behavior Modification [1973]
-     Psychotherapy [1967]
- N   ↓ Aversion Therapy [1973]
-     ↓ Exposure Therapy [1997]
-     Implosive Therapy [1973]
-     Reciprocal Inhibition Therapy [1973]
-     Response Cost [1997]

Behavior Therapy — (cont'd)
- N   Systematic Desensitization Therapy [1973]
- R   Anger Control [1997]
-     Anxiety Management [1997]
-     ↓ Behavior [1967]
-     Behavior Contracting [1978]
-     Counterconditioning [1973]
-     Eye Movement Desensitization Therapy [1997]
-     Paradoxical Techniques [1982]
-     Rational Emotive Therapy [1978]

Behavioral Assessment [1982]
PN 3733   **SC** 05671
SN Identification and measurement of response units and their controlling environmental and organismic variables for the purposes of understanding and altering human behavior.
- B   Behavior Analysis [2001]
-     Psychological Assessment [1997]
- N   Functional Analysis [2001]
- R   ↓ Behavior [1967]
-     ↓ Behavior Modification [1973]
-     ↓ Empirical Methods [1973]

Behavioral Contrast [1978]
PN 267   **SC** 05674
SN Change in response rate or latency following a change in reinforcement of one component of multiple operant discrimination schedules of reinforcement.
- R   ↓ Behavior [1967]
-     ↓ Reinforcement [1967]
-     Response Frequency [1973]
-     Response Latency [1967]
-     Stimulus Discrimination [1973]

Behavioral Ecology [1997]
PN 159   **SC** 57450
SN Study, usually based on naturalistic observations, of the interaction between the environment and the behavior of organisms within that environment.
- R   ↓ Ecological Factors [1973]
-     Ecological Psychology [1994]
-     Ecology [1973]
-     Environmental Psychology [1982]
-     Research Setting [2001]

Behavioral Genetics [1994]
PN 542   **SC** 57405
SN Scientific discipline concerned with the role of genes and gene action in the expression of behavior. Includes analysis of whole populations for specific traits, e.g., intelligence. Used for the scientific discipline or the behavioral genetic processes themselves.
- B   Genetics [1967]
- R   Biopsychosocial Approach [1991]
-     ↓ Genetic Disorders [1973]
-     Genetic Dominance [1973]
-     Genetic Recessiveness [1973]
-     Nature Nurture [1994]
-     Population Genetics [1973]
-     Psychobiology [1982]
-     Sociobiology [1982]

Behavioral Health
- **Use** Health Care Psychology

Behavioral Medicine
- **Use** Health Care Psychology

Behavioral Sciences [1997]
PN 124   **SC** 05680

Behavioral Sciences — (cont'd)
SN Group of scientific disciplines dealing with human and animal action and behavior. Use SOCIAL SCIENCES to access references from 1973-1996.
- B   Social Sciences [1967]
- N   ↓ Psychology [1967]
- R   ↓ Behavior [1967]
-     ↓ Sociology [1967]

Behaviorism [1967]
PN 1689   **SC** 05690
- B   History of Psychology [1967]
-     Psychological Theories [2001]
- R   ↓ Behavior [1967]
-     Positivism (Philosophy) [1997]
-     Skinner (Burrhus Frederic) [1991]
-     Watson (John Broadus) [1991]

Bekesy Audiometry
- **Use** Audiometry

Beliefs (Nonreligious)
- **Use** Attitudes

Beliefs (Religion)
- **Use** Religious Beliefs

Bem Sex Role Inventory [1988]
PN 64   **SC** 05727
- B   Nonprojective Personality Measures [1973]

Bemegride [1973]
PN 20   **SC** 05730
- B   Analeptic Drugs [1973]

Benactyzine [1973]
PN 26   **SC** 05740
- B   Cholinergic Blocking Drugs [1973]
-     Tranquilizing Drugs [1967]

Benadryl
- **Use** Diphenhydramine

Bender Gestalt Test [1967]
PN 387   **SC** 05770
- B   Projective Personality Measures [1973]
- R   ↓ Neuropsychological Assessment [1982]

Benign Neoplasms [1973]
PN 31   **SC** 05800
- B   Neoplasms [1967]

Benton Revised Visual Retention Test [1973]
PN 38   **SC** 05810
- B   Intelligence Measures [1967]
- R   ↓ Neuropsychological Assessment [1982]

Benzedrine
- **Use** Amphetamine

Benzodiazepine Agonists [1994]
PN 143   **SC** 05821
- R   ↓ Benzodiazepines [1978]

Benzodiazepine Antagonists [1985]
PN 402   **SC** 05822
- R   ↓ Benzodiazepines [1978]

Benzodiazepines [1978]
PN 2718   **SC** 05824
- B   Drugs [1967]
- N   Alprazolam [1988]

Benzodiazepines — (cont'd)

- **N**   Chlordiazepoxide   1973
  - Clonazepam   1991
  - Diazepam   1973
  - Flurazepam   1982
  - Lorazepam   1988
  - Midazolam   1991
  - Nitrazepam   1978
  - Oxazepam   1978
- **R**   ↓ Anticonvulsive Drugs   1973
  - Benzodiazepine Agonists   1994
  - Benzodiazepine Antagonists   1985
  - ↓ Hypnotic Drugs   1973
  - ↓ Minor Tranquilizers   1973
  - ↓ Muscle Relaxing Drugs   1973
  - ↓ Sedatives   1973
  - ↓ Tranquilizing Drugs   1967

Bereavement
Use   Grief

Beta Blockers
Use   Adrenergic Blocking Drugs

Between Groups Design   1985
PN 54   **SC** 05828
SN   Experimental design in which the subjects serve in only one treatment condition. Includes designs of matched or correlated groups and randomized groups.
- **B**   Experimental Design   1967

Beverages (Alcoholic)
Use   Alcoholic Beverages

Beverages (Nonalcoholic)   1978
PN 177   **SC** 05833
- **UF**   Coffee
  - Tea
- **R**   ↓ Alcoholic Beverages   1973
  - ↓ Drinking Behavior   1978
  - Nutrition   1973

Bias (Experimenter)
Use   Experimenter Bias

Bias (Response)
Use   Response Bias

Biased Sampling   1973
PN 189   **SC** 05860
SN   Inadequate selection of subject samples resulting in an inaccurate representation of the larger population.
- **B**   Sampling (Experimental)   1973
- **R**   Experiment Volunteers   1973

Bible   1973
PN 361   **SC** 05870
- **B**   Religious Literature   1973
- **R**   ↓ Christianity   1973
  - Judaism   1967
  - ↓ Religious Beliefs   1973

Bibliotherapy   1973
PN 352   **SC** 05890
SN   Use of reading as adjunct to psychotherapy.
- **B**   Treatment   1967
- **R**   Poetry Therapy   1994

Bicuculline   1994
PN 95   **SC** 05895

Bicuculline — (cont'd)
SN   Use GAMMA AMINOBUTYRIC ACID ANTAGO-NISTS to access references from 1985-1993.
- **B**   Analeptic Drugs   1973
  - Gamma Aminobutyric Acid Antagonists   1985

Big Five Personality Model
Use   Five Factor Personality Model

Bile   1973
PN 16   **SC** 05900
- **B**   Body Fluids   1973
- **R**   Taurine   1982

Bilingual Education   1978
PN 550   **SC** 05907
SN   Education in one's native language as well as the majority language of the country in which one is educated or education in two languages.
- **B**   Education   1967
- **R**   Bilingualism   1973
  - English as Second Language   1997
  - Foreign Language Learning   1967
  - Foreign Languages   1973
  - Multicultural Education   1988
  - ↓ Multilingualism   1973
  - ↓ Teaching   1967

Bilingualism   1973
PN 2252   **SC** 05910
- **B**   Multilingualism   1973
- **R**   Bilingual Education   1978
  - Code Switching   1988
  - Cross Cultural Communication   1997
  - English as Second Language   1997
  - ↓ Language   1967
  - Language Proficiency   1988

Binge Eating   1991
PN 609   **SC** 05915
SN   Eating excessive quantities of food often after stressful events. Compare BULIMIA.
- **B**   Feeding Practices   1973
- **R**   Bulimia   1985
  - ↓ Eating Disorders   1997
  - ↓ Symptoms   1967

Binocular Vision   1967
PN 1359   **SC** 05920
- **B**   Visual Perception   1967

Binomial Distribution   1973
PN 56   **SC** 05930
- **B**   Statistical Probability   1967
- **R**   ↓ Statistical Sample Parameters   1973

Bioavailability   1991
PN 147   **SC** 05935
SN   The degree and rate at which a drug enters the bloodstream and is circulated to specific organs or tissues, as measured by drug concentrations in body fluids or by pharmacologic or therapeutic response.
- **UF**   Bioequivalence
- **R**   Absorption (Physiological)   1973
  - ↓ Biochemistry   1967
  - ↓ Drug Dosages   1973
  - ↓ Drug Therapy   1967
  - ↓ Drugs   1967
  - ↓ Metabolism   1967
  - ↓ Pharmacology   1973

Biochemical Markers
Use   Biological Markers

Biochemistry   1967
PN 3825   **SC** 05940
SN   Study of the biological and physiological chemistry of living organisms. Used for the scientific discipline or the biochemical processes themselves.
- **B**   Chemistry   1967
- **N**   ↓ Neurochemistry   1973
- **R**   Bioavailability   1991
  - Biological Markers   1991
  - ↓ Physiology   1967

Bioequivalence
Use   Bioavailability

Biofeedback   1973
PN 1338   **SC** 05945
SN   Provision of immediate ongoing information regarding one's own physiological processes.
- **B**   Feedback   1967
- **N**   Biofeedback Training   1978
- **R**   ↓ Conditioning   1967
  - ↓ Reinforcement   1967
  - ↓ Stimulation   1967

Biofeedback Training   1978
PN 2250   **SC** 05946
SN   Self-directed process by which a person uses biofeedback information to gain voluntary control over processes or functions which are primarily under autonomic control. Used in experimental or treatment settings with human subjects.
- **B**   Behavior Modification   1973
  - Biofeedback   1973
- **R**   ↓ Alternative Medicine   1997
  - Autogenic Training   1973

Biographical Data   1978
PN 881   **SC** 05948
SN   Information identifying an individual's background, life history, or present status. Not used as a document type identifier.
- **R**   Biographical Inventories   1973
  - Demographic Characteristics   1967
  - ↓ Educational Background   1967
  - ↓ Family Background   1973
  - Life Experiences   1973
  - Patient History   1973

Biographical Inventories   1973
PN 115   **SC** 05950
SN   Sets of items listing information on an individual's background. Not used as a document type identifier.
- **B**   Inventories   1967
- **R**   Biographical Data   1978

Biography   1967
PN 666   **SC** 05960
SN   Recorded account of a person's life. From 1967-2000, the term was also used as a document type identifier; however, this usage has been discontinued due to the advent of Form/Content Type field identifiers. References from 1967-2000 can be accessed using either BIOGRAPHY or the Biography Form/Content Type field identifier.
- **B**   Prose   1973
- **N**   Autobiography   1973
- **R**   Narratives   1997
  - Psychohistory   1978

Biological Clocks (Animal)
Use   Animal Biological Rhythms

Biological Family 1988
PN 381   SC 05975
SN The genetic family members of a person in contrast to adoptive or foster families.
UF   Birth Parents
     Natural Family
B   Family 1967
     Family Members 1973
R   Family of Origin 1991

Biological Markers 1991
PN 1209   SC 05977
UF   Biochemical Markers
     Clinical Markers
R   ↓ Biochemistry 1967
     Interleukins 1994
     ↓ Medical Diagnosis 1973
     Physiological Correlates 1967
     Predisposition 1973
     Prognosis 1973
     ↓ Screening 1982
     Susceptibility (Disorders) 1973

Biological Psychiatry 1994
PN 78   SC 05978
SN A branch of psychiatry focusing on biological, physical, and neurological factors in the etiology and treatment of mental and behavioral disorders.
B   Psychiatry 1967
R   Neurobiology 1973
     Neuropsychiatry 1973
     Psychobiology 1982

Biological Rhythms 1967
PN 484   SC 05980
SN Rhythmic and periodic variations in physiological and psychological functions. Used for human or animal populations.
N   ↓ Animal Biological Rhythms 1973
     Human Biological Rhythms 1973
     Sleep Wake Cycle 1985
R   Lunar Synodic Cycle 1973
     Seasonal Variations 1973

Biological Symbiosis 1973
PN 390   SC 06000
SN Intimate relationship between organisms of two or more kinds, particularly one in which the symbiont benefits from the host. Includes parasitic behavior. Limited to animal populations.
UF   Parasitism
     Symbiosis (Biological)
R   ↓ Animals 1967
     ↓ Biology 1967
     Interspecies Interaction 1991

Biology 1967
PN 2209   SC 06010
SN Branch of science dealing with living organisms. Used for the scientific discipline or the biological processes themselves.
B   Sciences 1967
N   Botany 1973
     Neurobiology 1973
     Sociobiology 1982
     Zoology 1973
R   Biological Symbiosis 1973
     Biosynthesis 1973
     Phylogenesis 1973
     Psychobiology 1982

Biopsy 1973
PN 45   SC 06020
B   Medical Diagnosis 1973

Biopsy — (cont'd)
R   ↓ Surgery 1971

Biopsychosocial Approach 1991
PN 817   SC 06024
SN A systematic integration of biological, psychological, and social approaches to the study, treatment, and understanding of mental health and mental disorders.
UF   Biopsychosocial Model
R   Behavioral Genetics 1994
     Holistic Health 1985
     Interdisciplinary Treatment Approach 1973
     Psychobiology 1982
     Systems Theory 1988

Biopsychosocial Model
Use   Biopsychosocial Approach

Biosynthesis 1973
PN 86   SC 06030
SN Formation of chemical compounds of relatively complex structure from nutrients by enzyme-catalyzed reactions in living cells.
B   Metabolism 1967
R   ↓ Biology 1967

Bipolar Affective Disorder
Use   Bipolar Disorder

Bipolar Disorder 2001
PN 5680   SC 06034
SN The term MANIC DEPRESSIVE PSYCHOSIS was used to represent this concept from 1967-1988, and MANIC DEPRESSION was used from 1988-2000. In 2000, BIPOLAR DISORDER was created to replace these terms. MANIC DEPRESSIVE PSYCHOSIS and MANIC DEPRESSION were stripped from all records and replaced with BIPOLAR DISORDER.
UF   Bipolar Affective Disorder
     Bipolar Mood Disorder
     Manic Depression
     Manic Depressive Psychosis
B   Affective Disorders 2001
N   Cyclothymic Personality 1973
R   ↓ Affective Psychosis 1973
     ↓ Major Depression 1988
     ↓ Mania 1967

Bipolar Mood Disorder
Use   Bipolar Disorder

Biracial Children
Use   Interracial Offspring

Birds 1967
PN 5599   SC 06040
UF   Fowl
B   Vertebrates 1973
N   Blackbirds 1973
     Budgerigars 1973
     Canaries 1973
     Chickens 1967
     Doves 1973
     Ducks 1973
     Geese 1973
     Penguins 1973
     Pigeons 1967
     Quails 1973
     Robins 1973
     Sea Gulls 1973
R   Owls 1997

Birth 1967
PN 1954   SC 06050
UF   Childbirth
     Parturition
N   Natural Childbirth 1978
     Premature Birth 1973
R   Birth Injuries 1973
     Birth Rites 1973
     Birth Trauma 1973
     Birth Weight 1985
     Childbirth Training 1978
     Labor (Childbirth) 1973
     Midwifery 1985
     Obstetrical Complications 1978
     Perinatal Period 1994
     ↓ Pregnancy 1967
     ↓ Sexual Reproduction 1973

Birth Control 1971
PN 1268   SC 06060
UF   Contraception
     Population Control
B   Family Planning 1973
N   ↓ Contraceptive Devices 1973
     Rhythm Method 1973
     Tubal Ligation 1973
     Vasectomy 1973
R   Condoms 1991
     Induced Abortion 1971
     Overpopulation 1973
     Premarital Intercourse 1973
     Sexual Abstinence 1973
     ↓ Sterilization (Sex) 1973

Birth Control Attitudes
Use   Family Planning Attitudes

Birth Injuries 1973
PN 68   SC 06070
SN Physical injuries (such as brain damage) received during birth, mostly in, but not limited to, breech births, instrument deliveries, neonatal anoxia, or premature births. Used for both human and animal populations.
UF   Injuries (Birth)
B   Injuries 1973
R   ↓ Birth 1967
     Birth Trauma 1973
     ↓ Neonatal Disorders 1973
     Obstetrical Complications 1978

Birth Order 1967
PN 1671   SC 06080
B   Family Structure 1973

Birth Parents
Use   Biological Family

Birth Rate 1982
PN 143   SC 06087
SN Ratio of the number of live births to the number of individuals in a human population within a specified time period.
R   Fertility 1988
     ↓ Population 1973

Birth Rites 1973
PN 85   SC 06090
B   Rites of Passage 1973
R   ↓ Birth 1967
     Circumcision 2001

Birth Trauma [1973]
PN 89   SC 06100
SN Stress, as experienced by infants, of being born and bombarded with external stimuli that may have negative influences on subsequent psychological development. Limited to human populations.
  R ↓ Birth [1967]
    Birth Injuries [1973]

Birth Weight [1985]
PN 760   SC 06105
  UF Low Birth Weight
  B Body Weight [1967]
  R ↓ Birth [1967]
    Premature Birth [1973]

Bisexuality [1973]
PN 1002   SC 06110
  B Psychosexual Behavior [1967]
    Sexual Orientation [1997]
  R Lesbianism [1973]
    Male Homosexuality [1973]
    Transsexualism [1973]
    Transvestism [1973]

Bitterness
  Use Taste Perception

Black Power Movement [1973]
PN 38   SC 06130
  B Social Movements [1967]
  R ↓ Activist Movements [1973]

Blackbirds [1973]
PN 178   SC 06140
  B Birds [1967]

Blacks [1982]
PN 19485   SC 06150
SN In 1982, this term was created to replace the discontinued term NEGROES. In 2000, NEGROES was stripped from all records and replaced with BLACKS.
  UF African Americans
    Negroes
  B Racial and Ethnic Groups [2001]
  R Minority Groups [1967]

Blacky Pictures Test
SN Term was discontinued in 1997. In 2000, the term was stripped from all records containing it, and replaced with PROJECTIVE PERSONALITY MEASURES, its postable counterpart.
  Use Projective Personality Measures

Bladder [1973]
PN 55   SC 06170
  B Urogenital System [1973]

Blame [1994]
PN 289   SC 06175
SN To assign fault or responsibility for an event, state, or behavior, or the condition of fault or responsibility for something believed to deserve censure.
  R Accountability [1988]
    Attribution [1973]
    Guilt [1967]
    ↓ Responsibility [1973]
    Shame [1994]
    ↓ Social Perception [1967]

Blind [1967]
PN 2710   SC 06180

Blind — (cont'd)
  N Deaf Blind [1991]
  R ↓ Vision Disorders [1982]

Blink Reflex
  Use Eyeblink Reflex

Block Design Test (Kohs)
  Use Kohs Block Design Test

Blood [1967]
PN 1723   SC 06200
  B Body Fluids [1973]
  N ↓ Blood Plasma [1973]
  R Blood Alcohol Concentration [1994]
    Blood Groups [1973]
    Blood Volume [1973]
    ↓ Blood and Lymphatic Disorders [1973]
    ↓ Heart [1967]

Blood Alcohol Concentration [1994]
PN 134   SC 06205
  R ↓ Alcohol Abuse [1988]
    ↓ Alcohol Drinking Patterns [1967]
    ↓ Alcohol Intoxication [1973]
    ↓ Alcohols [1967]
    ↓ Blood [1967]
    Driving Under The Influence [1988]
    Drug Usage Screening [1988]

Blood and Lymphatic Disorders [1973]
PN 359   SC 06210
  UF Blood Disorders
    Hematologic Disorders
    Lymphatic Disorders
  B Physical Disorders [1997]
  N Anemia [1973]
    Hemophilia [1973]
    Leukemias [1973]
    Malaria [1973]
    Porphyria [1973]
    Rh Incompatibility [1973]
    Sickle Cell Disease [1994]
  R ↓ Blood [1967]

Blood Brain Barrier [1994]
PN 33   SC 06215
SN Functional barrier between brain blood vessels and brain tissues.
  R Blood Circulation [1973]
    ↓ Blood Flow [1973]
    ↓ Blood Vessels [1973]
    ↓ Brain [1967]
    ↓ Cardiovascular System [1967]
    Cerebrospinal Fluid [1973]
    ↓ Neurochemistry [1973]

Blood Cells [1973]
PN 163   SC 06220
  B Cells (Biology) [1973]
  N Erythrocytes [1973]
    ↓ Leucocytes [1973]

Blood Circulation [1973]
PN 162   SC 06230
  UF Circulation (Blood)
  R Arterial Pulse [1973]
    Blood Brain Barrier [1994]
    ↓ Blood Flow [1973]
    Blood Volume [1973]
    Cerebral Blood Flow [1994]

Blood Coagulation [1973]
PN 28   SC 06240
  UF Coagulation (Blood)

Blood Disorders
  Use Blood and Lymphatic Disorders

Blood Donation
  Use Tissue Donation

Blood Flow [1973]
PN 743   SC 06270
  N Cerebral Blood Flow [1994]
  R Blood Brain Barrier [1994]
    Blood Circulation [1973]
    Blood Volume [1973]

Blood Glucose
  Use Blood Sugar

Blood Groups [1973]
PN 73   SC 06300
SN Genetically determined classes of human erythrocytes based on specific antigens for which the groups are named.
  R Antigens [1982]
    ↓ Blood [1967]
    Erythrocytes [1973]
    ↓ Genetics [1967]

Blood Plasma [1973]
PN 3449   SC 06310
  UF Plasma (Blood)
  B Blood [1967]
  N Blood Serum [1973]

Blood Platelets [1973]
PN 1046   SC 06320
  UF Platelets (Blood)

Blood Pressure [1967]
PN 2751   SC 06330
  N Diastolic Pressure [1973]
    Systolic Pressure [1973]
  R ↓ Blood Pressure Disorders [1973]
    Blood Volume [1973]
    Cardiovascular Reactivity [1994]
    Cerebral Blood Flow [1994]
    ↓ Vasoconstrictor Drugs [1973]
    ↓ Vasodilator Drugs [1973]

Blood Pressure Disorders [1973]
PN 27   SC 06340
  B Cardiovascular Disorders [1967]
  N ↓ Hypertension [1973]
    Hypotension [1973]
    Syncope [1973]
  R ↓ Arteriosclerosis [1973]
    ↓ Blood Pressure [1967]
    Vasoconstriction [1973]
    Vasodilation [1973]

Blood Proteins [1973]
PN 108   SC 06350
  B Proteins [1973]
  N Hemoglobin [1973]
    ↓ Immunoglobulins [1973]
    Serum Albumin [1973]

Blood Serum [1973]
PN 1512   SC 06360
  UF Serum (Blood)
  B Blood Plasma [1973]

Blood Serum — (cont'd)
R   Antibodies 1973

Blood Sugar 1973
PN 358   SC 06370
UF   Blood Glucose
B   Glucose 1973

Blood Transfusion 1973
PN 43   SC 06380
UF   Transfusion (Blood)
B   Physical Treatment Methods 1973
R   Hemodialysis 1973
      Tissue Donation 1991

Blood Vessels 1973
PN 38   SC 06390
B   Cardiovascular System 1967
N   ↓ Arteries (Anatomy) 1973
      Capillaries (Anatomy) 1973
      Veins (Anatomy) 1973
R   Blood Brain Barrier 1994

Blood Volume 1973
PN 120   SC 06400
R   ↓ Blood 1967
      Blood Circulation 1973
      ↓ Blood Flow 1973
      ↓ Blood Pressure 1967

Blue Collar Workers 1973
PN 1134   SC 06410
SN Employees whose unskilled, semiskilled, or skilled occupations involve physical labor.
UF   Laborers (Construction and Industry)
B   Business and Industrial Personnel 1967
N   Industrial Foremen 1973
      Skilled Industrial Workers 1973
      Unskilled Industrial Workers 1973
R   Technical Service Personnel 1973

Boarding Schools 1988
PN 92   SC 06412
SN Elementary or secondary residential educational institutions for students enrolled in an instructional program. Primarily used for non-disordered populations.
B   Schools 1967
R   Institutional Schools 1978

Boards of Education 1978
PN 92   SC 06416
SN Governing bodies responsible for managing public school systems.
R   ↓ Education 1967
      Educational Administration 1967
      ↓ School Administrators 1973

Body Art
Use Cosmetic Techniques

Body Awareness 1982
PN 572   SC 06425
SN Perception of one's physical self or body at any particular time.
B   Awareness 1967
R   ↓ Body Image 1967
      Self Perception 1967
      ↓ Somesthetic Perception 1967

Body Dysmorphic Disorder 2001
PN 106   SC 06427

Body Dysmorphic Disorder — (cont'd)
SN A preoccupation with a slight or imagined defect in appearance that causes significant distress or impairment in social, occupational, or other areas of functioning. Compare BODY IMAGE DISTURBANCES. In 2000, this term was created to replace the discontinued term DYSMORPHOPHOBIA. DYSMORPHOPHOBIA was stripped from all records and replaced with BODY DYSMORPHIC DISORDER.
UF   Atypical Somatoform Disorder
      Dysmorphophobia
B   Somatoform Disorders 2001
R   ↓ Body Image Disturbances 1973
      Obsessive Compulsive Disorder 1985

Body Fluids 1973
PN 89   SC 06430
B   Anatomy 1967
N   Amniotic Fluid 1973
      Bile 1973
      ↓ Blood 1967
      Cerebrospinal Fluid 1973
      Mucus 1973
      Saliva 1973
      Sweat 1973
      Urine 1973
R   ↓ Physiology 1967

Body Height 1973
PN 377   SC 06440
UF   Height (Body)
B   Body Size 1985
R   Physique 1967

Body Image 1967
PN 2839   SC 06450
SN Mental representation of one's body according to feedback received from one's body, the environment, and other people.
N   ↓ Body Image Disturbances 1973
R   Body Awareness 1982

Body Image Disturbances 1973
PN 623   SC 06460
SN Distortions in the evaluative picture or mental representation an individual has of his/her body. Compare BODY DYSMORPHIC DISORDER.
B   Body Image 1967
N   Koro 1994
      Phantom Limbs 1973
R   Anorexia Nervosa 1973
      Body Dysmorphic Disorder 2001
      Castration Anxiety 1973

Body Language 1973
PN 339   SC 06470
SN Type of nonverbal communication in which thoughts, feelings, etc., are expressed through bodily movement or posture.
UF   Kinesics
B   Interpersonal Communication 1973
      Nonverbal Communication 1971
R   Gestures 1973
      Posture 1973

Body Rocking 1973
PN 55   SC 06480
UF   Rocking (Body)
B   Symptoms 1967
R   ↓ Behavior Disorders 1971

Body Rotation
Use Rotational Behavior

Body Size 1985
PN 940   SC 06485
SN Used for human or animal populations. For human populations consider also PHYSIQUE or SOMATOTYPES.
B   Size 1973
N   Body Height 1973
      ↓ Body Weight 1967
R   Physique 1967

Body Sway Testing 1973
PN 58   SC 06490
B   Measurement 1967
R   ↓ Neuropsychological Assessment 1982

Body Temperature 1973
PN 1445   SC 06500
UF   Temperature (Body)
B   Physiology 1967
N   Skin Temperature 1973
      Thermoregulation (Body) 1973
R   Hypothermia 1973

Body Types
Use Somatotypes

Body Weight 1967
PN 4290   SC 06520
UF   Weight (Body)
B   Body Size 1985
N   Birth Weight 1985
      Obesity 1967
      ↓ Underweight 1973
R   Obesity (Attitudes Toward) 1997
      Physique 1967
      Weight Control 1985

Bombesin 1988
PN 106   SC 06523
B   Peptides 1973

Bonding (Emotional)
Use Attachment Behavior

Bone Conduction Audiometry 1973
PN 32   SC 06530
B   Audiometry 1967
R   ↓ Auditory Stimulation 1967
      ↓ Perceptual Measures 1973

Bone Disorders 1973
PN 98   SC 06540
B   Musculoskeletal Disorders 1973
N   Osteoporosis 1991

Bone Marrow 1973
PN 185   SC 06550
B   Tissues (Body) 1973
R   Bones 1973

Bones 1973
PN 94   SC 06570
B   Connective Tissues 1973
      Musculoskeletal System 1973
R   Bone Marrow 1973
      Jaw 1973
      Spinal Column 1973

Bonobos 1997
PN 52   SC 06575
SN Members of the species Pan panicus. Although not members of the chimpanzee species, Bonobos are often referred to as pygmy chimpanzees.

Bonobos — (cont'd)
UF   Pygmy Chimpanzees
B   Primates (Nonhuman) [1973]
R   Chimpanzees [1973]

Bonuses [1973]
PN 33   **SC** 06580
B   Employee Benefits [1973]
R   Salaries [1973]

Books [1973]
PN 630   **SC** 06600
SN   Refers to books as a means of communication, as distinct from the document type identifier BOOK.
B   Printed Communications Media [1973]
N   ↓ Textbooks [1978]
R   Reading Materials [1973]

Borderline Mental Retardation [1973]
PN 290   **SC** 06610
SN   IQ 71-84. In 2000, this term replaced the discontinued term SLOW LEARNERS and the discontinued and deleted term BORDERLINE MENTALLY RETARDED. These terms were stripped from all records and replaced with BORDERLINE MENTAL RETARDATION.
UF   Slow Learners
B   Mental Retardation [1967]
R   Psychosocial Mental Retardation [1973]

Borderline Personality [2001]
PN 0   **SC** 06622
SN   Personality disorder with maladaptive patterns of behavior characterized by impulsive and unpredictable actions, mood instability, and unstable interpersonal relationships. Use BORDERLINE STATES to access references from 1978-2000.
B   Personality Disorders [1967]
R   Borderline States [1978]
     ↓ Self Destructive Behavior [1985]

Borderline States [1978]
PN 3633   **SC** 06624
SN   State in which individual has not broken with reality but may become psychotic if exposed to unfavorable circumstances.
R   Borderline Personality [2001]
     ↓ Mental Disorders [1967]
     ↓ Neurosis [1967]
     ↓ Psychosis [1967]

Boredom [1973]
PN 272   **SC** 06630
B   Emotional States [1973]
R   Monotony [1978]

Botany [1973]
PN 55   **SC** 06640
B   Biology [1967]
R   Phylogenesis [1973]

Bottle Feeding [1973]
PN 103   **SC** 06650
B   Feeding Practices [1973]

Boundaries (Psychological) [1997]
PN 162   **SC** 06660
SN   Psychological barriers that separate or divide, and, in some cases, protect the integrity of individuals or groups.
R   ↓ Group Dynamics [1967]
     Intergroup Dynamics [1973]
     ↓ Interpersonal Interaction [1967]
     Personal Space [1973]

Boundaries (Psychological) — (cont'd)
R   ↓ Personality Processes [1967]
     Territoriality [1967]

Boundary Violations (Sexual)
Use   Professional Client Sexual Relations

Bourgeois
Use   Middle Class

Bowel Disorders
Use   Colon Disorders

Boys
Use   Human Males

Brachial Plexus
Use   Spinal Nerves

Bradycardia [1973]
PN 115   **SC** 06730
B   Arrhythmias (Heart) [1973]

Bradykinesia [2001]
PN 0   **SC** 06735
SN   Abnormal slowness of movement, which is often a symptom of neurological disorders, particularly Parkinson's disease.
UF   Hypokinesia
B   Dyskinesia [1973]
R   Hyperkinesis [1973]
     Parkinsonism [1994]
     Parkinsons Disease [1973]

Braille [1978]
PN 148   **SC** 06737
B   Reading [1967]
R   Braille Instruction [1973]
     Reading Education [1973]
     Reading Materials [1973]
     ↓ Tactual Perception [1967]

Braille Instruction [1973]
PN 52   **SC** 06740
B   Curriculum [1967]
R   Braille [1978]
     Reading Education [1973]

Brain [1967]
PN 7059   **SC** 06750
N   ↓ Brain Stem [1973]
     ↓ Forebrain [1985]
     ↓ Hindbrain [1997]
     ↓ Mesencephalon [1973]
R   Blood Brain Barrier [1994]
     ↓ Brain Disorders [1967]
     Brain Size [1973]
     Brain Weight [1973]
     Cerebral Atrophy [1994]
     ↓ Cerebral Dominance [1973]
     ↓ Lateral Dominance [1967]
     Left Brain [1991]
     Ocular Dominance [1973]
     Right Brain [1991]

Brain Ablation
Use   Brain Lesions

Brain Concussion [1973]
PN 155   **SC** 06770
UF   Concussion (Brain)
B   Brain Damage [1967]

Brain Concussion — (cont'd)
B   Head Injuries [1973]

Brain Damage [1967]
PN 10406   **SC** 06780
SN   In 2000, this term replaced the discontinued and deleted term BRAIN DAMAGED. BRAIN DAMAGED was stripped from all records and replaced with BRAIN DAMAGE.
B   Brain Disorders [1967]
N   Brain Concussion [1973]
     Minimal Brain Disorders [1973]
     Traumatic Brain Injury [1997]
R   Cerebral Atrophy [1994]
     ↓ Congenital Disorders [1973]
     ↓ Disorders [1967]
     ↓ Epilepsy [1967]
     Global Amnesia [1997]
     ↓ Head Injuries [1973]
     ↓ Mental Retardation [1967]
     ↓ Neuropsychological Assessment [1982]

Brain Disorders [1967]
PN 2014   **SC** 06800
B   Central Nervous System Disorders [1973]
N   Acute Alcoholic Intoxication [1973]
     Anencephaly [1973]
     ↓ Aphasia [1967]
     Athetosis [1973]
     ↓ Brain Damage [1967]
     Brain Neoplasms [1973]
     Cerebral Palsy [1967]
     Cerebrovascular Accidents [1973]
     Chronic Alcoholic Intoxication [1973]
     Encephalitis [1973]
     ↓ Encephalopathies [1982]
     ↓ Epilepsy [1967]
     ↓ Epileptic Seizures [1973]
     Hydrocephaly [1973]
     Microcephaly [1973]
     Minimal Brain Disorders [1973]
     ↓ Organic Brain Syndromes [1973]
     Parkinsons Disease [1973]
R   ↓ Brain [1967]
     Cerebral Atrophy [1994]
     ↓ Convulsions [1967]
     ↓ Memory Disorders [1973]
     ↓ Mental Disorders [1967]
     Rett Syndrome [1994]

Brain Injury (Traumatic)
Use   Traumatic Brain Injury

Brain Lesions [1967]
PN 8857   **SC** 06830
SN   Not defined prior to 1982. From 1982, limited to experimentally induced lesions and used primarily for animal populations.
UF   Brain Ablation
     Cerebral Lesions
     Subcortical Lesions
B   Lesions [1967]
N   Hypothalamus Lesions [1973]
R   Decerebration [1973]
     Decortication (Brain) [1973]

Brain Mapping
Use   Stereotaxic Atlas

Brain Maps
Use   Stereotaxic Atlas

Brain Metabolism
Use   Neurochemistry

Brain Neoplasms 1973
PN   437   SC   06860
B   Brain Disorders 1967
         Nervous System Neoplasms 1973

Brain Self Stimulation 1985
PN   461   SC   06864
UF   Intracranial Self Stimulation
B   Brain Stimulation 1967
         Self Stimulation 1967

Brain Size 1973
PN   745   SC   06868
B   Size 1973
R   ↓ Brain 1967
         Brain Weight 1973
         Cerebral Atrophy 1994

Brain Stem 1973
PN   1308   SC   06870
B   Brain 1967
N   Locus Ceruleus 1982
         Medulla Oblongata 1973
         ↓ Pons 1973
         Reticular Formation 1967
R   ↓ Hindbrain 1997

Brain Stimulation 1967
PN   1917   SC   06880
B   Stereotaxic Techniques 1973
         Stimulation 1967
N   Brain Self Stimulation 1985
         Chemical Brain Stimulation 1973
         Electrical Brain Stimulation 1973
         Spreading Depression 1967
R   Physiological Arousal 1967

Brain Weight 1973
PN   148   SC   06882
R   ↓ Brain 1967
         Brain Size 1973
         Cerebral Atrophy 1994

Brainstorming 1982
PN   105   SC   06883
SN   Group problem-solving technique involving
spontaneous contribution of ideas from all group
members.
B   Group Problem Solving 1973
R   Choice Shift 1994
         ↓ Group Dynamics 1967

Brainwashing 1982
PN   60   SC   06884
SN   Indoctrination of an individual or group by
means of physical or psychological duress in order to
alter their political, social, religious, or moral beliefs.
UF   Thought Control
B   Persuasive Communication 1967
R   Attitude Change 1967
         Coercion 1994
         Propaganda 1973

Brand Names 1978
PN   714   SC   06885
B   Names 1985
R   ↓ Advertising 1967
         Brand Preferences 1994
         ↓ Consumer Behavior 1967
         ↓ Consumer Research 1973

Brand Names — (cont'd)
R   Marketing 1973
         Retailing 1991

Brand Preferences 1994
PN   280   SC   06887
SN   Includes loyalty to brand name products or prod-
uct switching.
B   Consumer Attitudes 1973
         Preferences 1967
R   ↓ Advertising 1967
         Brand Names 1978
         ↓ Consumer Behavior 1967
         ↓ Consumer Research 1973
         Marketing 1973

Bravery
Use   Courage

Breakthrough (Psychotherapeutic)
Use   Psychotherapeutic Breakthrough

Breakup (Relationship)
Use   Relationship Termination

Breast 1973
PN   254   SC   06920
B   Anatomy 1967

Breast Cancer Screening
Use   Cancer Screening

Breast Examination
Use   Self Examination (Medical)

Breast Feeding 1973
PN   559   SC   06930
B   Feeding Practices 1973
R   Weaning 1973

Breast Neoplasms 1973
PN   1460   SC   06940
UF   Mammary Neoplasms
B   Neoplasms 1967
R   Mammography 1994
         Mastectomy 1973

Breathing
Use   Respiration

Breeding (Animal)
Use   Animal Breeding

Brief Psychotherapy 1967
PN   2882   SC   06970
SN   Short-term or time-limited methods of psycho-
therapy.
UF   Short Term Psychotherapy
         Time Limited Psychotherapy
B   Psychotherapy 1967

Brief Reactive Psychosis
Use   Acute Psychosis

Bright Light Therapy
Use   Phototherapy

Brightness Constancy 1985
PN   24   SC   06975
SN   The tendency to perceive the brightness of stim-
uli as stable despite objective changes in illumination.
B   Brightness Perception 1973

Brightness Constancy — (cont'd)
B   Perceptual Constancy 1985

Brightness Contrast 1985
PN   205   SC   06977
B   Visual Contrast 1985

Brightness Perception 1973
PN   1296   SC   06980
UF   Luminance Threshold
B   Visual Perception 1967
N   Brightness Constancy 1985
R   ↓ Illumination 1967
         Luminance 1982

Bromides 1973
PN   35   SC   06990
SN   In 1997, this term replaced the discontinued
term LITHIUM BROMIDE. In 2000, LITHIUM BRO-
MIDE was stripped from all records and replaced with
BROMIDES.
UF   Lithium Bromide
B   Drugs 1967
R   Arecoline 1973
         Neostigmine 1973
         Scopolamine 1973

Bromocriptine 1988
PN   197   SC   06995
B   Alkaloids 1973
         Enzyme Inhibitors 1985
         Ergot Derivatives 1973

Bronchi 1973
PN   9   SC   07000
B   Respiratory System 1973

Bronchial Disorders 1973
PN   56   SC   07010
B   Respiratory Tract Disorders 1973

Brothers 1973
PN   183   SC   07020
B   Human Males 1973
         Siblings 1967

Bruxism 1985
PN   45   SC   07035
SN   Use NOCTURNAL TEETH GRINDING to
access references from 1973-1984.
UF   Teeth Grinding
N   Nocturnal Teeth Grinding 1973
R   Myofascial Pain 1991

Buddhism 1973
PN   335   SC   07040
B   Religious Affiliation 1973
N   Zen Buddhism 1973
R   Buddhists 1997

Buddhists 1997
PN   12   SC   07045
B   Religious Groups 1997
R   ↓ Buddhism 1973

Budgerigars 1973
PN   73   SC   07050
B   Birds 1967

Budgets 1997
PN   26   SC   07052
SN   Use COSTS AND COST ANALYSIS to access
references from 1973-1996.

Budgets — (cont'd)
- B   Costs and Cost Analysis 1973
- R   Cost Containment 1991
       Economics 1985
       Economy 1973
       Funding 1988
       Income (Economic) 1973
       Money 1967

Bufotenine 1973
PN 17   SC 07060
- B   Amines 1973
       Hallucinogenic Drugs 1967
       Vasoconstrictor Drugs 1973

Bulimia 1985
PN 3751   SC 07078
SN Disorder characterized primarily by binge eating and often accompanied by self-induced vomiting and/or misuse of laxatives.
- B   Eating Disorders 1997
- R   Anorexia Nervosa 1973
       Binge Eating 1991
       ↓ Somatoform Disorders 2001

Bulls
Use Cattle

Bupropion 1994
PN 113   SC 07081
- B   Antidepressant Drugs 1971

Burnout
Use Occupational Stress

Burns 1973
PN 350   SC 07090
- B   Injuries 1973
- R   Electrical Injuries 1973
       ↓ Wounds 1973

Buses
Use Motor Vehicles

Bush Babies
Use Lemurs

Business 1967
PN 1373   SC 07110
- UF   Commerce
       Industry
       Manufacturing
- R   Business Management 1973
       Business Organizations 1973
       Business Students 1973
       Entrepreneurship 1991
       ↓ Management 1967
       Ownership 1985
       Retailing 1991
       Self Employment 1994

Business and Industrial Personnel 1967
PN 5250   SC 07120
- UF   Businessmen
- UF   Industrial Personnel
- B   Personnel 1967
- N   Architects 1973
       ↓ Blue Collar Workers 1973
       Industrial Psychologists 1973
       Sales Personnel 1973
       Secretarial Personnel 1973
       ↓ Service Personnel 1991

Business and Industrial Personnel — (cont'd)
- N   Skilled Industrial Workers 1973
       ↓ Technical Personnel 1978
       ↓ White Collar Workers 1973
- R   ↓ Aerospace Personnel 1973
       ↓ Agricultural Workers 1973
       Engineers 1967
       ↓ Government Personnel 1973
       ↓ Nonprofessional Personnel 1982
       ↓ Professional Personnel 1978
       Scientists 1967
       Technical Service Personnel 1973

Business Education 1973
PN 376   SC 07123
- B   Curriculum 1967
- R   Business Management 1973
       Management Training 1973
       ↓ Personnel Management 1973
       ↓ Personnel Training 1967

Business Management 1973
PN 690   SC 07130
- B   Management 1967
- R   Business 1967
       Business Education 1973
       Entrepreneurship 1991
       ↓ Management Methods 1973
       ↓ Personnel Management 1973

Business Organizations 1973
PN 1997   SC 07140
- UF   Companies
       Corporations
- B   Organizations 1967
       Private Sector 1985
- R   Business 1967

Business Students 1973
PN 697   SC 07150
- B   Students 1967
- R   Business 1967

Businessmen
Use Business and Industrial Personnel

Buspirone 1991
PN 466   SC 07165
- B   Minor Tranquilizers 1973
- R   Serotonin Agonists 1988

Butterflies 1973
PN 119   SC 07170
- B   Insects 1967
- R   Larvae 1973

Butyrylperazine
SN Term was discontinued in 1997. In 2000, the term was stripped from all records containing it, and replaced with PHENOTHIAZINE DERIVATIVES, its nonpostable counterpart.
Use Phenothiazine Derivatives

Buying
Use Consumer Behavior

Cadres
Use Social Groups

Caffeine 1973
PN 1188   SC 07210

Caffeine — (cont'd)
- B   Alkaloids 1973
       CNS Stimulating Drugs 1973
       Diuretics 1973
       Heart Rate Affecting Drugs 1973
       Respiration Stimulating Drugs 1973
- R   ↓ Analeptic Drugs 1973

Cage Apparatus 1973
PN 70   SC 07220
- B   Apparatus 1967

Calcium 1973
PN 500   SC 07240
- B   Chemical Elements 1973
       Metallic Elements 1973
- N   Calcium Ions 1973

Calcium Channel Blockers
Use Channel Blockers

Calcium Ions 1973
PN 123   SC 07260
- B   Calcium 1973
       Electrolytes 1973

Calculators
Use Digital Computers

Calculus
Use Mathematics

California F Scale 1973
PN 32   SC 07290
- B   Nonprojective Personality Measures 1973

California Psychological Inventory 1967
PN 288   SC 07300
- B   Personality Measures 1967

California Test of Mental Maturity 1973
PN 9   SC 07310
- B   Intelligence Measures 1967

California Test of Personality 1973
PN 15   SC 07320
- B   Nonprojective Personality Measures 1973

Calories 1973
PN 324   SC 07330
- R   Energy Expenditure 1967

Cameras 1973
PN 39   SC 07350
- B   Apparatus 1967

Campaigns (Political)
Use Political Campaigns

Camping 1973
PN 101   SC 07370
- B   Recreation 1967
- R   Summer Camps (Recreation) 1973
- R   Vacationing 1973

Camps (Therapeutic)
Use Therapeutic Camps

Campuses 1973
PN 62   SC 07390
- B   School Facilities 1973

Canaries 1973
PN 53 SC 07410
B Birds 1967

Cancer Screening 1997
PN 215 SC 07415
UF Breast Cancer Screening
Prostate Cancer Screening
Skin Cancer Screening
B Health Screening 1997
R Health Promotion 1991
Mammography 1994
Physical Examination 1988
Self Examination (Medical) 1988

Cancers
Use Neoplasms

Candidates (Political)
Use Political Candidates

Canids 1997
PN 11 SC 07434
UF Coyotes
B Mammals 1973
N Dogs 1967
Foxes 1973
Wolves 1973

Cannabinoids 1982
PN 197 SC 07436
UF Nabilone
N Tetrahydrocannabinol 1973
R ↓ Cannabis 1973

Cannabis 1973
PN 391 SC 07440
UF Hemp (Cannabis)
B Drugs 1967
N Hashish 1973
Marihuana 1971
R Aphrodisiacs 1973
↓ Cannabinoids 1982
↓ Hallucinogenic Drugs 1967
↓ Narcotic Drugs 1973
Tetrahydrocannabinol 1973

Canonical Correlation
Use Multivariate Analysis

Capgras Syndrome 1985
PN 199 SC 07447
SN Clinical condition in which patient believes an acquaintance, a closely related person, or a close associate has been replaced by a double or an impostor.
B Psychosis 1967
Syndromes 1973
R Delusions 1967
↓ Symptoms 1967

Capillaries (Anatomy) 1973
PN 16 SC 07450
B Blood Vessels 1973

Capital Punishment 1973
PN 380 SC 07460
UF Death Penalty
Punishment (Capital)

Capitalism 1973
PN 174 SC 07470
B Political Economic Systems 1973

Capitalism — (cont'd)
R Entrepreneurship 1991
Ownership 1985

Capsaicin 1991
PN 143 SC 07475
B Fatty Acids 1973

Captivity (Animal)
Use Animal Captivity

Captopril 1991
PN 36 SC 07477
B Antihypertensive Drugs 1973
Enzyme Inhibitors 1985
R Angiotensin 1973

Carbachol 1973
PN 222 SC 07480
B Cholinomimetic Drugs 1973

Carbamazepine 1988
PN 703 SC 07483
B Analgesic Drugs 1973
Anticonvulsive Drugs 1973

Carbidopa 1988
PN 29 SC 07485
SN Use DECARBOXYLASES to access references from 1982-1987.
B Decarboxylase Inhibitors 1982
R DOPA 1973

Carbohydrate Metabolism 1973
PN 83 SC 07490
B Metabolism 1967
N Glucose Metabolism 1994
R Acetaldehyde 1982
Guanosine 1985

Carbohydrates 1973
PN 430 SC 07510
N Deoxyglucose 1991
↓ Sugars 1973

Carbon 1973
PN 10 SC 07520

Carbon Dioxide 1973
PN 281 SC 07530
R Respiration 1967

Carbon Monoxide 1973
PN 161 SC 07540
R ↓ Poisons 1973

Carbon Monoxide Poisoning 1973
PN 59 SC 07550
UF Carboxyhemoglobinemia
B Toxic Disorders 1973

Carbonic Anhydrase
SN Term was discontinued in 1997. In 2000, the term was stripped from all records containing it, and replaced with ENZYMES, its postable counterpart.
Use Enzymes

Carboxyhemoglobinemia
Use Carbon Monoxide Poisoning

Carcinogens 1973
PN 22 SC 07580

Carcinogens — (cont'd)
R ↓ Drugs 1967
Pollution 1973
Tobacco Smoking 1967

Carcinomas
Use Neoplasms

Cardiac Arrest
Use Heart Disorders

Cardiac Disorders
Use Heart Disorders

Cardiac Rate
Use Heart Rate

Cardiac Surgery
Use Heart Surgery

Cardiography 1973
PN 16 SC 07620
B Medical Diagnosis 1973
N Electrocardiography 1967

Cardiology 1973
PN 48 SC 07630
B Medical Sciences 1967
R ↓ Cardiovascular System 1967

Cardiotonic Drugs
SN Term was discontinued in 1997. In 2000, the term was stripped from all records containing it, and replaced with DRUGS, its postable counterpart.
Use Drugs

Cardiovascular Disorders 1967
PN 2585 SC 07640
UF Circulatory Disorders
Coronary Disorders
Raynauds Disease
Vascular Disorders
B Physical Disorders 1997
N Aneurysms 1973
↓ Arteriosclerosis 1973
↓ Blood Pressure Disorders 1973
↓ Cerebrovascular Disorders 1973
Embolisms 1973
↓ Heart Disorders 1973
↓ Hemorrhage 1973
↓ Hypertension 1973
↓ Ischemia 1973
↓ Thromboses 1973
R ↓ Cardiovascular System 1967
Coronary Prone Behavior 1982
↓ Dyspnea 1973
↓ Heart Rate Affecting Drugs 1973

Cardiovascular Reactivity 1994
PN 1014 SC 07645
SN Cardiovascular system responses to mental, physical, or environmental stress or other states due to intervention or natural occurrence.
R ↓ Blood Pressure 1967
↓ Cardiovascular System 1967
Heart Rate 1967
Physiological Arousal 1967
Physiological Correlates 1967
↓ Psychophysiology 1967
Stress Reactions 1973

Cardiovascular System 1967
PN 1756   SC 07650
  B   Anatomical Systems 1973
  N ↓ Blood Vessels 1973
     ↓ Heart 1967
  R   Blood Brain Barrier 1994
       Cardiology 1973
     ↓ Cardiovascular Disorders 1967
       Cardiovascular Reactivity 1994
       Spleen 1973

Career Aspirations
  Use Occupational Aspirations

Career Change 1978
PN 507   SC 07666
  UF   Job Change
  R   Career Development 1985
       Employment History 1978
       Job Satisfaction 1967
       Occupational Adjustment 1973
       Occupational Aspirations 1973
       Occupational Choice 1967
       Occupational Mobility 1973
     ↓ Occupations 1967
       Professional Development 1982

Career Choice
  Use Occupational Choice

Career Counseling
  Use Occupational Guidance

Career Development 1985
PN 2382   SC 07672
SN Formation of work identity or progression of
career decisions and/or events as influenced by life
or work experience, education, on-the-job training, or
other factors.
  UF   Career Transitions
       Management Development
  B   Development 1967
       Personnel Management 1973
  R   Career Change 1978
       Employment History 1978
     ↓ Management 1967
       Occupational Choice 1967
     ↓ Occupations 1967
       Personnel Placement 1973
       Personnel Promotion 1978
     ↓ Personnel Training 1967
       Professional Development 1982
       Professional Identity 1991
       Professional Specialization 1991

Career Education 1978
PN 700   SC 07675
SN Comprehensive educational programs focusing
on individual career development beginning in child-
hood and continuing through the adult years.
  UF   Career Exploration
  B   Curriculum 1967
  R   Occupational Guidance 1967

Career Exploration
  Use Career Education

Career Goals
  Use Occupational Aspirations

Career Guidance
  Use Occupational Guidance

Career Maturity
  Use Vocational Maturity

Career Preference
  Use Occupational Preference

Career Transitions
  Use Career Development

Careers
  Use Occupations

Caregiver Burden 1994
PN 1241   SC 07713
SN Used primarily for family or nonprofessional caregivers and the stress or associated emotional
responses experienced when caring for the mentally
or physically disabled. Consider OCCUPATIONAL
STRESS for professional caregivers, e.g., health care
personnel.
  R   Caregivers 1988
       Elder Care 1994
       Home Care 1985
       Homebound 1988
       Respite Care 1988
     ↓ Stress 1967

Caregivers 1988
PN 4671   SC 07715
SN Family members, professionals, or paraprofes-
sionals who provide care to the mentally or physically
disabled.
  UF   Family Caregivers
  R   Caregiver Burden 1994
       Elder Care 1994
     ↓ Health Care Services 1978
       Home Care 1985
       Home Care Personnel 1997
       Quality of Care 1988
       Respite Care 1988
     ↓ Treatment 1967

Carotid Arteries 1973
PN 129   SC 07720
  B   Arteries (Anatomy) 1973

Carp 1973
PN 44   SC 07740
  B   Fishes 1967
  N   Goldfish 1973

Cartoons (Humor) 1973
PN 250   SC 07780
  B   Humor 1967

Case History
  Use Patient History

Case Management 1991
PN 1007   SC 07788
SN Evaluation of health and social service needs of
individuals and development and delivery of service
or treatment. Includes attention to justification and
length of treatment, costs, and health insurance reim-
bursement.
  B   Management 1967
  N   Discharge Planning 1994
  R   Cost Containment 1991
     ↓ Health Care Administration 1997
       Health Care Costs 1994
     ↓ Health Care Delivery 1978
     ↓ Health Insurance 1973
       Health Service Needs 1997

Case Management — (cont'd)
  R   Intake Interview 1994
       Long Term Care 1994
     ↓ Managed Care 1994
       Needs Assessment 1985
       Outreach Programs 1997
       Social Casework 1967
     ↓ Treatment 1967
     ↓ Treatment Duration 1988
     ↓ Treatment Planning 1997

Case Report 1967
PN 21871   SC 07790
SN Used in records discussing issues involved in
the process of conducting exploratory studies of single or multiple clinical cases. From 1967-2000, the
term was also used as a mandatory document type
identifier; however, this usage has been discontinued
due to the advent of Form/Content Type field identifiers. References from 1967-2000 can be accessed
using either CASE REPORT or the Case Report
Form/Content Type field identifier.

Caseworkers
  Use Social Workers

Caste System 1973
PN 219   SC 07810
  B   Social Structure 1967
       Systems 1967

Castration 1967
PN 259   SC 07820
  B   Endocrine Gland Surgery 1973
       Sterilization (Sex) 1973
  N   Male Castration 1973
       Ovariectomy 1973

Castration Anxiety 1973
PN 149   SC 07830
  B   Anxiety Disorders 1997
  R ↓ Body Image Disturbances 1973

Cat Learning 1967
PN 120   SC 07840
SN Not defined prior to 1982. Use CAT LEARNING
or CATS to access references from 1967-1981. From
1982 used for discussions of hypotheses or theories
of learning in cats.
  B   Learning 1967
  R   Cats 1967

CAT Scan
  Use Tomography

Catabolism 1973
PN 18   SC 07850
SN Destructive metabolism involving release of
energy (heat) and resulting in breakdown of complex
materials within the organism.
  B   Metabolism 1967

Catabolites
  Use Metabolites

Catalepsy 1973
PN 346   SC 07860
SN Condition of muscular semirigidity and trance-
like postures. Cataleptic persons make no voluntary
motor movements and may display waxy flexibility.
  B   Movement Disorders 1985
       Symptoms 1967
  R   Autohypnosis 1973

Catalepsy — (cont'd)
- R   ↓ Hysteria [1967]
-     ↓ Schizophrenia [1967]
-     Suggestibility [1967]

Catamnesis
- **Use**   Posttreatment Followup

Cataplexy [1973]
- **PN** 67   **SC** 07880
- **SN**   Temporary loss of muscle tone or weakness following extreme emotion.
- B   Movement Disorders [1985]
-     Muscular Disorders [1973]
-     Neuromuscular Disorders [1973]
- R   Narcolepsy [1973]

Cataracts [1973]
- **PN** 71   **SC** 07890
- B   Eye Disorders [1973]

Catatonia [1973]
- **PN** 407   **SC** 07900
- **SN**   Reaction characterized by muscular rigidity or stupor sometimes punctuated by sudden violent outbursts, panic, or hallucinations.
- B   Symptoms [1967]
- R   Catatonic Schizophrenia [1973]

Catatonic Schizophrenia [1973]
- **PN** 119   **SC** 07910
- B   Schizophrenia [1967]
- R   Catatonia [1973]

Catecholamines [1973]
- **PN** 1862   **SC** 07920
- UF   Monoamines (Brain)
- B   Neurotransmitters [1985]
-     Sympathomimetic Amines [1973]
- N   Dopamine [1973]
-     Epinephrine [1967]
-     Norepinephrine [1973]
- R   ↓ Adrenergic Drugs [1973]
-     ↓ Decarboxylase Inhibitors [1982]
-     ↓ Dopamine Antagonists [1982]
-     Methyldopa [1973]

Categorizing
- **Use**   Classification (Cognitive Process)

Catharsis [1973]
- **PN** 214   **SC** 07940
- **SN**   Process of reliving painful experiences and feelings, and the associated emotional responses.
- UF   Abreaction
- B   Personality Processes [1967]
- R   ↓ Psychoanalysis [1967]

Catheterization [1973]
- **PN** 87   **SC** 07950
- B   Physical Treatment Methods [1973]

Cathexis [1973]
- **PN** 106   **SC** 07960
- **SN**   Psychoanalytic term designating the attachment of intense emotions to a particular object, person, or oneself.
- B   Personality Processes [1967]

Cathode Ray Tubes
- **Use**   Video Display Units

Catholicism (Roman)
- **Use**   Roman Catholicism

Catholics [1997]
- **PN** 104   **SC** 07975
- B   Christians [1997]
- R   Roman Catholicism [1973]

Cats [1967]
- **PN** 6548   **SC** 07980
- B   Felids [1997]
- R   Cat Learning [1967]

Cattell Culture Fair Intelligence Test
- **Use**   Culture Fair Intelligence Test

Cattell Infant Intelligence Scale
- **Use**   Infant Intelligence Scale

Cattle [1973]
- **PN** 477   **SC** 08010
- UF   Bulls
-     Cows
- B   Mammals [1973]

Caucasians
- **SN**   Term was discontinued in 1982. In 2000, the term was stripped from all records containing it, and replaced with WHITES, its postable counterpart.
- **Use**   Whites

Cauda Equina
- **Use**   Spinal Nerves

Caudate Nucleus [1973]
- **PN** 868   **SC** 08040
- B   Basal Ganglia [1973]
- R   Nucleus Accumbens [1982]

Causal Analysis [1994]
- **PN** 443   **SC** 08045
- **SN**   Systematic analysis of causal relationships among variables.
- B   Analysis [1967]
-     Methodology [1967]
- R   Attribution [1973]
-     ↓ Experimentation [1967]
-     Path Analysis [1991]
-     ↓ Statistical Regression [1985]
-     Structural Equation Modeling [1994]

Cecotrophy
- **Use**   Coprophagia

Celiac Plexus
- **Use**   Autonomic Ganglia

Celibacy
- **Use**   Sexual Abstinence

Cell Nucleus [1973]
- **PN** 17   **SC** 08070
- R   ↓ Cells (Biology) [1973]

Cells (Biology) [1973]
- **PN** 667   **SC** 08080
- B   Anatomy [1967]
- N   ↓ Blood Cells [1973]
-     ↓ Chromosomes [1973]
-     Cones (Eye) [1973]
-     Connective Tissue Cells [1973]
-     Epithelial Cells [1973]

Cells (Biology) — (cont'd)
- N   ↓ Neurons [1973]
-     Sperm [1973]
- R   Absorption (Physiological) [1973]
-     Cell Nucleus [1973]
-     Cytology [1973]
-     Cytoplasm [1973]
-     ↓ Physiology [1967]

Censorship [1978]
- **PN** 75   **SC** 08086
- R   ↓ Civil Rights [1978]
-     ↓ Communication [1967]
-     ↓ Communications Media [1973]
-     Freedom [1978]
-     Information [1967]
-     ↓ Laws [1967]
-     ↓ Social Issues [1991]

Centering [1991]
- **PN** 5   **SC** 08088
- **SN**   Focusing of attention and concentration on a particular stimulus or on the whole of the present environment and circumstances. Used primarily in, but not limited to, therapeutic settings.
- R   ↓ Consciousness States [1971]
-     Meditation [1973]
-     ↓ Psychotherapeutic Techniques [1967]
-     ↓ Self Management [1985]

Central Nervous System [1967]
- **PN** 2155   **SC** 08100
- B   Nervous System [1967]
- N   Extrapyramidal Tracts [1973]
-     Meninges [1973]
-     Neural Analyzers [1973]
-     ↓ Neural Pathways [1982]
-     ↓ Spinal Cord [1973]
- R   ↓ Central Nervous System Disorders [1973]

Central Nervous System Disorders [1973]
- **PN** 646   **SC** 08110
- B   Nervous System Disorders [1967]
- N   ↓ Brain Disorders [1967]
-     ↓ Chorea [1973]
-     Dysarthria [1973]
-     ↓ Meningitis [1973]
-     ↓ Myelitis [1973]
-     Neurosyphilis [1973]
-     Progressive Supranuclear Palsy [1997]
- R   ↓ Central Nervous System [1967]
-     Hemiplegia [1978]
-     Hypothermia [1973]
-     ↓ Paralysis [1973]
-     Paraplegia [1978]
-     Quadriplegia [1985]
-     ↓ Spinal Cord Injuries [1973]

Central Nervous System Drugs
- **Use**   CNS Affecting Drugs

Central Tendency Measures [1973]
- **PN** 28   **SC** 08130
- B   Statistical Analysis [1967]
-     Statistical Measurement [1973]
- N   Mean [1973]
-     Median [1973]
- R   ↓ Population (Statistics) [1973]
-     T Test [1973]
-     ↓ Variability Measurement [1973]

Central Vision
- **Use**   Foveal Vision

CER (Conditioning)
Use   Conditioned Emotional Responses

Cerebellar Cortex
Use   Cerebellum

Cerebellar Nuclei
Use   Cerebellum

Cerebellopontile Angle
Use   Cerebellum

Cerebellum [1973]
PN 1392   SC 08180
UF   Cerebellar Cortex
     Cerebellar Nuclei
     Cerebellopontile Angle
B   Hindbrain [1997]
N   Purkinje Cells [1994]

Cerebral Aqueduct
Use   Cerebral Ventricles

Cerebral Arteriosclerosis [1973]
PN 43   SC 08210
B   Arteriosclerosis [1973]
     Cerebrovascular Disorders [1973]
R   Cerebrovascular Accidents [1973]
     ↓ Senile Dementia [1973]

Cerebral Atrophy [1994]
PN 322   SC 08215
UF   Atrophy (Cerebral)
     Cortical Atrophy
R   ↓ Brain [1967]
     ↓ Brain Damage [1967]
     ↓ Brain Disorders [1967]
     Brain Size [1973]
     Brain Weight [1973]
     ↓ Cerebral Cortex [1967]
     ↓ Cerebral Dominance [1973]

Cerebral Blood Flow [1994]
PN 842   SC 08217
B   Blood Flow [1973]
R   Blood Circulation [1973]
     ↓ Blood Pressure [1967]
     ↓ Cerebral Cortex [1967]

Cerebral Cortex [1967]
PN 5155   SC 08220
UF   Cortex (Cerebral)
B   Telencephalon [1973]
N   Cerebral Ventricles [1973]
     Corpus Callosum [1973]
     ↓ Frontal Lobe [1973]
     Left Brain [1991]
     ↓ Limbic System [1973]
     ↓ Occipital Lobe [1973]
     ↓ Parietal Lobe [1973]
     Right Brain [1991]
     ↓ Temporal Lobe [1973]
R   Cerebral Atrophy [1994]
     Cerebral Blood Flow [1994]
     Interhemispheric Interaction [1985]

Cerebral Dominance [1973]
PN 4482   SC 08230
SN   The control of lower brain centers by the cerebrum or cerebral cortex. Compare LATERAL DOMINANCE.

Cerebral Dominance — (cont'd)
B   Dominance [1967]
N   ↓ Lateral Dominance [1967]
R   ↓ Brain [1967]
     Cerebral Atrophy [1994]
     Interhemispheric Interaction [1985]
     Left Brain [1991]
     Right Brain [1991]

Cerebral Hemorrhage [1973]
PN 226   SC 08250
B   Cerebrovascular Disorders [1973]
     Hemorrhage [1973]
R   Cerebrovascular Accidents [1973]

Cerebral Ischemia [1973]
PN 357   SC 08260
B   Cerebrovascular Disorders [1973]
     Ischemia [1973]
R   Cerebrovascular Accidents [1973]

Cerebral Lesions
Use   Brain Lesions

Cerebral Palsy [1967]
PN 1049   SC 08280
B   Brain Disorders [1967]
     Paralysis [1973]
R   Athetosis [1973]

Cerebral Vascular Disorders
Use   Cerebrovascular Disorders

Cerebral Ventricles [1973]
PN 711   SC 08310
UF   Cerebral Aqueduct
     Choroid Plexus
     Ependyma
     Ventricles (Cerebral)
B   Cerebral Cortex [1967]

Cerebrospinal Fluid [1973]
PN 1433   SC 08320
UF   Spinal Fluid
B   Body Fluids [1973]
R   Blood Brain Barrier [1994]

Cerebrovascular Accidents [1973]
PN 2696   SC 08330
UF   Apoplexy
     Stroke (Cerebrum)
B   Brain Disorders [1967]
     Cerebrovascular Disorders [1973]
R   Cerebral Arteriosclerosis [1973]
     Cerebral Hemorrhage [1973]
     Cerebral Ischemia [1973]
     Coma [1973]

Cerebrovascular Disorders [1973]
PN 478   SC 08340
UF   Cerebral Vascular Disorders
B   Cardiovascular Disorders [1967]
N   Cerebral Arteriosclerosis [1973]
     Cerebral Hemorrhage [1973]
     Cerebral Ischemia [1973]
     Cerebrovascular Accidents [1973]
R   Coma [1973]
     ↓ Hypertension [1973]
     Multi Infarct Dementia [1991]
     ↓ Nervous System Disorders [1967]
     ↓ Vascular Dementia [1997]

Certification (Professional)
Use   Professional Certification

Certification Examinations
Use   Professional Examinations

Certified Public Accountants
Use   Accountants

Cervical Plexus
Use   Spinal Nerves

Cervical Sprain Syndrome
Use   Whiplash

Cervix [1973]
PN 157   SC 08390
B   Uterus [1973]

Chance (Fortune) [1973]
PN 274   SC 08420
SN   The possibility of a favorable or unfavorable outcome in an uncertain situation.
UF   Luck
B   Probability [1967]
N   ↓ Statistical Probability [1967]
R   Uncertainty [1991]

Change (Organizational)
Use   Organizational Change

Change (Social)
Use   Social Change

Channel Blockers [1991]
PN 411   SC 08450
UF   Calcium Channel Blockers
B   Drugs [1967]
R   ↓ Vasodilator Drugs [1973]
     Verapamil [1991]

Chaos Theory [1997]
PN 126   SC 09455
B   Theories [1967]
R   ↓ Mathematical Modeling [1973]
     Predictability (Measurement) [1973]
     ↓ Prediction [1967]
     ↓ Probability [1967]
     ↓ Stochastic Modeling [1973]
     Uncertainty [1991]

Chaplains [1973]
PN 51   SC 08460
SN   Clergymen officially attached to branch of military, hospital, institution, court, or university.
B   Clergy [1973]
R   Lay Religious Personnel [1973]
     ↓ Military Personnel [1967]
     Ministers (Religion) [1973]
     Priests [1973]
     Rabbis [1973]

Character
Use   Personality

Character Development
Use   Personality Development

Character Disorders
Use   Personality Disorders

Character Formation
Use Personality Development

Charisma 1988
PN 171   SC 08515
B Personality Traits 1967
R Leadership Qualities 1997
Leadership Style 1973

Charitable Behavior 1973
PN 486   SC 08520
SN Generous or spontaneous goodness as manifested in actions for the benefit of others, especially of the needy, poor, or helpless.
B Interpersonal Interaction 1967
Prosocial Behavior 1982
R Altruism 1973
Assistance (Social Behavior) 1973
Sharing (Social Behavior) 1978
Tissue Donation 1991

Cheating 1973
PN 323   SC 08530
B Deception 1967
R Dishonesty 1973
Fraud 1994
Test Taking 1985

Chemical Brain Stimulation 1973
PN 961   SC 08540
B Brain Stimulation 1967
Stereotaxic Techniques 1973

Chemical Elements 1973
PN 208   SC 08550
SN In 1997, this term replaced the discontinued term NONMETALLIC ELEMENTS. In 2000, NONMETALLIC ELEMENTS was stripped from all records and replaced with CHEMICAL ELEMENTS.
UF Nonmetallic Elements
B Chemicals 1991
N ↓ Calcium 1973
R ↓ Electrolytes 1973
Food Additives 1978

Chemicals 1991
PN 326   SC 08555
SN May include compounds.
N ↓ Chemical Elements 1973
R ↓ Hazardous Materials 1991

Chemistry 1967
PN 402   SC 08560
SN Study of the atomic composition of substances, elements, and their reactions, and the formation, decomposition, and properties of molecules. Used for the scientific discipline or the chemical processes themselves.
B Sciences 1967
N ↓ Biochemistry 1967

Chemoreceptors 1973
PN 378   SC 08570
B Neural Receptors 1973
Sensory Neurons 1973
R Olfactory Mucosa 1973
Taste Buds 1973
Taste Disorders 2001
Vomeronasal Sense 1982

Chemotherapy
Use Drug Therapy

Chess 1973
PN 145   SC 08590
B Games 1967

Chest
Use Thorax

Chewing Tobacco
Use Smokeless Tobacco

Chi Square Test 1973
PN 171   SC 08620
B Nonparametric Statistical Tests 1967
R Statistical Significance 1973

Chicanos
Use Mexican Americans

Chickens 1967
PN 1937   SC 08630
B Birds 1967

Child Abuse 1971
PN 10575   SC 08650
SN Abuse of children or adolescents in a family, institutional, or other setting.
B Crime 1967
Family Violence 1982
N Battered Child Syndrome 1973
R Abandonment 1997
↓ Abuse Reporting 1997
Anatomically Detailed Dolls 1991
Attachment Disorders 2001
Child Abuse Reporting 1997
Child Neglect 1988
Child Welfare 1988
Emotional Abuse 1991
Failure to Thrive 1988
Munchausen Syndrome by Proxy 1997
Patient Abuse 1991
Pedophilia 1973
Physical Abuse 1991
↓ Sexual Abuse 1988

Child Abuse Reporting 1997
PN 143   SC 08652
SN Reporting of physical abuse, emotional abuse, sexual abuse, verbal abuse, or child neglect by the victim or other individuals.
B Abuse Reporting 1997
R ↓ Child Abuse 1971
Child Neglect 1988
Child Welfare 1988

Child Advocacy
Use Advocacy

Child Attitudes 1988
PN 1750   SC 08658
SN Attitudes of, not toward, children.
B Attitudes 1967

Child Behavior Checklist 1994
PN 118   SC 08659
B Nonprojective Personality Measures 1973

Child Care 1991
PN 916   SC 08660
SN Care of children of any age in any setting.
UF Babysitting
N Child Day Care 1973
Child Self Care 1988
R ↓ Childrearing Practices 1967

Child Care — (cont'd)
R Foster Care 1978

Child Care Workers 1978
PN 821   SC 08663
SN Mental health, educational, or social services personnel providing day care or residential care for children.
R Child Day Care 1973
Day Care Centers 1973
↓ Nonprofessional Personnel 1982
↓ Service Personnel 1991

Child Custody 1982
PN 1245   SC 08665
SN Legal guardianship of a child.
B Legal Processes 1973
R Child Support 1988
Child Visitation 1988
Divorce 1973
Guardianship 1988
Joint Custody 1988
↓ Living Arrangements 1991
Mediation 1988
↓ Parental Absence 1973
Protective Services 1997

Child Day Care 1973
PN 1548   SC 08670
SN Day care that provides for a child's physical needs and often his/her developmental or educational needs. Kinds of day care include day care centers and school-based programs.
UF Day Care (Child)
B Child Care 1991
R Child Care Workers 1978
Child Self Care 1988
Child Welfare 1988
Day Care Centers 1973
Quality of Care 1988

Child Discipline 1973
PN 844   SC 08680
UF Discipline (Child)
B Childrearing Practices 1967
Family Relations 1967
N Parental Permissiveness 1973
R ↓ Parent Child Relations 1967
Parental Role 1973

Child Guidance Clinics 1973
PN 257   SC 08690
SN Facilities which exist for the diagnosis and treatment of behavioral and emotional disorders in childhood.
UF Child Psychiatric Clinics
B Clinics 1967
R ↓ Community Facilities 1973
Community Mental Health Centers 1973
↓ Mental Health Programs 1973
↓ Mental Health Services 1978
Psychiatric Clinics 1973

Child Molestation
Use Pedophilia

Child Neglect 1988
PN 1270   SC 08695
SN Failure of parents or caretakers to provide basic care and emotional support necessary for normal development.
B Antisocial Behavior 1971
R Abandonment 1997
Attachment Disorders 2001

Child Neglect — (cont'd)
R ↓ Child Abuse 1971
     Child Abuse Reporting 1997
     Child Welfare 1988
     Emotional Abuse 1991
     Failure to Thrive 1988
     Munchausen Syndrome by Proxy 1997

Child Psychiatric Clinics
  Use   Child Guidance Clinics

Child Psychiatry 1967
PN 1921   SC 08710
SN Branch of psychiatry devoted to the study and treatment of behavioral, mental, and emotional disorders of children. Use a more specific term if possible.
  B   Psychiatry 1967
  R   Orthopsychiatry 1973

Child Psychology 1967
PN 722   SC 08720
SN Branch of developmental psychology devoted to the study of behavior, adjustment, and development and the treatment of behavioral, mental, and emotional disorders of children. Use a more specific term if possible.
  B   Developmental Psychology 1973

Child Psychotherapy 1967
PN 2504   SC 08730
  B   Psychotherapy 1967
  N   Play Therapy 1973
  R   Adolescent Psychotherapy 1994

Child Self Care 1988
PN 81   SC 08733
SN Responsibility for personal care without adult supervision usually before or after the school day. Primarily used for children under age 14.
  UF Latchkey Children
  B   Child Care 1991
  R   Child Day Care 1973
     Child Welfare 1988
     Self Care Skills 1978

Child Support 1988
PN 92   SC 08735
SN Legal obligation of parents or guardians to contribute to the economic maintenance of their children including provision of education, clothing, and food.
  R   Child Custody 1982
     Divorce 1973
     Joint Custody 1988
    ↓ Marital Separation 1973

Child Visitation 1988
PN 200   SC 08737
SN The right of or court-granted permission to parents, grandparents, or guardians to visit children.
  UF Visitation Rights
  B   Legal Processes 1973
  R   Child Custody 1982

Child Welfare 1988
PN 1131   SC 08738
  R   ↓ Adoption (Child) 1967
     Advocacy 1985
    ↓ Child Abuse 1971
     Child Abuse Reporting 1997
     Child Day Care 1973
     Child Neglect 1988
     Child Self Care 1988
     Foster Care 1978
     Protective Services 1997

Child Welfare — (cont'd)
  R   Social Casework 1967
    ↓ Social Services 1982

Childbirth
  Use Birth

Childbirth (Natural)
  Use Natural Childbirth

Childbirth Training 1978
PN 177   SC 08746
  B   Prenatal Care 1991
  R   ↓ Birth 1967
     Labor (Childbirth) 1973
     Natural Childbirth 1978
    ↓ Obstetrics 1978
    ↓ Pregnancy 1967

Childhood Development 1967
PN 9676   SC 08760
SN Process of physical, cognitive, personality, and psychosocial growth occurring from birth through age 12. Use a more specific term if possible.
  B   Human Development 1967
  N   ↓ Early Childhood Development 1973
  R   Adolescent Development 1973
     Developmental Age Groups 1973
    ↓ Developmental Stages 1973
    ↓ Motor Development 1973
     Object Relations 1982
    ↓ Perceptual Development 1973
    ↓ Physical Development 1973
    ↓ Psychogenesis 1973
    ↓ Psychomotor Development 1973
     Separation Individuation 1982
     Transitional Objects 1985

Childhood Memories
  Use Early Memories

Childhood Neurosis 1973
PN 185   SC 08770
  UF Infantile Neurosis
  B   Neurosis 1967

Childhood Play Behavior 1978
PN 3250   SC 08777
  UF Play Behavior (Childhood)
  B   Behavior 1967
  R   Anatomically Detailed Dolls 1991
     Childhood Play Development 1973
     Childrens Recreational Games 1973
     Doll Play 1973
    ↓ Games 1967
    ↓ Recreation 1967
     Role Playing 1967
     Toy Selection 1973
    ↓ Toys 1973

Childhood Play Development 1973
PN 706   SC 08780
  UF Play Development (Childhood)
  B   Psychosocial Development 1973
  R   Childhood Play Behavior 1978
     Childrens Recreational Games 1973
     Emotional Development 1973

Childhood Psychosis 1967
PN 592   SC 08790
  UF Infantile Psychosis
  B   Psychosis 1967
  N   Childhood Schizophrenia 1967

Childhood Psychosis — (cont'd)
  N   Early Infantile Autism 1973
     Symbiotic Infantile Psychosis 1973
  R   Autistic Children 1973
    ↓ Emotionally Disturbed 1973

Childhood Schizophrenia 1967
PN 695   SC 08800
  B   Childhood Psychosis 1967
     Schizophrenia 1967
  R   Early Infantile Autism 1973
     Symbiotic Infantile Psychosis 1973

Childlessness 1982
PN 187   SC 08805
SN State of having no children.
  B   Family Structure 1973
     Parenthood Status 1985
  R   Delayed Parenthood 1985
     Family Planning Attitudes 1973

Childrearing Attitudes 1973
PN 1196   SC 08810
  B   Attitudes 1967
  R   ↓ Family Relations 1967
    ↓ Parental Attitudes 1973

Childrearing Practices 1967
PN 5135   SC 08820
SN Limited to human populations.
  B   Family Relations 1967
  N   ↓ Child Discipline 1973
     Toilet Training 1973
     Weaning 1973
  R   ↓ Child Care 1991
     Father Child Relations 1973
    ↓ Feeding Practices 1973
     Mother Child Relations 1967
    ↓ Parent Child Relations 1967
     Parent Training 1978
    ↓ Parental Attitudes 1973
    ↓ Parental Characteristics 1994
     Parental Role 1973
     Parenting Skills 1997
    ↓ Sociocultural Factors 1967

Childrens Apperception Test 1973
PN 37   SC 08840
  B   Projective Personality Measures 1973

Childrens Manifest Anxiety Scale 1973
PN 31   SC 08850
  B   Nonprojective Personality Measures 1973

Childrens Personality Questionnaire 1973
PN 15   SC 08860
  B   Nonprojective Personality Measures 1973

Childrens Recreational Games 1973
PN 73   SC 08870
  B   Games 1967
     Recreation 1967
  R   Childhood Play Behavior 1978
     Childhood Play Development 1973
    ↓ Toys 1973

Chimpanzees 1973
PN 953   SC 08890
  B   Mammals 1973
     Primates (Nonhuman) 1973
  R   Bonobos 1997

Chinchillas 1973
PN 82   SC 08900
B   Mammals 1973
     Rodents 1973

Chinese Cultural Groups 1997
PN 386   SC 08902
SN Use ASIANS to access references from 1982-1996.
B   Asians 1982

Chiroptera
Use   Bats

Chloral Hydrate 1973
PN 28   SC 08910
B   Anticonvulsive Drugs 1973
     Hypnotic Drugs 1973
     Sedatives 1973

Chloralose
SN Term was discontinued in 1997. In 2000, the term was stripped from all records containing it, and replaced with HYPNOTIC DRUGS, its postable counterpart.
Use   Hypnotic Drugs

Chlordiazepoxide 1973
PN 849   SC 08930
UF   Librium
B   Amines 1973
     Benzodiazepines 1978
     Minor Tranquilizers 1973

Chloride Ions 1973
PN 65   SC 08940
B   Electrolytes 1973

Chlorimipramine 1973
PN 862   SC 08950
UF   Clomipramine
B   Amines 1973
     Serotonin Reuptake Inhibitors 1997
     Tricyclic Antidepressant Drugs 1997

Chlorisondamine
SN Term was discontinued in 1997. In 2000, the term was stripped from all records containing it, and replaced with AMINES, its postable counterpart.
Use   Amines

Chloroform 1973
PN 9   SC 08970
B   General Anesthetics 1973

Chlorophenylpiperazine
Use   Piperazines

Chlorpromazine 1967
PN 1377   SC 08990
UF   Thorazine
B   Amines 1973
     Antiemetic Drugs 1973
     Antihypertensive Drugs 1973
     CNS Depressant Drugs 1973
     Phenothiazine Derivatives 1973
     Sedatives 1973

Chlorprothixene 1973
PN 22   SC 09000
B   Amines 1973
     Antiemetic Drugs 1973
     Antihistaminic Drugs 1973

Chlorprothixene — (cont'd)
B   Antispasmodic Drugs 1973
     Minor Tranquilizers 1973
     Phenothiazine Derivatives 1973

Choice Behavior 1967
PN 6095   SC 09010
SN Motivational or judgmental processes involved in the decision or tendency to select one alternative over another or others. Also used for the choices themselves. Used for human or animal populations.
B   Behavior 1967
     Decision Making 1967
R   Classification (Cognitive Process) 1967
     Freedom 1978
     Human Mate Selection 1988
     Psychological Reactance 1978
     Therapist Selection 1994
     Uncertainty 1991
     Volition 1988

Choice Shift 1994
PN 23   SC 09013
SN In social psychology, the changes or shifts in choices made by groups during decision making processes that may differ from choices made by each group member acting on their own.
UF   Risky Shift
B   Group Decision Making 1978
R   Brainstorming 1982
     Group Discussion 1967
     ↓ Group Dynamics 1967
     ↓ Group Problem Solving 1973
     ↓ Risk Taking 1967

Cholecystokinin 1982
PN 764   SC 09015
SN Hormone secreted by upper intestinal mucosa on contact with gastric contents, it stimulates contraction of the gallbladder. Also, a neurotransmitter.
UF   Pancreozymin
B   Hormones 1967
     Neurotransmitters 1985
     Peptides 1973

Cholesterol 1973
PN 446   SC 09020
B   Steroids 1973

Choline 1973
PN 387   SC 09030
UF   Choline Chloride
B   Vitamins 1973
N   Lecithin 1991
R   Acetylcholine 1973
     Cholinesterase 1973
     Succinylcholine 1973

Choline Chloride
Use   Choline

Cholinergic Blocking Drugs 1973
PN 790   SC 09050
UF   Anticholinergic Drugs
     Cholinolytic Drugs
     Parasympatholytic Drugs
B   Drugs 1967
N   Atropine 1973
     Benactyzine 1973
     Levodopa 1973
     Nicotine 1973
     Orphenadrine 1973
     Scopolamine 1973
     Trihexyphenidyl 1973

Cholinergic Blocking Drugs — (cont'd)
R   ↓ Antiemetic Drugs 1973
     ↓ Antispasmodic Drugs 1973
     Cholinergic Nerves 1973
     Cholinesterase 1973
     ↓ Cholinomimetic Drugs 1973
     ↓ Hallucinogenic Drugs 1967
     ↓ Parasympathetic Nervous System 1973
     ↓ Phenothiazine Derivatives 1973

Cholinergic Drugs 1973
PN 545   SC 09060
UF   Muscarinic Drugs
B   Drugs 1967
N   Acetylcholine 1973
     Physostigmine 1973
     Pilocarpine 1973
R   ↓ Cholinomimetic Drugs 1973

Cholinergic Nerves 1973
PN 722   SC 09070
UF   Nerves (Cholinergic)
B   Autonomic Nervous System 1967
R   Acetylcholine 1973
     ↓ Cholinergic Blocking Drugs 1973
     ↓ Cholinomimetic Drugs 1973

Cholinesterase 1973
PN 97   SC 09080
B   Esterases 1973
R   Acetylcholinesterase 1973
     ↓ Choline 1973
     ↓ Cholinergic Blocking Drugs 1973
     ↓ Cholinesterase Inhibitors 1973

Cholinesterase Inhibitors 1973
PN 460   SC 09090
UF   Anticholinesterase Drugs
B   Enzyme Inhibitors 1985
N   Galanthamine 1973
     Neostigmine 1973
     Physostigmine 1973
R   Cholinesterase 1973
     ↓ Cholinomimetic Drugs 1973

Cholinolytic Drugs
Use   Cholinergic Blocking Drugs

Cholinomimetic Drugs 1973
PN 126   SC 09100
UF   Parasympathomimetic Drugs
B   Drugs 1967
N   Acetylcholine 1973
     Arecoline 1973
     Carbachol 1973
     Neostigmine 1973
     Physostigmine 1973
     Pilocarpine 1973
R   ↓ Analeptic Drugs 1973
     ↓ Cholinergic Blocking Drugs 1973
     ↓ Cholinergic Drugs 1973
     Cholinergic Nerves 1973
     ↓ Cholinesterase Inhibitors 1973
     ↓ Parasympathetic Nervous System 1973

Chorda Tympani Nerve
Use   Facial Nerve

Chorea 1973
PN 76   SC 09120
B   Central Nervous System Disorders 1973
     Movement Disorders 1985
N   Huntingtons Disease 1973

Chorea — (cont'd)
R ↓ Infectious Disorders 1973

Choroid
Use Eye (Anatomy)

Choroid Plexus
Use Cerebral Ventricles

Christianity 1973
PN 1625   SC 09150
B Religious Affiliation 1973
N ↓ Protestantism 1973
Roman Catholicism 1973
R Bible 1973
↓ Christians 1997

Christians 1997
PN 132   SC 09152
B Religious Groups 1997
N Catholics 1997
Protestants 1997
R ↓ Christianity 1973

Chromaticity 1997
PN 98   SC 09155
SN The collective aspects of a color stimulus deter-
mined by its hue (dominant wavelength of light) and
its saturation (purity).
N Color Saturation 1997
Hue 1973
R Achromatic Color 1973
↓ Color 1967
↓ Color Perception 1967
Luminance 1982

Chromosome Disorders 1973
PN 311   SC 09160
UF Karyotype Disorders
Mosaicism
B Genetic Disorders 1973
N ↓ Autosome Disorders 1973
Deletion (Chromosome) 1973
↓ Sex Chromosome Disorders 1973
Translocation (Chromosome) 1973
↓ Trisomy 1973
R ↓ Chromosomes 1973

Chromosomes 1973
PN 369   SC 09170
B Cells (Biology) 1973
N Autosomes 1973
Sex Chromosomes 1973
R ↓ Chromosome Disorders 1973
Genes 1973
Genetic Linkage 1994
↓ Genetics 1967
Mutations 1973

Chronic Alcoholic Intoxication 1973
PN 59   SC 09180
B Alcohol Intoxication 1973
Brain Disorders 1967
Chronic Illness 1991
R Toxic Encephalopathies 1973

Chronic Fatigue Syndrome 1997
PN 317   SC 09181
SN Syndrome thought to be caused by a viral
organism resulting in chronic fatigue, fever, pain, sore
throat, and, in some cases, depression.
B Chronic Illness 1991

Chronic Fatigue Syndrome — (cont'd)
R Syndromes 1973
↓ Encephalopathies 1982
Epstein Barr Viral Disorder 1994
Fatigue 1967
↓ Muscular Disorders 1973
↓ Viral Disorders 1973

Chronic Illness 1991
PN 1731   SC 09183
SN An illness or disorder that persists for a pro-
longed period of time. Used in conjunction with other
specific terms where appropriate.
N Chronic Alcoholic Intoxication 1973
Chronic Fatigue Syndrome 1997
↓ Chronic Mental Illness 1997
Chronic Pain 1985
R Chronicity (Disorders) 1982
↓ Disorders 1967
↓ Mental Disorders 1967
↓ Physical Disorders 1997
Severity (Disorders) 1982

Chronic Mental Illness 1997
PN 321   SC 09184
SN A mental illness that persists for a prolonged
period of time. Use a more specific term if possible.
UF Persistent Mental Illness
B Chronic Illness 1991
Mental Disorders 1967
N Chronic Psychosis 1973
R Chronicity (Disorders) 1982
Prognosis 1973
Severity (Disorders) 1982
↓ Treatment Resistant Disorders 1994

Chronic Pain 1985
PN 2655   SC 09185
B Chronic Illness 1991
Pain 1967
R Back Pain 1982
Myofascial Pain 1991
Somatoform Pain Disorder 1997

Chronic Psychosis 1973
PN 127   SC 09190
B Chronic Mental Illness 1997
Psychosis 1967

Chronic Schizophrenia
SN Term was discontinued in 1988. In 2000, the
term was stripped from all records containing it, and
replaced with SCHIZOPHRENIA, its postable counterpart.
Use Schizophrenia

Chronicity (Disorders) 1982
PN 1705   SC 09203
SN Used only when chronicity itself is a factor, vari-
able, or major focus of the research. Used in conjunc-
tion with other specific terms where appropriate.
R ↓ Chronic Illness 1991
↓ Chronic Mental Illness 1997
↓ Disorders 1967
↓ Mental Disorders 1967
↓ Physical Disorders 1997
Severity (Disorders) 1982

Churches
Use Religious Buildings

Cichlids 1973
PN 231   SC 09210

Cichlids — (cont'd)
B Fishes 1967

Cigarette Smoking
Use Tobacco Smoking

Cimetidine 1985
PN 40   SC 09225
B Antihistaminic Drugs 1973

Circadian Rhythms (Animal)
Use Animal Circadian Rhythms

Circadian Rhythms (Human)
Use Human Biological Rhythms

Circulation (Blood)
Use Blood Circulation

Circulatory Disorders
Use Cardiovascular Disorders

Circumcision 2001
PN 0   SC 09255
SN Term became postable in 2000. From 1973-
2000, BIRTH RITES and SURGERY were used
together to capture this concept.
UF Female Genital Mutilation
B Surgery 1971
R Birth Rites 1973
↓ Female Genitalia 1973
Gynecology 1978
↓ Male Genitalia 1973
↓ Religious Practices 1973
↓ Rites of Passage 1973

Cirrhosis (Liver) 1973
PN 111   SC 09260
B Liver Disorders 1973
R Jaundice 1973

Citalopram 1997
PN 175   SC 09265
B Antidepressant Drugs 1971
Serotonin Reuptake Inhibitors 1997

Cities
Use Urban Environments

Citizenship 1973
PN 164   SC 09280
SN Formal status or social quality of being a mem-
ber of a community, country, or some other political
designation.
R Immigration 1973
↓ Laws 1967
↓ Political Attitudes 1973

Civil Law 1994
PN 158   SC 09284
B Law (Government) 1973
R ↓ Civil Rights 1978
Disability Laws 1994
↓ Law Enforcement 1978
↓ Legal Processes 1973

Civil Rights 1978
PN 1368   SC 09288
SN Rights of personal liberty and equality guaran-
teed to citizens by constitution and legislation.
B Human Rights 1978
N ↓ Client Rights 1988

Civil Rights — (cont'd)
- R   Equal Education   1978
- Advocacy   1985
- Affirmative Action   1985
- Age Discrimination   1994
- Censorship   1978
- Civil Law   1994
- Civil Rights Movement   1973
- Democracy   1973
- Disability Discrimination   1997
- Disability Laws   1994
- Empowerment   1991
- Freedom   1978
- Informed Consent   1985
- ↓ Justice   1973
- ↓ Laws   1967
- ↓ Legal Processes   1973
- Race and Ethnic Discrimination   1994
- Sex Discrimination   1978
- ↓ Social Discrimination   1982
- Social Equality   1973
- ↓ Social Integration   1982
- ↓ Social Issues   1991
- ↓ Social Movements   1967

Civil Rights Movement   1973
PN 126   SC 09290
SN   Social and political effort to gain the constitutional rights of citizens, especially by minority groups whose rights have been denied. See SOCIAL MOVEMENTS for more specific terms.
- B   Social Movements   1967
- R   ↓ Activist Movements   1973
- ↓ Civil Rights   1978

Civil Servants
Use   Government Personnel

Clairvoyance   1973
PN 113   SC 09310
- B   Extrasensory Perception   1967
- N   Precognition   1973

Class Attitudes
Use   Socioeconomic Class Attitudes

Classical Conditioning   1967
PN 3963   SC 09330
SN   Learned behavior or the experimental paradigm or procedure used to develop and evoke classically conditioned responses.
- UF   Conditioning (Classical)
- Pavlovian Conditioning
- Respondent Conditioning
- B   Conditioning   1967
- N   Conditioned Emotional Responses   1967
- ↓ Conditioned Responses   1967
- Eyelid Conditioning   1973
- Higher Order Conditioning   1997
- Unconditioned Responses   1973
- R   Conditioned Stimulus   1973
- Learning Theory   1967
- Orienting Responses   1967
- Pavlov (Ivan)   1991
- Unconditioned Stimulus   1973

Classification (Cognitive Process)   1967
PN 6767   SC 09370
- UF   Categorizing
- Sorting (Cognition)
- B   Cognitive Processes   1967
- R   Choice Behavior   1967

Classification Systems
Use   Taxonomies

Classmates   1973
PN 47   SC 09400
- B   Students   1967

Classroom Behavior   1973
PN 3846   SC 09405
- B   Behavior   1967
- R   Classroom Behavior Modification   1973
- Classroom Discipline   1973
- Classroom Environment   1973

Classroom Behavior Modification   1973
PN 2035   SC 09410
- B   Behavior Modification   1973
- R   Classroom Behavior   1973
- Classroom Discipline   1973
- ↓ Education   1967

Classroom Discipline   1973
PN 1139   SC 09420
- UF   Discipline (Classroom)
- R   Classroom Behavior   1973
- Classroom Behavior Modification   1973
- ↓ Education   1967
- School Suspension   1973
- Teacher Student Interaction   1973

Classroom Environment   1973
PN 3390   SC 09430
SN   Physical, social, emotional, psychological, or intellectual characteristics of a classroom, especially as they contribute to the learning process. Includes classroom climate and class size.
- B   Academic Environment   1973
- R   Classroom Behavior   1973
- Classrooms   1967
- ↓ School Environment   1973

Classroom Instruction
Use   Teaching

Classroom Teachers
Use   Teachers

Classrooms   1967
PN 638   SC 09460
- B   School Facilities   1973
- R   Classroom Environment   1973

Claustrophobia   1973
PN 65   SC 09470
- B   Phobias   1967

Cleft Palate   1967
PN 147   SC 09480
- B   Congenital Disorders   1973
- Neonatal Disorders   1973
- R   ↓ Speech Disorders   1967

Clergy   1973
PN 518   SC 09490
- B   Religious Personnel   1973
- N   Chaplains   1973
- Ministers (Religion)   1973
- Priests   1973
- Rabbis   1973
- R   Evangelists   1973
- Lay Religious Personnel   1973

Clergy — (cont'd)
- R   Missionaries   1973
- ↓ Religious Groups   1997

Clerical Personnel   1973
PN 524   SC 09500
- UF   Keypunch Operators
- Typists
- B   White Collar Workers   1973
- R   Secretarial Personnel   1973

Clerical Secretarial Skills   1973
PN 201   SC 09510
- UF   Secretarial Skills
- B   Employee Skills   1973
- R   Proofreading   1988
- Typing   1991
- Word Processing   1991

Client Abuse
Use   Patient Abuse

Client Attitudes   1982
PN 5148   SC 09527
SN   Attitudes of clients that may affect compliance with a particular treatment modality, or preferences for a particular type of treatment. May include attitudes toward health care professionals.
- UF   Patient Attitudes
- B   Attitudes   1967
- Client Characteristics   1973
- N   Client Satisfaction   1994
- R   Clients   1973
- Therapist Selection   1994
- Treatment Compliance   1982

Client Centered Therapy   1967
PN 825   SC 09530
- UF   Nondirective Therapy
- Person Centered Psychotherapy
- Rogerian Therapy
- B   Psychotherapy   1967
- R   ↓ Humanistic Psychology   1985
- ↓ Psychotherapeutic Techniques   1967
- Rogers (Carl)   1991

Client Characteristics   1973
PN 9961   SC 09540
SN   Physical, psychological, emotional, and other traits of individual clients or patients influencing the outcome of the therapeutic process.
- UF   Patient Characteristics
- N   ↓ Client Attitudes   1982
- Health Behavior   1982
- Illness Behavior   1982
- Patient Violence   1994
- R   Client Participation   1997
- Client Treatment Matching   1997
- Clients   1973
- Cross Cultural Treatment   1994
- Patient History   1973
- Patient Selection   1997
- ↓ Treatment Planning   1997

Client Compliance
Use   Treatment Compliance

Client Counselor Interaction
Use   Psychotherapeutic Processes

Client Dropouts
Use   Treatment Dropouts

Client Education [1985]
PN 1460   SC 09555
SN Informing or instructing patients or clients on the specifics of their disorder and/or its treatment. For client educational level use EDUCATIONAL BACKGROUND.
UF Patient Education
     Pretraining (Therapy)
B Education [1967]
R ↓ Health Education [1973]
     Health Knowledge [1994]
     Health Promotion [1991]
     Psychoeducation [1994]
     ↓ Therapeutic Processes [1978]
     Treatment Compliance [1982]

Client Participation [1997]
PN 218   SC 09556
UF Patient Participation
B Participation [1973]
R ↓ Client Characteristics [1973]
     ↓ Client Rights [1988]
     Clients [1973]
     ↓ Patients [1967]
     Treatment Compliance [1982]

Client Records [1997]
PN 109   SC 57455
UF Patient Records
B Medical Records [1978]
R Patient History [1973]
     Privileged Communication [1973]

Client Rights [1988]
PN 814   SC 09557
SN Right of patient or client to be fully informed of benefits or risks of treatment procedures and to make informed decisions to accept or reject treatment.
UF Patient Rights
B Civil Rights [1978]
N Right to Treatment [1997]
R Advance Directives [1994]
     Client Participation [1997]
     Clients [1973]
     Empowerment [1991]
     Guardianship [1988]
     ↓ Human Rights [1978]
     Informed Consent [1985]
     Involuntary Treatment [1994]
     Life Sustaining Treatment [1997]
     Quality of Care [1988]
     ↓ Treatment [1967]
     Treatment Compliance [1982]
     Treatment Refusal [1994]
     Treatment Withholding [1988]

Client Satisfaction [1994]
PN 925   SC 09558
UF Patient Satisfaction
B Client Attitudes [1982]
     Satisfaction [1973]
R Clients [1973]

Client Transfer [1997]
PN 35   SC 57465
SN Transfer of client or patient care within or between treatment settings, therapists, or other health care providers.
UF Patient Transfer
R ↓ Facility Discharge [1988]
     ↓ Hospital Discharge [1973]
     Patient Selection [1997]
     Professional Referral [1973]
     Psychiatric Hospital Discharge [1978]

Client Transfer — (cont'd)
R ↓ Treatment [1967]
     Treatment Refusal [1994]
     Treatment Termination [1982]

Client Treatment Matching [1997]
PN 221   SC 57470
SN Treatment selection based on matching the client's characteristics and needs with appropriate treatment modalities.
UF Patient Treatment Matching
     Treatment Client Matching
R ↓ Client Characteristics [1973]
     Clinical Judgment (Not Diagnosis) [1973]
     Patient Selection [1997]
     ↓ Treatment [1967]
     Treatment Guidelines [2001]
     ↓ Treatment Outcomes [1982]
     ↓ Treatment Planning [1997]

Client Violence
Use Patient Violence

Clients [1973]
PN 1487   SC 09560
SN Persons receiving psychotherapy, counseling, or other mental health or social service. Consider also PATIENTS or one of its narrower terms.
UF Counselees
R ↓ Client Attitudes [1982]
     ↓ Client Characteristics [1973]
     Client Participation [1997]
     ↓ Client Rights [1988]
     Client Satisfaction [1994]
     Patient Selection [1997]

Climacteric Depression
Use Involutional Depression

Climacteric Paranoia
Use Involutional Paranoid Psychosis

Climate (Meteorological)
Use Atmospheric Conditions

Climate (Organizational)
Use Organizational Climate

Climax (Sexual)
Use Orgasm

Clinical Judgment (Medical Diagnosis)
Use Medical Diagnosis

Clinical Judgment (Not Diagnosis) [1973]
PN 3230   SC 09620
SN Analysis, evaluation, or prediction of disordered or abnormal behavior, symptoms, or other aspects of psychological functioning. Includes assessing the appropriateness of a particular treatment and the degree or likelihood of clinical improvement.
B Judgment [1967]
R Anatomically Detailed Dolls [1991]
     Client Treatment Matching [1997]
     ↓ Diagnosis [1967]
     Geriatric Assessment [1997]
     Intake Interview [1994]
     ↓ Measurement [1967]
     Prognosis [1973]
     ↓ Psychiatric Evaluation [1997]
     ↓ Psychodiagnosis [1967]
     ↓ Psychodiagnostic Typologies [1967]

Clinical Judgment (Not Diagnosis) — (cont'd)
     ↓ Psychological Assessment [1997]
R ↓ Treatment Planning [1997]

Clinical Judgment (Psychodiagnosis)
Use Psychodiagnosis

Clinical Markers
Use Biological Markers

Clinical Methods Training [1973]
PN 2179   SC 09640
SN Instruction and skills training in methods for management and treatment of mental and behavior disorders. Includes training of populations such as parents, teachers, clergy, and administrators as well as mental health or medical personnel.
UF Training (Clinical Methods)
B Education [1967]
N ↓ Clinical Psychology Graduate Training [2001]
     Clinical Psychology Internship [1973]
     ↓ Community Mental Health Training [1973]
     Psychiatric Training [1973]
     Psychoanalytic Training [1973]
     Psychotherapy Training [1973]
R Counselor Education [1973]
     Microcounseling [1978]
     Personal Therapy [1991]
     Practicum Supervision [1978]
     Theoretical Orientation [1982]

Clinical Psychologists [1973]
PN 1108   SC 09650
B Mental Health Personnel [1967]
     Psychologists [1967]
R Clinicians [1973]
     Hypnotherapists [1973]
     ↓ Psychotherapists [1973]

Clinical Psychology [1967]
PN 1926   SC 09660
B Applied Psychology [1973]
     Psychology [1967]
N Medical Psychology [1973]

Clinical Psychology Graduate Training [2001]
PN 0   SC 09675
SN In 2000, the truncated term CLINICAL PSYCHOLOGY GRAD TRAINING (which was used from 1973-2000) was deleted, removed from all records containing it, and mapped to its expanded form, CLINICAL PSYCHOLOGY GRADUATE TRAINING.
UF Training (Clinical Psychology Grad)
B Clinical Methods Training [1973]
     Graduate Psychology Education [1967]
     Postgraduate Training [1973]
N Clinical Psychology Internship [1973]
R Practicum Supervision [1978]

Clinical Psychology Internship [1973]
PN 347   SC 09680
B Clinical Methods Training [1973]
     Clinical Psychology Graduate Training [2001]
     Postgraduate Training [1973]
R Practicum Supervision [1978]

Clinical Supervision
Use Professional Supervision

Clinicians [1973]
PN 777   SC 09690
B Professional Personnel [1978]

Clinicians — (cont'd)
R   Clinical Psychologists 1973
    Counseling Psychologists 1988
    ↓ Medical Personnel 1967
    ↓ Mental Health Personnel 1967
    ↓ Physicians 1967
    Psychiatrists 1967
    ↓ Therapists 1967

Clinics 1967
PN   844   SC   09700
B   Treatment Facilities 1973
N   Child Guidance Clinics 1973
    Psychiatric Clinics 1973
    Walk In Clinics 1973
R   Community Mental Health Centers 1973
    ↓ Crisis Intervention Services 1973
    ↓ Hospitals 1967
    ↓ Treatment 1967

Cliques
Use   Social Groups

Clomipramine
Use   Chlorimipramine

Clonazepam 1991
PN   158   SC   09735
B   Anticonvulsive Drugs 1973
    Benzodiazepines 1978
    Minor Tranquilizers 1973

Clonidine 1973
PN   971   SC   09740
B   Antihypertensive Drugs 1973
    CNS Stimulating Drugs 1973

Closed Circuit Television 1973
PN   70   SC   09750
B   Television 1967

Closed Head Injuries
Use   Head Injuries

Closedmindedness
Use   Openmindedness

Closure (Perceptual)
Use   Perceptual Closure

Clothing 1967
PN   782   SC   09770
SN   Use CLOTHING FASHIONS to access references prior to 1991.
B   Fads and Fashions 1973
R   ↓ Physical Appearance 1982

Clozapine 1991
PN   1621   SC   09775
B   Neuroleptic Drugs 1973
    Sedatives 1973

Cloze Testing 1973
PN   256   SC   09780
SN   Tests or procedures assessing comprehension (e.g., reading or listening) in which the person being tested is required to provide missing components.
B   Testing Methods 1967
R   Sentence Completion Tests 1991

Clubs (Social Organizations) 1973
PN   101   SC   09790

Clubs (Social Organizations) — (cont'd)
B   Recreation 1967

Cluster Analysis 1973
PN   1067   SC   09800
UF   Clustering
B   Statistical Analysis 1967

Clustering
Use   Cluster Analysis

CNS Affecting Drugs 1973
PN   180   SC   09840
UF   Central Nervous System Drugs
B   Drugs 1967
N   ↓ CNS Depressant Drugs 1973
    ↓ CNS Stimulating Drugs 1973
R   ↓ Heart Rate Affecting Drugs 1973

CNS Depressant Drug Antagonists
Use   Analeptic Drugs

CNS Depressant Drugs 1973
PN   91   SC   09860
B   CNS Affecting Drugs 1973
N   Amobarbital 1973
    Barbital 1973
    Chlorpromazine 1967
    Glutethimide 1973
    Haloperidol 1973
    Scopolamine 1973
R   ↓ Analgesic Drugs 1973
    ↓ Anesthetic Drugs 1973
    ↓ Anticonvulsive Drugs 1973
    ↓ Barbiturates 1967
    ↓ Dopamine Antagonists 1982
    Flurazepam 1982
    ↓ Hypnotic Drugs 1973
    ↓ Muscle Relaxing Drugs 1973
    ↓ Narcotic Drugs 1973
    ↓ Sedatives 1973

CNS Stimulating Drugs 1973
PN   849   SC   09870
UF   Stimulants of CNS
B   CNS Affecting Drugs 1973
N   ↓ Amphetamine 1967
    ↓ Analeptic Drugs 1973
    Caffeine 1973
    Clonidine 1973
    Dextroamphetamine 1973
    Ephedrine 1973
    Methamphetamine 1973
    Methylphenidate 1973
    Pemoline 1978
    Pentylenetetrazol 1973
    Pipradrol 1973
    Piracetam 1982
R   ↓ Antidepressant Drugs 1971
    ↓ Emetic Drugs 1973
    ↓ Heart Rate Affecting Drugs 1973
    Smokeless Tobacco 1994

Coaches 1988
PN   357   SC   09880
SN   Use TEACHERS to access references from 1973-1987.
R   Athletic Training 1991
    ↓ Sports 1967

Coagulation (Blood)
Use   Blood Coagulation

Coalition Formation 1973
PN   257   SC   09910
SN   Temporary alliance of distinct parties, persons, or states for joint action.
B   Social Processes 1967
R   ↓ Social Movements 1967

Coast Guard Personnel 1988
PN   18   SC   00915
B   Military Personnel 1967

Cobalt 1973
PN   21   SC   09920
B   Metallic Elements 1973

Cocaine 1973
PN   4716   SC   09930
B   Alkaloids 1973
    Amines 1973
    Local Anesthetics 1973

Cochlea 1973
PN   541   SC   09940
UF   Organ of Corti
B   Labyrinth (Anatomy) 1973
R   Cochlear Implants 1994

Cochlear Implants 1994
PN   160   SC   09945
B   Hearing Aids 1973
    Prostheses 1973
    Surgery 1971
R   Cochlea 1973
    ↓ Deaf 1967
    Hearing Disorders 1982
    Partially Hearing Impaired 1973

Cochran Q Test 1973
PN   6   SC   09950
UF   Q Test
B   Nonparametric Statistical Tests 1967

Cockroaches 1973
PN   163   SC   09960
B   Insects 1967
R   Larvae 1973

Code Switching 1988
PN   129   SC   09965
SN   Alternating use of languages, dialects, or language styles in speech.
UF   Language Alternation
B   Oral Communication 1985
R   Bilingualism 1973
    Sociolinguistics 1985

Codeine 1973
PN   86   SC   09970
UF   Codeine Sulfate
    Methylmorphine
B   Alkaloids 1973
    Analgesic Drugs 1973
    Hypnotic Drugs 1973
    Opiates 1973

Codeine Sulfate
Use   Codeine

Codependency 1991
PN   236   SC   09985
R   ↓ Alcohol Abuse 1988
    Dependency (Personality) 1967
    Dependent Personality 1994

Codependency — (cont'd)
R ↓ Drug Abuse [1973]
    Dysfunctional Family [1991]
    ↓ Emotional Adjustment [1973]
    Enabling [1997]
    ↓ Family [1967]
    ↓ Family Relations [1967]
    ↓ Interpersonal Interaction [1967]
    ↓ Marital Relations [1967]
    ↓ Parent Child Relations [1967]
    ↓ Personality Traits [1967]

Coeds
Use College Students

Coeducation [1973]
PN 137   SC 10000
SN Education of male and female students at the same institution.
R ↓ Education [1967]
    Single Sex Environments [2001]

Coercion [1994]
PN 292   SC 10020
B Aggressive Behavior [1967]
   Social Influences [1967]
R Abuse of Power [1997]
   Authority [1967]
   Brainwashing [1982]
   ↓ Dominance [1967]
   Obedience [1973]
   ↓ Persuasive Communication [1967]
   ↓ Power [1967]
   ↓ Punishment [1967]
   ↓ Resistance [1997]
   Threat [1967]
   Torture [1988]
   ↓ Violence [1973]

Coffee
Use Beverages (Nonalcoholic)

Cognition [1967]
PN 5020   SC 10040
SN Act or process of knowing which includes awareness and judgment, perceiving, reasoning, and conceiving.
R ↓ Cognitive Development [1973]
   ↓ Cognitive Processes [1967]
   Intuition [1973]
   Metacognition [1991]
   Need for Cognition [1997]

Cognition Enhancing Drugs
Use Nootropic Drugs

Cognitions [1985]
PN 2861   SC 10045
SN The content of cognitive or thinking processes.
UF Thought Content
N ↓ Expectations [1967]
   Irrational Beliefs [1982]
R ↓ Attitudes [1967]
   Concepts [1967]
   Mind [1991]
   Rumination (Cognitive Process) [2001]
   Schema [1988]

Cognitive Ability [1973]
PN 15187   SC 10050
SN Level of functioning in intellectual tasks.
UF Cognitive Functioning

Cognitive Ability — (cont'd)
UF Executive Functioning
   Intellectual Functioning
B Ability [1967]
N Mathematical Ability [1973]
   Reading Ability [1973]
   ↓ Spatial Ability [1982]
   Verbal Ability [1967]
R Cognitive Assessment [1997]
   Cognitive Processing Speed [1997]
   Metacognition [1991]

Cognitive Assessment [1997]
PN 616   SC 10053
SN Used only for references that focus on the assessment process or the particular assessment itself.
UF Assessment (Cognitive)
B Psychological Assessment [1997]
R ↓ Cognitive Ability [1973]
   ↓ Cognitive Processes [1967]
   Intelligence [1967]
   ↓ Intelligence Measures [1967]
   Intelligence Quotient [1967]
   ↓ Neuropsychological Assessment [1982]
   ↓ Psychiatric Evaluation [1997]

Cognitive Behavior Therapy
Use Cognitive Therapy

Cognitive Complexity [1973]
PN 985   SC 10060
SN Conceptual, behavioral, or perceptual dimensions of thinking style that characterize an individual's differentiation or processing of stimuli.
UF Complexity (Cognitive)
B Cognitive Style [1967]

Cognitive Contiguity [1973]
PN 44   SC 10070
SN View of memory organization which holds that events that are experienced together tend to become associated with each other in memory.
UF Contiguity (Cognitive)
B Associative Processes [1967]

Cognitive Development [1973]
PN 14705   SC 10080
SN Acquisition of conscious thought, reasoning, symbol manipulation, and problem solving abilities beginning in infancy and following an orderly sequence. Compare INTELLECTUAL DEVELOPMENT.
B Psychogenesis [1973]
N ↓ Intellectual Development [1973]
   ↓ Language Development [1967]
   ↓ Perceptual Development [1973]
R Cognition [1967]
   ↓ Concept Formation [1967]
   Conservation (Concept) [1973]
   Constructivism [1994]
   Egocentrism [1978]
   Object Permanence [1985]
   Piaget (Jean) [1967]
   ↓ Speech Development [1973]
   Theory of Mind [2001]

Cognitive Discrimination [1973]
PN 1072   SC 10090
SN Ability to distinguish between examples vs non-examples of a concept, based on the presence or absence of its defining attributes.
UF Discrimination (Cognitive)
B Cognitive Processes [1967]

Cognitive Discrimination — (cont'd)
B Concept Formation [1967]
   Discrimination [1967]
R ↓ Lexical Access [1988]
   Lexical Decision [1988]
   Stroop Effect [1988]
   Visual Search [1982]

Cognitive Dissonance [1967]
PN 1247   SC 10100
SN Psychological conflict resulting from incongruous beliefs or attitudes held simultaneously, or from inconsistency between belief and behavior.
UF Dissonance (Cognitive)
R ↓ Cognitive Processes [1967]
   Psychological Reactance [1978]

Cognitive Functioning
Use Cognitive Ability

Cognitive Generalization [1967]
PN 621   SC 10110
SN Ability to evaluate the equivalence of an example of a concept or object across different contexts or modalities.
UF Generalization (Cognitive)
B Cognitive Processes [1967]
   Concept Formation [1967]
R ↓ Associative Processes [1967]
   Semantic Generalization [1973]

Cognitive Hypothesis Testing [1982]
PN 459   SC 10112
SN Problem-solving behavior in which the individual derives a set of rules (hypotheses) that are then sampled and tested until the one rule is discovered that consistently results in correct responding to the problem. Use HYPOTHESIS TESTING or other appropriate terms to access references prior to 1982.
UF Hypothesis Testing (Cognitive)
   Rule Learning
B Learning [1967]
   Problem Solving [1967]
R ↓ Concept Formation [1967]
   ↓ Reasoning [1967]

Cognitive Load
Use Human Channel Capacity

Cognitive Maps [1982]
PN 1068   SC 10117
SN Internal or symbolic representations of social or physical environments, means-end relationships, or spatial relationships.
B Cognitive Processes [1967]
R Direction Perception [1997]
   Schema [1988]
   Spatial Imagery [1982]
   ↓ Spatial Memory [1988]
   Spatial Organization [1973]
   Spatial Orientation (Perception) [1973]

Cognitive Mediation [1967]
PN 1144   SC 10120
SN Intervention of cognitive processes between observable stimuli and responses, resulting in a change in subsequent behavior.
UF Mediation (Cognitive)
B Cognitive Processes [1967]
R Naming [1988]

Cognitive Processes [1967]
PN 29349   SC 10130

Cognitive Processes — (cont'd)

SN Mental processes involved in the acquisition, processing, and utilization of knowledge or information.
- **UF** Human Information Processes
  Information Processes (Human)
- **N** ↓ Associative Processes   1967
  Classification (Cognitive Process)   1967
  Cognitive Discrimination   1973
  Cognitive Generalization   1967
  Cognitive Maps   1982
  Cognitive Mediation   1967
  ↓ Comprehension   1967
  Concentration   1982
  ↓ Concept Formation   1967
  ↓ Decision Making   1967
  ↓ Fantasy   1997
  ↓ Ideation   1973
  Imagination   1967
  Intuition   1973
  Mental Rotation   1991
  Metacognition   1991
  Naming   1988
  ↓ Problem Solving   1967
  Rumination (Cognitive Process)   2001
  Schema   1988
  Semantic Generalization   1973
  Social Cognition   1994
  ↓ Thinking   1967
  Transposition (Cognition)   1973
- **R** ↓ Artificial Intelligence   1982
  Cognition   1967
  Cognitive Assessment   1997
  Cognitive Dissonance   1967
  Cognitive Processing Speed   1997
  Cognitive Psychology   1985
  ↓ Conflict Resolution   1982
  Connectionism   1994
  Declarative Knowledge   1997
  Generation Effect (Learning)   1991
  Human Information Storage   1973
  ↓ Learning   1967
  ↓ Learning Strategies   1991
  ↓ Memory   1967
  Mind   1991
  Procedural Knowledge   1997
  Questioning   1982
  Reality Testing   1973
  ↓ Spatial Ability   1982
  ↓ Strategies   1967
  Word Associations   1967

Cognitive Processing Speed   1997

PN 325   **SC** 10133
- **UF** Information Processing Speed
- **R** ↓ Cognitive Ability   1973
  ↓ Cognitive Processes   1967
  ↓ Cognitive Style   1967
  Conceptual Tempo   1985
  Human Channel Capacity   1973
  Reaction Time   1967
  Response Latency   1967

Cognitive Psychology   1985

PN 1944   **SC** 10135
SN Branch of psychology concerned with aspects of behavior as they relate to mental processes.
- **B** Psychology   1967
- **R** ↓ Cognitive Processes   1967
  Connectionism   1994

Cognitive Rehabilitation   1985

PN 812   **SC** 10136

Cognitive Rehabilitation — (cont'd)

SN Procedures used to restore or enhance the cognitive functioning level of individuals with mental disability, injury, or disease (e.g., brain damaged stroke patients).
- **B** Neuropsychological Rehabilitation   1997
  Rehabilitation   1967
- **R** Memory Training   1994

Cognitive Restructuring   1985

PN 368   **SC** 10137
SN Cognitive technique for altering self-defeating thought patterns by first identifying and analyzing negative self-statements and then developing adaptive self-statements.
- **B** Cognitive Techniques   1985
- **R** ↓ Behavior Modification   1973
  Cognitive Therapy   1982

Cognitive Style   1967

PN 5965   **SC** 10140
SN Preferred or habitual style of learning or thinking.
- **UF** Learning Style
- **B** Personality Traits   1967
- **N** Cognitive Complexity   1973
  Conceptual Tempo   1985
  Field Dependence   1973
  Impulsiveness   1973
  Reflectiveness   1997
- **R** Cognitive Processing Speed   1997
  ↓ Learning Strategies   1991
  Neurolinguistic Programming   2001
  Perceptual Style   1973
  ↓ Personality   1967
  Schema   1988

Cognitive Techniques   1985

PN 1034   **SC** 10142
SN Methods directed at producing change in thought patterns that may result in changes in affect and behavior.
- **B** Treatment   1967
- **N** Cognitive Restructuring   1985
  Cognitive Therapy   1982
  Self Instructional Training   1985
- **R** Anxiety Management   1997
  Stress Management   1985

Cognitive Therapy   1982

PN 6269   **SC** 10144
SN Directive therapy based on the belief that the way one perceives and structures the world determines one's feelings and behavior. Treatment aims at altering cognitive schema and hence permitting the patient to change his/her distorted self-view and worldview.
- **UF** Cognitive Behavior Therapy
- **B** Cognitive Techniques   1985
- **R** Anxiety Management   1997
  ↓ Behavior Modification   1973
  Cognitive Restructuring   1985
  ↓ Psychotherapy   1967
  Rational Emotive Therapy   1978
  Self Instructional Training   1985
  ↓ Self Management   1985

Cohabitation   1973

PN 333   **SC** 10150
SN Primarily, but not exclusively, used for unmarried couples living together.
- **B** Living Arrangements   1991
- **R** Couples   1982
  ↓ Family   1967

Cohabitation — (cont'd)

- **R** Living Alone   1994
  Roommates   1973

Cohesion (Group)

Use Group Cohesion

Cohort Analysis   1988

PN 456   **SC** 10165
SN Analysis of the effects attributed to being a member of a group sharing a particular characteristic, experience, or event. Use AGE DIFFERENCES for effects attributable to normal biological, cognitive, or psychosocial maturation.
- **B** Analysis   1967
  Experimental Design   1967
  Methodology   1967
- **R** Age Differences   1967
  Generation Gap   1973

Coitus

Use Sexual Intercourse (Human)

Coitus (Animal)

Use Animal Mating Behavior

Cold Effects   1973

PN 670   **SC** 10200
- **B** Temperature Effects   1967

Colitis   1973

PN 43   **SC** 10220
- **B** Colon Disorders   1973
- **N** Ulcerative Colitis   1973
- **R** Gastrointestinal Ulcers   1967
  Irritable Bowel Syndrome   1991

Collaboration

Use Cooperation

Collective Behavior   1967

PN 2482   **SC** 10250
SN Behaviors which characterize groups or individuals acting in groups, usually working toward or achieving a specific goal. Used for human or animal populations.
- **B** Interpersonal Interaction   1967
- **N** Riots   1973
- **R** Contagion   1988
  Entrapment Games   1973
  ↓ Group Dynamics   1967
  Group Participation   1973
  Mass Hysteria   1973
  Social Demonstrations   1973
  ↓ Sociometry   1991

Collective Unconscious   1997

PN 38   **SC** 10255
SN Genetically determined part of the unconscious shared by all members of a species or race of people. Consider JUNGIAN PSYCHOLOGY to access references prior to 1997.
- **B** Jungian Psychology   1973
- **N** Archetypes   1991
- **R** Analytical Psychotherapy   1973
  Jung (Carl)   1973

College Academic Achievement   1967

PN 4993   **SC** 10260
- **B** Academic Achievement   1967

College Athletes   1994

PN 324   **SC** 10270

College Athletes — (cont'd)
- B   Athletes [1973]
-       College Students [1967]
- R   Athletic Participation [1973]
-       Athletic Performance [1991]
-       Athletic Training [1991]
-       ↓ Sports [1967]
-       ↓ Teams [1988]

College Degrees
- Use Educational Degrees

College Dropouts [1973]
PN 446   SC 10290
- B   School Dropouts [1967]

College Education
- Use Undergraduate Education

College Entrance Examination Board Scholastic Aptitude Test [2001]
PN 332   SC 10235
SN In 2000, the truncated term COLL ENT EXAM BD SCHOLASTIC APT TEST (which was used from 1973-2000) was deleted, removed from all records containing it, and mapped to its expanded form, COLLEGE ENTRANCE EXAMINATION SCHOLASTIC APTITUDE TEST.
- UF Preliminary Scholastic Aptitude Test
-       SAT
-       Scholastic Aptitude Test
- B   Aptitude Measures [1967]
-       Entrance Examinations [1973]

College Environment [1973]
PN 1216   SC 10300
SN Social or emotional climate or physical setting of a college or university.
- B   School Environment [1973]
- R   ↓ Colleges [1967]
-       Community Colleges [1978]

College Graduates [1982]
PN 321   SC 10304
- R   ↓ College Students [1967]
-       Educational Degrees [1973]
-       School Graduation [1991]
-       School to Work Transition [1994]

College Major
- Use Academic Specialization

College Students [1967]
PN 27563   SC 10320
SN Students attending an institution of higher education.
- UF Coeds
-       Undergraduates
- B   Students [1967]
- N   College Athletes [1994]
-       Community College Students [1973]
-       Education Students [1982]
-       Junior College Students [1973]
-       Nursing Students [1973]
-       ROTC Students [1973]
- R   College Graduates [1982]
-       Graduate Students [1967]
-       Postgraduate Students [1973]
-       Preservice Teachers [1982]
-       Reentry Students [1985]

College Teachers [1973]
PN 3589   SC 10330
- UF Professors
- B   Teachers [1967]

Colleges [1967]
PN 2475   SC 10350
- UF Junior Colleges
-       Universities
- B   Schools [1967]
- N   Community Colleges [1978]
- R   College Environment [1973]
-       ↓ Higher Education [1973]
-       Military Schools [1973]

Colon Disorders [1973]
PN 253   SC 10370
- UF Bowel Disorders
- B   Gastrointestinal Disorders [1973]
- N   ↓ Colitis [1973]
-       Constipation [1973]
-       Diarrhea [1973]
-       Fecal Incontinence [1973]
-       Irritable Bowel Syndrome [1991]

Color [1967]
PN 2459   SC 10380
SN Property of matter or light sources that corresponds to the relative reflectance or absorption of incident light and the wavelength of the incident light or light source. Color is described perceptually by the dimensions of hue, lightness, brightness, and saturation. Compare HUE.
- N   Achromatic Color [1973]
-       Eye Color [1991]
-       Hue [1973]
- R   ↓ Chromaticity [1997]
-       Color Saturation [1997]
-       ↓ Pigments [1973]
-       ↓ Visual Stimulation [1973]

Color Blindness [1973]
PN 263   SC 10390
- B   Eye Disorders [1973]
- R   ↓ Color Perception [1967]
-       ↓ Genetic Disorders [1973]

Color Constancy [1985]
PN 96   SC 10395
SN The tendency to perceive hue, brightness, and saturation as stable despite objective changes in context and illumination.
- B   Color Perception [1967]
-       Perceptual Constancy [1985]

Color Contrast [1985]
PN 173   SC 10397
- B   Color Perception [1967]
-       Visual Contrast [1985]

Color Perception [1967]
PN 3463   SC 10400
- UF Spectral Sensitivity
- B   Visual Perception [1967]
- N   Color Constancy [1985]
-       Color Contrast [1985]
- R   ↓ Chromaticity [1997]
-       Color Blindness [1973]
-       Color Saturation [1997]
-       Prismatic Stimulation [1973]

Color Pyramid Test
SN Term was discontinued in 1997. In 2000, the term was stripped from all records containing it, and replaced with PROJECTIVE PERSONALITY MEASURES, its postable counterpart.
- Use Projective Personality Measures

Color Saturation [1997]
PN 12   SC 10420
SN The degree of purity or richness of a color.
- UF Saturation (Color)
- B   Chromaticity [1997]
- R   Achromatic Color [1973]
-       ↓ Color [1967]
-       ↓ Color Perception [1967]
-       Hue [1973]
-       Luminance [1982]

Colostomy [1973]
PN 37   SC 10430
- B   Surgery [1971]

Columbia Mental Maturity Scale [1973]
PN 14   SC 10440
- B   Intelligence Measures [1967]

Coma [1973]
PN 284   SC 10450
- B   Symptoms [1967]
- R   Cerebrovascular Accidents [1973]
-       ↓ Cerebrovascular Disorders [1973]
-       ↓ Consciousness Disturbances [1973]
-       ↓ Epileptic Seizures [1973]
-       ↓ Injuries [1973]
-       Insulin Shock Therapy [1973]

Combat Experience [1991]
PN 668   SC 10452
SN Direct participation in war.
- R   ↓ Experiences (Events) [1973]
-       ↓ Military Personnel [1967]
-       Posttraumatic Stress Disorder [1985]
-       ↓ War [1967]

Comfort (Physical)
- Use Physical Comfort

Commerce
- Use Business

Commercials
- Use Television Advertising

Commissioned Officers [1973]
PN 244   SC 10470
SN Military officers who have received a formal certificate granting rank and authority and who thereby hold a position of command.
- UF Military Officers
-       Officers (Commissioned)
- B   Military Personnel [1967]
- R   ↓ Management Personnel [1973]
-       Volunteer Military Personnel [1973]

Commissurotomy [1985]
PN 272   SC 10475
- UF Split Brain
- B   Neurosurgery [1973]
- R   Corpus Callosum [1973]

Commitment [1985]
PN 1240   SC 10478

Commitment — (cont'd)
SN The process or extent of devoting one's efforts or resources to an activity, task, or interpersonal relationship.
N   Organizational Commitment 1991
R   ↓ Involvement 1973
       ↓ Motivation 1967

Commitment (Outpatient)
Use Outpatient Commitment

Commitment (Psychiatric) 1973
PN 1094   SC 10480
B   Hospitalization 1967
       Legal Processes 1973
N   Outpatient Commitment 1991
R   Court Referrals 1994
       Guardianship 1988
       Health Care Seeking Behavior 1997
       ↓ Institutional Release 1978
       Involuntary Treatment 1994
       ↓ Psychiatric Hospital Admission 1973
       Psychiatric Hospital Discharge 1978
       ↓ Psychiatric Hospitalization 1973
       Right to Treatment 1997
       Self Referral 1991

Communes 1973
PN 103   SC 10510
B   Communities 1967
N   Kibbutz 1973

Communicable Diseases
Use Infectious Disorders

Communication 1967
PN 4189   SC 10570
SN Conceptually broad term referring to the transmission of verbal or nonverbal information. Use a more specific term if possible.
UF Information Exchange
N   ↓ Animal Communication 1967
       ↓ Augmentative Communication 1994
       Electronic Communication 2001
       ↓ Interpersonal Communication 1973
       ↓ Nonverbal Communication 1971
       ↓ Persuasive Communication 1967
       Scientific Communication 1973
       ↓ Verbal Communication 1967
R   Censorship 1978
       ↓ Communication Skills 1973
       Communication Skills Training 1982
       ↓ Communication Systems 1973
       Communication Theory 1973
       ↓ Communications Media 1973
       ↓ Content Analysis 1978
       Emotional Content 1973
       Information 1967
       Messages 1973
       Privileged Communication 1973
       Rhetoric 1991
       Symbolism 1967
       ↓ Vocalization 1967
       ↓ Voice 1973

Communication (Privileged)
Use Privileged Communication

Communication (Professional)
Use Scientific Communication

Communication Apprehension
Use Speech Anxiety

Communication Disorders 1982
PN 690   SC 10533
SN Impaired ability to communicate usually due to speech, language, or hearing disorders.
N   Hearing Disorders 1982
       ↓ Language Disorders 1982
       ↓ Speech Disorders 1967
R   ↓ Augmentative Communication 1994
       ↓ Communication Skills 1973
       Communication Skills Training 1982
       Developmental Disabilities 1982
       ↓ Mental Disorders 1967
       ↓ Physical Disorders 1997
       Speech Anxiety 1985
       Speech Therapy 1967

Communication Skills 1973
PN 2928   SC 10540
SN Individual ability or competency in any type of communication. Limited to human populations.
UF Communicative Competence
B   Ability 1967
N   Language Proficiency 1988
       Rhetoric 1991
       Writing Skills 1985
R   ↓ Communication 1967
       ↓ Communication Disorders 1982
       Communication Skills Training 1982
       Pragmatics 1985
       Social Cognition 1994
       ↓ Verbal Communication 1967

Communication Skills Training 1982
PN 1250   SC 10542
SN Instruction, usually group oriented, to increase quality and capability of interpersonal communication.
B   Education 1967
R   Assertiveness Training 1978
       ↓ Behavior Modification 1973
       ↓ Communication 1967
       ↓ Communication Disorders 1982
       ↓ Communication Skills 1973
       Human Relations Training 1978
       Sensitivity Training 1973
       ↓ Skill Learning 1973
       Social Skills Training 1982

Communication Systems 1973
PN 752   SC 10550
SN Organized scheme for transmitting and receiving information.
B   Systems 1967
N   Internet 2001
       Telephone Systems 1973
R   ↓ Automated Information Processing 1973
       ↓ Communication 1967
       Electronic Communication 2001
       ↓ Information Systems 1991

Communication Theory 1973
PN 366   SC 10560
B   Theories 1967
R   ↓ Communication 1967
       Cybernetics 1967
       Information Theory 1967

Communications Media 1973
PN 731   SC 10580
UF Media (Communications)
N   ↓ Audiovisual Communications Media 1973

Communications Media — (cont'd)
N   ↓ Mass Media 1967
       ↓ Telecommunications Media 1973
R   Censorship 1978
       ↓ Communication 1967
       Electronic Communication 2001

Communicative Competence
Use Communication Skills

Communism 1973
PN 566   SC 10590
UF Marxism
B   Political Economic Systems 1973

Communities 1967
PN 2784   SC 10600
B   Social Environments 1973
N   ↓ Communes 1973
       Neighborhoods 1973
       Retirement Communities 1997
R   Community Development 1997

Community Attitudes 1973
PN 1181   SC 10620
SN Attitudes which characterize a group of individuals living in close proximity and organized into a social structure, however tenuous.
B   Attitudes 1967
R   Public Opinion 1973

Community College Students 1973
PN 1169   SC 10627
SN Students attending public postsecondary institutions offering 2-year degree programs and transfer components. Mandatory term in educational contexts.
B   College Students 1967
R   Junior College Students 1973

Community Colleges 1978
PN 386   SC 10630
B   Colleges 1967
R   College Environment 1973
       ↓ Community Facilities 1973

Community Development 1997
PN 82   SC 10635
UF Rural Development
       Urban Development
B   Development 1967
R   ↓ Communities 1967
       ↓ Community Services 1967
       Rural Environments 1967
       ↓ Urban Environments 1967
       Urban Planning 1973

Community Facilities 1973
PN 570   SC 10640
N   Community Mental Health Centers 1973
       ↓ Housing 1973
       Public Transportation 1973
       Shopping Centers 1973
       Suicide Prevention Centers 1973
R   Child Guidance Clinics 1973
       Community Colleges 1978
       ↓ Community Services 1967
       Day Care Centers 1973
       Group Homes 1982
       Halfway Houses 1973
       ↓ Libraries 1982
       ↓ Recreation Areas 1973
       ↓ Rehabilitation Centers 1973

Community Facilities — (cont'd)
- R   Religious Buildings [1973]
- ↓ Schools [1967]
-    Sheltered Workshops [1967]
-    Shelters [1991]
-    Urban Planning [1973]

Community Mental Health [1973]
PN 523   **SC** 10647
SN General psychological well-being or adjustment of persons in a given area.
- B   Mental Health [1967]
- R   Community Mental Health Centers [1973]
-    Community Mental Health Services [1978]
- ↓ Community Mental Health Training [1973]
-    Community Psychiatry [1973]
-    Community Psychology [1973]
-    Deinstitutionalization [1982]
- ↓ Mental Health Programs [1973]

Community Mental Health Centers [1973]
PN 1707   **SC** 10650
- UF   Mental Health Centers (Community)
- B   Community Facilities [1973]
-    Treatment Facilities [1973]
- R   Child Guidance Clinics [1973]
- ↓ Clinics [1967]
-    Community Mental Health [1973]
-    Community Mental Health Services [1978]
- ↓ Crisis Intervention Services [1973]
-    Day Care Centers [1973]
-    Hot Line Services [1973]
- ↓ Mental Health Programs [1973]
- ↓ Mental Health Services [1978]
-    Psychiatric Clinics [1973]
-    Suicide Prevention Centers [1973]

Community Mental Health Services [1978]
PN 3609   **SC** 10656
- B   Community Services [1967]
-    Mental Health Services [1978]
- R   Community Mental Health [1973]
-    Community Mental Health Centers [1973]
-    Community Psychiatry [1973]
-    Community Psychology [1973]
-    Deinstitutionalization [1982]
-    Group Homes [1982]
- ↓ Mental Health [1967]
- ↓ Mental Health Programs [1973]
-    Outreach Programs [1997]
-    Supported Employment [1994]

Community Mental Health Training [1973]
PN 300   **SC** 10660
- UF   Mental Health Training (Community)
-    Training (Community Mental Health)
- B   Clinical Methods Training [1973]
- N   Mental Health Inservice Training [1973]
- R   Community Mental Health [1973]
- ↓ Mental Health Programs [1973]

Community Psychiatry [1973]
PN 381   **SC** 10670
SN Branch of psychiatry concerned with the provision and delivery of community health care needs such as diagnosis; treatment; primary, secondary, and tertiary prevention; rehabilitation; and aftercare. Such services are usually delivered at community mental health centers.
- B   Psychiatry [1967]
- R   Community Mental Health [1973]
-    Community Mental Health Services [1978]
-    Community Psychology [1973]

Community Psychiatry — (cont'd)
- R   ↓ Mental Health [1967]
-    ↓ Mental Health Programs [1973]

Community Psychology [1973]
PN 776   **SC** 10680
SN Branch of psychology that emphasizes the analysis of social processes and interactions and design of social interventions within groups and the community.
- B   Applied Psychology [1973]
- R   Community Mental Health [1973]
-    Community Mental Health Services [1978]
-    Community Psychiatry [1973]
- ↓ Mental Health Programs [1973]

Community Services [1967]
PN 5697   **SC** 10690
- B   Social Services [1982]
- N   Community Mental Health Services [1978]
-    Community Welfare Services [1973]
- ↓ Crisis Intervention Services [1973]
-    Home Visiting Programs [1973]
-    Public Health Services [1973]
- R   Alcoholics Anonymous [1973]
-    Community Development [1997]
- ↓ Community Facilities [1973]
- ↓ Health Care Services [1978]
-    Independent Living Programs [1991]
-    Integrated Services [1997]
- ↓ Mental Health Programs [1973]
- ↓ Mental Health Services [1978]
-    Outreach Programs [1997]
- ↓ Self Help Techniques [1982]
-    Shelters [1991]
- ↓ Support Groups [1991]

Community Welfare Services [1973]
PN 212   **SC** 10700
- UF   Public Welfare Services
- B   Community Services [1967]
- R   Welfare Services (Government) [1973]

Commuting (Travel) [1985]
PN 83   **SC** 10705
- R   Geographical Mobility [1978]
- ↓ Transportation [1973]
-    Traveling [1973]

Comorbidity [1991]
PN 4103   **SC** 10707
SN Coexistence of two or more physical and/or mental disorders.
- R   ↓ Diagnosis [1967]
-    Differential Diagnosis [1967]
- ↓ Disorders [1967]
-    Dual Diagnosis [1991]
- ↓ Mental Disorders [1967]
-    Mental Disorders due to General Medical Conditions [2001]
- ↓ Physical Disorders [1997]
-    Psychopathology [1967]

Companies
   Use Business Organizations

Comparative Psychiatry
   Use Transcultural Psychiatry

Comparative Psychology [1967]
PN 1103   **SC** 10720

Comparative Psychology — (cont'd)
SN Branch of psychology devoted to the study of behavioral differences between organisms of different species. Prior to 1982, also used for comparative studies. From 1982, limited to the scientific discipline. Use SPECIES DIFFERENCES for comparative studies.
- B   Psychology [1967]

Compatibility (Interpersonal)
   Use Interpersonal Compatibility

Compensation (Defense Mechanism) [1973]
PN 68   **SC** 10740
SN Defense mechanism of covering up or making up for conscious or unconscious insecurity or feelings of failure.
- B   Defense Mechanisms [1967]

Compensatory Education [1973]
PN 228   **SC** 10745
SN Education designed to enhance intellectual and social skills of disadvantaged students, and to compensate for environmental, experiential, cultural, or economic deficits. Compare REMEDIAL EDUCATION.
- B   Curriculum [1967]
- R   ↓ Educational Programs [1973]
-    Project Follow Through [1973]
-    Project Head Start [1973]
- ↓ Remedial Education [1985]
-    Upward Bound [1973]

Competence [1982]
PN 3444   **SC** 10747
SN Possession of sufficient skills, knowledge, or qualities as required in a given situation.
- N   Professional Competence [1997]
- R   ↓ Ability [1967]
-    Accountability [1988]
- ↓ Achievement [1967]
-    Competency to Stand Trial [1985]
-    Minimum Competency Tests [1985]
- ↓ Performance [1967]
-    Social Skills [1978]

Competence (Social)
   Use Social Skills

Competency to Stand Trial [1985]
PN 371   **SC** 10749
- B   Legal Processes [1973]
- R   ↓ Competence [1982]
-    Criminal Responsibility [1991]
-    Forensic Evaluation [1994]
-    Mentally Ill Offenders [1985]

Competition [1967]
PN 3399   **SC** 10750
SN Used for human and animal populations.
- B   Social Behavior [1967]
- R   Rivalry [1973]

Complementary Medicine
   Use Alternative Medicine

Complexity (Cognitive)
   Use Cognitive Complexity

Complexity (Stimulus)
   Use Stimulus Complexity

Complexity (Task)
　Use　Task Complexity

Compliance 1973
PN 1705　　　　　SC 10810
SN　Limited to human populations.
　B　Social Behavior 1967
　N　Treatment Compliance 1982
　R　Obedience 1973
　　↓ Resistance 1997

Comprehension 1967
PN 3757　　　　　SC 10820
SN　Knowledge or understanding of communications, objects, events, or situations as relates to their meaning, significance, relationships, or general principles.
　UF　Understanding
　B　Cognitive Processes 1967
　N　Number Comprehension 1973
　　↓ Verbal Comprehension 1985
　R　Intuition 1973
　　↓ Meaning 1967
　　Meaningfulness 1967
　　Metacognition 1991
　　Theory of Mind 2001

Comprehension Tests 1973
PN 60　　　　　SC 10830
　B　Measurement 1967

Compressed Speech 1973
PN 145　　　　　SC 10840
　B　Speech Processing (Mechanical) 1973

Compulsions 1973
PN 611　　　　　SC 10850
　N　Compulsive Repetition 1973
　R　Obsessions 1967
　　Obsessive Compulsive Disorder 1985
　　Obsessive Compulsive Personality 1973
　　Perfectionism 1988

Compulsive Gambling
　Use　Pathological Gambling

Compulsive Neurosis
　Use　Obsessive Compulsive Disorder

Compulsive Personality Disorder
　Use　Obsessive Compulsive Personality

Compulsive Repetition 1973
PN 152　　　　　SC 10890
　UF　Repetition (Compulsive)
　B　Compulsions 1973

Compulsivity (Sexual)
　Use　Sexual Addiction

Computer Anxiety 2001
PN 0　　　　　SC 10897
　B　Anxiety 1967
　R　Computer Attitudes 1988
　　Computer Literacy 1991

Computer Applications 1973
PN 5932　　　　　SC 10900
SN　Application of computers, computer technology, or software to any area.
　N　↓ Artificial Intelligence 1982
　　Computer Assisted Design 1997

Computer Applications — (cont'd)
　N　Computer Assisted Diagnosis 1973
　　Computer Assisted Instruction 1973
　　Computer Assisted Testing 1988
　　↓ Computer Simulation 1973
　　Hypermedia 1997
　　Hypertext 1997
　R　Automated Speech Recognition 1994
　　↓ Computer Peripheral Devices 1985
　　Computer Searching 1991
　　↓ Computers 1967
　　Databases 1991
　　Decision Support Systems 1997
　　Electronic Communication 2001
　　↓ Information Systems 1991
　　Internet 2001
　　Microcomputers 1985
　　Virtual Reality 1997
　　Word Processing 1991

Computer Assisted Design 1997
PN 40　　　　　SC 10905
SN　Use of a computer system to design a product so that it can be displayed, manipulated, and revised or modified quickly and easily.
　B　Computer Applications 1973
　R　↓ Architecture 1973
　　↓ Computer Simulation 1973
　　↓ Computer Software 1967
　　↓ Computers 1967
　　↓ Environmental Planning 1982
　　Human Factors Engineering 1973
　　Human Machine Systems Design 1997
　　Product Design 1997

Computer Assisted Diagnosis 1973
PN 1145　　　　　SC 10910
　B　Computer Applications 1973
　　Diagnosis 1967
　R　Magnetic Resonance Imaging 1994
　　↓ Medical Diagnosis 1973
　　↓ Psychodiagnosis 1967
　　↓ Tomography 1988

Computer Assisted Instruction 1973
PN 4687　　　　　SC 10920
SN　Use of computers to present instructional materials to students and to assess performance. Compare TEACHING MACHINES.
　UF　Instruction (Computer Assisted)
　B　Computer Applications 1973
　　Teaching Methods 1967
　R　Individualized Instruction 1973
　　Programmed Instruction 2001
　　Teaching Machines 1973

Computer Assisted Testing 1988
PN 950　　　　　SC 10921
SN　Use of computers in test construction or administration, usually in an educational or employment setting. Not used for diagnosis.
　B　Computer Applications 1973
　　Testing 1967
　R　Adaptive Testing 1985

Computer Attitudes 1988
PN 796　　　　　SC 10922
　B　Attitudes 1967
　R　Computer Anxiety 2001
　　↓ Computers 1967

Computer Conferencing
　Use　Teleconferencing

Computer Games 1988
PN 409　　　　　SC 10923
　UF　Video Games
　B　Computers 1967
　　Games 1967
　R　↓ Computer Simulation 1973
　　↓ Recreation 1967
　　Simulation Games 1973
　　↓ Toys 1973

Computer Literacy 1991
PN 161　　　　　SC 10924
　B　Literacy 1973
　R　Computer Anxiety 2001
　　Computer Searching 1991
　　Computer Training 1994
　　↓ Computers 1967

Computer Peripheral Devices 1985
PN 140　　　　　SC 10925
SN　Computer peripheral components and hand-held microcomputer devices used for entering data, and collecting, displaying, receiving, and communicating information.
　B　Apparatus 1967
　N　Video Display Units 1985
　R　↓ Computer Applications 1973
　　↓ Computers 1967
　　Data Collection 1982
　　Electronic Communication 2001
　　Human Computer Interaction 1997
　　Human Machine Systems 1997
　　Keyboards 1985
　　↓ Visual Displays 1973

Computer Programming 2001
PN 239　　　　　SC 10928
SN　In 2000, this term was created to update the spelling from the discontinued term COMPUTER PROGRAMING. COMPUTER PROGRAMING was stripped from all records and replaced with COMPUTER PROGRAMMING.
　UF　Programming (Computer)
　R　Algorithms 1973
　　Computer Programming Languages 1973
　　↓ Computer Software 1967
　　↓ Computers 1967
　　↓ Data Processing 1967
　　Systems Analysis 1973

Computer Programming Languages 1973
PN 706　　　　　SC 10930
SN　In 2000, this term was created to update the spelling from the discontinued term COMPUTER PROGRAMING LANGUAGES. COMPUTER PROGRAMING LANGUAGES was stripped from all records and replaced with COMPUTER PROGRAMMING LANGUAGES.
　UF　FORTRAN
　　Programming Languages (Computer)
　R　Computer Programming 2001
　　Computer Training 1994
　　↓ Computers 1967
　　↓ Data Processing 1967

Computer Programs
　Use　Computer Software

Computer Searching 1991
PN 248　　　　　SC 10945
SN　Use of computerized interactive communication system to access and retrieve information.
　UF　Online Searching
　B　Automated Information Retrieval 1973

Computer Searching — (cont'd)
R   ↓ Computer Applications   1973
    Computer Literacy   1991
    ↓ Computers   1967
    Databases   1991
    Electronic Communication   2001
    Human Machine Systems   1997
    Information   1967
    Information Seeking   1973
    Information Services   1988

Computer Simulation   1973
PN 2134   **SC** 10950
B   Computer Applications   1973
    Simulation   1967
N   Neural Networks   1991
    Virtual Reality   1997
R   Computer Assisted Design   1997
    Computer Games   1988
    Decision Support Systems   1997
    Simulation Games   1973

Computer Software   1967
PN 4193   **SC** 10960
UF   Computer Programs
N   Decision Support Systems   1997
    Word Processing   1991
R   Computer Assisted Design   1997
    Computer Programming   2001
    ↓ Computers   1967
    ↓ Data Processing   1967
    Databases   1991
    Hypermedia   1997
    Hypertext   1997
    ↓ Systems   1967

Computer Training   1994
PN 165   **SC** 10963
B   Curriculum   1967
R   Computer Literacy   1991
    Computer Programming Languages   1973

Computerized Databases
Use Databases

Computers   1967
PN 3097   **SC** 10970
B   Apparatus   1967
N   Analog Computers   1973
    Computer Games   1988
    Digital Computers   1973
    Microcomputers   1985
R   ↓ Artificial Intelligence   1982
    Automated Information Coding   1973
    ↓ Automated Information Processing   1973
    ↓ Automated Information Retrieval   1973
    Automated Information Storage   1973
    Automation   1967
    ↓ Computer Applications   1973
    Computer Assisted Design   1997
    Computer Attitudes   1988
    Computer Literacy   1991
    ↓ Computer Peripheral Devices   1985
    Computer Programming   2001
    Computer Programming Languages   1973
    Computer Searching   1991
    ↓ Computer Software   1967
    Cybernetics   1967
    ↓ Data Processing   1967
    Databases   1991
    ↓ Expert Systems   1991
    Human Computer Interaction   1997
    Robotics   1985

Computers — (cont'd)
R   ↓ Systems   1967

Concentration   1982
PN 337   **SC** 10977
SN Cognitive effort directed to one object or area of study.
B   Cognitive Processes   1967
    Sustained Attention   1997
R   ↓ Attention   1967
    Distraction   1978
    Rumination (Cognitive Process)   2001
    Selective Attention   1973

Concentration Camps   1973
PN 359   **SC** 10980
R   Holocaust   1988
    Prisons   1967

Concept Formation   1967
PN 5479   **SC** 11000
SN Developmental or learning process involving identification of common properties of objects, events, or qualities, usually represented by words or symbols, and generalization of those properties to all appropriate objects, events, or qualities. In 1982, this term replaced the discontinued term CONCEPT LEARNING. In 2000, CONCEPT LEARNING was stripped from all records and replaced with CONCEPT FORMATION.
UF   Concept Learning
    Conceptualization
B   Cognitive Processes   1967
N   Cognitive Discrimination   1973
    Cognitive Generalization   1967
R   ↓ Cognitive Development   1973
    Cognitive Hypothesis Testing   1982
    Concepts   1967
    Conservation (Concept)   1973
    ↓ Discrimination Learning   1982
    Egocentrism   1978
    ↓ Generalization (Learning)   1982
    ↓ Learning   1967

Concept Learning
SN Term was discontinued in 1982. In 2000, the term was stripped from all records containing it, and replaced with CONCEPT FORMATION, its postable counterpart.
Use Concept Formation

Concept Validity
Use Statistical Validity

Concepts   1967
PN 2302   **SC** 11030
SN Generic ideas or categories derived from common properties of objects, events, or qualities, usually represented by words or symbols.
R   ↓ Cognitions   1985
    ↓ Concept Formation   1967
    Information   1967
    ↓ Mathematics (Concepts)   1967
    ↓ Terminology   1991

Conceptual Imagery   1973
PN 444   **SC** 11040
SN Mental representation of concepts or conceptual relationships.
UF   Imagery (Conceptual)
B   Imagery   1967
R   Imagination   1967
    Schema   1988

Conceptual Tempo   1985
PN 46   **SC** 11045
SN The dimension of cognitive style often measured by response latency or the time required to solve a problem.
B   Cognitive Style   1967
R   Attention Span   1973
    Cognitive Processing Speed   1997
    Impulsiveness   1973
    Perceptual Style   1973
    Reaction Time   1967
    Reflectiveness   1997

Conceptualization
Use Concept Formation

Concurrent Reinforcement Schedules   1988
PN 198   **SC** 11057
SN Simultaneous use of two or more reinforcement schedules.
B   Reinforcement Schedules   1967

Concurrent Validity
SN In 2000, the term was discontinued, and all records containing it were stripped of the term and replaced with STATISTICAL VALIDITY, its postable counterpart.
Use Statistical Validity

Concussion (Brain)
Use Brain Concussion

Conditioned Emotional Responses   1967
PN 607   **SC** 11070
UF   CER (Conditioning)
B   Classical Conditioning   1967
    Conditioned Responses   1967
    Emotional Responses   1967
    Operant Conditioning   1967

Conditioned Inhibition
Use Conditioned Suppression

Conditioned Place Preference
Use Place Conditioning

Conditioned Reflex
Use Conditioned Responses

Conditioned Responses   1967
PN 3459   **SC** 11090
UF   Conditioned Reflex
B   Classical Conditioning   1967
    Operant Conditioning   1967
    Responses   1967
N   Conditioned Emotional Responses   1967
    Conditioned Suppression   1973

Conditioned Stimulus   1973
PN 2142   **SC** 11100
SN In classical conditioning, that stimulus (e.g., a light) that acquires the capacity to elicit a conditioned response (e.g., salivation) as a result of that stimulus having been paired consistently with an unconditioned stimulus (e.g., food). In operant conditioning, those stimuli (S+,S-) which differentially signal the presence or absence of reinforcement. Compare CUES.
UF   Discriminative Stimulus
B   Conditioning   1967
R   ↓ Classical Conditioning   1967
    ↓ Latent Inhibition   1997
    ↓ Operant Conditioning   1967

Conditioned Stimulus — (cont'd)

R   Preconditioning [1994]
    Secondary Reinforcement [1967]
    ↓ Stimulation [1967]

Conditioned Suppression [1973]

PN 978   **SC** 11110
SN Learned behavior or the conditioning procedure in which the pairing of a neutral stimulus with an aversive stimulus, presented during the performance of a positively-reinforced behavior, results in a decrease of that behavior.
UF   Conditioned Inhibition
    Suppression (Conditioned)
B   Conditioned Responses [1967]
R   Prepulse Inhibition [1997]

Conditioning [1967]

PN 3020   **SC** 11120
B   Learning [1967]
N   Autoshaping [1978]
    ↓ Aversion Conditioning [1982]
    ↓ Classical Conditioning [1967]
    Conditioned Stimulus [1973]
    Counterconditioning [1973]
    ↓ Operant Conditioning [1967]
    Place Conditioning [1991]
    Preconditioning [1994]
    Unconditioned Stimulus [1973]
R   ↓ Biofeedback [1973]
    ↓ Latent Inhibition [1997]
    Primary Reinforcement [1973]
    ↓ Reinforcement [1967]
    Spontaneous Recovery (Learning) [1973]
    ↓ Stimulation [1967]

Conditioning (Avoidance)
Use   Avoidance Conditioning

Conditioning (Classical)
Use   Classical Conditioning

Conditioning (Escape)
Use   Escape Conditioning

Conditioning (Eyelid)
Use   Eyelid Conditioning

Conditioning (Operant)
Use   Operant Conditioning

Conditioning (Verbal)
Use   Verbal Learning

Condoms [1991]

PN 867   **SC** 11185
B   Contraceptive Devices [1973]
R   AIDS Prevention [1994]
    ↓ Birth Control [1971]
    ↓ Family Planning [1973]
    ↓ Prevention [1973]
    ↓ Venereal Diseases [1973]

Conduct Disorder [1991]

PN 1136   **SC** 11187
SN Repetitive and persistent aggressive or nonaggressive behavior in which basic rights of others or social norms are violated. Self esteem is generally low, and an inability to develop social relationships and lack of concern for others may or may not be present. Consider using BEHAVIOR DISORDERS prior to 1991.
R   ↓ Aggressive Behavior [1967]

Conduct Disorder — (cont'd)

R   ↓ Behavior Disorders [1971]
    ↓ Behavior Problems [1967]
    Explosive Disorder [2001]
    ↓ Impulse Control Disorders [1997]
    ↓ Mental Disorders [1967]
    Oppositional Defiant Disorder [1997]

Cones (Eye) [1973]

PN 507   **SC** 11190
B   Cells (Biology) [1973]
    Photoreceptors [1973]
    Retina [1967]
R   Fovea [1982]

Confabulation [1973]

PN 97   **SC** 11200
SN Giving untruthful answers to questions about situations or events that are not recalled due to loss of memory. Confabulation is not a conscious attempt to deceive.
B   Deception [1967]
    Thought Disturbances [1973]
R   False Memory [1997]
    Korsakoffs Psychosis [1973]

Confession (Religion) [1973]

PN 10   **SC** 11220
B   Religious Practices [1973]

Confidence (Self)
Use   Self Confidence

Confidence Limits (Statistics) [1973]

PN 182   **SC** 11230
B   Statistical Analysis [1967]
R   Effect Size (Statistical) [1985]
    ↓ Hypothesis Testing [1973]
    Predictability (Measurement) [1973]
    ↓ Statistical Measurement [1973]
    ↓ Statistical Sample Parameters [1973]
    Statistical Significance [1973]
    ↓ Statistical Tests [1973]

Confidentiality of Information
Use   Privileged Communication

Confirmatory Factor Analysis
Use   Factor Analysis

Conflict [1967]

PN 5107   **SC** 11250
SN Hostile encounter or antagonistic state or action.
B   Aggressive Behavior [1967]
    Interpersonal Interaction [1967]
N   Arguments [1973]
    Riots [1973]
    ↓ Violence [1973]
    ↓ War [1967]

Conflict Resolution [1982]

PN 2512   **SC** 11255
SN Process of reducing or removing antagonisms among individuals, groups, organizations, or political entities.
N   Mediation [1988]
R   ↓ Cognitive Processes [1967]
    Forgiveness [1988]
    ↓ Negotiation [1973]
    ↓ Social Interaction [1967]

Conformity (Personality) [1967]

PN 1267   **SC** 11270

Conformity (Personality) — (cont'd)

B   Personality Traits [1967]
    Social Behavior [1967]
R   Nonconformity (Personality) [1973]
    Openness to Experience [1997]

Confusion (Mental)
Use   Mental Confusion

Congenital Disorders [1973]

PN 902   **SC** 11290
SN The term CONGENITALLY HANDICAPPED was also used to capture this concept from 1973-1996, and CONGENITALLY DISABLED was used from 1997-2000. In 2000, CONGENITAL DISORDERS replaced the discontinued and deleted term CONGENITALLY DISABLED. CONGENITALLY DISABLED and CONGENITALLY HANDICAPPED were stripped from all records and replaced with CONGENITAL DISORDERS.
UF   Congenitally Handicapped
B   Disorders [1967]
N   Cleft Palate [1967]
    ↓ Drug Induced Congenital Disorders [1973]
    Hermaphroditism [1973]
    Microcephaly [1973]
    Prader Willi Syndrome [1991]
    Spina Bifida [1978]
R   Adventitious Disorders [2001]
    ↓ Brain Damage [1967]
    Cystic Fibrosis [1985]
    Deaf Blind [1991]
    Developmental Disabilities [1982]
    ↓ Genetic Disorders [1973]
    Hydrocephaly [1973]
    ↓ Mental Disorders [1967]
    Myotonia [1973]
    ↓ Neonatal Disorders [1973]
    ↓ Physical Disorders [1997]
    Prenatal Diagnosis [1988]
    ↓ Syphilis [1973]
    Teratogens [1988]

Congenitally Handicapped
SN The term was discontinued in 1997, when the term CONGENITALLY DISABLED was created to capture this concept. In 2000, with the deletion of the term CONGENITALLY DISABLED, CONGENITALLY HANDICAPPED was made a nonpostable term for the postable term CONGENITAL DISORDERS. CONGENITALLY DISABLED and CONGENITALLY HANDICAPPED were stripped from all records containing them and replaced with CONGENITAL DISORDERS.
Use   Congenital Disorders

Conjoint Measurement [1994]

PN 23   **SC** 11307
SN Statistical measurement of a variable that is composed of two or more components which affect the variable being measured.
B   Statistical Measurement [1973]
R   ↓ Experimental Design [1967]
    Psychometrics [1967]
    ↓ Statistical Analysis [1967]

Conjoint Therapy [1973]

PN 388   **SC** 11310
SN Type of marriage or family therapy in which partners or family members are seen in joint sessions.
UF   Triadic Therapy
B   Family Therapy [1967]
    Marriage Counseling [1973]
R   Couples Therapy [1994]

Conjoint Therapy — (cont'd)
R ↓ Group Psychotherapy ¹⁹⁶⁷
↓ Psychotherapeutic Techniques ¹⁹⁶⁷

Connectionism ¹⁹⁹⁴
PN 568   SC 11315
SN Theoretical principles that characterize all learning and behavior as connected to the stimulus-response paradigm and the theory that neural linkages, whether inherited or acquired, bond these behaviors.
R ↓ Associative Processes ¹⁹⁶⁷
↓ Cognitive Processes ¹⁹⁶⁷
Cognitive Psychology ¹⁹⁸⁵
↓ Learning ¹⁹⁶⁷
Learning Theory ¹⁹⁶⁷
Neural Networks ¹⁹⁹¹

Connective Tissue Cells ¹⁹⁷³
PN 13   SC 11320
B Cells (Biology) ¹⁹⁷³
R ↓ Connective Tissues ¹⁹⁷³

Connective Tissues ¹⁹⁷³
PN 25   SC 11330
B Tissues (Body) ¹⁹⁷³
N Bones ¹⁹⁷³
R Connective Tissue Cells ¹⁹⁷³

Connotations ¹⁹⁷³
PN 214   SC 11340
B Associative Processes ¹⁹⁶⁷
R Analogy ¹⁹⁹¹
↓ Figurative Language ¹⁹⁸⁵
Semantic Generalization ¹⁹⁷³
Word Meaning ¹⁹⁷³

Consanguineous Marriage ¹⁹⁷³
PN 32   SC 11350
B Endogamous Marriage ¹⁹⁷³

Conscience ¹⁹⁶⁷
PN 141   SC 11360
SN Cognitive and affective processes which govern the individual's standards of behavior, performance and morality.
B Psychoanalytic Personality Factors ¹⁹⁷³
Superego ¹⁹⁷³

Conscientiousness ¹⁹⁹⁷
PN 98   SC 11365
SN Extent to which an individual is purposeful, well-organized, strong-willed, and determined.
B Personality Traits ¹⁹⁶⁷
R Perfectionism ¹⁹⁸⁸
Persistence ¹⁹⁷³
↓ Responsibility ¹⁹⁷³
Self Monitoring (Personality) ¹⁹⁸⁵

Conscious (Personality Factor) ¹⁹⁷³
PN 378   SC 11370
SN That portion of personal mental functioning which is known to the individual or is observable by introspection. Use CONSCIOUS (PERSONALITY FACTORS) prior to 1988.
B Psychoanalytic Personality Factors ¹⁹⁷³

Consciousness Disturbances ¹⁹⁷³
PN 164   SC 11380
N Delirium ¹⁹⁷³
↓ Hypnosis ¹⁹⁶⁷
Place Disorientation ¹⁹⁷³
↓ Sleep Disorders ¹⁹⁷³

Consciousness Disturbances — (cont'd)
N Sleep Talking ¹⁹⁷³
Suggestibility ¹⁹⁶⁷
Time Disorientation ¹⁹⁷³
R Coma ¹⁹⁷³
↓ Consciousness States ¹⁹⁷¹
Dissociation ²⁰⁰¹
↓ Dissociative Disorders ²⁰⁰¹
↓ Mental Disorders ¹⁹⁶⁷
↓ Sleep ¹⁹⁶⁷

Consciousness Raising Groups ¹⁹⁷⁸
PN 127   SC 11387
SN Disciplined interaction of a small group of people whose exchange of feelings and experiences results in an increased awareness of social issues such as discriminatory social practices and stereotyped thinking.
B Human Potential Movement ¹⁹⁸²
R ↓ Encounter Group Therapy ¹⁹⁷³
↓ Group Dynamics ¹⁹⁶⁷
↓ Group Psychotherapy ¹⁹⁶⁷
Sensitivity Training ¹⁹⁷³

Consciousness States ¹⁹⁷¹
PN 3152   SC 11390
SN Conceptually broad term referring to variations in the degree and type of mental awareness. Use a more specific term if possible.
UF Deja Vu
N ↓ Awareness ¹⁹⁶⁷
Wakefulness ¹⁹⁷³
R Centering ¹⁹⁹¹
↓ Consciousness Disturbances ¹⁹⁷³
Dissociation ²⁰⁰¹
Mind ¹⁹⁹¹
Physiological Arousal ¹⁹⁶⁷
↓ Sleep ¹⁹⁶⁷

Conservation (Concept) ¹⁹⁷³
PN 1167   SC 11400
SN Knowledge of constancy of size, volume, or amount in spite of changed distance or shape; used as measure of cognitive development.
R ↓ Cognitive Development ¹⁹⁷³
↓ Concept Formation ¹⁹⁶⁷
Object Permanence ¹⁹⁸⁵
↓ Perceptual Development ¹⁹⁷³
Piaget (Jean) ¹⁹⁶⁷

Conservation (Ecological Behavior) ¹⁹⁷⁸
PN 625   SC 11403
B Behavior ¹⁹⁶⁷
R Ecology ¹⁹⁷³
Environmental Attitudes ¹⁹⁷⁸
Environmental Education ¹⁹⁹⁴

Conservatism ¹⁹⁷³
PN 472   SC 11405
UF Traditionalism
B Personality Traits ¹⁹⁶⁷
R Political Conservatism ¹⁹⁷³

Conservatism (Political)
Use Political Conservatism

Conservatorship
Use Guardianship

Consistency (Measurement) ¹⁹⁷³
PN 265   SC 11420
B Statistical Analysis ¹⁹⁶⁷
R Error of Measurement ¹⁹⁸⁵

Consistency (Measurement) — (cont'd)
R ↓ Prediction Errors ¹⁹⁷³
Statistical Reliability ¹⁹⁷³
Statistical Validity ¹⁹⁷³

Consonants ¹⁹⁷³
PN 910   SC 11430
B Letters (Alphabet) ¹⁹⁷³
Phonemes ¹⁹⁷³
R Syllables ¹⁹⁷³
Words (Phonetic Units) ¹⁹⁶⁷

Constant Time Delay ¹⁹⁹⁷
PN 10   SC 11435
SN Instruction involving a prompting technique in which dependence on the prompting is faded by a fixed time delay between the presentation of a target stimulus and the delivery of the controlling prompt.
B Prompting ¹⁹⁹⁷
R ↓ Behavior Modification ¹⁹⁷³
↓ Learning Strategies ¹⁹⁹¹
Task Analysis ¹⁹⁶⁷
↓ Teaching Methods ¹⁹⁶⁷

Constipation ¹⁹⁷³
PN 67   SC 11440
B Colon Disorders ¹⁹⁷³

Construct Validity
SN In 2000, the term was discontinued, and all records containing it were stripped of the term and replaced with STATISTICAL VALIDITY, its postable counterpart.
Use Statistical Validity

Constructionism
Use Constructivism

Constructivism ¹⁹⁹⁴
PN 1302   SC 11448
SN Theoretical perspective that characterizes perceptual experience and reality as constructed by the mind in the observation of the effects of independent actions on objects.
UF Constructionism
B Theories ¹⁹⁶⁷
R ↓ Cognitive Development ¹⁹⁷³
↓ Learning ¹⁹⁶⁷
↓ Perception ¹⁹⁶⁷
Phenomenology ¹⁹⁶⁷
Piaget (Jean) ¹⁹⁶⁷

Consultation (Professional)
Use Professional Consultation

Consultation Liaison Psychiatry ¹⁹⁹¹
PN 471   SC 11465
B Professional Consultation ¹⁹⁷³
Psychiatry ¹⁹⁶⁷

Consumer Attitudes ¹⁹⁷³
PN 3031   SC 11470
SN Attitudes of, not toward, consumers.
B Attitudes ¹⁹⁶⁷
N Brand Preferences ¹⁹⁹⁴
Consumer Satisfaction ¹⁹⁹⁴
R ↓ Consumer Research ¹⁹⁷³
Consumer Surveys ¹⁹⁷³
Public Relations ¹⁹⁷³
↓ Quality of Services ¹⁹⁹⁷

Consumer Behavior ¹⁹⁶⁷
PN 4579   SC 11480

Consumer Behavior — (cont'd)
UF   Buying
B   Behavior [1967]
N   Shopping [1997]
R   Brand Names [1978]
    Brand Preferences [1994]
    ↓ Consumer Research [1973]
    Consumer Satisfaction [1994]
    Consumer Surveys [1973]
    Retailing [1991]
    Shopping Centers [1973]

Consumer Fraud
Use   Fraud

Consumer Product Design
Use   Product Design

Consumer Protection [1973]
PN   116   **SC**   11490
R   Accountability [1988]
    ↓ Laws [1967]
    ↓ Legal Processes [1973]
    Product Design [1997]
    Warning Labels [1997]
    ↓ Warnings [1997]

Consumer Psychology [1973]
PN   247   **SC**   11500
SN   Subdiscipline in psychology that has as its emphasis the behavioral and psychological aspects of consumer behavior.
B   Applied Psychology [1973]

Consumer Research [1973]
PN   1134   **SC**   11510
SN   Marketing and advertising research assessing consumer needs, competition, and methods of sale for a product.
B   Experimentation [1967]
N   Consumer Surveys [1973]
R   ↓ Advertising [1967]
    Brand Names [1978]
    Brand Preferences [1994]
    ↓ Consumer Attitudes [1973]
    ↓ Consumer Behavior [1967]
    Consumer Satisfaction [1994]
    Mail Surveys [1994]
    Marketing [1973]
    Product Design [1997]
    Telephone Surveys [1994]

Consumer Satisfaction [1994]
PN   326   **SC**   11515
UF   Customer Satisfaction
B   Consumer Attitudes [1973]
    Satisfaction [1973]
R   ↓ Consumer Behavior [1967]
    ↓ Consumer Research [1973]
    Consumer Surveys [1973]
    Quality Control [1988]
    ↓ Quality of Services [1997]

Consumer Surveys [1973]
PN   229   **SC**   11520
SN   Surveys assessing consumer needs, product usage, and effectiveness of marketing and advertising.
B   Consumer Research [1973]
    Surveys [1967]
R   ↓ Consumer Attitudes [1973]
    ↓ Consumer Behavior [1967]
    Consumer Satisfaction [1994]

Consumer Surveys — (cont'd)
R   Mail Surveys [1994]
    Product Design [1997]
    Telephone Surveys [1994]

Contact Lenses [1973]
PN   38   **SC**   11540
B   Optical Aids [1973]

Contagion [1988]
PN   130   **SC**   11544
SN   Transmission of behavior, attitudes, or emotions to other persons through suggestions, verbal communication, imitation, or gestures. Not used for infectious disorders.
B   Social Behavior [1967]
R   ↓ Collective Behavior [1967]
    Mass Hysteria [1973]

Content Analysis [1978]
PN   2071   **SC**   11548
SN   Systematic, objective, quantitative or qualitative description of the manifest or latent content of communications.
B   Analysis [1967]
    Methodology [1967]
N   Discourse Analysis [1997]
R   ↓ Communication [1967]

Content Analysis (Test) [1967]
PN   229   **SC**   11550
SN   Systematic examination of a test, primarily to determine whether the test items constitute an adequate sample of the domain or subject matter to be tested.
B   Analysis [1967]
    Test Construction [1973]
    Testing [1967]

Contextual Associations [1967]
PN   4617   **SC**   11560
SN   In learning and memory, associations made to environmental or internal conditions during learning or memorization. In perception and communication, environmental conditions that affect such aspects as perceptual accuracy, comprehension, or meaning.
UF   Associations (Contextual)
B   Associative Processes [1967]
R   Place Conditioning [1991]
    ↓ Priming [1988]
    Semantic Priming [1994]
    Word Frequency [1973]
    Word Meaning [1973]

Contiguity (Cognitive)
Use   Cognitive Contiguity

Contingency Management [1973]
PN   974   **SC**   11580
SN   Behavior modification technique in which the stimuli and reinforcers that control a given behavior are manipulated to increase the likelihood of occurrence of the desired behavior.
B   Behavior Modification [1973]
N   Token Economy Programs [1973]
R   Noncontingent Reinforcement [1988]

Contingent Negative Variation [1982]
PN   267   **SC**   11583
SN   Cortical evoked potential of slow negativity recorded in the period between stimulus-presentation and responses and which is associated with states of attention or expectancy.
UF   Readiness Potential

Contingent Negative Variation — (cont'd)
B   Cortical Evoked Potentials [1973]

Continuing Education [1985]
PN   384   **SC**   11590
SN   Formal or informal courses, educational programs or services, usually at the postsecondary level, designed to advance or update adult learning for personal, academic, or occupational and professional purposes.
B   Adult Education [1973]
N   ↓ Inservice Training [1985]
R   Adult Learning [1997]
    ↓ Higher Education [1973]
    Individualized Instruction [1973]
    Professional Development [1982]
    Reentry Students [1985]

Continuous Reinforcement
Use   Reinforcement Schedules

Contour
Use   Form and Shape Perception

Contour Perception
Use   Form and Shape Perception

Contraception
Use   Birth Control

Contraceptive Devices [1973]
PN   211   **SC**   11630
B   Birth Control [1971]
N   Condoms [1991]
    Diaphragms (Birth Control) [1973]
    Intrauterine Devices [1973]
    Oral Contraceptives [1973]

Control (Emotional)
Use   Emotional Control

Control (Locus of)
Use   Internal External Locus of Control

Control (Self)
Use   Self Control

Control (Social)
Use   Social Control

Control Groups
Use   Experiment Controls

Controls (Instrument)
Use   Instrument Controls

Convergent Thinking
Use   Inductive Deductive Reasoning

Conversation [1973]
PN   2970   **SC**   11710
B   Interpersonal Communication [1973]
    Verbal Communication [1967]
R   Listening (Interpersonal) [1997]

Conversion Disorder [2001]
PN   448   **SC**   11717
SN   In 2000, this term replaced the discontinued term CONVERSION NEUROSIS. CONVERSION NEUROSIS was stripped from all records containing it and replaced with CONVERSION DISORDER.
UF   Conversion Hysteria

Conversion Disorder — (cont'd)
UF   Conversion Neurosis
       Hysterical Neurosis (Conversion)
B   Somatoform Disorders ²⁰⁰¹
N   Hysterical Paralysis ¹⁹⁷³
       Hysterical Vision Disturbances ¹⁹⁷³
       Pseudocyesis ¹⁹⁷³
R   ↓ Defense Mechanisms ¹⁹⁶⁷
       Histrionic Personality Disorder ¹⁹⁹¹
       Hypochondriasis ¹⁹⁷³
   ↓ Hysteria ¹⁹⁶⁷
       Somatization ¹⁹⁹⁴
       Somatoform Pain Disorder ¹⁹⁹⁷

Conversion Hysteria
Use Conversion Disorder

Conversion Neurosis
SN In 2000, the term was discontinued, and all records containing it were stripped of the term and replaced with CONVERSION DISORDER, its postable counterpart.
Use Conversion Disorder

Conviction (Criminal)
Use Criminal Conviction

Convulsions ¹⁹⁶⁷
PN 2368   SC 11750
UF   Seizures
B   Nervous System Disorders ¹⁹⁶⁷
       Symptoms ¹⁹⁶⁷
N   Audiogenic Seizures ¹⁹⁷⁸
R   ↓ Anticonvulsive Drugs ¹⁹⁷³
   ↓ Brain Disorders ¹⁹⁶⁷
   ↓ Epileptic Seizures ¹⁹⁷³
       Experimental Epilepsy ¹⁹⁷⁸
       Hydrocephaly ¹⁹⁷³
   ↓ Spasms ¹⁹⁷³

Cooperating Teachers ¹⁹⁷⁸
PN 122   SC 11756
SN Experienced elementary or secondary teachers employed to supervise student teachers or teacher interns in schools which, although not integral parts of teacher education institutions, provide experiences for the student teachers and teacher interns.
UF   Supervising Teachers
B   Teachers ¹⁹⁶⁷
R   Practicum Supervision ¹⁹⁷⁸
       Student Teachers ¹⁹⁷³
       Student Teaching ¹⁹⁷³
   ↓ Teacher Education ¹⁹⁶⁷

Cooperation ¹⁹⁶⁷
PN 4432   SC 11760
SN Used for human or animal populations.
UF   Collaboration
B   Interpersonal Interaction ¹⁹⁶⁷
       Prosocial Behavior ¹⁹⁸²
R   Agreeableness ¹⁹⁹⁷
       Cooperative Learning ¹⁹⁹⁴

Cooperative Education ¹⁹⁸²
PN 114   SC 11765
SN Combined complementary work and study experience or program coordinated by a teacher and designed by the school and the employer to achieve some occupational goal. Not to be confused with work study programs which serve as means for financial assistance.
B   Vocational Education ¹⁹⁷³
R   Curricular Field Experience ¹⁹⁸²
R   ↓ Educational Programs ¹⁹⁷³

Cooperative Education — (cont'd)
R   ↓ Experiential Learning ¹⁹⁹⁷

Cooperative Learning ¹⁹⁹⁴
PN 554   SC 11766
SN Learning in small groups where cooperation among group members determines rewards and performance.
B   Learning ¹⁹⁶⁷
R   Cooperation ¹⁹⁶⁷
       Group Instruction ¹⁹⁷³
       Individualized Instruction ¹⁹⁷³
       Peer Tutoring ¹⁹⁷³
       School Learning ¹⁹⁶⁷
   ↓ Teaching ¹⁹⁶⁷
   ↓ Teaching Methods ¹⁹⁶⁷
   ↓ Teams ¹⁹⁸⁸

Cooperative Therapy
Use Cotherapy

Coordination (Motor)
Use Motor Coordination

Coordination (Perceptual Motor)
Use Perceptual Motor Coordination

Coping Behavior ¹⁹⁶⁷
PN 16255   SC 11790
SN Use of conscious or unconscious strategies or mechanisms in adapting to stress, various disorders, or environmental demands.
B   Behavior ¹⁹⁶⁷
R   Adaptability (Personality) ¹⁹⁷³
       Adjustment Disorders ¹⁹⁹⁴
       Anosognosia ¹⁹⁹⁴
   ↓ Emotional Adjustment ¹⁹⁷³
   ↓ Emotional Control ¹⁹⁷³
       Hardiness ¹⁹⁹⁷
   ↓ Helplessness ¹⁹⁹⁷
       Illness Behavior ¹⁹⁸²

Copper ¹⁹⁷³
PN 81   SC 11800
B   Metallic Elements ¹⁹⁷³

Coprophagia ²⁰⁰¹
PN 0   SC 11805
SN Eating of feces. Used for both human and animal populations.
UF   Cecotrophy
B   Ingestion ²⁰⁰¹
R   Defecation ¹⁹⁶⁷
   ↓ Eating Disorders ¹⁹⁹⁷
       Fetishism ¹⁹⁷³
       Pica ¹⁹⁷³

Copulation
Use Sexual Intercourse (Human)

Copulation (Animal)
Use Animal Mating Behavior

Cornea ¹⁹⁷³
PN 42   SC 11830
B   Eye (Anatomy) ¹⁹⁶⁷

Coronary Disorders
Use Cardiovascular Disorders

Coronary Heart Disease
Use Heart Disorders

Coronary Prone Behavior ¹⁹⁸²
PN 2231   SC 11855
SN Constellation of behaviors or attitudes constituting a risk factor for coronary heart disease. Traits can include ambition, competitiveness, sense of time urgency, devotion to work over relaxation, positive attitude toward pressure, aggressiveness, impatience, need for recognition, and tendency toward hostility.
UF   Type A Personality
       Type B Personality
B   Behavior ¹⁹⁶⁷
R   At Risk Populations ¹⁹⁸⁵
   ↓ Cardiovascular Disorders ¹⁹⁶⁷
       Illness Behavior ¹⁹⁸²
   ↓ Personality ¹⁹⁶⁷
   ↓ Personality Traits ¹⁹⁶⁷
       Predisposition ¹⁹⁷³
       Stress Reactions ¹⁹⁷³
       Susceptibility (Disorders) ¹⁹⁷³

Coronary Thromboses ¹⁹⁷³
PN 7   SC 11860
B   Heart Disorders ¹⁹⁷³
       Thromboses ¹⁹⁷³
R   Myocardial Infarctions ¹⁹⁷³

Coronary Vessels
Use Arteries (Anatomy)

Corporal Punishment
Use Punishment

Corporations
Use Business Organizations

Corpus Callosum ¹⁹⁷³
PN 720   SC 11900
B   Cerebral Cortex ¹⁹⁶⁷
       Neural Pathways ¹⁹⁸²
R   Commissurotomy ¹⁹⁸⁵
       Interhemispheric Interaction ¹⁹⁸⁵
       Left Brain ¹⁹⁹¹
       Right Brain ¹⁹⁹¹

Corpus Striatum
Use Basal Ganglia

Correctional Institutions ¹⁹⁷³
PN 884   SC 11910
UF   Institutions (Correctional)
N   Prisons ¹⁹⁶⁷
       Reformatories ¹⁹⁷³
R   Halfway Houses ¹⁹⁷³
       Incarceration ¹⁹⁷³
       Institution Visitation ¹⁹⁷³
       Institutional Schools ¹⁹⁷⁸
       Maximum Security Facilities ¹⁹⁸⁵
       Penology ¹⁹⁷³

Corrective Lenses
Use Optical Aids

Correlation (Statistical)
Use Statistical Correlation

Cortex (Auditory)
Use Auditory Cortex

Cortex (Cerebral)
Use Cerebral Cortex

Cortex (Motor)
  Use Motor Cortex

Cortex (Somatosensory)
  Use Somatosensory Cortex

Cortex (Visual)
  Use Visual Cortex

Cortical Atrophy
  Use Cerebral Atrophy

Cortical Evoked Potentials [1973]
PN 1862   **SC** 11980
  B   Electrical Activity [1967]
        Evoked Potentials [1967]
  N   Contingent Negative Variation [1982]
  R   Auditory Evoked Potentials [1973]
        Olfactory Evoked Potentials [1973]
        Somatosensory Evoked Potentials [1973]
        Visual Evoked Potentials [1973]

Corticoids
  Use Corticosteroids

Corticosteroids [1973]
PN 489   **SC** 12000
  UF Adrenal Cortex Steroids
        Corticoids
  B   Steroids [1973]
  N   Aldosterone [1973]
        Corticosterone [1973]
        Cortisone [1973]
        Deoxycorticosterone [1973]
        Hydrocortisone [1973]
        Prednisolone [1973]
  R   ↓ Adrenal Cortex Hormones [1973]

Corticosterone [1973]
PN 1091   **SC** 12010
  B   Adrenal Cortex Hormones [1973]
        Corticosteroids [1973]

Corticotropin [1973]
PN 1367   **SC** 12020
  UF ACTH (Hormone)
        Adrenocorticotropin
  B   Pituitary Hormones [1973]
  R   Corticotropin Releasing Factor [1994]

Corticotropin Releasing Factor [1994]
PN 318   **SC** 12025
  UF ACTH Releasing Factor
  B   Hormones [1967]
        Peptides [1973]
  R   Corticotropin [1973]

Cortisol
  Use Hydrocortisone

Cortisone [1973]
PN 52   **SC** 12040
  B   Adrenal Cortex Hormones [1973]
        Corticosteroids [1973]

Cosmetic Techniques [2001]
PN 0   **SC** 12035
  UF Body Art
        Piercings
  UF Tattoos
  R   ↓ Fads and Fashions [1973]
        Initiation Rites [1973]

Cosmetic Techniques — (cont'd)
  R   ↓ Physical Appearance [1982]
        Plastic Surgery [1973]
        Rites (Nonreligious) [1973]
        Self Mutilation [1973]
        Skin (Anatomy) [1967]
        Subculture (Anthropological) [1973]

Cost Containment [1991]
PN 168   **SC** 12041
SN Policies or procedures to restrain or control expenses in any setting.
  R   Budgets [1997]
        ↓ Case Management [1991]
        ↓ Costs and Cost Analysis [1973]
        Diagnosis Related Groups [1988]
        Economics [1985]
        Fee for Service [1994]
        Health Care Costs [1994]
        ↓ Health Care Services [1978]
        Health Maintenance Organizations [1982]
        ↓ Managed Care [1994]
        Money [1967]
        ↓ Professional Fees [1978]
        Resource Allocation [1997]
        ↓ Treatment [1967]

Cost Effectiveness
  Use Costs and Cost Analysis

Costs and Cost Analysis [1973]
PN 3888   **SC** 12045
SN Applied to any subject and includes prices, expenses, or payments; also attachment of dollar estimates to the costs of an operation and its alternatives.
  UF Cost Effectiveness
        Price
  B   Analysis [1967]
  N   Budgets [1997]
        Health Care Costs [1994]
  R   Cost Containment [1991]
        Economics [1985]
        Economy [1973]
        Funding [1988]
        Money [1967]
        ↓ Professional Fees [1978]
        Resource Allocation [1997]
        Risk Management [1997]

Cotherapy [1982]
PN 192   **SC** 12047
SN Psychotherapeutic process in which a client or a group of clients are treated by more than one therapist. Use CONJOINT THERAPY to access references from 1973-1981.
  UF Cooperative Therapy
        Multiple Therapy
  B   Psychotherapeutic Techniques [1967]
  R   Psychiatric Training [1973]
        ↓ Psychotherapy [1967]
        Psychotherapy Training [1973]

Counselees
  Use Clients

Counseling [1967]
PN 8388   **SC** 12080
SN Conceptually broad term referring to a form of helping process which involves giving advice and information, in order to assist individuals or groups in coping with their problems. Use a more specific term if possible.
  N   Educational Counseling [1967]

Counseling — (cont'd)
  N   Genetic Counseling [1978]
        Group Counseling [1973]
        ↓ Marriage Counseling [1973]
        Microcounseling [1978]
        Occupational Guidance [1967]
        Pastoral Counseling [1967]
        Peer Counseling [1978]
        Premarital Counseling [1973]
        ↓ Psychotherapeutic Counseling [1973]
        Rehabilitation Counseling [1978]
        School Counseling [1982]
  R   Counseling Psychology [1973]
        ↓ Counselors [1967]
        Employee Assistance Programs [1985]
        ↓ Family Therapy [1967]
        Feminist Therapy [1994]
        ↓ Health Care Services [1978]
        ↓ Mental Health Services [1978]
        Social Casework [1967]
        Student Personnel Services [1978]
        ↓ Support Groups [1991]
        ↓ Treatment [1967]

Counseling (Group)
  Use Group Counseling

Counseling Psychologists [1988]
PN 239   **SC** 12065
  B   Psychologists [1967]
  R   Clinicians [1973]
        Counseling Psychology [1973]

Counseling Psychology [1973]
PN 977   **SC** 12070
  B   Applied Psychology [1973]
  R   ↓ Counseling [1907]
        Counseling Psychologists [1988]

Counselor Attitudes [1973]
PN 1123   **SC** 12090
SN Attitudes of, not toward, counselors.
  B   Attitudes [1967]
        Counselor Characteristics [1973]
  R   Counselor Role [1973]
        ↓ Counselors [1967]
        ↓ Health Personnel Attitudes [1985]
        Psychologist Attitudes [1991]

Counselor Characteristics [1973]
PN 2620   **SC** 12100
  UF Counselor Effectiveness
        Counselor Personality
  N   Counselor Attitudes [1973]
  R   ↓ Counselors [1967]

Counselor Client Interaction
  Use Psychotherapeutic Processes

Counselor Education [1973]
PN 3385   **SC** 12120
  B   Education [1967]
  R   ↓ Clinical Methods Training [1973]
        Counselor Trainees [1973]
        Microcounseling [1978]
        Practicum Supervision [1978]
        ↓ Psychology Education [1978]
  R   Psychotherapy Training [1973]
        Rehabilitation Education [1997]

Counselor Effectiveness
  Use Counselor Characteristics

Counselor Personality
Use Counselor Characteristics

Counselor Role 1973
PN 991   SC 12150
UF Role (Counselor)
B Roles 1967
R Counselor Attitudes 1973
↓ Counselors 1967
Therapist Role 1978

Counselor Trainees 1973
PN 1756   SC 12160
R Counselor Education 1973
↓ Counselors 1967
Therapist Trainees 1973

Counselors 1967
PN 2923   SC 12170
B Professional Personnel 1978
N Rehabilitation Counselors 1978
School Counselors 1973
Vocational Counselors 1973
R ↓ Counseling 1967
Counselor Attitudes 1973
↓ Counselor Characteristics 1973
Counselor Role 1973
Counselor Trainees 1973
↓ Health Personnel 1994
↓ Mental Health Personnel 1967
↓ Psychologists 1967
↓ Social Workers 1973
Sociologists 1973
↓ Therapists 1967

Counterconditioning 1973
PN 82   SC 12180
SN Technique used to extinguish a response to a
certain stimulus by conditioning an alternative, often
incompatible response to that stimulus.
B Conditioning 1967
R ↓ Aversion Therapy 1973
↓ Behavior Modification 1973
↓ Behavior Therapy 1967
Reciprocal Inhibition Therapy 1973

Countertransference 1973
PN 2708   SC 12190
SN Conscious or unconscious emotional reaction of
the therapist to the patient which may interfere with
the treatment.
B Psychotherapeutic Processes 1967
R Enactments 1997
Negative Therapeutic Reaction 1997
Professional Client Sexual Relations 1994
Psychotherapeutic Transference 1967

Countries 1967
PN 2047   SC 12195
SN Applies to cross-national studies when individ-
ual countries are not mentioned or are too numerous
to list.
N Developed Countries 1985
Developing Countries 1985
R Geography 1973

County Agricultural Agents
Use Agricultural Extension Workers

Couples 1982
PN 2910   SC 12205
SN Two individuals in an intimate relationship.
R Cohabitation 1973

Couples — (cont'd)
R Dyads 1973
↓ Family 1967
Romance 1997
Significant Others 1991
Social Dating 1973
↓ Spouses 1973

Couples Therapy 1994
PN 678   SC 12207
SN Used specifically for unmarried couples. Use
MARRIAGE COUNSELING for married couples.
R Conjoint Therapy 1973
↓ Marriage Counseling 1973
↓ Psychotherapy 1967
Sex Therapy 1978

Courage 1973
PN 69   SC 12210
UF Bravery
B Personality Traits 1967

Course Evaluation 1978
PN 483   SC 12215
SN Procedures, materials, or the process involved
in the assessment of quality or effectiveness of an
academic or vocational course or program by its stu-
dents or participants. Evaluation may include con-
tent, structure, or method of material presentation.
B Evaluation 1967
R ↓ Curriculum 1967
Educational Program Evaluation 1973
Educational Quality 1997
Teacher Effectiveness Evaluation 1978
↓ Teaching 1967

Course Objectives
Use Educational Objectives

Course of Illness
Use Disease Course

Court Ordered Treatment
Use Court Referrals

Court Referrals 1994
PN 163   SC 12219
SN Court ordered assessment, treatment, consulta-
tion, or other services for defendants, plaintiffs, or
criminals.
UF Court Ordered Treatment
B Adjudication 1967
R ↓ Commitment (Psychiatric) 1973
↓ Criminal Justice 1991
↓ Criminals 1967
Defendants 1985
Forensic Evaluation 1994
Insanity Defense 1985
Involuntary Treatment 1994
Mediation 1988
Mentally Ill Offenders 1985
Probation 1973
Professional Referral 1973
↓ Treatment 1967

Courts
Use Adjudication

Courtship (Animal)
Use Animal Courtship Behavior

Courtship (Human)
Use Human Courtship

Courtship Displays (Animal)
Use Animal Courtship Displays

Cousins 1973
PN 17   SC 12260
B Family Members 1973

Covert Sensitization 1988
PN 32   SC 12265
SN Form of aversion conditioning in which noxious
mental images, thoughts, or feelings are associated
with undesirable behavior by verbal cues. Frequently
used in therapeutic settings.
B Aversion Conditioning 1982
Aversion Therapy 1973
R Aversive Stimulation 1973

Cows
Use Cattle

Coyotes
Use Canids

Crabs 1973
PN 291   SC 12300
B Crustacea 1973

Crafts 1973
PN 43   SC 12310
UF Handicrafts
B Art 1967

Cramps (Muscle)
Use Muscular Disorders

Cranial Nerves 1973
PN 131   SC 12330
UF Accessory Nerve
Glossopharyngeal Nerve
Hypoglossal Nerve
Nerve (Accessory)
Nerves (Cranial)
Oculomotor Nerve
Trochlear Nerve
B Peripheral Nervous System 1973
N Abducens Nerve 1973
Acoustic Nerve 1973
Facial Nerve 1973
Olfactory Nerve 1973
Optic Nerve 1973
Trigeminal Nerve 1973
Vagus Nerve 1973

Cranial Spinal Cord 1973
PN 4   SC 12340
B Spinal Cord 1973

Craving 1997
PN 239   SC 12350
R ↓ Addiction 1973
↓ Appetite 1973
↓ Drug Abuse 1973
↓ Drug Usage 1971
↓ Emotional States 1973
Food 1978
↓ Needs 1967

Crayfish 1973
PN 112   SC 12360

Crayfish — (cont'd)
B   Crustacea   1973

Creative Arts Therapy   1994
PN 129   **SC** 12365
SN Therapeutic use of the arts in medicine, mental health, or education.
B   Treatment   1967
N   Art Therapy   1973
     Dance Therapy   1973
     Music Therapy   1973
     Poetry Therapy   1994
     Recreation Therapy   1973
R   Movement Therapy   1997
     ↓ Psychotherapeutic Techniques   1967

Creative Writing   1994
PN 225   **SC** 12370
SN Use LITERATURE to access references from 1973-1993.
UF   Writing (Creative)
B   Written Communication   1985
R   ↓ Literature   1967
     Narratives   1997
     Poetry   1973
     ↓ Prose   1973
     Rhetoric   1991
     Storytelling   1988

Creativity   1967
PN 7994   **SC** 12380
SN Ability to perceive new relationships, and to derive new ideas and solve problems by pursuing nontraditional patterns of thinking. Compare DIVERGENT THINKING.
UF   Innovativeness
     Originality
B   Personality Traits   1967
R   ↓ Ability   1967
     ↓ Artistic Ability   1973
     Divergent Thinking   1973
     Gifted   1967
     Intelligence   1967
     Openness to Experience   1997

Creativity Measurement   1973
PN 393   **SC** 12390
B   Measurement   1967

Credibility   1973
PN 877   **SC** 12400
R   ↓ Interpersonal Communication   1973
     Reputation   1997
     ↓ Social Perception   1967

Creutzfeldt Jakob Syndrome   1994
PN 67   **SC** 12410
B   Encephalopathies   1982
     Presenile Dementia   1973
     Syndromes   1973
     Viral Disorders   1973
R   ↓ Dementia   1985

Cri du Chat Syndrome
Use   Crying Cat Syndrome

Crib Death
Use   Sudden Infant Death

Crime   1967
PN 4985   **SC** 12430
UF   Felonies
UF   Misdemeanors

Crime — (cont'd)
B   Antisocial Behavior   1971
     Social Issues   1991
N   Arson   1985
     ↓ Child Abuse   1971
     Driving Under The Influence   1988
     Drug Distribution   1997
     Kidnapping   1988
     ↓ Sex Offenses   1982
     ↓ Theft   1973
     Vandalism   1978
R   ↓ Behavior Disorders   1971
     ↓ Behavior Problems   1967
     Crime Prevention   1985
     ↓ Crime Victims   1982
     ↓ Criminal Justice   1991
     Criminal Responsibility   1991
     ↓ Criminals   1967
     Fraud   1994
     Informants   1988
     ↓ Perpetrators   1988
     Self Defense   1985
     Stalking   2001
     Terrorism   1982
     Victimization   1973

Crime Prevention   1985
PN 626   **SC** 12432
SN Measures aimed at deterring the occurrence of crime or delinquent behavior.
B   Prevention   1973
R   ↓ Crime   1967
     ↓ Criminal Justice   1991
     ↓ Juvenile Delinquency   1967
     ↓ Law Enforcement   1978

Crime Victims   1982
PN 1325   **SC** 12434
SN Individuals subjected to and adversely affected by criminal activity. Use VICTIMIZATION to access references from 1973-1981.
N   Hostages   1988
R   ↓ Crime   1967
     Self Defense   1985
     Victimization   1973

Criminal Conviction   1973
PN 429   **SC** 12440
SN Declaration made by a court finding a person guilty and responsible for a criminal offense.
UF   Conviction (Criminal)
B   Criminal Justice   1991
R   ↓ Adjudication   1967
     ↓ Criminals   1967
     Legal Decisions   1991

Criminal Interrogation
Use   Legal Interrogation

Criminal Justice   1991
PN 791   **SC** 12445
SN Used for the system, discipline, or the actual process itself.
B   Justice   1973
     Legal Processes   1973
N   Criminal Conviction   1973
R   ↓ Adjudication   1967
     Court Referrals   1994
     ↓ Crime   1967
     Crime Prevention   1985
     Criminal Law   1973
     Forensic Psychiatry   1973
     Forensic Psychology   1985
     ↓ Law Enforcement   1978

Criminal Justice — (cont'd)
R   Legal Decisions   1991
     Penology   1973

Criminal Law   1973
PN 381   **SC** 12450
B   Law (Government)   1973
R   ↓ Criminal Justice   1991

Criminal Responsibility   1991
PN 268   **SC** 12453
SN State of mind that permits one to be held accountable for criminal acts.
B   Responsibility   1973
R   Accountability   1988
     ↓ Adjudication   1967
     Competency to Stand Trial   1985
     ↓ Crime   1967
     ↓ Criminals   1967
     Defendants   1985
     Insanity Defense   1985
     ↓ Perpetrators   1988

Criminally Insane
Use   Mentally Ill Offenders

Criminals   1967
PN 3807   **SC** 12460
UF   Offenders (Adult)
B   Perpetrators   1988
N   Female Criminals   1973
     Male Criminals   1973
     Mentally Ill Offenders   1985
R   Antisocial Personality   1973
     Court Referrals   1994
     ↓ Crime   1967
     Criminal Conviction   1973
     Criminal Responsibility   1991
     Defendants   1985
     Forensic Evaluation   1994
     ↓ Juvenile Delinquency   1967
     ↓ Prisoners   1967
     Recidivism   1973

Criminology   1973
PN 350   **SC** 12470
R   Penology   1973

Crises   1971
PN 918   **SC** 12490
N   Family Crises   1973
     Identity Crisis   1973
     Organizational Crises   1973
R   ↓ Crisis Intervention   1973
     ↓ Crisis Intervention Services   1973
     ↓ Disasters   1973
     ↓ Experiences (Events)   1973
     ↓ Stress   1967

Crisis (Reactions to)
Use   Stress Reactions

Crisis Intervention   1973
PN 1490   **SC** 12510
SN Brief therapeutic approach which is ameliorative rather than curative of acute psychiatric emergencies. Used in such contexts as emergency rooms of psychiatric or general hospitals, or in the home or place of crisis occurrence, this treatment approach focuses on interpersonal and intrapsychic factors and environmental modification of behavior.
B   Treatment   1967
N   Suicide Prevention   1973

Crisis Intervention — (cont'd)
R ↓ Crises 1971
    ↓ Crisis Intervention Services 1973

Crisis Intervention Services 1973
PN 598   SC 12520
SN Community organizations, programs, or mental health personnel which provide crisis care.
B Community Services 1967
    Mental Health Programs 1973
    Treatment 1967
N Hot Line Services 1973
    Suicide Prevention Centers 1973
R ↓ Clinics 1967
    Community Mental Health Centers 1973
    ↓ Crises 1971
    ↓ Crisis Intervention 1973
    Emergency Services 1973
    ↓ Treatment Facilities 1973
    Walk In Clinics 1973

Criterion Referenced Tests 1982
PN 303   SC 12525
SN Tests in which scores are measured against explicitly stated objectives rather than a group norm.
UF Mastery Tests
    Objective Referenced Tests
B Measurement 1967
R ↓ Achievement Measures 1967
    Performance Tests 1973

Critical Flicker Fusion Threshold 1967
PN 397   SC 12530
UF Flicker Fusion Frequency
B Visual Thresholds 1973
R ↓ Perceptual Measures 1973

Critical Period 1988
PN 70   SC 12533
R ↓ Development 1967
    Imprinting 1967

Critical Scores
Use Cutting Scores

Criticism 1973
PN 352   SC 12540
B Social Behavior 1967
    Social Influences 1967
R Social Approval 1967

Crocodilians 1973
PN 22   SC 12570
UF Alligators
B Reptiles 1967

Cross Cultural Communication 1997
PN 226   SC 12580
UF Intercultural Communication
    Interethnic Communication
B Interpersonal Communication 1973
R Bilingualism 1973
    Cross Cultural Differences 1967
    Cross Cultural Psychology 1997
    Cross Cultural Treatment 1994
    Cultural Assimilation 1973
    Cultural Sensitivity 1994
    Multicultural Education 1988
    Multiculturalism 1997
    Racial and Ethnic Differences 1982
    ↓ Racial and Ethnic Groups 2001

Cross Cultural Communication — (cont'd)
R Racial and Ethnic Relations 1982

Cross Cultural Differences 1967
PN 15428   SC 12590
SN Used for comparisons between populations with different psychological, sociological, or cultural mores. Used for comparisons both within and across countries. Compare REGIONAL DIFFERENCE and RACIAL AND ETHNIC DIFFERENCES.
UF Cultural Differences
B Sociocultural Factors 1967
R Cross Cultural Communication 1997
    Cross Cultural Psychology 1997
    Cross Cultural Treatment 1994
    Cultural Sensitivity 1994
    Ethnology 1967
    Multiculturalism 1997
    Racial and Ethnic Differences 1982
    ↓ Racial and Ethnic Groups 2001
    Regional Differences 2001

Cross Cultural Psychology 1997
PN 282   SC 12591
SN Branch of psychology that studies members of various cultural groups and their specific cultural experiences resulting in similarities and differences in human behavior.
B Psychology 1967
R Cross Cultural Communication 1997
    Cross Cultural Differences 1967
    Cultural Assimilation 1973
    ↓ Culture (Anthropological) 1967
    Ethnocentrism 1973
    Ethnology 1967
    ↓ Ethnospecific Disorders 1973
    Racial and Ethnic Differences 1982
    ↓ Racial and Ethnic Groups 2001
    ↓ Sociocultural Factors 1967
    Transcultural Psychiatry 1973

Cross Cultural Treatment 1994
PN 771   SC 12593
SN Treatment, in any context, where the racial, ethnic, or cultural background of the patient or client is different from that of the health care provider, e.g., therapist, counselor, or physician. Used primarily when the cultural or racial aspects of the treatment paradigm are the major focus.
B Treatment 1967
R ↓ Client Characteristics 1973
    Cross Cultural Communication 1997
    Cross Cultural Differences 1967
    Cultural Sensitivity 1994
    Racial and Ethnic Differences 1982
    ↓ Racial and Ethnic Groups 2001
    ↓ Therapist Characteristics 1973
    Transcultural Psychiatry 1973

Cross Disciplinary Research
Use Interdisciplinary Research

Crossed Eyes
Use Strabismus

Crowding 1978
PN 502   SC 12610
SN Conditions of high population density for a given area. Used for animal or human populations.
R Environmental Stress 1973
    Overpopulation 1973
    Personal Space 1973
    Social Density 1978

CRT
Use Video Display Units

Cruelty 1973
PN 58   SC 12620
B Antisocial Behavior 1971
    Personality Traits 1967
R ↓ Aggressive Behavior 1967

Crustacea 1973
PN 316   SC 12630
B Arthropoda 1973
N Crabs 1973
    Crayfish 1973

Crying 1973
PN 538   SC 12640
B Vocalization 1967
    Voice 1973
R Infant Vocalization 1973

Crying Cat Syndrome 1973
PN 26   SC 12650
UF Cri du Chat Syndrome
B Autosome Disorders 1973
    Mental Retardation 1967
    Neonatal Disorders 1973
    Syndromes 1973

Cuban Americans
Use Hispanics

Cued Recall 1994
PN 328   SC 12678
B Recall (Learning) 1967
R Cues 1967
    Forgetting 1973
    Free Recall 1973
    ↓ Memory 1967
    ↓ Prompting 1997

Cues 1967
PN 8007   SC 12680
SN Internal or external verbal or nonverbal signals which influence learning, performance, or behavior. Cues are often only obscure secondary stimuli which, though not fully detected, serve to facilitate learning, performance, or behavior. Compare CONDITIONED STIMULUS.
R ↓ Associative Processes 1967
    Cued Recall 1994
    Isolation Effect 1973
    ↓ Memory 1967
    Mnemonic Learning 1973
    ↓ Priming 1988
    ↓ Prompting 1997
    Semantic Priming 1994

Cultism 1973
PN 554   SC 12690
R Ethnology 1967
    Myths 1967
    Occultism 1978
    ↓ Religious Beliefs 1973
    Religious Experiences 1997
    Shamanism 1973
    ↓ Sociocultural Factors 1967

Cultural Assimilation 1973
PN 2642   SC 12700

Cultural Assimilation — (cont'd)

SN Contact of at least two autonomous cultural groups resulting in change in one or the other, or both groups. Includes the process of a minority group giving up its own cultural traits and absorbing those of a dominant society. In 1982, this term replaced the discontinued term ACCULTURATION. In 2000, ACCULTURATION was stripped from all records and replaced with CULTURAL ASSIMILATION.

UF Acculturation
     Assimilation (Cultural)
B Culture Change   1967
R Cross Cultural Communication   1997
     Cross Cultural Psychology   1997
     Cultural Sensitivity   1994
     Multiculturalism   1997

Cultural Deprivation   1973

PN 201   **SC** 12710
SN Inability of individuals to participate in their society's cultural achievements because of poverty, social discrimination, or other disadvantage. Consider also SOCIAL DEPRIVATION.

UF Culturally Disadvantaged
B Deprivation   1967
     Sociocultural Factors   1967
R Disadvantaged   1967
     Multiculturalism   1997
     Poverty Areas   1973
     ↓ Social Deprivation   1973
     ↓ Social Environments   1973

Cultural Differences

Use Cross Cultural Differences

Cultural Factors

Use Sociocultural Factors

Cultural Familial Mental Retardation

Use Psychosocial Mental Retardation

Cultural Pluralism

Use Multiculturalism

Cultural Psychiatry

Use Transcultural Psychiatry

Cultural Sensitivity   1994

PN 1240   **SC** 12728
SN Awareness and appreciation of the values, norms, and beliefs unique to a particular cultural, minority, ethnic, or racial group.

UF Ethnic Sensitivity
R Cross Cultural Communication   1997
     Cross Cultural Differences   1967
     Cross Cultural Treatment   1994
     Cultural Assimilation   1973
     ↓ Culture (Anthropological)   1967
     Ethnic Identity   1973
     Ethnic Values   1973
     Minority Groups   1967
     Multicultural Education   1988
     Multiculturalism   1997
     ↓ Racial and Ethnic Attitudes   1982
     Racial and Ethnic Differences   1982
     ↓ Racial and Ethnic Groups   2001
     Racial and Ethnic Relations   1982
     Sensitivity Training   1973
     ↓ Sociocultural Factors   1967

Cultural Test Bias   1973

PN 784   **SC** 12730

Cultural Test Bias — (cont'd)

SN Any significant differential performance on tests by different populations (e.g., Hispanics vs Blacks) as a result of test characteristics that are sensitive to cultural, subcultural, racial, or ethnic factors but which are irrelevant to the variable or construct being measured.

UF Test Bias (Cultural)
B Test Bias   1985
R Response Bias   1967
     Test Interpretation   1985

Culturally Disadvantaged

Use Cultural Deprivation

Culture (Anthropological)   1967

PN 5888   **SC** 12750
N ↓ Society   1967
     Subculture (Anthropological)   1973
R Cross Cultural Psychology   1997
     Cultural Sensitivity   1994
     Ethnology   1967
     ↓ Family Structure   1973
     Multiculturalism   1997
     ↓ Racial and Ethnic Groups   2001
     ↓ Sociocultural Factors   1967

Culture Change   1967

PN 495   **SC** 12760
SN Modification in behavior, values, customs, or artifacts over time or as the result of migration to a different cultural environment.

B Sociocultural Factors   1967
N Cultural Assimilation   1973
R Culture Shock   1973
     Ethnology   1967
     Multiculturalism   1997

Culture Fair Intelligence Test   1973

PN 32   **SC** 12770
UF Cattell Culture Fair Intelligence Test
B Intelligence Measures   1967

Culture Shock   1973

PN 182   **SC** 12780
SN Social, psychological, or emotional difficulties in adapting to a new culture or similar difficulties in adapting to one's own culture as the result of rapid social or cultural changes.

R ↓ Culture Change   1967
     Ethnology   1967

Curare   1973

PN 27   **SC** 12790
B Muscle Relaxing Drugs   1973
R ↓ Alkaloids   1973
     Tubocurarine   1973

Curiosity   1967

PN 304   **SC** 12800
UF Inquisitiveness
B Personality Traits   1967
R ↓ Exploratory Behavior   1967
     Openness to Experience   1997
     Questioning   1982

Curricular Field Experience   1982

PN 339   **SC** 12805
SN Organizationally or institutionally supervised educational activities, restricted primarily to high school and college, usually undertaken outside the classroom or campus in order to promote practical experience in a specific discipline.

UF Field Instruction

Curricular Field Experience — (cont'd)

UF Field Work (Educational)
B Experiential Learning   1997
R Cooperative Education   1982
     ↓ Curriculum   1967
     Educational Field Trips   1973
     ↓ Educational Programs   1973
     ↓ Practice   1967

Curriculum   1967

PN 6647   **SC** 12810
SN Set of courses constituting a framework for education in a given subject area.

B Education   1967
N Affective Education   1982
     Art Education   1973
     Braille Instruction   1973
     Business Education   1973
     Career Education   1978
     Compensatory Education   1973
     Computer Training   1994
     Driver Education   1973
     Foreign Language Education   1973
     ↓ Health Education   1973
     Home Economics   1985
     ↓ Language Arts Education   1973
     Mathematics Education   1973
     Music Education   1973
     Physical Education   1967
     ↓ Psychology Education   1978
     Science Education   1973
     Social Studies Education   1978
     ↓ Vocational Education   1973
R Course Evaluation   1978
     Curricular Field Experience   1982
     Curriculum Based Assessment   1994
     Curriculum Development   1973
     Educational Objectives   1978
     Educational Program Accreditation   1994
     Home Schooling   1994
     ↓ Nontraditional Education   1982

Curriculum Based Assessment   1994

PN 128   **SC** 12815
B Educational Measurement   1967
R ↓ Curriculum   1967

Curriculum Development   1973

PN 2439   **SC** 12820
SN Initiating, designing, implementing, and testing of activities designed to create new curricula or to change existing ones.

B Development   1967
R ↓ Curriculum   1967
     Educational Program Planning   1973
     ↓ Program Development   1991

Cursive Writing   1973

PN 62   **SC** 12830
UF Writing (Cursive)
B Handwriting   1967
R Orthography   1973

Cushings Syndrome   1973

PN 80   **SC** 12840
B Adrenal Gland Disorders   1973
     Metabolism Disorders   1973
     Syndromes   1973

Customer Satisfaction

Use Consumer Satisfaction

Cutaneous Receptive Fields 1985
PN 59   SC 12845
SN The area of skin being supplied by specific peripheral nerves and localized synaptic distribution in the CNS.
UF Dermatomes
B   Receptive Fields 1985

Cutaneous Sense 1967
PN 1311   SC 12850
SN Any of the senses, such as pressure, pain, warmth, cold, and touch, whose receptors lie within or beneath the skin or in the mucous membrane.
UF Haptic Perception
B   Somesthetic Perception 1967
N   ↓ Tactual Perception 1967

Cutting Scores 1985
PN 102   SC 12855
SN Points at which a continuum of scores may be divided into groups for such purposes as pass/fail decisions or test interpretations.
UF Critical Scores
B   Scoring (Testing) 1973
    Test Scores 1967
R   Score Equating 1985
    Test Interpretation 1985

Cybernetics 1967
PN 462   SC 12860
SN Study of control and communication between humans, machines, animals, and organizations and the parallels between information processing machines and human or animal intellectual or brain function.
R   ↓ Artificial Intelligence 1982
    Communication Theory 1973
    ↓ Computers 1967
    ↓ Expert Systems 1991
    Human Machine Systems 1997
    Robotics 1985

Cyclic Adenosine Monophosphate 1978
PN 246   SC 12875
B   Nucleotides 1978
R   Guanosine 1985

Cycloheximide 1973
PN 155   SC 12880
B   Antibiotics 1973

Cyclothymic Disorder
Use Cyclothymic Personality

Cyclothymic Personality 1973
PN 107   SC 12890
SN Affective disorder characterized by alternating and recurring periods of depression and elation, similar to manic depressive disorder but of a less severe nature.
UF Cyclothymic Disorder
B   Bipolar Disorder 2001
R   Hypomania 1973

Cynicism 1973
PN 121   SC 12900
B   Personality Traits 1967
R   Agreeableness 1997
    Fatalism 1973
    Hopelessness 1988
    Negativism 1973
    Pessimism 1973

Cysteine 1973
PN 21   SC 12910
B   Amino Acids 1973

Cystic Fibrosis 1985
PN 264   SC 12915
B   Digestive System Disorders 1973
    Lung Disorders 1973
    Metabolism Disorders 1973
R   ↓ Congenital Disorders 1973

Cytochrome Oxidase 1973
PN 80   SC 12920
B   Oxidases 1973

Cytology 1973
PN 116   SC 12930
R   ↓ Cells (Biology) 1973

Cytoplasm 1973
PN 17   SC 12940
R   ↓ Cells (Biology) 1973

Daily Activities 1994
PN 510   SC 12955
SN Daily patterns of behavior that are not reflective of functional ability. Compare ACTIVITIES OF DAILY LIVING.
R   Activities of Daily Living 1991
    Activity Level 1982
    Hobbies 1988
    ↓ Interests 1967
    Leisure Time 1973
    ↓ Lifestyle 1978
    ↓ Recreation 1967
    Self Care Skills 1978

Daily Biological Rhythms (Animal)
Use Animal Circadian Rhythms

Dance 1973
PN 334   SC 12970
UF Ballet
B   Arts 1973
    Recreation 1967
R   Dance Therapy 1973

Dance Therapy 1973
PN 279   SC 12980
B   Creative Arts Therapy 1994
R   Dance 1973
    Movement Therapy 1997
    Recreation Therapy 1973

Dangerousness 1988
PN 546   SC 12985
R   Patient Violence 1994
    ↓ Violence 1973

Dark Adaptation 1973
PN 410   SC 12990
UF Adaptation (Dark)
B   Sensory Adaptation 1967
    Visual Perception 1967
R   Light Adaptation 1982
    ↓ Perceptual Measures 1973
    ↓ Visual Thresholds 1973

Darwinism 1973
PN 297   SC 13000

Darwinism — (cont'd)
SN Biological theory of evolution formulated by C. Darwin, including the fundamental tenet of natural selection as the operating principle of organic change.
B   Theories 1967
N   Natural Selection 1997
R   Theory of Evolution 1967

Data Collection 1982
PN 1539   SC 13005
SN Systematic accumulation, generation, or assembly of information. Compare EXPERIMENTAL METHODS.
B   Methodology 1967
R   ↓ Computer Peripheral Devices 1985
    ↓ Data Processing 1967
    Information 1967
    ↓ Medical Records 1978
    ↓ Sampling (Experimental) 1973
    Statistical Data 1982
    ↓ Statistical Measurement 1973
    ↓ Surveys 1967

Data Pooling
Use Meta Analysis

Data Processing 1967
PN 315   SC 13020
N   Word Processing 1991
R   ↓ Automated Information Processing 1973
    Computer Programming 2001
    Computer Programming Languages 1973
    ↓ Computer Software 1967
    ↓ Computers 1967
    Data Collection 1982
    ↓ Expert Systems 1991
    Information 1967
    ↓ Information Systems 1991
    ↓ Medical Records 1978

Databases 1991
PN 381   SC 13024
SN Collection of computerized data stored in a computer or on magnetic tape or disks from which information can be accessed and retrieved.
UF Computerized Databases
    Online Databases
R   ↓ Automated Information Retrieval 1973
    Automated Information Storage 1973
    ↓ Computer Applications 1973
    Computer Searching 1991
    ↓ Computer Software 1967
    ↓ Computers 1967
    Decision Support Systems 1997
    Electronic Communication 2001
    ↓ Expert Systems 1991
    Human Machine Systems 1997
    Information 1967
    Information Services 1988
    ↓ Information Systems 1991

Date Rape
Use Acquaintance Rape

Dating (Social)
Use Social Dating

Daughters 1973
PN 1502   SC 13040
B   Family Members 1973
    Human Females 1973
    Offspring 1988

Day Camps (Recreation)
Use Summer Camps (Recreation)

Day Care (Child)
Use Child Day Care

Day Care (Treatment)
Use Partial Hospitalization

Day Care Centers 1973
PN 588　　　　**SC** 13070
SN Facilities for day care of individuals of any age.
　R Adult Day Care 1997
　　Child Care Workers 1978
　　Child Day Care 1973
　　↓ Community Facilities 1973
　　Community Mental Health Centers 1973

Day Hospital
Use Partial Hospitalization

Daydreaming 1973
PN 281　　　　**SC** 13080
　R ↓ Fantasy 1997
　　Fantasy (Defense Mechanism) 1967

DDT (Insecticide) 1973
PN 7　　　　**SC** 13090
　B Insecticides 1973

Deaf 1967
PN 4909　　　　**SC** 13100
SN Profoundly or severely hearing impaired. Consider also PARTIALLY HEARING IMPAIRED for severely hearing impaired.
　N Deaf Blind 1991
　R Cochlear Implants 1994
　　Hearing Disorders 1982
　　Lipreading 1973
　　Partially Hearing Impaired 1973

Deaf Blind 1991
PN 87　　　　**SC** 13103
　B Blind 1967
　　Deaf 1967
　　Multiple Disabilities 2001
　R ↓ Congenital Disorders 1973
　　Developmental Disabilities 1982

Deanol
SN Term was discontinued in 1997. In 2000, the term was stripped from all records containing it, and replaced with ANTIDEPRESSANT DRUGS, its postable counterpart.
Use Antidepressant Drugs

Death and Dying 1967
PN 6577　　　　**SC** 13110
　UF Dying
　　Mortality
　N Euthanasia 1973
　R Advance Directives 1994
　　Assisted Suicide 1997
　　Death Anxiety 1978
　　Death Attitudes 1973
　　Death Education 1982
　　Death Rites 1973
　　Grief 1973
　　Mortality Rate 1973
　　Near Death Experiences 1985
　　Palliative Care 1991
　　Psychological Autopsy 1988
　　Sudden Infant Death 1982

Death and Dying — (cont'd)
　R ↓ Suicide 1967
　　Terminal Cancer 1973
　　Terminally Ill Patients 1973
　　Treatment Withholding 1988

Death Anxiety 1978
PN 873　　　　**SC** 13115
　B Anxiety Disorders 1997
　R Death Attitudes 1973
　　↓ Death and Dying 1967

Death Attitudes 1973
PN 1787　　　　**SC** 13120
　B Attitudes 1967
　R Death Anxiety 1978
　　↓ Death and Dying 1967
　　Euthanasia 1973
　　↓ Religious Beliefs 1973

Death Education 1982
PN 315　　　　**SC** 13124
SN Education in the process of death and dying. Applies to patients or students of any age including helping professionals.
　UF Thanatology
　B Education 1967
　R ↓ Death and Dying 1967
　　↓ Treatment 1967

Death Instinct 1988
PN 189　　　　**SC** 13127
　UF Thanatos
　B Psychoanalytic Personality Factors 1973
　R Self Preservation 1997
　　Unconscious (Personality Factor) 1967

Death Penalty
Use Capital Punishment

Death Rate
Use Mortality Rate

Death Rites 1973
PN 158　　　　**SC** 13150
　UF Funerals
　B Rites of Passage 1973
　R ↓ Death and Dying 1967

Debates 1997
PN 48　　　　**SC** 13153
　UF Political Debates
　　Presidential Debates
　R Arguments 1973
　　Group Discussion 1967
　　↓ Persuasive Communication 1967
　　Political Campaigns 1973
　　Political Candidates 1973
　　Political Elections 1973
　　↓ Political Processes 1973
　　Public Speaking 1973
　　Rhetoric 1991

Debriefing (Experimental) 1991
PN 20　　　　**SC** 13154
SN At the conclusion of an experiment, the process that removes any deception and discloses the facts to subjects participating in the research by giving full details of the research purpose and procedures.
　UF Disclosure (Experimental)
　R ↓ Experimental Design 1967
　　Experimental Ethics 1978
　　↓ Experimental Subjects 1985

Debriefing (Experimental) — (cont'd)
　R ↓ Experimentation 1967
　　Informed Consent 1985

Decarboxylase Inhibitors 1982
PN 52　　　　**SC** 13157
　B Enzyme Inhibitors 1985
　N Carbidopa 1988
　R ↓ Antitremor Drugs 1973
　　↓ Catecholamines 1973
　　↓ Dopamine Antagonists 1982
　　↓ Enzymes 1973
　　↓ Serotonin Antagonists 1973

Decarboxylases 1973
PN 75　　　　**SC** 13160
　B Enzymes 1973

Decentralization 1978
PN 67　　　　**SC** 13166
SN Process of distributing or allocating administrative control over organizational functions to authorities that are more local.
　R Educational Administration 1967
　　Hospital Administration 1978
　　↓ Organizational Change 1973
　　Organizational Development 1973
　　Organizational Objectives 1973
　　Organizational Structure 1967

Deception 1967
PN 1928　　　　**SC** 13170
　UF Lying
　N Cheating 1973
　　Confabulation 1973
　　Faking 1973
　　Fraud 1994
　　Malingering 1973
　R Dishonesty 1973
　　Secrecy 1994
　　Sincerity 1973

Decerebration 1973
PN 120　　　　**SC** 13180
SN Elimination of cerebral functioning by transecting the brain stem or by cutting off the cerebral blood supply.
　B Neurosurgery 1973
　R ↓ Brain Lesions 1967

Decision Making 1967
PN 12599　　　　**SC** 13190
SN Cognitive process involving evaluation of the incentives, goals, and outcomes of alternative actions.
　B Cognitive Processes 1967
　N Choice Behavior 1967
　　↓ Group Decision Making 1978
　　Management Decision Making 1973
　R Decision Support Systems 1997
　　↓ Expert Systems 1991
　　↓ Judgment 1967
　　↓ Problem Solving 1967
　　Risk Analysis 1991
　　Uncertainty 1991
　　Volition 1988

Decision Support Systems 1997
PN 133　　　　**SC** 13193
SN Computer-based planning and decision making systems that provide data on the outcomes or results of alternative decision choices.
　B Computer Software 1967
　　Expert Systems 1991

Decision Support Systems — (cont'd)
R ↓ Artificial Intelligence [1982]
　 ↓ Computer Applications [1973]
　 ↓ Computer Simulation [1973]
　 Databases [1991]
　 ↓ Decision Making [1967]
　 ↓ Information Systems [1991]

Declarative Knowledge [1997]
PN 176　　　　　　　　　　SC 13194
SN Knowledge about "how" and "what" things are, which can be modified due to new experiences or internal thought processes. Compare PROCEDURAL KNOWLEDGE.
UF Factual Knowledge
R ↓ Cognitive Processes [1967]
　 Divergent Thinking [1973]
　 Information [1967]
　 ↓ Knowledge Level [1978]
　 ↓ Memory [1967]
　 Metacognition [1991]
　 ↓ Problem Solving [1967]
　 Procedural Knowledge [1997]
　 ↓ Reasoning [1967]

Decoding
Use Human Information Storage

Decompression Effects [1973]
PN 34　　　　　　　　　　SC 13200
R 　Acceleration Effects [1973]
　 ↓ Gravitational Effects [1967]
　 Physiological Stress [1967]
　 Spaceflight [1967]
　 Underwater Effects [1973]

Decortication (Brain) [1973]
PN 124　　　　　　　　　　SC 13210
SN Functional deactivation or physical removal of all or portions of the cortical substance of the brain. Primarily used for experimental contexts.
B 　Neurosurgery [1973]
R ↓ Brain Lesions [1967]

Deductive Reasoning
Use Inductive Deductive Reasoning

Deer [1973]
PN 213　　　　　　　　　　SC 13230
B 　Mammals [1973]

Defecation [1967]
PN 227　　　　　　　　　　SC 13240
B 　Excretion [1967]
R 　Coprophagia [2001]

Defendants [1985]
PN 410　　　　　　　　　　SC 13245
SN Persons who are being sued or prosecuted in a court of law.
R 　Court Referrals [1994]
　 Criminal Responsibility [1991]
　 ↓ Criminals [1967]
　 ↓ Law (Government) [1973]

Defense Mechanisms [1967]
PN 2964　　　　　　　　　　SC 13250
SN Any intrapsychic strategies that serve to provide relief from emotional conflict or frustration or from unreasonable or undesirable thoughts which lead to anxiety, distress, or depression.
B 　Personality Processes [1967]
N 　Compensation (Defense Mechanism) [1973]

Defense Mechanisms — (cont'd)
N 　Denial [1973]
　 Displacement (Defense Mechanism) [1973]
　 Fantasy (Defense Mechanism) [1967]
　 Grandiosity [1994]
　 Identification (Defense Mechanism) [1973]
　 Intellectualization [1973]
　 Introjection [1973]
　 Isolation (Defense Mechanism) [1973]
　 Projection (Defense Mechanism) [1967]
　 Projective Identification [1994]
　 Rationalization [1973]
　 Reaction Formation [1973]
　 Regression (Defense Mechanism) [1967]
　 Repression (Defense Mechanism) [1967]
　 Sublimation [1973]
　 Suppression (Defense Mechanism) [1973]
　 Withdrawal (Defense Mechanism) [1973]
R ↓ Conversion Disorder [2001]
　 Externalization [1973]
　 ↓ Internalization [1997]
　 ↓ Mental Disorders [1967]
　 ↓ Personality Disorders [1967]
　 Psychopathology [1967]

Defensive Behavior (Animal)
Use Animal Defensive Behavior

Defensiveness [1967]
PN 502　　　　　　　　　　SC 13260
B 　Personality Traits [1967]

Deformity
Use Physical Disfigurement

Degrees (Educational)
Use Educational Degrees

Dehydration [1988]
PN 69　　　　　　　　　　SC 13285
SN State of excessively reduced body water or water deficit.
R 　Homeostasis [1973]
　 Water Deprivation [1967]
　 Water Intake [1967]

Dehydrogenases [1973]
PN 79　　　　　　　　　　SC 13290
B 　Enzymes [1973]
N 　Alcohol Dehydrogenases [1973]
　 Lactate Dehydrogenase [1973]

Deinstitutionalization [1982]
PN 1229　　　　　　　　　　SC 13293
SN Programs emphasizing out-of-hospital treatment and community residence of clients, usually chronic psychiatric or handicapped patients, including those who may never have been hospitalized or who may or may not have experienced normal community life.
B 　Mental Health Programs [1973]
R 　Community Mental Health [1973]
　 Community Mental Health Services [1978]
　 Discharge Planning [1994]
　 Habilitation [1991]
　 ↓ Homeless [1988]
　 Homeless Mentally Ill [1997]
　 ↓ Institutional Release [1978]
　 ↓ Mainstreaming [1991]
　 Partial Hospitalization [1985]
　 ↓ Rehabilitation [1967]
　 Right to Treatment [1997]

Deja Vu
Use Consciousness States

Delay of Gratification [1978]
PN 259　　　　　　　　　　SC 13297
SN Voluntary postponement of need satisfaction or fulfillment of desires.
R ↓ Impulse Control Disorders [1997]
　 ↓ Motivation [1967]
　 ↓ Reinforcement [1967]
　 Reinforcement Delay [1985]
　 ↓ Rewards [1967]

Delayed Alternation [1994]
PN 36　　　　　　　　　　SC 13298
SN Alternation of rewards, usually in maze learning, with a delay between successive trials, forcing experimental subject to also alternate responses in order to receive the reward.
B 　Operant Conditioning [1967]
R ↓ Learning [1967]
　 Reinforcement Delay [1985]
　 Response Variability [1973]
　 ↓ Rewards [1967]
　 Spontaneous Alternation [1982]

Delayed Auditory Feedback [1973]
PN 127　　　　　　　　　　SC 13300
B 　Auditory Feedback [1973]
　 Delayed Feedback [1973]

Delayed Development [1973]
PN 1695　　　　　　　　　　SC 13310
SN Delays in any or all areas including cognitive, social, language, sensory, and emotional development.
B 　Development [1967]
N 　Failure to Thrive [1988]
　 Language Delay [1988]
　 Retarded Speech Development [1973]
R 　Developmental Age Groups [1973]
　 Developmental Disabilities [1982]
　 ↓ Human Development [1967]
　 ↓ Physical Development [1973]
　 ↓ Psychogenesis [1973]

Delayed Feedback [1973]
PN 158　　　　　　　　　　SC 13320
B 　Feedback [1967]
　 Perceptual Stimulation [1973]
N 　Delayed Auditory Feedback [1973]

Delayed Parenthood [1985]
PN 43　　　　　　　　　　SC 13325
SN Voluntary decision to postpone parenthood, usually for reasons involving personal development or career interests.
R 　Childlessness [1982]
　 ↓ Family Planning [1973]
　 Family Planning Attitudes [1973]
　 Parental Role [1973]

Delayed Reinforcement
Use Reinforcement Delay

Delayed Speech
Use Retarded Speech Development

Deletion (Chromosome) [1973]
PN 22　　　　　　　　　　SC 13340
B 　Chromosome Disorders [1973]

Delinquency (Juvenile)
Use Juvenile Delinquency

Delirium 1973
PN 783   SC 13360
B   Consciousness Disturbances 1973
     Symptoms 1967
R   Hyperthermia 1973

Delirium Tremens 1973
PN 127   SC 13370
SN Acute alcoholic, psychotic condition characterized by intense tremors, anxiety, hallucinations, and delusions.
B   Alcoholic Hallucinosis 1973
     Syndromes 1973

Delta Rhythm 1973
PN 86   SC 13380
SN Electrically measured impulses or waves of high amplitude and low frequency (1-3 cycles per second) observable in the electroencephalogram during sleep stages 3 and 4 (moderate to deep sleep).
B   Electrical Activity 1967
     Electroencephalography 1967

Delusions 1967
PN 1877   SC 13390
SN False personal beliefs held despite contradictory evidence and common sense.
B   Thought Disturbances 1973
R   Capgras Syndrome 1985
     Erotomania 1997
     Grandiosity 1994
     ↓ Schizophrenia 1967

Dementia 1985
PN 6933   SC 13395
B   Mental Disorders 1967
     Organic Brain Syndromes 1973
N   AIDS Dementia Complex 1997
     Dementia with Lewy Bodies 2001
     ↓ Presenile Dementia 1973
     ↓ Senile Dementia 1973
     ↓ Vascular Dementia 1997
R   Alzheimers Disease 1973
     Creutzfeldt Jakob Syndrome 1994
     Parkinsons Disease 1973
     Picks Disease 1973
     Pseudodementia 1985

Dementia (Multi Infarct)
Use Multi Infarct Dementia

Dementia (Presenile)
Use Presenile Dementia

Dementia (Senile)
Use Senile Dementia

Dementia of Alzheimers Type
Use Alzheimers Disease

Dementia Paralytica
Use General Paresis

Dementia Praecox
Use Schizophrenia

Dementia with Lewy Bodies 2001
PN 0   SC 13435

Dementia with Lewy Bodies — (cont'd)
SN Neurodegenerative disease marked by the presence of Lewy body cells in the cerebral cortex and brain stem. Symptoms often include dementia, parkinsonism, and striking fluctuations in cognitive performance.
UF   Lewy Body Disease
B   Dementia 1985
R   Alzheimers Disease 1973
     Parkinsonism 1994
     Parkinsons Disease 1973

Democracy 1973
PN 266   SC 13440
B   Political Economic Systems 1973
R   ↓ Civil Rights 1978

Democratic Party
Use Political Parties

Demographic Characteristics 1967
PN 15708   SC 13460
UF   Population Characteristics
R   Biographical Data 1978
     ↓ Population 1973
     Psychosocial Factors 1988

Demonic Possession
Use Spirit Possession

Demonstrations (Social)
Use Social Demonstrations

Dendrites 1973
PN 222   SC 13490
B   Neurons 1973

Denial 1973
PN 843   SC 13500
SN Exclusion from conscious awareness of unpleasant realities, which would produce anxiety if acknowledged.
B   Defense Mechanisms 1967
R   Anosognosia 1994

Density (Social)
Use Social Density

Dental Education 1973
PN 65   SC 13520
B   Graduate Education 1973

Dental Students 1973
PN 120   SC 13530
B   Students 1967
R   Graduate Students 1967

Dental Surgery 1973
PN 82   SC 13540
B   Dental Treatment 1973
     Surgery 1971

Dental Treatment 1973
PN 614   SC 13550
B   Physical Treatment Methods 1973
N   Dental Surgery 1973

Dentist Patient Interaction
Use Therapeutic Processes

Dentistry 1973
PN 120   SC 13560

Dentistry — (cont'd)
B   Medical Sciences 1967

Dentists 1973
PN 181   SC 13570
B   Medical Personnel 1967

Deoxycorticosterone 1973
PN 28   SC 13580
B   Adrenal Cortex Hormones 1973
     Corticosteroids 1973

Deoxyglucose 1991
PN 82   SC 13585
B   Carbohydrates 1973

Deoxyribonucleic Acid 1973
PN 320   SC 13590
UF   DNA (Deoxyribonucleic Acid)
B   Nucleic Acids 1973

Dependency (Drug)
Use Drug Dependency

Dependency (Personality) 1967
PN 1977   SC 13620
SN Lack of self-reliance, reflecting need for security, love, and protection from others.
B   Personality Traits 1967
R   Abandonment 1997
     Attachment Behavior 1985
     Codependency 1991
     Dependent Personality 1994
     Enabling 1997

Dependent Personality 1994
PN 48   SC 13625
SN Personality disorder characterized by pervasive patterns of dependent, passive, and submissive behavior.
B   Personality Disorders 1967
R   Codependency 1991
     Dependency (Personality) 1967

Dependent Variables 1973
PN 104   SC 13630
SN Statistical or experimental parameters whose values change as a consequence of changes in one or more other independent variables.
B   Statistical Variables 1973

Depersonalization 1973
PN 283   SC 13640
SN State in which an individual perceives or experiences a sensation of unreality concerning himself or his environment; seen in disorders such as schizophrenia, affective disorders, organic mental disorders, and personality disorders.
B   Dissociative Disorders 2001
     Symptoms 1967
R   Alienation 1971

Depression (Emotion) 1967
PN 15828   SC 13650
SN Mild depression that is not considered clinical depression. Prior to 1988, also used for major depression in clinical populations. For clinical depression, use MAJOR DEPRESSION.
B   Emotional States 1973
R   ↓ Major Depression 1988
     Sadness 1973
     ↓ Separation Reactions 1997

Depressive Reaction (Neurotic)
  Use Major Depression

Deprivation 1967
PN 1155   SC 13680
SN Removal, denial, or lack of something needed or desired.
  N   Cultural Deprivation 1973
      Food Deprivation 1967
      REM Dream Deprivation 1973
      Sleep Deprivation 1967
      ↓ Stimulus Deprivation 1973
      Water Deprivation 1967
  R   Environmental Stress 1973
      ↓ Motivation 1967
      Physiological Stress 1967
      Psychological Stress 1973
      ↓ Stress 1967

Depth Perception 1967
PN 1807   SC 13690
  B   Spatial Perception 1967
  N   Stereoscopic Vision 1973
  R   Eye Convergence 1982
      Linear Perspective 1982
      Motion Parallax 1997
      Ocular Accommodation 1982

Depth Psychology 1973
PN 171   SC 13700
SN Any of the psychological theories which study the unconscious processes of the personality.
  B   Psychology 1967

Dermatitis 1973
PN 80   SC 13710
  B   Skin Disorders 1973
  N   Eczema 1973
      Neurodermatitis 1973
  R   Allergic Skin Disorders 1973
      ↓ Infectious Disorders 1973
      ↓ Toxic Disorders 1973

Dermatomes
  Use Cutaneous Receptive Fields

Desegregation
  Use Social Integration

Desensitization (Systematic)
  Use Systematic Desensitization Therapy

Desertion
  Use Abandonment

Design (Experimental)
  Use Experimental Design

Design (Man Machine Systems)
  Use Human Machine Systems Design

Desipramine 1973
PN 891   SC 13760
  B   Tricyclic Antidepressant Drugs 1997

Desirability (Social)
  Use Social Desirability

Desires
  Use Motivation

Detection (Signal)
  Use Signal Detection (Perception)

Detention (Legal)
  Use Legal Detention

Determinism 1997
PN 73   SC 13815
SN A doctrine that assumes events or objects have antecedent causes that determine their nature.
  B   Philosophies 1967
  R   Epistemology 1973
      Idealism 1973
      Positivism 1973
      Volition 1988

Detoxification 1973
PN 702   SC 13820
  B   Alcohol Rehabilitation 1982
      Drug Rehabilitation 1973
  R   Alcohol Withdrawal 1994
      ↓ Drug Abstinence 1994
      ↓ Drug Therapy 1967
      ↓ Drug Withdrawal 1973
      Sobriety 1988

Developed Countries 1985
PN 179   SC 13823
  B   Countries 1967

Developing Countries 1985
PN 766   SC 13825
  UF   Third World Countries
      Underdeveloped Countries
  B   Countries 1967

Development 1967
PN 1927   SC 13830
  UF   Growth
      Ontogeny
  N   Animal Development 1978
      Career Development 1985
      Community Development 1997
      Curriculum Development 1973
      ↓ Delayed Development 1973
      ↓ Human Development 1967
      Organizational Development 1973
      ↓ Physical Development 1973
      Precocious Development 1973
      Professional Development 1982
      ↓ Program Development 1991
      ↓ Psychogenesis 1973
  R   Age Differences 1967
      Critical Period 1988
      Developmental Age Groups 1973
      ↓ Developmental Stages 1973
      Sex Linked Developmental Differences 1973

Developmental Age Groups 1973
PN 422   SC 13840
SN Groups defined by a chronological age span, and characterized by certain behavioral, psychological, and social attributes. Use AGE DIFFERENCES for age comparisons within or between groups.
  R   Adolescent Development 1973
      Adult Development 1978
      Age Differences 1967
      ↓ Aging 1991
      ↓ Childhood Development 1967
      ↓ Delayed Development 1973
      ↓ Development 1967
      ↓ Developmental Stages 1973

Developmental Age Groups — (cont'd)
  R   Emotional Development 1973
      ↓ Human Development 1967
      Mental Age 1973
      ↓ Motor Development 1973
      ↓ Physical Development 1973
      Precocious Development 1973
      ↓ Psychogenesis 1973

Developmental Differences
SN Term was discontinued in 1982. In 2000, the term was stripped from all records containing it, and replaced with AGE DIFFERENCES, its postable counterpart.
  Use Age Differences

Developmental Disabilities 1982
PN 4028   SC 13853
SN As encompassed in federal legislation for educational assistance to handicapped children, includes disabilities originating before age 18 that constitute substantial barriers to normal functioning. Use a more specific term if possible.
  B   Disorders 1967
  R   Aspergers Syndrome 1991
      ↓ Autism 1967
      ↓ Communication Disorders 1982
      ↓ Congenital Disorders 1973
      Deaf Blind 1991
      ↓ Delayed Development 1973
      ↓ Genetic Disorders 1973
      ↓ Human Development 1967
      ↓ Learning Disorders 1967
      ↓ Mental Retardation 1967
      ↓ Nervous System Disorders 1967
      ↓ Pervasive Developmental Disorders 2001

Developmental Measures 1994
PN 161   SC 13857
  N   Bayley Scales of Infant Development 1994

Developmental Psychology 1973
PN 1551   SC 13860
  B   Psychology 1967
  N   Adolescent Psychology 1973
      Child Psychology 1967
      Gerontology 1967
  R   ↓ Human Development 1967

Developmental Stages 1973
PN 2398   SC 13870
SN Phases in an individual's development characterized by certain physical, behavioral, mental, or social attributes, e.g., the latency stage of psychosexual development or the sensorimotor intelligence stage of cognitive development.
  N   Menopause 1973
      ↓ Prenatal Developmental Stages 1973
      Puberty 1973
  R   Adolescent Development 1973
      Adult Development 1978
      ↓ Aging 1991
      ↓ Childhood Development 1967
      ↓ Development 1967
      Developmental Age Groups 1973
      Erikson (Erik) 1991
      Generativity 2001
      ↓ Human Development 1967
      Object Permanence 1985
      ↓ Perceptual Development 1973
      ↓ Physical Development 1973
      Piaget (Jean) 1967
      ↓ Psychogenesis 1973
      ↓ Rites of Passage 1973

Deviant Behavior
  Use Antisocial Behavior

Deviation IQ
  Use Standard Scores

Deviations (Sexual)
  Use Paraphilias

Devices (Experimental)
  Use Apparatus

Dexamethasone 1985
  PN 707   **SC** 13905
  SN A synthetic analogue of cortisol.
  B   Glucocorticoids 1982
  R   Dexamethasone Suppression Test 1988

Dexamethasone Suppression Test 1988
  PN 646   **SC** 13907
  SN Laboratory analysis of hypersecretion of cortisol and the body's failure to suppress cortisol after the administration of dexamethasone. Used primarily for diagnosis of major depressive disorders.
  B   Medical Diagnosis 1973
  R   Dexamethasone 1985

Dexamphetamine
  Use Dextroamphetamine

Dexedrine
  Use Dextroamphetamine

Dexterity (Physical)
  Use Physical Dexterity

Dextroamphetamine 1973
  PN 1669   **SC** 13940
  UF Amphetamine (d-)
         Dexamphetamine
         Dexedrine
  B   Adrenergic Drugs 1973
         Amphetamine 1967
         Appetite Depressing Drugs 1973
         CNS Stimulating Drugs 1973
         Sympathomimetic Amines 1973

Diabetes 1973
  PN 1426   **SC** 13950
  B   Endocrine Disorders 1973
         Metabolism Disorders 1973
  N   Diabetes Insipidus 1973
         Diabetes Mellitus 1973

Diabetes Insipidus 1973
  PN 92   **SC** 13960
  B   Diabetes 1973
  R   ↓ Genetic Disorders 1973

Diabetes Mellitus 1973
  PN 1010   **SC** 13970
  B   Diabetes 1973

Diacetylmorphine
  Use Heroin

Diagnosis 1967
  PN 7575   **SC** 13990
  N   Computer Assisted Diagnosis 1973
         Differential Diagnosis 1967
         Educational Diagnosis 1978
         Galvanic Skin Response 1967

Diagnosis — (cont'd)
  N   ↓ Medical Diagnosis 1973
         ↓ Psychodiagnosis 1967
  R   Autopsy 1973
         Clinical Judgment (Not Diagnosis) 1973
         Comorbidity 1991
         Diagnosis Related Groups 1988
         ↓ Disorders 1967
         Dual Diagnosis 1991
         General Health Questionnaire 1991
         Geriatric Assessment 1997
         Intake Interview 1994
         International Classification of Diseases 2001
         Labeling 1978
         ↓ Measurement 1967
         ↓ Mental Disorders 1967
         Misdiagnosis 1997
         ↓ Neuropsychological Assessment 1982
         Pain Measurement 1997
         Patient History 1973
         ↓ Physical Disorders 1997
         Prognosis 1973
         Research Diagnostic Criteria 1994
         ↓ Screening 1982
         Severity (Disorders) 1982
         Symptom Checklists 1991

Diagnosis Related Groups 1988
  PN 67   **SC** 13985
  UF DRGs
  R   Cost Containment 1991
         ↓ Diagnosis 1967
         Health Care Costs 1994
         ↓ Health Insurance 1973
         Misdiagnosis 1997
         ↓ Professional Fees 1978

Diagnostic and Statistical Manual 1994
  PN 1176   **SC** 13988
  SN Used when the current Diagnostic and Statistical Manual or its revisions is the primary focus of the reference. Use PSYCHODIAGNOSTIC TYPOLOGIES to access references prior to 1994. Not used for specific psychodiagnostic categories.
  UF DSM
  B   Psychodiagnostic Typologies 1967
  R   International Classification of Diseases 2001
         ↓ Mental Disorders 1967
         ↓ Psychodiagnosis 1967
         Research Diagnostic Criteria 1994

Diagnostic Interview Schedule 1991
  PN 110   **SC** 13900
  B   Interview Schedules 2001
         Psychodiagnostic Interview 1973
  R   ↓ Psychodiagnostic Typologies 1967
         ↓ Screening 1982

Dialect 1973
  PN 321   **SC** 14000
  SN A variety of language characteristic of a geographical region or ethnic, occupational, socioeconomic, or other group.
  B   Language 1967
  N   Nonstandard English 1973
  R   Ethnolinguistics 1973

Dialectics 1973
  PN 361   **SC** 14010
  SN Intellectual investigation through deductive reasoning and juxtaposition of opposing or contradictory ideas.
  R   ↓ Reasoning 1967

Dialysis 1973
  PN 224   **SC** 14020
  B   Physical Treatment Methods 1973
  N   Hemodialysis 1973

Diaphragm (Anatomy) 1973
  PN 20   **SC** 14030
  B   Muscles 1967
         Respiratory System 1973
  R   Thorax 1973

Diaphragms (Birth Control) 1973
  PN 12   **SC** 14040
  B   Contraceptive Devices 1973

Diarrhea 1973
  PN 73   **SC** 14050
  B   Colon Disorders 1973
  R   Fecal Incontinence 1973

Diastolic Pressure 1973
  PN 217   **SC** 14060
  B   Blood Pressure 1967

Diazepam 1973
  PN 1957   **SC** 14070
  UF Valium
  B   Benzodiazepines 1978
         Minor Tranquilizers 1973
         Muscle Relaxing Drugs 1973

Dichoptic Stimulation 1982
  PN 119   **SC** 14075
  SN Simultaneous presentation of different stimuli to each eye independently.
  B   Visual Stimulation 1973

Dichotic Stimulation 1982
  PN 760   **SC** 14077
  SN Simultaneous presentation of different sounds to the two ears.
  B   Auditory Stimulation 1967

Dieldrin
  SN Term was discontinued in 1997. In 2000, the term was stripped from all records containing it, and replaced with INSECTICIDES, its postable counterpart.
  Use Insecticides

Diencephalon 1973
  PN 280   **SC** 14110
  B   Forebrain 1985
  N   ↓ Hypothalamus 1967
         Optic Chiasm 1973
         ↓ Thalamus 1967

Dietary Restraint 1994
  PN 336   **SC** 14112
  R   ↓ Appetite 1973
         Diets 1978
         ↓ Feeding Practices 1973
         Food Intake 1967

Dietary Supplements 2001
  PN 0   **SC** 14113
  SN Orally ingested products intended as supplements to the diet, including vitamins, herbs, amino acids, and concentrates, metabolites, and extracts of these substances.
  UF Nutritional Supplements
  R   ↓ Alternative Medicine 1997
         ↓ Amino Acids 1973

Dietary Supplements — (cont'd)
R   Diets [1978]
     Medicinal Herbs and Plants [2001]
     Nutrition [1973]
     ↓ Vitamins [1973]

Diets [1978]
PN 2957   SC 14114
SN Food and drink regularly consumed or pre-scribed for a special reason. Used for human or ani-mal populations.
B   Feeding Practices [1973]
R   Dietary Restraint [1994]
     Dietary Supplements [2001]
     ↓ Drinking Behavior [1978]
     Food [1978]
     Food Additives [1978]
     Food Allergies [1973]
     Food Deprivation [1967]
     Food Preferences [1973]
     Health Behavior [1982]
     Nutrition [1973]
     ↓ Nutritional Deficiencies [1973]
     Obesity [1973]
     ↓ Underweight [1973]
     Weight Control [1985]

Differential Aptitude Tests [1973]
PN 57   SC 14150
B   Aptitude Measures [1967]

Differential Diagnosis [1967]
PN 4820   SC 14160
SN Diagnosis aimed at distinguishing between physical and/or mental disorders of similar character by comparison of symptoms.
B   Diagnosis [1967]
R   Comorbidity [1991]
     Dual Diagnosis [1991]
     Educational Diagnosis [1978]
     ↓ Medical Diagnosis [1973]
     ↓ Psychodiagnosis [1967]

Differential Limen
Use Thresholds

Differential Personality Inventory
SN Term was discontinued in 1997. In 2000, the term was stripped from all records containing it, and replaced with NONPROJECTIVE PERSONALITY MEASURES, its postable counterpart.
Use Nonprojective Personality Measures

Differential Reinforcement [1973]
PN 868   SC 14190
SN Selective reinforcement of one response in a defined category (response class) of responses to the exclusion of any other members (responses) of that category. Has application in treatment as well as in experimental contexts.
B   Reinforcement [1967]
R   ↓ Discrimination Learning [1982]
     Omission Training [1985]

Difficulty Level (Test) [1973]
PN 297   SC 14200
UF   Test Difficulty
B   Test Construction [1973]
     Testing [1967]
R   Item Response Theory [1985]

Digestion [1973]
PN 86   SC 14210
B   Physiology [1967]
R   ↓ Digestive System [1967]
     ↓ Ingestion [2001]
     Salivation [1973]
     Swallowing [1988]

Digestive System [1967]
PN 359   SC 14220
B   Anatomical Systems [1973]
N   Esophagus [1973]
     ↓ Gastrointestinal System [1973]
     Liver [1973]
     Mouth (Anatomy) [1967]
     Pharynx [1973]
     Teeth (Anatomy) [1973]
     ↓ Tongue [1973]
R   Digestion [1973]
     ↓ Digestive System Disorders [1973]
     Salivary Glands [1973]

Digestive System Disorders [1973]
PN 92   SC 14230
B   Physical Disorders [1997]
N   Cystic Fibrosis [1985]
     ↓ Gastrointestinal Disorders [1973]
     Jaundice [1973]
     ↓ Liver Disorders [1973]
R   ↓ Digestive System [1967]
     ↓ Infectious Disorders [1973]
     ↓ Neoplasms [1967]
     ↓ Symptoms [1967]
     ↓ Toxic Disorders [1973]

Digit Span Testing [1973]
PN 236   SC 14240
SN Test of immediate recall involving presentation of a random series of numerals which the subject repeats after the series has been presented.
B   Measurement [1967]

Digital Computers [1973]
PN 166   SC 14250
SN Electronic or electromechanical machines that operate directly on binary digits when executing pro-grams and manipulating data (e.g., calculators).
UF   Calculators
B   Computers [1967]

Digits (Mathematics)
Use Numbers (Numerals)

Dihydroergotamine [1973]
PN 29   SC 14270
B   Adrenergic Blocking Drugs [1973]
     Analgesic Drugs [1973]
     Ergot Derivatives [1973]
     Vasoconstrictor Drugs [1973]

Dihydroxyphenylacetic Acid [1991]
PN 117   SC 14273
UF   DOPAC
B   Acids [1973]
     Dopamine Metabolites [1982]

Dihydroxytryptamine [1991]
PN 39   SC 14275
B   Serotonin Antagonists [1973]

Dilantin
Use Diphenylhydantoin

Dilation (Pupil)
Use Pupil Dilation

Diphenhydramine [1973]
PN 64   SC 14310
UF   Benadryl
B   Amines [1973]
     Antihistaminic Drugs [1973]
     Antitremor Drugs [1973]

Diphenylhydantoin [1973]
PN 197   SC 14320
UF   Dilantin
     Diphenylhydantoin Sodium
     Phenytoin
B   Anticonvulsive Drugs [1973]

Diphenylhydantoin Sodium
Use Diphenylhydantoin

Diptera [1973]
PN 306   SC 14350
UF   Flies
B   Insects [1967]
N   Drosophila [1973]
R   Larvae [1973]

Directed Discussion Method [1973]
PN 109   SC 14360
B   Teaching Methods [1967]
R   Lecture Method [1973]

Directed Reverie Therapy
SN Term discontinued in 2000. Use DIRECTED REVERIE THERAPY to access references from 1978-2000.
Use Guided Imagery

Direction Perception [1997]
PN 279   SC 14365
B   Spatial Perception [1967]
R   Cognitive Maps [1982]
     ↓ Motion Perception [1967]
     ↓ Perceptual Localization [1967]
     ↓ Spatial Memory [1988]
     Spatial Organization [1973]

Disabilities
Use Disorders

Disability Discrimination [1997]
PN 49   SC 57480
B   Social Discrimination [1982]
R   Affirmative Action [1985]
     ↓ Civil Rights [1978]
     Disability Laws [1994]
     ↓ Disabled (Attitudes Toward) [1997]
     ↓ Disorders [1973]
     ↓ Mental Disorders [1967]
     Mental Illness (Attitudes Toward) [1967]
     ↓ Physical Illness (Attitudes Toward) [1985]
     ↓ Prejudice [1967]
     Sensory Disabilities (Attitudes Toward) [2001]

Disability Evaluation [1988]
PN 139   SC 14367
SN Evaluation of one's ability to work in order to determine the need for insurance or health benefits.
R   ↓ Employee Benefits [1973]
     ↓ Insurance [1973]
     Social Security [1988]

Disability Laws ¹⁹⁹⁴

PN 262   **SC** 57410
SN Rules declared by federal or state governments and enacted by legislative bodies that affect populations with mental or physical disabilities or disorders. Used for the laws themselves, or the interpretation or application of the laws.
B   Laws ¹⁹⁶⁷
R   Civil Law ¹⁹⁹⁴
   ↓ Civil Rights ¹⁹⁷⁸
    Disability Discrimination ¹⁹⁹⁷
    Disabled Personnel ¹⁹⁹⁷

Disability Management ¹⁹⁹¹

PN 71   **SC** 14368
SN Process of returning an impaired or disabled worker to the workplace. Includes evaluation, assessment, early intervention, and rehabilitation.
B   Management ¹⁹⁶⁷
R   Disabled Personnel ¹⁹⁹⁷
    Employee Assistance Programs ¹⁹⁸⁵
   ↓ Prevention ¹⁹⁷³
   ↓ Rehabilitation ¹⁹⁶⁷
    Vocational Evaluation ¹⁹⁹¹
   ↓ Vocational Rehabilitation ¹⁹⁶⁷

Disabled (Attitudes Toward) ¹⁹⁹⁷

PN 1515   **SC** 14373
SN In 1997, this term replaced the discontinued term HANDICAPPED (ATTITUDES TOWARD). In 2000, HANDICAPPED (ATTITUDES TOWARD) was stripped from all records containing it and replaced with DISABLED (ATTITUDES TOWARD).
UF   Handicapped (Attitudes Toward)
B   Attitudes ¹⁹⁶⁷
N   Mental Illness (Attitudes Toward) ¹⁹⁶⁷
    Mental Retardation (Attitudes Toward) ²⁰⁰¹
    Physical Disabilities (Attitudes Toward) ²⁰⁰¹
    Sensory Disabilities (Attitudes Toward) ²⁰⁰¹
R   Disability Discrimination ¹⁹⁹⁷
   ↓ Physical Illness (Attitudes Toward) ¹⁹⁸⁵
    Stereotyped Attitudes ¹⁹⁶⁷

Disabled Personnel ¹⁹⁹⁷

PN 144   **SC** 14369
SN Employees with physical or mental disabilities or injuries resulting from work-related activities.
B   Personnel ¹⁹⁶⁷
R   Disability Laws ¹⁹⁹⁴
    Disability Management ¹⁹⁹¹
   ↓ Disorders ¹⁹⁶⁷
    Impaired Professionals ¹⁹⁸⁵
    Supported Employment ¹⁹⁹⁴
   ↓ Working Conditions ¹⁹⁷³
    Workmens Compensation Insurance ¹⁹⁷³

Disadvantaged ¹⁹⁶⁷

PN 3398   **SC** 14370
SN Individuals deprived of equal access to society's resources, especially as regards education, culture, and employment.
UF   Economically Disadvantaged
    Socially Disadvantaged
    Underprivileged
R   Cultural Deprivation ¹⁹⁷³
   ↓ Homeless ¹⁹⁸⁸
    Poverty ¹⁹⁷³
   ↓ Social Class ¹⁹⁶⁷
   ↓ Social Deprivation ¹⁹⁷³
   ↓ Socioeconomic Status ¹⁹⁶⁷

Disappointment ¹⁹⁷³

PN 51   **SC** 14380

Disappointment — (cont'd)

B   Emotional States ¹⁹⁷³
R   Dissatisfaction ¹⁹⁷³
   ↓ Separation Reactions ¹⁹⁹⁷

Disasters ¹⁹⁷³

PN 694   **SC** 14390
N   Natural Disasters ¹⁹⁷³
R   ↓ Accidents ¹⁹⁶⁷
   ↓ Crises ¹⁹⁷¹
   ↓ Stress ¹⁹⁶⁷

Discharge Planning ¹⁹⁹⁴

PN 67   **SC** 14395
B   Case Management ¹⁹⁹¹
    Treatment Planning ¹⁹⁹⁷
R   Aftercare ¹⁹⁷³
    Deinstitutionalization ¹⁹⁸²
   ↓ Facility Discharge ¹⁹⁸⁸
   ↓ Hospital Discharge ¹⁹⁷³
   ↓ Institutional Release ¹⁹⁷⁸
    Posttreatment Followup ¹⁹⁷³
    Psychiatric Hospital Discharge ¹⁹⁷⁸
    Treatment Termination ¹⁹⁸²

Discipline (Child)
Use   Child Discipline

Discipline (Classroom)
Use   Classroom Discipline

Disclosure (Experimental)
Use   Debriefing (Experimental)

Disclosure (Self)
Use   Self Disclosure

Discourse Analysis ¹⁹⁹⁷

PN 946   **SC** 14425
SN Analysis of written and spoken language.
B   Content Analysis ¹⁹⁷⁸
R   ↓ Grammar ¹⁹⁶⁷
   ↓ Language ¹⁹⁶⁷
   ↓ Linguistics ¹⁹⁷³
    Morphology (Language) ¹⁹⁷³
    Pragmatics ¹⁹⁸⁵
    Rhetoric ¹⁹⁹¹
   ↓ Semantics ¹⁹⁶⁷
   ↓ Syntax ¹⁹⁷¹
    Text Structure ¹⁹⁸²
   ↓ Verbal Communication ¹⁹⁶⁷

Discovery Teaching Method ¹⁹⁷³

PN 129   **SC** 14430
SN Unstructured or guided instruction which encourages independent exploration or discovery.
B   Teaching Methods ¹⁹⁶⁷
R   ↓ Experiential Learning ¹⁹⁹⁷
    Montessori Method ¹⁹⁷³
    Nondirected Discussion Method ¹⁹⁷³
    Open Classroom Method ¹⁹⁷³

Discrimination ¹⁹⁶⁷

PN 2586   **SC** 14450
SN Conceptually broad term referring to the general process of differentiation between qualities, entities, or people. Use a more specific term if possible.
N   Cognitive Discrimination ¹⁹⁷³
    Drug Discrimination ¹⁹⁸⁵
   ↓ Perceptual Discrimination ¹⁹⁷³
   ↓ Social Discrimination ¹⁹⁸²
    Stimulus Discrimination ¹⁹⁷³

Discrimination — (cont'd)

R   ↓ Discrimination Learning ¹⁹⁸²
   ↓ Perception ¹⁹⁶⁷
    Stereotyped Attitudes ¹⁹⁶⁷

Discrimination (Cognitive)
Use   Cognitive Discrimination

Discrimination (Social)
Use   Social Discrimination

Discrimination Learning ¹⁹⁸²

PN 2579   **SC** 14445
SN Learning paradigm in which responses to one stimulus (S+) are reinforced while responses to another stimulus (S-) are either not reinforced or are punished. Also, the learned discriminative responses themselves.
UF   Discriminative Learning
B   Learning ¹⁹⁶⁷
    Operant Conditioning ¹⁹⁶⁷
N   Drug Discrimination ¹⁹⁸⁵
    Matching to Sample ¹⁹⁹⁴
    Nonreversal Shift Learning ¹⁹⁷³
    Reversal Shift Learning ¹⁹⁶⁷
R   ↓ Concept Formation ¹⁹⁶⁷
    Differential Reinforcement ¹⁹⁷³
   ↓ Discrimination ¹⁹⁶⁷
    Extinction (Learning) ¹⁹⁶⁷
    Fading (Conditioning) ¹⁹⁸²
   ↓ Generalization (Learning) ¹⁹⁸²
    Kinship Recognition ¹⁹⁸⁸
    Stimulus Control ¹⁹⁶⁷
    Stimulus Discrimination ¹⁹⁷³

Discriminative Learning
Use   Discrimination Learning

Discriminative Stimulus
Use   Conditioned Stimulus

Discussion (Group)
Use   Group Discussion

Disease Course ¹⁹⁹¹

PN 2849   **SC** 14470
SN Stages or progression of physical or mental disorders. Compare PROGNOSIS.
UF   Course of Illness
    Disorder Course
R   ↓ Disorders ¹⁹⁶⁷
   ↓ Mental Disorders ¹⁹⁶⁷
   ↓ Physical Disorders ¹⁹⁹⁷
    Prognosis ¹⁹⁷³

Disease Outbreaks
Use   Epidemics

Diseases (Venereal)
Use   Venereal Diseases

Disgust ¹⁹⁹⁴

PN 67   **SC** 14495
B   Emotional States ¹⁹⁷³
R   ↓ Aversion ¹⁹⁶⁷

Dishonesty ¹⁹⁷³

PN 100   **SC** 14500
B   Personality Traits ¹⁹⁶⁷
R   Cheating ¹⁹⁷³
   ↓ Deception ¹⁹⁶⁷
    Fraud ¹⁹⁹⁴

Dishonesty — (cont'd)
R   Sincerity 1973

Dislike
Use   Aversion

Disorder Course
Use   Disease Course

Disorders 1967
PN 16202   SC 14520
SN Conceptually broad term referring primarily to physical illness. Also used when particular disorders are not specified. Use a more specific term if possible. For general discussions of health impairment consider also the term HEALTH. The term HANDICAPPED was also used to represent this concept from 1967-1996, and DISABLED was used from 1997-2000. In 2000, DISORDERS replaced the discontinued and deleted terms DISABLED and HANDICAPPED. DISABLED and HANDICAPPED were stripped from all records and replaced with DISORDERS.
UF   Disabilities
     Exceptional Children (Handicapped)
     Handicaps
N   Adventitious Disorders 2001
     ↓ Congenital Disorders 1973
     Developmental Disabilities 1982
     ↓ Emotionally Disturbed 1973
     ↓ Learning Disorders 1967
     ↓ Mental Disorders 1967
     ↓ Multiple Disabilities 2001
     ↓ Physical Disorders 1997
R   ↓ Brain Damage 1967
     ↓ Chronic Illness 1991
     Chronicity (Disorders) 1982
     Comorbidity 1991
     ↓ Diagnosis 1967
     Disability Discrimination 1997
     Disabled Personnel 1997
     Disease Course 1991
     Etiology 1967
     Health Complaints 1997
     Illness Behavior 1982
     ↓ Injuries 1973
     International Classification of Diseases 2001
     ↓ Mental Retardation 1967
     Onset (Disorders) 1973
     Predisposition 1973
     Premorbidity 1978
     Prenatal Exposure 1991
     Prognosis 1973
     Recovery (Disorders) 1973
     Relapse (Disorders) 1973
     ↓ Remission (Disorders) 1973
     Severity (Disorders) 1982
     Special Needs 1994
     Susceptibility (Disorders) 1973
     ↓ Symptoms 1967
     ↓ Syndromes 1973

Disorientation (Place)
Use   Place Disorientation

Disorientation (Time)
Use   Time Disorientation

Displacement (Defense Mechanism) 1973
PN 57   SC 14550
B   Defense Mechanisms 1967

Displays 1967
PN 359   SC 14560
SN Physical arrangements of stimuli to form a desired pattern; temporal, spatial, or otherwise.
N   Auditory Displays 1973
     Graphical Displays 1985
     Tactual Displays 1973
     ↓ Visual Displays 1973
R   ↓ Instrument Controls 1985

Disposition
Use   Personality

Disruptive Behavior
Use   Behavior Problems

Dissatisfaction 1973
PN 180   SC 14590
B   Emotional States 1973
R   Disappointment 1973
     Frustration 1967
     ↓ Satisfaction 1973

Dissociation 2001
PN 0   SC 14592
SN Used generally to describe the process whereby thoughts, attitudes, emotions, or a coordinated set of activities becomes separated from one's personality or mental processes. Compare DISSOCIATIVE DISORDERS. Consider DISSOCIATIVE PATTERNS from 1973-2000.
R   ↓ Amnesia 1967
     ↓ Consciousness Disturbances 1973
     ↓ Consciousness States 1971
     ↓ Dissociative Disorders 2001
     ↓ Neurosis 1967

Dissociative Disorders 2001
PN 0   SC 14593
SN A mental disorder characterized by disruptions and/or alterations in the normally integrated functions of consciousness, memory or identity. Compare DISSOCIATION. Consider DISSOCIATIVE PATTERNS to access records from 1973-2000.
UF   Dissociative Neurosis
     Dissociative Patterns
     Hysterical Neurosis (Dissociation)
B   Mental Disorders 1967
N   Depersonalization 1973
     Dissociative Identity Disorder 1997
     Fugue Reaction 1973
R   ↓ Amnesia 1967
     ↓ Consciousness Disturbances 1973
     Dissociation 2001
     ↓ Personality Disorders 1967

Dissociative Identity Disorder 1997
PN 1221   SC 14595
SN In 1997, this term was created to replace the discontinued term MULTIPLE PERSONALITY. In 2000, MULTIPLE PERSONALITY was stripped from all records and replaced with DISSOCIATIVE IDENTITY DISORDER.
UF   Multiple Personality
     Split Personality
B   Dissociative Disorders 2001

Dissociative Neurosis
SN Term discontinued in 1997.
Use   Dissociative Disorders

Dissociative Patterns
SN Term discontinued in 2000. Use DISSOCIATIVE PATTERNS to access references from 1973-2000.

Dissociative Patterns — (cont'd)
Use   Dissociative Disorders

Dissonance (Cognitive)
Use   Cognitive Dissonance

Distance Discrimination
Use   Distance Perception

Distance Perception 1973
PN 841   SC 14640
UF   Distance Discrimination
B   Spatial Perception 1967
N   Apparent Distance 1973
     Motion Parallax 1997
R   Eye Convergence 1982
     Linear Perspective 1982

Distortion (Perceptual)
Use   Perceptual Distortion

Distractibility 1973
PN 337   SC 14660
B   Symptoms 1967
R   ↓ Attention Deficit Disorder 1985
     Attention Deficit Disorder with
         Hyperactivity 2001
     Distraction 1978

Distraction 1978
PN 1192   SC 14663
SN Process or potential cause of interruption of attention.
R   ↓ Attention 1967
     Attention Span 1973
     Concentration 1982
     Distractibility 1973
     Divided Attention 1973
     Selective Attention 1973

Distress 1973
PN 4231   SC 14670
SN Negative emotional state characterized by physical and/or emotional discomfort, pain, or anguish. Compare STRESS.
UF   Anguish
B   Emotional States 1973
R   Agitation 1991
     ↓ Separation Reactions 1997
     ↓ Stress 1967
     Suffering 1973

Distress Calls (Animal)
Use   Animal Distress Calls

Distributed Practice 1973
PN 147   SC 14690
SN Practice schedule in which relatively short periods of practice are spaced with intermittent rest or periods of activity unrelated to the practiced task. Compare MASSED PRACTICE.
B   Learning Schedules 1967
     Practice 1967

Distribution (Frequency)
Use   Frequency Distribution

Distributive Justice
Use   Justice

Distrust
Use   Suspicion

Disulfiram 1978
PN 166   SC 14725
  UF Antabuse
  B   Emetic Drugs 1973

Diuresis 1973
PN 26   SC 14730
SN Increased flow of urine.
  B   Urination 1967
  R   ↓ Diuretics 1973

Diuretics 1973
PN 108   SC 14740
  B   Drugs 1967
  N   Acetazolamide 1973
      Caffeine 1973
      Theophylline 1973
  R   ↓ Antihypertensive Drugs 1973
      Diuresis 1973
      Probenecid 1982
      ↓ Urination 1967

Diurnal Variations
  Use Human Biological Rhythms

Divergent Thinking 1973
PN 603   SC 14760
SN Component of intelligence which is manifested
in the ability to generate a wide variety of original
ideas or solutions to a particular problem. Compare
CREATIVITY.
  B   Thinking 1967
  R   ↓ Abstraction 1967
      Creativity 1967
      Declarative Knowledge 1997
      ↓ Inductive Deductive Reasoning 1973
      Intelligence 1967
      Procedural Knowledge 1997

Divided Attention 1973
PN 651   SC 14765
SN Simultaneous attending to two or more stimuli or
through two or more perceptual modalities. Compare
SELECTIVE ATTENTION.
  B   Attention 1967
  R   Distraction 1978
      Selective Attention 1973

Division of Labor 1988
PN 388   SC 14767
  N   Animal Division of Labor 1973
  R   Economics 1985
      Household Management 1985
      ↓ Occupations 1967
      Sex Roles 1967
      Work Load 1982

Division of Labor (Animal)
  Use Animal Division of Labor

Divorce 1973
PN 3978   SC 14780
  B   Marital Separation 1973
  R   Child Custody 1982
      Child Support 1988
      Divorced Persons 1973
      ↓ Family 1967
      Joint Custody 1988
      Mediation 1988
      Remarriage 1985

Divorced Persons 1973
PN 718   SC 14790

Divorced Persons — (cont'd)
  R   Divorce 1973
      ↓ Family 1967
      ↓ Marital Separation 1973
      ↓ Marital Status 1973
      ↓ Parental Absence 1973

Dizygotic Twins
  Use Heterozygotic Twins

Dizziness
  Use Vertigo

DNA (Deoxyribonucleic Acid)
  Use Deoxyribonucleic Acid

Doctors
  Use Physicians

Dogmatism 1978
PN 519   SC 14830
  B   Personality Traits 1967
  R   Authoritarianism 1967
      Openmindedness 1978
      Relativism 1997

Dogs 1967
PN 1997   SC 14840
  B   Canids 1997

Doll Play 1973
PN 99   SC 14850
  B   Recreation 1967
  R   Anatomically Detailed Dolls 1991
      Childhood Play Behavior 1978

Dolphins 1973
PN 209   SC 14860
  B   Whales 1985
  R   Porpoises 1973

Domestic Service Personnel 1973
PN 36   SC 14870
  UF Maids
  B   Service Personnel 1991
  R   ↓ Nonprofessional Personnel 1982

Domestic Violence
  Use Family Violence

Domestication (Animal)
  Use Animal Domestication

Dominance 1967
PN 963   SC 14900
SN Conceptually broad term referring to relative
positions of objects, persons, things, or processes.
Use a more specific term if possible.
  N   Animal Dominance 1973
      ↓ Cerebral Dominance 1973
      Dominance Hierarchy 1973
      Genetic Dominance 1973
  R   Abuse of Power 1997
      Authoritarianism 1967
      Authority 1967
      Coercion 1994
      Emotional Superiority 1973
      Obedience 1973
      ↓ Power 1967
      ↓ Status 1967

Dominance (Animal)
  Use Animal Dominance

Dominance Hierarchy 1973
PN 954   SC 14890
SN Social structure of a group as it relates to the
relative social rank or dominance status of its mem-
bers. Used for human or animal populations.
  B   Dominance 1967
  R   Animal Dominance 1973
      ↓ Social Behavior 1967
      ↓ Social Structure 1967

Domination
  Use Authoritarianism

DOPA 1973
PN 88   SC 14940
  B   Amino Acids 1973
  R   Carbidopa 1988
      Dopamine 1973
      Levodopa 1973
      Methyldopa 1973

DOPAC
  Use Dihydroxyphenylacetic Acid

Dopamine 1973
PN 5637   SC 14950
  B   Catecholamines 1973
  R   DOPA 1973
      ↓ Dopamine Metabolites 1982
      ↓ Heart Rate Affecting Drugs 1973
      Homovanillic Acid 1978
      Levodopa 1973
      Methyldopa 1973
      Methylphenyltetrahydropyridine 1994

Dopamine Agonists 1985
PN 1011   SC 14951
  B   Drugs 1967
  N   ↓ Amphetamine 1967
      Apomorphine 1973
      Morphine 1973
      Quinpirole 1994

Dopamine Antagonists 1982
PN 1131   SC 14952
  B   Amine Oxidase Inhibitors 1973
  N   Sulpiride 1973
  R   ↓ CNS Depressant Drugs 1973
      ↓ Catecholamines 1973
      ↓ Decarboxylase Inhibitors 1982
      ↓ Narcotic Drugs 1973
      ↓ Tranquilizing Drugs 1967

Dopamine Metabolites 1982
PN 239   SC 14955
SN Molecules generated from the metabolism of
dopamine.
  B   Metabolites 1973
  N   Dihydroxyphenylacetic Acid 1991
      Homovanillic Acid 1978
  R   Acetaldehyde 1982
      Dopamine 1973
      ↓ Metabolism 1967

Dormitories 1973
PN 434   SC 14960
  UF Residence Halls
  B   Housing 1973
      School Facilities 1973

Dorsal Horns [1985]
PN 154 SC 14965
SN Longitudinal columns of gray matter (i.e., neuronal cell bodies) in the posterior spinal cord mainly serving sensory mechanisms.
B Spinal Cord [1973]
R ↓ Afferent Pathways [1982]
  Dorsal Roots [1973]

Dorsal Roots [1973]
PN 103 SC 14970
B Spinal Cord [1973]
R Dorsal Horns [1985]

Double Bind Interaction [1973]
PN 96 SC 14990
SN Simultaneous communication of conflicting messages in which the response to either message evokes rejection or disapproval.
B Interpersonal Communication [1973]
R Dysfunctional Family [1991]
  Schizophrenogenic Family [1967]
  Schizophrenogenic Mothers [1973]

Doubt [1973]
PN 65 SC 15000
B Emotional States [1973]
R Mental Confusion [1973]
  Suspicion [1973]
  Uncertainty [1991]

Doves [1973]
PN 176 SC 15010
B Birds [1967]

Downs Syndrome [1967]
PN 2503 SC 15020
UF Mongolism
B Autosome Disorders [1973]
  Mental Retardation [1967]
  Neonatal Disorders [1973]
  Syndromes [1973]
R Moderate Mental Retardation [2001]
  Trisomy 21 [1973]

Doxepin [1994]
PN 25 SC 15025
SN Use ANTIDEPRESSANT DRUGS or TRANQUILIZING DRUGS to access references from 1973-1993.
B Tranquilizing Drugs [1967]
  Tricyclic Antidepressant Drugs [1997]

Draftees [1973]
PN 55 SC 15030
SN Military personnel conscripted for service.
B Enlisted Military Personnel [1973]
R Army Personnel [1967]
  Navy Personnel [1967]

[1973]
  SC 15040
 heatre [1973]
 terature [1967]
 otion Pictures (Entertainment) [1973]
 riters [1991]

 Man Test
 to 1988, use Goodenough Harris Draw A
 st.
 uman Figures Drawing

Drawing [1967]
PN 2554 SC 15050
B Art [1967]

Dream Analysis [1973]
PN 1411 SC 15060
UF Dream Interpretation
B Psychoanalysis [1967]
  Psychotherapeutic Techniques [1967]
R ↓ Dreaming [1967]
  ↓ Parapsychology [1967]

Dream Content [1973]
PN 1199 SC 15070
R ↓ Dreaming [1967]
  Nightmares [1973]
  ↓ Sleep [1967]

Dream Interpretation
Use Dream Analysis

Dream Recall [1973]
PN 327 SC 15090
R ↓ Dreaming [1967]
  Lucid Dreaming [1994]

Dreaming [1967]
PN 1610 SC 15100
N Lucid Dreaming [1994]
  Nightmares [1973]
  REM Dreams [1973]
R Dream Analysis [1973]
  Dream Content [1973]
  Dream Recall [1973]
  ↓ Sleep [1967]

DRGs
Use Diagnosis Related Groups

Drinking (Alcohol)
Use Alcohol Drinking Patterns

Drinking Attitudes
Use Alcohol Drinking Attitudes

Drinking Behavior [1978]
PN 221 SC 15127
B Behavior [1967]
N ↓ Alcohol Drinking Patterns [1967]
  Animal Drinking Behavior [1973]
  Water Intake [1967]
R ↓ Alcoholic Beverages [1973]
  Beverages (Nonalcoholic) [1978]
  Diets [1978]
  Driving Under The Influence [1988]
  ↓ Fluid Intake [1985]
  ↓ Ingestion [2001]
  Sucking [1978]
  Thirst [1967]

Drinking Behavior (Animal)
Use Animal Drinking Behavior

Drive
Use Motivation

Driver Education [1973]
PN 179 SC 15150
B Curriculum [1967]
R Drivers [1973]

Driver Safety
Use Highway Safety

Drivers [1973]
PN 1257 SC 15170
R Automobiles [1973]
  Driver Education [1973]
  ↓ Driving Behavior [1967]
  Highway Safety [1973]
  Motor Traffic Accidents [1973]
  ↓ Motor Vehicles [1982]

Driving Behavior [1967]
PN 2503 SC 15180
SN Manner in which one operates a motor vehicle.
B Behavior [1967]
N Driving Under The Influence [1988]
R Drivers [1973]
  Highway Safety [1973]
  Motor Traffic Accidents [1973]
  Pedestrian Accidents [1973]
  Safety Belts [1973]

Driving Under The Influence [1988]
PN 795 SC 15185
UF Drunk Driving
B Crime [1967]
  Driving Behavior [1967]
R ↓ Accidents [1967]
  ↓ Alcohol Intoxication [1973]
  Blood Alcohol Concentration [1994]
  ↓ Drinking Behavior [1978]
  ↓ Drug Usage [1971]
  Highway Safety [1973]

Dropouts [1973]
PN 264 SC 15190
N Potential Dropouts [1973]
  ↓ School Dropouts [1967]
  Treatment Dropouts [1978]
R ↓ Education [1967]
  Experimental Attrition [1994]
  ↓ School Enrollment [1973]

Drosophila [1973]
PN 659 SC 15200
UF Fruit Fly
B Diptera [1973]
R Larvae [1973]

Drowsiness
Use Sleep Onset

Drug Abstinence [1994]
PN 410 SC 15215
SN Voluntary or involuntary abstinence from drugs. For alcohol abstinence, use SOBRIETY.
UF Abstinence (Drugs)
N Sobriety [1988]
R Detoxification [1973]
  ↓ Drug Abuse [1973]
  ↓ Drug Rehabilitation [1973]
  ↓ Drug Usage [1971]
  ↓ Drug Withdrawal [1973]
  Recovery (Disorders) [1973]
  Smoking Cessation [1988]

Drug Abuse [1973]
PN 12443 SC 15220
UF Substance Abuse
B Behavior Disorders [1971]
  Drug Usage [1971]
N ↓ Alcohol Abuse [1988]

Drug Abuse — (cont'd)
- N ↓ Drug Dependency 1973
- ↓ Inhalant Abuse 1985
- Polydrug Abuse 1994
- R ↓ Addiction 1973
- Codependency 1991
- Craving 1997
- ↓ Drug Abstinence 1994
- Drug Abuse Liability 1994
- Drug Abuse Prevention 1994
- ↓ Drug Addiction 1967
- Drug Distribution 1997
- ↓ Drug Legalization 1997
- Drug Overdoses 1978
- Drug Usage Screening 1988
- ↓ Drugs 1967
- Intravenous Drug Usage 1994
- Needle Exchange Programs 2001
- Needle Sharing 1994
- ↓ Social Issues 1991

Drug Abuse Liability 1994
PN 121   SC 15225
SN Properties of any psychoactive drug or substance which lead to self administration and potentiality for abuse, dependence, and addiction.
- UF Abuse Potential (Drugs)
- R ↓ Alcohol Abuse 1988
- ↓ Drug Abuse 1973
- ↓ Drug Addiction 1967
- ↓ Drug Dependency 1973
- ↓ Pharmacology 1973
- Psychopharmacology 1967

Drug Abuse Prevention 1994
PN 909   SC 15227
- UF Substance Abuse Prevention
- B Prevention 1973
- R ↓ Drug Abuse 1973
- Drug Education 1973
- Early Intervention 1982
- Preventive Medicine 1973
- Primary Mental Health Prevention 1973

Drug Addiction 1967
PN 4457   SC 15230
SN Physical and emotional dependence on a chemical substance. Compare DRUG DEPENDENCY.
- B Addiction 1973
- Drug Dependency 1973
- Side Effects (Drug) 1973
- N Heroin Addiction 1973
- R ↓ Drug Abuse 1973
- Drug Abuse Liability 1994
- Drug Overdoses 1978
- ↓ Drug Withdrawal 1973
- Intravenous Drug Usage 1994
- Methadone Maintenance 1978
- Polydrug Abuse 1994

Drug Administration Methods 1973
PN 1995   SC 15240
SN Techniques, procedures, and routes (e.g., oral, intravenous) of administration of drugs (in experimental or therapeutic contexts) including dosage forms (e.g., liquids, tablets), frequency, and duration of drug administration. Used only when methodological aspects of administering drugs are discussed.
- N ↓ Injections 1973
- R ↓ Drug Dosages 1973
- ↓ Drugs 1967

Drug Adverse Reactions
SN Term was discontinued in 1982. In 2000, the term was stripped from all records containing it, and replaced with SIDE EFFECTS (DRUG), its postable counterpart.
- Use Side Effects (Drug)

Drug Allergies 1973
PN 21   SC 15260
- B Allergic Disorders 1973
- Side Effects (Drug) 1973
- R Drug Sensitivity 1973

Drug Dependency 1973
PN 3945   SC 15270
SN Psychological craving for or habituation to the use of a chemical substance which may or may not be accompanied by physical dependency. Used for animal or human populations. Compare DRUG ADDICTION.
- UF Dependency (Drug)
- B Drug Abuse 1973
- Side Effects (Drug) 1973
- N ↓ Drug Addiction 1967
- R Drug Abuse Liability 1994
- Drug Usage Screening 1988
- Polydrug Abuse 1994

Drug Discrimination 1985
PN 1129   SC 15272
SN A discrimination learning paradigm used to study psychopharmacological and neuropharmacological phenomena. Also, the organism's ability to discriminate the presence, absence, or other qualitative aspects of a chemical substance.
- B Discrimination 1967
- Discrimination Learning 1982
- R ↓ Drugs 1967

Drug Dissociation
- Use State Dependent Learning

Drug Distribution 1997
PN 53   SC 15277
- B Crime 1967
- R ↓ Drug Abuse 1973
- ↓ Drug Laws 1973
- ↓ Drug Legalization 1997
- ↓ Drug Usage 1971

Drug Dosages 1973
PN 4800   SC 15280
- N Drug Overdoses 1978
- R Bioavailability 1991
- ↓ Drug Administration Methods 1973
- ↓ Drugs 1967

Drug Education 1973
PN 1486   SC 15290
- UF Alcohol Education
- B Health Education 1973
- R Drug Abuse Prevention 1994
- ↓ Drugs 1967

Drug Effects
SN Term discontinued in 1982. Prior to 1982, a mandatory term applied to all studies involving any use of chemical substances administered for non-treatment purposes to human or animal subjects. From 1982, use specific drug classes or names, or terms referring to the chemical substance introduced for nontreatment purposes. In 2000, the term was stripped from all records containing it, and replaced with DRUGS, its postable counterpart.

Drug Effects — (cont'd)
- Use Drugs

Drug Induced Congenital Disorders 1973
PN 87   SC 15310
- B Congenital Disorders 1973
- Toxic Disorders 1973
- N Fetal Alcohol Syndrome 1985
- R Thalidomide 1973

Drug Induced Hallucinations 1973
PN 62   SC 15320
- B Hallucinations 1967
- R Psychedelic Experiences 1973

Drug Interactions 1982
PN 4025   SC 15325
SN Chemical and/or pharmacological reactions of drugs in combination, including agonistic and antagonistic interactions. In 1982, this term was created to replace the discontinued terms DRUG POTENTIATION and DRUG SYNERGISM. In 2000, these terms were stripped from all records and replaced with DRUG INTERACTIONS.
- UF Drug Potentiation
- Drug Synergism
- Potentiation (Drugs)
- R ↓ Drugs 1967
- ↓ Neurotoxins 1982
- Polydrug Abuse 1994

Drug Laws 1973
PN 349   SC 15330
- B Laws 1967
- N ↓ Marihuana Laws 1973
- R Drug Distribution 1997
- ↓ Drug Legalization 1997
- ↓ Drugs 1967

Drug Legalization 1997
PN 10   SC 15333
- N Marihuana Legalization 1973
- R ↓ Drug Abuse 1973
- Drug Distribution 1997
- ↓ Drug Laws 1973
- ↓ Drug Usage 1971

Drug Overdoses 1978
PN 395   SC 15335
- B Drug Dosages 1973
- R ↓ Drug Abuse 1973
- ↓ Drug Addiction 1967
- ↓ Drug Therapy 1967
- ↓ Drug Usage 1971

Drug Potentiation
SN Term was discontinued in 1982. In 2000, the term was stripped from all records containing it, and replaced with DRUG INTERACTIONS, its postable counterpart.
- Use Drug Interactions

Drug Rehabilitation 1973
PN 8601   SC 15350
- UF Rehabilitation (Drug)
- B Rehabilitation 1967
- N ↓ Alcohol Rehabilitation 1982
- Detoxification 1973
- R ↓ Drug Abstinence 1994
- Drug Usage Screening 1988
- ↓ Drugs 1967
- Employee Assistance Programs 1985
- Methadone Maintenance 1978

Drug Rehabilitation — (cont'd)
- R ↓ Psychosocial Rehabilitation 1973
  - Rehabilitation Counseling 1978
  - Smoking Cessation 1988
  - Sobriety 1988
  - ↓ Twelve Step Programs 1997

Drug Sensitivity 1973
PN 1429   SC 15360
SN Behavioral or physical sensitivity, resistance, or reactivity to a particular chemical substance.
- UF   Sensitivity (Drugs)
- B   Side Effects (Drug) 1973
- R   Drug Allergies 1973
  - Drug Tolerance 1973

Drug Synergism
SN Term was discontinued in 1982. In 2000, the term was stripped from all records containing it, and replaced with DRUG INTERACTIONS, its postable counterpart.
- Use   Drug Interactions

Drug Testing
- Use   Drug Usage Screening

Drug Therapy 1967
PN 42827   SC 15380
SN Mandatory term applied to studies dealing with the use of drugs in the clinical treatment of diseases or psychological disorders. Used for human or animal populations. For the use of drugs in non-clinical contexts, use PHARMACOLOGY or PSYCHOPHARMACOLOGY.
- UF   Chemotherapy
  - Medication
  - Pharmacotherapy
  - Therapy (Drug)
- B   Physical Treatment Methods 1973
- N   Hormone Therapy 1994
  - ↓ Narcoanalysis 1973
  - Vitamin Therapy 1978
- R   Bioavailability 1991
  - Detoxification 1973
  - Drug Overdoses 1978
  - ↓ Drugs 1967
  - Maintenance Therapy 1997
  - Neuroleptic Malignant Syndrome 1988
  - ↓ Outpatient Treatment 1967
  - Prescribing (Drugs) 1991
  - Prescription Drugs 1991
  - Self Medication 1991
  - ↓ Side Effects (Drug) 1973
  - Sleep Treatment 1973
  - Tardive Dyskinesia 1988
  - Treatment Resistant Depression 1994

Drug Tolerance 1973
PN 2155   SC 15390
SN Condition in which, after repeated administration, a drug produces a decreased effect and must be administered in larger doses to produce the effect of the original dose.
- UF   Tolerance (Drug)
- R   Drug Sensitivity 1973
  - ↓ Drugs 1967
  - ↓ Side Effects (Drug) 1973

Drug Usage 1971
PN 6391   SC 15400
SN Act, amount, or mode of using any type of drug. Applies only to humans and should be used when neither abuse nor addiction are the subject matter, regardless of the legality of the particular drug.

Drug Usage — (cont'd)
- N ↓ Alcohol Drinking Patterns 1967
  - ↓ Drug Abuse 1973
  - Intravenous Drug Usage 1994
  - Marihuana Usage 1973
  - Tobacco Smoking 1967
- R ↓ Addiction 1973
  - Craving 1997
  - Driving Under The Influence 1988
  - ↓ Drug Abstinence 1994
  - Drug Distribution 1997
  - ↓ Drug Legalization 1997
  - Drug Overdoses 1978
  - Drug Usage Screening 1988
  - ↓ Drugs 1967
  - Needle Sharing 1994

Drug Usage Attitudes 1973
PN 1214   SC 15410
- B   Attitudes 1967
- N   Alcohol Drinking Attitudes 1973
  - Marihuana Legalization 1973
- R   Health Attitudes 1985

Drug Usage Screening 1988
PN 389   SC 15415
SN Procedures used to measure or detect prevalence of drug use through analysis of blood, urine, or other body fluids. Not used for measuring the clinical efficacy of therapeutic drugs.
- UF   Drug Testing
- B   Screening 1982
- R   Blood Alcohol Concentration 1994
  - ↓ Drug Abuse 1973
  - ↓ Drug Dependency 1973
  - ↓ Drug Rehabilitation 1973
  - ↓ Drug Usage 1971
  - ↓ Drugs 1967
  - ↓ Health Screening 1997
  - ↓ Medical Diagnosis 1973
  - Physical Examination 1988
  - Urinalysis 1973

Drug Withdrawal 1973
PN 3220   SC 15420
SN Processes and symptomatic effects resulting from abstinence from a chemical agent or medication. Used for human or animal populations. In 1982, this term replaced the discontinued term DRUG WITHDRAWAL EFFECTS. DRUG WITHDRAWAL EFFECTS was stripped from all records and replaced with DRUG WITHDRAWAL.
- UF   Drug Withdrawal Effects
  - Withdrawal (Drug)
- N   Alcohol Withdrawal 1994
  - Nicotine Withdrawal 1997
- R   Detoxification 1973
  - ↓ Drug Abstinence 1994
  - ↓ Drug Addiction 1967

Drug Withdrawal Effects
SN Term was discontinued in 1982. In 2000, the term was stripped from all records containing it, and replaced with DRUG WITHDRAWAL, its postable counterpart.
- Use   Drug Withdrawal

Drugs 1967
PN 18781   SC 15440

Drugs — (cont'd)
SN Conceptually broad term referring to any substance other than food administered for experimental or treatment purposes. Use specific drug classes or names if possible. In 1982, this term replaced the discontinued term DRUG EFFECTS, and in 1997 it replaced CARDIOTONIC DRUGS and NARCOANALYTIC DRUGS. In 2000, these terms were stripped from all records and replaced with DRUGS.
- UF   Cardiotonic Drugs
  - Drug Effects
  - Narcoanalytic Drugs
  - Psychoactive Drugs
  - Psychotropic Drugs
- N ↓ Adrenergic Blocking Drugs 1973
  - ↓ Adrenergic Drugs 1973
  - ↓ Alcohols 1967
  - ↓ Alkaloids 1973
  - ↓ Amines 1973
  - ↓ Analgesic Drugs 1973
  - ↓ Anesthetic Drugs 1973
  - ↓ Anti Inflammatory Drugs 1982
  - Antiandrogens 1982
  - ↓ Antibiotics 1973
  - ↓ Anticoagulant Drugs 1973
  - ↓ Anticonvulsive Drugs 1973
  - ↓ Antidepressant Drugs 1971
  - ↓ Antiemetic Drugs 1973
  - Antiestrogens 1982
  - ↓ Antihistaminic Drugs 1973
  - ↓ Antihypertensive Drugs 1973
  - Antineoplastic Drugs 1982
  - ↓ Antispasmodic Drugs 1973
  - ↓ Antitremor Drugs 1973
  - ↓ Antitubercular Drugs 1973
  - ↓ Antiviral Drugs 1994
  - ↓ Appetite Depressing Drugs 1973
  - ↓ Barbiturates 1967
  - ↓ Benzodiazepines 1978
  - Bromides 1973
  - ↓ Cannabis 1973
  - Channel Blockers 1991
  - ↓ Cholinergic Blocking Drugs 1973
  - ↓ Cholinergic Drugs 1973
  - ↓ Cholinomimetic Drugs 1973
  - ↓ CNS Affecting Drugs 1973
  - ↓ Diuretics 1973
  - ↓ Dopamine Agonists 1985
  - ↓ Emetic Drugs 1973
  - ↓ Enzyme Inhibitors 1985
  - ↓ Enzymes 1973
  - ↓ Ergot Derivatives 1973
  - ↓ Ganglion Blocking Drugs 1973
  - ↓ Hallucinogenic Drugs 1973
  - ↓ Heart Rate Affecting Drugs 1973
  - ↓ Hypnotic Drugs 1973
  - ↓ Muscle Relaxing Drugs 1973
  - ↓ Narcotic Agonists 1988
  - ↓ Narcotic Antagonists 1973
  - ↓ Narcotic Drugs 1973
  - Nonprescription Drugs 1991
  - ↓ Nootropic Drugs 1991
  - Prescription Drugs 1991
  - ↓ Psychedelic Drugs 1973
  - ↓ Psychotomimetic Drugs 1973
  - ↓ Respiration Stimulating Drugs 1973
  - ↓ Sedatives 1973
  - Serotonin Agonists 1988
  - ↓ Serotonin Antagonists 1973
  - ↓ Steroids 1973
  - ↓ Sympatholytic Drugs 1973
  - ↓ Sympathomimetic Drugs 1973
  - ↓ Tranquilizing Drugs 1967
  - ↓ Vasoconstrictor Drugs 1973
  - ↓ Vasodilator Drugs 1973

Drugs — (cont'd)
R ↓ Acids 1973
    Antibodies 1973
    Bioavailability 1991
    Carcinogens 1973
    ↓ Drug Abuse 1973
    ↓ Drug Administration Methods 1973
    Drug Discrimination 1985
    ↓ Drug Dosages 1973
    Drug Education 1973
    Drug Interactions 1982
    ↓ Drug Laws 1973
    ↓ Drug Rehabilitation 1973
    ↓ Drug Therapy 1967
    Drug Tolerance 1973
    ↓ Drug Usage 1971
    Drug Usage Screening 1988
    ↓ Hormones 1967
    ↓ Insecticides 1973
    ↓ Peptides 1973
    Placebo 1973
    Prenatal Exposure 1991
    Prescribing (Drugs) 1991
    ↓ Proteins 1973
    Self Medication 1991
    ↓ Side Effects (Drug) 1973
    Teratogens 1988
    Toxicity 1973
    ↓ Vitamins 1973

Drunk Driving
Use Driving Under The Influence

Drunkenness
Use Alcohol Intoxication

DSM
Use Diagnostic and Statistical Manual

Dual Careers 1982
PN 708   SC 15455
SN Situation in which both partners or spouses in a family pursue careers.
R ↓ Family 1967
    ↓ Family Structure 1973
    Family Work Relationship 1997
    Working Women 1978

Dual Diagnosis 1991
PN 658   SC 15457
SN Diagnosis based on the coexistence of two or more DSM disorders.
R Comorbidity 1991
    ↓ Diagnosis 1967
    Differential Diagnosis 1967
    ↓ Psychodiagnostic Typologies 1967

Dualism 1973
PN 776   SC 15460
SN Theory viewing mind and body as two separate and irreducible entities.
UF Mind Body
B Philosophies 1967
R Mind 1991

Duchennes Disease
Use Muscular Disorders

Ducks 1973
PN 316   SC 15480
B Birds 1967

Duodenum
Use Intestines

Duration (Response)
Use Response Duration

Duration (Stimulus)
Use Stimulus Duration

Duty to Warn 2001
PN 0   SC 15525
SN A health care professional's legal and ethical obligation to warn third parties of danger, violence, or the possibility of contracting a serious illness.
R ↓ Abuse Reporting 1997
    Accountability 1988
    Informants 1988
    Informed Consent 1985
    Privileged Communication 1973
    Professional Ethics 1973
    Professional Liability 1985
    ↓ Professional Standards 1973

Dwarfism (Pituitary)
Use Hypopituitarism

Dyads 1973
PN 2171   SC 15540
B Social Groups 1973
R Couples 1982

Dying
Use Death and Dying

Dying Patients
Use Terminally Ill Patients

Dynamics (Group)
Use Group Dynamics

Dynorphins 1985
PN 120   SC 15575
B Endogenous Opiates 1985
    Pituitary Hormones 1973

Dysarthria 1973
PN 266   SC 15580
SN Articulation disorder resulting from central nervous system disease, especially brain damage.
B Articulation Disorders 1973
    Central Nervous System Disorders 1973
R Muscular Dystrophy 1973
    ↓ Paralysis 1973

Dyscalculia
Use Acalculia

Dysfunctional Family 1991
PN 478   SC 15590
SN A family system in which relationships or communication are impaired.
R Codependency 1991
    Double Bind Interaction 1973
    ↓ Family 1967
    ↓ Family Relations 1967
    ↓ Family Structure 1973
    Marital Conflict 1973
    Schizophrenogenic Family 1967

Dyskinesia 1973
PN 708   SC 15600

Dyskinesia — (cont'd)
SN Abnormal involuntary motor processes that occur due to underlying disease processes.
B Movement Disorders 1985
    Symptoms 1967
N Bradykinesia 2001
    Tardive Dyskinesia 1988
R ↓ Neuromuscular Disorders 1973

Dyslexia 1973
PN 2271   SC 15610
SN Reading disorder involving an inability to understand what is read. Less severe than alexia.
B Alexia 1982
    Learning Disabilities 1973
    Reading Disabilities 1967
R Educational Diagnosis 1978
    ↓ Reading 1967

Dysmenorrhea 1973
PN 104   SC 15620
SN Difficult and painful menstruation.
B Menstrual Disorders 1973

Dysmetria
Use Ataxia

Dysmorphophobia
SN In 2000, the term was discontinued, and all records containing it were stripped of the term and replaced with BODY DYSMORPHIC DISORDER, its postable counterpart.
Use Body Dysmorphic Disorder

Dyspareunia 1973
PN 52   SC 15650
B Sexual Function Disturbances 1973
    Sexual Intercourse (Human) 1973
R Frigidity 1973
    Vaginismus 1973

Dysphasia 1978
PN 220   SC 15655
SN Impairment of language comprehension, formulation, or use due to brain damage. Used only for partial impairments.
B Aphasia 1967
N ↓ Alexia 1982

Dysphonia 1973
PN 220   SC 15660
SN Any speech disorder involving problems of voice quality, pitch, or intensity.
UF Voice Disorders
B Speech Disorders 1967

Dysphoria
Use Major Depression

Dyspnea 1973
PN 72   SC 15680
SN Difficulty in breathing which may or may not have an organic cause.
B Respiratory Distress 1973
    Respiratory Tract Disorders 1973
    Symptoms 1967
N Asthma 1967
R ↓ Cardiovascular Disorders 1967
    ↓ Lung Disorders 1973
    ↓ Somatoform Disorders 2001

Dyspraxia
Use Movement Disorders

Dysthymia
  Use Dysthymic Disorder

Dysthymic Disorder [1988]
PN 842   SC 15693
SN Chronic affective disorder characterized by either relatively mild depressive symptoms or marked loss of pleasure in usual activities. Consider DEPRESSION (EMOTION) to access references prior to 1988.
  UF Dysthymia
  B Major Depression [1988]
  R Anhedonia [1985]

Dystonia
  Use Muscular Disorders

Dystrophy (Muscular)
  Use Muscular Dystrophy

Eagerness
  Use Enthusiasm

Ear (Anatomy) [1967]
PN 491   SC 15720
  B Sense Organs [1973]
  N External Ear [1973]
    ↓ Labyrinth (Anatomy) [1973]
    Middle Ear [1973]
    ↓ Vestibular Apparatus [1967]
  R ↓ Ear Disorders [1973]

Ear Canal
  Use External Ear

Ear Disorders [1973]
PN 283   SC 15740
SN Disorders of the external, middle, or inner ear. Use HEARING DISORDERS for pathology involving auditory neural pathways beyond the inner ear. In 1997, this term replaced the discontinued term OTOSCLEROSIS. In 2000, OTOSCLEROSIS was stripped from all records and replaced with EAR DISORDERS.
  UF Otosclerosis
  B Sense Organ Disorders [1973]
  N ↓ Labyrinth Disorders [1973]
    Tinnitus [1973]
  R ↓ Auditory Perception [1967]
    ↓ Ear (Anatomy) [1967]
    Hearing Disorders [1982]

Ear Ossicles
  Use Middle Ear

Early Childhood Development [1973]
PN 2158   SC 15770
SN Process of physical, cognitive, personality, and psychosocial growth occurring from birth through age 5. Use a more specific term if possible.
  B Childhood Development [1967]
  N ↓ Infant Development [1973]
  R Early Experience [1967]
    Early Memories [1985]
    ↓ Physical Development [1973]
    ↓ Psychogenesis [1973]

Early Experience [1967]
PN 7545   SC 15780
SN Any occurrences early in an individual's life. Used for human or animal populations.
  B Experiences (Events) [1973]
  R Age Regression (Hypnotic) [1988]

Early Experience — (cont'd)
  R Anniversary Events [1994]
    Autobiographical Memory [1994]
    ↓ Early Childhood Development [1973]
    Early Memories [1985]
    Enactments [1997]
    Life Review [1991]

Early Infantile Autism [1973]
PN 481   SC 15790
  B Autism [1967]
    Childhood Psychosis [1967]
  R Autistic Children [1973]
    Childhood Schizophrenia [1967]
    Symbiotic Infantile Psychosis [1973]

Early Intervention [1982]
PN 2871   SC 15793
SN Action taken utilizing medical, family, school, social, or mental health resources and aimed at infants and children at risk for, or in the early stages of mental, physical, learning, or other disorders.
  R Drug Abuse Prevention [1994]
    ↓ Prenatal Care [1991]
    ↓ Prevention [1973]
    Primary Mental Health Prevention [1973]
    Special Education [1967]
    Special Needs [1994]
    ↓ Treatment [1967]

Early Memories [1985]
PN 863   SC 15796
SN Memories of events that occurred early in an individual's life.
  UF Childhood Memories
  B Memory [1967]
  R Age Regression (Hypnotic) [1988]
    Anniversary Events [1994]
    Autobiographical Memory [1994]
    ↓ Early Childhood Development [1973]
    Early Experience [1967]
    False Memory [1997]
    Life Review [1991]
    Reminiscence [1985]
    Repressed Memory [1997]

Earthworms [1973]
PN 26   SC 15800
  B Worms [1967]

Eating
  SN In 2000, the term was discontinued, and all records containing it were stripped of the term and replaced with INGESTION, its postable counterpart.
  Use Ingestion

Eating Attitudes [1994]
PN 388   SC 15823
  B Attitudes [1967]
  R ↓ Appetite [1973]
    Food Preferences [1973]
    Obesity (Attitudes Toward) [1997]

Eating Disorders [1997]
PN 3219   SC 15825
SN In 1997, this term was created to replace the discontinued term APPETITE DISORDERS. In 2000, APPETITE DISORDERS was stripped from all records and replaced with EATING DISORDERS.
  UF Appetite Disorders
  B Mental Disorders [1967]
  N Anorexia Nervosa [1973]
    Bulimia [1985]
    Hyperphagia [1973]

Eating Disorders — (cont'd)
  N Kleine Levin Syndrome [2001]
    Obesity [1973]
    Pica [1973]
  R Aphagia [1973]
    ↓ Appetite [1973]
    Binge Eating [1991]
    Coprophagia [2001]
    Nausea [1973]
    ↓ Nutritional Deficiencies [1973]
    ↓ Physical Disorders [1997]
    Rumination (Eating) [2001]
    ↓ Symptoms [1967]
    ↓ Underweight [1973]

Eating Patterns
  SN This term was discontinued in 1982, when the term EATING was used to capture the concept. In 2000, FEEDING PRACTICES replaced EATING as the postable counterpart. All records containing EATING PATTERNS were stripped of this term and replaced with FEEDING PRACTICES.
  Use Feeding Practices

Echinodermata [1973]
PN 35   SC 15840
  UF Starfish
  B Invertebrates [1973]

Echoencephalography [1973]
PN 9   SC 15850
  B Encephalography [1973]
    Medical Diagnosis [1973]

Echolalia [1973]
PN 104   SC 15870
  B Language Disorders [1982]
  R Gilles de la Tourette Disorder [1973]

Echolocation [1973]
PN 185   SC 15880
  R ↓ Animal Ethology [1967]
    ↓ Animal Vocalizations [1973]

Eclectic Psychology
  Use Theoretical Orientation

Eclectic Psychotherapy [1994]
PN 77   SC 15887
  B Psychotherapy [1967]
  R Interdisciplinary Treatment Approach [1973]
    Multimodal Treatment Approach [1991]

Ecological Factors [1973]
PN 972   SC 15890
SN Elements involved in relations between organisms and their natural environments.
  N Pollution [1973]
    Topography [1973]
  R Behavioral Ecology [1997]
    Ecological Psychology [1994]
    Ecology [1973]
    ↓ Environmental Effects [1973]

Ecological Psychology [1994]
PN 204   SC 15895
SN Branch of psychology that studies the frequency or nature of psychological processes or behavior as they occur in natural settings. Compare ENVIRONMENTAL PSYCHOLOGY.
  B Psychology [1967]
  R Behavioral Ecology [1997]
    ↓ Ecological Factors [1973]

Ecological Psychology — (cont'd)
R   Environmental Psychology 1982

Ecology 1973
PN 719   SC 15900
R   Behavioral Ecology 1997
     Conservation (Ecological Behavior) 1978
     ↓ Ecological Factors 1973
     ↓ Environment 1967
     Environmental Attitudes 1978
     Environmental Education 1994
     Pollution 1973

Economically Disadvantaged
Use Disadvantaged

Economics 1985
PN 2523   SC 15915
SN Social science dealing with the production, distribution, and consumption of goods and services. Used for the discipline or economic factors themselves.
B   Social Sciences 1967
R   Budgets 1997
     Cost Containment 1991
     ↓ Costs and Cost Analysis 1973
     ↓ Division of Labor 1988
     Economy 1973
     Health Care Costs 1994
     Money 1967
     ↓ Political Economic Systems 1973
     Resource Allocation 1997

Economy 1973
PN 815   SC 15920
R   Budgets 1997
     ↓ Costs and Cost Analysis 1973
     Economics 1985
     Money 1967
     ↓ Political Economic Systems 1973
     Taxation 1985

ECS Therapy
Use Electroconvulsive Shock Therapy

Ecstasy (Drug)
Use Methylenedioxymethamphetamine

ECT (Therapy)
Use Electroconvulsive Shock Therapy

Eczema 1973
PN 44   SC 15950
B   Dermatitis 1973
R   Allergic Skin Disorders 1973

Educable Mentally Retarded
SN In 2000, the term was discontinued, and all records containing it were stripped of the term and replaced with MILD MENTAL RETARDATION, its postable counterpart.
Use Mild Mental Retardation

Education 1967
PN 7869   SC 16000
SN Conceptually broad term referring to the process of imparting or obtaining knowledge, skills, and values. Use a more specific term if possible.
UF Educational Process
     Training
N   ↓ Adult Education 1973
     Bilingual Education 1978
     Client Education 1985

Education — (cont'd)
N   ↓ Clinical Methods Training 1973
     Communication Skills Training 1982
     Counselor Education 1973
     ↓ Curriculum 1967
     Death Education 1982
     Elementary Education 1973
     ↓ Family Life Education 1997
     ↓ Higher Education 1973
     Middle School Education 1985
     Multicultural Education 1988
     ↓ Nontraditional Education 1982
     Nursing Education 1973
     Paraprofessional Education 1973
     Parent Training 1978
     ↓ Personnel Training 1967
     Preschool Education 1973
     Private School Education 1973
     Public School Education 1973
     Religious Education 1973
     ↓ Remedial Education 1985
     Secondary Education 1973
     Social Work Education 1973
     Special Education 1967
     ↓ Teacher Education 1967
R   Ability Grouping 1973
     ↓ Academic Achievement 1967
     Academic Aptitude 1973
     Accreditation (Education Personnel) 1973
     Athletic Training 1991
     Boards of Education 1978
     Classroom Behavior Modification 1973
     Classroom Discipline 1973
     Coeducation 1973
     ↓ Dropouts 1973
     Educational Administration 1967
     Educational Aspirations 1973
     ↓ Educational Background 1967
     Educational Counseling 1967
     Educational Degrees 1973
     Educational Diagnosis 1978
     Educational Financial Assistance 1973
     Educational Incentives 1973
     ↓ Educational Laboratories 1973
     ↓ Educational Measurement 1967
     Educational Objectives 1978
     ↓ Educational Personnel 1973
     Educational Placement 1978
     Educational Program Accreditation 1994
     ↓ Educational Programs 1973
     ↓ Educational Psychology 1967
     Educational Quality 1997
     Educational Reform 1997
     Educational Television 1967
     Environmental Education 1994
     Equal Education 1978
     ↓ Extracurricular Activities 1973
     Grade Level 1994
     Home Schooling 1994
     Mainstreaming (Educational) 1978
     Psychoeducation 1994
     Questioning 1982
     School Adjustment 1967
     School Attendance 1973
     School Counseling 1982
     ↓ School Dropouts 1967
     ↓ School Enrollment 1973
     ↓ School Environment 1973
     ↓ School Facilities 1973
     School Graduation 1991
     School Integration 1982
     School Learning 1967
     School Readiness 1973
     School Transition 1997

Education — (cont'd)
R   School Truancy 1973
     School to Work Transition 1994
     ↓ Schools 1967
     Student Admission Criteria 1973
     Student Attitudes 1967
     ↓ Student Characteristics 1982
     Student Personnel Services 1978
     Student Records 1978
     ↓ Students 1967
     Study Habits 1973
     ↓ Teacher Characteristics 1973
     Teacher Student Interaction 1973
     Teacher Tenure 1973
     ↓ Teaching 1967
     ↓ Teaching Methods 1967
     Theories of Education 1973

Education Students 1982
PN 452   SC 15995
SN Students enrolled in a school or department of education.
B   College Students 1967
R   Preservice Teachers 1982
     Student Teachers 1973
     ↓ Teacher Education 1967

Educational Administration 1967
PN 2339   SC 16010
UF School Administration
     School Organization
B   Management 1967
R   Boards of Education 1978
     Decentralization 1978
     ↓ Education 1967
     Educational Reform 1997

Educational Administrators
Use School Administrators

Educational Aspirations 1973
PN 1010   SC 16020
SN Personal desire for achievement in a certain educational field or to a certain level or degree.
B   Aspirations 1967
R   Academic Specialization 1973
     ↓ Education 1967
     Educational Objectives 1978

Educational Attainment Level 1997
PN 749   SC 16025
SN Completion of a course of study or reaching a specific educational level.
UF Attainment Level (Education)
B   Educational Background 1967
R   ↓ Academic Achievement 1967
     Educational Degrees 1973
     School Graduation 1991
     School to Work Transition 1994

Educational Audiovisual Aids 1973
PN 256   SC 16030
UF Audiovisual Aids (Educational)
B   Audiovisual Communications Media 1973
     Instructional Media 1967
N   Motion Pictures (Educational) 1973
R   ↓ Audiovisual Instruction 1973
     Educational Television 1967
     Film Strips 1967
     Televised Instruction 1973
     Videotape Instruction 1973

Educational Background   1967
PN 3984   **SC** 16040
N   Educational Attainment Level   1997
      Parent Educational Background   1973
R   Biographical Data   1978
     ↓ Education   1967
      School Leavers   1988

Educational Background (Parents)
Use   Parent Educational Background

Educational Counseling   1967
PN 2517   **SC** 16060
SN   Assistance offered to school or college students on school program planning, course selection, or academic specialization. Compare SCHOOL COUNSELING.
UF   Educational Guidance
      Guidance (Educational)
B   Counseling   1967
R   ↓ Education   1967
      Occupational Guidance   1967
      Student Personnel Services   1978

Educational Degrees   1973
PN 692   **SC** 16070
UF   College Degrees
      Degrees (Educational)
      Graduate Degrees
      Undergraduate Degrees
R   College Graduates   1982
     ↓ Education   1967
      Educational Attainment Level   1997
      Educational Program Accreditation   1994
      High School Graduates   1978
     ↓ Higher Education   1973
      School Graduation   1991

Educational Diagnosis   1978
PN 2685   **SC** 16075
SN   Identification of cognitive, perceptual, emotional, and other factors which influence academic performance or school adjustment, usually for such purposes as placement of students in curricula or programs suited to their needs, and referral.
B   Diagnosis   1967
R   Differential Diagnosis   1967
      Dyslexia   1973
     ↓ Education   1967
     ↓ Educational Measurement   1967
      Educational Placement   1978
     ↓ Learning Disabilities   1973
     ↓ Learning Disorders   1967
     ↓ Psychodiagnosis   1967
      Psychological Report   1988
     ↓ Reading Disabilities   1967
      Woodcock Johnson Psychoeducational
       Battery   2001

Educational Environment
Use   School Environment

Educational Field Trips   1973
PN 67   **SC** 16080
UF   Field Trips (Educational)
B   Teaching Methods   1967
R   Curricular Field Experience   1982
     ↓ Experiential Learning   1997

Educational Financial Assistance   1973
PN 182   **SC** 16090
UF   Financial Assistance (Educational)
      Scholarships
      School Federal Aid

Educational Financial Assistance —
   (cont'd)
UF   School Financial Assistance
      Stipends
R   ↓ Education   1967
      Funding   1988
      Student Personnel Services   1978

Educational Guidance
Use   Educational Counseling

Educational Incentives   1973
PN 127   **SC** 16120
SN   Any type of incentive used or experienced in a school, classroom, or other educational context.
B   Incentives   1967
      Motivation   1967
R   ↓ Education   1967

Educational Inequality
Use   Equal Education

Educational Laboratories   1973
PN 166   **SC** 16130
UF   Laboratories (Educational)
B   School Facilities   1973
N   Language Laboratories   1973
R   ↓ Education   1967

Educational Measurement   1967
PN 5172   **SC** 16140
SN   Practices, procedures, methods, and tests used in the assessment of student characteristics or performance, such as academic achievement and school adjustment.
B   Testing   1967
N   Curriculum Based Assessment   1994
     ↓ Entrance Examinations   1973
      Grading (Educational)   1973
      Minimum Competency Tests   1985
R   ↓ Education   1967
      Educational Diagnosis   1978
     ↓ Screening   1982

Educational Objectives   1978
PN 1356   **SC** 16145
SN   Specific educational goals toward which one's efforts are directed, or goals proposed or established by educational authorities.
UF   Course Objectives
      Instructional Objectives
B   Goals   1967
R   ↓ Curriculum   1967
     ↓ Education   1967
      Educational Aspirations   1973
      Educational Quality   1997
      Educational Reform   1997
      Mastery Learning   1985

Educational Personnel   1973
PN 2660   **SC** 16150
UF   Faculty
B   Professional Personnel   1978
N   ↓ School Administrators   1973
      School Counselors   1973
      School Nurses   1973
      Teacher Aides   1973
     ↓ Teachers   1967
R   ↓ Education   1967
     ↓ Educational Psychologists   1973
     ↓ Mental Health Personnel   1967
      Missionaries   1973
      Professional Supervision   1988

Educational Personnel — (cont'd)
R   Speech Therapists   1973
     ↓ Volunteer Personnel   1973

Educational Placement   1978
PN 1797   **SC** 16155
SN   Assignment of students to classes, programs, or schools according to their abilities and readiness.
UF   Placement (Educational)
R   Ability Grouping   1973
     ↓ Education   1967
      Educational Diagnosis   1978
      Grade Level   1994
     ↓ Mainstreaming   1991
      Mainstreaming (Educational)   1978
      Remedial Reading   1973
     ↓ Screening   1982
      Special Education   1967

Educational Process
Use   Education

Educational Program Accreditation   1994
PN 102   **SC** 16165
SN   Recognition and approval of educational programs or institution's maintenance of standards to qualify graduates for professional practice or admission to higher or more specialized educational institutions.
UF   Accreditation (Educational Programs)
      School Accreditation
R   ↓ Curriculum   1967
     ↓ Education   1967
      Educational Degrees   1973
     ↓ Educational Programs   1973
      Educational Quality   1997
     ↓ Graduate Psychology Education   1967
     ↓ Higher Education   1973
     ↓ Psychology Education   1978

Educational Program Evaluation   1973
PN 2807   **SC** 16170
SN   Techniques, materials, or process of determining the worth or effectiveness of an educational program in relation to its goals or other criteria.
UF   Program Evaluation (Educational)
B   Program Evaluation   1985
R   Course Evaluation   1978
     ↓ Educational Programs   1973
      Educational Quality   1997

Educational Program Planning   1973
PN 1248   **SC** 16180
UF   Program Planning (Educational)
B   Program Development   1991
R   Curriculum Development   1973
     ↓ Educational Programs   1973

Educational Programs   1973
PN 6791   **SC** 16190
UF   Work Study Programs
N   Foreign Study   1973
      Literacy Programs   1997
      Project Follow Through   1973
      Project Head Start   1973
      Special Education   1967
      Upward Bound   1973
R   Compensatory Education   1973
      Cooperative Education   1982
      Curricular Field Experience   1982
     ↓ Education   1967
      Educational Program Accreditation   1994
      Educational Program Evaluation   1973
      Educational Program Planning   1973

Educational Programs — (cont'd)

- **R** Educational Reform [1997]
- Multicultural Education [1988]
- ↓ Nontraditional Education [1982]
- ↓ Program Development [1991]

Educational Psychologists [1973]

PN 442　　　　　**SC** 16200

SN Psychologists conducting research and formulating policies in areas of diagnosis and measurement, school adjustment, school learning, and special education.

- **B** Psychologists [1967]
- **N** School Psychologists [1973]
- **R** ↓ Educational Personnel [1973]

Educational Psychology [1967]

PN 1567　　　　　**SC** 16210

SN Branch of psychology that emphasizes the application of psychological theories and research findings to educational processes, especially in the areas of learning and motivation.

- **B** Applied Psychology [1973]
- **N** School Psychology [1973]
- **R** ↓ Education [1967]

Educational Quality [1997]

PN 112　　　　　**SC** 16205

- **UF** Quality of Education
- **R** Accreditation (Education Personnel) [1973]
- Course Evaluation [1978]
- ↓ Education [1967]
- Educational Objectives [1978]
- Educational Program Accreditation [1994]
- Educational Program Evaluation [1973]
- Educational Reform [1997]
- Equal Education [1978]
- Teacher Effectiveness Evaluation [1978]

Educational Reform [1997]

PN 358　　　　　**SC** 16217

- **R** ↓ Education [1967]
- Educational Administration [1967]
- Educational Objectives [1978]
- ↓ Educational Programs [1973]
- Educational Quality [1997]
- ↓ Policy Making [1988]

Educational Supervision

Use Professional Supervision

Educational Television [1967]

PN 173　　　　　**SC** 16220

- **B** Television [1967]
- **R** ↓ Education [1967]
- ↓ Educational Audiovisual Aids [1973]
- Televised Instruction [1973]

Educational Theory

Use Theories of Education

Educational Therapy [1997]

PN 11　　　　　**SC** 16225

SN Use SCHOOL COUNSELING to access references from 1982-1996.

- **R** Art Therapy [1973]
- Music Therapy [1973]
- Psychoeducation [1994]
- ↓ Psychotherapy [1967]
- ↓ Remedial Education [1985]
- School Counseling [1982]
- Special Education [1967]
- ↓ Teaching Methods [1967]

Educational Toys [1973]

PN 37　　　　　**SC** 16230

- **B** Toys [1973]

Edwards Personal Preference Schedule [1967]

PN 111　　　　　**SC** 16240

- **B** Nonprojective Personality Measures [1973]

Edwards Personality Inventory [1973]

PN 6　　　　　**SC** 16250

- **B** Nonprojective Personality Measures [1973]

Edwards Social Desirability Scale [1973]

PN 13　　　　　**SC** 16260

- **B** Nonprojective Personality Measures [1973]

EEG (Electrophysiology)

Use Electroencephalography

Effect Size (Statistical) [1985]

PN 250　　　　　**SC** 16272

SN A statistical estimate that represents the magnitude of a statistically significant result.

- **UF** Magnitude of Effect (Statistical)
- **B** Statistical Analysis [1967]
- **R** Confidence Limits (Statistics) [1973]
- Statistical Significance [1973]

Efferent Pathways [1982]

PN 382　　　　　**SC** 16275

SN Collections of fibers that typically carry neural impulses away from central nervous system connections toward muscular and glandular innervations.

- **UF** Motor Pathways
- **B** Neural Pathways [1982]
- Parasympathetic Nervous System [1973]
- **N** Extrapyramidal Tracts [1973]
- Pyramidal Tracts [1973]
- **R** ↓ Afferent Pathways [1982]
- Motor Neurons [1973]
- ↓ Motor Processes [1967]

Efficacy Expectations

Use Self Efficacy

Efficiency (Employee)

Use Employee Efficiency

Effort

Use Energy Expenditure

Egalitarianism [1985]

PN 109　　　　　**SC** 16287

- **B** Personality Traits [1967]
- **R** Authoritarianism [1967]
- ↓ Equity (Social) [1978]
- Resource Allocation [1997]

Ego [1967]

PN 3739　　　　　**SC** 16290

- **B** Psychoanalytic Personality Factors [1973]
- **R** ↓ Ego Development [1991]
- Ego Identity [1991]

Ego Development [1991]

PN 618　　　　　**SC** 16294

SN Gradual emergence development of a part of the id into the ego or an awareness of a child that he or she is a real distinct and separate entity.

- **B** Personality Development [1967]
- **N** Ego Identity [1991]

Ego Development — (cont'd)

- **R** Ego [1967]
- ↓ Psychoanalytic Theory [1967]

Ego Identity [1991]

PN 382　　　　　**SC** 16297

SN The experience of the self as a recognizable entity resulting from one's ego ideal, behavior and social roles, and adjustments to reality.

- **B** Ego Development [1991]
- **R** Ego [1967]
- Erikson (Erik) [1991]
- ↓ Personality Development [1967]
- ↓ Self Concept [1967]

Egocentrism [1978]

PN 641　　　　　**SC** 16300

SN Self-centered preoccupation or concern regarding one's own needs, wishes, desires, or preferences and usually accompanied by a disregard for the concerns of others. Also, in cognitive development, the inclination to believe that others maintain the same experiential perspective as oneself. Use EGOCENTRISM to access references to role taking or perspective taking from 1978-1981.

- **R** Agreeableness [1997]
- ↓ Cognitive Development [1973]
- ↓ Concept Formation [1967]
- Narcissism [1967]
- ↓ Personality [1967]
- ↓ Personality Traits [1967]
- Role Taking [1982]

Egotism [1973]

PN 139　　　　　**SC** 16310

- **B** Personality Traits [1967]
- **R** Emotional Superiority [1973]
- Grandiosity [1994]

Eidetic Imagery [1973]

PN 124　　　　　**SC** 16320

SN Clear and detailed memory for objects or events perceived, usually visually.

- **UF** Photographic Memory
- **B** Memory [1967]
- **R** Episodic Memory [1988]
- ↓ Spatial Memory [1988]
- ↓ Visual Memory [1994]

Ejaculation

Use Male Orgasm

EKG (Electrophysiology)

Use Electrocardiography

Elavil

Use Amitriptyline

Elbow (Anatomy) [1973]

PN 79　　　　　**SC** 16360

- **B** Joints (Anatomy) [1973]
- **R** Arm (Anatomy) [1973]

Elder Abuse [1988]

PN 344　　　　　**SC** 16363

SN Abuse or neglect of elderly persons in a family, institutional, or other setting.

- **B** Antisocial Behavior [1971]
- **R** ↓ Abuse Reporting [1997]
- Emotional Abuse [1991]
- ↓ Family Violence [1982]
- Patient Abuse [1991]
- Physical Abuse [1991]

Elder Abuse — (cont'd)
R ↓ Sexual Abuse 1988

Elder Care 1994
PN 538   SC 16364
SN Informal or formal support systems or programs for the care of the elderly or assistance to the families who have responsibilities for their care.
R   Adult Day Care 1997
     Caregiver Burden 1994
     Caregivers 1988
     Employee Assistance Programs 1985
   ↓ Employee Benefits 1973
     Home Care 1985
     Home Care Personnel 1997
     Home Visiting Programs 1973
     Homebound 1988
     Protective Services 1997

Elected Government Officials
Use Government Personnel

Elections (Political)
Use Political Elections

Elective Abortion
Use Induced Abortion

Elective Mutism 1973
PN 208   SC 16390
UF   Selective Mutism
B   Mental Disorders 1967
     Mutism 1973

Electra Complex 1973
PN 15   SC 16400
B   Psychoanalytic Personality Factors 1973

Electric Fishes 1973
PN 105   SC 16410
B   Fishes 1967

Electrical Activity 1967
PN 8159   SC 16420
SN Electrically measured responses or response patterns, usually of individual units (i.e., cells) or groups of cells, in any part of the nervous system. Includes neural or neuron impulses; neural depolarization or hyperpolarization; spike, resting, action, generator, graded, presynaptic, or postsynaptic potentials. Compare ELECTROPHYSIOLOGY.
B   Electrophysiology 1973
N   Alpha Rhythm 1973
   ↓ Cortical Evoked Potentials 1973
     Delta Rhythm 1973
   ↓ Evoked Potentials 1967
     Kindling 1985
     Postactivation Potentials 1985
     Theta Rhythm 1973
R   Electrocardiography 1967
   ↓ Electroencephalography 1967

Electrical Brain Stimulation 1973
PN 3404   SC 16430
B   Brain Stimulation 1967
     Electrical Stimulation 1973
     Electrophysiology 1973
     Stereotaxic Techniques 1973
R ↓ Evoked Potentials 1967
     Kindling 1985
     Postactivation Potentials 1985
   ↓ Self Stimulation 1967

Electrical Injuries 1973
PN 24   SC 16440
B   Injuries 1973
R   Burns 1973
     Shock 1967
   ↓ Wounds 1973

Electrical Stimulation 1973
PN 1819   SC 16460
B   Stimulation 1967
N   Electrical Brain Stimulation 1973
   ↓ Electroconvulsive Shock 1967
R   Experimental Epilepsy 1978
     Shock 1967

Electro Oculography 1973
PN 144   SC 16470
UF   EOG (Electrophysiology)
B   Electrophysiology 1973
     Medical Diagnosis 1973
     Ophthalmologic Examination 1973
R   Electroretinography 1967

Electrocardiography 1967
PN 347   SC 16480
UF   EKG (Electrophysiology)
B   Cardiography 1973
     Electrophysiology 1973
R ↓ Electrical Activity 1967

Electroconvulsive Shock 1967
PN 876   SC 16490
B   Electrical Stimulation 1973
N   Electroconvulsive Shock Therapy 1967
R   Shock 1967

Electroconvulsive Shock Therapy 1967
PN 2646   SC 16500
UF   ECS Therapy
     ECT (Therapy)
     Electroshock Therapy
B   Electroconvulsive Shock 1967
     Shock Therapy 1973

Electrodermal Response
Use Galvanic Skin Response

Electrodes 1967
PN 279   SC 16520
B   Apparatus 1967
R ↓ Stimulators (Apparatus) 1973

Electroencephalography 1967
PN 8453   SC 16530
SN Method of graphically recording the electrical activity (potentials) of the brain by means of intracranial electrodes or electrodes applied to the scalp. Used both for the method as well as the resulting electroencephalogram or the electrophysiological activity itself.
UF   EEG (Electrophysiology)
B   Electrophysiology 1973
     Encephalography 1973
     Medical Diagnosis 1973
N   Alpha Rhythm 1973
     Delta Rhythm 1973
     Theta Rhythm 1973
R ↓ Electrical Activity 1967
     Magnetoencephalography 1985
     Rheoencephalography 1973

Electrolytes 1973
PN 253   SC 16540

Electrolytes — (cont'd)
UF   Ions
N   Calcium Ions 1973
     Chloride Ions 1973
     Magnesium Ions 1973
     Potassium Ions 1973
     Sodium Ions 1973
     Zinc 1985
R ↓ Chemical Elements 1973

Electromyography 1967
PN 2329   SC 16550
UF   EMG (Electrophysiology)
B   Electrophysiology 1973
     Medical Diagnosis 1973

Electronic Communication 2001
PN 0   SC 16555
SN Conceptually broad term referring to the transmission or telecommunication of verbal or audiovisual information including, but not limited to electronic mail or email, Internet or local computer network Forums, Bulletin Boards, or other electronic messaging systems.
B   Communication 1967
R ↓ Automated Information Processing 1973
   ↓ Communication Systems 1973
   ↓ Communications Media 1973
   ↓ Computer Applications 1973
   ↓ Computer Peripheral Devices 1985
     Computer Searching 1991
     Databases 1991
     Information 1967
   ↓ Information Systems 1991
     Internet 2001
     Messages 1973
   ↓ Technology 1973

Electronystagmography 1973
PN 9   SC 16560
B   Electrophysiology 1973
     Medical Diagnosis 1973

Electrophysiology 1973
PN 1834   SC 16570
SN Branch of physiology concerned with the study of electrical phenomena within the living organism (i.e., nerve and muscle tissue). Used for the scientific discipline or the electrophysiological processes themselves. Compare ELECTRICAL ACTIVITY.
B   Physiology 1967
N ↓ Electrical Activity 1967
     Electrical Brain Stimulation 1973
     Electro Oculography 1973
     Electrocardiography 1967
   ↓ Electroencephalography 1967
     Electromyography 1967
     Electronystagmography 1973
     Electroplethysmography 1973
     Electroretinography 1967
     Galvanic Skin Response 1967
   ↓ Skin Electrical Properties 1973
     Skin Potential 1973
R ↓ Medical Diagnosis 1973

Electroplethysmography 1973
PN 6   SC 16580
B   Electrophysiology 1973
     Medical Diagnosis 1973
     Plethysmography 1973

Electroretinography 1967
PN 198   SC 16590
B   Electrophysiology 1973

Electroretinography — (cont'd)
- B   Medical Diagnosis   1973
-    Ophthalmologic Examination   1973
- R   Electro Oculography   1973

Electroshock Therapy
- Use   Electroconvulsive Shock Therapy

Electrosleep Treatment   1978
PN   15   SC   16605
SN   Therapeutic application of a low intensity, intermittent electrical current to the skull, often producing a state of relaxation, but not necessarily sleep.
- B   Physical Treatment Methods   1973
- R   ↓ Shock Therapy   1973
-    Sleep Treatment   1973

Elementarism
- Use   Reductionism

Elementary Education   1973
PN   1055   SC   16620
- B   Education   1967
- R   Elementary Schools   1973

Elementary School Students   1967
PN   29114   SC   16630
SN   Students in grades 1-6. Mandatory term in educational contexts.
- B   Students   1967
- N   Intermediate School Students   1973
-    Primary School Students   1973
- R   Grade Level   1994
-    Middle School Students   1985

Elementary School Teachers   1973
PN   5085   SC   16640
- B   Teachers   1967

Elementary Schools   1973
PN   812   SC   16650
- UF   Grammar Schools
-     Primary Schools
- B   Schools   1967
- R   Elementary Education   1973

Elephants   1973
PN   55   SC   16660
- B   Mammals   1973

Elimination (Excretion)
- Use   Excretion

Ellis (Albert)   1991
PN   23   SC   16680
SN   Identifies biographical or autobiographical studies and discussions of Ellis's works.
- R   ↓ Psychologists   1967
-    Rational Emotive Therapy   1978
-    Self Talk   1988

Embarrassment   1973
PN   238   SC   16690
- B   Emotional States   1973
- R   Shame   1994

Embedded Figures Testing   1967
PN   179   SC   16700
- B   Nonprojective Personality Measures   1973

Embolisms   1973
PN   36   SC   16710

Embolisms — (cont'd)
- B   Cardiovascular Disorders   1967
- R   ↓ Thromboses   1973

Embryo   1973
PN   218   SC   16720
- B   Prenatal Developmental Stages   1973

EMDR
- Use   Eye Movement Desensitization Therapy

Emergency Services   1973
PN   1560   SC   16730
- R   ↓ Crisis Intervention Services   1973
-    Natural Disasters   1973

Emetic Drugs   1973
PN   78   SC   16740
- UF   Vomit Inducing Drugs
- B   Drugs   1967
- N   Apomorphine   1973
-    Disulfiram   1978
- R   ↓ CNS Stimulating Drugs   1973
-    ↓ Narcotic Drugs   1973
-    Vomiting   1973

EMG (Electrophysiology)
- Use   Electromyography

Emotional Abuse   1991
PN   590   SC   16755
- UF   Psychological Abuse
- B   Antisocial Behavior   1971
- R   ↓ Child Abuse   1971
-    Child Neglect   1988
-    Elder Abuse   1988
-    Erotomania   1997
-    Partner Abuse   1991
-    Patient Abuse   1991
-    Physical Abuse   1991

Emotional Adjustment   1973
PN   8472   SC   16760
SN   Personal acceptance, adaptation, and relation to one's inner self and environment.
- UF   Emotional Maladjustment
-     Maladjustment (Emotional)
-     Personal Adjustment
-     Psychological Adjustment
- B   Adjustment   1967
- N   ↓ Emotional Control   1973
-    Identity Crisis   1973
- R   Adjustment Disorders   1994
-    Codependency   1991
-    Coping Behavior   1967
-    ↓ Emotionally Disturbed   1973
-    ↓ Emotions   1967
-    Hardiness   1997
-    ↓ Mental Disorders   1967
-    ↓ Mental Health   1967
-    ↓ Personality   1967
-    Psychopathology   1967

Emotional Content   1973
PN   1565   SC   16765
SN   Emotional themes, substance, form, or characteristics of feelings, especially as they are portrayed in various forms of communication (e.g., reading material, motion pictures) or as manifested in specific situations.
- R   ↓ Communication   1967
-    ↓ Emotions   1967

Emotional Control   1973
PN   670   SC   16770
SN   Directing or governing one's own or another's emotions. Not to be confused with EMOTIONAL MATURITY which involves the exhibition of emotional behavior appropriate to one's age.
- UF   Control (Emotional)
-     Emotional Restraint
- B   Emotional Adjustment   1973
- N   Anger Control   1997
- R   Coping Behavior   1967
-    Internal External Locus of Control   1967
-    Self Control   1973
-    Social Control   1988
-    Tantrums   1973

Emotional Development   1973
PN   2524   SC   16780
- B   Psychogenesis   1973
- R   Attachment Behavior   1985
-    Childhood Play Development   1973
-    Developmental Age Groups   1973
-    ↓ Emotions   1967
-    Object Relations   1982
-    ↓ Personality Development   1967
-    ↓ Physical Development   1973
-    Psychosexual Development   1982
-    ↓ Psychosocial Development   1973

Emotional Expressiveness
- Use   Emotionality (Personality)

Emotional Immaturity   1973
PN   46   SC   16800
SN   Tendency to exhibit emotional reactions considered inappropriate for one's age.
- UF   Immaturity (Emotional)
- B   Personality Traits   1967
- R   Emotional Maturity   1973

Emotional Inferiority   1973
PN   58   SC   16810
SN   Conscious or unconscious feelings of insecurity, insignificance, and inadequacy and of being unable to cope with life's demands.
- UF   Inferiority (Emotional)
- B   Personality Traits   1967
- R   Neuroticism   1973

Emotional Insecurity
- Use   Emotional Security

Emotional Instability   1973
PN   134   SC   16830
SN   Tendency to display unpredictable and rapidly changing emotions or moods.
- UF   Instability (Emotional)
- B   Personality Traits   1967
- R   Emotional Stability   1973
-    Neuroticism   1973

Emotional Maladjustment
- Use   Emotional Adjustment

Emotional Maturity   1973
PN   501   SC   16850
SN   Attainment of a level of emotional development and exhibition of emotional patterns commonly associated with persons of a specific age level. Not to be confused with EMOTIONAL CONTROL which involves the suppression or control of direction of one's emotions.
- UF   Maturity (Emotional)
- B   Personality Traits   1967

Emotional Maturity — (cont'd)
- R   Emotional Immaturity [1973]

Emotional Needs
- **Use** Psychological Needs

Emotional Responses [1967]
PN 6658   SC 16860
SN From 1982, limited to human populations. Use ANIMAL EMOTIONALITY for nonhuman subjects.
- B   Responses [1967]
- N   Conditioned Emotional Responses [1967]
- R   Animal Emotionality [1978]
-    ↓ Emotions [1967]
-    Laughter [1978]
-    Stranger Reactions [1988]

Emotional Restraint
- **Use** Emotional Control

Emotional Security [1973]
PN 464   SC 16880
SN Possession of inner resources enabling one to cope with unfamiliar or threatening situations, especially as engendered through early nurturance.
- UF   Emotional Insecurity
-    Insecurity (Emotional)
-    Security (Emotional)
- B   Personality Traits [1967]
- R   Emotional Stability [1973]

Emotional Stability [1973]
PN 360   SC 16890
SN Resistance to affective disruption or tendency toward evenness of feelings.
- UF   Stability (Emotional)
- B   Personality Traits [1967]
- R   Emotional Instability [1973]
-    Emotional Security [1973]
-    Hardiness [1997]
-    Neuroticism [1973]

Emotional States [1973]
PN 10265   SC 16900
- UF   Moods
- B   Emotions [1967]
- N   Affection [1973]
-    Alienation [1971]
-    Ambivalence [1973]
-    ↓ Anger [1967]
-    ↓ Anxiety [1967]
-    Apathy [1973]
-    ↓ Aversion [1967]
-    Boredom [1973]
-    Depression (Emotion) [1967]
-    Disappointment [1973]
-    Disgust [1994]
-    Dissatisfaction [1973]
-    Distress [1973]
-    Doubt [1973]
-    Embarrassment [1973]
-    Emotional Trauma [1967]
-    Enthusiasm [1973]
-    Euphoria [1973]
-    ↓ Fear [1967]
-    Frustration [1967]
-    Grief [1973]
-    Guilt [1967]
-    Happiness [1973]
-    ↓ Helplessness [1997]
-    Homesickness [1994]
-    Hope [1991]
-    Hopelessness [1988]

Emotional States — (cont'd)
- N   Jealousy [1973]
-    Loneliness [1973]
-    Love [1973]
-    ↓ Mania [1967]
-    Mental Confusion [1973]
-    Optimism [1973]
-    Pessimism [1973]
-    Pleasure [1973]
-    Pride [1973]
-    Restlessness [1973]
-    Sadness [1973]
-    Shame [1994]
-    Suffering [1973]
-    Suspicion [1973]
-    Sympathy [1973]
- R   Abandonment [1997]
-    Craving [1997]
-    ↓ Emotionally Disturbed [1973]
-    Irritability [1988]
-    Learned Helplessness [1978]
-    Morale [1978]
-    ↓ Personality [1967]

Emotional Superiority [1973]
PN 31   SC 16910
SN Feeling that one is better than others in ability, virtue, or worth.
- UF   Superiority (Emotional)
- B   Personality Traits [1967]
- R   ↓ Dominance [1967]
-    Egotism [1973]
-    Grandiosity [1994]

Emotional Trauma [1967]
PN 4160   SC 16920
- UF   Trauma (Emotional)
- B   Emotional States [1973]
- R   Adjustment Disorders [1994]
-    False Memory [1997]
-    Posttraumatic Stress Disorder [1985]
-    Repressed Memory [1997]
-    ↓ Separation Reactions [1997]

Emotionality (Animal)
- **Use** Animal Emotionality

Emotionality (Personality) [1973]
PN 1443   SC 16930
SN Personality trait characteristic of a person who tends to react strongly or excessively to emotional situations.
- UF   Emotional Expressiveness
- B   Personality Traits [1967]
- R   ↓ Emotions [1967]
-    Neuroticism [1973]

Emotionally Disturbed [1973]
PN 4318   SC 16940
- B   Disorders [1967]
- N   Autistic Children [1973]
- R   Acting Out [1967]
-    ↓ Childhood Psychosis [1967]
-    ↓ Emotional Adjustment [1973]
-    ↓ Emotional States [1973]
-    ↓ Emotions [1967]

Emotions [1967]
PN 9251   SC 16960
SN Conceptually broad term referring to the affective aspects of human consciousness. Use a more specific term if possible. Use ANIMAL EMOTIONALITY for nonhuman subjects.

Emotions — (cont'd)
- UF   Feelings
- N   ↓ Emotional States [1973]
- R   ↓ Emotional Adjustment [1973]
-    Emotional Content [1973]
-    Emotional Development [1973]
-    ↓ Emotional Responses [1967]
-    Emotionality (Personality) [1973]
-    ↓ Emotionally Disturbed [1973]
-    Expressed Emotion [1991]
-    Human Nature [1997]
-    Morale [1978]
-    ↓ Personality [1967]

Empathy [1967]
PN 3754   SC 16970
- B   Personality Traits [1967]
- R   Agreeableness [1997]

Emphysema (Pulmonary)
- **Use** Pulmonary Emphysema

Empirical Methods [1973]
PN 1082   SC 16990
SN Scientific methodology based on experimentation, systematic observation, or measurement, rather than theoretical formulation.
- B   Methodology [1967]
- N   ↓ Experimental Methods [1967]
-    Observation Methods [1967]
- R   ↓ Behavioral Assessment [1982]
-    Positivism (Philosophy) [1997]

Employability [1973]
PN 505   SC 17000
SN Potential usefulness of an individual as judged on the basis of job skills, functional literacy, emotional or social maturity, intellectual development, or personal values (e.g., personal responsibility).
- R   ↓ Employee Skills [1973]
-    ↓ Employment Status [1982]
-    ↓ Personnel [1967]
-    Supported Employment [1994]
-    Vocational Evaluation [1991]

Employee Absenteeism [1973]
PN 824   SC 17010
- UF   Absenteeism (Employee)
- R   ↓ Personnel [1967]

Employee Assistance Programs [1985]
PN 1195   SC 17015
SN Programs or services provided by the employer to help employees with personal or other matters, including retirement planning or alcohol rehabilitation.
- B   Employee Benefits [1973]
- R   ↓ Counseling [1967]
-    Disability Management [1991]
-    ↓ Drug Rehabilitation [1973]
-    Elder Care [1994]
-    ↓ Program Development [1991]
-    ↓ Support Groups [1991]

Employee Attitudes [1967]
PN 5188   SC 17020
SN Attitudes of, not toward, employees.
- B   Attitudes [1967]
-    Employee Characteristics [1988]
- N   Job Satisfaction [1967]
- R   Employee Motivation [1973]
-    Job Involvement [1978]
-    ↓ Job Performance [1967]
-    Organizational Commitment [1991]

Employee Attitudes — (cont'd)
R   Work (Attitudes Toward)   1973

Employee Benefits   1973
PN   384   SC   17030
SN   Benefits provided by an employer that may be voluntary or mandated by federal or state law.
N   Bonuses   1973
     Employee Assistance Programs   1985
     ↓ Employee Health Insurance   1973
     Employee Leave Benefits   1973
     Employee Pension Plans   1973
     Workmens Compensation Insurance   1973
R   Disability Evaluation   1988
     Elder Care   1994
     ↓ Personnel   1967
     Salaries   1973

Employee Characteristics   1988
PN   1236   SC   17035
N   ↓ Employee Attitudes   1967
     Employee Efficiency   1973
     Employee Motivation   1973
     Employee Productivity   1973
     ↓ Employee Skills   1973
     Job Experience Level   1973
     Job Knowledge   1997
R   Organizational Commitment   1991
     ↓ Personnel   1967
     Professional Competence   1997
     Professional Identity   1991

Employee Efficiency   1973
PN   166   SC   17040
UF   Efficiency (Employee)
B   Employee Characteristics   1988
     Job Performance   1967

Employee Health Insurance   1973
PN   61   SC   17050
B   Employee Benefits   1973
     Health Insurance   1973
N   Workmens Compensation Insurance   1973

Employee Interaction   1988
PN   1303   SC   17055
SN   Dynamics of interpersonal interactions between employees.
B   Interpersonal Interaction   1967
     Organizational Behavior   1978
N   Supervisor Employee Interaction   1997
R   ↓ Personnel   1967

Employee Leave Benefits   1973
PN   116   SC   17060
UF   Annual Leave
     Sick Leave
     Vacation Benefits
B   Employee Benefits   1973

Employee Motivation   1973
PN   1634   SC   17080
B   Employee Characteristics   1988
     Motivation   1967
R   ↓ Employee Attitudes   1967
     Job Involvement   1978

Employee Pension Plans   1973
PN   35   SC   17090
UF   Pension Plans (Employee)
B   Employee Benefits   1973

Employee Productivity   1973
PN   1338   SC   17110
UF   Productivity (Employee)
B   Employee Characteristics   1988
     Job Performance   1967

Employee Selection
Use   Personnel Selection

Employee Skills   1973
PN   536   SC   17130
B   Ability   1967
     Employee Characteristics   1988
N   Clerical Secretarial Skills   1973
R   Employability   1973
     Job Knowledge   1997
     Professional Competence   1997
     Supported Employment   1994
     Vocational Evaluation   1991

Employee Supervisor Interaction
Use   Supervisor Employee Interaction

Employee Termination
Use   Personnel Termination

Employee Turnover   1973
PN   1306   SC   17140
UF   Personnel Turnover
     Turnover
R   Employment History   1978
     Job Security   1978
     ↓ Occupational Tenure   1973
     ↓ Personnel   1967

Employees
Use   Personnel

Employer Attitudes   1973
PN   495   SC   17160
SN   Attitudes of, not toward, employers.
B   Attitudes   1967
R   Organizational Commitment   1991
     ↓ Personnel   1967
     Work (Attitudes Toward)   1973

Employment
Use   Employment Status

Employment Discrimination   1994
PN   202   SC   17173
SN   Prejudiced and differential treatment of employees or job applicants based on factors other than performance or qualifications.
UF   Job Discrimination
B   Social Discrimination   1982
R   Affirmative Action   1985
     Age Discrimination   1994
     Job Applicant Screening   1973
     ↓ Personnel Evaluation   1973
     ↓ Personnel Management   1973
     ↓ Personnel Selection   1967
     ↓ Prejudice   1967
     Race and Ethnic Discrimination   1994
     Racism   1973
     Sex Discrimination   1978
     Sexism   1988

Employment History   1978
PN   420   SC   17174
SN   Past record of an individual's working life, including periods of unemployment.
R   Career Change   1978

Employment History — (cont'd)
R   Career Development   1985
     Employee Turnover   1973
     ↓ Employment Status   1982
     Job Experience Level   1973
     Occupational Mobility   1973
     Occupational Success   1978
     ↓ Occupational Tenure   1973
     ↓ Occupations   1967
     ↓ Personnel   1967
     Personnel Promotion   1978
     Personnel Termination   1973
     Professional Development   1982
     Retirement   1973
     Unemployment   1967

Employment Interviews
Use   Job Applicant Interviews

Employment Processes
Use   Personnel Recruitment

Employment Status   1982
PN   3500   SC   17196
SN   Condition of employment including full- or part-time, temporary or permanent, and unemployment. Use OCCUPATIONS to access references from 1967-1981.
UF   Employment
N   Self Employment   1994
     Unemployment   1967
R   Employability   1973
     Employment History   1978
     Job Applicants   1985
     ↓ Occupational Tenure   1973
     Reemployment   1991
     Retirement   1973
     Supported Employment   1994
     Working Women   1978

Employment Tests   1973
PN   484   SC   17200
SN   Tests used in personnel selection to measure the suitability of an applicant for a given occupation.
B   Measurement   1967
R   Job Applicant Screening   1973

Empowerment   1991
PN   1188   SC   17203
SN   Promotion or attainment of autonomy and freedom of choice for individuals or groups.
R   Advocacy   1985
     Assertiveness   1973
     ↓ Civil Rights   1978
     ↓ Client Rights   1988
     ↓ Helplessness   1997
     Independence (Personality)   1973
     ↓ Involvement   1973
     ↓ Power   1967
     Self Determination   1994

Empty Nest   1991
PN   26   SC   17205
SN   Home environment after children have reached maturity and left home. Also, includes the concept of adult children returning to the home.
UF   Return to Home
R   Adult Offspring   1985
     ↓ Family   1967
     ↓ Family Relations   1967
     Family Size   1973
     ↓ Family Structure   1973
     Home Environment   1973
     Intergenerational Relations   1988

Empty Nest — (cont'd)
R   ↓ Living Arrangements ¹⁹⁹¹
    ↓ Parent Child Relations ¹⁹⁶⁷

Enabling ¹⁹⁹⁷
PN 17   SC 17207
B   Social Influences ¹⁹⁶⁷
R   Codependency ¹⁹⁹¹
    Dependency (Personality) ¹⁹⁶⁷
    ↓ Social Reinforcement ¹⁹⁶⁷

Enactments ¹⁹⁹⁷
PN 50   SC 17209
SN   Regressive or defensive interactions between a therapist and client or interaction between two or more people that reenacts past experiences or emotional conflicts of one or more of the persons involved.
UF   Reenactments
R   Acting Out ¹⁹⁶⁷
    Age Regression (Hypnotic) ¹⁹⁸⁸
    Countertransference ¹⁹⁷³
    Early Experience ¹⁹⁶⁷
    ↓ Interpersonal Interaction ¹⁹⁶⁷
    Projective Identification ¹⁹⁹⁴
    ↓ Psychotherapeutic Processes ¹⁹⁶⁷
    Psychotherapeutic Transference ¹⁹⁶⁷
    Reminiscence ¹⁹⁸⁵

Encephalitis ¹⁹⁷³
PN 296   SC 17210
B   Brain Disorders ¹⁹⁶⁷
    Viral Disorders ¹⁹⁷³
R   Encephalomyelitis ¹⁹⁷³
    ↓ Infectious Disorders ¹⁹⁷³

Encephalography ¹⁹⁷³
PN 20   SC 17220
B   Medical Diagnosis ¹⁹⁷³
N   Echoencephalography ¹⁹⁷³
    ↓ Electroencephalography ¹⁹⁶⁷
    Pneumoencephalography ¹⁹⁷³
    Rheoencephalography ¹⁹⁷³
R   ↓ Roentgenography ¹⁹⁷³

Encephalography (Air)
Use   Pneumoencephalography

Encephalomyelitis ¹⁹⁷³
PN 38   SC 17240
B   Myelitis ¹⁹⁷³
R   Encephalitis ¹⁹⁷³
    ↓ Infectious Disorders ¹⁹⁷³

Encephalopathies ¹⁹⁸²
PN 361   SC 17247
SN   Degenerative diseases of the brain.
B   Brain Disorders ¹⁹⁶⁷
N   Creutzfeldt Jakob Syndrome ¹⁹⁹⁴
    Toxic Encephalopathies ¹⁹⁷³
    Wernickes Syndrome ¹⁹⁷³
R   Chronic Fatigue Syndrome ¹⁹⁹⁷
    Thyrotoxicosis ¹⁹⁷³

Encoding
Use   Human Information Storage

Encopresis
Use   Fecal Incontinence

Encounter Group Therapy ¹⁹⁷³
PN 244   SC 17270

Encounter Group Therapy — (cont'd)
SN   Goal-oriented unstructured groups whose members seek heightened self-awareness and fulfillment of their human potential. The group leader (not necessarily a clinically trained therapist) participates freely in the group activity. Techniques used include role playing, sensory awareness, and physical contact.
B   Group Psychotherapy ¹⁹⁶⁷
    Human Potential Movement ¹⁹⁸²
N   Marathon Group Therapy ¹⁹⁷³
R   Consciousness Raising Groups ¹⁹⁷⁸
    Human Relations Training ¹⁹⁷⁸
    Sensitivity Training ¹⁹⁷³

Encouragement ¹⁹⁷³
PN 156   SC 17290
B   Social Interaction ¹⁹⁶⁷
R   ↓ Social Reinforcement ¹⁹⁶⁷

Endocrine Disorders ¹⁹⁷³
PN 180   SC 17300
B   Physical Disorders ¹⁹⁹⁷
N   ↓ Adrenal Gland Disorders ¹⁹⁷³
    ↓ Diabetes ¹⁹⁷³
    Endocrine Neoplasms ¹⁹⁷³
    ↓ Endocrine Sexual Disorders ¹⁹⁷³
    Parathyroid Disorders ¹⁹⁷³
    ↓ Pituitary Disorders ¹⁹⁷³
    ↓ Thyroid Disorders ¹⁹⁷³
R   ↓ Endocrine System ¹⁹⁷³
    Hypothermia ¹⁹⁷³
    Migraine Headache ¹⁹⁷³
    ↓ Secretion (Gland) ¹⁹⁷³
    ↓ Somatoform Disorders ²⁰⁰¹

Endocrine Gland Secretion ¹⁹⁷³
PN 103   SC 17310
B   Secretion (Gland) ¹⁹⁷³
N   Adrenal Gland Secretion ¹⁹⁷³
R   ↓ Endocrine Glands ¹⁹⁷³

Endocrine Gland Surgery ¹⁹⁷³
PN 8   SC 17320
B   Surgery ¹⁹⁷¹
N   Adrenalectomy ¹⁹⁷³
    ↓ Castration ¹⁹⁶⁷
    Hypophysectomy ¹⁹⁷³
    Pinealectomy ¹⁹⁷³
    Thyroidectomy ¹⁹⁷³

Endocrine Glands ¹⁹⁷³
PN 40   SC 17330
B   Endocrine System ¹⁹⁷³
    Glands ¹⁹⁶⁷
N   ↓ Adrenal Glands ¹⁹⁷³
    ↓ Gonads ¹⁹⁷³
    Parathyroid Glands ¹⁹⁷³
    Pineal Body ¹⁹⁷³
    ↓ Pituitary Gland ¹⁹⁷³
    Thyroid Gland ¹⁹⁷³
R   ↓ Endocrine Gland Secretion ¹⁹⁷³
    ↓ Hormones ¹⁹⁶⁷
    Pancreas ¹⁹⁷³

Endocrine Neoplasms ¹⁹⁷³
PN 22   SC 17340
B   Endocrine Disorders ¹⁹⁷³
    Neoplasms ¹⁹⁶⁷

Endocrine Sexual Disorders ¹⁹⁷³
PN 56   SC 17350
UF   Ovary Disorders

Endocrine Sexual Disorders — (cont'd)
UF   Testes Disorders
B   Endocrine Disorders ¹⁹⁷³
    Genital Disorders ¹⁹⁶⁷
N   ↓ Hypogonadism ¹⁹⁷³
    Testicular Feminization Syndrome ¹⁹⁷³
R   ↓ Adrenal Gland Disorders ¹⁹⁷³
    ↓ Gynecological Disorders ¹⁹⁷³
    Hermaphroditism ¹⁹⁷³
    ↓ Infertility ¹⁹⁷³
    ↓ Male Genital Disorders ¹⁹⁷³
    ↓ Pituitary Disorders ¹⁹⁷³
    ↓ Thyroid Disorders ¹⁹⁷³

Endocrine System ¹⁹⁷³
PN 293   SC 17360
B   Anatomical Systems ¹⁹⁷³
N   ↓ Endocrine Glands ¹⁹⁷³
R   ↓ Endocrine Disorders ¹⁹⁷³
    Pancreas ¹⁹⁷³

Endocrinology ¹⁹⁷³
PN 224   SC 17370
SN   Scientific discipline dealing with the study of endocrine glands and internal secretions.
B   Medical Sciences ¹⁹⁶⁷
N   Neuroendocrinology ¹⁹⁸⁵
R   Psychoneuroimmunology ¹⁹⁹¹

Endogamous Marriage ¹⁹⁷³
PN 20   SC 17380
B   Marriage ¹⁹⁶⁷
N   Consanguineous Marriage ¹⁹⁷³

Endogenous Depression ¹⁹⁷⁸
PN 1176   SC 17384
B   Major Depression ¹⁹⁸⁸

Endogenous Opiates ¹⁹⁸⁵
PN 438   SC 17385
UF   Opioids (Endogenous)
B   Opiates ¹⁹⁷³
    Peptides ¹⁹⁷³
N   Dynorphins ¹⁹⁸⁵
    ↓ Endorphins ¹⁹⁸²

Endorphins ¹⁹⁸²
PN 838   SC 17386
SN   Endogenous morphine-like brain polypeptides that can bind to opiate receptors.
B   Endogenous Opiates ¹⁹⁸⁵
    Neurotransmitters ¹⁹⁸⁵
    Proteins ¹⁹⁷³
N   Enkephalins ¹⁹⁸²
R   Analgesia ¹⁹⁸²

Endurance ¹⁹⁷³
PN 95   SC 17390
SN   Ability to withstand hardship, adversity, or stress. Used for human or animal populations.
N   Physical Endurance ¹⁹⁷³
    Psychological Endurance ¹⁹⁷³
R   ↓ Stress ¹⁹⁶⁷

Energy Expenditure ¹⁹⁶⁷
PN 1501   SC 17400
SN   Expenditure of mental or physical effort.
UF   Effort
R   Calories ¹⁹⁷³
    Metabolic Rates ¹⁹⁷³

Engineering Psychology ¹⁹⁶⁷
PN 535   SC 17410

Engineering Psychology — (cont'd)
SN Branch of applied psychology that emphasizes the study of machine design, the relationship between humans and machines, and the effects of machines on human behavior. Use a more specific term if possible.
B   Applied Psychology   1973
R ↓ Human Factors Engineering   1973

Engineers   1967
PN 698   **SC** 17420
B   Professional Personnel   1978
R ↓ Aerospace Personnel   1973
    ↓ Business and Industrial Personnel   1967
     Scientists   1967

English as Second Language   1997
PN 430   **SC** 17450
UF   ESL
R   Bilingual Education   1978
     Bilingualism   1973
     Foreign Language Education   1973
     Foreign Languages   1973
    ↓ Language   1967
    ↓ Language Arts Education   1973
     Language Proficiency   1988
    ↓ Multilingualism   1973

Enjoyment
Use Pleasure

Enkephalins   1982
PN 487   **SC** 17475
SN Endogenous morphine-like brain polypeptides closely related to endorphins.
B   Endorphins   1982
R   Analgesia   1982
    ↓ Peptides   1070

Enlisted Military Personnel   1973
PN 247   **SC** 17480
SN Military personnel ranking below commissioned officers.
B   Military Personnel   1967
N   Draftees   1973
     Noncommissioned Officers   1973
R   Volunteer Military Personnel   1973

Enlistment (Military)
Use Military Enlistment

Enrollment (School)
Use School Enrollment

Enteropeptidase
Use Kinases

Enthusiasm   1973
PN 51   **SC** 17530
UF   Eagerness
B   Emotional States   1973
R   Morale   1978
    ↓ Motivation   1967

Entrance Examinations   1973
PN 191   **SC** 17540
B   Educational Measurement   1967
N   College Entrance Examination Board
     Scholastic Aptitude Test   2001
R   Student Admission Criteria   1973

Entrapment Games   1973
PN 17   **SC** 17550

Entrapment Games — (cont'd)
B   Games   1967
R ↓ Collective Behavior   1967
     Game Theory   1967
     Non Zero Sum Games   1973
     Prisoners Dilemma Game   1973

Entrepreneurship   1991
PN 260   **SC** 17555
SN Initiation, organization, management, and assumption of the attendant risks of a business or enterprise.
R   Business   1967
     Business Management   1973
     Capitalism   1973
    ↓ Leadership   1967
    ↓ Management   1967
     Ownership   1985
    ↓ Private Sector   1985
     Self Employment   1994

Enuresis
Use Urinary Incontinence

Environment   1967
PN 6445   **SC** 17570
SN Totality of physical, social, psychological, or cultural conditions surrounding an organism.
N ↓ Facility Environment   1988
     Single Sex Environments   2001
    ↓ Social Environments   1973
    ↓ Therapeutic Environment   2001
R ↓ Architecture   1973
     Ecology   1973
     Environmental Adaptation   1973
     Environmental Attitudes   1978
     Environmental Education   1994
    ↓ Environmental Planning   1982
     Environmental Stress   1973
     Geography   1973
    ↓ Hazardous Materials   1991
     Nature Nurture   1994
     Person Environment Fit   1991
     Physical Comfort   1982
     Research Setting   2001
     Urban Planning   1973

Environmental Adaptation   1973
PN 460   **SC** 17590
SN Physiological or biological adaptation to conditions in the physical environment. For psychological, social, or emotional adaptation use ADJUSTMENT or one of its related terms.
UF   Adaptation (Environmental)
B   Adaptation   1967
R ↓ Environment   1967
     Person Environment Fit   1991

Environmental Attitudes   1978
PN 1388   **SC** 17594
SN Perceptions of or beliefs regarding the physical environment, including factors affecting its quality (e.g., overpopulation, pollution).
B   Attitudes   1967
R   Conservation (Ecological Behavior)   1978
     Ecology   1973
    ↓ Environment   1967
     Environmental Education   1994

Environmental Design
Use Environmental Planning

Environmental Education   1994
PN 113   **SC** 17598
SN Used for educational and noneducational settings.
R   Conservation (Ecological Behavior)   1978
     Ecology   1973
    ↓ Education   1967
    ↓ Environment   1967
     Environmental Attitudes   1978
     Pollution   1973

Environmental Effects   1973
PN 1327   **SC** 17600
N   Altitude Effects   1973
     Atmospheric Conditions   1973
    ↓ Gravitational Effects   1967
     Noise Effects   1973
     Seasonal Variations   1973
    ↓ Temperature Effects   1967
     Underwater Effects   1973
R ↓ Ecological Factors   1973
     Environmental Stress   1973
     Lunar Synodic Cycle   1973
     Physiological Stress   1967

Environmental Planning   1982
PN 578   **SC** 17607
SN Planning and design of environment with goals of efficient human-environment interaction and minimal ecological disruption.
UF   Environmental Design
N   Interior Design   1982
     Urban Planning   1973
R ↓ Architecture   1973
     Computer Assisted Design   1997
    ↓ Environment   1967
     Person Environment Fit   1991
    ↓ Recreation Areas   1973

Environmental Psychology   1982
PN 544   **SC** 17609
SN Branch of psychology that studies the relationship between environmental variables and behavior, including manipulation of one by the other.
B   Applied Psychology   1973
R   Behavioral Ecology   1997
     Ecological Psychology   1994

Environmental Stress   1973
PN 752   **SC** 17610
SN Naturally occurring or experimentally manipulated qualities of the physical environment which result in strain or disequilibrium. Consider also other specific terms (e.g., CROWDING, NOISE EFFECTS).
B   Stress   1967
R   Crowding   1978
    ↓ Deprivation   1967
    ↓ Environment   1967
    ↓ Environmental Effects   1973
     Overpopulation   1973
     Physiological Stress   1967
     Thermal Acclimatization   1973

Environmental Therapy
Use Milieu Therapy

Envy
Use Jealousy

Enzyme Inhibitors   1985
PN 315   **SC** 17625

Enzyme Inhibitors — (cont'd)
SN Any agent that slows or otherwise disrupts the activity of an enzyme, such as antienzymes or enzyme antibodies.
B Drugs [1967]
N Acetazolamide [1973]
   ↓ Amine Oxidase Inhibitors [1973]
   Bromocriptine [1988]
   Captopril [1991]
   ↓ Cholinesterase Inhibitors [1973]
   ↓ Decarboxylase Inhibitors [1982]
   Hydroxylase Inhibitors [1985]
   ↓ Monoamine Oxidase Inhibitors [1973]
   Theophylline [1973]
R ↓ Enzymes [1973]

Enzymes [1973]
PN 939   **SC** 17630
SN In 1997, this term replaced the discontinued terms ADOLASES and CARBONIC ANHYDRASE. In 2000, these terms were stripped from all records and replaced with ENZYMES.
UF Aldolases
   Carbonic Anhydrase
B Drugs [1967]
N Decarboxylases [1973]
   ↓ Dehydrogenases [1973]
   ↓ Esterases [1973]
   Hydroxylases [1973]
   Isozymes [1973]
   Kinases [1982]
   ↓ Oxidases [1973]
   Phosphatases [1973]
   Phosphorylases [1973]
   Proteinases [1973]
   ↓ Transferases [1973]
R ↓ Anti Inflammatory Drugs [1982]
   ↓ Decarboxylase Inhibitors [1982]
   ↓ Enzyme Inhibitors [1985]
   ↓ Proteins [1973]

EOG (Electrophysiology)
Use Electro Oculography

Ependyma
Use Cerebral Ventricles

Ephedrine [1973]
PN 52   **SC** 17660
B Adrenergic Drugs [1973]
   Alcohols [1967]
   Alkaloids [1973]
   CNS Stimulating Drugs [1973]
   Sympathomimetic Amines [1973]
   Vasoconstrictor Drugs [1973]
R ↓ Local Anesthetics [1973]

Epidemics [2001]
PN 0   **SC** 17665
SN Sudden increase in the incidence of a disease, injury, or other health-related event.
UF Disease Outbreaks
B Public Health [1988]
R Epidemiology [1973]
   Hygiene [1994]
   ↓ Infectious Disorders [1973]
   ↓ Injuries [1973]
   ↓ Syndromes [1973]

Epidemiology [1973]
PN 10399   **SC** 17670

Epidemiology — (cont'd)
SN Study of the occurrence, distribution, and containment of disease or mental disorders. Used for the scientific discipline as a whole or for specific epidemiological factors or findings (e.g., disease incidence or prevalence statistics).
B Medical Sciences [1967]
R Epidemics [2001]

Epilepsy [1967]
PN 4619   **SC** 17680
B Brain Disorders [1967]
N ↓ Epileptic Seizures [1973]
   Experimental Epilepsy [1978]
   Grand Mal Epilepsy [1973]
   Petit Mal Epilepsy [1973]
R ↓ Anticonvulsive Drugs [1973]
   Aura [1973]
   ↓ Brain Damage [1967]
   Fugue Reaction [1973]

Epileptic Seizures [1973]
PN 900   **SC** 17690
B Brain Disorders [1967]
   Epilepsy [1967]
N Experimental Epilepsy [1978]
R Coma [1973]
   ↓ Convulsions [1967]

Epinephrine [1967]
PN 856   **SC** 17700
UF Adrenaline
B Adrenergic Drugs [1973]
   Catecholamines [1973]
   Heart Rate Affecting Drugs [1973]
   Hormones [1967]
R Vasoconstriction [1973]
   Vasodilation [1973]

Episcopalians
Use Protestants

Episodic Memory [1988]
PN 543   **SC** 17705
B Memory [1967]
R Eidetic Imagery [1973]

Epistemology [1973]
PN 1575   **SC** 17710
SN Philosophical study of knowledge, including its origin, nature, and limits.
B Philosophies [1967]
R Determinism [1997]
   Hermeneutics [1991]
   Metaphysics [1973]
   Positivism (Philosophy) [1997]
   Relativism [1997]

Epithelial Cells [1973]
PN 13   **SC** 17720
B Cells (Biology) [1973]
R Skin (Anatomy) [1967]

Epithelium
Use Skin (Anatomy)

Epstein Barr Viral Disorder [1994]
PN 19   **SC** 17740
B Infectious Disorders [1973]
   Viral Disorders [1973]
R Chronic Fatigue Syndrome [1997]

Equal Education [1978]
PN 253   **SC** 17745
SN Provision of comparable educational opportunities to all individuals irrespective of race, national origin, religion, sex, socioeconomic status, or ability.
UF Educational Inequality
B Civil Rights [1978]
R ↓ Education [1967]
   Educational Quality [1997]
   School Integration [1982]
   Social Equality [1973]

Equality (Social)
Use Social Equality

Equilibrium [1973]
PN 515   **SC** 17760
SN Maintenance of postural balance. For physiological equilibrium consider HOMEOSTASIS.
UF Balance (Motor Processes)
R ↓ Perceptual Motor Processes [1967]
   Spatial Orientation (Perception) [1973]

Equimax Rotation [1973]
PN 2   **SC** 17770
B Orthogonal Rotation [1973]

Equipment
Use Apparatus

Equity (Payment) [1978]
PN 613   **SC** 17784
SN In society, group, or other interpersonal situations, the process of equal allocation of economic resources, rewards, or payoffs.
B Equity (Social) [1978]
R ↓ Justice [1973]
   Money [1967]
   Resource Allocation [1997]
   Salaries [1973]
   ↓ Social Behavior [1967]
   ↓ Social Processes [1967]

Equity (Social) [1978]
PN 771   **SC** 17786
SN In society, group, or other interpersonal situations, the maintenance of relationships in which the proportions of each member's societal and cultural contributions or benefits are approximately equal.
N Equity (Payment) [1978]
R Egalitarianism [1985]
   ↓ Justice [1973]
   Resource Allocation [1997]
   ↓ Social Behavior [1967]
   ↓ Social Processes [1967]

Erection (Penis) [1973]
PN 535   **SC** 17790
B Psychosexual Behavior [1967]
R Impotence [1973]

Ergonomics
Use Human Factors Engineering

Ergot Derivatives [1973]
PN 154   **SC** 17810
B Drugs [1967]
N Bromocriptine [1988]
   Dihydroergotamine [1973]
R ↓ Adrenergic Blocking Drugs [1973]
   ↓ Alkaloids [1973]
   Lysergic Acid Diethylamide [1967]
   Tyramine [1973]

Erikson (Erik) 1991
PN 163　　　　　　　　　**SC** 17815
SN Identifies biographical or autobiographical studies and discussions of Erikson's works.
　R ↓ Developmental Stages 1973
　　Ego Identity 1991
　　Generativity 2001
　　↓ Neopsychoanalytic School 1973
　　↓ Psychoanalysis 1967
　　↓ Psychoanalytic Theory 1967
　　↓ Psychologists 1967
　　↓ Psychosocial Development 1973

Eroticism 1973
PN 580　　　　　　　　　**SC** 17820
　B Sexual Arousal 1978
　R Autoeroticism 1997
　　Inhibited Sexual Desire 1997

Erotomania 1997
PN 26　　　　　　　　　**SC** 17823
　R ↓ Antisocial Behavior 1971
　　Attachment Behavior 1985
　　Delusions 1967
　　Emotional Abuse 1991
　　Grandiosity 1994
　　Hypersexuality 1973
　　Love 1973
　　Obsessions 1967
　　Partner Abuse 1991
　　↓ Psychosexual Behavior 1967
　　Sexual Fantasy 1997
　　Victimization 1973

Error Analysis 1973
PN 732　　　　　　　　　**SC** 17830
SN Collection, classification and/or analysis of mistakes, especially in task or test performance.
　B Analysis 1967
　R ↓ Errors 1967
　　Human Machine Systems 1997

Error of Measurement 1985
PN 386　　　　　　　　　**SC** 17835
SN Observed differences in obtained scores or measures due to chance variance.
　UF Error Variance
　　Standard Error of Measurement
　B Errors 1967
　　Statistical Analysis 1967
　R Consistency (Measurement) 1973
　　Least Squares 1985
　　↓ Scoring (Testing) 1973
　　Standard Deviation 1973
　　↓ Statistical Estimation 1985
　　↓ Statistical Measurement 1973
　　↓ Test Bias 1985
　　Test Reliability 1973
　　↓ Test Scores 1967

Error Variance
　Use Error of Measurement

Errors 1967
PN 2830　　　　　　　　　**SC** 17840
SN Inappropriate, inaccurate, or incorrect responses or performance. Also, factual errors or other informational inaccuracies and performance errors on the part of others to which a subject reacts.
　UF Mistakes
　N Error of Measurement 1985
　　↓ Prediction Errors 1973
　　↓ Refraction Errors 1973

Errors — (cont'd)
　R Error Analysis 1973
　　Halo Effect 1982
　　Proofreading 1988

Erythroblastosis Fetalis
　Use Rh Incompatibility

Erythrocytes 1973
PN 359　　　　　　　　　**SC** 17860
　UF Red Blood Cells
　B Blood Cells 1973
　R Blood Groups 1973

Escape
　Use Avoidance

Escape Behavior (Animal)
　Use Animal Escape Behavior

Escape Conditioning 1973
PN 445　　　　　　　　　**SC** 17890
SN Learned behavior or the operant conditioning procedure in which the subject learns a specific behavior that results in the termination of an ongoing aversive stimulus. Consider also NEGATIVE REINFORCEMENT. Compare AVOIDANCE CONDITIONING.
　UF Conditioning (Escape)
　B Operant Conditioning 1967

Eserine
　Use Physostigmine

Eskimos
SN In 2000, the term was discontinued, and all records containing it were stripped of the term and replaced with INUIT, its postable counterpart.
　Use Inuit

ESL
　Use English as Second Language

Esophagus 1973
PN 110　　　　　　　　　**SC** 17920
　B Digestive System 1967

ESP (Parapsychology)
　Use Extrasensory Perception

Essay Testing 1973
PN 83　　　　　　　　　**SC** 17940
　B Testing Methods 1967

Essential Hypertension 1973
PN 364　　　　　　　　　**SC** 17950
　B Hypertension 1973

Esterases 1973
PN 43　　　　　　　　　**SC** 17970
　B Enzymes 1973
　N Acetylcholinesterase 1973
　　Cholinesterase 1973
　R Hydroxylases 1973
　　Phosphatases 1973

Estimation 1967
PN 1542　　　　　　　　　**SC** 17980
SN Subjective judgment or inference about the character, quality, or nature of a person, process, or thing which may or may not involve the inspection or availability of data or pertinent information.

Estimation — (cont'd)
　N ↓ Statistical Estimation 1985
　　Time Estimation 1967
　R ↓ Expectations 1967
　　↓ Prediction 1967

Estradiol 1973
PN 1150　　　　　　　　　**SC** 18000
　B Estrogens 1973

Estrogen Antagonists
　Use Antiestrogens

Estrogen Replacement Therapy
　Use Hormone Therapy

Estrogens 1973
PN 974　　　　　　　　　**SC** 18010
　B Sex Hormones 1973
　N Estradiol 1973
　　Estrone 1973
　R Antiandrogens 1982
　　Antiestrogens 1982

Estrone 1973
PN 13　　　　　　　　　**SC** 18020
　B Estrogens 1973

Estrus 1973
PN 657　　　　　　　　　**SC** 18030
　R ↓ Animal Biological Rhythms 1973
　　Animal Sexual Receptivity 1973
　　↓ Menstrual Cycle 1973
　　↓ Menstruation 1973

Ethanal
　Use Acetaldehyde

Ethanol 1973
PN 4930　　　　　　　　　**SC** 18040
　UF Alcohol (Grain)
　　Ethyl Alcohol
　B Alcohols 1967
　R Fetal Alcohol Syndrome 1985

Ether (Anesthetic) 1973
PN 46　　　　　　　　　**SC** 18050
　UF Ethyl Ether (Anesthetic)
　B General Anesthetics 1973

Ethics 1967
PN 2048　　　　　　　　　**SC** 18060
SN For ethics in social or cultural situations, consider MORALITY.
　N Experimental Ethics 1978
　　Professional Ethics 1973
　R Euthanasia 1973
　　Integrity 1997
　　Morality 1967
　　↓ Religious Beliefs 1973
　　↓ Social Influences 1967
　　↓ Values 1967

Ethnic Differences
　Use Racial and Ethnic Differences

Ethnic Discrimination
　Use Race and Ethnic Discrimination

Ethnic Disorders
　Use Ethnospecific Disorders

Ethnic Groups
SN In 2000, the term was discontinued, and all records containing it were stripped of the term and replaced with RACIAL AND ETHNIC GROUPS, its postable counterpart.
   Use Racial and Ethnic Groups

Ethnic Identity 1973
PN 2769   **SC** 18090
SN Feelings, ties, or associations that an individual experiences as a member of a particular ethnic group.
  B   Sociocultural Factors 1967
  R   Cultural Sensitivity 1994
      Ingroup Outgroup 1997
      Reference Groups 1994
      ↓ Self Concept 1967
      ↓ Social Identity 1988

Ethnic Sensitivity
   Use Cultural Sensitivity

Ethnic Values 1973
PN 437   **SC** 18100
  B   Social Influences 1967
      Sociocultural Factors 1967
      Values 1967
  R   Cultural Sensitivity 1994
      ↓ Racial and Ethnic Groups 2001

Ethnocentrism 1973
PN 300   **SC** 18110
SN Exaggerated tendency to identify with one's own ethnic group, or the inclination to judge others in terms of standards and values of one's own group.
  B   Racial and Ethnic Attitudes 1982
  R   Cross Cultural Psychology 1997
      ↓ Social Identity 1988

Ethnography 1973
PN 984   **SC** 18120
SN Descriptive study of cultures and societies. Used for the scientific discipline or the descriptive analyses themselves. Consider also ETHNOLOGY.
  R   Anthropology 1967
      Ethnology 1967
      Folk Psychology 1997
      Kinship Structure 1973
      Race (Anthropological) 1973
      ↓ Rites of Passage 1973
      ↓ Sociocultural Factors 1967

Ethnolinguistics 1973
PN 213   **SC** 18130
SN A part of anthropological linguistics concerned with the interrelation between a language and the cultural behavior of those who speak it.
  B   Linguistics 1973
  R   ↓ Dialect 1973
      Ethnology 1967
      Metalinguistics 1994
      Psycholinguistics 1967
      Slang 1973
      Sociolinguistics 1985

Ethnology 1967
PN 1614   **SC** 18140
SN Conceptually broad term referring to the study of the origin, distribution, characteristics, and relations of the cultures or ethnic groups of the world. Also, a branch of anthropology dealing with the comparative or analytical study of human culture or societies. Use a more specific term if possible. Consider also ETHNOGRAPHY.

Ethnology — (cont'd)
  R   Animism 1973
      Anthropology 1967
      Cross Cultural Differences 1967
      Cross Cultural Psychology 1997
      Cultism 1973
      ↓ Culture (Anthropological) 1967
      ↓ Culture Change 1967
      Culture Shock 1973
      Ethnography 1973
      Ethnolinguistics 1973
      ↓ Ethnospecific Disorders 1973
      Folk Medicine 1973
      Folk Psychology 1997
      Folklore 1991
      Kinship 1985
      Kinship Structure 1973
      Myths 1967
      Race (Anthropological) 1973
      ↓ Racial and Ethnic Attitudes 1982
      Racial and Ethnic Differences 1982
      ↓ Racial and Ethnic Groups 2001
      Racial and Ethnic Relations 1982
      Shamanism 1973
      ↓ Sociocultural Factors 1967
      Taboos 1973
      Transcultural Psychiatry 1973
      Witchcraft 1973

Ethnospecific Disorders 1973
PN 61   **SC** 18150
  UF Ethnic Disorders
  N   Koro 1994
      Sickle Cell Disease 1994
  R   Cross Cultural Psychology 1997
      Ethnology 1967
      ↓ Mental Disorders 1967
      ↓ Personality Disorders 1967
      ↓ Physical Disorders 1997
      ↓ Racial and Ethnic Groups 2001
      Transcultural Psychiatry 1973

Ethology (Animal)
   Use Animal Ethology

Ethyl Alcohol
   Use Ethanol

Ethyl Ether (Anesthetic)
   Use Ether (Anesthetic)

Ethylaldehyde
   Use Acetaldehyde

Etiology 1967
PN 10948   **SC** 18190
SN Study of the causes and origins of psychological or physical conditions. Used for the science itself or the specific etiological findings and processes.
  UF Aetiology
      Pathogenesis
  R   ↓ Disorders 1967
      ↓ Mental Disorders 1967
      Patient History 1973
      ↓ Physical Disorders 1997

Etymology 1973
PN 68   **SC** 18200

Etymology — (cont'd)
SN Branch of linguistic science which traces the origin of words and morphemes to their earliest determinable base in a given language group and describes historical changes in words. Used for the discipline or specific etymological aspects of given words.
  UF Word Origins
  B   Linguistics 1973
  R   Words (Phonetic Units) 1967

Eugenics 1973
PN 65   **SC** 18210
SN Applied science or the biosocial movement which advocates the use of practices aimed at improving the genetic composition of a population. Usually refers to human populations. Compare ANIMAL BREEDING, ANIMAL DOMESTICATION, and SELECTIVE BREEDING.
  B   Genetic Engineering 1994
      Genetics 1967
      Sciences 1967
  R   ↓ Family Planning 1973
      Genetic Counseling 1978
      Reproductive Technology 1988
      Selective Breeding 1973
      ↓ Sterilization (Sex) 1973

Euphoria 1973
PN 135   **SC** 18230
  B   Emotional States 1973
  R   Happiness 1973
      Pleasure 1973

Eustachian Tube
   Use Middle Ear

Euthanasia 1973
PN 441   **SC** 18255
  UF Mercy Killing
  B   Death and Dying 1967
  R   Advance Directives 1994
      Assisted Suicide 1997
      Death Attitudes 1973
      ↓ Ethics 1967
      Professional Ethics 1973
      ↓ Treatment 1967
      Treatment Withholding 1988

Evaluation 1967
PN 4989   **SC** 18260
SN Conceptually broad term referring to the appraisal of the characteristics, significance, importance, or relative value of a person, organization, or thing.
  N   Course Evaluation 1978
      Forensic Evaluation 1994
      Geriatric Assessment 1997
      Needs Assessment 1985
      Peer Evaluation 1982
      ↓ Personnel Evaluation 1973
      ↓ Program Evaluation 1985
      ↓ Psychiatric Evaluation 1997
      Self Evaluation 1967
      Treatment Effectiveness Evaluation 1973
      Vocational Evaluation 1991
  R   Evaluation Criteria 2001
      Intake Interview 1994
      ↓ Measurement 1967
      ↓ Psychological Assessment 1997
      Psychological Report 1988

Evaluation (Psychiatric)
  Use Psychiatric Evaluation

Evaluation (Treatment Effectiveness)
  Use Treatment Effectiveness Evaluation

Evaluation Criteria 2001
PN 0   SC 18270
SN Specifications that may be used to appraise individuals, organizations, tests, values, or processes.
  UF Assessment Criteria
  R ↓ Evaluation 1967

Evangelists 1973
PN 63   SC 18320
  B Religious Personnel 1973
  R ↓ Clergy 1973
        Lay Religious Personnel 1973
        Missionaries 1973

Evidence (Legal)
  Use Legal Evidence

Evoked Potentials 1967
PN 3417   SC 18330
  B Electrical Activity 1967
  N Auditory Evoked Potentials 1973
        ↓ Cortical Evoked Potentials 1973
        Olfactory Evoked Potentials 1973
        Somatosensory Evoked Potentials 1973
        Visual Evoked Potentials 1973
  R Electrical Brain Stimulation 1973
        Sensory Gating 1991

Evolution (Theory of)
  Use Theory of Evolution

Exceptional Children (Gifted)
  Use Gifted

Exceptional Children (Handicapped)
  Use Disorders

Excitation (Physiological)
  Use Physiological Arousal

Excretion 1967
PN 598   SC 18370
  UF Elimination (Excretion)
  B Physiology 1967
  N Defecation 1967
        ↓ Urination 1967

Executive Functioning
  Use Cognitive Ability

Executives
  Use Top Level Managers

Exercise 1973
PN 3964   SC 18390
  UF Physical Exercise
  B Motor Processes 1967
  N Aerobic Exercise 1988
        Weightlifting 1994
        Yoga 1973
  R Health Behavior 1982
        Movement Therapy 1997
        Physical Fitness 1973
        Weight Control 1985

Exhaustion
  Use Fatigue

Exhibitionism 1973
PN 201   SC 18420
  B Paraphilias 1988
  R Voyeurism 1973

Existential Therapy 1973
PN 269   SC 18430
SN Form of psychotherapy that deals with the here and now of the patient's total situation rather than with his/her past; it emphasizes emotional experiences rather than rational thinking, and stresses a person's responsibility for his/her own existence.
  B Psychotherapy 1967
  R Logotherapy 1973

Existentialism 1967
PN 965   SC 18440
SN Philosophy based on the analysis of the individual's existence in the world which holds that human existence cannot be completely described in scientific terms. Existentialism also stresses the freedom and responsibility of the individual as well as the uniqueness of religious and ethical experiences and the analysis of subjective phenomena such as anxiety, guilt, and suffering.
  B Philosophies 1967
  R Relativism 1997
        ↓ Religious Beliefs 1973

Exogamous Marriage 1973
PN 95   SC 18450
  UF Interethnic Marriage
        Intermarriage
  B Marriage 1967
  N Interfaith Marriage 1973
        Interracial Marriage 1973

Expectant Fathers 1985
PN 99   SC 18455
  B Expectant Parents 1985
  R ↓ Fathers 1967

Expectant Mothers 1985
PN 293   SC 18456
  B Expectant Parents 1985
  R ↓ Mothers 1967

Expectant Parents 1985
PN 84   SC 18457
  N Expectant Fathers 1985
        Expectant Mothers 1985
  R ↓ Parents 1967

Expectations 1967
PN 9838   SC 18460
SN Anticipation of future behavior or events. Also refers to investigations of the effects of that anticipation on behavior.
  B Cognitions 1985
  N Experimenter Expectations 1973
        Parental Expectations 1997
        Role Expectations 1973
        Teacher Expectations 1978
  R ↓ Estimation 1967
        Future 1991
        Halo Effect 1982
        Hope 1991
        Self Efficacy 1985
        Self Fulfilling Prophecies 1997

Experience (Practice)
  Use Practice

Experience Level 1988
PN 2748   SC 18495
SN Amount of practical knowledge, skill, or practice as a result of direct participation in a particular activity.
  UF Expertise
  N Job Experience Level 1973
  R ↓ Knowledge Level 1978

Experience Level (Job)
  Use Job Experience Level

Experiences (Events) 1973
PN 4472   SC 18510
SN Perceptual, emotional, and/or cognitive consequences associated with specific events or contexts. Compare LIFE EXPERIENCES.
  N Anniversary Events 1994
        Early Experience 1967
        Life Experiences 1973
        Vicarious Experiences 1973
  R Combat Experience 1991
        ↓ Crises 1971
        Familiarity 1967
        Homesickness 1994
        Near Death Experiences 1985
        ↓ Practice 1967

Experiences (Life)
  Use Life Experiences

Experiential Learning 1997
PN 175   SC 18517
  B Learning 1967
        Teaching Methods 1967
  N Curricular Field Experience 1982
  R Apprenticeship 1973
        Cooperative Education 1982
        Discovery Teaching Method 1973
        Educational Field Trips 1973
        On the Job Training 1973
        School Learning 1967

Experiential Psychotherapy 1973
PN 262   SC 18520
SN Psychotherapeutic approach, having some roots in existentialism, that emphasizes the concrete, lived, and felt experience of the client.
  B Psychotherapy 1967

Experiment Controls 1973
PN 272   SC 18530
  UF Control Groups
  R ↓ Experimental Design 1967
        ↓ Experimental Subjects 1985
        ↓ Experimentation 1967
        ↓ Methodology 1967

Experiment Volunteers 1973
PN 367   SC 18540
  UF Volunteers (Experiment)
  B Experimental Subjects 1985
  R Biased Sampling 1973
        ↓ Experimental Design 1967
        Informed Consent 1985
        Random Sampling 1973

Experimental Apparatus
  Use Apparatus

Experimental Attrition [1994]
PN 71   **SC** 18555
SN Reduction in the number of experimental subjects over time as a result of resignation or other factors.
UF   Research Dropouts
R   ↓ Dropouts [1973]
    ↓ Experimental Subjects [1985]
    ↓ Experimentation [1967]

Experimental Design [1967]
PN 4439   **SC** 18560
SN General procedural plan for conducting an experiment or other research study in view of the specific data desired. This may include identification of the independent and dependent variables; selection of subjects and their assignment to specific experimental conditions/treatments; the sequence of experimental conditions/treatments; and a method of analysis. Consider also EXPERIMENTAL METHODS.
UF   Design (Experimental)
    Research Design
N   Between Groups Design [1985]
    Cohort Analysis [1988]
    Followup Studies [1973]
    ↓ Hypothesis Testing [1973]
    ↓ Longitudinal Studies [1973]
    Repeated Measures [1985]
R   Animal Models [1988]
    Conjoint Measurement [1994]
    Debriefing (Experimental) [1991]
    Experiment Controls [1973]
    Experiment Volunteers [1973]
    ↓ Experimental Methods [1967]
    ↓ Experimentation [1967]
    ↓ Methodology [1967]
    ↓ Population (Statistics) [1973]
    Psychometrics [1967]
    Research Setting [2001]
    ↓ Sampling (Experimental) [1973]
    ↓ Statistical Analysis [1967]
    ↓ Statistical Variables [1973]
    ↓ Test Construction [1973]

Experimental Environment
Use   Research Setting

Experimental Epilepsy [1978]
PN 183   **SC** 18564
SN Paroxysmal transient disruption of normal electrical activity in the brain induced by chemical, electrical, or physical stimulation of the brain or by repetitive sensory stimulation.
B   Epilepsy [1967]
    Epileptic Seizures [1973]
R   ↓ Convulsions [1967]
    ↓ Electrical Stimulation [1973]
    Kindling [1985]

Experimental Ethics [1978]
PN 989   **SC** 18566
B   Ethics [1967]
R   Animal Welfare [1985]
    Debriefing (Experimental) [1991]
    ↓ Experimentation [1967]
    Fraud [1994]
    Informed Consent [1985]
    Professional Ethics [1973]

Experimental Instructions [1967]
PN 2723   **SC** 18570
SN Directions given to a subject participating in an experiment.

Experimental Instructions — (cont'd)
UF   Instructions (Experimental)
R   ↓ Experimentation [1967]
    ↓ Methodology [1967]

Experimental Laboratories [1973]
PN 375   **SC** 18580
UF   Laboratories (Experimental)
R   ↓ Experimentation [1967]
    ↓ Methodology [1967]
    Research Setting [2001]

Experimental Methods [1967]
PN 4959   **SC** 18590
SN System of scientific investigation, usually based on a design and carried out under controlled conditions with the aim of testing a hypothesis, in which one or more variables is manipulated.
UF   Scientific Methods
B   Empirical Methods [1973]
N   ↓ Stimulus Presentation Methods [1973]
R   ↓ Experimental Design [1967]

Experimental Neurosis [1973]
PN 55   **SC** 18600
SN Acute neurotic-like state produced experimentally by requiring discrimination or problem solving responses which are beyond the subject's ability or level of learning. Such states are induced by the repeated delivery of aversive stimulation following failure.
B   Neurosis [1967]
R   Experimental Psychosis [1973]
    Learned Helplessness [1978]

Experimental Psychologists [1973]
PN 58   **SC** 18610
B   Psychologists [1967]

Experimental Psychology [1967]
PN 696   **SC** 18620
B   Psychology [1967]
R   ↓ Experimentation [1967]

Experimental Psychosis [1973]
PN 18   **SC** 18630
SN Experimentally induced psychotic-like state or condition usually achieved through drug administration. Not to be confused with inadvertent induction of psychotic conditions resulting from toxic side effects in drug therapy. Compare TOXIC PSYCHOSES.
B   Psychosis [1967]
R   Experimental Neurosis [1973]
    ↓ Hallucinogenic Drugs [1967]
    ↓ Psychotomimetic Drugs [1973]

Experimental Replication [1973]
PN 3649   **SC** 18640
SN Used in records discussing issues involved in the process of conducting a replication of an experiment. From 1973-2000, the term was also used as a mandatory document type identifier; however, this usage has been discontinued due to the advent of Form/Content Type field identifiers. References from 1973-2000 can be accessed using either EXPERIMENTAL REPLICATION or the Experimental Replication Form/Content Type field identifier.
UF   Replication (Experimental)
R   ↓ Experimentation [1967]
    ↓ Methodology [1967]

Experimental Subjects [1985]
PN 862   **SC** 18645

Experimental Subjects — (cont'd)
SN Any individual who is, knowingly or unknowingly, a member of an experiment or research population. Used only when methodological or procedural aspects are discussed regarding research subjects. Used primarily for human populations.
UF   Research Subjects
N   Experiment Volunteers [1973]
R   Debriefing (Experimental) [1991]
    Experiment Controls [1973]
    Experimental Attrition [1994]
    ↓ Experimentation [1967]

Experimentation [1967]
PN 18179   **SC** 18650
SN Conceptually broad term referring to any or all aspects of scientific research. Use a more specific term if possible.
UF   Investigation
    Research
N   ↓ Consumer Research [1973]
    Interdisciplinary Research [1985]
    Research Setting [2001]
R   Animal Models [1988]
    Causal Analysis [1994]
    Debriefing (Experimental) [1991]
    Experiment Controls [1973]
    Experimental Attrition [1994]
    ↓ Experimental Design [1967]
    Experimental Ethics [1978]
    Experimental Instructions [1967]
    Experimental Laboratories [1973]
    Experimental Psychology [1967]
    Experimental Replication [1973]
    ↓ Experimental Subjects [1985]
    Experimenters [1973]
    ↓ Measurement [1967]
    ↓ Methodology [1967]
    ↓ Population (Statistics) [1973]
    Privileged Communication [1973]
    Psychometrics [1967]
    Psychophysics [1967]
    ↓ Sampling (Experimental) [1973]
    ↓ Statistical Analysis [1967]
    ↓ Statistical Correlation [1967]
    Statistical Reliability [1973]
    Statistical Validity [1973]
    ↓ Statistical Variables [1973]
    ↓ Theories [1967]

Experimenter Bias [1967]
PN 506   **SC** 18660
SN Potential and unintentional influence on experimental outcomes caused by the experimenter.
UF   Bias (Experimenter)
R   Experimenter Expectations [1973]
    Experimenters [1973]
    Halo Effect [1982]

Experimenter Expectations [1973]
PN 152   **SC** 18670
SN Results from experimentation which are anticipated or desired by the researcher in order to confirm a hypothesis and which may serve as a potential factor in experimenter bias.
B   Expectations [1967]
R   Experimenter Bias [1967]
    Experimenters [1973]

Experimenters [1973]
PN 467   **SC** 18680
R   ↓ Experimentation [1967]
    Experimenter Bias [1967]
    Experimenter Expectations [1973]

Expert Systems 1991
PN 864   SC 18685
UF   Knowledge Based Systems
B   Artificial Intelligence 1982
    Systems 1967
N   Decision Support Systems 1997
R   ↓ Automated Information Processing 1973
    Automated Speech Recognition 1994
    ↓ Computers 1967
    Cybernetics 1967
    ↓ Data Processing 1967
    Databases 1991
    ↓ Decision Making 1967
    Human Machine Systems 1997
    ↓ Information Systems 1991
    ↓ Problem Solving 1967
    Robotics 1985

Expert Testimony 1973
PN 1150   SC 18690
SN   Legal testimony by persons who by virtue of their training, skills, or expertise are qualified to give evidence concerning some scientific, technical, or professional matter.
UF   Testimony (Expert)
B   Legal Testimony 1982
R   Forensic Evaluation 1994
    Forensic Psychiatry 1973
    Forensic Psychology 1985

Expertise
Use   Experience Level

Explicit Memory 1997
PN 191   SC 18695
B   Memory 1967

Exploratory Behavior 1967
PN 698   SC 18700
SN   Locomotor activity or perceptual processes involved in investigating and/or orienting oneself to an environment. From 1973, limited to human populations. From 1973, use ANIMAL EXPLORATORY BEHAVIOR to access references to nonhumans.
B   Behavior 1967
N   Animal Exploratory Behavior 1973
R   Curiosity 1967
    Information Seeking 1973
    ↓ Motivation 1967

Explosive Disorder 2001
PN 42   SC 18705
SN   Disorder characterized by discrete episodes of loss of control of aggressive impulses that may result in serious assault or destruction of property. In 2000, this term was created to replace the discontinued term EXPLOSIVE PERSONALITY. EXPLOSIVE PERSONALITY was stripped from all records and replaced with EXPLOSIVE DISORDER.
UF   Explosive Personality
    Intermittent Explosive Disorder
B   Impulse Control Disorders 1997
R   Anger Control 1997
    ↓ Antisocial Behavior 1971
    Conduct Disorder 1991
    ↓ Personality Disorders 1967

Explosive Personality
SN   In 2000, the term was discontinued, and all records containing it were stripped of the term and replaced with EXPLOSIVE DISORDER, its postable counterpart.
Use   Explosive Disorder

Exposure Therapy 1997
PN 187   SC 18715
B   Behavior Therapy 1967
N   Implosive Therapy 1973
    Systematic Desensitization Therapy 1973

Exposure Time (Stimulus)
Use   Stimulus Duration

Expressed Emotion 1991
PN 414   SC 18725
SN   Frequency and quality of negative emotions, e.g., anger or hostility, expressed by family members or significant others, that often lead to a high relapse rate, especially in schizophrenic patients.
R   ↓ Emotions 1967
    Relapse (Disorders) 1973
    ↓ Schizophrenia 1967

Expressions (Facial)
Use   Facial Expressions

Expressive Psychotherapy 1973
PN 83   SC 18740
SN   Psychotherapeutic method used to promote more effective personality functioning through uninhibited expression of feelings and open discussion of personal problems.
B   Psychotherapy 1967
R   Supportive Psychotherapy 1997

Expulsion (School)
Use   School Expulsion

Extended Family 1973
PN 235   SC 18760
B   Family 1967
    Family Structure 1973

Extension Workers (Agricultural)
Use   Agricultural Extension Workers

External Ear 1973
PN 58   SC 18780
UF   Ear Canal
B   Ear (Anatomy) 1967

External Rewards 1973
PN 327   SC 18790
SN   Tangible or overtly identifiable rewards given in return for service or attainment which may act as reinforcement for the activity rewarded. Compare PRIMARY REINFORCEMENT.
UF   Extrinsic Rewards
B   Rewards 1967
R   Extrinsic Motivation 1973
    Internal External Locus of Control 1967

Externalization 1973
PN 326   SC 18800
B   Personality Processes 1967
R   ↓ Defense Mechanisms 1967
    ↓ Internalization 1997
    ↓ Personality Development 1967

Extinction (Learning) 1967
PN 3332   SC 18810

Extinction (Learning) — (cont'd)
SN   Learned behavior or the experimental paradigm involving withholding reinforcement for a conditioned response and resulting in a gradual reduction and eventual elimination of responding or a return to a rate of responding comparable to levels prior to conditioning. Term may be used in either classical (Pavlovian) or operant (instrumental) conditioning contexts.
B   Learning 1967
R   ↓ Discrimination Learning 1982
    ↓ Reinforcement 1967

Extracurricular Activities 1973
PN 495   SC 18820
N   Fraternity Membership 1973
    School Club Membership 1973
    Sorority Membership 1973
R   Athletic Participation 1973
    Athletic Training 1991
    ↓ Education 1967

Extradimensional Shift Learning
Use   Nonreversal Shift Learning

Extramarital Intercourse 1973
PN 264   SC 18830
UF   Adultery
    Affairs (Sexual)
    Mate Swapping
B   Psychosexual Behavior 1967
    Sexual Intercourse (Human) 1973
R   ↓ Marital Relations 1967
    Monogamy 1997
    Promiscuity 1973

Extrapyramidal Symptoms 1994
PN 295   SC 18835
B   Symptoms 1967
R   ↓ Basal Ganglia 1973
    Extrapyramidal Tracts 1973
    ↓ Nervous System Disorders 1967

Extrapyramidal Tracts 1973
PN 121   SC 18840
B   Central Nervous System 1967
    Efferent Pathways 1982
    Spinal Cord 1973
R   Extrapyramidal Symptoms 1994

Extrasensory Perception 1967
PN 659   SC 18850
UF   ESP (Parapsychology)
B   Parapsychological Phenomena 1973
    Perception 1967
N   ↓ Clairvoyance 1973
    Psychokinesis 1973
R   Telepathy 1973

Extraversion 1967
PN 2612   SC 18854
SN   Personality trait which reflects the extent to which an individual likes people and prefers large gatherings; is assertive, active and talkative; enjoys excitement and stimulation; and tends to have a cheerful disposition.
B   Personality Traits 1967
R   Assertiveness 1973
    Five Factor Personality Model 1997
    Gregariousness 1973
    Introversion 1967
    Sensation Seeking 1978
    Sociability 1973

Extrinsic Motivation 1973
PN 470   SC 18860
SN Need or desire arising from outside the individual which causes action toward some goal.
B   Motivation 1967
R   External Rewards 1973
     ↓ Goals 1967
     Internal External Locus of Control 1967
     ↓ Needs 1967

Extrinsic Rewards
Use External Rewards

Eye (Anatomy) 1967
PN 1137   SC 18890
UF   Choroid
     Sclera
B   Sense Organs 1973
N   Cornea 1973
     Eye Color 1991
     Fovea 1982
     Iris (Eye) 1973
     Lens (Eye) 1973
     Pupil (Eye) 1973
     ↓ Retina 1967
R   ↓ Eye Disorders 1973
     ↓ Eye Movements 1967
     Ocular Dominance 1973
     Pupil Dilation 1973
     Retinal Image 1973
     ↓ Visual Perception 1967

Eye Accommodation
Use Ocular Accommodation

Eye Color 1991
PN 19   SC 18895
B   Color 1967
     Eye (Anatomy) 1967
R   Iris (Eye) 1973
     ↓ Pigments 1973

Eye Contact 1973
PN 580   SC 18900
SN Form of nonverbal communication in which two individuals meet each other's glance.
B   Interpersonal Communication 1973
     Nonverbal Communication 1971
R   ↓ Social Reinforcement 1967

Eye Convergence 1982
PN 221   SC 18902
SN Turning the eyes toward or away from each other when fixating on distal objects.
UF   Vergence Movements
B   Eye Movements 1967
R   ↓ Depth Perception 1967
     ↓ Distance Perception 1973
     Strabismus 1973

Eye Disorders 1973
PN 386   SC 18910
SN Diseases or defects of the eye. Use VISION DISORDERS for other pathology involving visual neural pathways.
B   Vision Disorders 1982
N   Amblyopia 1973
     Cataracts 1973
     Color Blindness 1973
     Glaucoma 1973
     Hemianopia 1973
     Nystagmus 1973
     ↓ Refraction Errors 1973
N   Strabismus 1973

Eye Disorders — (cont'd)
     Tunnel Vision 1973
R   Albinism 1973
     ↓ Eye (Anatomy) 1967
     Hysterical Vision Disturbances 1973
     Ocular Dominance 1973
     ↓ Visual Perception 1967

Eye Dominance
Use Ocular Dominance

Eye Examination
Use Ophthalmologic Examination

Eye Fixation 1982
PN 1271   SC 18924
SN Orienting one's eye(s) toward and stabilizing one's gaze on a specified visual stimulus.
UF   Gazing
     Ocular Fixation
     Visual Fixation
B   Visual Perception 1967
R   Visual Field 1967

Eye Movement Desensitization Therapy 1997
PN 157   SC 18927
SN Treatment methodology used in the reduction of the emotional impact of trauma-based symptomatology associated with anxiety, nightmares, flashbacks, or intrusive thought processes.
UF   EMDR
B   Psychotherapy 1967
R   ↓ Behavior Therapy 1967
     ↓ Eye Movements 1967

Eye Movements 1967
PN 5529   SC 18930
UF   Oculomotor Response
     Saccadic Eye Movements
N   Eye Convergence 1982
     Nystagmus 1973
     Rapid Eye Movement 1971
R   ↓ Eye (Anatomy) 1967
     Eye Movement Desensitization Therapy 1997
     REM Dreams 1973
     REM Sleep 1973
     Visual Search 1982

Eyeblink Reflex 1973
PN 628   SC 18940
UF   Blink Reflex
B   Reflexes 1971
R   Startle Reflex 1967

Eyelid Conditioning 1973
PN 623   SC 18950
SN Conditioned eye blinking or the classical conditioning paradigm resulting in conditioned eye blinking.
UF   Conditioning (Eyelid)
B   Classical Conditioning 1967

Eyewitnesses
Use Witnesses

Eysenck Personality Inventory 1973
PN 460   SC 18960
B   Nonprojective Personality Measures 1973

F Test 1973
PN 87   SC 18970
B   Parametric Statistical Tests 1973

F Test — (cont'd)
R   ↓ Variability Measurement 1973

Face (Anatomy) 1973
PN 531   SC 18980
B   Anatomy 1967
R   Facial Features 1973
     Head (Anatomy) 1973

Face Perception 1985
PN 2152   SC 18985
SN Used for human or animal populations.
UF   Face Recognition
B   Visual Perception 1967
R   ↓ Facial Expressions 1967
     Facial Features 1973
     Prosopagnosia 1994
     ↓ Social Perception 1967

Face Recognition
Use Face Perception

Facial Expressions 1967
PN 2300   SC 18990
UF   Expressions (Facial)
B   Nonverbal Communication 1971
N   Grimaces 1973
     Smiles 1973
R   Face Perception 1985
     Facial Features 1973

Facial Features 1973
PN 741   SC 18993
R   Face (Anatomy) 1973
     Face Perception 1985
     ↓ Facial Expressions 1967
     ↓ Physical Appearance 1982
     Physical Attractiveness 1973

Facial Muscles 1973
PN 276   SC 19000
B   Muscles 1967

Facial Nerve 1973
PN 143   SC 19010
UF   Chorda Tympani Nerve
     Nerve (Facial)
B   Cranial Nerves 1973

Facilitated Communication
Use Augmentative Communication

Facilitation (Social)
Use Social Facilitation

Facility Admission 1988
PN 143   SC 19024
UF   Facility Readmission
N   ↓ Hospital Admission 1973
R   ↓ Facility Discharge 1988
     ↓ Institutionalization 1967
     ↓ Treatment Facilities 1973

Facility Discharge 1988
PN 80   SC 19026
N   ↓ Hospital Discharge 1973
R   Client Transfer 1997
     Discharge Planning 1994
     ↓ Facility Admission 1988
     ↓ Institutionalization 1967
     ↓ Treatment Facilities 1973

Facility Environment 1988
PN 423   SC 19028
B   Environment 1967
     Therapeutic Environment 2001
N   Hospital Environment 1982
R   ↓ Treatment Facilities 1973

Facility Readmission
Use Facility Admission

Factitious Disorders 1988
PN 279   SC 19035
UF   Ganser Syndrome
B   Mental Disorders 1967
N   Munchausen Syndrome 1994
R   Malingering 1973
     Pseudodementia 1985

Factor Analysis 1967
PN 5364   SC 19040
SN   Use FACTOR ANALYSIS to access references
to the factor structure of psychometric measures
from 1967-1984.
UF   Confirmatory Factor Analysis
B   Multivariate Analysis 1982
N   Item Analysis (Statistical) 1973
     ↓ Statistical Rotation 1973
R   Factor Structure 1985
     Goodness of Fit 1988
     Path Analysis 1991
     ↓ Statistical Correlation 1967
     Statistical Significance 1973
     Structural Equation Modeling 1994

Factor Structure 1985
PN 3969   SC 19045
SN   The internal correlational structure of a set of
variables said to measure a given construct. Use
FACTOR ANALYSIS to access references prior to
1985.
R   ↓ Factor Analysis 1967
     ↓ Statistical Rotation 1973
     Structural Equation Modeling 1994

Factorial Validity
SN   In 2000, the term was discontinued, and all
records containing it were stripped of the term and
replaced with STATISTICAL VALIDITY, its postable
counterpart.
Use Statistical Validity

Factory Environments
Use Working Conditions

Factual Knowledge
Use Declarative Knowledge

Faculty
Use Educational Personnel

Fading (Conditioning) 1982
PN 136   SC 19087
SN   Gradual attenuation of dissimilarity of stimuli
dimensions contingent on the subject's mastery of
difference between those stimuli. The fading technique is used to facilitate errorless discrimination
learning.
B   Behavior Modification 1973
     Operant Conditioning 1967
R   ↓ Discrimination Learning 1982
     Stimulus Attenuation 1973
     Stimulus Discrimination 1973

Fads and Fashions 1973
PN 102   SC 19090
N   Clothing 1967
R   Cosmetic Techniques 2001
     Social Change 1967
     Trends 1991

Failure 1967
PN 1673   SC 19100
N   Academic Failure 1978
R   Academic Underachievement 1967
     ↓ Achievement 1967

Failure to Thrive 1988
PN 196   SC 19105
SN   Growth disorder of infants and children due to
nutritional and/or emotional deprivation and resulting
in loss of weight and delayed physical, emotional and
social development.
B   Delayed Development 1973
R   Attachment Disorders 2001
     ↓ Child Abuse 1971
     Child Neglect 1988
     ↓ Nutritional Deficiencies 1973

Fainting
Use Syncope

Fairbairnian Theory
Use Object Relations

Fairy Tales
Use Folklore

Faith Healing 1973
PN 322   SC 19120
UF   Psychic Healing
B   Alternative Medicine 1997
     Religious Practices 1973
R   Folk Medicine 1967
     Shamanism 1973
     Witchcraft 1973

Faking 1973
PN 426   SC 19130
B   Deception 1967
R   ↓ Behavior Disorders 1971

False Memory 1997
PN 400   SC 19135
UF   Pseudomemory
B   Memory 1967
R   Age Regression (Hypnotic) 1988
     ↓ Amnesia 1967
     Confabulation 1973
     Early Memories 1985
     Emotional Trauma 1967
     ↓ Hypnosis 1967
     ↓ Hypnotherapy 1973
     Repressed Memory 1997
     Suggestibility 1967

False Pregnancy
Use Pseudocyesis

Fame 1985
PN 65   SC 19145
R   Reputation 1997
     ↓ Social Perception 1967
     ↓ Status 1967

Familial Idiocy (Amaurotic)
Use Amaurotic Familial Idiocy

Familiarity 1967
PN 3591   SC 19160
SN   Knowledge of, or close acquaintance with, an
object, stimulus, person, environment, situation or
act.
R   ↓ Experiences (Events) 1973
     ↓ Practice 1967
     Stranger Reactions 1988

Family 1967
PN 6918   SC 19300
SN   Conceptually broad term. Use a more specific
term if possible.
N   Biological Family 1988
     Extended Family 1973
     Family of Origin 1991
     Interethnic Family 1988
     Interracial Family 1988
     Nuclear Family 1973
     Schizophrenogenic Family 1967
     Stepfamily 1991
R   Codependency 1991
     Cohabitation 1973
     Couples 1982
     Divorce 1973
     Divorced Persons 1973
     Dual Careers 1982
     Dysfunctional Family 1991
     Empty Nest 1991
     ↓ Family Background 1973
     Family Crises 1973
     ↓ Family Life Education 1997
     ↓ Family Members 1973
     ↓ Family Planning 1973
     ↓ Family Relations 1967
     Family Resemblance 1991
     ↓ Family Structure 1973
     Kinship 1985
     ↓ Living Arrangements 1991
     ↓ Marital Separation 1973
     ↓ Marital Status 1973
     ↓ Marriage 1967
     Transgenerational Patterns 1991
     Widowers 1973
     Widows 1973
     Working Women 1978

Family Background 1973
PN 3878   SC 19170
UF   Background (Family)
N   Family Socioeconomic Level 1973
     Parent Educational Background 1973
     Parental Occupation 1973
R   Biographical Data 1978
     ↓ Family 1967
     Family of Origin 1991
     ↓ Marital Status 1973

Family Caregivers
Use Caregivers

Family Counseling
Use Family Therapy

Family Crises 1973
PN 507   SC 19190
B   Crises 1971
R   ↓ Family 1967
     ↓ Stress 1967

Family Life
  Use Family Relations

Family Life Education 1997
PN 40   SC 19203
  UF Marriage and Family Education
  B   Education 1967
  N   Parent Training 1978
      Sex Education 1973
  R   ↓ Family 1967
      ↓ Family Relations 1967
      ↓ Family Therapy 1967
      Household Management 1985

Family Medicine 1988
PN 321   SC 19205
  B   Medical Sciences 1967
  R   Family Physicians 1973
      General Practitioners 1973

Family Members 1973
PN 7386   SC 19210
  N   Adopted Children 1973
      Adult Offspring 1985
      ↓ Ancestors 1973
      Biological Family 1988
      Cousins 1973
      Daughters 1973
      Foster Children 1973
      Grandchildren 1973
      Grandparents 1973
      Illegitimate Children 1973
      Inlaws 1997
      Orphans 1973
      ↓ Parents 1967
      ↓ Siblings 1967
      Sons 1973
      ↓ Spouses 1973
      Stepchildren 1973
  R   ↓ Family 1967
      Family Resemblance 1991
      Family of Origin 1991
      ↓ Offspring 1988
      Only Children 1982
      Significant Others 1991

Family of Origin 1991
PN 457   SC 19215
  SN Family in which an individual was raised. Compare BIOLOGICAL FAMILY.
  B   Family 1967
  R   Biological Family 1988
      ↓ Family Background 1973
      ↓ Family Members 1973
      ↓ Family Structure 1973
      Stepfamily 1991

Family Physicians 1973
PN 761   SC 19220
  B   Physicians 1967
  R   Family Medicine 1988
      General Practitioners 1973

Family Planning 1973
PN 569   SC 19230
  N   ↓ Birth Control 1971
  R   Condoms 1991
      Delayed Parenthood 1985
      Eugenics 1973
      ↓ Family 1967
      Fertility Enhancement 1973
      Induced Abortion 1971
      ↓ Sterilization (Sex) 1973

Family Planning Attitudes 1973
PN 871   SC 19240
  UF Birth Control Attitudes
  B   Attitudes 1967
  R   Childlessness 1982
      Delayed Parenthood 1985
      ↓ Family Relations 1967

Family Relations 1967
PN 18558   SC 19250
  SN Dynamics of interpersonal interaction and developmental processes taking place between and among members of a biological or socially defined family unit. See FAMILY MEMBERS for references to biological relatives in a family.
  UF Family Life
  N   ↓ Child Discipline 1973
      ↓ Childrearing Practices 1967
      ↓ Marital Relations 1967
      ↓ Parent Child Relations 1967
      Parental Role 1973
      Sibling Relations 1973
  R   Childrearing Attitudes 1973
      Codependency 1991
      Dysfunctional Family 1991
      Empty Nest 1991
      ↓ Family 1967
      ↓ Family Life Education 1997
      Family Planning Attitudes 1973
      ↓ Family Violence 1982
      Family Work Relationship 1997
      Intergenerational Relations 1988
      Marriage Attitudes 1973
      ↓ Relationship Satisfaction 2001
      Social Support Networks 1982
      Transgenerational Patterns 1991

Family Resemblance 1991
PN 57   SC 19255
  R   Assortative Mating 1991
      ↓ Family 1967
      ↓ Family Members 1973
      ↓ Genetics 1967
      Transgenerational Patterns 1991
      ↓ Twins 1967

Family Size 1973
PN 842   SC 19260
  B   Family Structure 1973
      Size 1973
  R   Empty Nest 1991
      ↓ Parenthood Status 1985

Family Socioeconomic Level 1973
PN 823   SC 19270
  B   Family Background 1973
      Socioeconomic Status 1967
  R   Parent Educational Background 1973
      Parental Occupation 1973

Family Structure 1973
PN 3206   SC 19280
  N   Birth Order 1967
      Childlessness 1982
      Extended Family 1973
      Family Size 1973
      Matriarchy 1973
      Monogamy 1997
      Nuclear Family 1973
      ↓ Parental Absence 1973
      Patriarchy 1973
      Polygamy 1973
      Schizophrenogenic Family 1967
      Stepfamily 1991

Family Structure — (cont'd)
  R   ↓ Culture (Anthropological) 1967
      Dual Careers 1982
      Dysfunctional Family 1991
      Empty Nest 1991
      ↓ Family 1967
      Family of Origin 1991
      Homosexual Parents 1994
      Kinship Structure 1973
      Living Alone 1994
      ↓ Living Arrangements 1991
      Only Children 1982
      ↓ Parenthood Status 1985
      ↓ Single Parents 1978
      ↓ Sociocultural Factors 1967
      Stepchildren 1973
      Stepparents 1973

Family Therapy 1967
PN 10590   SC 19290
  UF Family Counseling
  B   Psychotherapeutic Counseling 1973
  N   Conjoint Therapy 1973
  R   ↓ Counseling 1967
      ↓ Family Life Education 1997
      Social Casework 1967

Family Violence 1982
PN 2804   SC 19294
  SN Injurious or abusive behavior in family or other domestic interpersonal situations.
  UF Domestic Violence
  B   Violence 1973
  N   ↓ Child Abuse 1971
  R   Battered Females 1988
      Elder Abuse 1988
      ↓ Family Relations 1967
      Marital Conflict 1973
      Partner Abuse 1991
      Physical Abuse 1991
      ↓ Sexual Abuse 1988
      Shelters 1991

Family Work Relationship 1997
PN 395   SC 19297
  UF Job Family Relationship
      Work Family Relationship
  R   Dual Careers 1982
      ↓ Family Relations 1967
      Role Conflicts 1973
      Work (Attitudes Toward) 1973
      ↓ Working Conditions 1973
      Working Women 1978

Fans (Sports)
  Use Sports Spectators

Fantasies (Thought Disturbances) 1967
PN 472   SC 19310
  SN Thinking that severely distorts reality.
  B   Thought Disturbances 1973
  R   ↓ Fantasy 1997
      Magical Thinking 1973

Fantasy 1997
PN 245   SC 19315
  SN Use IMAGINATION to access references from 1982-1996.
  B   Cognitive Processes 1967
  N   Sexual Fantasy 1997
  R   Daydreaming 1973
      Fantasies (Thought Disturbances) 1967
      Fantasy (Defense Mechanism) 1967

Fantasy — (cont'd)

R   ↓ Ideation   1973
     Imagination   1967
     Magical Thinking   1973

Fantasy (Defense Mechanism)   1967

PN   787   SC   19320
SN   Daydreaming dominated by unconscious material and primary processes for the purpose of wish fulfillment or to alleviate social isolation.
B   Defense Mechanisms   1967
R   Daydreaming   1973
    ↓ Fantasy   1997
    Sexual Fantasy   1997

Farmers

Use   Agricultural Workers

Fascism   1973

PN   297   SC   19342
UF   Nazism
B   Political Economic Systems   1973
R   Holocaust   1988

Fat Metabolism

Use   Lipid Metabolism

Fatalism   1973

PN   71   SC   19360
B   Philosophies   1967
R   Cynicism   1973
    Nihilism   1973
    Pessimism   1973

Father Absence   1973

PN   623   SC   19370
SN   From 1982, limited to human populations. For animals consider ANIMAL PARENTAL BEHAVIOR.
B   Parental Absence   1973
R   Matriarchy   1973

Father Child Communication   1985

PN   93   SC   19375
SN   Verbal or nonverbal communication between father and child.
B   Parent Child Communication   1973
R   Father Child Relations   1973

Father Child Relations   1973

PN   2245   SC   19380
SN   From 1982, limited to human populations. For animals consider ANIMAL PARENTAL BEHAVIOR.
B   Parent Child Relations   1967
R   ↓ Childrearing Practices   1967
    Father Child Communication   1985
    ↓ Parental Attitudes   1973
    Parental Permissiveness   1973
    Parental Role   1973

Fathers   1967

PN   3375   SC   19390
SN   From 1982, limited to human populations. For animals consider ANIMAL PARENTAL BEHAVIOR.
B   Human Males   1973
    Parents   1967
N   Adolescent Fathers   1985
    Single Fathers   1994
R   Expectant Fathers   1985

Fatigue   1967

PN   1596   SC   19400
UF   Exhaustion
    Tiredness

Fatigue — (cont'd)

B   Symptoms   1967
R   Chronic Fatigue Syndrome   1997
    Hypersomnia   1994

Fatty Acids   1973

PN   368   SC   19410
B   Acids   1973
    Lipids   1973
N   Capsaicin   1991
    ↓ Phosphatides   1973
R   Prostaglandins   1982

Fear   1967

PN   5118   SC   19420
B   Emotional States   1973
N   Fear of Success   1978
    Panic   1973
R   Alarm Responses   1973
    ↓ Anxiety   1967
    Neophobia   1985
    ↓ Neurosis   1967
    ↓ Phobias   1967
    Shame   1994
    Social Anxiety   1985
    Stranger Reactions   1988

Fear of Public Speaking

Use   Speech Anxiety

Fear of Strangers

Use   Stranger Reactions

Fear of Success   1978

PN   397   SC   19424
SN   Need to inhibit maximum utilization of one's abilities in achievement situations due to expected negative consequences.
B   Fear   1967
    Motivation   1967
R   ↓ Achievement Motivation   1967
    ↓ Anxiety   1967
    ↓ Anxiety Disorders   1997
    Self Handicapping Strategy   1988

Fear Survey Schedule   1973

PN   52   SC   19430
B   Nonprojective Personality Measures   1973

Fecal Incontinence   1973

PN   347   SC   19440
UF   Encopresis
    Incontinence (Fecal)
B   Colon Disorders   1973
R   ↓ Behavior Disorders   1971
    Diarrhea   1973
    ↓ Symptoms   1967

Fee for Service   1994

PN   57   SC   19450
SN   Payment for health related services in which the health care provider is reimbursed for services by the client or health insurance carrier.
B   Health Insurance   1973
    Professional Fees   1978
R   Cost Containment   1991
    ↓ Health Care Delivery   1978
    ↓ Health Care Services   1978
    Health Maintenance Organizations   1982
    ↓ Managed Care   1994

Feedback   1967

PN   6233   SC   19460

Feedback — (cont'd)

SN   General concept denoting the return of information that may regulate or control subsequent behavior, cognition, perception, or performance. Use a more specific term if possible.
N   ↓ Biofeedback   1973
    ↓ Delayed Feedback   1973
    Knowledge of Results   1967
    ↓ Sensory Feedback   1973
R   ↓ Learning   1967
    ↓ Reinforcement   1967
    ↓ Stimulation   1967

Feeding Behavior (Animal)

Use   Animal Feeding Behavior

Feeding Practices   1973

PN   659   SC   19480
SN   Limited to human populations. In 2000, this term became the postable counterpart for the nonpostable term EATING PATTERNS. EATING PATTERNS was stripped from all records and replaced with FEEDING PRACTICES.
UF   Eating Patterns
    Mealtimes
N   Binge Eating   1991
    Bottle Feeding   1973
    Breast Feeding   1973
    Diets   1978
    Weaning   1973
R   Animal Feeding Behavior   1973
    ↓ Childrearing Practices   1967
    Dietary Restraint   1994
    ↓ Fluid Intake   1985
    Food Intake   1967
    ↓ Ingestion   2001

Feelings

Use   Emotions

Feet (Anatomy)   1973

PN   207   SC   19500
UF   Heels (Anatomy)
    Toes (Anatomy)
B   Anatomy   1967
    Musculoskeletal System   1973
R   Ankle   1973
    Leg (Anatomy)   1973

Felids   1997

PN   14   SC   19505
UF   Lions
    Tigers
B   Mammals   1973
N   Cats   1967

Felonies

Use   Crime

Female Animals   1973

PN   3677   SC   19520
B   Animals   1967

Female Criminals   1973

PN   437   SC   19530
B   Criminals   1967
    Human Females   1973

Female Delinquency   2001

PN   293   SC   19535

Female Delinquency — (cont'd)

SN In 2000, this term was created to replace the discontinued term FEMALE DELINQUENTS. FEMALE DELINQUENTS was stripped from all records and replaced with FEMALE DELINQUENCY.

B Juvenile Delinquency 1967
R ↓ Human Females 1973
Male Delinquency 2001

Female Genital Mutilation
Use Circumcision

Female Genitalia 1973
PN 252   **SC** 19550
SN Used for both human and animal populations.
UF Genitalia (Female)
B Urogenital System 1973
N Ovaries 1973
↓ Uterus 1973
Vagina 1973
R Circumcision 2001

Female Only Environments
Use Single Sex Environments

Female Orgasm 1973
PN 278   **SC** 19560
SN Used for both human and animal populations.
B Orgasm 1973
R Frigidity 1973
Masturbation 1973
↓ Sexual Intercourse (Human) 1973

Females (Human)
Use Human Females

Femininity 1967
PN 2019   **SC** 19580
B Personality Traits 1967
R Androgyny 1982
↓ Gender Identity 1985
Masculinity 1967
Sex Roles 1967

Feminism 1978
PN 3151   **SC** 19585
R Feminist Therapy 1994
↓ Sex Role Attitudes 1978
Womens Liberation Movement 1973

Feminist Therapy 1994
PN 215   **SC** 19587
SN An approach to psychotherapy, counseling, or consultation based on the assumptions and tenets of feminism.
B Psychotherapy 1967
R ↓ Counseling 1967
Feminism 1978

Feminization Syndrome (Testicular)
Use Testicular Feminization Syndrome

Femoral Nerve
Use Spinal Nerves

Fenfluramine 1973
PN 553   **SC** 19610
B Appetite Depressing Drugs 1973
Sympathomimetic Drugs 1973

Fentanyl 1985
PN 142   **SC** 19613

Fentanyl — (cont'd)
SN Synthetic opiate frequently used illicitly.
B Opiates 1973

Fertility 1988
PN 321   **SC** 19618
SN The quality or state of being capable of breeding or reproducing. Used for human and animal populations.
B Sexual Reproduction 1973
R Birth Rate 1982
Fertility Enhancement 1973
↓ Infertility 1973

Fertility Enhancement 1973
PN 32   **SC** 19620
R ↓ Family Planning 1973
Fertility 1988
↓ Hormones 1967
Oral Contraceptives 1973

Fertilization 1973
PN 97   **SC** 19630
R ↓ Pregnancy 1967
Reproductive Technology 1988
↓ Sexual Reproduction 1973

Fetal Alcohol Syndrome 1985
PN 357   **SC** 19635
B Drug Induced Congenital Disorders 1973
Syndromes 1973
R ↓ Alcoholism 1967
Ethanol 1973
↓ Mental Retardation 1967
↓ Prenatal Development 1973

Fetal Exposure
Use Prenatal Exposure

Fetishism 1973
PN 213   **SC** 19640
UF Sexual Fetishism
B Paraphilias 1988
R Coprophagia 2001
Sexual Masochism 1973
Sexual Sadism 1973
Transvestism 1973

Fetus 1967
PN 791   **SC** 19650
B Prenatal Developmental Stages 1973

Fever
Use Hyperthermia

Fibrillation (Heart) 1973
PN 32   **SC** 19680
UF Atrial Fibrillation
Auricular Fibrillation
Ventricular Fibrillation
B Arrhythmias (Heart) 1973

Fibromyalgia Syndrome
Use Muscular Disorders

Fiction
Use Literature

Field Dependence 1973
PN 2041   **SC** 19710

Field Dependence — (cont'd)
SN Aspect of cognitive style as seen in relative lack of autonomy from external referents, the inability to overcome embedding contexts, or the reliance on visual rather than gravitational cues in perception of the upright. Used also for reciprocal concept of field independence.
B Cognitive Style 1967

Field Instruction
Use Curricular Field Experience

Field Trips (Educational)
Use Educational Field Trips

Field Work (Educational)
Use Curricular Field Experience

Fighting
Use Aggressive Behavior

Figurative Language 1985
PN 351   **SC** 19736
SN Verbal expressions that signify one concept by using words that would normally be used to signify some other concept as a result of a conceptual analogy or qualitative similarity between the concepts.
UF Figures of Speech
Simile
B Language 1967
N Metaphor 1982
R Analogy 1991
Connotations 1973
Symbolism 1967
↓ Verbal Meaning 1973

Figure Ground Discrimination 1973
PN 672   **SC** 19740
SN Discrimination of a portion of a visual configuration as a coherent figure distinct from the background.
B Perceptual Discrimination 1973
R Form and Shape Perception 1967
Pattern Discrimination 1967
↓ Spatial Perception 1967

Figures of Speech
Use Figurative Language

Film Strips 1967
PN 535   **SC** 19750
SN Strips of film for still projection. Not used as a document type identifier.
B Audiovisual Communications Media 1973
R ↓ Educational Audiovisual Aids 1973

Filtered Noise 1973
PN 57   **SC** 19760
B Auditory Stimulation 1967

Filtered Speech 1973
PN 43   **SC** 19770
B Speech Processing (Mechanical) 1973

Financial Assistance (Educational)
Use Educational Financial Assistance

Fine Motor Skill Learning 1973
PN 154   **SC** 19790
B Perceptual Motor Learning 1967
Skill Learning 1973

Finger Tapping [1973]
PN 349   SC 19800
B   Motor Performance [1973]

Fingers (Anatomy) [1973]
PN 477   SC 19820
B   Musculoskeletal System [1973]
N   Thumb [1973]
R   Hand (Anatomy) [1967]

Fingerspelling [1973]
PN 73   SC 19830
B   Manual Communication [1978]
R   Sign Language [1973]

Fire Fighters [1991]
PN 145   SC 19845
R   Fire Prevention [1973]
    ↓ Government Personnel [1973]
    ↓ Paramedical Personnel [1973]
    ↓ Volunteer Personnel [1973]

Fire Prevention [1973]
PN 40   SC 19850
B   Prevention [1973]
R   Fire Fighters [1991]
    ↓ Safety [1967]

Firearms
Use   Weapons

Firesetting
Use   Arson

FIRO-B
Use   Fundamental Interpersonal Relation Orientation Behavior Ques

Fishes [1967]
PN 2143   SC 19870
B   Vertebrates [1973]
N   Bass (Fish) [1973]
    ↓ Carp [1973]
    Cichlids [1973]
    Electric Fishes [1973]
    Salmon [1973]
    Sticklebacks [1973]
R   Larvae [1973]

Five Factor Personality Model [1997]
PN 412   SC 19875
SN A model of personality dimensions that encompass five broad factors: neuroticism, extraversion, openness to experience, agreeableness, and conscientiousness.
UF   Big Five Personality Model
B   Personality Theory [1967]
R   Extraversion [1967]
    NEO Personality Inventory [1997]
    Neuroticism [1973]
    Openness to Experience [1997]
    ↓ Personality [1967]
    ↓ Personality Development [1967]
    ↓ Personality Traits [1967]

Fixed Interval Reinforcement [1973]
PN 749   SC 19880
UF   Interval Reinforcement
B   Reinforcement Schedules [1967]

Fixed Ratio Reinforcement [1973]
PN 784   SC 19890

Fixed Ratio Reinforcement — (cont'd)
UF   Ratio Reinforcement
B   Reinforcement Schedules [1967]

Flashbacks
Use   Hallucinations

Flexibility (Personality)
Use   Adaptability (Personality)

Flexion Reflex [1973]
PN 135   SC 19910
B   Reflexes [1971]

Flextime
Use   Work Scheduling

Flicker Fusion Frequency
Use   Critical Flicker Fusion Threshold

Flies
Use   Diptera

Flight Attendants
Use   Aerospace Personnel

Flight Instrumentation [1973]
PN 166   SC 19930
UF   Instrumentation (Flight)
B   Aviation [1967]
    Instrument Controls [1985]

Flight Simulation [1973]
PN 623   SC 19940
B   Simulation [1967]
R   Acceleration Effects [1973]
    ↓ Gravitational Effects [1967]

Flooding Therapy
Use   Implosive Therapy

Fluency
Use   Verbal Fluency

Fluid Intake [1985]
PN 925   SC 19965
SN Ingestion of liquids or solutions. Frequently used as an objective measure of physiological or motivational state or learning. Used for human or animal populations.
B   Ingestion [2001]
N   Water Intake [1967]
R   ↓ Drinking Behavior [1978]
    ↓ Feeding Practices [1973]
    Thirst [1967]

Fluoxetine [1991]
PN 1639   SC 19967
UF   Prozac
B   Antidepressant Drugs [1971]
    Serotonin Reuptake Inhibitors [1997]

Fluphenazine [1973]
PN 466   SC 19970
UF   Prolixin
B   Antiemetic Drugs [1973]
    Phenothiazine Derivatives [1973]

Flurazepam [1982]
PN 94   SC 19974

Flurazepam — (cont'd)
SN Organic heterocyclic compound, used as a benzodiazepine tranquilizer and a nonbarbiturate sedative.
B   Benzodiazepines [1978]
    Hypnotic Drugs [1973]
    Sedatives [1973]
R   ↓ CNS Depressant Drugs [1973]

Fluvoxamine [1994]
PN 344   SC 19975
B   Antidepressant Drugs [1971]
    Serotonin Reuptake Inhibitors [1997]

Focusing (Visual)
Use   Ocular Accommodation

Folic Acid [1973]
PN 94   SC 19980
B   Amino Acids [1973]

Folie A Deux [1973]
PN 94   SC 19990
UF   Shared Paranoid Disorder
B   Paranoia (Psychosis) [1967]
R   Involutional Paranoid Psychosis [1973]
    Paranoid Schizophrenia [1967]

Folk Medicine [1973]
PN 543   SC 20000
B   Alternative Medicine [1997]
R   Ethnology [1967]
    Faith Healing [1973]
    ↓ Medical Sciences [1967]
    Shamanism [1973]
    Transcultural Psychiatry [1973]

Folk Psychology [1997]
PN 53   SC 20005
SN Branch of psychology that deals with legends, beliefs, folklore, and customs of a race or people, especially primitive societies.
B   Psychology [1967]
R   Anthropology [1967]
    Ethnography [1973]
    Ethnology [1967]
    Folklore [1991]
    Social Psychology [1967]
    Transcultural Psychiatry [1973]

Folklore [1991]
PN 262   SC 20010
SN Use MYTHS to access references from 1973-1990.
UF   Fairy Tales
    Folktales
R   Ethnology [1967]
    Folk Psychology [1997]
    ↓ Literature [1967]
    Myths [1967]
    Storytelling [1988]

Folktales
Use   Folklore

Follicle Stimulating Hormone [1991]
PN 26   SC 20025
B   Gonadotropic Hormones [1973]

Followup (Posttreatment)
Use   Posttreatment Followup

Followup Studies 1973

PN 12261   SC 20040
SN Used in records discussing issues involved in the process of conducting studies with individuals or groups who are followed and reexamined to assess and compare present findings with the original observations or measurements. Differentiate from POST-TREATMENT FOLLOWUP which is used in the context of aftercare. From 1973-2000, the term was also used as a mandatory document type identifier; however, this usage has been discontinued due to the advent of Form/Content Type field identifiers. References from 1973-2000 can be accessed using either FOLLOWUP STUDIES or the Followup Studies Form/Content Type field identifier.
UF   Studies (Followup)
B   Experimental Design 1967
R   ↓ Longitudinal Studies 1973

Food 1978

PN 1417   SC 20045
R   Craving 1997
      Diets 1978
      Food Additives 1978
      Food Allergies 1973
      Food Intake 1967
      Food Preferences 1973
      Nutrition 1973

Food Additives 1978

PN 117   SC 20047
R   ↓ Chemical Elements 1973
      Diets 1978
      Food 1978
      Nutrition 1973

Food Allergies 1973

PN 66   SC 20050
B   Allergic Disorders 1973
R   Diets 1978
      Food 1978

Food Deprivation 1967

PN 2019   SC 20060
SN Absence of ad libitum food access. In experimental settings, food deprivation is used to achieve a definable level of motivation within the organism.
B   Deprivation 1967
      Stimulus Deprivation 1973
R   Diets 1978
      Hunger 1967
      ↓ Nutritional Deficiencies 1973
      Starvation 1973

Food Intake 1967

PN 6339   SC 20070
SN Ingestion of food. Frequently used as an objective measure of physiological or motivational state or learning. Used for human or animal populations.
B   Ingestion 2001
R   Animal Feeding Behavior 1973
      Dietary Restraint 1994
      ↓ Feeding Practices 1973
      Food 1978
      Rumination (Eating) 2001
      Sucking 1978
      Weight Control 1985

Food Preferences 1973

PN 1674   SC 20080
B   Preferences 1967
R   Diets 1978
      Eating Attitudes 1994
      Food 1978

Football 1973

PN 216   SC 20090
B   Recreation 1967
      Sports 1967

Foraging (Animal)
Use   Animal Foraging Behavior

Forced Choice (Testing Method) 1967

PN 249   SC 20100
SN Assessment method requiring a choice between equally unlikely or undesirable alternatives, designed to reduce the effects of social desirability on the selection of test answers.
UF   True False Tests
B   Testing Methods 1967

Forebrain 1985

PN 679   SC 20105
UF   Prosencephalon
B   Brain 1967
N   ↓ Diencephalon 1973
      Nucleus Basalis Magnocellularis 1994
      ↓ Telencephalon 1973

Foreign Language Education 1973

PN 885   SC 20110
SN Curriculum, teaching methods, and educational programs used in the instruction of a language that is not native to the learner.
UF   Immersion Programs
      Second Language Education
B   Curriculum 1967
R   English as Second Language 1997

Foreign Language Learning 1967

PN 2269   SC 20120
B   Learning 1967
R   Bilingual Education 1978
      Foreign Languages 1973
      ↓ Language Development 1967
      Language Laboratories 1973
      Language Proficiency 1988

Foreign Language Translation 1973

PN 2688   SC 20130
SN Rendering from one language to another. Use with foreign language test translations. Not used as a document type identifier.
R   Foreign Languages 1973

Foreign Languages 1973

PN 1222   SC 20140
SN Second or nonnative languages.
B   Language 1967
R   Bilingual Education 1978
      English as Second Language 1997
      Foreign Language Learning 1967
      Foreign Language Translation 1973

Foreign Nationals 1985

PN 106   SC 20145
SN Persons living in a country other than their own, generally with intent to return to their home country.
N   Foreign Students 1973
      Foreign Workers 1985
R   Immigration 1973

Foreign Organizations 1973

PN 34   SC 20150
SN Organizations located in or originating from a foreign country.
B   Organizations 1967

Foreign Organizations — (cont'd)
R   International Organizations 1973

Foreign Policy Making 1973

PN 244   SC 20160
UF   Policy Making (Foreign)
B   Government Policy Making 1973
R   Government 1967
      International Relations 1967
      Peace 1988
      ↓ War 1967

Foreign Students 1973

PN 866   SC 20168
SN Persons attending school or a training program in a country other than their own, generally with intent to return to their home country.
B   Foreign Nationals 1985
      Students 1967
R   Foreign Study 1973

Foreign Study 1973

PN 110   SC 20170
SN Pursuit of an educational program in a country other than one's own, generally with intent to return to the home country.
B   Educational Programs 1973
R   Foreign Students 1973

Foreign Workers 1985

PN 148   SC 20175
SN Persons employed in a country other than their own, generally with intent to return to their home country.
UF   Guest Workers
B   Foreign Nationals 1985
R   Migrant Farm Workers 1973

Foremen (Industrial)
Use   Industrial Foremen

Forensic Evaluation 1994

PN 477   SC 20185
B   Evaluation 1967
      Legal Processes 1973
      Psychiatric Evaluation 1997
R   Competency to Stand Trial 1985
      Court Referrals 1994
      ↓ Criminals 1967
      Expert Testimony 1973
      Forensic Psychiatry 1973
      Forensic Psychology 1985
      Insanity Defense 1985
      Mentally Ill Offenders 1985
      ↓ Psychodiagnosis 1967
      ↓ Psychological Assessment 1997
      Psychological Report 1988

Forensic Psychiatry 1973

PN 1170   SC 20190
SN Branch of psychiatry devoted to legal issues relating to disordered behavior and mental disorders, including legal responsibility, competency to stand trial, and commitment issues.
B   Psychiatry 1967
R   ↓ Criminal Justice 1991
      Expert Testimony 1973
      Forensic Evaluation 1994
      Forensic Psychology 1985
      Insanity Defense 1985

Forensic Psychology 1985

PN 766   SC 20195

Forensic Psychology — (cont'd)
UF Legal Psychology
B Psychology　1967
R ↓ Criminal Justice　1991
　　Expert Testimony　1973
　　Forensic Evaluation　1994
　　Forensic Psychiatry　1973
　　Psychological Autopsy　1988

Forgetting　1973
PN 878　　　　　**SC** 20200
SN Inability to recall, recollect, or reproduce previously learned material, behavior, or experience. Compare AMNESIA and MEMORY DECAY.
R ↓ Amnesia　1967
　　Cued Recall　1994
　　Free Recall　1973
　　Fugue Reaction　1973
　　↓ Interference (Learning)　1967
　　↓ Latent Inhibition　1997
　　↓ Learning　1967
　　↓ Memory　1967
　　Memory Decay　1973
　　Memory Training　1994
　　Reminiscence　1985
　　↓ Retention　1967
　　Serial Recall　1994
　　Suppression (Defense Mechanism)　1973

Forgiveness　1988
PN 221　　　　　**SC** 20205
R ↓ Conflict Resolution　1982
　　↓ Religious Beliefs　1973
　　↓ Social Interaction　1967

Form and Shape Perception　1967
PN 4210　　　　　**SC** 20210
SN Perception of the physical form or shape of objects through any of the senses, usually haptic or visual.
UF Contour
　　Contour Perception
　　Form Perception
　　Shape Perception
B Perception　1967
R Figure Ground Discrimination　1973
　　Motion Parallax　1997
　　Object Recognition　1997
　　Pattern Discrimination　1967

Form Classes (Language)　1973
PN 428　　　　　**SC** 20220
UF Words (Form Classes)
B Language　1967
　　Syntax　1971
N Adjectives　1973
　　Adverbs　1973
　　Nouns　1973
　　Pronouns　1973
　　Verbs　1973

Form Perception
Use Form and Shape Perception

Fornix　1982
PN 224　　　　　**SC** 20234
SN Arched white fiber tract extending from the hippocampal formation to the septum, anterior nucleus of the thalamus, and mammillary body.
UF Hippocampal Commissure
　　Trigonum Cerebrale
B Limbic System　1973
　　Neural Pathways　1982
R Medial Forebrain Bundle　1982

Fornix — (cont'd)
R Septal Nuclei　1982

FORTRAN
Use Computer Programming Languages

Forward Masking
Use Masking

Foster Care　1978
PN 1229　　　　　**SC** 20245
SN Family care provided by persons other than the natural or adoptive parents.
UF Foster Homes
R ↓ Child Care　1991
　　Child Welfare　1988
　　Foster Children　1973
　　Foster Parents　1973
　　Protective Services　1997

Foster Children　1973
PN 433　　　　　**SC** 20250
B Family Members　1973
R Foster Care　1978

Foster Homes
Use Foster Care

Foster Parents　1973
PN 335　　　　　**SC** 20260
B Parents　1967
R Foster Care　1978
　　Surrogate Parents (Humans)　1973

Fovea　1982
PN 166　　　　　**SC** 20265
SN Centrally located and depressed portion of the retina containing only cone photoreceptors.
B Eye (Anatomy)　1967
R Cones (Eye)　1973
　　Foveal Vision　1988
　　Visual Field　1967

Foveal Vision　1988
PN 249　　　　　**SC** 20267
UF Central Vision
B Visual Perception　1967
R Fovea　1982

Fowl
Use Birds

Foxes　1973
PN 76　　　　　**SC** 20290
B Canids　1997

Fragile X Syndrome　1994
PN 176　　　　　**SC** 20295
B Sex Linked Hereditary Disorders　1973
　　Syndromes　1973
R ↓ Mental Retardation　1967
　　↓ Sex Chromosome Disorders　1973

Fragmentation (Schizophrenia)　1973
PN 10　　　　　**SC** 20300
UF Loosening of Associations
B Thought Disturbances　1973
R ↓ Schizophrenia　1967

Frail
Use Health Impairments

Franck Drawing Completion Test　1973
PN 4　　　　　**SC** 20320
B Projective Personality Measures　1973
　　Projective Techniques　1967

Frankness
Use Honesty

Fraternal Twins
Use Heterozygotic Twins

Fraternity Membership　1973
PN 163　　　　　**SC** 20340
SN Belonging to a club traditionally restricted to males. Used also for fraternity organizations.
B Extracurricular Activities　1973

Fraud　1994
PN 53　　　　　**SC** 20345
UF Consumer Fraud
B Deception　1967
R Cheating　1973
　　↓ Crime　1967
　　Dishonesty　1973
　　Experimental Ethics　1978

Free Association　1994
PN 67　　　　　**SC** 20347
SN Spontaneous association of ideas or mental images restricted by consciousness. Primarily used in, but not restricted to, psychoanalysis or Jungian analysis as a method to gain access to the organization and content of a patient's mind.
UF Association (Free)
R ↓ Jungian Psychology　1973
　　↓ Psychoanalysis　1967
　　↓ Psychoanalytic Theory　1967
　　↓ Psychotherapeutic Techniques　1967
　　Unconscious (Personality Factor)　1967

Free Recall　1973
PN 1884　　　　　**SC** 20350
SN Method of measuring the retention of learned material in which a subject is asked to recall as much of the material as possible, in any order, without the aid of external cues. Compare SERIAL ANTICIPATION (LEARNING) and RECONSTRUCTION (LEARNING).
B Recall (Learning)　1967
R Cued Recall　1994
　　Forgetting　1973
　　↓ Memory　1967
　　Serial Recall　1994

Free Will
Use Volition

Freedom　1978
PN 415　　　　　**SC** 20354
R Censorship　1978
　　Choice Behavior　1967
　　↓ Civil Rights　1978
　　↓ Justice　1973
　　↓ Political Processes　1973
　　Psychological Reactance　1978
　　Volition　1988

Frequency (Pitch)
Use Pitch (Frequency)

Frequency (Response)
Use Response Frequency

Frequency (Stimulus)
Use Stimulus Frequency

Frequency Distribution 1973
PN 354 **SC** 20380
UF Distribution (Frequency)
B Statistical Analysis 1967
  Statistical Measurement 1973
N Normal Distribution 1973
  Skewed Distribution 1973
R Standard Deviation 1973

Freud (Sigmund) 1967
PN 3677 **SC** 20390
SN Identifies biographical or autobiographical studies and discussions of Freud's works.
R Freudian Psychoanalytic School 1973
  ↓ Neopsychoanalytic School 1973
  ↓ Psychoanalysis 1967
  ↓ Psychoanalytic Theory 1967
  ↓ Psychologists 1967

Freudian Psychoanalytic School 1973
PN 664 **SC** 20400
UF Psychoanalytic School (Freudian)
B History of Psychology 1967
  Psychoanalytic Theory 1967
  Psychological Theories 2001
R Freud (Sigmund) 1967
  Metapsychology 1994
  ↓ Neopsychoanalytic School 1973
  Psychoanalytic Interpretation 1967

Friendship 1967
PN 3076 **SC** 20410
B Interpersonal Interaction 1967
R Interpersonal Compatibility 1973
  Peer Pressure 1994
  ↓ Peer Relations 1967
  ↓ Relationship Satisfaction 2001
  ↓ Relationship Termination 1997
  Significant Others 1991
  Social Dating 1973
  Social Support Networks 1982

Frigidity 1973
PN 54 **SC** 20420
B Sexual Function Disturbances 1973
R Dyspareunia 1973
  Female Orgasm 1973
  Impotence 1973
  ↓ Orgasm 1973
  ↓ Symptoms 1967
  Vaginismus 1973

Frogs 1967
PN 844 **SC** 20430
B Amphibia 1973
R Larvae 1973

Frontal Lobe 1973
PN 3294 **SC** 20440
B Cerebral Cortex 1967
N Gyrus Cinguli 1973
  Motor Cortex 1973
  Prefrontal Cortex 1994

Frostig Developmental Test of Visual Perception 2001
PN 34 **SC** 20455

Frostig Developmental Test of Visual Perception — (cont'd)
SN In 2000, the truncated term FROSTIG DEVELOPMENT TEST VIS PERCEPT (which was used from 1973-2000) was deleted, removed from all records containing it, and mapped to its expanded form FROSTIG DEVELOPMENTAL TEST OF VISUAL PERCEPTION.
B Intelligence Measures 1967

Fruit Fly
Use Drosophila

Frustration 1967
PN 1255 **SC** 20470
B Emotional States 1973
R Dissatisfaction 1973
  Mental Confusion 1973

Fugue Reaction 1973
PN 38 **SC** 20480
SN Dissociative reaction characterized by extensive amnesia and a sudden change in one's lifestyle. Upon recovery, prefugue events are remembered but those that occurred during the fugue are forgotten.
B Dissociative Disorders 2001
R ↓ Epilepsy 1967
  Forgetting 1973

Fulfillment
Use Satisfaction

Functional Analysis 2001
PN 0 **SC** 20496
SN A part of behavioral assessment concerned with the experimental manipulation of environmental events that are maintaining or suppressing a target behavior.
B Behavioral Assessment 1982
R ↓ Analysis 1967
  ↓ Behavior Modification 1973
  ↓ Behavior Problems 1967
  ↓ Methodology 1967

Functional Knowledge
Use Procedural Knowledge

Functional Status
Use Ability Level

Functionalism 1973
PN 221 **SC** 20500
SN Doctrine or system of psychology which holds (contrary to structural psychology) that mental processes are the proper subject matter of psychology and that an essential feature of all psychological processes is the part they play in the adaptive functions of an organism.
B History of Psychology 1967
  Psychological Theories 2001
R James (William) 1991

Fundamental Interpersonal Relation Orientation Behavior Ques 2001
PN 56 **SC** 20515
SN In 2000, the truncated term FUND INTERPER RELA ORIENTAT BEH QUES (which was used from 1973-2000) was deleted, removed from all records containing it, and mapped to its expanded form FUNDAMENTAL INTERPERSONAL RELATION ORIENTATION BEHAVIOR QUES.
UF FIRO-B
B Nonprojective Personality Measures 1973

Fundamentalism 1973
PN 168 **SC** 20520
B Protestantism 1973

Funding 1988
PN 656 **SC** 20524
R Budgets 1997
  ↓ Costs and Cost Analysis 1973
  Educational Financial Assistance 1973
  ↓ Government Policy Making 1973
  ↓ Government Programs 1973
  Money 1967
  Resource Allocation 1997

Funerals
Use Death Rites

Furniture 1985
PN 29 **SC** 20527
R Human Factors Engineering 1973
  Interior Design 1982
  Physical Comfort 1982

Future 1991
PN 648 **SC** 20528
R ↓ Expectations 1967
  ↓ History 1973
  ↓ Prediction 1967
  Social Change 1967
  ↓ Time 1967
  Trends 1991

Fuzzy Set Theory 1991
PN 172 **SC** 20529
B Statistical Analysis 1967
  Theories 1967
R ↓ Mathematical Modeling 1973
  ↓ Psychophysical Measurement 1967
  ↓ Statistical Probability 1967

GABA Agonists
Use Gamma Aminobutyric Acid Agonists

GABA Antagonists
Use Gamma Aminobutyric Acid Antagonists

Galanin
Use Peptides

Galanthamine 1973
PN 19 **SC** 20530
B Amines 1973
  Cholinesterase Inhibitors 1973

Galvanic Skin Response 1967
PN 1875 **SC** 20550
SN Means of assessing sympathetic nervous system activity (i.e., arousal) by measuring onset of palmar sweat gland response.
UF Electrodermal Response
  GSR (Electrophysiology)
  Psychogalvanic Reflex
B Diagnosis 1967
  Electrophysiology 1973
  Medical Diagnosis 1973
R Skin Potential 1973
  ↓ Skin Resistance 1973

Gamblers Anonymous
Use Twelve Step Programs

Gambling 1973
PN 656   SC 20560
  B   Recreation 1967
       Risk Taking 1967
       Social Behavior 1967
  N   Pathological Gambling 1988
  R   ↓ Games 1967
       Risk Analysis 1991

Game Theory 1967
PN 515   SC 20570
SN Mathematical theory which attempts to analyze
and model the decision making process involved in
gain-loss situations.
  B   Theories 1967
  R   Entrapment Games 1973
       ↓ Games 1967
       Non Zero Sum Games 1973
       Prisoners Dilemma Game 1973
       Risk Analysis 1991
       ↓ Simulation 1967

Games 1967
PN 1850   SC 20580
  N   Chess 1973
       Childrens Recreational Games 1973
       Computer Games 1988
       Entrapment Games 1973
       Non Zero Sum Games 1973
       Prisoners Dilemma Game 1973
       Simulation Games 1973
  R   Childhood Play Behavior 1978
       ↓ Gambling 1973
       Game Theory 1967
       ↓ Recreation 1967
       ↓ Toys 1973

Gamma Aminobutyric Acid 1978
PN 1255   SC 20585
  B   Amino Acids 1973
       Neurotransmitters 1985
  R   ↓ Gamma Aminobutyric Acid Agonists 1985
       ↓ Gamma Aminobutyric Acid Antagonists 1985

Gamma Aminobutyric Acid Agonists 1985
PN 323   SC 20587
  UF   GABA Agonists
  N   Muscimol 1994
  R   Gamma Aminobutyric Acid 1978

Gamma Aminobutyric Acid Antagonists 1985
PN 265   SC 20589
  UF   GABA Antagonists
  B   Alkaloids 1973
  N   Bicuculline 1994
       Picrotoxin 1973
  R   Gamma Aminobutyric Acid 1978

Gamma Globulin 1973
PN 10   SC 20590
  B   Immunoglobulins 1973
  R   Antibodies 1973

Ganglia 1973
PN 232   SC 20600
  B   Nervous System 1967
  N   Autonomic Ganglia 1973
       ↓ Basal Ganglia 1973
       Spinal Ganglia 1973

Ganglion Blocking Drugs 1973
PN 15   SC 20610

Ganglion Blocking Drugs — (cont'd)
  B   Drugs 1967
  N   Hexamethonium 1973
       Mecamylamine 1973
       Nicotine 1973
  R   ↓ Antihypertensive Drugs 1973

Ganglion Cells (Retina) 1985
PN 145   SC 20615
  UF   Retinal Ganglion Cells
  B   Neurons 1973
       Retina 1967

Gangs (Juvenile)
  Use Juvenile Gangs

Ganser Syndrome
  Use Factitious Disorders

Gastrointestinal Disorders 1973
PN 546   SC 20630
  B   Digestive System Disorders 1973
  N   ↓ Colon Disorders 1973
       Gastrointestinal Ulcers 1967
       Vomiting 1973
  R   Influenza 1973
       ↓ Neoplasms 1967
       ↓ Somatoform Disorders 2001
       ↓ Toxic Disorders 1973

Gastrointestinal System 1973
PN 303   SC 20640
  B   Digestive System 1967
  N   Intestines 1973
       Stomach 1973
  R   Pancreas 1973

Gastrointestinal Ulcers 1967
PN 571   SC 20650
  UF   Peptic Ulcers
       Ulcers (Gastrointestinal)
  B   Gastrointestinal Disorders 1973
  R   ↓ Colitis 1973

Gastropods
  Use Mollusca

Gates MacGinitie Reading Tests 1973
PN 18   SC 20670
  UF   Gates Reading Readiness Tests
       Gates Reading Test
  B   Reading Measures 1973

Gates Reading Readiness Tests
  Use Gates MacGinitie Reading Tests

Gates Reading Test
  Use Gates MacGinitie Reading Tests

Gating (Sensory)
  Use Sensory Gating

Gaussian Distribution
  Use Normal Distribution

Gay Liberation Movement
  Use Homosexual Liberation Movement

Gay Males
  Use Male Homosexuality

Gay Parents
  Use Homosexual Parents

Gazing
  Use Eye Fixation

Geese 1973
PN 105   SC 20710
  B   Birds 1967

Gender Differences
  Use Human Sex Differences

Gender Identity 1985
PN 1518   SC 20717
SN Inner conviction that one is male or female or
inner sense of being masculine or feminine.
  UF   Sexual Identity (Gender)
  N   Transsexualism 1973
  R   Androgyny 1982
       Femininity 1967
       ↓ Gender Identity Disorder 1997
       Masculinity 1967
       ↓ Personality 1967
       Psychosexual Development 1982
       ↓ Self Concept 1967
       Sex Roles 1967
       ↓ Sexual Orientation 1997

Gender Identity Disorder 1997
PN 94   SC 20719
SN Consider GENDER IDENTITY to access refer-
ences from 1985-1996.
  B   Mental Disorders 1967
  N   Transsexualism 1973
  R   ↓ Gender Identity 1985
       Hermaphroditism 1973
       ↓ Sexual Orientation 1997
       Transvestism 1973

Gender Role Attitudes
  Use Sex Role Attitudes

Gender Roles
  Use Sex Roles

General Anesthetics 1973
PN 149   SC 20720
  B   Anesthetic Drugs 1973
  N   Chloroform 1973
       Ether (Anesthetic) 1973
       Methohexital 1973
       Thiopental 1973

General Aptitude Test Battery 1973
PN 58   SC 20730
  B   Aptitude Measures 1967

General Health Questionnaire 1991
PN 117   SC 20740
  B   Personality Measures 1967
       Questionnaires 1967
  R   ↓ Diagnosis 1967
       ↓ Health 1973
       ↓ Screening Tests 1982

General Paresis 1973
PN 36   SC 20750
  UF   Dementia Paralytica
       Paresis (General)
  B   Paralysis 1973
  R   Neurosyphilis 1973

General Paresis — (cont'd)
R ↓ Syphilis 1973

General Practitioners 1973
PN 1102   SC 20760
B Physicians 1967
R Family Medicine 1988
Family Physicians 1973

Generalization (Cognitive)
Use Cognitive Generalization

Generalization (Learning) 1982
PN 1415   SC 20775
SN Responding in a similar manner to different stimuli that have some common property as the result of a conditioned or learned similarity. Also known as secondary generalization. Also includes generalization of any learned behavior to a new context or setting. Compare TRANSFER (LEARNING) or STIMULUS GENERALIZATION.
B Learning 1967
N Response Generalization 1973
Stimulus Generalization 1967
R ↓ Concept Formation 1967
↓ Discrimination Learning 1982
↓ Transfer (Learning) 1967

Generalization (Response)
Use Response Generalization

Generalization (Semantic)
Use Semantic Generalization

Generalization (Stimulus)
Use Stimulus Generalization

Generalized Anxiety Disorder
Use Anxiety Disorders

Generation Effect (Learning) 1991
PN 93   SC 20802
SN In learning or memory contexts, the effect of generating a stimuli oneself rather than having it presented by external sources.
B Learning 1967
R ↓ Cognitive Processes 1967
↓ Memory 1967

Generation Gap 1973
PN 192   SC 20805
SN Differences in values, morals, attitudes, and behavior of young adults and older adults in contemporary society.
R Age Differences 1967
Cohort Analysis 1988
Intergenerational Relations 1988
↓ Parent Child Relations 1967
Transgenerational Patterns 1991

Generativity 2001
PN 0   SC 20807
SN The concern with passing on to the next generation knowledge and guidance which will outlive oneself. The conflict between generativity vs self-absorption is the seventh of E. Erikson's eight stages of man, and often occurs during middle adulthood.
R Adult Development 1978
↓ Aging 1991
↓ Developmental Stages 1973
Erikson (Erik) 1991
Intergenerational Relations 1988
↓ Prosocial Behavior 1982

Generativity — (cont'd)
R ↓ Psychosocial Development 1973

Generators (Apparatus) 1973
PN 30   SC 20810
B Apparatus 1967

Genes 1973
PN 1411   SC 20820
R ↓ Chromosomes 1973
Genetic Linkage 1994
↓ Genetics 1967

Genetic Counseling 1978
PN 428   SC 20826
SN Presentation and discussion, usually with prospective parents, of factors involved in potential inheritance of disorders.
B Counseling 1967
R Eugenics 1973
↓ Genetic Disorders 1973
↓ Genetic Engineering 1994
↓ Genetics 1967

Genetic Disorders 1973
PN 827   SC 20830
UF Hereditary Disorders
B Physical Disorders 1997
N Albinism 1973
Amaurotic Familial Idiocy 1973
↓ Chromosome Disorders 1973
Huntingtons Disease 1973
Phenylketonuria 1973
Porphyria 1973
Rh Incompatibility 1973
↓ Sex Linked Hereditary Disorders 1973
Sickle Cell Disease 1994
R Alopecia 1973
Anemia 1973
Behavioral Genetics 1994
Color Blindness 1973
↓ Congenital Disorders 1973
Developmental Disabilities 1982
Diabetes Insipidus 1973
Genetic Counseling 1978
↓ Genetic Engineering 1994
↓ Genetics 1967
Hypopituitarism 1973
Mutations 1973
Picks Disease 1973
Prenatal Diagnosis 1988
↓ Refraction Errors 1973

Genetic Dominance 1973
PN 54   SC 20840
B Dominance 1967
R Behavioral Genetics 1994
Genetic Recessiveness 1973
↓ Genetics 1967

Genetic Engineering 1994
PN 53   SC 20845
N Eugenics 1973
R Genetic Counseling 1978
↓ Genetic Disorders 1973
Genetic Linkage 1994
↓ Genetics 1967
Population Genetics 1973
Reproductive Technology 1988
Selective Breeding 1973

Genetic Linkage 1994
PN 444   SC 20847

Genetic Linkage — (cont'd)
SN Linkage of genes at different loci on the same chromosome and analysis of how genes are inherited together.
UF Linkage Analysis
R ↓ Chromosomes 1973
Genes 1973
↓ Genetic Engineering 1994
↓ Genetics 1967
Genotypes 1973

Genetic Recessiveness 1973
PN 33   SC 20850
UF Recessiveness (Genetic)
R Behavioral Genetics 1994
Genetic Dominance 1973
↓ Genetics 1967

Genetics 1967
PN 10969   SC 20860
SN Conceptually broad term referring both to the science of heredity and the biological process of transmission of characteristics from progenitor to offspring.
UF Heredity
N Behavioral Genetics 1994
Eugenics 1973
Population Genetics 1973
R ↓ Animal Breeding 1973
Animal Mate Selection 1982
Animal Strain Differences 1982
Assortative Mating 1991
Blood Groups 1973
↓ Chromosomes 1973
Family Resemblance 1991
Genes 1973
Genetic Counseling 1978
↓ Genetic Disorders 1973
Genetic Dominance 1973
↓ Genetic Engineering 1994
Genetic Linkage 1994
Genetic Recessiveness 1973
Genotypes 1973
Hybrids (Biology) 1973
Instinctive Behavior 1982
Mutations 1973
Natural Selection 1997
Nature Nurture 1994
↓ Nucleic Acids 1973
Phenotypes 1973
Predisposition 1973
Reproductive Technology 1988
Selective Breeding 1973
↓ Sexual Reproduction 1973
Species Differences 1982
Translocation (Chromosome) 1973
↓ Twins 1967

Geniculate Bodies (Thalamus) 1973
PN 447   SC 20870
B Thalamus 1967
R Visual Receptive Fields 1982

Genital Disorders 1967
PN 177   SC 20880
UF Sex Differentiation Disorders
Sexual Disorders (Physiological)
B Urogenital Disorders 1973
N ↓ Endocrine Sexual Disorders 1973
↓ Gynecological Disorders 1973
Hermaphroditism 1973
↓ Infertility 1973
↓ Male Genital Disorders 1973

Genital Disorders — (cont'd)
R   Sex [1967]

Genital Herpes
Use Herpes Genitalis

Genitalia (Female)
Use Female Genitalia

Genitalia (Male)
Use Male Genitalia

Geniuses
Use Gifted

Genocide [1988]
PN 119   SC 20915
SN Deliberate and systematic destruction of a racial, political, or cultural group.
B   Homicide [1967]
N   Holocaust [1988]

Genotypes [1973]
PN 776   SC 20920
R   Genetic Linkage [1994]
    ↓ Genetics [1967]
    Phenotypes [1973]

Genuineness
Use Sincerity

Geographic Regions
Use Geography

Geographical Differences
Use Regional Differences

Geographical Mobility [1978]
PN 416   SC 20924
SN Capacity or facility of individuals to move from one geographic region to another. Includes job- or study-related commuting.
UF Mobility (Geographical)
R   Commuting (Travel) [1985]
    ↓ Human Migration [1973]

Geography [1973]
PN 945   SC 20925
SN Science dealing with the description of the topographical features of the earth and the distribution of life on earth. Also, geographic areas or their features.
UF Geographic Regions
    Physical Divisions (Geographic)
    Physical Geography
    Political Divisions (Geographic)
B   Sciences [1967]
R   ↓ Countries [1967]
    ↓ Environment [1967]
    Regional Differences [2001]

Geomagnetism
Use Magnetism

Geometry
Use Mathematics

Gerbils [1973]
PN 662   SC 20940
B   Rodents [1973]

Geriatric Assessment [1997]
PN 272   SC 20945

Geriatric Assessment — (cont'd)
B   Evaluation [1967]
R   Activities of Daily Living [1991]
    Clinical Judgment (Not Diagnosis) [1973]
    ↓ Diagnosis [1967]
    Geriatric Patients [1973]
    Geriatric Psychiatry [1997]
    Geriatrics [1967]
    Gerontology [1967]
    ↓ Measurement [1967]
    Needs Assessment [1985]
    ↓ Psychiatric Evaluation [1997]
    ↓ Psychological Assessment [1997]
    ↓ Screening [1982]

Geriatric Patients [1973]
PN 4139   SC 20950
SN Older persons suffering from mental or physical diseases and disabilities and under some form of treatment.
B   Patients [1967]
R   Geriatric Assessment [1997]

Geriatric Psychiatry [1997]
PN 216   SC 20955
B   Psychiatry [1967]
R   ↓ Aging [1991]
    Geriatric Assessment [1997]
    Geriatric Psychotherapy [1973]
    Geriatrics [1967]
    Gerontology [1967]

Geriatric Psychotherapy [1973]
PN 288   SC 20960
B   Psychotherapy [1967]
R   ↓ Aging [1991]
    Animal Assisted Therapy [1994]
    Geriatric Psychiatry [1997]
    Geriatrics [1967]
    Gerontology [1967]
    Physiological Aging [1967]

Geriatrics [1967]
PN 1475   SC 20970
SN Medical subdiscipline which deals with the problems of old age and aging. Use GERIATRICS or GERONTOLOGY to access references on the aged (elderly) from 1967-1972.
B   Medical Sciences [1967]
R   Aged (Attitudes Toward) [1978]
    ↓ Aging [1991]
    Geriatric Assessment [1997]
    Geriatric Psychiatry [1997]
    Geriatric Psychotherapy [1973]
    Gerontology [1967]
    Physiological Aging [1967]

German Measles
Use Rubella

Gerontology [1967]
PN 1573   SC 21000
SN Scientific study of old age and the phenomena associated with old age. Use GERONTOLOGY or GERIATRICS to access references to the aged (elderly) from 1967-1972.
B   Developmental Psychology [1973]
R   Aged (Attitudes Toward) [1978]
    ↓ Aging [1991]
    Geriatric Assessment [1997]
    Geriatric Psychiatry [1997]
    Geriatric Psychotherapy [1973]
    Geriatrics [1967]

Gerontology — (cont'd)
R   Life Review [1991]

Gestalt Psychology [1967]
PN 692   SC 21010
SN School of psychology concerned with the study of the individual's perception of and response to configurational wholes.
B   History of Psychology [1967]
    Psychological Theories [2001]

Gestalt Therapy [1973]
PN 701   SC 21020
SN Type of psychotherapy which emphasizes treatment of the individual as a whole and focuses on sensory awareness of present experience.
B   Human Potential Movement [1982]
    Psychotherapy [1967]

Gestation
Use Pregnancy

Gestures [1973]
PN 850   SC 21040
B   Nonverbal Communication [1971]
R   Body Language [1973]

Ghettoes [1973]
PN 96   SC 21050
UF Urban Ghettoes
B   Urban Environments [1967]
R   Poverty Areas [1973]

Gifted [1967]
PN 4992   SC 21060
UF Exceptional Children (Gifted)
    Geniuses
    Intellectually Gifted
    Talented
R   ↓ Ability [1967]
    Creativity [1967]
    Intelligence [1967]
    Savants [2001]

Gilles de la Tourette Disorder [1973]
PN 1144   SC 21070
UF Tourette Syndrome
B   Neuromuscular Disorders [1973]
R   Echolalia [1973]

Gipsies
Use Gypsies

Girls
Use Human Females

Glands [1967]
PN 646   SC 21080
N   ↓ Endocrine Glands [1973]
    Mammary Glands [1973]
    Pancreas [1973]
    Salivary Glands [1973]
R   Pheromones [1973]

Glaucoma [1973]
PN 59   SC 21090
B   Eye Disorders [1973]

Global Amnesia [1997]
PN 37   SC 21095
SN Use AMNESIA to access references from 1967-1996.
B   Amnesia [1967]

Global Amnesia — (cont'd)
R ↓ Brain Damage 1967

Globulins 1973
PN 94   SC 21100
UF   Glycoproteins
B   Proteins 1973
N   Antibodies 1973
       ↓ Immunoglobulins 1973

Globus Pallidus 1973
PN 319   SC 21110
B   Basal Ganglia 1973

Glossolalia 1973
PN 44   SC 21130
SN   Unintelligible speech occurring in hypnotic or mediumistic trances, religious experiences, or some mental disorders.
R ↓ Mental Disorders 1967
       ↓ Religious Practices 1973

Glossopharyngeal Nerve
Use   Cranial Nerves

Glucagon 1973
PN 65   SC 21150
B   Hormones 1967

Glucocorticoids 1982
PN 388   SC 21155
SN   Any steroid-like compound capable of significantly influencing intermediary metabolism. Glucocorticoids are also clinically useful anti-inflammatory agents.
B   Adrenal Cortex Hormones 1973
       Anti Inflammatory Drugs 1982
N   Dexamethasone 1985

Glucose 1973
PN 1143   SC 21160
B   Sugars 1973
N   Blood Sugar 1973
R   Glucose Metabolism 1994
       Glycogen 1973

Glucose Metabolism 1994
PN 323   SC 21165
B   Carbohydrate Metabolism 1973
R ↓ Glucose 1973
       ↓ Neurochemistry 1973

Glue Sniffing 1973
PN 58   SC 21170
B   Inhalant Abuse 1985

Glutamic Acid 1973
PN 609   SC 21180
B   Amino Acids 1973
       Neurotransmitters 1985
R   Kainic Acid 1988

Glutamine 1973
PN 137   SC 21190
B   Amino Acids 1973

Glutethimide 1973
PN 16   SC 21210
B   CNS Depressant Drugs 1973
       Hypnotic Drugs 1973
       Sedatives 1973

Glycine 1973
PN 177   SC 21220
B   Amino Acids 1973
       Neurotransmitters 1985

Glycogen 1973
PN 47   SC 21230
R ↓ Glucose 1973

Glycoproteins
Use   Globulins

Goal Setting 1997
PN 341   SC 21237
R ↓ Aspirations 1967
       ↓ Goals 1967
       ↓ Motivation 1967

Goals 1967
PN 4075   SC 21240
SN   Aims toward which an individual or a group aspire or toward which effort is directed. Use a more specific term if possible.
UF   Objectives
N   Educational Objectives 1978
       Organizational Objectives 1973
R ↓ Aspirations 1967
       Extrinsic Motivation 1973
       Goal Setting 1997
       ↓ Incentives 1967
       Intention 1988
       Intrinsic Motivation 1973
       ↓ Motivation 1967
       ↓ Needs 1967

Goats 1973
PN 144   SC 21250
B   Mammals 1973

God Concepts 1973
PN 423   SC 21260
B   Religious Beliefs 1973

Goiters 1973
PN 18   SC 21270
B   Thyroid Disorders 1973
R   Hyperthyroidism 1973
       Hypothyroidism 1973

Goldfish 1973
PN 484   SC 21280
B   Carp 1973

Goldstein Scheerer Object Sort Test 1973
PN 4   SC 21290
B   Nonprojective Personality Measures 1973

Gonadotropic Hormones 1973
PN 351   SC 21300
UF   Gonadotropin
B   Hormones 1967
N   Follicle Stimulating Hormone 1991
       Luteinizing Hormone 1978
       Prolactin 1973
R ↓ Pituitary Hormones 1973
       ↓ Sex Hormones 1973

Gonadotropin
Use   Gonadotropic Hormones

Gonads 1973
PN 124   SC 21320

Gonads — (cont'd)
B   Endocrine Glands 1973
       Urogenital System 1973
N   Ovaries 1973
       Testes 1973

Gonorrhea 1973
PN 38   SC 21330
B   Bacterial Disorders 1973
       Venereal Diseases 1973

Goodenough Harris Draw A Person Test 1967
PN 128   SC 21340
B   Intelligence Measures 1967
R   Human Figures Drawing 1973

Goodness of Fit 1988
PN 269   SC 21350
B   Statistical Analysis 1967
R ↓ Factor Analysis 1967
       ↓ Mathematical Modeling 1973
       Maximum Likelihood 1985
       Statistical Significance 1973

Gorillas 1973
PN 233   SC 21370
B   Primates (Nonhuman) 1973

Gossip 1982
PN 102   SC 21375
SN   Idle personal talk or communication of unsubstantiated information.
UF   Rumors
B   Interpersonal Communication 1973
R   Messages 1973

Gough Adjective Check List 1973
PN 25   SC 21380
B   Nonprojective Personality Measures 1973

Government 1967
PN 775   SC 21390
UF   Government Bureaucracy
B   Public Sector 1985
R   Autonomy (Government) 1973
       Foreign Policy Making 1973
       Government Agencies 1973
       ↓ Government Personnel 1973
       ↓ Government Policy Making 1973
       ↓ Government Programs 1973
       Gun Control Laws 1973
       Job Corps 1973
       ↓ Law (Government) 1973
       ↓ Law Enforcement 1978
       ↓ Laws 1967
       ↓ Legal Processes 1973
       Legislative Processes 1973
       ↓ Marihuana Laws 1973
       Marihuana Legalization 1973
       Peace Corps 1973
       ↓ Political Economic Systems 1973
       ↓ Politics 1967
       Project Follow Through 1973
       Project Head Start 1973
       Taxation 1985
       Upward Bound 1973
       Volunteers in Service to America 1973
       Welfare Services (Government) 1973

Government Agencies 1973
PN 653   SC 21400
B   Organizations 1967

Government Agencies — (cont'd)
- **B**   Public Sector   1985
- **R**   Government   1967

Government Bureaucracy
- **Use**   Government

Government Personnel   1973
PN 1362   **SC** 21420
- **UF**   Civil Servants
-      Elected Government Officials
- **B**   Personnel   1967
- **N**   Agricultural Extension Workers   1973
-      ↓ Law Enforcement Personnel   1973
-      ↓ Military Personnel   1967
-      Police Personnel   1973
-      Public Health Service Nurses   1973
- **R**   ↓ Business and Industrial Personnel   1967
-      Fire Fighters   1991
-      Government   1967

Government Policy Making   1973
PN 4322   **SC** 21430
- **UF**   Policy Making (Government)
-      Public Policy
- **B**   Policy Making   1988
- **N**   Foreign Policy Making   1973
-      ↓ Laws   1967
-      Legislative Processes   1973
- **R**   Advocacy   1985
-      Funding   1988
-      Government   1967
-      Health Care Policy   1994
-      ↓ Legal Processes   1973
-      ↓ War   1967

Government Programs   1973
PN 1105   **SC** 21440
- **UF**   Programs (Government)
- **N**   Job Corps   1973
-      Medicaid   1994
-      Medicare   1988
-      Peace Corps   1973
-      Project Follow Through   1973
-      Project Head Start   1973
-      Social Security   1988
-      Upward Bound   1973
-      Volunteers in Service to America   1973
-      Welfare Services (Government)   1973
- **R**   Funding   1988
-      Government   1967
-      ↓ Program Development   1991
-      Shelters   1991
-      ↓ Social Services   1982

Grade Level   1994
PN 321   **SC** 21445
- **UF**   Academic Grade Level
- **R**   Ability Grouping   1973
-      Age Differences   1967
-      ↓ Education   1967
-      Educational Placement   1978
-      ↓ Elementary School Students   1967
-      High School Students   1967
-      Junior High School Students   1971
-      Kindergarten Students   1973
-      School Transition   1997
-      Special Education Students   1973
-      Transfer Students   1973

Gradepoint Average
- **Use**   Academic Achievement

Grading (Educational)   1973
PN 590   **SC** 21460
SN   Rating of achievement level by means of established scales or standards. Consider also SCORING (TESTING) or TEST SCORES.
- **B**   Educational Measurement   1967
- **R**   ↓ Scoring (Testing)   1973

Graduate Degrees
- **Use**   Educational Degrees

Graduate Education   1973
PN 648   **SC** 21480
- **B**   Higher Education   1973
- **N**   Dental Education   1973
-      ↓ Graduate Psychology Education   1967
-      ↓ Medical Education   1973
-      Rehabilitation Education   1997

Graduate Psychology Education   1967
PN 2702   **SC** 21490
- **UF**   Training (Graduate Psychology)
- **B**   Graduate Education   1973
-      Psychology Education   1978
- **N**   ↓ Clinical Psychology Graduate Training   2001
- **R**   Educational Program Accreditation   1994

Graduate Record Examination   1973
PN 142   **SC** 21500
- **B**   Aptitude Measures   1967

Graduate Schools   1973
PN 70   **SC** 21510
- **B**   Schools   1967
- **R**   ↓ Higher Education   1973
-      School Graduation   1991

Graduate Students   1967
PN 3270   **SC** 21520
SN   Students pursuing academic studies past the college level. Mandatory term in educational contexts.
- **B**   Students   1967
- **R**   ↓ College Students   1967
-      Dental Students   1967
-      Law Students   1978
-      Medical Students   1967
-      Postgraduate Students   1973

Graduation (School)
- **Use**   School Graduation

Grammar   1967
PN 2442   **SC** 21530
SN   Science of the structure of language including universal grammar, descriptive and prescriptive grammar, and the rules and principles of syntax, phonology, and semantics applied in verbal communication. Compare SYNTAX.
- **B**   Linguistics   1973
- **N**   Morphology (Language)   1973
-      ↓ Phonology   1973
-      ↓ Semantics   1967
-      ↓ Syntax   1971
-      Transformational Generative Grammar   1973
- **R**   Discourse Analysis   1997
-      ↓ Language   1967
-      ↓ Verbal Communication   1967
-      Words (Phonetic Units)   1967

Grammar Schools
- **Use**   Elementary Schools

Grand Mal Epilepsy   1973
PN 31   **SC** 21550
- **B**   Epilepsy   1967

Grandchildren   1973
PN 307   **SC** 21560
- **B**   Family Members   1973

Grandiosity   1994
PN 31   **SC** 21565
- **B**   Defense Mechanisms   1967
- **R**   Delusions   1967
-      Egotism   1973
-      Emotional Superiority   1973
-      Erotomania   1997
-      Narcissism   1967
-      Omnipotence   1994

Grandparents   1973
PN 778   **SC** 21570
- **B**   Ancestors   1973
-      Family Members   1973

Graphical Displays   1985
PN 796   **SC** 21575
SN   Pictorial rendering of data (e.g., bar graphs, continuous line graphs, and data plots). Consider VISUAL DISPLAYS to access references from 1973-1984.
- **B**   Displays   1967
- **R**   Statistical Data   1982
-      ↓ Statistical Measurement   1973

Graphology
- **Use**   Handwriting

Grasping   1997
PN 125   **SC** 21585
- **B**   Motor Processes   1967

Grasshoppers   1973
PN 89   **SC** 21590
- **B**   Insects   1967
- **R**   Larvae   1973

Gravitational Effects   1967
PN 241   **SC** 21600
- **B**   Environmental Effects   1973
- **N**   Weightlessness   1967
- **R**   Acceleration Effects   1973
-      Altitude Effects   1973
-      ↓ Aviation   1967
-      Decompression Effects   1973
-      Flight Simulation   1973
-      Spaceflight   1967
-      Underwater Effects   1973

Great Grandparents
- **Use**   Ancestors

Gregariousness   1973
PN 22   **SC** 21660
- **B**   Personality Traits   1967
- **R**   Extraversion   1967
-      Sociability   1973

Grief   1973
PN 4502   **SC** 21680
- **UF**   Bereavement
-      Mourning
- **B**   Emotional States   1973
- **R**   ↓ Death and Dying   1967
-      ↓ Separation Reactions   1997

Grief — (cont'd)
R   Suffering 1973

Grimaces 1973
PN 12   SC 21690
B   Facial Expressions 1967

Grooming Behavior (Animal)
Use   Animal Grooming Behavior

Gross Motor Skill Learning 1973
PN 175   SC 21700
B   Perceptual Motor Learning 1967
     Skill Learning 1973

Ground Transportation 1973
PN 122   SC 21710
B   Transportation 1973
N   ↓ Motor Vehicles 1982
     Railroad Trains 1973
R   Highway Safety 1973

Group Cohesion 1973
PN 1030   SC 21730
SN Mutual bonds formed among the members of a
group as a consequence of their combined efforts
toward a common goal or purpose.
UF   Cohesion (Group)
B   Group Dynamics 1967
R   Group Development 1997

Group Counseling 1973
PN 3220   SC 21740
UF   Counseling (Group)
B   Counseling 1967
R   ↓ Self Help Techniques 1982
     ↓ Support Groups 1991
     ↓ Twelve Step Programs 1997

Group Decision Making 1978
PN 1544   SC 21745
SN Process of arriving at a decision or judgment by
a group.
B   Decision Making 1967
N   Choice Shift 1994
R   Management Decision Making 1973

Group Development 1997
PN 159   SC 21747
SN Used in treatment and nontreatment settings.
B   Group Dynamics 1967
R   Group Cohesion 1973
     Group Participation 1973
     ↓ Group Psychotherapy 1967
     Group Size 1967
     Group Structure 1967

Group Discussion 1967
PN 2041   SC 21750
UF   Discussion (Group)
B   Group Dynamics 1967
     Interpersonal Communication 1973
R   Choice Shift 1994
     Debates 1997

Group Dynamics 1967
PN 7220   SC 21760
UF   Dynamics (Group)
N   Group Cohesion 1973
     Group Development 1997
     Group Discussion 1967
     Group Participation 1973
     Group Performance 1967

Group Dynamics — (cont'd)
N   Group Size 1967
     Group Structure 1967
     Intergroup Dynamics 1973
R   Boundaries (Psychological) 1997
     Brainstorming 1982
     Choice Shift 1994
     ↓ Collective Behavior 1967
     Consciousness Raising Groups 1978
     Group Instruction 1973
     ↓ Group Problem Solving 1973
     ↓ Group Psychotherapy 1967
     Human Relations Training 1978
     Ingroup Outgroup 1997
     ↓ Organizational Behavior 1978
     Peer Pressure 1994
     Reference Groups 1994
     Sensitivity Training 1973
     ↓ Sociometry 1991
     ↓ Teams 1988

Group Health Plans
Use   Health Maintenance Organizations

Group Homes 1982
PN 695   SC 21767
SN Housing for groups of patients, children, or oth-
ers who need or desire emotional and physical sup-
port.
B   Housing 1973
R   ↓ Community Facilities 1973
     Community Mental Health Services 1978
     ↓ Residential Care Institutions 1973
     Retirement Communities 1997
     Shelters 1991

Group Instruction 1973
PN 857   SC 21770
B   Teaching Methods 1967
R   Cooperative Learning 1994
     ↓ Group Dynamics 1967

Group Participation 1973
PN 1540   SC 21780
SN Involvement in a group's purpose or activities.
B   Group Dynamics 1967
     Interpersonal Interaction 1967
     Participation 1973
R   ↓ Collective Behavior 1967
     Group Development 1997

Group Performance 1967
PN 1650   SC 21790
SN Process and effectiveness of a group in accom-
plishing an intended goal.
B   Group Dynamics 1967
     Interpersonal Interaction 1967
     Performance 1967

Group Problem Solving 1973
PN 1223   SC 21800
SN Dynamics of group interaction during the pro-
cess of analyzing, defining, and attaining the solution
to a problem.
B   Problem Solving 1967
N   Brainstorming 1982
R   Choice Shift 1994
     ↓ Group Dynamics 1967

Group Psychotherapy 1967
PN 9451   SC 21810
UF   Group Therapy
B   Psychotherapy 1967

Group Psychotherapy — (cont'd)
N   ↓ Encounter Group Therapy 1973
     Therapeutic Community 1967
R   Conjoint Therapy 1973
     Consciousness Raising Groups 1978
     Group Development 1997
     ↓ Group Dynamics 1967
     ↓ Human Potential Movement 1982
     Psychodrama 1967
     Sensitivity Training 1973
     ↓ Support Groups 1991
     Transactional Analysis 1973
     ↓ Twelve Step Programs 1997

Group Size 1967
PN 1442   SC 21820
UF   Size (Group)
B   Group Dynamics 1967
     Size 1973
R   Group Development 1997

Group Structure 1967
PN 1063   SC 21830
SN Patterns of organization, behavior, and commu-
nication of a group that determine the interpersonal
relations of its members.
B   Group Dynamics 1967
R   Group Development 1997

Group Testing 1973
PN 213   SC 21840
B   Measurement 1967
R   Test Administration 1973

Group Therapy
Use   Group Psychotherapy

Groups (Organizations)
Use   Organizations

Groups (Social)
Use   Social Groups

Grown Children
Use   Adult Offspring

Growth
Use   Development

Growth Centers
Use   Human Potential Movement

Growth Hormone
Use   Somatotropin

Growth Hormone Inhibitor
Use   Somatostatin

GSR (Electrophysiology)
Use   Galvanic Skin Response

Guanethidine 1973
PN 36   SC 21930
B   Amines 1973
     Antihypertensive Drugs 1973
R   Norepinephrine 1973

Guanosine 1985
PN 63   SC 21929
R   ↓ Carbohydrate Metabolism 1973
     Cyclic Adenosine Monophosphate 1978

110

Guanosine — (cont'd)
R   ↓ Nucleic Acids   1973

Guardianship   1988
PN   145   SC   21932
SN   Court appointment of an individual to act as a guardian or conservator and to legally act and speak in the interest of a minor or a physically or mentally disabled adult.
UF   Conservatorship
B   Legal Processes   1973
R   Child Custody   1982
    ↓ Client Rights   1988
    ↓ Commitment (Psychiatric)   1973
    Informed Consent   1985
    Protective Services   1997

Guessing   1973
PN   221   SC   21933
SN   Responding to questions or test items on the basis of little or no knowledge of the correct answer.
R   Intuition   1973
    Questioning   1982
    ↓ Strategies   1967
    Test Taking   1985

Guest Workers
Use   Foreign Workers

Guidance (Educational)
Use   Educational Counseling

Guidance (Occupational)
Use   Occupational Guidance

Guidance Counseling
Use   School Counseling

Guided Fantasy
Use   Guided Imagery

Guided Imagery   2001
PN   0   SC   21957
SN   Mind-body technique involving the deliberate prompting of mental images, used in the treatment of mental disorders, for performance enhancement, and in helping patients cope with diseases and their symptoms.
UF   Directed Reverie Therapy
    Guided Fantasy
B   Psychotherapeutic Techniques   1967
    Psychotherapy   1967
R   ↓ Hypnotherapy   1973
    ↓ Imagery   1967
    Relaxation   1973
    ↓ Relaxation Therapy   1978

Guilford Zimmerman Temperament Survey   2001
PN   19   SC   21965
SN   In 2000, the truncated term GUILFORD ZIMMERMAN TEMPERAMENT SURV (which was used from 1973-2000) was deleted, removed from all records containing it, and mapped to its expanded form GUILFORD ZIMMERMAN TEMPERAMENT SURVEY.
B   Nonprojective Personality Measures   1973

Guilt   1967
PN   1827   SC   21970
B   Emotional States   1973
R   ↓ Anxiety   1967
    ↓ Anxiety Disorders   1997

Guilt — (cont'd)
R   Blame   1994
    Shame   1994

Guinea Pigs   1967
PN   865   SC   21980
B   Rodents   1973

Gulls
Use   Sea Gulls

Gun Control Laws   1973
PN   74   SC   22000
B   Laws   1967
R   Government   1967
    Weapons   1978

Gustatory Perception
Use   Taste Perception

Gymnastic Therapy
Use   Recreation Therapy

Gynecological Disorders   1973
PN   191   SC   22040
B   Genital Disorders   1967
    Urogenital Disorders   1973
N   ↓ Menstrual Disorders   1973
R   ↓ Endocrine Sexual Disorders   1973
    Hermaphroditism   1973
    ↓ Hypogonadism   1973
    ↓ Infertility   1973
    Pseudocyesis   1973
    Sterility   1973

Gynecologists   1973
PN   64   SC   22050
B   Physicians   1967
R   Obstetricians   1978
    Surgeons   1973

Gynecology   1978
PN   161   SC   22053
SN   Medical specialty dealing with the female endocrine system, reproductive physiology, and diseases of the genital tract. Used for the medical specialty or the specific gynecological issues or findings.
B   Medical Sciences   1967
R   Circumcision   2001
    ↓ Obstetrics   1978

Gypsies   1973
PN   58   SC   22055
UF   Gipsies
B   Racial and Ethnic Groups   2001
R   ↓ Human Migration   1973
    Minority Groups   1967

Gyrus Cinguli   1973
PN   298   SC   22060
B   Frontal Lobe   1973
    Limbic System   1973

Habilitation   1991
PN   66   SC   22065
SN   Establishment, not restoration, of fundamental capabilities, knowledge, experiences, and attitudes before or along with the usual rehabilitation procedures as a means of increasing patient awareness and developing their potential. Used primarily for physically or mentally disabled populations. Compare REHABILITATION.
R   Activities of Daily Living   1991

Habilitation — (cont'd)
R   Deinstitutionalization   1982
    Independent Living Programs   1991
    ↓ Mainstreaming   1991
    ↓ Rehabilitation   1967
    ↓ Skill Learning   1973

Habitat Selection
Use   Territoriality

Habitats (Animal)
Use   Animal Environments

Habits   1967
PN   399   SC   22080
UF   Mannerisms
N   Hair Pulling   1973
    Nail Biting   1973
    Thumbsucking   1973
    Tobacco Smoking   1967
R   ↓ Learning   1967

Habituation   1967
PN   2278   SC   22090
SN   Progressive attenuation of a response elicited by repetitive stimulation.
R   ↓ Sensory Adaptation   1967

Hair   1973
PN   187   SC   22100
B   Anatomy   1967
R   Alopecia   1973
    Scalp (Anatomy)   1973
    Skin (Anatomy)   1967

Hair Loss
Use   Alopecia

Hair Pulling   1973
PN   305   SC   22120
UF   Trichotillomania
B   Habits   1967
R   ↓ Behavior Disorders   1971
    ↓ Self Destructive Behavior   1985

Halcion
Use   Triazolam

Halfway Houses   1973
PN   228   SC   22140
SN   Facilities for psychiatric, drug, or alcohol rehabilitation patients or mentally retarded individuals who no longer need hospitalization or institutionalization, but who are not yet fully prepared to return to their communities.
B   Residential Care Institutions   1973
    Treatment Facilities   1973
R   ↓ Community Facilities   1973
    ↓ Correctional Institutions   1973
    ↓ Psychiatric Hospital Programs   1967
    Psychiatric Hospitals   1967

Hallucinations   1967
PN   1010   SC   22150
SN   Perceptions through any sense modality in the absence of an appropriate stimulus. (Usually indicative of abnormality but may be experienced occasionally by normal persons).
UF   Flashbacks
B   Perceptual Disturbances   1973
N   Auditory Hallucinations   1973
    Drug Induced Hallucinations   1973
    Hypnagogic Hallucinations   1973

Hallucinations — (cont'd)

N   Visual Hallucinations [1973]
R   ↓ Hallucinogenic Drugs [1967]
     ↓ Hallucinosis [1973]
     Near Death Experiences [1985]

Hallucinogenic Drugs [1967]

PN   437   **SC**   22160
B   Drugs [1967]
N   Bufotenine [1973]
     Lysergic Acid Diethylamide [1967]
     Mescaline [1973]
     Peyote [1973]
     Phencyclidine [1982]
     Psilocybin [1973]
R   ↓ Cannabis [1973]
     ↓ Cholinergic Blocking Drugs [1973]
     Experimental Psychosis [1973]
     ↓ Hallucinations [1967]
     ↓ Psychedelic Drugs [1973]
     ↓ Psychotomimetic Drugs [1973]
     Tetrahydrocannabinol [1973]

Hallucinosis [1973]

PN   36   **SC**   22170
SN   Mental disorder characterized by hallucinations occurring in a normal state of consciousness and attributable to specific organic factors.
B   Psychosis [1967]
N   ↓ Alcoholic Hallucinosis [1973]
R   ↓ Hallucinations [1967]

Halo Effect [1982]

PN   127   **SC**   22177
SN   Tendency to rate individuals too high or too low on the basis of one outstanding trait or an erroneous overall impression. Often the source of error in rating scales.
R   ↓ Errors [1967]
     ↓ Expectations [1967]
     Experimenter Bias [1967]
     Rating [1967]
     ↓ Social Perception [1967]

Haloperidol [1973]

PN   3049   **SC**   22180
B   CNS Depressant Drugs [1973]
     Sedatives [1973]
     Tranquilizing Drugs [1967]

Halstead Reitan Neuropsychological Battery [2001]

PN   106   **SC**   22185
SN   In 2000, the truncated term HALSTEAD REITAN NEUROPSYCH BATTERY (which was used from 1991-2000) was deleted, removed from all records containing it, and mapped to its expanded form HALSTEAD REITAN NEUROPSYCHOLOGICAL BATTERY. Use NEUROPSYCHOLOGICAL ASSESSMENT to access references from 1982-1990.
B   Neuropsychological Assessment [1982]

Hamsters [1973]

PN   1365   **SC**   22190
B   Rodents [1973]

Hand (Anatomy) [1967]

PN   1040   **SC**   22200
B   Anatomy [1967]
     Musculoskeletal System [1973]
R   Arm (Anatomy) [1973]
     ↓ Fingers (Anatomy) [1973]

Hand (Anatomy) — (cont'd)

R   Palm (Anatomy) [1973]
     Wrist [1973]

Handedness [1978]

PN   2541   **SC**   22210
SN   Learned or spontaneous differential dexterity with and tendency to use one hand rather than the other.
B   Lateral Dominance [1967]

Handicapped (Attitudes Toward)

SN   Term was discontinued in 1997. In 2000, the term was stripped from all records containing it, and replaced with DISABLED (ATTITUDES TOWARD), its postable counterpart.
Use   Disabled (Attitudes Toward)

Handicaps

Use   Disorders

Handicrafts

Use   Crafts

Handwriting [1967]

PN   907   **SC**   22250
UF   Graphology
     Writing (Handwriting)
B   Verbal Communication [1967]
     Written Language [1967]
N   Cursive Writing [1973]
     Handwriting Legibility [1973]
     Printing (Handwriting) [1973]

Handwriting Legibility [1973]

PN   64   **SC**   22260
UF   Legibility (Handwriting)
B   Handwriting [1967]
     Legibility [1978]

Happiness [1973]

PN   974   **SC**   22270
UF   Joy
B   Emotional States [1973]
R   Euphoria [1973]
     Pleasure [1973]

Haptic Perception

Use   Cutaneous Sense

Harassment [2001]

PN   0   **SC**   22282
B   Antisocial Behavior [1971]
N   Sexual Harassment [1985]
     Stalking [2001]
R   ↓ Perpetrators [1988]
     Threat [1967]
     Victimization [1973]

Harassment (Sexual)

Use   Sexual Harassment

Hardiness [1997]

PN   568   **SC**   22285
SN   Use PSYCHOLOGICAL ENDURANCE to access references from 1991-1996.
UF   Resilience (Psychological)
B   Personality Traits [1967]
R   Adaptability (Personality) [1973]
     Coping Behavior [1967]
     ↓ Emotional Adjustment [1973]
     Emotional Stability [1973]

Hardiness — (cont'd)

R   Psychological Endurance [1973]
     Psychological Stress [1973]

Hashish [1973]

PN   66   **SC**   22290
B   Cannabis [1973]
R   Marihuana [1971]
     Tetrahydrocannabinol [1973]

Hate [1973]

PN   239   **SC**   22300
B   Aversion [1967]
R   ↓ Anger [1967]
     Hostility [1967]

Hawaii Natives [2001]

PN   **SC**   22315
UF   Native Hawaiians
B   Pacific Islanders [2001]
R   Minority Groups [1967]

Hay Fever [1973]

PN   14   **SC**   22320
B   Allergic Disorders [1973]
     Respiratory Tract Disorders [1973]
R   ↓ Somatoform Disorders [2001]

Hazardous Materials [1991]

PN   190   **SC**   22325
UF   Asbestos
     Toxic Waste
N   ↓ Insecticides [1973]
     ↓ Poisons [1973]
     Teratogens [1988]
R   ↓ Accidents [1967]
     ↓ Chemicals [1991]
     ↓ Environment [1967]
     Occupational Exposure [1988]
     Pollution [1973]
     ↓ Safety [1967]
     Toxicity [1973]

Hazards [1973]

PN   270   **SC**   22330
R   ↓ Accidents [1967]
     Risk Perception [1997]
     ↓ Safety [1967]
     ↓ Safety Devices [1973]
     Warning Labels [1997]
     ↓ Warnings [1997]

Head (Anatomy) [1973]

PN   581   **SC**   22340
B   Anatomy [1967]
R   Face (Anatomy) [1973]
     Scalp (Anatomy) [1973]
     Skin (Anatomy) [1967]

Head Banging [1973]

PN   52   **SC**   22350
B   Self Destructive Behavior [1985]

Head Injuries [1973]

PN   2669   **SC**   22360
UF   Closed Head Injuries
B   Injuries [1973]
N   Brain Concussion [1973]
R   ↓ Brain Damage [1967]
     Traumatic Brain Injury [1997]
     Whiplash [1997]
     ↓ Wounds [1973]

Head Start
Use   Project Head Start

Headache   1973
PN 1111   **SC** 22380
B   Pain   1967
    Symptoms   1967
N   Migraine Headache   1973
    Muscle Contraction Headache   1973
R   ↓ Somatoform Disorders   2001

Health   1973
PN 9030   **SC** 22390
UF   Wellness
N   Holistic Health   1985
    ↓ Mental Health   1967
    ↓ Public Health   1988
R   General Health Questionnaire   1991
    Health Attitudes   1985
    Health Behavior   1982
    Health Complaints   1997
    Health Knowledge   1994
    Hygiene   1994
    Preventive Medicine   1973
    Public Health Services   1973
    Well Being   1994

Health Attitudes   1985
PN 3360   **SC** 22391
UF   Health Locus of Control
B   Attitudes   1967
R   ↓ Drug Usage Attitudes   1973
    ↓ Health   1973
    Health Behavior   1982
    Health Knowledge   1994
    Health Promotion   1991
    Lifestyle Changes   1997
    Obesity (Attitudes Toward)   1997
    ↓ Physical Illness (Attitudes Toward)   1985

Health Behavior   1982
PN 4665   **SC** 22392
SN   Individual lifestyle and behavior which may or may not enhance or maintain good health.
B   Behavior   1967
    Client Characteristics   1973
R   AIDS Prevention   1994
    Aerobic Exercise   1988
    Diets   1978
    ↓ Exercise   1973
    ↓ Health   1973
    Health Attitudes   1985
    Health Knowledge   1994
    Health Promotion   1991
    Holistic Health   1985
    Hygiene   1994
    ↓ Lifestyle   1978
    Lifestyle Changes   1997
    ↓ Prenatal Care   1991
    Preventive Medicine   1973
    Self Examination (Medical)   1988
    Self Referral   1991
    Weight Control   1985

Health Care Administration   1997
PN 135   **SC** 57485
B   Management   1967
N   Hospital Administration   1978
R   ↓ Case Management   1991
    ↓ Health Care Delivery   1978
    Health Care Policy   1994
    ↓ Health Care Services   1978
    ↓ Mental Health Programs   1973

Health Care Administration — (cont'd)
R   ↓ Mental Health Services   1978
    ↓ Treatment Facilities   1973

Health Care Costs   1994
PN 951   **SC** 22393
UF   Medical Care Costs
    Mental Health Care Costs
B   Costs and Cost Analysis   1973
R   ↓ Case Management   1991
    Cost Containment   1991
    Diagnosis Related Groups   1988
    Economics   1985
    ↓ Health Care Delivery   1978
    ↓ Health Care Services   1978
    Health Care Utilization   1985
    ↓ Health Insurance   1973
    Health Maintenance Organizations   1982
    ↓ Managed Care   1994
    ↓ Mental Health Services   1978
    ↓ Professional Fees   1978
    ↓ Treatment   1967

Health Care Delivery   1978
PN 5760   **SC** 22394
SN   Practices, policies, or referral processes that contribute to making mental and/or medical health care personnel, services, or facilities available to persons in need of such care.
N   Home Care   1985
    Hospice   1982
    ↓ Managed Care   1994
R   ↓ Case Management   1991
    Fee for Service   1994
    ↓ Health Care Administration   1997
    Health Care Costs   1994
    Health Care Policy   1994
    ↓ Health Care Services   1978
    Health Care Utilization   1985
    Health Maintenance Organizations   1982
    Health Service Needs   1997
    ↓ Mental Health Programs   1973
    ↓ Mental Health Services   1978
    Needs Assessment   1985
    Outreach Programs   1997
    Palliative Care   1991
    ↓ Prevention   1973
    Primary Health Care   1988
    Private Practice   1978
    Quality of Care   1988
    ↓ Quality of Services   1997
    ↓ Treatment   1967
    ↓ Treatment Planning   1997

Health Care Policy   1994
PN 916   **SC** 57415
UF   Mental Health Care Policy
B   Policy Making   1988
R   ↓ Government Policy Making   1973
    ↓ Health Care Administration   1997
    ↓ Health Care Delivery   1978
    ↓ Health Care Services   1978
    ↓ Health Insurance   1973
    Medicaid   1994
    Medicare   1988
    ↓ Mental Health Services   1978

Health Care Professionals
SN   Use MEDICAL PERSONNEL or MENTAL HEALTH PERSONNEL to access references prior to 1994.
Use   Health Personnel

Health Care Psychology   1985
PN 1148   **SC** 22398
UF   Behavioral Health
    Behavioral Medicine
    Health Psychology
N   Medical Psychology   1973
R   Interdisciplinary Treatment Approach   1973
    Psychosomatic Medicine   1978

Health Care Seeking Behavior   1997
PN 440   **SC** 22399
SN   Consider HELP SEEKING BEHAVIOR or HEALTH CARE UTILIZATION to access references from 1978-1984 and 1985-1996 respectively.
UF   Treatment Seeking Behavior
B   Help Seeking Behavior   1978
R   ↓ Commitment (Psychiatric)   1973
    ↓ Health Care Services   1978
    Health Care Utilization   1985
    Health Service Needs   1997
    ↓ Hospital Admission   1973
    ↓ Mental Health Services   1978
    Self Referral   1991
    ↓ Treatment   1967

Health Care Services   1978
PN 4204   **SC** 22396
B   Treatment   1967
N   Long Term Care   1994
    ↓ Mental Health Services   1978
    Palliative Care   1991
    Primary Health Care   1988
R   Caregivers   1988
    ↓ Community Services   1967
    Cost Containment   1991
    ↓ Counseling   1967
    Fee for Service   1994
    ↓ Health Care Administration   1997
    Health Care Costs   1994
    ↓ Health Care Delivery   1978
    Health Care Policy   1994
    Health Care Seeking Behavior   1997
    Health Care Utilization   1985
    Health Maintenance Organizations   1982
    Health Service Needs   1997
    Integrated Services   1997
    ↓ Managed Care   1994
    ↓ Mental Health Programs   1973
    Outreach Programs   1997
    ↓ Prenatal Care   1991
    ↓ Prevention   1973
    Quality of Care   1988
    ↓ Quality of Services   1997
    ↓ Rehabilitation   1967
    Self Referral   1991
    Social Casework   1967
    ↓ Social Services   1982

Health Care Utilization   1985
PN 4248   **SC** 22397
SN   Processes involved in or factors affecting usage of professional or nonprofessional health services or programs. Use HEALTH CARE SEEKING BEHAVIOR for factors involved in seeking treatment. Use HELP SEEKING BEHAVIOR to access references from 1978-1984.
UF   Assistance Seeking (Professional)
    Health Service Utilization
    Utilization (Health Care)
R   Health Care Costs   1994
    ↓ Health Care Delivery   1978
    Health Care Seeking Behavior   1997
    ↓ Health Care Services   1978
    ↓ Help Seeking Behavior   1978

Health Care Utilization — (cont'd)
R   Self Referral [1991]

Health Complaints [1997]
PN 127   SC 22402
R   ↓ Disorders [1967]
     ↓ Health [1973]
     Symptom Checklists [1991]
     ↓ Symptoms [1967]

Health Education [1973]
PN 3621   SC 22400
SN Instruction or programs in school, institutional,
or community settings which present material about
factors affecting health behavior and attitudes.
B   Curriculum [1967]
N   Drug Education [1973]
     Sex Education [1973]
R   AIDS Prevention [1994]
     Client Education [1985]
     Health Knowledge [1994]
     Health Promotion [1991]
     ↓ Prenatal Care [1991]
     ↓ Prevention [1973]
     Psychoeducation [1994]

Health Impairments [2001]
PN 509   SC 22415
SN In 2000, this term was created to replace the
discontinued and deleted term HEALTH IMPAIRED.
HEALTH IMPAIRED was stripped from all records
and replaced with HEALTH IMPAIRMENTS.
UF   Frail
B   Physical Disorders [1997]
R   Homebound [1988]

Health Insurance [1973]
PN 802   SC 22420
B   Insurance [1973]
N   ↓ Employee Health Insurance [1973]
     Fee for Service [1994]
     Health Maintenance Organizations [1982]
     Medicaid [1994]
     Medicare [1988]
R   ↓ Case Management [1991]
     Diagnosis Related Groups [1988]
     Health Care Costs [1994]
     Health Care Policy [1994]
     ↓ Hospitalization [1967]
     ↓ Managed Care [1994]

Health Knowledge [1994]
PN 1098   SC 22421
SN Knowledge or understanding of illness, health,
or mental health and health related issues.
B   Knowledge Level [1978]
R   Client Education [1985]
     ↓ Health [1973]
     Health Attitudes [1985]
     Health Behavior [1982]
     ↓ Health Education [1973]
     Health Promotion [1991]
     Mental Illness (Attitudes Toward) [1967]
     ↓ Physical Illness (Attitudes Toward) [1985]

Health Locus of Control
     Use Health Attitudes

Health Maintenance Organizations [1982]
PN 429   SC 22425
SN Organizations providing comprehensive, coordinated medical services to voluntarily enrolled members on a prepaid basis.

Health Maintenance Organizations —
   (cont'd)
UF   Group Health Plans
     HMO
B   Health Insurance [1973]
     Managed Care [1994]
     Organizations [1967]
R   Cost Containment [1991]
     Fee for Service [1994]
     Health Care Costs [1994]
     ↓ Health Care Delivery [1978]
     ↓ Health Care Services [1978]
     Health Promotion [1991]
     Preventive Medicine [1973]

Health Personnel [1994]
PN 1465   SC 57420
SN Personnel working in a medical or mental health
profession. Used for unspecified health care profes-
sionals or when both medical and mental health pro-
fessionals are discussed. Use a more specific term if
possible. Consider MEDICAL PERSONNEL OR
MENTAL HEALTH PERSONNEL to access refer-
ences prior to 1994.
UF   Health Care Professionals
B   Professional Personnel [1978]
N   ↓ Medical Personnel [1967]
     ↓ Mental Health Personnel [1967]
R   ↓ Counselors [1967]
     Home Care Personnel [1997]
     ↓ Social Workers [1973]
     ↓ Therapists [1967]

Health Personnel Attitudes [1985]
PN 4016   SC 22426
SN Attitudes of persons working in health or medi-
cal professions.
B   Attitudes [1967]
N   ↓ Therapist Attitudes [1978]
R   Counselor Attitudes [1973]
     Psychologist Attitudes [1991]

Health Promotion [1991]
PN 2030   SC 22423
SN Education or other types of interventions used
to improve and encourage both physical and mental
health. Consider using HEALTH EDUCATION to
access references from 1973-1990.
R   AIDS Prevention [1994]
     Cancer Screening [1997]
     Client Education [1985]
     Health Attitudes [1985]
     Health Behavior [1982]
     ↓ Health Education [1973]
     Health Knowledge [1994]
     Health Maintenance Organizations [1982]
     ↓ Health Screening [1997]
     Lifestyle Changes [1997]
     ↓ Prevention [1973]
     Preventive Medicine [1973]
     ↓ Public Health [1988]
     ↓ Screening [1982]

Health Psychology
     Use Health Care Psychology

Health Screening [1997]
PN 167   SC 22431
SN Consider PHYSICAL EXAMINATION to access
references from 1988-1996.
B   Screening [1982]
N   Cancer Screening [1997]
     HIV Testing [1997]
     Physical Examination [1988]

Health Screening — (cont'd)
R   Drug Usage Screening [1988]
     Health Promotion [1991]
     Mammography [1994]
     ↓ Medical Diagnosis [1973]
     Preventive Medicine [1973]
     ↓ Public Health [1988]

Health Service Needs [1997]
PN 479   SC 22432
UF   Mental Health Service Needs
B   Needs [1967]
R   ↓ Case Management [1991]
     ↓ Health Care Delivery [1978]
     Health Care Seeking Behavior [1997]
     ↓ Health Care Services [1978]
     Intake Interview [1994]
     ↓ Mental Health Services [1978]
     Needs Assessment [1985]

Health Service Utilization
     Use Health Care Utilization

Hearing Acuity
     Use Auditory Acuity

Hearing Aids [1973]
PN 481   SC 22430
B   Medical Therapeutic Devices [1973]
N   Cochlear Implants [1994]

Hearing Disorders [1982]
PN 2467   SC 22435
SN Disorders involving the hearing mechanisms,
specifically the sensorineural pathways. The term
AURALLY HANDICAPPED was also used to repre-
sent this concept from 1973-1996, and AURALLY
DISABLED was used from 1997-2000. In 2000,
HEARING DISORDERS replaced the discontinued
and deleted term AURALLY DISABLED. AURALLY
DISABLED and AURALLY HANDICAPPED were
stripped from all records and replaced with HEAR-
ING DISORDERS.
UF   Aurally Handicapped
     Sensorineural Hearing Loss
B   Communication Disorders [1982]
R   Cochlear Implants [1994]
     ↓ Deaf [1967]
     ↓ Ear Disorders [1973]

Hearing Impaired (Partially)
     Use Partially Hearing Impaired

Hearing Measures
     Use Speech and Hearing Measures

Heart [1967]
PN 462   SC 22460
B   Cardiovascular System [1967]
N   Heart Auricles [1973]
     Heart Valves [1973]
     Heart Ventricles [1973]
     Myocardium [1973]
R   ↓ Blood [1967]
     Vagus Nerve [1973]

Heart Attacks
     Use Heart Disorders

Heart Auricles [1973]
PN 11   SC 22470
UF   Atria (Heart)
     Auricles (Heart)

Heart Auricles — (cont'd)
B   Heart ¹⁹⁶⁷

Heart Beat
Use   Heart Rate

Heart Disorders ¹⁹⁷³
PN   1750   SC   22480
   UF   Cardiac Arrest
         Cardiac Disorders
         Coronary Heart Disease
         Heart Attacks
   B   Cardiovascular Disorders ¹⁹⁶⁷
   N   Angina Pectoris ¹⁹⁷³
        ↓ Arrhythmias (Heart) ¹⁹⁷³
        Coronary Thromboses ¹⁹⁷³
        Myocardial Infarctions ¹⁹⁷³
   R   Rheumatic Fever ¹⁹⁷³

Heart Rate ¹⁹⁶⁷
PN   5959   SC   22490
   UF   Cardiac Rate
         Heart Beat
         Heartbeat
   R   Cardiovascular Reactivity ¹⁹⁹⁴

Heart Rate Affecting Drugs ¹⁹⁷³
PN   63   SC   22500
   B   Drugs ¹⁹⁶⁷
   N   Caffeine ¹⁹⁷³
        Epinephrine ¹⁹⁶⁷
        Theophylline ¹⁹⁷³
        Verapamil ¹⁹⁹¹
   R   ↓ Analeptic Drugs ¹⁹⁷³
        ↓ Antihypertensive Drugs ¹⁹⁷³
        ↓ CNS Affecting Drugs ¹⁹⁷³
        ↓ CNS Stimulating Drugs ¹⁹⁷³
        ↓ Cardiovascular Disorders ¹⁹⁶⁷
        Dopamine ¹⁹⁷³
        ↓ Muscle Relaxing Drugs ¹⁹⁷³
        ↓ Vasoconstrictor Drugs ¹⁹⁷³
        ↓ Vasodilator Drugs ¹⁹⁷³

Heart Surgery ¹⁹⁷³
PN   527   SC   22510
   UF   Cardiac Surgery
   B   Surgery ¹⁹⁷¹
   R   Organ Transplantation ¹⁹⁷³

Heart Transplants
Use   Organ Transplantation

Heart Valves ¹⁹⁷³
PN   48   SC   22530
   UF   Valves (Heart)
   B   Heart ¹⁹⁶⁷

Heart Ventricles ¹⁹⁷³
PN   41   SC   22540
   UF   Ventricles (Heart)
   B   Heart ¹⁹⁶⁷

Heartbeat
Use   Heart Rate

Heat Effects ¹⁹⁷³
PN   600   SC   22560
   B   Temperature Effects ¹⁹⁶⁷

Hebephrenic Schizophrenia
SN   In 2000, the term was discontinued, and all records containing it were stripped of the term and replaced with SCHIZOPHRENIA (DISORGANIZED TYPE), its postable counterpart.
    Use   Schizophrenia (Disorganized Type)

Hedonism ¹⁹⁷³
PN   101   SC   22580
   R   ↓ Attitudes ¹⁹⁶⁷
        ↓ Philosophies ¹⁹⁶⁷

Heels (Anatomy)
Use   Feet (Anatomy)

Height (Body)
Use   Body Height

Helicopters ¹⁹⁷³
PN   73   SC   22610
   B   Aircraft ¹⁹⁷³

Helium ¹⁹⁷³
PN   28   SC   22620

Help Seeking Behavior ¹⁹⁷⁸
PN   1562   SC   22624
SN   Searching for or requesting help from others through formal or informal mechanisms. From 1978-1984 used primarily for the seeking or utilization of professional care or services. From 1997, use HEALTH CARE SEEKING BEHAVIOR to access references on help seeking in a treatment context.
   B   Social Behavior ¹⁹⁶⁷
   N   Health Care Seeking Behavior ¹⁹⁹⁷
   R   Assistance (Social Behavior) ¹⁹⁷³
        Health Care Utilization ¹⁹⁸⁵
        Self Referral ¹⁹⁹¹

Helping Behavior
Use   Assistance (Social Behavior)

Helplessness ¹⁹⁹⁷
PN   72   SC   22627
   B   Emotional States ¹⁹⁷³
   N   Learned Helplessness ¹⁹⁷⁸
   R   Coping Behavior ¹⁹⁶⁷
        Empowerment ¹⁹⁹¹
        Hopelessness ¹⁹⁸⁸
        Internal External Locus of Control ¹⁹⁶⁷
        ↓ Power ¹⁹⁶⁷
        Self Control ¹⁹⁷³
        Self Determination ¹⁹⁹⁴
        Self Efficacy ¹⁹⁸⁵

Helplessness (Learned)
Use   Learned Helplessness

Hematologic Disorders
Use   Blood and Lymphatic Disorders

Hematoma ¹⁹⁷³
PN   53   SC   22640
   B   Hemorrhage ¹⁹⁷³
        Symptoms ¹⁹⁶⁷
   R   ↓ Injuries ¹⁹⁷³

Hemianopia ¹⁹⁷³
PN   122   SC   22650
   UF   Hemiopia
   B   Eye Disorders ¹⁹⁷³
   R   ↓ Nervous System Disorders ¹⁹⁶⁷

Hemiopia
Use   Hemianopia

Hemiplegia ¹⁹⁷⁸
PN   255   SC   22675
SN   Paralysis of one side of the body resulting from disease or injury to the brain or spinal cord.
   B   Paralysis ¹⁹⁷³
   R   ↓ Central Nervous System Disorders ¹⁹⁷³
        ↓ Injuries ¹⁹⁷³
        ↓ Musculoskeletal Disorders ¹⁹⁷³
        Paraplegia ¹⁹⁷⁸
        Quadriplegia ¹⁹⁸⁵
        ↓ Spinal Cord Injuries ¹⁹⁷³

Hemispherectomy ¹⁹⁷³
PN   110   SC   22680
   B   Neurosurgery ¹⁹⁷³

Hemispheric Specialization
SN   Use CEREBRAL DOMINANCE to access references from 1973-1990.
    Use   Lateral Dominance

Hemodialysis ¹⁹⁷³
PN   505   SC   22690
   B   Dialysis ¹⁹⁷³
   R   Blood Transfusion ¹⁹⁷³

Hemoglobin ¹⁹⁷³
PN   81   SC   22700
   B   Blood Proteins ¹⁹⁷³
        Pigments ¹⁹⁷³

Hemophilia ¹⁹⁷³
PN   225   SC   22710
   B   Blood and Lymphatic Disorders ¹⁹⁷³
        Sex Linked Hereditary Disorders ¹⁹⁷³

Hemorrhage ¹⁹⁷³
PN   61   SC   22720
   B   Cardiovascular Disorders ¹⁹⁶⁷
        Symptoms ¹⁹⁶⁷
   N   Cerebral Hemorrhage ¹⁹⁷³
        Hematoma ¹⁹⁷³

Hemp (Cannabis)
Use   Cannabis

Henmon Nelson Tests of Mental Ability
SN   Term was discontinued in 1997. In 2000, the term was stripped from all records containing it, and replaced with INTELLIGENCE MEASURES, its postable counterpart.
    Use   Intelligence Measures

Heparin ¹⁹⁷³
PN   10   SC   22750
   B   Acids ¹⁹⁷³
        Anticoagulant Drugs ¹⁹⁷³

Hepatic Disorders
Use   Liver Disorders

Hepatitis ¹⁹⁷³
PN   180   SC   22770
   B   Liver Disorders ¹⁹⁷³
   N   Toxic Hepatitis ¹⁹⁷³
   R   ↓ Infectious Disorders ¹⁹⁷³
        Jaundice ¹⁹⁷³

Hereditary Disorders
  Use Genetic Disorders

Heredity
  Use Genetics

Hermaphroditism 1973
PN 92   SC 22800
  UF Intersexuality
      Pseudohermaphroditism
  B Congenital Disorders 1973
      Genital Disorders 1967
  R ↓ Endocrine Sexual Disorders 1973
      ↓ Gender Identity Disorder 1997
      ↓ Gynecological Disorders 1973
      ↓ Male Genital Disorders 1973
      Sterility 1973
      Testicular Feminization Syndrome 1973

Hermeneutics 1991
PN 348   SC 22805
  B Philosophies 1967
  R Epistemology 1973
      Metaphysics 1973
      Phenomenology 1967
      Positivism (Philosophy) 1997
      Rhetoric 1991
      ↓ Semiotics 1985

Heroin 1973
PN 620   SC 22810
  UF Diacetylmorphine
  B Alkaloids 1973
      Analgesic Drugs 1973
      Opiates 1973
      Sedatives 1973
  R Heroin Addiction 1973

Heroin Addiction 1973
PN 1277   SC 22820
  B Drug Addiction 1967
  R Heroin 1973
      Methadone Maintenance 1978

Herpes Genitalis 1988
PN 70   SC 22825
  UF Genital Herpes
  B Venereal Diseases 1973
      Viral Disorders 1973

Herpes Simplex 1973
PN 211   SC 22830
  B Skin Disorders 1973
      Viral Disorders 1973

Heterogeneity of Variance
  Use Variance Homogeneity

Heterosexism
  Use Homosexuality (Attitudes Toward)

Heterosexual Interaction
  Use Male Female Relations

Heterosexuality 1973
PN 1257   SC 22840
  B Psychosexual Behavior 1967
      Sexual Orientation 1997
  R Lesbianism 1973
      Male Female Relations 1988
      Male Homosexuality 1973
      Sex Linked Developmental Differences 1973

Heterosexuality — (cont'd)
  R Sexual Development 1973

Heterozygotic Twins 1973
PN 714   SC 22850
  UF Dizygotic Twins
      Fraternal Twins
  B Twins 1967

Heuristic Modeling 1973
PN 373   SC 22860
  B Simulation 1967
  R ↓ Mathematical Modeling 1973

Hexamethonium 1973
PN 29   SC 22870
  B Antihypertensive Drugs 1973
      Ganglion Blocking Drugs 1973

Hexobarbital 1973
PN 28   SC 22880
  B Anesthetic Drugs 1973
      Barbiturates 1967
      Hypnotic Drugs 1973
      Sedatives 1973

Hibernation 1973
PN 77   SC 22890
  B Animal Ethology 1967
  R ↓ Animal Biological Rhythms 1973

Hidden Figures Test 1973
PN 15   SC 22900
  B Intelligence Measures 1967

High Risk Populations
  Use At Risk Populations

High School Equivalency
  Use Adult Education

High School Graduates 1978
PN 292   SC 22924
  R Educational Degrees 1973
      High School Students 1967
      School Graduation 1991
      School to Work Transition 1994

**High School Personality
  Questionnaire** 2001
PN 31   SC 22927
  SN In 2000, the truncated term HIGH SCH PER-
  SONALITY QUESTIONNAIRE (which was used from
  1973-2000) was deleted, removed from all records
  containing it, and mapped to its expanded form HIGH
  SCHOOL PERSONALITY QUESTIONNAIRE.
  B Nonprojective Personality Measures 1973

High School Students 1967
PN 17407   SC 22930
  SN Students in grades 9-12. Mandatory term in
  educational contexts.
  B Students 1967
  R Grade Level 1994
      High School Graduates 1978
      Reentry Students 1985

High School Teachers 1973
PN 2447   SC 22940
  B Teachers 1967

High Schools 1973
PN 789   SC 22950
  B Schools 1967
  R Military Schools 1973
      Secondary Education 1973

Higher Education 1973
PN 1439   SC 22960
  SN College or university education beyond the suc-
  cessful completion of high school or grammar school,
  or the attainment of an approved equivalent.
  B Education 1967
  N ↓ Graduate Education 1973
      ↓ Postgraduate Training 1973
      Undergraduate Education 1978
  R ↓ Colleges 1967
      ↓ Continuing Education 1985
      Educational Degrees 1973
      Educational Program Accreditation 1994
      Graduate Schools 1973
      Professional Specialization 1991
      School Graduation 1991

Higher Order Conditioning 1997
PN 13   SC 22970
  SN A classical conditioning method in which the
  original conditioned stimulus is used as the uncondi-
  tioned stimulus in a new experimental setting.
  UF Second Order Conditioning
  B Classical Conditioning 1967

Highway Safety 1973
PN 817   SC 22980
  UF Automobile Safety
      Driver Safety
  B Safety 1967
  R Drivers 1973
      ↓ Driving Behavior 1967
      Driving Under The Influence 1988
      ↓ Ground Transportation 1973
      Motor Traffic Accidents 1973
      ↓ Transportation Accidents 1973

Hindbrain 1997
PN 14   SC 22985
  UF Rhombencephalon
  B Brain 1967
  N ↓ Cerebellum 1973
      Medulla Oblongata 1973
      ↓ Pons 1973
  R ↓ Brain Stem 1973
      Raphe Nuclei 1982

Hinduism 1973
PN 284   SC 22990
  B Religious Affiliation 1973
  R Hindus 1997

Hindus 1997
PN 28   SC 22995
  B Religious Groups 1997
  R Hinduism 1973

Hippies
  Use Subculture (Anthropological)

Hippocampal Commissure
  Use Fornix

Hippocampus 1967
PN 5654   SC 23010
  B Limbic System 1973
  R Medial Forebrain Bundle 1982

Hippocampus — (cont'd)
R   Septal Nuclei [1982]

Hips [1973]
PN 113   SC 23020
B   Musculoskeletal System [1973]

Hiring
Use   Personnel Selection

Hispanics [1982]
PN 5586   SC 23035
UF   Cuban Americans
    Latinos/Latinas
    Puerto Rican Americans
    Spanish Americans
B   Racial and Ethnic Groups [2001]
N   Mexican Americans [1973]
R   Minority Groups [1967]

Histamine [1973]
PN 219   SC 23050
B   Amines [1973]
    Neurotransmitters [1985]
R   ↓ Antihistaminic Drugs [1973]
    Histidine [1973]

Histidine [1973]
PN 35   SC 23060
B   Amino Acids [1973]
R   Histamine [1973]

Histology [1973]
PN 144   SC 23070
SN   Branch of anatomy dealing with the structure of cells, tissues, and organs in relation to their functions. Used for the scientific discipline or the organic structure itself.
R   Morphology [1973]
    ↓ Physiology [1967]
    ↓ Tissues (Body) [1973]

History [1973]
PN 8318   SC 23075
SN   Recording and/or explanation of previous events, experiences, trends, and treatments.
N   ↓ History of Psychology [1967]
R   Future [1991]
    Psychohistory [1978]
    Trends [1991]

History of Psychology [1967]
PN 6766   SC 23080
B   History [1973]
N   Associationism [1973]
    Behaviorism [1967]
    Freudian Psychoanalytic School [1973]
    Functionalism [1973]
    Gestalt Psychology [1967]
    ↓ Neopsychoanalytic School [1973]
    Structuralism [1973]
R   Phenomenology [1967]
    ↓ Psychological Theories [2001]
    ↓ Psychology [1967]
    ↓ Theories [1967]

Histrionic Personality Disorder [1991]
PN 272   SC 23082

Histrionic Personality Disorder — (cont'd)
SN   Personality disorder characterized by emotional instability, excitability, overreaction, self-dramatization, self-centeredness, and over-dependence on others. In 2000, the term's status changed from non-postable to postable. All records containing HYSTERICAL PERSONALITY were stripped of this term and replaced with HISTRIONIC PERSONALITY DISORDER.
UF   Hysterical Personality
B   Personality Disorders [1967]
R   ↓ Conversion Disorder [2001]
    ↓ Hysteria [1967]

HIV
Use   Human Immunodeficiency Virus

HIV Testing [1997]
PN 148   SC 23084
UF   AIDS Testing
B   Health Screening [1997]
    Medical Diagnosis [1973]
R   AIDS Prevention [1994]
    Acquired Immune Deficiency Syndrome [1988]
    ↓ Human Immunodeficiency Virus [1991]

HMO
Use   Health Maintenance Organizations

Hoarding Behavior (Animal)
Use   Animal Hoarding Behavior

Hobbies [1988]
PN 47   SC 23100
SN   Use RECREATION to access references from 1973-1988.
R   Daily Activities [1994]
    ↓ Interests [1967]
    Leisure Time [1973]
    ↓ Recreation [1967]

Hoffmanns Reflex [1973]
PN 41   SC 23110
SN   Flexing of the thumb and some other finger resulting from a sudden tapping of the nail of the index, middle, or ring finger. Also known as digital reflex, finger flexion reflex, snapping reflex, H reflex, or Hoffmann's (H) response.
B   Reflexes [1971]

Holidays [1988]
PN 63   SC 23113
SN   Days marked by general suspension of work in commemoration or celebration of an event.
R   Leisure Time [1973]
    ↓ Recreation [1967]
    Vacationing [1973]

Holistic Health [1985]
PN 545   SC 23115
SN   Personal practices or medical or psychological diagnosis and treatment based on the concept that humans are composed of body, mind, and spirit. An observed disorder or dysfunction in one component implies the need for treatment of the whole organism to restore health.
UF   Wholistic Health
B   Health [1973]
R   ↓ Alternative Medicine [1997]
    Biopsychosocial Approach [1991]
    Health Behavior [1982]
    ↓ Lifestyle [1978]
    Meditation [1973]

Holistic Health — (cont'd)
R   ↓ Physical Treatment Methods [1973]
    Preventive Medicine [1973]
    ↓ Psychotherapy [1967]

Holocaust [1988]
PN 334   SC 23117
SN   Nazi persecution and genocide of Jews and others in Europe between 1933 and 1945.
B   Genocide [1988]
R   AntiSemitism [1973]
    Concentration Camps [1973]
    Fascism [1973]
    Holocaust Survivors [1988]
    Jews [1997]
    Judaism [1967]

Holocaust Survivors [1988]
PN 448   SC 23118
B   Survivors [1994]
R   Holocaust [1988]
    Jews [1997]

Holtzman Inkblot Technique [1967]
PN 142   SC 23120
B   Projective Personality Measures [1973]
    Projective Techniques [1967]

Homatropine
SN   Term was discontinued in 1997. In 2000, the term was stripped from all records containing it, and replaced with ALKALOIDS, its postable counterpart.
Use   Alkaloids

Home Accidents [1973]
PN 50   SC 23140
B   Accidents [1967]

Home Birth
Use   Midwifery

Home Care [1985]
PN 1391   SC 23145
SN   Health and personal care provided in the home environment, usually by family members.
B   Health Care Delivery [1978]
R   Adult Day Care [1997]
    Caregiver Burden [1994]
    Caregivers [1988]
    Elder Care [1994]
    Home Care Personnel [1997]
    Home Visiting Programs [1973]
    Homebound [1988]
    Hospice [1982]
    Long Term Care [1994]
    ↓ Outpatient Treatment [1967]
    Quality of Care [1988]
    Respite Care [1988]

Home Care Personnel [1997]
PN 41   SC 23146
SN   Personnel providing personal care, nursing services, medical treatment, or followup care to patients in their homes.
UF   Home Health Aides
B   Paraprofessional Personnel [1973]
R   Caregivers [1988]
    Elder Care [1994]
    ↓ Health Personnel [1994]
    Home Care [1985]
    Home Visiting Programs [1973]
    ↓ Paramedical Personnel [1973]

Home Economics 1985
PN 59   SC 23147
- B   Curriculum 1967
- R   Household Management 1985

Home Environment 1973
PN 4180   SC 23150
- B   Social Environments 1973
- R   Empty Nest 1991
-     Living Alone 1994
-     ↓ Living Arrangements 1991
-     Single Sex Environments 2001

Home Health Aides
- Use   Home Care Personnel

Home Reared Mentally Retarded 1973
PN 50   SC 23160
- B   Mental Retardation 1967
- R   Institutionalized Mentally Retarded 1973

Home Schooling 1994
PN 32   SC 23165
- SN   Provision of compulsory education in the home.
- B   Nontraditional Education 1982
- R   ↓ Curriculum 1967
-     ↓ Education 1967
-     ↓ Teaching Methods 1967

Home Visiting Programs 1973
PN 579   SC 23170
- SN   Planned educational, health, or counseling procedures or activities that take place in the home.
- B   Community Services 1967
-     Mental Health Programs 1973
- R   Adult Day Care 1997
-     Elder Care 1994
-     Home Care 1985
-     Home Care Personnel 1997
-     Homebound 1988
-     ↓ Program Development 1991

Homebound 1988
PN 39   SC 23173
- SN   Individuals restricted to place of residence for health or disability reasons.
- R   Caregiver Burden 1994
-     Elder Care 1994
-     Health Impairments 2001
-     Home Care 1985
-     Home Visiting Programs 1973

Homeless 1988
PN 1860   SC 23174
- B   Social Issues 1991
- N   Homeless Mentally Ill 1997
- R   Deinstitutionalization 1982
-     Disadvantaged 1967
-     Poverty 1973
-     Shelters 1991
-     ↓ Social Deprivation 1973

Homeless Mentally Ill 1997
PN 191   SC 23171
- UF   Mentally Ill Homeless
- B   Homeless 1988
- R   Deinstitutionalization 1982
-     ↓ Mental Disorders 1967
-     Psychopathology 1967

Homemaking
- Use   Household Management

Homeopathic Medicine
- Use   Alternative Medicine

Homeostasis 1973
PN 308   SC 23180
- SN   Tendency of an organism to maintain a state of physiological equilibrium and the processes by which such a stable internal environment is maintained.
- UF   Autoregulation
- B   Physiology 1967
- R   Dehydration 1988
-     Instinctive Behavior 1982

Homesickness 1994
PN 37   SC 23183
- B   Emotional States 1973
- R   ↓ Experiences (Events) 1973
-     Life Experiences 1973
-     Loneliness 1973
-     Reminiscence 1985
-     Sadness 1973
-     ↓ Separation Reactions 1997

Homework 1988
PN 240   SC 23185
- SN   Assignment given to students or clients to be completed outside regular classroom period or therapeutic setting.
- R   Note Taking 1991
-     ↓ Psychotherapeutic Techniques 1967
-     Study Habits 1973

Homicide 1967
PN 2015   SC 23190
- UF   Murder
- B   Behavior Disorders 1971
- N   ↓ Genocide 1988
-     Infanticide 1978

Homing (Animal)
- Use   Animal Homing

Homographs 1973
PN 80   SC 23200
- SN   Words identical in spelling but different in derivation, pronunciation, and meaning.
- B   Vocabulary 1967
- R   Homonyms 1973
-     Orthography 1973
-     Words (Phonetic Units) 1967

Homonyms 1973
PN 81   SC 23210
- B   Semantics 1967
-     Vocabulary 1967
- R   Homographs 1973
-     Words (Phonetic Units) 1967

Homophobia
- Use   Homosexuality (Attitudes Toward)

Homosexual Liberation Movement 1973
PN 48   SC 23220
- UF   Gay Liberation Movement
- B   Social Movements 1967
- R   ↓ Activist Movements 1973

Homosexual Parents 1994
PN 100   SC 23225
- UF   Gay Parents
-     Lesbian Parents
- B   Parents 1967
- R   ↓ Family Structure 1973

Homosexual Parents — (cont'd)
- R   Lesbianism 1973
-     Male Homosexuality 1973
-     Significant Others 1991

Homosexuality 1967
PN 2205   SC 23230
- B   Psychosexual Behavior 1967
-     Sexual Orientation 1997
- N   Lesbianism 1973
-     Male Homosexuality 1973
- R   Homosexuality (Attitudes Toward) 1982
-     Transsexualism 1973
-     Transvestism 1973

Homosexuality (Attitudes Toward) 1982
PN 1244   SC 23233
- SN   Attitudes regarding sexual contact between persons of the same sex.
- UF   Heterosexism
-     Homophobia
- B   Attitudes 1967
- R   ↓ Homosexuality 1967
-     ↓ Sexual Orientation 1997
-     Stereotyped Attitudes 1967

Homovanillic Acid 1978
PN 602   SC 23235
- SN   Excretion product of dopamine metabolism.
- B   Acids 1973
-     Dopamine Metabolites 1982
- R   Dopamine 1973

Honesty 1973
PN 352   SC 23240
- UF   Frankness
- B   Personality Traits 1967
- R   Integrity 1997

Hope 1991
PN 301   SC 23247
- B   Emotional States 1973
- R   ↓ Expectations 1967
-     Hopelessness 1988
-     Optimism 1973
-     Positivism 1973
-     Trust (Social Behavior) 1967

Hopelessness 1988
PN 566   SC 23250
- SN   Feeling that one's physical, emotional, or social state is beyond improvement.
- B   Emotional States 1973
- R   Apathy 1973
-     Cynicism 1973
-     ↓ Helplessness 1997
-     Hope 1991
-     Pessimism 1973

Hormone Therapy 1994
PN 333   SC 23255
- UF   Estrogen Replacement Therapy
- B   Drug Therapy 1967
- R   ↓ Hormones 1967

Hormones 1967
PN 2790   SC 23260
- N   ↓ Adrenal Cortex Hormones 1973
-     ↓ Adrenal Medulla Hormones 1973
-     Cholecystokinin 1982
-     Corticotropin Releasing Factor 1994
-     Epinephrine 1967
-     Glucagon 1973

Hormones — (cont'd)

N ↓ Gonadotropic Hormones   1973
     Insulin   1973
     Melatonin   1973
     Parathyroid Hormone   1973
     ↓ Pituitary Hormones   1973
     ↓ Progestational Hormones   1985
     ↓ Sex Hormones   1973
     ↓ Thyroid Hormones   1973
R ↓ Anti Inflammatory Drugs   1982
     Antineoplastic Drugs   1982
     ↓ Drugs   1967
     ↓ Endocrine Glands   1973
     Fertility Enhancement   1973
     Hormone Therapy   1994
     Pheromones   1973
     Prostaglandins   1982
     ↓ Steroids   1973

Horses   1973
PN 236   **SC** 23270
B   Mammals   1973

Hospice   1982
PN 611   **SC** 23275
SN Supportive palliative care of terminally ill patients usually in their own home by a treatment team and family members; sometimes involves residential care.
B   Health Care Delivery   1978
R   Home Care   1985
     Palliative Care   1991
     Terminally Ill Patients   1973

Hospital Accreditation   1973
PN 19   **SC** 23280
SN Recognition of a hospital as maintaining standards set by a government agency.
R ↓ Hospitals   1967

Hospital Addiction Syndrome
Use Munchausen Syndrome

Hospital Administration   1978
PN 317   **SC** 23286
B   Health Care Administration   1997
R   Decentralization   1978
     ↓ Hospitals   1967
     ↓ Medical Records   1978

Hospital Admission   1973
PN 463   **SC** 23290
UF Admission (Hospital)
     Readmission (Hospital)
B   Facility Admission   1988
     Hospitalization   1967
N ↓ Psychiatric Hospital Admission   1973
R   Health Care Seeking Behavior   1997
     ↓ Hospital Discharge   1973
     ↓ Institutional Release   1978
     ↓ Psychiatric Hospitalization   1973

Hospital Attendants
Use Attendants (Institutions)

Hospital Discharge   1973
PN 512   **SC** 23303
B   Facility Discharge   1988
     Hospitalization   1967
     Institutional Release   1978
N   Psychiatric Hospital Discharge   1978
R   Client Transfer   1997
     Discharge Planning   1994

Hospital Discharge — (cont'd)
R ↓ Hospital Admission   1973
     ↓ Psychiatric Hospital Admission   1973
     Psychiatric Hospital Readmission   1973
     ↓ Psychiatric Hospitalization   1973
     Treatment Termination   1982

Hospital Environment   1982
PN 886   **SC** 23304
SN Physical, organizational, or psychological characteristics of a hospital, and their potential impact on hospital staff and patients.
B   Facility Environment   1988
R ↓ Hospitals   1967
     Intensive Care   1988

Hospital Programs   1978
PN 1512   **SC** 23306
SN Organized plans for care, including psychiatric treatment, or training in general medical hospital settings.
N ↓ Psychiatric Hospital Programs   1967
R   Intensive Care   1988
     Partial Hospitalization   1985
     ↓ Program Development   1991
     Psychiatric Units   1991

Hospital Psychiatric Units
Use Psychiatric Units

Hospital Staff
Use Medical Personnel

Hospitalization   1967
PN 1733   **SC** 23320
B   Institutionalization   1967
N ↓ Commitment (Psychiatric)   1973
     ↓ Hospital Admission   1973
     ↓ Hospital Discharge   1973
     ↓ Psychiatric Hospitalization   1973
R ↓ Health Insurance   1973
     Long Term Care   1994
     Patient Seclusion   1994
     Psychiatric Units   1991

Hospitalized Patients   1973
PN 5614   **SC** 23330
B   Patients   1967

Hospitals   1967
PN 1930   **SC** 23340
UF Infirmaries
B   Residential Care Institutions   1973
     Treatment Facilities   1973
N   Psychiatric Hospitals   1967
     Sanatoriums   1973
R ↓ Clinics   1967
     Hospital Accreditation   1973
     Hospital Administration   1978
     Hospital Environment   1982
     Intensive Care   1988
     Maximum Security Facilities   1985
     Nursing Homes   1973
     Psychiatric Clinics   1973
     Psychiatric Units   1991

Hostages   1988
PN 78   **SC** 23347
SN Use CRIME VICTIMS to access references from 1982-1987.
B   Crime Victims   1982
R   Kidnapping   1988
     Prisoners of War   1973

Hostages — (cont'd)
R   Terrorism   1982

Hostility   1967
PN 2331   **SC** 23350
UF Antagonism
     Resentment
B   Anger   1967
R   Hate   1973
     Retaliation   1991

Hot Line Services   1973
PN 420   **SC** 23360
SN Telephone information, counseling, and crisis intervention services.
UF Telephone Hot Lines
B   Crisis Intervention Services   1973
     Mental Health Programs   1973
R   Community Mental Health Centers   1973
     Information Services   1988
     Suicide Prevention Centers   1973

Household Management   1985
PN 609   **SC** 23365
SN Activities carried out for the regular maintenance of home and personal belongings.
UF Homemaking
     Housework
B   Management   1967
R ↓ Division of Labor   1988
     ↓ Family Life Education   1997
     Home Economics   1985
     Housewives   1973

Household Structure
Use Living Arrangements

Housewives   1973
PN 411   **SC** 23370
B   Wives   1973
R   Household Management   1985

Housework
Use Household Management

Housing   1973
PN 1303   **SC** 23380
B   Community Facilities   1973
N   Dormitories   1973
     Group Homes   1982
     Retirement Communities   1997
     Shelters   1991
R ↓ Living Arrangements   1991
     ↓ Social Programs   1973

Hue   1973
PN 292   **SC** 23390
SN One of the perceived dimensions of color corresponding to the wavelength of the light. Compare COLOR.
B   Chromaticity   1997
     Color   1967
R   Color Saturation   1997

Human Animal Interaction
Use Interspecies Interaction

Human Biological Rhythms   1973
PN 2328   **SC** 23400
SN Periodic variations in human physiological and psychological functions. Use BIOLOGICAL RHYTHMS to access references from 1967-1972.
UF Circadian Rhythms (Human)

Human Biological Rhythms — (cont'd)
- **UF** Diurnal Variations
- **B** Biological Rhythms 1967

Human Channel Capacity 1973
PN 1220   **SC** 23410
SN Number of signals or information volume which can be processed simultaneously.
- **UF** Cognitive Load
  - Mental Load
- **R** ↓ Attention 1967
  - Cognitive Processing Speed 1997
  - Human Information Storage 1973
  - Work Load 1982

Human Computer Interaction 1997
PN 759   **SC** 23415
SN Consider MAN MACHINE SYSTEMS to access references from 1973-1996.
- **R** ↓ Computer Peripheral Devices 1985
  - ↓ Computers 1967
  - Human Factors Engineering 1973
  - Human Machine Systems 1997
  - Human Machine Systems Design 1997
  - Keyboards 1985

Human Courtship 1973
PN 252   **SC** 23420
- **UF** Courtship (Human)
- **B** Psychosexual Behavior 1967
- **N** Social Dating 1973
- **R** Acquaintance Rape 1991
  - Human Mate Selection 1988
  - Male Female Relations 1988
  - Monogamy 1997
  - ↓ Relationship Termination 1997
  - Romance 1997

Human Development 1967
PN 2992   **SC** 23430
SN Conceptually broad term. Use a more specific term if possible.
- **UF** Maturation
- **B** Development 1967
- **N** Adolescent Development 1973
  - Adult Development 1978
  - ↓ Childhood Development 1967
- **R** Age Differences 1967
  - ↓ Aging 1991
  - ↓ Delayed Development 1973
  - Developmental Age Groups 1973
  - Developmental Disabilities 1982
  - ↓ Developmental Psychology 1973
  - ↓ Developmental Stages 1973
  - Life Expectancy 1982
  - Nature Nurture 1994
  - ↓ Physical Development 1973
  - ↓ Psychogenesis 1973

Human Factors Engineering 1973
PN 2317   **SC** 23440
- **UF** Ergonomics
- **R** Computer Assisted Design 1997
  - Engineering Psychology 1967
  - Furniture 1985
  - Human Computer Interaction 1997
  - Human Machine Systems 1997
  - ↓ Instrument Controls 1985
  - Quality Control 1988
  - ↓ Working Conditions 1973

Human Females 1973
PN 29000   **SC** 23450

Human Females — (cont'd)
SN Used for all-female populations when sex is pertinent to the focus of the study. For comparison of sexes use HUMAN SEX DIFFERENCES.
- **UF** Females (Human)
  - Girls
  - Women
- **N** Battered Females 1988
  - Daughters 1973
  - Female Criminals 1973
  - ↓ Mothers 1967
  - Sisters 1973
  - Widows 1973
  - ↓ Wives 1973
  - Working Women 1978
- **R** Female Delinquency 2001
  - ↓ Human Sex Differences 1967
  - Sex Linked Developmental Differences 1973

Human Figures Drawing 1973
PN 630   **SC** 23460
SN Projective measures or techniques designed to yield information from drawings of human figures and responses to questions about the drawings.
- **UF** Draw A Man Test
- **B** Projective Personality Measures 1973
- **R** Goodenough Harris Draw A Person Test 1967
  - Mirror Image 1991

Human Immunodeficiency Virus 1991
PN 6387   **SC** 23465
- **UF** HIV
- **B** Immunologic Disorders 1973
  - Viral Disorders 1973
- **N** Acquired Immune Deficiency Syndrome 1988
- **R** AIDS (Attitudes Toward) 1997
  - AIDS Dementia Complex 1997
  - AIDS Prevention 1994
  - HIV Testing 1997
  - ↓ Venereal Diseases 1973
  - Zidovudine 1994

Human Information Processes
Use Cognitive Processes

Human Information Storage 1973
PN 7182   **SC** 23480
SN Process of information perception, encoding, or storage, and retrieval of material from memory.
- **UF** Decoding
  - Encoding
  - Information Storage (Human)
- **R** ↓ Cognitive Processes 1967
  - Human Channel Capacity 1973
  - Information 1967
  - ↓ Lexical Access 1988
  - Lexical Decision 1988
  - ↓ Memory 1967
  - Word Recognition 1988

Human Machine Systems 1997
PN 1703   **SC** 23485
SN Systems based on the human engineering concept that views human operators and the machines they operate as functionally integrated parts of a larger goal-oriented system. In 1997, this term was created to replace the discontinued term MAN MACHINE SYSTEMS. In 2000, MAN MACHINE SYSTEMS was stripped from all records and replaced with HUMAN MACHINE SYSTEMS.
- **UF** Man Machine Systems
- **B** Systems 1967
- **R** ↓ Artificial Intelligence 1982
  - ↓ Computer Peripheral Devices 1985

Human Machine Systems — (cont'd)
- **R** Computer Searching 1991
  - Cybernetics 1967
  - Databases 1991
  - Error Analysis 1973
  - ↓ Expert Systems 1991
  - Human Computer Interaction 1997
  - Human Factors Engineering 1973
  - Human Machine Systems Design 1997
  - Systems Analysis 1973
  - Virtual Reality 1997

Human Machine Systems Design 1997
PN 1811   **SC** 23487
SN In 1997, this term was created to replace the discontinued term MAN MACHINE SYSTEMS DESIGN. In 2000, MAN MACHINE SYSTEMS DESIGN was stripped from all records and replaced with HUMAN MACHINE SYSTEMS DESIGN.
- **UF** Design (Man Machine Systems)
  - Man Machine Systems Design
- **R** Computer Assisted Design 1997
  - Human Computer Interaction 1997
  - Human Machine Systems 1997
  - ↓ Instrument Controls 1985
  - ↓ Systems 1967
  - Systems Analysis 1973

Human Males 1973
PN 9876   **SC** 23490
SN Used for all-male populations when sex is pertinent to the focus of the study. For comparison of sexes use HUMAN SEX DIFFERENCES.
- **UF** Boys
  - Males (Human)
  - Men
- **N** Brothers 1973
  - ↓ Fathers 1967
  - Husbands 1973
  - Male Criminals 1973
  - Sons 1973
  - Widowers 1973
- **R** ↓ Human Sex Differences 1967
  - Male Delinquency 2001
  - Sex Linked Developmental Differences 1973

Human Mate Selection 1988
PN 379   **SC** 23495
- **UF** Mate Selection
- **R** Assortative Mating 1991
  - Choice Behavior 1967
  - ↓ Human Courtship 1973
  - Interpersonal Attraction 1967
  - Interpersonal Compatibility 1973
  - ↓ Psychosexual Behavior 1967
  - Romance 1997

Human Migration 1973
PN 1184   **SC** 23500
SN Movement of residence from one place to another. Includes nomadism; labor or seasonal migration; patterns of rural, urban, or suburban migration; or voluntary or forced relocation.
- **UF** Migration (Human)
  - Population Shifts
- **B** Social Processes 1967
- **N** Refugees 1988
- **R** Geographical Mobility 1978
  - Gypsies 1973
  - Immigration 1973
  - Migrant Farm Workers 1973

Human Nature 1997
PN 95   **SC** 23502

Human Nature — (cont'd)
R   ↓ Behavior   1967
    ↓ Emotions   1967
    Instinctive Behavior   1982
    Mind   1991
    ↓ Personality   1967

Human Potential Movement   1982
PN   212   SC   23504
SN   Movement aimed at the enhancement of personal psychological growth. Formats used include Gestalt therapy, sensory awakening, sensory awareness, meditation, encounter groups, transactional analysis, assertiveness training, and humanistic psychology.
UF   Growth Centers
    Personal Growth Techniques
N   Assertiveness Training   1978
    Consciousness Raising Groups   1978
    ↓ Encounter Group Therapy   1973
    Gestalt Therapy   1973
    Human Relations Training   1978
    Sensitivity Training   1973
    Transactional Analysis   1973
R   ↓ Group Psychotherapy   1967
    Humanism   1973
    ↓ Humanistic Psychology   1985
    Maslow (Abraham Harold)   1991
    Meditation   1973
    Self Actualization   1973

Human Relations Training   1978
PN   480   SC   23506
SN   Techniques aimed at promoting awareness of feelings and needs of others in order to facilitate positive interpersonal interactions.
UF   T Groups
B   Human Potential Movement   1982
R   Assertiveness Training   1978
    Communication Skills Training   1982
    ↓ Encounter Group Therapy   1973
    ↓ Group Dynamics   1967
    Marathon Group Therapy   1973
    Parent Training   1978
    ↓ Personnel Training   1967
    Sensitivity Training   1973
    Social Skills Training   1982

Human Resources
Use   Personnel Management

Human Rights   1978
PN   524   SC   23508
SN   Fundamental rights of every human being to life, freedom, and equality. Often used for freedom from arbitrary governmental interference.
B   Social Issues   1991
N   ↓ Civil Rights   1978
R   ↓ Client Rights   1988
    Social Equality   1973
    ↓ Social Movements   1967
    ↓ Social Processes   1967
    Treatment Withholding   1988

Human Sex Differences   1967
PN   46377   SC   23510
UF   Gender Differences
    Sex Differences (Human)
N   Sex Linked Developmental Differences   1973
R   Androgyny   1982
    ↓ Human Females   1973
    ↓ Human Males   1973
    Sex   1967
    Sex Recognition   1997

Human Sex Differences — (cont'd)
R   Single Sex Environments   2001

Humanism   1973
PN   683   SC   23520
SN   Philosophy that asserts an individual's capacity for self-realization through reason and often rejects the supernatural.
B   Philosophies   1967
R   ↓ Human Potential Movement   1982
    ↓ Humanistic Psychology   1985

Humanistic Education
Use   Affective Education

Humanistic Psychology   1985
PN   533   SC   23527
SN   School of psychology emphasizing a holistic approach including self-actualization, creativity, and free choice.
B   Psychology   1967
N   Transpersonal Psychology   1988
R   Client Centered Therapy   1967
    ↓ Human Potential Movement   1982
    Humanism   1973
    Maslow (Abraham Harold)   1991
    Neurolinguistic Programming   2001
    Rogers (Carl)   1991
    Self Psychology   1988

Humor   1967
PN   1679   SC   23540
N   Cartoons (Humor)   1973
    Jokes   1973
R   Laughter   1978

Hunger   1967
PN   505   SC   23560
SN   Need or desire for food. May also be defined operationally in experimental settings as the duration of food deprivation or the organism's percentage of normal body weight following food deprivation. Compare APPETITE.
B   Appetite   1973
    Motivation   1967
R   Animal Feeding Behavior   1973
    Food Deprivation   1967
    Starvation   1973

Huntingtons Chorea
SN   Term was discontinued in 1997. In 2000, the term was stripped from all records containing it and replaced with HUNTINGTONS DISEASE, its postable counterpart.
Use   Huntingtons Disease

Huntingtons Disease   1973
PN   773   SC   23570
SN   In 1997, this term replaced the discontinued term HUNTINGTONS CHOREA. In 2000, HUNTINGTONS CHOREA was stripped from all records and replaced with HUNTINGTONS DISEASE.
UF   Huntingtons Chorea
B   Chorea   1973
    Genetic Disorders   1973

Husbands   1973
PN   1282   SC   23590
B   Human Males   1973
    Spouses   1973

Hybrids (Biology)   1973
PN   91   SC   23600

Hybrids (Biology) — (cont'd)
R   ↓ Genetics   1967

Hydralazine   1973
PN   8   SC   23620
B   Antihypertensive Drugs   1973
    Sympatholytic Drugs   1973

Hydrocephaly   1973
PN   270   SC   23630
B   Brain Disorders   1967
R   ↓ Congenital Disorders   1973
    ↓ Convulsions   1967
    ↓ Infectious Disorders   1973
    ↓ Mental Retardation   1967
    ↓ Neonatal Disorders   1973

Hydrocortisone   1973
PN   2157   SC   23640
UF   Cortisol
B   Adrenal Cortex Hormones   1973
    Corticosteroids   1973
R   ↓ Anti Inflammatory Drugs   1982

Hydrogen   1973
PN   12   SC   23650

Hydroxydopamine (6-)   1978
PN   637   SC   23656
UF   Oxidopamine
B   Adrenergic Blocking Drugs   1973

Hydroxyindoleacetic Acid (5-)   1985
PN   436   SC   23658
SN   Major metabolic product of serotonin.
B   Acids   1973
    Serotonin Metabolites   1978

Hydroxylamine   1973
PN   1   SC   23660
B   Amines   1973

Hydroxylase Inhibitors   1985
PN   24   SC   23665
B   Enzyme Inhibitors   1985
R   Hydroxylases   1973

Hydroxylases   1973
PN   274   SC   23670
B   Enzymes   1973
R   ↓ Esterases   1973
    Hydroxylase Inhibitors   1985
    Phosphatases   1973

Hydroxytryptamine (5-)
Use   Serotonin

Hydroxytryptophan (5-)   1991
PN   83   SC   23685
B   Tryptophan   1973

Hydroxyzine   1973
PN   26   SC   23690
B   Minor Tranquilizers   1973
R   ↓ Antihistaminic Drugs   1973

Hygiene   1994
PN   69   SC   23700
SN   Use HEALTH to access references from 1973-1993.
R   Activities of Daily Living   1991
    Epidemics   2001

Hygiene — (cont'd)
R ↓ Health 1973
     Health Behavior 1982
     Self Care Skills 1978

Hyoscine
Use Scopolamine

Hyoscyamine (dl-)
Use Atropine

Hyperactivity
Use Hyperkinesis

Hyperalgesia
Use Somatosensory Disorders

Hypercholesterolemia
Use Metabolism Disorders

Hyperesthesia
Use Somatosensory Disorders

Hyperglycemia 1985
PN 54   SC 23745
B Metabolism Disorders 1973
     Symptoms 1967

Hyperkinesis 1973
PN 5511   SC 23760
SN Excessive and usually inappropriate motor activity accompanied by poor attention span and restlessness. Consider also ATTENTION DEFICIT DISORDER.
UF Hyperactivity
B Nervous System Disorders 1967
     Symptoms 1967
R Ataxia 1973
     Attention Deficit Disorder with Hyperactivity 2001
     Bradykinesia 2001
     Minimal Brain Disorders 1973
     ↓ Neuromuscular Disorders 1973
     Oppositional Defiant Disorder 1997
     Restlessness 1973

Hypermedia 1997
PN 110   SC 23780
SN Computerized multimedia that contain images, video clips, and sounds in addition to or instead of text, and include highlighted elements that, when selected by the user, instruct the computer program to retrieve one or more of the computerized media.
B Computer Applications 1973
R ↓ Computer Software 1967
     Hypertext 1997

Hyperparathyroidism
Use Parathyroid Disorders

Hyperphagia 1973
PN 301   SC 23800
UF Polyphagia
B Eating Disorders 1997
     Symptoms 1967
R Kleine Levin Syndrome 2001
     Obesity 1973
     ↓ Somatoform Disorders 2001

Hypersensitivity (Immunologic)
Use Immunologic Disorders

Hypersexuality 1973
PN 69   SC 23820
UF Nymphomania
B Psychosexual Behavior 1967
R Erotomania 1997
     Promiscuity 1973
     Sex Drive 1973
     Sexual Addiction 1997

Hypersomnia 1994
PN 36   SC 23825
SN Excessive sleepiness.
B Sleep Disorders 1973
R Fatigue 1967
     Kleine Levin Syndrome 2001
     Narcolepsy 1973
     ↓ Symptoms 1967

Hypertension 1973
PN 2003   SC 23830
B Blood Pressure Disorders 1973
     Cardiovascular Disorders 1967
N Essential Hypertension 1973
R ↓ Antihypertensive Drugs 1973
     ↓ Cerebrovascular Disorders 1973

Hypertext 1997
PN 75   SC 23835
SN Computer-readable text that contains highlighted words or phrases that when selected by the user, instruct the computer program to retrieve one or more similar documents.
B Computer Applications 1973
R ↓ Computer Software 1967
     Hypermedia 1997

Hyperthermia 1973
PN 270   SC 23840
UF Fever
B Symptoms 1967
R Delirium 1973
     Thermoregulation (Body) 1973

Hyperthyroidism 1973
PN 128   SC 23850
B Thyroid Disorders 1973
R Goiters 1973
     Tachycardia 1973
     Thyrotoxicosis 1973
     ↓ Underweight 1973

Hyperventilation 1973
PN 276   SC 23860
B Respiratory Distress 1973
     Respiratory Tract Disorders 1973
     Symptoms 1967
R ↓ Somatoform Disorders 2001

Hypesthesia
Use Somatosensory Disorders

Hypnagogic Hallucinations 1973
PN 35   SC 23870
SN False sensory perceptions without actual appropriate stimuli, occurring while falling asleep.
B Hallucinations 1967
R ↓ Sleep Disorders 1973

Hypnoanalysis
Use Hypnotherapy

Hypnosis 1967
PN 3651   SC 23890

Hypnosis — (cont'd)
SN Trance-like state induced by effective suggestion and characterized by increased suggestibility to the hypnotist. For hypnosis used in treatment, use HYPNOTHERAPY.
B Consciousness Disturbances 1973
N Age Regression (Hypnotic) 1988
     Autohypnosis 1973
R False Memory 1997
     ↓ Hypnotherapy 1973
     Posthypnotic Suggestions 1994

Hypnotherapists 1973
PN 47   SC 23900
SN Persons conducting treatment by means of hypnosis.
B Hypnotists 1973
     Psychotherapists 1973
R Clinical Psychologists 1973
     Psychiatrists 1967
     Psychoanalysts 1973

Hypnotherapy 1973
PN 2697   SC 23910
SN Use of hypnosis in treatment.
UF Hypnoanalysis
B Psychotherapy 1967
N Age Regression (Hypnotic) 1988
R ↓ Alternative Medicine 1997
     False Memory 1997
     Guided Imagery 2001
     ↓ Hypnosis 1967
     Posthypnotic Suggestions 1994
     Progressive Relaxation Therapy 1978
     ↓ Psychoanalysis 1967
     ↓ Relaxation Therapy 1978

Hypnotic Drugs 1973
PN 738   SC 23920
SN In 1973, this term replaced the discontinued term CHLORALOSE. In 2000, CHLORALOSE was stripped from all records and replaced with HYPNOTIC DRUGS.
UF Chloralose
     Sleep Inducing Drugs
B Drugs 1967
N Amobarbital 1973
     Apomorphine 1973
     Barbital 1973
     Chloral Hydrate 1973
     Codeine 1973
     Flurazepam 1982
     Glutethimide 1973
     Hexobarbital 1973
     Meprobamate 1973
     Methaqualone 1973
     Nitrazepam 1978
     Pentobarbital 1973
     Phenobarbital 1973
     Secobarbital 1973
     Thalidomide 1973
     Thiopental 1973
     Triazolam 1988
R ↓ Analgesic Drugs 1973
     ↓ Anesthetic Drugs 1973
     ↓ Anticonvulsive Drugs 1973
     ↓ Antiemetic Drugs 1973
     ↓ Antihistaminic Drugs 1973
     ↓ Antihypertensive Drugs 1973
     ↓ Barbiturates 1967
     ↓ Benzodiazepines 1973
     ↓ CNS Depressant Drugs 1973
     ↓ Narcotic Drugs 1973
     ↓ Sedatives 1973

Hypnotic Susceptibility 1973
PN 1495   SC 23930
SN Personal characteristic or state of being receptive to hypnosis.
UF Susceptibility (Hypnotic)
B Personality Traits 1967
R Openness to Experience 1997
    Posthypnotic Suggestions 1994

Hypnotists 1973
PN 31   SC 23940
SN Persons conducting scientific experiments by means of hypnosis.
B Personnel 1967
N Hypnotherapists 1973

Hypoactive Sexual Desire Disorder
Use Inhibited Sexual Desire

Hypochondriasis 1973
PN 584   SC 23950
B Somatoform Disorders 2001
R ↓ Anxiety Disorders 1997
    ↓ Conversion Disorder 2001
    Somatization 1994
    Somatoform Pain Disorder 1997

Hypogastric Plexus
Use Autonomic Ganglia

Hypoglossal Nerve
Use Cranial Nerves

Hypoglycemia 1973
PN 236   SC 23980
B Metabolism Disorders 1973
    Symptoms 1967

Hypogonadism 1973
PN 48   SC 24000
B Endocrine Sexual Disorders 1973
N Klinefelters Syndrome 1973
    Turners Syndrome 1973
R ↓ Gynecological Disorders 1973
    Hypopituitarism 1973
    ↓ Male Genital Disorders 1973
    Sterility 1973

Hypokinesia
Use Bradykinesia

Hypomania 1973
PN 198   SC 24010
B Mania 1967
R Cyclothymic Personality 1973

Hyponatremia 1997
PN 49   SC 24015
SN Abnormally low blood sodium level.
B Metabolism Disorders 1973
R Polydipsia 1982
    ↓ Sodium 1973
    ↓ Toxic Disorders 1973

Hypoparathyroidism
Use Parathyroid Disorders

Hypophysectomy 1973
PN 120   SC 24030
UF Pituitary Gland Surgery
B Endocrine Gland Surgery 1973

Hypophysis Disorders
Use Pituitary Disorders

Hypopituitarism 1973
PN 67   SC 24050
UF Dwarfism (Pituitary)
    Pituitary Dwarfism
B Pituitary Disorders 1973
R ↓ Genetic Disorders 1973
    ↓ Hypogonadism 1973

Hypotension 1973
PN 119   SC 24060
B Blood Pressure Disorders 1973

Hypothalamo Hypophyseal System 1973
PN 409   SC 24070
B Hypothalamus 1967
    Pituitary Gland 1973
R Hypothalamo Pituitary Adrenal System 1997
    ↓ Pituitary Hormones 1973

Hypothalamo Pituitary Adrenal
    System 1997
PN 292   SC 24075
B Adrenal Glands 1973
    Hypothalamus 1967
    Pituitary Gland 1973
R Hypothalamo Hypophyseal System 1973

Hypothalamus 1967
PN 4272   SC 24080
UF Mammillary Bodies (Hypothalamic)
B Diencephalon 1973
N Hypothalamo Hypophyseal System 1973
    Hypothalamo Pituitary Adrenal System 1997
    Preoptic Area 1994
R Medial Forebrain Bundle 1982

Hypothalamus Lesions 1973
PN 891   SC 24090
SN Not defined prior to 1982. From 1982, limited to experimentally induced lesions and used primarily for animal populations.
B Brain Lesions 1967

Hypothermia 1973
PN 446   SC 24100
B Symptoms 1967
R ↓ Body Temperature 1973
    ↓ Central Nervous System Disorders 1973
    ↓ Endocrine Disorders 1973
    Thermoregulation (Body) 1973

Hypothesis Testing 1973
PN 920   SC 24110
SN Application of statistical tests to determine whether a research hypothesis should be accepted or rejected. From 1982, limited to discussions of statistical procedures. Use HYPOTHESIS TESTING or other appropriate terms to access references to COGNITIVE HYPOTHESIS TESTING prior to 1982.
B Experimental Design 1967
N Null Hypothesis Testing 1973
R Confidence Limits (Statistics) 1973
    Predictability (Measurement) 1973
    ↓ Prediction Errors 1973
    ↓ Probability 1961
    ↓ Statistical Analysis 1967
    Statistical Power 1991
    Statistical Significance 1973
    ↓ Theories 1967

Hypothesis Testing — (cont'd)
R Theory Formulation 1973
    Theory Verification 1973

Hypothesis Testing (Cognitive)
Use Cognitive Hypothesis Testing

Hypothyroidism 1973
PN 233   SC 24120
UF Myxedema
B Thyroid Disorders 1973
R Goiters 1973
    ↓ Infertility 1973
    ↓ Metabolism Disorders 1973
    Thyrotropin 1973
    Thyroxine 1973

Hypoxia
Use Anoxia

Hysterectomy 1973
PN 218   SC 24150
B Sterilization (Sex) 1973
    Surgery 1971
R Ovariectomy 1973

Hysteria 1967
PN 923   SC 24160
B Mental Disorders 1967
N Mass Hysteria 1973
R Catalepsy 1973
    ↓ Conversion Disorder 2001
    Histrionic Personality Disorder 1991
    Suggestibility 1967

Hysterical Blindness
Use Hysterical Vision Disturbances

Hysterical Neurosis (Conversion)
Use Conversion Disorder

Hysterical Neurosis (Dissociation)
Use Dissociative Disorders

Hysterical Paralysis 1973
PN 26   SC 24220
UF Paralysis (Hysterical)
B Conversion Disorder 2001

Hysterical Personality
SN In 2000, the term was discontinued, and all records containing it were stripped of the term and replaced with HISTRIONIC PERSONALITY DISORDER, its postable counterpart.
Use Histrionic Personality Disorder

Hysterical Vision Disturbances 1973
PN 24   SC 24240
UF Hysterical Blindness
    Vision Disturbances (Hysterical)
B Conversion Disorder 2001
R ↓ Eye Disorders 1973

Iatrogenic Effects
Use Side Effects (Treatment)

Ibotenic Acid 1991
PN 68   SC 24245
B Insecticides 1973
    Neurotoxins 1982
N Muscimol 1994

ICD
  Use International Classification of Diseases

Iconic Memory [1985]
PN 87   SC 24248
SN Brief sensory memory, usually lasting only fractions of a second.
  B Short Term Memory [1967]

Id [1973]
PN 78   SC 24250
  B Psychoanalytic Personality Factors [1973]
  R Unconscious (Personality Factor) [1967]

Ideal Self
  Use Self Concept

Idealism [1973]
PN 146   SC 24260
  B Philosophies [1967]
  R Determinism [1997]

Ideation [1973]
PN 304   SC 24270
SN Process of idea or image formation.
  B Cognitive Processes [1967]
  N Imagination [1967]
     Suicidal Ideation [1991]
  R ↓ Fantasy [1997]

Identical Twins
  Use Monozygotic Twins

Identification (Defense Mechanism) [1973]
PN 783   SC 24290
  B Defense Mechanisms [1967]
  R Introjection [1973]
     Projective Identification [1994]

Identity (Personal)
  Use Self Concept

Identity (Professional)
  Use Professional Identity

Identity Crisis [1973]
PN 302   SC 24320
  B Crises [1971]
     Emotional Adjustment [1973]
  R ↓ Personality Development [1967]
     ↓ Self Concept [1967]
     ↓ Stress [1967]

Idiocy (Amaurotic Familial)
  Use Amaurotic Familial Idiocy

Idiot Savants
SN In 2000, the term was discontinued, and all records containing it were stripped of the term and replaced with SAVANTS, its postable counterpart.
  Use Savants

Ileum
  Use Intestines

Illegitimate Children [1973]
PN 43   SC 24380
  B Family Members [1973]

Illinois Test of Psycholinguistic Abilities [2001]
PN 169   SC 24391

Illinois Test of Psycholinguistic Abilities — (cont'd)
SN In 2000, the truncated term ILLINOIS TEST PSYCHOLINGUIST ABIL (which was used from 1973-2000) was deleted, removed from all records containing it, and mapped to its expanded form ILLINOIS TEST OF PSYCHOLINGUISTIC ABILITIES.
  B Intelligence Measures [1967]

Illiteracy
  Use Literacy

Illness (Physical)
  Use Physical Disorders

Illness Behavior [1982]
PN 1392   SC 24415
SN Adaptive or nonadaptive behaviors exhibited by an individual during the course of an illness or dysfunction.
  B Behavior [1967]
     Client Characteristics [1973]
  R Anosognosia [1994]
     Coping Behavior [1967]
     Coronary Prone Behavior [1982]
     ↓ Disorders [1967]
     ↓ Physical Disorders [1997]
     ↓ Physical Illness (Attitudes Toward) [1985]
     Recovery (Disorders) [1973]
     Somatization [1994]
     ↓ Somatoform Disorders [2001]
     Treatment Compliance [1982]

Illumination [1967]
PN 4498   SC 24420
SN Visible portion of the electromagnetic radiation spectrum but may include ultraviolet and infrared light. May also refer more generally to ambient light. Compare LUMINANCE.
  UF Light
     Photic Threshold
  B Visual Stimulation [1973]
  N Photopic Stimulation [1973]
     Scotopic Stimulation [1973]
  R ↓ Brightness Perception [1973]
     Light Adaptation [1982]
     ↓ Light Refraction [1982]
     Luminance [1982]

Illumination Therapy
  Use Phototherapy

Illusion (Autokinetic)
  Use Autokinetic Illusion

Illusions (Perception) [1967]
PN 2658   SC 24440
SN Misperception or alteration of reality in subjective perception.
  UF Optical Illusions
  B Perception [1967]
  N Mueller Lyer Illusion [1988]
     ↓ Perceptual Aftereffect [1967]
     Spatial Distortion [1973]
  R ↓ Perceptual Distortion [1982]
     ↓ Perceptual Disturbances [1973]

Image (Retinal)
  Use Retinal Image

Imagery [1967]
PN 6296   SC 24470

Imagery — (cont'd)
  UF Visualization
  B Abstraction [1967]
  N Conceptual Imagery [1973]
     Spatial Imagery [1982]
  R Archetypes [1991]
     Guided Imagery [2001]
     Imagination [1967]

Imagery (Conceptual)
  Use Conceptual Imagery

Imagination [1967]
PN 2110   SC 24490
SN Process of forming mental images of objects, qualities, situations, or relationships, which are not immediately apparent to the senses.
  B Cognitive Processes [1967]
     Ideation [1973]
  R Conceptual Imagery [1973]
     ↓ Fantasy [1997]
     ↓ Imagery [1967]
     Magical Thinking [1973]
     Vicarious Experiences [1973]

Imaginativeness
  Use Openness to Experience

Imipramine [1973]
PN 1849   SC 24520
  UF Tofranil
  B Amines [1973]
     Tricyclic Antidepressant Drugs [1997]

Imitation (Learning) [1967]
PN 3600   SC 24530
SN Mimicking by human or animal subjects to learn a model's behavior or responses.
  UF Modeling Behavior
  B Social Learning [1973]
  R Observational Learning [1973]
     Role Models [1982]

Immaturity (Emotional)
  Use Emotional Immaturity

Immersion Programs
  Use Foreign Language Education

Immigrants
  Use Immigration

Immigration [1973]
PN 2782   SC 24560
SN Permanent resettlement in a country other than the country of one's origin.
  UF Immigrants
  B Social Processes [1967]
  R Citizenship [1973]
     ↓ Foreign Nationals [1985]
     ↓ Human Migration [1973]
     Refugees [1988]

Immunization [1973]
PN 250   SC 24570
  UF Vaccination
  B Physical Treatment Methods [1973]
  R Antibodies [1973]

Immunogens
  Use Antigens

Immunoglobulins [1973]
PN 246   SC 24580
- B   Blood Proteins [1973]
-     Globulins [1973]
- N   Gamma Globulin [1973]
- R   Antibodies [1973]
-     Antigens [1982]
-     ↓ Immunologic Disorders [1973]
-     Immunoreactivity [1994]
-     Interferons [1994]

Immunologic Disorders [1973]
PN 472   SC 24590
- UF   Autoimmune Disorders
-     Hypersensitivity (Immunologic)
- B   Physical Disorders [1997]
- N   ↓ Allergic Disorders [1973]
-     Anaphylactic Shock [1973]
-     ↓ Human Immunodeficiency Virus [1991]
-     Rh Incompatibility [1973]
- R   Asthma [1967]
-     ↓ Immunoglobulins [1973]

Immunology [1973]
PN 1915   SC 24600
SN   Medical science dealing with the study of immunity. Used for the scientific discipline or the immunological processes themselves.
- UF   Immunopathology
- B   Medical Sciences [1967]
- N   Psychoneuroimmunology [1991]
- R   Immunoreactivity [1994]

Immunopathology
Use   Immunology

Immunoreactivity [1994]
PN 794   SC 24613
SN   Use IMMUNOLOGY to access references from 1973-1993.
- R   ↓ Immunoglobulins [1973]
-     ↓ Immunology [1973]
-     Interleukins [1994]

Impaired Professionals [1985]
PN 277   SC 24615
SN   Professional personnel who are physically or psychologically disordered to the extent that such disorders interfere with the performance of professional duties or conflict with professional standards. Does not include handicaps that do not interfere with professional performance.
- R   Disabled Personnel [1997]
-     ↓ Medical Personnel [1967]
-     ↓ Mental Health Personnel [1967]
-     Personal Therapy [1991]
-     Professional Ethics [1973]
-     Professional Liability [1985]
-     ↓ Professional Personnel [1978]
-     ↓ Professional Standards [1973]

Implosive Therapy [1973]
PN 384   SC 24620
SN   Behavioral therapy involving flooding the client with anxiety through intense or prolonged real-life or imagined exposure to feared objects or situations, thereby demonstrating that they cause no harm. The aim is gradual extinction of anxiety or phobic responses.
- UF   Flooding Therapy
- B   Behavior Therapy [1967]
-     Exposure Therapy [1997]

Impotence [1973]
PN 489   SC 24630
- B   Sexual Function Disturbances [1973]
- R   Erection (Penis) [1973]
-     Frigidity [1973]
-     ↓ Male Orgasm [1973]
-     ↓ Orgasm [1973]
-     Premature Ejaculation [1973]

Impression Formation [1978]
PN 1394   SC 24634
SN   Process by which an individual transforms various perceptions and observations about another person or group into an overall impression or set of attitudes toward or about that person or group.
- B   Social Perception [1967]
- R   ↓ Attitudes [1967]
-     Attribution [1973]
-     Impression Management [1978]

Impression Management [1978]
PN 733   SC 24636
SN   Techniques of image cultivation or impression formation designed to obtain good evaluations of one's self and to win approval from others. Used for both individuals and groups.
- UF   Ingratiation
- R   Impression Formation [1978]
-     Self Monitoring (Personality) [1985]
-     ↓ Social Behavior [1967]
-     ↓ Social Perception [1967]
-     Uncertainty [1991]

Imprinting [1967]
PN 442   SC 24640
SN   Rapid learning process that takes place during early critical periods of development in social animals. Establishes the basis for patterns of social behavior. Used for both human and animal populations.
- B   Animal Ethology [1967]
-     Social Learning [1973]
- R   Critical Period [1988]
-     Species Recognition [1985]

Impulse Control Disorders [1997]
PN 61   SC 24645
SN   Mental disorders characterized by an intense need to gratify one's immediate desires and failure to resist the impulse or temptation.
- B   Mental Disorders [1967]
- N   Explosive Disorder [2001]
- R   ↓ Antisocial Behavior [1971]
-     Conduct Disorder [1991]
-     Delay of Gratification [1978]
-     Impulsiveness [1973]
-     Kleptomania [1973]
-     ↓ Paraphilias [1988]
-     Pathological Gambling [1988]
-     Pyromania [1973]
-     Self Control [1973]

Impulsiveness [1973]
PN 2076   SC 24650
- B   Cognitive Style [1967]
- R   ↓ Attention Deficit Disorder [1985]
-     Attention Deficit Disorder with Hyperactivity [2001]
-     Conceptual Tempo [1985]
-     ↓ Impulse Control Disorders [1997]
-     Kleptomania [1973]
-     Pathological Gambling [1988]
-     Pyromania [1973]
-     Reflectiveness [1997]

In Vitro Fertilization
Use   Reproductive Technology

Inadequate Personality [1973]
PN 4   SC 24660
SN   Inadequate responses to physical, social, and emotional demands; general ineptness and instability, despite absence of actual physical or mental deficit.
- B   Personality [1967]

Incarceration [1973]
PN 916   SC 24670
- B   Institutionalization [1967]
-     Law Enforcement [1978]
- R   ↓ Correctional Institutions [1973]
-     Institution Visitation [1973]
-     ↓ Institutional Release [1978]

Incentives [1967]
PN 1154   SC 24680
SN   Events or objects which increase or induce drives or determination. Popularly described as one's expectation of reward. May be used for human or animal populations. Compare REWARDS and REINFORCEMENT.
- B   Motivation [1967]
- N   Educational Incentives [1973]
-     Monetary Incentives [1973]
- R   ↓ Goals [1967]
-     ↓ Needs [1967]
-     ↓ Rewards [1967]
-     Temptation [1973]

Incest [1973]
PN 1895   SC 24690
- B   Paraphilias [1988]
-     Sexual Abuse [1988]
-     Sexual Intercourse (Human) [1973]
- R   Pedophilia [1973]
-     ↓ Perpetrators [1988]
-     ↓ Sex Offenses [1982]

Incidental Learning [1967]
PN 817   SC 24700
SN   Learning which takes place without the intent to learn or in the absence of formal instructions. From 1982, limited to human populations. Use LATENT LEARNING for animal populations.
- B   Learning [1967]
- N   Latent Learning [1973]

Income (Economic) [1973]
PN 576   SC 24710
SN   Monetary gain (such as wages, interest, dividends, profits) received by individuals or nations within a given period for labor or services rendered or from capital resources.
- R   Budgets [1997]
-     ↓ Income Level [1973]
-     Poverty [1973]
-     Salaries [1973]
-     ↓ Socioeconomic Status [1967]
-     Taxation [1985]

Income Level [1973]
PN 1144   SC 24720
SN   Total amount of monetary gain received within a given period that is associated with socioeconomic status.
- B   Socioeconomic Status [1967]
- N   Lower Income Level [1973]
-     Middle Income Level [1973]
-     Upper Income Level [1973]

Income Level — (cont'd)
R   Income (Economic) [1973]
    Salaries [1973]
    ↓ Social Class [1967]

Incompatibility (Rh)
   Use   Rh Incompatibility

Incomplete Man Test [1973]
PN   2   SC   24750
B   Projective Techniques [1967]

Incontinence (Fecal)
   Use   Fecal Incontinence

Incontinence (Urinary)
   Use   Urinary Incontinence

Incorporation (Psychological)
   Use   Internalization

Incubators (Apparatus) [1973]
PN   6   SC   24780
B   Apparatus [1967]

Independence (Personality) [1973]
PN   1988   SC   24790
UF   Autonomy (Personality)
B   Personality Traits [1967]
R   Empowerment [1991]
    Internal External Locus of Control [1967]
    ↓ Resistance [1997]
    Self Determination [1994]

Independent Living
   Use   Self Care Skills

Independent Living Programs [1991]
PN   176   SC   24798
SN   Community-based programs or services to assist disabled individuals to perform all or most of their daily functions, thus increasing self sufficiency and self determination and eliminating a need to depend on others.
R   Activities of Daily Living [1991]
    ↓ Community Services [1967]
    Habilitation [1991]
    ↓ Mainstreaming [1991]
    ↓ Program Development [1991]
    ↓ Rehabilitation [1967]
    Self Care Skills [1978]
    Supported Employment [1994]

Independent Party (Political)
   Use   Political Parties

Independent Study
   Use   Individualized Instruction

Independent Variables [1973]
PN   107   SC   24810
SN   Statistical or experimental parameters that are manipulated in an attempt to analyze their relative effect on specified dependent variables.
B   Statistical Variables [1973]

Indians (American)
   Use   American Indians

Indifference
   Use   Apathy

Indigenous Populations [2001]
PN   0   SC   24845
UF   Aboriginal Populations
    Maori
    Natives
B   Racial and Ethnic Groups [2001]
N   Alaska Natives [1997]
    American Indians [1967]
    Inuit [2001]
    ↓ Pacific Islanders [2001]
R   Minority Groups [1967]

Individual Counseling
   Use   Individual Psychotherapy

Individual Differences [1967]
PN   7548   SC   24860
SN   Any specific characteristic or quantitative difference in a quality or trait that can serve to distinguish one individual from another. Used for both human and animal populations.
R   ↓ Personality [1967]
    Personality Correlates [1967]
    ↓ Personality Theory [1967]

Individual Problem Solving
   Use   Problem Solving

Individual Psychology [1973]
PN   909   SC   24880
SN   Theory and practice of Adlerian psychology, stressing the unique wholeness of the individual and viewing the striving to overcome and master obstacles as the primary motivating force.
B   Neopsychoanalytic School [1973]
R   Adler (Alfred) [1967]
    Adlerian Psychotherapy [1997]

Individual Psychotherapy [1973]
PN   1585   SC   24890
SN   Psychotherapy occurring on a one-on-one basis as compared to a group setting or environment. Use ADLERIAN PSYCHOTHERAPY to access references on Adlerian individual psychotherapy.
UF   Individual Counseling
    Individual Therapy
    Psychotherapy (Individual)
B   Psychotherapy [1967]

Individual Psychotherapy (Adlerian)
   Use   Adlerian Psychotherapy

Individual Testing [1973]
PN   99   SC   24900
B   Measurement [1967]
R   Test Administration [1973]

Individual Therapy
   Use   Individual Psychotherapy

Individualism
   Use   Individuality

Individuality [1973]
PN   1162   SC   24930
UF   Individualism
B   Personality Traits [1967]
R   Nonconformity (Personality) [1973]
    Self Determination [1994]

Individualized Instruction [1973]
PN   1975   SC   24940

Individualized Instruction — (cont'd)
SN   Instruction adapted to individual needs or instruction in which a student works alone or only with a teacher. Also, self-initiated study with or without formal academic guidance or involvement.
UF   Independent Study
    Instruction (Individualized)
    Self Directed Learning
    Self Instruction
B   Teaching Methods [1967]
R   Computer Assisted Instruction [1973]
    ↓ Continuing Education [1985]
    Cooperative Learning [1994]
    ↓ Learning [1967]
    Open Classroom Method [1973]
    Programmed Instruction [2001]
    ↓ Tutoring [1973]

Induced Abortion [1971]
PN   1125   SC   24950
UF   Abortion (Induced)
    Elective Abortion
    Therapeutic Abortion
B   Surgery [1971]
R   Abortion Laws [1973]
    ↓ Birth Control [1971]
    ↓ Family Planning [1973]
    Spontaneous Abortion [1971]

Inductive Deductive Reasoning [1973]
PN   1265   SC   24960
UF   Convergent Thinking
    Deductive Reasoning
    Syllogistic Reasoning
B   Reasoning [1967]
N   Inference [1973]
R   Divergent Thinking [1973]
    Logical Thinking [1967]
    ↓ Problem Solving [1967]

Industrial Accidents [1973]
PN   518   SC   24970
B   Accidents [1967]
R   Occupational Exposure [1988]
    Occupational Safety [1973]
    Work Related Illnesses [1994]

Industrial Arts Education
   Use   Vocational Education

Industrial Foremen [1973]
PN   59   SC   24980
UF   Foremen (Industrial)
B   Blue Collar Workers [1973]
R   ↓ Management Personnel [1973]

Industrial Personnel
   Use   Business and Industrial Personnel

Industrial Psychologists [1973]
PN   111   SC   25000
B   Business and Industrial Personnel [1967]
    Psychologists [1967]
R   Social Psychologists [1973]

Industrial Psychology [1967]
PN   1437   SC   25010
UF   Organizational Psychology
B   Applied Psychology [1973]

Industrial Safety
   Use   Occupational Safety

Industrialization 1973
PN 421   SC 25030
B   Social Processes 1967
R   ↓ Technology 1973
     Urbanization 1973

Industry
Use Business

Infant Development 1973
PN 3592   SC 25060
B   Early Childhood Development 1973
N   Neonatal Development 1973
R   ↓ Physical Development 1973
     ↓ Psychogenesis 1973

Infant Intelligence Scale 1973
PN 3   SC 25070
UF   Cattell Infant Intelligence Scale
B   Intelligence Measures 1967

Infant Vocalization 1973
PN 578   SC 25080
UF   Babbling
     Vocalization (Infant)
B   Voice 1973
R   Crying 1973

Infanticide 1978
PN 322   SC 25085
UF   Neonaticide
B   Homicide 1967

Infantile Neurosis
Use Childhood Neurosis

Infantile Paralysis
Use Poliomyelitis

Infantile Psychosis
Use Childhood Psychosis

Infantilism 1973
PN 16   SC 25120
R   ↓ Mental Disorders 1967

Infants (Animal) 1978
PN 5334   SC 25134
UF   Neonates (Animal)
B   Animals 1967

Infarctions (Myocardial)
Use Myocardial Infarctions

Infections
Use Infectious Disorders

Infectious Disorders 1973
PN 409   SC 25160
UF   Communicable Diseases
     Infections
     Neuroinfections
B   Physical Disorders 1997
N   ↓ Bacterial Disorders 1973
     Epstein Barr Viral Disorder 1994
     ↓ Parasitic Disorders 1973
     ↓ Venereal Diseases 1973
     ↓ Viral Disorders 1973
R   ↓ Arthritis 1973
     ↓ Chorea 1973
     ↓ Dermatitis 1973
     ↓ Digestive System Disorders 1973

Infectious Disorders — (cont'd)
R   Encephalitis 1973
     Encephalomyelitis 1973
     Epidemics 2001
     ↓ Hepatitis 1973
     Hydrocephaly 1973
     Jaundice 1973
     ↓ Liver Disorders 1973
     ↓ Myelitis 1973

Inference 1973
PN 2396   SC 25180
B   Inductive Deductive Reasoning 1973
R   Analogy 1991
     Attribution 1973

Inferior Colliculus 1973
PN 218   SC 25190
B   Mesencephalon 1973

Inferiority (Emotional)
Use Emotional Inferiority

Infertility 1973
PN 671   SC 25210
B   Genital Disorders 1967
N   Sterility 1973
R   ↓ Endocrine Sexual Disorders 1973
     Fertility 1988
     ↓ Gynecological Disorders 1973
     Hypothyroidism 1973
     Klinefelters Syndrome 1973
     ↓ Male Genital Disorders 1973
     ↓ Venereal Diseases 1973

Infirmaries
Use Hospitals

Inflection 1973
PN 428   SC 25230
SN   A grammatically functional change in the pitch
or loudness of the voice. Also, the syntactic change
in words to designate such factors as case, gender,
or tense.
B   Prosody 1991
R   ↓ Phonology 1973
     ↓ Speech Characteristics 1973
     ↓ Syntax 1971

Influence (Interpersonal)
Use Interpersonal Influences

Influences (Social)
Use Social Influences

Influenza 1973
PN 125   SC 25260
B   Viral Disorders 1973
R   ↓ Gastrointestinal Disorders 1973
     ↓ Nervous System Disorders 1967
     ↓ Respiratory Tract Disorders 1973

Informants 1988
PN 79   SC 25270
SN   Persons who provide information against
another person who is suspected of committing a vio-
lation.
UF   Whistleblowing
R   ↓ Abuse Reporting 1997
     ↓ Crime 1967
     Duty to Warn 2001
     Labor Management Relations 1967

Informants — (cont'd)
R   ↓ Organizational Behavior 1978
     ↓ Social Behavior 1967

Information 1967
PN 4499   SC 25360
SN   Conceptually broad term referring to a body of
knowledge. Use a more specific term if possible. Differentiate from KNOWLEDGE LEVEL which is the
amount of information acquired or received by an
individual or group.
R   ↓ Automated Information Processing 1973
     Censorship 1978
     ↓ Communication 1967
     Computer Searching 1991
     Concepts 1967
     Data Collection 1982
     ↓ Data Processing 1967
     Databases 1991
     Declarative Knowledge 1997
     Electronic Communication 2001
     Human Information Storage 1973
     Information Seeking 1973
     Information Services 1988
     ↓ Information Specialists 1988
     ↓ Information Systems 1991
     Information Theory 1967
     ↓ Knowledge Level 1978
     ↓ Libraries 1982
     Messages 1973
     Privileged Communication 1973
     Procedural Knowledge 1997

Information (Messages)
Use Messages

Information Exchange
SN   Term discontinued in 2000. From 1973-1999,
the term was used to refer to a myriad of communicative and other exchanges. Consider HUMAN COM-
PUTER INTERACTION for exchanges between
humans and computers.
Use Communication

Information Processes (Human)
Use Cognitive Processes

Information Processing (Automated)
Use Automated Information Processing

Information Processing Speed
Use Cognitive Processing Speed

Information Retrieval (Automated)
Use Automated Information Retrieval

Information Seeking 1973
PN 1300   SC 25330
R   Computer Searching 1991
     ↓ Exploratory Behavior 1967
     Information 1967
     Questioning 1982

Information Services 1988
PN 170   SC 25335
R   ↓ Automated Information Retrieval 1973
     Computer Searching 1991
     Databases 1991
     Hot Line Services 1973
     Information 1967
     ↓ Information Systems 1991
     ↓ Libraries 1982

Information Specialists 1988
PN 24   SC 25338
B   Professional Personnel 1978
N   Librarians 1988
R   Information 1967

Information Storage (Human)
Use   Human Information Storage

Information Systems 1991
PN 720   SC 25345
SN Collection, organization, and storage of data or the operational functions used to process information.
UF Management Information Systems
B   Systems 1967
N   Internet 2001
R   ↓ Automated Information Processing 1973
    ↓ Automated Information Retrieval 1973
    Automated Information Storage 1973
    ↓ Communication Systems 1973
    ↓ Computer Applications 1973
    ↓ Data Processing 1967
    Databases 1991
    Decision Support Systems 1997
    Electronic Communication 2001
    ↓ Expert Systems 1991
    Information 1967
    Information Services 1988
    Word Processing 1991

Information Theory 1967
PN 524   SC 25350
SN Branch of science which deals statistically with the transmission of information and its measurable characteristics. Used for the scientific discipline or for application of information theory to specific areas of investigation.
B   Theories 1967
R   Communication Theory 1973
    Information 1967
    ↓ Stochastic Modeling 1973

Informed Consent 1985
PN 956   SC 25363
SN Process of making rational decisions regarding one's treatment or participation in experimental procedures.
R   ↓ Civil Rights 1978
    ↓ Client Rights 1988
    Debriefing (Experimental) 1991
    Duty to Warn 2001
    Experiment Volunteers 1973
    Experimental Ethics 1978
    Guardianship 1988
    Involuntary Treatment 1994
    ↓ Legal Processes 1973
    Professional Ethics 1973
    Treatment Compliance 1982
    Treatment Refusal 1994
    Treatment Withholding 1988

Ingestion 2001
PN 2244   SC 25364
SN Oral intake of food, liquids, medicine, etc. Used for both human and animal populations. In 2000, this term was created to replace the discontinued term EATING. EATING was stripped from all records and replaced with INGESTION.
UF Eating
B   Physiology 1967
N   Coprophagia 2001
    ↓ Fluid Intake 1985
    Food Intake 1967

Ingestion — (cont'd)
R   Animal Drinking Behavior 1973
    Animal Feeding Behavior 1973
    Digestion 1973
    ↓ Drinking Behavior 1978
    ↓ Feeding Practices 1973
    Pica 1973
    Swallowing 1988

Ingratiation
Use   Impression Management

Ingroup Outgroup 1997
PN 490   SC 25366
UF Outgroup Ingroup
B   Social Groups 1973
R   Ethnic Identity 1973
    ↓ Group Dynamics 1967
    Intergroup Dynamics 1973
    Self Perception 1967
    ↓ Social Identity 1988
    ↓ Social Networks 1994
    ↓ Social Perception 1967

Inhalant Abuse 1985
PN 230   SC 25367
SN Inhalation of vapors from volatile chemical substances (such as aerosol sprays, solvents, and anesthetics) in order to produce mind-altering effects.
UF Solvent Abuse
B   Drug Abuse 1973
N   Glue Sniffing 1973
R   ↓ Solvents 1982

Inhibited Sexual Desire 1997
PN 35   SC 25370
SN Lack of sexual interest or feelings.
UF Hypoactive Sexual Desire Disorder
B   Sexual Function Disturbances 1973
R   Eroticism 1973
    Libido 1973
    Sex Drive 1973
    ↓ Sexual Arousal 1978

Inhibition (Personality) 1973
PN 722   SC 25380
B   Personality Processes 1967

Inhibition (Proactive)
Use   Proactive Inhibition

Inhibition (Retroactive)
Use   Retroactive Inhibition

Initial Teaching Alphabet 1973
PN 17   SC 25410
B   Alphabets 1973
R   ↓ Language Arts Education 1973
    ↓ Reading 1967
    Reading Education 1973
    ↓ Teaching Methods 1967

Initiation Rites 1973
PN 66   SC 25420
B   Rites of Passage 1973
R   Cosmetic Techniques 2001

Initiative 1973
PN 108   SC 25430
B   Personality Traits 1967

Injections 1973
PN 236   SC 25440
B   Drug Administration Methods 1973
N   Intramuscular Injections 1973
    Intraperitoneal Injections 1973
    Intravenous Injections 1973
    Subcutaneous Injections 1973

Injuries 1973
PN 1984   SC 25450
UF Physical Trauma
    Trauma (Physical)
N   Birth Injuries 1973
    Burns 1973
    Electrical Injuries 1973
    ↓ Head Injuries 1973
    ↓ Spinal Cord Injuries 1973
    ↓ Wounds 1973
R   ↓ Accidents 1967
    Coma 1973
    ↓ Disorders 1967
    Epidemics 2001
    Hematoma 1973
    Hemiplegia 1978
    Paraplegia 1978
    Physical Disfigurement 1978
    ↓ Physical Disorders 1997
    Quadriplegia 1985
    ↓ Safety 1967
    Shock 1967

Injuries (Birth)
Use   Birth Injuries

Inlaws 1997
PN 15   SC 25465
B   Family Members 1973
R   ↓ Parents 1967
    ↓ Spouses 1973

Inmates (Prison)
Use   Prisoners

Innate Behavior (Animal)
Use   Instinctive Behavior

Inner City
Use   Urban Environments

Inner Ear
Use   Labyrinth (Anatomy)

Inner Speech
Use   Self Talk

Innovativeness
Use   Creativity

Inquisitiveness
Use   Curiosity

Insanity
Use   Mental Disorders

Insanity Defense 1985
PN 606   SC 25525
SN Legal defense designed to invoke an exemption from criminal responsibility on the basis of a mental disorder at the time of the alleged criminal offense.
B   Legal Processes 1973
R   Court Referrals 1994
    Criminal Responsibility 1991

Insanity Defense — (cont'd)
R   Forensic Evaluation 1994
      Forensic Psychiatry 1973
      ↓ Mental Disorders 1967
      Mentally Ill Offenders 1985

Insecticides 1973
PN 191   SC 25530
SN In 1997, this term replaced the discontinued term DIELDRIN. In 2000, DIELDRIN was stripped from all records and replaced with INSECTICIDES.
UF   Dieldrin
       Pesticides
B   Hazardous Materials 1991
N   DDT (Insecticide) 1973
       ↓ Ibotenic Acid 1991
       Parathion 1973
R   ↓ Drugs 1967
       ↓ Insects 1967
       ↓ Neurotoxins 1982
       Nicotine 1973
       ↓ Poisons 1973

Insects 1967
PN 1370   SC 25540
B   Arthropoda 1973
N   Ants 1973
       Bees 1973
       Beetles 1973
       Butterflies 1973
       Cockroaches 1973
       ↓ Diptera 1973
       Grasshoppers 1973
       Larvae 1973
       Mantis 1973
       Moths 1973
       Wasps 1982
R   ↓ Insecticides 1973

Insecurity (Emotional)
Use   Emotional Security

Insensitivity (Personality)
Use   Sensitivity (Personality)

Inservice Teacher Education 1973
PN 1452   SC 25570
SN Course or program designed to provide teachers with growth in job-related competencies or skills. Usually school sponsored.
B   Inservice Training 1985
       Teacher Education 1967
R   On the Job Training 1973
       Professional Development 1982

Inservice Training 1985
PN 378   SC 25575
B   Continuing Education 1985
       Personnel Training 1967
N   Inservice Teacher Education 1973
       Mental Health Inservice Training 1973
R   On the Job Training 1973
       Professional Development 1982

Inservice Training (Mental Health)
Use   Mental Health Inservice Training

Insight 1973
PN 443   SC 25590
B   Personality Processes 1967
R   Intuition 1973
       Perceptiveness (Personality) 1973

Insight (Psychotherapeutic Process) 1973
PN 217   SC 25600
B   Psychotherapeutic Processes 1967

Insight Therapy 1973
PN 157   SC 25610
SN Psychotherapeutic method which seeks to uncover the causes of the client's conflicts through conscious awareness (i.e., insight) into unconscious dynamics of feelings, responses, and behavior.
B   Psychotherapy 1967

Insomnia 1973
PN 1212   SC 25620
UF   Sleeplessness
B   Sleep Disorders 1973
       Symptoms 1967

Instability (Emotional)
Use   Emotional Instability

Instinctive Behavior 1982
PN 1184   SC 25638
SN Stereotyped, unlearned, largely stimulus-bound, adaptive behavior limited in its expression by the inherent properties of the nervous system and genetic factors. Used for human or animal populations. In 1982, this term was created to replace the discontinued terms ANIMAL INNATE BEHAVIOR and ANIMAL INSTINCTIVE BEHAVIOR. In 2000, these terms were stripped from all records and replaced with INSTINCTIVE BEHAVIOR.
UF   Animal Innate Behavior
       Animal Instinctive Behavior
       Innate Behavior (Animal)
B   Behavior 1967
R   ↓ Animal Defensive Behavior 1982
       Animal Distress Calls 1973
       ↓ Animal Ethology 1967
       Animal Exploratory Behavior 1973
       Animal Homing 1991
       Animal Motivation 1967
       Animal Predatory Behavior 1978
       ↓ Animal Sexual Behavior 1985
       Attack Behavior 1973
       ↓ Genetics 1967
       Homeostasis 1973
       Human Nature 1997
       ↓ Motivation 1967
       Neophobia 1985
       ↓ Nervous System 1967
       ↓ Physiology 1967
       ↓ Reflexes 1971
       Self Preservation 1997
       Species Recognition 1985
       Spontaneous Alternation 1982

Institution Visitation 1973
PN 114   SC 25650
SN Visiting a patient or convict in an institution (e.g., hospital, prison, or nursing home) by someone from outside the institution (e.g., friends or family).
UF   Visitation (Institution)
R   ↓ Correctional Institutions 1973
       Incarceration 1973
       ↓ Residential Care Institutions 1973

Institutional Release 1978
PN 177   SC 25664
SN Discharge or release of an individual from any type of correctional or therapeutic residential facility.
B   Institutionalization 1967
N   ↓ Hospital Discharge 1973
R   ↓ Commitment (Psychiatric) 1973

Institutional Release — (cont'd)
R   Deinstitutionalization 1982
      Discharge Planning 1994
      ↓ Hospital Admission 1973
      Incarceration 1973
      ↓ Psychiatric Hospital Admission 1973
      ↓ Psychiatric Hospitalization 1973

Institutional Schools 1978
PN 220   SC 25666
SN Schools that are part of larger residential institutions such as hospitals or prisons.
B   Schools 1967
R   Boarding Schools 1988
       ↓ Correctional Institutions 1973
       ↓ Residential Care Institutions 1973
       ↓ Treatment Facilities 1973

Institutionalization 1967
PN 1875   SC 25670
N   ↓ Hospitalization 1967
       Incarceration 1973
       ↓ Institutional Release 1978
R   ↓ Facility Admission 1988
       ↓ Facility Discharge 1988
       Orphanages 1973

Institutionalized Mentally Retarded 1973
PN 1347   SC 25680
B   Mental Retardation 1967
R   Home Reared Mentally Retarded 1973
       ↓ Residential Care Institutions 1973

Institutions (Correctional)
Use   Correctional Institutions

Institutions (Residential Care)
Use   Residential Care Institutions

Instruction
Use   Teaching

Instruction (Computer Assisted)
Use   Computer Assisted Instruction

Instruction (Individualized)
Use   Individualized Instruction

Instruction (Programmed)
Use   Programmed Instruction

Instructional Media 1967
PN 1225   SC 25740
SN Formats or technologies for conveyance of didactic content, including print, film, computers, phonographic records and magnetic tape.
B   Teaching 1967
N   Advance Organizers 1985
       ↓ Educational Audiovisual Aids 1973
       Reading Materials 1973
       Teaching Machines 1973
       ↓ Textbooks 1978

Instructional Objectives
Use   Educational Objectives

Instructions (Experimental)
Use   Experimental Instructions

Instructors
Use   Teachers

Instrument Controls [1985]

PN 91   **SC** 25765
SN May include knobs, handles, levers, latches, dials, switches, buttons, and any other mechanism used to control the operation of machines and instruments. Consider VISUAL DISPLAYS to access references from 1973-1984.
UF Controls (Instrument)
N Flight Instrumentation [1973]
R ↓ Displays [1967]
     Human Factors Engineering [1973]
     Human Machine Systems Design [1997]
     Keyboards [1985]

Instrumental Conditioning
Use Operant Conditioning

Instrumental Learning
Use Operant Conditioning

Instrumentality [1991]

PN 97   **SC** 25785
R ↓ Motivation [1967]
     ↓ Personality Traits [1967]
     Self Efficacy [1985]

Instrumentation (Flight)
Use Flight Instrumentation

Insulin [1973]

PN 740   **SC** 25800
B Hormones [1967]
R Insulin Shock Therapy [1973]

Insulin Shock Therapy [1973]

PN 33   **SC** 25820
B Shock Therapy [1973]
R Coma [1973]
     Insulin [1973]

Insurance [1973]

PN 156   **SC** 25830
N ↓ Health Insurance [1973]
     Life Insurance [1973]
     Social Security [1988]
R Disability Evaluation [1988]
     Risk Management [1997]

Insurance Agents
Use Sales Personnel

Intake Interview [1994]

PN 117   **SC** 25845
SN Initial evaluation, assessment, or screening of clients or patients to determine needs and appropriate health, mental health, rehabilitation, or other services.
B Interviews [1967]
R ↓ Case Management [1991]
     Clinical Judgment (Not Diagnosis) [1973]
     ↓ Diagnosis [1967]
     ↓ Evaluation [1967]
     Health Service Needs [1997]
     ↓ Interview Schedules [2001]
     Needs Assessment [1985]
     ↓ Psychiatric Evaluation [1997]
     ↓ Psychodiagnostic Interview [1973]
     ↓ Screening [1982]

Integrated Services [1997]

PN 433   **SC** 25847

Integrated Services — (cont'd)

SN Collaboration and cooperation among social service, education, health, or community service providers.
UF Interagency Services
R ↓ Community Services [1967]
     ↓ Health Care Services [1978]
     Interdisciplinary Treatment Approach [1973]
     ↓ Mental Health Programs [1973]
     ↓ Mental Health Services [1978]
     Multimodal Treatment Approach [1991]
     Public Health Services [1973]
     ↓ Social Programs [1973]
     ↓ Social Services [1982]

Integration (Racial)
Use Social Integration

Integrity [1997]

PN 75   **SC** 25855
B Personality Traits [1967]
R ↓ Ethics [1967]
     Honesty [1973]
     Morality [1967]
     ↓ Values [1967]

Intellectual Development [1973]

PN 1521   **SC** 25860
SN Acquisition of factual knowledge. Consider COGNITIVE DEVELOPMENT for acquisition of reasoning, thought, and problem solving abilities.
B Cognitive Development [1973]
N ↓ Language Development [1967]
R Intelligence [1967]

Intellectual Functioning
Use Cognitive Ability

Intellectualism [1973]

PN 17   **SC** 25870
SN Doctrine which attempts to explain emotion and volition in terms of cognitive processes.
B Philosophies [1967]

Intellectualization [1973]

PN 15   **SC** 25880
SN Defense mechanism in which distressful emotional content of a painful situation is avoided by focusing on intellectual (cognitive) aspects of the situation or by engaging in abstract thinking.
B Defense Mechanisms [1967]
R Isolation (Defense Mechanism) [1973]

Intellectually Gifted
Use Gifted

Intelligence [1967]

PN 8014   **SC** 25900
SN General ability to think, reason, learn, apply knowledge, or deal effectively with the environment. Consider also INTELLIGENCE QUOTIENT.
R ↓ Ability [1967]
     ↓ Artificial Intelligence [1982]
     Cognitive Assessment [1997]
     Creativity [1967]
     Divergent Thinking [1973]
     Gifted [1967]
     ↓ Intellectual Development [1973]
     Intelligence Quotient [1967]
     Mental Age [1973]
     ↓ Reasoning [1967]
     ↓ Thinking [1967]
     Wisdom [1994]

Intelligence Age
Use Mental Age

Intelligence Measures [1967]

PN 4195   **SC** 25910
SN In 1997, this term replaced the discontinued terms HENMON NELSON TESTS OF MENTAL ABILITY, LEITER ADULT INTELLIGENCE SCALE, TEMPORAL SPATIAL CONCEPT SCALE, and VANE KINDERGARTEN TEST. In 2000, these terms were stripped from all records and replaced with INTELLIGENCE MEASURES.
UF Henmon Nelson Tests of Mental Ability
     Leiter Adult Intelligence Scale
     Temporal Spatial Concept Scale
     Tests (Intelligence)
     Vane Kindergarten Test
B Measurement [1967]
N Benton Revised Visual Retention Test [1973]
     California Test of Mental Maturity [1973]
     Columbia Mental Maturity Scale [1973]
     Culture Fair Intelligence Test [1973]
     Frostig Developmental Test of Visual Perception [2001]
     Goodenough Harris Draw A Person Test [1967]
     Hidden Figures Test [1973]
     Illinois Test of Psycholinguistic Abilities [2001]
     Infant Intelligence Scale [1973]
     Kaufman Assessment Battery for Children [2001]
     Kohs Block Design Test [1973]
     Lorge Thorndike Intelligence Test [1973]
     Lowenfeld Mosaic Test [1973]
     Miller Analogies Test [1973]
     Peabody Picture Vocabulary Test [1973]
     Porteus Maze Test [1973]
     Raven Coloured Progressive Matrices [1973]
     Raven Progressive Matrices [1978]
     Remote Associates Test [1973]
     Slosson Intelligence Test [2001]
     Stanford Binet Intelligence Scale [1967]
     Wechsler Adult Intelligence Scale [1967]
     Wechsler Bellevue Intelligence Scale [1967]
     Wechsler Intelligence Scale for Children [2001]
     Wechsler Preschool Primary Scale [1988]
R Bayley Scales of Infant Development [1994]
     Cognitive Assessment [1997]

Intelligence Quotient [1967]

PN 3699   **SC** 25920
SN Relative intelligence of an individual expressed as a score on a standardized test of intelligence. Consider also INTELLIGENCE.
B Test Scores [1967]
R Cognitive Assessment [1997]
     Intelligence [1967]
     Mental Age [1973]

Intensity (Stimulus)
Use Stimulus Intensity

Intensive Care [1988]

PN 365   **SC** 25942
R Hospital Environment [1982]
     ↓ Hospital Programs [1978]
     ↓ Hospitals [1967]

Intention [1988]

PN 2185   **SC** 25945
SN Determination to act in a certain manner.
R ↓ Goals [1967]
     ↓ Motivation [1967]
     Planned Behavior [1997]

Intentional Learning 1973
PN 314   SC 25950
SN Purposive or motivated learning.
B Learning 1967

Interaction (Interpersonal)
Use Interpersonal Interaction

Interaction (Social)
Use Social Interaction

Interaction Analysis (Statistics) 1973
PN 121   SC 25990
B Statistical Analysis 1967
R Interaction Variance 1973

Interaction Variance 1973
PN 28   SC 26000
B Variability Measurement 1973
R Interaction Analysis (Statistics) 1973

Interagency Services
Use Integrated Services

Intercourse (Sexual)
Use Sexual Intercourse (Human)

Intercultural Communication
Use Cross Cultural Communication

Interdisciplinary Research 1985
PN 471   SC 26025
SN Any research effort coordinated or executed by members of two or more specialties, disciplines, or theoretical orientations.
UF Cross Disciplinary Research
Multidisciplinary Research
B Experimentation 1967
R Interdisciplinary Treatment Approach 1973

Interdisciplinary Treatment Approach 1973
PN 3008   SC 26030
SN Combination of two or more disciplines in the prevention, diagnosis, treatment, or rehabilitation of mental or physical disorders.
UF Multidisciplinary Treatment Approach
B Treatment 1967
R Biopsychosocial Approach 1991
Eclectic Psychotherapy 1994
↓ Health Care Psychology 1985
Integrated Services 1997
Interdisciplinary Research 1985
Multimodal Treatment Approach 1991
Partial Hospitalization 1985
↓ Teams 1988

Interest Inventories 1973
PN 483   SC 26040
B Inventories 1967

Interest Patterns
SN Term was discontinued in 1982. In 2000, the term was stripped from all records containing it and replaced with INTERESTS, its postable counterpart.
Use Interests

Interests 1967
PN 1309   SC 26080
SN In 1982, this term replaced the discontinued term INTEREST PATTERNS. In 2000, INTEREST PATTERNS was stripped from all records and replaced with INTERESTS.
UF Interest Patterns

Interests — (cont'd)
N Occupational Interests 1967
R Daily Activities 1994
Hobbies 1988

Interethnic Communication
Use Cross Cultural Communication

Interethnic Family 1988
PN 22   SC 26070
B Family 1967
R Interracial Adoption 1994
Interracial Family 1988
Racial and Ethnic Differences 1982

Interethnic Marriage
Use Exogamous Marriage

Interfaith Marriage 1973
PN 43   SC 26090
B Exogamous Marriage 1973

Interference (Learning) 1967
PN 3280   SC 26100
SN Inhibition of learning due to negative transfer effects of competing memories, thoughts, or learned behavior. Effects include slower learning and poorer memory.
B Learning 1967
N ↓ Latent Inhibition 1997
Proactive Inhibition 1973
Retroactive Inhibition 1973
R Forgetting 1973
↓ Memory 1967
↓ Retention 1967
Stroop Effect 1988

Interferons 1994
PN 86   SC 26103
B Proteins 1973
R Antineoplastic Drugs 1982
↓ Immunoglobulins 1973

Intergenerational Relations 1988
PN 1204   SC 26105
SN Contact between related or nonrelated persons of different generational age groups.
R Empty Nest 1991
↓ Family Relations 1967
Generation Gap 1973
Generativity 2001
Transgenerational Patterns 1991

Intergenerational Transmission
Use Transgenerational Patterns

Intergroup Dynamics 1973
PN 1143   SC 26110
B Group Dynamics 1967
R Boundaries (Psychological) 1997
Ingroup Outgroup 1997

Interhemispheric Interaction 1985
PN 716   SC 26112
SN Any neurophysiological, electrophysiological, or neurochemical exchange occurring between the cerebral hemispheres.
UF Interhemispheric Transfer
R ↓ Cerebral Cortex 1967
↓ Cerebral Dominance 1973
Corpus Callosum 1973
Left Brain 1991

Interhemispheric Interaction — (cont'd)
R Right Brain 1991

Interhemispheric Transfer
Use Interhemispheric Interaction

Interior Design 1982
PN 230   SC 26115
SN Practice or resultant product of planning and implementing the design of architectural interiors and furnishings.
B Architecture 1973
Environmental Planning 1982
R Aesthetic Preferences 1973
Aesthetics 1967
Furniture 1985

Interleukins 1994
PN 281   SC 26117
SN Compounds produced by lymphocytes that regulate immune system functioning and individual cell mediated immunity.
R Antigens 1982
Biological Markers 1991
Immunoreactivity 1994
Lymphocytes 1973

Intermarriage
Use Exogamous Marriage

Intermediate School Students 1973
PN 63   SC 26130
SN Includes the middle and/or upper elementary school grades, usually grades 4, 5, and 6. Use ELEMENTARY SCHOOL STUDENTS unless specific reference is made to population as intermediate school students. Use of a student term is mandatory in educational contexts.
B Elementary School Students 1967

Intermittent Explosive Disorder
Use Explosive Disorder

Intermittent Reinforcement
Use Reinforcement Schedules

Internal Consistency
Use Test Reliability

Internal External Locus of Control 1967
PN 9965   SC 26150
UF Control (Locus of)
Locus of Control
B Personality Traits 1967
R Attribution 1973
↓ Emotional Control 1973
External Rewards 1973
Extrinsic Motivation 1973
↓ Helplessness 1997
Independence (Personality) 1973
Internal Rewards 1973
Intrinsic Motivation 1973
Self Control 1973
Self Determination 1994

Internal Rewards 1973
PN 131   SC 26160
SN Satisfaction of a personal value or intrinsic criteria of behavior through action or attainment. Compare SECONDARY REINFORCEMENT.
UF Intrinsic Rewards
B Rewards 1967
R Internal External Locus of Control 1967

Internal Rewards — (cont'd)
R　　Intrinsic Motivation　1973

Internalization　1997
PN　310　　　　　　　　　　　　SC　26165
UF　Incorporation (Psychological)
B　　Personality Processes　1967
N　　Introjection　1973
R　↓ Defense Mechanisms　1967
　　　Externalization　1973
　　　Object Permanence　1985
　　　Object Relations　1982
　↓ Personality Development　1967
　↓ Psychotherapeutic Processes　1967

International Classification of Diseases　2001
PN　146　　　　　　　　　　　　SC　26168
SN　Used when the International Classification of Diseases or its revisions is the primary focus of the reference. Consider PSYCHODIAGNOSTIC TYPOL-OGIES to access references prior to 1997. Not used for specific psychodiagnostic categories. In 2000, the truncated term INTERNATIONAL CLASS OF DIS-EASES was deleted, and all records containing it were stripped of the term and replaced with INTER-NATIONAL CLASSIFICATION OF DISEASES, its expanded form.
UF　ICD
B　　Psychodiagnostic Typologies　1967
R　↓ Diagnosis　1967
　　　Diagnostic and Statistical Manual　1994
　↓ Disorders　1967
　↓ Mental Disorders　1967
　↓ Psychodiagnosis　1967
　　　Research Diagnostic Criteria　1994

International Organizations　1973
PN　364　　　　　　　　　　　　SC　26170
B　　Organizations　1967
R　　Foreign Organizations　1973

International Relations　1967
PN　1052　　　　　　　　　　　　SC　26180
R　　Foreign Policy Making　1973
　　　Peace　1988

Internet　2001
PN　0　　　　　　　　　　　　SC　26185
SN　A global system of linked computer networks that facilitates information retrieval and international communication.
UF　World Wide Web (WWW)
B　　Communication Systems　1973
　　　Information Systems　1991
R　↓ Automated Information Processing　1973
　↓ Computer Applications　1973
　　　Electronic Communication　2001
　↓ Telecommunications Media　1973

Internists　1973
PN　126　　　　　　　　　　　　SC　26190
B　　Physicians　1967

Internship (Medical)
Use　Medical Internship

Interobserver Reliability
Use　Interrater Reliability

Interocular Transfer　1985
PN　100　　　　　　　　　　　　SC　26207

Interocular Transfer — (cont'd)
SN　Any neurophysiological, electrophysiological, or perceptual interaction between the two eyes.
B　　Visual Perception　1967
R　　Ocular Dominance　1973
　↓ Perceptual Aftereffect　1967
　↓ Sensory Adaptation　1967

Interpersonal Attraction　1967
PN　2665　　　　　　　　　　　　SC　26210
UF　Attraction (Interpersonal)
B　　Interpersonal Interaction　1967
R　　Human Mate Selection　1988
　　　Likability　1988
　　　Physical Attractiveness　1973

Interpersonal Communication　1973
PN　7564　　　　　　　　　　　　SC　26220
B　　Communication　1967
　　　Interpersonal Interaction　1967
N　　Arguments　1973
　　　Body Language　1973
　　　Conversation　1973
　　　Cross Cultural Communication　1997
　　　Double Bind Interaction　1973
　　　Eye Contact　1973
　　　Gossip　1982
　　　Group Discussion　1967
　　　Interviewing　1973
　↓ Interviews　1967
　　　Job Applicant Interviews　1973
　　　Listening (Interpersonal)　1997
　↓ Negotiation　1973
　↓ Parent Child Communication　1973
R　　Credibility　1973
　　　Neurolinguistic Programming　2001
　　　Pragmatics　1985
　　　Scientific Communication　1973
　　　Self Disclosure　1973
　　　Self Reference　1994
　　　Speech Anxiety　1985

Interpersonal Compatibility　1973
PN　391　　　　　　　　　　　　SC　26230
UF　Compatibility (Interpersonal)
B　　Interpersonal Interaction　1967
R　　Friendship　1967
　　　Human Mate Selection　1988

Interpersonal Competence
Use　Social Skills

Interpersonal Distance
Use　Personal Space

Interpersonal Influences　1967
PN　3674　　　　　　　　　　　　SC　26240
SN　Effect one individual has on another with or without apparent intention or direct exercise of command.
UF　Influence (Interpersonal)
B　　Interpersonal Interaction　1967
　　　Social Influences　1967
N　　Peer Pressure　1994
R　↓ Persuasive Communication　1967
　　　Reference Groups　1994
　　　Suggestibility　1967

Interpersonal Interaction　1967
PN　17559　　　　　　　　　　　　SC　26250
UF　Interaction (Interpersonal)
　　　Rapport
B　　Social Interaction　1967

Interpersonal Interaction — (cont'd)
N　　Assistance (Social Behavior)　1973
　　　Charitable Behavior　1973
　↓ Collective Behavior　1967
　↓ Conflict　1967
　　　Cooperation　1967
　↓ Employee Interaction　1988
　　　Friendship　1967
　　　Group Participation　1973
　　　Group Performance　1967
　　　Interpersonal Attraction　1967
　↓ Interpersonal Communication　1973
　　　Interpersonal Compatibility　1973
　↓ Interpersonal Influences　1967
　　　Male Female Relations　1988
　↓ Participation　1973
　↓ Peer Relations　1967
　　　Persecution　1973
　　　Rivalry　1973
　　　Social Dating　1973
　　　Stranger Reactions　1988
R　　Affection　1973
　　　Boundaries (Psychological)　1997
　　　Codependency　1991
　　　Enactments　1997
　　　Intimacy　1973
　　　Mentor　1985
　　　Mirroring　1997
　　　Popularity　1988
　↓ Relationship Satisfaction　2001
　　　Retaliation　1991
　　　Social Cognition　1994
　↓ Social Networks　1994

Interpersonal Perception
Use　Social Perception

Interpersonal Psychotherapy　1997
PN　168　　　　　　　　　　　　SC　26263
SN　Technique formulated by H. S. Sullivan based on the study of the patient's interpersonal relationships both within and outside of the psychotherapeutic situation.
B　　Psychotherapy　1967
R　↓ Psychotherapeutic Techniques　1967

Interpersonal Relationship Satisfaction
Use　Relationship Satisfaction

Interracial Adoption　1994
PN　60　　　　　　　　　　　　SC　26265
UF　Transracial Adoption
B　　Adoption (Child)　1967
R　　Adopted Children　1973
　↓ Adoptees　1985
　　　Adoptive Parents　1973
　　　Interethnic Family　1988
　　　Interracial Family　1988

Interracial Family　1988
PN　39　　　　　　　　　　　　SC　26270
B　　Family　1967
R　　Interethnic Family　1988
　　　Interracial Adoption　1994
　　　Interracial Marriage　1973
　　　Interracial Offspring　1988
　　　Racial and Ethnic Differences　1982
　　　Racial and Ethnic Relations　1982

Interracial Marriage　1973
PN　147　　　　　　　　　　　　SC　26280
UF　Miscegenous Marriage
B　　Exogamous Marriage　1973

Interracial Marriage — (cont'd)
- R　Interracial Family 1988
　　Interracial Offspring 1988
　　Racial and Ethnic Relations 1982

Interracial Offspring 1988
PN　137　　　　　　　　　　SC　26282
- UF　Biracial Children
- B　Offspring 1988
- R　Interracial Family 1988
　　Interracial Marriage 1973
　　Racial and Ethnic Differences 1982
　　Racial and Ethnic Relations 1982

Interrater Reliability 1982
PN　1636　　　　　　　　　SC　26284
- SN　Statistically measured correspondence between judgments by observers of a common event.
- UF　Interobserver Reliability
- R　Observation Methods 1967
　　Rating 1967
　　Statistical Reliability 1973
　　Test Reliability 1973

Interresponse Time 1973
PN　273　　　　　　　　　　SC　26290
- SN　Interval between successive responses.
- B　Response Parameters 1973
　　Time 1967
- R　Response Frequency 1973

Intersensory Integration
- Use　Sensory Integration

Intersensory Processes 1978
PN　1033　　　　　　　　　SC　26295
- B　Perception 1967
- N　Sensory Integration 1991
- R　Perceptual Motor Development 1991
　↓ Perceptual Motor Processes 1967

Intersexuality
- Use　Hermaphroditism

Interspecies Interaction 1991
PN　761　　　　　　　　　　SC　26297
- SN　Social behavior involving members of two or more animal species including humans and animals.
- UF　Animal Human Interaction
　　Human Animal Interaction
- B　Social Behavior 1967
- R　Animal Assisted Therapy 1994
　↓ Animal Social Behavior 1967
　↓ Animals 1967
　　Biological Symbiosis 1973
　　Pets 1982
　　Species Differences 1982

Interstimulus Interval 1967
PN　2172　　　　　　　　　SC　26300
- SN　In conditioning contexts, the temporal interval separating the conditioned stimulus and uncondi-tioned stimulus or the temporal interval between the elements of a multiple component (i.e., compound) stimulus.
- B　Stimulus Intervals 1973
- R　Reinforcement Delay 1985

Intertrial Interval 1973
PN　983　　　　　　　　　　SC　26310
- SN　Temporal interval between successive discrete trials in conditioning or learning contexts.
- B　Stimulus Intervals 1973

Interval Reinforcement
- Use　Fixed Interval Reinforcement AND Variable Interval Reinforcement

Interview Schedules 2001
PN　0　　　　　　　　　　　SC　26325
- SN　Precoded questionnaires for gathering data, which are completed during interviews.
- B　Interviews 1967
- N　Diagnostic Interview Schedule 1991
　　Structured Clinical Interview 2001
- R　Intake Interview 1994
　↓ Psychiatric Evaluation 1997
　↓ Psychological Assessment 1997

Interviewers 1988
PN　186　　　　　　　　　　SC　26330
- R　Interviewing 1973
　↓ Interviews 1967

Interviewing 1973
PN　1435　　　　　　　　　SC　26340
- SN　Used for the methods, techniques, principles, and practice of interviewing.
- B　Interpersonal Communication 1973
- R　Interviewers 1988
　↓ Interviews 1967
　　Legal Interrogation 1994
　　Microcounseling 1978
　　Questioning 1982

Interviews 1967
PN　2609　　　　　　　　　SC　26350
- B　Interpersonal Communication 1973
- N　Intake Interview 1994
　↓ Interview Schedules 2001
　　Job Applicant Interviews 1973
　↓ Psychodiagnostic Interview 1973
- R　Interviewers 1988
　　Interviewing 1973
　↓ Measurement 1967
　　Questioning 1982

Intestines 1973
PN　152　　　　　　　　　　SC　26360
- UF　Duodenum
　　Ileum
- B　Gastrointestinal System 1973
- R　Absorption (Physiological) 1973

Intimacy 1973
PN　2643　　　　　　　　　SC　26370
- R　Affection 1973
　　Attachment Behavior 1985
　↓ Interpersonal Interaction 1967
　　Love 1973
　　Physical Contact 1982
　　Romance 1997

Intoxication
- Use　Toxic Disorders

Intoxication (Alcohol)
- Use　Alcohol Intoxication

Intra Aural Muscle Reflex
- Use　Acoustic Reflex

Intracranial Self Stimulation
- Use　Brain Self Stimulation

Intramuscular Injections 1973
PN　41　　　　　　　　　　　SC　26400
- B　Injections 1973

Intraperitoneal Injections 1973
PN　61　　　　　　　　　　　SC　26410
- B　Injections 1973

Intrauterine Devices 1973
PN　25　　　　　　　　　　　SC　26420
- B　Contraceptive Devices 1973

Intravenous Drug Usage 1994
PN　817　　　　　　　　　　SC　26425
- UF　IV Drug Usage
- B　Drug Usage 1971
- R　↓ Drug Abuse 1973
　↓ Drug Addiction 1967
　　Intravenous Injections 1973
　　Needle Exchange Programs 2001
　　Needle Sharing 1994

Intravenous Injections 1973
PN　507　　　　　　　　　　SC　26430
- B　Injections 1973
- R　Intravenous Drug Usage 1994
　　Needle Sharing 1994

Intrinsic Motivation 1973
PN　1349　　　　　　　　　SC　26440
- SN　Need or desire which arises from within the indi-vidual and causes action toward some goal.
- B　Motivation 1967
- R　↓ Goals 1967
　　Internal External Locus of Control 1967
　　Internal Rewards 1973
　　Need for Cognition 1997
　↓ Needs 1967

Intrinsic Rewards
- Use　Internal Rewards

Introjection 1973
PN　123　　　　　　　　　　SC　26460
- B　Defense Mechanisms 1967
　　Internalization 1997
- R　Identification (Defense Mechanism) 1973

Introspection 1973
PN　254　　　　　　　　　　SC　26470
- B　Personality Processes 1967
- R　Reflectiveness 1997
　　Self Monitoring (Personality) 1985
　　Self Perception 1967

Introversion 1967
PN　1166　　　　　　　　　SC　26480
- B　Personality Traits 1967
- R　Extraversion 1967

Intuition 1973
PN　603　　　　　　　　　　SC　26485
- B　Cognitive Processes 1967
- R　Cognition 1967
　↓ Comprehension 1967
　　Guessing 1973
　　Insight 1973

Inuit 2001
PN　253　　　　　　　　　　SC　26487
- SN　In 2000, this term was created to replace the discontinued term ESKIMOS. ESKIMOS was stripped from all records and replaced with INUIT.

Inuit — (cont'd)
- **UF** Eskimos
- **B** Indigenous Populations [2001]
- **R** Alaska Natives [1997]
  - American Indians [1967]
  - Minority Groups [1967]
  - ↓ Pacific Islanders [2001]

Inventories [1967]
PN 3937   **SC** 26490
- **B** Measurement [1967]
- **N** Biographical Inventories [1973]
  - Interest Inventories [1973]

Invertebrates [1973]
PN 216   **SC** 26540
- **B** Animals [1967]
- **N** ↓ Arthropoda [1973]
  - Echinodermata [1973]
  - ↓ Mollusca [1973]
  - ↓ Worms [1967]
- **R** ↓ Vertebrates [1973]

Investigation
- **Use** Experimentation

Involuntary Treatment [1994]
PN 238   **SC** 26555
- **B** Treatment [1967]
- **R** ↓ Client Rights [1988]
  - ↓ Commitment (Psychiatric) [1973]
  - Court Referrals [1994]
  - Informed Consent [1985]
  - Right to Treatment [1997]
  - Treatment Compliance [1982]
  - Treatment Dropouts [1978]
  - Treatment Refusal [1994]

Involutional Depression [1973]
PN 62   **SC** 26560
- **UF** Climacteric Depression
- **B** Affective Psychosis [1973]
  - Major Depression [1988]

Involutional Paranoid Psychosis [1973]
PN 7   **SC** 26570
- **UF** Climacteric Paranoia
- **B** Paranoia (Psychosis) [1967]
- **R** Folie A Deux [1973]
  - Paranoid Schizophrenia [1967]

Involvement [1973]
PN 2001   **SC** 26575
- **B** Social Behavior [1967]
- **N** Job Involvement [1978]
- **R** ↓ Commitment [1985]
  - Empowerment [1991]
  - ↓ Participation [1973]

Ions
- **Use** Electrolytes

Iowa Tests of Basic Skills [1973]
PN 50   **SC** 26590
- **B** Achievement Measures [1967]

Iproniazid [1973]
PN 16   **SC** 26600
- **B** Amine Oxidase Inhibitors [1973]
  - Antidepressant Drugs [1971]
  - Antihypertensive Drugs [1973]
  - Antitubercular Drugs [1973]

Iproniazid — (cont'd)
- **B** Monoamine Oxidase Inhibitors [1973]

Iris (Eye) [1973]
PN 53   **SC** 26630
- **B** Eye (Anatomy) [1967]
- **R** Eye Color [1991]

Iron [1973]
PN 126   **SC** 26640
- **B** Metallic Elements [1973]

Irradiation
- **Use** Radiation

Irrational Beliefs [1982]
PN 636   **SC** 26654
- **SN** Erroneous or distorted convictions or ideas firmly held despite objective and obvious contradictory proof or evidence.
- **B** Cognitions [1985]
- **R** ↓ Attitudes [1967]
  - Superstitions [1973]

Irritability [1988]
PN 186   **SC** 26658
- **SN** Used for human or animal populations.
- **B** Personality Traits [1967]
- **R** ↓ Emotional States [1973]

Irritable Bowel Syndrome [1991]
PN 166   **SC** 26659
- **SN** Functional disorder of the colon that is generally psychosomatic.
- **B** Colon Disorders [1973]
  - Syndromes [1973]
- **R** ↓ Colitis [1973]
  - ↓ Somatoform Disorders [2001]

Ischemia [1973]
PN 300   **SC** 26660
- **B** Cardiovascular Disorders [1967]
- **N** Cerebral Ischemia [1973]
- **R** Anoxia [1973]

Islam [1973]
PN 384   **SC** 26670
- **B** Religious Affiliation [1973]
- **R** Muslims [1997]

Isocarboxazid [1973]
PN 32   **SC** 26680
- **B** Amine Oxidase Inhibitors [1973]
  - Antidepressant Drugs [1971]
  - Monoamine Oxidase Inhibitors [1973]

Isoenzymes
- **Use** Isozymes

Isolation (Defense Mechanism) [1973]
PN 138   **SC** 26700
- **SN** Unconscious separation of an unacceptable impulse, idea, or act from its original memory source, removing the emotional charge associated with the original memory.
- **B** Defense Mechanisms [1967]
- **R** Intellectualization [1973]

Isolation (Social)
- **Use** Social Isolation

Isolation Effect [1973]
PN 212   **SC** 26720
- **SN** Facilitating effect of isolation of distinctive features of an item (e.g., type face, color) in learning. Prior to 1982 the term was not defined and was used inconsistently.
- **B** Associative Processes [1967]
- **R** Cues [1967]
  - Stimulus Salience [1973]
  - ↓ Verbal Learning [1967]

Isoniazid [1973]
PN 25   **SC** 26730
- **B** Antitubercular Drugs [1973]

Isoproterenol [1973]
PN 136   **SC** 26740
- **B** Alcohols [1967]
  - Sympathomimetic Drugs [1973]

Isozymes [1973]
PN 43   **SC** 26750
- **UF** Isoenzymes
- **B** Enzymes [1973]

Itching
- **Use** Pruritus

Item Analysis (Statistical) [1973]
PN 818   **SC** 26800
- **SN** Quantitative analysis of a test item, especially regarding its difficulty level and validity.
- **B** Factor Analysis [1967]
- **R** Adaptive Testing [1985]
  - Item Response Theory [1985]
  - Statistical Weighting [1985]
  - Test Items [1973]

Item Analysis (Test) [1967]
PN 1400   **SC** 26810
- **SN** Qualitative analysis of a test item, especially regarding its content and form.
- **B** Analysis [1967]
  - Test Construction [1973]
  - Testing [1967]
- **R** Item Content (Test) [1973]
  - Test Items [1973]

Item Bias
- **Use** Test Bias

Item Content (Test) [1973]
PN 445   **SC** 26820
- **SN** Topics or subject matter covered in test questions, units, or tasks.
- **B** Test Construction [1973]
  - Testing [1967]
- **R** Item Analysis (Test) [1967]
  - Test Forms [1988]
  - Test Items [1973]

Item Response Theory [1985]
PN 1171   **SC** 26825
- **SN** A statistical approach in psychological measurement. Also known as item characteristic curve theory.
- **UF** Latent Trait Theory
  - Logistic Models
  - Rasch Model
- **B** Testing [1967]
  - Theories [1967]
- **R** Difficulty Level (Test) [1973]
  - Item Analysis (Statistical) [1973]
  - Psychometrics [1967]

Item Response Theory — (cont'd)
R ↓ Test Scores [1967]

IV Drug Usage
Use Intravenous Drug Usage

Jails
Use Prisons

James (William) [1991]
PN 145   **SC** 26855
SN Identifies biographical or autobiographical studies and discussions of James's works.
R Functionalism [1973]
    ↓ Psychologists [1967]

Japanese Cultural Groups [1997]
PN 144   **SC** 26865
SN Use ASIANS to access references from 1982-1996.
B Asians [1982]

Jaundice [1973]
PN 30   **SC** 26870
B Digestive System Disorders [1973]
    Liver Disorders [1973]
R Cirrhosis (Liver) [1973]
    ↓ Hepatitis [1973]
    ↓ Infectious Disorders [1973]

Jaw [1973]
PN 236   **SC** 26880
UF Mandibula
    Maxilla
B Musculoskeletal System [1973]
R Bones [1973]

Jealousy [1973]
PN 579   **SC** 26890
UF Envy
B Emotional States [1973]
R ↓ Anger [1967]
    ↓ Anxiety [1967]

Jews [1997]
PN 255   **SC** 26900
SN Use JUDAISM to access references prior to 1997.
B Religious Groups [1997]
R AntiSemitism [1973]
    Holocaust [1988]
    Holocaust Survivors [1988]
    Judaism [1967]
    Minority Groups [1967]

Job Analysis [1967]
PN 1566   **SC** 26910
SN Analysis specifying job duties, responsibilities, and technical components.
B Analysis [1967]
    Personnel Management [1973]
R ↓ Job Characteristics [1985]
    Task Analysis [1967]
    Work Load [1982]

Job Applicant Attitudes [1973]
PN 206   **SC** 26920
SN Attitudes of, not toward, job applicants.
B Attitudes [1967]
R Job Applicants [1985]

Job Applicant Attitudes — (cont'd)
R Job Search [1985]
    Occupational Attitudes [1973]
    ↓ Personnel [1967]

Job Applicant Interviews [1973]
PN 705   **SC** 26930
UF Employment Interviews
B Interpersonal Communication [1973]
    Interviews [1967]
    Personnel Selection [1967]
R Job Search [1985]
    ↓ Personnel Evaluation [1973]
    ↓ Personnel Recruitment [1973]

Job Applicant Screening [1973]
PN 641   **SC** 26940
UF Testing (Job Applicants)
B Personnel Selection [1967]
    Screening [1982]
R Employment Discrimination [1994]
    Employment Tests [1973]
    Job Search [1985]
    ↓ Personnel Evaluation [1973]
    ↓ Personnel Recruitment [1973]

Job Applicants [1985]
PN 481   **SC** 26953
SN Persons seeking employment.
R ↓ Employment Status [1982]
    Job Applicant Attitudes [1973]
    Job Search [1985]
    ↓ Personnel [1967]

Job Change
Use Career Change

Job Characteristics [1985]
PN 2199   **SC** 26957
SN Responsibilities or tasks that characterize a specific job.
N Work Load [1982]
R Job Analysis [1967]
    ↓ Occupations [1967]
    Quality of Work Life [1988]

Job Corps [1973]
PN 34   **SC** 26960
SN U.S. Government program of vocational and psychosocial training and counseling for disadvantaged adolescents and adults.
B Government Programs [1973]
R Government [1967]

Job Discrimination
Use Employment Discrimination

Job Enrichment [1973]
PN 116   **SC** 26980
SN Formal or informal programs or techniques used to enhance the quality of a job or to further challenge the employee.
B Working Conditions [1973]
R Job Experience Level [1973]
    Job Satisfaction [1967]
    Occupational Guidance [1967]
    Occupational Mobility [1973]
    ↓ Personnel Training [1967]

Job Experience Level [1973]
PN 2017   **SC** 26990
UF Experience Level (Job)
B Employee Characteristics [1988]

Job Experience Level — (cont'd)
B Experience Level [1988]
R Employment History [1978]
    Job Enrichment [1973]
    Job Knowledge [1997]
    Occupational Status [1978]

Job Family Relationship
Use Family Work Relationship

Job Involvement [1978]
PN 1137   **SC** 26994
B Involvement [1973]
R ↓ Employee Attitudes [1967]
    Employee Motivation [1973]
    ↓ Job Performance [1967]
    Job Satisfaction [1967]
    Organizational Commitment [1991]
    Participative Management [1988]
    Work (Attitudes Toward) [1973]

Job Knowledge [1997]
PN 127   **SC** 26996
B Employee Characteristics [1988]
    Knowledge Level [1978]
R ↓ Employee Skills [1973]
    Job Experience Level [1973]
    ↓ Job Performance [1967]

Job Mobility
Use Occupational Mobility

Job Performance [1967]
PN 7799   **SC** 27010
B Performance [1967]
N Employee Efficiency [1973]
    Employee Productivity [1973]
R ↓ Employee Attitudes [1967]
    Job Involvement [1978]
    Job Knowledge [1997]
    Organizational Commitment [1991]
    ↓ Personnel [1967]
    ↓ Personnel Evaluation [1973]
    Personnel Promotion [1978]
    Work Load [1982]

Job Promotion
Use Personnel Promotion

Job Reentry
Use Reemployment

Job Satisfaction [1967]
PN 8379   **SC** 27040
SN Positive attitudes toward one's work when tangible and/or intangible rewards fulfill expectations.
UF Work Satisfaction
B Employee Attitudes [1967]
    Satisfaction [1973]
R Career Change [1978]
    Job Enrichment [1973]
    Job Involvement [1978]
    Organizational Commitment [1991]
    Quality of Work Life [1988]
    Role Satisfaction [1994]

Job Search [1985]
PN 379   **SC** 27043
SN Process of seeking employment. For consideration of career alternatives use CAREER EDUCATION.
R Job Applicant Attitudes [1973]
    Job Applicant Interviews [1973]

Job Search — (cont'd)
R   Job Applicant Screening 1973
      Job Applicants 1985
      Reemployment 1991
      Unemployment 1967

Job Security 1978
PN 185   SC 27045
SN Probable assurance of continued employment.
R   Employee Turnover 1973
      ↓ Occupational Tenure 1973
      Personnel Termination 1973
      Retirement 1973
      Unemployment 1967

Job Selection
Use Occupational Choice

Job Status
Use Occupational Status

Job Training
Use Personnel Training

Jobs
Use Occupations

Joint Custody 1988
PN 92   SC 27065
R   Child Custody 1982
      Child Support 1988
      Divorce 1973

Joint Disorders 1973
PN 89   SC 27070
B   Musculoskeletal Disorders 1973
N   ↓ Arthritis 1973
R   ↓ Joints (Anatomy) 1973

Joints (Anatomy) 1973
PN 157   SC 27080
B   Musculoskeletal System 1973
N   Ankle 1973
      Elbow (Anatomy) 1973
      Knee 1973
      Shoulder (Anatomy) 1973
      Wrist 1973
R   ↓ Joint Disorders 1973

Jokes 1973
PN 235   SC 27090
B   Humor 1967

Journalists 1973
PN 125   SC 27100
B   Professional Personnel 1978
R   ↓ News Media 1997

Joy
Use Happiness

Judaism 1967
PN 1471   SC 27130
B   Religious Affiliation 1973
R   AntiSemitism 1973
      Bible 1973
      Holocaust 1988
      Jews 1997
      Rabbis 1973

Judges 1985
PN 280   SC 27135
B   Legal Personnel 1985

Judgment 1967
PN 5612   SC 27140
SN Mental act of comparing or evaluating choices within a given set of values frequently with the purpose of choosing a course of action.
N   Clinical Judgment (Not Diagnosis) 1973
      Probability Judgment 1978
R   ↓ Decision Making 1967
      Judgment Disturbances 1973
      Uncertainty 1991
      Wisdom 1994

Judgment Disturbances 1973
PN 11   SC 27150
SN Maladaptive judgment resulting from wish-fulfilling, impulsive decisions based on need for immediate infantile gratification.
B   Thought Disturbances 1973
R   ↓ Judgment 1967

Judo 1973
PN 37   SC 27160
B   Recreation 1967
      Sports 1967
R   Martial Arts 1985

Jumping 1973
PN 118   SC 27170
B   Motor Performance 1973
      Motor Processes 1967

Jung (Carl) 1973
PN 705   SC 27180
SN Identifies biographical or autobiographical studies and discussions of Jung's works.
R   Analytical Psychotherapy 1973
      Archetypes 1991
      ↓ Collective Unconscious 1997
      ↓ Jungian Psychology 1973
      ↓ Psychologists 1967

Jungian Psychology 1973
PN 1992   SC 27190
SN Analytical psychology characterized by theories of the collective unconscious, the archetype, the complex, and psychological types.
UF Analytic Psychology
B   Neopsychoanalytic School 1973
N   ↓ Collective Unconscious 1997
R   Analytical Psychotherapy 1973
      Archetypes 1991
      Free Association 1994
      Jung (Carl) 1973

Jungian Psychotherapy
Use Analytical Psychotherapy

Junior College Students 1973
PN 200   SC 27200
SN Students in 2-year colleges. Mandatory term in educational contexts.
B   College Students 1967
R   Community College Students 1973

Junior Colleges
Use Colleges

Junior High School Students 1971
PN 10127   SC 27220

Junior High School Students — (cont'd)
SN Students in 7th and 8th grade. Sometimes includes students in 9th grade. Mandatory term in educational contexts.
B   Students 1967
R   Grade Level 1994
      Middle School Students 1985

Junior High School Teachers 1973
PN 1441   SC 27230
B   Teachers 1967

Junior High Schools 1973
PN 286   SC 27240
B   Schools 1967
R   Secondary Education 1973

Juries 1985
PN 871   SC 27245
SN Bodies of persons sworn to give a verdict in a court of law. Also used for mock and simulated juries. Use ADJUDICATION to access references from 1973-1984.
R   ↓ Adjudication 1967
      Jury Selection 1994
      ↓ Legal Personnel 1985

Jury Selection 1994
PN 23   SC 27252
SN Use JURIES to access references from 1985-1993.
R   ↓ Adjudication 1967
      Juries 1985

Justice 1973
PN 1498   SC 27260
SN Used for the impartial and fair settlement of conflict and differences, or the designation of rewards or punishment.
UF Distributive Justice
N   ↓ Criminal Justice 1991
R   ↓ Civil Rights 1978
      Equity (Payment) 1978
      ↓ Equity (Social) 1978
      Freedom 1978
      ↓ Law (Government) 1973
      ↓ Law Enforcement 1978
      Morality 1967
      Reward Allocation 1988
      Social Equality 1973
      ↓ Social Issues 1991

Juvenile Court
Use Adjudication

Juvenile Delinquency 1967
PN 6564   SC 27280
SN Behavior of children or adolescents that is antisocial, dangerous, or criminal, and usually subject to legal action. The age at which juveniles become adults varies across countries and cultures, but usually ranges from 15-18 years. In 2000, this term became the postable counterpart for the discontinued term JUVENILE DELINQUENTS. JUVENILE DELINQUENTS was stripped from all records and replaced with JUVENILE DELINQUENCY.
UF Delinquency (Juvenile)
      Offenders (Juvenile)
B   Antisocial Behavior 1971
      Behavior Disorders 1971
N   Female Delinquency 2001
      Male Delinquency 2001
R   Antisocial Personality 1973
      Crime Prevention 1985

Juvenile Delinquency — (cont'd)
R   ↓ Criminals   1967
     Juvenile Gangs   1973
     Predelinquent Youth   1978

Juvenile Gangs   1973
PN   417   SC   27300
UF   Gangs (Juvenile)
R   ↓ Juvenile Delinquency   1967

Kainic Acid   1988
PN   155   SC   27305
B   Acids   1973
R   Glutamic Acid   1973
     ↓ Neurotoxins   1982

Kangaroos   1973
PN   17   SC   27310
B   Marsupials   1973

Karate
Use   Martial Arts

Karyotype Disorders
Use   Chromosome Disorders

Kaufman Assessment Battery for Children   2001
PN   168   SC   27323
SN   In 2000, the truncated term KAUFMAN ASSESSMENT BATTERY CHILDREN (which was used from 1988-2000) was deleted, removed from all records containing it, and mapped to its expanded form KAUFMAN ASSESSMENT BATTERY FOR CHILDREN.
B   Intelligence Measures   1967

Ketamine   1997
PN   98   SC   27327
B   Anesthetic Drugs   1973

Keyboards   1985
PN   78   SC   27328
B   Apparatus   1967
R   ↓ Computer Peripheral Devices   1985
     Human Computer Interaction   1997
     ↓ Instrument Controls   1985
     Typing   1991

Keypunch Operators
Use   Clerical Personnel

Kibbutz   1973
PN   341   SC   27340
B   Communes   1973

Kidnapping   1988
PN   92   SC   27345
B   Crime   1967
R   Hostages   1988

Kidney Diseases   1988
PN   421   SC   27347
UF   Renal Diseases
B   Urogenital Disorders   1973

Kidney Transplants
Use   Organ Transplantation

Kidneys   1973
PN   265   SC   27360

Kidneys — (cont'd)
B   Urogenital System   1973

Kinases   1982
PN   284   SC   27366
SN   Enzymes that catalyze the conversion of proenzymes to active enzymes or the transfer of phosphate groups to form triphosphates (ATP).
UF   Enteropeptidase
B   Enzymes   1973

Kindergarten Students   1973
PN   3241   SC   27370
SN   Students in kindergarten. Mandatory term in educational contexts.
B   Students   1967
R   Grade Level   1994
     ↓ Preschool Students   1982

Kindergartens   1973
PN   244   SC   27380
B   Schools   1967

Kindling   1985
PN   303   SC   27385
SN   Afterdischarges and generalized convulsions produced by repeated brain stimulation, usually electrical. Often used as an experimental model of epilepsy.
B   Electrical Activity   1967
R   Electrical Brain Stimulation   1973
     Experimental Epilepsy   1978

Kinesics
Use   Body Language

Kinesthetic Perception   1967
PN   1081   SC   27390
SN   Sensory modality involving awareness of body movement, position, and posture, and movement of body parts, such as muscles, tendons, and joints. Used for human or animal populations.
B   Somesthetic Perception   1967
R   Spatial Orientation (Perception)   1973

Kinship   1985
PN   485   SC   27395
SN   The state of being related such as by birth, common ancestry, or marriage. Used for human or animal populations.
R   Ethnology   1967
     ↓ Family   1967
     Kinship Recognition   1988
     Kinship Structure   1973

Kinship Recognition   1988
PN   325   SC   27399
R   ↓ Discrimination Learning   1982
     Kinship   1985
     Species Recognition   1985

Kinship Structure   1973
PN   189   SC   27400
R   Ethnography   1973
     Ethnology   1967
     ↓ Family Structure   1973
     Kinship   1985
     ↓ Sociocultural Factors   1967

Kirton Adaption Innovation Inventory   2001
PN   6   SC   27411

Kirton Adaption Innovation Inventory — (cont'd)
SN   In 2000, the truncated term KIRTON ADAPTION INNOVATION INVEN (which was used from 1997-2000) was deleted and mapped to its expanded form KIRTON ADAPTION INNOVATION INVENTORY.
B   Personality Measures   1967

Kleine Levin Syndrome   2001
PN   0   SC   27415
SN   A condition characterized by recurrent hypersomnia and hyperphagia and marked by such symptoms as mental confusion, excessive sleep restlessness, and hallucinations.
B   Eating Disorders   1997
     Sleep Disorders   1973
     Syndromes   1973
R   Hyperphagia   1973
     Hypersomnia   1994

Kleptomania   1973
PN   58   SC   27420
R   ↓ Impulse Control Disorders   1997
     Impulsiveness   1973
     ↓ Personality Disorders   1967

Klinefelters Syndrome   1973
PN   77   SC   27430
B   Hypogonadism   1973
     Male Genital Disorders   1973
     Neonatal Disorders   1973
     Sex Chromosome Disorders   1973
     Syndromes   1973
R   ↓ Infertility   1973
     ↓ Mental Retardation   1967

Knee   1973
PN   102   SC   27440
B   Joints (Anatomy)   1973
R   Leg (Anatomy)   1973

Knowledge Based Systems
Use   Expert Systems

Knowledge Level   1978
PN   8997   SC   27446
SN   Range of received or acquired information, understanding, or awareness. Limited to human populations.
N   Health Knowledge   1994
     Job Knowledge   1997
R   Declarative Knowledge   1997
     ↓ Experience Level   1988
     Information   1967
     Procedural Knowledge   1997
     Wisdom   1994

Knowledge of Results   1967
PN   556   SC   27450
B   Feedback   1967

Kohlberg (Lawrence)   1991
PN   80   SC   27455
SN   Identifies biographical or autobiographical studies and discussions of Kohlberg's works.
R   Moral Development   1973
     ↓ Psychologists   1967

Kohs Block Design Test   1973
PN   28   SC   27460
UF   Block Design Test (Kohs)
B   Intelligence Measures   1967

Kolmogorov Smirnov Test 1973
PN 4   SC 27470
 B   Nonparametric Statistical Tests 1967

Korean Cultural Groups 1997
PN 164   SC 27483
SN Use ASIANS to access references prior to
1982-1996.
 B   Asians 1982

Koro 1994
PN 32   SC 27485
SN A mental disorder characterized by fear or delu-
sions of the shrinkage of the penis, labia, or breasts
into the abdomen or chest. Observed primarily in
Southern Chinese and some African cultures.
 B   Body Image Disturbances 1973
        Ethnospecific Disorders 1973
        Mental Disorders 1967

Korsakoffs Psychosis 1973
PN 465   SC 27490
 B   Alcoholic Hallucinosis 1973
 R   Confabulation 1973

Kuder Occupational Interest Survey 1973
PN 45   SC 27510
 B   Occupational Interest Measures 1973

Kuder Preference Record 1973
PN 19   SC 27520
 B   Preference Measures 1973

Kupfer Detre Self Rating Scale
SN Term was discontinued in 1997. In 2000, the
term was stripped from all records containing it, and
replaced with NONPROJECTIVE PERSONALITY
MEASURES, its postable counterpart.
 Use   Nonprojective Personality Measures

Kwashiorkor 1973
PN 7   SC 27550
 B   Protein Deficiency Disorders 1973

L Dopa
 Use   Levodopa

Labeling 1978
PN 1250   SC 27565
SN In social or therapeutic settings, designating the
condition of an individual or group by a simplistic
word or phrase which may serve to indicate status,
stigma, or other characteristics.
 R   ↓ Attitudes 1967
        ↓ Diagnosis 1967
        ↓ Names 1985
        ↓ Psychodiagnostic Typologies 1967
        ↓ Social Perception 1967
        Stereotyped Attitudes 1967
        Stigma 1991

Labor (Childbirth) 1973
PN 357   SC 27570
 R   ↓ Birth 1967
        Childbirth Training 1978
        Midwifery 1985
        Obstetrical Complications 1978

Labor Management Relations 1967
PN 671   SC 27580
 UF   Labor Relations
 B   Personnel Management 1973

Labor Management Relations — (cont'd)
 R   Informants 1988
        Labor Unions 1973
        ↓ Management 1967
        Mediation 1988
        ↓ Organizational Behavior 1978
        Strikes 1973
        Supervisor Employee Interaction 1997

Labor Relations
 Use   Labor Management Relations

Labor Union Members 1973
PN 236   SC 27600
 R   ↓ Personnel 1967

Labor Unions 1973
PN 427   SC 27610
 B   Organizations 1967
 R   Labor Management Relations 1967

Laboratories (Educational)
 Use   Educational Laboratories

Laboratories (Experimental)
 Use   Experimental Laboratories

Laborers (Construction and Industry)
 Use   Blue Collar Workers

Laborers (Farm)
 Use   Agricultural Workers

Labyrinth (Anatomy) 1973
PN 116   SC 27660
SN The bony structure of the inner ear that houses
the membranous labyrinth (i.e., the cochlea, vesti-
bule, semicircular canals, utricle, and saccule). May
also refer to these latter membranous structures.
 UF   Inner Ear
 B   Ear (Anatomy) 1967
 N   Cochlea 1973
 R   ↓ Vestibular Apparatus 1967

Labyrinth (Apparatus)
 Use   Mazes

Labyrinth Disorders 1973
PN 48   SC 27680
 B   Ear Disorders 1973
 N   Menieres Disease 1973
        Motion Sickness 1973
 R   ↓ Somesthetic Perception 1967
        Vertigo 1973

Lactate Dehydrogenase 1973
PN 20   SC 27690
 B   Dehydrogenases 1973

Lactation 1973
PN 572   SC 27700
 B   Secretion (Gland) 1973
 R   Postnatal Period 1973

Lactic Acid 1991
PN 69   SC 27720
 UF   Sodium Lactate
 B   Acids 1973

Landscapes
 Use   Topography

Language 1967
PN 7754   SC 27740
 N   ↓ Dialect 1973
        ↓ Figurative Language 1985
        Foreign Languages 1973
        ↓ Form Classes (Language) 1973
        Phrases 1973
        Profanity 1991
        Rhetoric 1991
        Sentences 1967
        Sign Language 1973
        Spelling 1973
        ↓ Vocabulary 1967
        ↓ Written Language 1967
 R   Bilingualism 1973
        Discourse Analysis 1997
        English as Second Language 1997
        ↓ Grammar 1967
        ↓ Language Development 1967
        ↓ Linguistics 1973
        ↓ Literacy 1973
        Metalinguistics 1994
        Monolingualism 1973
        ↓ Multilingualism 1973
        Neurolinguistics 1991
        Symbolism 1967
        ↓ Verbal Communication 1967

Language Alternation
 Use   Code Switching

Language Arts Education 1973
PN 1894   SC 27750
SN Education in subjects aimed at development of
comprehension and use of written and oral language.
 B   Curriculum 1967
 N   Phonics 1973
        Reading Education 1973
        Spelling 1973
 R   English as Second Language 1997
        Initial Teaching Alphabet 1973
        ↓ Literacy 1973
        Literacy Programs 1997

Language Delay 1988
PN 303   SC 27755
 B   Delayed Development 1973
        Language Development 1967
 R   ↓ Language Disorders 1982
        Retarded Speech Development 1973

Language Development 1967
PN 10507   SC 27760
SN Acquisition of the rules governing the structure
of language (e.g., syntax) and meaning. Use
SPEECH DEVELOPMENT for acquisition of speech
sound production. Compare VERBAL LEARNING.
 B   Cognitive Development 1973
        Intellectual Development 1973
 N   Language Delay 1988
 R   Foreign Language Learning 1967
        ↓ Language 1967
        ↓ Language Disorders 1982
        Metalinguistics 1994
        Reading Development 1997
        ↓ Speech Development 1973
        ↓ Verbal Communication 1967
        Vygotsky (Lev) 1991

Language Disorders 1982
PN 2634   SC 27763

Language Disorders — (cont'd)
SN Disorders, usually due to cognitive or neurological dysfunction, resulting in problems in symbolization or in delays in language and speech development.
- **B** Communication Disorders [1982]
- **N** ↓ Aphasia [1967]
  Echolalia [1973]
  ↓ Mutism [1973]
- **R** Language Delay [1988]
  ↓ Language Development [1967]
  Neurolinguistics [1991]
  ↓ Speech Disorders [1967]

Language Laboratories [1973]
PN 6　　　　　　　　　　**SC** 27770
- **B** Educational Laboratories [1973]
- **R** Foreign Language Learning [1967]
  Learning Centers (Educational) [1973]

Language Proficiency [1988]
PN 929　　　　　　　　**SC** 27773
SN Accuracy and fluency of verbal communication in a second language learning or bilingual context. Includes concept of Limited English Proficiency, which is knowledge of English without sufficient proficiency to communicate or participate in an English-speaking society. Consider VERBAL FLUENCY for other contexts.
- **UF** Limited English Proficiency
- **B** Communication Skills [1973]
  Verbal Communication [1967]
- **R** Bilingualism [1973]
  English as Second Language [1997]
  Foreign Language Learning [1967]
  Verbal Ability [1967]
  Verbal Fluency [1973]

Larvae [1973]
PN 287　　　　　　　　**SC** 27780
- **B** Insects [1967]
- **R** Ants [1973]
  Bees [1973]
  Beetles [1973]
  Butterflies [1973]
  Cockroaches [1973]
  ↓ Diptera [1973]
  Drosophila [1973]
  ↓ Fishes [1967]
  Frogs [1967]
  Grasshoppers [1973]
  Mantis [1973]
  Moths [1973]
  Salamanders [1973]
  Toads [1973]
  Wasps [1982]

Laryngeal Disorders [1973]
PN 98　　　　　　　　　**SC** 27790
- **B** Respiratory Tract Disorders [1973]

Larynx [1973]
PN 152　　　　　　　　**SC** 27800
- **B** Respiratory System [1973]
- **N** Vocal Cords [1973]

Laser Irradiation [1973]
PN 30　　　　　　　　　**SC** 27810
- **B** Radiation [1967]

Latchkey Children
　Use Child Self Care

Latency (Response)
　Use Response Latency

Latent Inhibition [1997]
PN 150　　　　　　　　**SC** 27825
- **B** Interference (Learning) [1967]
- **N** Proactive Inhibition [1973]
  Retroactive Inhibition [1973]
- **R** Conditioned Stimulus [1973]
  ↓ Conditioning [1967]
  Forgetting [1973]
  ↓ Memory [1967]
  Prepulse Inhibition [1997]

Latent Learning [1973]
PN 106　　　　　　　　**SC** 27830
SN Learning that is not immediately manifested in performance but which remains dormant until activated by some contingency. From 1982, limited to animal populations. Use INCIDENTAL LEARNING for human populations.
- **B** Incidental Learning [1967]

Latent Trait Theory
　Use Item Response Theory

Lateral Dominance [1967]
PN 6511　　　　　　　　**SC** 27840
SN The tendency for the right or left hemisphere to be dominant over the other for most functions, leading to a differential primacy, functional asymmetry, or preference for one side of the body. Compare CEREBRAL DOMINANCE.
- **UF** Hemispheric Specialization
- **B** Cerebral Dominance [1973]
- **N** Handedness [1978]
  Ocular Dominance [1973]
- **R** ↓ Brain [1967]
  Left Brain [1991]
  Right Brain [1991]

Latinos/Latinas
　Use Hispanics

Laughter [1978]
PN 257　　　　　　　　**SC** 27855
- **B** Vocalization [1967]
- **R** ↓ Emotional Responses [1967]
  ↓ Humor [1967]
  ↓ Nonverbal Communication [1971]
  Smiles [1973]

Law (Government) [1973]
PN 233　　　　　　　　**SC** 27860
SN Science and philosophy of law as sanctioned by governmental authority. For specific laws or statutes, use LAWS.
- **N** Civil Law [1994]
  Criminal Law [1973]
- **R** Defendants [1985]
  Government [1967]
  ↓ Justice [1973]
  ↓ Law Enforcement [1978]
  ↓ Laws [1967]
  Political Psychology [1997]

Law Enforcement [1978]
PN 657　　　　　　　　**SC** 27865
- **B** Legal Processes [1973]
- **N** ↓ Adjudication [1967]
  Incarceration [1973]
  Legal Arrest [1973]
  Legal Detention [1973]

Law Enforcement — (cont'd)
- **R** Civil Law [1994]
  Crime Prevention [1985]
  ↓ Criminal Justice [1991]
  Government [1967]
  ↓ Justice [1973]
  ↓ Law (Government) [1973]
  ↓ Laws [1967]
  ↓ Legal Evidence [1991]
  Legal Interrogation [1994]
  Parole [1973]
  Probation [1973]

Law Enforcement Personnel [1973]
PN 391　　　　　　　　**SC** 27870
- **B** Government Personnel [1973]
  Legal Personnel [1985]
- **N** Parole Officers [1973]
  Police Personnel [1973]
  Prison Personnel [1973]
  Probation Officers [1973]
- **R** Attorneys [1973]
  ↓ Social Workers [1973]

Law Students [1978]
PN 173　　　　　　　　**SC** 27875
- **B** Students [1967]
- **R** Attorneys [1973]
  Graduate Students [1967]

Laws [1967]
PN 4122　　　　　　　　**SC** 27880
SN Rules of conduct made obligatory by some legal or controlling authority; includes statutes enacted by a legislative body.
- **B** Government Policy Making [1973]
- **N** Abortion Laws [1973]
  Disability Laws [1994]
  ↓ Drug Laws [1973]
  Gun Control Laws [1973]
- **R** ↓ Abuse Reporting [1997]
  Censorship [1978]
  Citizenship [1973]
  ↓ Civil Rights [1978]
  Consumer Protection [1973]
  Government [1967]
  ↓ Law (Government) [1973]
  ↓ Law Enforcement [1978]
  Legal Decisions [1991]
  ↓ Legal Processes [1973]
  Legislative Processes [1973]

Lawyers
　Use Attorneys

Lay Religious Personnel [1973]
PN 79　　　　　　　　**SC** 27900
SN Participants or members of a religious group or organization who perform various functional and ceremonial tasks not requiring a member of the clergy.
- **B** Religious Personnel [1973]
- **R** Chaplains [1973]
  ↓ Clergy [1973]
  Evangelists [1973]
  Missionaries [1973]

Lead (Metal) [1973]
PN 213　　　　　　　　**SC** 27910
- **B** Metallic Elements [1973]

Lead Poisoning [1973]
PN 313　　　　　　　　**SC** 27920
- **B** Toxic Disorders [1973]

Lead Poisoning — (cont'd)
R   Pica [1973]

Leadership [1967]
PN   5146   SC   27930
B   Social Behavior [1967]
N   Leadership Qualities [1997]
    Leadership Style [1973]
R   Abuse of Power [1997]
    Authority [1967]
    Entrepreneurship [1991]
    ↓ Management [1967]

Leadership Qualities [1997]
PN   228   SC   27935
B   Leadership [1967]
R   Charisma [1988]
    Leadership Style [1973]
    ↓ Management [1967]
    ↓ Personality Traits [1967]

Leadership Style [1973]
PN   2561   SC   27940
B   Leadership [1967]
    Social Behavior [1967]
R   Charisma [1988]
    Leadership Qualities [1997]

Learned Helplessness [1978]
PN   1524   SC   27945
SN   Learned expectation that one's responses are independent of reward and, hence, do not predict or control the occurrence of rewards. Learned helplessness derives from a history, experimentally induced or naturally occurring, of having received punishment/aversive stimulation regardless of responses made. Such circumstances result in an impaired ability to learn. Used for human or animal populations.
UF   Helplessness (Learned)
B   Helplessness [1997]
R   Attribution [1973]
    ↓ Emotional States [1973]
    Experimental Neurosis [1973]

Learning [1967]
PN   14561   SC   28030
SN   Conceptually broad term referring to the process of acquiring knowledge, skills, or behaviors by instruction, study, or experience. Use a more specific term if possible. Used for both human and animal populations.
N   Adult Learning [1997]
    Cat Learning [1967]
    Cognitive Hypothesis Testing [1982]
    ↓ Conditioning [1967]
    Cooperative Learning [1994]
    ↓ Discrimination Learning [1982]
    ↓ Experiential Learning [1997]
    Extinction (Learning) [1967]
    Foreign Language Learning [1967]
    ↓ Generalization (Learning) [1982]
    Generation Effect (Learning) [1991]
    ↓ Incidental Learning [1967]
    Intentional Learning [1973]
    ↓ Interference (Learning) [1967]
    Mastery Learning [1985]
    Maze Learning [1967]
    Mnemonic Learning [1973]
    Nonverbal Learning [1973]
    Observational Learning [1973]
    Overlearning [1967]
    ↓ Perceptual Motor Learning [1967]
    Probability Learning [1967]

Learning — (cont'd)
N   Rat Learning [1967]
    Relearning [1973]
    School Learning [1967]
    Sequential Learning [1973]
    ↓ Serial Learning [1967]
    ↓ Skill Learning [1973]
    ↓ Social Learning [1973]
    Spatial Learning [1994]
    Spontaneous Recovery (Learning) [1973]
    State Dependent Learning [1982]
    ↓ Transfer (Learning) [1967]
    Trial and Error Learning [1973]
    ↓ Verbal Learning [1967]
R   ↓ Cognitive Processes [1967]
    ↓ Concept Formation [1967]
    Connectionism [1994]
    Constructivism [1994]
    Delayed Alternation [1994]
    ↓ Feedback [1967]
    Forgetting [1973]
    ↓ Habits [1967]
    Individualized Instruction [1973]
    Learning Ability [1973]
    ↓ Learning Disorders [1967]
    Learning Rate [1973]
    ↓ Learning Schedules [1967]
    ↓ Learning Strategies [1991]
    Learning Theory [1967]
    ↓ Memory [1967]
    Metacognition [1991]
    Primacy Effect [1973]
    ↓ Prompting [1997]
    Recency Effect [1973]
    ↓ Reinforcement [1967]
    ↓ Retention [1967]
    ↓ Serial Position Effect [1982]
    Spontaneous Alternation [1982]
    ↓ Strategies [1967]
    Time On Task [1988]

Learning Ability [1973]
PN   1094   SC   27960
SN   Capacity to acquire a behavior, skill, or knowledge from experience, formal instruction, or conditioning. Used for animal or human populations.
B   Ability [1967]
R   ↓ Learning [1967]

Learning Centers (Educational) [1973]
PN   64   SC   27970
B   School Facilities [1973]
R   Language Laboratories [1973]

Learning Disabilities [1973]
PN   12349   SC   27980
SN   According to U.S. federal legislation, disabilities involved in understanding or using language, manifested in impaired listening, thinking, talking, reading, writing, or arithmetic skills. Includes perceptual handicaps, brain injury, minimal brain dysfunction, and developmental aphasia. Compare LEARNING DISORDERS.
B   Learning Disorders [1967]
N   Dyslexia [1973]
R   Acalculia [1973]
    Agraphia [1973]
    ↓ Aphasia [1967]
    Educational Diagnosis [1978]
    Minimal Brain Disorders [1973]
    ↓ Perceptual Disturbances [1973]

Learning Disorders [1967]
PN   1338   SC   27990

Learning Disorders — (cont'd)
SN   According to U.S. federal legislation, learning problems that are due to visual, hearing, or motor handicaps, mental retardation, emotional disturbance or environmental, cultural, or economic disadvantage. Compare LEARNING DISABILITIES.
B   Disorders [1967]
N   ↓ Learning Disabilities [1973]
    ↓ Reading Disabilities [1967]
R   Developmental Disabilities [1982]
    Educational Diagnosis [1978]
    ↓ Learning [1967]
    ↓ Mental Disorders [1967]
    ↓ Physical Disorders [1997]

Learning Rate [1973]
PN   562   SC   28000
R   ↓ Learning [1967]
    ↓ Serial Position Effect [1982]

Learning Schedules [1967]
PN   100   SC   28010
UF   Schedules (Learning)
N   Distributed Practice [1973]
    Massed Practice [1973]
R   ↓ Learning [1967]

Learning Strategies [1991]
PN   1938   SC   28013
SN   Techniques, methods, or tactics used for learning. Limited to human populations.
UF   Strategies (Learning)
B   Strategies [1967]
N   Mnemonic Learning [1973]
    Observational Learning [1973]
    ↓ Social Learning [1973]
    Trial and Error Learning [1973]
R   Advance Organizers [1985]
    ↓ Cognitive Processes [1967]
    ↓ Cognitive Style [1967]
    Constant Time Delay [1997]
    ↓ Learning [1967]
    Memory Training [1994]
    Metacognition [1991]
    Note Taking [1991]
    ↓ Prompting [1997]
    Study Habits [1973]
    Time Management [1994]

Learning Style
    Use Cognitive Style

Learning Theory [1967]
PN   1869   SC   28020
B   Theories [1967]
R   ↓ Classical Conditioning [1967]
    Connectionism [1994]
    ↓ Learning [1967]
    ↓ Operant Conditioning [1967]

Learys Interpersonal Check List [1973]
PN   15   SC   28040
SN   Use LEARYS INTERPERSONAL CHECK LIST or LEARY INTERPERSONAL CHECK LIST to access references from 1973-1977.
B   Nonprojective Personality Measures [1973]

Least Preferred Coworker Scale [1973]
PN   62   SC   28050
B   Preference Measures [1973]

Least Squares [1985]
PN   174   SC   28055

Least Squares — (cont'd)
SN Method of estimating the curve-of-best-fit or regression line of a set of points representing statistical data.
- **B**   Statistical Estimation 1985
- **R**   Error of Measurement 1985
- ↓ Statistical Regression 1985

Lecithin 1991
PN 8   **SC** 28058
- **B**   Choline 1973
-      Phosphatides 1973

Lecture Method 1973
PN 627   **SC** 28060
- **B**   Teaching Methods 1967
- **R**   Directed Discussion Method 1973

Left Brain 1991
PN 412   **SC** 28070
SN Used only when the left hemisphere of the brain is the focus of the document.
- **B**   Cerebral Cortex 1967
- **R** ↓ Brain 1967
- ↓ Cerebral Dominance 1973
-     Corpus Callosum 1973
-     Interhemispheric Interaction 1985
- ↓ Lateral Dominance 1967
-     Ocular Dominance 1973
-     Right Brain 1991

Leg (Anatomy) 1973
PN 287   **SC** 28080
- **B**   Musculoskeletal System 1973
- **R**   Ankle 1973
-      Feet (Anatomy) 1973
-      Knee 1973
-      Thigh 1973

Legal Arrest 1973
PN 451   **SC** 28090
SN Taking custody, under legal authority, of a person for the purpose of holding or detaining him/her to answer criminal charges or civil demands.
- **UF** Arrest (Law)
- **B**   Law Enforcement 1978

Legal Decisions 1991
PN 496   **SC** 28095
SN Used for discussions of the implications or the effects of specific judicial decisions. Not used for the actual process of judicial decision making. Consider CASE LAW for descriptions, not discussions, of laws resulting from court decisions.
- **R** ↓ Adjudication 1967
-     Criminal Conviction 1973
- ↓ Criminal Justice 1991
- ↓ Laws 1967
- ↓ Legal Processes 1973
-     Legislative Processes 1973

Legal Detention 1973
PN 101   **SC** 28100
SN Being detained (e.g., in jail) by law enforcers for having committed or for being suspected of having committed a crime, especially immediately prior to a legal court disposition.
- **UF** Detention (Legal)
- **B**   Law Enforcement 1978
- **R**   Legal Interrogation 1994

Legal Evidence 1991
PN 269   **SC** 28103

Legal Evidence — (cont'd)
SN Testimony, records, documents, objects, and diagrams submitted to a court during a hearing or trial.
- **UF** Evidence (Legal)
- **B**   Legal Processes 1973
- **N** ↓ Legal Testimony 1982
- **R** ↓ Adjudication 1967
- ↓ Law Enforcement 1978
-     Legal Interrogation 1994
-     Witnesses 1985

Legal Interrogation 1994
PN 104   **SC** 28104
- **UF** Criminal Interrogation
-      Police Interrogation
- **B**   Legal Processes 1973
- **R**   Interviewing 1973
- ↓ Law Enforcement 1978
-     Legal Detention 1973
- ↓ Legal Evidence 1991
- ↓ Legal Testimony 1982
-     Polygraphs 1973
-     Questioning 1982
-     Witnesses 1985

Legal Liability (Professional)
Use Professional Liability

Legal Personnel 1985
PN 189   **SC** 28107
- **UF** Paralegal Personnel
- **B**   Professional Personnel 1978
- **N**   Attorneys 1973
-      Judges 1985
- ↓ Law Enforcement Personnel 1973
- **R**   Juries 1985

Legal Processes 1973
PN 5681   **SC** 28110
SN Broad concept encompassing psychological and behavioral aspects of the law--its formation, enforcement, impact, and implications. Also includes reference to the legal justice system and legislative processes as they relate to psychology.
- **N** ↓ Adoption (Child) 1967
-     Child Custody 1982
-     Child Visitation 1988
- ↓ Commitment (Psychiatric) 1973
-     Competency to Stand Trial 1985
- ↓ Criminal Justice 1991
-     Forensic Evaluation 1994
-     Guardianship 1988
-     Insanity Defense 1985
- ↓ Law Enforcement 1978
- ↓ Legal Evidence 1991
-     Legal Interrogation 1994
- ↓ Legal Testimony 1982
-     Legislative Processes 1973
-     Parole 1973
-     Probation 1973
- **R**   Advance Directives 1994
-     Civil Law 1994
- ↓ Civil Rights 1978
-     Consumer Protection 1973
-     Government 1967
- ↓ Government Policy Making 1973
-     Informed Consent 1985
- ↓ Laws 1967
-     Legal Decisions 1991
-     Professional Liability 1985
-     Protective Services 1997
-     Risk Management 1997

Legal Processes — (cont'd)
- **R** ↓ Social Issues 1991

Legal Psychology
Use Forensic Psychology

Legal Testimony 1982
PN 754   **SC** 28115
SN Evidence presented by a witness under oath or affirmation (as distinguished from evidence derived from other sources) either orally or written as deposition or affidavit.
- **B**   Legal Evidence 1991
-     Legal Processes 1973
- **N**   Expert Testimony 1973
- **R**   Legal Interrogation 1994
-     Witnesses 1985

Legalization (Marihuana)
Use Marihuana Legalization

Legibility 1978
PN 49   **SC** 28127
- **N**   Handwriting Legibility 1973
- **R**   Readability 1978
- ↓ Written Language 1967

Legibility (Handwriting)
Use Handwriting Legibility

Legislative Processes 1973
PN 602   **SC** 28140
- **B**   Government Policy Making 1973
-     Legal Processes 1973
- **R**   Advocacy 1985
-     Government 1967
- ↓ Laws 1967
-     Legal Decisions 1991

Leisure Time 1973
PN 1779   **SC** 28150
- **R**   Daily Activities 1994
-     Hobbies 1988
-     Holidays 1988
- ↓ Recreation 1967
-     Relaxation 1973

Leiter Adult Intelligence Scale
SN Term was discontinued in 1997. In 2000, the term was stripped from all records containing it, and replaced with INTELLIGENCE MEASURES, its postable counterpart.
- **Use** Intelligence Measures

Lemniscal System 1985
PN 15   **SC** 28165
SN Long ascending sensory neural pathways projecting to the diencephalon. This system includes the medial lemniscus, lateral lemniscus, spinothalamic tracts, and secondary trigeminal projections.
- **B**   Afferent Pathways 1982
- **N**   Spinothalamic Tracts 1973
- **R**   Reticular Formation 1967

Lemurs 1973
PN 305   **SC** 28170
- **UF** Bush Babies
- **B**   Mammals 1973

Length of Stay
Use Treatment Duration

Lens (Eye) 1973
PN 57　　　　　　　　　　　　SC 28180
　B　Eye (Anatomy) 1967
　R　↓ Light Refraction 1982
　　　Ocular Accommodation 1982

Lesbian Parents
　Use　Homosexual Parents

Lesbianism 1973
PN 2244　　　　　　　　　　SC 28190
　B　Homosexuality 1967
　R　Bisexuality 1973
　　　Heterosexuality 1973
　　　Homosexual Parents 1994
　　　Male Homosexuality 1973

Lesions 1967
PN 2151　　　　　　　　　　SC 28200
　SN　Not defined prior to 1982. From 1982, limited to experimentally induced lesions and used primarily for animal populations.
　UF　Ablation
　　　Sectioning (Lesion)
　N　↓ Brain Lesions 1967
　　　Neural Lesions 1973
　R　↓ Surgery 1971

Lesson Plans 1973
PN 148　　　　　　　　　　　SC 28220
　B　Teaching Methods 1967

Letters (Alphabet) 1973
PN 1741　　　　　　　　　　SC 28230
　B　Alphabets 1973
　N　Consonants 1973
　　　Vowels 1973

Leucine 1973
PN 48　　　　　　　　　　　SC 28240
　B　Amino Acids 1973

Leucocytes 1973
PN 321　　　　　　　　　　　SC 28250
　UF　Leukocytes
　　　White Blood Cells
　B　Blood Cells 1973
　N　Lymphocytes 1973

Leukemias 1973
PN 363　　　　　　　　　　　SC 28260
　B　Blood and Lymphatic Disorders 1973
　　　Neoplasms 1967

Leukocytes
　Use　Leucocytes

Leukotomy
　Use　Psychosurgery

Level of Functioning
　Use　Ability Level

Levodopa 1973
PN 702　　　　　　　　　　　SC 28290
　UF　L Dopa
　B　Antitremor Drugs 1973
　　　Cholinergic Blocking Drugs 1973
　R　DOPA 1973
　　　Dopamine 1973

Lewy Body Disease
　Use　Dementia with Lewy Bodies

Lexical Access 1988
PN 1424　　　　　　　　　　SC 29293
　N　Lexical Decision 1988
　R　Cognitive Discrimination 1973
　　　Human Information Storage 1973
　　　Semantic Memory 1988
　　　↓ Verbal Memory 1994
　　　Word Meaning 1973
　　　Words (Phonetic Units) 1967

Lexical Decision 1988
PN 1309　　　　　　　　　　SC 29296
　B　Lexical Access 1988
　R　Cognitive Discrimination 1973
　　　Human Information Storage 1973
　　　Semantic Memory 1988
　　　↓ Verbal Memory 1994
　　　Word Meaning 1973
　　　Words (Phonetic Units) 1967

Liberalism 1973
PN 178　　　　　　　　　　　SC 28298
　B　Personality Traits 1967
　R　Political Liberalism 1973

Liberalism (Political)
　Use　Political Liberalism

Libido 1973
PN 209　　　　　　　　　　　SC 28310
　B　Psychoanalytic Personality Factors 1973
　R　Inhibited Sexual Desire 1997
　　　Sex Drive 1973

Librarians 1988
PN 53　　　　　　　　　　　SC 28314
　B　Information Specialists 1988
　R　↓ Professional Personnel 1978

Libraries 1982
PN 104　　　　　　　　　　　SC 28317
　N　School Libraries 1973
　R　↓ Community Facilities 1973
　　　Information 1967
　　　Information Services 1988

Libraries (School)
　Use　School Libraries

Librium
　Use　Chlordiazepoxide

Licensing (Professional)
　Use　Professional Licensing

Licensure Examinations
　Use　Professional Examinations

Licking 1988
PN 170　　　　　　　　　　　SC 28345
　SN　Used for human or animal populations.
　UF　Animal Licking Behavior
　B　Animal Ethology 1967
　　　Motor Processes 1967
　R　Animal Drinking Behavior 1973
　　　Animal Grooming Behavior 1978
　　　Animal Maternal Behavior 1973

Lidocaine 1973
PN 170　　　　　　　　　　　SC 28350
　UF　Xylocaine
　B　Local Anesthetics 1973

Life Change
　Use　Life Experiences

Life Expectancy 1982
PN 481　　　　　　　　　　　SC 28352
　SN　Anticipated number of years of life for an individual, based on statistical probability. Use AGED and PHYSIOLOGICAL AGING together to access references from 1973-1981. Used for both human and animal populations.
　UF　Life Span
　　　Longevity
　R　↓ Aging 1991
　　　↓ Human Development 1967
　　　Physiological Aging 1967

Life Experiences 1973
PN 6333　　　　　　　　　　SC 28355
　SN　Specific events which are commonly considered noteworthy or memorable (e.g., college graduation, wedding) or are considered unusual or otherwise significant (e.g., life change due to illness). Compare EXPERIENCES (EVENTS).
　UF　Experiences (Life)
　　　Life Change
　B　Experiences (Events) 1973
　R　Age Regression (Hypnotic) 1988
　　　Anniversary Events 1994
　　　Autobiographical Memory 1994
　　　Biographical Data 1978
　　　Homesickness 1994
　　　Life Review 1991
　　　Life Satisfaction 1985

Life Insurance 1973
PN 21　　　　　　　　　　　SC 28360
　B　Insurance 1973

Life Review 1991
PN 234　　　　　　　　　　　SC 28361
　SN　Reflection on and return to past life experiences in order to think about and reintegrate them into present life circumstances. Usually performed in a treatment or intervention setting. Not limited to elderly populations. Consider using REMINISCENCE to access references from 1985-1990.
　R　Anniversary Events 1994
　　　Autobiographical Memory 1994
　　　Early Experience 1967
　　　Early Memories 1985
　　　Gerontology 1967
　　　Life Experiences 1973
　　　Narratives 1997
　　　Reminiscence 1985
　　　↓ Treatment 1967

Life Satisfaction 1985
PN 2211　　　　　　　　　　SC 28362
　B　Satisfaction 1973
　R　Life Experiences 1973
　　　Lifestyle Changes 1997
　　　↓ Quality of Life 1985
　　　Role Satisfaction 1994
　　　Well Being 1994

Life Span
　Use　Life Expectancy

Life Sustaining Treatment 1997
PN 104   SC 28368
- B Treatment 1967
- R Advance Directives 1994
-   Assisted Suicide 1997
-   ↓ Client Rights 1988
-   Medical Treatment (General) 1973
-   Palliative Care 1991
-   Terminally Ill Patients 1973
-   Treatment Refusal 1994
-   Treatment Withholding 1988

Lifesaving
- Use Artificial Respiration

Lifestyle 1978
PN 2300   SC 28375
SN Typical way of life or manner of living character-
istic of an individual or groups.
- N Lifestyle Changes 1997
- R Daily Activities 1994
-   Health Behavior 1982
-   Holistic Health 1985
-   ↓ Personality 1967
-   ↓ Personality Processes 1967
-   ↓ Quality of Life 1985

Lifestyle Changes 1997
PN 164   SC 28380
- B Lifestyle 1978
- R Behavior Change 1973
-   Health Attitudes 1985
-   Health Behavior 1982
-   Health Promotion 1991
-   Life Satisfaction 1985
-   ↓ Quality of Life 1985
-   Well Being 1994

Light
- Use Illumination

Light Adaptation 1982
PN 254   SC 28393
SN Change in the general level of sensitivity of the
photoreceptors as a result of exposure to light.
- UF Adaptation (Light)
- B Sensory Adaptation 1967
- R Dark Adaptation 1973
-   ↓ Illumination 1967
-   ↓ Visual Thresholds 1973

Light Refraction 1982
PN 34   SC 28395
SN Deflection of light from a straight path when
passing obliquely through the interface of two media
that have different densities.
- N ↓ Refraction Errors 1973
- R ↓ Illumination 1967
-   Lens (Eye) 1973

Likability 1988
PN 119   SC 28387
- B Personality Traits 1967
- R Agreeableness 1997
-   Interpersonal Attraction 1967
-   Peer Pressure 1994
-   Social Approval 1967
-   ↓ Social Perception 1967

Likert Scales 1994
PN 72   SC 28388

Likert Scales — (cont'd)
- B Rating Scales 1967
- R Attitude Measurement 1973
-   ↓ Attitude Measures 1967
-   Self Report 1982
-   Semantic Differential 1967
-   ↓ Surveys 1967

Liking
- Use Affection

Limbic System 1973
PN 1260   SC 28410
- B Cerebral Cortex 1967
-   Neural Pathways 1982
- N Amygdaloid Body 1973
-   Fornix 1982
-   Gyrus Cinguli 1973
-   Hippocampus 1967
-   Medial Forebrain Bundle 1982
-   Olfactory Bulb 1973
-   Septal Nuclei 1982
- R Nucleus Accumbens 1982
-   Raphe Nuclei 1982

Limen
- Use Thresholds

Limited English Proficiency
- Use Language Proficiency

Linear Perspective 1982
PN 153   SC 28427
SN Apparent convergence of parallel contours that
are projected into the plane of sight of the observer.
- UF Visual Perspective
- B Vision 1967
- R ↓ Depth Perception 1967
-   ↓ Distance Perception 1973
-   ↓ Size Discrimination 1967
-   ↓ Visual Stimulation 1973

Linear Regression 1973
PN 299   SC 28430
- B Statistical Correlation 1967
-   Statistical Regression 1985
- R Multiple Regression 1982

Linguistics 1973
PN 2648   SC 28450
- N Ethnolinguistics 1973
-   Etymology 1973
-   ↓ Grammar 1967
-   Metalinguistics 1994
-   Neurolinguistics 1991
-   Orthography 1973
-   Psycholinguistics 1967
-   Sociolinguistics 1985
- R Discourse Analysis 1997
-   ↓ Language 1967
-   Pragmatics 1985
-   ↓ Prosody 1991
-   ↓ Semiotics 1985
-   ↓ Verbal Communication 1967

Linkage Analysis
- Use Genetic Linkage

Lions
- Use Felids

Lipid Metabolism 1973
PN 137   SC 28460
- UF Fat Metabolism
- B Metabolism 1967
- R ↓ Lipids 1973

Lipid Metabolism Disorders 1973
PN 45   SC 28470
- B Metabolism Disorders 1973
- N Amaurotic Familial Idiocy 1973

Lipids 1973
PN 644   SC 28480
- N ↓ Fatty Acids 1973
- R Lipid Metabolism 1973
-   ↓ Steroids 1973

Lipoproteins 1973
PN 195   SC 28490
- R ↓ Proteins 1973

Lipreading 1973
PN 326   SC 28500
- UF Speechreading
- R ↓ Deaf 1967
-   Speech Perception 1967
-   ↓ Visual Perception 1967

Lips (Face) 1973
PN 112   SC 28510
- R Mouth (Anatomy) 1967

Liquor 1973
PN 41   SC 28520
- B Alcoholic Beverages 1973

Listening
- Use Auditory Perception

Listening (Interpersonal) 1997
PN 124   SC 28535
- B Interpersonal Communication 1973
- R ↓ Attention 1967
-   ↓ Auditory Perception 1967
-   Conversation 1967
-   Listening Comprehension 1973
-   Social Skills 1978

Listening Comprehension 1973
PN 1390   SC 28540
- B Verbal Comprehension 1985
- R Listening (Interpersonal) 1997

Literacy 1973
PN 1905   SC 28550
- UF Illiteracy
- N Computer Literacy 1991
- R ↓ Language 1967
-   ↓ Language Arts Education 1973
-   Literacy Programs 1997
-   Reading Development 1997
-   Reading Education 1973
-   ↓ Reading Skills 1973
-   Writing Skills 1985

Literacy Programs 1997
PN 124   SC 28555
- B Educational Programs 1973
- R ↓ Adult Education 1973
-   ↓ Language Arts Education 1973
-   ↓ Literacy 1973
-   Reading Education 1973

Literacy Programs — (cont'd)
R ↓ Reading Skills 1973
↓ Social Services 1982
Writing Skills 1985

Literature 1967
PN 5167 SC 28560
UF Fiction
B Arts 1973
N Poetry 1973
↓ Prose 1973
R Creative Writing 1994
Drama 1973
Folklore 1991
Metaphor 1982
Myths 1967
Narratives 1997
Postmodernism 1997
↓ Religious Literature 1973
Writers 1991

Literature Review 1967
PN 21799 SC 28580
SN Used in records discussing issues involved in the process of conducting surveys of previously published material. From 1967-2000, the term was also used as a mandatory document type identifier; however, this usage has been discontinued due to the advent of Form/Content Type record field identifiers. References from 1967-2000 can be accessed using either LITERATURE REVIEW or the Literature Review Form/Content Type field identifier. In 1973, this term replaced the discontinued term REVIEW (OF LITERATURE). In 2000, REVIEW (OF LITERATURE) was stripped from all records and replaced with LITERATURE REVIEW.
UF Review (of Literature)
R Meta Analysis 1985

Lithium 1973
PN 3078 SC 28590
SN Used for documents that do not specify the type of lithium used, e.g., carbonate, chloride or bromide. Use a more specific term if possible.
B Metallic Elements 1973
N Lithium Carbonate 1973
R ↓ Antidepressant Drugs 1971
↓ Tricyclic Antidepressant Drugs 1997

Lithium Bromide
SN Term was discontinued in 1997. In 2000, the term was stripped from all records containing it, and replaced with BROMIDES, its postable counterpart.
Use Bromides

Lithium Carbonate 1973
PN 710 SC 28610
B Antidepressant Drugs 1971
Lithium 1973

Litter Size 1985
PN 107 SC 28615
SN Used for animal populations only.
B Size 1973
R ↓ Animal Breeding 1973

Liver 1973
PN 335 SC 28620
B Digestive System 1967

Liver Disorders 1973
PN 229 SC 28630

Liver Disorders — (cont'd)
UF Hepatic Disorders
B Digestive System Disorders 1973
N Cirrhosis (Liver) 1973
↓ Hepatitis 1973
Jaundice 1973
R ↓ Infectious Disorders 1973
↓ Neoplasms 1967
↓ Toxic Disorders 1973

Living Alone 1994
PN 38 SC 28633
SN Use LIVING ARRANGEMENTS to access references from 1991-1993.
B Living Arrangements 1991
R Cohabitation 1973
↓ Family Structure 1973
Home Environment 1973
↓ Marital Status 1973
Single Persons 1973

Living Arrangements 1991
PN 798 SC 28635
UF Household Structure
N Cohabitation 1973
Living Alone 1994
R Child Custody 1982
Empty Nest 1991
↓ Family 1967
↓ Family Structure 1973
Home Environment 1973
↓ Housing 1973
↓ Marital Status 1973
Retirement Communities 1997
Roommates 1973
Shelters 1991
Single Sex Environments 2001

Living Wills
Use Advance Directives

Lizards 1973
PN 430 SC 28640
B Reptiles 1967

Lobectomy
Use Psychosurgery

Lobotomy
Use Psychosurgery

Local Anesthetics 1973
PN 89 SC 28660
B Anesthetic Drugs 1973
N Cocaine 1973
Lidocaine 1973
Quinine 1973
R Ephedrine 1973
Methoxamine 1973

Localization (Perceptual)
Use Perceptual Localization

Localization (Sound)
Use Auditory Localization

Locus Ceruleus 1982
PN 379 SC 28687
SN Pigmented nucleus in the brain stem that synthesizes norepinephrine.

Locus Ceruleus — (cont'd)
B Brain Stem 1973
R Reticular Formation 1967

Locus of Control
Use Internal External Locus of Control

Logic (Philosophy) 1973
PN 292 SC 28700
B Philosophies 1967

Logical Thinking 1967
PN 1612 SC 28710
UF Ratiocination
B Thinking 1967
R Analogy 1991
↓ Inductive Deductive Reasoning 1973

Logistic Models
Use Item Response Theory

Logotherapy 1973
PN 301 SC 28720
SN Existential analysis based on spiritual values and emphasizing search for the meaning of human existence.
B Psychotherapy 1967
R Existential Therapy 1973

Loneliness 1973
PN 1293 SC 28730
B Emotional States 1973
R Abandonment 1997
Homesickness 1994

Long Term Care 1994
PN 548 SC 28735
SN Delivery of health or mental health services over a prolonged or extended period. Care can be in an institutional setting or in the community, e.g., at home, and delivered by health care professionals, family, or friends.
B Health Care Services 1978
Treatment Duration 1988
R Adult Day Care 1997
↓ Case Management 1991
Home Care 1985
↓ Hospitalization 1967
↓ Mental Health Services 1978
Nursing Homes 1973
Palliative Care 1991

Long Term Memory 1973
PN 1752 SC 28740
SN Retention of events or learned material for relatively long periods, presumed to be based on permanent encoding and storage of information transferred from short term memory. Consider also RETENTION.
B Memory 1967

Long Term Potentiation
Use Postactivation Potentials

Longevity
Use Life Expectancy

Longitudinal Studies 1973
PN 13874 SC 28760

Longitudinal Studies — (cont'd)
SN Used in records discussing issues involved in the process of conducting observations or measurements of the same individual or group over an extended period. From 1973-2000, the term was also used as a mandatory document type identifier; however, this usage has been discontinued due to the advent of Form/Content Type field identifiers. References from 1973-2000 can be accessed using either LONGITUDINAL STUDIES or the Longitudinal Studies Form/Content Type field identifier.
UF Studies (Longitudinal)
B Experimental Design 1967
N Prospective Studies 1997
R Followup Studies 1973
Retrospective Studies 1997

Loosening of Associations
Use Fragmentation (Schizophrenia)

Lorazepam 1988
PN 332   **SC** 28765
B Benzodiazepines 1978
Minor Tranquilizers 1973

Lordosis (Animal)
Use Animal Sexual Receptivity

Lorge Thorndike Intelligence Test 1973
PN 14   **SC** 28770
B Intelligence Measures 1967

Loudness 1967
PN 461   **SC** 28780
UF Sound Pressure Level
B Auditory Stimulation 1967
N Noise Levels (Work Areas) 1973

Loudness Discrimination 1973
PN 172   **SC** 28790
B Loudness Perception 1973

Loudness Perception 1973
PN 295   **SC** 28800
B Auditory Perception 1967
N Loudness Discrimination 1973

Love 1973
PN 1612   **SC** 28830
B Emotional States 1973
R Affection 1973
Attachment Behavior 1985
Erotomania 1997
Intimacy 1973
Romance 1997

Low Birth Weight
Use Birth Weight

Lowenfeld Mosaic Test 1973
PN 11   **SC** 28840
B Intelligence Measures 1967

Lower Class 1973
PN 897   **SC** 28850
B Social Class 1967
Socioeconomic Status 1967

Lower Class Attitudes 1973
PN 61   **SC** 28860
SN Attitudes of, not toward, the lower class.
B Socioeconomic Class Attitudes 1973

Lower Income Level 1973
PN 1717   **SC** 28870
B Income Level 1973
R Poverty 1973

Loxapine 1982
PN 49   **SC** 28875
SN Organic heterocyclic compound used as a tranquilizing agent.
UF Oxilapine
B Minor Tranquilizers 1973

Loyalty 1973
PN 199   **SC** 28880
B Personality Traits 1967

LSD (Drug)
Use Lysergic Acid Diethylamide

Lucid Dreaming 1994
PN 32   **SC** 28893
B Dreaming 1967
R Dream Recall 1973
REM Dreams 1973
REM Sleep 1973
↓ Sleep 1967

Luck
Use Chance (Fortune)

Lumbar Spinal Cord 1973
PN 117   **SC** 28900
B Spinal Cord 1973

Lumbrosacral Plexus
Use Spinal Nerves

Luminance 1982
PN 1202   **SC** 28930
SN Product of multiplying the physical intensity of a light wave by the spectral sensitivity of the typical observer's visual system for that specific wavelength. Compare ILLUMINATION.
R ↓ Brightness Perception 1973
↓ Chromaticity 1997
Color Saturation 1997
↓ Illumination 1967
Stimulus Intensity 1967
↓ Visual Thresholds 1973

Luminance Threshold
Use Brightness Perception AND Visual Thresholds

Lunar Synodic Cycle 1973
PN 107   **SC** 28950
SN Successive phases of the moon reflecting its motion around the earth.
R ↓ Biological Rhythms 1967
↓ Environmental Effects 1973

Lung 1973
PN 112   **SC** 28960
B Respiratory System 1973

Lung Disorders 1973
PN 336   **SC** 28970
UF Pulmonary Disorders
B Respiratory Tract Disorders 1973
N Cystic Fibrosis 1985
Pneumonia 1973
Pulmonary Emphysema 1973
Pulmonary Tuberculosis 1973

Lung Disorders — (cont'd)
R ↓ Dyspnea 1973

Lupus 1973
PN 242   **SC** 28980
B Skin Disorders 1973
R ↓ Tuberculosis 1973

Luria Nebraska Neuropsychological Battery 2001
PN 76   **SC** 28983
SN In 2000, the truncated term LURIA NEBRASKA NEUROPSYCH BATTERY (which was used from 1991-2000) was deleted, removed from all records containing it, and mapped to its expanded form LURIA NEBRASKA NEUROPSYCHOLOGICAL BATTERY. Use NEUROPSYCHOLOGICAL ASSESSMENT to access references from 1982-1990.
B Neuropsychological Assessment 1982

Luteinizing Hormone 1978
PN 434   **SC** 28985
B Gonadotropic Hormones 1973
R ↓ Pituitary Hormones 1973
↓ Sex Hormones 1973

Lutherans
Use Protestants

Lying
Use Deception

Lymphatic Disorders
Use Blood and Lymphatic Disorders

Lymphocytes 1973
PN 595   **SC** 29060
B Leucocytes 1973
R Interleukins 1994

Lysergic Acid Diethylamide 1967
PN 802   **SC** 29070
UF LSD (Drug)
B Acids 1973
Amine Oxidase Inhibitors 1973
Hallucinogenic Drugs 1967
Psychedelic Drugs 1973
Psychotomimetic Drugs 1973
Serotonin Antagonists 1973
R ↓ Ergot Derivatives 1973

Machiavellianism 1973
PN 370   **SC** 29087
SN Extent to which an individual feels that any means, however unscrupulous, can justifiably be used to achieve power.
B Personality Traits 1967

Magazines 1973
PN 401   **SC** 29090
B Printed Communications Media 1973

Magical Thinking 1973
PN 131   **SC** 29100
SN Belief that one's utterances, thoughts, or behavior can have a controlling influence on specific events or prevent their occurrence by means that operate beyond the normal laws of cause and effect.
B Thinking 1967
Thought Disturbances 1973
R Fantasies (Thought Disturbances) 1967
↓ Fantasy 1997
Imagination 1967

Magical Thinking — (cont'd)
  R   Omnipotence [1994]

Magnesium [1973]
PN 166   SC 29110
  B   Metallic Elements [1973]
  N   Magnesium Ions [1973]

Magnesium Ions [1973]
PN 14   SC 29120
  B   Electrolytes [1973]
        Magnesium [1973]

Magnet Schools
  Use   Nontraditional Education

Magnetic Resonance Imaging [1994]
PN 902   SC 29133
  UF   MRI
  B   Tomography [1988]
  R   Computer Assisted Diagnosis [1973]
        Magnetoencephalography [1985]

Magnetism [1985]
PN 399   SC 29135
  UF   Geomagnetism
  R   Magnetoencephalography [1985]
        Physics [1973]

Magnetoencephalography [1985]
PN 211   SC 29136
  R   ↓ Electroencephalography [1967]
        Magnetic Resonance Imaging [1994]
        Magnetism [1985]

Magnitude Estimation [1991]
PN 140   SC 29138
SN Unidimensional scaling method in statistics and
psychophysics for quantitative judgment and ratio
estimation.
  B   Psychophysical Measurement [1967]
        Statistical Estimation [1985]
  R   Scaling (Testing) [1967]

Magnitude of Effect (Statistical)
  Use   Effect Size (Statistical)

Maids
  Use   Domestic Service Personnel

Mail Surveys [1994]
PN 92   SC 29141
  B   Surveys [1967]
  R   ↓ Consumer Research [1973]
        Consumer Surveys [1973]
      ↓ Methodology [1967]
      ↓ Questionnaires [1967]
        Telephone Surveys [1994]

Mainstreaming [1991]
PN 221   SC 29144
SN Integration or transition into society of individuals who have been considered for institutionalization
or other type of isolation, but are now considered
able to learn from education or community involvement.
  N   Mainstreaming (Educational) [1978]
  R   Deinstitutionalization [1982]
        Educational Placement [1978]
        Habilitation [1991]
        Independent Living Programs [1991]
      ↓ Rehabilitation [1967]

Mainstreaming — (cont'd)
  R   School to Work Transition [1994]
      ↓ Social Integration [1982]
        Special Education [1967]
        Special Needs [1994]

Mainstreaming (Educational) [1978]
PN 2880   SC 29145
SN Integration of students with special education
needs into classes or schools with regular students.
  B   Mainstreaming [1991]
  R   ↓ Education [1967]
        Educational Placement [1978]
        School Integration [1982]
        Special Education [1967]

Maintenance Therapy [1997]
PN 148   SC 29142
SN Treatment or therapy that is designed to maintain patients in a stable condition and to promote
either gradual healing or to prevent the relapse of a
disorder or condition. Used primarily, but not exclusively, in drug therapy settings.
  R   Aftercare [1973]
      ↓ Drug Therapy [1967]
        Methadone Maintenance [1978]
      ↓ Outpatient Treatment [1967]
        Relapse Prevention [1994]
      ↓ Treatment Duration [1988]

Major Depression [1988]
PN 27919   SC 29143
SN Affective disorder marked by dysphoric mood,
inactivity, lack of interest, insomnia, feelings of worth-
lessness, diminished ability to think, and thoughts of
suicide. Consider DEPRESSION (EMOTION) to
access references prior to 1988. Use DEPRESSION
(EMOTION) for nonclinical depression. In 1988, this
term replaced the discontinued term PSYCHOTIC
DEPRESSIVE REACTION, and in 2000 it replaced
the term NEUROTIC DEPRESSIVE REACTION. In
2000, these terms were stripped from all records and
replaced with MAJOR DEPRESSION.
  UF   Agitated Depression
        Depressive Reaction (Neurotic)
        Dysphoria
        Melancholia
        Neurotic Depressive Reaction
        Psychotic Depressive Reaction
        Unipolar Depression
  B   Affective Disorders [2001]
  N   Anaclitic Depression [1973]
        Dysthymic Disorder [1988]
        Endogenous Depression [1978]
        Involutional Depression [1973]
        Postpartum Depression [1973]
        Reactive Depression [1973]
        Recurrent Depression [1994]
        Treatment Resistant Depression [1994]
  R   ↓ Bipolar Disorder [2001]
        Depression (Emotion) [1967]
      ↓ Neurosis [1967]
        Pseudodementia [1985]
        Seasonal Affective Disorder [1991]

Major Tranquilizers
  Use   Neuroleptic Drugs

Maladjustment (Emotional)
  Use   Emotional Adjustment

Maladjustment (Social)
  Use   Social Adjustment

Malaria [1973]
PN 55   SC 29180
  B   Blood and Lymphatic Disorders [1973]
        Parasitic Disorders [1973]
  R   ↓ Nervous System Disorders [1967]

Male Animals [1973]
PN 3820   SC 29190
  B   Animals [1967]

Male Castration [1973]
PN 681   SC 29200
SN Used for both human and animal populations.
  B   Castration [1967]

Male Criminals [1973]
PN 1086   SC 29210
  B   Criminals [1967]
        Human Males [1973]

Male Delinquency [2001]
PN 1055   SC 29215
SN In 2000, this term was created to replace the
discontinued term MALE DELINQUENTS. MALE
DELINQUENTS was stripped from all records and
replaced with MALE DELINQUENCY.
  B   Juvenile Delinquency [1967]
  R   Female Delinquency [2001]
      ↓ Human Males [1973]

Male Female Relations [1988]
PN 1816   SC 29225
SN Relationships or interactions between the sexes.
Limited to human populations.
  UF   Heterosexual Interaction
  B   Interpersonal Interaction [1967]
  R   Heterosexuality [1973]
      ↓ Human Courtship [1973]
      ↓ Marital Relations [1967]
      ↓ Relationship Satisfaction [2001]
      ↓ Relationship Termination [1997]
        Social Dating [1973]
        Social Skills [1978]

Male Genital Disorders [1973]
PN 44   SC 29230
  B   Genital Disorders [1967]
  N   Klinefelters Syndrome [1973]
        Testicular Feminization Syndrome [1973]
  R   ↓ Endocrine Sexual Disorders [1973]
        Hermaphroditism [1973]
      ↓ Hypogonadism [1973]
      ↓ Infertility [1973]
        Sterility [1973]

Male Genitalia [1973]
PN 151   SC 29240
SN Used for both human and animal populations.
  UF   Genitalia (Male)
  B   Urogenital System [1973]
  N   Penis [1973]
        Prostate [1973]
        Testes [1973]
  R   Circumcision [2001]

Male Homosexuality [1973]
PN 3615   SC 29250
  UF   Gay Males
  B   Homosexuality [1967]
  R   Bisexuality [1973]
        Heterosexuality [1973]
        Homosexual Parents [1994]
        Lesbianism [1973]

Male Only Environments
  Use Single Sex Environments

Male Orgasm 1973
PN 279   **SC** 29260
SN Used for both human and animal populations.
  UF Ejaculation
  B   Orgasm 1973
  N   Nocturnal Emission 1973
      Premature Ejaculation 1973
  R   Impotence 1973
      Masturbation 1973
      ↓ Sexual Intercourse (Human) 1973

Males (Human)
  Use Human Males

Malignant Neoplasms
  Use Neoplasms

Malingering 1973
PN 622   **SC** 29290
SN Feigning or exaggerating illness or symptoms usually in order to escape work, evoke sympathy, or gain compensation.
  B   Deception 1967
  R   ↓ Factitious Disorders 1988
      ↓ Mental Disorders 1967
      Munchausen Syndrome 1994
      ↓ Physical Disorders 1997
      ↓ Somatoform Disorders 2001

Malnutrition
  Use Nutritional Deficiencies

Malpractice
  Use Professional Liability

Mammals 1973
PN 1432   **SC** 29310
  B   Vertebrates 1973
  N   Bats 1973
      ↓ Canids 1997
      Cattle 1973
      Chimpanzees 1973
      Chinchillas 1973
      Deer 1973
      Elephants 1973
      ↓ Felids 1997
      Goats 1973
      Horses 1973
      Lemurs 1973
      ↓ Marsupials 1973
      ↓ Primates (Nonhuman) 1973
      Rabbits 1967
      ↓ Rodents 1973
      Seals (Animal) 1973
      Sheep 1973
      ↓ Whales 1985

Mammary Glands 1973
PN 15   **SC** 29320
  B   Glands 1967

Mammary Neoplasms
  Use Breast Neoplasms

Mammillary Bodies (Hypothalamic)
  Use Hypothalamus

Mammography 1994
PN 178   **SC** 29345

Mammography — (cont'd)
  B   Roentgenography 1973
  R   Breast Neoplasms 1973
      Cancer Screening 1997
      ↓ Health Screening 1997
      ↓ Medical Diagnosis 1973
      Physical Examination 1988
      Preventive Medicine 1973

Man Machine Systems
SN Term was discontinued in 1997. In 2000, the term was stripped from all records containing it, and replaced with HUMAN MACHINE SYSTEMS, its postable counterpart.
  Use Human Machine Systems

Man Machine Systems Design
SN Term was discontinued in 1997. In 2000, the term was stripped from all records containing it, and replaced with HUMAN MACHINE SYSTEMS DESIGN, its postable counterpart.
  Use Human Machine Systems Design

Managed Care 1994
PN 1236   **SC** 29365
SN Competitive prepaid plan of health care delivery to contain costs and provide access to quality health care. Use CASE MANAGEMENT to access references from 1991-1993.
  B   Health Care Delivery 1978
  N   Health Maintenance Organizations 1982
  R   ↓ Case Management 1991
      Cost Containment 1991
      Fee for Service 1994
      Health Care Costs 1994
      ↓ Health Care Services 1978
      ↓ Health Insurance 1973
      Quality of Care 1988
      ↓ Treatment Planning 1997

Management 1967
PN 2089   **SC** 29420
SN Conceptually broad term referring to the process of manipulation of human or material resources to accomplish given goals. Use a more specific term if possible.
  N   Business Management 1973
      ↓ Case Management 1991
      Disability Management 1991
      Educational Administration 1967
      ↓ Health Care Administration 1997
      Household Management 1985
      ↓ Personnel Management 1973
      Risk Management 1997
      ↓ Self Management 1985
      Stress Management 1985
      Time Management 1994
  R   Accountability 1988
      Business 1967
      Career Development 1985
      Entrepreneurship 1991
      Labor Management Relations 1967
      ↓ Leadership 1967
      Leadership Qualities 1997
      Management Decision Making 1973
      ↓ Management Methods 1973
      ↓ Management Personnel 1973
      Management Planning 1973
      Management Training 1973
      ↓ Work Teams 2001

Management Decision Making 1973
PN 1441   **SC** 29370
  B   Decision Making 1967

Management Decision Making — (cont'd)
  R   ↓ Group Decision Making 1978
      ↓ Management 1967
      ↓ Management Methods 1973
      Management Planning 1973
      Participative Management 1988

Management Development
  Use Career Development

Management Information Systems
  Use Information Systems

Management Methods 1973
PN 3024   **SC** 29380
  N   Participative Management 1988
      Self Managing Work Teams 2001
  R   Business Management 1973
      ↓ Management 1967
      Management Decision Making 1973
      Management Planning 1973
      Supervisor Employee Interaction 1997
      ↓ Teams 1988
      Work Scheduling 1973
      ↓ Work Teams 2001

Management Personnel 1973
PN 7887   **SC** 29390
  UF Administrators
      Supervisors
  B   White Collar Workers 1973
  N   Middle Level Managers 1973
      Top Level Managers 1973
  R   Commissioned Officers 1973
      Industrial Foremen 1973
      ↓ Management 1967
      ↓ School Administrators 1973
      Supervisor Employee Interaction 1997

Management Planning 1973
PN 376   **SC** 29400
  UF Planning (Management)
  R   ↓ Management 1967
      Management Decision Making 1973
      ↓ Management Methods 1973
      Marketing 1973

Management Training 1973
PN 1272   **SC** 29410
  B   Personnel Training 1967
  R   Business Education 1973
      ↓ Management 1967
      Wilderness Experience 1991

Manager Employee Interaction
  Use Supervisor Employee Interaction

Mandibula
  Use Jaw

Mania 1967
PN 1935   **SC** 29450
  B   Affective Disorders 2001
      Emotional States 1973
  N   Hypomania 1973
  R   ↓ Bipolar Disorder 2001

Manic Depression
SN In 2000, the term was discontinued, and all records containing it were stripped of the term and replaced with BIPOLAR DISORDER, its postable counterpart.

Manic Depression — (cont'd)
  Use Bipolar Disorder

Manic Depressive Psychosis
  SN This term was discontinued in 1988, when the term MANIC DEPRESSION was created to capture this concept. In 2000, MANIC DEPRESSION was discontinued and made nonpostable for the new term BIPOLAR DISORDER. MANIC DEPRESSIVE PSYCHOSIS and MANIC DEPRESSION were stripped from all records containing them and replaced with BIPOLAR DISORDER.
  Use Bipolar Disorder

Mann Whitney U Test [1973]
  PN 16   **SC** 29470
  B Nonparametric Statistical Tests [1967]

Mannerisms
  Use Habits

Manpower
  SN Use PERSONNEL to access references from 1967-1981.
  Use Personnel Supply

Mantis [1973]
  PN 28   **SC** 29500
  UF Praying Mantis
  B Insects [1967]
  R Larvae [1973]

Manual Communication [1978]
  PN 146   **SC** 29505
  SN Form of communication used by the deaf in which sign language and finger spelling are substituted for speech. Also, an unsystematic or informal method of communication with gestures.
  B Augmentative Communication [1994]
  Nonverbal Communication [1971]
  Verbal Communication [1967]
  N Fingerspelling [1973]
  Sign Language [1973]

Manufacturing
  Use Business

Maori
  Use Indigenous Populations

Maprotiline [1982]
  PN 200   **SC** 29527
  B Tricyclic Antidepressant Drugs [1997]

Marathon Group Therapy [1973]
  PN 130   **SC** 29540
  SN Encounter group that meets for extended sessions and that aims to develop the ability to express oneself emotionally and to initiate intimate interpersonal interactions.
  B Encounter Group Therapy [1973]
  R Human Relations Training [1978]
  Sensitivity Training [1973]

Marihuana [1971]
  PN 733   **SC** 29550
  UF Marijuana
  B Cannabis [1973]
  R Hashish [1973]
  ↓ Marihuana Laws [1973]
  Marihuana Usage [1973]
  Tetrahydrocannabinol [1973]

Marihuana Laws [1973]
  PN 24   **SC** 29560
  B Drug Laws [1973]
  N Marihuana Legalization [1973]
  R Government [1967]
  Marihuana [1971]
  Marihuana Usage [1973]

Marihuana Legalization [1973]
  PN 35   **SC** 29570
  UF Legalization (Marihuana)
  B Drug Legalization [1997]
  Marihuana Laws [1973]
  R ↓ Drug Usage Attitudes [1973]
  Government [1967]

Marihuana Usage [1973]
  PN 1114   **SC** 29580
  B Drug Usage [1971]
  R Marihuana [1971]
  ↓ Marihuana Laws [1973]

Marijuana
  Use Marihuana

Marine Personnel [1973]
  PN 211   **SC** 29600
  B Military Personnel [1967]

Marital Adjustment
  Use Marital Relations

Marital Conflict [1973]
  PN 1499   **SC** 29620
  B Marital Relations [1967]
  R Dysfunctional Family [1991]
  ↓ Family Violence [1982]
  ↓ Relationship Termination [1997]

Marital Fidelity
  Use Monogamy

Marital Relations [1967]
  PN 7074   **SC** 29640
  UF Marital Adjustment
  B Family Relations [1967]
  N Marital Conflict [1973]
  Marital Satisfaction [1988]
  R Codependency [1991]
  Extramarital Intercourse [1973]
  Male Female Relations [1988]
  Postpartum Depression [1973]
  ↓ Relationship Termination [1997]
  Romance [1997]

Marital Satisfaction [1988]
  PN 1418   **SC** 29645
  B Marital Relations [1967]
  Relationship Satisfaction [2001]
  Satisfaction [1973]
  R ↓ Relationship Termination [1997]
  Role Satisfaction [1994]

Marital Separation [1973]
  PN 813   **SC** 29650
  UF Separation (Marital)
  B Relationship Termination [1997]
  N Divorce [1973]
  R Child Support [1988]
  Divorced Persons [1973]
  ↓ Family [1967]
  ↓ Marital Status [1973]

Marital Separation — (cont'd)
  R ↓ Parental Absence [1973]

Marital Status [1973]
  PN 1995   **SC** 29660
  N Never Married [1994]
  R Divorced Persons [1973]
  ↓ Family [1967]
  ↓ Family Background [1973]
  Living Alone [1994]
  ↓ Living Arrangements [1991]
  ↓ Marital Separation [1973]
  ↓ Marriage [1967]
  Remarriage [1985]
  ↓ Single Parents [1978]
  Single Persons [1973]
  Widowers [1973]
  Widows [1973]

Marital Therapy
  Use Marriage Counseling

Marketing [1973]
  PN 2323   **SC** 29670
  R ↓ Advertising [1967]
  Brand Names [1978]
  Brand Preferences [1994]
  ↓ Consumer Research [1973]
  Management Planning [1973]
  Product Design [1997]
  ↓ Quality of Services [1997]
  Retailing [1991]

Markov Chains [1973]
  PN 208   **SC** 29680
  SN Statistical model representing conditional and sequential probabilities to determine the future values of a random variable.
  B Simulation [1967]
  Stochastic Modeling [1973]

Marlowe Crowne Social Desirability Scale [2001]
  PN 49   **SC** 29691
  SN In 2000, the truncated term MARLOWE CROWNE SOC DESIRABIL SCALE (which was used from 1973-2000) was deleted, removed from all records containing it, and mapped to its expanded form MARLOWE CROWNE SOCIAL DESIRABILITY SCALE.
  B Nonprojective Personality Measures [1973]

Marriage [1967]
  PN 1834   **SC** 29700
  N ↓ Endogamous Marriage [1973]
  ↓ Exogamous Marriage [1973]
  Monogamy [1997]
  Polygamy [1973]
  Remarriage [1985]
  R ↓ Family [1967]
  ↓ Marital Status [1973]
  Marriage Rites [1973]
  Romance [1997]

Marriage and Family Education
  Use Family Life Education

Marriage Attitudes [1973]
  PN 736   **SC** 29710
  SN General attitudes toward marriage and divorce, or attitudes toward a specific marital relationship.
  B Attitudes [1967]
  R ↓ Family Relations [1967]

Marriage Counseling 1973
PN 2884   SC 29720
  UF Marital Therapy
      Marriage Therapy
  B Counseling 1967
  N Conjoint Therapy 1973
  R Couples Therapy 1994
    ↓ Psychotherapeutic Counseling 1973
    ↓ Psychotherapy 1967
    Sex Therapy 1978

Marriage Rites 1973
PN 46   SC 29730
  B Rites of Passage 1973
  R ↓ Marriage 1967

Marriage Therapy
  Use Marriage Counseling

Married Couples
  Use Spouses

Marsupials 1973
PN 47   SC 29760
  B Mammals 1973
  N Kangaroos 1973
    Opossums 1973

Martial Arts 1985
PN 126   SC 29765
  UF Karate
  B Recreation 1967
    Sports 1967
  R Judo 1973
    Meditation 1973
    Self Defense 1985

Marxism
  Use Communism

Masculinity 1967
PN 2192   SC 29780
  B Personality Traits 1967
  R Androgyny 1982
    Femininity 1967
    ↓ Gender Identity 1985
    Sex Roles 1967

Masking 1967
PN 649   SC 29790
SN Changes in perceptual sensitivity to a stimulus due to the presence of a second stimulus in close temporal proximity.
  UF Backward Masking
    Forward Masking
  N Auditory Masking 1973
    Visual Masking 1973
  R ↓ Perceptual Stimulation 1973

Maslow (Abraham Harold) 1991
PN 57   SC 29795
SN Identifies biographical or autobiographical studies and discussions of Maslow's works.
  R ↓ Human Potential Movement 1982
    ↓ Humanistic Psychology 1985
    ↓ Psychologists 1967
    Self Actualization 1973

Masochism 1973
PN 320   SC 29800
SN Pleasure derived from being physically or psychologically abused.

Masochism — (cont'd)
  B Sadomasochism 1973
  N Sexual Masochism 1973
  R Masochistic Personality 1973
    ↓ Sadism 1973
    ↓ Self Destructive Behavior 1985

Masochistic Personality 1973
PN 65   SC 29810
SN Personality marked by self-destructiveness or self-defeating behavior, a conscious or unconscious need to suffer, and seeking out opportunities for suffering or self-injury.
  B Sadomasochistic Personality 1973
  R ↓ Masochism 1973
    ↓ Self Destructive Behavior 1985
    Sexual Masochism 1973

Mass Hysteria 1973
PN 67   SC 29820
  B Hysteria 1967
  R ↓ Collective Behavior 1967
    Contagion 1988

Mass Media 1967
PN 1958   SC 29830
  B Communications Media 1973
  N ↓ Motion Pictures 1973
    ↓ News Media 1997
    ↓ Printed Communications Media 1973
    Radio 1973
    ↓ Television 1967
  R ↓ Advertising 1967

Massage 2001
PN 0   SC 29835
SN Systematic manipulation of body tissues. Used in both therapeutic and non-therapeutic situations.
  B Tactual Stimulation 1973
  R ↓ Alternative Medicine 1997
    Physical Contact 1982
    Physical Therapy 1973
    ↓ Physical Treatment Methods 1973

Massed Practice 1973
PN 157   SC 29840
SN Practice schedule with trials that are closely spaced and continuous over a long period. Compare DISTRIBUTED PRACTICE.
  B Learning Schedules 1967
    Practice 1967

Mastectomy 1973
PN 239   SC 29850
  B Amputation 1973
  R Breast Neoplasms 1973

Mastery Learning 1985
PN 224   SC 29855
SN Educational approach involving specification of educational objectives and success criteria and individual pacing in attaining them.
  B Learning 1967
  R Educational Objectives 1978
    School Learning 1967
    Sequential Learning 1973
    ↓ Teaching Methods 1967

Mastery Tests
  Use Criterion Referenced Tests

Masticatory Muscles 1973
PN 42   SC 29860

Masticatory Muscles — (cont'd)
  B Muscles 1967

Masturbation 1973
PN 325   SC 29870
  B Psychosexual Behavior 1967
  R Autoeroticism 1997
    Female Orgasm 1973
    ↓ Male Orgasm 1973

Matching Test
  Use Matching to Sample

Matching to Sample 1994
PN 404   SC 29873
  UF Matching Test
  B Discrimination Learning 1982
  R ↓ Memory 1967
    ↓ Recognition (Learning) 1967

Mate Selection
  Use Animal Mate Selection OR Human Mate Selection

Mate Swapping
  Use Extramarital Intercourse

Materialism 1973
PN 251   SC 29890
  B Philosophies 1967

Maternal Behavior (Animal)
  Use Animal Maternal Behavior

Maternal Behavior (Human)
  Use Mother Child Relations

Maternal Investment
  Use Parental Investment

Mates (Humans)
  Use Spouses

Mathematical Ability 1973
PN 1943   SC 29930
  UF Numerical Ability
  B Cognitive Ability 1973
    Nonverbal Ability 1988
  R ↓ Mathematics (Concepts) 1967
    Mathematics Anxiety 1985

Mathematical Modeling 1973
PN 4541   SC 29940
SN Use of mathematical formulas or equations to analyze or systematize data for description in quantitative terms.
  B Simulation 1967
  N Structural Equation Modeling 1994
  R Chaos Theory 1997
    Fuzzy Set Theory 1991
    Goodness of Fit 1988
    Heuristic Modeling 1973
    ↓ Stochastic Modeling 1973

Mathematical Psychology 1973
PN 146   SC 29950
SN Discipline that attempts to systematize the data of psychology by means of mathematical and statistical models and applications.
  B Psychology 1967

Mathematicians 1973
PN 37   SC 29960
B   Professional Personnel 1978
R   Physicists 1973
      Scientists 1967

Mathematics 1982
PN 1195   SC 29965
SN Science of numbers and the operations per-
formed on them. Compare MATHEMATICS (CON-
CEPTS).
UF   Algebra
      Arithmetic
      Calculus
      Geometry
B   Sciences 1967
N   Statistics 1982
R   Mathematics Anxiety 1985

Mathematics (Concepts) 1967
PN 2461   SC 29970
SN Specific principles that are cognitively internal-
ized or are to be learned concerning numbers, their
relations, and mathematical operations performed on
them. Compare MATHEMATICS.
N   Algorithms 1973
      Number Systems 1973
      Numbers (Numerals) 1967
R   Concepts 1967
      Mathematical Ability 1973
      Mathematics Achievement 1973
      Mathematics Education 1973
      ↓ Statistical Analysis 1967

Mathematics Achievement 1973
PN 3767   SC 29980
B   Academic Achievement 1967
R   ↓ Mathematics (Concepts) 1967
      Mathematics Anxiety 1985
      Mathematics Education 1973
      Science Achievement 1997

Mathematics Anxiety 1985
PN 264   SC 29985
SN Fear or tension associated with the study or per-
formance of arithmetic and mathematical tasks.
B   Anxiety 1967
R   ↓ Anxiety Disorders 1997
      Mathematical Ability 1973
      ↓ Mathematics 1982
      Mathematics Achievement 1973

Mathematics Education 1973
PN 3542   SC 29990
B   Curriculum 1967
R   ↓ Mathematics (Concepts) 1967
      Mathematics Achievement 1973
      Science Achievement 1997

Mating Behavior (Animal)
Use   Animal Mating Behavior

Matriarchy 1973
PN 31   SC 30010
B   Family Structure 1973
R   Father Absence 1973
      Patriarchy 1973
      ↓ Sex Role Attitudes 1978
      Sex Roles 1967

Matriculation
Use   School Enrollment

Maturation
Use   Human Development

Maturity (Emotional)
Use   Emotional Maturity

Maturity (Physical)
Use   Physical Maturity

Maturity (Vocational)
Use   Vocational Maturity

Maudsley Personality Inventory 1973
PN 15   SC 30060
B   Nonprojective Personality Measures 1973

Maxilla
Use   Jaw

Maximum Likelihood 1985
PN 265   SC 30075
SN Method of estimating population parameters
from sample data by selecting parameter values that
maximize the likelihood of the occurrence of the
observed sample results.
B   Statistical Estimation 1985
R   Goodness of Fit 1988

Maximum Security Facilities 1985
PN 121   SC 30077
R   ↓ Correctional Institutions 1973
      ↓ Hospitals 1967

Maze Learning 1967
PN 2286   SC 30080
SN Learning the correct route through a maze to
obtain reinforcement. Used for human or animal pop-
ulations.
B   Learning 1967
R   Spatial Learning 1994

Maze Pathways 1973
PN 129   SC 30090
SN Use when specifically referring to pathway
choice, discrimination, or spatial organization of path-
way. Used for human or animal populations. When
comparing types of mazes, use MAZES.
UF   Runways (Maze)
B   Mazes 1967

Mazes 1967
PN 292   SC 30110
SN System of pathways consisting of a number of
blind alleys and one or more correct paths leading to
a goal/reinforcement. Used to study learning and
motivation in humans and animals.
UF   Labyrinth (Apparatus)
B   Apparatus 1967
N   Maze Pathways 1973
      T Mazes 1973

MCPP
Use   Piperazines

MDMA
Use   Methylenedioxymethamphetamine

Mealtimes
Use   Feeding Practices

Mean 1973
PN 237   SC 30160

Mean — (cont'd)
B   Central Tendency Measures 1973
R   Standard Scores 1985

Meaning 1967
PN 2855   SC 30170
SN Generally refers to the significance, sense, con-
notation, or denotation conveyed by any form of infor-
mation.
N   Nonverbal Meaning 1973
      ↓ Verbal Meaning 1973
R   ↓ Comprehension 1967
      Meaningfulness 1967

Meaningfulness 1967
PN 1211   SC 30180
R   ↓ Comprehension 1967
      ↓ Meaning 1967

Measles 1973
PN 14   SC 30190
B   Viral Disorders 1973
R   Rubella 1973

Measurement 1967
PN 18816   SC 30200
SN Conceptually broad term referring to the process and tools used in psychological assessment of
human subjects. Use specific test names or procedures if possible. For other types of measurement
that do not involve psychological tests, consider
METHODOLOGY, EVALUATION, or other appropriate terms.
UF   Assessment
      Tests
N   ↓ Achievement Measures 1967
      ↓ Aptitude Measures 1967
      Attitude Measurement 1973
      ↓ Attitude Measures 1967
      Body Sway Testing 1973
      Comprehension Tests 1973
      Creativity Measurement 1973
      Criterion Referenced Tests 1982
      Digit Span Testing 1973
      Employment Tests 1973
      Group Testing 1973
      Individual Testing 1973
      ↓ Intelligence Measures 1967
      ↓ Inventories 1967
      Multidimensional Scaling 1982
      Needs Assessment 1985
      ↓ Occupational Interest Measures 1973
      Pain Measurement 1997
      ↓ Perceptual Measures 1973
      Performance Tests 1973
      ↓ Personality Measures 1967
      Posttesting 1973
      ↓ Preference Measures 1973
      Pretesting 1973
      Professional Examinations 1994
      Profiles (Measurement) 1973
      Projective Testing Technique 1973
      ↓ Psychiatric Evaluation 1997
      ↓ Psychological Assessment 1997
      Psychometrics 1967
      ↓ Questionnaires 1967
      ↓ Rating Scales 1967
      ↓ Reading Measures 1973
      ↓ Retention Measures 1973
      ↓ Screening 1982
      ↓ Screening Tests 1982
      ↓ Selection Tests 1973
      ↓ Sensorimotor Measures 1973
      Sociometric Tests 1967

Measurement — (cont'd)

- N ↓ Speech and Hearing Measures [1973]
  - Standardized Tests [1985]
  - ↓ Statistical Measurement [1973]
  - Subtests [1973]
  - ↓ Surveys [1967]
  - Symptom Checklists [1991]
  - ↓ Testing [1967]
  - Verbal Tests [1973]
- R Clinical Judgment (Not Diagnosis) [1973]
  - ↓ Diagnosis [1967]
  - ↓ Evaluation [1967]
  - ↓ Experimentation [1967]
  - Geriatric Assessment [1997]
  - ↓ Interviews [1967]
  - ↓ Methodology [1967]
  - Piagetian Tasks [1973]
  - ↓ Prediction Errors [1973]
  - Response Bias [1967]
  - Semantic Differential [1967]
  - Sociograms [1973]
  - ↓ Statistical Analysis [1967]
  - ↓ Test Construction [1973]
  - Test Norms [1973]
  - ↓ Test Scores [1967]
  - ↓ Testing Methods [1967]
  - Testwiseness [1978]

Mecamylamine [1973]
PN 135   SC 30220
- B Amines [1973]
  - Antihypertensive Drugs [1973]
  - Ganglion Blocking Drugs [1973]

Mechanical Aptitude [1973]
PN 70   SC 30230
- B Nonverbal Ability [1988]

Mechanoreceptors [1973]
PN 193   SC 30250
- B Neural Receptors [1973]
  - Sensory Neurons [1973]

Media (Communications)
Use Communications Media

Medial Forebrain Bundle [1982]
PN 167   SC 30286
SN Complex group of nerve fibers arising from basal olfactory regions, the periamygdaloid region, and the septal nuclei passing to, and through, the lateral preoptic and hypothalamic regions. This bundle provides the chief pathway for reciprocal connections between the hypothalamus and the biogenic amine systems of the brain stem.
- B Limbic System [1973]
- R Amygdaloid Body [1973]
  - Fornix [1982]
  - Hippocampus [1967]
  - ↓ Hypothalamus [1967]
  - Septal Nuclei [1982]

Median [1973]
PN 18   SC 30290
- B Central Tendency Measures [1973]

Median Nerve
Use Spinal Nerves

Mediated Responses [1967]
PN 90   SC 30310

Mediated Responses — (cont'd)
SN Intervening or anticipatory responses aroused by stimuli and subsequently responsible for the initiation of behavior.
- B Responses [1967]

Mediation [1988]
PN 983   SC 30315
SN Intervention by independent and impartial third party or parties to promote reconciliation, settlement, or compromise between conflicting parties.
- B Conflict Resolution [1982]
- R Child Custody [1982]
  - Court Referrals [1994]
  - Divorce [1973]
  - Labor Management Relations [1967]
  - ↓ Negotiation [1973]

Mediation (Cognitive)
Use Cognitive Mediation

Medicaid [1994]
PN 159   SC 30323
SN Government health care program for impoverished citizens administered by most local public assistance offices. Compare MEDICARE.
- B Government Programs [1973]
  - Health Insurance [1973]
- R Health Care Policy [1994]
  - Medicare [1988]
  - Social Security [1988]
  - Welfare Services (Government) [1973]

Medical Care Costs
Use Health Care Costs

Medical Diagnosis [1973]
PN 3121   SC 30330
SN Diagnosis of mental or physical disorders through use of medical methods or tests. Compare PSYCHODIAGNOSIS.
- UF Clinical Judgment (Medical Diagnosis)
- B Diagnosis [1967]
- N Biopsy [1973]
  - ↓ Cardiography [1973]
  - Dexamethasone Suppression Test [1988]
  - Echoencephalography [1973]
  - Electro Oculography [1973]
  - ↓ Electroencephalography [1967]
  - Electromyography [1967]
  - Electronystagmography [1973]
  - Electroplethysmography [1973]
  - Electroretinography [1967]
  - ↓ Encephalography [1973]
  - Galvanic Skin Response [1967]
  - HIV Testing [1997]
  - ↓ Ophthalmologic Examination [1973]
  - ↓ Plethysmography [1973]
  - Pneumoencephalography [1973]
  - Prenatal Diagnosis [1988]
  - Rheoencephalography [1973]
  - ↓ Roentgenography [1973]
  - ↓ Tomography [1988]
  - Urinalysis [1973]
- R Autopsy [1973]
  - Biological Markers [1991]
  - Computer Assisted Diagnosis [1973]
  - Differential Diagnosis [1967]
  - Drug Usage Screening [1988]
  - ↓ Electrophysiology [1973]
  - ↓ Health Screening [1997]
  - Mammography [1994]
  - Patient History [1973]
  - Physical Examination [1988]

Medical Diagnosis — (cont'd)
- R Prognosis [1973]
  - Psychological Report [1988]

Medical Education [1973]
PN 2877   SC 30340
- B Graduate Education [1973]
- N Medical Internship [1973]
  - Medical Residency [1973]
  - Psychiatric Training [1973]
- R Nursing Education [1973]

Medical History
Use Patient History

Medical Internship [1973]
PN 134   SC 30350
- UF Internship (Medical)
- B Medical Education [1973]
  - Postgraduate Training [1973]

Medical Model [1978]
PN 615   SC 30355
SN Conceptual approach to disorders originally applied to the study and treatment of physical illness. Also known as the disease or faulty mechanism model.
- B Models [1967]

Medical Patients [1973]
PN 3777   SC 30360
- B Patients [1967]

Medical Personnel [1967]
PN 2737   SC 30370
- UF Hospital Staff
- B Health Personnel [1994]
- N Dentists [1973]
  - Military Medical Personnel [1973]
  - ↓ Nurses [1967]
  - Optometrists [1973]
  - ↓ Paramedical Personnel [1973]
  - Pharmacists [1991]
  - Physical Therapists [1973]
  - ↓ Physicians [1967]
  - ↓ Psychiatric Hospital Staff [1973]
- R Clinicians [1973]
  - Impaired Professionals [1985]
  - ↓ Medical Sciences [1967]
  - ↓ Mental Health Personnel [1967]
  - Scientists [1967]

Medical Personnel Supply [1973]
PN 21   SC 30380
SN Manpower needs and availability of medical personnel.
- B Personnel Supply [1973]

Medical Psychology [1973]
PN 259   SC 30390
SN Subspecialty of clinical psychology concerned with physical health and illness.
- B Clinical Psychology [1967]
  - Health Care Psychology [1985]
- R ↓ Medical Sciences [1967]

Medical Records [1978]
PN 453   SC 30395
SN Use MEDICAL RECORDS KEEPING to access references from 1978-1996.
- N Client Records [1997]
- R Data Collection [1982]
  - ↓ Data Processing [1967]

Medical Records — (cont'd)
- R   Hospital Administration [1978]
-     Patient History [1973]
- ↓ Treatment [1967]

Medical Regimen Compliance
- **Use**   Treatment Compliance

Medical Residency [1973]
PN 1424   SC 30400
SN   Required hospital training in a medical specialty for a graduate and licensed physician.
- **UF**   Psychiatric Residency
-     Residency (Medical)
- **B**   Medical Education [1973]
-     Postgraduate Training [1973]

Medical Sciences [1967]
PN 1769   SC 30410
- **UF**   Medicine (Science of)
- **B**   Sciences [1967]
- **N**   Anesthesiology [1973]
-     Cardiology [1973]
-     Dentistry [1973]
-     ↓ Endocrinology [1973]
-     Epidemiology [1973]
-     Family Medicine [1988]
-     Geriatrics [1967]
-     Gynecology [1978]
-     ↓ Immunology [1973]
-     Neurology [1967]
-     ↓ Obstetrics [1978]
-     Ophthalmology [1973]
-     ↓ Pathology [1973]
-     Pediatrics [1973]
-     ↓ Psychiatry [1967]
-     Psychosomatic Medicine [1978]
-     Radiology [1973]
-     ↓ Surgery [1971]
-     Veterinary Medicine [1973]
- **R**   Folk Medicine [1973]
-     ↓ Medical Personnel [1967]
-     Medical Psychology [1973]
-     ↓ Neurosciences [1973]
-     ↓ Paramedical Sciences [1973]

Medical Students [1967]
PN 3273   SC 30420
- **B**   Students [1967]
- **R**   Graduate Students [1967]

Medical Therapeutic Devices [1973]
PN 423   SC 30430
SN   Equipment designed for rehabilitation or treatment of abnormal or undesirable conditions.
- **UF**   Therapeutic Devices (Medical)
- **N**   Artificial Pacemakers [1973]
-     ↓ Hearing Aids [1973]
-     ↓ Optical Aids [1973]
-     ↓ Prostheses [1973]
- **R**   ↓ Augmentative Communication [1994]
-     Mobility Aids [1978]

Medical Treatment (General) [1973]
PN 2035   SC 30440
SN   Use for medical treatment as a broad topic.
- **B**   Treatment [1967]
- **R**   ↓ Alternative Medicine [1997]
-     Life Sustaining Treatment [1997]
-     ↓ Physical Treatment Methods [1973]

Medicare [1988]
PN 157   SC 30445

Medicare — (cont'd)
SN   Government health care program for the aged administered through the Social Security Administration or the US Health Care Financing Administration. Compare MEDICAID.
- **B**   Government Programs [1973]
-     Health Insurance [1973]
- **R**   Health Care Policy [1994]
-     Medicaid [1994]
-     Social Security [1988]

Medication
- **Use**   Drug Therapy

Medicinal Herbs and Plants [2001]
PN 0   SC 30455
SN   Herbs and plants whose roots, leaves, seeds, bark, or other constituents possess therapeutic qualities when administered in a treatment capacity.
- **R**   ↓ Alternative Medicine [1997]
-     Dietary Supplements [2001]

Medicine (Science of)
- **Use**   Medical Sciences

Medics
SN   Term was discontinued in 1997. In 2000, the term was stripped from all records containing it, and replaced with PARAMEDICAL PERSONNEL, its postable counterpart.
- **Use**   Paramedical Personnel

Meditation [1973]
PN 1186   SC 30480
SN   Family of contemplative techniques all of which involve a conscious attempt to focus one's attention in a nonanalytical way and to refrain from ruminating, discursive thought. Sometimes considered a spiritual or religious practice.
- **B**   Religious Practices [1973]
- **R**   ↓ Alternative Medicine [1997]
-     Centering [1991]
-     Holistic Health [1985]
-     ↓ Human Potential Movement [1982]
-     Martial Arts [1985]
-     Prayer [1973]
-     ↓ Relaxation Therapy [1978]

Medulla Oblongata [1973]
PN 441   SC 30490
- **B**   Brain Stem [1973]
-     Hindbrain [1997]

Melancholia
SN   Use DEPRESSION (EMOTION) to access references from 1973-1987.
- **Use**   Major Depression

Melancholy
- **Use**   Sadness

Melanin [1973]
PN 36   SC 30530
- **B**   Pigments [1973]
- **R**   Melanocyte Stimulating Hormone [1985]
-     Melatonin [1973]
-     ↓ Tyrosine [1973]

Melanocyte Stimulating Hormone [1985]
PN 83   SC 30535
- **UF**   Melanotropin
- **B**   Peptides [1973]
-     Pituitary Hormones [1973]

Melanocyte Stimulating Hormone — (cont'd)
- **R**   Melanin [1973]
-     Melatonin [1973]

Melanotropin
- **Use**   Melanocyte Stimulating Hormone

Melatonin [1973]
PN 620   SC 30540
- **B**   Hormones [1967]
- **R**   Melanin [1973]
-     Melanocyte Stimulating Hormone [1985]
-     Pineal Body [1973]

Mellaril
- **Use**   Thioridazine

Membranes [1973]
PN 194   SC 30560
- **B**   Tissues (Body) [1973]
- **N**   Meninges [1973]
-     ↓ Nasal Mucosa [1973]
-     Nictitating Membrane [1973]

Memory [1967]
PN 23097   SC 30570
- **N**   Autobiographical Memory [1994]
-     Early Memories [1985]
-     Eidetic Imagery [1973]
-     Episodic Memory [1988]
-     Explicit Memory [1997]
-     False Memory [1997]
-     Long Term Memory [1973]
-     Memory Decay [1973]
-     Memory Trace [1973]
-     Reminiscence [1985]
-     Repressed Memory [1997]
-     ↓ Short Term Memory [1967]
-     ↓ Spatial Memory [1988]
-     Spontaneous Recovery (Learning) [1973]
-     ↓ Verbal Memory [1994]
-     ↓ Visual Memory [1994]
- **R**   ↓ Amnesia [1967]
-     ↓ Cognitive Processes [1967]
-     Cued Recall [1994]
-     Cues [1967]
-     Declarative Knowledge [1997]
-     Forgetting [1973]
-     Free Recall [1973]
-     Generation Effect (Learning) [1991]
-     Human Information Storage [1973]
-     ↓ Interference (Learning) [1967]
-     ↓ Latent Inhibition [1997]
-     ↓ Learning [1967]
-     Matching to Sample [1994]
-     ↓ Memory Disorders [1973]
-     Memory Training [1994]
-     Metacognition [1991]
-     Note Taking [1991]
-     Procedural Knowledge [1997]
-     ↓ Prompting [1997]
-     ↓ Recall (Learning) [1967]
-     Relearning [1973]
-     ↓ Retention [1967]
-     Rote Learning [1973]
-     Serial Recall [1994]

Memory Decay [1973]
PN 287   SC 30580
SN   Fading of memory traces over time. Compare FORGETTING and AMNESIA.
- **B**   Memory [1967]

Memory Decay — (cont'd)
R   Forgetting [1973]
    Memory Training [1994]

Memory Disorders [1973]
PN 1322   SC 30590
B   Thought Disturbances [1973]
N   ↓ Amnesia [1967]
R   ↓ Brain Disorders [1967]
    ↓ Memory [1967]
    Memory Training [1994]
    ↓ Mental Disorders [1967]
    ↓ Physical Disorders [1997]

Memory Enhancing Drugs
Use   Nootropic Drugs

Memory for Designs Test [1973]
PN 32   SC 30610
B   Nonprojective Personality Measures [1973]
R   ↓ Neuropsychological Assessment [1982]

Memory Trace [1973]
PN 363   SC 30620
SN   Hypothetical change in nerve cells or brain activity that accompanies the storage of information.
B   Memory [1967]

Memory Training [1994]
PN 224   SC 30623
R   Cognitive Rehabilitation [1985]
    Forgetting [1973]
    ↓ Learning Strategies [1991]
    ↓ Memory [1967]
    Memory Decay [1973]
    ↓ Memory Disorders [1973]
    Mnemonic Learning [1973]
    ↓ Neuropsychological Rehabilitation [1997]
    ↓ Practice [1967]
    ↓ Recall (Learning) [1967]
    ↓ Recognition (Learning) [1967]
    ↓ Retention [1967]

Men
Use   Human Males

Menarche [1973]
PN 171   SC 30630
B   Menstruation [1973]
R   Puberty [1973]

Menieres Disease [1973]
PN 54   SC 30640
B   Labyrinth Disorders [1973]
    Syndromes [1973]
R   Vertigo [1973]

Meninges [1973]
PN 26   SC 30650
B   Central Nervous System [1967]
    Membranes [1973]

Meningitis [1973]
PN 50   SC 30660
B   Central Nervous System Disorders [1973]
N   Bacterial Meningitis [1973]

Meningomyelocele
Use   Spina Bifida

Menopause [1973]
PN 795   SC 30670

Menopause — (cont'd)
B   Developmental Stages [1973]
R   ↓ Menstrual Cycle [1973]

Menstrual Cycle [1973]
PN 1083   SC 30680
N   ↓ Menstruation [1973]
    Ovulation [1973]
    Premenstrual Tension [1973]
R   Estrus [1973]
    Menopause [1973]

Menstrual Disorders [1973]
PN 163   SC 30690
B   Gynecological Disorders [1973]
N   Amenorrhea [1973]
    Dysmenorrhea [1973]
R   Premenstrual Tension [1973]

Menstruation [1973]
PN 324   SC 30700
B   Menstrual Cycle [1973]
N   Menarche [1973]
R   Estrus [1973]

Mental Age [1973]
PN 253   SC 30710
SN   Intelligence level expressed in units of chronological age and determined by comparison with other individuals of the same age using intelligence test scores.
UF   Intelligence Age
R   Developmental Age Groups [1973]
    Intelligence [1967]
    Intelligence Quotient [1967]

Mental Confusion [1973]
PN 379   SC 30720
UF   Confusion (Mental)
B   Emotional States [1973]
R   Doubt [1973]
    Frustration [1967]
    ↓ Thought Disturbances [1973]
    Wandering Behavior [1991]

Mental Deficiency
Use   Mental Retardation

Mental Disorders [1967]
PN 24605   SC 30740
SN   Conceptually broad term referring to all forms of psychopathology. Use a more specific term if possible.
UF   Insanity
    Mental Illness
    Nervous Breakdown
    Psychiatric Disorders
B   Disorders [1967]
N   Adjustment Disorders [1994]
    ↓ Affective Disorders [2001]
    Alexithymia [1982]
    ↓ Anxiety Disorders [1997]
    ↓ Autism [1967]
    ↓ Chronic Mental Illness [1997]
    ↓ Dementia [1985]
    ↓ Dissociative Disorders [2001]
    ↓ Eating Disorders [1997]
    Elective Mutism [1973]
    ↓ Factitious Disorders [1988]
    ↓ Gender Identity Disorder [1997]
    ↓ Hysteria [1967]
    ↓ Impulse Control Disorders [1997]
    Koro [1994]

Mental Disorders — (cont'd)
N   Mental Disorders due to General Medical Conditions [2001]
    ↓ Neurosis [1967]
    ↓ Paraphilias [1988]
    ↓ Personality Disorders [1967]
    ↓ Pervasive Developmental Disorders [2001]
    Pseudodementia [1985]
    ↓ Psychosis [1967]
    Schizoaffective Disorder [1994]
R   Adaptive Behavior [1991]
    ↓ Attention Deficit Disorder [1985]
    Attention Deficit Disorder with Hyperactivity [2001]
    ↓ Behavior Disorders [1971]
    Borderline States [1978]
    ↓ Brain Disorders [1967]
    ↓ Chronic Illness [1991]
    Chronicity (Disorders) [1982]
    ↓ Communication Disorders [1982]
    Comorbidity [1991]
    Conduct Disorder [1991]
    ↓ Congenital Disorders [1973]
    ↓ Consciousness Disturbances [1973]
    ↓ Defense Mechanisms [1967]
    ↓ Diagnosis [1967]
    Diagnostic and Statistical Manual [1994]
    Disability Discrimination [1997]
    Disease Course [1991]
    ↓ Emotional Adjustment [1973]
    ↓ Ethnospecific Disorders [1973]
    Etiology [1967]
    Glossolalia [1973]
    Homeless Mentally Ill [1997]
    Infantilism [1973]
    Insanity Defense [1985]
    International Classification of Diseases [2001]
    ↓ Learning Disorders [1967]
    Malingering [1973]
    ↓ Memory Disorders [1973]
    Mental Illness (Attitudes Toward) [1967]
    ↓ Mental Retardation [1967]
    Mentally Ill Offenders [1985]
    Microcephaly [1973]
    Narcissism [1967]
    Onset (Disorders) [1973]
    ↓ Organic Brain Syndromes [1973]
    ↓ Perceptual Disturbances [1973]
    ↓ Personality Processes [1967]
    ↓ Physical Disorders [1997]
    Porphyria [1973]
    Predisposition [1973]
    Premorbidity [1978]
    Prognosis [1973]
    Psychiatric Patients [1967]
    Psychiatric Symptoms [1997]
    ↓ Psychodiagnosis [1967]
    ↓ Psychological Assessment [1997]
    Psychopathology [1967]
    Recovery (Disorders) [1973]
    Relapse (Disorders) [1973]
    ↓ Remission (Disorders) [1973]
    Research Diagnostic Criteria [1994]
    Rett Syndrome [1994]
    ↓ Sadomasochism [1973]
    Savants [2001]
    Schizophrenogenic Family [1967]
    Severity (Disorders) [1982]
    ↓ Sexual Function Disturbances [1973]
    ↓ Sleep Disorders [1973]
    Special Needs [1994]
    Structured Clinical Interview [2001]
    ↓ Suicide [1967]
    Susceptibility (Disorders) [1973]

Mental Disorders — (cont'd)
R   ↓ Symptoms 1967
    ↓ Syndromes 1973
    ↓ Thought Disturbances 1973
    ↓ Toxic Disorders 1973
    ↓ Treatment Resistant Disorders 1994
    Work Related Illnesses 1994

Mental Disorders due to General Medical Conditions 2001
PN   0   SC   30745
SN   Used for disorders characterized by the presence of mental symptoms judged to be the direct physiological consequence of a general medical condition. Use only for disorders described by this or more specific phraseology. This could include "Catatonic Disorder due to a General Medical Condition," "Dementia due to a General Medical Condition," etc. For a more specific disorder, also use a term for the symptom (e.g., CATATONIA, DEMENTIA). Compare COMORBIDITY.
B   Mental Disorders 1967
R   Comorbidity 1991

Mental Health 1967
PN   8546   SC   30750
B   Health 1973
N   Community Mental Health 1973
R   Community Mental Health Services 1978
    Community Psychiatry 1973
    ↓ Emotional Adjustment 1973
    ↓ Mental Health Personnel 1967
    ↓ Mental Health Programs 1973
    ↓ Mental Health Services 1978
    Primary Mental Health Prevention 1973
    Well Being 1994

Mental Health Care Costs
Use   Health Care Costs

Mental Health Care Policy
Use   Health Care Policy

Mental Health Centers (Community)
Use   Community Mental Health Centers

Mental Health Consultation
SN   Term was discontinued in 1982. In 2000, the term was stripped from all records containing it, and replaced with PROFESSIONAL CONSULTATION, its postable counterpart.
Use   Professional Consultation

Mental Health Inservice Training 1973
PN   441   SC   30780
UF   Inservice Training (Mental Health)
    Training (Mental Health Inservice)
B   Community Mental Health Training 1973
    Inservice Training 1985
R   ↓ Mental Health Programs 1973
    Professional Development 1982

Mental Health Personnel 1967
PN   5256   SC   30790
B   Health Personnel 1994
N   Clinical Psychologists 1973
    ↓ Psychiatric Hospital Staff 1973
    Psychiatric Nurses 1973
    Psychiatric Social Workers 1973
    Psychiatrists 1967
    ↓ Psychotherapists 1973
    School Psychologists 1973
R   Clinicians 1973

Mental Health Personnel — (cont'd)
R   ↓ Counselors 1967
    ↓ Educational Personnel 1973
    Impaired Professionals 1985
    ↓ Medical Personnel 1967
    ↓ Mental Health 1967
    Mental Health Personnel Supply 1973
    Occupational Therapists 1973
    ↓ Paraprofessional Personnel 1973
    Personal Therapy 1991
    Professional Supervision 1988
    ↓ Psychologists 1967
    ↓ Social Workers 1973
    ↓ Therapists 1967

Mental Health Personnel Supply 1973
PN   104   SC   30800
B   Personnel Supply 1973
R   ↓ Mental Health Personnel 1967

Mental Health Program Evaluation 1973
PN   1264   SC   30810
SN   Methodology or procedures for assessment of any mental health program in relation to previously established goals or other criteria. Also used for the formal evaluations themselves. For effectiveness of particular treatment modes, use the specific type of treatment (e.g., DRUG THERAPY). For efficacy of treatment for a particular disorder, use the specific disorder (e.g., MANIA).
UF   Program Evaluation (Mental Health)
B   Program Evaluation 1985
R   ↓ Mental Health Programs 1973
    Psychotherapeutic Outcomes 1973
    ↓ Treatment 1967
    Treatment Effectiveness Evaluation 1973
    ↓ Treatment Outcomes 1982

Mental Health Programs 1973
PN   2168   SC   30820
SN   Programs for the maintenance of mental health.
UF   Programs (Mental Health)
N   ↓ Crisis Intervention Services 1973
    Deinstitutionalization 1982
    Home Visiting Programs 1973
    Hot Line Services 1973
    Suicide Prevention Centers 1973
R   Child Guidance Clinics 1973
    Community Mental Health 1973
    Community Mental Health Centers 1973
    Community Mental Health Services 1978
    ↓ Community Mental Health Training 1973
    Community Psychiatry 1973
    Community Psychology 1973
    ↓ Community Services 1967
    ↓ Health Care Administration 1997
    ↓ Health Care Delivery 1978
    ↓ Health Care Delivery 1978
    Integrated Services 1997
    ↓ Mental Health 1967
    Mental Health Inservice Training 1973
    Mental Health Program Evaluation 1973
    ↓ Mental Health Services 1978
    Outreach Programs 1997
    Partial Hospitalization 1985
    Primary Mental Health Prevention 1973
    ↓ Program Development 1991
    Psychiatric Clinics 1973
    Public Health Services 1973

Mental Health Service Needs
Use   Health Service Needs

Mental Health Services 1978
PN   7856   SC   30825
SN   Services available for maintenance of mental health and treatment of mental disorders.
B   Health Care Services 1978
N   Community Mental Health Services 1978
R   Child Guidance Clinics 1973
    Community Mental Health Centers 1973
    ↓ Community Services 1967
    ↓ Counseling 1967
R   ↓ Health Care Administration 1997
    Health Care Costs 1994
    ↓ Health Care Delivery 1978
    Health Care Policy 1994
    Health Care Seeking Behavior 1997
    Health Service Needs 1997
    Integrated Services 1997
    Long Term Care 1994
    ↓ Mental Health 1967
    ↓ Mental Health Programs 1973
    Outreach Programs 1997
    ↓ Prevention 1973
    ↓ Psychiatric Hospital Programs 1967
    Quality of Care 1988
    ↓ Quality of Services 1997
    School Counseling 1982
    Social Casework 1967
    ↓ Social Services 1982
    Student Personnel Services 1978
    ↓ Support Groups 1991
    ↓ Twelve Step Programs 1997

Mental Health Training (Community)
Use   Community Mental Health Training

Mental Hospitals
Use   Psychiatric Hospitals

Mental Illness
Use   Mental Disorders

Mental Illness (Attitudes Toward) 1967
PN   1553   SC   30860
B   Disabled (Attitudes Toward) 1997
R   Disability Discrimination 1997
    Health Knowledge 1994
    ↓ Mental Disorders 1967

Mental Load
Use   Human Channel Capacity

Mental Retardation 1967
PN   15328   SC   30870
SN   Impaired intellectual (IQ below 70) and adaptive functioning manifested during the developmental period. Use a more specific term if possible. Use for both the concept of the disorder itself and for populations of mentally retarded persons. In 2000, this term replaced the discontinued and deleted term MENTALLY RETARDED. MENTALLY RETARDED was stripped from all records and replaced with MENTAL RETARDATION.
UF   Amentia
    Mental Deficiency
    Oligophrenia
    Retardation (Mental)
N   Amaurotic Familial Idiocy 1973
    Anencephaly 1973
    Borderline Mental Retardation 1973
    Crying Cat Syndrome 1973
    Downs Syndrome 1967
    Home Reared Mentally Retarded 1973
    Institutionalized Mentally Retarded 1973
    Mild Mental Retardation 2001

Mental Retardation — (cont'd)

N　Moderate Mental Retardation ²⁰⁰¹
　　Profound Mental Retardation ²⁰⁰¹
　　Psychosocial Mental Retardation ¹⁹⁷³
　　Severe Mental Retardation ²⁰⁰¹
R　Adaptive Behavior ¹⁹⁹¹
　　↓ Brain Damage ¹⁹⁶⁷
　　Developmental Disabilities ¹⁹⁸²
　　↓ Disorders ¹⁹⁶⁷
　　Fetal Alcohol Syndrome ¹⁹⁸⁵
　　Fragile X Syndrome ¹⁹⁹⁴
　　Hydrocephaly ¹⁹⁷³
　　Klinefelters Syndrome ¹⁹⁷³
　　↓ Mental Disorders ¹⁹⁶⁷
　　Mental Retardation (Attitudes Toward) ²⁰⁰¹
　　Microcephaly ¹⁹⁷³
　　Phenylketonuria ¹⁹⁷³
　　Prader Willi Syndrome ¹⁹⁹¹
　　Rett Syndrome ¹⁹⁹⁴
　　Savants ²⁰⁰¹

Mental Retardation (Attitudes Toward) ²⁰⁰¹

PN 593　　　　　　**SC** 30881
SN　In 2000, the truncated term MENTAL RETARDATION (ATTIT TOWARD) (which was used from 1973-2000) was deleted, removed from all records containing it, and mapped to its expanded form MENTAL RETARDATION (ATTITUDES TOWARD).
B　Disabled (Attitudes Toward) ¹⁹⁹⁷
R　↓ Mental Retardation ¹⁹⁶⁷

Mental Rotation ¹⁹⁹¹

PN 308　　　　　　**SC** 30883
B　Cognitive Processes ¹⁹⁶⁷
R　Mirror Image ¹⁹⁹¹
　　↓ Spatial Ability ¹⁹⁸²
　　Spatial Imagery ¹⁹⁸²
　　Spatial Organization ¹⁹⁷³
　　↓ Spatial Perception ¹⁹⁶⁷

Mentally Ill Homeless

Use　Homeless Mentally Ill

Mentally Ill Offenders ¹⁹⁸⁵

PN 1368　　　　　　**SC** 30885
UF　Criminally Insane
B　Criminals ¹⁹⁶⁷
R　Competency to Stand Trial ¹⁹⁸⁵
　　Court Referrals ¹⁹⁹⁴
　　Forensic Evaluation ¹⁹⁹⁴
　　Insanity Defense ¹⁹⁸⁵
　　↓ Mental Disorders ¹⁹⁶⁷

Mentor ¹⁹⁸⁵

PN 753　　　　　　**SC** 30895
SN　An individual who befriends and facilitates the development of a less experienced individual, especially within a profession, business, trade, or academic environment.
R　Adult Development ¹⁹⁷⁸
　　Apprenticeship ¹⁹⁷³
　　↓ Interpersonal Interaction ¹⁹⁶⁷
　　Occupational Aspirations ¹⁹⁷³
　　Occupational Guidance ¹⁹⁶⁷
　　Peer Counseling ¹⁹⁷⁸
　　Professional Development ¹⁹⁸²
　　Significant Others ¹⁹⁹¹
　　↓ Social Influences ¹⁹⁶⁷
　　Supervisor Employee Interaction ¹⁹⁹⁷
　　Vocational Counselors ¹⁹⁷³

Meperidine ¹⁹⁷³

PN 66　　　　　　**SC** 30900
B　Amines ¹⁹⁷³
　　Analgesic Drugs ¹⁹⁷³
　　Antispasmodic Drugs ¹⁹⁷³
　　Narcotic Drugs ¹⁹⁷³
　　Sedatives ¹⁹⁷³

Mephenesin

SN　Term was discontinued in 1997. In 2000, the term was stripped from all records containing it, and replaced with MUSCLE RELAXING DRUGS, its postable counterpart.
Use　Muscle Relaxing Drugs

Meprobamate ¹⁹⁷³

PN 59　　　　　　**SC** 30920
B　Hypnotic Drugs ¹⁹⁷³
　　Muscle Relaxing Drugs ¹⁹⁷³
　　Sedatives ¹⁹⁷³
　　Tranquilizing Drugs ¹⁹⁶⁷

Mercury (Metal) ¹⁹⁷³

PN 74　　　　　　**SC** 30930
B　Metallic Elements ¹⁹⁷³

Mercury Poisoning ¹⁹⁷³

PN 88　　　　　　**SC** 30940
B　Toxic Disorders ¹⁹⁷³

Mercy Killing

Use　Euthanasia

Mescaline ¹⁹⁷³

PN 113　　　　　　**SC** 30950
B　Alkaloids ¹⁹⁷³
　　Hallucinogenic Drugs ¹⁹⁶⁷
　　Psychotomimetic Drugs ¹⁹⁷³
R　Peyote ¹⁹⁷³

Mesencephalon ¹⁹⁷³

PN 1608　　　　　　**SC** 30960
UF　Midbrain
　　Red Nucleus
B　Brain ¹⁹⁶⁷
N　Inferior Colliculus ¹⁹⁷³
　　Optic Lobe ¹⁹⁷³
　　Substantia Nigra ¹⁹⁹⁴
　　Superior Colliculus ¹⁹⁷³
　　↓ Tegmentum ¹⁹⁹¹

Mesoridazine ¹⁹⁷³

PN 35　　　　　　**SC** 30970
B　Phenothiazine Derivatives ¹⁹⁷³

Messages ¹⁹⁷³

PN 1275　　　　　　**SC** 30980
SN　Informational content of communications transmitted between persons or systems.
UF　Information (Messages)
R　↓ Communication ¹⁹⁶⁷
　　Electronic Communication ²⁰⁰¹
　　Gossip ¹⁹⁸²
　　Information ¹⁹⁶⁷

Meta Analysis ¹⁹⁸⁵

PN 2315　　　　　　**SC** 30985

Meta Analysis — (cont'd)

SN　Statistical analysis of a large collection of results from individual studies for the purpose of integrating findings. From 1985-2000, the term was also used as a document type identifier; however, this usage has been discontinued due to the advent of Form/Content Typefield identifiers. References from 1985-2000 can be accessed using either META ANALYSIS or the Meta Analysis Form/Content Type field identifier.
UF　Data Pooling
B　Methodology ¹⁹⁶⁷
　　Statistical Analysis ¹⁹⁶⁷
R　Literature Review ¹⁹⁶⁷

Metabolic Rates ¹⁹⁷³

PN 202　　　　　　**SC** 30990
R　Energy Expenditure ¹⁹⁶⁷
　　↓ Metabolism ¹⁹⁶⁷
　　↓ Physiology ¹⁹⁶⁷

Metabolism ¹⁹⁶⁷

PN 2452　　　　　　**SC** 31000
SN　Biochemical changes in the cells, digestive system, and body tissues by which energy is provided, new material is incorporated, and substances, such as drugs, are disposed.
B　Physiology ¹⁹⁶⁷
N　Anabolism ¹⁹⁷³
　　Basal Metabolism ¹⁹⁷³
　　Biosynthesis ¹⁹⁷³
　　↓ Carbohydrate Metabolism ¹⁹⁷³
　　Catabolism ¹⁹⁷³
　　Lipid Metabolism ¹⁹⁷³
　　↓ Metabolites ¹⁹⁷³
　　Protein Metabolism ¹⁹⁷³
R　Bioavailability ¹⁹⁹¹
　　↓ Dopamine Metabolites ¹⁹⁸²
　　Metabolic Rates ¹⁹⁷³
　　↓ Metabolism Disorders ¹⁹⁷³
　　↓ Norepinephrine Metabolites ¹⁹⁸²
　　Thermoregulation (Body) ¹⁹⁷³

Metabolism Disorders ¹⁹⁷³

PN 421　　　　　　**SC** 31020
UF　Hypercholesterolemia
B　Physical Disorders ¹⁹⁹⁷
N　Cushings Syndrome ¹⁹⁷³
　　Cystic Fibrosis ¹⁹⁸⁵
　　↓ Diabetes ¹⁹⁷³
　　Hyperglycemia ¹⁹⁸⁵
　　Hypoglycemia ¹⁹⁷³
　　Hyponatremia ¹⁹⁹⁷
　　↓ Lipid Metabolism Disorders ¹⁹⁷³
　　Phenylketonuria ¹⁹⁷³
　　Porphyria ¹⁹⁷³
R　Hypothyroidism ¹⁹⁷³
　　↓ Metabolism ¹⁹⁶⁷
　　↓ Nutritional Deficiencies ¹⁹⁷³

Metabolites ¹⁹⁷³

PN 903　　　　　　**SC** 31030
SN　Biochemical products of metabolism.
UF　Anabolites
　　Catabolites
B　Metabolism ¹⁹⁶⁷
N　↓ Dopamine Metabolites ¹⁹⁸²
　　↓ Norepinephrine Metabolites ¹⁹⁸²
　　↓ Serotonin Metabolites ¹⁹⁷⁸

Metacognition ¹⁹⁹¹

PN 1322　　　　　　**SC** 31040

Metacognition — (cont'd)

SN Awareness, monitoring, and knowledge of one's own cognitive processes and activities including memory and comprehension.

UF Metamemory
B Cognitive Processes 1967
R ↓ Awareness 1967
Cognition 1967
↓ Cognitive Ability 1973
↓ Comprehension 1967
Declarative Knowledge 1997
↓ Learning 1967
↓ Learning Strategies 1991
↓ Memory 1967
Metalinguistics 1994
Procedural Knowledge 1997
School Learning 1967

Metalinguistics 1994
PN 105   **SC** 31045
SN Branch of linguistics concerned with how language is used, the role of language in culture, and the use of particular linguistic forms.
B Linguistics 1973
R Ethnolinguistics 1973
↓ Language 1967
↓ Language Development 1967
Metacognition 1991
Pragmatics 1985
Psycholinguistics 1967
Sociolinguistics 1985
Verbal Ability 1967
↓ Verbal Communication 1967

Metallic Elements 1973
PN 302   **SC** 31050
B Metals 1991
N Aluminum 1994
Barium 1973
↓ Calcium 1973
Cobalt 1973
Copper 1973
Iron 1973
Lead (Metal) 1973
↓ Lithium 1973
↓ Magnesium 1973
Mercury (Metal) 1973
↓ Potassium 1973
↓ Sodium 1973
Zinc 1985

Metals 1991
PN 38   **SC** 31052
SN May include alloys.
N ↓ Metallic Elements 1973

Metamemory
Use Metacognition

Metaphor 1982
PN 1672   **SC** 31057
SN Figures of speech used to suggest an analogy between one kind of object or idea and another.
B Figurative Language 1985
R Analogy 1991
↓ Literature 1967
Myths 1967
↓ Semantics 1967
Symbolism 1967

Metaphysics 1973
PN 296   **SC** 31060
SN Branch of philosophy concerned with the fundamental nature of things and existence.

Metaphysics — (cont'd)
B Philosophies 1967
R Epistemology 1973
Hermeneutics 1991
Reality 1973
Relativism 1997

Metapsychology 1994
PN 121   **SC** 31070
B Psychology 1967
R Freudian Psychoanalytic School 1973
Object Relations 1982
↓ Psychoanalytic Theory 1967

Methadone 1973
PN 644   **SC** 31080
B Analgesic Drugs 1973
Narcotic Drugs 1973
R Methadone Maintenance 1978

Methadone Maintenance 1978
PN 1455   **SC** 31083
SN Rehabilitation of heroin addicts by substituting methadone for heroin, enabling the addict to lead a relatively normal life. Methadone maintenance does not actually treat the addiction.
R ↓ Drug Addiction 1967
↓ Drug Rehabilitation 1973
Heroin Addiction 1973
Maintenance Therapy 1997
Methadone 1973

Methamphetamine 1973
PN 523   **SC** 31090
UF Methedrine
B Amphetamine 1967
CNS Stimulating Drugs 1973
Vasoconstrictor Drugs 1973
R Methylenedioxymethamphetamine 1991

Methanol 1973
PN 30   **SC** 31100
UF Methyl Alcohol
B Alcohols 1967

Methaqualone 1973
PN 44   **SC** 31110
UF Quaalude
B Hypnotic Drugs 1973
Sedatives 1973

Methedrine
Use Methamphetamine

Methionine 1973
PN 110   **SC** 31130
B Amino Acids 1973

Methodists
Use Protestants

Methodology 1967
PN 15083   **SC** 31140
SN Conceptually broad term that refers generally to strategies, techniques, or procedures used in applied, descriptive, or empirical studies. Compare EXPERIMENTAL METHODS.
UF Research Methods
N Causal Analysis 1994
Cohort Analysis 1988
↓ Content Analysis 1978
Data Collection 1982
↓ Empirical Methods 1973

Methodology — (cont'd)
N Meta Analysis 1985
Self Report 1982
R Experiment Controls 1973
↓ Experimental Design 1967
Experimental Instructions 1967
Experimental Laboratories 1973
Experimental Replication 1973
↓ Experimentation 1967
Functional Analysis 2001
Mail Surveys 1994
↓ Measurement 1967
↓ Surveys 1967
Telephone Surveys 1994
Theory Formulation 1973
Theory Verification 1973

Methohexital 1973
PN 41   **SC** 31150
B Barbiturates 1967
General Anesthetics 1973

Methoxamine 1973
PN 22   **SC** 31160
B Adrenergic Drugs 1973
Alcohols 1967
Sympathomimetic Amines 1973
Vasoconstrictor Drugs 1973
R ↓ Local Anesthetics 1973

Methoxyhydroxyphenylglycol (3,4) 1991
PN 155   **SC** 31165
UF MHPG
B Norepinephrine Metabolites 1982

Methyl Alcohol
Use Methanol

Methylatropine
Use Atropine

Methyldiphenylhydramine
Use Orphenadrine

Methyldopa 1973
PN 51   **SC** 31190
B Antihypertensive Drugs 1973
R ↓ Catecholamines 1973
DOPA 1973
Dopamine 1973

Methylenedioxymethamphetamine 1991
PN 201   **SC** 31195
UF Ecstasy (Drug)
MDMA
R Methamphetamine 1973

Methylmorphine
Use Codeine

Methylphenidate 1973
PN 1255   **SC** 31210
UF Ritalin
B Amines 1973
Antidepressant Drugs 1971
CNS Stimulating Drugs 1973
R ↓ Analeptic Drugs 1973

Methylphenyltetrahydropyridine 1994
PN 31   **SC** 31213
UF MPTP
B Neurotoxins 1982

Methylphenyltetrahydropyridine — (cont'd)
R   Dopamine [1973]

Methysergide
Use   Serotonin Antagonists

Metrazole
Use   Pentylenetetrazol

Metronomes [1973]
PN 23   SC 31230
B   Apparatus [1967]

Metropolitan Readiness Tests [1978]
PN 40   SC 31240
SN   Use METROPOLITAN READING READINESS
TEST to access references from 1973-1977.
B   Reading Measures [1973]

Mexican Americans [1973]
PN 2953   SC 31250
SN   Populations of Mexican descent residing perma-
nently in the U.S.
UF   Chicanos
B   Hispanics [1982]

MHPG
Use   Methoxyhydroxyphenylglycol (3,4)

Mianserin [1982]
PN 299   SC 31266
SN   Organic heterocyclic compound having antiser-
otonin properties and used as an antihistamine.
B   Antidepressant Drugs [1971]
Antihistaminic Drugs [1973]
Serotonin Antagonists [1973]

Mice [1973]
PN 11336   SC 31270
B   Rodents [1973]

Microcephaly [1973]
PN 59   SC 31280
SN   Smallness of the head produced by incomplete
development of the brain often associated with below
normal mental and cognitive development.
B   Brain Disorders [1967]
Congenital Disorders [1973]
R   ↓ Mental Disorders [1967]
↓ Mental Retardation [1967]
↓ Neonatal Disorders [1973]

Microcomputers [1985]
PN 930   SC 31282
UF   Personal Computers
B   Computers [1967]
R   ↓ Computer Applications [1973]

Microcounseling [1978]
PN 94   SC 31284
SN   Short-term technique for teaching basic inter-
viewing skills using role playing, videotape analysis,
and feedback in prepracticum training.
B   Counseling [1967]
R   ↓ Clinical Methods Training [1973]
Counselor Education [1973]
Interviewing [1973]
Paraprofessional Education [1973]

Microorganisms [1985]
PN 61   SC 31287

Microorganisms — (cont'd)
SN   Single-celled microscopic or ultramicroscopic
organisms.
UF   Bacteria
Single Cell Organisms
N   Protozoa [1973]

Microscopes [1973]
PN 9   SC 31290
B   Apparatus [1967]

Micturition
Use   Urination

Midazolam [1991]
PN 210   SC 31303
B   Benzodiazepines [1978]
Minor Tranquilizers [1973]

Midbrain
Use   Mesencephalon

Middle Class [1973]
PN 769   SC 31320
UF   Bourgeois
B   Social Class [1967]

Middle Class Attitudes [1973]
PN 57   SC 31330
SN   Attitudes of, not toward, the middle class.
B   Socioeconomic Class Attitudes [1973]

Middle Ear [1973]
PN 134   SC 31340
UF   Ear Ossicles
Eustachian Tube
Tympanic Membrane
B   Ear (Anatomy) [1967]

Middle Income Level [1973]
PN 98   SC 31350
B   Income Level [1973]

Middle Level Managers [1973]
PN 630   SC 31360
SN   Second-line managers or supervisors primarily
responsible for daily work flow and production in a
business or industrial organization.
B   Management Personnel [1973]
R   Top Level Managers [1973]

Middle School Education [1985]
PN 223   SC 31364
SN   Education for grades six through eight (sometimes five through eight) using methods and materials specifically focusing on the needs and
characteristics of early adolescents.
B   Education [1967]

Middle School Students [1985]
PN 1537   SC 31367
SN   Students in 6th, 7th, and 8th grades. Sometimes
may include students in 5th grade. Use ELEMEN-
TARY SCHOOL STUDENTS or JUNIOR HIGH
SCHOOL STUDENTS, as appropriate, unless spe-
cific reference is made to the population as middle
school students. Application of a student term is
mandatory in educational contexts.
R   ↓ Elementary School Students [1967]
Junior High School Students [1971]

Midwifery [1985]
PN 76   SC 31368

Midwifery — (cont'd)
UF   Home Birth
B   Obstetrics [1978]
R   ↓ Birth [1967]
Labor (Childbirth) [1973]

Migraine Headache [1973]
PN 1248   SC 31370
B   Headache [1973]
R   ↓ Endocrine Disorders [1973]
Nausea [1973]
↓ Somatoform Disorders [2001]

Migrant Farm Workers [1973]
PN 109   SC 31380
B   Agricultural Workers [1973]
R   Foreign Workers [1985]
↓ Human Migration [1973]

Migration (Human)
Use   Human Migration

Migratory Behavior (Animal) [1973]
PN 667   SC 31400
UF   Animal Navigation
B   Animal Ethology [1967]
R   Animal Homing [1991]

Mild Mental Retardation [2001]
PN 3392   SC 31405
SN   IQ 50-70. In 2000, this term was created to
replace the discontinued term EDUCABLE MEN-
TALLY RETARDED and the discontinued and deleted
term MILDLY MENTALLY RETARDED. These terms
were stripped from all records and replaced with
MILD MENTAL RETARDATION.
UF   Educable Mentally Retarded
B   Mental Retardation [1967]

Milieu Therapy [1988]
PN 208   SC 31420
SN   Modification or manipulation of patient's per-
sonal life circumstances or environment through con-
trolled and stimulatory environments. Treatment
setting can be a hospital, therapeutic community or
home. Use THERAPEUTIC COMMUNITY to access
references from 1973-1987.
UF   Environmental Therapy
Socioenvironmental Therapy
B   Treatment [1967]
R   Sociotherapy [1973]
Therapeutic Community [1967]
↓ Therapeutic Environment [2001]

Militancy [1973]
PN 61   SC 31430
B   Social Behavior [1967]

Military Enlistment [1973]
PN 269   SC 31440
UF   Enlistment (Military)
R   Military Recruitment [1973]

Military Medical Personnel [1973]
PN 166   SC 31450
B   Medical Personnel [1967]
Military Personnel [1967]

Military Officers
Use   Commissioned Officers

Military Personnel [1967]
PN 2980   SC 31470

Military Personnel — (cont'd)
- **UF**   Servicemen
- **B**   Government Personnel 1973
- **N**   Air Force Personnel 1967
       Army Personnel 1967
       Coast Guard Personnel 1988
       Commissioned Officers 1973
     ↓ Enlisted Military Personnel 1973
       Marine Personnel 1973
       Military Medical Personnel 1973
       Military Psychologists 1997
       National Guardsmen 1973
       Navy Personnel 1967
       ROTC Students 1973
       Volunteer Military Personnel 1973
- **R**   Astronauts 1973
       Chaplains 1973
       Combat Experience 1991
       Military Veterans 1973

Military Psychologists 1997
PN 8   **SC** 31475
- **B**   Military Personnel 1967
       Psychologists 1967
- **R**   Military Psychology 1967

Military Psychology 1967
PN 513   **SC** 31480
- **B**   Applied Psychology 1973
- **R**   Military Psychologists 1997

Military Recruitment 1973
PN 232   **SC** 31490
- **UF**   Recruitment (Military)
- **B**   Personnel Recruitment 1973
- **R**   Military Enlistment 1973

Military Schools 1973
PN 156   **SC** 31500
- **B**   Schools 1967
- **R** ↓ Colleges 1967
       High Schools 1973

Military Training 1973
PN 1279   **SC** 31510
- **B**   Personnel Training 1967

Military Veterans 1973
PN 2854   **SC** 31520
- **UF**   Veterans (Military)
- **R** ↓ Military Personnel 1967
      ↓ Personnel 1967

Miller Analogies Test 1973
PN 13   **SC** 31530
- **B**   Intelligence Measures 1967

Millon Clinical Multiaxial Inventory 1988
PN 372   **SC** 31540
- **B**   Nonprojective Personality Measures 1973

Mind 1991
PN 1401   **SC** 31550
- **SN**   Conceptually broad term referring to the organized totality of conscious and unconscious mental processes or psychic activities of an individual.
- **R** ↓ Cognitions 1985
      ↓ Cognitive Processes 1967
      ↓ Consciousness States 1971
       Dualism 1973
       Human Nature 1997
      ↓ Perception 1967
       Theory of Mind 2001

Mind — (cont'd)
- **R**   Unconscious (Personality Factor) 1967

Mind Blindness
- **Use**   Theory of Mind

Mind Body
- **Use**   Dualism

Mini Mental State Examination 1994
PN 179   **SC** 31548
- **B**   Neuropsychological Assessment 1982

Minimal Brain Disorders 1973
PN 486   **SC** 31560
- **SN**   In 2000, this term replaced the discontinued and deleted term MINIMALLY BRAIN DAMAGED. MINIMALLY BRAIN DAMAGED was stripped from all records and replaced with MINIMAL BRAIN DISORDERS.
- **B**   Brain Damage 1967
       Brain Disorders 1967
- **R** ↓ Attention Deficit Disorder 1985
       Attention Deficit Disorder with
         Hyperactivity 2001
       Hyperkinesis 1973
      ↓ Learning Disabilities 1973

Minimum Competency Tests 1985
PN 123   **SC** 31585
- **UF**   Basic Skills Testing
- **B**   Educational Measurement 1967
- **R** ↓ Competence 1982

Ministers (Religion) 1973
PN 492   **SC** 31590
- **UF**   Pastors
- **B**   Clergy 1973
- **R**   Chaplains 1973
       Missionaries 1973

Minks 1973
PN 34   **SC** 31600
- **B**   Rodents 1973

**Minnesota Multiphasic Personality
      Inventory** 2001
PN 4179   **SC** 31611
- **SN**   In 2000, the truncated term MINN MULTIPHASIC PERSONALITY INVEN (which was used from 1967-2000) was deleted, removed from all records containing it, and mapped to its expanded form MINNESOTA MULTIPHASIC PERSONALITY INVENTORY.
- **UF**   MMPI
- **B**   Nonprojective Personality Measures 1973

Minnesota Teacher Attitude Inventory
- **SN**   Term was discontinued in 1997. In 2000, the term was stripped from all records containing it, and replaced with ATTITUDE MEASURES, its postable counterpart.
- **Use**   Attitude Measures

Minor Tranquilizers 1973
PN 177   **SC** 31630
- **B**   Tranquilizing Drugs 1967
- **N**   Alprazolam 1988
       Buspirone 1991
       Chlordiazepoxide 1973
       Chlorprothixene 1973
       Clonazepam 1991
       Diazepam 1973

Minor Tranquilizers — (cont'd)
- **N**   Hydroxyzine 1973
       Lorazepam 1988
       Loxapine 1982
       Midazolam 1991
       Oxazepam 1978
- **R** ↓ Benzodiazepines 1978

Minority Group Discrimination
- **SN**   Term was discontinued in 1982. From 1982-1993, SOCIAL DISCRIMINATION was used to capture this concept, and then in 1994, RACE AND ETHNIC DISCRIMINATION was created as the new postable terminology. In 2000, MINORITY GROUP DISCRIMINATION was stripped from all records containing it, and replaced with RACE AND ETHNIC DISCRIMINATION, its postable counterpart.
- **Use**   Race and Ethnic Discrimination

Minority Groups 1967
PN 3178   **SC** 31640
- **SN**   Includes ethnic and linguistic minority groups and in/out social groups.
- **B**   Social Groups 1973
- **R**   Affirmative Action 1985
       Alaska Natives 1997
       American Indians 1967
       Arabs 1988
      ↓ Asians 1982
       Blacks 1982
       Cultural Sensitivity 1994
       Gypsies 1973
       Hawaii Natives 2001
      ↓ Hispanics 1982
      ↓ Indigenous Populations 2001
       Inuit 2001
       Jews 1997
       Multiculturalism 1997
      ↓ Pacific Islanders 2001
       Race and Ethnic Discrimination 1994
      ↓ Racial and Ethnic Groups 2001
      ↓ Social Identity 1988

Mirror Image 1991
PN 166   **SC** 31645
- **R**   Human Figures Drawing 1973
       Mental Rotation 1991
      ↓ Perceptual Discrimination 1973
       Self Perception 1967
      ↓ Visual Perception 1967

Mirroring 1997
PN 19   **SC** 31647
- **SN**   Reflecting or emulating another person's behavior or other qualities in interactional or psychotherapeutic contexts. Also a technique in psychodrama.
- **B**   Psychotherapeutic Techniques 1967
- **R** ↓ Interpersonal Interaction 1967
       Psychodrama 1967
      ↓ Psychotherapeutic Processes 1967
       Self Psychology 1988

Misanthropy 1973
PN 38   **SC** 31650
- **UF**   Misogyny
- **B**   Personality Traits 1967

Misarticulation
- **Use**   Articulation Disorders

Misbehavior
- **Use**   Behavior Problems

Miscarriage
Use Spontaneous Abortion

Miscegenous Marriage
Use Interracial Marriage

Misconduct
Use Behavior Problems

Misdemeanors
Use Crime

Misdiagnosis 1997
PN 60 **SC** 31705
R ↓ Diagnosis 1967
Diagnosis Related Groups 1988
Patient History 1973
Professional Liability 1985
↓ Psychodiagnostic Typologies 1967
↓ Screening 1982

Misogyny
Use Misanthropy

Missionaries 1973
PN 134 **SC** 31720
B Religious Personnel 1973
R ↓ Clergy 1973
↓ Educational Personnel 1973
Evangelists 1973
Lay Religious Personnel 1973
Ministers (Religion) 1973
Nuns 1973
Priests 1973

Mistakes
Use Errors

MMPI
Use Minnesota Multiphasic Personality Inventory

Mnemonic Learning 1973
PN 865 **SC** 31750
SN Use of artificial ways (e.g., imagery) to facilitate learning, memory, recognition, and recall of material learned.
B Learning 1967
Learning Strategies 1991
R Cues 1967
Memory Training 1994
Note Taking 1991

Mobility (Geographical)
Use Geographical Mobility

Mobility (Occupational)
Use Occupational Mobility

Mobility (Social)
Use Social Mobility

Mobility Aids 1978
PN 222 **SC** 31774
UF Seeing Eye Dogs
Tactual Maps
Wheelchairs
R ↓ Medical Therapeutic Devices 1973
Physical Mobility 1994

Moclobemide 1997
PN 111 **SC** 31780
B Antidepressant Drugs 1971

Moclobemide — (cont'd)
B Monoamine Oxidase Inhibitors 1973

Modeling
Use Simulation

Modeling Behavior
Use Imitation (Learning)

Models 1967
PN 27261 **SC** 31805
SN Quantitative or descriptive representations of how systems function, or criteria used for comparison purposes. Not to be used for role models.
N Animal Models 1988
Medical Model 1978

Moderate Mental Retardation 2001
PN 1709 **SC** 31807
SN IQ 35-49. In 2000, this term was created to replace the discontinued term TRAINABLE MENTALLY RETARDED and the discontinued and deleted term MODERATELY MENTALLY RETARDED. These terms were stripped from all records and replaced with MODERATE MENTAL RETARDATION.
UF Trainable Mentally Retarded
B Mental Retardation 1967
R Downs Syndrome 1967

Modern Language Aptitude Test 1973
PN 7 **SC** 31820
B Aptitude Measures 1967

Molindone 1982
PN 36 **SC** 31833
SN Organic heterocyclic indole having antiserotonin properties and used as an antidepressant, sedative, and tranquilizer.
B Antidepressant Drugs 1971
Neuroleptic Drugs 1973
Sedatives 1973
Serotonin Antagonists 1973

Mollusca 1973
PN 381 **SC** 31840
UF Gastropods
B Invertebrates 1973
N Octopus 1973
Snails 1973

Monetary Incentives 1973
PN 573 **SC** 31850
SN Money expected or promised in return for service or attainment which may encourage the continued occurrence of the activity being rewarded.
B Incentives 1967
Motivation 1967
R Monetary Rewards 1973
↓ Needs 1967

Monetary Rewards 1973
PN 444 **SC** 31860
SN Money given in return for service or attainment which may act as reinforcement for the activity being rewarded.
B Rewards 1967
R Monetary Incentives 1973

Money 1967
PN 1280 **SC** 31870
R Budgets 1997
Cost Containment 1991
↓ Costs and Cost Analysis 1973

Money — (cont'd)
R Economics 1985
Economy 1973
Equity (Payment) 1978
Funding 1988
↓ Professional Fees 1978
Resource Allocation 1997

Mongolism
Use Downs Syndrome

Monitoring 1973
PN 984 **SC** 31890
SN Systematic observation or recording of events, processes, or individuals.
B Attention 1967
N Self Monitoring 1982
Vigilance 1967
R Selective Attention 1973
↓ Tracking 1967

Monkeys 1967
PN 10628 **SC** 31900
B Primates (Nonhuman) 1973

Monoamine Oxidase Inhibitors 1973
PN 969 **SC** 31920
B Enzyme Inhibitors 1985
N Iproniazid 1973
Isocarboxazid 1973
Moclobemide 1997
Nialamide 1973
Pargyline 1973
Phenelzine 1973
Pheniprazine 1973
Tranylcypromine 1973
R ↓ Amine Oxidase Inhibitors 1973
↓ Antidepressant Drugs 1971
Monoamine Oxidases 1973
↓ Tricyclic Antidepressant Drugs 1997

Monoamine Oxidases 1973
PN 601 **SC** 31930
B Oxidases 1973
R ↓ Monoamine Oxidase Inhibitors 1973

Monoamines (Brain)
Use Catecholamines

Monocular Vision 1973
PN 698 **SC** 31940
B Visual Perception 1967
R Motion Parallax 1997

Monogamy 1997
PN 62 **SC** 31945
SN Used for human or animal populations.
UF Marital Fidelity
B Family Structure 1973
Marriage 1967
Psychosexual Behavior 1967
R Extramarital Intercourse 1973
↓ Human Courtship 1973
Polygamy 1973

Monolingualism 1973
PN 163 **SC** 31950
R ↓ Language 1967

Monotony 1978
PN 59 **SC** 31955
SN Quality of task or stimulation characterized by tedious or wearisome sameness and uniformity.

Monotony — (cont'd)
  R   Boredom 1973

Monozygotic Twins 1973
PN 1069   SC 31960
  UF   Identical Twins
  B   Twins 1967

Montessori Method 1973
PN 78   SC 31970
SN Method of early childhood education developed by M. Montessori, stressing individual instruction and guidance and emphasizing practical life activities.
  B   Teaching Methods 1967
  R   Discovery Teaching Method 1973
       Open Classroom Method 1973

Mood Disorders
  Use Affective Disorders

Moodiness 1973
PN 32   SC 31980
  B   Personality Traits 1967

Moods
  Use Emotional States

Mooney Problem Check List 1973
PN 11   SC 32000
  B   Nonprojective Personality Measures 1973

Moral Development 1973
PN 3355   SC 32006
SN Process of acquiring ethical judgment.
  B   Psychogenesis 1973
  R   Kohlberg (Lawrence) 1991
       Morality 1967
       ↓ Personality Development 1967
       ↓ Psychosocial Development 1973

Morale 1978
PN 603   SC 32008
SN Prevailing spirit or attitude of an individual or group characterized by self confidence and motivation and sense of purpose.
  R   ↓ Emotional States 1973
       ↓ Emotions 1967
       Enthusiasm 1973

Morality 1967
PN 3602   SC 32010
SN Subjective or objective standards of right or wrong, based on societal norms or ethical principles. In 1982, this term replaced the discontinued term MORALS. In 2000, MORALS was stripped from all records and replaced with MORALITY.
  UF   Morals
  R   ↓ Ethics 1967
       Integrity 1997
       ↓ Justice 1973
       Moral Development 1973
       Personal Values 1973
       ↓ Religious Beliefs 1973
       Reputation 1997
       Shame 1994
       Social Values 1973
       ↓ Values 1967

Morals
SN Term was discontinued in 1982. In 2000, the term was stripped from all records contining it, and replaced with MORALITY, its postable counterpart.
  Use Morality

Mores
  Use Values

Morita Therapy 1994
PN 26   SC 32035
  B   Psychotherapeutic Techniques 1967

Morphemes 1973
PN 282   SC 32050
SN Minimum meaningful linguistic units that contain no smaller meaningful units.
  R   Morphology (Language) 1973
       Phonetics 1967

Morphine 1973
PN 3553   SC 32060
  B   Alkaloids 1973
       Analgesic Drugs 1973
       Dopamine Agonists 1985
       Opiates 1973

Morphology 1973
PN 1042   SC 32070
SN Branch of biology that deals with the structure and form of plants and animals. Used for the scientific discipline or the morphological structure itself.
  R   ↓ Anatomy 1967
       Histology 1973
       ↓ Physiology 1967

Morphology (Language) 1973
PN 620   SC 32080
SN Study of morphemes, including both their phonology and semantics. Used for the linguistic discipline or the specific morphological principles or characteristics of words. Compare MORPHEMES.
  B   Grammar 1967
  R   Discourse Analysis 1997
       Morphemes 1973
       ↓ Phonology 1973
       ↓ Prosody 1991
       ↓ Semantics 1967
       ↓ Syntax 1971
       Words (Phonetic Units) 1967

Mortality
  Use Death and Dying

Mortality Rate 1973
PN 1790   SC 32100
  UF   Death Rate
  R   ↓ Death and Dying 1967
       ↓ Population 1973

Mosaicism
  Use Chromosome Disorders

Moslems
  Use Muslims

Mother Absence 1973
PN 255   SC 32120
SN From 1982, limited to human populations. For animals use ANIMAL MATERNAL DEPRIVATION.
  B   Parental Absence 1973
  R   Patriarchy 1973

Mother Child Communication 1985
PN 1107   SC 32125
SN Verbal or nonverbal communication between mother and child.
  B   Parent Child Communication 1973
  R   Mother Child Relations 1967

Mother Child Relations 1967
PN 9604   SC 32130
SN From 1982, limited to human populations. For animals consider ANIMAL MATERNAL BEHAVIOR.
  UF   Maternal Behavior (Human)
  B   Parent Child Relations 1967
  R   ↓ Childrearing Practices 1967
       Mother Child Communication 1985
       ↓ Parental Attitudes 1973
       Parental Permissiveness 1973
       Parental Role 1973
       Postpartum Depression 1973
       Schizophrenogenic Mothers 1973
       Separation Individuation 1982
       Symbiotic Infantile Psychosis 1973

Mothers 1967
PN 13449   SC 32140
SN From 1982, limited to human populations. For animals consider ANIMAL MATERNAL BEHAVIOR.
  B   Human Females 1973
       Parents 1967
  N   Adolescent Mothers 1985
       Schizophrenogenic Mothers 1973
       Single Mothers 1994
       Unwed Mothers 1973
  R   Expectant Mothers 1985
       Primipara 2001

Moths 1973
PN 145   SC 32150
  B   Insects 1967
  R   Larvae 1973

Motion Parallax 1997
PN 37   SC 32155
SN Monocular distance cues for motion perception based on observer movements and the resultant movements of objects in the visual field.
  B   Distance Perception 1973
       Motion Perception 1967
  R   ↓ Depth Perception 1967
       Form and Shape Perception 1967
       Monocular Vision 1973

Motion Perception 1967
PN 4609   SC 32160
  UF   Movement Perception
  B   Spatial Perception 1967
  N   ↓ Apparent Movement 1967
       Motion Parallax 1997
  R   Direction Perception 1997

Motion Pictures 1973
PN 426   SC 32170
SN Use a more specific term if possible. Not used as a document type identifier.
  B   Audiovisual Communications Media 1973
       Mass Media 1967
  N   Motion Pictures (Educational) 1973
       Motion Pictures (Entertainment) 1973

Motion Pictures (Educational) 1973
PN 157   SC 32180
SN Films produced for educational purposes. Not used as a document type identifier.
  B   Educational Audiovisual Aids 1973
       Motion Pictures 1973

Motion Pictures (Entertainment) 1973
PN 834   SC 32190
SN Not used as a document type identifier.
  UF   Movies
  B   Motion Pictures 1973

Motion Pictures (Entertainment) — (cont'd)
R　Drama [1973]
　　Photographic Art [1973]

Motion Sickness [1973]
PN 340　　　　　　　　　　SC 32200
B　Labyrinth Disorders [1973]

Motivation [1967]
PN 12569　　　　　　　　　SC 32210
UF　Desires
　　Drive
N　↓ Achievement Motivation [1967]
　　Affiliation Motivation [1967]
　　Animal Motivation [1967]
　　Educational Incentives [1973]
　　Employee Motivation [1973]
　　Extrinsic Motivation [1973]
　　Fear of Success [1978]
　　Hunger [1967]
　　↓ Incentives [1967]
　　Intrinsic Motivation [1973]
　　Monetary Incentives [1973]
　　Procrastination [1985]
　　Sex Drive [1973]
　　Temptation [1973]
　　Thirst [1967]
R　Activity Level [1982]
　　↓ Aspirations [1967]
　　↓ Commitment [1985]
　　Delay of Gratification [1978]
　　↓ Deprivation [1967]
　　Enthusiasm [1973]
　　↓ Exploratory Behavior [1967]
　　Goal Setting [1997]
　　↓ Goals [1967]
　　Instinctive Behavior [1982]
　　Instrumentality [1991]
　　Intention [1988]
　　Motivation Training [1973]
　　↓ Needs [1967]
　　Persistence [1973]
　　Planned Behavior [1997]
　　↓ Reinforcement [1967]
　　Satiation [1967]

Motivation Training [1973]
PN 126　　　　　　　　　　SC 32220
UF　Training (Motivation)
R　↓ Motivation [1967]

Motor Coordination [1973]
PN 1267　　　　　　　　　 SC 32230
UF　Coordination (Motor)
B　Motor Processes [1967]
R　↓ Motor Performance [1973]
　　Motor Skills [1973]
　　↓ Perceptual Motor Coordination [1973]
　　↓ Physical Agility [1973]

Motor Cortex [1973]
PN 817　　　　　　　　　　SC 32240
UF　Cortex (Motor)
B　Frontal Lobe [1973]

Motor Development [1973]
PN 1804　　　　　　　　　 SC 32250
B　Physical Development [1973]
N　Perceptual Motor Development [1991]
　　↓ Psychomotor Development [1973]
R　Animal Development [1978]
　　↓ Childhood Development [1967]

Motor Development — (cont'd)
R　Developmental Age Groups [1973]
　　↓ Motor Processes [1967]
　　Physical Mobility [1994]

Motor Disorders
Use　Nervous System Disorders

Motor Evoked Potentials
Use　Somatosensory Evoked Potentials

Motor Neurons [1973]
PN 599　　　　　　　　　　SC 32290
B　Neurons [1973]
R　↓ Efferent Pathways [1982]

Motor Pathways
Use　Efferent Pathways

Motor Performance [1973]
PN 5061　　　　　　　　　 SC 32300
B　Motor Processes [1967]
　　Performance [1967]
N　Finger Tapping [1973]
　　Jumping [1973]
　　Running [1973]
　　Walking [1973]
R　Motor Coordination [1973]

Motor Processes [1967]
PN 10064　　　　　　　　　SC 32310
N　Activity Level [1982]
　　Animal Locomotion [1982]
　　↓ Exercise [1973]
　　Grasping [1997]
　　Jumping [1973]
　　Licking [1988]
　　Motor Coordination [1973]
　　↓ Motor Performance [1973]
　　Motor Skills [1973]
　　↓ Physical Agility [1973]
　　Physical Mobility [1994]
　　Rotational Behavior [1994]
　　Sucking [1978]
　　Swallowing [1988]
　　Swimming [1973]
　　Tonic Immobility [1978]
　　Tool Use [1991]
　　Wandering Behavior [1991]
R　↓ Efferent Pathways [1982]
　　↓ Motor Development [1973]
　　Muscle Tone [1985]
　　↓ Perceptual Motor Processes [1967]
　　Physical Restraint [1982]
　　Posture [1973]

Motor Skill Learning
Use　Perceptual Motor Learning

Motor Skills [1973]
PN 1352　　　　　　　　　 SC 32330
B　Motor Processes [1967]
　　Nonverbal Ability [1988]
R　Motor Coordination [1973]
　　↓ Tracking [1967]

Motor Traffic Accidents [1973]
PN 1408　　　　　　　　　 SC 32340
UF　Automobile Accidents
　　Traffic Accidents (Motor)
B　Transportation Accidents [1973]
R　Drivers [1973]

Motor Traffic Accidents — (cont'd)
R　↓ Driving Behavior [1967]
　　Highway Safety [1973]
　　Pedestrian Accidents [1973]

Motor Vehicles [1982]
PN 278　　　　　　　　　　SC 32350
SN　Automotive vehicles not operated on rails.
UF　Buses
　　Motorcycles
　　Trucks
B　Ground Transportation [1973]
N　Automobiles [1973]
R　Drivers [1973]

Motorcycles
Use　Motor Vehicles

Mourning
Use　Grief

Mouse Killing
Use　Muricide

Mouth (Anatomy) [1967]
PN 384　　　　　　　　　　SC 32370
B　Digestive System [1967]
R　Lips (Face) [1973]
　　Salivary Glands [1973]
　　Teeth (Anatomy) [1973]
　　↓ Tongue [1973]

Movement Disorders [1985]
PN 594　　　　　　　　　　SC 32375
SN　Physically- or psychologically-based abnormalities in motor processes relating primarily to posture, coordination, or locomotion.
UF　Dyspraxia
B　Nervous System Disorders [1967]
N　Apraxia [1973]
　　Ataxia [1973]
　　Athetosis [1973]
　　Catalepsy [1973]
　　Cataplexy [1973]
　　↓ Chorea [1973]
　　↓ Dyskinesia [1973]
　　Myasthenia Gravis [1973]
　　Myoclonia [1973]
　　↓ Paralysis [1973]
　　↓ Spasms [1973]
　　Tics [1973]
　　Torticollis [1973]
　　Tremor [1973]
R　↓ Muscular Disorders [1973]
　　↓ Musculoskeletal Disorders [1973]
　　↓ Neuromuscular Disorders [1973]
　　↓ Symptoms [1967]

Movement Perception
Use　Motion Perception

Movement Therapy [1997]
PN 81　　　　　　　　　　 SC 32385
SN　Therapeutic technique utilizing bodily movements and rhythmic exercises used to improve psychological and/or physical functioning of patients or clients.
B　Treatment [1967]
R　Art Therapy [1973]
　　↓ Creative Arts Therapy [1994]
　　Dance Therapy [1973]
　　↓ Exercise [1973]
　　Music Therapy [1973]

Movement Therapy — (cont'd)
R   Recreation Therapy 1973

Movies
Use   Motion Pictures (Entertainment)

MPTP
Use   Methylphenyltetrahydropyridine

MRI
Use   Magnetic Resonance Imaging

Mucus 1973
PN 22   SC 32440
B   Body Fluids 1973

Mueller Lyer Illusion 1988
PN 84   SC 32439
B   Illusions (Perception) 1967

Multi Infarct Dementia 1991
PN 290   SC 32442
UF   Dementia (Multi Infarct)
B   Vascular Dementia 1997
R   ↓ Cerebrovascular Disorders 1973

Multicultural Education 1988
PN 501   SC 32441
SN   Educational program involving two or more ethnic or cultural groups designed to help participants
define their own ethnic or cultural identity and to
appreciate that of others. The primary purposes are
to reduce prejudice and stereotyping, and to promote
cultural pluralism.
B   Education 1967
R   Bilingual Education 1978
     Cross Cultural Communication 1997
     Cultural Sensitivity 1994
     ↓ Educational Programs 1973
     Multiculturalism 1997

Multiculturalism 1997
PN 531   SC 57500
UF   Cultural Pluralism
R   Cross Cultural Communication 1997
     Cross Cultural Differences 1967
     Cultural Assimilation 1973
     Cultural Deprivation 1973
     Cultural Sensitivity 1994
     ↓ Culture (Anthropological) 1967
     ↓ Culture Change 1967
     Minority Groups 1967
     Multicultural Education 1988
     ↓ Racial and Ethnic Attitudes 1982
     Racial and Ethnic Differences 1982
     ↓ Racial and Ethnic Groups 2001
     Racial and Ethnic Relations 1982
     ↓ Sociocultural Factors 1967

Multidimensional Scaling 1982
PN 643   SC 32443
SN   Set of psychological data analysis techniques
that represent perceived stimuli in multidimensional
spatial or pictorial configurations.
B   Measurement 1967
R   ↓ Analysis 1967
     ↓ Rating Scales 1967
     Scaling (Testing) 1967

Multidisciplinary Research
Use   Interdisciplinary Research

Multidisciplinary Treatment Approach
Use   Interdisciplinary Treatment Approach

Multidrug Abuse
Use   Polydrug Abuse

Multilingualism 1973
PN 110   SC 32450
N   Bilingualism 1973
R   Bilingual Education 1978
     English as Second Language 1997
     ↓ Language 1967

Multimodal Treatment Approach 1991
PN 660   SC 32455
SN   Use of different therapeutic techniques based
on the theoretical principles from one medical or psy-
chological specialty or discipline. Compare INTER-
DISCIPLINARY TREATMENT APPROACH.
B   Treatment 1967
R   Eclectic Psychotherapy 1994
     Integrated Services 1997
     Interdisciplinary Treatment Approach 1973

Multiple Births 1973
PN 40   SC 32460
SN   Birth of more than one child at the same time to
the same parents. Also used to refer to the children
themselves. Use a more specific term if possible.
Limited to human populations.
B   Siblings 1967
N   Triplets 1973
     ↓ Twins 1967

Multiple Choice (Testing Method) 1973
PN 675   SC 32470
B   Testing Methods 1967

Multiple Disabilities 2001
PN 884   SC 32473
SN   The term MULTIPLY HANDICAPPED was used
to represent this concept from 1973-1996, and MUL-
TIPLY DISABLED was used from 1997-2000. In
2000, MULTIPLE DISABILITIES was created to
replace the discontinued and deleted term MULTIPLY
DISABLED. MULTIPLY DISABLED and MULTIPLY
HANDICAPPED were stripped from all records and
replaced with MULTIPLE DISABILITIES.
UF   Multiply Handicapped
B   Disorders 1967
N   Deaf Blind 1991

Multiple Personality
SN   Term was discontinued in 1997. In 2000, the
term was stripped from all records containing it, and
replaced with DISSOCIATIVE IDENTITY DISOR-
DER, its postable counterpart.
Use   Dissociative Identity Disorder

Multiple Regression 1982
PN 291   SC 32485
SN   Method of analyzing the collective and separate
influences of two or more independent variables on
the variation of a criterion variable.
B   Multivariate Analysis 1982
     Statistical Regression 1985
R   Analysis of Covariance 1973
     Analysis of Variance 1967
     Linear Regression 1973
     Nonlinear Regression 1973
     Path Analysis 1991
     ↓ Statistical Correlation 1967

Multiple Sclerosis 1973
PN 1194   SC 32490
B   Sclerosis (Nervous System) 1973
R   ↓ Myelitis 1973

Multiple Therapy
Use   Cotherapy

Multiply Handicapped
SN   The term was discontinued in 1997, when the
term MULTIPLY DISABLED was created to capture
this concept. In 2000, with the deletion of the term
MULTIPLY DISABLED, MULTIPLY HANDICAPPED
was made a nonpostable term for the new postable
term MULTIPLE DISABILITIES. MULTIPLY HANDI-
CAPPED and MULTIPLY DISABLED were stripped
from all records containing them and replaced with
MULTIPLE DISABILITIES.
Use   Multiple Disabilities

Multivariate Analysis 1982
PN 937   SC 32513
SN   Any statistical technique designed to measure
the influence of many independent variables acting
simultaneously on more than one dependent vari-
able.
UF   Canonical Correlation
B   Statistical Analysis 1967
N   ↓ Factor Analysis 1967
     Multiple Regression 1982
     Path Analysis 1991
R   Analysis of Covariance 1973
     Analysis of Variance 1967
     ↓ Statistical Correlation 1967
     ↓ Statistical Regression 1985

Munchausen Syndrome 1994
PN 46   SC 32517
SN   A disorder characterized by plausible presenta-
tions of physical symptoms or an acute illness that
are under the individual's control, and often resulting
in multiple, unnecessary hospitalizations. Use FACTI-
TIOUS DISORDERS to access references from
1988-1993.
UF   Hospital Addiction Syndrome
B   Factitious Disorders 1988
R   Malingering 1973
     Munchausen Syndrome by Proxy 1997
     ↓ Somatoform Disorders 2001

Munchausen Syndrome by Proxy 1997
PN 72   SC 32519
SN   A phenomenon in which symptoms of an acute
illness are fabricated by an individual other than the
patient (e.g., a caregiver or parent) resulting in habitual seeking of medical care.
R   ↓ Child Abuse 1971
     Child Neglect 1988
     Munchausen Syndrome 1994

Murder
Use   Homicide

Muricide 1988
PN 38   SC 32523
UF   Mouse Killing
B   Animal Aggressive Behavior 1973

Muscarinic Drugs
Use   Cholinergic Drugs

Muscimol 1994
PN 103   SC 32525

Muscimol — (cont'd)
SN Use GAMMA AMINOBUTYRIC ACID AGO-
NISTS to access references from 1985-1993.
  UF Pantherine
  B Gamma Aminobutyric Acid Agonists [1985]
    Ibotenic Acid [1991]

Muscle Contraction Headache [1973]
PN 500   **SC** 32530
  UF Tension Headache
  B Headache [1973]

Muscle Contractions [1973]
PN 589   **SC** 32540
  UF Rigidity (Muscles)
  R Muscle Relaxation [1973]
    Muscle Tone [1985]
    ↓ Muscles [1967]
    Parkinsonism [1994]
    ↓ Reflexes [1971]

Muscle Cramps
  Use Muscular Disorders

Muscle Relaxation [1973]
PN 452   **SC** 32557
  R Muscle Contractions [1973]
    ↓ Muscles [1967]
    Progressive Relaxation Therapy [1978]
    Relaxation [1973]
    ↓ Relaxation Therapy [1978]

Muscle Relaxation Therapy
  Use Relaxation Therapy

Muscle Relaxing Drugs [1973]
PN 170   **SC** 32560
SN In 1997, this term replaced the discontinued
term MEPHENESIN. In 2000, MEPHENESIN was
stripped from all records and replaced with MUSCLE
RELAXING DRUGS.
  UF Mephenesin
    Neuromuscular Blocking Drugs
  B Drugs [1967]
  N Baclofen [1991]
    Curare [1973]
    Diazepam [1973]
    Meprobamate [1973]
    Orphenadrine [1973]
    Papaverine [1973]
    Succinylcholine [1973]
    Theophylline [1973]
    Tubocurarine [1973]
  R ↓ Anesthetic Drugs [1973]
    ↓ Anticonvulsive Drugs [1973]
    ↓ Antihypertensive Drugs [1973]
    ↓ Antispasmodic Drugs [1973]
    ↓ Benzodiazepines [1978]
    ↓ CNS Depressant Drugs [1973]
    ↓ Heart Rate Affecting Drugs [1973]
    ↓ Tranquilizing Drugs [1967]
    Vasodilation [1973]

Muscle Spasms [1973]
PN 70   **SC** 32570
  B Spasms [1973]
  R ↓ Muscles [1967]

Muscle Tone [1985]
PN 73   **SC** 32575
  R ↓ Motor Processes [1967]
    Muscle Contractions [1973]
    ↓ Reflexes [1971]

Muscles [1967]
PN 1613   **SC** 32580
  B Musculoskeletal System [1973]
  N Abdominal Wall [1973]
    Diaphragm (Anatomy) [1973]
    Facial Muscles [1973]
    Masticatory Muscles [1973]
    Oculomotor Muscles [1973]
  R Muscle Contractions [1973]
    Muscle Relaxation [1973]
    Muscle Spasms [1973]
    ↓ Tissues (Body) [1973]

Muscular Atrophy [1973]
PN 33   **SC** 32590
  UF Atrophy (Muscular)
  B Muscular Disorders [1973]

Muscular Disorders [1973]
PN 724   **SC** 32600
  UF Cramps (Muscle)
    Duchennes Disease
    Dystonia
    Fibromyalgia Syndrome
    Muscle Cramps
  B Musculoskeletal Disorders [1973]
  N Cataplexy [1973]
    Muscular Atrophy [1973]
    Muscular Dystrophy [1973]
    Myasthenia Gravis [1973]
    Myoclonia [1973]
    Myofascial Pain [1991]
    Myotonia [1973]
    Torticollis [1973]
  R Chronic Fatigue Syndrome [1997]
    ↓ Movement Disorders [1985]
    ↓ Neuromuscular Disorders [1973]

Muscular Dystrophy [1973]
PN 154   **SC** 32610
  UF Dystrophy (Muscular)
  B Muscular Disorders [1973]
    Neuromuscular Disorders [1973]
  R Dysarthria [1973]
    ↓ Peripheral Nerve Disorders [1973]

Musculocutaneous Nerve
  Use Spinal Nerves

Musculoskeletal Disorders [1973]
PN 440   **SC** 32630
  UF Skeletomuscular Disorders
    Temporomandibular Joint Syndrome
  B Physical Disorders [1997]
  N ↓ Bone Disorders [1973]
    ↓ Joint Disorders [1973]
    ↓ Muscular Disorders [1973]
  R Hemiplegia [1978]
    ↓ Movement Disorders [1985]
    ↓ Musculoskeletal System [1973]
    ↓ Neuromuscular Disorders [1973]
    ↓ Paralysis [1973]
    Paraplegia [1978]
    Poliomyelitis [1973]
    Quadriplegia [1985]
    ↓ Tuberculosis [1973]

Musculoskeletal System [1973]
PN 115   **SC** 32640
  B Anatomical Systems [1973]
  N Arm (Anatomy) [1973]
    Bones [1973]
    Feet (Anatomy) [1973]

Musculoskeletal System — (cont'd)
  N ↓ Fingers (Anatomy) [1973]
    Hand (Anatomy) [1967]
    Hips [1973]
    Jaw [1973]
    ↓ Joints (Anatomy) [1973]
    Leg (Anatomy) [1973]
    ↓ Muscles [1967]
    Skull [1973]
    Spinal Column [1973]
    Tendons [1973]
    Thorax [1973]
  R ↓ Musculoskeletal Disorders [1973]
    ↓ Nose [1973]

Music [1967]
PN 4004   **SC** 32650
  UF Songs
  B Arts [1973]
  N Musical Instruments [1973]
    Rock Music [1991]
  R Music Perception [1997]
    Musicians [1991]
    ↓ Rhythm [1991]
    Singing [1997]
    Tempo [1997]

Music Education [1973]
PN 1069   **SC** 32660
  B Curriculum [1967]

Music Perception [1997]
PN 379   **SC** 32665
  B Auditory Perception [1967]
  R ↓ Music [1967]
    Musical Ability [1973]
    ↓ Pitch Perception [1973]
    ↓ Rhythm [1991]
    Singing [1997]
    Tempo [1997]

Music Therapy [1973]
PN 1071   **SC** 32670
  B Creative Arts Therapy [1994]
  R Educational Therapy [1973]
    Movement Therapy [1997]
    Recreation Therapy [1973]

Musical Ability [1973]
PN 815   **SC** 32680
  B Artistic Ability [1973]
  R Music Perception [1997]

Musical Instruments [1973]
PN 220   **SC** 32690
  UF Piano
  B Music [1967]

Musicians [1991]
PN 496   **SC** 32695
  B Artists [1973]
  R ↓ Music [1967]

Muslims [1997]
PN 102   **SC** 32700
SN Use ISLAM to access references prior to 1997.
  UF Moslems
  B Religious Groups [1997]
  R Islam [1973]

Mutations [1973]
PN 594   **SC** 32710

Mutations — (cont'd)
SN Individual, strain, or species genetic variation resulting from an abrupt or unusual change in gene structure. Also, an externally induced or naturally occurring change in gene characteristics that is propagated in subsequent divisions of the cell.
R ↓ Chromosomes 1973
  ↓ Genetic Disorders 1973
  ↓ Genetics 1967
  Translocation (Chromosome) 1973

Mutilation (Self)
Use Self Mutilation

Mutism 1973
PN 223   SC 32730
B Language Disorders 1982
N Elective Mutism 1973

Mutual Storytelling Technique 1973
PN 48   SC 32740
UF Storytelling Technique
B Psychotherapeutic Techniques 1967

Myasthenia 1973
PN 8   SC 32750
SN Anomaly of the muscles, resulting in muscular debility, weakness, lack of tone, fatigue, or exhaustion.
B Asthenia 1973

Myasthenia Gravis 1973
PN 55   SC 32760
B Movement Disorders 1985
  Muscular Disorders 1973
  Neuromuscular Disorders 1973
  Peripheral Nerve Disorders 1973

Myelin Sheath 1973
PN 86   SC 32780
B Nerve Tissues 1973

Myelitis 1973
PN 9   SC 32790
B Central Nervous System Disorders 1973
N Encephalomyelitis 1973
  Poliomyelitis 1973
R ↓ Infectious Disorders 1973
  Multiple Sclerosis 1973

Myelomeningocele
Use Spina Bifida

Myenteric Plexus
Use Autonomic Ganglia

Myers Briggs Type Indicator 1973
PN 450   SC 32810
B Nonprojective Personality Measures 1973

Myocardial Infarctions 1973
PN 933   SC 32820
UF Infarctions (Myocardial)
B Heart Disorders 1973
R Angina Pectoris 1973
  Coronary Thromboses 1973

Myocardium 1973
PN 20   SC 32830
B Heart 1967

Myoclonia 1973
PN 176   SC 32840
B Movement Disorders 1985
  Muscular Disorders 1973

Myofascial Pain 1991
PN 84   SC 32845
B Muscular Disorders 1973
  Pain 1967
R ↓ Bruxism 1985
  Chronic Pain 1985
  ↓ Somatoform Disorders 2001
  ↓ Syndromes 1973

Myopia 1973
PN 121   SC 32850
UF Nearsightedness
B Refraction Errors 1973

Myotonia 1973
PN 37   SC 32860
B Muscular Disorders 1973
R ↓ Congenital Disorders 1973

Mysticism 1967
PN 424   SC 32870
UF Visions (Mysticism)
B Philosophies 1967
R Occultism 1978
  ↓ Parapsychology 1967
  ↓ Religious Beliefs 1973
  Religious Experiences 1997
  ↓ Religious Practices 1973
  Witchcraft 1973

Myths 1967
PN 1376   SC 32890
R Animism 1973
  Archetypes 1991
  Cultism 1973
  Ethnology 1967
  Folklore 1991
  ↓ Literature 1967
  Metaphor 1982
  Storytelling 1988
  Transcultural Psychiatry 1973

Myxedema
Use Hypothyroidism

N-Methyl-D-Aspartate 1994
PN 1150   SC 32905
UF NMDA
B Aspartic Acid 1973

Nabilone
Use Cannabinoids

NAch
Use Achievement Motivation

Nail Biting 1973
PN 75   SC 32920
B Habits 1967

Nalorphine 1973
PN 47   SC 32940
B Narcotic Antagonists 1973

Naloxone 1978
PN 1799   SC 32944
B Narcotic Antagonists 1973

Naltrexone 1988
PN 637   SC 32945
B Narcotic Antagonists 1973

Names 1985
PN 436   SC 32947
N Brand Names 1978
R Labeling 1978
  Nouns 1973

Naming 1988
PN 1454   SC 32948
SN Process of identifying an object or concept with a word or phrase.
B Cognitive Processes 1967
R Cognitive Mediation 1967
  Object Recognition 1997

Napping 1994
PN 46   SC 32949
B Sleep 1967
R Sleep Onset 1973
  Sleep Wake Cycle 1985

Narcissism 1967
PN 1710   SC 32950
SN Self-love in which all sources of pleasure are unrealistically believed to emanate from within oneself, resulting in a false sense of omnipotence, and in which the libido is no longer attached to external love objects, but is redirected to one's self.
B Personality Traits 1967
R Autoeroticism 1997
  Egocentrism 1978
  Grandiosity 1994
  ↓ Mental Disorders 1967
  Narcissistic Personality 1973
  Selfishness 1973

Narcissistic Personality 1973
PN 929   SC 32960
SN Personality disorder characterized by excessive self-love, egocentrism, grandiosity, exhibitionism, excessive needs for attention, and sensitivity to criticism.
B Personality Disorders 1967
R Antisocial Personality 1973
  Narcissism 1967

Narcoanalysis 1973
PN 18   SC 32970
SN Sleep-like state induced by medication or hypnosis and used in the treatment of mental disorders.
B Drug Therapy 1967
  Physical Treatment Methods 1973
N Sleep Treatment 1973

Narcoanalytic Drugs
SN Term was discontinued in 1997. In 2000, the term was stripped from all records containing it, and replaced with DRUGS, its postable counterpart.
Use Drugs

Narcolepsy 1973
PN 316   SC 32990
UF Paroxysmal Sleep
B Sleep Disorders 1973
R Cataplexy 1973
  Hypersomnia 1994

Narcosis 1973
PN 74   SC 33000
B Toxic Disorders 1973

Narcosis — (cont'd)
R   ↓ Narcotic Drugs   1973

Narcotic Agonists   1988
PN   673   SC   32995
   UF   Opiate Agonists
   B   Drugs   1967
   N   Pentazocine   1991
   R   ↓ Narcotic Drugs   1973

Narcotic Antagonists   1973
PN   904   SC   33010
   UF   Opiate Antagonists
       Opioid Antagonists
   B   Drugs   1967
   N   Nalorphine   1973
       Naloxone   1978
       Naltrexone   1988
   R   ↓ Narcotic Drugs   1973

Narcotic Drugs   1973
PN   462   SC   33020
   B   Drugs   1967
   N   Apomorphine   1973
       Atropine   1973
       Meperidine   1973
       Methadone   1973
       ↓ Opiates   1973
   R   ↓ Analgesic Drugs   1973
       ↓ Anesthetic Drugs   1973
       ↓ Anticonvulsive Drugs   1973
       ↓ CNS Depressant Drugs   1973
       ↓ Cannabis   1973
       ↓ Dopamine Antagonists   1982
       ↓ Emetic Drugs   1973
       ↓ Hypnotic Drugs   1973
       Narcosis   1973
       ↓ Narcotic Agonists   1988
       ↓ Narcotic Antagonists   1973
       ↓ Tranquilizing Drugs   1967

Narcotics Anonymous
   Use   Twelve Step Programs

Narratives   1997
PN   1444   SC   33025
SN   Construction or reconstruction of an event or story. Not a document type identifier.
   B   Verbal Communication   1967
   R   ↓ Biography   1967
       Creative Writing   1994
       Life Review   1991
       ↓ Literature   1967
       Storytelling   1988

Nasal Mucosa   1973
PN   43   SC   33030
   B   Membranes   1973
       Nose   1973
   N   Olfactory Mucosa   1973

National Guardsmen   1973
PN   56   SC   33040
   B   Military Personnel   1967
   R   Air Force Personnel   1967
       Army Personnel   1967
       Volunteer Military Personnel   1973
       ↓ Volunteer Personnel   1973

Nationalism   1967
PN   315   SC   33050
   B   Political Attitudes   1973

Native Alaskans
   Use   Alaska Natives

Native Americans
   Use   American Indians

Native Hawaiians
   Use   Hawaii Natives

Natives
   Use   Indigenous Populations

Natural Childbirth   1978
PN   47   SC   33056
   UF   Childbirth (Natural)
   B   Birth   1967
   R   Childbirth Training   1978

Natural Disasters   1973
PN   656   SC   33060
SN   Calamity caused by natural forces resulting in substantial damage, loss, and distress.
   B   Disasters   1973
   R   Emergency Services   1973
       ↓ Stress   1967

Natural Family
   Use   Biological Family

Natural Selection   1997
PN   90   SC   33073
SN   Natural evolutionary process that results in the survival of organisms best suited to changing living conditions through the perpetuation of desirable genetic qualities and the elimination of undesirable ones. Consider DARWINISM to access references from 1973-1996.
   B   Darwinism   1973
   R   ↓ Genetics   1967
       Theory of Evolution   1967

Naturalistic Observation
   Use   Observation Methods

Nature Nurture   1994
PN   370   SC   33075
SN   Debatable issue concerning the controversial role of genetics or heredity versus environment or experience in normal or abnormal developmental processes.
   R   Behavioral Genetics   1994
       ↓ Environment   1967
       ↓ Genetics   1967
       ↓ Human Development   1967
       Predisposition   1973
       ↓ Psychogenesis   1973

Nausea   1973
PN   244   SC   33080
   B   Symptoms   1967
   R   ↓ Antiemetic Drugs   1973
       ↓ Eating Disorders   1997
       Migraine Headache   1973
       Vomiting   1973

Navigators (Aircraft)
   Use   Aerospace Personnel

Navy Personnel   1967
PN   1133   SC   33100
   B   Military Personnel   1967
   R   Draftees   1973

Nazism
   Use   Fascism

Near Death Experiences   1985
PN   301   SC   33105
SN   Psychological and sensory phenomena reported by persons who were near clinical death.
   B   Parapsychological Phenomena   1973
   R   ↓ Death and Dying   1967
       ↓ Experiences (Events)   1973
       ↓ Hallucinations   1967
       Out of Body Experiences   1988

Nearsightedness
   Use   Myopia

Neck (Anatomy)   1973
PN   192   SC   33120
   B   Anatomy   1967

Need Achievement
   Use   Achievement Motivation

Need for Affiliation
   Use   Affiliation Motivation

Need for Approval   1997
PN   26   SC   33160
   B   Personality Traits   1967
   R   ↓ Needs   1967
       Social Acceptance   1967
       Social Approval   1967
       Social Desirability   1967

Need for Cognition   1997
PN   45   SC   33167
   B   Personality Traits   1967
   R   Cognition   1967
       Intrinsic Motivation   1973
       ↓ Needs   1967

Need Satisfaction   1973
PN   596   SC   33170
   B   Satisfaction   1973
   R   ↓ Needs   1967
       Psychological Needs   1997

Needle Exchange Programs   2001
PN   0   SC   33173
   B   Social Programs   1973
   R   AIDS Prevention   1994
       ↓ Drug Abuse   1973
       Intravenous Drug Usage   1994
       Needle Sharing   1994
       Outreach Programs   1997

Needle Sharing   1994
PN   179   SC   33175
   R   ↓ Drug Abuse   1973
       ↓ Drug Usage   1971
       Intravenous Drug Usage   1994
       Intravenous Injections   1973
       Needle Exchange Programs   2001
       Sharing (Social Behavior)   1978

Needs   1967
PN   3605   SC   33180
   N   Health Service Needs   1997
       Psychological Needs   1997
   R   ↓ Achievement Motivation   1967
       Affiliation Motivation   1967
       Craving   1997

Needs — (cont'd)
R　Extrinsic Motivation　1973
　↓ Goals　1967
　↓ Incentives　1967
　Intrinsic Motivation　1973
　Monetary Incentives　1973
　↓ Motivation　1967
　Need Satisfaction　1973
　Need for Approval　1997
　Need for Cognition　1997
　Needs Assessment　1985
　Nurturance　1985
　Special Needs　1994

Needs Assessment　1985
PN　1474　　　　　　　　SC　33185
SN　Systematic identification of needs of an individual or a group.
B　Evaluation　1967
　Measurement　1967
R　↓ Case Management　1991
　Geriatric Assessment　1997
　↓ Health Care Delivery　1978
　Health Service Needs　1997
　Intake Interview　1994
　↓ Needs　1967
　↓ Psychological Assessment　1997
　Psychological Needs　1997
　Special Needs　1994
　↓ Surveys　1967
　↓ Treatment Planning　1997

Negative and Positive Symptoms
Use　Positive and Negative Symptoms

Negative Reinforcement　1973
PN　368　　　　　　　　SC　33200
SN　A stimulus or stimulus situation that, when withdrawn or discontinued following a response, increases the probability of occurrence of that response. Consider also ESCAPE CONDITIONING.
B　Reinforcement　1967

Negative Therapeutic Reaction　1997
PN　14　　　　　　　　SC　33205
SN　In psychoanalysis, after a period of successful and constructive treatment, the worsening of a patient's symptoms and neurotic behavior.
B　Psychotherapeutic Processes　1967
R　Countertransference　1973
　↓ Psychoanalysis　1967
　Psychotherapeutic Resistance　1973
　Psychotherapeutic Transference　1967

Negative Transfer　1973
PN　194　　　　　　　　SC　33210
SN　Previous learning or practice that hinders the acquisition of new material or skills as the result of dissimilar characteristics of the prior and current learning situation.
B　Transfer (Learning)　1967

Negativism　1973
PN　349　　　　　　　　SC　33220
SN　State of mind or behavior characterized by extreme skepticism and persistent opposition or resistance to outside suggestions or advice.
B　Personality Traits　1967
R　Cynicism　1973
　Pessimism　1973

Negotiation　1973
PN　1442　　　　　　　　SC　33230

Negotiation — (cont'd)
B　Interpersonal Communication　1973
N　Bargaining　1973
R　↓ Conflict Resolution　1982
　Mediation　1988

Negroes
SN　Term was discontinued in 1982. In 2000, the term was stripped from all records containing it, and replaced with BLACKS, its postable counterpart.
Use　Blacks

Neighborhoods　1973
PN　792　　　　　　　　SC　33260
B　Communities　1967

Nembutal
Use　Pentobarbital

NEO Personality Inventory　1997
PN　94　　　　　　　　SC　33275
B　Personality Measures　1967
R　Five Factor Personality Model　1997

NeoFreudian School
Use　Neopsychoanalytic School

Neologisms　1973
PN　38　　　　　　　　SC　33290
B　Vocabulary　1967
R　Words (Phonetic Units)　1967

Neonatal Development　1973
PN　705　　　　　　　　SC　33320
SN　Process of physical, cognitive, personality, and psychosocial growth occurring during the first month of life. Use a more specific term if possible.
B　Infant Development　1973
R　Neonatal Period　2001
　↓ Physical Development　1973
　↓ Psychogenesis　1973

Neonatal Disorders　1973
PN　133　　　　　　　　SC　33330
B　Physical Disorders　1997
N　Amaurotic Familial Idiocy　1973
　Anencephaly　1973
　Cleft Palate　1967
　Crying Cat Syndrome　1973
　Downs Syndrome　1967
　Klinefelters Syndrome　1973
　Phenylketonuria　1973
　Turners Syndrome　1973
R　↓ Apnea　1973
　Birth Injuries　1973
　↓ Congenital Disorders　1973
　Hydrocephaly　1973
　Microcephaly　1973
　Rh Incompatibility　1973
　Sleep Apnea　1991

Neonatal Period　2001
PN　0　　　　　　　　SC　33340
SN　Usually the period from age 0 through 1 month. Compare PERINATAL PERIOD. Used for both human and animal populations.
R　Neonatal Development　1973

Neonates (Animal)
Use　Infants (Animal)

Neonaticide
Use　Infanticide

Neophobia　1985
PN　145　　　　　　　　SC　33368
SN　Fearful or cautious exploration or reaction to novel objects, situations, or stimuli. Usually examined in subhuman species.
R　Animal Exploratory Behavior　1973
　Avoidance　1967
　↓ Fear　1967
　Instinctive Behavior　1982
　Stimulus Novelty　1973

Neoplasms　1967
PN　5448　　　　　　　　SC　33370
UF　Cancers
　Carcinomas
　Malignant Neoplasms
　Sarcomas
　Tumors
B　Physical Disorders　1997
N　Benign Neoplasms　1973
　Breast Neoplasms　1973
　Endocrine Neoplasms　1973
　Leukemias　1973
　↓ Nervous System Neoplasms　1973
　Terminal Cancer　1973
R　Antineoplastic Drugs　1982
　↓ Digestive System Disorders　1973
　↓ Gastrointestinal Disorders　1973
　↓ Liver Disorders　1973

Neopsychoanalytic School　1973
PN　52　　　　　　　　SC　33380
SN　School of psychoanalysis originating with Jung and Adler which differs from Freudian psychoanalysis in emphasizing the importance of social and cultural factors in development of an individual's personality.
UF　NeoFreudian School
B　History of Psychology　1967
　Psychological Theories　2001
N　Individual Psychology　1973
　↓ Jungian Psychology　1973
R　Erikson (Erik)　1991
　Freud (Sigmund)　1967
　Freudian Psychoanalytic School　1973
　↓ Psychoanalytic Theory　1967

Neostigmine　1973
PN　40　　　　　　　　SC　33390
UF　Proserine
B　Cholinesterase Inhibitors　1973
　Cholinomimetic Drugs　1973
R　Bromides　1973

Nerve (Abducens)
Use　Abducens Nerve

Nerve (Accessory)
Use　Cranial Nerves

Nerve (Acoustic)
Use　Acoustic Nerve

Nerve (Facial)
Use　Facial Nerve

Nerve Cells
Use　Neurons

Nerve Endings　1973
PN　35　　　　　　　　SC　33450

Nerve Endings — (cont'd)
- **B**   Nervous System [1967]
- **N**   ↓ Neural Receptors [1973]
  - Proprioceptors [1973]
  - Synapses [1973]
  - Thermoreceptors [1973]

Nerve Growth Factor [1994]
PN 198   **SC** 33455
SN Polypeptide proteins that stimulate growth and development of peripheral, sympathetic, and sensory neurons.
- **B**   Peptides [1973]
- **R**   ↓ Amino Acids [1973]
  - ↓ Nervous System [1967]
  - Neural Development [1985]
  - ↓ Neurons [1973]

Nerve Tissues [1973]
PN 112   **SC** 33460
- **B**   Nervous System [1967]
  - Tissues (Body) [1973]
- **N**   Myelin Sheath [1973]
- **R**   ↓ Neurons [1973]

Nerves (Adrenergic)
- **Use** Adrenergic Nerves

Nerves (Cholinergic)
- **Use** Cholinergic Nerves

Nerves (Cranial)
- **Use** Cranial Nerves

Nerves (Peripheral)
- **Use** Peripheral Nervous System

Nerves (Spinal)
- **Use** Spinal Nerves

Nervous Breakdown
- **Use** Mental Disorders

Nervous System [1967]
PN 699   **SC** 33530
- **B**   Anatomical Systems [1973]
- **N**   ↓ Central Nervous System [1967]
  - ↓ Ganglia [1973]
  - ↓ Nerve Endings [1973]
  - ↓ Nerve Tissues [1973]
  - ↓ Neurons [1973]
  - ↓ Peripheral Nervous System [1973]
  - ↓ Receptive Fields [1985]
- **R**   Afferent Stimulation [1973]
  - Instinctive Behavior [1982]
  - Nerve Growth Factor [1994]
  - ↓ Nervous System Disorders [1967]
  - Neural Development [1985]
  - Neural Networks [1991]
  - Neural Plasticity [1994]
  - ↓ Stereotaxic Techniques [1973]

Nervous System Disorders [1967]
PN 4902   **SC** 33540
- **UF** Motor Disorders
  - Neuroinfections
  - Neurological Disorders
  - Neuropathy
- **B**   Physical Disorders [1997]
- **N**   Autonomic Nervous System Disorders [1973]
  - ↓ Central Nervous System Disorders [1973]
  - ↓ Convulsions [1967]

Nervous System Disorders — (cont'd)
- **N**   Hyperkinesis [1973]
  - ↓ Movement Disorders [1985]
  - ↓ Nervous System Neoplasms [1973]
  - ↓ Neuromuscular Disorders [1973]
  - ↓ Peripheral Nerve Disorders [1973]
  - ↓ Sclerosis (Nervous System) [1973]
- **R**   ↓ Cerebrovascular Disorders [1973]
  - Developmental Disabilities [1982]
  - Extrapyramidal Symptoms [1994]
  - Hemianopia [1973]
  - Influenza [1973]
  - Malaria [1973]
  - ↓ Nervous System [1967]
  - Nystagmus [1973]
  - Parkinsonism [1994]
  - Somatosensory Disorders [2001]
  - ↓ Symptoms [1967]
  - ↓ Tuberculosis [1973]

Nervous System Neoplasms [1973]
PN 26   **SC** 33550
- **B**   Neoplasms [1967]
  - Nervous System Disorders [1967]
- **N**   Brain Neoplasms [1973]

Nervous System Plasticity
- **Use** Neural Plasticity

Nervousness [1973]
PN 60   **SC** 33560
- **B**   Personality Traits [1967]

Nest Building [1973]
PN 598   **SC** 33570
- **B**   Animal Ethology [1967]
- **R**   ↓ Animal Mating Behavior [1967]

Networks (Social)
- **Use** Social Networks

Neural Analyzers [1973]
PN 24   **SC** 33600
SN The peripheral sensory receptors or nerve endings (e.g., visual analyzer, acoustic analyzer) that select and transform stimuli and their associated projections and terminations in the central nervous system where synthesis of the transformations occurs.
- **B**   Central Nervous System [1967]

Neural Development [1985]
PN 2073   **SC** 33605
SN Functional and morphological development of central and peripheral nervous systems and supportive tissue.
- **UF** Neural Regeneration
  - Reinnervation
- **B**   Physical Development [1973]
- **R**   Animal Development [1978]
  - Nerve Growth Factor [1994]
  - ↓ Nervous System [1967]
  - Neural Plasticity [1994]
  - Neural Transplantation [1985]

Neural Lesions [1973]
PN 955   **SC** 33610
SN Not defined prior to 1982. From 1982, limited to experimentally induced neural lesions and used primarily for animal populations.
- **B**   Lesions [1967]

Neural Networks [1991]
PN 2716   **SC** 33612

Neural Networks — (cont'd)
SN Computer simulation that duplicates the neural structure and cognitive processes of the human or animal brain.
- **B**   Artificial Intelligence [1982]
  - Computer Simulation [1973]
- **R**   Connectionism [1994]
  - ↓ Nervous System [1967]
  - Neuroanatomy [1967]

Neural Pathways [1982]
PN 1466   **SC** 33615
SN Collections of central or peripheral neural fibers having a common neurological function and serving to connect neuroanatomical systems such as sensory or motor mechanisms or central nervous system nuclei.
- **B**   Central Nervous System [1967]
  - Peripheral Nervous System [1973]
- **N**   ↓ Afferent Pathways [1982]
  - Corpus Callosum [1973]
  - ↓ Efferent Pathways [1982]
  - Fornix [1982]
  - ↓ Limbic System [1973]
  - Optic Chiasm [1973]
  - Optic Tract [1982]
  - Reticular Formation [1967]

Neural Plasticity [1994]
PN 759   **SC** 33617
SN Change in reactivity of the nervous system and its components as a result of constant successive activations.
- **UF** Nervous System Plasticity
- **R**   ↓ Nervous System [1967]
  - Neural Development [1985]
  - Postactivation Potentials [1985]
  - ↓ Receptive Fields [1985]

Neural Receptors [1973]
PN 5406   **SC** 33620
- **UF** Receptors (Neural)
- **B**   Nerve Endings [1973]
- **N**   Baroreceptors [1973]
  - Chemoreceptors [1973]
  - Mechanoreceptors [1973]
  - Nociceptors [1985]
  - ↓ Photoreceptors [1973]
  - Proprioceptors [1973]
  - Thermoreceptors [1973]
- **R**   Receptor Binding [1985]

Neural Regeneration
- **Use** Neural Development

Neural Transplantation [1985]
PN 344   **SC** 33628
- **R**   Neural Development [1985]
  - Organ Transplantation [1973]
  - Tissue Donation [1991]

Neuralgia [1973]
PN 74   **SC** 33630
- **B**   Pain [1967]
  - Peripheral Nerve Disorders [1973]
- **N**   Trigeminal Neuralgia [1973]

Neurasthenic Neurosis [1973]
PN 128   **SC** 33640
- **B**   Neurosis [1967]
- **R**   ↓ Asthenia [1973]

Neuroanatomy 1967
PN 3017   SC 33660
SN Branch of neurology concerned with the anatomy of the nervous system. Used for the scientific discipline or the anatomical structures themselves.
B   Neurosciences 1973
R   ↓ Anatomy 1967
     Neural Networks 1991

Neurobiology 1973
PN 1658   SC 33670
SN Biology of the nervous system. Used for the scientific discipline or the neurobiological processes themselves.
B   Biology 1967
     Neurosciences 1973
R   Biological Psychiatry 1994

Neurochemistry 1973
PN 8511   SC 33680
SN Chemical makeup and metabolism of nervous tissue. Used for the scientific discipline or the neurochemical processes themselves.
UF   Brain Metabolism
B   Biochemistry 1967
     Neurosciences 1973
N   Neuroendocrinology 1985
     Receptor Binding 1985
R   Blood Brain Barrier 1994
     Glucose Metabolism 1994

Neurodermatitis 1973
PN 29   SC 33690
B   Dermatitis 1973
     Somatoform Disorders 2001
R   Allergic Skin Disorders 1973

Neuroendocrinology 1985
PN 1102   SC 33695
SN Study of the biological, chemical, and physical relations between the nervous system and endocrine glands. Used for the scientific discipline or neuroendocrinological processes themselves.
B   Endocrinology 1973
     Neurochemistry 1973
     Neurophysiology 1973

Neuroinfections
   Use Infectious Disorders AND Nervous System Disorders

Neurokinins 1997
PN 25   SC 33705
B   Amino Acids 1973
     Anti Inflammatory Drugs 1982
     Neurotransmitters 1985
     Peptides 1973
N   Substance P 1985

Neuroleptic Drugs 1973
PN 6667   SC 33710
SN In 1982, this term replaced the discontinued terms ANTIPSYCHOTIC DRUGS and ANTISCHIZOPHRENIC DRUGS. In 2000, these terms were stripped from all records and replaced with NEUROLEPTIC DRUGS.
UF   Antipsychotic Drugs
     Antischizophrenic Drugs
     Major Tranquilizers
B   Tranquilizing Drugs 1967
N   Clozapine 1991
     Molindone 1982
     Nialamide 1973
     Reserpine 1967

Neuroleptic Drugs — (cont'd)
N   Risperidone 1997
     Spiroperidol 1991
     Sulpiride 1973
     Tetrabenazine 1973
R   Neuroleptic Malignant Syndrome 1988
     Prostaglandins 1982
     Tardive Dyskinesia 1988

Neuroleptic Malignant Syndrome 1988
PN 420   SC 33715
B   Syndromes 1973
     Toxic Disorders 1973
R   ↓ Drug Therapy 1967
     ↓ Neuroleptic Drugs 1973
     ↓ Side Effects (Drug) 1973

Neurolinguistic Programming 2001
PN 98   SC 33718
SN R. Bandler's model of techniques and strategies for interpersonal communication based on elements of transformational grammar and preferred sensory representations for learning and self expression. Also, self intervention method in humanistic psychology aimed at personal growth and human potential. In 2000, this term was created to update the spelling from the discontinued term NEUROLINGUISTIC PROGRAMING. NEUROLINGUISTIC PROGRAMING was stripped from all records and replaced with NEUROLINGUISTIC PROGRAMMING.
R   ↓ Cognitive Style 1967
     ↓ Humanistic Psychology 1985
     ↓ Interpersonal Communication 1973
     Neurolinguistics 1991
     Perceptual Style 1973

Neurolinguistics 1991
PN 182   SC 33719
SN Study of the neurological mechanisms involved in the development, acquisition, and use of language. Used for the scientific discipline or the neurolinguistic processes themselves.
B   Linguistics 1973
R   ↓ Language 1967
     ↓ Language Disorders 1982
     Neurolinguistic Programming 2001
     Psycholinguistics 1967
     ↓ Verbal Communication 1967

Neurological Disorders
   Use Nervous System Disorders

Neurologists 1973
PN 108   SC 33730
UF   Neuropathologists
B   Physicians 1967
R   Surgeons 1973

Neurology 1967
PN 5599   SC 33740
SN Scientific discipline dealing with the anatomy, physiology, and organic diseases of the nervous system. Used for the scientific discipline or the neurological findings themselves.
B   Medical Sciences 1967
     Neurosciences 1973
R   Neuropathology 1973
     ↓ Neurosurgery 1973

Neuromuscular Blocking Drugs
   Use Muscle Relaxing Drugs

Neuromuscular Disorders 1973
PN 228   SC 33760

Neuromuscular Disorders — (cont'd)
B   Nervous System Disorders 1967
N   Cataplexy 1973
     Gilles de la Tourette Disorder 1973
     Muscular Dystrophy 1973
     Myasthenia Gravis 1973
     ↓ Paralysis 1973
     Parkinsons Disease 1973
R   ↓ Dyskinesia 1973
     Hyperkinesis 1973
     ↓ Movement Disorders 1985
     ↓ Muscular Disorders 1973
     ↓ Musculoskeletal Disorders 1973
     ↓ Sclerosis (Nervous System) 1973
     ↓ Spinal Cord Injuries 1973

Neurons 1973
PN 4189   SC 33770
UF   Nerve Cells
B   Cells (Biology) 1973
     Nervous System 1967
N   Axons 1973
     Dendrites 1973
     Ganglion Cells (Retina) 1985
     Motor Neurons 1973
     Purkinje Cells 1994
     ↓ Sensory Neurons 1973
R   Nerve Growth Factor 1994
     ↓ Nerve Tissues 1973
     Visual Receptive Fields 1982

Neuropathologists
   Use Neurologists

Neuropathology 1973
PN 2739   SC 33790
SN Branch of medicine dealing with morphological and other aspects of nervous system disorders. Used for the scientific discipline or the neuropathological findings themselves.
B   Neurosciences 1973
     Pathology 1973
R   Neurology 1967

Neuropathy
   Use Nervous System Disorders

Neuropeptides
   Use Peptides

Neurophysiology 1973
PN 4396   SC 33810
SN Physiology of the nervous system. Used for the scientific discipline or the neurophysiological processes themselves.
B   Neurosciences 1973
     Physiology 1967
N   Neuroendocrinology 1985
     Receptor Binding 1985

Neuropsychiatrists
   Use Psychiatrists

Neuropsychiatry 1973
PN 805   SC 33830
SN Medical specialty that combines psychiatry and neurology. Used for the scientific discipline or the neuropsychiatric findings themselves.
B   Neurosciences 1973
     Psychiatry 1967
R   Biological Psychiatry 1994

Neuropsychological Assessment [1982]
PN 5452   **SC** 33835
SN Use of tests, including intelligence, motor, and lateralization measures, to diagnose brain damage or other neurological dysfunction.
B Psychological Assessment [1997]
N Halstead Reitan Neuropsychological
         Battery [2001]
     Luria Nebraska Neuropsychological
         Battery [2001]
     Mini Mental State Examination [1994]
     Wechsler Memory Scale [1988]
     Wisconsin Card Sorting Test [1994]
R Bender Gestalt Test [1967]
     Benton Revised Visual Retention Test [1973]
     Body Sway Testing [1973]
     ↓ Brain Damage [1967]
     Cognitive Assessment [1997]
     ↓ Diagnosis [1967]
     Memory for Designs Test [1973]
     ↓ Neuropsychological Rehabilitation [1997]
     ↓ Testing [1967]
     Traumatic Brain Injury [1997]

Neuropsychological Rehabilitation [1997]
PN 268   **SC** 33837
B Rehabilitation [1967]
N Cognitive Rehabilitation [1985]
R Memory Training [1994]
     ↓ Neuropsychological Assessment [1982]

Neuropsychology [1973]
PN 6385   **SC** 33840
SN Branch of clinical psychology emphasizing the relationship between brain and behavior, including the diagnosis of brain pathology using cognitive or psychological tests. Used for the discipline or the neuropsychological functions themselves.
B Neurosciences [1973]
     Physiological Psychology [1967]
R Psychoneuroimmunology [1991]

Neurosciences [1973]
PN 598   **SC** 33850
SN Scientific disciplines concerned with the development, structure, function, chemistry, and pathology of the nervous system.
B Sciences [1967]
N Neuroanatomy [1967]
     Neurobiology [1973]
     ↓ Neurochemistry [1973]
     Neurology [1967]
     Neuropathology [1973]
     ↓ Neurophysiology [1973]
     Neuropsychiatry [1973]
     Neuropsychology [1973]
R ↓ Medical Sciences [1967]

Neurosis [1967]
PN 4727   **SC** 33860
SN Psychoanalytic term referring to mental conditions characterized primarily by anxiety, fears, obsessive thoughts, compulsions, dissociation, and depression. Neuroses have no organic origins and are believed to be a product of unconscious processes resulting from internal conflicts. Compare PSYCHOSIS.
UF Psychoneurosis
B Mental Disorders [1967]
N Childhood Neurosis [1973]
     Experimental Neurosis [1973]
     Neurasthenic Neurosis [1973]
     Occupational Neurosis [1973]

Neurosis — (cont'd)
N Traumatic Neurosis [1973]
R Anhedonia [1985]
     ↓ Anxiety [1967]
     Borderline States [1978]
     Dissociation [2001]
     ↓ Fear [1967]
     ↓ Major Depression [1988]
     Obsessive Compulsive Disorder [1985]

Neurosurgeons
Use Surgeons

Neurosurgery [1973]
PN 809   **SC** 33890
B Surgery [1971]
N Commissurotomy [1985]
     Decerebration [1973]
     Decortication (Brain) [1973]
     Hemispherectomy [1973]
     ↓ Psychosurgery [1973]
     Pyramidotomy [1973]
     Sympathectomy [1973]
     Tractotomy [1973]
     Vagotomy [1973]
R Neurology [1967]

Neurosyphilis [1973]
PN 37   **SC** 33900
B Central Nervous System Disorders [1973]
     Syphilis [1973]
R General Paresis [1973]

Neurotensin [1985]
PN 165   **SC** 33905
B Neurotransmitters [1985]
     Peptides [1973]

Neurotic Depressive Reaction
SN In 2000, the term was discontinued, and all records containing it were stripped of the term and replaced with MAJOR DEPRESSION, its postable counterpart.
Use Major Depression

Neuroticism [1973]
PN 1860   **SC** 33915
SN Personality trait that contrasts adjustment or emotional stability with maladjustment. Experience of anxiety, anger, disgust, sadness, embarrassment, and a variety of other negative emotions.
B Personality Traits [1967]
R Emotional Inferiority [1973]
     Emotional Instability [1973]
     Emotional Stability [1973]
     Emotionality (Personality) [1973]
     Five Factor Personality Model [1997]

Neurotoxins [1982]
PN 1163   **SC** 33920
SN Bacterial, chemical, or pharmacological substances that are destructive to nerve tissue.
B Poisons [1973]
N ↓ Ibotenic Acid [1991]
     Methylphenyltetrahydropyridine [1994]
R Antibodies [1973]
     Drug Interactions [1982]
     ↓ Insecticides [1973]
     Kainic Acid [1988]
     ↓ Toxic Disorders [1973]
     Toxicity [1973]

Neurotransmitters [1985]
PN 1182   **SC** 33924
SN Chemical substances, synthesized and released by nerve cells, or glandular hormones that excite or inhibit other nerve, muscle, or gland cells by producing a brief alteration in the postsynaptic membrane of the receiving cell. Use a more specific term if possible.
N Acetylcholine [1973]
     ↓ Aspartic Acid [1973]
     ↓ Catecholamines [1973]
     Cholecystokinin [1982]
     ↓ Endorphins [1982]
     Gamma Aminobutyric Acid [1978]
     Glutamic Acid [1973]
     Glycine [1973]
     Histamine [1973]
     ↓ Neurokinins [1997]
     Neurotensin [1985]
     Serotonin [1973]
     Substance P [1985]
R ↓ Amino Acids [1973]
     ↓ Peptides [1973]

Neutrality (Psychotherapeutic)
Use Psychotherapeutic Neutrality

Never Married [1994]
PN 43   **SC** 33926
B Marital Status [1973]
R ↓ Single Parents [1978]
     Single Persons [1973]
     Unwed Mothers [1973]

News Media [1997]
PN 194   **SC** 33945
B Mass Media [1967]
N Newspapers [1973]
R Journalists [1973]
     Radio [1973]
     ↓ Television [1967]

Newsletters (Professional)
Use Scientific Communication

Newspapers [1973]
PN 533   **SC** 33960
B News Media [1997]
     Printed Communications Media [1973]

Niacin
Use Nicotinic Acid

Niacinamide
Use Nicotinamide

Nialamide [1973]
PN 40   **SC** 33990
B Amine Oxidase Inhibitors [1973]
     Antidepressant Drugs [1971]
     Monoamine Oxidase Inhibitors [1973]
     Neuroleptic Drugs [1973]

Nicotinamide [1973]
PN 34   **SC** 34000
UF Niacinamide
     Nicotinic Acid Amide
B Vitamins [1973]
R Nicotinic Acid [1973]
     Pellagra [1973]

Nicotine [1973]
PN 2164   **SC** 34010

Nicotine — (cont'd)
- **UF** Tobacco (Drug)
- **B** Alkaloids 1973
  - Cholinergic Blocking Drugs 1973
  - Ganglion Blocking Drugs 1973
- **R** ↓ Insecticides 1973
  - Nicotine Withdrawal 1997
  - Smokeless Tobacco 1994
  - Tobacco Smoking 1967

Nicotine Withdrawal 1997
- **PN** 85 **SC** 34015
- **B** Drug Withdrawal 1973
- **R** Nicotine 1973
  - Smokeless Tobacco 1994
  - Smoking Cessation 1988
  - Tobacco Smoking 1967

Nicotinic Acid 1973
- **PN** 76 **SC** 34020
- **UF** Niacin
- **B** Acids 1973
  - Vasodilator Drugs 1973
  - Vitamins 1973
- **R** Nicotinamide 1973

Nicotinic Acid Amide
- **Use** Nicotinamide

Nictitating Membrane 1973
- **PN** 315 **SC** 34040
- **SN** Fold of transparent or semitransparent mucous membrane present in many vertebrates that can be drawn over the eye like a third eyelid. This membrane cleans and moistens the cornea without occluding light.
- **B** Membranes 1973

Night Terrors
- **Use** Sleep Disorders

Nightmares 1973
- **PN** 326 **SC** 34050
- **B** Dreaming 1967
- **R** Dream Content 1973

Nihilism 1973
- **PN** 17 **SC** 34060
- **B** Philosophies 1967
- **R** Fatalism 1973
  - Pessimism 1973

Nitrazepam 1978
- **PN** 56 **SC** 34066
- **B** Anticonvulsive Drugs 1973
  - Benzodiazepines 1978
  - Hypnotic Drugs 1973
  - Sedatives 1973

Nitrogen 1973
- **PN** 232 **SC** 34070

NMDA
- **Use** N-Methyl-D-Aspartate

Nociception
- **Use** Pain Perception

Nociceptors 1985
- **PN** 334 **SC** 34080
- **UF** Pain Receptors
- **B** Neural Receptors 1973

Nociceptors — (cont'd)
- **B** Sensory Neurons 1973

Nocturnal Behavior (Animal)
- **Use** Animal Nocturnal Behavior

Nocturnal Emission 1973
- **PN** 6 **SC** 34100
- **B** Male Orgasm 1973

Nocturnal Teeth Grinding 1973
- **PN** 47 **SC** 34110
- **SN** Use NOCTURNAL TEETH GRINDING to access references to BRUXISM from 1973-1984.
- **B** Bruxism 1985
- **R** ↓ Sleep 1967

Noise (Sound)
- **Use** Auditory Stimulation

Noise Effects 1973
- **PN** 1508 **SC** 34150
- **SN** Behavioral, physiological, or psychological effects of environmental or experimentally manipulated noise on an organism.
- **B** Environmental Effects 1973
- **R** Acoustics 1997
  - Pollution 1973

Noise Levels (Work Areas) 1973
- **PN** 257 **SC** 34160
- **B** Loudness 1967
  - Working Conditions 1973

Nomenclature (Psychological)
- **Use** Psychological Terminology

Nomifensine 1982
- **PN** 133 **SC** 34175
- **SN** Organic heterocyclic compound used as an antiparkinson agent and antidepressive agent.
- **B** Antidepressant Drugs 1971
  - Antitremor Drugs 1973

Non Zero Sum Games 1973
- **PN** 34 **SC** 34180
- **SN** Quantitative games in which all players may win points as opposed to zero sum games in which points won by one player must be lost by another or others.
- **B** Games 1967
- **R** Entrapment Games 1973
  - Game Theory 1967
  - Prisoners Dilemma Game 1973

Noncommissioned Officers 1973
- **PN** 40 **SC** 34200
- **SN** Subordinate military officers (e.g., sergeants) appointed from enlisted personnel.
- **UF** Officers (Noncommissioned)
- **B** Enlisted Military Personnel 1973

Nonconformity (Personality) 1973
- **PN** 82 **SC** 34210
- **B** Personality Traits 1967
- **R** Conformity (Personality) 1967
  - Individuality 1973

Noncontingent Reinforcement 1988
- **PN** 92 **SC** 34215
- **SN** Presentation of reinforcement (punishment or positive rewards) independently of behavior.

Noncontingent Reinforcement — (cont'd)
- **B** Reinforcement 1967
- **R** Autoshaping 1978
  - ↓ Contingency Management 1973

Nondirected Discussion Method 1973
- **PN** 18 **SC** 34220
- **SN** Teaching method which encourages students' spontaneity and restricts the leader's role to that of a moderator.
- **B** Teaching Methods 1967
- **R** Discovery Teaching Method 1973

Nondirective Therapy
- **Use** Client Centered Therapy

Nongraded Schools 1973
- **PN** 11 **SC** 34250
- **SN** Schools that group students according to such characteristics as academic achievement, mental and physical ability, or emotional development, rather than by age or grade level.
- **B** Schools 1967

Nonlinear Regression 1973
- **PN** 66 **SC** 34260
- **B** Statistical Correlation 1967
  - Statistical Regression 1985
- **R** Multiple Regression 1982

Nonmetallic Elements
- **SN** Term was discontinued in 1997. In 2000, the term was stripped from all records containing it, and replaced with CHEMICAL ELEMENTS, its postable counterpart.
- **Use** Chemical Elements

Nonparametric Statistical Tests 1967
- **PN** 334 **SC** 34280
- **B** Statistical Tests 1973
- **N** Chi Square Test 1973
  - Cochran Q Test 1973
  - Kolmogorov Smirnov Test 1973
  - Mann Whitney U Test 1973
  - Sign Test 1973
  - Wilcoxon Sign Rank Test 1973

Nonprescription Drugs 1991
- **PN** 114 **SC** 34285
- **SN** Drugs or medication sold legally without prescription.
- **UF** Over The Counter Drugs
- **B** Drugs 1967
- **R** Prescription Drugs 1991
  - Self Medication 1991

Nonprofessional Personnel 1982
- **PN** 118 **SC** 34290
- **SN** Conceptually broad term. Use a more specific term if possible. Use PARAPROFESSIONAL PERSONNEL to access references from 1973-1981.
- **B** Personnel 1967
- **N** ↓ Agricultural Workers 1973
- **R** ↓ Business and Industrial Personnel 1967
  - Child Care Workers 1978
  - Domestic Service Personnel 1973
  - ↓ Paraprofessional Personnel 1973
  - ↓ Professional Personnel 1978
  - ↓ Service Personnel 1991
  - Technical Service Personnel 1973

Nonprofit Organizations 1973
- **PN** 219 **SC** 34300

Nonprofit Organizations — (cont'd)

B   Organizations   1967

Nonprojective Personality Measures   1973
PN 1229   **SC** 34304
SN Direct assessment of personality traits through scoring of a subject's responses to questions on structured, standardized tests. Use a more specific term if possible. In 1997, this term replaced the discontinued terms AUTHORITARIANISM REBELLION SCALE, DIFFERENTIAL PERSONALITY INVENTORY, KUPFER DETRE SELF RATING SCALE, and WHITE BETZ A B SCALE. In 2000, these terms were stripped from all records and replaced with NONPROJECTIVE PERSONALITY MEASURES.
UF   Authoritarianism Rebellion Scale
      Differential Personality Inventory
      Kupfer Detre Self Rating Scale
      White Betz A B Scale
B   Personality Measures   1967
N   Bannister Repertory Grid   1973
      Barrett Lennard Relationship Inventory   2001
      Barron Welsh Art Scale   1973
      Beck Depression Inventory   1988
      Bem Sex Role Inventory   1988
      California F Scale   1973
      California Test of Personality   1973
      Child Behavior Checklist   1994
      Childrens Manifest Anxiety Scale   1973
      Childrens Personality Questionnaire   1973
      Edwards Personal Preference Schedule   1967
      Edwards Personality Inventory   1973
      Edwards Social Desirability Scale   1973
      Embedded Figures Testing   1967
      Eysenck Personality Inventory   1973
      Fear Survey Schedule   1973
      Fundamental Interpersonal Relation Orientation Behavior Ques   2001
      Goldstein Scheerer Object Sort Test   1973
      Gough Adjective Check List   1973
      Guilford Zimmerman Temperament Survey   2001
      High School Personality Questionnaire   2001
      Learys Interpersonal Check List   1973
      Marlowe Crowne Social Desirability Scale   2001
      Maudsley Personality Inventory   1973
      Memory for Designs Test   1973
      Millon Clinical Multiaxial Inventory   1988
      Minnesota Multiphasic Personality Inventory   2001
      Mooney Problem Check List   1973
      Myers Briggs Type Indicator   1973
      Omnibus Personality Inventory   1973
      Personal Orientation Inventory   1973
      Psychological Screening Inventory   1973
      Repression Sensitization Scale   1973
      Rod and Frame Test   1973
      Rokeach Dogmatism Scale   1973
      Rotter Internal External Locus of Control Scale   2001
      Sixteen Personality Factors Questionnaire   2001
      State Trait Anxiety Inventory   1973
      Taylor Manifest Anxiety Scale   1973
      Tennessee Self Concept Scale   1973
      Vineland Social Maturity Scale   1973
      Welsh Figure Preference Test   1973
      Zungs Self Rating Depression Scale   1973

Nonrapid Eye Movement Sleep
Use   NREM Sleep

NonREM Sleep
Use   NREM Sleep

Nonreversal Shift Learning   1973
PN 44   **SC** 34330
SN Experimental technique used for the demonstration of mediating processes in concept formation that assesses the ability to shift dimensions in stimulus discrimination tasks, as, for example, from size to color.
UF   Extradimensional Shift Learning
B   Discrimination Learning   1982

Nonsense Syllable Learning   1967
PN 167   **SC** 34340
SN Verbal learning paradigm in which collections or lists of letters, which have no obvious meaning (e.g., XAB, GZL), are used as stimulus items. Also, the actual acquisition, retention, and retrieval of such stimulus items.
B   Verbal Learning   1967

Nonstandard English   1973
PN 274   **SC** 34350
B   Dialect   1973
R   Slang   1973

Nontraditional Careers   1985
PN 333   **SC** 34352
SN Occupations in which certain groups (usually males or females) have traditionally been underrepresented.
B   Occupations   1967
R   Occupational Choice   1967
      Sex Roles   1967

Nontraditional Education   1982
PN 494   **SC** 34355
SN Alternative educational programs within or without the formal educational system that provide flexible and innovative teaching, curriculum, grading, or degree requirements.
UF   Alternative Schools
      Magnet Schools
      Open Universities
B   Education   1967
N   Home Schooling   1994
R   ↓ Curriculum   1967
      ↓ Educational Programs   1973
      ↓ Teaching Methods   1967

Nonverbal Ability   1988
PN 293   **SC** 34357
SN Ability in nonlanguage areas such as spatial relations, mathematics, or music.
B   Ability   1967
N   ↓ Artistic Ability   1973
      Mathematical Ability   1973
      Mechanical Aptitude   1973
      Motor Skills   1973
      ↓ Spatial Ability   1982
R   Academic Aptitude   1973
      ↓ Nonverbal Communication   1971

Nonverbal Communication   1971
PN 3431   **SC** 34360
B   Communication   1967
N   Body Language   1973
      Eye Contact   1973
      ↓ Facial Expressions   1967
      Gestures   1973
      ↓ Manual Communication   1978
R   Laughter   1978
      ↓ Nonverbal Ability   1988

Nonverbal Learning   1973
PN 206   **SC** 34370
SN Acquisition, retention, and retrieval of knowledge or skills that do not involve verbally presented information or language, such as perceptual responses or motor activities.
B   Learning   1967

Nonverbal Meaning   1973
PN 64   **SC** 34380
B   Meaning   1967

Nonverbal Reinforcement   1973
PN 31   **SC** 34390
B   Social Reinforcement   1967

Nonviolence   1991
PN 42   **SC** 34393
B   Social Interaction   1967
R   Pacifism   1973
      ↓ Political Attitudes   1973
      ↓ Violence   1973

Nootropic Drugs   1991
PN 290   **SC** 34395
UF   Cognition Enhancing Drugs
      Memory Enhancing Drugs
B   Drugs   1967
N   Piracetam   1982

Noradrenaline
Use   Norepinephrine

Norepinephrine   1973
PN 2986   **SC** 34410
UF   Noradrenaline
B   Adrenal Medulla Hormones   1973
      Catecholamines   1973
      Vasoconstrictor Drugs   1973
R   Guanethidine   1973
      ↓ Norepinephrine Metabolites   1982

Norepinephrine Metabolites   1982
PN 297   **SC** 34413
SN Molecules generated from the metabolism of norepinephrine.
B   Metabolites   1973
N   Methoxyhydroxyphenylglycol (3,4)   1991
R   ↓ Metabolism   1967
      Norepinephrine   1973

Normal Distribution   1973
PN 142   **SC** 34420
UF   Gaussian Distribution
B   Frequency Distribution   1973
R   ↓ Statistical Sample Parameters   1973

Normalization (Test)
Use   Test Standardization

Norms (Social)
Use   Social Norms

Norms (Statistical)
Use   Statistical Norms

Norms (Test)
Use   Test Norms

Nortriptyline   1994
PN 130   **SC** 34485

Nortriptyline — (cont'd)
SN Use ANTIDEPRESSANT DRUGS to access references from 1978-1993.
   B   Tricyclic Antidepressant Drugs ¹⁹⁹⁷

Norway Rats ¹⁹⁷³
PN 120   **SC** 34500
   B   Rats ¹⁹⁶⁷

Nose ¹⁹⁷³
PN 86   **SC** 34510
   B   Respiratory System ¹⁹⁷³
   N ↓ Nasal Mucosa ¹⁹⁷³
   R ↓ Musculoskeletal System ¹⁹⁷³

Note Taking ¹⁹⁹¹
PN 96   **SC** 34515
   R   Homework ¹⁹⁸⁸
       ↓ Learning Strategies ¹⁹⁹¹
       ↓ Memory ¹⁹⁶⁷
          Mnemonic Learning ¹⁹⁷³
       ↓ Strategies ¹⁹⁶⁷
          Study Habits ¹⁹⁷³
       ↓ Written Communication ¹⁹⁸⁵

Nouns ¹⁹⁷³
PN 738   **SC** 34520
   B   Form Classes (Language) ¹⁹⁷³
   R ↓ Names ¹⁹⁸⁵

Novel Stimuli
   Use   Stimulus Novelty

Novelty Seeking
   Use   Sensation Seeking

Novocaine
SN Term was discontinued in 1982. In 2000, the term was stripped from all records containing it, and replaced with PROCAINE, its postable counterpart.
   Use   Procaine

NREM Sleep ¹⁹⁷³
PN 657   **SC** 34550
   UF   Nonrapid Eye Movement Sleep
         NonREM Sleep
         Slow Wave Sleep
   B   Sleep ¹⁹⁶⁷

Nuclear Family ¹⁹⁷³
PN 206   **SC** 34560
   B   Family ¹⁹⁶⁷
         Family Structure ¹⁹⁷³

Nuclear Technology ¹⁹⁸⁵
PN 415   **SC** 34565
   B   Technology ¹⁹⁷³

Nuclear War ¹⁹⁸⁵
PN 534   **SC** 34567
   B   War ¹⁹⁶⁷

Nucleic Acids ¹⁹⁷³
PN 65   **SC** 34570
   B   Acids ¹⁹⁷³
   N   Adenosine ¹⁹⁷³
         Deoxyribonucleic Acid ¹⁹⁷³
       ↓ Nucleotides ¹⁹⁷⁸
         Ribonucleic Acid ¹⁹⁷³
   R ↓ Genetics ¹⁹⁶⁷
         Guanosine ¹⁹⁸⁵

Nucleotides ¹⁹⁷⁸
PN 173   **SC** 34573
   B   Nucleic Acids ¹⁹⁷³
   N   Cyclic Adenosine Monophosphate ¹⁹⁷⁸

Nucleus Accumbens ¹⁹⁸²
PN 1244   **SC** 34574
SN One of the largest nuclei in the septal region lying anteriorly and medially to the junction of the caudate nucleus and putamen and laterally to the septal nuclei.
   R   Caudate Nucleus ¹⁹⁷³
       ↓ Limbic System ¹⁹⁷³
         Septal Nuclei ¹⁹⁸²

Nucleus Basalis Magnocellularis ¹⁹⁹⁴
PN 94   **SC** 57425
   B   Forebrain ¹⁹⁸⁵
   R ↓ Basal Ganglia ¹⁹⁷³

Nudity ¹⁹⁷³
PN 49   **SC** 34575
   R   Obscenity ¹⁹⁷⁸
       ↓ Physical Appearance ¹⁹⁸²
         Pornography ¹⁹⁷³

Null Hypothesis Testing ¹⁹⁷³
PN 175   **SC** 34580
SN Application of statistical tests to determine whether a null hypothesis should be accepted or rejected. Limited to discussions of statistical procedures.
   B   Hypothesis Testing ¹⁹⁷³

Number Comprehension ¹⁹⁷³
PN 439   **SC** 34590
SN Knowledge or understanding of the meaning, significance, and relationships symbolized by numerals.
   B   Comprehension ¹⁹⁶⁷

Number Systems ¹⁹⁷³
PN 56   **SC** 34600
   B   Mathematics (Concepts) ¹⁹⁶⁷
         Systems ¹⁹⁶⁷
   R   Numbers (Numerals) ¹⁹⁶⁷

Numbers (Numerals) ¹⁹⁶⁷
PN 1047   **SC** 34610
SN Symbol of a member of an abstract mathematical system which is subject to rules of succession, addition, and multiplication.
   UF   Digits (Mathematics)
   B   Mathematics (Concepts) ¹⁹⁶⁷
         Written Language ¹⁹⁶⁷
   R   Number Systems ¹⁹⁷³
         Numerosity Perception ¹⁹⁶⁷

Numerical Ability
   Use   Mathematical Ability

Numerosity Perception ¹⁹⁶⁷
PN 428   **SC** 34630
SN Perception of quantities in stimulus sets in visual, auditory, or other perceptual modes.
   B   Perception ¹⁹⁶⁷
   R   Numbers (Numerals) ¹⁹⁶⁷

Nuns ¹⁹⁷³
PN 136   **SC** 34640
   B   Religious Personnel ¹⁹⁷³
   R   Missionaries ¹⁹⁷³

Nurse Patient Interaction
   Use   Therapeutic Processes

Nursery School Students ¹⁹⁷³
PN 397   **SC** 34650
SN Students attending a nursery school, usually ages 2, 3, and 4. Mandatory term in educational contexts.
   B   Preschool Students ¹⁹⁸²

Nursery Schools ¹⁹⁷³
PN 141   **SC** 34660
   B   Schools ¹⁹⁶⁷

Nurses ¹⁹⁶⁷
PN 5363   **SC** 34670
   B   Medical Personnel ¹⁹⁶⁷
   N   Psychiatric Nurses ¹⁹⁷³
         Public Health Service Nurses ¹⁹⁷³
         School Nurses ¹⁹⁷³

Nursing ¹⁹⁷³
PN 2474   **SC** 34680
   B   Paramedical Sciences ¹⁹⁷³

Nursing Education ¹⁹⁷³
PN 1153   **SC** 34690
   B   Education ¹⁹⁶⁷
   R ↓ Medical Education ¹⁹⁷³

Nursing Homes ¹⁹⁷³
PN 2891   **SC** 34700
SN Establishments where maintenance and personal or nursing care are provided for persons (as the aged or chronically ill) who are unable to care for themselves.
   B   Residential Care Institutions ¹⁹⁷³
         Treatment Facilities ¹⁹⁷³
   R ↓ Hospitals ¹⁹⁶⁷
         Long Term Care ¹⁹⁹⁴
         Psychiatric Units ¹⁹⁹¹
         Retirement Communities ¹⁹⁹⁷
         Sanatoriums ¹⁹⁷³

Nursing Students ¹⁹⁷³
PN 1482   **SC** 34710
   B   College Students ¹⁹⁶⁷

Nurturance ¹⁹⁸⁵
PN 277   **SC** 34714
SN Need, tendency, or process of providing care and support to others. For animal populations, use ANIMAL MATERNAL BEHAVIOR or ANIMAL PARENTAL BEHAVIOR.
   B   Personality Traits ¹⁹⁶⁷
         Social Behavior ¹⁹⁶⁷
   R ↓ Needs ¹⁹⁶⁷
       ↓ Parent Child Relations ¹⁹⁶⁷

Nutrition ¹⁹⁷³
PN 1738   **SC** 34720
   R   Beverages (Nonalcoholic) ¹⁹⁷⁸
         Dietary Supplements ²⁰⁰¹
         Diets ¹⁹⁷⁸
         Food ¹⁹⁷⁸
         Food Additives ¹⁹⁷⁸
       ↓ Nutritional Deficiencies ¹⁹⁷³
       ↓ Physiology ¹⁹⁶⁷

Nutritional Deficiencies ¹⁹⁷³
PN 1003   **SC** 34730
   UF   Malnutrition
   B   Physical Disorders ¹⁹⁹⁷

Nutritional Deficiencies — (cont'd)
- **N** ↓ Protein Deficiency Disorders [1973]
  - Starvation [1973]
  - ↓ Vitamin Deficiency Disorders [1973]
- **R** ↓ Alcoholic Psychosis [1973]
  - ↓ Alcoholism [1967]
  - Anorexia Nervosa [1973]
  - Diets [1978]
  - ↓ Eating Disorders [1997]
  - Failure to Thrive [1988]
  - Food Deprivation [1967]
  - ↓ Metabolism Disorders [1973]
  - Nutrition [1973]
  - ↓ Underweight [1973]

Nutritional Supplements
- **Use** Dietary Supplements

Nymphomania
- **Use** Hypersexuality

Nystagmus [1973]
PN 578   SC 34760
SN Eye movement reflex stabilizing the retinal image of a visual stimulus to compensate for head or stimulus movement. Also, eye movement defects resulting from neurological, muscular, or genetic disorders.
- **UF** Optokinetic Nystagmus
  - Vestibular Nystagmus
- **B** Eye Disorders [1973]
  - Eye Movements [1967]
  - Reflexes [1971]
- **R** ↓ Nervous System Disorders [1967]

Obedience [1973]
PN 311   SC 34770
SN Limited to human populations.
- **UF** Submissiveness
- **B** Personality Traits [1967]
- **R** Coercion [1994]
  - ↓ Compliance [1973]
  - ↓ Dominance [1967]
  - ↓ Resistance [1997]

Obesity [1973]
PN 3654   SC 34780
- **UF** Overweight
- **B** Body Weight [1967]
  - Eating Disorders [1997]
  - Symptoms [1967]
- **R** Diets [1978]
  - Hyperphagia [1973]
  - Obesity (Attitudes Toward) [1997]
  - ↓ Somatoform Disorders [2001]

Obesity (Attitudes Toward) [1997]
PN 41   SC 34783
- **B** Attitudes [1967]
- **R** ↓ Body Weight [1967]
  - Eating Attitudes [1994]
  - Health Attitudes [1985]
  - Obesity [1973]
  - Weight Control [1985]

Object Permanence [1985]
PN 199   SC 34788
SN Knowledge of the continued existence of an object even when it is not directly perceived.
- **R** ↓ Cognitive Development [1973]
  - Conservation (Concept) [1973]
  - ↓ Developmental Stages [1973]
  - ↓ Internalization [1997]

Object Permanence — (cont'd)
- **R** ↓ Perceptual Constancy [1985]

Object Recognition [1997]
PN 749   SC 34789
- **B** Perception [1967]
  - Recognition (Learning) [1967]
- **R** Form and Shape Perception [1967]
  - Naming [1988]
  - ↓ Perceptual Discrimination [1973]

Object Relations [1982]
PN 3393   SC 34786
SN Psychoanalytic description of emotional attachments formed with other persons, as opposed to interest and love for oneself; individual's mode of relation to others and self.
- **UF** Fairbairnian Theory
  - Winnicottian Theory
- **R** Anaclitic Depression [1973]
  - Attachment Behavior [1985]
  - ↓ Childhood Development [1967]
  - Emotional Development [1973]
  - ↓ Internalization [1997]
  - Metapsychology [1994]
  - ↓ Psychoanalytic Theory [1967]
  - ↓ Psychosocial Development [1973]
  - Self Psychology [1988]
  - Separation Individuation [1982]
  - Transitional Objects [1985]

Objective Referenced Tests
- **Use** Criterion Referenced Tests

Objectives
- **Use** Goals

Objectives (Organizational)
- **Use** Organizational Objectives

Objectivity [1973]
PN 518   SC 34810
- **B** Personality Traits [1967]
- **R** Subjectivity [1994]

Oblique Rotation [1973]
PN 60   SC 34820
- **B** Statistical Rotation [1973]

Obscenity [1978]
PN 82   SC 34826
- **R** Nudity [1973]
  - Pornography [1973]
  - Profanity [1991]

Observation Methods [1967]
PN 2548   SC 34830
SN In research, any techniques used in the intentional examination of persons or processes in natural or manipulated settings for the purpose of obtaining facts or reporting conclusions.
- **UF** Naturalistic Observation
- **B** Empirical Methods [1973]
- **R** Interrater Reliability [1982]
  - Self Monitoring [1982]

Observational Learning [1973]
PN 767   SC 34840
SN Learning by observation of others by human or animal subjects or learning by visualization of behavior without actually performing an act and experiencing its consequences. Compare SOCIAL LEARNING.
- **B** Learning [1967]

Observational Learning — (cont'd)
- **B** Learning Strategies [1991]
- **R** Imitation (Learning) [1967]
  - ↓ Social Learning [1973]

Observers [1973]
PN 575   SC 34850
SN Individuals who examine, record, or rate specified events, behaviors, or processes in experimental, social, or therapeutic situations.
- **R** ↓ Audiences [1967]

Obsessions [1967]
PN 708   SC 34860
- **B** Thought Disturbances [1973]
- **R** ↓ Compulsions [1973]
  - Erotomania [1997]
  - Obsessive Compulsive Disorder [1985]
  - Obsessive Compulsive Personality [1973]

Obsessive Compulsive Disorder [1985]
PN 3508   SC 34865
SN Disorder characterized by recurrent obsessions or compulsions that may interfere with the individual's daily functioning or serve as a source of distress. In 2000, this term replaced the discontinued term OBSESSIVE COMPULSIVE NEUROSIS. OBSESSIVE COMPULSIVE NEUROSIS was stripped from all records and replaced with OBSESSIVE COMPULSIVE DISORDER.
- **UF** Compulsive Neurosis
  - Obsessive Compulsive Neurosis
  - Obsessive Neurosis
- **B** Anxiety Disorders [1997]
- **R** Body Dysmorphic Disorder [2001]
  - ↓ Compulsions [1973]
  - ↓ Neurosis [1967]
  - Obsessions [1967]
  - Obsessive Compulsive Personality [1973]

Obsessive Compulsive Neurosis
SN In 2000, the term was discontinued, and all records containing it were stripped of the term and replaced with OBSESSIVE COMPULSIVE DISORDER, its postable counterpart.
- **Use** Obsessive Compulsive Disorder

Obsessive Compulsive Personality [1973]
PN 274   SC 34880
SN Personality disorder characterized by perfectionism, indecisiveness, excessive devotion to work, inability to express warm emotions, and insistence that things be done in accord with one's own preferences.
- **UF** Anankastic Personality
  - Compulsive Personality Disorder
- **B** Personality Disorders [1967]
- **R** ↓ Compulsions [1973]
  - Obsessions [1967]
  - Obsessive Compulsive Disorder [1985]

Obsessive Neurosis
- **Use** Obsessive Compulsive Disorder

Obstetrical Complications [1978]
PN 575   SC 34895
- **R** ↓ Birth [1967]
  - Birth Injuries [1973]
  - Labor (Childbirth) [1973]
  - ↓ Obstetrics [1978]
  - Postsurgical Complications [1973]
  - ↓ Pregnancy [1967]
  - Premature Birth [1973]

Obstetricians 1978
PN 55   SC 34900
B   Physicians 1967
R   Gynecologists 1973
    Surgeons 1973

Obstetrics 1978
PN 197   SC 34910
SN Use OBSTETRICS GYNECOLOGY to access references from 1973-1977.
B   Medical Sciences 1967
N   Midwifery 1985
R   Childbirth Training 1978
    Gynecology 1978
    Obstetrical Complications 1978
    ↓ Prenatal Care 1991

Obturator Nerve
Use   Spinal Nerves

Occipital Lobe 1973
PN 507   SC 34930
B   Cerebral Cortex 1967
N   Visual Cortex 1967

Occultism 1978
PN 150   SC 34935
R   Cultism 1973
    Mysticism 1967
    ↓ Parapsychological Phenomena 1973
    ↓ Parapsychology 1967
    ↓ Religious Beliefs 1973
    Spirit Possession 1997
    Witchcraft 1973

Occupation (Parental)
Use   Parental Occupation

Occupational Adjustment 1973
PN 1159   SC 34950
SN Personal adaptation to one's vocation.
UF   Vocational Adjustment
B   Adjustment 1967
R   Adjustment Disorders 1994
    Career Change 1978
    Occupational Neurosis 1973
    ↓ Occupations 1967
    School to Work Transition 1994
    Work Adjustment Training 1991

Occupational Aspirations 1973
PN 2073   SC 34960
UF   Career Aspirations
    Career Goals
    Vocational Aspirations
B   Aspirations 1967
R   Career Change 1978
    Mentor 1985
    ↓ Occupations 1967
    Professional Development 1982

Occupational Attitudes 1973
PN 1875   SC 34970
SN Attitudes toward specific occupations or careers.
B   Attitudes 1967
R   Job Applicant Attitudes 1973
    ↓ Occupations 1967
    Vocational Maturity 1978
    Work (Attitudes Toward) 1973

Occupational Choice 1967
PN 3863   SC 34980

Occupational Choice — (cont'd)
UF   Career Choice
    Job Selection
    Vocational Choice
R   Career Change 1978
    Career Development 1985
    Nontraditional Careers 1985
    Occupational Preference 1973
    ↓ Occupations 1967
    Professional Specialization 1991
    Reemployment 1991
    Vocational Maturity 1978

Occupational Exposure 1988
PN 416   SC 34985
SN Exposure to conditions, substances, or apparatus in the workplace that may be harmful to health.
R   ↓ Hazardous Materials 1991
    Industrial Accidents 1973
    Occupational Safety 1973
    ↓ Occupations 1967
    Work Related Illnesses 1994
    ↓ Working Conditions 1973

Occupational Guidance 1967
PN 4415   SC 34990
SN Assistance in career selection or development; assessment of interests, abilities, or aptitude; compilation of occupational and economic information; and referral to placement services.
UF   Career Counseling
    Career Guidance
    Guidance (Occupational)
    Vocational Counseling
    Vocational Guidance
B   Counseling 1967
R   Assessment Centers 1982
    Career Education 1978
    Educational Counseling 1967
    Job Enrichment 1973
    Mentor 1985
    Occupational Success Prediction 1973
    ↓ Occupations 1967
    Student Personnel Services 1978
    Vocational Counselors 1973

Occupational Interest Measures 1973
PN 709   SC 35000
B   Measurement 1967
N   Kuder Occupational Interest Survey 1973
    Strong Vocational Interest Blank 1967

Occupational Interests 1967
PN 1730   SC 35010
UF   Vocational Interests
B   Interests 1967
R   ↓ Occupations 1967
    Vocational Maturity 1978

Occupational Mobility 1973
PN 556   SC 35020
SN The capacity or actual tendency toward upward progression in occupational status or occupational attainment.
UF   Job Mobility
    Mobility (Occupational)
    Vocational Mobility
R   Career Change 1978
    Employment History 1978
    Job Enrichment 1973
    ↓ Occupational Tenure 1973
    ↓ Occupations 1967

Occupational Neurosis 1973
PN 24   SC 35030
SN Neurotic disorder developed as a consequence of occupational stress, inappropriate occupational choice, overwork, job dissatisfaction, or other job-related stress.
B   Neurosis 1967
R   Occupational Adjustment 1973
    Occupational Stress 1973

Occupational Preference 1973
PN 943   SC 35040
UF   Career Preference
    Vocational Preference
B   Preferences 1967
R   Occupational Choice 1967
    ↓ Occupations 1967
    Professional Specialization 1991
    Vocational Maturity 1978

Occupational Safety 1973
PN 714   SC 35050
UF   Industrial Safety
B   Safety 1967
    Working Conditions 1973
R   Industrial Accidents 1973
    Occupational Exposure 1988
    ↓ Occupations 1967
    Work Related Illnesses 1994

Occupational Status 1978
PN 1785   SC 35056
SN Occupational rank or position achieved by employee, usually based on abilities or competence. Also, social prestige attributed to specific occupations.
UF   Job Status
    Prestige (Occupational)
B   Status 1967
R   Job Experience Level 1973
    ↓ Occupational Tenure 1973
    ↓ Occupations 1967
    Personnel Promotion 1978

Occupational Stress 1973
PN 6803   SC 35060
UF   Burnout
B   Stress 1967
R   Occupational Neurosis 1973
    ↓ Occupations 1967
    Quality of Work Life 1988
    Work Related Illnesses 1994

Occupational Success 1978
PN 1132   SC 35067
B   Achievement 1967
R   Employment History 1978
    Occupational Success Prediction 1973
    ↓ Occupations 1967
    Personnel Promotion 1978

Occupational Success Prediction 1973
PN 740   SC 35070
B   Personnel Evaluation 1973
    Prediction 1967
R   Occupational Guidance 1967
    Occupational Success 1978

Occupational Tenure 1973
PN 481   SC 35080
UF   Tenure (Occupational)
N   Teacher Tenure 1973
R   Employee Turnover 1973
    Employment History 1978

Occupational Tenure — (cont'd)
R   ↓ Employment Status   1982
    Job Security   1978
    Occupational Mobility   1973
    Occupational Status   1978
    ↓ Occupations   1967
    Personnel Termination   1973

Occupational Therapists   1973
PN   573   SC   35090
B   Therapists   1967
R   ↓ Mental Health Personnel   1967
    ↓ Paraprofessional Personnel   1973
    ↓ Psychiatric Hospital Staff   1973

Occupational Therapy   1967
PN   1922   SC   35100
SN   Method of treatment for physical or mental disorders that involves engagement of patients in useful or creative activities or work as a means of improving functional skills in the areas of work, daily living, or vocational activities.
B   Rehabilitation   1967
R   Physical Therapy   1973

Occupations   1967
PN   3846   SC   35110
SN   Conceptually broad term referring to work specialties as defined by duties and required skills. Use OCCUPATIONS to access references on employment status from 1967-1981. Use a more specific term if possible.
UF   Careers
    Jobs
    Vocations
N   Nontraditional Careers   1985
R   Career Change   1978
    Career Development   1985
    ↓ Division of Labor   1988
    Employment History   1978
    ↓ Job Characteristics   1985
    Occupational Adjustment   1973
    Occupational Aspirations   1973
    Occupational Attitudes   1973
    Occupational Choice   1967
    Occupational Exposure   1988
    Occupational Guidance   1967
    Occupational Interests   1967
    Occupational Mobility   1973
    Occupational Preference   1973
    Occupational Safety   1973
    Occupational Status   1978
    Occupational Stress   1973
    Occupational Success   1978
    ↓ Occupational Tenure   1973
    ↓ Personnel   1967
    ↓ Professional Personnel   1978
    ↓ Vocational Education   1973
    Vocational Maturity   1978
    Working Women   1978

Octopus   1973
PN   52   SC   35120
B   Mollusca   1973

Ocular Accommodation   1982
PN   288   SC   35127
SN   Process of focusing an image on the retina by means of a flattening or bulging of the lens.
UF   Eye Accommodation
    Focusing (Visual)
B   Reflexes   1971
R   ↓ Depth Perception   1967

Ocular Accommodation — (cont'd)
R   Lens (Eye)   1973
    ↓ Refraction Errors   1973

Ocular Dominance   1973
PN   296   SC   35130
UF   Eye Dominance
B   Lateral Dominance   1967
R   ↓ Brain   1967
    ↓ Eye (Anatomy)   1967
    ↓ Eye Disorders   1973
    Interocular Transfer   1985
    Left Brain   1991
    Right Brain   1991

Ocular Fixation
Use   Eye Fixation

Oculomotor Muscles   1973
PN   119   SC   35140
B   Muscles   1967

Oculomotor Nerve
Use   Cranial Nerves

Oculomotor Response
Use   Eye Movements

Odor Aversion Conditioning
Use   Aversion Conditioning

Odor Discrimination   1973
PN   979   SC   35170
B   Olfactory Perception   1967
    Perceptual Discrimination   1973
R   Olfactory Thresholds   1973

Oedipal Complex   1973
PN   1029   SC   35180
B   Psychoanalytic Personality Factors   1973

Offenders (Adult)
Use   Criminals

Offenders (Juvenile)
Use   Juvenile Delinquency

Office Environment
Use   Working Conditions

Officers (Commissioned)
Use   Commissioned Officers

Officers (Noncommissioned)
Use   Noncommissioned Officers

Offspring   1988
PN   1661   SC   35230
SN   Used specifically for children, regardless of age, whose parents had significant experiences or conditions, e.g., alcoholism, fame, or political persecution. Not used as an age identifier. Limited to human populations.
N   Adult Offspring   1985
    Daughters   1973
    Interracial Offspring   1988
    Sons   1973
R   ↓ Family Members   1973

Olfactory Bulb   1973
PN   666   SC   35247

Olfactory Bulb — (cont'd)
B   Limbic System   1973

Olfactory Evoked Potentials   1973
PN   94   SC   35250
B   Evoked Potentials   1967
R   ↓ Cortical Evoked Potentials   1973

Olfactory Impairment
Use   Anosmia

Olfactory Mucosa   1973
PN   65   SC   35260
B   Nasal Mucosa   1973
R   Chemoreceptors   1973

Olfactory Nerve   1973
PN   123   SC   35270
B   Cranial Nerves   1973

Olfactory Perception   1967
PN   2243   SC   35280
UF   Smell Perception
B   Perception   1967
N   Odor Discrimination   1973
    Olfactory Thresholds   1973
R   Anosmia   1973
    Taste Perception   1967
    Vomeronasal Sense   1982

Olfactory Stimulation   1978
PN   1039   SC   35285
B   Perceptual Stimulation   1973

Olfactory Thresholds   1973
PN   188   SC   35290
B   Olfactory Perception   1967
    Thresholds   1967
R   Odor Discrimination   1973
    ↓ Perceptual Measures   1973

Oligophrenia
Use   Mental Retardation

Oligophrenia (Phenylpyruvic)
Use   Phenylketonuria

Omission Training   1985
PN   14   SC   35315
SN   Removal of positive reinforcement upon occurrence of undesirable behavior. Has applications in both therapeutic and experimental contexts.
B   Behavior Modification   1973
    Operant Conditioning   1967
R   Differential Reinforcement   1973
    Time Out   1985

Omnibus Personality Inventory   1973
PN   12   SC   35320
B   Nonprojective Personality Measures   1973

Omnipotence   1994
PN   28   SC   35325
B   Personality Traits   1967
R   Authority   1967
    Grandiosity   1994
    Magical Thinking   1973
    ↓ Power   1967

On the Job Training   1973
PN   176   SC   35330
B   Personnel Training   1967

On the Job Training — (cont'd)
- R ↓ Experiential Learning 1997
  - Inservice Teacher Education 1973
  - ↓ Inservice Training 1985

Online Databases
- Use Databases

Online Searching
- Use Computer Searching

Only Children 1982
PN 100   SC 35335
SN Children having no siblings.
- R ↓ Family Members 1973
  - ↓ Family Structure 1973

Onomatopoeia and Images Test
SN Term was discontinued in 1997. In 2000, the term was stripped from all records containing it, and replaced with PROJECTIVE PERSONALITY MEASURES, its postable counterpart.
- Use Projective Personality Measures

Onset (Disorders) 1973
PN 2964   SC 35350
SN Beginning or first appearance of a mental or physical disorder.
- R ↓ Disorders 1967
  - ↓ Mental Disorders 1967
  - ↓ Physical Disorders 1997
  - Premorbidity 1978

Ontogeny
- Use Development

Open Classroom Method 1973
PN 369   SC 35370
SN Approach to teaching and learning emphasizing the student's right to make decisions and viewing the teacher as a facilitator of learning rather than a transmitter of knowledge. May include grouping of students across grades, independent study, individualized rates of progression, open-plan schools without interior walls, or unstructured time and curricula.
- B Teaching Methods 1967
- R Discovery Teaching Method 1973
  - Individualized Instruction 1973
  - Montessori Method 1973
  - Team Teaching Method 1973

Open Field Behavior (Animal)
- Use Animal Open Field Behavior

Open Universities
- Use Nontraditional Education

Openmindedness 1978
PN 168   SC 35376
SN Willingness to consider new and unconventional ideas, and readiness to reexamine social, political, and religious values.
- UF Closedmindedness
- B Personality Traits 1967
- R Agreeableness 1997
  - Authoritarianism 1967
  - Dogmatism 1978

Openness to Experience 1997
PN 77   SC 35378

Openness to Experience — (cont'd)
SN A broad experiential trait manifested in active imagination, aesthetic sensitivity, attentiveness to inner feelings, preference for variety, intellectual curiosity, and independence of judgment.
- UF Imaginativeness
- B Personality Traits 1967
- R Adaptability (Personality) 1973
  - Conformity (Personality) 1967
  - Creativity 1967
  - Curiosity 1967
  - Five Factor Personality Model 1997
  - Hypnotic Susceptibility 1973
  - Rigidity (Personality) 1967
  - ↓ Tolerance 1973

Operant Conditioning 1967
PN 6787   SC 35380
SN Learned behavior or the experimental paradigm in which reinforcers (positive or negative) or punishers immediately and contingently follow the performance of some behavior, the frequency of which changes as a direct consequence of such contingent reinforcement.
- UF Conditioning (Operant)
  - Instrumental Conditioning
  - Instrumental Learning
- B Conditioning 1967
- N Avoidance Conditioning 1967
  - Conditioned Emotional Responses 1967
  - ↓ Conditioned Responses 1967
  - Delayed Alternation 1994
  - ↓ Discrimination Learning 1982
  - Escape Conditioning 1973
  - Fading (Conditioning) 1982
  - Omission Training 1985
  - Time Out 1985
- R ↓ Adjunctive Behavior 1982
  - ↓ Behavior Modification 1973
  - Conditioned Stimulus 1973
  - Learning Theory 1967
  - Polydipsia 1982
  - ↓ Reinforcement 1967
  - ↓ Self Stimulation 1967
  - Skinner (Burrhus Frederic) 1991
  - Unconditioned Stimulus 1973

Operation (Surgery)
- Use Surgery

Ophidiophobia 1973
PN 259   SC 35400
SN Fear of snakes.
- UF Snake Phobia
- B Phobias 1967

Ophthalmologic Examination 1973
PN 68   SC 35410
- UF Eye Examination
- B Medical Diagnosis 1973
- N Electro Oculography 1973
  - Electroretinography 1967

Ophthalmology 1973
PN 42   SC 35420
- B Medical Sciences 1967
- R Optometry 1973

Opiate Agonists
- Use Narcotic Agonists

Opiate Antagonists
- Use Narcotic Antagonists

Opiates 1973
PN 2680   SC 35430
- UF Opioids
  - Opium Alkaloids
  - Opium Derivatives
- B Narcotic Drugs 1973
- N Codeine 1973
  - ↓ Endogenous Opiates 1985
  - Fentanyl 1985
  - Heroin 1973
  - Morphine 1973
  - Papaverine 1973

Opinion (Public)
- Use Public Opinion

Opinion Attitude and Interest Survey
SN Term was discontinued in 1997. In 2000, the term was stripped from all records containing it, and replaced with ATTITUDE MEASURES, its postable counterpart.
- Use Attitude Measures

Opinion Change
- Use Attitude Change

Opinion Questionnaires
- Use Attitude Measures

Opinion Surveys
- Use Attitude Measures

Opinions
- Use Attitudes

Opioid Antagonists
- Use Narcotic Antagonists

Opioids
- Use Opiates

Opioids (Endogenous)
- Use Endogenous Opiates

Opium Alkaloids
- Use Alkaloids AND Opiates

Opium Derivatives
- Use Opiates

Opossums 1973
PN 81   SC 35530
- B Marsupials 1973

Oppositional Defiant Disorder 1997
PN 187   SC 35535
SN A psychopathological disorder, usually beginning in childhood, consisting of negativism, disobedience, and hostile behavior toward authority figures.
- R ↓ Attention Deficit Disorder 1985
  - Attention Deficit Disorder with Hyperactivity 2001
  - ↓ Behavior Disorders 1971
  - Conduct Disorder 1991
  - Hyperkinesis 1973

Optic Chiasm 1973
PN 74   SC 35540
- B Diencephalon 1973
  - Neural Pathways 1982
- R Optic Nerve 1973

Optic Lobe 1973
PN 129   SC 35550
B   Mesencephalon 1973

Optic Nerve 1973
PN 214   SC 35560
B   Cranial Nerves 1973
R   Optic Chiasm 1973

Optic Tract 1982
PN 70   SC 35563
SN Portion of the optic pathway that extends posteriorly from the optic chiasm in two nerve fiber bundles to synapse near the superior colliculi and in the lateral geniculate body of the thalamus.
B   Neural Pathways 1982

Optical Aids 1973
PN 165   SC 35565
UF   Corrective Lenses
B   Medical Therapeutic Devices 1973
N   Contact Lenses 1973

Optical Illusions
Use Illusions (Perception)

Optimism 1973
PN 763   SC 35580
SN Attitude characterized by a positive and cheerful disposition and inclination to anticipate the most favorable outcome of events or actions.
B   Emotional States 1973
       Personality Traits 1967
R   Hope 1991
       Pessimism 1973
       Positivism 1973

Optokinetic Nystagmus
Use Nystagmus

Optometrists 1973
PN 36   SC 35590
B   Medical Personnel 1967

Optometry 1973
PN 143   SC 35600
B   Paramedical Sciences 1973
R   Ophthalmology 1973

Oral Communication 1985
PN 4243   SC 35610
SN Expression of information in oral form. Use VERBAL COMMUNICATION to access references from 1967-1984.
UF   Speech
       Verbalization
B   Verbal Communication 1967
N   Code Switching 1988
       Oral Reading 1973
       Public Speaking 1973
       Self Talk 1988
       Singing 1997
       ↓ Speech Characteristics 1973
R   Rhetoric 1991
       Verbal Ability 1967
       Verbal Fluency 1973
       ↓ Vocalization 1967
       ↓ Voice 1973

Oral Contraceptives 1973
PN 283   SC 35620
B   Contraceptive Devices 1973
R   Fertility Enhancement 1973

Oral Reading 1973
PN 1084   SC 35630
SN Reading aloud by individuals or groups or the condition of being read to by others.
UF   Reading Aloud
B   Oral Communication 1985
       Reading 1967

Organ Donation
Use Tissue Donation

Organ of Corti
Use Cochlea

Organ Transplantation 1973
PN 838   SC 35660
UF   Heart Transplants
       Kidney Transplants
       Renal Transplantation
       Transplants (Organ)
B   Surgery 1971
R   Heart Surgery 1973
       Neural Transplantation 1985
       Tissue Donation 1991

Organic Brain Syndromes 1973
PN 763   SC 35670
B   Brain Disorders 1967
       Syndromes 1973
N   ↓ Alcoholic Psychosis 1973
       Alzheimers Disease 1973
       ↓ Dementia 1985
       Toxic Psychoses 1973
R   ↓ Mental Disorders 1967
       Postpartum Depression 1973

Organic Therapies
SN In 2000, the term was discontinued, and all records containing it were stripped of the term and replaced with PHYSICAL TREATMENT METHODS, its postable counterpart.
Use Physical Treatment Methods

Organizational Behavior 1978
PN 6345   SC 35695
SN Behavior of organizations and of individuals within organizational settings.
B   Social Behavior 1967
N   ↓ Employee Interaction 1988
       Organizational Effectiveness 1985
R   ↓ Group Dynamics 1967
       Informants 1988
       Labor Management Relations 1967
       ↓ Organizational Characteristics 1997
       Organizational Commitment 1991
       Organizational Structure 1967
       ↓ Organizations 1967
       ↓ Sociometry 1991

Organizational Change 1973
PN 2725   SC 35700
UF   Change (Organizational)
N   Organizational Merger 1973
R   Decentralization 1978
       Organizational Climate 1973
       Organizational Crises 1973
       Organizational Development 1973

Organizational Characteristics 1997
PN 607   SC 35705
N   Organizational Climate 1973
       Organizational Structure 1967
R   ↓ Organizational Behavior 1978

Organizational Characteristics — (cont'd)
R   Organizational Commitment 1991
       Organizational Objectives 1973
       Quality of Work Life 1988

Organizational Climate 1973
PN 3381   SC 35710
SN Social or environmental characteristics of an organization which affect the behavior or performance of its members.
UF   Climate (Organizational)
B   Organizational Characteristics 1997
R   ↓ Organizational Change 1973
       Organizational Crises 1973
       Organizational Structure 1967
       Quality of Work Life 1988
       ↓ Working Conditions 1973

Organizational Commitment 1991
PN 1146   SC 35715
SN Commitment of organizations and of individuals within organizational settings.
B   Commitment 1985
R   ↓ Employee Attitudes 1967
       ↓ Employee Characteristics 1988
       Employer Attitudes 1973
       Job Involvement 1978
       ↓ Job Performance 1967
       Job Satisfaction 1967
       ↓ Organizational Behavior 1978
       ↓ Organizational Characteristics 1997
       Organizational Effectiveness 1985
       Organizational Objectives 1973

Organizational Crises 1973
PN 178   SC 35720
B   Crises 1971
R   ↓ Organizational Change 1973
       Organizational Climate 1973
       ↓ Stress 1967

Organizational Development 1973
PN 1718   SC 35730
SN Application of behavioral, management, or other techniques to organizations in order to integrate individuals' or members' needs with organizational goals and objectives.
B   Development 1967
R   Decentralization 1978
       ↓ Organizational Change 1973
       Organizational Objectives 1973
       Organizational Structure 1967

Organizational Effectiveness 1985
PN 1263   SC 35735
SN Measure of the ability of an organization to meet the needs of its environment, including personnel needs.
UF   Organizational Performance
B   Organizational Behavior 1978
R   Organizational Commitment 1991
       Organizational Objectives 1973
       Quality Control 1988

Organizational Goals
Use Organizational Objectives

Organizational Merger 1973
PN 120   SC 35750
B   Organizational Change 1973
R   Organizational Structure 1967

Organizational Objectives 1973
PN 644   SC 35760
UF   Objectives (Organizational)
     Organizational Goals
B   Goals 1967
R   Decentralization 1978
     ↓ Organizational Characteristics 1997
     Organizational Commitment 1991
     Organizational Development 1973
     Organizational Effectiveness 1985
     Quality Control 1988

Organizational Performance
Use Organizational Effectiveness

Organizational Policy Making
Use Policy Making

Organizational Psychology
Use Industrial Psychology

Organizational Structure 1967
PN 3256   SC 35770
B   Organizational Characteristics 1997
R   Decentralization 1978
     ↓ Organizational Behavior 1978
     Organizational Climate 1973
     Organizational Development 1973
     Organizational Merger 1973
     ↓ Organizations 1967
     Self Managing Work Teams 2001
     ↓ Work Teams 2001

Organizations 1967
PN 2266   SC 35780
UF   Agencies (Groups)
     Associations (Groups)
     Groups (Organizations)
N   Business Organizations 1973
     Foreign Organizations 1973
     Government Agencies 1973
     Health Maintenance Organizations 1982
     International Organizations 1973
     Labor Unions 1973
     Nonprofit Organizations 1973
     Professional Organizations 1973
     Religious Organizations 1991
R   ↓ Organizational Behavior 1978
     Organizational Structure 1967

Orgasm 1973
PN 94   SC 35790
UF   Climax (Sexual)
B   Psychosexual Behavior 1967
N   Female Orgasm 1973
     ↓ Male Orgasm 1973
R   Frigidity 1973
     Impotence 1973
     Sexual Satisfaction 1994

Orientals
Use Asians

Orientation (Perceptual)
Use Perceptual Orientation

Orientation (Spatial)
Use Spatial Orientation (Perception)

Orienting Reflex 1967
PN 889   SC 35820

Orienting Reflex — (cont'd)
SN   Innate physiological responses, such as pupil dilation, galvanic skin response, and EEG activity, to novel stimuli.
B   Reflexes 1971
     Sensory Adaptation 1967

Orienting Responses 1967
PN 1074   SC 35830
SN   Behavioral reactions in an organism, such as arrest of movement or head turning, to novel stimuli; behavioral correlate of orienting reflex.
B   Responses 1967
     Sensory Adaptation 1967
R   ↓ Classical Conditioning 1967

Originality
Use Creativity

Orphanages 1973
PN 72   SC 35850
B   Residential Care Institutions 1973
R   ↓ Institutionalization 1967
     Orphans 1973

Orphans 1973
PN 128   SC 35860
B   Family Members 1973
R   Orphanages 1973

Orphenadrine 1973
PN 14   SC 35870
UF   Methyldiphenylhydramine
B   Amines 1973
     Antihistaminic Drugs 1973
     Antispasmodic Drugs 1973
     Antitremor Drugs 1973
     Cholinergic Blocking Drugs 1973
     Muscle Relaxing Drugs 1973

Orthogonal Rotation 1973
PN 99   SC 35880
B   Statistical Rotation 1973
N   Equimax Rotation 1973
     Quartimax Rotation 1973
     Varimax Rotation 1973

Orthography 1973
PN 1084   SC 35890
SN   Art and formal rules of writing and spelling according to accepted usage. Also used to refer to the representation of the sounds of a language by written symbols.
B   Linguistics 1973
R   ↓ Alphabets 1973
     Cursive Writing 1973
     Homographs 1973
     Proofreading 1988
     Spelling 1973
     ↓ Written Language 1967

Orthopedically Handicapped
Use Physical Disorders

Orthopsychiatry 1973
PN 16   SC 35910
SN   Interdisciplinary approach combining psychiatry, psychology, pediatrics, and other related fields for prevention and early treatment of mental disorders, particularly in children and adolescents.
B   Psychiatry 1967
R   Child Psychiatry 1967

Oscilloscopes 1973
PN 26   SC 35920
B   Apparatus 1967

Osteoporosis 1991
PN 88   SC 35930
B   Bone Disorders 1973

Otosclerosis
SN   Term discontinued in 1997. In 2000, the term was stripped from all records containing it, and replaced with EAR DISORDERS, its postable counterpart.
Use Ear Disorders

Out of Body Experiences 1988
PN 73   SC 35945
B   Parapsychological Phenomena 1973
R   Near Death Experiences 1985

Outcomes (Psychotherapeutic)
Use Psychotherapeutic Outcomes

Outcomes (Treatment)
Use Treatment Outcomes

Outgroup Ingroup
Use Ingroup Outgroup

Outpatient Commitment 1991
PN 46   SC 35957
SN   Legally mandated psychiatric or psychological treatment on an outpatient basis.
UF   Commitment (Outpatient)
B   Commitment (Psychiatric) 1973
     Outpatient Treatment 1967
R   Aftercare 1973
     Partial Hospitalization 1985

Outpatient Psychiatric Clinics
Use Psychiatric Clinics

Outpatient Treatment 1967
PN 2949   SC 35970
SN   Treatment in private practice, clinic, or hospital for ambulatory, non-hospitalized patients. Compare PARTIAL HOSPITALIZATION.
UF   Ambulatory Care
B   Treatment 1967
N   Outpatient Commitment 1991
R   Aftercare 1973
     ↓ Drug Therapy 1967
     Home Care 1985
     Maintenance Therapy 1997
     Outpatients 1973
     Psychiatric Clinics 1973

Outpatients 1973
PN 1814   SC 35980
B   Patients 1967
R   ↓ Outpatient Treatment 1967

Outreach Programs 1997
PN 172   SC 35983
B   Social Programs 1973
     Social Services 1982
R   ↓ Case Management 1991
     Community Mental Health Services 1978
     ↓ Community Services 1967
     ↓ Health Care Delivery 1978
     ↓ Health Care Services 1978
     ↓ Mental Health Programs 1973
     ↓ Mental Health Services 1978

Outreach Programs — (cont'd)
R   Needle Exchange Programs 2001
      Social Casework 1967
      ↓ Support Groups 1991

Outward Bound
   Use   Wilderness Experience

Ovariectomy 1973
PN 868   SC 35990
   B   Castration 1967
   R   Hysterectomy 1973

Ovaries 1973
PN 140   SC 36000
   B   Female Genitalia 1973
      Gonads 1973

Ovary Disorders
   Use   Endocrine Sexual Disorders

Over The Counter Drugs
   Use   Nonprescription Drugs

Overachievement (Academic)
   Use   Academic Overachievement

Overcorrection 1985
PN 44   SC 36025
SN   Therapeutic technique involving restitution and/ or intensive practice of appropriate behavior following the occurrence of disruptive or inappropriate behavior.
   B   Behavior Modification 1973
   R   Overlearning 1967
      ↓ Practice 1967

Overlearning 1967
PN 224   SC 36030
SN   Learning in which practice continues beyond the point of mastery of the material or task.
   B   Learning 1967
   R   Overcorrection 1985

Overpopulation 1973
PN 189   SC 36040
   B   Population 1973
   R   ↓ Birth Control 1971
      Crowding 1978
      Environmental Stress 1973
      Social Density 1978

Overweight
   Use   Obesity

Ovulation 1973
PN 143   SC 36060
   B   Menstrual Cycle 1973

Owls 1997
PN 33   SC 36063
   R   ↓ Birds 1967

Ownership 1985
PN 349   SC 36065
   UF   Possession
      Property
   R   Business 1967
      Capitalism 1973
      Entrepreneurship 1991
      ↓ Private Sector 1985
      Self Employment 1994

Oxazepam 1978
PN 114   SC 36075
   B   Anticonvulsive Drugs 1973
      Benzodiazepines 1978
      Minor Tranquilizers 1973

Oxidases 1973
PN 66   SC 36080
   B   Enzymes 1973
   N   Cytochrome Oxidase 1973
      Monoamine Oxidases 1973

Oxidopamine
   Use   Hydroxydopamine (6-)

Oxilapine
   Use   Loxapine

Oxygen 1973
PN 308   SC 36090

Oxygenation 1973
PN 83   SC 36100
   B   Physiology 1967

Oxytocin 1973
PN 365   SC 36120
   B   Pituitary Hormones 1973

Pacemakers (Artificial)
   Use   Artificial Pacemakers

Pacific Islanders 2001
PN 0   SC 36133
   B   Indigenous Populations 2001
   N   Hawaii Natives 2001
   R   Alaska Natives 1997
      American Indians 1967
      Inuit 2001
      Minority Groups 1967

Pacifism 1973
PN 34   SC 36140
   B   Philosophies 1967
   R   Nonviolence 1991

Pain 1967
PN 4643   SC 36150
   UF   Aches
   B   Symptoms 1967
   N   Aphagia 1973
      Back Pain 1982
      Chronic Pain 1985
      ↓ Headache 1973
      Myofascial Pain 1991
      ↓ Neuralgia 1973
      Somatoform Pain Disorder 1997
   R   ↓ Analgesic Drugs 1973
      Pain Management 1994
      Pain Measurement 1997
      ↓ Pain Perception 1973
      Pain Thresholds 1973
      ↓ Physical Disorders 1997
      ↓ Spasms 1973
      Suffering 1973

Pain (Psychogenic)
   Use   Somatoform Pain Disorder

Pain Disorder
   Use   Somatoform Pain Disorder

Pain Management 1994
PN 1215   SC 36165
   B   Treatment 1967
   R   Analgesia 1982
      ↓ Analgesic Drugs 1973
      ↓ Pain 1967
      Pain Measurement 1997
      ↓ Pain Perception 1973
      Pain Thresholds 1973
      Palliative Care 1991
      ↓ Physical Treatment Methods 1973
      Somatoform Pain Disorder 1997

Pain Measurement 1997
PN 190   SC 36167
SN   Tests, scales, or other techniques used to assess or evaluate pain in human or animal populations. Used only when the methodology is the focus of the reference.
   B   Measurement 1967
   R   Analgesia 1982
      ↓ Diagnosis 1967
      ↓ Pain 1967
      Pain Management 1994
      ↓ Pain Perception 1973
      Pain Thresholds 1973
      ↓ Perceptual Measures 1973

Pain Perception 1973
PN 3731   SC 36170
   UF   Nociception
   B   Somesthetic Perception 1967
   N   Analgesia 1982
      Pain Thresholds 1973
   R   ↓ Pain 1967
      Pain Management 1994
      Pain Measurement 1997
      Somatosensory Disorders 2001

Pain Receptors
   Use   Nociceptors

Pain Relieving Drugs
   Use   Analgesic Drugs

Pain Thresholds 1973
PN 946   SC 36190
   B   Pain Perception 1973
      Thresholds 1967
   R   ↓ Pain 1967
      Pain Management 1994
      Pain Measurement 1997
      ↓ Perceptual Measures 1973

Painting (Art) 1973
PN 547   SC 36200
   B   Art 1967

Paired Associate Learning 1967
PN 2762   SC 36210
   B   Verbal Learning 1967
   R   Word Associations 1967

Palestinians
   Use   Arabs

Palliative Care 1991
PN 495   SC 36219
   B   Health Care Services 1978
   R   Advance Directives 1994
      Assisted Suicide 1997
      ↓ Death and Dying 1967
      ↓ Health Care Delivery 1978

Palliative Care — (cont'd)
R　Hospice [1982]
　　Life Sustaining Treatment [1997]
　　Long Term Care [1994]
　　Pain Management [1994]
　　Terminally Ill Patients [1973]

Palm (Anatomy) [1973]
PN 39　　　　　　　　SC 36220
B　Anatomy [1967]
R　Hand (Anatomy) [1967]

Palsy
Use　Paralysis

Pancreas [1973]
PN 102　　　　　　　SC 36240
B　Glands [1967]
R　↓ Endocrine Glands [1973]
　　↓ Endocrine System [1973]
　　↓ Gastrointestinal System [1973]

Pancreozymin
Use　Cholecystokinin

Panic [1973]
PN 978　　　　　　　SC 36260
SN　Prior to 1988, also used for PANIC DISORDER.
B　Fear [1967]
R　↓ Anxiety [1967]
　　Panic Disorder [1988]

Panic Disorder [1988]
PN 3742　　　　　　　SC 36265
SN　Consider PANIC to access references from 1973-1987.
B　Anxiety Disorders [1997]
R　↓ Anxiety [1967]
　　Panic [1973]

Pantherine
Use　Muscimol

Papaverine [1973]
PN 34　　　　　　　　SC 36270
B　Alkaloids [1973]
　　Analgesic Drugs [1973]
　　Antispasmodic Drugs [1973]
　　Muscle Relaxing Drugs [1973]
　　Opiates [1973]

Parachlorophenylalanine [1978]
PN 184　　　　　　　SC 36275
B　Phenylalanine [1973]
　　Serotonin Antagonists [1973]

Paradigmatic Techniques
Use　Paradoxical Techniques

Paradoxical Sleep
Use　REM Sleep

Paradoxical Techniques [1982]
PN 433　　　　　　　SC 36282
SN　Techniques designed to disrupt dysfunctional behavior patterns through systematically encouraging them, thus allaying anticipatory anxiety, creating resistance to the symptomatic behavior, or enabling clients to achieve voluntary control over this behavior.
UF　Paradigmatic Techniques
　　Reframing

Paradoxical Techniques — (cont'd)
UF　Symptom Prescription
B　Psychotherapeutic Techniques [1967]
R　↓ Behavior Therapy [1967]
　　↓ Psychotherapy [1967]

Paragraphs [1973]
PN 70　　　　　　　　SC 36300
B　Written Language [1967]

Paraldehyde
SN　Term discontinued in 1997. In 2000, the term was stripped from all records containing it, and replaced with ANTICONVULSIVE DRUGS, its postable counterpart.
Use　Anticonvulsive Drugs

Paralegal Personnel
Use　Legal Personnel

Paralysis [1973]
PN 303　　　　　　　SC 36320
UF　Palsy
B　Movement Disorders [1985]
　　Neuromuscular Disorders [1973]
N　Cerebral Palsy [1967]
　　General Paresis [1973]
　　Hemiplegia [1978]
　　Paraplegia [1978]
　　Parkinsons Disease [1973]
　　Quadriplegia [1985]
R　↓ Central Nervous System Disorders [1973]
　　Dysarthria [1973]
　　↓ Musculoskeletal Disorders [1973]
　　↓ Peripheral Nerve Disorders [1973]
　　Poliomyelitis [1973]
　　↓ Sclerosis (Nervous System) [1973]
　　↓ Spinal Cord Injuries [1973]

Paralysis (Hysterical)
Use　Hysterical Paralysis

Paralysis (Infantile)
Use　Poliomyelitis

Paralysis Agitans
Use　Parkinsons Disease

Paramedical Personnel [1973]
PN 259　　　　　　　SC 36360
SN　In 1997, this term replaced the discontinued term MEDICS. In 2000, MEDICS was stripped from all records and replaced with PARAMEDICAL PERSONNEL.
UF　Medics
B　Medical Personnel [1967]
　　Paraprofessional Personnel [1973]
N　Attendants (Institutions) [1973]
　　Psychiatric Aides [1973]
R　Fire Fighters [1991]
　　Home Care Personnel [1997]
　　↓ Paramedical Sciences [1973]
　　↓ Psychiatric Hospital Staff [1973]

Paramedical Sciences [1973]
PN 9　　　　　　　　SC 36370
N　Audiology [1973]
　　Nursing [1973]
　　Optometry [1973]
　　↓ Pharmacology [1973]
　　Physical Therapy [1973]

Paramedical Sciences — (cont'd)
R　↓ Medical Sciences [1967]
　　↓ Paramedical Personnel [1973]

Parameter Estimation
Use　Statistical Estimation

Parameters (Response)
Use　Response Parameters

Parameters (Stimulus)
Use　Stimulus Parameters

Parametric Statistical Tests [1973]
PN 112　　　　　　　SC 36400
B　Statistical Tests [1973]
N　F Test [1973]
　　T Test [1973]

Paranoia [1988]
PN 197　　　　　　　SC 36410
SN　Mild paranoia in nonpsychotic persons.
B　Personality Traits [1967]
R　Paranoid Personality [1973]

Paranoia (Psychosis) [1967]
PN 879　　　　　　　SC 36420
SN　Gradual development of an elaborate and complex delusional system, usually involving persecutory or grandiose delusions with few other signs of personality or thought disturbance.
UF　Acute Paranoid Disorder
　　Atypical Paranoid Disorder
　　Paranoid Disorder
B　Psychosis [1967]
N　Folie A Deux [1973]
　　Involutional Paranoid Psychosis [1973]
R　Paranoid Personality [1973]
　　Paranoid Schizophrenia [1967]

Paranoid Disorder
Use　Paranoia (Psychosis)

Paranoid Personality [1973]
PN 165　　　　　　　SC 36430
SN　Nonpsychotic personality disorder marked by hypersensitivity, jealousy, and unwarranted suspicion with tendency to blame others for one's shortcomings.
UF　Paranoid Personality Disorder
B　Personality Disorders [1967]
R　Paranoia [1988]
　　↓ Paranoia (Psychosis) [1967]
　　Paranoid Schizophrenia [1967]

Paranoid Personality Disorder
Use　Paranoid Personality

Paranoid Schizophrenia [1967]
PN 1287　　　　　　　SC 36440
SN　Type of schizophrenia characterized by grandiosity, suspiciousness, and delusions of persecution, often with hallucinations.
B　Schizophrenia [1967]
R　Folie A Deux [1973]
　　Involutional Paranoid Psychosis [1973]
　　↓ Paranoia (Psychosis) [1967]
　　Paranoid Personality [1973]
　　↓ Psychosis [1967]

Paraphilias [1988]
PN 1341　　　　　　　SC 36443

Paraphilias — (cont'd)

SN Sexual urges, fantasies, or behaviors generally involving themes of suffering, humiliation, sexual activity with non-consenting partners, or an orientation toward non-human objects for sexual arousal. In 2000, the term's status changed from nonpostable to postable. All records containing SEXUAL DEVIATIONS were stripped of this term and replaced with PARAPHILIAS.

UF   Deviations (Sexual)
      Perversions (Sexual)
      Sexual Deviations

B   Mental Disorders   1967
      Psychosexual Behavior   1967

N   Exhibitionism   1973
      Fetishism   1973
      Incest   1973
      Pedophilia   1973
      Sexual Masochism   1973
      Sexual Sadism   1973
      Transvestism   1973
      Voyeurism   1973

R   ↓ Impulse Control Disorders   1997
      Pornography   1973
      ↓ Sex Offenses   1982
      ↓ Sexual Abuse   1988
      Sexual Addiction   1997

Paraplegia   1978

PN 157   **SC** 36446
SN Paralysis of the lower limbs and trunk.
B   Paralysis   1973
R   ↓ Central Nervous System Disorders   1973
      Hemiplegia   1978
      ↓ Injuries   1973
      ↓ Musculoskeletal Disorders   1973
      Quadriplegia   1985
      ↓ Spinal Cord Injuries   1973

Paraprofessional Education   1973

PN 592   **SC** 36450
SN Training or education of aides, such as paramedical and paralegal personnel, who assist professional persons.
B   Education   1967
R   Microcounseling   1978

Paraprofessional Personnel   1973

PN 1108   **SC** 36460
SN Persons with minimal or special training in a profession working as aides or assistants to professionals. Use PARAPROFESSIONAL PERSONNEL to access references to nonprofessional personnel from 1973-1981.
B   Personnel   1967
N   Home Care Personnel   1997
      ↓ Paramedical Personnel   1973
      Teacher Aides   1973
R   ↓ Mental Health Personnel   1967
      ↓ Nonprofessional Personnel   1982
      Occupational Therapists   1973
      ↓ Professional Personnel   1978
      Volunteer Civilian Personnel   1973
      ↓ Volunteer Personnel   1973

Parapsychological Phenomena   1973

PN 1245   **SC** 36470
B   Parapsychology   1967
N   ↓ Extrasensory Perception   1967
      Near Death Experiences   1985
      Out of Body Experiences   1988
      Telepathy   1973
R   Occultism   1978
      Religious Experiences   1997

Parapsychological Phenomena — (cont'd)

R   Spirit Possession   1997
      Superstitions   1973

Parapsychology   1967

PN 981   **SC** 36480
N   ↓ Parapsychological Phenomena   1973
R   Astrology   1973
      Dream Analysis   1973
      Mysticism   1967
      Occultism   1978
      Witchcraft   1973

Parasitic Disorders   1973

PN 127   **SC** 36490
B   Infectious Disorders   1973
N   Malaria   1973

Parasitism

Use   Biological Symbiosis

Parasuicide

Use   Attempted Suicide

Parasympathetic Nervous System   1973

PN 74   **SC** 36500
B   Autonomic Nervous System   1967
N   ↓ Efferent Pathways   1982
      Vagus Nerve   1973
R   ↓ Cholinergic Blocking Drugs   1973
      ↓ Cholinomimetic Drugs   1973

Parasympatholytic Drugs

Use   Cholinergic Blocking Drugs

Parasympathomimetic Drugs

Use   Cholinomimetic Drugs

Parathion   1973

PN 8   **SC** 36530
B   Insecticides   1973

Parathyroid Disorders   1973

PN 51   **SC** 36540
UF   Hyperparathyroidism
      Hypoparathyroidism
B   Endocrine Disorders   1973

Parathyroid Glands   1973

PN 9   **SC** 36550
B   Endocrine Glands   1973
R   Parathyroid Hormone   1973

Parathyroid Hormone   1973

PN 14   **SC** 36560
B   Hormones   1967
R   Parathyroid Glands   1973

Parent Attitude Research Instrument   1973

PN 13   **SC** 36570
B   Attitude Measures   1967

Parent Child Communication   1973

PN 1770   **SC** 36580
SN From 1982, limited to human populations. For animals consider ANIMAL PARENTAL BEHAVIOR or ANIMAL MATERNAL BEHAVIOR.
B   Interpersonal Communication   1973
N   Father Child Communication   1985
      Mother Child Communication   1985
R   ↓ Parent Child Relations   1967
      ↓ Parental Characteristics   1994

Parent Child Relations   1967

PN 11585   **SC** 36590
SN From 1982, limited to human populations. For animals consider ANIMAL PARENTAL BEHAVIOR or ANIMAL MATERNAL BEHAVIOR.
UF   Parental Influence
B   Family Relations   1967
N   Father Child Relations   1973
      Mother Child Relations   1967
      ↓ Parental Attitudes   1973
      Parental Permissiveness   1973
R   Attachment Behavior   1985
      Attachment Disorders   2001
      ↓ Child Discipline   1973
      ↓ Childrearing Practices   1967
      Codependency   1991
      Empty Nest   1991
      Generation Gap   1973
      Nurturance   1985
      ↓ Parent Child Communication   1973
      Parent School Relationship   1982
      Parent Training   1978
      ↓ Parental Characteristics   1994
      Parental Expectations   1997
      Parental Investment   1997
      Parental Role   1973
      Parenting Skills   1997
      Transgenerational Patterns   1991

Parent Educational Background   1973

PN 778   **SC** 36600
UF   Educational Background (Parents)
B   Educational Background   1967
      Family Background   1973
      Parental Characteristics   1994
R   Family Socioeconomic Level   1973
      Parental Occupation   1973

Parent Effectiveness Training

Use   Parent Training

Parent School Relationship   1982

PN 1239   **SC** 36605
SN Interaction between parents and school and/or educational personnel, such as parent-teacher conferences.
UF   PTA
R   ↓ Parent Child Relations   1967
      Parent Training   1978
      ↓ Teacher Attitudes   1967

Parent Training   1978

PN 3120   **SC** 36606
SN Educational materials, information, or instruction for parents.
UF   Parent Effectiveness Training
B   Education   1967
      Family Life Education   1997
R   ↓ Childrearing Practices   1967
      Human Relations Training   1978
      ↓ Parent Child Relations   1967
      Parent School Relationship   1982
      Parental Role   1973
      Parenting Skills   1997

Parental Absence   1973

PN 538   **SC** 36610
SN From 1982, limited to human populations. For animals consider ANIMAL PARENTAL BEHAVIOR or ANIMAL MATERNAL BEHAVIOR.
B   Family Structure   1973
N   Father Absence   1973
      Mother Absence   1973
R   Anaclitic Depression   1973

Parental Absence — (cont'd)
R   Child Custody [1982]
     Divorced Persons [1973]
     ↓ Marital Separation [1973]
     ↓ Parental Characteristics [1994]
     ↓ Single Parents [1978]
     Widowers [1973]
     Widows [1973]

Parental Attitudes [1973]
PN   7554   SC   36620
SN   Attitudes of, not toward, parents.
B   Attitudes [1967]
     Parent Child Relations [1967]
     Parental Characteristics [1994]
N   Parental Expectations [1997]
R   Childrearing Attitudes [1973]
     ↓ Childrearing Practices [1967]
     Father Child Relations [1973]
     Mother Child Relations [1967]
     Parental Permissiveness [1973]
     Parental Role [1973]

Parental Authoritarianism
Use Parental Permissiveness

Parental Behavior (Animal)
Use Animal Parental Behavior

Parental Characteristics [1994]
PN   1798   SC   36637
N   Parent Educational Background [1973]
     ↓ Parental Attitudes [1973]
     Parental Occupation [1973]
     Parental Permissiveness [1973]
     Parental Role [1973]
     Parenting Skills [1997]
R   ↓ Childrearing Practices [1967]
     ↓ Parent Child Communication [1973]
     ↓ Parent Child Relations [1967]
     ↓ Parental Absence [1973]
     Parental Investment [1997]
     ↓ Parents [1967]

Parental Expectations [1997]
PN   149   SC   36639
SN   Expectations or aspirations for a level of behav-
ior, achievement, or performance (e.g., in school, life
or career) that parents have for their children.
B   Expectations [1967]
     Parental Attitudes [1973]
R   ↓ Parent Child Relations [1967]
     Parental Investment [1997]
     Parental Role [1973]
     ↓ Parents [1967]

Parental Influence
Use Parent Child Relations

Parental Investment [1997]
PN   217   SC   36645
SN   Parental provision of resources and/or care to
offspring. Used for both human and animal popula-
tions.
UF   Maternal Investment
     Paternal Investment
R   ↓ Animal Parental Behavior [1982]
     ↓ Parent Child Relations [1967]
     ↓ Parental Characteristics [1994]
     Parental Expectations [1997]

Parental Occupation [1973]
PN   379   SC   36650

Parental Occupation — (cont'd)
UF   Occupation (Parental)
B   Family Background [1973]
     Parental Characteristics [1994]
R   Family Socioeconomic Level [1973]
     Parent Educational Background [1973]

Parental Permissiveness [1973]
PN   384   SC   36660
UF   Authoritarianism (Parental)
     Parental Authoritarianism
     Permissiveness (Parental)
B   Child Discipline [1973]
     Parent Child Relations [1967]
     Parental Characteristics [1994]
R   Father Child Relations [1973]
     Mother Child Relations [1967]
     ↓ Parental Attitudes [1973]
     Parental Role [1973]

Parental Role [1973]
PN   2662   SC   36670
SN   Descriptions, perceptions, and attitudes about
the social, psychological, behavioral, or emotional
role of parents.
B   Family Relations [1967]
     Parental Characteristics [1994]
     Roles [1967]
R   ↓ Child Discipline [1973]
     ↓ Childrearing Practices [1967]
     Delayed Parenthood [1985]
     Father Child Relations [1973]
     Mother Child Relations [1967]
     ↓ Parent Child Relations [1967]
     Parent Training [1978]
     ↓ Parental Attitudes [1973]
     Parental Expectations [1997]
     Parental Permissiveness [1973]

Parenthood Status [1985]
PN   801   SC   36675
SN   State of having or not having children, or, the
number of children one has.
N   Childlessness [1982]
R   Family Size [1973]
     ↓ Family Structure [1973]

Parenting Skills [1997]
PN   454   SC   36677
B   Parental Characteristics [1994]
R   ↓ Childrearing Practices [1967]
     ↓ Parent Child Relations [1967]
     Parent Training [1978]

Parents [1967]
PN   11850   SC   36680
SN   From 1982, limited to human populations. For
animals consider ANIMAL PARENTAL BEHAVIOR or
ANIMAL MATERNAL BEHAVIOR.
B   Ancestors [1973]
     Family Members [1973]
N   Adoptive Parents [1973]
     ↓ Fathers [1967]
     Foster Parents [1973]
     Homosexual Parents [1994]
     ↓ Mothers [1967]
     ↓ Single Parents [1978]
     Stepparents [1973]
     Surrogate Parents (Humans) [1973]
R   ↓ Expectant Parents [1985]
     Inlaws [1997]
     ↓ Parental Characteristics [1994]
     Parental Expectations [1997]

Parents — (cont'd)
R   ↓ Spouses [1973]

Paresis (General)
Use General Paresis

Paresthesia
Use Somatosensory Disorders

Pargyline [1973]
PN   79   SC   36700
B   Antihypertensive Drugs [1973]
     Monoamine Oxidase Inhibitors [1973]

Parietal Lobe [1973]
PN   1071   SC   36710
B   Cerebral Cortex [1967]
N   Somatosensory Cortex [1973]

Parkinsonism [1994]
PN   276   SC   36715
SN   Clinical state, usually drug induced, character-
ized by tremors, muscle rigidity, postural reflex dys-
function, and akinesia. Compare PARKINSONS
DISEASE.
R   Apraxia [1973]
     Bradykinesia [2001]
     Dementia with Lewy Bodies [2001]
     Muscle Contractions [1973]
     ↓ Nervous System Disorders [1967]
     Parkinsons Disease [1973]
     ↓ Reflexes [1971]
     ↓ Symptoms [1967]
     Tremor [1973]

Parkinsons Disease [1973]
PN   2901   SC   36720
SN   A disease characterized as a progressive motor
disability manifested by tremors, shaking, muscular
rigidity, and lack of postural reflexes.
UF   Paralysis Agitans
B   Brain Disorders [1967]
     Neuromuscular Disorders [1973]
     Paralysis [1973]
R   Amantadine [1978]
     ↓ Antitremor Drugs [1973]
     Bradykinesia [2001]
     ↓ Dementia [1985]
     Dementia with Lewy Bodies [2001]
     Parkinsonism [1994]
     Tremor [1973]

Parks (Recreational)
Use Recreation Areas

Parochial School Education
Use Private School Education

Parole [1973]
PN   281   SC   36750
SN   Conditional release of a prisoner serving an
indeterminate or unexpired sentence.
UF   Parolees
B   Legal Processes [1973]
R   ↓ Law Enforcement [1978]
     Probation [1973]

Parole Officers [1973]
PN   47   SC   36760
B   Law Enforcement Personnel [1973]
R   Probation Officers [1973]

Parolees
Use Parole

Paroxetine [1994]
PN 512   **SC** 36770
B   Antidepressant Drugs [1971]
      Serotonin Reuptake Inhibitors [1997]

Paroxysmal Sleep
Use Narcolepsy

Partial Hospitalization [1985]
PN 1141   **SC** 36775
SN Ambulatory treatment program of intensive, multidisciplinary care. Involves stabilization, rehabilitation, and/or maintenance of patients through more comprehensive treatment than is possible in an outpatient setting. Compare OUTPATIENT TREATMENT.
UF   Day Care (Treatment)
      Day Hospital
B   Treatment [1967]
R   Aftercare [1973]
      Deinstitutionalization [1982]
      ↓ Hospital Programs [1978]
      Interdisciplinary Treatment Approach [1973]
      ↓ Mental Health Programs [1973]
      Outpatient Commitment [1991]
      ↓ Rehabilitation [1967]

Partial Reinforcement
Use Reinforcement Schedules

Partially Hearing Impaired [1973]
PN 2511   **SC** 36790
UF   Hearing Impaired (Partially)
R   Cochlear Implants [1994]
      ↓ Deaf [1967]

Partially Sighted [1973]
PN 128   **SC** 36800

Participation [1973]
PN 2239   **SC** 36810
SN Taking part in an activity. Use a more specific term if possible.
B   Interpersonal Interaction [1967]
N   Athletic Participation [1973]
      Client Participation [1997]
      Group Participation [1973]
      Participative Management [1988]
R   ↓ Involvement [1973]

Participative Management [1988]
PN 449   **SC** 36820
SN Management technique permitting nonmanagement personnel to be involved in the governance, management, or policy-making processes of an institution or organization.
UF   Quality Circles
B   Management Methods [1973]
      Participation [1973]
R   Job Involvement [1978]
      Management Decision Making [1973]
      Quality Control [1988]
      Self Managing Work Teams [2001]

Partner Abuse [1991]
PN 1288   **SC** 36825
SN Includes married and unmarried persons.
UF   Spouse Abuse
B   Antisocial Behavior [1971]
R   ↓ Abuse Reporting [1997]

Partner Abuse — (cont'd)
R   Battered Females [1988]
      Emotional Abuse [1991]
      Erotomania [1997]
      ↓ Family Violence [1982]
      Physical Abuse [1991]
      ↓ Sexual Abuse [1988]
      ↓ Violence [1973]

Parturition
Use Birth

Passive Aggressive Personality [1973]
PN 46   **SC** 36850
B   Personality Disorders [1967]

Passive Avoidance
Use Avoidance Conditioning

Passiveness [1973]
PN 221   **SC** 36870
B   Personality Traits [1967]

Pastoral Counseling [1967]
PN 1268   **SC** 36880
SN Provision of counseling by religious personnel.
B   Counseling [1967]
R   ↓ Psychotherapy [1967]

Pastors
Use Ministers (Religion)

Paternal Investment
Use Parental Investment

Path Analysis [1991]
PN 99   **SC** 36895
SN Quantification of the causal relationships that exist among variables.
B   Multivariate Analysis [1982]
R   Causal Analysis [1994]
      ↓ Factor Analysis [1967]
      Multiple Regression [1982]

Pathogenesis
Use Etiology

Pathological Gambling [1988]
PN 536   **SC** 36905
UF   Compulsive Gambling
B   Gambling [1973]
R   ↓ Addiction [1973]
      ↓ Behavior Disorders [1971]
      ↓ Impulse Control Disorders [1997]
      Impulsiveness [1973]

Pathologists [1973]
PN 14   **SC** 36920
B   Physicians [1967]
R   Surgeons [1973]

Pathology [1973]
PN 634   **SC** 36930
B   Medical Sciences [1967]
N   Neuropathology [1973]
      Psychopathology [1967]

Patient Abuse [1991]
PN 85   **SC** 36935
UF   Client Abuse
B   Antisocial Behavior [1971]

Patient Abuse — (cont'd)
R   ↓ Child Abuse [1971]
      Elder Abuse [1988]
      Emotional Abuse [1991]
      Patient Violence [1994]
      ↓ Patients [1967]
      Physical Abuse [1991]
      Professional Client Sexual Relations [1994]
      Professional Liability [1985]
      ↓ Professional Standards [1973]
      ↓ Sexual Abuse [1988]
      ↓ Therapeutic Processes [1978]
      ↓ Treatment [1967]

Patient Attitudes
Use Client Attitudes

Patient Care Planning
Use Treatment Planning

Patient Characteristics
Use Client Characteristics

Patient Dropouts
Use Treatment Dropouts

Patient Education
Use Client Education

Patient History [1973]
PN 2523   **SC** 36955
UF   Case History
      Medical History
      Psychiatric History
R   Biographical Data [1978]
      ↓ Client Characteristics [1973]
      Client Records [1997]
      ↓ Diagnosis [1967]
      Etiology [1967]
      ↓ Medical Diagnosis [1973]
      ↓ Medical Records [1978]
      Misdiagnosis [1997]
      Premorbidity [1978]
      Prognosis [1973]
      ↓ Psychodiagnosis [1967]
      ↓ Treatment [1967]

Patient Participation
Use Client Participation

Patient Records
Use Client Records

Patient Rights
Use Client Rights

Patient Satisfaction
Use Client Satisfaction

Patient Seclusion [1994]
PN 70   **SC** 36959
UF   Seclusion (Patient)
B   Social Isolation [1967]
R   ↓ Hospitalization [1967]
      Patient Violence [1994]
      ↓ Patients [1967]
      ↓ Psychiatric Hospitalization [1973]
      Psychiatric Hospitals [1967]
      Psychiatric Units [1991]

Patient Selection [1997]
PN 27   **SC** 57505

Patient Selection — (cont'd)

SN Selection of patients or clients for participation in research studies or for specific treatment modalities.
- **R** ↓ Client Characteristics [1973]
  - Client Transfer [1997]
  - Client Treatment Matching [1997]
  - Clients [1973]
  - ↓ Patients [1967]
  - Therapist Selection [1994]

Patient Therapist Interaction
- **Use** Psychotherapeutic Processes

Patient Therapist Sexual Relations
- **Use** Professional Client Sexual Relations

Patient Transfer
- **Use** Client Transfer

Patient Treatment Matching
- **Use** Client Treatment Matching

Patient Violence [1994]

PN 328   **SC** 36965

SN Violence or behavioral disruptions by psychiatric or medical patients directed toward other patients, institutional staff, or themselves.
- **UF** Client Violence
- **B** Client Characteristics [1973]
  - Violence [1973]
- **R** Dangerousness [1988]
  - Patient Abuse [1991]
  - Patient Seclusion [1994]
  - ↓ Patients [1967]
  - Physical Restraint [1982]
  - ↓ Therapeutic Processes [1978]

Patients [1967]

PN 1983   **SC** 36970

SN Persons under medical care. Use a more specific term if possible. Consider also CLIENTS.
- **N** Geriatric Patients [1973]
  - Hospitalized Patients [1973]
  - Medical Patients [1973]
  - Outpatients [1973]
  - Psychiatric Patients [1967]
  - Surgical Patients [1973]
  - Terminally Ill Patients [1973]
- **R** Client Participation [1997]
  - Patient Abuse [1991]
  - Patient Seclusion [1994]
  - Patient Selection [1997]
  - Patient Violence [1994]

Patriarchy [1973]

PN 155   **SC** 36980
- **B** Family Structure [1973]
- **R** Matriarchy [1973]
  - Mother Absence [1973]
  - ↓ Sex Role Attitudes [1978]
  - Sex Roles [1967]

Pattern Discrimination [1967]

PN 3193   **SC** 37000

SN Distinguishing temporal, spatial, or pictorial/symbolic regularities (patterns) of visual, auditory, or other types of stimuli. Includes the concept of pattern perception.
- **B** Perceptual Discrimination [1973]
- **R** ↓ Auditory Perception [1967]
  - Figure Ground Discrimination [1973]
  - Form and Shape Perception [1967]

Pattern Discrimination — (cont'd)
- **R** Perceptual Closure [1973]
  - ↓ Rhythm [1991]
  - Texture Perception [1982]
  - Visual Acuity [1982]
  - Visual Search [1982]

Pavlov (Ivan) [1991]

PN 61   **SC** 37005

SN Identifies biographical or autobiographical studies and discussions of Pavlov's works.
- **R** ↓ Classical Conditioning [1967]
  - ↓ Psychologists [1967]

Pavlovian Conditioning
- **Use** Classical Conditioning

Pay
- **Use** Salaries

PCP
- **Use** Phencyclidine

Peabody Picture Vocabulary Test [1973]

PN 287   **SC** 37030
- **B** Intelligence Measures [1967]

Peace [1988]

PN 365   **SC** 37038
- **B** Social Interaction [1967]
  - Social Issues [1991]
- **R** Foreign Policy Making [1973]
  - International Relations [1967]
  - ↓ Social Movements [1967]
  - ↓ War [1967]

Peace Corps [1973]

PN 22   **SC** 37040
- **B** Government Programs [1973]
- **R** Government [1967]

Pearson Product Moment Correlation Coefficient
- **Use** Statistical Correlation

Pecking Order
- **Use** Animal Dominance

Pederasty
- **Use** Pedophilia

Pedestrian Accidents [1973]

PN 93   **SC** 37090
- **B** Accidents [1967]
- **R** ↓ Driving Behavior [1967]
  - Motor Traffic Accidents [1973]
  - Pedestrians [1973]

Pedestrians [1973]

PN 163   **SC** 37100
- **R** Pedestrian Accidents [1973]

Pediatricians [1973]

PN 417   **SC** 37110
- **B** Physicians [1967]

Pediatrics [1973]

PN 1317   **SC** 37120
- **B** Medical Sciences [1967]

Pedophilia [1973]

PN 541   **SC** 37130
- **UF** Child Molestation
  - Pederasty
- **B** Paraphilias [1988]
- **R** ↓ Child Abuse [1971]
  - Incest [1973]
  - ↓ Sex Offenses [1982]
  - ↓ Sexual Abuse [1988]

Peer Counseling [1978]

PN 643   **SC** 37135

SN Supervised performance of limited counselor functions by a person of approximately the same age or status as the counselee.
- **B** Counseling [1967]
- **R** Mentor [1985]
  - ↓ Peer Relations [1967]
  - Peer Tutoring [1973]
  - Peers [1978]

Peer Evaluation [1982]

PN 919   **SC** 37137

SN Appraisal by one's peers.
- **UF** Peer Review
- **B** Evaluation [1967]
- **R** ↓ Peer Relations [1967]
  - ↓ Personnel Evaluation [1973]
  - Professional Competence [1997]
  - ↓ Professional Fees [1978]
  - ↓ Professional Standards [1973]

Peer Pressure [1994]

PN 155   **SC** 37138
- **B** Interpersonal Influences [1967]
  - Peer Relations [1967]
- **R** Friendship [1967]
  - ↓ Group Dynamics [1967]
  - Likability [1988]
  - Peers [1978]
  - ↓ Persuasive Communication [1967]
  - Social Acceptance [1967]
  - Social Approval [1967]
  - Temptation [1973]

Peer Relations [1967]

PN 7384   **SC** 37140
- **B** Interpersonal Interaction [1967]
- **N** Peer Pressure [1994]
- **R** Friendship [1967]
  - Peer Counseling [1978]
  - Peer Evaluation [1982]
  - Peers [1978]
  - Reference Groups [1994]
  - ↓ Relationship Termination [1997]
  - ↓ Sociometry [1991]

Peer Review
- **Use** Peer Evaluation

Peer Tutoring [1973]

PN 783   **SC** 37150

SN Teaching method in which students provide individual instruction for other students, not necessarily of the same age or grade level.
- **B** Tutoring [1973]
- **R** Cooperative Learning [1994]
  - Peer Counseling [1978]
  - Peers [1978]

Peers [1978]

PN 1365   **SC** 37154
- **R** Peer Counseling [1978]

Peers — (cont'd)
R   Peer Pressure 1994
     ↓ Peer Relations 1967
     Peer Tutoring 1973
     Significant Others 1991

Pellagra 1973
PN 10   SC 37160
B   Vitamin Deficiency Disorders 1973
R   Nicotinamide 1973

Pemoline 1978
PN 85   SC 37175
B   CNS Stimulating Drugs 1973

Penguins 1973
PN 60   SC 37180
B   Birds 1967

Penicillins 1973
PN 67   SC 37190
B   Antibiotics 1973

Penis 1973
PN 252   SC 37200
B   Male Genitalia 1973

Penis Envy 1973
PN 66   SC 37210
R   ↓ Psychoanalytic Personality Factors 1973

Penitentiaries
Use Prisons

Penology 1973
PN 196   SC 37230
R   ↓ Correctional Institutions 1973
     ↓ Criminal Justice 1991
     Criminology 1973

Pension Plans (Employee)
Use Employee Pension Plans

Pentazocine 1991
PN 27   SC 37245
B   Analgesic Drugs 1973
     Narcotic Agonists 1988

Pentobarbital 1973
PN 703   SC 37250
UF   Nembutal
     Sodium Pentobarbital
B   Anesthetic Drugs 1973
     Anticonvulsive Drugs 1973
     Barbiturates 1967
     Hypnotic Drugs 1973
     Sedatives 1973

Pentothal
Use Thiopental

Pentylenetetrazol 1973
PN 264   SC 37270
UF   Metrazole
     Pentylenetetrazole
B   CNS Stimulating Drugs 1973
R   ↓ Analeptic Drugs 1973

Pentylenetetrazole
Use Pentylenetetrazol

Peptic Ulcers
Use Gastrointestinal Ulcers

Peptides 1973
PN 2489   SC 37330
UF   Galanin
     Neuropeptides
N   Angiotensin 1973
     Bombesin 1988
     Cholecystokinin 1982
     Corticotropin Releasing Factor 1994
     ↓ Endogenous Opiates 1985
     Melanocyte Stimulating Hormone 1985
     Nerve Growth Factor 1994
     ↓ Neurokinins 1997
     Neurotensin 1985
     Somatostatin 1991
     Substance P 1985
R   ↓ Drugs 1967
     Enkephalins 1982
     ↓ Neurotransmitters 1985
     ↓ Proteins 1973

Perception 1967
PN 5406   SC 37350
SN   Conceptually broad term referring to the process of obtaining cognitive or sensory information about the environment. Use a more specific term if possible.
UF   Sensation
N   ↓ Auditory Perception 1967
     ↓ Extrasensory Perception 1967
     Form and Shape Perception 1967
     ↓ Illusions (Perception) 1967
     ↓ Intersensory Processes 1978
     Numerosity Perception 1967
     Object Recognition 1997
     ↓ Olfactory Perception 1967
     Perceptual Closure 1973
     ↓ Perceptual Constancy 1985
     ↓ Perceptual Discrimination 1973
     ↓ Perceptual Distortion 1982
     ↓ Perceptual Localization 1967
     ↓ Perceptual Motor Learning 1967
     ↓ Perceptual Motor Processes 1967
     ↓ Perceptual Orientation 1973
     Perceptual Style 1973
     Risk Perception 1997
     Role Perception 1973
     Self Perception 1967
     Sensory Gating 1991
     ↓ Social Perception 1967
     ↓ Somesthetic Perception 1967
     ↓ Spatial Perception 1967
     Subliminal Perception 1973
     Taste Perception 1967
     ↓ Time Perception 1967
     ↓ Visual Perception 1967
R   Apperception 1973
     ↓ Attention 1967
     Constructivism 1994
     ↓ Discrimination 1967
     Mind 1991
     ↓ Perceptual Development 1973
     ↓ Perceptual Disturbances 1973
     ↓ Perceptual Measures 1973
     ↓ Perceptual Stimulation 1973
     ↓ Priming 1988
     ↓ Rhythm 1991
     Sensory Neglect 1994
     Signal Detection (Perception) 1967

Perceptiveness (Personality) 1973
PN 37   SC 37360

Perceptiveness (Personality) — (cont'd)
SN   Demonstrating insight or sympathetic understanding or keen powers of observation.
B   Personality Traits 1967
R   Insight 1973
     Sensitivity (Personality) 1967
     ↓ Social Perception 1967

Perceptual Aftereffect 1967
PN 1111   SC 37370
SN   Subjective perceptual alterations resulting from prolonged exposure to preceding sensory stimulation.
UF   Aftereffect (Perceptual)
B   Illusions (Perception) 1967
N   Afterimage 1967
R   Interocular Transfer 1985

Perceptual Closure 1973
PN 136   SC 37380
SN   Perception of units which together form a closed unit or whole, being organized together and perceived as a whole.
UF   Closure (Perceptual)
     Perceptual Fill
B   Perception 1967
R   Pattern Discrimination 1967

Perceptual Constancy 1985
PN 125   SC 37385
SN   Stable perception of a stimulus in any sensory modality despite changes in its objective properties.
B   Perception 1967
N   Brightness Constancy 1985
     Color Constancy 1985
     Size Constancy 1985
R   Object Permanence 1985

Perceptual Development 1973
PN 2992   SC 37390
SN   The acquisition of sensory skills or abilities in the natural course of physical and psychological maturation.
B   Cognitive Development 1973
N   Perceptual Motor Development 1991
R   ↓ Childhood Development 1967
     Conservation (Concept) 1973
     ↓ Developmental Stages 1973
     ↓ Perception 1967
     ↓ Physical Development 1973
     ↓ Psychomotor Development 1973

Perceptual Discrimination 1973
PN 1027   SC 37400
B   Discrimination 1967
     Perception 1967
N   Auditory Acuity 1988
     Auditory Discrimination 1967
     Figure Ground Discrimination 1973
     Odor Discrimination 1973
     Pattern Discrimination 1967
     Visual Discrimination 1967
R   Mirror Image 1991
     Object Recognition 1997
     Stroop Effect 1988

Perceptual Distortion 1982
PN 177   SC 37410
SN   Lack of correspondence between the common perception of a stimulus and the perception by an individual. Perceptual distortion does not involve hallucinatory or illusory components, but rather is a function of individual differences.
UF   Distortion (Perceptual)

Perceptual Distortion — (cont'd)
- **B**   Perception 1967
- **N**   Spatial Distortion 1973
- **R**   ↓ Illusions (Perception) 1967
  - ↓ Perceptual Disturbances 1973
  - Sensory Neglect 1994

Perceptual Disturbances 1973
PN 509   **SC** 37420
- **N**   ↓ Agnosia 1973
  - ↓ Hallucinations 1967
- **R**   ↓ Aphasia 1967
  - ↓ Illusions (Perception) 1967
  - ↓ Learning Disabilities 1973
  - ↓ Mental Disorders 1967
  - ↓ Perception 1967
  - ↓ Perceptual Distortion 1982
  - Sensory Neglect 1994

Perceptual Fill
Use Perceptual Closure

Perceptual Localization 1967
PN 875   **SC** 37440
SN Discrimination of the physical displacement or spatial location of a stimulus in any sensory modality.
- **UF** Localization (Perceptual)
- **B**   Perception 1967
- **N**   Auditory Localization 1973
- **R**   Direction Perception 1997
  - ↓ Tracking 1967

Perceptual Measures 1973
PN 718   **SC** 37450
- **B**   Measurement 1967
- **N**   Rod and Frame Test 1973
  - Stroop Color Word Test 1973
- **R**   ↓ Audiometry 1967
  - Auditory Thresholds 1973
  - Bone Conduction Audiometry 1973
  - Critical Flicker Fusion Threshold 1967
  - Dark Adaptation 1973
  - Olfactory Thresholds 1973
  - Pain Measurement 1997
  - Pain Thresholds 1973
  - ↓ Perception 1967
  - ↓ Psychophysical Measurement 1967
  - ↓ Sensorimotor Measures 1973
  - ↓ Speech and Hearing Measures 1973
  - ↓ Thresholds 1967
  - Vibrotactile Thresholds 1973
  - ↓ Visual Thresholds 1973

Perceptual Motor Coordination 1973
PN 1191   **SC** 37460
- **UF** Coordination (Perceptual Motor)
- **B**   Perceptual Motor Processes 1967
- **N**   Physical Dexterity 1973
- **R**   Motor Coordination 1973
  - Perceptual Motor Development 1991

Perceptual Motor Development 1991
PN 329   **SC** 37470
SN Use MOTOR DEVELOPMENT and PERCEPTUAL DEVELOPMENT to access references from 1973-1990.
- **UF** Sensorimotor Development
- **B**   Motor Development 1973
  - Perceptual Development 1973
- **R**   Animal Development 1978
  - ↓ Intersensory Processes 1978
  - ↓ Perceptual Motor Coordination 1973
  - ↓ Perceptual Motor Learning 1967

Perceptual Motor Development — (cont'd)
- **R**   ↓ Perceptual Motor Processes 1967
  - ↓ Psychomotor Development 1973

Perceptual Motor Learning 1967
PN 1804   **SC** 37480
- **UF** Motor Skill Learning
- **B**   Learning 1967
  - Perception 1967
- **N**   Fine Motor Skill Learning 1973
  - Gross Motor Skill Learning 1973
- **R**   Perceptual Motor Development 1991
  - ↓ Skill Learning 1973
  - ↓ Tracking 1967

Perceptual Motor Measures
Use Sensorimotor Measures

Perceptual Motor Processes 1967
PN 6086   **SC** 37490
- **UF** Psychomotor Processes
  - Sensorimotor Processes
- **B**   Perception 1967
- **N**   ↓ Perceptual Motor Coordination 1973
  - Sensory Integration 1991
  - ↓ Tracking 1967
- **R**   ↓ Equilibrium 1973
  - ↓ Intersensory Processes 1978
  - ↓ Motor Processes 1967
  - Perceptual Motor Development 1991

Perceptual Neglect
Use Sensory Neglect

Perceptual Orientation 1973
PN 904   **SC** 37500
SN Awareness of one's position in time and space.
- **UF** Orientation (Perceptual)
- **B**   Perception 1967
- **N**   Spatial Orientation (Perception) 1973
- **R**   Time Perspective 1978

Perceptual Stimulation 1973
PN 490   **SC** 37510
- **B**   Stimulation 1967
- **N**   ↓ Auditory Stimulation 1967
  - ↓ Delayed Feedback 1973
  - Olfactory Stimulation 1978
  - ↓ Sensory Feedback 1973
  - ↓ Somesthetic Stimulation 1973
  - Taste Stimulation 1967
  - ↓ Visual Stimulation 1973
- **R**   Afferent Stimulation 1973
  - ↓ Masking 1967
  - ↓ Perception 1967
  - Sensory Gating 1991

Perceptual Style 1973
PN 520   **SC** 37520
SN Manner in which sensory information or stimuli are organized meaningfully by an individual.
- **B**   Perception 1967
- **R**   ↓ Cognitive Style 1967
  - Conceptual Tempo 1985
  - Neurolinguistic Programming 2001
  - Schema 1988

Perfectionism 1988
PN 289   **SC** 37523
- **B**   Personality Traits 1967
- **R**   ↓ Compulsions 1973
  - Conscientiousness 1997

Performance 1967
PN 5769   **SC** 37525
SN Conceptually broad term, having application across broad disciplines and subject matter contexts in which execution or accomplishment of a specified task or objective is of concern. Use terms describing specific activity or performance when possible.
- **N**   Athletic Performance 1991
  - Group Performance 1967
  - ↓ Job Performance 1967
  - ↓ Motor Performance 1973
- **R**   ↓ Ability 1967
  - ↓ Achievement 1967
  - ↓ Competence 1982
  - Performance Anxiety 1994

Performance Anxiety 1994
PN 112   **SC** 37527
- **B**   Anxiety 1967
- **R**   ↓ Anxiety Disorders 1997
  - ↓ Performance 1967

Performance Tests 1973
PN 722   **SC** 37530
SN Tests requiring nonverbal responses, for example, the manipulation of objects or the performance of motor skills.
- **B**   Measurement 1967
- **R**   Criterion Referenced Tests 1982

Performing Arts
Use Arts

Periaqueductal Gray 1985
PN 300   **SC** 37550
SN Mesencephalic cells in the gray area surrounding the cerebral aqueduct important for visceral and limbic mechanisms.
- **B**   Tegmentum 1991

Perinatal Period 1994
PN 295   **SC** 37555
SN Usually the period just preceding or just following birth. Compare NEONATAL PERIOD. Used for both human and animal populations.
- **R**   ↓ Birth 1967
  - Postnatal Period 1973
  - ↓ Pregnancy 1967
  - ↓ Prenatal Development 1973

Peripheral Nerve Disorders 1973
PN 119   **SC** 37560
- **B**   Nervous System Disorders 1967
- **N**   Myasthenia Gravis 1973
  - ↓ Neuralgia 1973
- **R**   Muscular Dystrophy 1973
  - ↓ Paralysis 1973
  - ↓ Peripheral Nervous System 1973

Peripheral Nervous System 1973
PN 356   **SC** 37570
SN Anatomical systems of structures outside the brain and spinal cord composed of neural tissue. Use PERIPHERAL NERVES to access references from 1973-1993.
- **UF** Nerves (Peripheral)
- **B**   Nervous System 1967
- **N**   ↓ Autonomic Nervous System 1967
  - ↓ Cranial Nerves 1973
  - ↓ Neural Pathways 1982
  - Spinal Nerves 1973
- **R**   Autonomic Ganglia 1973
  - ↓ Peripheral Nerve Disorders 1973

Peripheral Vision 1988
PN 337　　　　　　　　　　　SC 37580
　B　Visual Perception 1967
　R　Visual Field 1967

Permissiveness (Parental)
　Use Parental Permissiveness

Perpetrators 1988
PN 2143　　　　　　　　　　SC 37595
　N　↓ Criminals 1967
　R　↓ Crime 1967
　　　Criminal Responsibility 1991
　　↓ Harassment 2001
　　　Incest 1973
　　　Stalking 2001
　　　Victimization 1973

Perphenazine 1973
PN 131　　　　　　　　　　　SC 37600
　B　Antiemetic Drugs 1973
　　　Phenothiazine Derivatives 1973

Persecution 1973
PN 128　　　　　　　　　　　SC 37610
　B　Antisocial Behavior 1971
　　　Interpersonal Interaction 1967
　R　Torture 1988
　　　Victimization 1973

Perseverance
　Use Persistence

Perseveration 1967
PN 227　　　　　　　　　　　SC 37630
SN Persistent repetition of a response to different
and perhaps inappropriate stimuli which may be due
to a refusal or an inability to interrupt one's behavior
or to change from one task to another. Also, pathological repetition of thoughts, acts, or verbalizations.
　B　Thought Disturbances 1973

Persistence 1973
PN 985　　　　　　　　　　　SC 37640
SN Maintenance of particular behavior despite
effort, opposition, or cessation of initiating stimulus.
Used for human or animal populations.
　UF Perseverance
　B　Personality Traits 1967
　R　Conscientiousness 1997
　　↓ Motivation 1967

Persistent Mental Illness
　Use Chronic Mental Illness

Person Centered Psychotherapy
　Use Client Centered Therapy

Person Environment Fit 1991
PN 518　　　　　　　　　　　SC 37645
SN Compatibility between individuals and their sur-
roundings.
　R　↓ Adjustment 1967
　　↓ Environment 1967
　　　Environmental Adaptation 1973
　　↓ Environmental Planning 1982
　　↓ Personality 1967
　　↓ Systems 1967
　　↓ Working Conditions 1973

Personal Adjustment
　Use Emotional Adjustment

Personal Computers
　Use Microcomputers

Personal Construct Theory
　Use Personality Theory

Personal Defense
　Use Self Defense

Personal Growth Techniques
　Use Human Potential Movement

Personal Orientation Inventory 1973
PN 118　　　　　　　　　　　SC 37670
　B　Nonprojective Personality Measures 1973

Personal Space 1973
PN 1114　　　　　　　　　　SC 37680
SN Minimal spatial distance preferred by an individ-
ual in his/her relations with others.
　UF Interpersonal Distance
　R　Boundaries (Psychological) 1997
　　　Crowding 1978
　　　Physical Contact 1982
　　↓ Social Behavior 1967
　　　Social Density 1978

Personal Therapy 1991
PN 79　　　　　　　　　　　SC 37685
SN Therapy for professionals working in the mental
health field, for example, psychologists, psychiatrists,
or social workers.
　B　Treatment 1967
　R　↓ Clinical Methods Training 1973
　　　Impaired Professionals 1985
　　↓ Mental Health Personnel 1967
　　↓ Professional Consultation 1973
　　　Professional Supervision 1988
　　　Psychoanalytic Training 1973
　　　Self Analysis 1994

Personal Values 1973
PN 2293　　　　　　　　　　SC 37690
SN Set of ideals that an individual deems worth-
while and that influence his/her behavior.
　B　Values 1967
　R　Anomie 1978
　　　Morality 1967

Personality 1967
PN 10068　　　　　　　　　　SC 37870
SN Conceptually broad term referring to the totality
of an individual's behavioral or emotional characteris-
tics. Use a more specific term if possible.
　UF Character
　　　Disposition
　　　Temperament
　N　Inadequate Personality 1973
　　↓ Personality Traits 1967
　　↓ Psychoanalytic Personality Factors 1973
　R　↓ Cognitive Style 1967
　　　Coronary Prone Behavior 1982
　　　Egocentrism 1978
　　↓ Emotional Adjustment 1973
　　↓ Emotional States 1973
　　↓ Emotions 1967
　　　Five Factor Personality Model 1997
　　↓ Gender Identity 1985
　　　Human Nature 1997
　　　Individual Differences 1967
　　↓ Lifestyle 1978
　　　Person Environment Fit 1991
　　　Personality Change 1967

Personality — (cont'd)
　R　Personality Correlates 1967
　　↓ Personality Development 1967
　　↓ Personality Disorders 1967
　　↓ Personality Processes 1967
　　↓ Personality Theory 1967
　　　Predisposition 1973
　　　Psychodynamics 1973
　　　Self Actualization 1973
　　↓ Self Concept 1967
　　　Self Disclosure 1973
　　　Self Evaluation 1967
　　　Self Monitoring (Personality) 1985
　　　Self Perception 1967
　　　Somatotypes 1973
　　　Teacher Personality 1973

Personality Assessment
　Use Personality Measures

Personality Change 1967
PN 1297　　　　　　　　　　SC 37720
SN Process or fact of change associated either with
development and maturity, or as the result of stress,
illness, treatment, or other factors.
　B　Personality Processes 1967
　R　Behavior Change 1973
　　↓ Personality 1967
　　↓ Personality Development 1967

Personality Correlates 1967
PN 4485　　　　　　　　　　SC 37740
SN Description of numerous or unspecified person-
ality traits which bear a mutual or reciprocal relation-
ship to a particular phenomenon or behavior.
　R　Individual Differences 1967
　　↓ Personality 1967

Personality Development 1967
PN 5462　　　　　　　　　　SC 37750
　UF Character Development
　　　Character Formation
　B　Psychosocial Development 1973
　N　↓ Ego Development 1991
　　　Separation Individuation 1982
　R　Ego Identity 1991
　　　Emotional Development 1973
　　　Externalization 1973
　　　Five Factor Personality Model 1997
　　　Identity Crisis 1973
　　↓ Internalization 1997
　　　Moral Development 1973
　　↓ Personality 1967
　　　Personality Change 1967
　　↓ Personality Theory 1967

Personality Disorders 1967
PN 4165　　　　　　　　　　SC 37760
SN In 1997, this term replaced the discontinued
term ASTHENIC PERSONALITY. In 2000,
ASTHENIC PERSONALITY was stripped from all
records and replaced with PERSONALITY DISOR-
DERS.
　UF Asthenic Personality
　　　Character Disorders
　B　Mental Disorders 1967
　N　Antisocial Personality 1973
　　　Avoidant Personality 1994
　　　Borderline Personality 2001
　　　Dependent Personality 1994
　　　Histrionic Personality Disorder 1991
　　　Narcissistic Personality 1973
　　　Obsessive Compulsive Personality 1973
　　　Paranoid Personality 1973

Personality Disorders — (cont'd)

- **N**   Passive Aggressive Personality 1973
- ↓ Sadomasochistic Personality 1973
- Schizoid Personality 1973
- Schizotypal Personality 1991
- **R**   ↓ Defense Mechanisms 1967
- ↓ Dissociative Disorders 2001
- ↓ Ethnospecific Disorders 1973
- Explosive Disorder 2001
- Kleptomania 1973
- ↓ Personality 1967
- ↓ Personality Processes 1967
- ↓ Personality Theory 1967
- Pyromania 1973

Personality Factors
Use Personality Traits

Personality Factors (Psychoanalytic)
Use Psychoanalytic Personality Factors

Personality Measures 1967
PN 8647   **SC** 37790
- **UF** Personality Assessment
- Personality Tests
- Tests (Personality)
- **B**   Measurement 1967
- **N**   California Psychological Inventory 1967
- General Health Questionnaire 1991
- Kirton Adaption Innovation Inventory 2001
- NEO Personality Inventory 1997
- ↓ Nonprojective Personality Measures 1973
- ↓ Projective Personality Measures 1973
- Rokeach Dogmatism Scale 1973
- Sensation Seeking Scale 1973
- Sentence Completion Tests 1991

Personality Processes 1967
PN 1380   **SC** 37800
SN Conceptually broad term referring to the interaction among personality structures (e.g., ego, id) or pattern of characteristic tendencies, often but not exclusively from a psychoanalytic perspective. Use a more specific term if possible.
- **N**   Catharsis 1973
- Cathexis 1973
- ↓ Defense Mechanisms 1967
- Externalization 1973
- Inhibition (Personality) 1973
- Insight 1973
- ↓ Internalization 1997
- Introspection 1973
- Personality Change 1967
- **R**   Boundaries (Psychological) 1997
- ↓ Lifestyle 1978
- ↓ Mental Disorders 1967
- ↓ Personality 1967
- ↓ Personality Disorders 1967
- ↓ Psychoanalytic Personality Factors 1973
- ↓ Psychoanalytic Theory 1967
- Reality Testing 1973

Personality Tests
Use Personality Measures

Personality Theory 1967
PN 2987   **SC** 37850
- **UF** Personal Construct Theory
- **N**   Five Factor Personality Model 1997
- **R**   Individual Differences 1967
- ↓ Personality 1967
- ↓ Personality Development 1967
- ↓ Personality Disorders 1967

Personality Theory — (cont'd)
- **R**   Self Perception 1967
- Self Psychology 1988

Personality Traits 1967
PN 20867   **SC** 37860
- **UF** Personality Factors
- **B**   Personality 1967
- **N**   Adaptability (Personality) 1973
- Aggressiveness 1973
- Agreeableness 1997
- Altruism 1973
- Androgyny 1982
- Assertiveness 1973
- Authoritarianism 1967
- Charisma 1988
- ↓ Cognitive Style 1967
- Conformity (Personality) 1967
- Conscientiousness 1997
- Conservatism 1973
- Courage 1973
- Creativity 1967
- Cruelty 1973
- Curiosity 1967
- Cynicism 1973
- Defensiveness 1967
- Dependency (Personality) 1967
- Dishonesty 1973
- Dogmatism 1978
- Egalitarianism 1985
- Egotism 1973
- Emotional Immaturity 1973
- Emotional Inferiority 1973
- Emotional Instability 1973
- Emotional Maturity 1973
- Emotional Security 1973
- Emotional Stability 1973
- Emotional Superiority 1973
- Emotionality (Personality) 1973
- Empathy 1967
- Extraversion 1967
- Femininity 1967
- Gregariousness 1973
- Hardiness 1997
- Honesty 1973
- Hypnotic Susceptibility 1973
- Independence (Personality) 1973
- Individuality 1973
- Initiative 1973
- Integrity 1997
- Internal External Locus of Control 1967
- Introversion 1967
- Irritability 1988
- Liberalism 1973
- Likability 1988
- Loyalty 1973
- Machiavellianism 1973
- Masculinity 1967
- Misanthropy 1973
- Moodiness 1973
- Narcissism 1967
- Need for Approval 1997
- Need for Cognition 1997
- Negativism 1973
- Nervousness 1973
- Neuroticism 1973
- Nonconformity (Personality) 1973
- Nurturance 1985
- Obedience 1973
- Objectivity 1973
- Omnipotence 1994
- Openmindedness 1978
- Openness to Experience 1997
- Optimism 1973

Personality Traits — (cont'd)
- **N**   Paranoia 1988
- Passiveness 1973
- Perceptiveness (Personality) 1973
- Perfectionism 1988
- Persistence 1973
- Pessimism 1973
- Positivism 1973
- Psychoticism 1978
- Repression Sensitization 1973
- Rigidity (Personality) 1967
- ↓ Risk Taking 1967
- Self Control 1973
- Selfishness 1973
- Sensation Seeking 1978
- Sensitivity (Personality) 1967
- Seriousness 1973
- Sexuality 1973
- Sincerity 1973
- Sociability 1973
- Subjectivity 1994
- Suggestibility 1967
- Timidity 1973
- ↓ Tolerance 1973
- **R**   Codependency 1991
- Coronary Prone Behavior 1982
- Egocentrism 1978
- Five Factor Personality Model 1997
- Instrumentality 1991
- Leadership Qualities 1997

Personnel 1967
PN 4225   **SC** 37980
SN Conceptually broad term referring to the body of persons employed by a given organization or associated with a particular occupation. Use a more specific term if possible.
- **UF** Employees
- Workers
- **N**   ↓ Artists 1973
- ↓ Business and Industrial Personnel 1967
- Disabled Personnel 1997
- ↓ Government Personnel 1973
- ↓ Hypnotists 1973
- ↓ Nonprofessional Personnel 1982
- ↓ Paraprofessional Personnel 1973
- ↓ Professional Personnel 1978
- ↓ Religious Personnel 1973
- ↓ Social Workers 1973
- ↓ Volunteer Personnel 1973
- **R**   Affirmative Action 1985
- Employability 1973
- Employee Absenteeism 1973
- ↓ Employee Benefits 1973
- ↓ Employee Characteristics 1988
- ↓ Employee Interaction 1988
- Employee Turnover 1973
- Employer Attitudes 1973
- Employment History 1978
- Job Applicant Attitudes 1973
- Job Applicants 1985
- ↓ Job Performance 1967
- Labor Union Members 1973
- Military Veterans 1973
- ↓ Occupations 1967
- ↓ Personnel Management 1973
- ↓ Personnel Supply 1973
- ↓ Personnel Training 1967
- Reemployment 1991
- Retirement 1973
- ↓ Teams 1988
- Unemployment 1967
- Work (Attitudes Toward) 1973
- ↓ Working Conditions 1973

Personnel — (cont'd)
R Working Women ¹⁹⁷⁸

Personnel Development
Use Personnel Training

Personnel Evaluation ¹⁹⁷³
PN 2698 **SC** 37900
B Evaluation ¹⁹⁶⁷
Personnel Management ¹⁹⁷³
N Occupational Success Prediction ¹⁹⁷³
Teacher Effectiveness Evaluation ¹⁹⁷⁸
R Assessment Centers ¹⁹⁸²
Employment Discrimination ¹⁹⁹⁴
Job Applicant Interviews ¹⁹⁷³
Job Applicant Screening ¹⁹⁷³
↓ Job Performance ¹⁹⁶⁷
Peer Evaluation ¹⁹⁸²
Personnel Promotion ¹⁹⁷⁸
↓ Personnel Selection ¹⁹⁶⁷
Professional Competence ¹⁹⁹⁷

Personnel Management ¹⁹⁷³
PN 1579 **SC** 37910
UF Human Resources
B Management ¹⁹⁶⁷
N Career Development ¹⁹⁸⁵
Job Analysis ¹⁹⁶⁷
Labor Management Relations ¹⁹⁶⁷
↓ Personnel Evaluation ¹⁹⁷³
Personnel Placement ¹⁹⁷³
Personnel Promotion ¹⁹⁷⁸
↓ Personnel Recruitment ¹⁹⁷³
↓ Personnel Selection ¹⁹⁶⁷
Personnel Termination ¹⁹⁷³
R Affirmative Action ¹⁹⁸⁵
Business Education ¹⁹⁷³
Business Management ¹⁹⁷³
Employment Discrimination ¹⁹⁹⁴
↓ Personnel ¹⁹⁶⁷
Resource Allocation ¹⁹⁹⁷
Supervisor Employee Interaction ¹⁹⁹⁷
Supported Employment ¹⁹⁹⁴

Personnel Placement ¹⁹⁷³
PN 325 **SC** 37920
UF Placement (Personnel)
B Personnel Management ¹⁹⁷³
R Assessment Centers ¹⁹⁸²
Career Development ¹⁹⁸⁵

Personnel Promotion ¹⁹⁷⁸
PN 420 **SC** 37925
UF Job Promotion
B Personnel Management ¹⁹⁷³
R Assessment Centers ¹⁹⁸²
Career Development ¹⁹⁸⁵
Employment History ¹⁹⁷⁸
↓ Job Performance ¹⁹⁶⁷
Occupational Status ¹⁹⁷⁸
Occupational Success ¹⁹⁷⁸
↓ Personnel Evaluation ¹⁹⁷³

Personnel Recruitment ¹⁹⁷³
PN 462 **SC** 37930
UF Employment Processes
Recruitment (Personnel)
B Personnel Management ¹⁹⁷³
N Military Recruitment ¹⁹⁷³
Teacher Recruitment ¹⁹⁷³
R Affirmative Action ¹⁹⁸⁵
Job Applicant Interviews ¹⁹⁷³
Job Applicant Screening ¹⁹⁷³

Personnel Selection ¹⁹⁶⁷
PN 3183 **SC** 37940
UF Employee Selection
Hiring
Selection (Personnel)
B Personnel Management ¹⁹⁷³
N Job Applicant Interviews ¹⁹⁷³
Job Applicant Screening ¹⁹⁷³
R Affirmative Action ¹⁹⁸⁵
Assessment Centers ¹⁹⁸²
Employment Discrimination ¹⁹⁹⁴
↓ Personnel Evaluation ¹⁹⁷³
↓ Screening ¹⁹⁸²

Personnel Supply ¹⁹⁷³
PN 112 **SC** 37950
SN Availability of manpower or human resources required for an occupation or service in order to meet demands.
UF Manpower
N Medical Personnel Supply ¹⁹⁷³
Mental Health Personnel Supply ¹⁹⁷³
R ↓ Personnel ¹⁹⁶⁷

Personnel Termination ¹⁹⁷³
PN 457 **SC** 37960
UF Employee Termination
B Personnel Management ¹⁹⁷³
R Employment History ¹⁹⁷⁸
Job Security ¹⁹⁷⁸
↓ Occupational Tenure ¹⁹⁷³
Retirement ¹⁹⁷³
Unemployment ¹⁹⁶⁷

Personnel Training ¹⁹⁶⁷
PN 3754 **SC** 37970
UF Job Training
Personnel Development
Training (Personnel)
B Education ¹⁹⁶⁷
N Apprenticeship ¹⁹⁷³
↓ Inservice Training ¹⁹⁸⁵
Management Training ¹⁹⁷³
Military Training ¹⁹⁷³
On the Job Training ¹⁹⁷³
R Business Education ¹⁹⁷³
Career Development ¹⁹⁸⁵
Human Relations Training ¹⁹⁷⁸
Job Enrichment ¹⁹⁷³
↓ Personnel ¹⁹⁶⁷
Sensitivity Training ¹⁹⁷³

Personnel Turnover
Use Employee Turnover

Perspective Taking
Use Role Taking

Perspiration
Use Sweat

Persuasion Therapy ¹⁹⁷³
PN 13 **SC** 38000
SN Limited directive therapy in which the client is encouraged to follow the therapist's advice to deal with current crises.
B Psychotherapy ¹⁹⁶⁷

Persuasive Communication ¹⁹⁶⁷
PN 2552 **SC** 38010
SN Communication, in written or oral form, aimed at influencing others to accept a position, belief, or course of action.

Persuasive Communication — (cont'd)
B Communication ¹⁹⁶⁷
N Brainwashing ¹⁹⁸²
R Coercion ¹⁹⁹⁴
Debates ¹⁹⁹⁷
↓ Interpersonal Influences ¹⁹⁶⁷
Peer Pressure ¹⁹⁹⁴
Propaganda ¹⁹⁷³
Rhetoric ¹⁹⁹¹

Pervasive Developmental Disorders ²⁰⁰¹
PN 0 **SC** 38016
SN Broad term for disorders, usually first diagnosed in children prior to age 4, characterized by severe and profound impairment in social interaction, communication, and the presence of stereotyped behaviors, interests, and activities. Compare DEVELOPMENTAL DISABILITIES.
B Mental Disorders ¹⁹⁶⁷
N Aspergers Syndrome ¹⁹⁹¹
↓ Autism ¹⁹⁶⁷
Rett Syndrome ¹⁹⁹⁴
R Developmental Disabilities ¹⁹⁸²
Stereotyped Behavior ¹⁹⁷³

Perversions (Sexual)
Use Paraphilias

Pessimism ¹⁹⁷³
PN 381 **SC** 38020
SN Attitude characterized by a gloomy and desperate temperament and inclination to emphasize and expect the worst possible outcome of events and actions.
B Emotional States ¹⁹⁷³
Personality Traits ¹⁹⁶⁷
R Cynicism ¹⁹⁷³
Fatalism ¹⁹⁷³
Hopelessness ¹⁹⁸⁸
Negativism ¹⁹⁷³
Nihilism ¹⁹⁷³
Optimism ¹⁹⁷³

Pesticides
Use Insecticides

Pet Therapy
Use Animal Assisted Therapy

Petit Mal Epilepsy ¹⁹⁷³
PN 44 **SC** 38030
B Epilepsy ¹⁹⁶⁷

Pets ¹⁹⁸²
PN 510 **SC** 38035
SN Domesticated animals kept primarily for pleasure rather than utility.
R Animal Assisted Therapy ¹⁹⁹⁴
Animal Domestication ¹⁹⁷⁸
↓ Animals ¹⁹⁶⁷
Interspecies Interaction ¹⁹⁹¹

Peyote ¹⁹⁷³
PN 7 **SC** 38050
B Alkaloids ¹⁹⁷³
Hallucinogenic Drugs ¹⁹⁶⁷
Psychotomimetic Drugs ¹⁹⁷³
R Mescaline ¹⁹⁷³

Phantom Limbs ¹⁹⁷³
PN 143 **SC** 38060
B Body Image Disturbances ¹⁹⁷³
R ↓ Amputation ¹⁹⁷³

Pharmacists 1991
PN 115   SC 38065
  B   Medical Personnel 1967

Pharmacology 1973
PN 1341   SC 38070
SN The study of the chemistry, actions, and effects of drugs on living organisms or tissues. Used for intended effects of drugs; for adverse or undesired effects of drugs, use SIDE EFFECTS (DRUG). For the use of drugs in a treatment capacity, use DRUG THERAPY.
  B   Paramedical Sciences 1973
  N   Psychopharmacology 1967
  R   Bioavailability 1991
       Drug Abuse Liability 1994

Pharmacotherapy
  Use Drug Therapy

Pharyngeal Disorders 1973
PN 23   SC 38090
  B   Respiratory Tract Disorders 1973

Pharynx 1973
PN 41   SC 38100
  B   Digestive System 1967
       Respiratory System 1973

Phenaglycodol
SN Term discontinued in 1997. In 2000, the term was stripped from all records containing it, and replaced with SEDATIVES, its postable counterpart.
  Use Sedatives

Phencyclidine 1982
PN 697   SC 38125
SN Piperadine having hallucinogenic, anesthetic, and analgesic properties.
  UF   PCP
  B   Analgesic Drugs 1973
       Anesthetic Drugs 1973
       Hallucinogenic Drugs 1967

Phenelzine 1973
PN 300   SC 38130
  B   Antidepressant Drugs 1971
       Monoamine Oxidase Inhibitors 1973

Phenethylamines 1985
PN 115   SC 38135
  UF   Phenylethylamines
  B   Amines 1973
  R   ↓ Amphetamine 1967

Pheniprazine 1973
PN 6   SC 38140
  B   Antidepressant Drugs 1971
       Antihypertensive Drugs 1973
       Monoamine Oxidase Inhibitors 1973

Phenmetrazine 1973
PN 13   SC 38150
  B   Appetite Depressing Drugs 1973
       Sympathomimetic Amines 1973

Phenobarbital 1973
PN 327   SC 38160
  B   Anticonvulsive Drugs 1973
       Barbiturates 1967
       Hypnotic Drugs 1973
       Sedatives 1973

Phenomenology 1967
PN 2116   SC 38180
  B   Philosophies 1967
  R   Constructivism 1994
       Hermeneutics 1991
       ↓ History of Psychology 1967

Phenothiazine Derivatives 1973
PN 220   SC 38190
SN In 1997, this term replaced the discontinued terms BUTYRYLPERAZINE and TRIFLUPRO-MAZINE. In 2000, these terms were stripped from all records and replaced with PHENOTHIAZINE DERIV-ATIVES.
  UF   Butyrylperazine
       Triflupromazine
  B   Tranquilizing Drugs 1967
  N   Chlorpromazine 1967
       Chlorprothixene 1973
       Fluphenazine 1973
       Mesoridazine 1973
       Perphenazine 1973
       Prochlorperazine 1973
       Promazine 1973
       Thioridazine 1973
       Trifluoperazine 1973
  R   ↓ Cholinergic Blocking Drugs 1973

Phenotypes 1973
PN 622   SC 38200
  R   Assortative Mating 1991
       ↓ Genetics 1967
       Genotypes 1973

Phenoxybenzamine 1973
PN 73   SC 38210
  B   Adrenergic Blocking Drugs 1973
       Amines 1973
       Antihypertensive Drugs 1973

Phenylalanine 1973
PN 164   SC 38220
  B   Alanines 1973
  N   Parachlorophenylalanine 1978

Phenylethylamines
  Use Phenethylamines

Phenylketonuria 1973
PN 198   SC 38230
  UF   Oligophrenia (Phenylpyruvic)
       PKU (Hereditary Disorder)
  B   Genetic Disorders 1973
       Metabolism Disorders 1973
       Neonatal Disorders 1973
  R   ↓ Mental Retardation 1967

Phenytoin
  Use Diphenylhydantoin

Pheromones 1973
PN 799   SC 38240
SN Chemical substances released by an organism that may influence the behavior of other organisms of the same species in characteristic ways.
  R   ↓ Animal Mating Behavior 1967
       Animal Scent Marking 1985
       ↓ Glands 1967
       ↓ Hormones 1967

Phi Coefficient 1973
PN 22   SC 38250
  B   Statistical Correlation 1967

Philosophies 1967
PN 5135   SC 38270
  N   Animism 1973
       Asceticism 1973
       Determinism 1997
       Dualism 1973
       Epistemology 1973
       Existentialism 1967
       Fatalism 1973
       Hermeneutics 1991
       Humanism 1973
       Idealism 1973
       Intellectualism 1973
       Logic (Philosophy) 1973
       Materialism 1973
       Metaphysics 1973
       Mysticism 1967
       Nihilism 1973
       Pacifism 1973
       Phenomenology 1967
       Positivism (Philosophy) 1997
       Postmodernism 1997
       Pragmatism 1973
       Realism (Philosophy) 1973
       Reductionism 1973
       Relativism 1997
  R   Hedonism 1973

Philosophy of Life
  Use World View

Phobias 1967
PN 2639   SC 38280
SN Disorders characterized by persistent, unrealistic, intense fear of an object, activity, or situation. In 1988, this term replaced the discontinued term PHOBIC NEUROSIS. In 2000, PHOBIC NEUROSIS was stripped from all records and replaced with PHOBIAS.
  UF   Arachnophobia
       Phobic Neurosis
       Spider Phobia
  B   Anxiety Disorders 1997
  N   Acrophobia 1973
       Agoraphobia 1973
       Claustrophobia 1973
       Ophidiophobia 1973
       School Phobia 1973
       Social Phobia 1985
  R   ↓ Anxiety 1967
       ↓ Fear 1967

Phobic Neurosis
SN Term discontinued in 1988. In 2000, the term was stripped from all records containing it, and replaced with PHOBIAS, its postable counterpart.
  Use Phobias

Phonemes 1973
PN 1226   SC 38300
SN Members of the set of the smallest units of speech that serve to distinguish one utterance from another, such as the "p" of pat and the "f" of fat. Used both for the concept of phonemes as well as the discipline of phonemics. Compare PHONOLOGY.
  B   Phonology 1973
  N   Consonants 1973
  R   Phonetics 1967
       ↓ Prosody 1991
       Vowels 1973

Phonetics 1967
PN 1207   SC 38310

Phonetics — (cont'd)
SN Science, study, analysis, and classification of sounds including their production in speech, transmission and perception. Used for the linguistic discipline or the specific phonetic characteristics of utterances themselves.
B   Phonology 1973
R   Articulation (Speech) 1967
      Morphemes 1973
      ↓ Phonemes 1973
      Syllables 1973

Phonics 1973
PN 216   **SC** 38320
SN Science of sound. Also, a method of teaching beginners to read and pronounce words by hearing the phonetic value of letters, letter groups, and especially syllables.
B   Language Arts Education 1973
R   Reading Education 1973

Phonology 1973
PN 2812   **SC** 38330
SN Study of the ways in which speech sounds (phonemes) and phonetic features form systems and patterns at a given point in time or from a historical perspective. Used for the linguistic discipline or the specific phonological processes or factors themselves. Compare PHONEMES.
B   Grammar 1967
N   ↓ Phonemes 1973
      Phonetics 1967
      ↓ Prosody 1991
      Syllables 1973
      Vowels 1973
R   Inflection 1973
      Morphology (Language) 1973
      ↓ Semantics 1967
      ↓ Syntax 1971

Phosphatases 1973
PN 116   **SC** 38340
B   Enzymes 1973
R   ↓ Esterases 1973
      Hydroxylases 1973

Phosphatides 1973
PN 261   **SC** 38350
UF Phospholipids
B   Fatty Acids 1973
N   Lecithin 1991

Phospholipids
Use Phosphatides

Phosphorus 1973
PN 66   **SC** 38370

Phosphorylases 1973
PN 27   **SC** 38380
B   Enzymes 1973

Photic Threshold
Use Illumination AND Visual Thresholds

Photographic Art 1973
PN 54   **SC** 38400
B   Art 1967
R   Motion Pictures (Entertainment) 1973

Photographic Memory
Use Eidetic Imagery

Photographs 1967
PN 811   **SC** 38410
SN Use for photographs as stimuli. Not used as a document type identifier.
B   Audiovisual Communications Media 1973
R   Pictorial Stimuli 1978

Photopic Stimulation 1973
PN 249   **SC** 38420
SN Presentation of light at intensity levels characteristic of daylight illumination, activating cone photoreceptors in the retina.
B   Illumination 1967
R   Scotopic Stimulation 1973

Photoreceptors 1973
PN 383   **SC** 38430
B   Neural Receptors 1973
      Sensory Neurons 1973
N   Cones (Eye) 1973
      Rods (Eye) 1973
R   Visual Receptive Fields 1982

Phototherapy 1991
PN 337   **SC** 38435
UF Bright Light Therapy
      Illumination Therapy
B   Physical Treatment Methods 1973
R   ↓ Alternative Medicine 1997
      ↓ Psychotherapy 1967
      Seasonal Affective Disorder 1991

Phrases 1973
PN 217   **SC** 38440
SN Groups of words that function as an element in grammatical structure.
B   Language 1967
R   ↓ Syntax 1971

Phrenic Nerve
Use Spinal Nerves

Phylogenesis 1973
PN 241   **SC** 38460
R   ↓ Biology 1967
      Botany 1973

Physical Abuse 1991
PN 1726   **SC** 38465
B   Antisocial Behavior 1971
R   ↓ Abuse Reporting 1997
      Battered Child Syndrome 1973
      Battered Females 1988
      ↓ Child Abuse 1971
      Elder Abuse 1988
      Emotional Abuse 1991
      ↓ Family Violence 1982
      Partner Abuse 1991
      Patient Abuse 1991
      ↓ Sexual Abuse 1988
      ↓ Violence 1973

Physical Agility 1973
PN 95   **SC** 38470
UF Agility (Physical)
B   Motor Processes 1967
N   Physical Dexterity 1973
R   Motor Coordination 1973
      Physical Mobility 1994

Physical Appearance 1982
PN 671   **SC** 38473

Physical Appearance — (cont'd)
SN Externally visible characteristics or features of a person.
N   Physique 1967
R   Clothing 1967
      Cosmetic Techniques 2001
      Facial Features 1973
      Nudity 1973
      Physical Attractiveness 1973
      Somatotypes 1973

Physical Attractiveness 1973
PN 1619   **SC** 38475
R   Facial Features 1973
      Interpersonal Attraction 1967
      ↓ Physical Appearance 1982

Physical Comfort 1982
PN 203   **SC** 38477
SN Perceived degree of physical well-being in response to internal or environmental conditions.
UF Comfort (Physical)
R   ↓ Environment 1967
      Furniture 1985
      ↓ Satisfaction 1973

Physical Contact 1982
PN 848   **SC** 38478
SN Bodily contact. Used for human or animal populations.
UF Touching
B   Social Interaction 1967
R   Affection 1973
      ↓ Animal Social Behavior 1967
      Intimacy 1973
      Massage 2001
      Personal Space 1973
      ↓ Tactual Perception 1967

Physical Development 1973
PN 1845   **SC** 38480
UF Physical Growth
B   Development 1967
N   ↓ Motor Development 1973
      Neural Development 1985
      ↓ Prenatal Development 1973
      Sexual Development 1973
R   Adolescent Development 1973
      Age Differences 1967
      Aging (Attitudes Toward) 1985
      Animal Development 1978
      ↓ Childhood Development 1967
      ↓ Delayed Development 1973
      Developmental Age Groups 1973
      ↓ Developmental Stages 1973
      ↓ Early Childhood Development 1973
      Emotional Development 1973
      ↓ Human Development 1967
      ↓ Infant Development 1973
      Neonatal Development 1973
      ↓ Perceptual Development 1973
      Physical Maturity 1973
      Precocious Development 1973
      ↓ Psychogenesis 1973
      Sex Linked Developmental Differences 1973

Physical Dexterity 1973
PN 171   **SC** 38490
UF Dexterity (Physical)
B   Perceptual Motor Coordination 1973
      Physical Agility 1973
R   Physical Mobility 1994

Physical Disabilities (Attitudes Toward) [2001]
PN 600   **SC** 38485
SN In 2000, the truncated terms PHYSICAL DIS-
ABILITIES (ATTIT TOWARD) (which was used from
1997-2000) and PHYSICAL HANDICAPS (ATTIT
TOWARD) (which was used from 1973-1996) were
deleted, stripped from all records containing them,
and mapped to the expanded form PHYSICAL DIS-
ABILITIES (ATTITUDES TOWARD).
  UF   Physical Handicaps (Attitudes Toward)
  B   Disabled (Attitudes Toward) [1997]

Physical Disfigurement [1978]
PN 204   **SC** 38492
  UF   Deformity
  R   ↓ Injuries [1973]
        ↓ Physical Disorders [1997]

Physical Disorders [1997]
PN 3749   **SC** 38493
SN Consider DISORDERS to access references
prior to 1997. The term PHYSICALLY HANDI-
CAPPED was also used to represent this concept
from 1967-1996, and PHYSICALLY DISABLED was
used from 1997-2000. In 2000, PHYSICAL DISOR-
DERS replaced the discontinued and deleted term
PHYSICALLY DISABLED. PHYSICALLY DISABLED
and PHYSICALLY HANDICAPPED were stripped
from all records and replaced with PHYSICAL DIS-
ORDERS.
  UF   Illness (Physical)
        Orthopedically Handicapped
        Physical Illness
        Physically Handicapped
  B   Disorders [1967]
  N   ↓ Blood and Lymphatic Disorders [1973]
        ↓ Cardiovascular Disorders [1967]
        ↓ Digestive System Disorders [1973]
        ↓ Endocrine Disorders [1973]
        ↓ Genetic Disorders [1973]
        Health Impairments [2001]
        ↓ Immunologic Disorders [1973]
        ↓ Infectious Disorders [1973]
        ↓ Metabolism Disorders [1973]
        ↓ Musculoskeletal Disorders [1973]
        ↓ Neonatal Disorders [1973]
        ↓ Neoplasms [1967]
        ↓ Nervous System Disorders [1967]
        ↓ Nutritional Deficiencies [1973]
        ↓ Respiratory Tract Disorders [1973]
        ↓ Sense Organ Disorders [1973]
        ↓ Sensory System Disorders [2001]
        ↓ Skin Disorders [1973]
        ↓ Toxic Disorders [1973]
        ↓ Urogenital Disorders [1973]
        ↓ Vision Disorders [1982]
  R   Anesthesia (Feeling) [1973]
        Back Pain [1982]
        ↓ Chronic Illness [1991]
        Chronicity (Disorders) [1982]
        ↓ Communication Disorders [1982]
        Comorbidity [1991]
        ↓ Congenital Disorders [1973]
        ↓ Diagnosis [1967]
        Disease Course [1991]
        ↓ Eating Disorders [1997]
        ↓ Ethnospecific Disorders [1973]
        Etiology [1967]
        Illness Behavior [1982]
        ↓ Injuries [1973]
        ↓ Learning Disorders [1967]
        Malingering [1973]

Physical Disorders — (cont'd)
  R   ↓ Memory Disorders [1973]
        ↓ Mental Disorders [1967]
        Onset (Disorders) [1973]
        ↓ Pain [1967]
        Physical Disfigurement [1978]
        Predisposition [1973]
        Premorbidity [1978]
        Prenatal Exposure [1991]
        Prognosis [1973]
        Recovery (Disorders) [1973]
        Relapse (Disorders) [1973]
        ↓ Remission (Disorders) [1973]
        Rett Syndrome [1994]
        Severity (Disorders) [1982]
        ↓ Sexual Function Disturbances [1973]
        ↓ Sleep Disorders [1973]
        Special Needs [1994]
        Susceptibility (Disorders) [1973]
        ↓ Symptoms [1967]
        ↓ Syndromes [1973]
        ↓ Treatment Resistant Disorders [1994]
        Work Related Illnesses [1994]

Physical Divisions (Geographic)
  Use   Geography

Physical Education [1967]
PN 1514   **SC** 38500
  B   Curriculum [1967]

Physical Endurance [1973]
PN 262   **SC** 38510
  B   Endurance [1973]
  R   Physical Fitness [1973]
        Physical Strength [1973]
        Physiological Stress [1967]

Physical Examination [1988]
PN 409   **SC** 38515
SN Examination or screening of an individual's
overall physical health.
  B   Health Screening [1997]
  R   Cancer Screening [1997]
        Drug Usage Screening [1988]
        Mammography [1994]
        ↓ Medical Diagnosis [1973]
        Preventive Medicine [1973]
        Self Examination (Medical) [1988]

Physical Exercise
  Use   Exercise

Physical Fitness [1973]
PN 1273   **SC** 38530
  R   Aerobic Exercise [1988]
        ↓ Exercise [1973]
        Physical Endurance [1973]
        Physical Strength [1973]

Physical Geography
  Use   Geography

Physical Growth
  Use   Physical Development

Physical Handicaps (Attitudes Toward)
  SN The term was discontinued in 1997, when the
term PHYSICAL DISABILITIES (ATTIT TOWARD)
was created to capture this concept. In 2000, these
two truncated terms were deleted and mapped to
their expanded forms: PHYSICAL HANDICAPS
(ATTITUDES TOWARD) and PHYSICAL DISABILI-
TIES (ATTITUDES TOWARD). All records containing
the truncated versions of the terms were stripped of
these terms and replaced with PHYSICAL DISABILI-
TIES (ATTITUDES TOWARD), the valid postable version of the term.
  Use   Physical Disabilities (Attitudes Toward)

Physical Illness
  Use   Physical Disorders

Physical Illness (Attitudes Toward) [1985]
PN 1406   **SC** 38557
SN Attitudes toward one's own or other's physical ill-
ness.
  B   Attitudes [1967]
  N   AIDS (Attitudes Toward) [1997]
  R   Disability Discrimination [1997]
        ↓ Disabled (Attitudes Toward) [1997]
        Health Attitudes [1985]
        Health Knowledge [1994]
        Illness Behavior [1982]

Physical Maturity [1973]
PN 96   **SC** 38560
SN Attainment of a stage of physical development
commonly associated with persons of a given age
level.
  UF   Maturity (Physical)
  R   ↓ Physical Development [1973]

Physical Mobility [1994]
PN 233   **SC** 38563
SN Ability to move within one's environment. May
be used for mobility problems associated with aging
or handicapping conditions. Used for human popula-
tions only.
  B   Motor Processes [1967]
  R   Activities of Daily Living [1991]
        Activity Level [1982]
        Mobility Aids [1978]
        ↓ Motor Development [1973]
        ↓ Physical Agility [1973]
        Physical Dexterity [1973]

Physical Restraint [1982]
PN 931   **SC** 38566
SN Use of any physical means to restrict the move-
ment of a client or subject, human or animal.
  UF   Restraint (Physical)
  R   ↓ Motor Processes [1967]
        Patient Violence [1994]
        ↓ Physical Treatment Methods [1973]
        ↓ Treatment [1967]

Physical Strength [1973]
PN 432   **SC** 38570
  UF   Strength (Physical)
  R   Physical Endurance [1973]
        Physical Fitness [1973]

Physical Therapists [1973]
PN 113   **SC** 38580
  B   Medical Personnel [1967]
        Therapists [1967]

Physical Therapy [1973]
PN 471   SC 38590
SN Treatment of disorder or injury by physical means, such as light, heat, cold, water, electricity, or by mechanical apparatus or kinesitherapy.
- UF Physiotherapy
- B Paramedical Sciences [1973]
  Rehabilitation [1967]
- R Massage [2001]
  Occupational Therapy [1967]

Physical Trauma
Use Injuries

Physical Treatment Methods [1973]
PN 768   SC 38610
SN In 2000, this term became the postable counterpart for the discontinued term ORGANIC THERAPIES. ORGANIC THERAPIES was stripped from all records and replaced with PHYSICAL TREATMENT METHODS.
- UF Organic Therapies
  Treatment Methods (Physical)
- B Treatment [1967]
- N Acupuncture [1973]
  Artificial Respiration [1973]
  Blood Transfusion [1973]
  Catheterization [1973]
  ↓ Dental Treatment [1973]
  ↓ Dialysis [1973]
  ↓ Drug Therapy [1967]
  Electrosleep Treatment [1978]
  Immunization [1973]
  ↓ Narcoanalysis [1973]
  Phototherapy [1991]
  ↓ Psychosurgery [1973]
  Radiation Therapy [1973]
  ↓ Shock Therapy [1973]
  ↓ Surgery [1971]
- R ↓ Alternative Medicine [1997]
  Holistic Health [1985]
  Massage [2001]
  Medical Treatment (General) [1973]
  Pain Management [1994]
  Physical Restraint [1982]

Physically Handicapped
SN The term was discontinued in 1997, when the term PHYSICALLY DISABLED was created to capture this concept. In 2000, with the deletion of the term PHYSICALLY DISABLED, PHYSICALLY HANDICAPPED was made a nonpostable term for the postable term PHYSICAL DISORDERS. PHYSICALLY DISABLED and PHYSICALLY HANDICAPPED were stripped from all records containing them and replaced with PHYSICAL DISORDERS.
Use Physical Disorders

Physician Patient Interaction
Use Therapeutic Processes

Physicians [1967]
PN 5144   SC 38640
- UF Doctors
- B Medical Personnel [1967]
- N Family Physicians [1973]
  General Practitioners [1973]
  Gynecologists [1973]
  Internists [1973]
  Neurologists [1973]
  Obstetricians [1978]
  Pathologists [1973]
  Pediatricians [1973]
  Psychiatrists [1967]

Physicians — (cont'd)
- N Surgeons [1973]
- R Clinicians [1973]

Physicists [1973]
PN 31   SC 38650
- B Professional Personnel [1978]
- R ↓ Aerospace Personnel [1973]
  Mathematicians [1973]
  Scientists [1967]

Physics [1973]
PN 765   SC 38660
- B Sciences [1967]
- R Magnetism [1985]
  Relativism [1997]

Physiological Aging [1967]
PN 3555   SC 38670
SN Biological changes which occur in an organism with the passage of time.
- UF Aging (Physiological)
- B Aging [1991]
- R Adult Development [1978]
  Aged (Attitudes Toward) [1978]
  Aging (Attitudes Toward) [1985]
  Geriatric Psychotherapy [1973]
  Geriatrics [1967]
  Life Expectancy [1982]
  ↓ Physiology [1967]
  ↓ Senile Dementia [1973]

Physiological Arousal [1967]
PN 3870   SC 38680
SN Condition of alertness and readiness to respond as evidenced by physiological signs such as heart rate or blood pressure.
- UF Arousal (Physiological)
  Excitation (Physiological)
- R ↓ Brain Stimulation [1967]
  Cardiovascular Reactivity [1994]
  ↓ Consciousness States [1971]
  Physiological Stress [1967]
  ↓ Physiology [1967]
  ↓ Sexual Arousal [1978]

Physiological Correlates [1967]
PN 6957   SC 38690
SN Numerous or unspecified physiological processes which accompany a particular psychological or physical action, state, or characteristic.
- R Biological Markers [1991]
  Cardiovascular Reactivity [1994]
  Physiological Stress [1967]
  ↓ Physiology [1967]
  ↓ Symptoms [1967]

Physiological Psychology [1967]
PN 473   SC 38700
SN Branch of psychology concerned with the physiological correlates of cognitive, emotional, and behavioral processes. Use PHYSIOLOGY, PSYCHOPHYSIOLOGY, or a more specific term for the specific physiological processes themselves.
- B Psychology [1967]
- N Neuropsychology [1973]
- R ↓ Psychophysiology [1967]

Physiological Stress [1967]
PN 1973   SC 38710
- B Stress [1967]
- R Acceleration Effects [1973]
  Decompression Effects [1973]
  ↓ Deprivation [1967]

Physiological Stress — (cont'd)
- R ↓ Environmental Effects [1973]
  Environmental Stress [1973]
  Physical Endurance [1973]
  Physiological Arousal [1967]
  Physiological Correlates [1967]
  ↓ Physiology [1967]
  Pollution [1973]
  Thermal Acclimatization [1973]

Physiology [1967]
PN 1945   SC 38720
SN Conceptually broad term referring both to a branch of biological science and the functions and processes of living organisms. Use a more specific term if possible.
- N Absorption (Physiological) [1973]
  ↓ Appetite [1973]
  ↓ Body Temperature [1973]
  Digestion [1973]
  ↓ Electrophysiology [1973]
  ↓ Excretion [1967]
  Homeostasis [1973]
  ↓ Ingestion [2001]
  ↓ Metabolism [1967]
  ↓ Neurophysiology [1973]
  Oxygenation [1973]
  ↓ Psychophysiology [1967]
  ↓ Reflexes [1971]
  ↓ Secretion (Gland) [1973]
  ↓ Sexual Reproduction [1973]
  Thermal Acclimatization [1973]
- R ↓ Anatomy [1967]
  ↓ Biochemistry [1967]
  ↓ Body Fluids [1973]
  ↓ Cells (Biology) [1973]
  Histology [1973]
  Instinctive Behavior [1982]
  Metabolic Rates [1973]
  Morphology [1973]
  Nutrition [1973]
  Physiological Aging [1967]
  Physiological Arousal [1967]
  Physiological Correlates [1967]
  Physiological Stress [1967]

Physiotherapy
Use Physical Therapy

Physique [1967]
PN 511   SC 38740
SN Overall body structure and appearance, including size, musculature, and posture. Limited primarily to human populations. Consider also BODY SIZE or SOMATOTYPES.
- B Physical Appearance [1982]
- R Body Height [1973]
  ↓ Body Size [1985]
  ↓ Body Weight [1967]
  Posture [1973]
  Somatotypes [1973]

Physostigmine [1973]
PN 547   SC 38750
- UF Eserine
- B Alkaloids [1973]
  Amines [1973]
  Cholinergic Drugs [1973]
  Cholinesterase Inhibitors [1973]
  Cholinomimetic Drugs [1973]

Piaget (Jean) [1967]
PN 1253   SC 38755

Piaget (Jean) — (cont'd)
SN   Identifies biographical or autobiographical studies and discussions of Piaget's works.
   R   ↓ Cognitive Development   1973
        Conservation (Concept)   1973
        Constructivism   1994
        ↓ Developmental Stages   1973
        Piagetian Tasks   1973
        ↓ Psychologists   1967

Piagetian Tasks   1973
PN   795   SC   38757
SN   In measurement context, tasks used to assess children's cognitive abilities, based on Piaget's theory of cognitive development.
   R   ↓ Measurement   1967
        Piaget (Jean)   1967

Piano
   Use   Musical Instruments

Pica   1973
PN   117   SC   38770
   B   Eating Disorders   1997
   R   ↓ Adjunctive Behavior   1982
        Coprophagia   2001
        ↓ Ingestion   2001
        Lead Poisoning   1973
        Toxicomania   1973

Picketing
   Use   Social Demonstrations

Picks Disease   1973
PN   117   SC   38790
   B   Presenile Dementia   1973
   R   Alzheimers Disease   1973
        ↓ Dementia   1985
        ↓ Genetic Disorders   1973

Picrotoxin   1973
PN   214   SC   38800
   B   Analeptic Drugs   1973
        Gamma Aminobutyric Acid Antagonists   1985

Pictorial Stimuli   1978
PN   3539   SC   38805
SN   Drawings, pictures, or other visual stimuli not composed of letters or digits.
   R   Photographs   1967
        ↓ Stimulus Presentation Methods   1973
        ↓ Visual Displays   1973
        ↓ Visual Stimulation   1973

Piercings
   Use   Cosmetic Techniques

Pigeons   1967
PN   4911   SC   38810
   B   Birds   1967

Pigments   1973
PN   252   SC   38820
   N   Hemoglobin   1973
        Melanin   1973
        Rhodopsin   1985
   R   Animal Coloration   1985
        ↓ Color   1967
        Eye Color   1991

Pigs   1973
PN   636   SC   38830

Pigs — (cont'd)
   B   Vertebrates   1973

Pilocarpine   1973
PN   152   SC   38840
   B   Alkaloids   1973
        Cholinergic Drugs   1973
        Cholinomimetic Drugs   1973

Pilots (Aircraft)
   Use   Aircraft Pilots

Pimozide   1973
PN   447   SC   38860
   B   Tranquilizing Drugs   1967

Pineal Body   1973
PN   240   SC   38870
   B   Endocrine Glands   1973
   R   Melatonin   1973

Pinealectomy   1973
PN   74   SC   38880
   B   Endocrine Gland Surgery   1973

Piperazines   1994
PN   110   SC   38885
   UF   Chlorophenylpiperazine
        MCPP
   N   Trazodone   1988

Pipradrol   1973
PN   14   SC   38890
   B   Antidepressant Drugs   1971
        CNS Stimulating Drugs   1973

Piracetam   1982
PN   157   SC   38900
   B   Antiemetic Drugs   1973
        CNS Stimulating Drugs   1973
        Nootropic Drugs   1991

Pitch (Frequency)   1967
PN   2286   SC   38910
SN   Perceived changes in auditory stimuli that are a function of the sound's frequency usually measured in hertz. Also, in linguistics, a phonetic element marking the fundamental frequency of a component of speech.
   UF   Frequency (Pitch)
        Tone (Frequency)
   B   Auditory Stimulation   1967
   N   Speech Pitch   1973
        Ultrasound   1973

Pitch Discrimination   1973
PN   575   SC   38920
   B   Pitch Perception   1973

Pitch Perception   1973
PN   457   SC   38930
   B   Auditory Perception   1967
   N   Pitch Discrimination   1973
   R   Music Perception   1997

Pituitary Disorders   1973
PN   51   SC   38940
   UF   Hypophysis Disorders
   B   Endocrine Disorders   1973
   N   Hypopituitarism   1973
   R   ↓ Adrenal Gland Disorders   1973
        ↓ Endocrine Sexual Disorders   1973

Pituitary Disorders — (cont'd)
   R   ↓ Thyroid Disorders   1973

Pituitary Dwarfism
   Use   Hypopituitarism

Pituitary Gland   1973
PN   366   SC   38960
   B   Endocrine Glands   1973
   N   Hypothalamo Hypophyseal System   1973
        Hypothalamo Pituitary Adrenal System   1997

Pituitary Gland Surgery
   Use   Hypophysectomy

Pituitary Hormones   1973
PN   265   SC   38980
   B   Hormones   1967
   N   Corticotropin   1973
        Dynorphins   1985
        Melanocyte Stimulating Hormone   1985
        Oxytocin   1973
        Somatotropin   1973
        Thyrotropin   1973
        Vasopressin   1973
   R   ↓ Gonadotropic Hormones   1973
        Hypothalamo Hypophyseal System   1973
        Luteinizing Hormone   1978

PKU (Hereditary Disorder)
   Use   Phenylketonuria

Place Conditioning   1991
PN   506   SC   39005
SN   Learned behavior or the conditioning procedure in which a stimulus is paired with an environment, location, or physical position.
   UF   Conditioned Place Preference
   B   Conditioning   1967
   R   ↓ Animal Environments   1967
        Contextual Associations   1967

Place Disorientation   1973
PN   52   SC   39010
SN   Impaired awareness of place, often characteristic of organic mental disorders.
   UF   Disorientation (Place)
   B   Consciousness Disturbances   1973
   R   Wandering Behavior   1991

Placebo   1973
PN   941   SC   39020
SN   Any effect of therapeutic intervention that cannot be attributed to the specific action of a drug or the treatment. Also, the specific substance used as a control in experiments testing the effect of a particular drug. Term is used selectively for studies of the placebo effect or other methodological issues.
   R   ↓ Drugs   1967

Placement (Educational)
   Use   Educational Placement

Placement (Personnel)
   Use   Personnel Placement

Placenta   1973
PN   62   SC   39040
   R   ↓ Pregnancy   1967
        ↓ Uterus   1973

Planarians 1973
PN 31   SC 39060
  B   Worms 1967

Planned Behavior 1997
PN 233   SC 39065
SN Based on I. Ajzen's theory that behavioral intentions are determined by one's perceived control over the behavior, attitude toward the behavior, and subjective norms.
  R   ↓ Attitudes 1967
      ↓ Behavior 1967
      Intention 1988
      ↓ Motivation 1967

Planning (Management)
  Use   Management Planning

Plasma (Blood)
  Use   Blood Plasma

Plastic Surgery 1973
PN 135   SC 39090
  B   Surgery 1971
  R   Cosmetic Techniques 2001

Platelets (Blood)
  Use   Blood Platelets

Play
  Use   Recreation

Play (Animal)
  Use   Animal Play

Play Behavior (Childhood)
  Use   Childhood Play Behavior

Play Development (Childhood)
  Use   Childhood Play Development

Play Therapy 1973
PN 980   SC 39150
  B   Child Psychotherapy 1967

Playgrounds 1973
PN 129   SC 39160
  B   Recreation Areas 1973
  R   ↓ School Facilities 1973

Pleasure 1973
PN 738   SC 39170
  UF   Enjoyment
  B   Emotional States 1973
  R   Anhedonia 1985
      Euphoria 1973
      Happiness 1973

Plethysmography 1973
PN 72   SC 39180
  B   Medical Diagnosis 1973
  N   Electroplethysmography 1973

PMS
  Use   Premenstrual Tension

Pneumoencephalography 1973
PN 28   SC 39190
  UF   Air Encephalography
      Encephalography (Air)
  B   Encephalography 1973

Pneumoencephalography — (cont'd)
  B   Medical Diagnosis 1973
      Roentgenography 1973

Pneumonia 1973
PN 49   SC 39200
  B   Lung Disorders 1973
  R   ↓ Bacterial Disorders 1973
      ↓ Viral Disorders 1973

Poetry 1973
PN 901   SC 39210
  B   Literature 1967
  R   Creative Writing 1994

Poetry Therapy 1994
PN 38   SC 39215
  B   Creative Arts Therapy 1994
  R   Bibliotherapy 1973
      ↓ Psychotherapeutic Techniques 1967

Point Biserial Correlation 1973
PN 20   SC 39220
  B   Statistical Correlation 1967

Poisoning
  Use   Toxic Disorders

Poisons 1973
PN 458   SC 39240
  UF   Toxins
  B   Hazardous Materials 1991
  N   ↓ Neurotoxins 1982
  R   Carbon Monoxide 1973
      ↓ Insecticides 1973
      Prenatal Exposure 1991
      Teratogens 1988

Poisson Distribution
  Use   Skewed Distribution

Police Interrogation
  Use   Legal Interrogation

Police Personnel 1973
PN 2403   SC 39270
  B   Government Personnel 1973
      Law Enforcement Personnel 1973

Policy Making 1988
PN 1931   SC 39278
  UF   Organizational Policy Making
  N   ↓ Government Policy Making 1973
      Health Care Policy 1994
  R   Educational Reform 1997

Policy Making (Foreign)
  Use   Foreign Policy Making

Policy Making (Government)
  Use   Government Policy Making

Poliomyelitis 1973
PN 53   SC 39300
  UF   Infantile Paralysis
      Paralysis (Infantile)
  B   Myelitis 1973
      Viral Disorders 1973
  R   ↓ Musculoskeletal Disorders 1973
      ↓ Paralysis 1973
      ↓ Respiratory Tract Disorders 1973

Political Assassination 1973
PN 68   SC 39320
  UF   Assassination (Political)

Political Attitudes 1973
PN 2631   SC 39330
  B   Attitudes 1967
      Politics 1967
  N   Nationalism 1967
      Political Conservatism 1973
      Political Liberalism 1973
      Political Radicalism 1973
  R   Citizenship 1973
      Nonviolence 1991
      Political Socialization 1988
      Voting Behavior 1973

Political Campaigns 1973
PN 262   SC 39340
  UF   Campaigns (Political)
  B   Political Processes 1973
  R   Debates 1997
      Political Candidates 1973
      Political Elections 1973
      Political Issues 1973
      Political Parties 1973
      Politicians 1978

Political Candidates 1973
PN 395   SC 39350
  UF   Candidates (Political)
  B   Politics 1967
  R   Debates 1997
      Political Campaigns 1973
      Political Elections 1973
      Politicians 1978

Political Conservatism 1973
PN 250   SC 39360
  UF   Conservatism (Political)
  B   Political Attitudes 1973
  R   Conservatism 1973

Political Debates
  Use   Debates

Political Divisions (Geographic)
  Use   Geography

Political Economic Systems 1973
PN 345   SC 39370
  B   Systems 1967
  N   Capitalism 1973
      Communism 1973
      Democracy 1973
      Fascism 1973
      Socialism 1973
      Totalitarianism 1973
  R   Economics 1985
      Economy 1973
      Government 1967
      Political Psychology 1997

Political Elections 1973
PN 379   SC 39380
  UF   Elections (Political)
  B   Political Processes 1973
  R   Debates 1997
      Political Campaigns 1973
      Political Candidates 1973
      Political Parties 1973
      Politicians 1978

Political Elections — (cont'd)
  R   Voting Behavior [1973]

Political Involvement
  Use Political Participation

Political Issues [1973]
PN 615   **SC** 39390
  B   Politics [1967]
  R   Political Campaigns [1973]
      ↓ Social Issues [1991]
      Voting Behavior [1973]

Political Liberalism [1973]
PN 194   **SC** 39400
  UF Liberalism (Political)
  B   Political Attitudes [1973]
  R   Liberalism [1973]

Political Participation [1988]
PN 349   **SC** 39405
  UF Political Involvement
  B   Politics [1967]
  N   Voting Behavior [1973]
  R   Political Psychology [1997]
      Social Demonstrations [1973]
      ↓ Social Movements [1967]

Political Parties [1973]
PN 319   **SC** 39410
  UF Democratic Party
      Independent Party (Political)
      Republican Party
  B   Politics [1967]
  R   Political Campaigns [1973]
      Political Elections [1973]

Political Processes [1973]
PN 1069   **SC** 39420
  B   Politics [1967]
  N   Political Campaigns [1973]
      Political Elections [1973]
      Voting Behavior [1973]
  R   Debates [1997]
      Freedom [1978]
      Political Psychology [1997]
      Political Revolution [1973]
      ↓ Social Processes [1967]

Political Psychology [1997]
PN 73   **SC** 39425
  B   Applied Psychology [1973]
  R   ↓ Law (Government) [1973]
      ↓ Political Economic Systems [1973]
      ↓ Political Participation [1988]
      ↓ Political Processes [1973]
      ↓ Politics [1967]
      Public Opinion [1973]
      Voting Behavior [1973]

Political Radicalism [1973]
PN 132   **SC** 39430
  UF Radicalism (Political)
  B   Political Attitudes [1973]

Political Refugees
  Use Refugees

Political Revolution [1973]
PN 141   **SC** 39440
  UF Revolutions (Political)
  B   Radical Movements [1973]

Political Revolution — (cont'd)
  R   ↓ Political Processes [1973]
      Terrorism [1982]

Political Socialization [1988]
PN 138   **SC** 39443
SN Transmission of political norms through social agents, e.g., school, parents, peers, or mass media.
  B   Socialization [1967]
  R   ↓ Political Attitudes [1973]

Politicians [1978]
PN 746   **SC** 39445
  R   Political Campaigns [1973]
      Political Candidates [1973]
      Political Elections [1973]
      ↓ Politics [1967]

Politics [1967]
PN 2204   **SC** 39450
  N   ↓ Political Attitudes [1973]
      Political Candidates [1973]
      Political Issues [1973]
      ↓ Political Participation [1988]
      Political Parties [1973]
      ↓ Political Processes [1973]
  R   Government [1967]
      Political Psychology [1997]
      Politicians [1978]

Pollution [1973]
PN 350   **SC** 39460
  B   Ecological Factors [1973]
  R   Atmospheric Conditions [1973]
      Carcinogens [1973]
      Ecology [1973]
      Environmental Education [1994]
      ↓ Hazardous Materials [1991]
      Noise Effects [1973]
      Physiological Stress [1967]
      ↓ Temperature Effects [1967]

Polydipsia [1982]
PN 406   **SC** 39465
SN Noncontingent excessive drinking behavior usually produced and maintained by operant schedules of reinforcement involving food as a reinforcer. Also used for disordered human populations.
  B   Adjunctive Behavior [1982]
  R   Animal Drinking Behavior [1973]
      Hyponatremia [1997]
      ↓ Operant Conditioning [1967]

Polydrug Abuse [1994]
PN 173   **SC** 39467
  UF Multidrug Abuse
  B   Drug Abuse [1973]
  R   ↓ Alcohol Abuse [1988]
      ↓ Drug Addiction [1967]
      ↓ Drug Dependency [1973]
      Drug Interactions [1982]

Polygamy [1973]
PN 104   **SC** 39470
SN Used for human or animal populations.
  B   Family Structure [1973]
      Marriage [1967]
  R   Monogamy [1997]

Polygraphs [1973]
PN 271   **SC** 39480
  B   Apparatus [1967]
  R   Legal Interrogation [1994]

Polyphagia
  Use Hyperphagia

Pons [1973]
PN 548   **SC** 39510
  B   Brain Stem [1973]
      Hindbrain [1997]
  N   Raphe Nuclei [1982]

Popularity [1988]
PN 272   **SC** 39520
SN Use SOCIAL APPROVAL to access references from 1973-1987.
  R   ↓ Interpersonal Interaction [1967]
      Reputation [1997]
      Social Acceptance [1967]
      Social Approval [1967]
      ↓ Social Influences [1967]
      ↓ Social Perception [1967]

Population [1973]
PN 390   **SC** 39530
SN Total number of organisms (human or animal) inhabiting a given locality.
  N   Overpopulation [1973]
      ↓ Population (Statistics) [1973]
  R   Birth Rate [1982]
      Demographic Characteristics [1967]
      Mortality Rate [1973]
      Social Density [1978]

Population (Statistics) [1973]
PN 687   **SC** 39540
SN All the objects or people of a given class.
  B   Population [1973]
  N   ↓ Statistical Samples [1973]
  R   ↓ Central Tendency Measures [1973]
      ↓ Experimental Design [1967]
      ↓ Experimentation [1967]
      ↓ Sampling (Experimental) [1973]
      ↓ Statistical Analysis [1967]
      Statistical Reliability [1973]
      ↓ Statistical Variables [1973]

Population Characteristics
  Use Demographic Characteristics

Population Control
  Use Birth Control

Population Density
  Use Social Density

Population Genetics [1973]
PN 137   **SC** 39570
SN Study of the genetic composition of human or animal populations; gene interactions and alterations that promote population changes and evolution.
  B   Genetics [1967]
  R   Assortative Mating [1991]
      Behavioral Genetics [1994]
      ↓ Genetic Engineering [1994]

Population Shifts
  Use Human Migration

Pornography [1973]
PN 474   **SC** 39580
  UF X Rated Materials
  R   Nudity [1973]
      Obscenity [1978]
      ↓ Paraphilias [1988]
      ↓ Psychosexual Behavior [1967]

Pornography — (cont'd)
R   Sex ¹⁹⁶⁷ → N/A

R   Sex ¹⁹⁶⁷
↓ Sex Offenses ¹⁹⁸²

Porphyria ¹⁹⁷³
PN   38   SC   39590
B   Blood and Lymphatic Disorders ¹⁹⁷³
    Genetic Disorders ¹⁹⁷³
    Metabolism Disorders ¹⁹⁷³
R   ↓ Mental Disorders ¹⁹⁶⁷

Porpoises ¹⁹⁷³
PN   8   SC   39600
B   Whales ¹⁹⁸⁵
R   Dolphins ¹⁹⁷³

Porteus Maze Test ¹⁹⁷³
PN   21   SC   39610
B   Intelligence Measures ¹⁹⁶⁷

Positive and Negative Symptoms ¹⁹⁹⁷
PN   524   SC   39618
UF   Negative and Positive Symptoms
B   Symptoms ¹⁹⁶⁷
R   ↓ Schizophrenia ¹⁹⁶⁷

Positive Reinforcement ¹⁹⁷³
PN   905   SC   39620
SN   Presentation of a positive reinforcer contingent on the performance of some behavior. Also, the positively reinforcing object or event itself which, when made to follow the performance of some behavior, results in an increase in the frequency of occurrence of that behavior. Compare REWARDS.
B   Reinforcement ¹⁹⁶⁷
N   Praise ¹⁹⁷³

Positive Transfer ¹⁹⁷³
PN   170   SC   39630
SN   Previous learning or practice which aids the acquisition of new material or skills as the result of common characteristics shared by the prior and current learning situation.
B   Transfer (Learning) ¹⁹⁶⁷

Positivism ¹⁹⁷³
PN   267   SC   39640
SN   Personal quality or state of being positive or confident. Compare OPTIMISM.
B   Personality Traits ¹⁹⁶⁷
R   Determinism ¹⁹⁹⁷
    Hope ¹⁹⁹¹
    Optimism ¹⁹⁷³

Positivism (Philosophy) ¹⁹⁹⁷
PN   23   SC   39642
SN   Philosophical view that scientific knowledge comes only from direct observation and application of empirical methods.
B   Philosophies ¹⁹⁶⁷
R   Behaviorism ¹⁹⁶⁷
    ↓ Empirical Methods ¹⁹⁷³
    Epistemology ¹⁹⁷³
    Hermeneutics ¹⁹⁹¹
    Reductionism ¹⁹⁷³

Positron Emission Tomography
Use   Tomography

Possession
Use   Ownership

Postactivation Potentials ¹⁹⁸⁵
PN   565   SC   39650
SN   Enhancement of synaptic and cellular responses induced by brief high frequency electrical stimulation.
UF   Long Term Potentiation
    Short Term Potentiation
B   Electrical Activity ¹⁹⁶⁷
R   Electrical Brain Stimulation ¹⁹⁷³
    Neural Plasticity ¹⁹⁹⁴

Postganglionic Autonomic Fibers
Use   Autonomic Ganglia

Postgraduate Students ¹⁹⁷³
PN   143   SC   39684
SN   Students involved in study or research after having completed a master's or doctoral degree. Such students are not necessarily pursuing a degree. Mandatory term in educational contexts.
B   Students ¹⁹⁶⁷
R   ↓ College Students ¹⁹⁶⁷
    Graduate Students ¹⁹⁶⁷

Postgraduate Training ¹⁹⁷³
PN   284   SC   39685
SN   Studies or research beyond master's or doctoral degree.
B   Higher Education ¹⁹⁷³
N   ↓ Clinical Psychology Graduate Training ²⁰⁰¹
    Clinical Psychology Internship ¹⁹⁷³
    Medical Internship ¹⁹⁷³
    Medical Residency ¹⁹⁷³
R   Professional Specialization ¹⁹⁹¹

Posthypnotic Suggestions ¹⁹⁹⁴
PN   61   SC   39687
R   ↓ Hypnosis ¹⁹⁶⁷
    ↓ Hypnotherapy ¹⁹⁷³
    Hypnotic Susceptibility ¹⁹⁷³
    ↓ Relaxation Therapy ¹⁹⁷⁸
    Suggestibility ¹⁹⁶⁷

Postmodernism ¹⁹⁹⁷
PN   357   SC   39689
B   Philosophies ¹⁹⁶⁷
R   ↓ Arts ¹⁹⁷³
    ↓ Literature ¹⁹⁶⁷

Postnatal Dysphoria
Use   Postpartum Depression

Postnatal Period ¹⁹⁷³
PN   1650   SC   39690
R   Lactation ¹⁹⁷³
    Perinatal Period ¹⁹⁹⁴
    Postpartum Depression ¹⁹⁷³
    ↓ Pregnancy ¹⁹⁶⁷

Postpartum Depression ¹⁹⁷³
PN   812   SC   39700
UF   Postnatal Dysphoria
    Postpartum Psychosis
B   Major Depression ¹⁹⁸⁸
R   ↓ Acute Psychosis ¹⁹⁷³
    Acute Schizophrenia ¹⁹⁷³
    Attachment Behavior ¹⁹⁸⁵
    ↓ Marital Relations ¹⁹⁶⁷
    Mother Child Relations ¹⁹⁶⁷
    ↓ Organic Brain Syndromes ¹⁹⁷³
    Postnatal Period ¹⁹⁷³

Postpartum Psychosis
Use   Postpartum Depression

Postsurgical Complications ¹⁹⁷³
PN   215   SC   39710
UF   Surgical Complications
R   Obstetrical Complications ¹⁹⁷⁸
    Recovery (Disorders) ¹⁹⁷³
    Relapse (Disorders) ¹⁹⁷³
    ↓ Surgery ¹⁹⁷¹
    ↓ Treatment Outcomes ¹⁹⁸²

Posttesting ¹⁹⁷³
PN   105   SC   39720
SN   Measurement performed after experimental manipulation, treatment, or program intervention. Comparison of pretest and posttest scores gives a measure of effectiveness of independent variables such as treatments or programs.
B   Measurement ¹⁹⁶⁷
R   Repeated Measures ¹⁹⁸⁵
    ↓ Testing Methods ¹⁹⁶⁷

Posttraumatic Stress Disorder ¹⁹⁸⁵
PN   5183   SC   39727
SN   Acute, chronic, or delayed reactions to traumatic events such as military combat, assault, or natural disaster. Use TRAUMATIC NEUROSIS or STRESS REACTIONS to access references from 1973-1984.
B   Anxiety Disorders ¹⁹⁹⁷
R   Adjustment Disorders ¹⁹⁹⁴
    Combat Experience ¹⁹⁹¹
    Emotional Trauma ¹⁹⁶⁷
    Stress Reactions ¹⁹⁷³
    Traumatic Neurosis ¹⁹⁷³

Posttreatment Followup ¹⁹⁷³
PN   800   SC   39730
SN   Periodic check-ups of patients. Usually part of a comprehensive aftercare treatment. Differentiate from FOLLOWUP STUDIES which is a mandatory term identifying a type of methodology used in research.
UF   Catamnesis
    Followup (Posttreatment)
R   Aftercare ¹⁹⁷³
    Discharge Planning ¹⁹⁹⁴
    ↓ Treatment ¹⁹⁶⁷
    ↓ Treatment Planning ¹⁹⁹⁷

Posture ¹⁹⁷³
PN   1307   SC   39740
R   Body Language ¹⁹⁷³
    ↓ Motor Processes ¹⁹⁶⁷
    Physique ¹⁹⁶⁷

Potassium ¹⁹⁷³
PN   219   SC   39750
B   Metallic Elements ¹⁹⁷³
N   Potassium Ions ¹⁹⁷³

Potassium Ions ¹⁹⁷³
PN   74   SC   39770
B   Electrolytes ¹⁹⁷³
    Potassium ¹⁹⁷³

Potential (Achievement)
Use   Achievement Potential

Potential Dropouts ¹⁹⁷³
PN   142   SC   39790
B   Dropouts ¹⁹⁷³

Potentiation (Drugs)
Use Drug Interactions

Poverty 1973
PN 1203   **SC** 39820
B Social Issues 1991
R Disadvantaged 1967
   ↓ Homeless 1988
   Income (Economic) 1973
   Lower Income Level 1973
   ↓ Socioeconomic Status 1967

Poverty Areas 1973
PN 108   **SC** 39830
UF Slums
B Social Environments 1973
R Cultural Deprivation 1973
   Ghettoes 1973

Power 1967
PN 3961   **SC** 39840
SN Social control an individual has over others.
B Social Influences 1967
N Abuse of Power 1997
R Authority 1967
   Coercion 1994
   ↓ Dominance 1967
   Empowerment 1991
   ↓ Helplessness 1997
   Omnipotence 1994

Practical Knowledge
Use Procedural Knowledge

Practice 1967
PN 4487   **SC** 39850
SN In 1982, this term replaced the discontinued term PRACTICE EFFECTS. In 2000, PRACTICE EFFECTS was stripped from all records and replaced with PRACTICE.
UF Experience (Practice)
   Practice Effects
   Rehearsal
N Distributed Practice 1973
   Massed Practice 1973
R Curricular Field Experience 1982
   ↓ Experiences (Events) 1973
   Familiarity 1967
   Memory Training 1994
   Overcorrection 1985
   Test Coaching 1997

Practice Effects
SN Term discontinued in 1982. In 2000, the term was stripped from all records containing it, and replaced with PRACTICE, its postable counterpart.
Use Practice

Practicum Supervision 1978
PN 827   **SC** 39865
SN Supervision of students involved in practical application of learned material.
R ↓ Clinical Methods Training 1973
   ↓ Clinical Psychology Graduate Training 2001
   Clinical Psychology Internship 1973
   Cooperating Teachers 1978
   Counselor Education 1973
   ↓ Teacher Education 1967

Prader Willi Syndrome 1991
PN 102   **SC** 39867
B Congenital Disorders 1973
   Syndromes 1973

Prader Willi Syndrome — (cont'd)
R ↓ Mental Retardation 1967

Pragmatics 1985
PN 898   **SC** 39868
SN Study of the rules governing the use of language in context. Also used for the actual social interaction aspects of communication.
B Semiotics 1985
   Verbal Communication 1967
R ↓ Communication Skills 1973
   Discourse Analysis 1997
   ↓ Interpersonal Communication 1973
   ↓ Linguistics 1973
   Metalinguistics 1994

Pragmatism 1973
PN 119   **SC** 39870
B Philosophies 1967

Praise 1973
PN 502   **SC** 39880
B Positive Reinforcement 1973
   Verbal Reinforcement 1973

Prayer 1973
PN 139   **SC** 39890
B Religious Practices 1973
R Meditation 1973

Praying Mantis
Use Mantis

Precocious Development 1973
PN 91   **SC** 39910
B Development 1967
R Developmental Age Groups 1973
   ↓ Physical Development 1973
   ↓ Psychogenesis 1973

Precognition 1973
PN 124   **SC** 39920
B Clairvoyance 1973

Preconditioning 1994
PN 22   **SC** 39923
SN Presentation of two stimuli in a consecutive manner without reinforcement to determine if a subject will respond to both stimuli in a conditioning paradigm.
UF Sensory Preconditioning
B Conditioning 1967
R Conditioned Stimulus 1973

Predatory Behavior (Animal)
Use Animal Predatory Behavior

Predelinquent Youth 1978
PN 107   **SC** 39927
SN Children considered at risk for developing delinquent behavior because their sociocultural and family backgrounds and early behavior patterns parallel those of juvenile delinquents.
R ↓ Juvenile Delinquency 1967

Predictability (Measurement) 1973
PN 271   **SC** 39930
SN Statistical procedures used to forecast the value of the criterion variables (such as behavior, performance, or outcomes) on the basis of selected predictor variables.
B Statistical Analysis 1967
   Statistical Measurement 1973

Predictability (Measurement) — (cont'd)
R Chaos Theory 1997
   Confidence Limits (Statistics) 1973
   ↓ Hypothesis Testing 1973
   ↓ Prediction 1967
   ↓ Prediction Errors 1973
   ↓ Probability 1967
   ↓ Statistical Estimation 1985

Prediction 1967
PN 8602   **SC** 39940
N Academic Achievement Prediction 1967
   Occupational Success Prediction 1973
R Chaos Theory 1997
   ↓ Estimation 1967
   Future 1991
   Predictability (Measurement) 1973
   ↓ Prediction Errors 1973
   Prognosis 1973
   Self Fulfilling Prophecies 1997

Prediction Errors 1973
PN 85   **SC** 39950
B Errors 1967
N Type I Errors 1973
   Type II Errors 1973
R Consistency (Measurement) 1973
   ↓ Hypothesis Testing 1973
   ↓ Measurement 1967
   Predictability (Measurement) 1973
   ↓ Prediction 1967
   ↓ Statistical Analysis 1967
   Statistical Power 1991
   Statistical Reliability 1973
   Statistical Validity 1973
   ↓ Statistical Variables 1973

Predictive Validity
SN In 2000, the term was discontinued, and all records containing it were stripped of the term and replaced with STATISTICAL VALIDITY, its postable counterpart.
Use Statistical Validity

Predisposition 1973
PN 2441   **SC** 39970
SN Proneness toward disorders or propensity toward certain behaviors due to physical, psychological, social, or situational factors. Consider also SUSCEPTIBILITY (DISORDERS).
R At Risk Populations 1985
   Biological Markers 1991
   Coronary Prone Behavior 1982
   ↓ Disorders 1967
   ↓ Genetics 1967
   ↓ Mental Disorders 1967
   Nature Nurture 1994
   ↓ Personality 1967
   ↓ Physical Disorders 1997
   Premorbidity 1978
   Response Bias 1967
   Risk Factors 2001
   Susceptibility (Disorders) 1973

Prednisolone 1973
PN 42   **SC** 39980
B Adrenal Cortex Hormones 1973
   Corticosteroids 1973

Preference Measures 1973
PN 689   **SC** 39990
B Measurement 1967
N Kuder Preference Record 1973

Preference Measures — (cont'd)
- N   Least Preferred Coworker Scale   1973
- R   ↓ Attitude Measures   1967
-     ↓ Preferences   1967

Preferences   1967
PN   6804   SC   39995
- N   Aesthetic Preferences   1973
-     Brand Preferences   1994
-     Food Preferences   1973
-     Occupational Preference   1973
- R   ↓ Preference Measures   1973
-     Preferred Rewards   1973

Preferred Rewards   1973
PN   143   SC   40030
- B   Rewards   1967
- R   ↓ Preferences   1967

Prefrontal Cortex   1994
PN   1023   SC   40035
- B   Frontal Lobe   1973

Preganglionic Autonomic Fibers
- Use   Autonomic Ganglia

Pregnancy   1967
PN   4985   SC   40050
- UF   Gestation
- N   Adolescent Pregnancy   1988
- R   ↓ Birth   1967
-     Childbirth Training   1978
-     Fertilization   1973
-     Obstetrical Complications   1978
-     Perinatal Period   1994
-     Placenta   1973
-     Postnatal Period   1973
-     ↓ Prenatal Care   1991
-     Primipara   2001
-     Reproductive Technology   1988
-     ↓ Sexual Reproduction   1973
-     Sexual Risk Taking   1997

Pregnancy (False)
- Use   Pseudocyesis

Prejudice   1967
PN   1658   SC   40070
- B   Social Influences   1967
- N   ↓ Religious Prejudices   1973
- R   Age Discrimination   1994
-     AntiSemitism   1973
-     ↓ Attitudes   1967
-     Disability Discrimination   1997
-     Employment Discrimination   1994
-     Race and Ethnic Discrimination   1994
-     ↓ Racial and Ethnic Attitudes   1982
-     Racial and Ethnic Relations   1982
-     Racism   1973
-     Sex Discrimination   1978
-     Sexism   1988
-     Stereotyped Attitudes   1967
-     Stigma   1991

Preliminary Scholastic Aptitude Test
- Use   College Entrance Examination Board
-     Scholastic Aptitude Test

Premarital Counseling   1973
PN   157   SC   40090
- B   Counseling   1967
- R   ↓ Psychotherapeutic Counseling   1973

Premarital Intercourse   1973
PN   297   SC   40100
- B   Sexual Intercourse (Human)   1973
- R   ↓ Birth Control   1971
-     Promiscuity   1973
-     Social Dating   1973
-     Unwed Mothers   1973
-     Virginity   1973

Premature Birth   1973
PN   1541   SC   40110
- B   Birth   1967
- R   Birth Weight   1985
-     Obstetrical Complications   1978

Premature Ejaculation   1973
PN   149   SC   40120
- B   Male Orgasm   1973
-     Sexual Function Disturbances   1973
- R   Impotence   1973

Premenstrual Syndrome
- Use   Premenstrual Tension

Premenstrual Tension   1973
PN   980   SC   40130
- SN   Physiological, emotional, and mental stress related to the period of time immediately preceding menstruation.
- UF   PMS
-     Premenstrual Syndrome
- B   Menstrual Cycle   1973
- R   ↓ Menstrual Disorders   1973
-     ↓ Somatoform Disorders   2001

Premorbidity   1978
PN   722   SC   40135
- SN   Condition of an individual before onset of illness or disorder.
- R   At Risk Populations   1985
-     ↓ Disorders   1967
-     ↓ Mental Disorders   1967
-     Onset (Disorders)   1973
-     Patient History   1973
-     ↓ Physical Disorders   1997
-     Predisposition   1973
-     Susceptibility (Disorders)   1973

Prenatal Care   1991
PN   341   SC   40137
- SN   Medical, health, and educational services provided or obtained during pregnancy. Includes maternal health behavior affecting prenatal development.
- N   Childbirth Training   1978
- R   Early Intervention   1982
-     Health Behavior   1982
-     ↓ Health Care Services   1978
-     ↓ Health Education   1973
-     ↓ Obstetrics   1978
-     ↓ Pregnancy   1967
-     ↓ Prenatal Development   1973
-     Prenatal Diagnosis   1988
-     ↓ Prevention   1973
-     Preventive Medicine   1973

Prenatal Development   1973
PN   2149   SC   40140
- SN   Development of an organism prior to birth. Used for human or animal populations.
- B   Physical Development   1973
- N   ↓ Prenatal Developmental Stages   1973
- R   Animal Development   1978
-     Fetal Alcohol Syndrome   1985
-     Perinatal Period   1994

Prenatal Development — (cont'd)
- R   ↓ Prenatal Care   1991
-     Prenatal Diagnosis   1988
-     Prenatal Exposure   1991
-     ↓ Psychogenesis   1973
-     Teratogens   1988

Prenatal Developmental Stages   1973
PN   34   SC   40150
- B   Developmental Stages   1973
-     Prenatal Development   1973
- N   Embryo   1973
-     Fetus   1967

Prenatal Diagnosis   1988
PN   183   SC   40152
- SN   Techniques or procedures used to detect or identify specific abnormalities or characteristics of the fetus.
- UF   Amniocentesis
- B   Medical Diagnosis   1973
- R   ↓ Congenital Disorders   1973
-     ↓ Genetic Disorders   1973
-     ↓ Prenatal Care   1991
-     ↓ Prenatal Development   1973
-     Reproductive Technology   1988

Prenatal Exposure   1991
PN   1801   SC   40156
- SN   Exposure to chemicals or other environmental factors prior to birth. Used for human and animal populations.
- UF   Fetal Exposure
- R   ↓ Alcoholic Beverages   1973
-     ↓ Disorders   1967
-     ↓ Drugs   1967
-     ↓ Physical Disorders   1997
-     ↓ Poisons   1973
-     ↓ Prenatal Development   1973
-     Teratogens   1988
-     Thalidomide   1973
-     Tobacco Smoking   1967

Preoptic Area   1994
PN   166   SC   40158
- SN   Consider HYPOTHALAMUS to access references prior to 1994.
- B   Hypothalamus   1967

Prepulse Inhibition   1997
PN   199   SC   40159
- SN   Markedly reduced startle response resulting from a weaker stimulus preceding a stronger startle-inducing stimulus.
- R   Conditioned Suppression   1973
-     ↓ Latent Inhibition   1997
-     Sensory Gating   1991
-     Startle Reflex   1967

Presbyterians
- Use   Protestants

Preschool Education   1973
PN   1566   SC   40170
- B   Education   1967
- R   Project Head Start   1973

Preschool Students   1982
PN   2515   SC   40173
- SN   Students from infancy to entrance in kindergarten or 1st grade. Mandatory term in educational contexts.
- B   Students   1967

Preschool Students — (cont'd)
N   Nursery School Students 1973
R   Kindergarten Students 1973

Preschool Teachers 1985
PN 491   SC 40176
B   Teachers 1967

Prescribing (Drugs) 1991
PN 584   SC 40177
R   ↓ Drug Therapy 1967
     ↓ Drugs 1967
     ↓ Treatment 1967

Prescription Drugs 1991
PN 212   SC 40178
B   Drugs 1967
R   ↓ Drug Therapy 1967
     Nonprescription Drugs 1991
     Self Medication 1991

Presenile Dementia 1973
PN 204   SC 40180
UF   Dementia (Presenile)
B   Dementia 1985
N   Alzheimers Disease 1973
     Creutzfeldt Jakob Syndrome 1994
     Picks Disease 1973
R   ↓ Senile Dementia 1973

Preservice Teachers 1982
PN 805   SC 40205
SN   Education students or graduates prior to
employment as teachers.
B   Teachers 1967
R   ↓ College Students 1967
     Education Students 1982
     Student Teachers 1973
     ↓ Teacher Education 1967

Presidential Debates
Use Debates

Pressoreceptors
Use Baroreceptors

Pressors (Drugs)
Use Vasoconstrictor Drugs

Pressure Sensation 1973
PN 82   SC 40270
R   Somatosensory Disorders 2001
     ↓ Somesthetic Perception 1967

Prestige (Occupational)
Use Occupational Status

Pretesting 1973
PN 155   SC 40280
SN   Running preliminary trials to establish a base-
line. Comparison of pretest and posttest scores gives
a measure of effectiveness of independent variables
such as treatments or programs.
B   Measurement 1967
R   Repeated Measures 1985
     ↓ Testing Methods 1967

Pretraining (Therapy)
Use Client Education

Prevention 1973
PN 7692   SC 40290

Prevention — (cont'd)
SN   Conceptually broad term referring to any pro-
cess that acts to deter undesirable occurrences. Use
a more specific term if possible.
N   Accident Prevention 1973
     AIDS Prevention 1994
     Crime Prevention 1985
     Drug Abuse Prevention 1994
     Fire Prevention 1973
     Preventive Medicine 1973
     Primary Mental Health Prevention 1973
     Relapse Prevention 1994
     Suicide Prevention 1973
R   Condoms 1991
     Disability Management 1991
     Early Intervention 1982
     ↓ Health Care Delivery 1978
     ↓ Health Care Services 1978
     ↓ Health Education 1973
     Health Promotion 1991
     ↓ Mental Health Services 1978
     ↓ Prenatal Care 1991
     Risk Management 1997
     Risk Perception 1997
     ↓ Safety 1967
     Suicide Prevention Centers 1973
     ↓ Treatment 1967

Preventive Medicine 1973
PN 631   SC 40300
B   Prevention 1973
     Treatment 1967
R   ↓ Alternative Medicine 1997
     Drug Abuse Prevention 1994
     ↓ Health 1973
     Health Behavior 1982
     Health Maintenance Organizations 1982
     Health Promotion 1991
     ↓ Health Screening 1997
     Holistic Health 1985
     Mammography 1994
     Physical Examination 1988
     ↓ Prenatal Care 1991
     Relapse Prevention 1994

Price
Use Costs and Cost Analysis

Pride 1973
PN 118   SC 40310
B   Emotional States 1973

Priests 1973
PN 205   SC 40320
B   Clergy 1973
R   Chaplains 1973
     Missionaries 1973

Primacy Effect 1973
PN 233   SC 40328
SN   Component of the serial position effect which is
manifested by a greater ease in learning items that
occur at the beginning of a series rather than those
toward the middle. Compare RECENCY EFFECT.
B   Serial Position Effect 1982
R   ↓ Learning 1967
     Recency Effect 1973

Primal Therapy 1978
PN 49   SC 40329

Primal Therapy — (cont'd)
SN   Combination of intensive individual therapy and
group psychotherapy with emphasis on experiencing
and expression of blocked traumatic events or feelings (primals) and their integration into total life functioning.
B   Psychotherapy 1967
R   ↓ Psychotherapeutic Techniques 1967

Primary Health Care 1988
PN 1994   SC 40331
SN   Health care provided by a medical professional
with whom a patient has initial contact when entering
the health care system and by whom a patient may
be referred to a specialist.
B   Health Care Services 1978
R   ↓ Health Care Delivery 1978

Primary Mental Health Prevention 1973
PN 1488   SC 40330
SN   Mental health programs designed to prevent
onset or occurrence of mental illness in high risk or
target populations.
B   Prevention 1973
R   Drug Abuse Prevention 1994
     Early Intervention 1982
     ↓ Mental Health 1967
     ↓ Mental Health Programs 1973
     Relapse Prevention 1994

Primary Reinforcement 1973
PN 54   SC 40340
SN   Presentation of a primary reinforcer. Also,
objects or events which do not require prior pairing
with other reinforcers in order to maintain reinforcing
properties. Also known as unconditioned reinforcers
or unconditioned stimuli. Compare EXTERNAL
REWARDS.
B   Reinforcement 1967
R   ↓ Conditioning 1967
     Unconditioned Stimulus 1973

Primary School Students 1973
PN 512   SC 40350
SN   Students in kindergarten through 3rd grade. Use
ELEMENTARY SCHOOL STUDENTS or KINDER-
GARTEN STUDENTS unless specific reference is
made to population as primary school students. Use
of a student term is mandatory in educational con-
texts.
B   Elementary School Students 1967

Primary Schools
Use Elementary Schools

Primates (Nonhuman) 1973
PN 1676   SC 40370
UF   Apes
B   Mammals 1973
N   Baboons 1973
     Bonobos 1997
     Chimpanzees 1973
     Gorillas 1973
     Monkeys 1967

Primidone 1973
PN 18   SC 40380
B   Anticonvulsive Drugs 1973
R   ↓ Barbiturates 1967

Priming 1988
PN 1904   SC 40385
N   Semantic Priming 1994
R   Contextual Associations 1967

Priming — (cont'd)
R   Cues ¹⁹⁶⁷
    ↓ Perception ¹⁹⁶⁷
    ↓ Prompting ¹⁹⁹⁷
    ↓ Semantics ¹⁹⁶⁷

Primipara ²⁰⁰¹
PN 0   **SC** 40325
SN   Pregnant with, or having borne, only one child or offspring.
R   ↓ Mothers ¹⁹⁶⁷
    ↓ Pregnancy ¹⁹⁶⁷

Printed Communications Media ¹⁹⁷³
PN 432   **SC** 40390
B   Mass Media ¹⁹⁶⁷
N   ↓ Books ¹⁹⁷³
    Magazines ¹⁹⁷³
    Newspapers ¹⁹⁷³

Printing (Handwriting) ¹⁹⁷³
PN 44   **SC** 40400
B   Handwriting ¹⁹⁶⁷

Prismatic Stimulation ¹⁹⁷³
PN 191   **SC** 40410
SN   Visual stimulation technique in which special lenses are used to spatially distort or invert visual images or the visual field. Also includes prisms that differentially refract light of different wavelengths to produce an array or spectrum of colors.
B   Visual Stimulation ¹⁹⁷³
R   ↓ Color Perception ¹⁹⁶⁷
    Spatial Distortion ¹⁹⁷³

Prison Personnel ¹⁹⁷³
PN 488   **SC** 40420
B   Law Enforcement Personnel ¹⁹⁷³
R   Attendants (Institutions) ¹⁹⁷³

Prisoners ¹⁹⁶⁷
PN 3734   **SC** 40430
UF   Inmates (Prison)
N   Prisoners of War ¹⁹⁷³
R   ↓ Criminals ¹⁹⁶⁷

Prisoners Dilemma Game ¹⁹⁷³
PN 389   **SC** 40440
SN   Nonzero-sum game in which individual outcomes are determined by joint actions of two players. Incentives for both cooperation and competition exist, and no communication is permitted between the two players.
B   Games ¹⁹⁶⁷
R   Entrapment Games ¹⁹⁷³
    Game Theory ¹⁹⁶⁷
    Non Zero Sum Games ¹⁹⁷³

Prisoners of War ¹⁹⁷³
PN 189   **SC** 40450
B   Prisoners ¹⁹⁶⁷
R   Hostages ¹⁹⁸⁸

Prisons ¹⁹⁶⁷
PN 1178   **SC** 40460
UF   Jails
    Penitentiaries
B   Correctional Institutions ¹⁹⁷³
R   Concentration Camps ¹⁹⁷³
    Reformatories ¹⁹⁷³

Privacy ¹⁹⁷³
PN 500   **SC** 40467

Privacy — (cont'd)
R   Privileged Communication ¹⁹⁷³
    Secrecy ¹⁹⁹⁴
    ↓ Social Behavior ¹⁹⁶⁷

Private Practice ¹⁹⁷⁸
PN 524   **SC** 40469
SN   Employment of professional personnel in independent for-profit practices (as opposed to public offices or nonprofit settings) in which there is direct contact with clients and payment for services rendered. Private practitioners may function in individual practices, partnerships, or incorporated business settings.
R   ↓ Health Care Delivery ¹⁹⁷⁸

Private School Education ¹⁹⁷³
PN 535   **SC** 40470
SN   Schools or formal education in schools supported and administered by organizations not affiliated with the government.
UF   Parochial School Education
B   Education ¹⁹⁶⁷
R   Religious Education ¹⁹⁷³

Private Sector ¹⁹⁸⁵
PN 385   **SC** 40475
SN   Any type of non-government organization, service, or sphere of involvement.
N   Business Organizations ¹⁹⁷³
R   Entrepreneurship ¹⁹⁹¹
    Ownership ¹⁹⁸⁵

Privileged Communication ¹⁹⁷³
PN 986   **SC** 40480
SN   Confidential communication between doctors, lawyers, or therapists and their clients which, by legal sanction, may not be revealed to others. Also, any documents or recorded statements of such communication which can be legally withheld from public inspection.
UF   Communication (Privileged)
    Confidentiality of Information
R   ↓ Abuse Reporting ¹⁹⁹⁷
    Anonymity ¹⁹⁷³
    Client Records ¹⁹⁹⁷
    ↓ Communication ¹⁹⁶⁷
    Duty to Warn ²⁰⁰¹
    ↓ Experimentation ¹⁹⁶⁷
    Information ¹⁹⁶⁷
    Privacy ¹⁹⁷³

Proactive Inhibition ¹⁹⁷³
PN 712   **SC** 40490
SN   The theory that previous learning of material can interfere with the retention of newly-learned material. Also, the actual proactive interference itself.
UF   Inhibition (Proactive)
B   Interference (Learning) ¹⁹⁶⁷
    Latent Inhibition ¹⁹⁹⁷

Probability ¹⁹⁶⁷
PN 1687   **SC** 40500
SN   The likelihood of the chance occurrence of specific events. May include the mathematical study of probability theory.
N   ↓ Chance (Fortune) ¹⁹⁷³
    Response Probability ¹⁹⁷³
    ↓ Statistical Probability ¹⁹⁶⁷
R   Chaos Theory ¹⁹⁹⁷
    ↓ Hypothesis Testing ¹⁹⁷³
    Predictability (Measurement) ¹⁹⁷³
    Probability Judgment ¹⁹⁷⁸
    Probability Learning ¹⁹⁶⁷

Probability Judgment ¹⁹⁷⁸
PN 952   **SC** 40505
SN   Process of ascertaining or estimating the degree of likelihood that certain specified conditions or events have, can, or will occur.
B   Judgment ¹⁹⁶⁷
R   ↓ Probability ¹⁹⁶⁷
    Probability Learning ¹⁹⁶⁷

Probability Learning ¹⁹⁶⁷
PN 585   **SC** 40510
SN   Experimental paradigm in which subjects are asked to guess or estimate whether an experimentally controlled event will occur or choose which of various alternative events will occur. As learning occurs, the proportion of correct responses tends to approach the actual probability proportion of event occurrences. Used for the experimental paradigm or task as well as the learned behavior itself.
B   Learning ¹⁹⁶⁷
R   ↓ Probability ¹⁹⁶⁷
    Probability Judgment ¹⁹⁷⁸

Probation ¹⁹⁷³
PN 459   **SC** 40520
SN   Period of suspended sentence of a convicted offender following good behavior and during which the offender is not incarcerated but is under the supervision of a probation officer.
B   Legal Processes ¹⁹⁷³
R   Court Referrals ¹⁹⁹⁴
    ↓ Law Enforcement ¹⁹⁷⁸
    Parole ¹⁹⁷³

Probation Officers ¹⁹⁷³
PN 209   **SC** 40530
B   Law Enforcement Personnel ¹⁹⁷³
R   Parole Officers ¹⁹⁷³

Probenecid ¹⁹⁸²
PN 15   **SC** 40535
SN   Agent that promotes the urinary excretion of uric acid.
R   ↓ Diuretics ¹⁹⁷³

Problem Drinking
SN   Term discontinued in 1988. In 2000, the term was stripped from all records containing it, and replaced with ALCOHOL ABUSE, its postable counterpart.
Use   Alcohol Abuse

Problem Solving ¹⁹⁶⁷
PN 11582   **SC** 40550
SN   Process of determining a correct sequence of alternatives leading to a desired goal or to successful completion or performance of a task.
UF   Individual Problem Solving
B   Cognitive Processes ¹⁹⁶⁷
N   Anagram Problem Solving ¹⁹⁷³
    Cognitive Hypothesis Testing ¹⁹⁸²
    ↓ Group Problem Solving ¹⁹⁷³
R   ↓ Decision Making ¹⁹⁶⁷
    Declarative Knowledge ¹⁹⁹⁷
    ↓ Expert Systems ¹⁹⁹¹
    ↓ Inductive Deductive Reasoning ¹⁹⁷³
    ↓ Reasoning ¹⁹⁶⁷

Procaine ¹⁹⁸²
PN 87   **SC** 40560
SN   In 1982, this term replaced the discontinued term NOVOCAINE. In 2000, NOVOCAINE was stripped from all records and replaced with PROCAINE.
UF   Novocaine

Procaine — (cont'd)
- **B** Analgesic Drugs [1973]
  - Anesthetic Drugs [1973]

Procedural Knowledge [1997]
PN 190   **SC** 40565
SN Knowledge regarding how to do things. Compare DECLARATIVE KNOWLEDGE.
- **UF** Functional Knowledge
  - Practical Knowledge
- **R** ↓ Cognitive Processes [1967]
  - Declarative Knowledge [1997]
  - Divergent Thinking [1973]
  - Information [1967]
  - ↓ Knowledge Level [1978]
  - ↓ Memory [1967]
  - Metacognition [1991]
  - ↓ Reasoning [1967]

Process Psychosis [1973]
PN 65   **SC** 40570
- **UF** Process Schizophrenia
- **B** Psychosis [1967]

Process Schizophrenia
- **Use** Process Psychosis AND Schizophrenia

Prochlorperazine [1973]
PN 16   **SC** 40640
- **B** Antiemetic Drugs [1973]
  - Phenothiazine Derivatives [1973]

Procrastination [1985]
PN 169   **SC** 40645
SN Habitual, often counterproductive postponing. Use STUDY HABITS to access references in educational contexts from 1973-1984.
- **B** Motivation [1967]

Product Design [1997]
PN 154   **SC** 40647
SN Process of conceptualizing, planning, researching, developing, and field testing products or goods.
- **UF** Consumer Product Design
- **R** ↓ Advertising [1967]
  - Computer Assisted Design [1997]
  - Consumer Protection [1973]
  - ↓ Consumer Research [1973]
  - Consumer Surveys [1973]
  - Marketing [1973]

Productivity (Employee)
- **Use** Employee Productivity

Profanity [1991]
PN 12   **SC** 40655
- **B** Language [1967]
- **R** Obscenity [1978]

Professional Certification [1973]
PN 695   **SC** 40660
SN In general, certification constitutes permission to use a particular professional title contingent on fulfilling requisite educational and training programs.
- **UF** Certification (Professional)
- **N** Accreditation (Education Personnel) [1973]
- **R** Professional Development [1982]
  - Professional Examinations [1994]
  - ↓ Professional Licensing [1973]
  - ↓ Professional Personnel [1978]

Professional Client Sexual Relations [1994]
PN 279   **SC** 40665
SN Sexual relations, intimacy, or affectionate behavior between a professional (e.g., therapist, lawyer, religious personnel, or educator) and their clients or patients.
- **UF** Boundary Violations (Sexual)
  - Patient Therapist Sexual Relations
  - Sexual Boundary Violations
  - Therapist Patient Sexual Relations
- **R** Countertransference [1973]
  - Patient Abuse [1991]
  - Professional Ethics [1973]
  - ↓ Professional Standards [1973]
  - ↓ Psychosexual Behavior [1967]
  - ↓ Psychotherapeutic Processes [1967]
  - Psychotherapeutic Transference [1967]
  - ↓ Sexual Abuse [1988]
  - Sexual Harassment [1985]
  - ↓ Therapeutic Processes [1978]

Professional Communication
- **Use** Scientific Communication

Professional Competence [1997]
PN 381   **SC** 40675
- **B** Competence [1982]
- **R** ↓ Employee Characteristics [1988]
  - ↓ Employee Skills [1973]
  - Peer Evaluation [1982]
  - ↓ Personnel Evaluation [1973]
  - Professional Development [1982]
  - Professional Liability [1985]
  - ↓ Professional Standards [1973]

Professional Consultation [1973]
PN 3838   **SC** 40680
SN Advisory services offered by specialists in a particular field which may be client or colleague oriented or focus on policy setting, planning, and programs of an organization. In 1982, this term replaced the discontinued term MENTAL HEALTH CONSULTATION. In 2000, MENTAL HEALTH CONSULTATION was stripped from all records and replaced with PROFESSIONAL CONSULTATION.
- **UF** Consultation (Professional)
  - Mental Health Consultation
- **N** Consultation Liaison Psychiatry [1991]
- **R** Personal Therapy [1991]
  - ↓ Professional Personnel [1978]
  - Professional Supervision [1988]

Professional Development [1982]
PN 2226   **SC** 40715
SN Participation in activities which promote professional career development.
- **B** Development [1967]
- **R** Career Change [1978]
  - Career Development [1985]
  - ↓ Continuing Education [1985]
  - Employment History [1978]
  - Inservice Teacher Education [1973]
  - ↓ Inservice Training [1985]
  - Mental Health Inservice Training [1973]
  - Mentor [1985]
  - Occupational Aspirations [1973]
  - ↓ Professional Certification [1973]
  - Professional Competence [1997]
  - Professional Identity [1991]
  - ↓ Professional Personnel [1978]
  - Professional Specialization [1991]
  - ↓ Professional Standards [1973]

Professional Ethics [1973]
PN 5620   **SC** 40720
SN Moral principles of conducting professional research or practices.
- **B** Ethics [1967]
- **R** ↓ Abuse Reporting [1997]
  - Assisted Suicide [1997]
  - Duty to Warn [2001]
  - Euthanasia [1973]
  - Experimental Ethics [1978]
  - Impaired Professionals [1985]
  - Informed Consent [1985]
  - Professional Client Sexual Relations [1994]
  - Professional Liability [1985]
  - ↓ Professional Personnel [1978]
  - ↓ Professional Standards [1973]

Professional Examinations [1994]
PN 114   **SC** 40723
SN Required examinations for licensure or certification in order to practice a profession.
- **UF** Certification Examinations
  - Licensure Examinations
  - State Board Examinations
- **B** Measurement [1967]
- **R** Accreditation (Education Personnel) [1973]
  - ↓ Professional Certification [1973]
  - ↓ Professional Licensing [1973]

Professional Fees [1978]
PN 356   **SC** 40724
- **N** Fee for Service [1994]
- **R** Cost Containment [1991]
  - ↓ Costs and Cost Analysis [1973]
  - Diagnosis Related Groups [1988]
  - Health Care Costs [1994]
  - Money [1967]
  - Peer Evaluation [1982]
  - ↓ Professional Personnel [1978]
  - Salaries [1973]

Professional Identity [1991]
PN 632   **SC** 40725
SN Concept of self and role within a professional domain.
- **UF** Identity (Professional)
- **B** Social Identity [1988]
- **R** Career Development [1985]
  - ↓ Employee Characteristics [1988]
  - Professional Development [1982]
  - ↓ Professional Personnel [1978]
  - Role Perception [1973]
  - ↓ Self Concept [1967]

Professional Liability [1985]
PN 926   **SC** 40727
SN Legal liabilities relating to the conduct of one's profession.
- **UF** Legal Liability (Professional)
  - Malpractice
- **B** Professional Standards [1973]
- **R** Accountability [1988]
  - Duty to Warn [2001]
  - Impaired Professionals [1985]
  - ↓ Legal Processes [1973]
  - Misdiagnosis [1997]
  - Patient Abuse [1991]
  - Professional Competence [1997]
  - Professional Ethics [1973]
  - ↓ Responsibility [1973]
  - Risk Management [1997]

Professional Licensing [1973]
PN 508   **SC** 40730

Professional Licensing — (cont'd)

SN Permission from an authority (e.g., government review board) to use a particular professional title as well as to practice the profession. Professional licensing laws also specify what activities constitute the legal or legitimate practice of the profession. One does not necessarily need to be certified (professionally) in order to be licensed.
UF Licensing (Professional)
N Accreditation (Education Personnel) 1973
R ↓ Professional Certification 1973
    Professional Examinations 1994
    ↓ Professional Personnel 1978

Professional Newsletters
Use Scientific Communication

Professional Organizations 1973
PN 2093   **SC** 40760
B Organizations 1967
R ↓ Professional Personnel 1978

Professional Orientation
Use Theoretical Orientation

Professional Personnel 1978
PN 1949   **SC** 40765
SN Conceptually broad term referring to members of professions requiring prolonged and specialized training. Use a more specific term if possible.
B Personnel 1967
N ↓ Aerospace Personnel 1973
    Anthropologists 1973
    Clinicians 1973
    ↓ Counselors 1967
    ↓ Educational Personnel 1973
    Engineers 1967
    ↓ Health Personnel 1994
    ↓ Information Specialists 1988
    Journalists 1973
    ↓ Legal Personnel 1985
    Mathematicians 1973
    Physicists 1973
    ↓ Psychologists 1967
    Scientists 1967
    Sociologists 1973
    ↓ Therapists 1967
R ↓ Business and Industrial Personnel 1967
    Impaired Professionals 1985
    Librarians 1988
    ↓ Nonprofessional Personnel 1982
    ↓ Occupations 1967
    ↓ Paraprofessional Personnel 1973
    ↓ Professional Certification 1973
    ↓ Professional Consultation 1973
    Professional Development 1982
    Professional Ethics 1973
    ↓ Professional Fees 1978
    Professional Identity 1991
    ↓ Professional Licensing 1973
    Professional Organizations 1973
    Professional Referral 1973
    Professional Specialization 1991
    ↓ Professional Standards 1973
    Professional Supervision 1988
    ↓ Religious Personnel 1973

Professional Referral 1973
PN 1769   **SC** 40770
SN Act of directing a client to a professional or agency for assessment, treatment, or consultation.
UF Referral (Professional)
R Client Transfer 1997

Professional Referral — (cont'd)
R Court Referrals 1994
    ↓ Professional Personnel 1978
    Self Referral 1991

Professional Specialization 1991
PN 420   **SC** 40775
SN Training in or choice of a speciality within a profession.
UF Specialization (Professional)
R Academic Specialization 1973
    Career Development 1985
    ↓ Higher Education 1973
    Occupational Choice 1967
    Occupational Preference 1973
    ↓ Postgraduate Training 1973
    Professional Development 1982
    ↓ Professional Personnel 1978

Professional Standards 1973
PN 2509   **SC** 40780
SN Minimally acceptable levels of quality professional care or services maintained in order to promote the welfare of those who make use of such services.
UF Standards (Professional)
N Professional Liability 1985
R Accountability 1988
    Duty to Warn 2001
    Impaired Professionals 1985
    Patient Abuse 1991
    Peer Evaluation 1982
    Professional Client Sexual Relations 1994
    Professional Competence 1997
    Professional Development 1982
    Professional Ethics 1973
    ↓ Professional Personnel 1978
    ↓ Quality of Services 1997
    Treatment Guidelines 2001

Professional Supervision 1988
PN 1831   **SC** 40785
SN Processes or techniques of supervision of fully trained educational or mental health personnel.
UF Clinical Supervision
    Educational Supervision
    Supervision (Professional)
R ↓ Educational Personnel 1973
    ↓ Mental Health Personnel 1967
    Personal Therapy 1991
    ↓ Professional Consultation 1973
    ↓ Professional Personnel 1978

Professors
Use College Teachers

Profiles (Measurement) 1973
PN 1461   **SC** 40800
SN Usually a composite of scores obtained through psychological testing utilizing instruments which yield separate measures and which comprises a picture or profile of the individual's characteristics across several areas.
B Measurement 1967

Profound Mental Retardation 2001
PN 1384   **SC** 40805
SN IQ below 20. In 2000, this term replaced the discontinued and deleted term PROFOUNDLY MENTALLY RETARDED. PROFOUNDLY MENTALLY RETARDED was stripped from all records and replaced with PROFOUND MENTAL RETARDATION.
B Mental Retardation 1967

Progestational Hormones 1985
PN 83   **SC** 40815
UF Progestins
B Hormones 1967
N Progesterone 1973

Progesterone 1973
PN 938   **SC** 40820
B Progestational Hormones 1985
    Sex Hormones 1973
    Steroids 1973

Progestins
Use Progestational Hormones

Prognosis 1973
PN 2599   **SC** 40830
SN Prediction of the course, duration, and outcome of a disorder. Compare DISEASE COURSE.
R Biological Markers 1991
    ↓ Chronic Mental Illness 1997
    Clinical Judgment (Not Diagnosis) 1973
    ↓ Diagnosis 1967
    Disease Course 1991
    ↓ Disorders 1967
    ↓ Medical Diagnosis 1973
    ↓ Mental Disorders 1967
    Patient History 1973
    ↓ Physical Disorders 1997
    ↓ Prediction 1967
    ↓ Psychodiagnosis 1967
    Severity (Disorders) 1982
    ↓ Treatment 1967

Program Development 1991
PN 1670   **SC** 40832
SN Formulation and/or implementation of programs in any setting.
UF Program Planning
B Development 1967
N Educational Program Planning 1973
R Curriculum Development 1973
    ↓ Educational Programs 1973
    Employee Assistance Programs 1985
    ↓ Government Programs 1973
    Home Visiting Programs 1973
    ↓ Hospital Programs 1978
    Independent Living Programs 1991
    ↓ Mental Health Programs 1973
    ↓ Program Evaluation 1985
    ↓ Psychiatric Hospital Programs 1967
    ↓ Social Programs 1973

Program Evaluation 1985
PN 2494   **SC** 40835
SN Assessment of programs in any setting.
B Evaluation 1967
N Educational Program Evaluation 1973
    Mental Health Program Evaluation 1973
R ↓ Program Development 1991

Program Evaluation (Educational)
Use Educational Program Evaluation

Program Evaluation (Mental Health)
Use Mental Health Program Evaluation

Program Planning
Use Program Development

Program Planning (Educational)
Use Educational Program Planning

Programmed Instruction   2001
PN 939   **SC** 40870
SN In 2000, this term was created to update the spelling from the discontinued term PROGRAMED INSTRUCTION. PROGRAMED INSTRUCTION was stripped from all records and replaced with PRO-GRAMMED INSTRUCTION.
- **UF** Instruction (Programmed)
- **B** Teaching Methods   1967
- **R** Computer Assisted Instruction   1973
  Individualized Instruction   1973
  Programmed Textbooks   2001
  ↓ Prompting   1997
  Teaching Machines   1973

Programmed Textbooks   2001
PN 40   **SC** 40900
SN Textbooks prepared for use with programmed instruction. Not used as a document type identifier. In 2000, this term was created to update the spelling from the discontinued term PROGRAMED TEXT-BOOKS. PROGRAMED TEXTBOOKS was stripped from all records and replaced with PROGRAMMED TEXTBOOKS.
- **B** Textbooks   1978
- **R** Programmed Instruction   2001

Programming (Computer)
SN Use COMPUTER SOFTWARE to access references from 1973-1993.
- **Use** Computer Programming

Programming Languages (Computer)
- **Use** Computer Programming Languages

Programs (Government)
- **Use** Government Programs

Programs (Mental Health)
- **Use** Mental Health Programs

Progressive Relaxation Therapy   1978
PN 558   **SC** 40945
SN Therapeutic procedures which teach clients to tense and relax muscle groups, focusing on the sensations involved in relaxation. This method provides clients with practice in recognizing the sensation of tension which will serve as a cue to produce a state of muscle relaxation.
- **B** Relaxation Therapy   1978
- **R** ↓ Hypnotherapy   1973
  Muscle Relaxation   1973
  Systematic Desensitization Therapy   1973

Progressive Supranuclear Palsy   1997
PN 32   **SC** 40947
SN A progressive neurological disorder characterized by ophthalmoplegia, dystonia, memory impairment, personality disorders, and dementia. Etiology is unknown.
- **B** Central Nervous System Disorders   1973
- **R** ↓ Basal Ganglia   1973
  ↓ Senile Dementia   1973

Project Follow Through   1973
PN 41   **SC** 40950
SN U.S. Government educational program for disadvantaged elementary school students to supplement Project Head Start and encourage academic and psychosocial growth.
- **B** Educational Programs   1973
  Government Programs   1973
- **R** Compensatory Education   1973
  Government   1967

Project Head Start   1973
PN 515   **SC** 40960
SN U.S. Government program for disadvantaged 3-5 yr olds aimed at improving children's educational potential by encouraging their psychosocial development and by providing economic assistance to their families.
- **UF** Head Start
- **B** Educational Programs   1973
  Government Programs   1973
- **R** Compensatory Education   1973
  Government   1967
  Preschool Education   1973
  School Readiness   1973

Projection (Defense Mechanism)   1967
PN 489   **SC** 40970
- **B** Defense Mechanisms   1967
- **R** Projective Identification   1994

Projective Identification   1994
PN 204   **SC** 40975
- **B** Defense Mechanisms   1967
- **R** Enactments   1997
  Identification (Defense Mechanism)   1973
  Projection (Defense Mechanism)   1967

Projective Personality Measures   1973
PN 916   **SC** 40980
SN Tests which derive an indirect and global assessment of personality through the analysis of meaning or structure freely imposed by the subject upon unstructured or ambiguous materials. Use a more specific term if possible. Compare NON-PROJECTIVE PERSONALITY MEASURES. In 1997, this term replaced the discontinued terms BLACKY PICTURES TEST, COLOR PYRAMID TEST, and ONOMATOPOEIA AND IMAGES TEST. In 2000, these terms were stripped from all records and replaced with PROJECTIVE PERSONALITY MEASURES.
- **UF** Blacky Pictures Test
  Color Pyramid Test
  Onomatopoeia and Images Test
- **B** Personality Measures   1967
  Projective Techniques   1967
- **N** Bender Gestalt Test   1967
  Childrens Apperception Test   1973
  Franck Drawing Completion Test   1973
  Holtzman Inkblot Technique   1967
  Human Figures Drawing   1973
  Rorschach Test   1967
  Rosenzweig Picture Frustration Study   1967
  Rotter Incomplete Sentences Blank   1973
  Sentence Completion Tests   1991
  Szondi Test   1973
  Thematic Apperception Test   1967
  Zulliger Z Test   1973
- **R** Psychoanalytic Interpretation   1967

Projective Techniques   1967
PN 1601   **SC** 40990
SN Utilization of ambiguous or unstructured stimuli designed to elicit responses which are believed to reveal an individual's attitudes, defense modes or motivations, and personality structure. Also, the specific tests or techniques themselves. Use a more specific term if possible.
- **UF** Projective Tests
- **N** Franck Drawing Completion Test   1973
  Holtzman Inkblot Technique   1967
  Incomplete Man Test   1973
  ↓ Projective Personality Measures   1973
- **R** Psychoanalytic Interpretation   1967

Projective Testing Technique   1973
PN 362   **SC** 41000
SN Administration, construction, scoring, and interpretation of projective tests.
- **B** Measurement   1967

Projective Tests
- **Use** Projective Techniques

Prolactin   1973
PN 1420   **SC** 41020
- **B** Gonadotropic Hormones   1973

Proline   1982
PN 19   **SC** 41027
- **B** Amino Acids   1973

Prolixin
- **Use** Fluphenazine

Promazine   1973
PN 24   **SC** 41040
- **B** Phenothiazine Derivatives   1973

Promethazine   1973
PN 37   **SC** 41050
- **B** Antiemetic Drugs   1973
  Antihistaminic Drugs   1973
  Sedatives   1973

Promiscuity   1973
PN 104   **SC** 41060
- **UF** Sexual Delinquency
- **B** Psychosexual Behavior   1967
- **R** Extramarital Intercourse   1973
  Hypersexuality   1973
  Premarital Intercourse   1973
  Prostitution   1973
  Sexual Addiction   1997

Prompting   1997
PN 65   **SC** 41065
- **N** Constant Time Delay   1997
- **R** ↓ Behavior Modification   1973
  Cued Recall   1994
  Cues   1967
  ↓ Learning   1967
  ↓ Learning Strategies   1991
  ↓ Memory   1967
  ↓ Priming   1988
  Programmed Instruction   2001
  ↓ Teaching Methods   1967

Pronouns   1973
PN 378   **SC** 41070
- **B** Form Classes (Language)   1973

Pronunciation   1973
PN 472   **SC** 41080
- **B** Speech Characteristics   1973
- **R** Articulation (Speech)   1967

Proofreading   1988
PN 52   **SC** 41085
- **R** Clerical Secretarial Skills   1973
  ↓ Errors   1967
  Orthography   1973
  ↓ Reading   1967
  Verbal Ability   1967
  ↓ Written Communication   1985

Propaganda 1973
PN 73   SC 41090
B   Social Influences 1967
R   Brainwashing 1982
     ↓ Persuasive Communication 1967

Property
Use Ownership

Propranolol 1973
PN 579   SC 41100
B   Adrenergic Blocking Drugs 1973
     Alcohols 1967

Proprioceptors 1973
PN 155   SC 41110
B   Nerve Endings 1973
     Neural Receptors 1973
     Sensory Neurons 1973

Prose 1973
PN 886   SC 41120
B   Literature 1967
N   ↓ Biography 1967
R   Creative Writing 1994
     Text Structure 1982

Prosencephalon
Use Forebrain

Proserine
Use Neostigmine

Prosocial Behavior 1982
PN 1248   SC 41133
SN Positive social behavior generally concerned
with promotion of the welfare of others. Limited to
human populations.
B   Social Behavior 1967
N   Altruism 1973
     Assistance (Social Behavior) 1973
     Charitable Behavior 1973
     Cooperation 1967
     Sharing (Social Behavior) 1978
     Trust (Social Behavior) 1967
R   ↓ Antisocial Behavior 1971
     Generativity 2001

Prosody 1991
PN 374   SC 41134
SN Physical characteristics of speech that indicate
linguistic features such as stress, intonation, inten-
sity, and duration of speech sounds. Use INFLEC-
TION to access references from 1988-1990.
B   Phonology 1973
N   Inflection 1973
R   ↓ Linguistics 1973
     Morphology (Language) 1973
     ↓ Phonemes 1973
     Sentence Structure 1973
     ↓ Speech Characteristics 1973

Prosopagnosia 1994
PN 83   SC 41135
SN A visual agnosia usually due to brain damage
and characterized by an inability to recognize familiar
faces, and in some cases, one's own face.
B   Agnosia 1973
R   Face Perception 1985

Prospective Studies 1997
PN 256   SC 41137

Prospective Studies — (cont'd)
SN Used in records discussing issues involved in
the process of conducting studies of observations of
the same individual or group over an extended period
of time, usually to generate prognostic data or incidence rates related to a particular disorder, event, or
behavior. From 1997-2000, the term was also used
as a mandatory document type identifier; however,
this usage has been discontinued due to the advent
of Form/Content Type field identifiers. References
from 1997-2000 can be accessed using either PRO-
SPECTIVE STUDIES or the Prospective Studies
Form/Content Type field identifier.
B   Longitudinal Studies 1973
R   Retrospective Studies 1997

Prostaglandins 1982
PN 195   SC 41136
SN Physiologically potent compounds of ubiquitous
occurrence formed from essential fatty acids and
affecting the nervous system, female reproductive
organs, and metabolism.
R   ↓ Anti Inflammatory Drugs 1982
     ↓ Fatty Acids 1973
     ↓ Hormones 1967
     ↓ Neuroleptic Drugs 1973
     ↓ Sympathomimetic Drugs 1973

Prostate 1973
PN 101   SC 41140
B   Male Genitalia 1973

Prostate Cancer Screening
Use Cancer Screening

Prostheses 1973
PN 244   SC 41150
UF   Artificial Limbs
B   Medical Therapeutic Devices 1973
N   Cochlear Implants 1994
R   ↓ Amputation 1973

Prostitution 1973
PN 569   SC 41160
B   Psychosexual Behavior 1967
R   Promiscuity 1973

Protective Services 1997
PN 245   SC 41170
B   Social Services 1982
R   Child Custody 1982
     Child Welfare 1988
     Elder Care 1994
     Foster Care 1978
     Guardianship 1988
     ↓ Legal Processes 1973
     Shelters 1991
     Social Casework 1967

Protein Deficiency Disorders 1973
PN 39   SC 41180
B   Nutritional Deficiencies 1973
N   Kwashiorkor 1973

Protein Metabolism 1973
PN 181   SC 41190
B   Metabolism 1967

Protein Sensitization
Use Anaphylactic Shock

Proteinases 1973
PN 34   SC 41210

Proteinases — (cont'd)
B   Enzymes 1973

Proteins 1973
PN 1937   SC 41220
N   ↓ Blood Proteins 1973
     ↓ Endorphins 1982
     ↓ Globulins 1973
     Interferons 1994
R   ↓ Amino Acids 1973
     ↓ Drugs 1967
     ↓ Enzymes 1973
     Lipoproteins 1973
     ↓ Peptides 1973

Protest (Student)
Use Student Activism

Protestantism 1973
PN 481   SC 41250
B   Christianity 1973
N   Fundamentalism 1973
R   Protestants 1997

Protestants 1997
PN 120   SC 41253
UF   Baptists
     Episcopalians
     Lutherans
     Methodists
     Presbyterians
B   Christians 1997
R   ↓ Protestantism 1973

Protozoa 1973
PN 19   SC 41255
B   Microorganisms 1985

Prozac
Use Fluoxetine

Pruritus 1973
PN 47   SC 41260
UF   Itching
B   Skin Disorders 1973
     Symptoms 1967
R   Scratching 1973

Pseudocyesis 1973
PN 72   SC 41270
UF   False Pregnancy
     Pregnancy (False)
     Pseudopregnancy
B   Conversion Disorder 2001
R   ↓ Gynecological Disorders 1973

Pseudodementia 1985
PN 101   SC 41280
SN Dementia-like disorder in the absence of
organic brain disease.
B   Mental Disorders 1967
R   ↓ Dementia 1985
     ↓ Factitious Disorders 1988
     ↓ Major Depression 1988

Pseudohermaphroditism
Use Hermaphroditism

Pseudomemory
Use False Memory

Pseudopregnancy
  Use Pseudocyesis

Pseudopsychopathic Schizophrenia
SN Term discontinued in 1988. In 2000, the term was stripped from all records containing it, and replaced with SCHIZOPHRENIA, its postable counterpart.
  Use Schizophrenia

Psilocybin 1973
PN 40   **SC** 41310
  B   Hallucinogenic Drugs 1967

Psychedelic Drugs 1973
PN 102   **SC** 41320
  B   Drugs 1967
  N   Lysergic Acid Diethylamide 1967
  R   ↓ Hallucinogenic Drugs 1967
          ↓ Psychotomimetic Drugs 1973

Psychedelic Experiences 1973
PN 44   **SC** 41330
  R   Drug Induced Hallucinations 1973

Psychiatric Aides 1973
PN 86   **SC** 41340
  B   Paramedical Personnel 1973
          Psychiatric Hospital Staff 1973

Psychiatric Classifications (Taxon)
  Use Psychodiagnostic Typologies

Psychiatric Clinics 1973
PN 563   **SC** 41370
  UF   Outpatient Psychiatric Clinics
  B   Clinics 1967
  R   Child Guidance Clinics 1973
          Community Mental Health Centers 1973
          ↓ Hospitals 1967
          ↓ Mental Health Programs 1973
          ↓ Outpatient Treatment 1967
          Walk In Clinics 1973

Psychiatric Disorders
  Use Mental Disorders

Psychiatric Evaluation 1997
PN 279   **SC** 41385
  UF   Evaluation (Psychiatric)
  B   Evaluation 1967
          Measurement 1967
  N   Forensic Evaluation 1994
  R   Clinical Judgment (Not Diagnosis) 1973
          Cognitive Assessment 1997
          Geriatric Assessment 1997
          Intake Interview 1994
          ↓ Interview Schedules 2001
          ↓ Psychodiagnosis 1967
          ↓ Psychodiagnostic Interview 1973
          ↓ Psychological Assessment 1997
          Psychological Report 1988
          ↓ Screening 1982
          ↓ Screening Tests 1982

Psychiatric History
  Use Patient History

Psychiatric Hospital Admission 1973
PN 1030   **SC** 41390
  UF   Admission (Psychiatric Hospital)
  B   Hospital Admission 1973

Psychiatric Hospital Admission — (cont'd)
  B   Psychiatric Hospitalization 1973
  N   Psychiatric Hospital Readmission 1973
  R   ↓ Commitment (Psychiatric) 1973
          ↓ Hospital Discharge 1973
          ↓ Institutional Release 1978
          Psychiatric Hospital Discharge 1978

Psychiatric Hospital Discharge 1978
PN 740   **SC** 41395
  B   Hospital Discharge 1973
          Psychiatric Hospitalization 1973
  R   Client Transfer 1997
          ↓ Commitment (Psychiatric) 1973
          Discharge Planning 1994
          ↓ Psychiatric Hospital Admission 1973
          Psychiatric Hospital Readmission 1973
          Treatment Termination 1982

Psychiatric Hospital Programs 1967
PN 1695   **SC** 41400
SN Organized plans for care or training in psychiatric hospitals.
  B   Hospital Programs 1978
  N   Therapeutic Community 1967
  R   Halfway Houses 1973
          ↓ Mental Health Services 1978
          ↓ Program Development 1991
          Token Economy Programs 1973

Psychiatric Hospital Readmission 1973
PN 628   **SC** 41410
  UF   Readmission (Psychiatric Hospital)
  B   Psychiatric Hospital Admission 1973
          Psychiatric Hospitalization 1973
  R   ↓ Hospital Discharge 1973
          Psychiatric Hospital Discharge 1978

Psychiatric Hospital Staff 1973
PN 765   **SC** 41420
  B   Medical Personnel 1967
          Mental Health Personnel 1967
  N   Psychiatric Aides 1973
  R   Attendants (Institutions) 1973
          Occupational Therapists 1973
          ↓ Paramedical Personnel 1973
          Psychiatric Nurses 1973
          Psychiatrists 1967

Psychiatric Hospitalization 1973
PN 4057   **SC** 41430
  B   Hospitalization 1967
  N   ↓ Psychiatric Hospital Admission 1973
          Psychiatric Hospital Discharge 1978
          Psychiatric Hospital Readmission 1973
  R   ↓ Commitment (Psychiatric) 1973
          ↓ Hospital Admission 1973
          ↓ Hospital Discharge 1973
          ↓ Institutional Release 1978
          Patient Seclusion 1994

Psychiatric Hospitals 1967
PN 3648   **SC** 41440
  UF   Asylums
          Mental Hospitals
          State Hospitals
  B   Hospitals 1967
  R   Halfway Houses 1973
          Patient Seclusion 1994
          Psychiatric Units 1991
          Sanatoriums 1973

Psychiatric Nurses 1973
PN 898   **SC** 41450
  B   Mental Health Personnel 1967
          Nurses 1967
  R   ↓ Psychiatric Hospital Staff 1973

Psychiatric Patients 1967
PN 19735   **SC** 41460
  B   Patients 1967
  R   ↓ Mental Disorders 1967
          Psychiatric Symptoms 1997
          Psychopathology 1967

Psychiatric Report
  Use Psychological Report

Psychiatric Residency
  Use Medical Residency AND Psychiatric Training

Psychiatric Social Workers 1973
PN 64   **SC** 41470
  B   Mental Health Personnel 1967
          Social Workers 1973

Psychiatric Symptoms 1997
PN 1885   **SC** 41475
  UF   Psychotic Symptoms
  B   Symptoms 1967
  R   ↓ Mental Disorders 1967
          Psychiatric Patients 1967
          Psychopathology 1967
          Symptom Checklists 1991
          Symptom Remission 1973

Psychiatric Training 1973
PN 1838   **SC** 41480
  UF   Psychiatric Residency
          Training (Psychiatric)
  B   Clinical Methods Training 1973
          Medical Education 1973
  R   Cotherapy 1982
          Psychoanalytic Training 1973
          Psychotherapy Training 1973

Psychiatric Units 1991
PN 544   **SC** 41485
SN Units in a general hospital or inpatient care facility specializing in psychiatric care of acutely disturbed patients.
  UF   Hospital Psychiatric Units
  R   ↓ Hospital Programs 1978
          ↓ Hospitalization 1967
          ↓ Hospitals 1967
          Nursing Homes 1973
          Patient Seclusion 1994
          Psychiatric Hospitals 1967
          ↓ Residential Care Institutions 1973

Psychiatrists 1967
PN 4194   **SC** 41490
  UF   Neuropsychiatrists
  B   Mental Health Personnel 1967
          Physicians 1967
  R   Clinicians 1973
          Hypnotherapists 1973
          ↓ Psychiatric Hospital Staff 1973
          Psychoanalysts 1973
          ↓ Psychologists 1967
          ↓ Psychotherapists 1973

Psychiatry 1967
PN 6863   **SC** 41500
  B   Medical Sciences 1967

Psychiatry — (cont'd)

- **N**   Adolescent Psychiatry [1985]
  - Biological Psychiatry [1994]
  - Child Psychiatry [1967]
  - Community Psychiatry [1973]
  - Consultation Liaison Psychiatry [1991]
  - Forensic Psychiatry [1973]
  - Geriatric Psychiatry [1997]
  - Neuropsychiatry [1973]
  - Orthopsychiatry [1973]
  - Social Psychiatry [1967]
  - Transcultural Psychiatry [1973]
- **R**   ↓ Psychology [1967]
  - ↓ Treatment [1967]

Psychic Healing
    Use   Faith Healing

Psychoactive Drugs
    Use   Drugs

Psychoanalysis [1967]
PN 18400   **SC** 41520
- **UF**   Psychoanalytic Therapy
- **B**   Psychotherapy [1967]
- **N**   Adlerian Psychotherapy [1997]
  - Dream Analysis [1973]
  - Self Analysis [1994]
- **R**   Catharsis [1973]
  - Erikson (Erik) [1991]
  - Free Association [1994]
  - Freud (Sigmund) [1967]
  - ↓ Hypnotherapy [1973]
  - Negative Therapeutic Reaction [1997]
  - ↓ Psychoanalytic Theory [1967]
  - Psychotherapeutic Neutrality [1997]
  - ↓ Psychotherapeutic Processes [1967]
  - Transactional Analysis [1973]

Psychoanalysts [1973]
PN 2371   **SC** 41530
- **UF**   Analysts
- **B**   Psychotherapists [1973]
- **R**   Hypnotherapists [1973]
  - Psychiatrists [1967]

Psychoanalytic Interpretation [1967]
PN 6368   **SC** 41540
SN Description or formulation of the meaning or significance of any particular event, condition, or process (e.g., patient's productions, art, literature, or historical biographies) from a psychoanalytic perspective.
- **B**   Theoretical Interpretation [1988]
- **R**   Freudian Psychoanalytic School [1973]
  - ↓ Projective Personality Measures [1973]
  - ↓ Projective Techniques [1967]
  - ↓ Psychoanalytic Theory [1967]
  - Psychohistory [1978]

Psychoanalytic Personality Factors [1973]
PN 536   **SC** 41550
- **UF**   Personality Factors (Psychoanalytic)
- **B**   Personality [1967]
- **N**   Conscience [1967]
  - Conscious (Personality Factor) [1973]
  - Death Instinct [1988]
  - Ego [1967]
  - Electra Complex [1973]
  - Id [1973]
  - Libido [1973]
  - Oedipal Complex [1973]
  - Subconscious [1973]

Psychoanalytic Personality Factors — (cont'd)
- **N**   ↓ Superego [1973]
  - Unconscious (Personality Factor) [1967]
- **R**   Penis Envy [1973]
  - ↓ Personality Processes [1967]

Psychoanalytic School (Freudian)
    Use   Freudian Psychoanalytic School

Psychoanalytic Theory [1967]
PN 12792   **SC** 41570
- **N**   Freudian Psychoanalytic School [1973]
- **R**   ↓ Ego Development [1991]
  - Erikson (Erik) [1991]
  - Free Association [1994]
  - Freud (Sigmund) [1967]
  - Metapsychology [1994]
  - ↓ Neopsychoanalytic School [1973]
  - Object Relations [1982]
  - ↓ Personality Processes [1967]
  - ↓ Psychoanalysis [1967]
  - Psychoanalytic Interpretation [1967]
  - Self Psychology [1988]

Psychoanalytic Therapy
    Use   Psychoanalysis

Psychoanalytic Training [1973]
PN 712   **SC** 41590
- **UF**   Training (Psychoanalytic)
- **B**   Clinical Methods Training [1973]
- **R**   Personal Therapy [1991]
  - Psychiatric Training [1973]
  - Psychotherapy Training [1973]
  - Self Analysis [1994]

Psychobiology [1982]
PN 874   **SC** 41595
SN Scientific discipline emphasizing the holistic functioning of the individual in the environment in relation to normal or abnormal behavior.
- **B**   Sciences [1967]
- **R**   Behavioral Genetics [1994]
  - Biological Psychiatry [1994]
  - ↓ Biology [1967]
  - Biopsychosocial Approach [1991]
  - ↓ Psychology [1967]

Psychodiagnosis [1967]
PN 14972   **SC** 41600
SN Diagnosis of mental disorders through the use of psychological methods or tests. Compare MEDICAL DIAGNOSIS.
- **UF**   Clinical Judgment (Psychodiagnosis)
- **B**   Diagnosis [1967]
- **N**   ↓ Psychodiagnostic Interview [1973]
- **R**   Clinical Judgment (Not Diagnosis) [1973]
  - Computer Assisted Diagnosis [1973]
  - Diagnostic and Statistical Manual [1994]
  - Differential Diagnosis [1967]
  - Educational Diagnosis [1978]
  - Forensic Evaluation [1994]
  - International Classification of Diseases [2001]
  - ↓ Mental Disorders [1967]
  - Patient History [1973]
  - Prognosis [1973]
  - ↓ Psychiatric Evaluation [1997]
  - ↓ Psychodiagnostic Typologies [1967]
  - ↓ Psychological Assessment [1997]
  - Psychological Report [1988]
  - Research Diagnostic Criteria [1994]
  - Structured Clinical Interview [2001]

Psychodiagnostic Interview [1973]
PN 1677   **SC** 41630
- **B**   Interviews [1967]
  - Psychodiagnosis [1967]
- **N**   Diagnostic Interview Schedule [1991]
  - Structured Clinical Interview [2001]
- **R**   Intake Interview [1994]
  - ↓ Psychiatric Evaluation [1997]
  - ↓ Psychological Assessment [1997]

Psychodiagnostic Typologies [1967]
PN 5566   **SC** 41640
SN Systematic classification of mental, cognitive, emotional, or behavioral disorders.
- **UF**   Psychiatric Classifications (Taxon)
  - Typologies (Psychodiagnostic)
- **N**   Diagnostic and Statistical Manual [1994]
  - International Classification of Diseases [2001]
  - Research Diagnostic Criteria [1994]
- **R**   Clinical Judgment (Not Diagnosis) [1973]
  - Diagnostic Interview Schedule [1991]
  - Dual Diagnosis [1991]
  - Labeling [1978]
  - Misdiagnosis [1997]
  - ↓ Psychodiagnosis [1967]
  - Structured Clinical Interview [2001]
  - Taxonomies [1973]

Psychodrama [1967]
PN 890   **SC** 41650
SN Projective technique and method of group psychotherapy in which personality make-up, interpersonal relations, conflicts, and emotional problems are explored through dramatization of meaningful situations.
- **B**   Psychotherapeutic Techniques [1967]
  - Psychotherapy [1967]
- **R**   ↓ Group Psychotherapy [1967]
  - Mirroring [1997]
  - Role Playing [1967]

Psychodynamics [1973]
PN 6162   **SC** 41660
SN Human behavior and emotions in terms of conscious and unconscious motivations.
- **UF**   Psychological Correlates
- **R**   ↓ Personality [1967]
  - Psychosocial Factors [1988]
  - ↓ Social Behavior [1967]
  - ↓ Social Interaction [1967]

Psychoeducation [1994]
PN 656   **SC** 41665
- **R**   Client Education [1985]
  - ↓ Education [1967]
  - Educational Therapy [1997]
  - ↓ Health Education [1973]
  - ↓ Treatment [1967]

Psychogalvanic Reflex
    Use   Galvanic Skin Response

Psychogenesis [1973]
PN 914   **SC** 41670
SN Development of mental functions, traits, or states.
- **UF**   Psychological Development
- **B**   Development [1967]
- **N**   ↓ Cognitive Development [1973]
  - Emotional Development [1973]
  - Moral Development [1973]
  - ↓ Psychosocial Development [1973]
- **R**   Adolescent Development [1973]
  - Adult Development [1978]

Psychogenesis — (cont'd)
R   Age Differences 1967
    ↓ Childhood Development 1967
    ↓ Delayed Development 1973
    Developmental Age Groups 1973
    ↓ Developmental Stages 1973
    ↓ Early Childhood Development 1973
    ↓ Human Development 1967
    ↓ Infant Development 1973
    Nature Nurture 1994
    Neonatal Development 1973
    ↓ Physical Development 1973
    Precocious Development 1973
    ↓ Prenatal Development 1973
    Sex Linked Developmental Differences 1973
    Sexual Development 1973

Psychogenic Pain
SN   Term discontinued in 1997. In 2000, the term was stripped from all records containing it, and replaced with SOMATOFORM PAIN DISORDER, its postable counterpart.
Use   Somatoform Pain Disorder

Psychohistory 1978
PN   1076   SC   41685
SN   Psychological, often psychoanalytical, interpretation of historical events and personalities. Includes psychobiographies, historical group fantasies and processes, studies of childhood from an historical perspective and historical psychodynamics.
R   ↓ Biography 1967
    ↓ History 1973
    Psychoanalytic Interpretation 1967

Psychoimmunology
Use   Psychoneuroimmunology

Psychokinesis 1973
PN   211   SC   41690
UF   Telekinesis
B   Extrasensory Perception 1967

Psycholinguistics 1967
PN   2134   SC   41700
SN   Discipline that combines the techniques of linguistics and psychology in the study of the relationship of language and behavior and cognitive processes. Used for the discipline as well as specific psycholinguistic processes themselves.
B   Linguistics 1973
R   Ethnolinguistics 1973
    Metalinguistics 1994
    Neurolinguistics 1991
    Vygotsky (Lev) 1991

Psychological Abuse
Use   Emotional Abuse

Psychological Adjustment
Use   Emotional Adjustment

Psychological Assessment 1997
PN   1628   SC   41706
SN   Assessment of a patient/client by interviews, observations, or psychological tests to evaluate personality, adjustment, abilities, interests, cognitive functioning or functioning in other areas of life. Used for references that focus on the assessment process or the assessment itself.
UF   Assessment (Psychological)
B   Measurement 1967
N   ↓ Behavioral Assessment 1982
    Cognitive Assessment 1997

Psychological Assessment — (cont'd)
N   ↓ Neuropsychological Assessment 1982
R   Clinical Judgment (Not Diagnosis) 1973
    ↓ Evaluation 1967
    Forensic Evaluation 1994
    Geriatric Assessment 1997
    ↓ Interview Schedules 2001
    ↓ Mental Disorders 1967
    Needs Assessment 1985
    ↓ Psychiatric Evaluation 1997
    ↓ Psychodiagnosis 1967
    ↓ Psychodiagnostic Interview 1973
    Psychological Report 1988
    Psychopathology 1967
    Structured Clinical Interview 2001

Psychological Autopsy 1988
PN   93   SC   41705
SN   Psychological profile developed after an individual's death by examination of personal letters or by interviewing acquaintances and relatives. Such autopsies are usually done following suicidal deaths and suspicious cases of death.
R   Autopsy 1973
    ↓ Death and Dying 1967
    Forensic Psychology 1985
    ↓ Suicide 1967

Psychological Correlates
Use   Psychodynamics

Psychological Development
Use   Psychogenesis

Psychological Endurance 1973
PN   459   SC   41710
B   Endurance 1973
R   Hardiness 1997
    Psychological Stress 1973
    Stress Reactions 1973

Psychological Interpretation
Use   Theoretical Interpretation

Psychological Needs 1997
PN   153   SC   41715
UF   Emotional Needs
B   Needs 1967
R   Need Satisfaction 1973
    Needs Assessment 1985

Psychological Reactance 1978
PN   260   SC   41716
SN   Decrease in the attractiveness of an activity, behavior, or attitude as a result of having been forced or induced by external sources to engage in the activity or behavior, or to maintain the attitude. Such reactions may appear as emotional dissatisfaction, involvement and performance decrements, or negative attitude.
UF   Reactance
R   Choice Behavior 1967
    Cognitive Dissonance 1967
    Freedom 1978

Psychological Report 1988
PN   122   SC   41718
UF   Psychiatric Report
R   Educational Diagnosis 1978
    ↓ Evaluation 1967
    Forensic Evaluation 1994
    ↓ Medical Diagnosis 1973
    ↓ Psychiatric Evaluation 1997

Psychological Report — (cont'd)
R   ↓ Psychodiagnosis 1967
    ↓ Psychological Assessment 1997

Psychological Screening Inventory 1973
PN   43   SC   41720
B   Nonprojective Personality Measures 1973
    Screening Tests 1982
    Selection Tests 1973

Psychological Stress 1973
PN   4061   SC   41730
B   Stress 1967
R   ↓ Deprivation 1967
    Hardiness 1997
    Psychological Endurance 1973

Psychological Terminology 1973
PN   1247   SC   41740
SN   Definitions, analysis, evaluation, or review of individual terms or nomenclature in the field of psychology. Compare GLOSSARY.
UF   Nomenclature (Psychological)
    Terminology (Psychological)
B   Terminology 1991
R   Scientific Communication 1973

Psychological Testing
Use   Psychometrics

Psychological Theories 2001
PN   7   SC   41746
B   Theories 1967
N   Associationism 1973
    Behaviorism 1967
    Freudian Psychoanalytic School 1973
    Functionalism 1973
    Gestalt Psychology 1967
    ↓ Neopsychoanalytic School 1973
    Structuralism 1973
R   ↓ History of Psychology 1967
    ↓ Psychology 1967

Psychologist Attitudes 1991
PN   462   SC   41747
SN   Attitudes of, not toward, psychologists.
B   Attitudes 1967
R   Counselor Attitudes 1973
    ↓ Health Personnel Attitudes 1985
    ↓ Psychologists 1967
    ↓ Therapist Attitudes 1978

Psychologists 1967
PN   6190   SC   41750
B   Professional Personnel 1978
N   Clinical Psychologists 1973
    Counseling Psychologists 1988
    ↓ Educational Psychologists 1973
    Experimental Psychologists 1973
    Industrial Psychologists 1973
    Military Psychologists 1997
    Social Psychologists 1973
R   Adler (Alfred) 1967
    ↓ Counselors 1967
    Ellis (Albert) 1991
    Erikson (Erik) 1991
    Freud (Sigmund) 1967
    James (William) 1991
    Jung (Carl) 1973
    Kohlberg (Lawrence) 1991
    Maslow (Abraham Harold) 1991
    ↓ Mental Health Personnel 1967
    Pavlov (Ivan) 1991

Psychologists — (cont'd)
R   Piaget (Jean) 1967
     Psychiatrists 1967
     Psychologist Attitudes 1991
     ↓ Psychotherapists 1973
     Rogers (Carl) 1991
     Scientists 1967
     Skinner (Burrhus Frederic) 1991
     ↓ Social Workers 1973
     Vygotsky (Lev) 1991
     Watson (John Broadus) 1991

Psychology 1967
PN 8386   SC 41760
B   Behavioral Sciences 1997
N   ↓ Applied Psychology 1973
     ↓ Clinical Psychology 1967
     Cognitive Psychology 1985
     Comparative Psychology 1967
     Cross Cultural Psychology 1997
     Depth Psychology 1973
     ↓ Developmental Psychology 1973
     Ecological Psychology 1994
     Experimental Psychology 1967
     Folk Psychology 1997
     Forensic Psychology 1985
     ↓ Humanistic Psychology 1985
     Mathematical Psychology 1973
     Metapsychology 1994
     ↓ Physiological Psychology 1967
     Self Psychology 1988
R   ↓ History of Psychology 1967
     ↓ Psychiatry 1967
     Psychobiology 1982
     ↓ Psychological Theories 2001
     ↓ Psychophysiology 1967

Psychology Education 1978
PN 2688   SC 41765
B   Curriculum 1967
N   ↓ Graduate Psychology Education 1967
R   Counselor Education 1973
     Educational Program Accreditation 1994
     Theoretical Orientation 1982

Psychometrics 1967
PN 4105   SC 41770
SN   Subdiscipline within psychology dealing with the
development and application of statistical techniques
to the analysis of psychological data. Also, psycho-
logical measurement in which numerical estimates
are obtained of a specific aspect of performance.
UF   Psychological Testing
B   Measurement 1967
R   Conjoint Measurement 1994
     ↓ Experimental Design 1967
     ↓ Experimentation 1967
     Item Response Theory 1985
     Psychophysics 1967
     ↓ Statistical Analysis 1967
     Test Interpretation 1985
     ↓ Testing 1967

Psychomotor Development 1973
PN 353   SC 41780
B   Motor Development 1973
N   ↓ Speech Development 1973
R   ↓ Childhood Development 1967
     ↓ Perceptual Development 1973
     Perceptual Motor Development 1991

Psychomotor Processes
Use Perceptual Motor Processes

Psychoneuroimmunology 1991
PN 463   SC 41795
SN   Study of the interrelationship among immune
responses, psychological processes, and the ner-
vous system. Used for the scientific discipline or the
psychoneuroimmunologic processes themselves.
UF   Psychoimmunology
B   Immunology 1973
     Psychophysiology 1967
R   ↓ Endocrinology 1973
     Neuropsychology 1973

Psychoneurosis
Use Neurosis

Psychopath
Use Antisocial Personality

Psychopathology 1967
PN 10226   SC 41820
SN   Study of mental disorders, emotional problems,
or maladaptive behaviors. Used for the scientific dis-
cipline or for unspecified dysfunctions.
B   Pathology 1973
R   ↓ Antisocial Behavior 1971
     Comorbidity 1991
     ↓ Defense Mechanisms 1967
     ↓ Emotional Adjustment 1973
     Homeless Mentally III 1997
     ↓ Mental Disorders 1967
     Psychiatric Patients 1967
     Psychiatric Symptoms 1997
     ↓ Psychological Assessment 1997

Psychopathy
SN   Term discontinued in 1997. In 2000, the term
was stripped from all records containing it, and
replaced with ANTISOCIAL PERSONALITY, its postable counterpart.
Use Antisocial Personality

Psychopharmacology 1967
PN 2492   SC 41840
SN   The study of the effect of drugs on behavior or
other psychological processes. For the use of drugs
in a treatment capacity, use DRUG THERAPY.
B   Pharmacology 1973
R   Drug Abuse Liability 1994

Psychophysical Measurement 1967
PN 1672   SC 41850
SN   Techniques or methodology used to assess per-
ceptual sensitivities and functions of any sensory
modality as related to the parameters of stimulation.
N   Magnitude Estimation 1991
R   Fuzzy Set Theory 1991
     ↓ Perceptual Measures 1973
     Signal Detection (Perception) 1967
     Threshold Determination 1973

Psychophysics 1967
PN 1006   SC 41860
R   ↓ Experimentation 1967
     Psychometrics 1967

Psychophysiologic Disorders
Use Somatoform Disorders

Psychophysiology 1967
PN 3090   SC 41880
SN   Study of the physiological correlates of mental,
somatic, and behavioral processes.
B   Physiology 1967
N   Psychoneuroimmunology 1991

Psychophysiology — (cont'd)
R   Cardiovascular Reactivity 1994
     ↓ Physiological Psychology 1967
     ↓ Psychology 1967

Psychosexual Behavior 1967
PN 9014   SC 41890
SN   Human sexual behavior which includes both
mental and somatic aspects of sexuality.
UF   Sexual Behavior
B   Behavior 1967
N   Bisexuality 1973
     Erection (Penis) 1973
     Extramarital Intercourse 1973
     Heterosexuality 1973
     ↓ Homosexuality 1967
     ↓ Human Courtship 1973
     Hypersexuality 1973
     Masturbation 1973
     Monogamy 1997
     ↓ Orgasm 1973
     ↓ Paraphilias 1988
     Promiscuity 1973
     Prostitution 1973
     Seduction 1994
     Sex Roles 1967
     Sexual Abstinence 1973
     ↓ Sexual Arousal 1978
     ↓ Sexual Function Disturbances 1973
     ↓ Sexual Intercourse (Human) 1973
     Sexual Risk Taking 1997
     Transsexualism 1973
     Transvestism 1973
     Virginity 1973
R   Affection 1973
     Assortative Mating 1991
     Autoeroticism 1997
     Erotomania 1997
     Human Mate Selection 1988
     Pornography 1973
     Professional Client Sexual Relations 1994
     Psychosexual Development 1982
     Romance 1997
     Sex 1967
     Sex Linked Developmental Differences 1973
     Sexual Addiction 1997
     Sexual Attitudes 1973
     Sexual Development 1973
     Sexual Fantasy 1997
     ↓ Sexual Orientation 1997
     Sexual Satisfaction 1994

Psychosexual Development 1982
PN 1555   SC 41895
SN   Psychological maturation and development of
sexual identity, desires, beliefs, and attitudes
throughout the life cycle.
B   Psychosocial Development 1973
R   Emotional Development 1973
     ↓ Gender Identity 1985
     ↓ Psychosexual Behavior 1967
     Sex 1967
     Sexual Attitudes 1973
     Sexual Development 1973
     Sexuality 1973

Psychosis 1967
PN 8075   SC 41910
B   Mental Disorders 1967
N   ↓ Acute Psychosis 1973
     ↓ Affective Psychosis 1973
     ↓ Alcoholic Psychosis 1973
     Capgras Syndrome 1985
     ↓ Childhood Psychosis 1967

Psychosis — (cont'd)
- **N** Chronic Psychosis [1973]
  - Experimental Psychosis [1973]
  - ↓ Hallucinosis [1973]
  - ↓ Paranoia (Psychosis) [1967]
  - Process Psychosis [1973]
  - Reactive Psychosis [1973]
  - ↓ Schizophrenia [1967]
  - Senile Psychosis [1973]
  - Toxic Psychoses [1973]
- **R** Borderline States [1978]
  - Paranoid Schizophrenia [1967]

Psychosocial Development [1973]
PN 7483   **SC** 41920
SN Process of psychological and social maturation occurring at any time during the life cycle.
- **UF** Social Development
- **B** Psychogenesis [1973]
- **N** Childhood Play Development [1973]
  - ↓ Personality Development [1967]
  - Psychosexual Development [1982]
- **R** Aging (Attitudes Toward) [1985]
  - Emotional Development [1973]
  - Erikson (Erik) [1991]
  - Generativity [2001]
  - Moral Development [1973]
  - Object Relations [1982]

Psychosocial Factors [1988]
PN 10384   **SC** 41925
- **R** Demographic Characteristics [1967]
  - Psychodynamics [1973]
  - Risk Factors [2001]
  - ↓ Social Influences [1967]
  - ↓ Sociocultural Factors [1967]

Psychosocial Mental Retardation [1973]
PN 47   **SC** 41930
SN Reversible mental retardation due to environmental and/or social factors with no organic etiological component.
- **UF** Cultural Familial Mental Retardation
- **B** Mental Retardation [1967]
- **R** Borderline Mental Retardation [1973]

Psychosocial Readjustment [1973]
PN 1158   **SC** 41940
SN Attainment of attitudes and skills which will facilitate an individual's reintegration or functioning in society, usually following traumatic or unusual personal experiences. In 1982, this term replaced the discontinued term PSYCHOSOCIAL RESOCIALIZATION. In 2000, PSYCHOSOCIAL RESOCIALIZATION was stripped from all records and replaced with PSYCHOSOCIAL READJUSTMENT.
- **UF** Psychosocial Resocialization
  - Readjustment (Psychosocial)
  - Resocialization (Psychosocial)
- **R** ↓ Psychosocial Rehabilitation [1973]
  - ↓ Treatment [1967]

Psychosocial Rehabilitation [1973]
PN 1712   **SC** 41950
SN Programs, techniques, or processes of treatment by which individuals, institutionalized or otherwise removed from normal community life (e.g., prisoners), acquire psychological and social skills and attitudes which facilitate community reentry.
- **UF** Rehabilitation (Psychosocial)
- **B** Rehabilitation [1967]
- **N** Therapeutic Social Clubs [1973]
  - ↓ Vocational Rehabilitation [1967]

Psychosocial Rehabilitation — (cont'd)
- **R** ↓ Drug Rehabilitation [1973]
- **R** Psychosocial Readjustment [1973]
  - Rehabilitation Counseling [1978]

Psychosocial Resocialization
SN Term was discontinued in 1982. In 2000, the term was stripped from all records containing it, and replaced with PSYCHOSOCIAL READJUSTMENT, its postable counterpart.
- **Use** Psychosocial Readjustment

Psychosomatic Disorders
SN Term discontinued in 2000. Use PSYCHOSOMATIC DISORDERS to access records from 1967-2000.
- **Use** Somatoform Disorders

Psychosomatic Medicine [1978]
PN 517   **SC** 41975
SN Medical specialty dealing with the diagnosis and treatment of psychosomatic disorders.
- **B** Medical Sciences [1967]
- **R** ↓ Health Care Psychology [1985]
  - Somatization Disorder [2001]
  - ↓ Somatoform Disorders [2001]

Psychosurgery [1973]
PN 272   **SC** 41980
- **UF** Leukotomy
  - Lobectomy
  - Lobotomy
- **B** Neurosurgery [1973]
  - Physical Treatment Methods [1973]
- **N** Thalamotomy [1973]
- **R** Sympathectomy [1973]
  - Tractotomy [1973]

Psychotherapeutic Breakthrough [1973]
PN 35   **SC** 41990
- **UF** Breakthrough (Psychotherapeutic)
- **B** Psychotherapeutic Processes [1967]

Psychotherapeutic Counseling [1973]
PN 899   **SC** 42000
- **B** Counseling [1967]
  - Psychotherapy [1967]
- **N** ↓ Family Therapy [1967]
- **R** ↓ Marriage Counseling [1973]
  - Premarital Counseling [1973]

Psychotherapeutic Methods
- **Use** Psychotherapeutic Techniques

Psychotherapeutic Neutrality [1997]
PN 35   **SC** 42025
- **UF** Neutrality (Psychotherapeutic)
- **R** ↓ Psychoanalysis [1967]
  - ↓ Psychotherapeutic Processes [1967]
  - ↓ Psychotherapeutic Techniques [1967]

Psychotherapeutic Outcomes [1973]
PN 2971   **SC** 42030
SN Limited to treatment results that are a direct function of specific characteristics of clients or therapists or a function of unique or specifically-described circumstances of the treatment itself.
- **UF** Outcomes (Psychotherapeutic)
- **B** Treatment Outcomes [1982]
- **R** Mental Health Program Evaluation [1973]
  - Treatment Dropouts [1978]
  - Treatment Effectiveness Evaluation [1973]

Psychotherapeutic Processes [1967]
PN 17281   **SC** 42040
SN Experiential, attitudinal, emotional, or behavioral phenomena occurring during the course of psychotherapy. Applies to the client or psychotherapist individually or to their interaction.
- **UF** Client Counselor Interaction
  - Counselor Client Interaction
  - Patient Therapist Interaction
  - Therapist Patient Interaction
- **B** Therapeutic Processes [1978]
- **N** Countertransference [1973]
  - Insight (Psychotherapeutic Process) [1973]
  - Negative Therapeutic Reaction [1997]
  - Psychotherapeutic Breakthrough [1973]
  - Psychotherapeutic Resistance [1973]
  - Psychotherapeutic Transference [1967]
  - Therapeutic Alliance [1994]
- **R** Enactments [1997]
  - ↓ Internalization [1997]
  - Mirroring [1997]
  - Professional Client Sexual Relations [1994]
  - ↓ Psychoanalysis [1967]
  - Psychotherapeutic Neutrality [1997]
  - ↓ Psychotherapy [1967]
  - ↓ Treatment Outcomes [1982]

Psychotherapeutic Resistance [1973]
PN 842   **SC** 42050
SN Conscious or unconscious defensive attempts by the client to prevent repressed material from coming to consciousness.
- **UF** Resistance (Psychotherapeutic)
- **B** Psychotherapeutic Processes [1967]
  - Resistance [1997]
- **R** Negative Therapeutic Reaction [1997]
  - Treatment Refusal [1994]

Psychotherapeutic Techniques [1967]
PN 10744   **SC** 42060
- **UF** Psychotherapeutic Methods
  - Therapeutic Techniques (Psychother)
- **B** Treatment [1967]
- **N** Animal Assisted Therapy [1994]
  - Autogenic Training [1973]
  - Cotherapy [1982]
  - Dream Analysis [1973]
  - Guided Imagery [2001]
  - Mirroring [1997]
  - Morita Therapy [1994]
  - Mutual Storytelling Technique [1973]
  - Paradoxical Techniques [1982]
  - Psychodrama [1967]
- **R** Age Regression (Hypnotic) [1988]
  - Centering [1991]
  - Client Centered Therapy [1967]
  - Conjoint Therapy [1973]
  - ↓ Creative Arts Therapy [1994]
  - Free Association [1994]
  - Homework [1988]
  - Interpersonal Psychotherapy [1997]
  - Poetry Therapy [1994]
  - Primal Therapy [1978]
  - Psychotherapeutic Neutrality [1997]
  - ↓ Psychotherapy [1967]
  - Rational Emotive Therapy [1978]
  - Reality Therapy [1973]
  - ↓ Relaxation Therapy [1978]
  - Role Playing [1967]
  - ↓ Self Help Techniques [1982]
  - Self Talk [1988]
  - ↓ Twelve Step Programs [1997]
  - Wilderness Experience [1991]

Psychotherapeutic Transference [1967]
PN 3160   SC 42070
SN Unconscious projection of feelings, thoughts, and wishes to the therapist that were originally associated with important figures from the client's past.
UF   Transference (Psychotherapeutic)
B   Psychotherapeutic Processes [1967]
R   Countertransference [1973]
    Enactments [1997]
    Negative Therapeutic Reaction [1997]
    Professional Client Sexual Relations [1994]
    Therapeutic Alliance [1994]

Psychotherapist Attitudes [1973]
PN 791   SC 42080
SN Attitudes of, not toward, psychotherapists.
B   Therapist Attitudes [1978]
R   ↓ Psychotherapists [1973]
    Therapist Role [1978]

Psychotherapist Trainees
Use   Therapist Trainees

Psychotherapists [1973]
PN 3344   SC 42100
B   Mental Health Personnel [1967]
    Therapists [1967]
N   Hypnotherapists [1973]
    Psychoanalysts [1973]
R   Clinical Psychologists [1973]
    Psychiatrists [1967]
    ↓ Psychologists [1967]
    Psychotherapist Attitudes [1973]

Psychotherapy [1967]
PN 18098   SC 42110
UF   Reconstructive Psychotherapy
B   Treatment [1967]
N   Adlerian Psychotherapy [1997]
    Adolescent Psychotherapy [1994]
    Analytical Psychotherapy [1973]
    Autogenic Training [1973]
    ↓ Behavior Therapy [1967]
    Brief Psychotherapy [1967]
    ↓ Child Psychotherapy [1967]
    Client Centered Therapy [1967]
    Eclectic Psychotherapy [1994]
    Existential Therapy [1973]
    Experiential Psychotherapy [1973]
    Expressive Psychotherapy [1973]
    Eye Movement Desensitization Therapy [1997]
    Feminist Therapy [1994]
    Geriatric Psychotherapy [1973]
    Gestalt Therapy [1973]
    ↓ Group Psychotherapy [1967]
    Guided Imagery [2001]
    ↓ Hypnotherapy [1973]
    Individual Psychotherapy [1973]
    Insight Therapy [1973]
    Interpersonal Psychotherapy [1997]
    Logotherapy [1973]
    Persuasion Therapy [1973]
    Primal Therapy [1978]
    ↓ Psychoanalysis [1967]
    Psychodrama [1967]
    ↓ Psychotherapeutic Counseling [1973]
    Rational Emotive Therapy [1978]
    Reality Therapy [1973]
    Relationship Therapy [1973]
    Supportive Psychotherapy [1997]
    Transactional Analysis [1973]
R   Cognitive Therapy [1982]
    Cotherapy [1982]

Psychotherapy — (cont'd)
R   Couples Therapy [1994]
    Educational Therapy [1997]
    Holistic Health [1985]
    ↓ Marriage Counseling [1973]
    Paradoxical Techniques [1982]
    Pastoral Counseling [1967]
    Phototherapy [1991]
    ↓ Psychotherapeutic Processes [1967]
    ↓ Psychotherapeutic Techniques [1967]
    Recreation Therapy [1973]
    Spontaneous Remission [1973]
    Theoretical Orientation [1982]

Psychotherapy (Individual)
Use   Individual Psychotherapy

Psychotherapy Training [1973]
PN 1472   SC 42120
UF   Training (Psychotherapy)
B   Clinical Methods Training [1973]
R   Cotherapy [1982]
    Counselor Education [1973]
    Psychiatric Training [1973]
    Psychoanalytic Training [1973]

Psychotic Depressive Reaction
SN Term was discontinued in 1988. In 2000, the term was stripped from all records containing it, and replaced with MAJOR DEPRESSION, its postable counterpart.
Use   Major Depression

Psychotic Episode (Acute)
Use   Acute Psychosis

Psychotic Symptoms
Use   Psychiatric Symptoms

Psychoticism [1978]
PN 499   SC 42145
B   Personality Traits [1967]

Psychotomimetic Drugs [1973]
PN 48   SC 42150
B   Drugs [1967]
N   Lysergic Acid Diethylamide [1967]
    Mescaline [1973]
    Peyote [1973]
R   Experimental Psychosis [1973]
    ↓ Hallucinogenic Drugs [1967]
    ↓ Psychedelic Drugs [1973]

Psychotropic Drugs
Use   Drugs

PTA
Use   Parent School Relationship

Puberty [1973]
PN 599   SC 42160
B   Developmental Stages [1973]
R   Menarche [1973]

Pubescence
Use   Sexual Development

Public Attitudes
Use   Public Opinion

Public Health [1988]
PN 614   SC 42185

Public Health — (cont'd)
B   Health [1973]
N   Epidemics [2001]
R   Health Promotion [1991]
    ↓ Health Screening [1997]
    Public Health Services [1973]

Public Health Service Nurses [1973]
PN 133   SC 42190
B   Government Personnel [1973]
    Nurses [1967]
R   Public Health Services [1973]

Public Health Services [1973]
PN 731   SC 42200
B   Community Services [1967]
R   ↓ Health [1973]
    Integrated Services [1997]
    ↓ Mental Health Programs [1973]
    ↓ Public Health [1988]
    Public Health Service Nurses [1973]

Public Opinion [1973]
PN 1849   SC 42210
UF   Opinion (Public)
    Public Attitudes
B   Attitudes [1967]
R   Community Attitudes [1973]
    Political Psychology [1997]
    Public Relations [1973]

Public Policy
Use   Government Policy Making

Public Relations [1973]
PN 191   SC 42220
SN The business of attempting to influence or persuade individuals or the public to have an understanding or concern for, or positive disposition toward, a particular person, organization, idea, policy, practice, or activity.
R   ↓ Advertising [1967]
    ↓ Consumer Attitudes [1973]
    Public Opinion [1973]

Public School Education [1973]
PN 1123   SC 42230
SN Education in free tax-supported schools controlled by a local governmental authority.
B   Education [1967]

Public Sector [1985]
PN 559   SC 42235
SN Any type of government-related or public organization, service, or sphere of involvement.
N   Government [1967]
    Government Agencies [1973]

Public Speaking [1973]
PN 517   SC 42240
SN Formal or informal speech in a group or public setting.
B   Oral Communication [1985]
R   Debates [1997]
    Speech Anxiety [1985]

Public Transportation [1973]
PN 116   SC 42250
B   Community Facilities [1973]
    Transportation [1973]
R   Air Transportation [1973]
    Railroad Trains [1973]

Public Welfare Services
Use Community Welfare Services

Puerto Rican Americans
Use Hispanics

Pulmonary Disorders
Use Lung Disorders

Pulmonary Emphysema 1973
PN 38   SC 42290
  UF Emphysema (Pulmonary)
  B Lung Disorders 1973

Pulmonary Tuberculosis 1973
PN 14   SC 42300
  B Bacterial Disorders 1973
     Lung Disorders 1973
     Tuberculosis 1973

Pulse (Arterial)
Use Arterial Pulse

Punishment 1967
PN 2747   SC 42320
SN Presentation of a punisher contingent on the performance of some behavior. Also, the punishing event or object itself which, when following the performance of some behavior, results in a reduction in the occurrence or frequency of that behavior. Compare AVERSIVE STIMULATION. Used for both human and animal populations.
  UF Corporal Punishment
  B Reinforcement 1967
  N Response Cost 1997
  R Coercion 1994
     Threat 1967

Punishment (Capital)
Use Capital Punishment

Pupil (Eye) 1973
PN 141   SC 42340
  B Eye (Anatomy) 1967

Pupil Dilation 1973
PN 307   SC 42360
  UF Dilation (Pupil)
  R ↓ Eye (Anatomy) 1967

Purdue Perceptual Motor Survey 1973
PN 8   SC 42380
  B Sensorimotor Measures 1973

Purkinje Cells 1994
PN 111   SC 42385
  B Cerebellum 1973
     Neurons 1973

Puromycin 1973
PN 36   SC 42390
  B Amines 1973
     Antibiotics 1973

Putamen 1985
PN 215   SC 42405
SN The largest and most lateral part of the basal ganglia which, together with the caudate nucleus and globus pallidus, forms the corpus striatum.
  B Basal Ganglia 1973

Pygmalion Effect
Use Self Fulfilling Prophecies

Pygmy Chimpanzees
Use Bonobos

Pyramidal Tracts 1973
PN 114   SC 42410
  B Efferent Pathways 1982
     Spinal Cord 1973

Pyramidotomy 1973
PN 10   SC 42420
  B Neurosurgery 1973
  R Tractotomy 1973

Pyromania 1973
PN 39   SC 42430
  R ↓ Impulse Control Disorders 1997
     Impulsiveness 1973
     ↓ Personality Disorders 1967

Q Sort Testing Technique 1967
PN 176   SC 42440
  B Testing Methods 1967

Q Test
Use Cochran Q Test

Quaalude
Use Methaqualone

Quadriplegia 1985
PN 100   SC 42470
SN Paralysis of both arms and both legs.
  B Paralysis 1973
  R ↓ Central Nervous System Disorders 1973
     Hemiplegia 1978
     ↓ Injuries 1973
     ↓ Musculoskeletal Disorders 1973
     Paraplegia 1978
     ↓ Spinal Cord Injuries 1973

Quails 1973
PN 366   SC 42480
  B Birds 1967

Quality Circles
Use Participative Management

Quality Control 1988
PN 344   SC 42483
SN Efforts or techniques directed at the detection of imperfections or shortcomings in products or services.
  R Accountability 1988
     Consumer Satisfaction 1994
     Human Factors Engineering 1973
     Organizational Effectiveness 1985
     Organizational Objectives 1973
     Participative Management 1988
     ↓ Quality of Services 1997

Quality of Care 1988
PN 1518   SC 42484
SN Quality of medical or mental health care.
  B Quality of Services 1997
  R Accountability 1988
     Caregivers 1988
     Child Day Care 1973
     ↓ Client Rights 1988
     ↓ Health Care Delivery 1978

Quality of Care — (cont'd)
  R ↓ Health Care Services 1978
     Home Care 1985
     ↓ Managed Care 1994
     ↓ Mental Health Services 1978
     ↓ Treatment 1967

Quality of Education
Use Educational Quality

Quality of Life 1985
PN 4162   SC 42485
  N Quality of Work Life 1988
  R Life Satisfaction 1985
     ↓ Lifestyle 1978
     Lifestyle Changes 1997
     Well Being 1994

Quality of Services 1997
PN 404   SC 57510
SN Used for health care and non-health care services. Consider QUALITY of CARE for health care services.
  UF Service Quality
  N Quality of Care 1988
  R ↓ Advertising 1967
     ↓ Consumer Attitudes 1973
     Consumer Satisfaction 1994
     ↓ Health Care Delivery 1978
     ↓ Health Care Services 1978
     Marketing 1973
     ↓ Mental Health Services 1978
     ↓ Professional Standards 1973
     Quality Control 1988
     Retailing 1991
     Treatment Guidelines 2001

Quality of Work Life 1988
PN 386   SC 42487
SN Includes aspects such as salary, benefits, safety, and efficiency, as well as variety and challenge, responsibility, contribution, and recognition.
  B Quality of Life 1985
  R ↓ Job Characteristics 1985
     Job Satisfaction 1967
     Occupational Stress 1973
     ↓ Organizational Characteristics 1997
     Organizational Climate 1973
     ↓ Working Conditions 1973

Quartimax Rotation 1973
PN 4   SC 42490
  B Orthogonal Rotation 1973

Questioning 1982
PN 1350   SC 42495
  R ↓ Cognitive Processes 1967
     Curiosity 1967
     ↓ Education 1967
     Guessing 1973
     Information Seeking 1973
     Interviewing 1973
     ↓ Interviews 1967
     Legal Interrogation 1994
     ↓ Teaching Methods 1967

Questionnaires 1967
PN 5737   SC 42500
  B Measurement 1967
  N General Health Questionnaire 1991
  R Mail Surveys 1994
     ↓ Surveys 1967
     Telephone Surveys 1994

Quinidine
SN Term was discontinued in 1997. In 2000, the term was stripped from all records containing it, and replaced with ALKALOIDS, its postable counterpart.
  Use Alkaloids

Quinine [1973]
PN 164   SC 42560
  B   Alkaloids [1973]
       Analgesic Drugs [1973]
       Local Anesthetics [1973]

Quinpirole [1994]
PN 111   SC 42570
  B   Antihypertensive Drugs [1973]
       Dopamine Agonists [1985]

Rabbis [1973]
PN 42   SC 42580
  B   Clergy [1973]
  R   Chaplains [1973]
       Judaism [1967]

Rabbits [1967]
PN 2757   SC 42590
  B   Mammals [1973]

Race (Anthropological) [1973]
PN 484   SC 42600
  R   Ethnography [1973]
       Ethnology [1967]
       ↓ Racial and Ethnic Attitudes [1982]
       Racial and Ethnic Differences [1982]
       ↓ Racial and Ethnic Groups [2001]
       ↓ Sociocultural Factors [1967]
       ↓ Whites [1982]

Race and Ethnic Discrimination [1994]
PN 569   SC 42605
SN Use SOCIAL DISCRIMINATION to access references from 1982-1993. In 1994, this term replaced the discontinued terms MINORITY GROUP DISCRIMINATION and RACIAL DISCRIMINATION. In 2000, these terms were stripped from all records and replaced with RACE AND ETHNIC DISCRIMINATION.
  UF   Ethnic Discrimination
       Minority Group Discrimination
       Racial Discrimination
  B   Social Discrimination [1982]
  R   Affirmative Action [1985]
       ↓ Civil Rights [1978]
       Employment Discrimination [1994]
       Minority Groups [1967]
       ↓ Prejudice [1967]
       ↓ Racial and Ethnic Attitudes [1982]
       Racial and Ethnic Differences [1982]
       Racism [1973]

Race Attitudes
SN Term was discontinued in 1982. In 2000, the term was stripped from all records containing it, and replaced with RACIAL AND ETHNIC ATTITUDES, its postable counterpart.
  Use Racial and Ethnic Attitudes

Race Relations
SN Term was discontinued in 1982. In 2000, the term was stripped from all records containing it, and replaced with RACIAL AND EHNIC RELATIONS, its postable counterpart.
  Use Racial and Ethnic Relations

Racial and Ethnic Attitudes [1982]
PN 3021   SC 42617
SN Attitudes about race or ethnicity or toward members of a given racial or ethnic group. In 1982, this term was created to replace the discontinued term RACE ATTITUDES. In 2000, RACE ATTITUDES was stripped from all records and replaced with RACIAL AND ETHNIC ATTITUDES.
  UF   Race Attitudes
  B   Attitudes [1967]
  N   AntiSemitism [1973]
       Ethnocentrism [1973]
       Racism [1973]
  R   Cultural Sensitivity [1994]
       Ethnology [1967]
       Multiculturalism [1997]
       ↓ Prejudice [1967]
       Race (Anthropological) [1973]
       Race and Ethnic Discrimination [1994]
       ↓ Racial and Ethnic Groups [2001]
       Racial and Ethnic Relations [1982]
       Stereotyped Attitudes [1967]

Racial and Ethnic Differences [1982]
PN 12784   SC 42618
SN Differences between two or more racial or ethnic groups. Use CROSS CULTURAL DIFFERENCES for cultural comparisons, and use REGIONAL DIFFERENCES for geographical comparisons. In 1982, this term replaced the discontinued term RACIAL DIFFERENCES. In 2000, RACIAL DIFFERENCES was stripped from all records and replaced with RACIAL AND ETHNIC DIFFERENCES.
  UF   Ethnic Differences
       Racial Differences
  R   Cross Cultural Communication [1997]
       Cross Cultural Differences [1967]
       Cross Cultural Psychology [1997]
       Cross Cultural Treatment [1994]
       Cultural Sensitivity [1994]
       Ethnology [1967]
       Interethnic Family [1988]
       Interracial Family [1988]
       Interracial Offspring [1988]
       Multiculturalism [1997]
       Race (Anthropological) [1973]
       Race and Ethnic Discrimination [1994]
       ↓ Racial and Ethnic Groups [2001]
       Racism [1973]

Racial and Ethnic Groups [2001]
PN 4363   SC 42616
SN In 2000, this term was created to replace the discontinued term ETHNIC GROUPS. ETHNIC GROUPS was stripped from all records and replaced with RACIAL AND ETHNIC GROUPS.
  UF   Ethnic Groups
  N   Arabs [1988]
       ↓ Asians [1982]
       Blacks [1982]
       Gypsies [1973]
       ↓ Hispanics [1982]
       ↓ Indigenous Populations [2001]
       ↓ Whites [1982]
  R   Cross Cultural Communication [1997]
       Cross Cultural Differences [1967]
       Cross Cultural Psychology [1997]
       Cross Cultural Treatment [1994]
       Cultural Sensitivity [1994]
       ↓ Culture (Anthropological) [1967]
       Ethnic Values [1973]
       Ethnology [1967]
       ↓ Ethnospecific Disorders [1973]
       Minority Groups [1967]
       Multiculturalism [1997]

Racial and Ethnic Groups — (cont'd)
  R   Race (Anthropological) [1973]
       ↓ Racial and Ethnic Attitudes [1982]
       Racial and Ethnic Differences [1982]
       ↓ Religious Groups [1997]
       ↓ Sociocultural Factors [1967]
       Tribes [1973]

Racial and Ethnic Relations [1982]
PN 1206   SC 42619
SN Contact and interaction between and among different racial and ethnic groups. In 1982, this term was created to replace the discontinued term RACE RELATIONS. In 2000, RACE RELATIONS was stripped from all records and replaced with RACIAL AND ETHNIC RELATIONS.
  UF   Race Relations
  B   Social Behavior [1967]
  R   Cross Cultural Communication [1997]
       Cultural Sensitivity [1994]
       Ethnology [1967]
       Interracial Family [1988]
       Interracial Marriage [1973]
       Interracial Offspring [1988]
       Multiculturalism [1997]
       ↓ Prejudice [1967]
       ↓ Racial and Ethnic Attitudes [1982]
       School Integration [1982]
       ↓ Social Discrimination [1982]
       Social Equality [1973]
       ↓ Social Integration [1982]

Racial Differences
SN Term was discontinued in 1982. In 2000, the term was stripped from all records containing it, and replaced with RACIAL AND ETHNIC DIFFERENCES, its postable counterpart.
  Use Racial and Ethnic Differences

Racial Discrimination
SN Term was discontinued in 1982. From 1982-1993, SOCIAL DISCRIMINATION was used to capture this concept, and then in 1994, RACE AND ETHNIC DISCRIMINATION was created as the new postable terminology. In 2000, RACIAL DISCRIMINATION was stripped from all records containing it, and replaced with RACE AND ETHNIC DISCRIMINATION, its postable counterpart.
  Use Race and Ethnic Discrimination

Racial Integration
SN Term was discontinued in 1982. In 2000, the term was stripped from all records containing it, and replaced with SOCIAL INTEGRATION, its postable counterpart.
  Use Social Integration

Racial Segregation (Schools)
  Use School Integration

Racism [1973]
PN 1120   SC 42660
SN Belief that racial differences produce inherent superiority of a particular race.
  B   Racial and Ethnic Attitudes [1982]
  R   AntiSemitism [1973]
       Employment Discrimination [1994]
       ↓ Prejudice [1967]
       Race and Ethnic Discrimination [1994]
       Racial and Ethnic Differences [1982]
       ↓ Social Discrimination [1982]
       ↓ Social Issues [1991]

Radial Nerve
Use Spinal Nerves

Radiation 1967
PN 550   **SC** 42680
  UF Irradiation
  N   Laser Irradiation 1973
  R   Radiation Therapy 1973
    ↓ Roentgenography 1973

Radiation Therapy 1973
PN 219   **SC** 42690
  UF X Ray Therapy
  B   Physical Treatment Methods 1973
  R   ↓ Radiation 1967

Radical Movements 1973
PN 69   **SC** 42700
  N   Political Revolution 1973
  R   ↓ Social Movements 1967
    Terrorism 1982

Radicalism (Political)
Use Political Radicalism

Radio 1973
PN 294   **SC** 42730
  B   Audiovisual Communications Media 1973
    Mass Media 1967
    Telecommunications Media 1973
  R   ↓ News Media 1997

Radiography
Use Roentgenography

Radiology 1973
PN 64   **SC** 42740
  B   Medical Sciences 1967

Rage
Use Anger

Railroad Trains 1973
PN 139   **SC** 42760
  UF Trains (Railroad)
  B   Ground Transportation 1973
  R   Public Transportation 1973

Random Sampling 1973
PN 191   **SC** 42780
  B   Sampling (Experimental) 1973
  R   Experiment Volunteers 1973

Rank Difference Correlation 1973
PN 29   **SC** 42790
  UF Spearman Rho
  B   Statistical Correlation 1967

Rank Order Correlation 1973
PN 107   **SC** 42800
  B   Statistical Correlation 1967

Rape 1973
PN 2251   **SC** 42810
  B   Sexual Abuse 1988
    Sexual Intercourse (Human) 1973
  N   Acquaintance Rape 1991

Raphe Nuclei 1982
PN 430   **SC** 42815

Raphe Nuclei — (cont'd)
SN Serotonin synthesizing neurons in and near the median plane of the brain stem lying dorsally in the pons. These nuclei are sometimes grouped with the reticular formation and are thought to function as part of the limbic system.
  B   Pons 1973
  R   ↓ Hindbrain 1997
    ↓ Limbic System 1973
    Reticular Formation 1967

Rapid Eye Movement 1971
PN 311   **SC** 42820
  UF REM
  B   Eye Movements 1967
  R   REM Dream Deprivation 1973
    REM Dreams 1973
    REM Sleep 1973

Rapid Eye Movement Dreams
Use REM Dreams

Rapid Eye Movement Sleep
Use REM Sleep

Rapid Heart Rate
Use Tachycardia

Rapport
Use Interpersonal Interaction

Rasch Model
Use Item Response Theory

Rat Learning 1967
PN 2096   **SC** 42860
SN Not defined prior to 1982. Use RAT LEARNING or RATS to access references from 1967-1981. From 1982 used for discussions of hypotheses or theories of learning in rats.
  B   Learning 1967

Rating 1967
PN 1886   **SC** 42880
SN Measurement technique involving relative evaluation or estimate of characteristics or qualities of a person, process, or thing. Used when rating as a technique is the object of interest.
  B   Testing 1967
  R   Halo Effect 1982
    Interrater Reliability 1982

Rating Scales 1967
PN 9831   **SC** 42890
  B   Measurement 1967
  N   Likert Scales 1994
  R   Multidimensional Scaling 1982

Ratio Reinforcement
Use Fixed Ratio Reinforcement AND Variable Ratio Reinforcement

Ratiocination
Use Logical Thinking

Rational Emotive Therapy 1978
PN 1069   **SC** 42915
SN A therapy developed by Albert Ellis that stresses cognitive, philosophic, and value-oriented aspects of personality and views the goal of treatment as the client's development of rational as opposed to irrational beliefs about his/her problem.
  B   Psychotherapy 1967

Rational Emotive Therapy — (cont'd)
  R   ↓ Behavior Therapy 1967
    Cognitive Therapy 1982
    Ellis (Albert) 1991
    ↓ Psychotherapeutic Techniques 1967

Rationalization 1973
PN 131   **SC** 42920
  B   Defense Mechanisms 1967

Rats 1967
PN 58705   **SC** 42930
  UF Albino Rats
    White Rats
  B   Rodents 1973
  N   Norway Rats 1973

Rauwolfia
SN Term was discontinued in 1997. In 2000, the term was stripped from all records containing it and replaced with ALKALOIDS, its postable counterpart.
Use Alkaloids

Raven Coloured Progressive Matrices 1973
PN 115   **SC** 42950
  B   Intelligence Measures 1967

Raven Progressive Matrices 1978
PN 215   **SC** 42960
SN Use RAVENS PROGRESSIVE MATRICES to access references from 1973-1977.
  B   Intelligence Measures 1967

Raynauds Disease
Use Cardiovascular Disorders

RDC
Use Research Diagnostic Criteria

Reactance
Use Psychological Reactance

Reaction Formation 1973
PN 27   **SC** 42990
SN Defense mechanism that leads to the formation of behaviors and attitudes opposite to the repressed anxiety-inducing behavior or feelings.
  B   Defense Mechanisms 1967

Reaction Time 1967
PN 8627   **SC** 43000
SN Minimal time interval between the onset of a stimulus and the beginning of a subject's response to that stimulus. Compare RESPONSE LATENCY.
  UF Response Lag
    Response Speed
    Response Time
    RT (Response)
    Speed (Response)
  B   Response Parameters 1973
  R   Cognitive Processing Speed 1997
    Conceptual Tempo 1985

Reactive Attachment Disorder
Use Attachment Disorders

Reactive Depression 1973
PN 265   **SC** 43020
  B   Major Depression 1988

Reactive Psychosis 1973
PN 201   **SC** 43030
  UF Reactive Schizophrenia

Reactive Psychosis — (cont'd)
UF Traumatic Psychosis
B   Psychosis 1967

Reactive Schizophrenia
Use Reactive Psychosis AND Schizophrenia

Readability 1978
PN 421   **SC** 43045
SN Textual difficulty or other qualitative aspects of reading material that facilitate comprehension. May include clarity of graphic displays.
B   Written Language 1967
R   ↓ Legibility 1978
     ↓ Reading 1967
     Reading Comprehension 1973
     Reading Materials 1973

Readaptation
Use Adaptation

Readiness Potential
Use Contingent Negative Variation

Reading 1967
PN 3982   **SC** 43080
N   Braille 1978
     Oral Reading 1973
     Remedial Reading 1973
     Silent Reading 1973
R   Dyslexia 1973
     Initial Teaching Alphabet 1973
     Proofreading 1988
     Readability 1978
     Reading Ability 1973
     Reading Achievement 1973
     Reading Comprehension 1973
     Reading Development 1997
     ↓ Reading Disabilities 1967
     Reading Education 1973
     Reading Materials 1973
     Reading Readiness 1973
     ↓ Reading Skills 1973
     Reading Speed 1973
     Sight Vocabulary 1973

Reading Ability 1973
PN 3577   **SC** 43090
SN Perceptual and intellectual capacity or efficiency in reading.
B   Cognitive Ability 1973
R   Academic Aptitude 1973
     ↓ Reading 1967
     Reading Development 1997
     ↓ Reading Skills 1973

Reading Achievement 1973
PN 3523   **SC** 43100
B   Academic Achievement 1967
R   ↓ Reading 1967

Reading Aloud
Use Oral Reading

Reading Comprehension 1973
PN 5336   **SC** 43110
B   Reading Skills 1973
     Verbal Comprehension 1985
R   Readability 1978
     ↓ Reading 1967

Reading Development 1997
PN 400   **SC** 43115

Reading Development — (cont'd)
R   ↓ Language Development 1967
     ↓ Literacy 1973
     ↓ Reading 1967
     Reading Ability 1973
     Reading Readiness 1973
     ↓ Reading Skills 1973

Reading Disabilities 1967
PN 2993   **SC** 43120
B   Learning Disorders 1967
N   Dyslexia 1973
R   ↓ Alexia 1982
     Educational Diagnosis 1978
     ↓ Reading 1967

Reading Education 1973
PN 3820   **SC** 43130
B   Language Arts Education 1973
R   Braille 1978
     Braille Instruction 1973
     Initial Teaching Alphabet 1973
     ↓ Literacy 1973
     Literacy Programs 1997
     Phonics 1973
     ↓ Reading 1967
     Remedial Reading 1973

Reading Materials 1973
PN 1193   **SC** 43140
UF Basal Readers
B   Instructional Media 1967
R   ↓ Books 1973
     Braille 1978
     Readability 1978
     ↓ Reading 1967
     Text Structure 1982
     ↓ Textbooks 1978

Reading Measures 1973
PN 689   **SC** 43150
B   Measurement 1967
N   Gates MacGinitie Reading Tests 1973
     Metropolitan Readiness Tests 1978

Reading Readiness 1973
PN 398   **SC** 43160
SN Developmental level at which language skills; cognitive, perceptual and motor abilities; experience; and interest combine to enable a child to profit from specific reading activities. Compare SCHOOL READINESS.
R   ↓ Reading 1967
     Reading Development 1997

Reading Skills 1973
PN 2024   **SC** 43170
SN Proficiency in reading developed through practice and influenced by ability. Includes word recognition, pronunciation, and comprehension.
B   Ability 1967
N   Reading Comprehension 1973
     Reading Speed 1973
R   ↓ Literacy 1973
     Literacy Programs 1997
     ↓ Reading 1967
     Reading Ability 1973
     Reading Development 1997
     Sight Vocabulary 1973
     Word Recognition 1988

Reading Speed 1973
PN 704   **SC** 43180

Reading Speed — (cont'd)
B   Reading Skills 1973
R   ↓ Reading 1967

Readjustment (Psychosocial)
Use Psychosocial Readjustment

Readmission (Hospital)
Use Hospital Admission

Readmission (Psychiatric Hospital)
Use Psychiatric Hospital Readmission

Realism (Philosophy) 1973
PN 167   **SC** 43220
B   Philosophies 1967

Reality 1973
PN 1167   **SC** 43230
R   Metaphysics 1973
     Reality Testing 1973
     Reality Therapy 1973

Reality Testing 1973
PN 252   **SC** 43240
SN Cognitive process of evaluation and judgment for differentiation between objective perceptions originating outside of the self and subjective stimuli or fantasies.
R   ↓ Cognitive Processes 1967
     ↓ Personality Processes 1967
     Reality 1973

Reality Therapy 1973
PN 414   **SC** 43250
SN Method of psychotherapeutic treatment based on assumption of client's personal responsibility for his/her behavior. Therapist actively guides client to accurate self-perception for fulfillment of needs of self-worth and respect for others.
B   Psychotherapy 1967
R   ↓ Psychotherapeutic Techniques 1967
     Reality 1973

Reasoning 1967
PN 4308   **SC** 43260
B   Thinking 1967
N   ↓ Inductive Deductive Reasoning 1973
R   Analogy 1991
     Cognitive Hypothesis Testing 1982
     Declarative Knowledge 1997
     Dialectics 1973
     Intelligence 1967
     ↓ Problem Solving 1967
     Procedural Knowledge 1997

Recall (Learning) 1967
PN 10438   **SC** 43290
B   Retention 1967
N   Cued Recall 1994
     Free Recall 1973
     Serial Recall 1994
R   ↓ Memory 1967
     Memory Training 1994
     Reminiscence 1985

Recency Effect 1973
PN 341   **SC** 43298
SN Component of the serial position effect which is manifested by a greater ease in learning items which occur at the end of a series rather than those toward the middle.
B   Serial Position Effect 1982

Recency Effect — (cont'd)
R   ↓ Learning   1967
     Primacy Effect   1973

Receptive Fields   1985
PN   117   SC   43299
SN   Spatially discrete patterns of peripheral and central neuronal innervation of sensory mechanisms.
B   Nervous System   1967
N   Cutaneous Receptive Fields   1985
     Visual Receptive Fields   1982
R   ↓ Afferent Pathways   1982
     Neural Plasticity   1994
     Sensory Neglect   1994
   ↓ Sensory Neurons   1973

Receptor Binding   1985
PN   2680   SC   43297
SN   Affinity processes occurring between chemical substances and specific cellular sites in the body (e.g., blood platelet or neural receptor binding of an adrenergic drug.) Consider also NEURAL RECEPTORS.
B   Neurochemistry   1973
     Neurophysiology   1973
R   ↓ Neural Receptors   1973

Receptors (Neural)
Use   Neural Receptors

Recessiveness (Genetic)
Use   Genetic Recessiveness

Recidivism   1973
PN   1425   SC   43320
SN   Repetition or recurrence of previous condition or behavior pattern (e.g., behavior disorder or criminal or delinquent behavior), especially when recurrence leads to recommitment or a second conviction.
B   Antisocial Behavior   1971
R   ↓ Criminals   1967

Reciprocal Inhibition Therapy   1973
PN   66   SC   43330
SN   Form of behavior therapy which seeks to evoke one response in order to bring about a suppression or decrease in the strength of a simultaneous response. Used to weaken unadaptive habits, particularly anxiety responses.
B   Behavior Therapy   1967
R   Counterconditioning   1973
     Systematic Desensitization Therapy   1973

Reciprocity   1973
PN   846   SC   43340
B   Social Behavior   1967
R   Retaliation   1991

Recognition (Learning)   1967
PN   7059   SC   43350
B   Retention   1967
N   Object Recognition   1997
R   Matching to Sample   1994
     Memory Training   1994
     Word Recognition   1988

Reconstruction (Learning)   1973
PN   138   SC   43360
SN   Recalling memorized items in the order in which they were originally presented. Compare FREE RECALL.
B   Retention   1967

Reconstructive Psychotherapy
Use   Psychotherapy

Recorders (Tape)
Use   Tape Recorders

Recovery (Disorders)   1973
PN   2924   SC   43390
R   ↓ Disorders   1967
   ↓ Drug Abstinence   1994
     Illness Behavior   1982
   ↓ Mental Disorders   1967
   ↓ Physical Disorders   1997
     Postsurgical Complications   1973
     Relapse Prevention   1994
   ↓ Remission (Disorders)   1973
     Sobriety   1988
   ↓ Treatment Outcomes   1982

Recreation   1967
PN   2014   SC   43400
UF   Play
N   Athletic Participation   1973
     Baseball   1973
     Basketball   1973
     Camping   1973
     Childrens Recreational Games   1973
     Clubs (Social Organizations)   1973
     Dance   1973
     Doll Play   1973
     Football   1973
   ↓ Gambling   1973
     Judo   1973
     Martial Arts   1985
     Soccer   1994
     Summer Camps (Recreation)   1973
     Swimming   1973
     Television Viewing   1973
     Tennis   1973
     Traveling   1973
     Vacationing   1973
     Weightlifting   1994
R   Childhood Play Behavior   1978
     Computer Games   1988
     Daily Activities   1994
   ↓ Games   1967
     Hobbies   1988
     Holidays   1988
     Leisure Time   1973
     Relaxation   1973
   ↓ Sports   1967
   ↓ Toys   1973
     Wilderness Experience   1991

Recreation Areas   1973
PN   304   SC   43410
UF   Parks (Recreational)
N   Playgrounds   1973
R   ↓ Community Facilities   1973
   ↓ Environmental Planning   1982
     Urban Planning   1973

Recreation Therapy   1973
PN   467   SC   43420
UF   Activity Therapy
     Gymnastic Therapy
B   Creative Arts Therapy   1994
R   Art Therapy   1973
     Dance Therapy   1973
     Movement Therapy   1997
     Music Therapy   1973
   ↓ Psychotherapy   1967
     Therapeutic Camps   1978

Recreational Day Camps
Use   Summer Camps (Recreation)

Recruitment (Military)
Use   Military Recruitment

Recruitment (Personnel)
Use   Personnel Recruitment

Recruitment (Teachers)
Use   Teacher Recruitment

Recurrence (Disorders)
Use   Relapse (Disorders)

Recurrent Depression   1994
PN   155   SC   43465
B   Major Depression   1988
R   Relapse (Disorders)   1973
     Seasonal Affective Disorder   1991

Red Blood Cells
Use   Erythrocytes

Red Nucleus
Use   Mesencephalon

Reductionism   1973
PN   189   SC   43480
UF   Atomism
     Elementarism
B   Philosophies   1967
R   Positivism (Philosophy)   1997

Reemployment   1991
PN   178   SC   43485
SN   Returning to work following a period of absence, e.g., unemployment or retirement.
UF   Job Reentry
     Return to Work
R   ↓ Employment Status   1982
     Job Search   1985
     Occupational Choice   1967
   ↓ Personnel   1967
     Retirement   1973
     Unemployment   1967

Reenactments
Use   Enactments

Reentry Students   1985
PN   331   SC   43495
SN   Persons reentering school or an educational program after an extended absence; for example, middle-aged adults enrolled in undergraduate programs.
B   Students   1967
R   ↓ Adult Education   1973
     Adult Learning   1997
   ↓ College Students   1967
   ↓ Continuing Education   1985
     High School Students   1967
   ↓ School Dropouts   1967

Reference Groups   1994
PN   105   SC   43497
SN   Social groups used as sources for personal and behavioral identification, motivation, and evaluation of one's own status.
B   Social Groups   1973
R   Ethnic Identity   1973
   ↓ Group Dynamics   1967
   ↓ Interpersonal Influences   1967

Reference Groups — (cont'd)
- R ↓ Peer Relations 1967
  - ↓ Self Concept 1967
  - ↓ Social Identity 1988
  - ↓ Social Influences 1967
  - Social Support Networks 1982
  - ↓ Socialization 1967

Referral (Professional)
- Use Professional Referral

Referral (Self)
- Use Self Referral

Reflectiveness 1997
PN 125   SC 43505
SN Use IMPULSIVENESS to access references from 1985-1996.
- B Cognitive Style 1967
- R Conceptual Tempo 1985
  - Impulsiveness 1973
  - Introspection 1973
  - Reminiscence 1985
  - Self Monitoring (Personality) 1985
  - Self Perception 1967

Reflexes 1971
PN 1489   SC 43530
SN Simple automatic involuntary neuromuscular responses to stimuli.
- UF Unconditioned Reflex
- B Physiology 1967
- N Achilles Tendon Reflex 1973
  - Acoustic Reflex 1973
  - Babinski Reflex 1973
  - Eyeblink Reflex 1973
  - Flexion Reflex 1973
  - Hoffmanns Reflex 1973
  - Nystagmus 1973
  - Ocular Accommodation 1982
  - Orienting Reflex 1967
  - Startle Reflex 1967
  - Yawning 1988
- R Instinctive Behavior 1982
  - Muscle Contractions 1973
  - Muscle Tone 1985
  - Parkinsonism 1994

Reformatories 1973
PN 49   SC 43540
SN Specific type of correctional institution to which young or first offenders are committed for training and reformation.
- B Correctional Institutions 1973
- R Prisons 1967

Refraction Errors 1973
PN 94   SC 43550
- B Errors 1967
  - Eye Disorders 1973
  - Light Refraction 1982
- N Myopia 1973
- R Amblyopia 1973
  - ↓ Genetic Disorders 1973
  - Ocular Accommodation 1982

Reframing
- Use Paradoxical Techniques

Refugees 1988
PN 923   SC 43555

Refugees — (cont'd)
SN Uprooted, homeless, voluntary or involuntary migrants who flee their native country, usually to escape danger or persecution because of their race, religion, or political views, and who no longer possess protection of their former government. Use HUMAN MIGRATION to access references from 1982-1987.
- UF Political Refugees
- B Human Migration 1973
- R Immigration 1973
  - ↓ Social Processes 1967

Refusal (Treatment)
- Use Treatment Refusal

Regional Differences 2001
PN 0   SC 43558
SN Used for comparisons between similar populations whose attributes differ primarily due to their geographical region of residence. Used for comparisons both within and across countries. Compare CROSS CULTURAL DIFFERENCES.
- UF Geographical Differences
- R Cross Cultural Differences 1967
  - Geography 1973
  - ↓ Sociocultural Factors 1967

Regression (Defense Mechanism) 1967
PN 532   SC 43560
- B Defense Mechanisms 1967

Regression Analysis
- Use Statistical Regression

Regression Artifact
- Use Statistical Regression

Regurgitation
- Use Vomiting

Rehabilitation 1967
PN 5474   SC 43580
SN Treatment designed to restore or bring a client to a condition of health or useful and constructive activity. Used for populations including sensory handicapped, retarded, delinquent, criminal, or disordered. Use a more specific term if possible.
- B Treatment 1967
- N Cognitive Rehabilitation 1985
  - ↓ Drug Rehabilitation 1973
  - ↓ Neuropsychological Rehabilitation 1997
  - Occupational Therapy 1967
  - Physical Therapy 1973
  - ↓ Psychosocial Rehabilitation 1973
- R Activities of Daily Living 1991
  - Adaptive Behavior 1991
  - Animal Assisted Therapy 1994
  - Deinstitutionalization 1982
  - Disability Management 1991
  - Habilitation 1991
  - ↓ Health Care Services 1978
  - Independent Living Programs 1991
  - ↓ Mainstreaming 1991
  - Partial Hospitalization 1985
  - ↓ Rehabilitation Centers 1973
  - Rehabilitation Counseling 1978
  - Self Care Skills 1978
  - ↓ Support Groups 1991
  - ↓ Twelve Step Programs 1997
  - Wilderness Experience 1991

Rehabilitation (Drug)
- Use Drug Rehabilitation

Rehabilitation (Psychosocial)
- Use Psychosocial Rehabilitation

Rehabilitation (Vocational)
- Use Vocational Rehabilitation

Rehabilitation Centers 1973
PN 281   SC 43620
- N Sheltered Workshops 1967
- R ↓ Community Facilities 1973
  - ↓ Rehabilitation 1967

Rehabilitation Counseling 1978
PN 678   SC 43624
- B Counseling 1967
- R ↓ Alcohol Rehabilitation 1982
  - ↓ Drug Rehabilitation 1973
  - ↓ Psychosocial Rehabilitation 1973
  - ↓ Rehabilitation 1967
  - Rehabilitation Education 1997
  - ↓ Vocational Rehabilitation 1967
  - Work Adjustment Training 1991

Rehabilitation Counselors 1978
PN 677   SC 43626
- B Counselors 1967
- R Rehabilitation Education 1997
  - ↓ Social Workers 1973

Rehabilitation Education 1997
PN 64   SC 43627
SN Graduate education to train students in rehabilitation processes or counseling in such areas as drug rehabilitation, vocational rehabilitation, or occupational rehabilitation.
- B Graduate Education 1973
- R Counselor Education 1973
  - Rehabilitation Counseling 1978
  - Rehabilitation Counselors 1978

Rehearsal
- Use Practice

Reinforcement 1967
PN 6628   SC 43630
SN Presentation of a reinforcer contingent on the performance of some behavior. Also, the reinforcing event or object itself (i.e., the reinforcer) which, when made to follow the performance of some behavior, results in a change in the frequency of occurrence of that behavior. Compare REWARDS and INCENTIVES.
- N Differential Reinforcement 1973
  - Negative Reinforcement 1973
  - Noncontingent Reinforcement 1988
  - ↓ Positive Reinforcement 1973
  - Primary Reinforcement 1973
  - ↓ Punishment 1967
  - Reinforcement Amounts 1973
  - ↓ Reinforcement Schedules 1967
  - ↓ Rewards 1967
  - Secondary Reinforcement 1967
  - Self Reinforcement 1973
  - ↓ Social Reinforcement 1967
- R Autoshaping 1978
  - Behavioral Contrast 1978
  - ↓ Biofeedback 1973
  - ↓ Conditioning 1967
  - Delay of Gratification 1978
  - Extinction (Learning) 1967

Reinforcement — (cont'd)
R   ↓ Feedback   1967
     ↓ Learning   1967
     ↓ Motivation   1967
     ↓ Operant Conditioning   1967
     ↓ Self Stimulation   1967
     Vicarious Experiences   1973

Reinforcement (Vicarious)
Use   Vicarious Experiences

Reinforcement Amounts   1973
PN   983   SC   43640
B   Reinforcement   1967
R   Reinforcement Delay   1985

Reinforcement Delay   1985
PN   355   SC   43645
SN   Time delay between the occurrence of a conditioned response and the administration of reinforcement in an operant conditioning paradigm. Consider INTERSTIMULUS INTERVAL for classical conditioning studies.
UF   Delayed Reinforcement
B   Reinforcement Schedules   1967
R   Delay of Gratification   1978
     Delayed Alternation   1994
     Interstimulus Interval   1967
     Reinforcement Amounts   1973
     ↓ Stimulus Intervals   1973

Reinforcement Schedules   1967
PN   4912   SC   43650
UF   Continuous Reinforcement
     Intermittent Reinforcement
     Partial Reinforcement
     Schedules (Reinforcement)
B   Reinforcement   1967
N   Concurrent Reinforcement Schedules   1988
     Fixed Interval Reinforcement   1973
     Fixed Ratio Reinforcement   1973
     Reinforcement Delay   1985
     Variable Interval Reinforcement   1973
     Variable Ratio Reinforcement   1973

Reinnervation
Use   Neural Development

Rejection (Social)
Use   Social Acceptance

Relapse (Disorders)   1973
PN   2313   SC   43660
SN   Recurrence of symptoms after apparent cure or period of improvement.
UF   Recurrence (Disorders)
R   ↓ Disorders   1967
     Expressed Emotion   1991
     ↓ Mental Disorders   1967
     ↓ Physical Disorders   1997
     Postsurgical Complications   1973
     Recurrent Depression   1994
     Relapse Prevention   1994
     ↓ Treatment Outcomes   1982

Relapse Prevention   1994
PN   395   SC   43670
B   Prevention   1973
R   Maintenance Therapy   1997
     Preventive Medicine   1973
     Primary Mental Health Prevention   1973
     Recovery (Disorders)   1973
     Relapse (Disorders)   1973

Relapse Prevention — (cont'd)
R   ↓ Remission (Disorders)   1973
     ↓ Treatment   1967
     ↓ Treatment Outcomes   1982

Relationship Satisfaction   2001
PN   0   SC   43675
SN   Used for satisfaction in relationships, including those between married and unmarried individuals, same-sex couples, relatives, and friends.
UF   Interpersonal Relationship Satisfaction
B   Satisfaction   1973
N   Marital Satisfaction   1988
R   ↓ Family Relations   1967
     Friendship   1967
     ↓ Interpersonal Interaction   1967
     Male Female Relations   1988
     ↓ Relationship Termination   1997
     Role Satisfaction   1994

Relationship Termination   1997
PN   108   SC   43680
SN   Voluntary or involuntary ending of a relationship.
UF   Breakup (Relationship)
N   ↓ Marital Separation   1973
R   Abandonment   1997
     Attachment Disorders   2001
     Friendship   1967
     ↓ Human Courtship   1973
     Male Female Relations   1988
     Marital Conflict   1973
     ↓ Marital Relations   1967
     Marital Satisfaction   1988
     ↓ Peer Relations   1967
     ↓ Relationship Satisfaction   2001
     Romance   1997
     Separation Anxiety   1973
     ↓ Separation Reactions   1997
     Social Dating   1973

Relationship Therapy   1973
PN   43   SC   43690
SN   Psychotherapeutic approach in which the relationship between the therapist and client serves as the basis for the therapy. The therapist provides a supportive setting in which the client can grow and develop and gradually reach differentiation from the therapist and come to perceive his/her own self as separate and distinct.
B   Psychotherapy   1967

Relativism   1997
PN   43   SC   43694
B   Philosophies   1967
R   Dogmatism   1978
     Epistemology   1973
     Existentialism   1967
     Metaphysics   1973
     Physics   1973

Relaxation   1973
PN   1007   SC   43697
SN   Tranquil and restful state, activity, or pastime of lessened muscle tension, stress, or attention.
R   Guided Imagery   2001
     Leisure Time   1973
     Muscle Relaxation   1973
     ↓ Recreation   1967
     Yoga   1973

Relaxation Therapy   1978
PN   2269   SC   43700

Relaxation Therapy — (cont'd)
SN   Therapy emphasizing relaxation and teaching a person or patient how to relax in order to reduce psychological tensions.
UF   Muscle Relaxation Therapy
B   Treatment   1967
N   Progressive Relaxation Therapy   1978
R   Anxiety Management   1997
     Autogenic Training   1973
     ↓ Behavior Modification   1973
     Guided Imagery   2001
     ↓ Hypnotherapy   1973
     Meditation   1973
     Muscle Relaxation   1973
     Posthypnotic Suggestions   1994
     ↓ Psychotherapeutic Techniques   1967
     Systematic Desensitization Therapy   1973

Relearning   1973
PN   129   SC   43710
B   Learning   1967
R   ↓ Memory   1967

Reliability (Statistical)
SN   Term was discontinued in 1973. In 2000, the term was stripped from all records containing it, and replaced with STATISTICAL RELIABILITY, its postable counterpart.
Use   Statistical Reliability

Reliability (Test)
Use   Test Reliability

Religion   1967
PN   3345   SC   43740
SN   Conceptually broad term. Use a more specific term if possible.
UF   Theology
R   Asceticism   1973
     ↓ Religious Beliefs   1973
     Religious Buildings   1973
     Religious Education   1973
     Religious Experiences   1997
     ↓ Religious Literature   1973
     Religious Organizations   1991
     ↓ Religious Personnel   1973
     ↓ Religious Practices   1973
     ↓ Religious Prejudices   1973
     Spirituality   1988

Religiosity   1973
PN   1918   SC   43750
SN   Degree of one's religious involvement, devotion to religious beliefs, or adherence to religious observances.
B   Religious Beliefs   1973
R   Spirituality   1988

Religious Affiliation   1973
PN   1233   SC   43760
B   Religious Beliefs   1973
N   ↓ Buddhism   1973
     ↓ Christianity   1973
     Hinduism   1973
     Islam   1973
     Judaism   1967
     Shamanism   1973
R   ↓ Religious Groups   1997
     ↓ Religious Practices   1973

Religious Beliefs   1973
PN   3715   SC   43770
UF   Beliefs (Religion)

Religious Beliefs — (cont'd)
- N   Atheism [1973]
-     God Concepts [1973]
-     Religiosity [1973]
-     ↓ Religious Affiliation [1973]
-     Sin [1973]
- R   Asceticism [1973]
-     ↓ Attitudes [1967]
-     Bible [1973]
-     Cultism [1973]
-     Death Attitudes [1973]
-     ↓ Ethics [1967]
-     Existentialism [1967]
-     Forgiveness [1988]
-     Morality [1967]
-     Mysticism [1967]
-     Occultism [1978]
-     Religion [1967]
-     Religious Education [1973]
-     Religious Experiences [1997]
-     ↓ Religious Literature [1973]
-     ↓ Religious Practices [1973]
-     ↓ Religious Prejudices [1973]
-     Spirit Possession [1997]
-     Spirituality [1988]
-     Superstitions [1973]
-     Witchcraft [1973]

Religious Buildings [1973]
PN 43   SC 43780
- UF   Churches
- R   ↓ Architecture [1973]
-     ↓ Community Facilities [1973]
-     Religion [1967]

Religious Education [1973]
PN 540   SC 43790
- B   Education [1967]
- R   Private School Education [1973]
-     Religion [1967]
-     ↓ Religious Beliefs [1973]
-     ↓ Religious Personnel [1973]
-     Seminaries [1973]

Religious Experiences [1997]
PN 133   SC 43795
- R   Cultism [1973]
-     Mysticism [1967]
-     ↓ Parapsychological Phenomena [1973]
-     Religion [1967]
-     ↓ Religious Beliefs [1973]
-     Spirituality [1988]

Religious Groups [1997]
PN 132   SC 43797
SN Groups and their members sharing common religious beliefs and belonging to the same religious affiliation.
- N   Buddhists [1997]
-     ↓ Christians [1997]
-     Hindus [1997]
-     Jews [1997]
-     Muslims [1997]
- R   ↓ Clergy [1973]
-     ↓ Racial and Ethnic Groups [2001]
-     ↓ Religious Affiliation [1973]
-     Religious Organizations [1991]
-     ↓ Religious Practices [1973]

Religious Literature [1973]
PN 122   SC 43800
- N   Bible [1973]
- R   ↓ Literature [1967]

Religious Literature — (cont'd)
- R   Religion [1967]
-     ↓ Religious Beliefs [1973]

Religious Occupations
Use Religious Personnel

Religious Organizations [1991]
PN 234   SC 43815
SN Any type of agency, organization, or institution operated by religious groups or persons. Includes, but not limited to, church, social service, educational, fraternal, recreational, missionary, or rehabilitation organizations.
- B   Organizations [1967]
- R   Religion [1967]
-     ↓ Religious Groups [1997]

Religious Personnel [1973]
PN 295   SC 43820
- UF   Religious Occupations
- B   Personnel [1967]
- N   ↓ Clergy [1973]
-     Evangelists [1973]
-     Lay Religious Personnel [1973]
-     Missionaries [1973]
-     Nuns [1973]
-     Seminarians [1973]
- R   ↓ Professional Personnel [1978]
-     Religion [1967]
-     Religious Education [1973]
-     ↓ Volunteer Personnel [1973]

Religious Practices [1973]
PN 1232   SC 43830
- UF   Rites (Religion)
-     Rituals (Religion)
-     Worship
- N   Asceticism [1973]
-     Confession (Religion) [1973]
-     Faith Healing [1973]
-     Meditation [1973]
-     Prayer [1973]
-     Yoga [1973]
- R   Circumcision [2001]
-     Glossolalia [1973]
-     Mysticism [1967]
-     Religion [1967]
-     ↓ Religious Affiliation [1973]
-     ↓ Religious Beliefs [1973]
-     ↓ Religious Groups [1997]

Religious Prejudices [1973]
PN 43   SC 43840
- B   Prejudice [1967]
- N   AntiSemitism [1973]
- R   Religion [1967]
-     ↓ Religious Beliefs [1973]

REM
Use Rapid Eye Movement

REM Dream Deprivation [1973]
PN 25   SC 43860
- B   Deprivation [1967]
- R   Rapid Eye Movement [1971]

REM Dreams [1973]
PN 94   SC 43870
- UF   Rapid Eye Movement Dreams
- B   Dreaming [1967]
- R   ↓ Eye Movements [1967]
-     Lucid Dreaming [1994]

REM Dreams — (cont'd)
- R   REM Sleep [1973]
-     Rapid Eye Movement [1971]

REM Sleep [1973]
PN 1836   SC 43880
- UF   Paradoxical Sleep
-     Rapid Eye Movement Sleep
- B   Sleep [1967]
- R   ↓ Eye Movements [1967]
-     Lucid Dreaming [1994]
-     REM Dreams [1973]
-     Rapid Eye Movement [1971]

Remarriage [1985]
PN 445   SC 43885
- B   Marriage [1967]
- R   Divorce [1973]
-     ↓ Marital Status [1973]
-     Stepfamily [1991]

Remedial Education [1985]
PN 587   SC 43887
SN Specialized instruction designed to raise academic competence of students with below-normal achievement or learning difficulties. Compare COMPENSATORY EDUCATION.
- B   Education [1967]
- N   Remedial Reading [1973]
- R   Compensatory Education [1973]
-     Educational Therapy [1997]
-     Special Education [1967]

Remedial Reading [1973]
PN 795   SC 43890
SN Specialized instruction designed to correct faulty reading habits or to improve imperfectly learned reading skills.
- B   Reading [1967]
-     Remedial Education [1985]
- R   Educational Placement [1978]
-     Reading Education [1973]

Remembering
Use Retention

Reminiscence [1985]
PN 651   SC 43905
SN Process of recalling past experiences.
- B   Memory [1967]
- R   Anniversary Events [1994]
-     Autobiographical Memory [1994]
-     Early Memories [1985]
-     Enactments [1997]
-     Forgetting [1973]
-     Homesickness [1994]
-     Life Review [1991]
-     ↓ Recall (Learning) [1967]
-     Reflectiveness [1997]
-     ↓ Retention [1967]

Remission (Disorders) [1973]
PN 591   SC 43910
SN Diminution or disappearance of symptoms.
- N   Spontaneous Remission [1973]
-     Symptom Remission [1973]
- R   ↓ Disorders [1967]
-     ↓ Mental Disorders [1967]
-     ↓ Physical Disorders [1997]
-     Recovery (Disorders) [1973]
-     Relapse Prevention [1994]
-     ↓ Treatment Outcomes [1982]

Remote Associates Test 1973
PN 16 SC 43920
 B Intelligence Measures 1967

Renal Diseases
 Use Kidney Diseases

Renal Transplantation
 Use Organ Transplantation

Repairmen
 Use Technical Service Personnel

Repeated Measures 1985
PN 218 SC 43935
SN Experimental design in which the subjects serve in all experimental, treatment, or control conditions.
 UF Within Subjects Design
 B Experimental Design 1967
  Testing 1967
 R Posttesting 1973
  Pretesting 1973

Repetition (Compulsive)
 Use Compulsive Repetition

Replication (Experimental)
 Use Experimental Replication

Repressed Memory 1997
PN 358 SC 43955
 B Memory 1967
 R Age Regression (Hypnotic) 1988
  ↓ Amnesia 1967
  Early Memories 1985
  Emotional Trauma 1967
  False Memory 1997
  Repression (Defense Mechanism) 1967

Repression (Defense Mechanism) 1967
PN 819 SC 43960
 B Defense Mechanisms 1967
 R Repressed Memory 1997
  Suppression (Defense Mechanism) 1973

Repression Sensitization 1973
PN 271 SC 43968
SN Personality continuum which characterizes individual's defensive response to threat, with avoidance (repression or denial) at one extreme and approach (worry or intellectualization) at the other.
 UF Sensitization Repression
 B Personality Traits 1967

Repression Sensitization Scale 1973
PN 28 SC 43970
 B Nonprojective Personality Measures 1973

Reproductive Technology 1988
PN 343 SC 43975
 UF Artificial Insemination
  In Vitro Fertilization
  Test Tube Babies
 R Eugenics 1973
  Fertilization 1973
  ↓ Genetic Engineering 1994
  ↓ Genetics 1967
  ↓ Pregnancy 1967
  Prenatal Diagnosis 1988
  Selective Breeding 1973
  ↓ Sexual Reproduction 1973

Reptiles 1967
PN 68 SC 43980
 B Vertebrates 1973
 N Crocodilians 1973
  Lizards 1973
  Snakes 1973
  Turtles 1973

Republican Party
 Use Political Parties

Reputation 1997
PN 47 SC 43995
 R Credibility 1973
  Fame 1985
  Morality 1967
  Popularity 1988
  Social Approval 1967
  Social Cognition 1994
  ↓ Social Perception 1967
  ↓ Status 1967

Research
 Use Experimentation

Research Design
 Use Experimental Design

Research Diagnostic Criteria 1994
PN 28 SC 44013
SN Used when the Research Diagnostic Criteria or its revisions are the focus of the reference. Use PSYCHODIAGNOSTIC TYPOLOGIES to access references prior to 1994. Not used for specific psychodiagnostic categories.
 UF RDC
 B Psychodiagnostic Typologies 1967
 R ↓ Diagnosis 1967
  Diagnostic and Statistical Manual 1994
  International Classification of Diseases 2001
  ↓ Mental Disorders 1967
  ↓ Psychodiagnosis 1967

Research Dropouts
 Use Experimental Attrition

Research Methods
 Use Methodology

Research Setting 2001
PN 0 SC 44024
 UF Experimental Environment
 B Experimentation 1967
 R Behavioral Ecology 1997
  ↓ Environment 1967
  ↓ Experimental Design 1967
  Experimental Laboratories 1973

Research Subjects
 Use Experimental Subjects

Resentment
 Use Hostility

Reserpine 1967
PN 314 SC 44040
 UF Serpasil
 B Alkaloids 1973
  Antihypertensive Drugs 1973
  Neuroleptic Drugs 1973
  Sedatives 1973
  Sympatholytic Drugs 1973

Residence Halls
 Use Dormitories

Residency (Medical)
 Use Medical Residency

Residential Care Attendants
 Use Attendants (Institutions)

Residential Care Institutions 1973
PN 4545 SC 44080
SN Facilities where individuals or patients live and receive appropriate treatment or care.
 UF Institutions (Residential Care)
 N Halfway Houses 1973
  ↓ Hospitals 1967
  Nursing Homes 1973
  Orphanages 1973
 R Group Homes 1982
  Institution Visitation 1973
  Institutional Schools 1978
  Institutionalized Mentally Retarded 1973
  Psychiatric Units 1991
  Retirement Communities 1997
  ↓ Treatment Facilities 1973

Resilience (Psychological)
 Use Hardiness

Resistance 1997
PN 193 SC 44087
 N Psychotherapeutic Resistance 1973
 R Assertiveness 1973
  Avoidance 1967
  Coercion 1994
  ↓ Compliance 1973
  Independence (Personality) 1973
  Obedience 1973
  School Refusal 1994
  Temptation 1973
  Treatment Refusal 1994

Resistance (Psychotherapeutic)
 Use Psychotherapeutic Resistance

Resocialization (Psychosocial)
 Use Psychosocial Readjustment

Resonance
 Use Vibration

Resource Allocation 1997
PN 261 SC 44125
 UF Allocation of Resources
 R Cost Containment 1991
  ↓ Costs and Cost Analysis 1973
  Economics 1985
  Egalitarianism 1985
  Equity (Payment) 1978
  ↓ Equity (Social) 1978
  Funding 1988
  Money 1967
  ↓ Personnel Management 1973
  Reward Allocation 1988

Resource Teachers 1973
PN 104 SC 44130
SN Teachers with special competencies who supplement regular curricula or programs or who assist other teachers in specified areas.
 B Teachers 1967
 R Special Education Teachers 1973

Respiration   1967
PN 2431   SC 44140
UF   Breathing
R   Artificial Respiration   1973
     Carbon Dioxide   1973
     ↓ Respiration Stimulating Drugs   1973
     ↓ Respiratory Distress   1973
     ↓ Respiratory System   1973
     ↓ Respiratory Tract Disorders   1973
     Yawning   1988

Respiration Stimulating Drugs   1973
PN 11   SC 44160
B   Drugs   1967
N   Caffeine   1973
R   Respiration   1967

Respiratory Distress   1973
PN 110   SC 44170
B   Symptoms   1967
N   ↓ Apnea   1973
     ↓ Dyspnea   1973
     Hyperventilation   1973
R   Anoxia   1973
     Respiration   1967

Respiratory System   1973
PN 91   SC 44180
B   Anatomical Systems   1973
N   Bronchi   1973
     Diaphragm (Anatomy)   1973
     ↓ Larynx   1973
     Lung   1973
     ↓ Nose   1973
     Pharynx   1973
     Thorax   1973
     Trachea   1973
R   Artificial Respiration   1973
     Respiration   1967

Respiratory Tract Disorders   1973
PN 414   SC 44190
B   Physical Disorders   1997
N   ↓ Apnea   1973
     Bronchial Disorders   1973
     ↓ Dyspnea   1973
     Hay Fever   1973
     Hyperventilation   1973
     Laryngeal Disorders   1973
     ↓ Lung Disorders   1973
     Pharyngeal Disorders   1973
R   Artificial Respiration   1973
     Influenza   1973
     Poliomyelitis   1973
     Respiration   1967

Respite Care   1988
PN 213   SC 44195
SN   Provision of care, relief, or support to caregivers of physically or mentally disabled persons.
R   Caregiver Burden   1994
     Caregivers   1988
     Home Care   1985

Respondent Conditioning
Use   Classical Conditioning

Response Amplitude   1973
PN 739   SC 44210
UF   Amplitude (Response)
B   Response Parameters   1973

Response Bias   1967
PN 1875   SC 44220
SN   Tendency to respond with different styles or criteria as a result of motivational or physical influences. Response bias frequently serves as a source of measurement error in psychophysical, personality, and other types of measurement.
UF   Bias (Response)
R   Cultural Test Bias   1973
     ↓ Measurement   1967
     Predisposition   1973
     ↓ Test Bias   1985
     Test Taking   1985

Response Consistency
Use   Response Variability

Response Cost   1997
PN 19   SC 44228
SN   Punishment procedure in which positive reinforcer is lost when a specified behavior is performed.
B   Behavior Therapy   1967
     Punishment   1967
R   Token Economy Programs   1973

Response Duration   1973
PN 419   SC 44230
UF   Duration (Response)
B   Response Parameters   1973

Response Frequency   1973
PN 1766   SC 44240
SN   Number of responses measured during a fixed time period.
UF   Frequency (Response)
     Response Rate
B   Response Parameters   1973
R   Behavioral Contrast   1978
     Interresponse Time   1973

Response Generalization   1973
PN 428   SC 44250
SN   Learning phenomenon in which an emitted response is functionally identical to the originally-conditioned response but which, unlike the conditioned response, was never specifically conditioned. Compare GENERALIZATION (LEARNING) and STIMULUS GENERALIZATION.
UF   Generalization (Response)
B   Generalization (Learning)   1982
     Response Parameters   1973

Response Lag
Use   Reaction Time

Response Latency   1967
PN 2219   SC 44270
SN   Duration of the interval between a stimulus and the onset of the elicited response. Compare REACTION TIME.
UF   Latency (Response)
B   Response Parameters   1973
R   Behavioral Contrast   1978
     Cognitive Processing Speed   1997

Response Parameters   1973
PN 1210   SC 44280
UF   Parameters (Response)
N   Interresponse Time   1973
     Reaction Time   1967
     Response Amplitude   1973
     Response Duration   1973
     Response Frequency   1973

Response Parameters — (cont'd)
N   Response Generalization   1973
     Response Latency   1967
     Response Probability   1973
     Response Set   1967
     Response Variability   1973
R   ↓ Responses   1967

Response Probability   1973
PN 204   SC 44290
B   Probability   1967
     Response Parameters   1973

Response Rate
Use   Response Frequency

Response Set   1967
PN 612   SC 44300
SN   Cognitive state of concentration or behavioral readiness to respond. Also, deliberate or inadvertent style or tendency to respond to test items in characteristic ways (e.g., with socially desirable answers) that detract from the validity of the obtained measures.
UF   Set (Response)
B   Response Parameters   1973

Response Speed
Use   Reaction Time

Response Time
Use   Reaction Time

Response Variability   1973
PN 633   SC 44330
UF   Response Consistency
     Variability (Response)
B   Response Parameters   1973
R   Delayed Alternation   1994
     Spontaneous Alternation   1982

Responses   1967
PN 2755   SC 44340
N   ↓ Conditioned Responses   1967
     ↓ Emotional Responses   1967
     Mediated Responses   1967
     Orienting Responses   1967
     Unconditioned Responses   1973
R   ↓ Response Parameters   1973

Responsibility   1973
PN 2525   SC 44345
B   Social Behavior   1967
N   Accountability   1988
     Criminal Responsibility   1991
R   Blame   1994
     Conscientiousness   1997
     Professional Liability   1985

Restlessness   1973
PN 162   SC 44350
B   Emotional States   1973
     Symptoms   1967
R   Agitation   1991
     Akathisia   1991
     Hyperkinesis   1973

Restraint (Physical)
Use   Physical Restraint

Restricted Environmental Stimulation
Use   Stimulus Deprivation

Retail Stores
  Use Retailing

Retailing 1991
PN 369   **SC** 44362
  UF Retail Stores
  R ↓ Advertising 1967
      Brand Names 1978
      Business 1967
      ↓ Consumer Behavior 1967
      Marketing 1973
      ↓ Quality of Services 1997
      Sales Personnel 1973
      Self Employment 1994
      Shopping 1997
      Shopping Centers 1973

Retaliation 1991
PN 89   **SC** 44364
SN Use RECIPROCITY to access references from 1973-1990.
  UF Revenge
  B Social Behavior 1967
  R ↓ Aggressive Behavior 1967
      Attack Behavior 1973
      Hostility 1967
      ↓ Interpersonal Interaction 1967
      Reciprocity 1973

Retardation (Mental)
  Use Mental Retardation

Retarded Speech Development 1973
PN 139   **SC** 44390
SN Speech development that is below normal for a specific age level.
  UF Delayed Speech
  B Delayed Development 1973
      Speech Development 1973
  R Language Delay 1988
      ↓ Speech Disorders 1967

Retention 1967
PN 4899   **SC** 44400
SN Persistence of a learned act, information, or experience as measured by reproduction, recall, recognition, or relearning. Consider also LONG TERM MEMORY or SHORT TERM MEMORY. Used for both human and animal populations.
  UF Remembering
  N ↓ Recall (Learning) 1967
      ↓ Recognition (Learning) 1967
      Reconstruction (Learning) 1973
  R Forgetting 1973
      ↓ Interference (Learning) 1967
      ↓ Learning 1967
      ↓ Memory 1967
      Memory Training 1994
      Reminiscence 1985
      ↓ Retention Measures 1973

Retention (School)
  Use School Retention

Retention Measures 1973
PN 145   **SC** 44410
  B Measurement 1967
  N Wechsler Memory Scale 1988
  R ↓ Retention 1967

Reticular Formation 1967
PN 512   **SC** 44420
  B Brain Stem 1973

Reticular Formation — (cont'd)
  B Neural Pathways 1982
  R ↓ Lemniscal System 1985
      Locus Ceruleus 1982
      Raphe Nuclei 1982

Retina 1967
PN 1434   **SC** 44430
  B Eye (Anatomy) 1967
  N Cones (Eye) 1973
      Ganglion Cells (Retina) 1985
      Rods (Eye) 1973
  R Retinal Eccentricity 1991

Retinal Eccentricity 1991
PN 139   **SC** 44435
  R ↓ Retina 1967
      Retinal Image 1973
      Spatial Organization 1973
      ↓ Visual Perception 1967
      Visual Receptive Fields 1982
      ↓ Visual Thresholds 1973

Retinal Ganglion Cells
  Use Ganglion Cells (Retina)

Retinal Image 1973
PN 561   **SC** 44450
  UF Image (Retinal)
  R ↓ Eye (Anatomy) 1967
      Retinal Eccentricity 1991

Retinal Vessels
  Use Arteries (Anatomy)

Retirement 1973
PN 1360   **SC** 44470
  R Employment History 1978
      ↓ Employment Status 1982
      Job Security 1978
      ↓ Personnel 1967
      Personnel Termination 1973
      Reemployment 1991
      Retirement Communities 1997
      Unemployment 1967

Retirement Communities 1997
PN 46   **SC** 44473
  B Communities 1967
      Housing 1973
  R Group Homes 1982
      ↓ Living Arrangements 1991
      Nursing Homes 1973
      ↓ Residential Care Institutions 1973
      Retirement 1973

Retroactive Inhibition 1973
PN 533   **SC** 44480
SN The theory that learning new material can interfere with the retention of previously learned material. Also, the actual retroactive interference itself.
  UF Inhibition (Retroactive)
  B Interference (Learning) 1967
      Latent Inhibition 1997

Retrospective Studies 1997
PN 228   **SC** 44481

Retrospective Studies — (cont'd)
SN Used in records discussing issues involved in the process of conducting studies which utilize data about experiences or events that occurred in the past, usually to study etiologic hypotheses or causative factors related to a disorder, behavior, or phenomenon. From 1997-2000, the term was also used as a document type identifier; however, this usage has been discontinued due to the advent of Form/Content Type field identifiers. References from 1997-2000 can be accessed using either RETROSPECTIVE STUDIES or the Retrospective Studies Form/Content Type field identifier.
  R ↓ Longitudinal Studies 1973
      Prospective Studies 1997

Rett Syndrome 1994
PN 117   **SC** 44482
  B Pervasive Developmental Disorders 2001
      Syndromes 1973
  R Aspergers Syndrome 1991
      ↓ Brain Disorders 1967
      ↓ Mental Disorders 1967
      ↓ Mental Retardation 1967
      ↓ Physical Disorders 1997

Return to Home
  Use Empty Nest

Return to Work
  Use Reemployment

Revenge
  Use Retaliation

Reversal Shift Learning 1967
PN 673   **SC** 44490
SN Experimental technique for demonstration of mediating processes in concept formation which assesses ability to learn to reverse responses in stimulus discrimination task, so that the subject is required to respond to a formerly negative stimulus and not to respond to the formerly positive discriminative stimulus.
  B Discrimination Learning 1982

Review (of Literature)
SN Term was discontinued in 1973. In 2000, the term was stripped from all records containing it, and replaced with LITERATURE REVIEW, its postable counterpart.
  Use Literature Review

Revolutions (Political)
  Use Political Revolution

Reward Allocation 1988
PN 173   **SC** 44515
  R ↓ Justice 1973
      Resource Allocation 1997
      ↓ Rewards 1967
      ↓ Social Perception 1967

Rewards 1967
PN 3011   **SC** 44520
SN Events or objects subjectively deemed to be pleasant to a recipient. Compare INCENTIVES, REINFORCEMENT, and POSITIVE REINFORCEMENT.
  B Reinforcement 1967
  N External Rewards 1973
      Internal Rewards 1973
      Monetary Rewards 1973
      Preferred Rewards 1973

Rewards — (cont'd)
R   Delay of Gratification [1978]
    Delayed Alternation [1994]
  ↓ Incentives [1967]
    Reward Allocation [1988]

Rh Incompatibility [1973]
PN 6   SC 44530
UF   Erythroblastosis Fetalis
    Incompatibility (Rh)
B   Blood and Lymphatic Disorders [1973]
    Genetic Disorders [1973]
    Immunologic Disorders [1973]
R   ↓ Neonatal Disorders [1973]

Rheoencephalography [1973]
PN 19   SC 44540
B   Encephalography [1973]
    Medical Diagnosis [1973]
R   ↓ Electroencephalography [1967]

Rhetoric [1991]
PN 361   SC 44545
B   Communication Skills [1973]
    Language [1967]
R   ↓ Communication [1967]
    Creative Writing [1994]
    Debates [1997]
    Discourse Analysis [1997]
    Hermeneutics [1991]
  ↓ Oral Communication [1985]
  ↓ Persuasive Communication [1967]
  ↓ Written Communication [1985]

Rheumatic Fever [1973]
PN 22   SC 44550
R   ↓ Bacterial Disorders [1973]
  ↓ Heart Disorders [1973]
    Rheumatoid Arthritis [1973]

Rheumatism
Use   Arthritis

Rheumatoid Arthritis [1973]
PN 753   SC 44570
B   Arthritis [1973]
R   Rheumatic Fever [1973]

Rhodopsin [1985]
PN 11   SC 44575
SN   A red pigment localized in the outer segments of rod cells in the retina.
B   Pigments [1973]
R   Rods (Eye) [1973]

Rhombencephalon
Use   Hindbrain

Rhythm [1991]
PN 288   SC 44577
N   Speech Rhythm [1973]
R   ↓ Auditory Perception [1967]
  ↓ Music [1967]
    Music Perception [1997]
    Pattern Discrimination [1967]
  ↓ Perception [1967]
    Speech Perception [1967]
    Tempo [1997]

Rhythm Method [1973]
PN 4   SC 44580
B   Birth Control [1971]

Ribonucleic Acid [1973]
PN 488   SC 44600
UF   RNA (Ribonucleic Acid)
B   Nucleic Acids [1973]

Right Brain [1991]
PN 571   SC 44610
SN   Used only when the right hemisphere of the brain is the focus of the document.
B   Cerebral Cortex [1967]
R   ↓ Brain [1967]
  ↓ Cerebral Dominance [1973]
    Corpus Callosum [1973]
  ↓ Interhemispheric Interaction [1985]
  ↓ Lateral Dominance [1967]
    Left Brain [1991]
    Ocular Dominance [1973]

Right to Treatment [1997]
PN 13   SC 44615
B   Client Rights [1988]
R   Advocacy [1985]
  ↓ Commitment (Psychiatric) [1973]
    Deinstitutionalization [1982]
    Involuntary Treatment [1994]
    Self Referral [1991]

Rigidity (Muscles)
Use   Muscle Contractions

Rigidity (Personality) [1967]
PN 243   SC 44620
B   Personality Traits [1967]
R   Openness to Experience [1997]

Riots [1973]
PN 122   SC 44640
B   Collective Behavior [1967]
    Conflict [1967]
R   ↓ Violence [1973]

Risk Analysis [1991]
PN 1540   SC 44643
B   Analysis [1967]
R   ↓ Decision Making [1967]
  ↓ Gambling [1973]
    Game Theory [1967]
    Risk Management [1997]
    Risk Perception [1997]
  ↓ Risk Taking [1967]
  ↓ Statistical Probability [1967]

Risk Factors [2001]
PN 0   SC 44642
SN   Personal behaviors or lifestyles, environmental effects, or inborn characteristics which epidemiological evidence has shown to be associated with the increased rate of a behavior or health-related condition.
R   At Risk Populations [1985]
    Predisposition [1973]
    Psychosocial Factors [1988]
  ↓ Sociocultural Factors [1967]
    Susceptibility (Disorders) [1973]
  ↓ Symptoms [1967]

Risk Management [1997]
PN 297   SC 44644
SN   Reducing and preventing loss, damage, harm, or danger to a business, group, or individual through safety and protective measures. Used for clinical and nonclinical environments.
B   Management [1967]

Risk Management — (cont'd)
R   Accident Prevention [1973]
  ↓ Costs and Cost Analysis [1973]
  ↓ Insurance [1973]
  ↓ Legal Processes [1973]
  ↓ Prevention [1973]
    Professional Liability [1985]
    Risk Analysis [1991]
  ↓ Risk Taking [1967]
  ↓ Safety [1967]

Risk Perception [1997]
PN 676   SC 44646
SN   Awareness of, or attitudes toward, potential risk. Primarily used for risk associated with disease or behavior.
B   Perception [1967]
R   Hazards [1973]
  ↓ Prevention [1973]
    Risk Analysis [1991]
  ↓ Risk Taking [1967]
  ↓ Safety [1967]
    Sexual Risk Taking [1997]

Risk Populations
Use   At Risk Populations

Risk Taking [1967]
PN 4123   SC 44650
B   Personality Traits [1967]
    Social Behavior [1967]
N   ↓ Gambling [1973]
    Sexual Risk Taking [1997]
R   Choice Shift [1994]
    Risk Analysis [1991]
    Risk Management [1997]
    Risk Perception [1997]

Risky Shift
Use   Choice Shift

Risperidone [1997]
PN 591   SC 44657
B   Neuroleptic Drugs [1973]

Ritalin
Use   Methylphenidate

Ritanserin [1997]
PN 47   SC 44665
B   Serotonin Antagonists [1973]

Rites (Nonreligious) [1973]
PN 585   SC 44670
UF   Rituals (Nonreligious)
R   Cosmetic Techniques [2001]
  ↓ Rites of Passage [1973]

Rites (Religion)
Use   Religious Practices

Rites of Passage [1973]
PN 139   SC 44690
B   Sociocultural Factors [1967]
N   Birth Rites [1973]
    Death Rites [1973]
    Initiation Rites [1973]
    Marriage Rites [1973]
R   Circumcision [2001]
  ↓ Developmental Stages [1973]
    Ethnography [1973]
    Rites (Nonreligious) [1973]

Rites of Passage — (cont'd)
  R   Taboos 1973

Rituals (Nonreligious)
  Use   Rites (Nonreligious)

Rituals (Religion)
  Use   Religious Practices

Rivalry 1973
PN 50   **SC** 44720
  B   Interpersonal Interaction 1967
  R   Competition 1967

RNA (Ribonucleic Acid)
  Use   Ribonucleic Acid

Robbery
  Use   Theft

Robins 1973
PN 49   **SC** 44750
  B   Birds 1967

Robotics 1985
PN 422   **SC** 44755
  R   ↓ Artificial Intelligence 1982
      ↓ Computers 1967
      Cybernetics 1967
      ↓ Expert Systems 1991

Rock Music 1991
PN 113   **SC** 44757
  B   Music 1967

Rocking (Body)
  Use   Body Rocking

Rod and Frame Test 1973
PN 128   **SC** 44770
  B   Nonprojective Personality Measures 1973
      Perceptual Measures 1973

Rodents 1973
PN 1029   **SC** 44780
  UF   Voles
  B   Mammals 1973
  N   Beavers 1973
      Chinchillas 1973
      Gerbils 1973
      Guinea Pigs 1967
      Hamsters 1973
      Mice 1973
      Minks 1973
      ↓ Rats 1967
      Squirrels 1973

Rods (Eye) 1973
PN 251   **SC** 44790
  B   Photoreceptors 1973
      Retina 1967
  R   Rhodopsin 1985

Roentgenography 1973
PN 162   **SC** 44800
  UF   Radiography
      X Ray Diagnosis
  B   Medical Diagnosis 1973
  N   Angiography 1973
      Mammography 1994
      Pneumoencephalography 1973

Roentgenography — (cont'd)
  R   ↓ Encephalography 1973
      ↓ Radiation 1967
      ↓ Tomography 1988

Rogerian Therapy
  Use   Client Centered Therapy

Rogers (Carl) 1991
PN 105   **SC** 44805
SN   Identifies biographical or autobiographical studies and discussions of Rogers's works.
  R   Client Centered Therapy 1967
      ↓ Humanistic Psychology 1985
      ↓ Psychologists 1967

Rokeach Dogmatism Scale 1973
PN 31   **SC** 44810
  B   Nonprojective Personality Measures 1973
      Personality Measures 1967

Role (Counselor)
  Use   Counselor Role

Role Conflicts 1973
PN 2167   **SC** 44830
  UF   Role Strain
  R   Family Work Relationship 1997
      Role Satisfaction 1994
      ↓ Roles 1967

Role Expectations 1973
PN 997   **SC** 44840
SN   Functional patterns or types of behavior expected from an individual in a specific social or professional position or situation.
  B   Expectations 1967
  R   Role Satisfaction 1994
      ↓ Roles 1967

Role Models 1982
PN 468   **SC** 44845
SN   Real or theoretical persons consciously or unconsciously perceived as being a standard for emulation in one or more of their roles.
  R   Imitation (Learning) 1967
      Role Perception 1973
      ↓ Roles 1967
      Significant Others 1991
      ↓ Social Influences 1967

Role Perception 1973
PN 2269   **SC** 44850
SN   Views or understanding of one's own or others' function or behavior in particular situations.
  B   Perception 1967
  R   Professional Identity 1991
      Role Models 1982
      Role Satisfaction 1994
      Role Taking 1982
      ↓ Roles 1967

Role Playing 1967
PN 1454   **SC** 44860
SN   Psychological or behavioral enactment of social roles other than one's own, typically seen in child's play, or used as an experimental, instructional, or psychotherapeutic technique. Compare ROLE TAKING.
  R   Childhood Play Behavior 1978
      Psychodrama 1967
      ↓ Psychotherapeutic Techniques 1967
      Role Taking 1982

Role Playing — (cont'd)
  R   ↓ Roles 1967

Role Satisfaction 1994
PN 123   **SC** 44863
  B   Satisfaction 1973
  R   Job Satisfaction 1967
      Life Satisfaction 1985
      Marital Satisfaction 1988
      ↓ Relationship Satisfaction 2001
      Role Conflicts 1973
      Role Expectations 1973
      Role Perception 1973
      ↓ Roles 1967
      ↓ Self Concept 1967

Role Strain
  Use   Role Conflicts

Role Taking 1982
PN 662   **SC** 44865
SN   Perceiving, understanding, or experiencing the social, emotional or physical aspects of a situation from a standpoint of another person or persons. Use EGOCENTRISM to access references from 1978-1981. Compare ROLE PLAYING.
  UF   Perspective Taking
  R   Egocentrism 1978
      Role Perception 1973
      Role Playing 1967
      ↓ Roles 1967
      Symbolic Interactionism 1988

Roles 1967
PN 4665   **SC** 44870
  N   Counselor Role 1973
      Parental Role 1973
      Sex Roles 1967
      Therapist Role 1978
  R   Role Conflicts 1973
      Role Expectations 1973
      Role Models 1982
      Role Perception 1973
      Role Playing 1967
      Role Satisfaction 1994
      Role Taking 1982

Roman Catholicism 1973
PN 756   **SC** 44880
  UF   Catholicism (Roman)
  B   Christianity 1973
  R   Catholics 1997

Romance 1997
PN 320   **SC** 44883
  R   Affection 1973
      Couples 1982
      ↓ Human Courtship 1973
      Human Mate Selection 1988
      Intimacy 1973
      Love 1973
      ↓ Marital Relations 1967
      ↓ Marriage 1967
      ↓ Psychosexual Behavior 1967
      ↓ Relationship Termination 1997
      Significant Others 1991
      Social Dating 1973

Roommates 1973
PN 130   **SC** 44890
SN   Individuals residing in common abodes.
  R   Cohabitation 1973
      ↓ Living Arrangements 1991

Rorschach Test 1967
PN 2620   SC 44900
B   Projective Personality Measures 1973

Rosenzweig Picture Frustration Study 1967
PN 51   SC 44910
B   Projective Personality Measures 1973

Rotary Pursuit 1967
PN 194   SC 44920
B   Tracking 1967
R   ↓ Attention 1967

Rotation Methods (Statistical)
Use Statistical Rotation

Rotational Behavior 1994
PN 140   SC 44935
SN Used primarily for animal populations.
UF   Body Rotation
B   Motor Processes 1967
R   Activity Level 1982

ROTC Students 1973
PN 71   SC 44940
B   College Students 1967
     Military Personnel 1967
R   Volunteer Military Personnel 1973
     ↓ Volunteer Personnel 1973

Rote Learning 1973
PN 126   SC 44950
SN Verbatim memorization of information which
requires no understanding.
R   ↓ Memory 1967

Rotter Incomplete Sentences Blank 1973
PN 18   SC 44960
B   Projective Personality Measures 1973

**Rotter Internal External Locus of Control
    Scale** 2001
PN 152   SC 44971
SN In 2000, the truncated term ROTTER INTERN
EXTERN LOCUS CONT SCAL (which was used
from 1973-2000) was deleted, removed from all
records containing it, and mapped to its expanded
form ROTTER INTERNAL EXTERNAL LOCUS OF
CONTROL SCALE.
B   Nonprojective Personality Measures 1973

RT (Response)
Use Reaction Time

Rubella 1973
PN 38   SC 45000
UF   German Measles
B   Viral Disorders 1973
R   Measles 1973

Rule Learning
Use Cognitive Hypothesis Testing

Rumination (Cognitive Process) 2001
PN 0   SC 45007
SN Constant preoccupation with particular thoughts
which may provoke anxiety and distress. Can be
associated with obsessive compulsive disorder and
depression.
B   Cognitive Processes 1967
R   ↓ Cognitions 1985
     Concentration 1982

Rumination (Cognitive Process) — (cont'd)
R   ↓ Thought Disturbances 1973

Rumination (Eating) 2001
PN 0   SC 45008
SN Characterized by regurgitating partially digested
food and chewing it again. Often used to describe an
eating disorder of infancy or early childhood.
R   ↓ Eating Disorders 1997
     Food Intake 1967
     Vomiting 1973

Rumors
Use Gossip

Runaway Behavior 1973
PN 378   SC 45015
B   Antisocial Behavior 1971
R   Shelters 1991

Running 1973
PN 691   SC 45020
B   Motor Performance 1973

Runways (Maze)
Use Maze Pathways

Rural Development
Use Community Development

Rural Environments 1967
PN 4592   SC 45040
B   Social Environments 1973
R   Community Development 1997

Saccadic Eye Movements
Use Eye Movements

Saccharin 1973
PN 467   SC 45050
R   ↓ Sugars 1973

SAD
Use Seasonal Affective Disorder

Sadism 1973
PN 81   SC 45070
B   Sadomasochism 1973
N   Sexual Sadism 1973
R   ↓ Masochism 1973

Sadness 1973
PN 412   SC 45090
UF   Melancholy
B   Emotional States 1973
R   Depression (Emotion) 1967
     Homesickness 1994
     ↓ Separation Reactions 1997

Sadomasochism 1973
PN 135   SC 45100
SN Derivation of pleasure from infliction of physical
or mental pain on others and oneself, with presence
of high degree of destructiveness.
N   ↓ Masochism 1973
     ↓ Sadism 1973
R   ↓ Mental Disorders 1967
     ↓ Sadomasochistic Personality 1973

Sadomasochistic Personality 1973
PN 11   SC 45110

Sadomasochistic Personality — (cont'd)
B   Personality Disorders 1967
N   Masochistic Personality 1973
R   ↓ Sadomasochism 1973

Safety 1967
PN 1093   SC 45120
N   ↓ Aviation Safety 1973
     Highway Safety 1973
     Occupational Safety 1973
     Water Safety 1973
R   Accident Prevention 1973
     Accident Proneness 1973
     ↓ Accidents 1967
     Fire Prevention 1973
     ↓ Hazardous Materials 1991
     Hazards 1973
     ↓ Injuries 1973
     ↓ Prevention 1973
     Risk Management 1997
     Risk Perception 1997
     ↓ Safety Devices 1973
     Warning Labels 1997
     ↓ Warnings 1997

Safety Belts 1973
PN 267   SC 45130
UF   Seat Belts
B   Safety Devices 1973
R   ↓ Driving Behavior 1967
     ↓ Transportation Accidents 1973

Safety Devices 1973
PN 218   SC 45140
N   Safety Belts 1973
R   Hazards 1973
     ↓ Safety 1967
     Warning Labels 1997
     ↓ Warnings 1997

Safety Warnings
Use Warnings

Salamanders 1973
PN 217   SC 45150
B   Amphibia 1973
R   Larvae 1973

Salaries 1973
PN 1328   SC 45160
UF   Pay
     Wages
R   Bonuses 1973
     ↓ Employee Benefits 1973
     Equity (Payment) 1978
     Income (Economic) 1973
     ↓ Income Level 1973
     ↓ Professional Fees 1978

Sales Personnel 1973
PN 1021   SC 45170
UF   Insurance Agents
B   Business and Industrial Personnel 1967
     White Collar Workers 1973
R   Retailing 1991
     ↓ Service Personnel 1991

Salience (Stimulus)
Use Stimulus Salience

Saliva 1973
PN 336   SC 45200
B   Body Fluids 1973

Saliva — (cont'd)
R   Salivation ¹⁹⁷³

Salivary Glands ¹⁹⁷³
PN 43   SC 45210
B   Glands ¹⁹⁶⁷
R   ↓ Digestive System ¹⁹⁶⁷
       Mouth (Anatomy) ¹⁹⁶⁷

Salivation ¹⁹⁷³
PN 216   SC 45220
B   Secretion (Gland) ¹⁹⁷³
R   Digestion ¹⁹⁷³
       Saliva ¹⁹⁷³

Salmon ¹⁹⁷³
PN 77   SC 45230
B   Fishes ¹⁹⁶⁷

Saltiness
Use   Taste Perception

Same Sex Environments
Use   Single Sex Environments

Sample Size ¹⁹⁹⁷
PN 80   SC 45245
B   Statistical Sample Parameters ¹⁹⁷³
R   ↓ Sampling (Experimental) ¹⁹⁷³

Sampling (Experimental) ¹⁹⁷³
PN 759   SC 45250
SN   Systematic selection of part of a larger population of individual responses, individuals, or groups for use in empirical study or research. Results about the entire population are then generalized from this smaller sample.
N   Biased Sampling ¹⁹⁷³
       Random Sampling ¹⁹⁷³
R   Data Collection ¹⁹⁸²
       ↓ Experimental Design ¹⁹⁶⁷
       ↓ Experimentation ¹⁹⁶⁷
       ↓ Population (Statistics) ¹⁹⁷³
       Sample Size ¹⁹⁹⁷
       ↓ Statistical Analysis ¹⁹⁶⁷
       Statistical Power ¹⁹⁹¹
       Statistical Reliability ¹⁹⁷³
       ↓ Statistical Samples ¹⁹⁷³
       ↓ Statistical Variables ¹⁹⁷³

Sanatoriums ¹⁹⁷³
PN 12   SC 45260
B   Hospitals ¹⁹⁶⁷
R   Nursing Homes ¹⁹⁷³
       Psychiatric Hospitals ¹⁹⁶⁷

Sarcomas
Use   Neoplasms

SAT
Use   College Entrance Examination Board Scholastic Aptitude Test

Satiation ¹⁹⁶⁷
PN 859   SC 45280
SN   Primarily limited to gratification or satisfaction of a physiologically-based motivation (e.g., need for food and water) but may also refer to gratification of a psychic goal or motivation. Consider also SATISFACTION or NEED SATISFACTION for the latter concept.
R   ↓ Appetite ¹⁹⁷³

Satiation — (cont'd)
R   ↓ Motivation ¹⁹⁶⁷

Satisfaction ¹⁹⁷³
PN 4489   SC 45290
UF   Fulfillment
N   Client Satisfaction ¹⁹⁹⁴
       Consumer Satisfaction ¹⁹⁹⁴
       Job Satisfaction ¹⁹⁶⁷
       Life Satisfaction ¹⁹⁸⁵
       Marital Satisfaction ¹⁹⁸⁸
       Need Satisfaction ¹⁹⁷³
       ↓ Relationship Satisfaction ²⁰⁰¹
       Role Satisfaction ¹⁹⁹⁴
       Sexual Satisfaction ¹⁹⁹⁴
R   Dissatisfaction ¹⁹⁷³
       Physical Comfort ¹⁹⁸²

Saturation (Color)
Use   Color Saturation

Savants ²⁰⁰¹
PN 102   SC 45297
SN   In 2000, this term was created to replace the discontinued term IDIOT SAVANTS. IDIOT SAVANTS was stripped from all records and replaced with SAVANTS.
UF   Idiot Savants
R   Gifted ¹⁹⁶⁷
       ↓ Mental Disorders ¹⁹⁶⁷
       ↓ Mental Retardation ¹⁹⁶⁷

Scaling (Testing) ¹⁹⁶⁷
PN 1470   SC 45360
B   Testing ¹⁹⁶⁷
       Testing Methods ¹⁹⁶⁷
R   Magnitude Estimation ¹⁹⁹¹
       Multidimensional Scaling ¹⁹⁸²

Scalp (Anatomy) ¹⁹⁷³
PN 61   SC 45370
B   Anatomy ¹⁹⁶⁷
R   Hair ¹⁹⁷³
       Head (Anatomy) ¹⁹⁷³
       Skin (Anatomy) ¹⁹⁶⁷

Scalp Disorders
Use   Skin Disorders

Scent Marking (Animal)
Use   Animal Scent Marking

Schedules (Learning)
Use   Learning Schedules

Schedules (Reinforcement)
Use   Reinforcement Schedules

Scheduling (Work)
Use   Work Scheduling

Schema ¹⁹⁸⁸
PN 2066   SC 45425
SN   Cognitive structure used for comprehension, perception, and interpretation of stimuli.
UF   Scripts
B   Cognitive Processes ¹⁹⁶⁷
R   ↓ Cognitions ¹⁹⁸⁵
       Cognitive Maps ¹⁹⁸²
       ↓ Cognitive Style ¹⁹⁶⁷
       Conceptual Imagery ¹⁹⁷³
       Perceptual Style ¹⁹⁷³

Schema — (cont'd)
R   Social Cognition ¹⁹⁹⁴

Schizoaffective Disorder ¹⁹⁹⁴
PN 849   SC 45427
SN   Mental disorder characterized by the presence of both affective disorder and schizophrenia-like symptoms.
B   Mental Disorders ¹⁹⁶⁷
R   ↓ Affective Disorders ²⁰⁰¹
       ↓ Schizophrenia ¹⁹⁶⁷

Schizoid Personality ¹⁹⁷³
PN 427   SC 45430
SN   Personality disorder characterized by alienation, shyness, oversensitivity, seclusiveness, egocentricity, avoidance of intimate relationships, autistic thinking, and withdrawal from and lack of response to the environment.
B   Personality Disorders ¹⁹⁶⁷
R   ↓ Schizophrenia ¹⁹⁶⁷
       Schizotypal Personality ¹⁹⁹¹

Schizophrenia ¹⁹⁶⁷
PN 31238   SC 45440
SN   In 1988, this term replaced the terms CHRONIC SCHIZOPHRENIA, PSEUDOPSYCHOPATHIC SCHIZOPHRENIA, and SIMPLE SCHIZOPHRENIA. In 2000, these terms were stripped from all records and replaced with SCHIZOPHRENIA.
UF   Chronic Schizophrenia
       Dementia Praecox
       Process Schizophrenia
       Pseudopsychopathic Schizophrenia
       Reactive Schizophrenia
       Schizophrenia (Residual Type)
       Simple Schizophrenia
B   Psychosis ¹⁹⁶⁷
N   Acute Schizophrenia ¹⁹⁷³
       Catatonic Schizophrenia ¹⁹⁷³
       Childhood Schizophrenia ¹⁹⁶⁷
       Paranoid Schizophrenia ¹⁹⁶⁷
       Schizophrenia (Disorganized Type) ¹⁹⁷³
       Schizophreniform Disorder ¹⁹⁹⁴
       Undifferentiated Schizophrenia ¹⁹⁷³
R   Anhedonia ¹⁹⁸⁵
       Catalepsy ¹⁹⁷³
       Delusions ¹⁹⁶⁷
       Expressed Emotion ¹⁹⁹¹
       Fragmentation (Schizophrenia) ¹⁹⁷³
       Positive and Negative Symptoms ¹⁹⁹⁷
       Schizoaffective Disorder ¹⁹⁹⁴
       Schizoid Personality ¹⁹⁷³
       Schizotypal Personality ¹⁹⁹¹

Schizophrenia (Disorganized Type) ¹⁹⁷³
PN 122   SC 45445
SN   In 2000, the term's status changed from nonpostable to postable. All records containing the term HEBEPHRENIC SCHIZOPHRENIA were stripped of this term and replaced with SCHIZOPHRENIA (DISORGANIZED TYPE).
UF   Hebephrenic Schizophrenia
B   Schizophrenia ¹⁹⁶⁷

Schizophrenia (Residual Type)
Use   Schizophrenia

Schizophreniform Disorder ¹⁹⁹⁴
PN 145   SC 45447
SN   Use ACUTE SCHIZOPHRENIA to access references from 1988-1993.
B   Schizophrenia ¹⁹⁶⁷

Schizophrenogenic Family [1967]
PN 298   SC 45450
B   Family [1967]
      Family Structure [1973]
R   Double Bind Interaction [1973]
      Dysfunctional Family [1991]
      ↓ Mental Disorders [1967]
      Schizophrenogenic Mothers [1973]

Schizophrenogenic Mothers [1973]
PN 36   SC 45460
B   Mothers [1967]
R   Double Bind Interaction [1973]
      Mother Child Relations [1967]
      Schizophrenogenic Family [1967]

Schizotypal Personality [1991]
PN 403   SC 45465
SN Personality disorder characterized by eccentric thoughts and appearance, inappropriate affect and behavior, extreme social anxiety, and limited interpersonal interaction. Consider using SCHIZOID PERSONALITY to access references from 1973-1990.
B   Personality Disorders [1967]
R   Schizoid Personality [1973]
      ↓ Schizophrenia [1967]

Scholarships
Use Educational Financial Assistance

Scholastic Achievement
Use Academic Achievement

Scholastic Aptitude
Use Academic Aptitude

Scholastic Aptitude Test
Use College Entrance Examination Board Scholastic Aptitude Test

School Accreditation
Use Educational Program Accreditation

School Achievement
Use Academic Achievement

School Adjustment [1967]
PN 3644   SC 45510
SN Process of adjusting to school environment and to the role of a student.
UF   Student Adjustment
B   Adjustment [1967]
R   Adjustment Disorders [1994]
      ↓ Education [1967]
      School Transition [1997]

School Administration
Use Educational Administration

School Administrators [1973]
PN 2434   SC 45530
UF   Administrators (School)
      Educational Administrators
B   Educational Personnel [1973]
N   School Principals [1973]
      School Superintendents [1973]
R   Boards of Education [1978]
      ↓ Management Personnel [1973]

School and College Ability Test
SN Term was discontinued in 1997. In 2000, the term was stripped from all records containing it, and replaced with APTITUDE MEASURES, its postable counterpart.
Use Aptitude Measures

School Attendance [1973]
PN 1165   SC 45560
SN Regular presence of students in school or classes or absenteeism due to factors other than truancy. Compare SCHOOL ENROLLMENT.
UF   Attendance (School)
R   ↓ Education [1967]
      ↓ School Enrollment [1973]
      School Refusal [1994]
      School Retention [1994]
      Student Attrition [1991]

School Club Membership [1973]
PN 31   SC 45570
B   Extracurricular Activities [1973]

School Counseling [1982]
PN 2945   SC 45579
SN Counseling services provided by counselors or teacher counselors in order to help school, college, or university students cope with adjustment problems. Compare EDUCATIONAL COUNSELING.
UF   Guidance Counseling
      School Guidance
B   Counseling [1967]
R   ↓ Education [1967]
      Educational Therapy [1997]
      ↓ Mental Health Services [1978]
      School Counselors [1973]
      Student Personnel Services [1978]

School Counselors [1973]
PN 1697   SC 45580
B   Counselors [1967]
      Educational Personnel [1973]
R   School Counseling [1982]
      School Psychologists [1973]
      Vocational Counselors [1973]

School Dropouts [1967]
PN 1287   SC 45590
B   Dropouts [1973]
N   College Dropouts [1973]
R   ↓ Education [1967]
      Reentry Students [1985]
      School Refusal [1994]
      School Retention [1994]
      Student Attrition [1991]

School Enrollment [1973]
PN 483   SC 45600
SN Number of students registered to attend school, college or university. Also, the act of enrolling in school. Compare SCHOOL ATTENDANCE.
UF   Enrollment (School)
      Matriculation
N   School Expulsion [1973]
      School Suspension [1973]
      Student Attrition [1991]
R   ↓ Dropouts [1973]
      ↓ Education [1967]
      School Attendance [1973]
      School Retention [1994]
      School Truancy [1973]

School Environment [1973]
PN 4049   SC 45610
SN School characteristics, including overall social and physical atmosphere or school climate.
UF   Educational Environment
B   Academic Environment [1973]
N   College Environment [1973]
R   Classroom Environment [1973]
      ↓ Education [1967]
      ↓ School Facilities [1973]
      ↓ Schools [1967]

School Expulsion [1973]
PN 62   SC 45620
UF   Expulsion (School)
B   School Enrollment [1973]
R   School Suspension [1973]
      Student Attrition [1991]

School Facilities [1973]
PN 131   SC 45630
N   Campuses [1973]
      Classrooms [1967]
      Dormitories [1973]
      ↓ Educational Laboratories [1973]
      Learning Centers (Educational) [1973]
      School Libraries [1973]
R   ↓ Education [1967]
      Playgrounds [1973]
      ↓ School Environment [1973]
      ↓ Schools [1967]

School Federal Aid
Use Educational Financial Assistance

School Financial Assistance
Use Educational Financial Assistance

School Graduation [1991]
PN 139   SC 45653
SN Completion of a course of study resulting in the award or acceptance of a diploma or degree.
UF   Graduation (School)
R   ↓ Academic Achievement [1967]
      College Graduates [1982]
      ↓ Education [1967]
      Educational Attainment Level [1997]
      Educational Degrees [1973]
      Graduate Schools [1973]
      High School Graduates [1978]
      ↓ Higher Education [1973]
      School Transition [1997]
      School to Work Transition [1994]

School Guidance
Use School Counseling

School Integration [1982]
PN 592   SC 45658
SN Incorporation of students of different racial, ethnic, or other types of groups into the same school. In 1982, this term was created to replace the discontinued term SCHOOL INTEGRATION (RACIAL). In 2000, SCHOOL INTEGRATION (RACIAL) was stripped from all records and replaced with SCHOOL INTEGRATION.
UF   Racial Segregation (Schools)
      School Integration (Racial)
B   Social Integration [1982]
R   ↓ Activist Movements [1973]
      ↓ Education [1967]
      Equal Education [1978]
      Mainstreaming (Educational) [1978]

School Integration — (cont'd)
R   Racial and Ethnic Relations 1982

School Integration (Racial)
SN Term was discontinued in 1982. In 2000, the term was stripped from all records containing it, and replaced with SCHOOL INTEGRATION, its postable counterpart.
Use School Integration

School Learning 1967
PN 4587   **SC** 45670
SN Learning in an academic environment. For educational performance use ACADEMIC ACHIEVEMENT or one of its narrower terms.
B   Learning 1967
R   ↓ Academic Achievement 1967
     Cooperative Learning 1994
    ↓ Education 1967
    ↓ Experiential Learning 1997
     Mastery Learning 1985
     Metacognition 1991

School Leavers 1988
PN 69   **SC** 45675
SN British term referring to persons who have recently left school, generally after the completion of a basic education program and satisfaction of government requirements.
R   ↓ Educational Background 1967
     School Retention 1994
     Student Attrition 1991

School Libraries 1973
PN 88   **SC** 45680
UF Libraries (School)
B   Libraries 1982
     School Facilities 1973

School Nurses 1973
PN 71   **SC** 45690
B   Educational Personnel 1973
     Nurses 1967

School Organization
Use Educational Administration

School Phobia 1973
PN 262   **SC** 45710
B   Phobias 1967
R   School Refusal 1994
     Separation Anxiety 1973
     Student Attitudes 1967

School Principals 1973
PN 2410   **SC** 45720
B   School Administrators 1973

School Psychologists 1973
PN 1751   **SC** 45730
SN Psychologists usually associated with elementary or secondary schools who provide counseling, testing, or diagnostic services to students, teachers, or parents.
B   Educational Psychologists 1973
     Mental Health Personnel 1967
R   School Counselors 1973

School Psychology 1973
PN 1213   **SC** 45740
SN Branch of psychology that emphasizes training and certification of school psychologists.
B   Educational Psychology 1967

School Readiness 1973
PN 538   **SC** 45750
SN Developmental level at which a child is prepared to adjust to school and the student role. Compare READING READINESS.
R   ↓ Education 1967
     Project Head Start 1973

School Refusal 1994
PN 102   **SC** 45755
SN Unwillingness of students to attend school or classes.
R   ↓ Resistance 1997
     School Attendance 1973
    ↓ School Dropouts 1967
     School Phobia 1973
     School Truancy 1973
     Separation Anxiety 1973
     Student Attitudes 1967

School Retention 1994
PN 236   **SC** 45757
SN Retention of students in school or educational programs.
UF Retention (School)
R   School Attendance 1973
    ↓ School Dropouts 1967
    ↓ School Enrollment 1973
     School Leavers 1988
     School Truancy 1973
     Student Attrition 1991
    ↓ Students 1967

School Superintendents 1973
PN 453   **SC** 45760
SN Administrators who coordinate and direct the operations and activities of a school system at the district, city, or state level.
UF Superintendents (School)
B   School Administrators 1973

School Suspension 1973
PN 157   **SC** 45770
SN Temporary, forced withdrawal of a student from school, usually for disciplinary reasons.
UF Suspension (School)
B   School Enrollment 1973
R   Classroom Discipline 1973
     School Expulsion 1973

School to Work Transition 1994
PN 245   **SC** 45775
SN Transition following school graduation or termination and entry into the work force. Used for normal and disordered populations.
R   College Graduates 1982
    ↓ Education 1967
     Educational Attainment Level 1997
     High School Graduates 1978
    ↓ Mainstreaming 1991
     Occupational Adjustment 1973
     School Graduation 1991
    ↓ Vocational Rehabilitation 1967

School Transition 1997
PN 129   **SC** 45777
SN Movement or advancement from one grade, school, or program to the next.
R   ↓ Academic Achievement 1967
    ↓ Education 1967
     Grade Level 1994
     School Adjustment 1967
     School Graduation 1991

School Truancy 1973
PN 227   **SC** 45780
SN Student's deliberate, often chronic absence from school without an accepted medical or other justifiable reason.
B   Truancy 1973
R   ↓ Education 1967
    ↓ School Enrollment 1973
     School Refusal 1994
     School Retention 1994

Schools 1967
PN 1968   **SC** 45790
N   Boarding Schools 1988
    ↓ Colleges 1967
     Elementary Schools 1973
     Graduate Schools 1973
     High Schools 1973
     Institutional Schools 1978
     Junior High Schools 1973
     Kindergartens 1973
     Military Schools 1973
     Nongraded Schools 1973
     Nursery Schools 1973
     Seminaries 1973
     Technical Schools 1973
R   ↓ Community Facilities 1973
    ↓ Education 1967
    ↓ School Environment 1973
    ↓ School Facilities 1973

Sciatic Nerve
Use Spinal Nerves

SCID
Use Structured Clinical Interview

Science Achievement 1997
PN 176   **SC** 45815
B   Academic Achievement 1967
R   Mathematics Achievement 1973
     Mathematics Education 1973
     Science Education 1973

Science Education 1973
PN 3628   **SC** 45820
B   Curriculum 1967
R   Science Achievement 1997

Sciences 1967
PN 2109   **SC** 45825
N   ↓ Biology 1967
    ↓ Chemistry 1967
     Eugenics 1973
     Geography 1973
    ↓ Mathematics 1982
    ↓ Medical Sciences 1967
    ↓ Neurosciences 1973
     Physics 1973
     Psychobiology 1982
    ↓ Social Sciences 1967
R   ↓ Technology 1973

Scientific Communication 1973
PN 3749   **SC** 45830
SN Formal or informal communication among professionals.
UF Communication (Professional)
     Newsletters (Professional)
     Professional Communication
     Professional Newsletters
B   Communication 1967
R   ↓ Interpersonal Communication 1973

Scientific Communication — (cont'd)
R   Psychological Terminology [1973]
   ↓ Terminology [1991]

Scientific Methods
Use   Experimental Methods

Scientists [1967]
PN 1166   **SC** 45850
SN Conceptually broad term. Use a more specific term if possible.
B   Professional Personnel [1978]
R   ↓ Aerospace Personnel [1973]
   Anthropologists [1973]
   ↓ Business and Industrial Personnel [1967]
   Engineers [1967]
   Mathematicians [1973]
   ↓ Medical Personnel [1967]
   Physicists [1973]
   ↓ Psychologists [1967]
   Sociologists [1973]

Sclera
Use   Eye (Anatomy)

Sclerosis (Nervous System) [1973]
PN 218   **SC** 45870
B   Nervous System Disorders [1967]
N   Multiple Sclerosis [1973]
R   ↓ Neuromuscular Disorders [1973]
   ↓ Paralysis [1973]

Scopolamine [1973]
PN 1165   **SC** 45880
UF   Hyoscine
   Scopolamine Hydrobromide
B   Alkaloids [1973]
   Amines [1973]
   Analgesic Drugs [1973]
   Cholinergic Blocking Drugs [1973]
   CNS Depressant Drugs [1973]
   Sedatives [1973]
R   Bromides [1973]

Scopolamine Hydrobromide
Use   Scopolamine

Score Equating [1985]
PN 210   **SC** 45895
SN Techniques, procedures, or methods used to allow comparision of scores obtained from various editions of the same test or from different tests measuring the same trait.
UF   Test Equating
R   Cutting Scores [1985]
   ↓ Scoring (Testing) [1973]
   Standard Scores [1985]

Scores (Test)
Use   Test Scores

Scoring (Testing) [1973]
PN 1934   **SC** 45910
SN Assignment of numerical values or other types of codes, or the application of comments to test results in order to evaluate a test performance in reference to some established standard or other criterion. Compare GRADING (EDUCATIONAL) or TEST SCORES.
B   Testing [1967]
N   Cutting Scores [1985]
R   Error of Measurement [1985]
   Grading (Educational) [1973]

Scoring (Testing) — (cont'd)
R   Score Equating [1985]
   Standard Scores [1985]
   Statistical Weighting [1985]
   Test Interpretation [1985]
   ↓ Test Scores [1967]

Scotopic Stimulation [1973]
PN 132   **SC** 45940
SN Presentation of light at intensity levels characteristic of nighttime illumination, activating rod photoreceptors in the retina.
B   Illumination [1967]
R   Photopic Stimulation [1973]

Scratching [1973]
PN 64   **SC** 45950
B   Symptoms [1967]
R   Pruritus [1973]

Screening [1982]
PN 1678   **SC** 45960
SN Preliminary use of testing procedures or instruments to identify individuals at risk for a particular problem, or in need of a more thorough evaluation, or to determine an individual's suitability for a specific treatment, education, or occupation.
B   Measurement [1967]
N   Drug Usage Screening [1988]
   ↓ Health Screening [1997]
   Job Applicant Screening [1973]
R   Biological Markers [1991]
   ↓ Diagnosis [1967]
   Diagnostic Interview Schedule [1991]
   ↓ Educational Measurement [1967]
   Educational Placement [1978]
   Geriatric Assessment [1997]
   Health Promotion [1991]
   Intake Interview [1994]
   Misdiagnosis [1997]
   ↓ Personnel Selection [1967]
   ↓ Psychiatric Evaluation [1997]
   ↓ Screening Tests [1982]
   Symptom Checklists [1991]

Screening Tests [1982]
PN 2022   **SC** 45980
B   Measurement [1967]
N   Psychological Screening Inventory [1973]
R   General Health Questionnaire [1991]
   ↓ Psychiatric Evaluation [1997]
   ↓ Screening [1982]

Scripts
Use   Schema

Sculpturing [1973]
PN 62   **SC** 45990
B   Art [1967]

Sea Gulls [1973]
PN 185   **SC** 46010
UF   Gulls
B   Birds [1967]

Seals (Animal) [1973]
PN 141   **SC** 46020
B   Mammals [1973]

Seasonal Affective Disorder [1991]
PN 474   **SC** 46025
UF   SAD

Seasonal Affective Disorder — (cont'd)
UF   Winter Depression
B   Affective Disorders [2001]
R   ↓ Major Depression [1988]
   Phototherapy [1991]
   Recurrent Depression [1994]

Seasonal Variations [1973]
PN 1485   **SC** 46030
SN Periodic changes in behavioral, psychological, or physiological responses in relation to seasonal changes. Used for human or animal populations.
B   Environmental Effects [1973]
R   ↓ Biological Rhythms [1967]
   ↓ Temperature Effects [1967]

Seat Belts
Use   Safety Belts

Seclusion (Patient)
Use   Patient Seclusion

Secobarbital [1973]
PN 53   **SC** 46040
UF   Seconal
B   Barbiturates [1967]
   Hypnotic Drugs [1973]
   Sedatives [1973]

Seconal
Use   Secobarbital

Second Language Education
Use   Foreign Language Education

Second Order Conditioning
Use   Higher Order Conditioning

Secondary Education [1973]
PN 1118   **SC** 46060
SN Education provided by comprehensive schools, grammar schools, junior high or high schools, typically for grades 7-12.
B   Education [1967]
R   High Schools [1973]
   Junior High Schools [1973]

Secondary Reinforcement [1967]
PN 361   **SC** 46070
SN Presentation of a secondary reinforcer. Also, objects or events which acquire reinforcing properties only through having been consistently paired or associated with other reinforcers. Also known as conditioned reinforcers. Compare INTERNAL REWARDS.
UF   Token Reinforcement
B   Reinforcement [1967]
R   Conditioned Stimulus [1973]

Secrecy [1994]
PN 97   **SC** 46075
R   Anonymity [1973]
   ↓ Deception [1967]
   Privacy [1973]
   Self Disclosure [1973]

Secretarial Personnel [1973]
PN 157   **SC** 46080
B   Business and Industrial Personnel [1967]
   White Collar Workers [1973]
R   Clerical Personnel [1973]

Secretarial Skills
  Use Clerical Secretarial Skills

Secretion (Gland) 1973
PN 157   SC 46100
  B Physiology 1967
  N ↓ Endocrine Gland Secretion 1973
     Lactation 1973
     Salivation 1973
     Sweating 1973
  R ↓ Endocrine Disorders 1973

Sectioning (Lesion)
  Use Lesions

Security (Emotional)
  Use Emotional Security

Sedatives 1973
PN 507   SC 46130
SN In 1997, this term replaced the discontinued term PHENAGLYCODOL. In 2000, PHENAGLY-CODOL was stripped from all records and replaced with SEDATIVES.
  UF Phenaglycodol
  B Drugs 1967
  N Alprazolam 1988
     Amobarbital 1973
     Atropine 1973
     Barbital 1973
     Chloral Hydrate 1973
     Chlorpromazine 1967
     Clozapine 1991
     Flurazepam 1982
     Glutethimide 1973
     Haloperidol 1973
     Heroin 1973
     Hexobarbital 1973
     Meperidine 1973
     Meprobamate 1973
     Methaqualone 1973
     Molindone 1982
     Nitrazepam 1978
     Pentobarbital 1973
     Phenobarbital 1973
     Promethazine 1973
     Reserpine 1967
     Scopolamine 1973
     Secobarbital 1973
     Thalidomide 1973
     Thiopental 1973
     Triazolam 1988
  R ↓ Analgesic Drugs 1973
     ↓ Anesthetic Drugs 1973
     ↓ Anticonvulsive Drugs 1973
     ↓ Antiemetic Drugs 1973
     ↓ Antihistaminic Drugs 1973
     ↓ Antihypertensive Drugs 1973
     ↓ Barbiturates 1967
     ↓ Benzodiazepines 1978
     ↓ CNS Depressant Drugs 1973
     ↓ Hypnotic Drugs 1973
     ↓ Tranquilizing Drugs 1967

Seduction 1994
PN 56   SC 46133
  B Psychosexual Behavior 1967

Seeing Eye Dogs
  Use Mobility Aids

Segregation (Racial)
  Use Social Integration

Seizures
  Use Convulsions

Selection (Personnel)
  Use Personnel Selection

Selection (Therapist)
  Use Therapist Selection

Selection Tests 1973
PN 484   SC 46170
SN Tests developed to assess specific traits or skills with the purpose of screening or selecting individuals for occupational or educational placement.
  B Measurement 1967
  N Psychological Screening Inventory 1973

Selective Attention 1973
PN 2444   SC 46175
SN Focusing of awareness on a limited range of stimuli. Compare DIVIDED ATTENTION.
  B Attention 1967
  R Concentration 1982
     Distraction 1978
     Divided Attention 1973
     ↓ Monitoring 1973
     Sensory Gating 1991
     Vigilance 1967

Selective Breeding 1973
PN 327   SC 46180
SN Systematic approach to the development of genotype-dependent differences in a physical or behavioral trait. Compare ANIMAL BREEDING, ANIMAL DOMESTICATION, and EUGENICS.
  B Animal Breeding 1973
  R Animal Domestication 1978
     Eugenics 1973
     ↓ Genetic Engineering 1994
     ↓ Genetics 1967
     Reproductive Technology 1988

Selective Mutism
  Use Elective Mutism

Self Acceptance
  Use Self Perception

Self Actualization 1973
PN 2206   SC 46190
SN According to A. Maslow's theory, the process of striving to fulfull one's talents, capacities, and potentialities for maximum self realization, ideally with integration of physical, social, intellectual, and emotional needs.
  UF Actualization (Self)
     Self Realization
  R Affective Education 1982
     ↓ Human Potential Movement 1982
     Maslow (Abraham Harold) 1991
     ↓ Personality 1967
     Self Determination 1994
     ↓ Self Help Techniques 1982

Self Analysis 1994
PN 69   SC 46195
SN A psychotherapist's application of psychoanalytic principles to his or her personal feelings, drives, and behaviors.
  B Psychoanalysis 1967
  R Personal Therapy 1991
     Psychoanalytic Training 1973

Self Assessment
  Use Self Evaluation

Self Care Skills 1978
PN 1769   SC 46215
SN Skills such as personal hygiene, feeding, independent housekeeping, public transportation use, which are often taught in rehabilitation programs for persons with mental, physical, or emotional handicaps.
  UF Independent Living
  B Ability 1967
  R Activities of Daily Living 1991
     Adaptive Behavior 1991
     Child Self Care 1988
     Daily Activities 1994
     Hygiene 1994
     Independent Living Programs 1991
     ↓ Rehabilitation 1967
     ↓ Skill Learning 1973
     Special Education 1967

Self Concept 1967
PN 19194   SC 46220
  UF Ideal Self
     Identity (Personal)
     Self Image
  N Academic Self Concept 1997
     Self Confidence 1994
     Self Esteem 1973
  R Affective Education 1982
     Ego Identity 1991
     Ethnic Identity 1973
     ↓ Gender Identity 1985
     Identity Crisis 1973
     ↓ Personality 1967
     Professional Identity 1991
     Reference Groups 1994
     Role Satisfaction 1994
     Self Congruence 1978
     Self Perception 1967
     ↓ Social Identity 1988
     Symbolic Interactionism 1988

Self Confidence 1994
PN 495   SC 46230
SN Use SELF ESTEEM to access references from 1973-1993.
  UF Confidence (Self)
  B Self Concept 1967
  R Academic Self Concept 1997
     Self Efficacy 1985
     Self Esteem 1973
     Self Perception 1967

Self Congruence 1978
PN 262   SC 46235
SN State of harmony between actual and ideal selves, or congruence between experience, personality, and self-concept.
  R ↓ Self Concept 1967

Self Consciousness
  Use Self Perception

Self Control 1973
PN 3394   SC 46240
SN The ability to repress or the practice of repressing one's behavior, impulsive reactions, emotions, or desires.
  UF Control (Self)
     Willpower
  B Personality Traits 1967
  R Anger Control 1997

Self Control — (cont'd)

R ↓ Emotional Control 1973
   ↓ Helplessness 1997
   ↓ Impulse Control Disorders 1997
   Internal External Locus of Control 1967
   Temptation 1973

Self Defeating Behavior 1988

PN 163   SC 46243
SN Behavior that blocks one's own goals and wishes, e.g., the tendency to compete so aggressively that one cannot hold a job.
B   Behavior 1967
R   ↓ Self Destructive Behavior 1985
    Self Handicapping Strategy 1988

Self Defense 1985

PN 108   SC 46245
SN Protecting one's self or property against crime.
UF Personal Defense
R   ↓ Crime 1967
    ↓ Crime Victims 1982
    Martial Arts 1985
    Self Preservation 1997
    ↓ Violence 1973

Self Destructive Behavior 1985

PN 1176   SC 46244
B   Behavior 1967
N   Attempted Suicide 1973
    Head Banging 1973
    Self Inflicted Wounds 1973
    Self Mutilation 1973
    ↓ Suicide 1967
R   ↓ Behavior Disorders 1971
    Borderline Personality 2001
    Hair Pulling 1973
    ↓ Masochism 1973
    Masochistic Personality 1973
    Self Defeating Behavior 1988

Self Determination 1994

PN 305   SC 46246
SN The power of individuals to determine their own destiny or actions.
R   Empowerment 1991
    ↓ Helplessness 1997
    Independence (Personality) 1973
    Individuality 1973
    Internal External Locus of Control 1967
    Self Actualization 1973
    ↓ Self Management 1985
    Volition 1988
    World View 1988

Self Directed Learning

Use Individualized Instruction

Self Disclosure 1973

PN 3141   SC 46250
UF Disclosure (Self)
R   Anonymity 1973
    ↓ Interpersonal Communication 1973
    ↓ Personality 1967
    Secrecy 1994

Self Efficacy 1985

PN 4205   SC 46255
SN Cognitive mechanism based on expectations or beliefs about one's ability to perform actions necessary to produce a given effect. Also, a theoretical component of behavior change in various therapeutic treatments.

Self Efficacy — (cont'd)

UF Efficacy Expectations
R   Academic Self Concept 1997
    ↓ Expectations 1967
    ↓ Helplessness 1997
    Instrumentality 1991
    Self Confidence 1994
    Self Evaluation 1967
    Self Fulfilling Prophecies 1997
    Self Perception 1967

Self Employment 1994

PN 30   SC 46257
B   Employment Status 1982
R   Business 1967
    Entrepreneurship 1991
    Ownership 1985
    Retailing 1991

Self Esteem 1973

PN 11385   SC 46260
UF Self Respect
B   Self Concept 1967
R   Self Confidence 1994
    Self Perception 1967

Self Evaluation 1967

PN 4566   SC 46270
UF Self Assessment
B   Evaluation 1967
R   ↓ Personality 1967
    Self Efficacy 1985
    ↓ Self Management 1985
    Self Monitoring 1982
    Self Report 1982
    Social Comparison 1985

Self Examination (Medical) 1988

PN 236   SC 46273
SN Self examination for detection of medical conditions or disorders, e.g., breast or testicular cancer. Also used for self administration of medical diagnostic procedures.
UF Breast Examination
R   Cancer Screening 1997
    Health Behavior 1982
    Physical Examination 1988

Self Fulfilling Prophecies 1997

PN 40   SC 46271
SN Expectations or predictions that turn out just as one prophesized. The fulfillment of expectations is usually due to behavior that optimizes the outcome.
UF Pygmalion Effect
R   Attribution 1973
    ↓ Expectations 1967
    ↓ Prediction 1967
    Self Efficacy 1985
    Social Cognition 1994
    ↓ Social Perception 1967

Self Handicapping Strategy 1988

PN 124   SC 46274
SN Conscious or unconscious efforts to lessen one's chances of performing well at a task in which one is ego-involved and fears failure so that poor performance or lack of ability may be attributed to circumstance.
R   Fear of Success 1978
    Self Defeating Behavior 1988

Self Help Techniques 1982

PN 1601   SC 46275

Self Help Techniques — (cont'd)

SN Techniques, materials, or processes designed to assist individuals in solving their own problems. Consider also SUPPORT GROUPS.
N   ↓ Self Management 1985
R   ↓ Behavior Modification 1973
    ↓ Community Services 1967
    Group Counseling 1973
    ↓ Psychotherapeutic Techniques 1967
    Self Actualization 1973
    Self Monitoring 1982
    Self Referral 1991
    Social Support Networks 1982
    ↓ Support Groups 1991
    ↓ Treatment 1967
    ↓ Twelve Step Programs 1997

Self Hypnosis

Use Autohypnosis

Self Image

Use Self Concept

Self Inflicted Wounds 1973

PN 439   SC 46290
SN Any injury to body tissue (including bones) resulting from self directed physical violence. Compare SELF MUTILATION.
B   Self Destructive Behavior 1985
    Wounds 1973
R   Self Mutilation 1973

Self Instruction

Use Individualized Instruction

Self Instructional Training 1985

PN 207   SC 46294
SN Cognitive technique for overcoming cognitive deficits in areas such as problem solving, verbal mediation, and information seeking. Overt verbalizations of thought processes are modeled for and imitated by the client. Covert self-verbalizations follow which result in the client gaining verbal control over behavior.
B   Cognitive Techniques 1985
    Self Management 1985
R   Cognitive Therapy 1982

Self Management 1985

PN 1559   SC 46295
SN Self-regulated modification and/or maintenance of behavior by self-governing of behavioral consequences. Used with disordered or normal populations of all ages.
B   Behavior Modification 1973
    Management 1967
    Self Help Techniques 1982
N   Self Instructional Training 1985
R   Centering 1991
    Cognitive Therapy 1982
    Self Determination 1994
    Self Evaluation 1967
    Self Monitoring 1982
    Self Reinforcement 1973
    Time Management 1994

Self Managing Work Teams 2001

PN 0   SC 46299
SN Autonomous groups of employees who share the responsibility for and have been given the authority to oversee and control all work processes.
B   Management Methods 1973
    Work Teams 2001
R   Organizational Structure 1967

Self Managing Work Teams — (cont'd)
R   Participative Management   1988

Self Medication   1991
PN   173   SC   46298
R   ↓ Drug Therapy   1967
    ↓ Drugs   1967
     Nonprescription Drugs   1991
     Prescription Drugs   1991

Self Monitoring   1982
PN   1250   SC   46296
SN   Systematic observation and recording of one's own behavior usually for the purpose of changing the behavior by means of behavior modification techniques.
UF   Self Observation
B   Monitoring   1973
R   ↓ Behavior Modification   1973
     Observation Methods   1967
     Self Evaluation   1967
     ↓ Self Help Techniques   1982
     ↓ Self Management   1985
     Self Report   1982

Self Monitoring (Personality)   1985
PN   469   SC   46297
SN   The process of subjectively observing and comparing one's own behaviors and expressions with those of others in social interactions for the purpose of regulating and controlling one's own verbal and nonverbal behaviors.
R   Conscientiousness   1997
     Impression Management   1978
     Introspection   1973
     ↓ Personality   1967
     Reflectiveness   1997
     Self Perception   1967
     Social Comparison   1985
     ↓ Social Interaction   1967

Self Mutilation   1973
PN   663   SC   46300
SN   Act of inflicting permanent physical damage to oneself, such as cutting off or destroying a limb or other part of the body. Compare SELF INFLICTED WOUNDS.
UF   Autotomy
     Mutilation (Self)
B   Behavior Disorders   1971
     Self Destructive Behavior   1985
R   Cosmetic Techniques   2001
     Self Inflicted Wounds   1973

Self Observation
Use   Self Monitoring

Self Perception   1967
PN   11434   SC   46310
SN   Physical and social awareness and perceptions of oneself.
UF   Self Acceptance
     Self Consciousness
B   Perception   1967
R   Academic Self Concept   1997
     Aging (Attitudes Toward)   1985
     Body Awareness   1982
     Ingroup Outgroup   1997
     Introspection   1973
     Mirror Image   1991
     ↓ Personality   1967
     ↓ Personality Theory   1967
     Reflectiveness   1997

Self Perception — (cont'd)
R   ↓ Self Concept   1967
     Self Confidence   1994
     Self Efficacy   1985
     Self Esteem   1973
     Self Monitoring (Personality)   1985
     Self Reference   1994
     Self Report   1982

Self Preservation   1997
PN   64   SC   46312
UF   Survival Instinct
R   Death Instinct   1988
     Instinctive Behavior   1982
     Self Defense   1985
     Theory of Evolution   1967

Self Psychology   1988
PN   1233   SC   46315
SN   Psychological theory and approach to psychotherapy focusing on interpretation of behavior in reference to self. Includes the psychoanalytic concept of an individual's need to organize the psyche into a cohesive whole, the self.
B   Psychology   1967
R   ↓ Humanistic Psychology   1985
     Mirroring   1997
     Object Relations   1982
     ↓ Personality Theory   1967
     ↓ Psychoanalytic Theory   1967

Self Realization
Use   Self Actualization

Self Reference   1994
PN   144   SC   46323
R   ↓ Interpersonal Communication   1973
     Self Perception   1967
     ↓ Social Perception   1967

Self Referral   1991
PN   79   SC   46325
SN   Act of directing oneself to an agency, service, or professional for assessment, diagnosis, treatment, or consultation.
UF   Referral (Self)
R   ↓ Commitment (Psychiatric)   1973
     Health Behavior   1982
     Health Care Seeking Behavior   1997
     ↓ Health Care Services   1978
     Health Care Utilization   1985
     ↓ Help Seeking Behavior   1978
     Professional Referral   1973
     Right to Treatment   1997
     ↓ Self Help Techniques   1982

Self Reinforcement   1973
PN   1326   SC   46330
SN   Used for human and animal populations.
B   Reinforcement   1967
R   ↓ Self Management   1985
     ↓ Self Stimulation   1967

Self Report   1982
PN   4194   SC   46335
SN   Method for obtaining information through the elicitation of overt verbal responses, oral or written, from the subject/client by the use of questions or directives. Used only when self-report is discussed in reference to methodological considerations.
B   Methodology   1967
R   Likert Scales   1994
     Self Evaluation   1967

Self Report — (cont'd)
R   Self Monitoring   1982
     Self Perception   1967

Self Respect
Use   Self Esteem

Self Stimulation   1967
PN   1995   SC   46350
B   Stimulation   1967
N   Brain Self Stimulation   1985
R   Electrical Brain Stimulation   1973
     ↓ Operant Conditioning   1967
     ↓ Reinforcement   1967
     Self Reinforcement   1973
     Stereotyped Behavior   1973

Self Talk   1988
PN   338   SC   46355
SN   Vocalized or unvocalized speech that is directed to oneself or an imaginary recipient.
UF   Inner Speech
B   Oral Communication   1985
R   Ellis (Albert)   1991
     ↓ Psychotherapeutic Techniques   1967
     Subvocalization   1973

Selfishness   1973
PN   86   SC   46360
B   Personality Traits   1967
R   Narcissism   1967

Semantic Differential   1967
PN   854   SC   46370
SN   Technique or test which uses subjective ratings of an idea, concept, or object by means of scaling opposite adjectives in order to study connotative meaning. Also used to assess interactions between people and situations and for attitude assessment.
R   ↓ Attitude Measures   1967
     Likert Scales   1994
     ↓ Measurement   1967

Semantic Generalization   1973
PN   166   SC   46380
SN   Conditioning of a reaction to a nonverbal stimulus and subsequent generalization of the response to verbal signs representative of the original stimulus. The types include generalization from object to sign, from sign to sign, and from sign to object.
UF   Generalization (Semantic)
B   Cognitive Processes   1967
R   Cognitive Generalization   1967
     Connotations   1973

Semantic Memory   1988
PN   947   SC   46385
SN   Organized knowledge about words, their meanings, and their relations.
B   Verbal Memory   1994
R   ↓ Lexical Access   1988
     Lexical Decision   1988
     Semantic Priming   1994
     ↓ Semantics   1967

Semantic Priming   1994
PN   450   SC   46387
B   Priming   1988
R   Contextual Associations   1967
     Cues   1967
     Semantic Memory   1988
     ↓ Semantics   1967

Semantics [1967]

PN 5019　　　　　　　　　　**SC** 46390
SN Linguistic science dealing with the relations between language symbols (words, expressions, phrases) and the objects or concepts to which they refer. Also includes the study of changes in the meanings of words. Used for the discipline or the specific semantic characteristics of linguistic symbols.
B　Grammar [1967]
N　Antonyms [1973]
　　Homonyms [1973]
　　Synonyms [1973]
R　Discourse Analysis [1997]
　　Metaphor [1982]
　　Morphology (Language) [1973]
　　↓ Phonology [1973]
　　↓ Priming [1988]
　　Semantic Memory [1988]
　　Semantic Priming [1994]
　　↓ Syntax [1971]
　　↓ Verbal Meaning [1973]
　　↓ Vocabulary [1967]
　　Words (Phonetic Units) [1967]

Semicircular Canals [1973]

PN 50　　　　　　　　　　**SC** 46400
B　Vestibular Apparatus [1967]

Seminarians [1973]

PN 198　　　　　　　　　　**SC** 46410
B　Religious Personnel [1973]
　　Students [1967]

Seminaries [1973]

PN 28　　　　　　　　　　**SC** 46420
SN Institutions for training for ministry, priesthood, or rabbinate.
B　Schools [1967]
R　Religious Education [1973]

Semiotics [1985]

PN 357　　　　　　　　　　**SC** 46425
SN Analysis of signs and symbols, especially their syntactic, semantic, and pragmatic functions in language.
N　Pragmatics [1985]
R　Hermeneutics [1991]
　　↓ Linguistics [1973]
　　Symbolism [1967]

Senile Dementia [1973]

PN 892　　　　　　　　　　**SC** 46440
UF　Dementia (Senile)
B　Dementia [1985]
　　Syndromes [1973]
N　Senile Psychosis [1973]
R　Alzheimers Disease [1973]
　　Cerebral Arteriosclerosis [1973]
　　Physiological Aging [1967]
　　↓ Presenile Dementia [1973]
　　Progressive Supranuclear Palsy [1997]

Senile Psychosis [1973]

PN 16　　　　　　　　　　**SC** 46450
B　Psychosis [1967]
　　Senile Dementia [1973]

Sensation

Use　Perception

Sensation Seeking [1978]

PN 853　　　　　　　　　　**SC** 46477

Sensation Seeking — (cont'd)

SN Need for novel experience or stimulation in order to reach optimal levels of arousal. Limited to human populations.
UF　Novelty Seeking
　　Stimulation Seeking (Personality)
B　Personality Traits [1967]
R　Extraversion [1967]

Sensation Seeking Scale [1973]

PN 80　　　　　　　　　　**SC** 46480
B　Personality Measures [1967]

Sense Organ Disorders [1973]

PN 36　　　　　　　　　　**SC** 46490
B　Physical Disorders [1997]
　　Sensory System Disorders [2001]
N　Anosmia [1973]
　　↓ Ear Disorders [1973]
　　Taste Disorders [2001]
　　↓ Vision Disorders [1982]
R　Anesthesia (Feeling) [1973]
　　↓ Sense Organs [1973]

Sense Organs [1973]

PN 82　　　　　　　　　　**SC** 46500
B　Anatomy [1967]
N　↓ Ear (Anatomy) [1967]
　　↓ Eye (Anatomy) [1967]
　　Taste Buds [1973]
R　↓ Sense Organ Disorders [1973]
　　↓ Sensory System Disorders [2001]
　　Taste Disorders [2001]

Sensitivity (Drugs)

Use　Drug Sensitivity

Sensitivity (Personality) [1967]

PN 1230　　　　　　　　　　**SC** 46520
UF　Insensitivity (Personality)
B　Personality Traits [1967]
R　Perceptiveness (Personality) [1973]

Sensitivity Training [1973]

PN 1074　　　　　　　　　　**SC** 46530
SN Group training that focuses on interpersonal relations within the group and enhancement of self-confidence, self-perception, behavioral skills, and role flexibility.
B　Human Potential Movement [1982]
R　Communication Skills Training [1982]
　　Consciousness Raising Groups [1978]
　　Cultural Sensitivity [1994]
　　↓ Encounter Group Therapy [1973]
　　↓ Group Dynamics [1967]
　　↓ Group Psychotherapy [1967]
　　Human Relations Training [1978]
　　Marathon Group Therapy [1973]
　　↓ Personnel Training [1967]
　　Social Skills Training [1982]

Sensitization (Protein)

Use　Anaphylactic Shock

Sensitization Repression

Use　Repression Sensitization

Sensorially Handicapped

SN The term was discontinued in 1997, when the term SENSORIALLY DISABLED was created to capture this concept. In 2000, with the deletion of the term SENSORIALLY DISABLED, SENSORIALLY HANDICAPPED was made a nonpostable term for the new postable term SENSORY SYSTEM DISORDERS. SENSORIALLY HANDICAPPED and SENSORIALLY DISABLED were stripped from all records containing them and replaced with SENSORY SYSTEM DISORDERS.
Use　Sensory System Disorders

Sensorimotor Development

Use　Perceptual Motor Development

Sensorimotor Measures [1973]

PN 316　　　　　　　　　　**SC** 46550
UF　Perceptual Motor Measures
B　Measurement [1967]
N　Purdue Perceptual Motor Survey [1973]
R　↓ Perceptual Measures [1973]

Sensorimotor Processes

Use　Perceptual Motor Processes

Sensorineural Hearing Loss

Use　Hearing Disorders

Sensory Adaptation [1967]

PN 2003　　　　　　　　　　**SC** 46560
SN Change in sensitivity of sensory systems or components as a result of ongoing or prolonged stimulation.
UF　Adaptation (Sensory)
B　Adaptation [1967]
　　Thresholds [1967]
N　Dark Adaptation [1973]
　　Light Adaptation [1982]
　　Orienting Reflex [1967]
　　Orienting Responses [1967]
R　Habituation [1967]
　　Interocular Transfer [1985]
　　Sensory Integration [1991]

Sensory Deprivation [1967]

PN 1140　　　　　　　　　　**SC** 46570
SN Restriction of sensory or environmental stimulation through surgical or other techniques. Used primarily for animal populations. Consider STIMULUS DEPRIVATION for human populations.
B　Stimulus Deprivation [1973]

Sensory Disabilities (Attitudes Toward) [2001]

PN 0　　　　　　　　　　**SC** 46576
SN In 2000, the truncated terms SENSORY DISABILITIES (ATTIT TOWARD) (which was used from 1997-2000) and SENSORY HANDICAPS (ATTIT TOWARD) (which was used from 1973-1996) were deleted, stripped from all records containing them, and mapped to the expanded form SENSORY DISABILITIES (ATTITUDES TOWARD).
UF　Sensory Handicaps (Attitudes Toward)
B　Disabled (Attitudes Toward) [1997]
R　Disability Discrimination [1997]

Sensory Feedback [1973]

PN 384　　　　　　　　　　**SC** 46580
SN Return of afferent neural signals or information from sensory receptors. Sensory feedback may function in the regulation of behavior in general but is especially important in the control of bodily movement. Use a more specific term if possible.

Sensory Feedback — (cont'd)
B Feedback 1967
Perceptual Stimulation 1973
N ↓ Auditory Feedback 1973
Visual Feedback 1973

Sensory Gating 1991
PN 255 **SC** 46585
SN The internal process of blocking one or more sensory stimuli while attention is focused on another sensory stimuli or sensory channel.
UF Gating (Sensory)
B Perception 1967
R ↓ Awareness 1967
↓ Evoked Potentials 1967
↓ Perceptual Stimulation 1973
Prepulse Inhibition 1997
Selective Attention 1973

Sensory Handicaps (Attitudes Toward)
SN The term was discontinued in 1997, when the term SENSORY DISABILITIES (ATTIT TOWARD) was created to capture this concept. In 2000, these two truncated terms were deleted and mapped to their expanded forms: SENSORY HANDICAPS (ATTITUDES TOWARD) and SENSORY DISABILITIES (ATTITUDES TOWARD). All records containing the truncated versions of the terms were stripped of these terms and replaced with SENSORY DISABILITIES (ATTITUDES TOWARD), the valid postable version of the term.
Use Sensory Disabilities (Attitudes Toward)

Sensory Integration 1991
PN 434 **SC** 46595
SN Neural processes of organizing sensory inputs from the environment and producing an adaptive response. In treatment, the environment's sensory input is manipulated to facilitate environmental interaction.
UF Intersensory Integration
B Intersensory Processes 1978
Perceptual Motor Processes 1967
R ↓ Sensory Adaptation 1967
↓ Treatment 1967

Sensory Neglect 1994
PN 548 **SC** 46597
UF Perceptual Neglect
Spatial Neglect
Visual Neglect
R ↓ Perception 1967
↓ Perceptual Distortion 1982
↓ Perceptual Disturbances 1973
↓ Receptive Fields 1985

Sensory Neurons 1973
PN 903 **SC** 46610
B Neurons 1973
N Auditory Neurons 1973
Baroreceptors 1973
Chemoreceptors 1973
Mechanoreceptors 1973
Nociceptors 1985
↓ Photoreceptors 1973
Proprioceptors 1973
Taste Buds 1973
Thermoreceptors 1973
R ↓ Afferent Pathways 1982
↓ Receptive Fields 1985
Taste Disorders 2001

Sensory Pathways
Use Afferent Pathways

Sensory Preconditioning
Use Preconditioning

Sensory System Disorders 2001
PN 89 **SC** 46599
SN Disorders of the sense organs or of the somatosensory system. The term SENSORIALLY HANDICAPPED was used to represent this concept from 1994-1996, and SENSORIALLY DISABLED was used from 1997-2000. In 2000, SENSORY SYSTEM DISORDERS was created to replace the discontinued and deleted term SENSORIALLY DISABLED. SENSORIALLY DISABLED and SENSORIALLY HANDICAPPED were stripped from all records and replaced with SENSORY SYSTEM DISORDERS.
UF Sensorially Handicapped
B Physical Disorders 1997
N ↓ Sense Organ Disorders 1973
Somatosensory Disorders 2001
R ↓ Sense Organs 1973
Somatosensory Cortex 1973

Sentence Completion Tests 1991
PN 33 **SC** 46617
B Personality Measures 1967
Projective Personality Measures 1973
R Cloze Testing 1973

Sentence Comprehension 1973
PN 1925 **SC** 46620
B Verbal Comprehension 1985

Sentence Structure 1973
PN 1791 **SC** 46630
SN Specific characteristics of a sentence's construction, including such aspects as its syntax, length, and complexity. Compare SYNTAX.
R ↓ Prosody 1991
↓ Syntax 1971
Text Structure 1982

Sentences 1967
PN 1723 **SC** 46640
SN Grammatically and syntactically arranged words that constitute a grammatically complete and meaningful unit.
B Language 1967

Sentencing
Use Adjudication

Separation (Marital)
Use Marital Separation

Separation Anxiety 1973
PN 798 **SC** 46660
B Anxiety Disorders 1997
Separation Reactions 1997
R Abandonment 1997
Attachment Behavior 1985
Attachment Disorders 2001
↓ Relationship Termination 1997
School Phobia 1973
School Refusal 1994
Stranger Reactions 1988

Separation Individuation 1982
PN 1364 **SC** 46665
SN Normal process begun in infancy of disengagement from one's mother and development of a separate, individual identity. Limited to human populations.
B Personality Development 1967

Separation Individuation — (cont'd)
R Attachment Behavior 1985
R ↓ Childhood Development 1967
Mother Child Relations 1967
Object Relations 1982
Transitional Objects 1985

Separation Reactions 1997
PN 139 **SC** 46670
N Separation Anxiety 1973
R Abandonment 1997
Alienation 1971
Anaclitic Depression 1973
Apathy 1973
Attachment Behavior 1985
Attachment Disorders 2001
Depression (Emotion) 1967
Disappointment 1973
Distress 1973
Emotional Trauma 1967
Grief 1973
Homesickness 1994
↓ Relationship Termination 1997
Sadness 1973
Withdrawal (Defense Mechanism) 1973

Septal Nuclei 1982
PN 563 **SC** 46676
SN Subcallosal nuclei that form an integral part of the limbic system. These nuclei contribute to the medial forebrain bundle and have processes synapsing in the hippocampus.
UF Septum
B Limbic System 1973
R Fornix 1982
Hippocampus 1967
Medial Forebrain Bundle 1982
Nucleus Accumbens 1982

Septum
Use Septal Nuclei

Sequential Learning 1973
PN 414 **SC** 46690
SN Type of learning in which a particular task is completed before the next task is given. The learning of each subsequent task is dependent on the previous task completed.
B Learning 1967
R Mastery Learning 1985

Serial Anticipation (Learning) 1973
PN 126 **SC** 46700
SN Learning paradigm which involves the initial presentation of a list of items or a series of events with a short interval between the items or elements in the series. Upon subsequent presentation of the list/series, the subject attempts to guess or anticipate the next item/element in the sequence. Thus, each item/element serves as a cue for the recall of the next. Compare FREE RECALL.
UF Anticipation (Serial Learning)
B Serial Learning 1967
R ↓ Verbal Learning 1967

Serial Learning 1967
PN 1361 **SC** 46720
SN Learning, usually memorization, of items in a list according to a prescribed order.
B Learning 1967
N Serial Anticipation (Learning) 1973
R ↓ Serial Position Effect 1982
Serial Recall 1994
↓ Verbal Learning 1967

Serial Position Effect 1982
PN 282   SC 46724
SN Effect of the relative position of an item in a series on the rate of learning that item.
- N Primacy Effect 1973
- Recency Effect 1973
- R ↓ Learning 1967
- Learning Rate 1973
- ↓ Serial Learning 1967
- Serial Recall 1994

Serial Recall 1994
PN 186   SC 46727
- B Recall (Learning) 1967
- R Forgetting 1973
- Free Recall 1973
- ↓ Memory 1967
- ↓ Serial Learning 1967
- ↓ Serial Position Effect 1982

Seriousness 1973
PN 18   SC 46730
- B Personality Traits 1967

Serotonin 1973
PN 5180   SC 46740
- UF Hydroxytryptamine (5-)
- B Amines 1973
- Neurotransmitters 1985
- Vasoconstrictor Drugs 1973
- R ↓ Adrenergic Drugs 1973
- Serotonin Agonists 1988
- ↓ Serotonin Antagonists 1973
- ↓ Serotonin Metabolites 1978
- ↓ Serotonin Precursors 1978

Serotonin Agonists 1988
PN 1218   SC 46745
- B Drugs 1967
- R Buspirone 1991
- Serotonin 1973
- ↓ Serotonin Antagonists 1973

Serotonin Antagonists 1973
PN 1909   SC 46750
- UF Methysergide
- B Drugs 1967
- N Dihydroxytryptamine 1991
- Lysergic Acid Diethylamide 1967
- Mianserin 1982
- Molindone 1982
- Parachlorophenylalanine 1978
- Ritanserin 1997
- Tetrabenazine 1973
- R ↓ Decarboxylase Inhibitors 1982
- Serotonin 1973
- Serotonin Agonists 1988
- ↓ Serotonin Precursors 1978
- ↓ Serotonin Reuptake Inhibitors 1997

Serotonin Metabolites 1978
PN 164   SC 46754
- B Metabolites 1973
- N Hydroxyindoleacetic Acid (5-) 1985
- R Serotonin 1973
- ↓ Serotonin Precursors 1978

Serotonin Precursors 1978
PN 97   SC 46756
- N ↓ Tryptophan 1973
- R Serotonin 1973
- ↓ Serotonin Antagonists 1973
- ↓ Serotonin Metabolites 1978

Serotonin Reuptake Inhibitors 1997
PN 646   SC 46758
SN Consider using SEROTONIN ANTAGONISTS to access references from 1973-1996.
- N Chlorimipramine 1973
- Citalopram 1997
- Fluoxetine 1991
- Fluvoxamine 1994
- Paroxetine 1994
- Zimeldine 1988
- R ↓ Serotonin Antagonists 1973

Serpasil
Use Reserpine

Sertraline 1997
PN 303   SC 46765
- B Antidepressant Drugs 1971

Serum (Blood)
Use Blood Serum

Serum Albumin 1973
PN 34   SC 46780
- B Blood Proteins 1973

Service Personnel 1991
PN 321   SC 46785
SN Employees who have direct contact with the public; generally nonprofessional and nonsales personnel. Includes hotel, airline, and restaurant personnel, but does not include health care personnel.
- B Business and Industrial Personnel 1967
- N Domestic Service Personnel 1973
- Technical Service Personnel 1973
- R Child Care Workers 1978
- ↓ Nonprofessional Personnel 1982
- Sales Personnel 1973
- ↓ Technical Personnel 1978

Service Quality
Use Quality of Services

Servicemen
Use Military Personnel

Set (Response)
Use Response Set

Severe Mental Retardation 2001
PN 2141   SC 46800
SN IQ 20-34. In 2000, this term replaced the discontinued and deleted term SEVERELY MENTALLY RETARDED. SEVERELY MENTALLY RETARDED was stripped from all records and replaced with SEVERE MENTAL RETARDATION.
- B Mental Retardation 1967

Severity (Disorders) 1982
PN 4053   SC 46824
SN Degree of severity of mental or physical disorder.
- R ↓ Chronic Illness 1991
- ↓ Chronic Mental Illness 1997
- Chronicity (Disorders) 1982
- ↓ Diagnosis 1967
- ↓ Disorders 1967
- ↓ Mental Disorders 1967
- ↓ Physical Disorders 1997
- Prognosis 1973

Sex 1967
PN 851   SC 46950

Sex — (cont'd)
SN Conceptually broad term referring to the structural, functional, or behavioral characteristics of males and females of a given species. Use a more specific term if possible. For comparisons of the sexes use HUMAN SEX DIFFERENCES or ANIMAL SEX DIFFERENCES.
- R Animal Sex Differences 1967
- ↓ Animal Sexual Behavior 1985
- ↓ Genital Disorders 1967
- ↓ Human Sex Differences 1967
- Pornography 1973
- ↓ Psychosexual Behavior 1967
- Psychosexual Development 1982
- Sex Change 1988
- Sex Chromosomes 1973
- Sex Discrimination 1978
- Sex Drive 1973
- Sex Education 1973
- ↓ Sex Hormones 1973
- ↓ Sex Offenses 1982
- Sex Recognition 1997
- ↓ Sex Role Attitudes 1978
- Sex Therapy 1978
- Sexual Attitudes 1973
- Sexual Development 1973
- Sexual Harassment 1985
- ↓ Sexual Reproduction 1973
- Sexuality 1973

Sex Change 1988
PN 115   SC 46828
- UF Sexual Reassignment
- B Surgery 1971
- R Sex 1967
- Transsexualism 1973

Sex Chromosome Disorders 1973
PN 162   SC 46830
- B Chromosome Disorders 1973
- N Klinefelters Syndrome 1973
- R Fragile X Syndrome 1994
- ↓ Sex Linked Hereditary Disorders 1973

Sex Chromosomes 1973
PN 94   SC 46840
- B Chromosomes 1973
- R Sex 1967

Sex Differences (Animal)
Use Animal Sex Differences

Sex Differences (Human)
Use Human Sex Differences

Sex Differentiation Disorders
Use Genital Disorders

Sex Discrimination 1978
PN 1015   SC 46875
SN Prejudiced and differential treatment on the basis of sex rather than on the basis of merit.
- B Social Discrimination 1982
- R Affirmative Action 1985
- ↓ Civil Rights 1978
- Employment Discrimination 1994
- ↓ Prejudice 1967
- Sex 1967
- Sexism 1988

Sex Drive 1973
PN 300   SC 46880
- B Motivation 1967

Sex Drive — (cont'd)
- R   Hypersexuality [1973]
  Inhibited Sexual Desire [1997]
  Libido [1973]
  Sex [1967]
  ↓ Sexual Arousal [1978]

Sex Education [1973]
PN 1250   SC 46890
- B   Family Life Education [1997]
  Health Education [1973]
- R   Sex [1967]

Sex Hormones [1973]
PN 604   SC 46900
- B   Hormones [1967]
- N   ↓ Androgens [1973]
  ↓ Estrogens [1973]
  Progesterone [1973]
- R   ↓ Gonadotropic Hormones [1973]
  Luteinizing Hormone [1978]
  Sex [1967]

Sex Linked Developmental Differences [1973]
PN 1365   SC 46920
SN Differential variation between males and females in specified areas of development. Limited to human populations.
- B   Human Sex Differences [1967]
- R   Adolescent Development [1973]
  ↓ Development [1967]
  Heterosexuality [1973]
  ↓ Human Females [1973]
  ↓ Human Males [1973]
  ↓ Physical Development [1973]
  ↓ Psychogenesis [1973]
  ↓ Psychosexual Behavior [1967]
  Sexual Development [1973]

Sex Linked Hereditary Disorders [1973]
PN 134   SC 46930
SN Disorders occurring in either sex and which are transmitted by genes in the sex chromosomes.
- B   Genetic Disorders [1973]
- N   Fragile X Syndrome [1994]
  Hemophilia [1973]
  Testicular Feminization Syndrome [1973]
  Turners Syndrome [1973]
- R   ↓ Sex Chromosome Disorders [1973]

Sex Offenses [1982]
PN 2092   SC 46933
- B   Crime [1967]
- N   ↓ Sexual Abuse [1988]
- R   Incest [1973]
  ↓ Paraphilias [1988]
  Pedophilia [1973]
  Pornography [1973]
  Sex [1967]
  Sexual Harassment [1985]

Sex Recognition [1997]
PN 30   SC 46934
- R   Animal Sex Differences [1967]
  ↓ Human Sex Differences [1967]
  Sex [1967]

Sex Role Attitudes [1978]
PN 5996   SC 46935
SN Attitudes toward culturally- or socially-prescribed patterns of behavior for males and females.
- UF   Gender Role Attitudes

Sex Role Attitudes — (cont'd)
- B   Attitudes [1967]
- N   Sexism [1988]
- R   Feminism [1978]
  Matriarchy [1973]
  Patriarchy [1973]
  Sex [1967]
  Sex Roles [1967]
  Stereotyped Attitudes [1967]

Sex Roles [1967]
PN 9426   SC 46940
SN Behavioral patterns in a given society which are deemed appropriate to one sex or the other.
- UF   Gender Roles
- B   Psychosexual Behavior [1967]
  Roles [1967]
- R   Androgyny [1982]
  ↓ Division of Labor [1988]
  Femininity [1967]
  ↓ Gender Identity [1985]
  Masculinity [1967]
  Matriarchy [1973]
  Nontraditional Careers [1985]
  Patriarchy [1973]
  ↓ Sex Role Attitudes [1978]
  Social Norms [1985]

Sex Therapy [1978]
PN 1007   SC 46945
SN Treatment of specific sexual function disturbances or therapy aimed at improving sexual relationships.
- B   Treatment [1967]
- R   Couples Therapy [1994]
  ↓ Marriage Counseling [1973]
  Sex [1967]

Sexism [1988]
PN 444   SC 46955
- B   Sex Role Attitudes [1978]
- R   Employment Discrimination [1994]
  ↓ Prejudice [1967]
  Sex Discrimination [1978]

Sexual Abstinence [1973]
PN 111   SC 46960
- UF   Abstinence (Sexual)
  Celibacy
- B   Psychosexual Behavior [1967]
- R   ↓ Birth Control [1971]
  Virginity [1973]

Sexual Abuse [1988]
PN 7018   SC 46965
- B   Antisocial Behavior [1971]
  Sex Offenses [1982]
- N   Incest [1973]
  ↓ Rape [1973]
- R   ↓ Abuse Reporting [1997]
  Anatomically Detailed Dolls [1991]
  ↓ Child Abuse [1971]
  Elder Abuse [1988]
  ↓ Family Violence [1982]
  ↓ Paraphilias [1988]
  Partner Abuse [1991]
  Patient Abuse [1991]
  Pedophilia [1973]
  Physical Abuse [1991]
  Professional Client Sexual Relations [1994]
  Sexual Harassment [1985]

Sexual Addiction [1997]
PN 114   SC 46967
- UF   Compulsivity (Sexual)
  Sexual Compulsivity
- B   Addiction [1973]
- R   Hypersexuality [1973]
  ↓ Paraphilias [1988]
  Promiscuity [1973]
  ↓ Psychosexual Behavior [1967]

Sexual Arousal [1978]
PN 1058   SC 46970
SN Physiological and/or emotional state of sexual excitation.
- UF   Arousal (Sexual)
- B   Psychosexual Behavior [1967]
- N   Eroticism [1973]
- R   Inhibited Sexual Desire [1997]
  Physiological Arousal [1967]
  Sex Drive [1973]
  Sexual Fantasy [1997]
  Sexual Satisfaction [1994]

Sexual Attitudes [1973]
PN 2988   SC 46980
SN Opinions or beliefs about sexual development and behavior.
- B   Attitudes [1967]
- R   ↓ Psychosexual Behavior [1967]
  Psychosexual Development [1982]
  Sex [1967]
  ↓ Sexual Orientation [1997]
  Sexual Risk Taking [1997]
  Sexual Satisfaction [1994]

Sexual Behavior
- Use   Psychosexual Behavior

Sexual Boundary Violations
- Use   Professional Client Sexual Relations

Sexual Compulsivity
- Use   Sexual Addiction

Sexual Delinquency
- Use   Promiscuity

Sexual Development [1973]
PN 776   SC 47010
SN Prior to 1982 used for maturation of cognitive, emotional, and physical aspects of sexuality in humans or animals. From 1982 consider PSYCHOSEXUAL DEVELOPMENT for references on cognitive and emotional aspects.
- UF   Pubescence
- B   Physical Development [1973]
- R   Adolescent Development [1973]
  Heterosexuality [1973]
  ↓ Psychogenesis [1973]
  ↓ Psychosexual Behavior [1967]
  Psychosexual Development [1982]
  Sex [1967]
  Sex Linked Developmental Differences [1973]

Sexual Deviations
SN In 2000, the term was discontinued, and all records containing it were stripped of the term and replaced with PARAPHILIAS, its postable counterpart.
- Use   Paraphilias

Sexual Disorders (Physiological)
- Use   Genital Disorders

Sexual Fantasy [1997]
PN 70   **SC** 47035
B   Fantasy [1997]
R   Erotomania [1997]
    Fantasy (Defense Mechanism) [1967]
    ↓ Psychosexual Behavior [1967]
    ↓ Sexual Arousal [1978]
    Sexuality [1973]

Sexual Fetishism
Use   Fetishism

Sexual Function Disturbances [1973]
PN 2046   **SC** 47050
B   Psychosexual Behavior [1967]
N   Dyspareunia [1973]
    Frigidity [1973]
    Impotence [1973]
    Inhibited Sexual Desire [1997]
    Premature Ejaculation [1973]
    Vaginismus [1973]
R   ↓ Mental Disorders [1967]
    ↓ Physical Disorders [1997]
    ↓ Somatoform Disorders [2001]
    ↓ Urogenital Disorders [1973]

Sexual Harassment [1985]
PN 845   **SC** 47055
SN Physical or psychological sexual threats or attempts to willfully subject a person to involuntary sexual activity usually for the purpose of social control.
UF   Harassment (Sexual)
B   Harassment [2001]
R   Professional Client Sexual Relations [1994]
    Sex [1967]
    ↓ Sex Offenses [1982]
    ↓ Sexual Abuse [1988]
    Victimization [1973]

Sexual Identity (Gender)
Use   Gender Identity

Sexual Intercourse (Human) [1973]
PN 840   **SC** 47060
UF   Coitus
    Copulation
    Intercourse (Sexual)
B   Psychosexual Behavior [1967]
N   Dyspareunia [1973]
    Extramarital Intercourse [1973]
    Incest [1973]
    Premarital Intercourse [1973]
    ↓ Rape [1973]
R   Female Orgasm [1973]
    ↓ Male Orgasm [1973]
    ↓ Sexual Reproduction [1973]
    Sexual Satisfaction [1994]

Sexual Masochism [1973]
PN 49   **SC** 47070
B   Masochism [1973]
    Paraphilias [1988]
R   Fetishism [1973]
    Masochistic Personality [1973]
    Sexual Sadism [1973]

Sexual Orientation [1997]
PN 393   **SC** 47072
N   Bisexuality [1973]
    Heterosexuality [1973]
    ↓ Homosexuality [1967]
R   ↓ Gender Identity [1985]

Sexual Orientation — (cont'd)
R   ↓ Gender Identity Disorder [1997]
    Homosexuality (Attitudes Toward) [1982]
    ↓ Psychosexual Behavior [1967]
    Sexual Attitudes [1973]

Sexual Reassignment
Use   Sex Change

Sexual Receptivity (Animal)
Use   Animal Sexual Receptivity

Sexual Reproduction [1973]
PN 1211   **SC** 47090
B   Physiology [1967]
N   Fertility [1988]
R   ↓ Animal Breeding [1973]
    Animal Mate Selection [1982]
    ↓ Animal Mating Behavior [1967]
    ↓ Birth [1967]
    Fertilization [1973]
    ↓ Genetics [1967]
    ↓ Pregnancy [1967]
    Reproductive Technology [1988]
    Sex [1967]
    ↓ Sexual Intercourse (Human) [1973]
    Sperm [1973]

Sexual Risk Taking [1997]
PN 1012   **SC** 47095
B   Psychosexual Behavior [1967]
    Risk Taking [1967]
R   AIDS Prevention [1994]
    ↓ Pregnancy [1967]
    Risk Perception [1997]
    Sexual Attitudes [1973]
    ↓ Venereal Diseases [1973]

Sexual Sadism [1973]
PN 49   **SC** 47100
B   Paraphilias [1988]
    Sadism [1973]
R   Fetishism [1973]
    Sexual Masochism [1973]

Sexual Satisfaction [1994]
PN 170   **SC** 47110
B   Satisfaction [1973]
R   ↓ Orgasm [1973]
    ↓ Psychosexual Behavior [1967]
    ↓ Sexual Arousal [1978]
    Sexual Attitudes [1973]
    ↓ Sexual Intercourse (Human) [1973]
    Sexuality [1973]

Sexuality [1973]
PN 2690   **SC** 47120
B   Personality Traits [1967]
R   Affection [1973]
    Psychosexual Development [1982]
    Sex [1967]
    Sexual Fantasy [1997]
    Sexual Satisfaction [1994]

Sexually Transmitted Diseases
Use   Venereal Diseases

Shamanism [1973]
PN 230   **SC** 47130
B   Religious Affiliation [1973]
R   Cultism [1973]
    Ethnology [1967]

Shamanism — (cont'd)
R   Faith Healing [1973]
    Folk Medicine [1973]
    Transcultural Psychiatry [1973]
    ↓ Treatment [1967]
    Witchcraft [1973]

Shame [1994]
PN 581   **SC** 47140
SN Use GUILT to access references from 1973-1993.
B   Emotional States [1973]
R   ↓ Anxiety [1967]
    Blame [1994]
    Embarrassment [1973]
    ↓ Fear [1967]
    Guilt [1967]
    Morality [1967]

Shape Perception
Use   Form and Shape Perception

Shared Paranoid Disorder
Use   Folie A Deux

Sharing (Social Behavior) [1978]
PN 388   **SC** 47155
B   Prosocial Behavior [1982]
R   Altruism [1973]
    Charitable Behavior [1973]
    Needle Sharing [1994]

Sheep [1973]
PN 624   **SC** 47170
B   Mammals [1973]

Sheltered Workshops [1967]
PN 335   **SC** 47180
SN Places which provide handicapped individuals with job training and work experience.
B   Rehabilitation Centers [1973]
R   ↓ Community Facilities [1973]
    Supported Employment [1994]

Shelters [1991]
PN 269   **SC** 47185
B   Housing [1973]
R   Battered Females [1988]
    ↓ Community Facilities [1973]
    ↓ Community Services [1967]
    ↓ Family Violence [1982]
    ↓ Government Programs [1973]
    Group Homes [1982]
    ↓ Homeless [1988]
    ↓ Living Arrangements [1991]
    Protective Services [1997]
    Runaway Behavior [1973]
    ↓ Social Services [1982]

Shifts (Workday)
Use   Workday Shifts

Shock [1967]
PN 3026   **SC** 47200
B   Symptoms [1967]
R   Anaphylactic Shock [1973]
    Electrical Injuries [1973]
    ↓ Electrical Stimulation [1973]
    ↓ Electroconvulsive Shock [1967]
    ↓ Injuries [1973]
    ↓ Shock Therapy [1973]
    Shock Units [1973]

Shock — (cont'd)
R   Syncope [1973]

Shock Therapy [1973]
PN 42   SC 47210
B   Physical Treatment Methods [1973]
N   Electroconvulsive Shock Therapy [1967]
     Insulin Shock Therapy [1973]
R   ↓ Alternative Medicine [1997]
     ↓ Aversion Therapy [1973]
     Electrosleep Treatment [1978]
     Shock [1967]

Shock Units [1973]
PN 25   SC 47220
B   Stimulators (Apparatus) [1973]
R   Shock [1967]

Shoplifting [1973]
PN 130   SC 47230
B   Theft [1973]

Shopping [1997]
PN 81   SC 47240
SN   Use CONSUMER BEHAVIOR to access references prior to 1997.
B   Consumer Behavior [1967]
R   Retailing [1991]
     Shopping Centers [1973]

Shopping Centers [1973]
PN 130   SC 47250
B   Community Facilities [1973]
R   ↓ Consumer Behavior [1967]
     Retailing [1991]
     Shopping [1997]

Short Term Memory [1967]
PN 6166   SC 47260
SN   Retention of information for very brief periods, usually seconds; also referred to as working memory. Consider also RETENTION.
UF   Working Memory
B   Memory [1967]
N   Iconic Memory [1985]

Short Term Potentiation
Use Postactivation Potentials

Short Term Psychotherapy
Use Brief Psychotherapy

Shoulder (Anatomy) [1973]
PN 81   SC 47290
B   Joints (Anatomy) [1973]
R   Arm (Anatomy) [1973]

Shuttle Box Grids
SN   Term was discontinued in 1997. In 2000, the term was stripped from all records containing it, and replaced with SHUTTLE BOXES, its postable counterpart.
Use Shuttle Boxes

Shuttle Box Hurdles
SN   Term was discontinued in 1997. In 2000, the term was stripped from all records containing it, and replaced with SHUTTLE BOXES, its postable counterpart.
Use Shuttle Boxes

Shuttle Boxes [1973]
PN 85   SC 47320

Shuttle Boxes — (cont'd)
SN   In 1997, this term replaced the discontinued terms SHUTTLE BOX GRIDS and SHUTTLE BOX HURDLES. In 2000, these terms were stripped from all records and replaced with SHUTTLE BOXES.
UF   Shuttle Box Grids
     Shuttle Box Hurdles
B   Apparatus [1967]

Shyness
Use Timidity

Siamese Twins [1973]
PN 7   SC 47340
B   Twins [1967]

Sibling Relations [1973]
PN 1203   SC 47350
B   Family Relations [1967]

Siblings [1967]
PN 2161   SC 47360
B   Family Members [1973]
N   Brothers [1973]
     ↓ Multiple Births [1973]
     Sisters [1973]

Sick Leave
Use Employee Leave Benefits

Sickle Cell Disease [1994]
PN 173   SC 47380
B   Blood and Lymphatic Disorders [1973]
     Ethnospecific Disorders [1973]
     Genetic Disorders [1973]
R   Anemia [1973]

Side Effects (Drug) [1973]
PN 8866   SC 47390
SN   Acute or chronic and often undesirable effects of drugs occurring in addition to the intended or therapeutic objective. In 1982, this term replaced the discontinued term DRUG ADVERSE REACTIONS. In 2000, DRUG ADVERSE REACTIONS was stripped from all records and replaced with SIDE EFFECTS (DRUG).
UF   Drug Adverse Reactions
B   Side Effects (Treatment) [1988]
N   ↓ Drug Addiction [1967]
     Drug Allergies [1973]
     ↓ Drug Dependency [1973]
     Drug Sensitivity [1973]
R   Akathisia [1991]
     ↓ Drug Therapy [1967]
     Drug Tolerance [1973]
     ↓ Drugs [1967]
     Neuroleptic Malignant Syndrome [1988]
     Tardive Dyskinesia [1988]

Side Effects (Treatment) [1988]
PN 697   SC 47392
SN   Acute or chronic and often undesirable effects of treatment other than drug therapy occurring in addition to the intended or therapeutic objective. For side effects of drug therapy use SIDE EFFECTS (DRUG).
UF   Iatrogenic Effects
N   ↓ Side Effects (Drug) [1973]
R   ↓ Treatment [1967]
     ↓ Treatment Outcomes [1982]

Sight Vocabulary [1973]
PN 142   SC 47400
SN   Words that one recognizes immediately while reading.

Sight Vocabulary — (cont'd)
B   Vocabulary [1967]
R   ↓ Reading [1967]
     ↓ Reading Skills [1973]
     Word Recognition [1988]

Sign Language [1973]
PN 1219   SC 47410
SN   System of hand gestures for communication in which the gestures function as words.
B   Language [1967]
     Manual Communication [1978]
R   Fingerspelling [1973]

Sign Rank Test
Use Wilcoxon Sign Rank Test

Sign Test [1973]
PN 5   SC 47430
B   Nonparametric Statistical Tests [1967]
R   Statistical Significance [1973]

Signal Detection (Perception) [1967]
PN 2726   SC 47440
SN   Psychophysical technique that permits the estimation of the bias of the observer as well as the detectability of the signal (i.e., stimulus) in any sensory modality. Compare THRESHOLDS.
UF   Detection (Signal)
R   ↓ Attention [1967]
     ↓ Perception [1967]
     ↓ Psychophysical Measurement [1967]
     Threshold Determination [1973]
     Visual Search [1982]

Signal Intensity
Use Stimulus Intensity

Significance (Statistical)
Use Statistical Significance

Significant Others [1991]
PN 462   SC 47465
SN   Includes teachers, peers, family members, friends, and unmarried persons or couples.
R   Couples [1982]
     ↓ Family Members [1973]
     Friendship [1967]
     Homosexual Parents [1994]
     Mentor [1985]
     Peers [1978]
     Role Models [1982]
     Romance [1997]
     Social Support Networks [1982]
     ↓ Spouses [1973]

Silent Reading [1973]
PN 255   SC 47470
B   Reading [1967]

Similarity (Stimulus)
Use Stimulus Similarity

Simile
Use Figurative Language

Simple Schizophrenia
SN   Term was discontinued in 1988. In 2000, the term was stripped from all records containing it, and replaced with SCHIZOPHRENIA, its postable counterpart.
Use Schizophrenia

Simulation 1967
PN 2527   SC 47510
UF   Modeling
     Simulators
N   ↓ Computer Simulation 1973
     Flight Simulation 1973
     Heuristic Modeling 1973
     Markov Chains 1973
     ↓ Mathematical Modeling 1973
     Simulation Games 1973
     ↓ Stochastic Modeling 1973
R   Game Theory 1967

Simulation Games 1973
PN 463   SC 47520
B   Games 1967
     Simulation 1967
R   Computer Games 1988
     ↓ Computer Simulation 1973

Simulators
Use   Simulation

Sin 1973
PN 66   SC 47540
B   Religious Beliefs 1973

Sincerity 1973
PN 48   SC 47550
UF   Genuineness
B   Personality Traits 1967
R   ↓ Deception 1967
     Dishonesty 1973

Singing 1997
PN 95   SC 47552
SN   Use ANIMAL VOCALIZATIONS for singing in animal populations.
B   Oral Communication 1985
R   ↓ Music 1967
     Music Perception 1997
     ↓ Vocalization 1967
     ↓ Voice 1973

Single Cell Organisms
Use   Microorganisms

Single Fathers 1994
PN 28   SC 47554
SN   Use SINGLE PARENTS to access references from 1978-1993.
B   Fathers 1967
     Single Parents 1978
R   Single Persons 1973

Single Mothers 1994
PN 268   SC 47555
SN   Use SINGLE PARENTS to access references from 1978-1993.
B   Mothers 1967
     Single Parents 1978
R   Single Persons 1973
     Unwed Mothers 1973
     Working Women 1978

Single Parents 1978
PN 949   SC 47556
SN   Parents rearing children alone.
B   Parents 1967
N   Single Fathers 1994
     Single Mothers 1994
R   ↓ Family Structure 1973
     ↓ Marital Status 1973

Single Parents — (cont'd)
R   Never Married 1994
     ↓ Parental Absence 1973
     Single Persons 1973
     Unwed Mothers 1973

Single Persons 1973
PN 406   SC 47560
SN   Persons who are not married.
R   Living Alone 1994
     ↓ Marital Status 1973
     Never Married 1994
     Single Fathers 1994
     Single Mothers 1994
     ↓ Single Parents 1978

Single Sex Environments 2001
PN 0   SC 47565
SN   Used for both human and animal populations. Use only when gender is pertinent to the focus of the study.
UF   Female Only Environments
     Male Only Environments
     Same Sex Environments
B   Environment 1967
R   ↓ Academic Environment 1973
     ↓ Animal Environments 1967
     Animal Sex Differences 1967
     Coeducation 1973
     Home Environment 1973
     ↓ Human Sex Differences 1967
     ↓ Living Arrangements 1991

Sisters 1973
PN 159   SC 47570
B   Human Females 1973
     Siblings 1967

Sixteen Personality Factors Questionnaire 2001
PN 416   SC 47591
SN   In 2000, the truncated term SIXTEEN PERSONALITY FACTORS QUESTION (which was used from 1973-2000) was deleted, removed from all records containing it, and mapped to its expanded form SIXTEEN PERSONALITY FACTORS QUESTIONNAIRE.
B   Nonprojective Personality Measures 1973

Size 1973
PN 839   SC 47610
SN   Relative physical dimensions of objects or stimuli.
B   Stimulus Parameters 1967
N   ↓ Body Size 1985
     Brain Size 1973
     Family Size 1973
     Group Size 1967
     Litter Size 1985
     Size Constancy 1985
     ↓ Size Discrimination 1967

Size (Apparent)
Use   Apparent Size

Size (Group)
Use   Group Size

Size Constancy 1985
PN 39   SC 47635
SN   The tendency for the perceived size of stimuli to remain constant despite objective changes in context and stimulus parameters.

Size Constancy — (cont'd)
B   Perceptual Constancy 1985
     Size 1973
R   ↓ Size Discrimination 1967

Size Discrimination 1967
PN 912   SC 47640
B   Size 1973
     Spatial Perception 1967
N   Apparent Size 1973
R   Linear Perspective 1982
     Size Constancy 1985

Skeletomuscular Disorders
Use   Musculoskeletal Disorders

Skewed Distribution 1973
PN 86   SC 47680
UF   Poisson Distribution
B   Frequency Distribution 1973

Skill Learning 1973
PN 2183   SC 47690
B   Learning 1967
N   Fine Motor Skill Learning 1973
     Gross Motor Skill Learning 1973
R   Communication Skills Training 1982
     Habilitation 1991
     ↓ Perceptual Motor Learning 1967
     Self Care Skills 1978
     Social Skills Training 1982

Skilled Industrial Workers 1973
PN 247   SC 47700
SN   Blue collar workers who perform skilled labor in an industrial setting.
B   Blue Collar Workers 1973
     Business and Industrial Personnel 1967

Skills
Use   Ability

Skin (Anatomy) 1967
PN 829   SC 47720
UF   Epithelium
B   Tissues (Body) 1973
R   Absorption (Physiological) 1973
     Cosmetic Techniques 2001
     Epithelial Cells 1973
     Hair 1973
     Head (Anatomy) 1973
     Scalp (Anatomy) 1973

Skin Cancer Screening
Use   Cancer Screening

Skin Conduction
Use   Skin Resistance

Skin Disorders 1973
PN 476   SC 47740
UF   Scalp Disorders
B   Physical Disorders 1997
N   Allergic Skin Disorders 1973
     Alopecia 1973
     ↓ Dermatitis 1973
     Herpes Simplex 1973
     Lupus 1973
     Pruritus 1973
R   Albinism 1973
     ↓ Somatoform Disorders 2001
     Sweating 1973

Skin Disorders — (cont'd)
  R   ↓ Tuberculosis   1973

Skin Electrical Properties   1973
PN   93   SC   47750
SN   General electrodermal characteristics and responses as measured on the skin surface. Use a more specific term if possible.
  B   Electrophysiology   1973
  N   Skin Potential   1973
     ↓ Skin Resistance   1973

Skin Potential   1973
PN   93   SC   47760
SN   Degree of electrical charge of the skin.
  B   Electrophysiology   1973
     Skin Electrical Properties   1973
  R   Galvanic Skin Response   1967
     ↓ Skin Resistance   1973

Skin Resistance   1973
PN   1317   SC   47770
SN   Resistance of the skin to the flow of electric current; reciprocal of skin conductance.
  UF   Skin Conduction
  B   Skin Electrical Properties   1973
  N   Basal Skin Resistance   1973
  R   Galvanic Skin Response   1967
     Skin Potential   1973

Skin Temperature   1973
PN   606   SC   47780
  B   Body Temperature   1973

Skinner (Burrhus Frederic)   1991
PN   176   SC   47785
SN   Identifies biographical or autobiographical studies and discussions of Skinner's works.
  R   Behaviorism   1967
     ↓ Operant Conditioning   1967
     ↓ Psychologists   1967
     Skinner Boxes   1973

Skinner Boxes   1973
PN   21   SC   47790
  B   Apparatus   1967
  R   Skinner (Burrhus Frederic)   1991

Skull   1973
PN   25   SC   47800
  B   Musculoskeletal System   1973

Slang   1973
PN   51   SC   47810
  B   Vocabulary   1967
  R   Ethnolinguistics   1973
     Nonstandard English   1973

Sleep   1967
PN   5525   SC   47820
  N   Napping   1994
     NREM Sleep   1973
     REM Sleep   1973
  R   ↓ Consciousness Disturbances   1973
     ↓ Consciousness States   1971
     Dream Content   1973
     ↓ Dreaming   1967
     Lucid Dreaming   1994
     Nocturnal Teeth Grinding   1973
     Sleep Apnea   1991
     Sleep Deprivation   1967
     ↓ Sleep Disorders   1973
     Sleep Onset   1973

Sleep — (cont'd)
  R   Sleep Talking   1973
     Sleep Treatment   1973
     Sleep Wake Cycle   1985

Sleep Apnea   1991
PN   194   SC   47825
SN   Temporary absence of breathing or prolonged respiratory failure occurring during sleep.
  B   Apnea   1973
  R   ↓ Neonatal Disorders   1973
     ↓ Sleep   1967
     Sudden Infant Death   1982

Sleep Deprivation   1967
PN   1246   SC   47830
  B   Deprivation   1967
  R   ↓ Sleep   1967
     ↓ Sleep Disorders   1973

Sleep Disorders   1973
PN   1626   SC   47840
  UF   Night Terrors
  B   Consciousness Disturbances   1973
  N   Hypersomnia   1994
     Insomnia   1973
     Kleine Levin Syndrome   2001
     Narcolepsy   1973
     Sleepwalking   1973
  R   Hypnagogic Hallucinations   1973
     ↓ Mental Disorders   1967
     ↓ Physical Disorders   1997
     ↓ Sleep   1967
     Sleep Deprivation   1967

Sleep Inducing Drugs
  Use   Hypnotic Drugs

Sleep Onset   1973
PN   647   SC   47860
  UF   Drowsiness
  R   Napping   1994
     ↓ Sleep   1967

Sleep Talking   1973
PN   15   SC   47870
  B   Consciousness Disturbances   1973
  R   ↓ Sleep   1967

Sleep Treatment   1973
PN   51   SC   47880
SN   Prolonged sleep or rest used in the treatment of mental disorders. Such sleep may be induced by drugs, hypnosis, or other means. For sleep withdrawal therapy, which is the deprivation of sleep for therapeutic purposes, use SLEEP DEPRIVATION.
  B   Narcoanalysis   1973
  R   ↓ Drug Therapy   1967
     Electrosleep Treatment   1978
     ↓ Sleep   1967

Sleep Wake Cycle   1985
PN   1145   SC   47885
  B   Biological Rhythms   1967
  R   Napping   1994
     ↓ Sleep   1967
     Wakefulness   1973

Sleeplessness
  Use   Insomnia

Sleepwalking   1973
PN   126   SC   47890
SN   In 1982, this term replaced the discontinued term SOMNAMBULISM. In 2000, SOMNAMBULISM was stripped from all records and replaced with SLEEPWALKING.
  UF   Somnambulism
  B   Sleep Disorders   1973

Slosson Intelligence Test   2001
PN   67   SC   47901
SN   In 2000, the truncated term SLOSSON INTELLIGENCE TEST FOR CHILD (which was used from 1991-2000) was deleted, removed from all records containing it, and mapped to its new form SLOSSON INTELLIGENCE TEST.
  B   Intelligence Measures   1967

Slow Learners
SN   In 2000, the term was discontinued, and all records containing it were stripped of the term and replaced with BORDERLINE MENTAL RETARDATION, its postable counterpart.
  Use   Borderline Mental Retardation

Slow Wave Sleep
  Use   NREM Sleep

Slums
  Use   Poverty Areas

Smell Perception
  Use   Olfactory Perception

Smiles   1973
PN   288   SC   47950
  B   Facial Expressions   1967
  R   Laughter   1978

Smokeless Tobacco   1994
PN   85   SC   47960
  UF   Chewing Tobacco
     Snuff
     Tobacco (Smokeless)
  R   ↓ CNS Stimulating Drugs   1973
     Nicotine   1973
     Nicotine Withdrawal   1997
     Tobacco Smoking   1967

Smoking (Tobacco)
  Use   Tobacco Smoking

Smoking Cessation   1988
PN   1908   SC   47980
SN   Used for cigarette smoking rehabilitation programs or stopping the habit of smoking. Use DRUG REHABILITATION and TOBACCO SMOKING to access references prior to 1988.
  R   ↓ Drug Abstinence   1994
     ↓ Drug Rehabilitation   1973
     Nicotine Withdrawal   1997
     Tobacco Smoking   1967

Snails   1973
PN   430   SC   47990
  UF   Aplysia
  B   Mollusca   1973

Snake Phobia
  Use   Ophidiophobia

Snakes   1973
PN   303   SC   48010

Snakes — (cont'd)
  B   Reptiles [1967]

Snuff
  Use Smokeless Tobacco

Sobriety [1988]
PN 549   **SC** 48020
  UF Alcohol Abstinence
  B   Drug Abstinence [1994]
  R   Alcohol Drinking Attitudes [1973]
      ↓ Alcohol Rehabilitation [1982]
      Alcohol Withdrawal [1994]
      ↓ Alcoholism [1967]
      Detoxification [1973]
      ↓ Drug Rehabilitation [1973]
      Recovery (Disorders) [1973]

Soccer [1994]
PN 88   **SC** 48025
  B   Recreation [1967]
      Sports [1967]

Sociability [1973]
PN 388   **SC** 48030
  B   Personality Traits [1967]
  R   Extraversion [1967]
      Gregariousness [1973]

Social Acceptance [1967]
PN 1948   **SC** 48040
  SN Degree to which an individual is incorporated by others in their activities or is welcomed to interact with others informally. Limited to human populations.
  UF Acceptance (Social)
      Rejection (Social)
      Social Rejection
  B   Social Behavior [1967]
  R   Need for Approval [1997]
      Peer Pressure [1994]
      Popularity [1988]
      Social Approval [1967]
      Stigma [1991]
      ↓ Tolerance [1973]

Social Adaptation
  Use Social Adjustment

Social Adjustment [1973]
PN 5754   **SC** 48060
  UF Adaptation (Social)
      Maladjustment (Social)
      Social Adaptation
      Social Maladjustment
  B   Adjustment [1967]
      Social Behavior [1967]
  R   Adjustment Disorders [1994]

Social Anxiety [1985]
PN 699   **SC** 48065
  SN Apprehension or fear of social interaction or social situations in general. Compare SOCIAL PHOBIA.
  B   Anxiety [1967]
  R   ↓ Anxiety Disorders [1997]
      Avoidant Personality [1994]
      ↓ Fear [1967]
      ↓ Social Interaction [1967]
      ↓ Social Isolation [1967]
      Speech Anxiety [1985]

Social Approval [1967]
PN 1726   **SC** 48070

Social Approval — (cont'd)
  SN Favorable direct or indirect judgment by member or members of a given social group of another member or members, based on conduct, physical makeup, or other characteristics.
  UF Approval (Social)
  B   Social Behavior [1967]
      Social Influences [1967]
  R   Criticism [1973]
      Likability [1988]
      Need for Approval [1997]
      Peer Pressure [1994]
      Popularity [1988]
      Reputation [1997]
      Social Acceptance [1967]
      ↓ Social Reinforcement [1967]
      Stigma [1991]

Social Behavior [1967]
PN 5800   **SC** 48080
  B   Behavior [1967]
  N   ↓ Aggressive Behavior [1967]
      ↓ Animal Social Behavior [1967]
      Competition [1967]
      ↓ Compliance [1973]
      Conformity (Personality) [1967]
      Contagion [1988]
      Criticism [1973]
      ↓ Gambling [1973]
      ↓ Help Seeking Behavior [1978]
      Interspecies Interaction [1991]
      ↓ Involvement [1973]
      ↓ Leadership [1967]
      Leadership Style [1973]
      Militancy [1973]
      Nurturance [1985]
      ↓ Organizational Behavior [1978]
      ↓ Prosocial Behavior [1982]
      Racial and Ethnic Relations [1982]
      Reciprocity [1973]
      ↓ Responsibility [1973]
      Retaliation [1991]
      ↓ Risk Taking [1967]
      Social Acceptance [1967]
      Social Adjustment [1973]
      Social Approval [1967]
      Social Cognition [1994]
      Social Demonstrations [1973]
      Social Drinking [1973]
      Social Facilitation [1973]
      ↓ Social Interaction [1967]
      ↓ Social Perception [1967]
      ↓ Social Reinforcement [1967]
      Social Skills [1978]
  R   ↓ Antisocial Behavior [1971]
      Dominance Hierarchy [1973]
      Equity (Payment) [1978]
      ↓ Equity (Social) [1978]
      Impression Management [1978]
      Informants [1988]
      Personal Space [1973]
      Privacy [1973]
      Psychodynamics [1973]
      Social Change [1967]
      ↓ Social Influences [1967]

Social Casework [1967]
PN 4435   **SC** 48090
  UF Social Work
  B   Treatment [1967]
  R   ↓ Case Management [1991]
      Child Welfare [1988]
      ↓ Counseling [1967]
      ↓ Family Therapy [1967]

Social Casework — (cont'd)
  R   ↓ Health Care Services [1978]
      ↓ Mental Health Services [1978]
      Outreach Programs [1997]
      Protective Services [1997]
      ↓ Social Services [1982]

Social Caseworkers
  Use Social Workers

Social Change [1967]
PN 3834   **SC** 48110
  UF Change (Social)
  R   ↓ Fads and Fashions [1973]
      Future [1991]
      ↓ Social Behavior [1967]
      ↓ Social Influences [1967]
      ↓ Social Movements [1967]
      ↓ Social Processes [1967]
      ↓ Social Programs [1973]
      Trends [1991]

Social Class [1967]
PN 2517   **SC** 48120
  B   Social Structure [1967]
      Socioeconomic Status [1967]
  N   Lower Class [1973]
      Middle Class [1973]
      Upper Class [1973]
  R   Disadvantaged [1967]
      ↓ Income Level [1973]
      ↓ Socioeconomic Class Attitudes [1973]

Social Class Attitudes
  Use Socioeconomic Class Attitudes

Social Clubs (Therapeutic)
  Use Therapeutic Social Clubs

Social Cognition [1994]
PN 1802   **SC** 48143
  SN Cognitive processes and activity that accompany and mediate social interaction.
  B   Cognitive Processes [1967]
      Social Behavior [1967]
  R   ↓ Communication Skills [1973]
      ↓ Interpersonal Interaction [1967]
      Reputation [1997]
      Schema [1988]
      Self Fulfilling Prophecies [1997]
      ↓ Social Interaction [1967]
      ↓ Social Perception [1967]
      Social Skills Training [1982]

Social Comparison [1985]
PN 997   **SC** 48145
  SN Subjective evaluation of personal characteristics (e.g., ability level, personality traits, accomplishments) of oneself or another person in relation to the perceived characteristics of others.
  B   Social Perception [1967]
  R   Self Evaluation [1967]
      Self Monitoring (Personality) [1985]
      ↓ Social Influences [1967]

Social Control [1988]
PN 598   **SC** 48148
  SN Power of institutions, organizations, or laws of society to influence or regulate behavior or attitudes of groups or individuals. Consider POWER to access references that describe the control an individual has over other persons.
  UF Control (Social)

Social Control — (cont'd)
- **B** Social Processes [1967]
- **R** ↓ Emotional Control [1973]
  - ↓ Social Influences [1967]

Social Dating [1973]
PN 1280   **SC** 48150
- **UF** Dating (Social)
- **B** Human Courtship [1973]
  - Interpersonal Interaction [1967]
- **R** Acquaintance Rape [1991]
  - Couples [1982]
  - Friendship [1967]
  - Male Female Relations [1988]
  - Premarital Intercourse [1973]
  - ↓ Relationship Termination [1997]
  - Romance [1997]

Social Demonstrations [1973]
PN 76   **SC** 48160
- **UF** Demonstrations (Social)
  - Picketing
- **B** Social Behavior [1967]
- **R** ↓ Collective Behavior [1967]
  - ↓ Political Participation [1988]
  - ↓ Social Movements [1967]
  - Student Activism [1973]

Social Density [1978]
PN 497   **SC** 48165
- **SN** Number of animals or humans per given space unit. For specifically high density conditions use CROWDING.
- **UF** Density (Social)
  - Population Density
- **R** Crowding [1978]
  - Overpopulation [1973]
  - Personal Space [1973]
  - ↓ Population [1973]
  - ↓ Social Environments [1973]

Social Deprivation [1973]
PN 291   **SC** 48170
- **SN** Limited access to society's resources due to poverty, neglect, social discrimination, or other disadvantage. For a lack of social contact use SOCIAL ISOLATION. Consider also CULTURAL DEPRIVATION.
- **B** Social Processes [1967]
  - Stimulus Deprivation [1973]
- **N** ↓ Social Isolation [1967]
- **R** Cultural Deprivation [1973]
  - Disadvantaged [1967]
  - ↓ Homeless [1988]

Social Desirability [1967]
PN 1417   **SC** 48180
- **UF** Desirability (Social)
- **B** Social Influences [1967]
- **R** Need for Approval [1997]

Social Development
Use Psychosocial Development

Social Discrimination [1982]
PN 1071   **SC** 48185
- **SN** Prejudiced and differential treatment based on religion, sex, race, ethnicity, disability, or other personal characteristics rather than on the basis of merit. Use a more specific term if possible.
- **UF** Discrimination (Social)
- **B** Discrimination [1967]
  - Social Issues [1991]
- **N** Age Discrimination [1994]

Social Discrimination — (cont'd)
- **N** Disability Discrimination [1997]
  - Employment Discrimination [1994]
  - Race and Ethnic Discrimination [1994]
  - Sex Discrimination [1978]
- **R** Affirmative Action [1985]
  - ↓ Civil Rights [1978]
  - Racial and Ethnic Relations [1982]
  - Racism [1973]
  - ↓ Social Integration [1982]
  - Stereotyped Attitudes [1967]
  - Stigma [1991]

Social Drinking [1973]
PN 496   **SC** 48190
- **SN** Consumption of alcoholic beverages in social settings.
- **B** Alcohol Drinking Patterns [1967]
  - Social Behavior [1967]

Social Environments [1973]
PN 2507   **SC** 48200
- **B** Environment [1967]
- **N** ↓ Academic Environment [1973]
  - ↓ Animal Environments [1967]
  - ↓ Communities [1967]
  - Home Environment [1973]
  - Poverty Areas [1973]
  - Rural Environments [1967]
  - Suburban Environments [1967]
  - Towns [1973]
  - ↓ Urban Environments [1967]
  - ↓ Working Conditions [1973]
- **R** Cultural Deprivation [1973]
  - Social Density [1978]

Social Equality [1973]
PN 851   **SC** 48210
- **UF** Equality (Social)
- **B** Social Issues [1991]
- **R** Affirmative Action [1985]
  - ↓ Civil Rights [1978]
  - Equal Education [1978]
  - ↓ Human Rights [1978]
  - ↓ Justice [1973]
  - Racial and Ethnic Relations [1982]
  - ↓ Social Integration [1982]

Social Facilitation [1973]
PN 443   **SC** 48220
- **UF** Facilitation (Social)
- **B** Social Behavior [1967]
- **R** ↓ Social Influences [1967]

Social Groups [1973]
PN 1160   **SC** 48230
- **UF** Cadres
  - Cliques
  - Groups (Social)
- **N** Dyads [1973]
  - Ingroup Outgroup [1997]
  - Minority Groups [1967]
  - Reference Groups [1994]
- **R** ↓ Social Networks [1994]

Social Identity [1988]
PN 1980   **SC** 48235
- **SN** An aspect of self image based on in-group preference or ethnocentrism and a perception of belonging to a social or cultural group.
- **N** Professional Identity [1991]
- **R** Ethnic Identity [1973]
  - Ethnocentrism [1973]

Social Identity — (cont'd)
- **R** Ingroup Outgroup [1997]
  - Minority Groups [1967]
  - Reference Groups [1994]
  - ↓ Self Concept [1967]

Social Immobility
Use Social Mobility

Social Influences [1967]
PN 5700   **SC** 48250
- **UF** Influences (Social)
- **N** Coercion [1994]
  - Criticism [1973]
  - Enabling [1997]
  - Ethnic Values [1973]
  - ↓ Interpersonal Influences [1967]
  - ↓ Power [1967]
  - ↓ Prejudice [1967]
  - Propaganda [1973]
  - Social Approval [1967]
  - Social Desirability [1967]
  - Social Norms [1985]
  - Social Values [1973]
  - Superstitions [1973]
  - Taboos [1973]
- **R** Authority [1967]
  - ↓ Ethics [1967]
  - Mentor [1985]
  - Popularity [1988]
  - Psychosocial Factors [1988]
  - Reference Groups [1994]
  - Role Models [1982]
  - ↓ Social Behavior [1967]
  - Social Change [1967]
  - Social Comparison [1985]
  - Social Control [1988]
  - Social Facilitation [1973]
  - ↓ Social Movements [1967]
  - ↓ Social Reinforcement [1967]

Social Integration [1982]
PN 1110   **SC** 48258
- **SN** Process of uniting diverse groups (e.g., racial, ethnic, religious, or disabled) of a society or organization. In 1982, this term was created to replace the discontinued term RACIAL INTEGRATION. In 2000, RACIAL INTEGRATION was stripped from all records and replaced with SOCIAL INTEGRATION.
- **UF** Desegregation
  - Integration (Racial)
  - Racial Integration
  - Segregation (Racial)
- **B** Social Issues [1991]
  - Social Processes [1967]
- **N** School Integration [1982]
- **R** ↓ Activist Movements [1973]
  - ↓ Civil Rights [1978]
  - ↓ Mainstreaming [1991]
  - Racial and Ethnic Relations [1982]
  - ↓ Social Discrimination [1982]
  - Social Equality [1973]

Social Interaction [1967]
PN 7584   **SC** 48260
- **UF** Interaction (Social)
- **B** Social Behavior [1967]
- **N** Encouragement [1973]
  - ↓ Interpersonal Interaction [1967]
  - Nonviolence [1991]
  - Peace [1988]
  - Physical Contact [1982]
  - Victimization [1973]
- **R** ↓ Aggressive Behavior [1967]

Social Interaction — (cont'd)

R ↓ Conflict Resolution 1982
   Forgiveness 1988
   Psychodynamics 1973
   Self Monitoring (Personality) 1985
   Social Anxiety 1985
   Social Cognition 1994
   ↓ Social Networks 1994
   Social Support Networks 1982
   Symbolic Interactionism 1988

Social Isolation 1967

PN 2965   SC 48270
SN Voluntary or involuntary absence of contact with others. Used for human or animal populations.
UF Isolation (Social)
B   Social Deprivation 1973
    Stimulus Deprivation 1973
N   Patient Seclusion 1994
R   Animal Maternal Deprivation 1988
    Social Anxiety 1985

Social Issues 1991

PN 1079   SC 48275
SN Social concerns, including but not limited to problems or conditions perceived to have social causes, definitions, consequences, or possible solutions.
UF Social Problems
N   ↓ Crime 1967
    ↓ Homeless 1988
    ↓ Human Rights 1978
    Peace 1988
    Poverty 1973
    ↓ Social Discrimination 1982
    Social Equality 1973
    ↓ Social Integration 1982
    Unemployment 1967
    ↓ War 1967
R   Adolescent Pregnancy 1988
    Censorship 1978
    ↓ Civil Rights 1978
    ↓ Drug Abuse 1973
    ↓ Justice 1973
    ↓ Legal Processes 1973
    Political Issues 1973
    Racism 1973
    ↓ Social Movements 1967
    ↓ Social Processes 1967
    ↓ Social Programs 1973

Social Learning 1973

PN 1509   SC 48280
B   Learning 1967
    Learning Strategies 1991
N   Imitation (Learning) 1967
    Imprinting 1967
R   Observational Learning 1973
    ↓ Social Reinforcement 1967

Social Maladjustment

Use Social Adjustment

Social Mobility 1967

PN 363   SC 48300
SN Change in social status by an individual or a group.
UF Mobility (Social)
    Social Immobility
    Upward Mobility
B   Social Processes 1967

Social Movements 1967

PN 1020   SC 48310
N   ↓ Activist Movements 1973
    Black Power Movement 1973
    Civil Rights Movement 1973
    Homosexual Liberation Movement 1973
    Womens Liberation Movement 1973
R   ↓ Civil Rights 1978
    Coalition Formation 1973
    ↓ Human Rights 1978
    Peace 1988
    ↓ Political Participation 1988
    ↓ Radical Movements 1973
    Social Change 1967
    Social Demonstrations 1973
    ↓ Social Influences 1967
    ↓ Social Issues 1991
    ↓ Social Programs 1973

Social Networks 1994

PN 770   SC 48313
SN A formal or informal linkage, association, or network of individuals or groups that share common interests, contacts, knowledge, or resources. Compare SOCIAL SUPPORT NETWORKS and SUPPORT GROUPS.
UF Networks (Social)
N   Social Support Networks 1982
R   Ingroup Outgroup 1997
    ↓ Interpersonal Interaction 1967
    ↓ Social Groups 1973
    ↓ Social Interaction 1967
    Sociograms 1973
    ↓ Sociometry 1991
    ↓ Support Groups 1991

Social Norms 1985

PN 1519   SC 48315
SN Rules for social conduct, or standards which comprise a cultural definition of desirable or acceptable behavior. Also, patterns or traits seen as typical in the behavior of a social group.
UF Norms (Social)
B   Social Influences 1967
R   Sex Roles 1967
    Social Values 1973

Social Perception 1967

PN 16297   SC 48320
SN Awareness of social phenomena, including attitudes or behaviors of persons or groups, especially as they relate to one's self.
UF Interpersonal Perception
B   Perception 1967
    Social Behavior 1967
N   Attribution 1973
    Impression Formation 1978
    Social Comparison 1985
R   Anonymity 1973
    Blame 1994
    Credibility 1973
    Face Perception 1985
    Fame 1985
    Halo Effect 1982
    Impression Management 1978
    Ingroup Outgroup 1997
    Labeling 1978
    Likability 1988
    Perceptiveness (Personality) 1973
    Popularity 1988
    Reputation 1997
    Reward Allocation 1988
    Self Fulfilling Prophecies 1997
    Self Reference 1994

Social Perception — (cont'd)

R   Social Cognition 1994
    Stereotyped Attitudes 1967
    Stigma 1991
    Stranger Reactions 1988
    Theory of Mind 2001

Social Phobia 1985

PN 986   SC 48325
SN Extreme apprehension or fear of social interaction or social situations in general. Compare SOCIAL ANXIETY.
B   Phobias 1967
R   Avoidant Personality 1994

Social Problems

Use Social Issues

Social Processes 1967

PN 2875   SC 48330
N   Anomie 1978
    Coalition Formation 1973
    ↓ Human Migration 1973
    Immigration 1973
    Industrialization 1973
    Social Control 1988
    ↓ Social Deprivation 1973
    ↓ Social Integration 1982
    Social Mobility 1967
    ↓ Socialization 1967
    ↓ Status 1967
    Urbanization 1973
R   Equity (Payment) 1978
    ↓ Equity (Social) 1978
    ↓ Human Rights 1978
    ↓ Political Processes 1973
    Refugees 1988
    Social Change 1967
    ↓ Social Issues 1991
    ↓ Sociocultural Factors 1967
    Trends 1991

Social Programs 1973

PN 648   SC 48340
N   Needle Exchange Programs 2001
    Outreach Programs 1997
R   ↓ Housing 1973
    Integrated Services 1997
    ↓ Program Development 1991
    Social Change 1967
    ↓ Social Issues 1991
    ↓ Social Movements 1967
    ↓ Social Services 1982

Social Psychiatry 1967

PN 225   SC 48350
SN Branch of psychiatry concerned with the role of ecological, social, cultural, and economic factors in the etiology, incidence, and manifestations of mental disorders. Differentiate from COMMUNITY PSYCHIATRY, which emphasizes the practical and clinical applications of social psychiatry.
B   Psychiatry 1967
R   Social Psychology 1967

Social Psychologists 1973

PN 114   SC 48360
B   Psychologists 1967
R   Industrial Psychologists 1973
    Sociologists 1973

Social Psychology 1967

PN 3330   SC 48370

Social Psychology — (cont'd)

SN Branch of psychology concerned with the study of individuals in groups and the interpersonal interactions within and between groups.
- **B** Applied Psychology   1973
- **R** Folk Psychology   1997
  - Social Psychiatry   1967

Social Reinforcement   1967

PN 1332   **SC** 48380
- **B** Reinforcement   1967
  - Social Behavior   1967
- **N** Nonverbal Reinforcement   1973
  - ↓ Verbal Reinforcement   1973
- **R** Enabling   1997
  - Encouragement   1973
  - Eye Contact   1973
  - Social Approval   1967
  - ↓ Social Influences   1967
  - ↓ Social Learning   1973

Social Rejection

Use Social Acceptance

Social Sciences   1967

PN 2140   **SC** 48390
SN Group of scientific disciplines which study social institutions, their functioning, and the interpersonal relationships and behavior of individuals of those institutions.
- **B** Sciences   1967
- **N** Anthropology   1967
  - ↓ Behavioral Sciences   1997
  - Economics   1985
  - ↓ Sociology   1967
- **R** Theoretical Orientation   1982

Social Security   1988

PN 117   **SC** 48392
SN Government program providing for economic security and social welfare of individuals or families upon retirement, death, or disability. Used for US and non-US programs.
- **B** Government Programs   1973
  - Insurance   1973
- **R** Disability Evaluation   1988
  - Medicaid   1994
  - Medicare   1988

Social Services   1982

PN 2790   **SC** 48393
SN Activities designed to promote social welfare, usually associated with government or a helping organization (e.g., a church).
- **N** ↓ Community Services   1967
  - Outreach Programs   1997
  - Protective Services   1997
- **R** Child Welfare   1988
  - ↓ Government Programs   1973
  - ↓ Health Care Services   1978
  - Integrated Services   1997
  - Literacy Programs   1997
  - ↓ Mental Health Services   1978
  - Shelters   1991
  - Social Casework   1967
  - ↓ Social Programs   1973
  - ↓ Support Groups   1991

Social Skills   1978

PN 5092   **SC** 48395
- **UF** Competence (Social)
  - Interpersonal Competence
- **B** Ability   1967
  - Social Behavior   1967

Social Skills — (cont'd)

- **R** Adaptive Behavior   1991
  - Affective Education   1982
  - ↓ Competence   1982
  - Listening (Interpersonal)   1997
  - Male Female Relations   1988
  - Social Skills Training   1982

Social Skills Training   1982

PN 2370   **SC** 48397
SN Instruction, usually group oriented, to increase quality and capability of interpersonal interaction.
- **R** Assertiveness Training   1978
  - ↓ Behavior Modification   1973
  - Communication Skills Training   1982
  - Human Relations Training   1978
  - Sensitivity Training   1973
  - ↓ Skill Learning   1973
  - Social Cognition   1994
  - Social Skills   1978

Social Stigma

Use Stigma

Social Stress   1973

PN 868   **SC** 48400
- **B** Stress   1967

Social Structure   1967

PN 2030   **SC** 48410
- **B** Society   1967
- **N** Caste System   1973
  - ↓ Social Class   1967
- **R** Dominance Hierarchy   1973
  - ↓ Status   1967

Social Studies Education   1978

PN 564   **SC** 48415
SN Social sciences education in elementary, junior high, and high schools. Includes history, current events, and political science.
- **B** Curriculum   1967

Social Support Networks   1982

PN 11679   **SC** 48417
SN Family members or friends who provide social, emotional, or psychological support or comfort to an individual. Consider also SUPPORT GROUPS.
- **B** Social Networks   1994
- **R** Assistance (Social Behavior)   1973
  - ↓ Family Relations   1967
  - Friendship   1967
  - Reference Groups   1994
  - ↓ Self Help Techniques   1982
  - Significant Others   1991
  - ↓ Social Interaction   1967
  - ↓ Support Groups   1991

Social Values   1973

PN 1960   **SC** 48420
- **B** Social Influences   1967
  - Values   1967
- **R** Anomie   1978
  - Morality   1967
  - Social Norms   1985
  - ↓ Society   1967

Social Work

Use Social Casework

Social Work Education   1973

PN 1028   **SC** 48440
- **B** Education   1967

Social Workers   1973

PN 3197   **SC** 48450
- **UF** Caseworkers
  - Social Caseworkers
- **B** Personnel   1967
- **N** Psychiatric Social Workers   1973
- **R** ↓ Counselors   1967
  - ↓ Health Personnel   1994
  - ↓ Law Enforcement Personnel   1973
  - ↓ Mental Health Personnel   1967
  - ↓ Psychologists   1967
  - Rehabilitation Counselors   1978
  - Sociologists   1973
  - ↓ Therapists   1967
  - Vocational Counselors   1973

Socialism   1973

PN 258   **SC** 48460
- **B** Political Economic Systems   1973

Socialization   1967

PN 3820   **SC** 48470
SN Process by which individuals acquire social skills and other characteristics necessary to function effectively in society or in a particular group.
- **B** Social Processes   1967
- **N** Political Socialization   1988
- **R** Reference Groups   1994

Socially Disadvantaged

Use Disadvantaged

Society   1967

PN 1336   **SC** 48490
- **B** Culture (Anthropological)   1967
- **N** ↓ Social Structure   1967
  - ↓ Socioeconomic Status   1967
- **R** Social Values   1973

Sociobiology   1982

PN 505   **SC** 48495
SN Systematic study of the biological basis of all aspects of social behavior. Used for both human and animal populations.
- **B** Biology   1967
  - Sociology   1967
- **R** Behavioral Genetics   1994

Sociocultural Factors   1967

PN 11756   **SC** 48500
- **UF** Cultural Factors
- **N** Cross Cultural Differences   1967
  - Cultural Deprivation   1973
  - ↓ Culture Change   1967
  - Ethnic Identity   1973
  - Ethnic Values   1973
  - ↓ Rites of Passage   1973
- **R** ↓ Childrearing Practices   1967
  - Cross Cultural Psychology   1997
  - Cultism   1973
  - Cultural Sensitivity   1994
  - ↓ Culture (Anthropological)   1967
  - Ethnography   1973
  - Ethnology   1967
  - ↓ Family Structure   1973
  - Kinship Structure   1973
  - Multiculturalism   1997
  - Psychosocial Factors   1988
  - Race (Anthropological)   1973
  - ↓ Racial and Ethnic Groups   2001
  - Regional Differences   2001
  - Risk Factors   2001
  - ↓ Social Processes   1967

Socioeconomic Class Attitudes [1973]
PN 268   **SC** 48510
SN Attitudes of, not toward, members of a particular socioeconomic class.
- **UF** Class Attitudes
- **UF** Social Class Attitudes
- **B** Attitudes [1967]
- **N** Lower Class Attitudes [1973]
  - Middle Class Attitudes [1973]
  - Upper Class Attitudes [1973]
- **R** ↓ Social Class [1967]
  - ↓ Socioeconomic Status [1967]

Socioeconomic Status [1967]
PN 8431   **SC** 48520
SN The combination of one's social class and income level. Includes socioeconomic differences between individuals or groups.
- **B** Society [1967]
  - Status [1967]
- **N** Family Socioeconomic Level [1973]
  - ↓ Income Level [1973]
  - Lower Class [1973]
  - ↓ Social Class [1967]
- **R** Disadvantaged [1967]
  - Income (Economic) [1973]
  - Poverty [1973]
  - ↓ Socioeconomic Class Attitudes [1973]

Socioenvironmental Therapy
- **Use** Milieu Therapy

Sociograms [1973]
PN 50   **SC** 48530
SN Diagrams in which interactions between group members are analyzed on the basis of mutual attractions or antipathies.
- **B** Sociometry [1991]
- **R** ↓ Measurement [1967]
  - ↓ Social Networks [1994]

Sociolinguistics [1985]
PN 413   **SC** 48535
SN The study of the sociological aspects of language, concerned with the part language plays in maintaining the social roles in a community.
- **B** Linguistics [1973]
- **R** Code Switching [1988]
  - Ethnolinguistics [1973]
  - Metalinguistics [1994]
  - ↓ Sociology [1967]
  - Symbolic Interactionism [1988]

Sociologists [1973]
PN 106   **SC** 48540
- **B** Professional Personnel [1978]
- **R** Anthropologists [1973]
  - ↓ Counselors [1967]
  - Scientists [1967]
  - Social Psychologists [1973]
  - ↓ Social Workers [1973]

Sociology [1967]
PN 1724   **SC** 48550
- **B** Social Sciences [1967]
- **N** Sociobiology [1982]
- **R** ↓ Behavioral Sciences [1997]
  - Sociolinguistics [1985]
  - Symbolic Interactionism [1988]

Sociometric Tests [1967]
PN 417   **SC** 48560

Sociometric Tests — (cont'd)
SN Tests or techniques used to identify preferences, likes, or dislikes of group members with respect to each other, as well as to identify various patterns of group structure or interaction.
- **B** Measurement [1967]
  - Sociometry [1991]

Sociometry [1991]
PN 219   **SC** 48565
SN Used for the scientific discipline or the sociometric processes and properties themselves.
- **N** Sociograms [1973]
  - Sociometric Tests [1967]
- **R** ↓ Collective Behavior [1967]
  - ↓ Group Dynamics [1967]
  - ↓ Organizational Behavior [1978]
  - ↓ Peer Relations [1967]
  - ↓ Social Networks [1994]

Sociopath
- **Use** Antisocial Personality

Sociopathology
- **Use** Antisocial Behavior

Sociotherapy [1973]
PN 95   **SC** 48580
SN Any therapy in which the main emphasis is on socioenvironmental and interpersonal factors. Sometimes used to refer to a therapeutic community.
- **B** Treatment [1967]
- **R** Milieu Therapy [1988]
  - Therapeutic Community [1967]

Sodium [1973]
PN 921   **SC** 48590
- **B** Metallic Elements [1973]
- **N** Sodium Ions [1973]
- **R** Hyponatremia [1997]

Sodium Ions [1973]
PN 87   **SC** 48610
- **B** Electrolytes [1973]
  - Sodium [1973]

Sodium Lactate
- **Use** Lactic Acid

Sodium Pentobarbital
- **Use** Pentobarbital

Solvent Abuse
- **Use** Inhalant Abuse

Solvents [1982]
PN 309   **SC** 48625
SN Substances that react chemically with a solid to bring it into solution. Also, liquids that dissolve another substance (solute) without any change in chemical composition.
- **N** Toluene [1991]
- **R** ↓ Acids [1973]
  - ↓ Alcohols [1967]
  - ↓ Inhalant Abuse [1985]

Somatization [1994]
PN 617   **SC** 57430
SN Process of organically manifesting and expressing cognitive and emotional disturbances through bodily symptoms. Primarily used in nonclinical contexts.
- **R** ↓ Conversion Disorder [2001]

Somatization — (cont'd)
- **R** Hypochondriasis [1973]
  - Illness Behavior [1982]
  - Somatization Disorder [2001]
  - ↓ Somatoform Disorders [2001]
  - Somatoform Pain Disorder [1997]
  - ↓ Symptoms [1967]

Somatization Disorder [2001]
PN 0   **SC** 48627
SN Pattern of recurring polysymptomatic somatic complaints resulting in medical treatment or impaired daily function. Usually begins before age 30 and extends over a period of years. Consider PSYCHOSOMATIC DISORDERS to access records from 1967-2000.
- **B** Somatoform Disorders [2001]
- **R** Psychosomatic Medicine [1978]
  - Somatization [1994]

Somatoform Disorders [2001]
PN 0   **SC** 48628
SN Disorders characterized by bodily symptoms caused by psychological factors. Consider PSYCHOSOMATIC DISORDERS to access references from 1967-2000.
- **UF** Psychophysiologic Disorders
  - Psychosomatic Disorders
- **N** Body Dysmorphic Disorder [2001]
  - ↓ Conversion Disorder [2001]
  - Hypochondriasis [1973]
  - Neurodermatitis [1973]
  - Somatization Disorder [2001]
  - Somatoform Pain Disorder [1997]
- **R** Anorexia Nervosa [1973]
  - Asthma [1967]
  - Bulimia [1985]
  - ↓ Dyspnea [1973]
  - ↓ Endocrine Disorders [1973]
  - ↓ Gastrointestinal Disorders [1973]
  - Hay Fever [1973]
  - ↓ Headache [1973]
  - Hyperphagia [1973]
  - Hyperventilation [1973]
  - Illness Behavior [1982]
  - Irritable Bowel Syndrome [1991]
  - Malingering [1973]
  - Migraine Headache [1973]
  - Munchausen Syndrome [1994]
  - Myofascial Pain [1991]
  - Obesity [1973]
  - Premenstrual Tension [1973]
  - Psychosomatic Medicine [1978]
  - ↓ Sexual Function Disturbances [1973]
  - ↓ Skin Disorders [1973]
  - Somatization [1994]
  - ↓ Symptoms [1967]
  - ↓ Urinary Function Disorders [1973]
  - ↓ Urogenital Disorders [1973]

Somatoform Pain Disorder [1997]
PN 257   **SC** 48629
SN In 1997, this term was created to replace the discontinued term PSYCHOGENIC PAIN. In 2000, PSYCHOGENIC PAIN was stripped from all records and replaced with SOMATOFORM PAIN DISORDER.
- **UF** Pain (Psychogenic)
  - Pain Disorder
  - Psychogenic Pain
- **B** Pain [1967]
  - Somatoform Disorders [2001]
- **R** Chronic Pain [1985]
  - ↓ Conversion Disorder [2001]

Somatoform Pain Disorder — (cont'd)
- R   Hypochondriasis ¹⁹⁷³ → Pain Management ¹⁹⁹⁴
  - Somatization ¹⁹⁹⁴

Somatosensory Cortex ¹⁹⁷³
PN   673   SC   48630
- UF   Cortex (Somatosensory)
- B   Parietal Lobe ¹⁹⁷³
- R   ↓ Sensory System Disorders ²⁰⁰¹

Somatosensory Disorders ²⁰⁰¹
PN   0   SC   48635
SN   Disorders of sensory information received from the skin and deep tissue of the body that are associated with impaired or abnormal somatic sensation. Such disorders may affect proprioception, tactile, thermal, and pressure sensation, and pain perception.
- UF   Hyperalgesia
  - Hyperesthesia
  - Hypesthesia
  - Paresthesia
- B   Sensory System Disorders ²⁰⁰¹
- R   ↓ Nervous System Disorders ¹⁹⁶⁷
  - ↓ Pain Perception ¹⁹⁷³
  - Pressure Sensation ¹⁹⁷³
  - ↓ Somesthetic Perception ¹⁹⁶⁷
  - Temperature Perception ¹⁹⁷³

Somatosensory Evoked Potentials ¹⁹⁷³
PN   810   SC   48640
- UF   Motor Evoked Potentials
- B   Evoked Potentials ¹⁹⁶⁷
- R   ↓ Cortical Evoked Potentials ¹⁹⁷³

Somatostatin ¹⁹⁹¹
PN   163   SC   48645
- UF   Growth Hormone Inhibitor
- B   Peptides ¹⁹⁷³
- R   Somatotropin ¹⁹⁷³

Somatotropin ¹⁹⁷³
PN   757   SC   48650
- UF   Growth Hormone
- B   Pituitary Hormones ¹⁹⁷³
- R   Somatostatin ¹⁹⁹¹

Somatotypes ¹⁹⁷³
PN   189   SC   48660
SN   Body types as derived from any of various classifications of body build and which usually imply a correlation with personality characteristics.
- UF   Body Types
- R   ↓ Personality ¹⁹⁶⁷
  - ↓ Physical Appearance ¹⁹⁸²
  - Physique ¹⁹⁶⁷

Somesthetic Perception ¹⁹⁶⁷
PN   895   SC   48670
SN   Awareness of bodily condition or stimuli, including kinesthetic and cutaneous perception.
- B   Perception ¹⁹⁶⁷
- N   ↓ Cutaneous Sense ¹⁹⁶⁷
  - Kinesthetic Perception ¹⁹⁶⁷
  - ↓ Pain Perception ¹⁹⁷³
  - Temperature Perception ¹⁹⁷³
  - Weight Perception ¹⁹⁶⁷
- R   Body Awareness ¹⁹⁸²
  - ↓ Labyrinth Disorders ¹⁹⁷³
  - Pressure Sensation ¹⁹⁷³
  - Somatosensory Disorders ²⁰⁰¹

Somesthetic Stimulation ¹⁹⁷³
PN   669   SC   48680
- UF   Vestibular Stimulation
- B   Perceptual Stimulation ¹⁹⁷³
- N   ↓ Tactual Stimulation ¹⁹⁷³
- R   Weightlessness ¹⁹⁶⁷

Somnambulism
SN   Term was discontinued in 1982. In 2000, the term was stripped from all records containing it, and replaced with SLEEPWALKING, its postable counterpart.
- Use   Sleepwalking

Sonar ¹⁹⁷³
PN   40   SC   48700
- B   Apparatus ¹⁹⁶⁷

Songs
- Use   Music

Sons ¹⁹⁷³
PN   943   SC   48710
- B   Family Members ¹⁹⁷³
  - Human Males ¹⁹⁷³
  - Offspring ¹⁹⁸⁸

Sorority Membership ¹⁹⁷³
PN   120   SC   48720
SN   Belonging to a club traditionally restricted to females. Used also for sorority organizations.
- B   Extracurricular Activities ¹⁹⁷³

Sorting (Cognition)
- Use   Classification (Cognitive Process)

Sound
- Use   Auditory Stimulation

Sound Localization
- Use   Auditory Localization

Sound Pressure Level
- Use   Loudness

Sound Waves
- Use   Acoustics

Sourness
- Use   Taste Perception

Spacecraft ¹⁹⁷³
PN   50   SC   48820
- R   Air Transportation ¹⁹⁷³
  - Astronauts ¹⁹⁷³

Spaceflight ¹⁹⁶⁷
PN   272   SC   48830
- B   Aviation ¹⁹⁶⁷
- R   Acceleration Effects ¹⁹⁷³
  - Decompression Effects ¹⁹⁷³
  - ↓ Gravitational Effects ¹⁹⁶⁷
  - Weightlessness ¹⁹⁶⁷

Spanish Americans
SN   Term was discontinued in 1982. In 2000, SPANISH AMERICANS was stripped from all records containing it and replaced with HISPANICS its postable counterpart.
- Use   Hispanics

Spasms ¹⁹⁷³
PN   111   SC   48850

Spasms — (cont'd)
- B   Movement Disorders ¹⁹⁸⁵
  - Symptoms ¹⁹⁶⁷
- N   Muscle Spasms ¹⁹⁷³
- R   ↓ Anticonvulsive Drugs ¹⁹⁷³
  - ↓ Antispasmodic Drugs ¹⁹⁷³
  - ↓ Convulsions ¹⁹⁶⁷
  - ↓ Pain ¹⁹⁶⁷

Spatial Ability ¹⁹⁸²
PN   1918   SC   48855
SN   Potential or actual performance on tasks involving mental manipulation of objects or judgments of spatial relationships with respect to actual or imagined bodily orientation.
- B   Cognitive Ability ¹⁹⁷³
  - Nonverbal Ability ¹⁹⁸⁸
- N   ↓ Visuospatial Ability ¹⁹⁹⁷
- R   ↓ Cognitive Processes ¹⁹⁶⁷
  - Mental Rotation ¹⁹⁹¹
  - Spatial Imagery ¹⁹⁸²
  - Spatial Learning ¹⁹⁹⁴
  - Spatial Orientation (Perception) ¹⁹⁷³

Spatial Discrimination
- Use   Spatial Perception

Spatial Distortion ¹⁹⁷³
PN   171   SC   48870
SN   Alterations of an organism's normal spatial perception in any sensory modality. Distortions may be induced by such means as optical lenses, prisms, mirror displays or images, and left-right inversion of sound stimuli.
- B   Illusions (Perception) ¹⁹⁶⁷
  - Perceptual Distortion ¹⁹⁸²
  - Spatial Perception ¹⁹⁶⁷
- R   Prismatic Stimulation ¹⁹⁷³

Spatial Frequency ¹⁹⁸²
PN   1488   SC   48872
SN   Number of alternating cycles (e.g., patterns of vertical stripes of light and dark light) occurring in a specified visual angle as, for example, in sine wave or square wave displays.
- B   Stimulus Parameters ¹⁹⁶⁷
- R   Temporal Frequency ¹⁹⁸⁵
  - ↓ Visual Displays ¹⁹⁷³
  - ↓ Visual Stimulation ¹⁹⁷³

Spatial Imagery ¹⁹⁸²
PN   431   SC   48875
SN   Mental representation of spatial relationships.
- B   Imagery ¹⁹⁶⁷
- R   Cognitive Maps ¹⁹⁸²
  - Mental Rotation ¹⁹⁹¹
  - ↓ Spatial Ability ¹⁹⁸²
  - ↓ Spatial Memory ¹⁹⁸⁸
  - Spatial Organization ¹⁹⁷³
  - Spatial Orientation (Perception) ¹⁹⁷³

Spatial Learning ¹⁹⁹⁴
PN   731   SC   48876
- B   Learning ¹⁹⁶⁷
- R   Maze Learning ¹⁹⁶⁷
  - ↓ Spatial Ability ¹⁹⁸²
  - ↓ Spatial Memory ¹⁹⁸⁸
  - ↓ Spatial Perception ¹⁹⁶⁷

Spatial Memory ¹⁹⁸⁸
PN   1585   SC   48877
- B   Memory ¹⁹⁶⁷
- N   Visuospatial Memory ¹⁹⁹⁷
- R   Cognitive Maps ¹⁹⁸²

Spatial Memory — (cont'd)
Direction Perception 1997
Eidetic Imagery 1973
Spatial Imagery 1982
Spatial Learning 1994
↓ Visual Memory 1994

Spatial Neglect
Use Sensory Neglect

Spatial Organization 1973
PN 2951 **SC** 48880
SN Perception of spatial relationships. Also, the actual pattern or physical arrangement of objects or stimuli, including the dimensions of proximity, continuation, and relative position.
B Spatial Perception 1967
R Cognitive Maps 1982
Direction Perception 1997
Mental Rotation 1991
Retinal Eccentricity 1991
Spatial Imagery 1982

Spatial Orientation (Perception) 1973
PN 3792 **SC** 48890
SN Ability to perceive or orient oneself or external stimuli in space with respect to environmentally or egocentrically defined reference points.
UF Orientation (Spatial)
B Perceptual Orientation 1973
Spatial Perception 1967
R Cognitive Maps 1982
Equilibrium 1973
Kinesthetic Perception 1967
↓ Spatial Ability 1982
Spatial Imagery 1982

Spatial Perception 1967
PN 4550 **SC** 48900
UF Spatial Discrimination
B Perception 1967
N ↓ Depth Perception 1967
Direction Perception 1997
↓ Distance Perception 1973
↓ Motion Perception 1967
↓ Size Discrimination 1967
Spatial Distortion 1973
Spatial Organization 1973
Spatial Orientation (Perception) 1973
R Figure Ground Discrimination 1973
Mental Rotation 1991
Spatial Learning 1994
Visual Acuity 1982

Spearman Brown Test 1973
PN 12 **SC** 48910
B Statistical Tests 1973
R Statistical Reliability 1973

Spearman Rho
Use Rank Difference Correlation

Special Education 1967
PN 12657 **SC** 48930
SN Educational programs and services for students with disabilities or gifted students whose characteristics and educational needs differ from those who can be taught through standard methods and materials.
B Education 1967
Educational Programs 1973
R Ability Grouping 1973
Adaptive Behavior 1991
R Early Intervention 1982

Special Education — (cont'd)
Educational Placement 1978
Educational Therapy 1997
↓ Mainstreaming 1991
Mainstreaming (Educational) 1978
↓ Remedial Education 1985
Self Care Skills 1978
Special Needs 1994

Special Education Students 1973
PN 3832 **SC** 49010
B Students 1967
R Grade Level 1994

Special Education Teachers 1973
PN 2014 **SC** 49020
B Teachers 1967
R Resource Teachers 1973

Special Needs 1994
PN 546 **SC** 49025
SN Unspecified disorder, disability, or other problem that requires special services or intervention practices. Use a more specific term if possible.
R ↓ Disorders 1967
Early Intervention 1982
↓ Mainstreaming 1991
↓ Mental Disorders 1967
↓ Needs 1967
Needs Assessment 1985
↓ Physical Disorders 1997
Special Education 1967

Specialization (Academic)
Use Academic Specialization

Specialization (Professional)
Use Professional Specialization

Species Differences 1982
PN 1864 **SC** 49035
SN Anatomical, physiological, and/or behavioral variations between members of different species. May be used for comparisons between human and animal populations. Consider COMPARATIVE PSYCHOLOGY to access references from 1967-1981. Compare ANIMAL STRAIN DIFFERENCES.
R ↓ Animals 1967
↓ Genetics 1967
Interspecies Interaction 1991

Species Recognition 1985
PN 342 **SC** 49037
SN Ability of members of a given species to identify and recognize other members of the same species.
B Animal Ethology 1967
R Imprinting 1967
Instinctive Behavior 1982
Kinship Recognition 1988

Spectral Sensitivity
Use Color Perception

Speech
Use Oral Communication

Speech and Hearing Measures 1973
PN 578 **SC** 49060
SN Consider also AUDIOLOGY and AUDIOMETRY.
UF Hearing Measures
Speech Measures
B Measurement 1967

Speech and Hearing Measures — (cont'd)
N Wepman Auditory Discrimination Test 2001
R ↓ Perceptual Measures 1973

Speech Anxiety 1985
PN 356 **SC** 49065
SN Anxiety or fear associated with actual or anticipated oral communication with others.
UF Communication Apprehension
Fear of Public Speaking
B Anxiety 1967
R ↓ Anxiety Disorders 1997
↓ Communication Disorders 1982
↓ Interpersonal Communication 1973
Public Speaking 1973
Social Anxiety 1985

Speech Characteristics 1973
PN 3795 **SC** 49070
B Oral Communication 1985
N Articulation (Speech) 1967
Pronunciation 1973
Speech Pauses 1973
Speech Pitch 1973
Speech Rate 1973
Speech Rhythm 1973
R Acoustics 1997
Inflection 1973
↓ Prosody 1991

Speech Development 1973
PN 1604 **SC** 49080
B Psychomotor Development 1973
N Retarded Speech Development 1973
R ↓ Cognitive Development 1973
↓ Language Development 1967

Speech Disorders 1967
PN 2166 **SC** 49090
SN The term SPEECH HANDICAPPED was also used to represent this concept from 1973-1996, and SPEECH DISABLED was used from 1997-2000. In 2000, SPEECH DISORDERS replaced the discontinued and deleted term SPEECH DISABLED. SPEECH DISABLED and SPEECH HANDICAPPED were stripped from all records and replaced with SPEECH DISORDERS.
UF Speech Handicapped
B Communication Disorders 1982
N ↓ Articulation Disorders 1973
Dysphonia 1973
Stuttering 1967
R Apraxia 1973
↓ Augmentative Communication 1994
Cleft Palate 1967
↓ Language Disorders 1982
Retarded Speech Development 1973

Speech Handicapped
SN The term was discontinued in 1997, when the term SPEECH DISABLED was created to capture this concept. In 2000, with the deletion of the term SPEECH DISABLED, SPEECH HANDICAPPED was made a nonpostable term for the new postable term SPEECH DISORDERS. SPEECH HANDICAPPED and SPEECH DISABLED were stripped from all records containing them and replaced with SPEECH DISORDERS.
Use Speech Disorders

Speech Measures
Use Speech and Hearing Measures

Speech Pauses 1973
PN 268   SC 49120
  B   Speech Characteristics 1973

Speech Perception 1967
PN 4890   SC 49130
  B   Auditory Perception 1967
  R   Automated Speech Recognition 1994
      Lipreading 1973
      ↓ Rhythm 1991
      Word Recognition 1988

Speech Pitch 1973
PN 301   SC 49140
  B   Pitch (Frequency) 1967
      Speech Characteristics 1973

Speech Processing (Mechanical) 1973
PN 225   SC 49150
  N   Automated Speech Recognition 1994
      Compressed Speech 1973
      Filtered Speech 1973
      Synthetic Speech 1973
  R   ↓ Auditory Stimulation 1967
      ↓ Verbal Communication 1967

Speech Rate 1973
PN 646   SC 49160
  UF   Accelerated Speech
  B   Speech Characteristics 1973
  R   Tempo 1997
      Verbal Fluency 1973

Speech Rhythm 1973
PN 190   SC 49170
  B   Rhythm 1991
      Speech Characteristics 1973
  R   Tempo 1997

Speech Therapists 1973
PN 390   SC 49180
  B   Therapists 1967
  R   ↓ Educational Personnel 1973

Speech Therapy 1967
PN 2068   SC 49190
  B   Treatment 1967
  R   ↓ Augmentative Communication 1994
      ↓ Communication Disorders 1982

Speechreading
  Use   Lipreading

Speed
  Use   Velocity

Speed (Response)
  Use   Reaction Time

Spelling 1973
PN 1694   SC 49220
SN   Instruction, ability, or performance in the formation of words from letters according to accepted orthographic standards.
  B   Language 1967
      Language Arts Education 1973
  R   Orthography 1973

Sperm 1973
PN 153   SC 49230
  B   Cells (Biology) 1973
  R   ↓ Sexual Reproduction 1973

Sperm Donation
  Use   Tissue Donation

Spider Phobia
  Use   Phobias

Spiders
  Use   Arachnida

Spina Bifida 1978
PN 313   SC 49245
SN   Birth defect involving inadequate closure of the bony casement of the spinal cord, through which the spinal membranes, with or without spinal cord tissue, may protrude.
  UF   Meningomyelocele
      Myelomeningocele
  B   Congenital Disorders 1973

Spinal Column 1973
PN 72   SC 49250
  B   Musculoskeletal System 1973
  R   Bones 1973
      ↓ Spinal Cord 1973

Spinal Cord 1973
PN 1013   SC 49260
  B   Central Nervous System 1967
  N   Cranial Spinal Cord 1973
      Dorsal Horns 1985
      Dorsal Roots 1973
      Extrapyramidal Tracts 1973
      Lumbar Spinal Cord 1973
      Pyramidal Tracts 1973
      Spinothalamic Tracts 1973
      Ventral Roots 1973
  R   Spinal Column 1973

Spinal Cord Injuries 1973
PN 759   SC 49270
  B   Injuries 1973
  N   Whiplash 1997
  R   ↓ Central Nervous System Disorders 1973
      Hemiplegia 1978
      ↓ Neuromuscular Disorders 1973
      ↓ Paralysis 1973
      Paraplegia 1978
      Quadriplegia 1985

Spinal Fluid
  Use   Cerebrospinal Fluid

Spinal Ganglia 1973
PN 35   SC 49290
  B   Ganglia 1973

Spinal Nerves 1973
PN 368   SC 49300
  UF   Brachial Plexus
      Cauda Equina
      Cervical Plexus
      Femoral Nerve
      Lumbrosacral Plexus
      Median Nerve
      Musculocutaneous Nerve
      Nerves (Spinal)
      Obturator Nerve
      Phrenic Nerve
      Radial Nerve
      Sciatic Nerve
      Thoracic Nerves
      Ulnar Nerve
  B   Peripheral Nervous System 1973

Spinothalamic Tracts 1973
PN 51   SC 49310
  B   Afferent Pathways 1982
      Lemniscal System 1985
      Spinal Cord 1973

Spiperone
  Use   Spiroperidol

Spirit Possession 1997
PN 39   SC 49314
  UF   Demonic Possession
  R   Occultism 1978
      ↓ Parapsychological Phenomena 1973
      ↓ Religious Beliefs 1973

Spirituality 1988
PN 1873   SC 49315
SN   Degree of involvement or state of awareness or devotion to a higher being or life philosophy. Not always related to conventional religious beliefs.
  R   Religion 1967
      Religiosity 1973
      ↓ Religious Beliefs 1973
      Religious Experiences 1997

Spiroperidol 1991
PN 41   SC 49317
  UF   Spiperone
  B   Neuroleptic Drugs 1973

Spleen 1973
PN 67   SC 49320
  R   ↓ Cardiovascular System 1967

Split Brain
  Use   Commissurotomy

Split Personality
  Use   Dissociative Identity Disorder

Spontaneous Abortion 1971
PN 268   SC 49350
  UF   Abortion (Spontaneous)
      Miscarriage
  R   Induced Abortion 1971

Spontaneous Alternation 1982
PN 174   SC 49352
SN   Instinctive successive alternation of responses between alternatives in a situation involving discrete choices or exploration.
  R   Animal Exploratory Behavior 1973
      Delayed Alternation 1994
      Instinctive Behavior 1982
      ↓ Learning 1967
      Response Variability 1973

Spontaneous Recovery (Learning) 1973
PN 91   SC 49357
SN   Recurrence of a conditioned response following experimental extinction. The response is weaker than when originally conditioned and will extinguish rapidly if not reinforced.
  B   Learning 1967
      Memory 1967
  R   ↓ Conditioning 1967

Spontaneous Remission 1973
PN 63   SC 49360
  B   Remission (Disorders) 1973
  R   ↓ Psychotherapy 1967
      ↓ Treatment 1967

Sport Performance
  Use Athletic Performance

Sport Psychology [1982]
PN 732   **SC** 49365
SN Branch of psychology that investigates and applies psychological and physiological principles relating to athletic activity. Also used for psychological processes and their manifestations in such activity.
  B   Applied Psychology [1973]

Sport Training
  Use Athletic Training

Sports [1967]
PN 2555   **SC** 49370
  N   Baseball [1973]
      Basketball [1973]
      Football [1973]
      Judo [1973]
      Martial Arts [1985]
      Soccer [1994]
      Swimming [1973]
      Tennis [1973]
      Weightlifting [1994]
  R ↓ Athletes [1973]
      Athletic Participation [1973]
      Athletic Performance [1991]
      Athletic Training [1991]
      Coaches [1988]
      College Athletes [1994]
      ↓ Recreation [1967]
      Sports Spectators [1997]
      ↓ Teams [1988]
      Wilderness Experience [1991]

Sports Spectators [1997]
PN 69   **SC** 49373
  UF Fans (Sports)
  B   Audiences [1967]
  R ↓ Sports [1967]

Spouse Abuse
  Use Partner Abuse

Spouses [1973]
PN 6687   **SC** 49380
SN Married persons.
  UF Married Couples
      Mates (Humans)
  B   Family Members [1973]
  N   Husbands [1973]
      ↓ Wives [1973]
  R   Couples [1982]
      Inlaws [1997]
      ↓ Parents [1967]
      Significant Others [1991]

Spreading Depression [1967]
PN 143   **SC** 49390
SN Cerebral cortex cellular depolarization and a depressed electrical activity in depolarized cortical areas resulting from application of intense localized electrical stimulation or local application of a chemical or localized trauma to the cerebral cortex.
  B   Brain Stimulation [1967]

Squirrels [1973]
PN 334   **SC** 49400
  B   Rodents [1973]

Stability (Emotional)
  Use Emotional Stability

Stage Plays
  Use Theatre

Stalking [2001]
PN 0   **SC** 49435
SN Willful, malicious, and repeated nonconsensual contact with and harassing of another individual.
  B   Harassment [2001]
  R ↓ Crime [1967]
      ↓ Perpetrators [1988]
      Victimization [1973]

Stammering
SN Term was discontinued in 1982. In 2000, the term was stripped from all records containing it, and replaced with STUTTERING, its postable counterpart.
  Use Stuttering

Standard Deviation [1973]
PN 122   **SC** 49450
  B   Variability Measurement [1973]
  R   Error of Measurement [1985]
      ↓ Frequency Distribution [1973]
      Standard Scores [1985]
      Variance Homogeneity [1985]

Standard Error of Measurement
  Use Error of Measurement

Standard Scores [1985]
PN 79   **SC** 49455
SN Test scores measuring the distance of individual scores from the mean of the normative group, expressed in terms of the standard deviation.
  UF Deviation IQ
      Stanines
      Z Scores
  B   Test Scores [1967]
  R   Mean [1973]
      Score Equating [1985]
      ↓ Scoring (Testing) [1973]
      Standard Deviation [1973]

Standardization (Test)
  Use Test Standardization

Standardized Tests [1985]
PN 473   **SC** 49465
SN Tests with established norms, administration and scoring procedures, and validity and reliability data.
  B   Measurement [1967]
  R   Test Norms [1973]
      Test Standardization [1973]

Standards (Professional)
  Use Professional Standards

Stanford Achievement Test [1973]
PN 59   **SC** 49480
  B   Achievement Measures [1967]

Stanford Binet Intelligence Scale [1967]
PN 353   **SC** 49490
  B   Intelligence Measures [1967]

Stanines
  Use Standard Scores

Stapedius Reflex
  Use Acoustic Reflex

Starfish
  Use Echinodermata

Startle Reflex [1967]
PN 1110   **SC** 49510
  B   Reflexes [1971]
  R   Acoustic Reflex [1973]
      Alarm Responses [1973]
      Eyeblink Reflex [1973]
      Prepulse Inhibition [1997]

Starvation [1973]
PN 100   **SC** 49520
  B   Nutritional Deficiencies [1973]
  R   Food Deprivation [1967]
      Hunger [1967]

State Board Examinations
  Use Professional Examinations

State Dependent Learning [1982]
PN 118   **SC** 49525
SN Learning phenomenon wherein the transfer of a response that was learned in the context of specific internal or external cues is dependent on the constancy of the stimulus complex in the new situation to which the behavior is to transfer.
  UF Drug Dissociation
  B   Learning [1967]

State Hospitals
  Use Psychiatric Hospitals

State Trait Anxiety Inventory [1973]
PN 208   **SC** 49540
  B   Nonprojective Personality Measures [1973]

Statistical Analysis [1967]
PN 7234   **SC** 49550
SN Application of statistical procedures to the interpretation of numerical data.
  B   Analysis [1967]
  N ↓ Central Tendency Measures [1973]
      Cluster Analysis [1973]
      Confidence Limits (Statistics) [1973]
      Consistency (Measurement) [1973]
      Effect Size (Statistical) [1985]
      Error of Measurement [1985]
      ↓ Frequency Distribution [1973]
      Fuzzy Set Theory [1991]
      Goodness of Fit [1988]
      Interaction Analysis (Statistics) [1973]
      Meta Analysis [1985]
      ↓ Multivariate Analysis [1982]
      Predictability (Measurement) [1973]
      ↓ Statistical Correlation [1967]
      Statistical Data [1982]
      ↓ Statistical Estimation [1985]
      Statistical Norms [1971]
      ↓ Statistical Probability [1967]
      ↓ Statistical Regression [1985]
      Statistical Reliability [1973]
      Statistical Significance [1973]
      ↓ Statistical Tests [1973]
      Statistical Validity [1973]
      Statistical Weighting [1985]
      Time Series [1985]
      ↓ Variability Measurement [1973]
  R   Conjoint Measurement [1994]
      ↓ Experimental Design [1967]

Statistical Analysis — (cont'd)

R ↓ Experimentation [1967]
  ↓ Hypothesis Testing [1973]
  ↓ Mathematics (Concepts) [1967]
  ↓ Measurement [1967]
  ↓ Population (Statistics) [1973]
  ↓ Prediction Errors [1973]
  Psychometrics [1967]
  ↓ Sampling (Experimental) [1973]
  ↓ Statistical Measurement [1973]
  ↓ Statistical Variables [1973]
  Uncertainty [1991]

Statistical Correlation [1967]

PN 3304   SC 49560

UF Correlation (Statistical)
  Pearson Product Moment Correlation Coefficient
B Statistical Analysis [1967]
N Linear Regression [1973]
  Nonlinear Regression [1973]
  Phi Coefficient [1973]
  Point Biserial Correlation [1973]
  Rank Difference Correlation [1973]
  Rank Order Correlation [1973]
  Tetrachoric Correlation [1973]
R ↓ Experimentation [1967]
  ↓ Factor Analysis [1967]
  Multiple Regression [1982]
  ↓ Multivariate Analysis [1982]
  Statistical Data [1982]
  ↓ Statistical Regression [1985]
  Statistical Significance [1973]
  Statistical Validity [1973]
  ↓ Statistical Variables [1973]
  ↓ Variability Measurement [1973]

Statistical Data [1982]

PN 645   SC 49564

SN Sets of quantitative values that summarize, through mathematical operation, or express the parameters that represent a population or some other sample (e.g., response frequency).
B Statistical Analysis [1967]
R Data Collection [1982]
  Graphical Displays [1985]
  ↓ Statistical Correlation [1967]
  ↓ Statistical Measurement [1973]
  Statistical Tables [1982]
  ↓ Statistical Variables [1973]
  Time Series [1985]

Statistical Estimation [1985]

PN 1028   SC 49567

SN Any inferential mathematical derivation of an estimate of a parameter from one or more samples. Includes interval estimation.
UF Parameter Estimation
B Estimation [1967]
  Statistical Analysis [1967]
N Least Squares [1985]
  Magnitude Estimation [1991]
  Maximum Likelihood [1985]
R Error of Measurement [1985]
  Predictability (Measurement) [1973]

Statistical Measurement [1973]

PN 657   SC 49570

SN Process of or products derived from the collection or manipulation of statistical data in order to derive basic summarizing quantitative values which describe a set of measurements.
B Measurement [1967]

Statistical Measurement — (cont'd)

N ↓ Central Tendency Measures [1973]
  Conjoint Measurement [1994]
  ↓ Frequency Distribution [1973]
  Predictability (Measurement) [1973]
  Statistical Norms [1971]
  ↓ Statistical Probability [1967]
  ↓ Variability Measurement [1973]
  Variance Homogeneity [1985]
R Confidence Limits (Statistics) [1973]
  Data Collection [1982]
  Error of Measurement [1985]
  Graphical Displays [1985]
  ↓ Statistical Analysis [1967]
  Statistical Data [1982]
  Statistical Significance [1973]
  ↓ Statistical Tests [1973]

Statistical Norms [1971]

PN 288   SC 49580

UF Norms (Statistical)
B Statistical Analysis [1967]
  Statistical Measurement [1973]
R ↓ Statistical Sample Parameters [1973]

Statistical Power [1991]

PN 195   SC 49585

SN The ability of a statistic to reject a false hypothesis.
B Statistical Probability [1967]
R ↓ Hypothesis Testing [1973]
  ↓ Prediction Errors [1973]
  ↓ Sampling (Experimental) [1973]
  Statistical Significance [1973]
  ↓ Statistical Tests [1973]
  Type I Errors [1973]
  Type II Errors [1973]

Statistical Probability [1967]

PN 1013   SC 49590

UF Bayes Theorem
B Chance (Fortune) [1973]
  Probability [1967]
  Statistical Analysis [1967]
  Statistical Measurement [1973]
N Binomial Distribution [1973]
  Statistical Power [1991]
R Fuzzy Set Theory [1991]
  Risk Analysis [1991]

Statistical Regression [1985]

PN 515   SC 49595

SN Statistical comparison of the frequency distributions of one variable while the other(s) are held constant for the purpose of discovering predictive and functional relationships between variables. Use ANALYSIS OF VARIANCE or more specific terms prior to 1985.
UF Regression Analysis
  Regression Artifact
B Statistical Analysis [1967]
N Linear Regression [1973]
  Multiple Regression [1982]
  Nonlinear Regression [1973]
R Analysis of Variance [1967]
  Causal Analysis [1994]
  Least Squares [1985]
  ↓ Multivariate Analysis [1982]
  ↓ Statistical Correlation [1967]

Statistical Reliability [1973]

PN 2421   SC 49600

Statistical Reliability — (cont'd)

SN In 1973, this term was created to replace the discontinued term RELIABILITY (STATISTICAL). In 2000, RELIABILITY (STATISTICAL) was stripped from all records and replaced with STATISTICAL RELIABILITY.
UF Reliability (Statistical)
B Statistical Analysis [1967]
R Consistency (Measurement) [1973]
  ↓ Experimentation [1967]
  Interrater Reliability [1982]
  ↓ Population (Statistics) [1973]
  ↓ Prediction Errors [1973]
  ↓ Sampling (Experimental) [1973]
  Spearman Brown Test [1973]
  Statistical Validity [1973]

Statistical Rotation [1973]

PN 71   SC 49610

UF Rotation Methods (Statistical)
B Factor Analysis [1967]
N Oblique Rotation [1973]
  ↓ Orthogonal Rotation [1973]
R Factor Structure [1985]

Statistical Sample Parameters [1973]

PN 405   SC 49620

SN Quantities and qualities describing a statistical population.
B Statistical Samples [1973]
N Sample Size [1997]
R Binomial Distribution [1973]
  Confidence Limits (Statistics) [1973]
  Normal Distribution [1973]
  Statistical Norms [1971]

Statistical Samples [1973]

PN 283   SC 49630

SN Portion of a population taken as representative of the whole population.
B Population (Statistics) [1973]
N ↓ Statistical Sample Parameters [1973]
R ↓ Sampling (Experimental) [1973]

Statistical Significance [1973]

PN 652   SC 49640

UF Significance (Statistical)
B Statistical Analysis [1967]
R Chi Square Test [1973]
  Confidence Limits (Statistics) [1973]
  Effect Size (Statistical) [1985]
  ↓ Factor Analysis [1967]
  Goodness of Fit [1988]
  ↓ Hypothesis Testing [1973]
  Sign Test [1973]
  ↓ Statistical Correlation [1967]
  ↓ Statistical Measurement [1973]
  Statistical Power [1991]
  ↓ Statistical Tests [1973]
  T Test [1973]

Statistical Tables [1982]

PN 121   SC 49647

SN Systematically organized displays of statistical values or distributions or summary data derived from statistical calculation. The table of critical values of the F distribution is an example of the first category, and a contingency table showing test score means as related to the variables of sex and age is an example of the second category.
R Statistical Data [1982]
  ↓ Statistical Variables [1973]

Statistical Tests 1973
PN 600   SC 49650
SN Specific mathematical techniques used to analyze data in order to assess the probability that a set of results could have occurred by chance and hence to test for the probable correctness of empirical hypotheses.
UF Tests (Statistical)
B Statistical Analysis 1967
N ↓ Nonparametric Statistical Tests 1967
↓ Parametric Statistical Tests 1973
Spearman Brown Test 1973
R Confidence Limits (Statistics) 1973
↓ Statistical Measurement 1973
Statistical Power 1991
Statistical Significance 1973

Statistical Validity 1973
PN 11688   SC 49660
SN In 2000, this term became the postable counterpart for the terms CONCURRENT VALIDITY, CONSTRUCT VALIDITY, FACTORIAL VALIDITY, and PREDICTIVE VALIDITY. These terms were stripped from all records and replaced with STATISTICAL VALIDITY.
UF Concept Validity
Concurrent Validity
Construct Validity
Factorial Validity
Predictive Validity
Validity (Statistical)
B Statistical Analysis 1967
R Consistency (Measurement) 1973
↓ Experimentation 1967
↓ Prediction Errors 1973
↓ Statistical Correlation 1967
Statistical Reliability 1973
↓ Statistical Variables 1973

Statistical Variables 1973
PN 786   SC 49670
N Dependent Variables 1973
Independent Variables 1973
R ↓ Experimental Design 1967
↓ Experimentation 1967
↓ Population (Statistics) 1973
↓ Prediction Errors 1973
↓ Sampling (Experimental) 1973
↓ Statistical Analysis 1967
↓ Statistical Correlation 1967
Statistical Data 1982
Statistical Tables 1982
Statistical Validity 1973

Statistical Weighting 1985
PN 175   SC 49671
SN A coefficient or mathematical constant that determines the relative contribution of a statistic to a total numeric value. Also, the process of assigning such statistical weights.
UF Weight (Statistics)
B Statistical Analysis 1967
R Item Analysis (Statistical) 1973
↓ Scoring (Testing) 1973
Test Interpretation 1985
↓ Test Scores 1967

Statistics 1982
PN 716   SC 49672
SN Subdiscipline of mathematics that deals with the gathering and evaluation of numerical data for making inferences from the data. Also used as a document type identifier.
B Mathematics 1982

Status 1967
PN 1907   SC 49675
SN General term used to indicate relative social position or rank.
B Social Processes 1967
N Occupational Status 1978
↓ Socioeconomic Status 1967
R Authority 1967
↓ Dominance 1967
Fame 1985
Reputation 1997
↓ Social Structure 1967

Stealing
Use Theft

Stelazine
Use Trifluoperazine

Stellate Ganglion
Use Autonomic Ganglia

Stepchildren 1973
PN 257   SC 49720
B Family Members 1973
R ↓ Family Structure 1973
Stepfamily 1991

Stepfamily 1991
PN 269   SC 49725
B Family 1967
Family Structure 1973
R Family of Origin 1991
Remarriage 1985
Stepchildren 1973
Stepparents 1973

Stepparents 1973
PN 440   SC 49730
B Parents 1967
R ↓ Family Structure 1973
Stepfamily 1991

Stereopsis
Use Stereoscopic Vision

Stereoscopic Presentation 1973
PN 183   SC 49750
SN Simultaneous presentation of separate two-dimensional pictures (taken from slightly different angles) to each eye of one subject, resulting in a perception of depth.
B Stimulus Presentation Methods 1973
Visual Stimulation 1973

Stereoscopic Vision 1973
PN 755   SC 49760
UF Stereopsis
B Depth Perception 1967
Visual Perception 1967

Stereotaxic Atlas 1973
PN 752   SC 49770
UF Brain Mapping
Brain Maps
R ↓ Stereotaxic Techniques 1973

Stereotaxic Techniques 1973
PN 142   SC 49780
SN Methods, procedures, or apparatus which permit precise spatial positioning of electrodes or other probes into the brain for experimental or surgical purposes.

Stereotaxic Techniques — (cont'd)
B Surgery 1971
N ↓ Brain Stimulation 1967
Chemical Brain Stimulation 1973
Electrical Brain Stimulation 1973
R Afferent Stimulation 1973
↓ Nervous System 1967
Stereotaxic Atlas 1973

Stereotyped Attitudes 1967
PN 5039   SC 49790
SN Oversimplified, rigid, often negative preconceptions of individuals, groups, or social classes who identify with a particular ethnicity, gender, religion, sexual orientation, or other group. Compare STIGMA.
UF Stereotyping
B Attitudes 1967
R ↓ Disabled (Attitudes Toward) 1997
↓ Discrimination 1967
Homosexuality (Attitudes Toward) 1982
Labeling 1978
↓ Prejudice 1967
↓ Racial and Ethnic Attitudes 1982
↓ Sex Role Attitudes 1978
↓ Social Discrimination 1982
↓ Social Perception 1967
Stigma 1991

Stereotyped Behavior 1973
PN 2182   SC 49795
SN Highly repetitive, often non-functional, rhythmic behaviors that occur at a high frequency. Used for animal or disordered human populations.
B Behavior 1967
R ↓ Animal Ethology 1967
↓ Pervasive Developmental Disorders 2001
↓ Self Stimulation 1967
↓ Symptoms 1967

Stereotyping
Use Stereotyped Attitudes

Sterility 1973
PN 44   SC 49810
B Infertility 1973
R ↓ Gynecological Disorders 1973
Hermaphroditism 1973
↓ Hypogonadism 1973
↓ Male Genital Disorders 1973
Testicular Feminization Syndrome 1973
Turners Syndrome 1973
↓ Venereal Diseases 1973

Sterilization (Sex) 1973
PN 114   SC 49820
N ↓ Castration 1967
Hysterectomy 1973
Tubal Ligation 1973
Vasectomy 1973
R ↓ Birth Control 1971
Eugenics 1973
↓ Family Planning 1973

Steroids 1973
PN 738   SC 49830
B Drugs 1967
N Cholesterol 1973
↓ Corticosteroids 1973
Progesterone 1973
R ↓ Anti Inflammatory Drugs 1982
Antiandrogens 1982
Antiestrogens 1982

Steroids — (cont'd)
- R   Antineoplastic Drugs   1982
- ↓ Hormones   1967
- ↓ Lipids   1973

Sticklebacks   1973
PN   178   SC   49840
- B   Fishes   1967

Stigma   1991
PN   664   SC   49843
SN   Perception of a distinguishing personal characteristic or condition, e.g., a physical or psychological disorder, race, or religion, which carries or is believed to carry a physical, psychological, or social disadvantage.
- UF   Social Stigma
- R   ↓ Attitudes   1967
- Labeling   1978
- ↓ Prejudice   1967
- Social Acceptance   1967
- Social Approval   1967
- ↓ Social Discrimination   1982
- ↓ Social Perception   1967
- Stereotyped Attitudes   1967

Stimulants of CNS
- Use   CNS Stimulating Drugs

Stimulation   1967
PN   1321   SC   49850
- N   Afferent Stimulation   1973
- Aversive Stimulation   1973
- ↓ Brain Stimulation   1967
- ↓ Electrical Stimulation   1973
- ↓ Perceptual Stimulation   1973
- ↓ Self Stimulation   1967
- Subliminal Stimulation   1985
- Verbal Stimuli   1982
- R   ↓ Biofeedback   1973
- Conditioned Stimulus   1973
- ↓ Conditioning   1967
- ↓ Feedback   1967
- Stimulus Ambiguity   1967
- Stimulus Change   1973
- Stimulus Control   1967
- ↓ Stimulus Deprivation   1973
- Stimulus Discrimination   1973
- Stimulus Generalization   1967
- ↓ Stimulus Parameters   1967
- ↓ Stimulus Presentation Methods   1973
- Unconditioned Stimulus   1973

Stimulation Seeking (Personality)
- Use   Sensation Seeking

Stimulators (Apparatus)   1973
PN   53   SC   49860
- B   Apparatus   1967
- N   Shock Units   1973
- R   Electrodes   1967
- Vibrators (Apparatus)   1973

Stimulus (Unconditioned)
- Use   Unconditioned Stimulus

Stimulus Ambiguity   1967
PN   844   SC   49890
- UF   Ambiguity (Stimulus)
- R   ↓ Stimulation   1967
- Stimulus Generalization   1967
- Stroop Effect   1988

Stimulus Attenuation   1973
PN   119   SC   49900
SN   Controlled, progressive, or otherwise manipulated reduction in the intensity, clarity, salience, or other such distinguishing qualities of a stimulus.
- B   Stimulus Parameters   1967
- R   Fading (Conditioning)   1982

Stimulus Change   1973
PN   470   SC   49910
- R   ↓ Stimulation   1967

Stimulus Complexity   1971
PN   1735   SC   49920
- UF   Complexity (Stimulus)
- B   Stimulus Parameters   1967

Stimulus Control   1967
PN   1400   SC   49930
SN   Change in the probability of occurrence of a conditioned response as a direct function of the onset, offset, or changes in a conditioned stimulus.
- R   ↓ Discrimination Learning   1982
- ↓ Stimulation   1967
- Stimulus Generalization   1967

Stimulus Deprivation   1973
PN   161   SC   49940
- UF   Restricted Environmental Stimulation
- B   Deprivation   1967
- N   Food Deprivation   1967
- Sensory Deprivation   1967
- ↓ Social Deprivation   1973
- ↓ Social Isolation   1967
- Water Deprivation   1967
- R   ↓ Stimulation   1967

Stimulus Discrimination   1973
PN   2098   SC   49950
- B   Discrimination   1967
- R   Behavioral Contrast   1978
- ↓ Discrimination Learning   1982
- Fading (Conditioning)   1982
- ↓ Stimulation   1967
- Stimulus Generalization   1967

Stimulus Duration   1973
PN   2620   SC   49960
- UF   Duration (Stimulus)
- Exposure Time (Stimulus)
- B   Stimulus Parameters   1967

Stimulus Frequency   1973
PN   1321   SC   49980
SN   Number of stimulus presentations within a given trial or per unit time.
- UF   Frequency (Stimulus)
- B   Stimulus Parameters   1967
- R   Temporal Frequency   1985

Stimulus Generalization   1967
PN   842   SC   49990
SN   Responding in a similar manner to different stimuli which have some common physical property. Also known as primary generalization. Compare GENERALIZATION (LEARNING) and RESPONSE GENERALIZATION.
- UF   Generalization (Stimulus)
- B   Generalization (Learning)   1982
- R   ↓ Stimulation   1967
- Stimulus Ambiguity   1967
- Stimulus Control   1967
- Stimulus Discrimination   1973

Stimulus Intensity   1967
PN   3206   SC   50000
- UF   Intensity (Stimulus)
- Signal Intensity
- B   Stimulus Parameters   1967
- R   Luminance   1982

Stimulus Intervals   1973
PN   1232   SC   50010
SN   Temporal intervals between stimuli presented in any sensory modality. Use INTERSTIMULUS INTERVAL in conditioning contexts.
- B   Stimulus Parameters   1967
- N   Interstimulus Interval   1967
- Intertrial Interval   1973
- R   Reinforcement Delay   1985

Stimulus Novelty   1973
PN   1928   SC   50020
SN   New, unexpected, or unfamiliar quality of a stimulus.
- UF   Novel Stimuli
- B   Stimulus Parameters   1967
- R   Neophobia   1985

Stimulus Offset   1985
PN   75   SC   50023
- B   Stimulus Parameters   1967

Stimulus Onset   1982
PN   496   SC   50025
- B   Stimulus Parameters   1967

Stimulus Parameters   1967
PN   5847   SC   50030
SN   Applied when quantifiable or descriptive characteristics of stimuli in a study are emphasized. Use a more specific term if possible.
- UF   Parameters (Stimulus)
- N   ↓ Size   1973
- Spatial Frequency   1982
- Stimulus Attenuation   1973
- Stimulus Complexity   1971
- Stimulus Duration   1973
- Stimulus Frequency   1973
- Stimulus Intensity   1967
- ↓ Stimulus Intervals   1973
- Stimulus Novelty   1973
- Stimulus Offset   1985
- Stimulus Onset   1982
- Stimulus Salience   1973
- Stimulus Similarity   1967
- Stimulus Variability   1973
- Temporal Frequency   1985
- R   Acoustics   1997
- ↓ Stimulation   1967

Stimulus Pattern
- Use   Stimulus Variability

Stimulus Presentation Methods   1973
PN   2501   SC   50050
SN   Methodological, procedural, or technical aspects of stimulus presentation. Use a more specific term if possible, e.g., VISUAL STIMULATION for visual stimulus presentation.
- B   Experimental Methods   1967
- N   Stereoscopic Presentation   1973
- Tachistoscopic Presentation   1973
- R   Pictorial Stimuli   1978
- ↓ Stimulation   1967
- Verbal Stimuli   1982

Stimulus Salience [1973]
PN 900   **SC** 50060
SN Relative prominence or distinctiveness of a stimulus.
  UF Salience (Stimulus)
  B Stimulus Parameters [1967]
  R Isolation Effect [1973]

Stimulus Similarity [1967]
PN 2166   **SC** 50070
SN Conceptual or physical resemblance of two or more stimuli.
  UF Similarity (Stimulus)
  B Stimulus Parameters [1967]

Stimulus Variability [1973]
PN 1470   **SC** 50080
  UF Stimulus Pattern
    Variability (Stimulus)
  B Stimulus Parameters [1967]

Stipends
  Use Educational Financial Assistance

Stochastic Modeling [1973]
PN 520   **SC** 50100
SN Statistical modeling for sequences of events whose probabilities are constantly changing.
  B Simulation [1967]
  N Markov Chains [1973]
  R Chaos Theory [1997]
    Information Theory [1967]
    ↓ Mathematical Modeling [1973]
    Time Series [1985]

Stomach [1973]
PN 135   **SC** 50120
  B Gastrointestinal System [1973]

Storytelling [1988]
PN 1226   **SC** 50125
  B Verbal Communication [1967]
  R Creative Writing [1994]
    Folklore [1991]
    Myths [1967]
    Narratives [1997]

Storytelling Technique
  Use Mutual Storytelling Technique

Strabismus [1973]
PN 189   **SC** 50140
  UF Crossed Eyes
  B Eye Disorders [1973]
  R Amblyopia [1973]
    Eye Convergence [1982]

Strain Differences (Animal)
  Use Animal Strain Differences

Stranger Reactions [1988]
PN 239   **SC** 50148
SN Emotional or behavioral responses to unfamiliar persons. Used for all age groups.
  UF Fear of Strangers
    Xenophobia
  B Interpersonal Interaction [1967]
  R Attachment Behavior [1985]
    ↓ Emotional Responses [1967]
    Familiarity [1967]
    ↓ Fear [1967]
    Separation Anxiety [1973]
    ↓ Social Perception [1967]

Strategies [1967]
PN 5889   **SC** 50150
SN Methods, techniques, or tactics used in accomplishing a given goal or task.
  N ↓ Learning Strategies [1991]
  R ↓ Cognitive Processes [1967]
    Guessing [1973]
    ↓ Learning [1967]
    Note Taking [1991]

Strategies (Learning)
  Use Learning Strategies

Strength (Physical)
  Use Physical Strength

Stress [1967]
PN 17900   **SC** 50170
SN Refers to the emotional, psychological, or physical effects as well as the sources of agitation, strain, tension, or pressure. Compare DISTRESS. Used for both human and animal populations.
  N Environmental Stress [1973]
    Occupational Stress [1973]
    Physiological Stress [1967]
    Psychological Stress [1973]
    Social Stress [1973]
    Stress Reactions [1973]
  R Adjustment Disorders [1994]
    ↓ Adrenal Cortex Hormones [1973]
    ↓ Anxiety [1967]
    Caregiver Burden [1994]
    ↓ Crises [1971]
    ↓ Deprivation [1967]
    ↓ Disasters [1973]
    Distress [1973]
    ↓ Endurance [1973]
    Family Crises [1973]
    Identity Crisis [1973]
    Natural Disasters [1973]
    Organizational Crises [1973]
    Stress Management [1985]

Stress Management [1985]
PN 1853   **SC** 50175
SN Techniques or services designed to alleviate the effects and/or causes of stress.
  B Management [1967]
  R Anxiety Management [1997]
    ↓ Behavior Modification [1973]
    ↓ Cognitive Techniques [1985]
    ↓ Stress [1967]
    ↓ Treatment [1967]

Stress Reactions [1973]
PN 5362   **SC** 50180
SN Reactions to stressful events in everyday life or in experimental settings. Differentiate from POST-TRAUMATIC STRESS DISORDER which refers to reactions that seriously impair a person's functioning.
  UF Crisis (Reactions to)
  B Stress [1967]
  R Adjustment Disorders [1994]
    Cardiovascular Reactivity [1994]
    Coronary Prone Behavior [1982]
    Posttraumatic Stress Disorder [1985]
    Psychological Endurance [1973]

Striate Cortex
  Use Visual Cortex

Strikes [1973]
PN 123   **SC** 50190

Strikes — (cont'd)
  R Labor Management Relations [1967]

Stroboscopic Movement
  Use Apparent Movement

Stroke (Cerebrum)
  Use Cerebrovascular Accidents

Strong Vocational Interest Blank [1967]
PN 220   **SC** 50220
  B Occupational Interest Measures [1973]

Stroop Color Word Test [1973]
PN 373   **SC** 50250
  B Perceptual Measures [1973]
  R Stroop Effect [1988]

Stroop Effect [1988]
PN 390   **SC** 50255
SN Interference in information or perceptual processing due to presentation of stimuli that are contradictory in different dimensions as a measure of cognitive control, e.g., stimulus word "red" printed in the color green.
  R Cognitive Discrimination [1973]
    ↓ Interference (Learning) [1967]
    ↓ Perceptual Discrimination [1973]
    Stimulus Ambiguity [1967]
    Stroop Color Word Test [1973]

Structural Equation Modeling [1994]
PN 485   **SC** 50257
  B Mathematical Modeling [1973]
  R Causal Analysis [1994]
    ↓ Factor Analysis [1967]
    Factor Structure [1985]

Structuralism [1973]
PN 216   **SC** 50260
  B History of Psychology [1967]
    Psychological Theories [2001]

Structured Clinical Interview [2001]
PN 0   **SC** 50263
  UF SCID
  B Interview Schedules [2001]
    Psychodiagnostic Interview [1973]
  R ↓ Mental Disorders [1967]
    ↓ Psychodiagnosis [1967]
    ↓ Psychodiagnostic Typologies [1967]
    ↓ Psychological Assessment [1997]

Structured Overview
  Use Advance Organizers

Strychnine [1973]
PN 124   **SC** 50270
  B Alkaloids [1973]
    Analeptic Drugs [1973]

Student Activism [1973]
PN 228   **SC** 50280
  UF Activism (Student)
    Protest (Student)
    Student Protest
  B Activist Movements [1973]
  R Social Demonstrations [1973]

Student Adjustment
  Use School Adjustment

Student Admission Criteria 1973
PN 712　　　　　　　　　　SC 50290
　UF　Admission Criteria (Student)
　R　Academic Aptitude 1973
　　↓ Education 1967
　　↓ Entrance Examinations 1973

Student Attitudes 1967
PN 14779　　　　　　　　　SC 50300
　SN　Attitudes of, not toward, students.
　B　Attitudes 1967
　　Student Characteristics 1982
　R　↓ Education 1967
　　School Phobia 1973
　　School Refusal 1994

Student Attrition 1991
PN 151　　　　　　　　　　SC 50301
　SN　Reduction in students enrolled in school as a
result of transfers or dropouts.
　B　School Enrollment 1973
　R　School Attendance 1973
　　↓ School Dropouts 1967
　　School Expulsion 1973
　　School Leavers 1988
　　School Retention 1994
　　↓ Students 1967

Student Characteristics 1982
PN 3341　　　　　　　　　SC 50303
　SN　Distinguishing traits or qualities of a student.
　N　Student Attitudes 1967
　R　↓ Education 1967
　　↓ Students 1967

Student Personnel Services 1978
PN 1527　　　　　　　　　SC 50305
　SN　Services offered by schools, colleges, or univer-
sities related to health, housing, employment, or
other student concerns.
　R　↓ Counseling 1967
　　↓ Education 1967
　　Educational Counseling 1967
　　Educational Financial Assistance 1973
　　↓ Mental Health Services 1978
　　Occupational Guidance 1967
　　School Counseling 1982

Student Protest
　Use　Student Activism

Student Records 1978
PN 67　　　　　　　　　　SC 50315
　UF　Academic Records
　R　↓ Education 1967

Student Teachers 1973
PN 1346　　　　　　　　　SC 50320
　SN　Students engaged in practice teaching under
the supervision of a cooperating master teacher as
partial fulfillment of an education degree.
　B　Teachers 1967
　R　Cooperating Teachers 1978
　　Education Students 1982
　　Preservice Teachers 1982

Student Teaching 1973
PN 277　　　　　　　　　　SC 50330
　SN　College students teaching under the supervision
of a regular teacher in a real school situation. Part of
the graduation requirement for education majors.
　UF　Teaching Internship
　B　Teacher Education 1967

Student Teaching — (cont'd)
　R　Cooperating Teachers 1978

Students 1967
PN 6504　　　　　　　　　SC 50340
　SN　Persons attending school. Application of a stu-
dent term is mandatory in educational contexts. Use
a more specific term if possible.
　N　Business Students 1973
　　Classmates 1973
　　↓ College Students 1967
　　Dental Students 1973
　　↓ Elementary School Students 1967
　　Foreign Students 1973
　　Graduate Students 1967
　　High School Students 1967
　　Junior High School Students 1971
　　Kindergarten Students 1973
　　Law Students 1978
　　Medical Students 1967
　　Postgraduate Students 1973
　　↓ Preschool Students 1982
　　Reentry Students 1985
　　Seminarians 1973
　　Special Education Students 1973
　　Transfer Students 1973
　　Vocational School Students 1973
　R　↓ Education 1967
　　School Retention 1994
　　Student Attrition 1991
　　↓ Student Characteristics 1982

Students T Test
　Use　T Test

Studies (Followup)
　Use　Followup Studies

Studies (Longitudinal)
　Use　Longitudinal Studies

Study Habits 1973
PN 1658　　　　　　　　　SC 50380
　UF　Study Skills
　R　Advance Organizers 1985
　　↓ Education 1967
　　Homework 1988
　　↓ Learning Strategies 1991
　　Note Taking 1991
　　Test Taking 1985
　　Time Management 1994

Study Skills
　Use　Study Habits

Stuttering 1967
PN 2196　　　　　　　　　SC 50390
　SN　In 1982, this term replaced the discontinued
term STAMMERING. In 2000, STAMMERING was
stripped from all records and replaced with STUT-
TERING.
　UF　Stammering
　B　Speech Disorders 1967

Subconscious 1973
PN 79　　　　　　　　　　SC 50410
　B　Psychoanalytic Personality Factors 1973

Subcortical Lesions
　Use　Brain Lesions

Subculture (Anthropological) 1973
PN 517　　　　　　　　　　SC 50430

Subculture (Anthropological) — (cont'd)
　UF　Hippies
　B　Culture (Anthropological) 1967
　R　Cosmetic Techniques 2001

Subcutaneous Injections 1973
PN 42　　　　　　　　　　SC 50440
　B　Injections 1973

Subjectivity 1994
PN 464　　　　　　　　　　SC 50450
　SN　Use OBJECTIVITY to access references from
1973-1993.
　B　Personality Traits 1967
　R　Objectivity 1973

Sublimation 1973
PN 95　　　　　　　　　　SC 50460
　B　Defense Mechanisms 1967

Subliminal Perception 1973
PN 331　　　　　　　　　　SC 50470
　SN　Perceptual response to a stimulus that is below
the threshold for conscious detection.
　B　Perception 1967
　R　Subliminal Stimulation 1985

Subliminal Stimulation 1985
PN 278　　　　　　　　　　SC 50475
　SN　Below-threshold stimulation.
　B　Stimulation 1967
　R　Subliminal Perception 1973

Submarines 1973
PN 36　　　　　　　　　　SC 50480
　B　Water Transportation 1973

Submissiveness
　Use　Obedience

Submucous Plexus
　Use　Autonomic Ganglia

Substance Abuse
　Use　Drug Abuse

Substance Abuse Prevention
　Use　Drug Abuse Prevention

Substance P 1985
PN 280　　　　　　　　　　SC 50527
　B　Neurokinins 1997
　　Neurotransmitters 1985
　　Peptides 1973

Substantia Nigra 1994
PN 140　　　　　　　　　　SC 50530
　SN　Use MESENCEPHALON to access references
from 1973-1993.
　B　Mesencephalon 1973
　R　↓ Basal Ganglia 1973

Subtests 1973
PN 1264　　　　　　　　　SC 50540
　B　Measurement 1967
　R　↓ Testing Methods 1967

Suburban Environments 1967
PN 573　　　　　　　　　　SC 50550
　B　Social Environments 1973

Subvocalization   1973
PN 92   **SC** 50555
SN Covert speech behavior which involves movement of the tongue, mouth, and larynx without producing audible sounds.
    B   Vocalization   1967
    R   Self Talk   1988

Success
    Use   Achievement

Successive Contrast
    Use   Afterimage

Succinylcholine   1973
PN 13   **SC** 50580
    B   Muscle Relaxing Drugs   1973
    R   ↓ Choline   1973

Sucking   1978
PN 381   **SC** 50585
    B   Motor Processes   1967
    R   Animal Drinking Behavior   1973
         Animal Feeding Behavior   1973
         ↓ Drinking Behavior   1978
         Food Intake   1967
         Weaning   1973

Sudden Infant Death   1982
PN 165   **SC** 50587
SN Unexpected death of an apparently healthy infant during sleep.
    UF   Crib Death
    R   ↓ Apnea   1973
         ↓ Death and Dying   1967
         Sleep Apnea   1991
         ↓ Syndromes   1973

Suffering   1973
PN 347   **SC** 50590
    B   Emotional States   1973
    R   Distress   1973
         Grief   1973
         ↓ Pain   1967
         Torture   1988

Suffocation
    Use   Anoxia

Sugars   1973
PN 881   **SC** 50600
    B   Carbohydrates   1973
    N   ↓ Glucose   1973
    R   Saccharin   1973

Suggestibility   1967
PN 765   **SC** 50610
    B   Consciousness Disturbances   1973
         Personality Traits   1967
    R   Catalepsy   1973
         False Memory   1997
         ↓ Hysteria   1967
         ↓ Interpersonal Influences   1967
         Posthypnotic Suggestions   1994

Suicidal Ideation   1991
PN 1230   **SC** 50605
SN Thoughts of or an unusual preoccupation with suicide.
    B   Ideation   1973
    R   Attempted Suicide   1973
         ↓ Suicide   1967

Suicide   1967
PN 7966   **SC** 50620
    B   Self Destructive Behavior   1985
    N   Assisted Suicide   1997
    R   Attempted Suicide   1973
         ↓ Death and Dying   1967
         ↓ Mental Disorders   1967
         Psychological Autopsy   1988
         Suicidal Ideation   1991
         Suicide Prevention   1973

Suicide (Attempted)
    Use   Attempted Suicide

Suicide Prevention   1973
PN 1153   **SC** 50640
    B   Crisis Intervention   1973
         Prevention   1973
    R   Attempted Suicide   1973
         ↓ Suicide   1967
         Suicide Prevention Centers   1973

Suicide Prevention Centers   1973
PN 96   **SC** 50650
    B   Community Facilities   1973
         Crisis Intervention Services   1973
         Mental Health Programs   1973
    R   Community Mental Health Centers   1973
         Hot Line Services   1973
         ↓ Prevention   1973
         Suicide Prevention   1973

Sulpiride   1973
PN 401   **SC** 50660
    B   Antidepressant Drugs   1971
         Antiemetic Drugs   1973
         Dopamine Antagonists   1982
         Neuroleptic Drugs   1973

Summer Camps (Recreation)   1973
PN 131   **SC** 50670
    UF   Day Camps (Recreation)
         Recreational Day Camps
    B   Recreation   1967
    R   Camping   1973
         Vacationing   1973

Superego   1973
PN 362   **SC** 50690
    B   Psychoanalytic Personality Factors   1973
    N   Conscience   1967

Superintendents (School)
    Use   School Superintendents

Superior Colliculus   1973
PN 540   **SC** 50700
    B   Mesencephalon   1973

Superiority (Emotional)
    Use   Emotional Superiority

Superstitions   1973
PN 145   **SC** 50720
    B   Social Influences   1967
    R   Astrology   1973
         ↓ Attitudes   1967
         Irrational Beliefs   1982
         ↓ Parapsychological Phenomena   1973
         ↓ Religious Beliefs   1973
         Taboos   1973

Supervising Teachers
    Use   Cooperating Teachers

Supervision (Professional)
    Use   Professional Supervision

Supervisor Employee Interaction   1997
PN 477   **SC** 50729
    UF   Employee Supervisor Interaction
         Manager Employee Interaction
    B   Employee Interaction   1988
    R   Labor Management Relations   1967
         ↓ Management Methods   1973
         ↓ Management Personnel   1973
         Mentor   1985
         ↓ Personnel Management   1973

Supervisors
    Use   Management Personnel

Support Groups   1991
PN 1331   **SC** 50740
SN Groups, organizations, or institutions providing social and emotional support to an individual. Consider SOCIAL SUPPORT NETWORKS to access references from 1982-1990. Compare SOCIAL NETWORKS and SELF HELP TECHNIQUES.
    N   ↓ Twelve Step Programs   1997
    R   ↓ Community Services   1967
         ↓ Counseling   1967
         Employee Assistance Programs   1985
         Group Counseling   1973
         ↓ Group Psychotherapy   1967
         ↓ Mental Health Services   1978
         Outreach Programs   1997
         ↓ Rehabilitation   1967
         ↓ Self Help Techniques   1982
         ↓ Social Networks   1994
         ↓ Social Services   1982
         Social Support Networks   1982

Supported Employment   1994
PN 258   **SC** 50745
SN Competitive employment in an integrated setting for persons with disabilities who require ongoing support to perform their jobs.
    B   Vocational Rehabilitation   1967
    R   Community Mental Health Services   1978
         Disabled Personnel   1997
         Employability   1973
         ↓ Employee Skills   1973
         ↓ Employment Status   1982
         Independent Living Programs   1991
         ↓ Personnel Management   1973
         Sheltered Workshops   1967
         Work Adjustment Training   1991

Supportive Psychotherapy   1997
PN 72   **SC** 50750
SN Psychotherapy aimed at supporting or reinforcing strengths and coping mechanisms, rather than interpreting or uncovering deeper psychological conflicts. May entail guidance, reassurance, advice, encouragement, and assistance. Use PSYCHOTHERAPY to access references from 1973-1996.
    B   Psychotherapy   1967
    R   Expressive Psychotherapy   1973

Suppression (Conditioned)
    Use   Conditioned Suppression

Suppression (Defense Mechanism)   1973
PN 131   **SC** 50770
    B   Defense Mechanisms   1967

Suppression (Defense Mechanism) — (cont'd)
R　Forgetting　1973
　　Repression (Defense Mechanism)　1967

Surgeons　1973
PN　137　　　　　　　　　　SC　50780
UF　Neurosurgeons
B　Physicians　1967
R　Gynecologists　1973
　　Neurologists　1973
　　Obstetricians　1978
　　Pathologists　1973

Surgery　1971
PN　1976　　　　　　　　　SC　50790
UF　Operation (Surgery)
B　Medical Sciences　1967
　　Physical Treatment Methods　1973
N　↓ Amputation　1973
　　Circumcision　2001
　　Cochlear Implants　1994
　　Colostomy　1973
　　Dental Surgery　1973
　　↓ Endocrine Gland Surgery　1973
　　Heart Surgery　1973
　　Hysterectomy　1973
　　Induced Abortion　1971
　　↓ Neurosurgery　1973
　　Organ Transplantation　1973
　　Plastic Surgery　1973
　　Sex Change　1988
　　↓ Stereotaxic Techniques　1973
　　Vasectomy　1973
R　Afferent Stimulation　1973
　　Biopsy　1973
　　↓ Lesions　1967
　　Postsurgical Complications　1973

Surgical Complications
Use　Postsurgical Complications

Surgical Patients　1973
PN　1629　　　　　　　　　SC　50810
B　Patients　1967

Surrogate Parents (Humans)　1973
PN　120　　　　　　　　　　SC　50820
B　Parents　1967
R　Foster Parents　1973

Surveys　1967
PN　2526　　　　　　　　　SC　50830
B　Measurement　1967
N　Consumer Surveys　1973
　　Mail Surveys　1994
　　Telephone Surveys　1994
R　Data Collection　1982
　　Likert Scales　1994
　　↓ Methodology　1967
　　Needs Assessment　1985
　　↓ Questionnaires　1967

Survival Instinct
Use　Self Preservation

Survivors　1994
PN　1058　　　　　　　　　SC　50850
SN　Family members, significant others, or individuals surviving traumatic life events. Not used as a general population type identifier.
N　Holocaust Survivors　1988

Susceptibility (Disorders)　1973
PN　1312　　　　　　　　　SC　50880
SN　Vulnerability to mental or physical disorders due to genetic, immunologic, or other characteristics. Consider also PREDISPOSITION.
UF　Vulnerability (Disorders)
R　At Risk Populations　1985
　　Biological Markers　1991
　　Coronary Prone Behavior　1982
　　↓ Disorders　1967
　　↓ Mental Disorders　1967
　　↓ Physical Disorders　1997
　　Predisposition　1973
　　Premorbidity　1978
　　Risk Factors　2001

Susceptibility (Hypnotic)
Use　Hypnotic Susceptibility

Suspension (School)
Use　School Suspension

Suspicion　1973
PN　133　　　　　　　　　　SC　50910
UF　Distrust
B　Emotional States　1973
R　Doubt　1973
　　Uncertainty　1991

Sustained Attention　1997
PN　162　　　　　　　　　　SC　50915
SN　Focusing or attending to one or more stimuli over an extended period.
B　Attention　1967
N　Attention Span　1973
　　Concentration　1982
　　Vigilance　1967

Swallowing　1988
PN　84　　　　　　　　　　SC　50920
B　Motor Processes　1967
R　Digestion　1973
　　↓ Ingestion　2001

Sweat　1973
PN　34　　　　　　　　　　SC　50930
UF　Perspiration
B　Body Fluids　1973
R　Sweating　1973

Sweating　1973
PN　67　　　　　　　　　　SC　50940
B　Secretion (Gland)　1973
R　↓ Skin Disorders　1973
　　Sweat　1973

Sweetness
Use　Taste Perception

Swimming　1973
PN　657　　　　　　　　　SC　50970
B　Motor Processes　1967
　　Recreation　1967
　　Sports　1967

Syllables　1973
PN　866　　　　　　　　　SC　50990
B　Phonology　1973
R　Consonants　1973
　　Phonetics　1967
　　Vowels　1973

Syllogistic Reasoning
Use　Inductive Deductive Reasoning

Symbiosis (Biological)
Use　Biological Symbiosis

Symbiotic Infantile Psychosis　1973
PN　23　　　　　　　　　　SC　51020
B　Childhood Psychosis　1967
R　Childhood Schizophrenia　1967
　　Early Infantile Autism　1973
　　Mother Child Relations　1967

Symbolic Interactionism　1988
PN　232　　　　　　　　　SC　51025
SN　Sociological theory that assumes that self concept is created through interpretation of symbolic gestures, words, actions, and appearances expressed by others during social interaction.
R　Role Taking　1982
　　↓ Self Concept　1967
　　↓ Social Interaction　1967
　　Sociolinguistics　1985
　　↓ Sociology　1967

Symbolism　1967
PN　2439　　　　　　　　SC　51030
R　↓ Communication　1967
　　↓ Figurative Language　1985
　　↓ Language　1967
　　Metaphor　1982
　　↓ Semiotics　1985

Sympathectomy　1973
PN　51　　　　　　　　　　SC　51050
B　Neurosurgery　1973
R　↓ Psychosurgery　1973

Sympathetic Nervous System　1973
PN　387　　　　　　　　　SC　51060
B　Autonomic Nervous System　1967
N　Baroreceptors　1973
R　↓ Adrenergic Blocking Drugs　1973
　　↓ Adrenergic Drugs　1973
　　↓ Sympatholytic Drugs　1973
　　↓ Sympathomimetic Drugs　1973

Sympatholytic Drugs　1973
PN　25　　　　　　　　　　SC　51080
UF　Antiadrenergic Drugs
B　Drugs　1967
N　Hydralazine　1973
　　Reserpine　1967
R　↓ Adrenergic Blocking Drugs　1973
　　↓ Sympathetic Nervous System　1973
　　↓ Sympathomimetic Drugs　1973

Sympathomimetic Amines　1973
PN　12　　　　　　　　　　SC　51090
B　Amines　1973
　　Sympathomimetic Drugs　1973
N　↓ Amphetamine　1967
　　↓ Catecholamines　1973
　　Dextroamphetamine　1973
　　Ephedrine　1973
　　Methoxamine　1973
　　Phenmetrazine　1973
　　Tyramine　1973

Sympathomimetic Drugs　1973
PN　93　　　　　　　　　　SC　51100
B　Drugs　1967
N　Fenfluramine　1973

Sympathomimetic Drugs — (cont'd)
- **N** Isoproterenol 1973
- ↓ Sympathomimetic Amines 1973
- **R** ↓ Adrenergic Drugs 1973
- Prostaglandins 1982
- ↓ Sympathetic Nervous System 1973
- ↓ Sympatholytic Drugs 1973

Sympathy 1973
PN 145   SC 51110
- **B** Emotional States 1973

Symptom Checklists 1991
PN 252   SC 51124
- **B** Measurement 1967
- **R** ↓ Diagnosis 1967
- Health Complaints 1997
- Psychiatric Symptoms 1997
- ↓ Screening 1982
- ↓ Symptoms 1967

Symptom Prescription
- **Use** Paradoxical Techniques

Symptom Remission 1973
PN 108   SC 51130
- **B** Remission (Disorders) 1973
- **R** Psychiatric Symptoms 1997
- ↓ Symptoms 1967

Symptoms 1967
PN 14611   SC 51140
- **N** Acting Out 1967
- Anhedonia 1985
- Anoxia 1973
- Aphagia 1973
- Apraxia 1973
- ↓ Asthenia 1973
- Ataxia 1973
- Aura 1973
- Automatism 1973
- Body Rocking 1973
- Catalepsy 1973
- Catatonia 1973
- Coma 1973
- ↓ Convulsions 1967
- Delirium 1973
- Depersonalization 1973
- Distractibility 1973
- ↓ Dyskinesia 1973
- ↓ Dyspnea 1973
- Extrapyramidal Symptoms 1994
- Fatigue 1967
- ↓ Headache 1973
- Hematoma 1973
- ↓ Hemorrhage 1973
- Hyperglycemia 1985
- Hyperkinesis 1973
- Hyperphagia 1973
- Hyperthermia 1973
- Hyperventilation 1973
- Hypoglycemia 1973
- Hypothermia 1973
- Insomnia 1973
- Nausea 1973
- Obesity 1973
- ↓ Pain 1967
- Positive and Negative Symptoms 1997
- Pruritus 1973
- Psychiatric Symptoms 1997
- ↓ Respiratory Distress 1973
- Restlessness 1973
- Scratching 1973

Symptoms — (cont'd)
- **N** Shock 1967
- ↓ Spasms 1973
- Syncope 1973
- Tics 1973
- Tremor 1973
- ↓ Underweight 1973
- Vertigo 1973
- Vomiting 1973
- **R** Akathisia 1991
- ↓ Behavior Disorders 1971
- Binge Eating 1991
- Capgras Syndrome 1985
- ↓ Digestive System Disorders 1973
- ↓ Disorders 1967
- ↓ Eating Disorders 1997
- Fecal Incontinence 1973
- Frigidity 1973
- Health Complaints 1997
- Hypersomnia 1994
- ↓ Mental Disorders 1967
- ↓ Movement Disorders 1985
- ↓ Nervous System Disorders 1967
- Parkinsonism 1994
- ↓ Physical Disorders 1997
- Physiological Correlates 1967
- Risk Factors 2001
- Somatization 1994
- ↓ Somatoform Disorders 2001
- Stereotyped Behavior 1973
- Symptom Checklists 1991
- Symptom Remission 1973
- Urinary Incontinence 1973
- Wandering Behavior 1991

Synapses 1973
PN 1324   SC 51150
- **B** Nerve Endings 1973

Syncope 1973
PN 76   SC 51160
- **UF** Fainting
- **B** Blood Pressure Disorders 1973
- Symptoms 1967
- **R** Shock 1967
- Vertigo 1973

Syndromes 1973
PN 2933   SC 51170
- **N** Acquired Immune Deficiency Syndrome 1988
- Addisons Disease 1973
- Aspergers Syndrome 1991
- Battered Child Syndrome 1973
- Capgras Syndrome 1985
- Chronic Fatigue Syndrome 1997
- Creutzfeldt Jakob Syndrome 1994
- Crying Cat Syndrome 1973
- Cushings Syndrome 1973
- Delirium Tremens 1973
- Downs Syndrome 1967
- Fetal Alcohol Syndrome 1985
- Fragile X Syndrome 1994
- Irritable Bowel Syndrome 1991
- Kleine Levin Syndrome 2001
- Klinefelters Syndrome 1973
- Menieres Disease 1973
- Neuroleptic Malignant Syndrome 1988
- ↓ Organic Brain Syndromes 1973
- Prader Willi Syndrome 1991
- Rett Syndrome 1994
- ↓ Senile Dementia 1973
- Testicular Feminization Syndrome 1973
- Turners Syndrome 1973

Syndromes — (cont'd)
- **N** Wernickes Syndrome 1973
- **R** ↓ Disorders 1967
- Epidemics 2001
- ↓ Mental Disorders 1967
- Myofascial Pain 1991
- ↓ Physical Disorders 1997
- Sudden Infant Death 1982

Synonyms 1973
PN 110   SC 51190
- **B** Semantics 1967
- Vocabulary 1967
- **R** Words (Phonetic Units) 1967

Syntax 1971
PN 2958   SC 51220
- **SN** Study and rules of the relation of morphemes to one another as expressions of ideas and as structural components of sentences; the study and science of sentence construction; and, the actual grouping and specific combination and relationship of words in a sentence. Compare GRAMMAR and SENTENCE STRUCTURE.
- **B** Grammar 1967
- **N** ↓ Form Classes (Language) 1973
- **R** Discourse Analysis 1997
- Inflection 1973
- Morphology (Language) 1973
- ↓ Phonology 1973
- Phrases 1973
- ↓ Semantics 1967
- Sentence Structure 1973
- Transformational Generative Grammar 1973

Synthetic Speech 1973
PN 341   SC 51230
- **SN** Sounds having similar characteristics and functional properties of natural speech but which are made by means other than natural vocalization mechanisms (e.g., computer-generated speech sounds).
- **B** Speech Processing (Mechanical) 1973

Syphilis 1973
PN 59   SC 51240
- **B** Venereal Diseases 1973
- **N** Neurosyphilis 1973
- **R** ↓ Congenital Disorders 1973
- General Paresis 1973

Systematic Desensitization Therapy 1973
PN 1557   SC 51250
- **UF** Desensitization (Systematic)
- **B** Behavior Therapy 1967
- Exposure Therapy 1997
- **R** Progressive Relaxation Therapy 1978
- Reciprocal Inhibition Therapy 1973
- ↓ Relaxation Therapy 1978

Systems 1967
PN 895   SC 51270
- **SN** Conceptually broad term referring to interrelated elements acting as or constituting a unified whole. Use a more specific term if possible.
- **N** ↓ Anatomical Systems 1973
- Caste System 1973
- ↓ Communication Systems 1973
- ↓ Expert Systems 1991
- Human Machine Systems 1997
- ↓ Information Systems 1991
- Number Systems 1973
- ↓ Political Economic Systems 1973
- **R** ↓ Computer Software 1967

Systems — (cont'd)
R ↓ Computers 1967
Human Machine Systems Design 1997
Person Environment Fit 1991
Systems Analysis 1973
Systems Theory 1988

Systems Analysis 1973
PN 575   SC 51260
B   Analysis 1967
R   Computer Programming 2001
Human Machine Systems 1997
Human Machine Systems Design 1997
↓ Systems 1967
Systems Theory 1988
Task Analysis 1967

Systems Theory 1988
PN 2634   SC 51265
SN   Examination of organizations, structures, or procedures from a macroscopic perspective that integrates constituent parts into a whole.
B   Theories 1967
R   Biopsychosocial Approach 1991
↓ Systems 1967
Systems Analysis 1973

Systolic Pressure 1973
PN 297   SC 51280
B   Blood Pressure 1967

Szondi Test 1973
PN 35   SC 51290
B   Projective Personality Measures 1973

T Groups
Use Human Relations Training

T Mazes 1973
PN 66   SC 51310
B   Mazes 1967

T Test 1973
PN 111   SC 51320
UF   Students T Test
B   Parametric Statistical Tests 1973
R   ↓ Central Tendency Measures 1973
Statistical Significance 1973

Taboos 1973
PN 132   SC 51330
B   Social Influences 1967
R   Animism 1973
Ethnology 1967
↓ Rites of Passage 1973
Superstitions 1973
Transcultural Psychiatry 1973

Tachistoscopes 1973
PN 40   SC 51340
SN   Apparatus used in experimental studies for presentation of visual stimuli for controlled stimulus intervals, intensities, and durations.
B   Apparatus 1967

Tachistoscopic Presentation 1973
PN 458   SC 51350
B   Stimulus Presentation Methods 1973
Visual Stimulation 1973

Tachycardia 1973
PN 83   SC 51360

Tachycardia — (cont'd)
UF   Rapid Heart Rate
B   Arrhythmias (Heart) 1973
R   Hyperthyroidism 1973

Tactual Discrimination
Use Tactual Perception

Tactual Displays 1973
PN 91   SC 51380
SN   Materials or apparatus designed to present information or patterns by means of touch or manipulation. Also, any information or patterns conveyed by such means.
B   Displays 1967
Tactual Stimulation 1973

Tactual Maps
Use Mobility Aids

Tactual Perception 1967
PN 1945   SC 51390
SN   Awareness of the qualities or characteristics of objects, substances, or surfaces by means of touch.
UF   Tactual Discrimination
Touch
B   Cutaneous Sense 1967
N   Texture Perception 1982
Vibrotactile Thresholds 1973
R   Anesthesia (Feeling) 1973
Braille 1978
Physical Contact 1982

Tactual Stimulation 1973
PN 1331   SC 51400
SN   Perceptual arousal or excitation of an organism by means of touch.
B   Somesthetic Stimulation 1973
N   Massage 2001
Tactual Displays 1973

Tailored Testing
Use Adaptive Testing

Talent
Use Ability

Talented
Use Gifted

Tantrums 1973
PN 62   SC 51440
B   Behavior Problems 1967
R   ↓ Anger 1967
↓ Emotional Control 1973

Tape Recorders 1973
PN 81   SC 51450
UF   Recorders (Tape)
B   Apparatus 1967
N   Videotape Recorders 1973

Tardive Dyskinesia 1988
PN 902   SC 51460
B   Dyskinesia 1973
R   ↓ Drug Therapy 1967
↓ Neuroleptic Drugs 1973
↓ Side Effects (Drug) 1973

Task Analysis 1967
PN 1499   SC 51470
B   Analysis 1967

Task Analysis — (cont'd)
R   Constant Time Delay 1997
Job Analysis 1967
Systems Analysis 1973
Task Complexity 1973

Task Complexity 1973
PN 3926   SC 51480
UF   Complexity (Task)
Task Difficulty
R   Task Analysis 1967

Task Difficulty
Use Task Complexity

Taste Aversion Conditioning
Use Aversion Conditioning

Taste Buds 1973
PN 193   SC 51500
B   Sense Organs 1973
Sensory Neurons 1973
Tongue 1973
R   Chemoreceptors 1973
Taste Disorders 2001

Taste Discrimination
Use Taste Perception

Taste Disorders 2001
PN 0   SC 51515
SN   Disorders involving abnormal gustatory function or perception.
B   Sense Organ Disorders 1973
R   Anosmia 1973
Chemoreceptors 1973
↓ Sense Organs 1973
↓ Sensory Neurons 1973
Taste Buds 1973
↓ Tongue 1973

Taste Perception 1967
PN 3284   SC 51520
UF   Bitterness
Gustatory Perception
Saltiness
Sourness
Sweetness
Taste Discrimination
B   Perception 1967
R   ↓ Olfactory Perception 1967

Taste Stimulation 1967
PN 871   SC 51530
B   Perceptual Stimulation 1973

Tattoos
Use Cosmetic Techniques

Taurine 1982
PN 43   SC 51545
SN   Suspected neurotransmitter or membrane stabilizer located in the posterior pituitary gland as well as other mammalian tissue.
B   Acids 1973
R   Bile 1973

Taxation 1985
PN 147   SC 51547
R   Economy 1973
Government 1967
Income (Economic) 1973

Taxonomies 1973
PN 3400   SC 51550
  UF Classification Systems
      Typologies (General)
  R ↓ Psychodiagnostic Typologies 1967

Tay Sachs Disease
  Use Amaurotic Familial Idiocy

Taylor Manifest Anxiety Scale 1973
PN 34   SC 51570
SN Use MA SCALE (TEST) to access references
from 1967-1972.
  B Nonprojective Personality Measures 1973

Tea
  Use Beverages (Nonalcoholic)

Teacher Accreditation
  Use Accreditation (Education Personnel)

Teacher Aides 1973
PN 140   SC 51600
SN Paraprofessional school personnel who assist
teachers in the instructional process or other class-
room duties.
  B Educational Personnel 1973
      Paraprofessional Personnel 1973

Teacher Attitudes 1967
PN 9284   SC 51610
SN Attitudes of, not toward, teachers.
  B Attitudes 1967
      Teacher Characteristics 1973
  N Teacher Expectations 1978
  R Parent School Relationship 1982
      Teacher Personality 1973
      Teacher Student Interaction 1973

Teacher Characteristics 1973
PN 4527   SC 51615
  UF Teacher Effectiveness
  N ↓ Teacher Attitudes 1967
      Teacher Personality 1973
  R ↓ Education 1967
      Teacher Effectiveness Evaluation 1978
      Teacher Expectations 1978
      Teacher Student Interaction 1973
      ↓ Teachers 1967
      ↓ Teaching 1967

Teacher Education 1967
PN 3962   SC 51620
  UF Teacher Training
  B Education 1967
  N Inservice Teacher Education 1973
      Student Teaching 1973
  R Cooperating Teachers 1978
      Education Students 1982
      Practicum Supervision 1978
      Preservice Teachers 1982

Teacher Effectiveness
  Use Teacher Characteristics

Teacher Effectiveness Evaluation 1978
PN 1374   SC 51625
SN Techniques, materials, or the procedural
aspects of judging teachers' performance by peers,
students, or others based on stated criteria. Use
PERSONNEL EVALUATION and TEACHERS (or a
more specific term, e.g., COLLEGE TEACHERS) to
access references from 1973-1977.

Teacher Effectiveness Evaluation —
  (cont'd)
  B Personnel Evaluation 1973
  R Course Evaluation 1978
      Educational Quality 1997
      ↓ Teacher Characteristics 1973

Teacher Expectations 1978
PN 721   SC 51627
  B Expectations 1967
      Teacher Attitudes 1967
  R ↓ Teacher Characteristics 1973
      Teacher Student Interaction 1973

Teacher Personality 1973
PN 490   SC 51630
  B Teacher Characteristics 1973
  R ↓ Personality 1967
      ↓ Teacher Attitudes 1967
      Teacher Student Interaction 1973

Teacher Recruitment 1973
PN 43   SC 51640
SN Process of attracting candidates to the teaching
profession or finding teachers to fill vacancies.
  UF Recruitment (Teachers)
  B Personnel Recruitment 1973

Teacher Student Interaction 1973
PN 4886   SC 51650
  R Classroom Discipline 1973
      ↓ Education 1967
      ↓ Teacher Attitudes 1967
      ↓ Teacher Characteristics 1973
      Teacher Expectations 1978
      Teacher Personality 1973

Teacher Tenure 1973
PN 126   SC 51670
  UF Tenure (Teacher)
  B Occupational Tenure 1973
  R ↓ Education 1967

Teacher Training
  Use Teacher Education

Teachers 1967
PN 7913   SC 51690
  UF Classroom Teachers
      Instructors
      Tutors
  B Educational Personnel 1973
  N College Teachers 1973
      Cooperating Teachers 1978
      Elementary School Teachers 1973
      High School Teachers 1973
      Junior High School Teachers 1973
      Preschool Teachers 1985
      Preservice Teachers 1982
      Resource Teachers 1973
      Special Education Teachers 1973
      Student Teachers 1973
      Vocational Education Teachers 1988
  R ↓ Teacher Characteristics 1973

Teaching 1967
PN 4191   SC 51700
  UF Classroom Instruction
      Instruction
  N ↓ Instructional Media 1967
      ↓ Teaching Methods 1967
  R Bilingual Education 1978

Teaching — (cont'd)
  R Cooperative Learning 1994
      Course Evaluation 1978
      ↓ Education 1967
      ↓ Teacher Characteristics 1973

Teaching Internship
  Use Student Teaching

Teaching Machines 1973
PN 59   SC 51730
SN Mechanical, electronic, or electrically controlled
apparatus for the presentation of programmed
instructional material or texts for independent, self-
paced education. Compare COMPUTER ASSISTED
INSTRUCTION.
  B Instructional Media 1967
  R Computer Assisted Instruction 1973
      Programmed Instruction 2001

Teaching Methods 1967
PN 18071   SC 51740
  B Teaching 1967
  N Advance Organizers 1985
      ↓ Audiovisual Instruction 1973
      Computer Assisted Instruction 1973
      Directed Discussion Method 1973
      Discovery Teaching Method 1973
      Educational Field Trips 1973
      ↓ Experiential Learning 1997
      Group Instruction 1973
      Individualized Instruction 1973
      Lecture Method 1973
      Lesson Plans 1973
      Montessori Method 1973
      Nondirected Discussion Method 1973
      Open Classroom Method 1973
      Programmed Instruction 2001
      Team Teaching Method 1973
      ↓ Tutoring 1973
  R Constant Time Delay 1997
      Cooperative Learning 1994
      ↓ Education 1967
      Educational Therapy 1997
      Home Schooling 1994
      Initial Teaching Alphabet 1973
      Mastery Learning 1985
      ↓ Nontraditional Education 1982
      ↓ Prompting 1997
      Questioning 1982

Team Teaching Method 1973
PN 157   SC 51750
  B Teaching Methods 1967
  R Open Classroom Method 1973
      ↓ Teams 1988

Teams 1988
PN 1856   SC 51751
  N ↓ Work Teams 2001
  R Athletic Performance 1991
      Athletic Training 1991
      College Athletes 1994
      Cooperative Learning 1994
      ↓ Group Dynamics 1967
      Interdisciplinary Treatment Approach 1973
      ↓ Management Methods 1973
      ↓ Personnel 1967
      ↓ Sports 1967
      Team Teaching Method 1973

Technical Education Teachers
  Use Vocational Education Teachers

Technical Personnel 1978
PN 420   SC 51755
 B   Business and Industrial Personnel 1967
 N   Technical Service Personnel 1973
 R   ↓ Service Personnel 1991

Technical Schools 1973
PN 168   SC 51760
SN Schools that teach specific job skills, usually at
the postsecondary level, often emphasizing underlying sciences and supporting mathematics as well as
skills, methods, materials, and processes of a specialized field of technology.
 UF   Vocational Schools
 B   Schools 1967

Technical Service Personnel 1973
PN 132   SC 51770
 UF   Repairmen
 B   Service Personnel 1991
      Technical Personnel 1978
 R   ↓ Blue Collar Workers 1973
      ↓ Business and Industrial Personnel 1967
      ↓ Nonprofessional Personnel 1982

Technology 1973
PN 2661   SC 51805
 N   Nuclear Technology 1985
 R   Electronic Communication 2001
      Industrialization 1973
      ↓ Sciences 1967

Teenage Fathers
 Use Adolescent Fathers

Teenage Mothers
 Use Adolescent Mothers

Teenage Pregnancy
 Use Adolescent Pregnancy

Teeth (Anatomy) 1973
PN 215   SC 51820
 B   Digestive System 1967
 R   Mouth (Anatomy) 1967

Teeth Grinding
 Use Bruxism

Tegmentum 1991
PN 355   SC 51835
 UF   Ventral Tegmental Area
 B   Mesencephalon 1973
 N   Periaqueductal Gray 1985

Telecommunications Media 1973
PN 425   SC 51840
 B   Communications Media 1973
 N   Radio 1973
      Telephone Systems 1973
      ↓ Television 1967
      Television Advertising 1973
 R   Internet 2001
      Teleconferencing 1997
      Telemetry 1973

Teleconferencing 1997
PN 135   SC 51845
SN Communication between persons remote from
one another by means of a telecommunication sys-
tem with audio and/or visual links.
 UF   Computer Conferencing

Teleconferencing — (cont'd)
 R   ↓ Telecommunications Media 1973
      Telephone Systems 1973
      ↓ Television 1967

Telekinesis
 Use Psychokinesis

Telemetry 1973
PN 46   SC 51860
SN Process of measuring and transmitting quantita-
tive information and recording at a remote location.
 R   ↓ Telecommunications Media 1973

Telencephalon 1973
PN 392   SC 51870
 B   Forebrain 1985
 N   ↓ Basal Ganglia 1973
      ↓ Cerebral Cortex 1967

Telepathy 1973
PN 124   SC 51880
 B   Parapsychological Phenomena 1973
 R   ↓ Extrasensory Perception 1967

Telephone Hot Lines
 Use Hot Line Services

Telephone Surveys 1994
PN 117   SC 51895
 B   Surveys 1967
 R   ↓ Consumer Research 1973
      Consumer Surveys 1973
      Mail Surveys 1994
      ↓ Methodology 1967
      ↓ Questionnaires 1967
      Telephone Systems 1973

Telephone Systems 1973
PN 665   SC 51900
 B   Communication Systems 1973
      Telecommunications Media 1973
 R   Teleconferencing 1997
      Telephone Surveys 1994

Televised Instruction 1973
PN 187   SC 51910
 B   Audiovisual Instruction 1973
 R   ↓ Educational Audiovisual Aids 1973
      Educational Television 1967

Television 1967
PN 1876   SC 51920
 B   Audiovisual Communications Media 1973
      Mass Media 1967
      Telecommunications Media 1973
 N   Closed Circuit Television 1973
      Educational Television 1967
      Television Advertising 1973
 R   ↓ Apparatus 1967
      ↓ News Media 1997
      Teleconferencing 1997
      Video Display Units 1985

Television Advertising 1973
PN 788   SC 51930
 UF   Commercials
 B   Advertising 1967
      Audiovisual Communications Media 1973
      Telecommunications Media 1973
      Television 1967

Television Viewing 1973
PN 1977   SC 51940
 B   Recreation 1967

Temperament
 Use Personality

Temperature (Body)
 Use Body Temperature

Temperature Effects 1967
PN 1310   SC 51990
 UF   Thermal Factors
 B   Environmental Effects 1973
 N   Cold Effects 1973
      Heat Effects 1973
 R   Atmospheric Conditions 1973
      Pollution 1973
      Seasonal Variations 1973
      Thermal Acclimatization 1973

Temperature Perception 1973
PN 340   SC 52000
 B   Somesthetic Perception 1967
 R   Somatosensory Disorders 2001

Tempo 1997
PN 86   SC 52005
 R   ↓ Music 1967
      Music Perception 1997
      ↓ Rhythm 1991
      Speech Rate 1973
      Speech Rhythm 1973
      ↓ Time Perception 1967

Temporal Frequency 1985
PN 620   SC 52015
SN Number of alternating cycles (e.g., patterns of
vertical stripes of light and dark light) occurring during
a specified time interval. Usually expressed in terms
of cycles per second (Hz) as, for example, in sine or
square wave visual displays.
 B   Stimulus Parameters 1967
 R   Spatial Frequency 1982
      Stimulus Frequency 1973
      ↓ Visual Displays 1973
      ↓ Visual Stimulation 1973

Temporal Lobe 1973
PN 2407   SC 52010
 B   Cerebral Cortex 1967
 N   Auditory Cortex 1967

Temporal Spatial Concept Scale
SN Term was discontinued in 1997. In 2000, the
term was stripped from all records containing it, and
replaced with INTELLIGENCE MEASURES, its postable counterpart.
 Use Intelligence Measures

Temporomandibular Joint Syndrome
 Use Musculoskeletal Disorders

Temptation 1973
PN 118   SC 52030
 B   Motivation 1967
 R   ↓ Incentives 1967
      Peer Pressure 1994
      ↓ Resistance 1997
      Self Control 1973

Tendons 1973
PN 14   SC 52050

Tendons — (cont'd)
- B   Musculoskeletal System   1973

Tennessee Self Concept Scale   1973
- PN   49   SC   52060
- B   Nonprojective Personality Measures   1973

Tennis   1973
- PN   207   SC   52070
- B   Recreation   1967
-     Sports   1967

Tension Headache
- Use   Muscle Contraction Headache

Tenure (Occupational)
- Use   Occupational Tenure

Tenure (Teacher)
- Use   Teacher Tenure

Teratogens   1988
- PN   256   SC   52105
- SN   Drugs or other agents that cause developmental malformations.
- B   Hazardous Materials   1991
- R   ↓ Congenital Disorders   1973
-     ↓ Drugs   1967
-     ↓ Poisons   1973
-     ↓ Prenatal Development   1973
-     Prenatal Exposure   1991
-     Thalidomide   1973
-     Toxicity   1973

Terminal Cancer   1973
- PN   437   SC   52110
- B   Neoplasms   1967
- R   ↓ Death and Dying   1967
-     Terminally Ill Patients   1973

Terminally Ill Patients   1973
- PN   1682   SC   52120
- UF   Dying Patients
- B   Patients   1967
- R   Advance Directives   1994
-     Assisted Suicide   1997
-     ↓ Death and Dying   1967
-     Hospice   1982
-     Life Sustaining Treatment   1997
-     Palliative Care   1991
-     Terminal Cancer   1973

Terminology   1991
- PN   419   SC   52125
- SN   Definitions, analysis, evaluation, or review of individual terms or nomenclature in any field.
- N   Psychological Terminology   1973
- R   Concepts   1967
-     Scientific Communication   1973

Terminology (Psychological)
- Use   Psychological Terminology

Territoriality   1967
- PN   1795   SC   52140
- SN   Behavioral patterns characteristic of defense or occupation of a territory. Used for both human and animal populations.
- UF   Habitat Selection
- B   Animal Ethology   1967
- R   ↓ Animal Aggressive Behavior   1973
-     Animal Courtship Displays   1973

Territoriality — (cont'd)
- R   Animal Dominance   1973
-     Animal Homing   1991
-     Animal Scent Marking   1985
-     Boundaries (Psychological)   1997

Terrorism   1982
- PN   282   SC   52150
- SN   Violence or threats of violence in order to achieve political, economic, or social goals.
- B   Antisocial Behavior   1971
- R   ↓ Crime   1967
-     Hostages   1988
-     Political Revolution   1973
-     ↓ Radical Movements   1973
-     ↓ Violence   1973

Test Administration   1973
- PN   1860   SC   52180
- SN   Instructions, timing, preparation of test materials, testing conditions, mode of presentation, and other factors involved in the administration of tests.
- UF   Administration (Test)
- B   Testing   1967
- R   Group Testing   1973
-     Individual Testing   1973
-     ↓ Testing Methods   1967

Test Anxiety   1967
- PN   1995   SC   52190
- SN   Fear or tension in anticipation of formal examination frequently resulting in performance decrement and contributing to measurement error.
- B   Anxiety   1967
- R   ↓ Anxiety Disorders   1997
-     Test Taking   1985

Test Bias   1985
- PN   503   SC   52196
- SN   Any significant differential performance on tests by different populations (e.g., males versus females) as a result of test characteristics which are irrelevant to the variable or construct being measured.
- UF   Item Bias
- B   Test Construction   1973
-     Testing   1967
- N   Cultural Test Bias   1973
- R   Error of Measurement   1985
-     Response Bias   1967

Test Bias (Cultural)
- Use   Cultural Test Bias

Test Coaching   1997
- PN   17   SC   52205
- R   ↓ Practice   1967
-     Test Taking   1985
-     ↓ Testing   1967
-     Testwiseness   1978
-     ↓ Tutoring   1973

Test Construction   1973
- PN   11223   SC   52210
- SN   Planning, selection, writing, editing, and statistical analysis of test items, and design of instructions for test administration and scoring.
- N   Content Analysis (Test)   1967
-     Difficulty Level (Test)   1973
-     Item Analysis (Test)   1967
-     Item Content (Test)   1973
-     ↓ Test Bias   1985
-     Test Forms   1988
-     Test Items   1973
-     Test Reliability   1973

Test Construction — (cont'd)
- N   Test Standardization   1973
-     Test Validity   1973
- R   Adaptive Testing   1985
-     ↓ Experimental Design   1967
-     ↓ Measurement   1967

Test Difficulty
- Use   Difficulty Level (Test)

Test Equating
- Use   Score Equating

Test Forms   1988
- PN   1843   SC   52214
- SN   Includes different versions or schedules of a test.
- B   Test Construction   1973
-     Testing   1967
- R   Item Content (Test)   1973

Test Interpretation   1985
- PN   961   SC   52215
- SN   Judgment and explanation of the significance, meaning, application, or limitation of an assessment instrument and an obtained score or scores.
- B   Testing   1967
- R   Cultural Test Bias   1973
-     Cutting Scores   1985
-     Psychometrics   1967
-     ↓ Scoring (Testing)   1973
-     Statistical Weighting   1985
-     ↓ Test Scores   1967
-     Test Validity   1973

Test Items   1973
- PN   1208   SC   52220
- B   Test Construction   1973
-     Testing   1967
- R   Item Analysis (Statistical)   1973
-     Item Analysis (Test)   1967
-     Item Content (Test)   1973

Test Normalization
- Use   Test Standardization

Test Norms   1973
- PN   1363   SC   52240
- UF   Norms (Test)
- R   ↓ Measurement   1967
-     Standardized Tests   1985

Test Reliability   1973
- PN   13160   SC   52250
- SN   Consistency, dependability, and reproducibility of test scores, expressed as a reliability coefficient.
- UF   Internal Consistency
-     Reliability (Test)
- B   Test Construction   1973
-     Testing   1967
- R   Error of Measurement   1985
-     Interrater Reliability   1982
-     Test Standardization   1973

Test Scores   1967
- PN   4027   SC   52260
- SN   Quantitative values or evaluations assigned to describe test performance of individuals. Compare SCORING (TESTING) and GRADING (EDUCATIONAL).
- UF   Scores (Test)
- N   Cutting Scores   1985
-     Intelligence Quotient   1967

Test Scores — (cont'd)
- **N** Standard Scores [1985]
- **R** Error of Measurement [1985]
  Item Response Theory [1985]
  ↓ Measurement [1967]
  ↓ Scoring (Testing) [1973]
  Statistical Weighting [1985]
  Test Interpretation [1985]

Test Standardization [1973]
- **PN** 868   **SC** 52270
- **UF** Normalization (Test)
  Standardization (Test)
  Test Normalization
- **B** Test Construction [1973]
  Testing [1967]
- **R** Standardized Tests [1985]
  Test Reliability [1973]
  Test Validity [1973]

Test Taking [1985]
- **PN** 657   **SC** 52275
- **SN** Strategies, attitudes, behaviors, or other factors associated with taking any type of test.
- **R** Cheating [1973]
  Guessing [1973]
  Response Bias [1967]
  Study Habits [1973]
  Test Anxiety [1967]
  Test Coaching [1997]
  ↓ Testing [1967]
  Testwiseness [1978]

Test Tube Babies
- **Use** Reproductive Technology

Test Validity [1973]
- **PN** 20025   **SC** 52280
- **SN** Extent to which a test measures what it was designed to measure. Includes criterion-oriented and content validity.
- **UF** Validity (Test)
- **B** Test Construction [1973]
  Testing [1967]
- **R** Test Interpretation [1985]
  Test Standardization [1973]

Testes [1973]
- **PN** 171   **SC** 52290
- **B** Gonads [1973]
  Male Genitalia [1973]

Testes Disorders
- **Use** Endocrine Sexual Disorders

Testicular Feminization Syndrome [1973]
- **PN** 8   **SC** 52310
- **UF** Feminization Syndrome (Testicular)
- **B** Endocrine Sexual Disorders [1973]
  Male Genital Disorders [1973]
  Sex Linked Hereditary Disorders [1973]
  Syndromes [1973]
- **R** Hermaphroditism [1973]
  Sterility [1973]

Testimony (Expert)
- **Use** Expert Testimony

Testing [1967]
- **PN** 3316   **SC** 52330

Testing — (cont'd)
- **SN** Administration of tests, and analysis and interpretation of test scores in order to measure differences between individuals or between test performances of the same individual on different occasions.
- **B** Measurement [1967]
- **N** Computer Assisted Testing [1988]
  Content Analysis (Test) [1967]
  Difficulty Level (Test) [1973]
  ↓ Educational Measurement [1967]
  Item Analysis (Test) [1967]
  Item Content (Test) [1973]
  Item Response Theory [1985]
  Rating [1967]
  Repeated Measures [1985]
  Scaling (Testing) [1967]
  ↓ Scoring (Testing) [1973]
  Test Administration [1973]
  ↓ Test Bias [1985]
  Test Forms [1988]
  Test Interpretation [1985]
  Test Items [1973]
  Test Reliability [1973]
  Test Standardization [1973]
  Test Validity [1973]
- **R** ↓ Neuropsychological Assessment [1982]
  Psychometrics [1967]
  Test Coaching [1997]
  Test Taking [1985]
  Testwiseness [1978]

Testing (Job Applicants)
- **Use** Job Applicant Screening

Testing Methods [1967]
- **PN** 1187   **SC** 52370
- **N** Adaptive Testing [1985]
  Cloze Testing [1973]
  Essay Testing [1973]
  Forced Choice (Testing Method) [1967]
  Multiple Choice (Testing Method) [1973]
  Q Sort Testing Technique [1967]
  Scaling (Testing) [1967]
- **R** ↓ Measurement [1967]
  Posttesting [1973]
  Pretesting [1973]
  Subtests [1973]
  Test Administration [1973]

Testosterone [1973]
- **PN** 2037   **SC** 52380
- **B** Androgens [1973]

Tests
- **Use** Measurement

Tests (Achievement)
- **Use** Achievement Measures

Tests (Aptitude)
- **Use** Aptitude Measures

Tests (Intelligence)
- **Use** Intelligence Measures

Tests (Personality)
- **Use** Personality Measures

Tests (Statistical)
- **Use** Statistical Tests

Testwiseness [1978]
- **PN** 114   **SC** 52415
- **SN** High degree of sophistication in test-taking skills resulting in advantage over others with same knowledge or ability.
- **R** ↓ Measurement [1967]
  Test Coaching [1997]
  Test Taking [1985]
  ↓ Testing [1967]

Tetrabenazine [1973]
- **PN** 40   **SC** 52430
- **B** Neuroleptic Drugs [1973]
  Serotonin Antagonists [1973]

Tetrachoric Correlation [1973]
- **PN** 13   **SC** 52450
- **B** Statistical Correlation [1967]

Tetrahydrocannabinol [1973]
- **PN** 652   **SC** 52470
- **B** Alcohols [1967]
  Cannabinoids [1982]
- **R** ↓ Cannabis [1973]
  ↓ Hallucinogenic Drugs [1967]
  Hashish [1973]
  Marihuana [1971]

Text Structure [1982]
- **PN** 1783   **SC** 52473
- **SN** Arrangement of sentence or paragraph segments, concepts, or physical format of reading material.
- **R** Discourse Analysis [1997]
  ↓ Prose [1973]
  Reading Materials [1973]
  Sentence Structure [1973]
  ↓ Verbal Communication [1967]

Textbooks [1978]
- **PN** 876   **SC** 52475
- **SN** Books focusing on principles of a specific subject and used as basis of instruction. Not used as a document type identifier. Use BOOK to access references that are in themselves textbooks. Use TEXTBOOKS when textbooks are the object of discussion or study (e.g., analyses of best format for textbook chapters).
- **B** Books [1973]
  Instructional Media [1967]
- **N** Programmed Textbooks [2001]
- **R** Reading Materials [1973]

Texture Perception [1982]
- **PN** 542   **SC** 52485
- **SN** Perception of the surface characteristics (frequently patterned) or appearance of objects or substances, usually through the visual or haptic senses.
- **B** Tactual Perception [1967]
  Visual Perception [1967]
- **R** Pattern Discrimination [1967]

Thalamic Nuclei [1973]
- **PN** 432   **SC** 52500
- **B** Thalamus [1967]

Thalamotomy [1973]
- **PN** 30   **SC** 52510
- **B** Psychosurgery [1973]

Thalamus [1967]
- **PN** 1119   **SC** 52520
- **B** Diencephalon [1973]
- **N** Geniculate Bodies (Thalamus) [1973]

Thalamus — (cont'd)
N   Thalamic Nuclei [1973]

Thalidomide [1973]
PN   14   SC   52530
B   Amines [1973]
     Hypnotic Drugs [1973]
     Sedatives [1973]
R   ↓ Drug Induced Congenital Disorders [1973]
     Prenatal Exposure [1991]
     Teratogens [1988]

Thanatology
Use   Death Education

Thanatos
Use   Death Instinct

Theatre [1973]
PN   273   SC   52540
UF   Stage Plays
B   Arts [1973]
N   Drama [1973]

Theft [1973]
PN   463   SC   52550
UF   Robbery
     Stealing
B   Crime [1967]
N   Shoplifting [1973]

Thematic Apperception Test [1967]
PN   554   SC   52560
B   Projective Personality Measures [1973]

Theology
Use   Religion

Theophylline [1973]
PN   89   SC   52580
B   Alkaloids [1973]
     Diuretics [1973]
     Enzyme Inhibitors [1985]
     Heart Rate Affecting Drugs [1973]
     Muscle Relaxing Drugs [1973]
R   ↓ Analeptic Drugs [1973]
     Vasodilation [1973]

Theoretical Interpretation [1988]
PN   824   SC   52582
SN   Description or analysis of any particular event, condition, or process from a specific psychological perspective. Usually used in conjunction with other index terms, e.g., humanistic psychology.
UF   Psychological Interpretation
N   Psychoanalytic Interpretation [1967]
R   ↓ Theories [1967]

Theoretical Orientation [1982]
PN   3549   SC   52584
SN   Adherence to a particular school of thought, theoretical movement, or practice in a scientific or other area of knowledge.
UF   Eclectic Psychology
     Professional Orientation
R   ↓ Clinical Methods Training [1973]
     ↓ Psychology Education [1978]
     ↓ Psychotherapy [1967]
     ↓ Social Sciences [1967]
     ↓ Theories [1967]
     ↓ Therapist Characteristics [1973]

Theories [1967]
PN   22447   SC   52590
SN   Conceptually broad term referring to the systematic deductive derivation of secondary principles explaining observed phenomena. Use a more specific term if possible.
N   Chaos Theory [1997]
     Communication Theory [1973]
     Constructivism [1994]
     ↓ Darwinism [1973]
     Fuzzy Set Theory [1991]
     Game Theory [1967]
     Information Theory [1967]
     Item Response Theory [1985]
     Learning Theory [1967]
     ↓ Psychological Theories [2001]
     Systems Theory [1988]
     Theories of Education [1973]
     Theory of Evolution [1967]
R   ↓ Experimentation [1967]
     ↓ History of Psychology [1967]
     ↓ Hypothesis Testing [1973]
     ↓ Theoretical Interpretation [1988]
     Theoretical Orientation [1982]
     Theory Formulation [1973]
     Theory Verification [1973]

Theories of Education [1973]
PN   688   SC   52587
SN   Principles and supporting data concerning the educational process, with application for educational practice.
UF   Educational Theory
B   Theories [1967]
R   ↓ Education [1967]

Theory Formulation [1973]
PN   1463   SC   52600
SN   Advancement of propositions and formulation of hypotheses concerning description, explanation, or interpretation of facts. Applies both to principles of theory formulation and presentation of new theories.
R   ↓ Hypothesis Testing [1973]
     ↓ Methodology [1967]
     ↓ Theories [1967]
     Theory Verification [1973]

Theory of Evolution [1967]
PN   2683   SC   52610
SN   Theories explaining the origins of living organisms and the process by which they evolved into their present forms. For C. Darwin's theory of evolution, use DARWINISM.
UF   Evolution (Theory of)
B   Theories [1967]
R   ↓ Darwinism [1973]
     Natural Selection [1997]
     Self Preservation [1997]

Theory of Mind [2001]
PN   0   SC   52615
SN   Ability to attribute mental states, cognitions, attitudes, beliefs, and emotions to oneself and other individuals. Used for both human and animal populations.
UF   Mind Blindness
R   ↓ Autism [1967]
     ↓ Cognitive Development [1973]
     ↓ Comprehension [1967]
     Mind [1991]
     ↓ Social Perception [1967]

Theory Verification [1973]
PN   1598   SC   52620

Theory Verification — (cont'd)
SN   Process of proving or disproving theoretical assumptions using empirical data. Applies both to principles of theory testing and their applications.
UF   Verification (of Theories)
R   ↓ Hypothesis Testing [1973]
     ↓ Methodology [1967]
     ↓ Theories [1967]
     Theory Formulation [1973]

Therapeutic Abortion
Use   Induced Abortion

Therapeutic Alliance [1994]
PN   464   SC   52633
UF   Working Alliance
B   Psychotherapeutic Processes [1967]
R   Psychotherapeutic Transference [1967]
     ↓ Treatment [1967]

Therapeutic Camps [1978]
PN   132   SC   52635
SN   Camps, usually for children, staffed by mental health personnel and offering treatment programs as well as outdoor activities fostering personal growth and accomplishment.
UF   Camps (Therapeutic)
B   Treatment Facilities [1973]
R   Recreation Therapy [1973]
     Wilderness Experience [1991]

Therapeutic Community [1967]
PN   1414   SC   52640
SN   Institutional or residential treatment setting emphasizing social and environmental factors in therapy and management and rehabilitation, usually of psychiatric or drug rehabilitation patients.
B   Group Psychotherapy [1967]
     Psychiatric Hospital Programs [1967]
R   Milieu Therapy [1988]
     Sociotherapy [1973]

Therapeutic Devices (Medical)
Use   Medical Therapeutic Devices

Therapeutic Environment [2001]
PN   0   SC   52621
UF   Treatment Environment
B   Environment [1967]
N   ↓ Facility Environment [1988]
R   Milieu Therapy [1988]
     ↓ Therapeutic Processes [1978]
     ↓ Treatment Facilities [1973]

Therapeutic Outcomes
Use   Treatment Outcomes

Therapeutic Processes [1978]
PN   5558   SC   52655
SN   Experiential, attitudinal, emotional, or behavioral phenomena occurring during the course of treatment. Applies to the patient or therapist (i.e., nurse, doctor, etc.) individually or to their interaction.
UF   Dentist Patient Interaction
     Nurse Patient Interaction
     Physician Patient Interaction
N   ↓ Psychotherapeutic Processes [1967]
R   Client Education [1985]
     Patient Abuse [1991]
     Patient Violence [1994]
     Professional Client Sexual Relations [1994]
     ↓ Therapeutic Environment [2001]
     Therapist Selection [1994]
     ↓ Treatment [1967]

Therapeutic Processes — (cont'd)
R ↓ Treatment Outcomes 1982
    Treatment Termination 1982

Therapeutic Social Clubs 1973
PN 70   SC 52660
SN Associations of persons, usually patients or former patients, who engage in regular social activities stressing self-help and psychosocial rehabilitation.
  UF Social Clubs (Therapeutic)
  B   Psychosocial Rehabilitation 1973
  R   ↓ Treatment 1967

Therapeutic Techniques (Psychother)
  Use Psychotherapeutic Techniques

Therapist Attitudes 1978
PN 1237   SC 52680
SN Attitudes of, not toward, therapists.
  B   Health Personnel Attitudes 1985
     Therapist Characteristics 1973
  N   Psychotherapist Attitudes 1973
  R   Psychologist Attitudes 1991
     Therapist Role 1978

Therapist Characteristics 1973
PN 3424   SC 52690
SN Traits or qualities of therapists, including but not limited to effectiveness, experience level, and personality.
  UF Therapist Effectiveness
     Therapist Experience
     Therapist Personality
  N   ↓ Therapist Attitudes 1978
  R   Cross Cultural Treatment 1994
     Theoretical Orientation 1982
     Therapist Selection 1994
     ↓ Therapists 1967

Therapist Effectiveness
  Use Therapist Characteristics

Therapist Experience
  Use Therapist Characteristics

Therapist Patient Interaction
  Use Psychotherapeutic Processes

Therapist Patient Sexual Relations
  Use Professional Client Sexual Relations

Therapist Personality
  Use Therapist Characteristics

Therapist Role 1978
PN 1087   SC 52735
  B   Roles 1967
  R   Counselor Role 1973
     Psychotherapist Attitudes 1973
     ↓ Therapist Attitudes 1978

Therapist Selection 1994
PN 25   SC 52737
SN Motivational and judgmental processes involved in the decision to choose a particular therapist or counselor.
  UF Selection (Therapist)
  R   Choice Behavior 1967
     ↓ Client Attitudes 1982
     Patient Selection 1997
     ↓ Therapeutic Processes 1978

Therapist Selection — (cont'd)
  R   ↓ Therapist Characteristics 1973
     ↓ Therapists 1967
     ↓ Treatment 1967

Therapist Trainees 1973
PN 867   SC 52740
  UF Psychotherapist Trainees
  R   Counselor Trainees 1973
     ↓ Therapists 1967

Therapists 1967
PN 1773   SC 52750
SN Conceptually broad term referring to persons trained in the treatment of problems including mental disorders and behavior disorders. Use a more specific term if possible.
  B   Professional Personnel 1978
  N   Occupational Therapists 1973
     Physical Therapists 1973
     ↓ Psychotherapists 1973
     Speech Therapists 1973
  R   Clinicians 1973
     ↓ Counselors 1967
     ↓ Health Personnel 1994
     ↓ Mental Health Personnel 1967
     ↓ Social Workers 1973
     ↓ Therapist Characteristics 1973
     Therapist Selection 1994
     Therapist Trainees 1973

Therapy
  Use Treatment

Therapy (Drug)
  Use Drug Therapy

Thermal Acclimatization 1973
PN 57   SC 52830
SN Adjustment to ambient temperature ranges that may be different from the organism's typical experience or that may be typical but cyclical in nature (e.g., seasonal changes in temperature). Compare THERMOREGULATION (BODY).
  UF Acclimatization (Thermal)
  B   Adaptation 1967
     Physiology 1967
  R   Atmospheric Conditions 1973
     Environmental Stress 1973
     Physiological Stress 1967
     ↓ Temperature Effects 1967
     Thermoregulation (Body) 1973

Thermal Factors
  Use Temperature Effects

Thermoreceptors 1973
PN 40   SC 52840
  B   Nerve Endings 1973
     Neural Receptors 1973
     Sensory Neurons 1973

Thermoregulation (Body) 1973
PN 589   SC 52850
SN Homeostatic behavioral or physiological responses that maintain body temperature within a viable range. Compare THERMAL ACCLIMATIZATION.
  B   Body Temperature 1973
  R   Hyperthermia 1973
     Hypothermia 1973
     ↓ Metabolism 1967
     Thermal Acclimatization 1973

Theta Rhythm 1973
PN 296   SC 52860
SN Electrically measured impulses or waves of low amplitude and a frequency of 4-7 cycles per second observable in the electroencephalogram during stage 1 sleep.
  B   Electrical Activity 1967
     Electroencephalography 1967

Thigh 1973
PN 8   SC 52870
  B   Anatomy 1967
  R   Leg (Anatomy) 1973

Thinking 1967
PN 4056   SC 52880
SN Cognitive process involved in the manipulation of concepts and ideas.
  B   Cognitive Processes 1967
  N   ↓ Abstraction 1967
     Autistic Thinking 1973
     Divergent Thinking 1973
     Logical Thinking 1967
     Magical Thinking 1973
     ↓ Reasoning 1967
  R   Intelligence 1967

Thiopental 1973
PN 33   SC 52890
  UF Pentothal
  B   Barbiturates 1967
     General Anesthetics 1973
     Hypnotic Drugs 1973
     Sedatives 1973

Thioridazine 1973
PN 315   SC 52900
  UF Mellaril
  B   Phenothiazine Derivatives 1973

Thiothixene 1973
PN 103   SC 52910
  B   Tranquilizing Drugs 1967

Third World Countries
  Use Developing Countries

Thirst 1967
PN 268   SC 52920
  B   Motivation 1967
  R   Animal Drinking Behavior 1973
     ↓ Drinking Behavior 1978
     ↓ Fluid Intake 1985
     Water Deprivation 1967

Thoracic Nerves
  Use Spinal Nerves

Thorax 1973
PN 115   SC 52960
  UF Chest
  B   Musculoskeletal System 1973
     Respiratory System 1973
  R   Diaphragm (Anatomy) 1973

Thorazine
  Use Chlorpromazine

Thought Content
  Use Cognitions

Thought Control
Use　Brainwashing

Thought Disturbances 1973
PN 1037　　　　　　　　　　**SC** 52980
SN　Disturbances of thinking that affect thought content, language, and/or communication marked by delusions, incoherence, and profound loosening of associations.
N　Autistic Thinking 1973
　　Confabulation 1973
　　Delusions 1967
　　Fantasies (Thought Disturbances) 1967
　　Fragmentation (Schizophrenia) 1973
　　Judgment Disturbances 1973
　　Magical Thinking 1973
　　↓ Memory Disorders 1973
　　Obsessions 1967
　　Perseveration 1967
R　Mental Confusion 1973
　　↓ Mental Disorders 1967
　　Rumination (Cognitive Process) 2001

Threat 1967
PN 1768　　　　　　　　　　**SC** 52990
R　Coercion 1994
　　↓ Harassment 2001
　　↓ Punishment 1967
　　Threat Postures 1973

Threat Postures 1973
PN 99　　　　　　　　　　　**SC** 53000
B　Animal Aggressive Behavior 1973
　　Animal Defensive Behavior 1982
R　Animal Predatory Behavior 1978
　　Threat 1967

Threshold Determination 1973
PN 392　　　　　　　　　　**SC** 53010
SN　Methods and apparatus used in the measurement of both absolute and difference thresholds for any sensory modality.
R　↓ Psychophysical Measurement 1967
　　Signal Detection (Perception) 1967
　　↓ Thresholds 1967

Thresholds 1967
PN 1392　　　　　　　　　　**SC** 53020
SN　The minimal level (e.g., intensity) of stimulation, the minimal difference between any stimuli, or the minimal stimulus change that is perceptually detectable or to which a sensory receptor or other neuron will respond. Compare SIGNAL DETECTION (PERCEPTION).
UF　Differential Limen
　　Limen
N　Auditory Thresholds 1973
　　Olfactory Thresholds 1973
　　Pain Thresholds 1973
　　↓ Sensory Adaptation 1967
　　Vibrotactile Thresholds 1973
　　↓ Visual Thresholds 1973
R　↓ Perceptual Measures 1973
　　Threshold Determination 1973

Thromboses 1973
PN 39　　　　　　　　　　　**SC** 53040
B　Cardiovascular Disorders 1967
N　Coronary Thromboses 1973
R　Embolisms 1973

Thumb 1973
PN 22　　　　　　　　　　　**SC** 53050

Thumb — (cont'd)
B　Fingers (Anatomy) 1973

Thumbsucking 1973
PN 69　　　　　　　　　　　**SC** 53060
B　Habits 1967
R　↓ Behavior Disorders 1971

Thymoleptic Drugs
Use　Tranquilizing Drugs

Thyroid Disorders 1973
PN 170　　　　　　　　　　**SC** 53090
B　Endocrine Disorders 1973
N　Goiters 1973
　　Hyperthyroidism 1973
　　Hypothyroidism 1973
　　Thyrotoxicosis 1973
R　↓ Endocrine Sexual Disorders 1973
　　↓ Pituitary Disorders 1973

Thyroid Extract
SN　Term was discontinued in 1997. In 2000, the term was stripped from all records containing it, and replaced with THYROID HORMONES, its postable counterpart.
Use　Thyroid Hormones

Thyroid Gland 1973
PN 107　　　　　　　　　　**SC** 53110
B　Endocrine Glands 1973

Thyroid Hormones 1973
PN 307　　　　　　　　　　**SC** 53120
SN　In 1997, this term replaced the discontinued term THYROID EXTRACT. In 2000, THYROID EXTRACT was stripped from all records and replaced with THYROID HORMONES.
UF　Thyroid Extract
B　Hormones 1967
N　Thyroxine 1973
　　Triiodothyronine 1973

Thyroid Stimulating Hormone
Use　Thyrotropin

Thyroidectomy 1973
PN 31　　　　　　　　　　　**SC** 53140
B　Endocrine Gland Surgery 1973

Thyrotoxicosis 1973
PN 32　　　　　　　　　　　**SC** 53150
B　Thyroid Disorders 1973
　　Toxic Disorders 1973
R　↓ Encephalopathies 1982
　　Hyperthyroidism 1973
　　Toxic Psychoses 1973

Thyrotropic Hormone
Use　Thyrotropin

Thyrotropin 1973
PN 790　　　　　　　　　　**SC** 53170
UF　Thyroid Stimulating Hormone
　　Thyrotropic Hormone
B　Pituitary Hormones 1973
R　Hypothyroidism 1973

Thyroxine 1973
PN 228　　　　　　　　　　**SC** 53180
B　Thyroid Hormones 1973
R　Hypothyroidism 1973

Tic Douloureux
Use　Trigeminal Neuralgia

Tics 1973
PN 451　　　　　　　　　　**SC** 53200
B　Movement Disorders 1985
　　Symptoms 1967

Tigers
Use　Felids

Time 1967
PN 4568　　　　　　　　　　**SC** 53210
SN　Continuum in which events or experiences are expressed in terms of the past, the present, and the future. For effects of time-of-day or season consider also SEASONAL VARIATIONS and BIOLOGICAL RHYTHMS or their associated terms.
N　Interresponse Time 1973
R　Future 1991
　　Time Disorientation 1973
　　Time Management 1994
　　↓ Time Perception 1967
　　Time Perspective 1978
　　Trends 1991

Time Disorientation 1973
PN 88　　　　　　　　　　　**SC** 53230
UF　Disorientation (Time)
B　Consciousness Disturbances 1973
R　↓ Time 1967

Time Estimation 1967
PN 1013　　　　　　　　　　**SC** 53240
SN　Estimation of duration or passage of time.
B　Estimation 1967
　　Time Perception 1967
R　Time Management 1994

Time Limited Psychotherapy
Use　Brief Psychotherapy

Time Management 1994
PN 156　　　　　　　　　　**SC** 51435
B　Management 1967
R　↓ Learning Strategies 1991
　　↓ Self Management 1985
　　Study Habits 1973
　　↓ Time 1967
　　Time Estimation 1967
　　Time On Task 1988
　　↓ Time Perception 1967
　　Time Perspective 1978

Time On Task 1988
PN 499　　　　　　　　　　**SC** 53244
SN　Period of active involvement in a learning or production activity.
R　↓ Attention 1967
　　↓ Learning 1967
　　Time Management 1994

Time Out 1985
PN 166　　　　　　　　　　**SC** 53245
SN　Removal of the availability of gratification and reinforcement for any behavior following the occurrence of an undesired response. Has application in therapeutic, experimental, educational, and childrearing contexts.
B　Behavior Modification 1973
　　Operant Conditioning 1967
R　Omission Training 1985

Time Perception ¹⁹⁶⁷

PN 1921   **SC** 53250
SN Perception of duration, simultaneity, or succession in the passage of time. Prior to the introduction of TIME PERSPECTIVE in 1978, TIME PERCEPTION was used for this concept also.
B   Perception ¹⁹⁶⁷
N   Time Estimation ¹⁹⁶⁷
R   Tempo ¹⁹⁹⁷
     ↓ Time ¹⁹⁶⁷
     Time Management ¹⁹⁹⁴
     Time Perspective ¹⁹⁷⁸

Time Perspective ¹⁹⁷⁸

PN 907   **SC** 53255
SN Mental representation of temporal relationships or the capacity to remember events in their actual chronology. Also, one's outlook on the past, present, and/or future in relation to subjective qualities of time passage. To access references prior to 1978 use TIME PERCEPTION.
R   ↓ Perceptual Orientation ¹⁹⁷³
     ↓ Time ¹⁹⁶⁷
     Time Management ¹⁹⁹⁴
     ↓ Time Perception ¹⁹⁶⁷

Time Series ¹⁹⁸⁵

PN 342   **SC** 53257
SN A set of observational data ordered in time, typically with observations made at regular intervals.
B   Statistical Analysis ¹⁹⁶⁷
R   Statistical Data ¹⁹⁸²
     ↓ Stochastic Modeling ¹⁹⁷³

Timers (Apparatus) ¹⁹⁷³

PN 48   **SC** 53260
B   Apparatus ¹⁹⁶⁷

Timidity ¹⁹⁷³

PN 507   **SC** 53270
UF   Shyness
B   Personality Traits ¹⁹⁶⁷

Tinnitus ¹⁹⁷³

PN 162   **SC** 53280
B   Ear Disorders ¹⁹⁷³

Tiredness
Use Fatigue

Tissue Donation ¹⁹⁹¹

PN 225   **SC** 53295
SN Donation of organs, blood, sperm, or other tissues for medical use.
UF   Blood Donation
     Organ Donation
     Sperm Donation
R   Blood Transfusion ¹⁹⁷³
     Charitable Behavior ¹⁹⁷³
     Neural Transplantation ¹⁹⁸⁵
     Organ Transplantation ¹⁹⁷³

Tissues (Body) ¹⁹⁷³

PN 145   **SC** 53300
B   Anatomy ¹⁹⁶⁷
N   Bone Marrow ¹⁹⁷³
     ↓ Connective Tissues ¹⁹⁷³
     ↓ Membranes ¹⁹⁷³
     ↓ Nerve Tissues ¹⁹⁷³
     Skin (Anatomy) ¹⁹⁶⁷
R   Histology ¹⁹⁷³
     ↓ Muscles ¹⁹⁶⁷

Toads ¹⁹⁷³

PN 186   **SC** 53320
B   Amphibia ¹⁹⁷³
R   Larvae ¹⁹⁷³

Tobacco (Drug)
Use Nicotine

Tobacco (Smokeless)
Use Smokeless Tobacco

Tobacco Smoking ¹⁹⁶⁷

PN 6718   **SC** 53340
UF   Cigarette Smoking
     Smoking (Tobacco)
B   Drug Usage ¹⁹⁷¹
     Habits ¹⁹⁶⁷
R   Carcinogens ¹⁹⁷³
     Nicotine ¹⁹⁷³
     Nicotine Withdrawal ¹⁹⁹⁷
     Prenatal Exposure ¹⁹⁹¹
     Smokeless Tobacco ¹⁹⁹⁴
     Smoking Cessation ¹⁹⁸⁸

Toes (Anatomy)
Use Feet (Anatomy)

Tofranil
Use Imipramine

Toilet Training ¹⁹⁷³

PN 121   **SC** 53400
B   Childrearing Practices ¹⁹⁶⁷

Token Economy Programs ¹⁹⁷³

PN 650   **SC** 53410
SN Group treatment based on operant conditioning in which elements in a patient's environment are arranged so that reinforcement is made contingent on the patient's behavior. When the desired behavior occurs, a token is given which may be exchanged for a reinforcing agent (e.g., goods or services).
B   Contingency Management ¹⁹⁷³
R   ↓ Psychiatric Hospital Programs ¹⁹⁶⁷
     Response Cost ¹⁹⁹⁷

Token Reinforcement
Use Secondary Reinforcement

Tolerance ¹⁹⁷³

PN 397   **SC** 53440
B   Personality Traits ¹⁹⁶⁷
N   Tolerance for Ambiguity ¹⁹⁶⁷
R   Agreeableness ¹⁹⁹⁷
     Openness to Experience ¹⁹⁹⁷
     Social Acceptance ¹⁹⁶⁷

Tolerance (Drug)
Use Drug Tolerance

Tolerance for Ambiguity ¹⁹⁶⁷

PN 422   **SC** 53460
SN Willingness to accept situations having conflicting or multiple interpretations or outcomes.
UF   Ambiguity (Tolerance)
B   Tolerance ¹⁹⁷³

Toluene ¹⁹⁹¹

PN 38   **SC** 53465
B   Solvents ¹⁹⁸²

Tomography ¹⁹⁸⁸

PN 2043   **SC** 53470
UF   CAT Scan
     Positron Emission Tomography
B   Medical Diagnosis ¹⁹⁷³
N   Magnetic Resonance Imaging ¹⁹⁹⁴
R   Computer Assisted Diagnosis ¹⁹⁷³
     ↓ Roentgenography ¹⁹⁷³

Tone (Frequency)
Use Pitch (Frequency)

Tongue ¹⁹⁷³

PN 354   **SC** 53490
B   Digestive System ¹⁹⁶⁷
N   Taste Buds ¹⁹⁷³
R   Mouth (Anatomy) ¹⁹⁶⁷
     Taste Disorders ²⁰⁰¹

Tonic Immobility ¹⁹⁷⁸

PN 338   **SC** 53495
SN Adaptive escape or alarm response in certain species in which the animal adopts a motionless posture as if feigning death.
B   Motor Processes ¹⁹⁶⁷
R   Alarm Responses ¹⁹⁷³
     ↓ Animal Defensive Behavior ¹⁹⁸²

Tool Use ¹⁹⁹¹

PN 183   **SC** 53497
SN Used for human or animal populations.
UF   Animal Tool Use
B   Motor Processes ¹⁹⁶⁷
R   ↓ Animal Ethology ¹⁹⁶⁷

Top Level Managers ¹⁹⁷³

PN 1388   **SC** 53500
SN Executives in business or industry who are responsible for the major strategic and policy decisions.
UF   Executives
B   Management Personnel ¹⁹⁷³
R   Middle Level Managers ¹⁹⁷³

Topography ¹⁹⁷³

PN 161   **SC** 53510
UF   Landscapes
B   Ecological Factors ¹⁹⁷³

Torticollis ¹⁹⁷³

PN 82   **SC** 53520
UF   Wryneck
B   Movement Disorders ¹⁹⁸⁵
     Muscular Disorders ¹⁹⁷³

Tortoises
Use Turtles

Torture ¹⁹⁸⁸

PN 250   **SC** 53535
B   Antisocial Behavior ¹⁹⁷¹
R   ↓ Aggressive Behavior ¹⁹⁶⁷
     Coercion ¹⁹⁹⁴
     Persecution ¹⁹⁷³
     Suffering ¹⁹⁷³
     Victimization ¹⁹⁷³
     ↓ Violence ¹⁹⁷³

Totalitarianism ¹⁹⁷³

PN 57   **SC** 53540
B   Political Economic Systems ¹⁹⁷³

Touch
Use Tactual Perception

Touching
Use Physical Contact

Tourette Syndrome
Use Gilles de la Tourette Disorder

Towns 1973
PN 66   **SC** 53560
B Social Environments 1973

Toxic Disorders 1973
PN 431   **SC** 53570
UF Intoxication
Poisoning
B Physical Disorders 1997
N Acute Alcoholic Intoxication 1973
Barbiturate Poisoning 1973
Carbon Monoxide Poisoning 1973
↓ Drug Induced Congenital Disorders 1973
Lead Poisoning 1973
Mercury Poisoning 1973
Narcosis 1973
Neuroleptic Malignant Syndrome 1988
Thyrotoxicosis 1973
Toxic Encephalopathies 1973
Toxic Hepatitis 1973
Toxic Psychoses 1973
R ↓ Alcohol Intoxication 1973
↓ Alcoholism 1967
↓ Dermatitis 1973
↓ Digestive System Disorders 1973
↓ Gastrointestinal Disorders 1973
Hyponatremia 1997
↓ Liver Disorders 1973
↓ Mental Disorders 1967
↓ Neurotoxins 1982
Toxicity 1973
Toxicomania 1973

Toxic Encephalopathies 1973
PN 94   **SC** 53580
B Encephalopathies 1982
Toxic Disorders 1973
R Acute Alcoholic Intoxication 1973
Chronic Alcoholic Intoxication 1973
Toxic Psychoses 1973

Toxic Hepatitis 1973
PN 7   **SC** 53590
B Hepatitis 1973
Toxic Disorders 1973

Toxic Psychoses 1973
PN 139   **SC** 53600
SN Psychotic states or conditions resulting from ingestion of toxic agents or by the presence of toxins within the body. Compare EXPERIMENTAL PSY-CHOSIS.
B Organic Brain Syndromes 1973
Psychosis 1967
Toxic Disorders 1973
R ↓ Alcohol Intoxication 1973
↓ Alcoholic Psychosis 1973
Thyrotoxicosis 1973
Toxic Encephalopathies 1973

Toxic Waste
Use Hazardous Materials

Toxicity 1973
PN 918   **SC** 53610
R ↓ Drugs 1967
↓ Hazardous Materials 1991
↓ Neurotoxins 1982
Teratogens 1988
↓ Toxic Disorders 1973

Toxicomania 1973
PN 16   **SC** 53620
R Pica 1973
↓ Toxic Disorders 1973

Toxins
Use Poisons

Toy Selection 1973
PN 199   **SC** 53650
R Childhood Play Behavior 1978
↓ Toys 1973

Toys 1973
PN 424   **SC** 53660
N Anatomically Detailed Dolls 1991
Educational Toys 1973
R Childhood Play Behavior 1978
Childrens Recreational Games 1973
Computer Games 1988
↓ Games 1967
↓ Recreation 1967
Toy Selection 1973

Trachea 1973
PN 39   **SC** 53680
B Respiratory System 1973

Tracking 1967
PN 505   **SC** 53700
SN Following the movement of a moving stimulus or the contours (or shape) of a stationary target by means of direct physical contact or through any sensory modality. Used for human or animal populations.
B Perceptual Motor Processes 1967
N Rotary Pursuit 1967
Visual Tracking 1973
R ↓ Attention 1967
↓ Monitoring 1973
Motor Skills 1973
↓ Perceptual Localization 1967
↓ Perceptual Motor Learning 1967

Tractotomy 1973
PN 21   **SC** 53710
B Neurosurgery 1973
R ↓ Psychosurgery 1973
Pyramidotomy 1973

Traditionalism
Use Conservatism

Traffic Accidents (Motor)
Use Motor Traffic Accidents

Trainable Mentally Retarded
SN In 2000, the term was discontinued, and all records containing it were stripped of the term and replaced with MODERATE MENTAL RETARDA-TION, its postable counterpart.
Use Moderate Mental Retardation

Training
Use Education

Training (Athletic)
Use Athletic Training

Training (Clinical Methods)
Use Clinical Methods Training

Training (Clinical Psychology Grad)
Use Clinical Psychology Graduate Training

Training (Community Mental Health)
Use Community Mental Health Training

Training (Graduate Psychology)
Use Graduate Psychology Education

Training (Mental Health Inservice)
Use Mental Health Inservice Training

Training (Motivation)
Use Motivation Training

Training (Personnel)
Use Personnel Training

Training (Psychiatric)
Use Psychiatric Training

Training (Psychoanalytic)
Use Psychoanalytic Training

Training (Psychotherapy)
Use Psychotherapy Training

Trains (Railroad)
Use Railroad Trains

Tranquilizing Drugs 1967
PN 2161   **SC** 53900
UF Antianxiety Drugs
Anxiety Reducing Drugs
Anxiolytic Drugs
Ataractic Drugs
Ataraxic Drugs
Thymoleptic Drugs
B Drugs 1967
N Amitriptyline 1973
Benactyzine 1973
Doxepin 1994
Haloperidol 1973
Meprobamate 1973
↓ Minor Tranquilizers 1973
↓ Neuroleptic Drugs 1973
↓ Phenothiazine Derivatives 1973
Pimozide 1973
Thiothixene 1973
R ↓ Anticonvulsive Drugs 1973
↓ Antiemetic Drugs 1973
↓ Antihypertensive Drugs 1973
↓ Benzodiazepines 1978
↓ Dopamine Antagonists 1982
↓ Muscle Relaxing Drugs 1973
↓ Narcotic Drugs 1973
↓ Sedatives 1973

Transactional Analysis 1973
PN 979   **SC** 53910
SN Type of psychotherapy developed by E. Berne based on the theory that all interactions between individuals reflect the inner relationships of the "Parent", "Adult", and "Child" ego states.
B Human Potential Movement 1982
Psychotherapy 1967

Transactional Analysis — (cont'd)
R   ↓ Group Psychotherapy   1967
     ↓ Psychoanalysis   1967

Transaminases   1973
PN 31   SC 53920
UF   Aminotransferases
B   Transferases   1973

Transcultural Psychiatry   1973
PN 401   SC 53930
SN   Comparative study of mental illness and mental health among various societies or cultures, including epidemiology and symptomatology.
UF   Comparative Psychiatry
     Cultural Psychiatry
B   Psychiatry   1967
R   ↓ Alternative Medicine   1997
     Cross Cultural Psychology   1997
     Cross Cultural Treatment   1994
     Ethnology   1967
     ↓ Ethnospecific Disorders   1973
     Folk Medicine   1973
     Folk Psychology   1997
     Myths   1967
     Shamanism   1973
     Taboos   1973

Transducers   1973
PN 26   SC 53940
B   Apparatus   1967

Transfer (Learning)   1967
PN 3132   SC 53950
SN   Effect of previous learning on the acquisition of new material or skills as a function of the relative similarity between the prior and current learning situations. Compare GENERALIZATION (LEARNING).
B   Learning   1967
N   Negative Transfer   1973
     Positive Transfer   1973
R   ↓ Generalization (Learning)   1982

Transfer Students   1973
PN 156   SC 53955
SN   Students transferring from one school or educational program to another.
B   Students   1967
R   Grade Level   1994

Transferases   1973
PN 281   SC 53960
B   Enzymes   1973
N   Transaminases   1973

Transference (Psychotherapeutic)
   Use   Psychotherapeutic Transference

Transformational Generative
     Grammar   1973
PN 104   SC 53980
SN   Transformational grammar relates the deep syntactic structures of a language to the surface structures by means of transformational rules. Generative grammar represents, through abstract formulas, all and only the grammatical utterances of a language.
B   Grammar   1967
R   ↓ Syntax   1971

Transfusion (Blood)
   Use   Blood Transfusion

Transgendered
   Use   Transsexualism

Transgenerational Patterns   1991
PN 600   SC 54005
SN   Patterns of behavior, for example, pregnancy in adolescence, drug abuse, or child abuse, that appear in successive generations.
UF   Intergenerational Transmission
R   ↓ Family   1967
     ↓ Family Relations   1967
     Family Resemblance   1991
     Generation Gap   1973
     Intergenerational Relations   1988
     ↓ Parent Child Relations   1967
     Trends   1991

Transistors (Apparatus)
SN   Term was discontinued in 1997. In 2000, the term was stripped from all records containing it, and replaced with APPARATUS, its postable counterpart.
   Use   Apparatus

Transitional Objects   1985
PN 231   SC 54015
SN   Psychoanalytic concept referring to any material object having a special value that serves an anxiety-reducing function. Such attachment is a normal phenomenon during transition from one phase to another in separation-individuation.
R   ↓ Childhood Development   1967
     Object Relations   1982
     Separation Individuation   1982

Translocation (Chromosome)   1973
PN 33   SC 54020
B   Chromosome Disorders   1973
R   ↓ Genetics   1967
     Mutations   1973

Transpersonal Psychology   1988
PN 323   SC 54025
SN   Subdiscipline of humanistic psychology which studies higher states of consciousness and transcendental experiences.
B   Humanistic Psychology   1985

Transplants (Organ)
   Use   Organ Transplantation

Transportation   1973
PN 159   SC 54040
N   Air Transportation   1973
     ↓ Ground Transportation   1973
     Public Transportation   1973
     ↓ Water Transportation   1973
R   Commuting (Travel)   1985
     ↓ Transportation Accidents   1973

Transportation Accidents   1973
PN 157   SC 54050
B   Accidents   1967
N   Air Traffic Accidents   1973
     Motor Traffic Accidents   1973
R   Accident Prevention   1973
     Air Traffic Control   1973
     ↓ Aviation Safety   1973
     Highway Safety   1973
     Safety Belts   1973
     ↓ Transportation   1973

Transposition (Cognition)   1973
PN 46   SC 54060

Transposition (Cognition) — (cont'd)
SN   Condition in learning in which subjects react to relationships between stimuli rather than to each stimulus itself.
B   Cognitive Processes   1967

Transracial Adoption
   Use   Interracial Adoption

Transsexualism   1973
PN 719   SC 54070
SN   The urge to belong to the opposite sex that may include surgical procedures to modify the sex organs in order to appear as the opposite sex.
UF   Transgendered
B   Gender Identity   1985
     Gender Identity Disorder   1997
     Psychosexual Behavior   1967
R   Bisexuality   1973
     ↓ Homosexuality   1967
     Sex Change   1988
     Transvestism   1973

Transvestism   1973
PN 215   SC 54080
SN   The act of dressing like and adopting the behavior of the opposite sex, often for sexual gratification.
B   Paraphilias   1988
     Psychosexual Behavior   1967
R   Bisexuality   1973
     Fetishism   1973
     ↓ Gender Identity Disorder   1997
     ↓ Homosexuality   1967
     Transsexualism   1973

Tranylcypromine   1973
PN 176   SC 54090
B   Antidepressant Drugs   1971
     Monoamine Oxidase Inhibitors   1973

Trauma (Emotional)
   Use   Emotional Trauma

Trauma (Physical)
   Use   Injuries

Traumatic Brain Injury   1997
PN 1223   SC 54115
SN   Brain injury resulting from an accident, surgery, or other trauma. Consider BRAIN DAMAGE or BRAIN DAMAGED to access references prior to 1997.
UF   Brain Injury (Traumatic)
B   Brain Damage   1967
R   ↓ Head Injuries   1973
     ↓ Neuropsychological Assessment   1982

Traumatic Neurosis   1973
PN 152   SC 54130
SN   Use TRAUMATIC NEUROSIS or STRESS REACTIONS to access references to POSTTRAUMATIC STRESS DISORDER from 1973-1984.
B   Neurosis   1967
R   Posttraumatic Stress Disorder   1985

Traumatic Psychosis
   Use   Reactive Psychosis

Traveling   1973
PN 290   SC 54150
B   Recreation   1967
R   Commuting (Travel)   1985
     Vacationing   1973

Trazodone ¹⁹⁸⁸
PN 222   **SC** 54152
 B Antidepressant Drugs ¹⁹⁷¹
    Piperazines ¹⁹⁹⁴

Treatment ¹⁹⁶⁷
PN 21436   **SC** 54190
SN Conceptually broad term referring to psychological or physical measures designed to ameliorate or cure an abnormal or undesirable condition. Use a more specific term if possible.
 UF Therapy
 N Aftercare ¹⁹⁷³
  ↓ Alternative Medicine ¹⁹⁹⁷
  ↓ Behavior Modification ¹⁹⁷³
   Bibliotherapy ¹⁹⁷³
  ↓ Cognitive Techniques ¹⁹⁸⁵
  ↓ Creative Arts Therapy ¹⁹⁹⁴
  ↓ Crisis Intervention ¹⁹⁷³
  ↓ Crisis Intervention Services ¹⁹⁷³
   Cross Cultural Treatment ¹⁹⁹⁴
  ↓ Health Care Services ¹⁹⁷⁸
   Interdisciplinary Treatment Approach ¹⁹⁷³
   Involuntary Treatment ¹⁹⁹⁴
   Life Sustaining Treatment ¹⁹⁹⁷
   Medical Treatment (General) ¹⁹⁷³
   Milieu Therapy ¹⁹⁸⁸
   Movement Therapy ¹⁹⁹⁷
   Multimodal Treatment Approach ¹⁹⁹¹
  ↓ Outpatient Treatment ¹⁹⁶⁷
   Pain Management ¹⁹⁹⁴
   Partial Hospitalization ¹⁹⁸⁵
   Personal Therapy ¹⁹⁹¹
  ↓ Physical Treatment Methods ¹⁹⁷³
   Preventive Medicine ¹⁹⁷³
  ↓ Psychotherapeutic Techniques ¹⁹⁶⁷
  ↓ Psychotherapy ¹⁹⁶⁷
  ↓ Rehabilitation ¹⁹⁶⁷
  ↓ Relaxation Therapy ¹⁹⁷⁸
   Sex Therapy ¹⁹⁷⁸
   Social Casework ¹⁹⁶⁷
   Sociotherapy ¹⁹⁷³
   Speech Therapy ¹⁹⁶⁷
   Treatment Guidelines ²⁰⁰¹
 R Caregivers ¹⁹⁸⁸
  ↓ Case Management ¹⁹⁹¹
  ↓ Client Rights ¹⁹⁸⁸
   Client Transfer ¹⁹⁹⁷
   Client Treatment Matching ¹⁹⁹⁷
  ↓ Clinics ¹⁹⁶⁷
   Cost Containment ¹⁹⁹¹
  ↓ Counseling ¹⁹⁶⁷
   Court Referrals ¹⁹⁹⁴
   Death Education ¹⁹⁸²
   Early Intervention ¹⁹⁸²
   Euthanasia ¹⁹⁷³
   Health Care Costs ¹⁹⁹⁴
  ↓ Health Care Delivery ¹⁹⁷⁸
   Health Care Seeking Behavior ¹⁹⁹⁷
   Life Review ¹⁹⁹¹
  ↓ Medical Records ¹⁹⁷⁸
   Mental Health Program Evaluation ¹⁹⁷³
   Patient Abuse ¹⁹⁹¹
   Patient History ¹⁹⁷³
   Physical Restraint ¹⁹⁸²
   Posttreatment Followup ¹⁹⁷³
   Prescribing (Drugs) ¹⁹⁹¹
  ↓ Prevention ¹⁹⁷³
   Prognosis ¹⁹⁷³
  ↓ Psychiatry ¹⁹⁶⁷
   Psychoeducation ¹⁹⁹⁴
   Psychosocial Readjustment ¹⁹⁷³
   Quality of Care ¹⁹⁸⁸
   Relapse Prevention ¹⁹⁹⁴

Treatment — (cont'd)
 R ↓ Self Help Techniques ¹⁹⁸²
   Sensory Integration ¹⁹⁹¹
   Shamanism ¹⁹⁷³
  ↓ Side Effects (Treatment) ¹⁹⁸⁸
   Spontaneous Remission ¹⁹⁷³
   Stress Management ¹⁹⁸⁵
   Therapeutic Alliance ¹⁹⁹⁴
  ↓ Therapeutic Processes ¹⁹⁷⁸
   Therapeutic Social Clubs ¹⁹⁷³
   Therapist Selection ¹⁹⁹⁴
   Treatment Compliance ¹⁹⁸²
  ↓ Treatment Duration ¹⁹⁸⁸
   Treatment Effectiveness Evaluation ¹⁹⁷³
  ↓ Treatment Facilities ¹⁹⁷³
  ↓ Treatment Outcomes ¹⁹⁸²
  ↓ Treatment Planning ¹⁹⁹⁷
  ↓ Treatment Resistant Disorders ¹⁹⁹⁴
   Treatment Termination ¹⁹⁸²
   Treatment Withholding ¹⁹⁸⁸
  ↓ Twelve Step Programs ¹⁹⁹⁷

Treatment Client Matching
 Use Client Treatment Matching

Treatment Compliance ¹⁹⁸²
PN 3715   **SC** 54153
SN Adherence by a patient or client to professional advice or a systematic plan of treatment.
 UF Client Compliance
    Medical Regimen Compliance
 B Compliance ¹⁹⁷³
 R ↓ Client Attitudes ¹⁹⁸²
   Client Education ¹⁹⁸⁵
   Client Participation ¹⁹⁹⁷
  ↓ Client Rights ¹⁹⁸⁸
   Illness Behavior ¹⁹⁸²
   Informed Consent ¹⁹⁸⁵
   Involuntary Treatment ¹⁹⁹⁴
  ↓ Treatment ¹⁹⁶⁷
   Treatment Dropouts ¹⁹⁷⁸
  ↓ Treatment Duration ¹⁹⁸⁸
   Treatment Refusal ¹⁹⁹⁴
   Treatment Withholding ¹⁹⁸⁸

Treatment Dropouts ¹⁹⁷⁸
PN 1155   **SC** 54155
SN Persons who drop out of treatment, or discontinuation of treatment without the consent of the person in charge of treatment or before scheduled termination. Compare TREATMENT TERMINATION.
 UF Client Dropouts
    Patient Dropouts
 B Dropouts ¹⁹⁷³
 R Involuntary Treatment ¹⁹⁹⁴
   Psychotherapeutic Outcomes ¹⁹⁷³
   Treatment Compliance ¹⁹⁸²
  ↓ Treatment Duration ¹⁹⁸⁸
  ↓ Treatment Outcomes ¹⁹⁸²
   Treatment Refusal ¹⁹⁹⁴
   Treatment Termination ¹⁹⁸²

Treatment Duration ¹⁹⁸⁸
PN 1511   **SC** 54157
SN Length of hospital or institutional stay and length or number of treatment or therapy sessions. Used for any treatment modality.
 UF Length of Stay
 N Long Term Care ¹⁹⁹⁴
 R ↓ Case Management ¹⁹⁹¹
   Maintenance Therapy ¹⁹⁹⁷
  ↓ Treatment ¹⁹⁶⁷
   Treatment Compliance ¹⁹⁸²
   Treatment Dropouts ¹⁹⁷⁸

Treatment Duration — (cont'd)
 R ↓ Treatment Outcomes ¹⁹⁸²
  ↓ Treatment Planning ¹⁹⁹⁷
   Treatment Termination ¹⁹⁸²

Treatment Effectiveness Evaluation ¹⁹⁷³
PN 4360   **SC** 54160
SN Methodology or procedures for assessment of treatment success in relation to previously established goals or other criteria. Also used for formal evaluations themselves. For effectiveness of particular treatment modes, use the specific type of treatment (e.g., DRUG THERAPY). For efficacy of treatment for a particular disorder, use the specific disorder (e.g., MANIA) and the specific type of treatment.
 UF Evaluation (Treatment Effectiveness)
 B Evaluation ¹⁹⁶⁷
 R Mental Health Program Evaluation ¹⁹⁷³
    Psychotherapeutic Outcomes ¹⁹⁷³
  ↓ Treatment ¹⁹⁶⁷
  ↓ Treatment Outcomes ¹⁹⁸²

Treatment Environment
 Use Therapeutic Environment

Treatment Facilities ¹⁹⁷³
PN 430   **SC** 54170
 N ↓ Clinics ¹⁹⁶⁷
   Community Mental Health Centers ¹⁹⁷³
   Halfway Houses ¹⁹⁷³
  ↓ Hospitals ¹⁹⁶⁷
   Nursing Homes ¹⁹⁷³
   Therapeutic Camps ¹⁹⁷⁸
 R ↓ Crisis Intervention Services ¹⁹⁷³
  ↓ Facility Admission ¹⁹⁸⁸
  ↓ Facility Discharge ¹⁹⁸⁸
  ↓ Facility Environment ¹⁹⁸⁸
  ↓ Health Care Administration ¹⁹⁹⁷
   Institutional Schools ¹⁹⁷⁸
  ↓ Residential Care Institutions ¹⁹⁷³
  ↓ Therapeutic Environment ²⁰⁰¹
  ↓ Treatment ¹⁹⁶⁷

Treatment Guidelines ²⁰⁰¹
PN 0   **SC** 54175
 B Treatment ¹⁹⁶⁷
 R Client Treatment Matching ¹⁹⁹⁷
  ↓ Professional Standards ¹⁹⁷³
  ↓ Quality of Services ¹⁹⁹⁷
  ↓ Treatment Planning ¹⁹⁹⁷

Treatment Methods (Physical)
 Use Physical Treatment Methods

Treatment Outcomes ¹⁹⁸²
PN 6511   **SC** 54185
SN Limited to treatment results that are a function of unique or specifically-described circumstances or characteristics (e.g., race) of the clients/patients, the treatment provider, or the treatment itself. For effectiveness of particular treatment modes, use the specific type of treatment (e.g., DRUG THERAPY). For efficacy of treatment for a particular disorder, use the specific disorder (e.g., MANIA) and the specific type of treatment.
 UF Outcomes (Treatment)
    Therapeutic Outcomes
 N Psychotherapeutic Outcomes ¹⁹⁷³
 R Client Treatment Matching ¹⁹⁹⁷
    Mental Health Program Evaluation ¹⁹⁷³
    Postsurgical Complications ¹⁹⁷³
  ↓ Psychotherapeutic Processes ¹⁹⁶⁷
   Recovery (Disorders) ¹⁹⁷³

Treatment Outcomes — (cont'd)
- R   Relapse (Disorders) [1973]
-     Relapse Prevention [1994]
- ↓ Remission (Disorders) [1973]
- ↓ Side Effects (Treatment) [1988]
- ↓ Therapeutic Processes [1978]
- ↓ Treatment [1967]
-     Treatment Dropouts [1978]
- ↓ Treatment Duration [1988]
-     Treatment Effectiveness Evaluation [1973]
-     Treatment Termination [1982]

Treatment Planning [1997]
PN 510   SC 54189
- UF   Patient Care Planning
- N   Discharge Planning [1994]
- R   Aftercare [1973]
- ↓ Case Management [1991]
- ↓ Client Characteristics [1973]
-     Client Treatment Matching [1997]
-     Clinical Judgment (Not Diagnosis) [1973]
- ↓ Health Care Delivery [1978]
- ↓ Managed Care [1994]
-     Needs Assessment [1985]
-     Posttreatment Followup [1973]
- ↓ Treatment [1967]
- ↓ Treatment Duration [1988]
-     Treatment Guidelines [2001]

Treatment Refusal [1994]
PN 221   SC 54186
SN   Patient or client refusal of or resistance to medical, psychological, or psychiatric treatment. Consider TREATMENT WITHHOLDING for life sustaining contexts.
- UF   Refusal (Treatment)
- R   Advance Directives [1994]
-     Assisted Suicide [1997]
- ↓ Client Rights [1988]
-     Client Transfer [1997]
-     Informed Consent [1985]
-     Involuntary Treatment [1994]
-     Life Sustaining Treatment [1997]
-     Psychotherapeutic Resistance [1973]
- ↓ Resistance [1997]
-     Treatment Compliance [1982]
-     Treatment Dropouts [1978]
-     Treatment Termination [1982]
-     Treatment Withholding [1988]

Treatment Resistant Depression [1994]
PN 359   SC 57440
- UF   Tricyclic Resistant Depression
- B   Major Depression [1988]
-     Treatment Resistant Disorders [1994]
- R   ↓ Drug Therapy [1967]

Treatment Resistant Disorders [1994]
PN 614   SC 57445
SN   Used for any disorder that is resistant to any type of psychological or medical treatment.
- N   Treatment Resistant Depression [1994]
- R   ↓ Chronic Mental Illness [1997]
- ↓ Mental Disorders [1967]
- ↓ Physical Disorders [1997]
- ↓ Treatment [1967]

Treatment Seeking Behavior
- Use   Health Care Seeking Behavior

Treatment Termination [1982]
PN 926   SC 54187

Treatment Termination — (cont'd)
SN   Completion of medical or psychological/behavioral treatment programs. Compare TREATMENT DROPOUTS.
- R   Client Transfer [1997]
-     Discharge Planning [1994]
- ↓ Hospital Discharge [1973]
-     Psychiatric Hospital Discharge [1978]
- ↓ Therapeutic Processes [1978]
- ↓ Treatment [1967]
-     Treatment Dropouts [1978]
- ↓ Treatment Duration [1988]
- ↓ Treatment Outcomes [1982]
-     Treatment Refusal [1994]
-     Treatment Withholding [1988]

Treatment Withholding [1988]
PN 186   SC 54188
SN   Limiting or restricting medical treatment for seriously ill persons. Includes do-not-resuscitate orders. Compare TREATMENT TERMINATION.
- R   Advance Directives [1994]
-     Assisted Suicide [1997]
- ↓ Client Rights [1988]
- ↓ Death and Dying [1967]
-     Euthanasia [1973]
- ↓ Human Rights [1978]
-     Informed Consent [1985]
-     Life Sustaining Treatment [1997]
- ↓ Treatment [1967]
-     Treatment Compliance [1982]
-     Treatment Refusal [1994]
-     Treatment Termination [1982]

Tremor [1973]
PN 276   SC 54200
- B   Movement Disorders [1985]
-     Symptoms [1967]
- R   ↓ Antitremor Drugs [1973]
-     Parkinsonism [1994]
-     Parkinsons Disease [1973]

Trends [1991]
PN 1097   SC 54204
SN   Used specifically for analysis of past, present, or future patterns in technology, economics, and social or developmental processes.
- R   ↓ Fads and Fashions [1973]
-     Future [1991]
- ↓ History [1973]
-     Social Change [1967]
- ↓ Social Processes [1967]
- ↓ Time [1967]
-     Transgenerational Patterns [1991]

Triadic Therapy
- Use   Conjoint Therapy

Trial and Error Learning [1973]
PN 65   SC 54210
- B   Learning [1967]
-     Learning Strategies [1991]

Triazolam [1988]
PN 232   SC 54215
- UF   Halcion
- B   Hypnotic Drugs [1973]
-     Sedatives [1973]

Tribes [1973]
PN 525   SC 54220
- R   Alaska Natives [1997]
-     American Indians [1967]

Tribes — (cont'd)
- R   ↓ Racial and Ethnic Groups [2001]

Trichotillomania
- Use   Hair Pulling

Tricyclic Antidepressant Drugs [1997]
PN 208   SC 54226
- B   Antidepressant Drugs [1971]
- N   Amitriptyline [1973]
-     Chlorimipramine [1973]
-     Desipramine [1973]
-     Doxepin [1994]
-     Imipramine [1973]
-     Maprotiline [1982]
-     Nortriptyline [1994]
- R   ↓ Adrenergic Blocking Drugs [1973]
- ↓ Lithium [1973]
- ↓ Monoamine Oxidase Inhibitors [1973]

Tricyclic Resistant Depression
- Use   Treatment Resistant Depression

Trifluoperazine [1973]
PN 121   SC 54230
- UF   Stelazine
- B   Phenothiazine Derivatives [1973]

Triflupromazine
SN   Term discontinued in 1997. In 2000, the term was stripped from all records containing it, and replaced with PHENOTHIAZINE DERIVATIVES, its postable counterpart.
- Use   Phenothiazine Derivatives

Trigeminal Nerve [1973]
PN 184   SC 54250
- B   Cranial Nerves [1973]

Trigeminal Neuralgia [1973]
PN 47   SC 54260
- UF   Tic Douloureux
- B   Neuralgia [1973]

Trigonum Cerebrale
- Use   Fornix

Trihexyphenidyl [1973]
PN 60   SC 54270
- B   Alcohols [1967]
-     Amines [1973]
-     Antispasmodic Drugs [1973]
-     Antitremor Drugs [1973]
-     Cholinergic Blocking Drugs [1973]

Triiodothyronine [1973]
PN 140   SC 54280
- B   Thyroid Hormones [1973]

Triplets [1973]
PN 35   SC 54310
- B   Multiple Births [1973]

Trisomy [1973]
PN 66   SC 54320
- B   Chromosome Disorders [1973]
- N   Trisomy 21 [1973]

Trisomy 21 [1973]
PN 61   SC 54340
- B   Autosome Disorders [1973]
-     Trisomy [1973]

Trisomy 21 — (cont'd)
R   Downs Syndrome [1967]

Trochlear Nerve
Use   Cranial Nerves

Truancy [1973]
PN   85   SC   54360
N   School Truancy [1973]

Trucks
Use   Motor Vehicles

True False Tests
Use   Forced Choice (Testing Method)

Trust (Social Behavior) [1967]
PN   1368   SC   54370
B   Prosocial Behavior [1982]
R   Hope [1991]

Tryptamine [1973]
PN   105   SC   54380
B   Amines [1973]
    Vasoconstrictor Drugs [1973]

Tryptophan [1973]
PN   959   SC   54390
B   Amino Acids [1973]
    Serotonin Precursors [1978]
N   Hydroxytryptophan (5-) [1991]

Tubal Ligation [1973]
PN   47   SC   54400
B   Birth Control [1971]
    Sterilization (Sex) [1973]

Tuberculosis [1973]
PN   130   SC   54410
B   Bacterial Disorders [1973]
N   Pulmonary Tuberculosis [1973]
R   Addisons Disease [1973]
    ↓ Antitubercular Drugs [1973]
    Lupus [1973]
    ↓ Musculoskeletal Disorders [1973]
    ↓ Nervous System Disorders [1967]
    ↓ Skin Disorders [1973]

Tubocurarine [1973]
PN   15   SC   54420
B   Alkaloids [1973]
    Muscle Relaxing Drugs [1973]
R   Curare [1973]

Tumors
Use   Neoplasms

Tunnel Vision [1973]
PN   14   SC   54440
SN   Disorder characterized by severe limitation or total lack of peripheral vision.
B   Eye Disorders [1973]
R   ↓ Vision [1967]

Turners Syndrome [1973]
PN   142   SC   54460
B   Hypogonadism [1973]
    Neonatal Disorders [1973]
    Sex Linked Hereditary Disorders [1973]
    Syndromes [1973]
R   Sterility [1973]

Turnover
Use   Employee Turnover

Turtles [1973]
PN   197   SC   54480
UF   Tortoises
B   Reptiles [1967]

Tutoring [1973]
PN   754   SC   54490
B   Teaching Methods [1967]
N   Peer Tutoring [1973]
R   Individualized Instruction [1973]
    Test Coaching [1997]

Tutors
Use   Teachers

Twelve Step Programs [1997]
PN   109   SC   54505
UF   Gamblers Anonymous
    Narcotics Anonymous
B   Support Groups [1991]
N   Alcoholics Anonymous [1973]
R   ↓ Drug Rehabilitation [1973]
    Group Counseling [1973]
    ↓ Group Psychotherapy [1967]
    ↓ Mental Health Services [1978]
    ↓ Psychotherapeutic Techniques [1967]
    ↓ Rehabilitation [1967]
    ↓ Self Help Techniques [1982]
    ↓ Treatment [1967]

Twins [1967]
PN   1571   SC   54510
B   Multiple Births [1973]
N   Heterozygotic Twins [1973]
    Monozygotic Twins [1973]
    Siamese Twins [1973]
R   Family Resemblance [1991]
    ↓ Genetics [1967]

Tympanic Membrane
Use   Middle Ear

Type A Personality
Use   Coronary Prone Behavior

Type B Personality
Use   Coronary Prone Behavior

Type I Errors [1973]
PN   289   SC   54530
B   Prediction Errors [1973]
R   Statistical Power [1991]

Type II Errors [1973]
PN   80   SC   54540
B   Prediction Errors [1973]
R   Statistical Power [1991]

Typing [1991]
PN   64   SC   54550
SN   Use CLERICAL SECRETARIAL SKILLS to access references from 1973-1990.
R   Clerical Secretarial Skills [1973]
    Keyboards [1985]
    Word Processing [1991]

Typists
Use   Clerical Personnel

Typologies (General)
Use   Taxonomies

Typologies (Psychodiagnostic)
Use   Psychodiagnostic Typologies

Tyramine [1973]
PN   84   SC   54580
B   Adrenergic Drugs [1973]
    Sympathomimetic Amines [1973]
    Vasoconstrictor Drugs [1973]
R   ↓ Ergot Derivatives [1973]

Tyrosine [1973]
PN   346   SC   54590
B   Amino Acids [1973]
N   Alpha Methylparatyrosine [1978]
R   Melanin [1973]

Ulcerative Colitis [1973]
PN   162   SC   54620
B   Colitis [1973]

Ulcers (Gastrointestinal)
Use   Gastrointestinal Ulcers

Ulnar Nerve
Use   Spinal Nerves

Ultrasound [1973]
PN   321   SC   54650
SN   Sound waves with frequencies above the range of human hearing.
B   Pitch (Frequency) [1967]

Uncertainty [1991]
PN   829   SC   54655
SN   May be used for uncertainty reduction processes; uncertainty in decision making, choice, or judgment; or in statistical contexts.
R   ↓ Chance (Fortune) [1973]
    Chaos Theory [1997]
    Choice Behavior [1967]
    ↓ Decision Making [1967]
    Doubt [1973]
    Impression Management [1978]
    ↓ Judgment [1967]
    ↓ Statistical Analysis [1967]
    Suspicion [1973]

Unconditioned Reflex
Use   Reflexes

Unconditioned Responses [1973]
PN   135   SC   54680
B   Classical Conditioning [1967]
    Responses [1967]

Unconditioned Stimulus [1973]
PN   1283   SC   54690
UF   Stimulus (Unconditioned)
B   Conditioning [1967]
R   ↓ Classical Conditioning [1967]
    ↓ Operant Conditioning [1967]
    Primary Reinforcement [1973]
    ↓ Stimulation [1967]

Unconscious (Personality Factor) [1967]
PN   1527   SC   54700
B   Psychoanalytic Personality Factors [1973]
R   Archetypes [1991]
    Death Instinct [1988]

Unconscious (Personality Factor) — (cont'd)
- **R** Free Association 1994
  - Id 1973
  - Mind 1991

Underachievement (Academic)
- **Use** Academic Underachievement

Underdeveloped Countries
- **Use** Developing Countries

Undergraduate Degrees
- **Use** Educational Degrees

Undergraduate Education 1978
PN 1123　　　　　　　　　　SC 54725
- **UF** College Education
- **B** Higher Education 1973

Undergraduates
- **Use** College Students

Underprivileged
- **Use** Disadvantaged

Understanding
- **Use** Comprehension

Underwater Effects 1973
PN 190　　　　　　　　　　SC 54760
- **B** Environmental Effects 1973
- **R** Decompression Effects 1973
  - ↓ Gravitational Effects 1967

Underweight 1973
PN 58　　　　　　　　　　SC 54770
- **B** Body Weight 1967
  - Symptoms 1967
- **N** Anorexia Nervosa 1973
- **R** Diets 1978
  - ↓ Eating Disorders 1997
  - Hyperthyroidism 1973
  - ↓ Nutritional Deficiencies 1973

Undifferentiated Schizophrenia 1973
PN 93　　　　　　　　　　SC 54780
- **B** Schizophrenia 1967

Unemployment 1967
PN 1504　　　　　　　　　　SC 54790
- **B** Employment Status 1982
  - Social Issues 1991
- **R** Employment History 1978
  - Job Search 1985
  - Job Security 1978
  - ↓ Personnel 1967
  - Personnel Termination 1973
  - Reemployment 1991
  - Retirement 1973

Unipolar Depression
- **SN** Use DEPRESSION (EMOTION) to access references from 1982-1987.
- **Use** Major Depression

Universities
- **Use** Colleges

Unskilled Industrial Workers 1973
PN 81　　　　　　　　　　SC 54880

Unskilled Industrial Workers — (cont'd)
- **SN** Blue collar workers who perform unskilled labor in an industrial setting.
- **B** Blue Collar Workers 1973

Unwed Mothers 1973
PN 225　　　　　　　　　　SC 54890
- **SN** Consider also ADOLESCENT MOTHERS.
- **B** Mothers 1967
- **R** Never Married 1994
  - Premarital Intercourse 1973
  - Single Mothers 1994
  - ↓ Single Parents 1978

Upper Class 1973
PN 130　　　　　　　　　　SC 54900
- **B** Social Class 1967

Upper Class Attitudes 1973
PN 12　　　　　　　　　　SC 54910
- **SN** Attitudes of, not toward, the upper class.
- **B** Socioeconomic Class Attitudes 1973

Upper Income Level 1973
PN 66　　　　　　　　　　SC 54920
- **B** Income Level 1973

Upward Bound 1973
PN 45　　　　　　　　　　SC 54930
- **SN** U.S. Government educational and counseling program for disadvantaged high school and college students.
- **B** Educational Programs 1973
  - Government Programs 1973
- **R** Compensatory Education 1973
  - Government 1967

Upward Mobility
- **Use** Social Mobility

Urban Development
- **Use** Community Development

Urban Environments 1967
PN 6522　　　　　　　　　　SC 54940
- **UF** Cities
  - Inner City
- **B** Social Environments 1973
- **N** Ghettoes 1973
- **R** Community Development 1997
  - Urban Planning 1973

Urban Ghettoes
- **Use** Ghettoes

Urban Planning 1973
PN 187　　　　　　　　　　SC 54960
- **B** Environmental Planning 1982
- **R** ↓ Architecture 1973
  - Community Development 1997
  - ↓ Community Facilities 1973
  - ↓ Environment 1967
  - ↓ Recreation Areas 1973
  - ↓ Urban Environments 1967

Urbanization 1973
PN 177　　　　　　　　　　SC 54970
- **B** Social Processes 1967
- **R** Industrialization 1973

Uric Acid 1973
PN 63　　　　　　　　　　SC 55010

Uric Acid — (cont'd)
- **B** Acids 1973

Urinalysis 1973
PN 230　　　　　　　　　　SC 55020
- **B** Medical Diagnosis 1973
- **R** Drug Usage Screening 1988

Urinary Function Disorders 1973
PN 135　　　　　　　　　　SC 55040
- **B** Urogenital Disorders 1973
- **N** Urinary Incontinence 1973
- **R** ↓ Somatoform Disorders 2001

Urinary Incontinence 1973
PN 902　　　　　　　　　　SC 55050
- **UF** Bedwetting
  - Enuresis
  - Incontinence (Urinary)
- **B** Urinary Function Disorders 1973
- **R** ↓ Behavior Disorders 1971
  - ↓ Symptoms 1967

Urination 1967
PN 250　　　　　　　　　　SC 55070
- **UF** Micturition
- **B** Excretion 1967
- **N** Diuresis 1973
- **R** ↓ Diuretics 1973

Urine 1973
PN 848　　　　　　　　　　SC 55080
- **B** Body Fluids 1973

Urogenital Disorders 1973
PN 262　　　　　　　　　　SC 55090
- **B** Physical Disorders 1997
- **N** ↓ Genital Disorders 1967
  - ↓ Gynecological Disorders 1973
  - Kidney Diseases 1988
  - ↓ Urinary Function Disorders 1973
- **R** ↓ Sexual Function Disturbances 1973
  - ↓ Somatoform Disorders 2001
  - ↓ Urogenital System 1973
  - ↓ Venereal Diseases 1973

Urogenital System 1973
PN 62　　　　　　　　　　SC 55100
- **B** Anatomical Systems 1973
- **N** Bladder 1973
  - ↓ Female Genitalia 1973
  - ↓ Gonads 1973
  - Kidneys 1973
  - ↓ Male Genitalia 1973
- **R** ↓ Urogenital Disorders 1973

Uterus 1973
PN 69　　　　　　　　　　SC 55110
- **B** Female Genitalia 1973
- **N** Cervix 1973
- **R** Placenta 1973

Utilization (Health Care)
- **Use** Health Care Utilization

Vacation Benefits
- **Use** Employee Leave Benefits

Vacationing 1973
PN 137　　　　　　　　　　SC 55130
- **B** Recreation 1967
- **R** Camping 1973

Vacationing — (cont'd)
R   Holidays [1988]
     Summer Camps (Recreation) [1973]
     Traveling [1973]

Vaccination
Use   Immunization

Vagina [1973]
PN   200   SC   55150
B   Female Genitalia [1973]

Vaginismus [1973]
PN   74   SC   55160
B   Sexual Function Disturbances [1973]
R   Dyspareunia [1973]
     Frigidity [1973]

Vagotomy [1973]
PN   142   SC   55170
B   Neurosurgery [1973]

Vagus Nerve [1973]
PN   190   SC   55180
B   Cranial Nerves [1973]
     Parasympathetic Nervous System [1973]
R   ↓ Heart [1967]

Validity (Statistical)
Use   Statistical Validity

Validity (Test)
Use   Test Validity

Valium
Use   Diazepam

Valproic Acid [1991]
PN   369   SC   55215
B   Anticonvulsive Drugs [1973]

Values [1967]
PN   5836   SC   55220
SN   Qualities, principles or behaviors considered to be morally or intrinsically valuable or desirable. Use a more specific term if possible.
UF   Mores
N   Ethnic Values [1973]
     Personal Values [1973]
     Social Values [1973]
R   ↓ Ethics [1967]
     Integrity [1997]
     Morality [1967]
     World View [1988]

Valves (Heart)
Use   Heart Valves

Vandalism [1978]
PN   105   SC   55235
SN   Willful or malicious destruction or defacement of public or private property.
B   Crime [1967]

Vane Kindergarten Test
SN   Term discontinued in 1997. In 2000, the term was stripped from all records containing it, and replaced with INTELLIGENCE MEASURES, its postable counterpart.
Use   Intelligence Measures

Variability (Response)
Use   Response Variability

Variability (Stimulus)
Use   Stimulus Variability

Variability Measurement [1973]
PN   270   SC   55270
B   Statistical Analysis [1967]
     Statistical Measurement [1973]
N   Analysis of Covariance [1973]
     Analysis of Variance [1967]
     Interaction Variance [1973]
     Standard Deviation [1973]
R   ↓ Central Tendency Measures [1973]
     F Test [1973]
     ↓ Statistical Correlation [1967]

Variable Interval Reinforcement [1973]
PN   701   SC   55280
UF   Interval Reinforcement
B   Reinforcement Schedules [1967]

Variable Ratio Reinforcement [1973]
PN   178   SC   55290
UF   Ratio Reinforcement
B   Reinforcement Schedules [1967]

Variance Homogeneity [1985]
PN   98   SC   55295
SN   Extent to which the variance in two or more statistical samples is similar or different.
UF   Heterogeneity of Variance
B   Statistical Measurement [1973]
R   Analysis of Variance [1967]
     Standard Deviation [1973]

Varimax Rotation [1973]
PN   50   SC   55330
B   Orthogonal Rotation [1973]

Vascular Dementia [1997]
PN   284   SC   55333
B   Dementia [1985]
N   Multi Infarct Dementia [1991]
R   ↓ Cerebrovascular Disorders [1973]

Vascular Disorders
Use   Cardiovascular Disorders

Vasectomy [1973]
PN   78   SC   55350
B   Birth Control [1971]
     Sterilization (Sex) [1973]
     Surgery [1971]

Vasoconstriction [1973]
PN   95   SC   55360
R   ↓ Blood Pressure Disorders [1973]
     Epinephrine [1967]

Vasoconstrictor Drugs [1973]
PN   34   SC   55370
UF   Pressors (Drugs)
     Vasopressor Drugs
B   Drugs [1967]
N   ↓ Amphetamine [1967]
     Angiotensin [1973]
     Bufotenine [1973]
     Dihydroergotamine [1973]
     Ephedrine [1973]
     Methamphetamine [1973]

Vasoconstrictor Drugs — (cont'd)
N   Methoxamine [1973]
     Norepinephrine [1973]
     Serotonin [1973]
     Tryptamine [1973]
     Tyramine [1973]
R   ↓ Blood Pressure [1967]
     ↓ Heart Rate Affecting Drugs [1973]
     ↓ Vasodilator Drugs [1973]
     Vasopressin [1973]

Vasodilation [1973]
PN   71   SC   55380
R   ↓ Blood Pressure Disorders [1973]
     Epinephrine [1967]
     ↓ Muscle Relaxing Drugs [1973]
     Theophylline [1973]

Vasodilator Drugs [1973]
PN   189   SC   55390
B   Drugs [1967]
N   Nicotinic Acid [1973]
     Verapamil [1991]
R   ↓ Antihypertensive Drugs [1973]
     ↓ Blood Pressure [1967]
     Channel Blockers [1991]
     ↓ Heart Rate Affecting Drugs [1973]
     ↓ Vasoconstrictor Drugs [1973]

Vasopressin [1973]
PN   846   SC   55400
B   Pituitary Hormones [1973]
R   ↓ Vasoconstrictor Drugs [1973]

Vasopressor Drugs
Use   Vasoconstrictor Drugs

Veins (Anatomy) [1973]
PN   37   SC   55420
B   Blood Vessels [1973]

Velocity [1973]
PN   1084   SC   55430
UF   Speed
R   Vibration [1967]

Venereal Diseases [1973]
PN   683   SC   55440
UF   Diseases (Venereal)
     Sexually Transmitted Diseases
B   Infectious Disorders [1973]
N   Gonorrhea [1973]
     Herpes Genitalis [1988]
     ↓ Syphilis [1973]
R   Acquired Immune Deficiency Syndrome [1988]
     Condoms [1991]
     ↓ Human Immunodeficiency Virus [1991]
     ↓ Infertility [1973]
     Sexual Risk Taking [1997]
     Sterility [1973]
     ↓ Urogenital Disorders [1973]

Ventral Roots [1973]
PN   27   SC   55460
B   Spinal Cord [1973]

Ventral Tegmental Area
Use   Tegmentum

Ventricles (Cerebral)
Use   Cerebral Ventricles

Ventricles (Heart)
　Use　Heart Ventricles

Ventricular Fibrillation
　Use　Fibrillation (Heart)

Verapamil 1991
PN 73　　　　　　　　　　**SC** 55495
　B　Heart Rate Affecting Drugs 1973
　　　Vasodilator Drugs 1973
　R　Channel Blockers 1991

Verbal Ability 1967
PN 2914　　　　　　　　　**SC** 55500
　B　Cognitive Ability 1973
　R　Academic Aptitude 1973
　　　Language Proficiency 1988
　　　Metalinguistics 1994
　　　↓ Oral Communication 1985
　　　Proofreading 1988
　　　↓ Verbal Communication 1967
　　　↓ Verbal Memory 1994
　　　Writing Skills 1985
　　　↓ Written Communication 1985

Verbal Communication 1967
PN 9869　　　　　　　　　**SC** 55520
　SN　Communication through spoken or written language. Use narrower terms if possible.
　B　Communication 1967
　N　Articulation (Speech) 1967
　　　Conversation 1973
　　　↓ Handwriting 1967
　　　Language Proficiency 1988
　　　↓ Manual Communication 1978
　　　Narratives 1997
　　　↓ Oral Communication 1985
　　　Pragmatics 1985
　　　Storytelling 1988
　　　↓ Written Communication 1985
　R　↓ Communication Skills 1973
　　　Discourse Analysis 1997
　　　↓ Grammar 1967
　　　↓ Language 1967
　　　↓ Language Development 1967
　　　↓ Linguistics 1973
　　　Metalinguistics 1994
　　　Neurolinguistics 1991
　　　↓ Speech Processing (Mechanical) 1973
　　　Text Structure 1982
　　　Verbal Ability 1967
　　　↓ Vocabulary 1967
　　　↓ Vocalization 1967

Verbal Comprehension 1985
PN 1282　　　　　　　　　**SC** 55525
　B　Comprehension 1967
　N　Listening Comprehension 1973
　　　Reading Comprehension 1973
　　　Sentence Comprehension 1973

Verbal Conditioning
　Use　Verbal Learning

Verbal Fluency 1973
PN 1604　　　　　　　　　**SC** 55540
　SN　Ability to produce and manipulate words in thought or speech.
　UF　Fluency
　R　Language Proficiency 1988
　　　↓ Oral Communication 1985
　　　Speech Rate 1973

Verbal Learning 1967
PN 3631　　　　　　　　　**SC** 55550
　SN　Acquisition, retention, and retrieval of verbal stimulus materials such as nonsense syllables, words, or sentences. Compare LANGUAGE DEVELOPMENT.
　UF　Conditioning (Verbal)
　　　Verbal Conditioning
　B　Learning 1967
　N　Nonsense Syllable Learning 1967
　　　Paired Associate Learning 1967
　R　Isolation Effect 1973
　　　Serial Anticipation (Learning) 1973
　　　↓ Serial Learning 1967
　　　↓ Verbal Memory 1994

Verbal Meaning 1973
PN 782　　　　　　　　　**SC** 55560
　SN　Connotative or denotative meaning associated with any verbally informative unit (e.g., morpheme, word, sentence, or phrase).
　B　Meaning 1967
　N　Word Meaning 1973
　R　↓ Figurative Language 1985
　　　↓ Semantics 1967

Verbal Memory 1994
PN 724　　　　　　　　　**SC** 55565
　B　Memory 1967
　N　Semantic Memory 1988
　R　↓ Lexical Access 1988
　　　Lexical Decision 1988
　　　Verbal Ability 1967
　　　↓ Verbal Learning 1967

Verbal Reinforcement 1973
PN 706　　　　　　　　　**SC** 55570
　B　Social Reinforcement 1967
　N　Praise 1973

Verbal Stimuli 1982
PN 1185　　　　　　　　　**SC** 55575
　SN　Aural or visual presentation of syllables or words or nonword letter combinations.
　B　Stimulation 1967
　R　↓ Stimulus Presentation Methods 1973

Verbal Tests 1973
PN 162　　　　　　　　　**SC** 55580
　SN　Tests designed to assess verbal ability or in which performance depends upon verbal ability.
　B　Measurement 1967

Verbalization
　Use　Oral Communication

Verbs 1973
PN 949　　　　　　　　　**SC** 55600
　B　Form Classes (Language) 1973

Verdict Determination
　Use　Adjudication

Vergence Movements
　Use　Eye Convergence

Verification (of Theories)
　Use　Theory Verification

Vernier Acuity
　Use　Visual Acuity

Vertebrates 1973
PN 226　　　　　　　　　**SC** 55620
　B　Animals 1967
　N　↓ Amphibia 1973
　　　↓ Birds 1967
　　　↓ Fishes 1967
　　　↓ Mammals 1973
　　　Pigs 1973
　　　↓ Reptiles 1967
　R　↓ Invertebrates 1973

Vertigo 1973
PN 136　　　　　　　　　**SC** 55630
　UF　Dizziness
　B　Symptoms 1967
　R　↓ Labyrinth Disorders 1973
　　　Menieres Disease 1973
　　　Syncope 1973

Vestibular Apparatus 1967
PN 620　　　　　　　　　**SC** 55660
　SN　Major organ of equilibrium which acts as a sensory receptor that detects the position and changes in the position of the head in space.
　B　Ear (Anatomy) 1967
　N　Semicircular Canals 1973
　R　↓ Labyrinth (Anatomy) 1973

Vestibular Nystagmus
　Use　Nystagmus

Vestibular Stimulation
　Use　Somesthetic Stimulation

Veterans (Military)
　Use　Military Veterans

Veterinary Medicine 1973
PN 61　　　　　　　　　**SC** 55680
　B　Medical Sciences 1967

Vibration 1967
PN 422　　　　　　　　　**SC** 55690
　UF　Resonance
　R　Velocity 1973

Vibrators (Apparatus) 1973
PN 19　　　　　　　　　**SC** 55700
　B　Apparatus 1967
　R　↓ Stimulators (Apparatus) 1973

Vibrotactile Thresholds 1973
PN 312　　　　　　　　　**SC** 55710
　SN　The minimal level of vibratory stimulation, the minimal difference between any such stimuli, or the minimal vibratory stimulus change that is tactually perceptible.
　B　Tactual Perception 1967
　　　Thresholds 1967
　R　↓ Perceptual Measures 1973

Vicarious Experiences 1973
PN 280　　　　　　　　　**SC** 55713
　UF　Reinforcement (Vicarious)
　　　Vicarious Reinforcement
　B　Experiences (Events) 1973
　R　Imagination 1967
　　　↓ Reinforcement 1967

Vicarious Reinforcement
　Use　Vicarious Experiences

Victimization 1973
PN 5527   SC 55716
SN Process or state of having been personally subjected to crime, deception, fraud, or other detrimental circumstances as a result of the deeds of others.
B   Social Interaction 1967
R   ↓ Crime 1967
      ↓ Crime Victims 1982
      Erotomania 1997
      ↓ Harassment 2001
      ↓ Perpetrators 1988
      Persecution 1973
      Sexual Harassment 1985
      Stalking 2001
      Torture 1988

Video Display Terminals
Use   Video Display Units

Video Display Units 1985
PN 540   SC 55718
SN Electronic devices used to present information or stimulation through visual means. Use VISUAL DISPLAYS to access references from 1973-1984.
UF   Cathode Ray Tubes
      CRT
      Video Display Terminals
B   Computer Peripheral Devices 1985
      Visual Displays 1973
R   ↓ Television 1967
      ↓ Visual Stimulation 1973

Video Games
Use   Computer Games

Videotape Instruction 1973
PN 637   SC 55720
SN Audiovisual teaching method which employs presentation of feedback as an aid to learning.
B   Audiovisual Instruction 1973
R   ↓ Educational Audiovisual Aids 1973

Videotape Recorders 1973
PN 98   SC 55730
SN Device for recording on magnetic tape and having varied applications (e.g., teaching aid, analysis of research data).
B   Tape Recorders 1973

Videotapes 1973
PN 1485   SC 55740
SN Audiovisual tape recordings used in both noneducational and educational settings. Not used as a document type identifier.
B   Audiovisual Communications Media 1973

Vietnamese Cultural Groups 1997
PN 88   SC 57748
SN Use ASIANS to access references from 1982-1996.
B   Asians 1982

Vigilance 1967
PN 1404   SC 55750
SN Intentional and conscious alertness characterized by a readiness to respond to environmental changes. Compare ATTENTION.
B   Attention 1967
      Monitoring 1973
      Sustained Attention 1997
R   Attention Span 1973
      Selective Attention 1973

Vineland Social Maturity Scale 1973
PN 23   SC 55760
B   Nonprojective Personality Measures 1973

Violence 1973
PN 6841   SC 55770
B   Antisocial Behavior 1971
      Conflict 1967
N   ↓ Family Violence 1982
      Patient Violence 1994
R   Coercion 1994
      Dangerousness 1988
      Nonviolence 1991
      Partner Abuse 1991
      Physical Abuse 1991
      Riots 1973
      Self Defense 1985
      Terrorism 1982
      Torture 1988
      ↓ War 1967

Viral Disorders 1973
PN 413   SC 55780
B   Infectious Disorders 1973
N   Creutzfeldt Jakob Syndrome 1994
      Encephalitis 1973
      Epstein Barr Viral Disorder 1994
      Herpes Genitalis 1988
      Herpes Simplex 1973
      ↓ Human Immunodeficiency Virus 1991
      Influenza 1973
      Measles 1973
      Poliomyelitis 1973
      Rubella 1973
R   Chronic Fatigue Syndrome 1997
      Pneumonia 1973

Virginity 1973
PN 87   SC 55810
B   Psychosexual Behavior 1967
R   Premarital Intercourse 1973
      Sexual Abstinence 1973

Virtual Reality 1997
PN 249   SC 55815
B   Computer Simulation 1973
R   ↓ Computer Applications 1973
      Human Machine Systems 1997

Vision 1967
PN 3291   SC 55820
N   Linear Perspective 1982
      ↓ Visual Perception 1967
R   Tunnel Vision 1973
      Visual Cortex 1967
      Visual Evoked Potentials 1973
      Visual Hallucinations 1973
      Visual Tracking 1973

Vision Disorders 1982
PN 2672   SC 55825
SN Disorders involving the visual system, including visual neural pathways. The term VISUALLY HANDICAPPED was also used to represent this concept from 1967-1996, and VISUALLY DISABLED was used from 1997-2000. In 2000, VISION DISORDERS replaced the discontinued and deleted term VISUALLY DISABLED. VISUALLY DISABLED and VISUALLY HANDICAPPED were stripped from all records and replaced with VISION DISORDERS.
UF   Visually Handicapped
B   Physical Disorders 1997
      Sense Organ Disorders 1973
N   ↓ Eye Disorders 1973

Vision Disorders — (cont'd)
R   ↓ Blind 1967

Vision Disturbances (Hysterical)
Use   Hysterical Vision Disturbances

Visions (Mysticism)
Use   Mysticism

Visitation (Institution)
Use   Institution Visitation

Visitation Rights
Use   Child Visitation

VISTA Volunteers
Use   Volunteers in Service to America

Visual Acuity 1982
PN 945   SC 55897
SN The ability or capacity of an observer to perceive fine detail. Consider VISUAL THRESHOLDS or VISUAL DISCRIMINATION to access references prior to 1982.
UF   Vernier Acuity
B   Visual Perception 1967
R   Pattern Discrimination 1967
      ↓ Spatial Perception 1967

Visual Contrast 1985
PN 1069   SC 55898
SN Perceived difference in color, brightness, or other qualities of two or more simultaneously or successively presented visual stimuli despite a lack of objective differences.
B   Visual Perception 1967
N   Brightness Contrast 1985
      Color Contrast 1985

Visual Cortex 1967
PN 2605   SC 55900
UF   Cortex (Visual)
      Striate Cortex
B   Occipital Lobe 1973
R   ↓ Vision 1967
      Visual Receptive Fields 1982

Visual Discrimination 1967
PN 6213   SC 55910
SN Ability to recognize quantitative or qualitative differences between visual shapes, forms, and patterns. Use VISUAL DISCRIMINATION or VISUAL THRESHOLDS to access references on visual acuity prior to 1982.
B   Perceptual Discrimination 1973
      Visual Perception 1967
R   Visual Search 1982
      Visual Tracking 1973

Visual Displays 1973
PN 2688   SC 55920
SN Presentation of visual information in the form of charts, graphs, maps, signs, symbols, or patterns. Prior to 1985, used for visual devices such as cathode-ray tubes or instrument panels. From 1985, consider also VIDEO DISPLAY UNITS, INSTRUMENT CONTROLS, or GRAPHICAL DISPLAYS.
B   Displays 1967
      Visual Stimulation 1973
N   Video Display Units 1985
R   ↓ Computer Peripheral Devices 1985
      Pictorial Stimuli 1978
      Spatial Frequency 1982

Visual Displays — (cont'd)
R   Temporal Frequency   1985

Visual Evoked Potentials   1973
PN 2691   SC 55930
B   Evoked Potentials   1967
R   ↓ Cortical Evoked Potentials   1973
     ↓ Vision   1967

Visual Feedback   1973
PN 501   SC 55940
SN Return of information on specified behavioral
functions or parameters by means of visual stimulation. Such stimulation may serve to regulate or control subsequent behavior, cognition, perception, or
performance.
B   Sensory Feedback   1973
     Visual Stimulation   1973

Visual Field   1967
PN 3081   SC 55950
B   Visual Perception   1967
R   Eye Fixation   1982
     Fovea   1982
     Peripheral Vision   1988

Visual Fixation
Use Eye Fixation

Visual Hallucinations   1973
PN 280   SC 55960
B   Hallucinations   1967
R   ↓ Vision   1967

Visual Masking   1973
PN 978   SC 55970
SN Changes in perceptual sensitivity to a visual
stimulus due to the presence of a second stimulus in
close temporal proximity.
B   Masking   1967
R   ↓ Visual Stimulation   1973

Visual Memory   1994
PN 677   SC 55973
B   Memory   1967
N   Visuospatial Memory   1997
R   Eidetic Imagery   1973
     ↓ Spatial Memory   1988
     ↓ Visual Perception   1967

Visual Neglect
Use Sensory Neglect

Visual Perception   1967
PN 16632   SC 55980
B   Perception   1967
     Vision   1967
N   Autokinetic Illusion   1967
     Binocular Vision   1967
     ↓ Brightness Perception   1973
     ↓ Color Perception   1967
     Dark Adaptation   1973
     Eye Fixation   1982
     Face Perception   1985
     Foveal Vision   1988
     Interocular Transfer   1985
     Monocular Vision   1973
     Peripheral Vision   1988
     Stereoscopic Vision   1973
     Texture Perception   1982
     Visual Acuity   1982
     ↓ Visual Contrast   1985
     Visual Discrimination   1967

Visual Perception — (cont'd)
N   Visual Field   1967
     ↓ Visual Thresholds   1973
     ↓ Visuospatial Ability   1997
R   ↓ Eye (Anatomy)   1967
     ↓ Eye Disorders   1973
     Lipreading   1973
     Mirror Image   1991
     Retinal Eccentricity   1991
     ↓ Visual Memory   1994
     Visual Receptive Fields   1982
     Visual Tracking   1973

Visual Perspective
Use Linear Perspective

Visual Receptive Fields   1982
PN 575   SC 55985
SN Area of the retina which, when stimulated,
affects a specific ganglion cell or lateral geniculate
body cell, with zones in each field responding in a
complementary way to various properties of visual
stimuli such as color or onset/offset. Also, those
zones in the visual cortex which respond in a complementary way to straight-edge orientation-specific
stimuli.
B   Receptive Fields   1985
R   Geniculate Bodies (Thalamus)   1973
     ↓ Neurons   1973
     ↓ Photoreceptors   1973
     Retinal Eccentricity   1991
     Visual Cortex   1967
     ↓ Visual Perception   1967

Visual Search   1982
PN 1478   SC 55987
SN Perceptual processes associated with detecting
and/or locating specified visual targets which are
usually not continuously visible. Compare VISUAL
TRACKING.
R   Cognitive Discrimination   1973
     ↓ Eye Movements   1967
     Pattern Discrimination   1967
     Signal Detection (Perception)   1967
     Visual Discrimination   1967
     ↓ Visual Thresholds   1973

Visual Spatial Ability
Use Visuospatial Ability

Visual Spatial Memory
Use Visuospatial Memory

Visual Stimulation   1973
PN 7844   SC 55990
B   Perceptual Stimulation   1973
N   Dichoptic Stimulation   1982
     ↓ Illumination   1967
     Prismatic Stimulation   1973
     Stereoscopic Presentation   1973
     Tachistoscopic Presentation   1973
     ↓ Visual Displays   1973
     Visual Feedback   1973
R   ↓ Color   1967
     Linear Perspective   1982
     Pictorial Stimuli   1978
     Spatial Frequency   1982
     Temporal Frequency   1985
     Video Display Units   1985
     Visual Masking   1973

Visual Thresholds   1973
PN 2161   SC 56000

Visual Thresholds — (cont'd)
SN The minimal level of stimulation, the minimal dif-
ference between any stimuli, or the minimal stimulus
change that is visually detectable.
UF   Luminance Threshold
     Photic Threshold
B   Thresholds   1967
     Visual Perception   1967
N   Critical Flicker Fusion Threshold   1967
R   Dark Adaptation   1973
     Light Adaptation   1982
     Luminance   1982
     ↓ Perceptual Measures   1973
     Retinal Eccentricity   1991
     Visual Search   1982

Visual Tracking   1973
PN 1234   SC 56010
SN Perceptual processes associated with following
a specified visual target with the eyes along its path
of movement. Usually involves a continuously visible
target. Compare VISUAL SEARCH.
B   Tracking   1967
R   ↓ Vision   1967
     Visual Discrimination   1967
     ↓ Visual Perception   1967

Visualization
Use Imagery

Visually Handicapped
SN The term was discontinued in 1997, when the
term VISUALLY DISABLED was created to capture
this concept. In 2000, with the deletion of the term
VISUALLY DISABLED, VISUALLY HANDICAPPED
was made a nonpostable term for the postable term
VISION DISORDERS. VISUALLY DISABLED and
VISUALLY HANDICAPPED were stripped from all
records containing them and replaced with VISION
DISORDERS.
Use Vision Disorders

Visuospatial Ability   1997
PN 526   SC 56025
UF   Visual Spatial Ability
B   Spatial Ability   1982
     Visual Perception   1967
N   Visuospatial Memory   1997

Visuospatial Memory   1997
PN 208   SC 56027
UF   Visual Spatial Memory
B   Spatial Memory   1988
     Visual Memory   1994
     Visuospatial Ability   1997

Vitamin C
Use Ascorbic Acid

Vitamin Deficiency Disorders   1973
PN 155   SC 56040
B   Nutritional Deficiencies   1973
N   Pellagra   1973
     Wernickes Syndrome   1973
R   ↓ Vitamins   1973

Vitamin Therapy   1978
PN 270   SC 56045
B   Drug Therapy   1967
R   ↓ Vitamins   1973

Vitamins   1973
PN 462   SC 56050

Vitamins — (cont'd)
- **N** Ascorbic Acid [1973]
- ↓ Choline [1973]
  - Nicotinamide [1973]
  - Nicotinic Acid [1973]
- **R** Dietary Supplements [2001]
- ↓ Drugs [1967]
- ↓ Vitamin Deficiency Disorders [1973]
  - Vitamin Therapy [1978]

Vocabulary [1967]
PN 2121   **SC** 56060
- **UF** Words (Vocabulary)
- **B** Language [1967]
- **N** Anagrams [1973]
  - Antonyms [1973]
  - Homographs [1973]
  - Homonyms [1973]
  - Neologisms [1973]
  - Sight Vocabulary [1973]
  - Slang [1973]
  - Synonyms [1973]
- **R** ↓ Semantics [1967]
- ↓ Verbal Communication [1967]

Vocal Cords [1973]
PN 50   **SC** 56070
- **B** Larynx [1973]

Vocalization [1967]
PN 776   **SC** 56075
SN Production of sounds by means of vocal cord vibrations.
- **N** ↓ Animal Vocalizations [1973]
  - Crying [1973]
  - Laughter [1978]
  - Subvocalization [1973]
- ↓ Voice [1973]
- **R** ↓ Animal Communication [1967]
- ↓ Communication [1967]
- ↓ Oral Communication [1985]
  - Singing [1997]
- ↓ Verbal Communication [1967]

Vocalization (Infant)
Use Infant Vocalization

Vocalizations (Animal)
Use Animal Vocalizations

Vocational Adjustment
Use Occupational Adjustment

Vocational Aspirations
Use Occupational Aspirations

Vocational Choice
Use Occupational Choice

Vocational Counseling
Use Occupational Guidance

Vocational Counselors [1973]
PN 260   **SC** 56140
SN Persons engaged in career guidance, usually in social service, school, government agency, industrial, or employment center settings.
- **B** Counselors [1967]
- **R** Mentor [1985]
  - Occupational Guidance [1967]
  - School Counselors [1973]
- ↓ Social Workers [1973]

Vocational Education [1973]
PN 1498   **SC** 56150
SN Formal training in or out of school, designed to teach skills and knowledge required for occupational proficiency, especially for paraprofessional, trade, or clerical occupations.
- **UF** Industrial Arts Education
- **B** Curriculum [1967]
- **N** Cooperative Education [1982]
- **R** ↓ Occupations [1967]

Vocational Education Teachers [1988]
PN 49   **SC** 56155
- **UF** Technical Education Teachers
- **B** Teachers [1967]

Vocational Evaluation [1991]
PN 146   **SC** 56157
SN Assessment of vocational aptitude, job skills, and performance potential using simulated or real work experiences and measures. Used for disabled or disordered populations.
- **B** Evaluation [1967]
  - Vocational Rehabilitation [1967]
- **R** Disability Management [1991]
  - Employability [1973]
- ↓ Employee Skills [1973]
  - Work Adjustment Training [1991]

Vocational Guidance
Use Occupational Guidance

Vocational Interests
Use Occupational Interests

Vocational Maturity [1978]
PN 927   **SC** 56175
SN Ability to make age-appropriate vocational decisions and choices, usually predictive of good vocational adjustment.
- **UF** Career Maturity
  - Maturity (Vocational)
- **R** Occupational Attitudes [1973]
  - Occupational Choice [1967]
  - Occupational Interests [1967]
  - Occupational Preference [1973]
- ↓ Occupations [1967]

Vocational Mobility
Use Occupational Mobility

Vocational Preference
Use Occupational Preference

Vocational Rehabilitation [1967]
PN 3157   **SC** 56210
SN Planning and providing necessary services required for successful job placement and subsequent vocational adjustment of handicapped clients.
- **UF** Rehabilitation (Vocational)
- **B** Psychosocial Rehabilitation [1973]
- **N** Supported Employment [1994]
  - Vocational Evaluation [1991]
  - Work Adjustment Training [1991]
- **R** Disability Management [1991]
  - Rehabilitation Counseling [1978]
  - School to Work Transition [1994]

Vocational School Students [1973]
PN 360   **SC** 56220
- **B** Students [1967]

Vocational Schools
Use Technical Schools

Vocations
Use Occupations

Voice [1973]
PN 799   **SC** 56250
- **B** Vocalization [1967]
- **N** Crying [1973]
  - Infant Vocalization [1973]
- **R** ↓ Communication [1967]
- ↓ Oral Communication [1985]
  - Singing [1997]

Voice Disorders
Use Dysphonia

Voles
Use Rodents

Volition [1988]
PN 462   **SC** 56257
SN Process of deciding on a course of action voluntarily or without direct external influence.
- **UF** Free Will
- **R** Choice Behavior [1967]
- ↓ Decision Making [1967]
  - Determinism [1997]
  - Freedom [1978]
  - Self Determination [1994]

Volt Meters
SN Term discontinued in 1997. In 2000, the term was stripped from all records containing it, and replaced with APPARATUS, its postable counterpart.
Use Apparatus

Volunteer Civilian Personnel [1973]
PN 179   **SC** 56280
SN Civilians rendering services free of charge on behalf of various social causes (e.g., mental health, community services, politics).
- **B** Volunteer Personnel [1973]
- **R** ↓ Paraprofessional Personnel [1973]

Volunteer Military Personnel [1973]
PN 35   **SC** 56290
- **B** Military Personnel [1967]
  - Volunteer Personnel [1973]
- **R** Commissioned Officers [1973]
- ↓ Enlisted Military Personnel [1973]
  - National Guardsmen [1973]
  - ROTC Students [1973]

Volunteer Personnel [1973]
PN 1000   **SC** 56300
- **B** Personnel [1967]
- **N** Volunteer Civilian Personnel [1973]
  - Volunteer Military Personnel [1973]
- **R** ↓ Educational Personnel [1973]
  - Fire Fighters [1991]
  - National Guardsmen [1973]
- ↓ Paraprofessional Personnel [1973]
  - ROTC Students [1973]
- ↓ Religious Personnel [1973]

Volunteers (Experiment)
Use Experiment Volunteers

Volunteers in Service to America [1973]
PN 2   **SC** 56320

Volunteers in Service to America — (cont'd)
SN National corps of volunteers whose mission is to address poverty and poverty-related human, social, and environmental problems in the USA. Part of ACTION, a U.S. Government agency.
UF VISTA Volunteers
B Government Programs [1973]
R Government [1967]

Vomeronasal Sense [1982]
PN 131   **SC** 56327
SN Perceptual system activated by chemical stimuli which trigger vomeronasal nerve activity.
R Chemoreceptors [1973]
↓ Olfactory Perception [1967]

Vomit Inducing Drugs
Use Emetic Drugs

Vomiting [1973]
PN 467   **SC** 56340
UF Regurgitation
B Gastrointestinal Disorders [1973]
Symptoms [1967]
R ↓ Antiemetic Drugs [1973]
↓ Emetic Drugs [1973]
Nausea [1973]
Rumination (Eating) [2001]

Voting Behavior [1973]
PN 853   **SC** 56350
B Behavior [1967]
Political Participation [1988]
Political Processes [1973]
R ↓ Political Attitudes [1973]
Political Elections [1973]
Political Issues [1973]
Political Psychology [1997]

Vowels [1973]
PN 1016   **SC** 56360
B Letters (Alphabet) [1973]
Phonology [1973]
R ↓ Phonemes [1973]
Syllables [1973]
Words (Phonetic Units) [1967]

Voyeurism [1973]
PN 56   **SC** 56370
B Paraphilias [1988]
R Exhibitionism [1973]

Vulnerability (Disorders)
Use Susceptibility (Disorders)

Vygotsky (Lev) [1991]
PN 389   **SC** 56375
SN Identifies biographical or autobiographical studies and discussions of Vygotsky's works. Sometimes spelled Vigotsky or Vygotski.
R ↓ Language Development [1967]
Psycholinguistics [1967]
↓ Psychologists [1967]

Wages
Use Salaries

Wakefulness [1973]
PN 1029   **SC** 56410
B Consciousness States [1971]
R Sleep Wake Cycle [1985]

Walk In Clinics [1973]
PN 47   **SC** 56430
SN Facilities in hospitals or other community locations which typically provide immediate access to counseling and referral; are often staffed by volunteers and nondegreed counselors and focus on minority, indigent, or youthful populations.
B Clinics [1967]
R ↓ Crisis Intervention Services [1973]
Psychiatric Clinics [1973]

Walking [1973]
PN 603   **SC** 56440
B Motor Performance [1973]

Wandering Behavior [1991]
PN 54   **SC** 56450
SN Aimless activity usually resulting from a confused mental state.
B Behavior [1967]
Motor Processes [1967]
R Mental Confusion [1973]
Place Disorientation [1973]
↓ Symptoms [1967]

War [1967]
PN 2692   **SC** 56460
B Conflict [1967]
Social Issues [1991]
N Nuclear War [1985]
R Combat Experience [1991]
Foreign Policy Making [1973]
↓ Government Policy Making [1973]
Peace [1988]
↓ Violence [1973]

Warning Labels [1997]
PN 24   **SC** 56464
B Warnings [1997]
R Accident Prevention [1973]
↓ Accidents [1967]
Consumer Protection [1973]
Hazards [1973]
↓ Safety [1967]
↓ Safety Devices [1973]

Warning Signs
Use Warnings

Warnings [1997]
PN 84   **SC** 56470
UF Safety Warnings
Warning Signs
N Warning Labels [1997]
R Accident Prevention [1973]
↓ Accidents [1967]
Consumer Protection [1973]
Hazards [1973]
↓ Safety [1967]
↓ Safety Devices [1973]

Wasps [1982]
PN 276   **SC** 56475
SN Any of numerous social or solitary winged hymenopterous insects.
B Insects [1967]
R Larvae [1973]

Water Deprivation [1967]
PN 726   **SC** 56480
SN Absence of ad libitum water access. In experimental settings, water deprivation is used to achieve a definable level of motivation within the organism.
B Deprivation [1967]

Water Deprivation — (cont'd)
B Stimulus Deprivation [1973]
R Dehydration [1988]
Thirst [1967]

Water Intake [1967]
PN 2007   **SC** 56490
SN Ingestion of water. Frequently used as an objective measure of physiological or motivational state or learning. Used for human or animal populations.
B Drinking Behavior [1978]
Fluid Intake [1985]
R Animal Drinking Behavior [1973]
Dehydration [1988]

Water Safety [1973]
PN 129   **SC** 56500
SN Programs or activities for accident prevention in aquatic environments.
B Safety [1967]

Water Transportation [1973]
PN 167   **SC** 56510
B Transportation [1973]
N Submarines [1973]

Watson (John Broadus) [1991]
PN 27   **SC** 56515
SN Identifies biographical or autobiographical studies and discussions of Watson's works.
R Behaviorism [1967]
↓ Psychologists [1967]

Weaning [1973]
PN 248   **SC** 56520
SN Process of acclimating an infant or child to a substitute for the mother's milk. Used for human or animal populations.
B Childrearing Practices [1967]
Feeding Practices [1973]
R Breast Feeding [1973]
Sucking [1978]

Weapons [1978]
PN 458   **SC** 56525
UF Firearms
R Gun Control Laws [1973]

Weather
Use Atmospheric Conditions

Wechsler Adult Intelligence Scale [1967]
PN 1666   **SC** 56530
B Intelligence Measures [1967]

Wechsler Bellevue Intelligence Scale [1967]
PN 44   **SC** 56540
B Intelligence Measures [1967]

**Wechsler Intelligence Scale for
Children** [2001]
PN 2250   **SC** 56551
SN In 2000, the truncated term WECHSLER INTELLIGENCE SCALE CHILDREN (which was used from 1967-2000) was deleted, removed from all records containing it, and mapped to its expanded form WECHSLER INTELLIGENCE SCALE FOR CHILDREN.
B Intelligence Measures [1967]

Wechsler Memory Scale [1988]
PN 191   **SC** 56553
B Neuropsychological Assessment [1982]

Wechsler Memory Scale — (cont'd)
  B   Retention Measures 1973

Wechsler Preschool Primary Scale 1988
  PN 100   SC 56555
  B   Intelligence Measures 1967

Weight (Body)
  Use Body Weight

Weight (Statistics)
  Use Statistical Weighting

Weight Control 1985
  PN 1353   SC 56565
  SN Deliberate regulation of one's weight through diet, exercise, or other means. Also, the relative weight change resulting from such regulation practices. Used for human populations only.
  R   Aerobic Exercise 1988
     ↓ Body Weight 1967
       Diets 1978
     ↓ Exercise 1973
       Food Intake 1967
       Health Behavior 1982
       Obesity (Attitudes Toward) 1997

Weight Perception 1967
  PN 269   SC 56570
  SN Awareness of mass or weight.
  B   Somesthetic Perception 1967

Weightlessness 1967
  PN 65   SC 56580
  B   Gravitational Effects 1967
  R ↓ Somesthetic Stimulation 1973
       Spaceflight 1967

Weightlifting 1994
  PN 65   SC 56585
  B   Exercise 1973
       Recreation 1967
       Sports 1967

Welfare Services (Government) 1973
  PN 736   SC 56600
  B   Government Programs 1973
  R   Community Welfare Services 1973
       Government 1967
       Medicaid 1994

Well Being 1994
  PN 3019   SC 56603
  R ↓ Adjustment 1967
     ↓ Health 1973
       Life Satisfaction 1985
       Lifestyle Changes 1997
     ↓ Mental Health 1967
     ↓ Quality of Life 1985

Wellness
  Use Health

Welsh Figure Preference Test 1973
  PN 5   SC 56610
  B   Nonprojective Personality Measures 1973

Wepman Auditory Discrimination Test 2001
  PN 7   SC 56619

Wepman Auditory Discrimination Test — (cont'd)
  SN In 2000, the truncated term WEPMAN TEST OF AUDITORY DISCRIM (which was used from 1973-2000) was deleted, removed from all records containing it, and mapped to its expanded form WEPMAN AUDITORY DISCRIMINATION TEST.
  B   Speech and Hearing Measures 1973

Wernickes Syndrome 1973
  PN 109   SC 56630
  SN Use APHASIA for Wernicke's aphasia.
  B   Alcoholic Hallucinosis 1973
       Encephalopathies 1982
       Syndromes 1973
       Vitamin Deficiency Disorders 1973

Whales 1985
  PN 67   SC 56665
  B   Mammals 1973
  N   Dolphins 1973
       Porpoises 1973

Wheelchairs
  Use Mobility Aids

Whiplash 1997
  PN 35   SC 56669
  SN Soft tissue injury of cervical spine due to sudden hyperextension or hyperflexion or hyperrotation of neck or limbs.
  UF Cervical Sprain Syndrome
  B   Spinal Cord Injuries 1973
  R ↓ Head Injuries 1973

Whistleblowing
  Use Informants

White Betz A B Scale
  SN Term discontinued in 1997. In 2000, the term was stripped from all records containing it, and replaced with NONPROJECTIVE PERSONALITY MEASURES, its postable counterpart.
  Use Nonprojective Personality Measures

White Blood Cells
  Use Leucocytes

White Collar Workers 1973
  PN 484   SC 56690
  SN Individuals employed in technical, professional, sales, administrative, or clerical positions.
  B   Business and Industrial Personnel 1967
  N   Accountants 1973
       Clerical Personnel 1973
     ↓ Management Personnel 1973
       Sales Personnel 1973
       Secretarial Personnel 1973

White Noise 1973
  PN 350   SC 56700
  SN Noise composed of random mixture of sounds of different wavelengths.
  B   Auditory Stimulation 1967

White Rats
  Use Rats

Whites 1982
  PN 10039   SC 56720

Whites — (cont'd)
  SN In 1982, this term was created to replace the discontinued term CAUCASIANS. In 2000, CAUCASIANS was stripped from all records and replaced with WHITES.
  UF Caucasians
  B   Racial and Ethnic Groups 2001
  N   Anglos 1988
  R   Race (Anthropological) 1973

Wholistic Health
  Use Holistic Health

Wide Range Achievement Test 1973
  PN 171   SC 56730
  B   Achievement Measures 1967

Widowers 1973
  PN 399   SC 56740
  B   Human Males 1973
  R ↓ Family 1967
     ↓ Marital Status 1973
     ↓ Parental Absence 1973

Widows 1973
  PN 843   SC 56750
  B   Human Females 1973
  R ↓ Family 1967
     ↓ Marital Status 1973
     ↓ Parental Absence 1973

Wilcoxon Sign Rank Test 1973
  PN 16   SC 56760
  UF Sign Rank Test
  B   Nonparametric Statistical Tests 1967

Wilderness Experience 1991
  PN 128   SC 56763
  SN Outdoor environment and activities used to promote experiential learning or to treat and rehabilitate individuals with physical, emotional, or behavioral problems.
  UF Outward Bound
  R   Management Training 1973
     ↓ Psychotherapeutic Techniques 1967
     ↓ Recreation 1967
     ↓ Rehabilitation 1967
     ↓ Sports 1967
       Therapeutic Camps 1978

Willpower
  Use Self Control

Wilson Patterson Conservatism Scale 1973
  PN 16   SC 56780
  B   Attitude Measures 1967

Wine 1973
  PN 62   SC 56810
  B   Alcoholic Beverages 1973

Winnicottian Theory
  Use Object Relations

Winter Depression
  Use Seasonal Affective Disorder

Wisconsin Card Sorting Test 1994
  PN 176   SC 56835
  B   Neuropsychological Assessment 1982

Wisdom 1994
PN 89   SC 56837
R   Intelligence 1967
     ↓ Judgment 1967
     ↓ Knowledge Level 1978

Witchcraft 1973
PN 125   SC 56840
R   Ethnology 1967
     Faith Healing 1973
     Mysticism 1967
     Occultism 1978
     ↓ Parapsychology 1967
     ↓ Religious Beliefs 1973
     Shamanism 1973

Withdrawal (Defense Mechanism) 1973
PN 209   SC 56860
SN   Psychoanalytic term describing the escape from
or avoidance of emotionally or psychologically painful
situations.
     B   Defense Mechanisms 1967
     R   ↓ Separation Reactions 1997

Withdrawal (Drug)
     Use   Drug Withdrawal

Within Subjects Design
     Use   Repeated Measures

Witnesses 1985
PN 1341   SC 56885
SN   Persons giving evidence in a court of law or
observing traumatic events in a nonlegal context.
Also used for analog studies of eyewitness identification performance, perception of witness credibility,
and other studies of witness characteristics having
legal implications.
     UF   Eyewitnesses
     R   ↓ Legal Evidence 1991
          Legal Interrogation 1994
          ↓ Legal Testimony 1982

Wives 1973
PN 2179   SC 56900
     B   Human Females 1973
          Spouses 1973
     N   Housewives 1973

Wolves 1973
PN 131   SC 56910
     B   Canids 1997

Women
     Use   Human Females

Womens Liberation Movement 1973
PN 421   SC 56920
     B   Social Movements 1967
     R   ↓ Activist Movements 1973
          Feminism 1978

**Woodcock Johnson Psychoeducational
   Battery** 2001
PN 46   SC 56926
SN   In 2000, the truncated term WOODCOCK
JOHNSON PSYCHOED BATTERY (which was used
from 1994-2000) was deleted, removed from all
records containing it, and mapped to its expanded
form WOODCOCK JOHNSON PSYCHOEDUCA-
TIONAL BATTERY.
     B   Achievement Measures 1967
     R   Educational Diagnosis 1978

Word Associations 1967
PN 1870   SC 56930
     UF   Associations (Word)
     R   ↓ Associative Processes 1967
          ↓ Cognitive Processes 1967
          Paired Associate Learning 1967

Word Blindness
     Use   Alexia

Word Deafness
     Use   Aphasia

Word Frequency 1973
PN 862   SC 56970
SN   Statistical probability of the occurrence of a
given word in a given natural language.
     R   Contextual Associations 1967

Word Meaning 1973
PN 2476   SC 56980
SN   Connotative or denotative significance of a
word.
     B   Verbal Meaning 1973
     R   Connotations 1973
          Contextual Associations 1967
          ↓ Lexical Access 1988
          Lexical Decision 1988

Word Origins
     Use   Etymology

Word Processing 1991
PN 155   SC 56993
SN   Use of computer software to compose, edit, and
produce text.
     B   Computer Software 1967
          Data Processing 1967
     R   Clerical Secretarial Skills 1973
          ↓ Computer Applications 1973
          ↓ Information Systems 1991
          Typing 1991

Word Recognition 1988
PN 2814   SC 56995
     R   ↓ Associative Processes 1967
          Human Information Storage 1973
          ↓ Reading Skills 1973
          ↓ Recognition (Learning) 1967
          Sight Vocabulary 1973
          Speech Perception 1967
          Words (Phonetic Units) 1967

Words (Form Classes)
     Use   Form Classes (Language)

Words (Phonetic Units) 1967
PN 6401   SC 57020
SN   Spoken or written symbolic representation of an
idea, frequently viewed as the smallest grammatically
independent unit.
     R   Antonyms 1973
          Consonants 1973
          Etymology 1973
          ↓ Grammar 1967
          Homographs 1973
          Homonyms 1973
          ↓ Lexical Access 1988
          Lexical Decision 1988
          Morphology (Language) 1973
          Neologisms 1973
          ↓ Semantics 1967
          Synonyms 1973

Words (Phonetic Units) — (cont'd)
     R   Vowels 1973
          Word Recognition 1988

Words (Vocabulary)
     Use   Vocabulary

Work (Attitudes Toward) 1973
PN 2873   SC 57037
SN   General work values. Use EMPLOYEE ATTI-
TUDES for specific job situations and OCCUPA-
TIONAL ATTITUDES for specific careers.
     UF   Work Ethic
     B   Attitudes 1967
     R   ↓ Employee Attitudes 1967
          Employer Attitudes 1973
          Family Work Relationship 1997
          Job Involvement 1978
          Occupational Attitudes 1973
          ↓ Personnel 1967

Work Adjustment Training 1991
PN 49   SC 57045
SN   Training or programs to help disabled individuals increase work productivity, handle day to day
demands of competitive employment, develop work
tolerance, and to encourage interpersonal work relationships.
     B   Vocational Rehabilitation 1967
     R   ↓ Adjustment 1967
          Occupational Adjustment 1973
          Rehabilitation Counseling 1978
          Supported Employment 1994
          Vocational Evaluation 1991

Work Environments
     Use   Working Conditions

Work Ethic
     Use   Work (Attitudes Toward)

Work Family Relationship
     Use   Family Work Relationship

Work Load 1982
PN 866   SC 57055
SN   Amount of work or working time expected from,
assigned to, or performed by an individual.
     B   Job Characteristics 1985
     R   ↓ Division of Labor 1988
          Human Channel Capacity 1973
          Job Analysis 1967
          ↓ Job Performance 1967
          Work Scheduling 1973
          ↓ Working Conditions 1973

Work Related Illnesses 1994
PN 226   SC 57057
SN   Includes both physical and mental illnesses,
injuries, or disorders. Consider OCCUPATIONAL
STRESS for work related stress.
     R   Industrial Accidents 1973
          ↓ Mental Disorders 1967
          Occupational Exposure 1988
          Occupational Safety 1973
          Occupational Stress 1973
          ↓ Physical Disorders 1997
          ↓ Working Conditions 1973
          Workmens Compensation Insurance 1973

Work Rest Cycles 1973
PN 130   SC 57060

Work Rest Cycles — (cont'd)
SN Strictly scheduled periods of working and resting based on observations that any increase in number of working hours beyond an optimal point diminishes production and efficiency.
B   Working Conditions 1973
R   Work Scheduling 1973

Work Satisfaction
Use Job Satisfaction

Work Scheduling 1973
PN 433   **SC** 57070
SN Individual or organizational distribution of workload or work hours. Consider also WORKDAY SHIFTS.
UF Flextime
      Scheduling (Work)
R ↓ Management Methods 1973
      Work Load 1982
      Work Rest Cycles 1973

Work Study Programs
Use Educational Programs

Work Teams 2001
PN 0   **SC** 57077
B   Teams 1988
N   Self Managing Work Teams 2001
R ↓ Management 1967
    ↓ Management Methods 1973
      Organizational Structure 1967

Work Week Length 1973
PN 80   **SC** 57080
SN Actual number of hours or workdays an employee is required to work during a consecutive 7-day period.
B   Working Conditions 1973

Workday Shifts 1973
PN 608   **SC** 57090
SN Regularly scheduled daily working hours or scheduled working shifts with core hours being in morning, evening, or late night/predawn. Consider also WORK SCHEDULING.
UF Shifts (Workday)
B   Working Conditions 1973

Workers
Use Personnel

Working Alliance
Use Therapeutic Alliance

Working Conditions 1973
PN 5258   **SC** 57120
SN Factors which contribute to the global milieu of the workplace. Includes physical environment characteristics, job content and work load, and psychosocial factors such as personnel composition, norms, attitudes, motivation, and employee services.
UF Factory Environments
      Office Environment
      Work Environments
B   Social Environments 1973
N   Job Enrichment 1973
      Noise Levels (Work Areas) 1973
      Occupational Safety 1973
N   Work Rest Cycles 1973
      Work Week Length 1973
      Workday Shifts 1973
      Working Space 1973

Working Conditions — (cont'd)
R   Disabled Personnel 1997
      Family Work Relationship 1997
      Human Factors Engineering 1973
      Occupational Exposure 1988
      Organizational Climate 1973
      Person Environment Fit 1991
    ↓ Personnel 1967
      Quality of Work Life 1988
      Work Load 1982
      Work Related Illnesses 1994

Working Memory
Use Short Term Memory

Working Space 1973
PN 92   **SC** 57130
SN Physical characteristics of job setting, including such factors as amount of space, noise level, or lighting conditions.
B   Working Conditions 1973

Working Women 1978
PN 2788   **SC** 57135
B   Human Females 1973
R   Dual Careers 1982
    ↓ Employment Status 1982
    ↓ Family 1967
      Family Work Relationship 1997
    ↓ Occupations 1967
    ↓ Personnel 1967
      Single Mothers 1994

Workmens Compensation Insurance 1973
PN 200   **SC** 57140
SN Insurance that provides medical benefits for employees who are injured in work-related accidents and provides continued income during disability.
B   Employee Benefits 1973
      Employee Health Insurance 1973
R   Disabled Personnel 1997
      Work Related Illnesses 1994

World View 1988
PN 1232   **SC** 57150
UF Philosophy of Life
R ↓ Attitudes 1967
      Self Determination 1994
    ↓ Values 1967

World Wide Web (WWW)
Use Internet

Worms 1967
PN 145   **SC** 57160
B   Invertebrates 1973
N   Earthworms 1973
      Planarians 1973

Worry
Use Anxiety

Worship
Use Religious Practices

Wounds 1973
PN 34   **SC** 57180
B   Injuries 1973
N   Self Inflicted Wounds 1973
R   Burns 1973
      Electrical Injuries 1973
    ↓ Head Injuries 1973

Wrist 1973
PN 110   **SC** 57190
B   Joints (Anatomy) 1973
R   Arm (Anatomy) 1973
      Hand (Anatomy) 1967

Writers 1991
PN 537   **SC** 57195
UF Authors
B   Artists 1973
R   Drama 1973
    ↓ Literature 1967

Writing (Creative)
SN Use LITERATURE to access references from 1973-1993.
Use Creative Writing

Writing (Cursive)
Use Cursive Writing

Writing (Handwriting)
Use Handwriting

Writing Skills 1985
PN 1918   **SC** 57225
SN Proficiency in writing as developed through practice and influenced by ability.
B   Communication Skills 1973
R ↓ Literacy 1973
      Literacy Programs 1997
      Verbal Ability 1967
    ↓ Written Communication 1985

Written Communication 1985
PN 3317   **SC** 57227
SN Expression of information in written form.
B   Verbal Communication 1967
N   Creative Writing 1994
R   Note Taking 1991
      Proofreading 1988
      Rhetoric 1991
      Verbal Ability 1967
      Writing Skills 1985

Written Language 1967
PN 1651   **SC** 57230
SN System of signs and symbols used to convey information.
B   Language 1967
N ↓ Alphabets 1973
    ↓ Handwriting 1967
      Numbers (Numerals) 1967
      Paragraphs 1973
      Readability 1978
R ↓ Legibility 1978
      Orthography 1973

Wryneck
Use Torticollis

X Rated Materials
Use Pornography

X Ray Diagnosis
Use Roentgenography

X Ray Therapy
Use Radiation Therapy

Xenophobia
Use Stranger Reactions

Xylocaine
Use Lidocaine

Yawning [1988]
PN 124   **SC** 57300
  B Reflexes [1971]
  R Respiration [1967]

Yoga [1973]
PN 271   **SC** 57310
  B Exercise [1973]
      Religious Practices [1973]
  R Relaxation [1973]

Yohimbine [1988]
PN 229   **SC** 57315
  B Adrenergic Blocking Drugs [1973]

Z Scores
Use Standard Scores

Zen Buddhism [1973]
PN 140   **SC** 57370
  B Buddhism [1973]

Zidovudine [1994]
PN 47   **SC** 57371
  UF Azidothymidine
      AZT
  B Antiviral Drugs [1994]
  R Acquired Immune Deficiency Syndrome [1988]
     ↓ Human Immunodeficiency Virus [1991]

Zimeldine [1988]
PN 46   **SC** 57373
  B Antidepressant Drugs [1971]
      Serotonin Reuptake Inhibitors [1997]

Zinc [1985]
PN 124   **SC** 57375
  B Electrolytes [1973]
      Metallic Elements [1973]

Zoo Environment
Use Animal Captivity

Zoology [1973]
PN 24   **SC** 57380
  B Biology [1967]

Zulliger Z Test [1973]
PN 11   **SC** 57390
  B Projective Personality Measures [1973]

Zungs Self Rating Depression Scale [1973]
PN 72   **SC** 57400
  B Nonprojective Personality Measures [1973]

ROTATED ALPHABETICAL TERMS SECTION

Abandonment
Abdomen
Abdominal Wall
Abducens Nerve
Illinois Test of Psycholinguistic **Abilities**
Ability
Ability Grouping
Ability Level
Ability Tests *USE Aptitude Measures*
Artistic **Ability**
Cognitive **Ability**
Henmon Nelson Tests of Mental Ability *USE Intelligence Measures*
Learning **Ability**
Mathematical **Ability**
Musical **Ability**
Nonverbal **Ability**
Numerical Ability *USE Mathematical Ability*
Reading **Ability**
School and College Ability Test *USE Aptitude Measures*
Spatial **Ability**
Verbal **Ability**
Visual Spatial Ability *USE Visuospatial Ability*
Visuospatial **Ability**
Ablation *USE Lesions*
Brain Ablation *USE Brain Lesions*
Aboriginal Populations
USE Indigenous Populations
Abortion Laws
Elective Abortion *USE Induced Abortion*
Induced **Abortion**
Spontaneous **Abortion**
Therapeutic Abortion *USE Induced Abortion*
Maslow **(Abraham** Harold)
Abreaction *USE Catharsis*
Father **Absence**
Mother **Absence**
Parental **Absence**
Employee **Absenteeism**
Absorption (Physiological)
Alcohol Abstinence *USE Sobriety*
Drug **Abstinence**
Sexual **Abstinence**
Abstraction
Abuse of Power
Abuse Reporting
Alcohol **Abuse**
Child **Abuse**
Child **Abuse** Reporting
Client Abuse *USE Patient Abuse*
Drug **Abuse**
Drug **Abuse** Liability
Drug **Abuse** Prevention
Elder **Abuse**
Emotional **Abuse**
Inhalant **Abuse**
Multidrug Abuse *USE Polydrug Abuse*
Partner **Abuse**
Patient **Abuse**
Physical **Abuse**
Polydrug **Abuse**
Psychological Abuse *USE Emotional Abuse*
Sexual **Abuse**
Solvent Abuse *USE Inhalant Abuse*
Spouse Abuse *USE Partner Abuse*
Substance Abuse *USE Drug Abuse*
Substance Abuse Prevention
USE Drug Abuse Prevention
Academic Achievement
Academic Achievement Motivation
Academic Achievement Prediction
Academic Aptitude
Academic Environment
Academic Failure

Academic Grade Level *USE Grade Level*
Academic Overachievement
Academic Records *USE Student Records*
Academic Self Concept
Academic Specialization
Academic Underachievement
College **Academic** Achievement
Acalculia
Accelerated Speech *USE Speech Rate*
Acceleration Effects
Self Acceptance *USE Self Perception*
Social **Acceptance**
Lexical **Access**
Accessory Nerve *USE Cranial Nerves*
Accident Prevention
Accident Proneness
Accidents
Air Traffic **Accidents**
Automobile Accidents *USE Motor Traffic Accidents*
Cerebrovascular **Accidents**
Home **Accidents**
Industrial **Accidents**
Motor Traffic **Accidents**
Pedestrian **Accidents**
Transportation **Accidents**
Thermal **Acclimatization**
Eye Accommodation
USE Ocular Accommodation
Ocular **Accommodation**
Accomplishment *USE Achievement*
Accountability
Accountants
Certified Public Accountants *USE Accountants*
Accreditation (Education Personnel)
Educational Program **Accreditation**
Hospital **Accreditation**
School Accreditation *USE Educational Program Accreditation*
Teacher Accreditation *USE Accreditation (Education Personel)*
Acculturation *USE Cultural Assimilation*
Nucleus **Accumbens**
Acetaldehyde
Acetazolamide
Acetic Aldehyde *USE Acetaldehyde*
Acetylcholine
Acetylcholinesterase
Acetylsalicylic Acid *USE Aspirin*
Aches *USE Pain*
Achievement
Achievement Measures
Achievement Motivation
Achievement Potential
Academic **Achievement**
Academic **Achievement** Motivation
Academic **Achievement** Prediction
College Academic **Achievement**
Mathematics **Achievement**
Need Achievement *USE Achievement Motivation*
Reading **Achievement**
Scholastic Achievement *USE Academic Achievement*
School Achievement *USE Academic Achievement*
Science **Achievement**
Stanford **Achievement** Test
Wide Range **Achievement** Test
Achilles Tendon Reflex
Achromatic Color
Acetylsalicylic Acid *USE Aspirin*
Ascorbic **Acid**
Aspartic **Acid**
Deoxyribonucleic **Acid**
Dihydroxyphenylacetic **Acid**
Folic **Acid**
Gamma Aminobutyric **Acid**
Gamma Aminobutyric **Acid** Agonists

Gamma Aminobutyric **Acid** Antagonists
Glutamic **Acid**
Homovanillic **Acid**
Hydroxyindoleacetic **Acid** (5-)
Ibotenic **Acid**
Kainic **Acid**
Lactic **Acid**
Lysergic **Acid** Diethylamide
Nicotinic **Acid**
Nicotinic Acid Amide *USE Nicotinamide*
Ribonucleic **Acid**
Uric **Acid**
Valproic **Acid**
Acids
Amino **Acids**
Fatty **Acids**
Nucleic **Acids**
Acoustic Nerve
Acoustic Reflex
Acoustic Stimuli *USE Auditory Stimulation*
Acoustics
Acquaintance Rape
Acquired Immune Deficiency Syndrome
Acrophobia
ACTH Releasing Factor
USE Corticotropin Releasing Factor
Acting Out
Affirmative **Action**
Active Avoidance
USE Avoidance Conditioning
Student **Activism**
Activist Movements
Activities of Daily Living
Daily **Activities**
Extracurricular **Activities**
Activity Level
Activity Therapy *USE Recreation Therapy*
Electrical **Activity**
Self **Actualization**
Auditory **Acuity**
Hearing Acuity *USE Auditory Acuity*
Vernier Acuity *USE Visual Acuity*
Visual **Acuity**
Acupuncture
Acute Alcoholic Intoxication
Acute Paranoid Disorder
USE Paranoia (Psychosis)
Acute Psychosis
Acute Psychotic Episode
USE Acute Psychosis
Acute Schizophrenia
Adaptability (Personality)
Adaptation
Dark **Adaptation**
Environmental **Adaptation**
Light **Adaptation**
Sensory **Adaptation**
Social Adaptation *USE Social Adjustment*
Kirton **Adaption** Innovation Inventory
Adaptive Behavior
Adaptive Testing
Addiction
Alcohol Addiction *USE Alcoholism*
Drug **Addiction**
Heroin **Addiction**
Hospital Addiction Syndrome
USE Munchausen Syndrome
Sexual **Addiction**
Addisons Disease
Food **Additives**
Adenosine
Cyclic **Adenosine** Monophosphate
ADHD *USE Attention Deficit Disorder with Hyperactivity*
Gough **Adjective** Check List

Adjectives
Adjudication
Adjunctive Behavior
Adjustment
Adjustment Disorders
Emotional **Adjustment**
Marital Adjustment *USE Marital Relations*
Occupational **Adjustment**
Personal Adjustment *USE Emotional Adjustment*
Psychological Adjustment *USE Emotional Adjustment*
School **Adjustment**
Social **Adjustment**
Student Adjustment *USE School Adjustment*
Vocational Adjustment *USE Occupational Adjustment*
Work **Adjustment** Training
Adler (Alfred)
Adlerian Psychotherapy
Drug **Administration** Methods
Educational **Administration**
Health Care **Administration**
Hospital **Administration**
School Administration
USE Educational Administration
Test **Administration**
Administrators
USE Management Personnel
Educational Administrators *USE School Administrators*
School **Administrators**
Facility **Admission**
Hospital **Admission**
Psychiatric Hospital **Admission**
Student **Admission** Criteria
Adolescent Attitudes
Adolescent Development
Adolescent Fathers
Adolescent Mothers
Adolescent Pregnancy
Adolescent Psychiatry
Adolescent Psychology
Adolescent Psychotherapy
Adopted Children
Adoptees
Adoption (Child)
Interracial **Adoption**
Transracial Adoption *USE Interracial Adoption*
Adoptive Parents
Adrenal Cortex Hormones
Adrenal Cortex Steroids
USE Corticosteroids
Adrenal Gland Disorders
Adrenal Gland Secretion
Adrenal Glands
Adrenal Medulla Hormones
Hypothalamo Pituitary **Adrenal** System
Adrenalectomy
Adrenaline *USE Epinephrine*
Adrenergic Blocking Drugs
Adrenergic Drugs
Adrenergic Nerves
Adrenocorticotropin *USE Corticotropin*
Adrenolytic Drugs *USE Adrenergic Drugs*
Adult Attitudes
Adult Children *USE Adult Offspring*
Adult Day Care
Adult Development
Adult Education
Adult Learning
Adult Offspring
Leiter Adult Intelligence Scale
USE Intelligence Measures
Wechsler **Adult** Intelligence Scale
Adultery *USE Extramarital Intercourse*
Advance Directives
Advance Organizers
Adventitious Disorders

Adventitiously Handicapped
    USE Adventitious Disorders
Adverbs
Drug **Adverse** Reactions
    USE Side Effects (Drug)
Advertising
Television **Advertising**
Advocacy
Child **Advocacy** *USE Advocacy*
Aerobic Exercise
Aerospace Personnel
Aesthetic Preferences
Aesthetics
Aetiology *USE Etiology*
CNS **Affecting** Drugs
Heart Rate **Affecting** Drugs
Affection
Affective Disorders
Affective Disturbances
    USE Affective Disorders
Affective Education
Affective Psychosis
Bipolar Affective Disorder *USE Bipolar Disorder*
Seasonal **Affective** Disorder
Afferent Pathways
Afferent Stimulation
Afferentation *USE Afferent Stimulation*
Affiliation Motivation
Need for Affiliation *USE Affiliation Motivation*
Religious **Affiliation**
Affirmative Action
African Americans *USE Blacks*
Aftercare
Perceptual **Aftereffect**
Afterimage
Age Differences
Age Discrimination
Age Regression (Hypnotic)
Developmental **Age** Groups
Intelligence Age *USE Mental Age*
Mental **Age**
Aged (Attitudes Toward)
Government **Agencies**
County Agricultural Agents *USE Agricultural Extension Workers*
Insurance Agents *USE Sales Personnel*
Aggressive Behavior
Animal **Aggressive** Behavior
Passive **Aggressive** Personality
Aggressiveness
Physical **Agility**
Aging
Aging (Attitudes Toward)
Physiological **Aging**
Paralysis Agitans *USE Parkinsons Disease*
Agitated Depression
    USE Major Depression
Agitation
Agnosia
Agonistic Behavior
    USE Aggressive Behavior
Benzodiazepine **Agonists**
Dopamine **Agonists**
GABA Agonists *USE Gamma Aminobutyric Acid Agonists*
Gamma Aminobutyric Acid **Agonists**
Narcotic **Agonists**
Opiate Agonists *USE Narcotic Agonists*
Serotonin **Agonists**
Agoraphobia
Agrammatism *USE Aphasia*
Agraphia
Agreeableness
Agricultural Extension Workers
Agricultural Workers
County Agricultural Agents

USE Agricultural Extension Workers
School Federal Aid *USE Educational Financial Assistance*
Home Health Aides *USE Home Care Personnel*
Psychiatric **Aides**
Teacher **Aides**
AIDS (Attitudes Toward)
AIDS *USE Acquired Immune Deficiency Syndrome*
AIDS Dementia Complex
AIDS Prevention
AIDS Testing *USE HIV Testing*
Educational Audiovisual **Aids**
Hearing **Aids**
Mobility **Aids**
Optical **Aids**
Air Encephalography
    USE Pneumoencephalography
Air Force Personnel
Air Traffic Accidents
Air Traffic Control
Air Transportation
Aircraft
Aircraft Crew *USE Aerospace Personnel*
Aircraft Pilots
Airplanes *USE Aircraft*
Akathisia
Akinesia *USE Apraxia*
Alanines
Alanon *USE Alcohol Rehabilitation*
Alarm Responses
Alaska Natives
Native Alaskans *USE Alaska Natives*
Alateen *USE Alcohol Rehabilitation*
Ellis **(Albert)**
Albinism
Albino Rats *USE Rats*
Serum **Albumin**
Alcohol Abstinence *USE Sobriety*
Alcohol Abuse
Alcohol Addiction *USE Alcoholism*
Alcohol Dehydrogenases
Alcohol Drinking Attitudes
Alcohol Drinking Patterns
Alcohol Education *USE Drug Education*
Alcohol Intoxication
Alcohol Rehabilitation
Alcohol Withdrawal
Blood **Alcohol** Concentration
Ethyl Alcohol *USE Ethanol*
Fetal **Alcohol** Syndrome
Methyl Alcohol *USE Methanol*
Alcoholic Beverages
Alcoholic Hallucinosis
Alcoholic Psychosis
Acute **Alcoholic** Intoxication
Chronic **Alcoholic** Intoxication
Alcoholics Anonymous
Alcoholism
Alcohols
Acetic Aldehyde *USE Acetaldehyde*
Aldolases *USE Enzymes*
Aldosterone
Alexia
Alexithymia
Adler **(Alfred)**
Algebra *USE Mathematics*
Algorithms
Alienation
Alkaloids
Opium Alkaloids *USE Alkaloids*
Opium Alkaloids *USE Opiates*
Allergens *USE Antigens*
Allergic Disorders
Allergic Skin Disorders
Drug **Allergies**

Food **Allergies**
Therapeutic **Alliance**
Working Alliance *USE Therapeutic Alliance*
Alligators *USE Crocodilians*
Allocation of Resources
    USE Resource Allocation
Resource **Allocation**
Reward **Allocation**
Allport Vernon Lindzey Study Values
    USE Attitude Measures
Living **Alone**
Alopecia
Reading Aloud *USE Oral Reading*
Alpha Methylparatyrosine
Alpha Methyltyrosine
    USE Alpha Methylparatyrosine
Alpha Rhythm
Initial Teaching **Alphabet**
Letters **(Alphabet)**
Alphabets
Alprazolam
Delayed **Alternation**
Language Alternation *USE Code Switching*
Spontaneous **Alternation**
Alternative Medicine
Alternative Schools
    USE Nontraditional Education
Altitude Effects
Altruism
Aluminum
Alzheimers Disease
Dementia of Alzheimers Type *USE Alzheimers Disease*
Amantadine
Amatadine *USE Amantadine*
Amaurotic Familial Idiocy
Stimulus **Ambiguity**
Tolerance for **Ambiguity**
Ambition *USE Aspirations*
Ambivalence
Amblyopia
Ambulatory Care
    USE Outpatient Treatment
Amenorrhea
Amentia *USE Mental Retardation*
Volunteers in Service to **America**
American Indians
African Americans *USE Blacks*
Asian Americans *USE Asians*
Cuban Americans *USE Hispanics*
Japanese **Americans**
Mexican **Americans**
Native Americans *USE American Indians*
Puerto Rican Americans *USE Hispanics*
Spanish Americans *USE Hispanics*
Nicotinic Acid Amide *USE Nicotinamide*
Amine Oxidase Inhibitors
Amines
Sympathomimetic **Amines**
Amino Acids
Gamma **Aminobutyric** Acid
Gamma **Aminobutyric** Acid Agonists
Gamma **Aminobutyric** Acid Antagonists
Aminotransferases *USE Transaminases*
Amitriptyline
Amnesia
Global **Amnesia**
Amniocentesis *USE Prenatal Diagnosis*
Amniotic Fluid
Amobarbital
Amobarbital Sodium *USE Amobarbital*
Reinforcement **Amounts**
Amphetamine
Amphetamine Sulfate *USE Amphetamine*
Amphibia
Amplifiers (Apparatus)

Response **Amplitude**
Amputation
Amygdaloid Body
Amytal *USE Amobarbital*
Anabolism
Anabolites *USE Metabolites*
Anaclitic Depression
Anagram Problem Solving
Anagrams
Analeptic Drugs
Analgesia
Analgesic Drugs
Analog Computers
Miller **Analogies** Test
Analogy
Analysis
Analysis of Covariance
Analysis of Variance
Behavior **Analysis**
Causal **Analysis**
Cluster **Analysis**
Cohort **Analysis**
Confirmatory Factor Analysis *USE Factor Analysis*
Content **Analysis**
Content **Analysis** (Test)
Costs and Cost **Analysis**
Discourse **Analysis**
Dream **Analysis**
Error **Analysis**
Factor **Analysis**
Functional **Analysis**
Interaction **Analysis** (Statistics)
Item **Analysis** (Statistical)
Item **Analysis** (Test)
Job **Analysis**
Linkage Analysis *USE Genetic Linkage*
Meta **Analysis**
Multivariate **Analysis**
Path **Analysis**
Regression Analysis *USE Statistical Regression*
Risk **Analysis**
Self **Analysis**
Statistical **Analysis**
Systems **Analysis**
Task **Analysis**
Transactional **Analysis**
Analysts *USE Psychoanalysts*
Analytic Psychology
    USE Jungian Psychology
Analytical Psychotherapy
Neural **Analyzers**
Anankastic Personality
    USE Obsessive Compulsive
    Personality
Anaphylactic Shock
Anatomical Systems
Anatomically Detailed Dolls
Anatomy
Arm **(Anatomy)**
Arteries **(Anatomy)**
Back **(Anatomy)**
Capillaries **(Anatomy)**
Diaphragm **(Anatomy)**
Ear **(Anatomy)**
Elbow **(Anatomy)**
Eye **(Anatomy)**
Face **(Anatomy)**
Feet **(Anatomy)**
Fingers **(Anatomy)**
Hand **(Anatomy)**
Head **(Anatomy)**
Joints **(Anatomy)**
Labyrinth **(Anatomy)**
Leg **(Anatomy)**
Mouth **(Anatomy)**

Neck **(Anatomy)**
Palm **(Anatomy)**
Scalp **(Anatomy)**
Shoulder **(Anatomy)**
Skin **(Anatomy)**
Teeth **(Anatomy)**
Veins **(Anatomy)**
Ancestors
Androgen Antagonists *USE Antiandrogens*
Androgens
Androgyny
Anemia
Anencephaly
Anesthesia (Feeling)
Anesthesiology
Anesthetic Drugs
Ether **(Anesthetic)**
General **Anesthetics**
Local **Anesthetics**
Aneurysms
Anger
Anger Control
Angina Pectoris
Angiography
Angiotensin
Cerebellopontile Angle *USE Cerebellum*
Anglos
Angst *USE Anxiety*
Anguish *USE Distress*
Anhedonia
Carbonic Anhydrase *USE Enzymes*
Animal Aggressive Behavior
Animal Assisted Therapy
Animal Behavior *USE Animal Ethology*
Animal Biological Rhythms
Animal Breeding
Animal Captivity
Animal Circadian Rhythms
Animal Coloration
Animal Communication
Animal Courtship Behavior
Animal Courtship Displays
Animal Defensive Behavior
Animal Development
Animal Distress Calls
Animal Division of Labor
Animal Domestication
Animal Dominance
Animal Drinking Behavior
Animal Emotionality
Animal Environments
Animal Escape Behavior
Animal Ethology
Animal Exploratory Behavior
Animal Feeding Behavior
Animal Foraging Behavior
Animal Grooming Behavior
Animal Hoarding Behavior
Animal Homing
Animal Human Interaction
  USE Interspecies Interaction
Animal Innate Behavior
  USE Instinctive Behavior
Animal Instinctive Behavior
  USE Instinctive Behavior
Animal Licking Behavior *USE Licking*
Animal Locomotion
Animal Mate Selection
Animal Maternal Behavior
Animal Maternal Deprivation
Animal Mating Behavior
Animal Models
Animal Motivation
Animal Navigation
  USE Migratory Behavior (Animal)

Animal Nocturnal Behavior
Animal Open Field Behavior
Animal Parental Behavior
Animal Paternal Behavior
Animal Play
Animal Predatory Behavior
Animal Rearing
Animal Scent Marking
Animal Sex Differences
Animal Sexual Behavior
Animal Sexual Receptivity
Animal Social Behavior
Animal Strain Differences
Animal Tool Use *USE Tool Use*
Animal Vocalizations
Animal Welfare
Human Animal Interaction
  USE Interspecies Interaction
Infants **(Animal)**
Migratory Behavior **(Animal)**
Seals **(Animal)**
Animals
Female **Animals**
Male **Animals**
Animism
Ankle
Anniversary Events
Anniversary Reactions
  USE Anniversary Events
Annual Leave
  USE Employee Leave Benefits
Anodynes *USE Analgesic Drugs*
Anomie
Anonymity
Alcoholics **Anonymous**
Gamblers Anonymous *USE Twelve Step Programs*
Narcotics Anonymous *USE Twelve Step Programs*
Anorexia Nervosa
Anorexigenic Drugs
  USE Appetite Depressing Drugs
Anosmia
Anosognosia
Anoxia
Antabuse *USE Disulfiram*
Antagonism *USE Hostility*
Androgen Antagonists *USE Antiandrogens*
Benzodiazepine **Antagonists**
CNS Depressant Drug Antagonists *USE Analeptic Drugs*
Dopamine **Antagonists**
Estrogen Antagonists *USE Antiestrogens*
GABA Antagonists
  USE Gamma Aminobutyric Acid
    Antagonists
Gamma Aminobutyric Acid **Antagonists**
Narcotic **Antagonists**
Opiate Antagonists *USE Narcotic Antagonists*
Opioid Antagonists *USE Narcotic Antagonists*
Serotonin **Antagonists**
Culture **(Anthropological)**
Race **(Anthropological)**
Subculture **(Anthropological)**
Anthropologists
Anthropology
Anti Inflammatory Drugs
Antiadrenergic Drugs
  USE Sympatholytic Drugs
Antiandrogens
Antianxiety Drugs *USE Tranquilizing Drugs*
Antibiotics
Antibodies
Anticholinergic Drugs
  USE Cholinergic Blocking Drugs
Anticholinesterase Drugs
  USE Cholinesterase Inhibitors
Serial **Anticipation** (Learning)

Anticoagulant Drugs
Anticonvulsive Drugs
Antidepressant Drugs
Tricyclic **Antidepressant** Drugs
Antiemetic Drugs
Antiepileptic Drugs
    USE Anticonvulsive Drugs
Antiestrogens
Antigens
Antihistaminic Drugs
Antihypertensive Drugs
Antinauseant Drugs *USE Antiemetic Drugs*
Antineoplastic Drugs
Antiparkinsonian Drugs
    USE Antitremor Drugs
Antipathy *USE Aversion*
Antipsychotic Drugs
    USE Neuroleptic Drugs
Antipyretic Drugs
    USE Anti Inflammatory Drugs
Antischizophrenic Drugs
    USE Neuroleptic Drugs
AntiSemitism
Antisocial Behavior
Antisocial Personality
Antispasmodic Drugs
Antitremor Drugs
Antitubercular Drugs
Antiviral Drugs
Antonyms
Ants
Anxiety
Anxiety Disorders
Anxiety Management
Anxiety Neurosis *USE Anxiety Disorders*
Anxiety Reducing Drugs
    USE Tranquilizing Drugs
Castration **Anxiety**
Childrens Manifest **Anxiety** Scale
Computer **Anxiety**
Death **Anxiety**
Generalized Anxiety Disorder *USE Anxiety Disorders*
Mathematics **Anxiety**
Performance **Anxiety**
Separation **Anxiety**
Social **Anxiety**
Speech **Anxiety**
State Trait **Anxiety** Inventory
Taylor Manifest **Anxiety** Scale
Test **Anxiety**
Anxiolytic Drugs *USE Tranquilizing Drugs*
Anxiousness *USE Anxiety*
Aorta
Apathy
Apes *USE Primates (Nonhuman)*
Aphagia
Aphasia
Aphrodisiacs
Aplysia *USE Snails*
Apnea
Sleep **Apnea**
Apomorphine
Apomorphine Hydrochloride
    USE Apomorphine
Apoplexy *USE Cerebrovascular Accidents*
Apparatus
Amplifiers **(Apparatus)**
Cage **Apparatus**
Experimental Apparatus *USE Apparatus*
Generators **(Apparatus)**
Incubators **(Apparatus)**
Stimulators **(Apparatus)**
Timers **(Apparatus)**
Vestibular **Apparatus**
Vibrators **(Apparatus)**

Apparent Distance
Apparent Movement
Apparent Size
Physical **Appearance**
Apperception
Childrens **Apperception** Test
Thematic **Apperception** Test
Appetite
Appetite Depressing Drugs
Appetite Disorders *USE Eating Disorders*
Job **Applicant** Attitudes
Job **Applicant** Interviews
Job **Applicant** Screening
Job **Applicants**
Computer **Applications**
Applied Psychology
Apprehension *USE Anxiety*
Communication Apprehension *USE Speech Anxiety*
Apprenticeship
Biopsychosocial **Approach**
Interdisciplinary Treatment **Approach**
Multidisciplinary Treatment Approach *USE Interdisciplinary Treatment*
    Approach
Multimodal Treatment **Approach**
Need for **Approval**
Social **Approval**
Apraxia
Aptitude *USE Ability*
Aptitude Measures
Academic **Aptitude**
College Entrance
Examination Board Scholastic **Aptitude** Test
Differential **Aptitude** Tests
General **Aptitude** Test Battery
Mechanical **Aptitude**
Modern Language **Aptitude** Test
Preliminary Scholastic Aptitude Test
    USE College Entrance Examination
    Board Scholastic Aptitude Test
Scholastic Aptitude *USE Academic Aptitude*
Scholastic Aptitude Test
    USE College Entrance Examination
    Board Scholastic Aptitude Test
Cerebral Aqueduct *USE Cerebral Ventricles*
Arabs
Arachnida
Arachnophobia *USE Phobias*
Archetypes
Architects
Architecture
Preoptic **Area**
Ventral Tegmental Area *USE Tegmentum*
Noise Levels (Work **Areas)**
Poverty **Areas**
Recreation **Areas**
Arecoline
Arecoline Hydrobromide *USE Arecoline*
Arguments
Arithmetic *USE Mathematics*
Arm (Anatomy)
Army General Classification Test
Army Personnel
Physiological **Arousal**
Sexual **Arousal**
Living **Arrangements**
Cardiac Arrest *USE Heart Disorders*
Legal **Arrest**
Arrhythmias (Heart)
Arson
Art
Art Education
Art Therapy
Barron Welsh **Art** Scale
Body Art *USE Cosmetic Techniques*
Painting **(Art)**

Photographic **Art**
Arterial Pulse
Arteries (Anatomy)
Carotid **Arteries**
Arteriosclerosis
Cerebral **Arteriosclerosis**
Arthritis
Rheumatoid **Arthritis**
Arthropoda
Articulation (Speech)
Articulation Disorders
Regression Artifact *USE Statistical Regression*
Artificial Insemination
USE Reproductive Technology
Artificial Intelligence
Artificial Limbs *USE Prostheses*
Artificial Pacemakers
Artificial Respiration
Artistic Ability
Artists
Arts
Creative **Arts** Therapy
Industrial Arts Education *USE Vocational Education*
Language **Arts** Education
Martial **Arts**
Performing Arts *USE Arts*
Artwork *USE Art*
Asbestos *USE Hazardous Materials*
Asceticism
Ascorbic Acid
Asian Americans *USE Asians*
Asians
Aspartic Acid
Aspergers Syndrome
Asphyxia *USE Anoxia*
Aspiration Level
Aspirations
Career Aspirations *USE Occupational Aspirations*
Educational **Aspirations**
Occupational **Aspirations**
Vocational Aspirations *USE Occupational Aspirations*
Aspirin
Political **Assassination**
Assertiveness
Assertiveness Training
Assessment *USE Measurement*
Assessment Centers
Assessment Criteria
USE Evaluation Criteria
Behavioral **Assessment**
Cognitive **Assessment**
Curriculum Based **Assessment**
Geriatric **Assessment**
Kaufman **Assessment** Battery for Children
Needs **Assessment**
Neuropsychological **Assessment**
Personality Assessment *USE Personality Measures*
Psychological **Assessment**
Self Assessment *USE Self Evaluation*
Cultural **Assimilation**
Assistance (Social Behavior)
Educational Financial **Assistance**
Employee **Assistance** Programs
School Financial Assistance
USE Educational Financial Assistance
Assisted Suicide
Animal **Assisted** Therapy
Computer **Assisted** Design
Computer **Assisted** Diagnosis
Computer **Assisted** Instruction
Computer **Assisted** Testing
Paired **Associate** Learning
Remote **Associates** Test
Free **Association**
Associationism

Contextual **Associations**
Loosening of Associations
USE Fragmentation (Schizophrenia)
Word **Associations**
Associative Processes
Assortative Mating
Assortive Mating *USE Assortative Mating*
Asthenia
Asthenic Personality
USE Personality Disorders
Asthma
Astrology
Astronauts
Asylums *USE Psychiatric Hospitals*
Ataractic Drugs *USE Tranquilizing Drugs*
Ataraxic Drugs *USE Tranquilizing Drugs*
Ataxia
Atheism
Atherosclerosis
Athetosis
Athletes
College **Athletes**
Athletic Participation
Athletic Performance
Athletic Training
Stereotaxic **Atlas**
Atmospheric Conditions
Atomism *USE Reductionism*
Atrial Fibrillation *USE Fibrillation (Heart)*
Cerebral **Atrophy**
Cortical Atrophy *USE Cerebral Atrophy*
Muscular **Atrophy**
Atropine
Attachment Behavior
Attachment Disorders
Reactive Attachment Disorder
USE Attachment Disorders
Attack Behavior
Heart Attacks *USE Heart Disorders*
Educational **Attainment** Level
Attempted Suicide
School **Attendance**
Attendants (Institutions)
Flight Attendants *USE Aerospace Personnel*
Hospital Attendants *USE Attendants (Institutions)*
Residential Care Attendants *USE Attendants (Institutions)*
Attention
Attention Deficit Disorder
Attention Deficit Disorder with Hyperactivity
Attention Span
Divided **Attention**
Selective **Attention**
Sustained **Attention**
Stimulus **Attenuation**
Attitude Change
Attitude Formation
Attitude Measurement
Attitude Measures
Attitude Similarity
Minnesota Teacher Attitude Inventory *USE Attitude Measures*
Opinion Attitude and Interest Survey
USE Attitude Measures
Parent **Attitude** Research Instrument
Attitudes
Adolescent **Attitudes**
Adult **Attitudes**
Aged **(Attitudes** Toward)
Aging **(Attitudes** Toward)
AIDS **(Attitudes** Toward)
Alcohol Drinking **Attitudes**
Birth Control Attitudes *USE Family Planning Attitudes*
Child **Attitudes**
Childrearing **Attitudes**
Class Attitudes
USE Socioeconomic Class Attitudes

Client **Attitudes**
Community **Attitudes**
Computer **Attitudes**
Consumer **Attitudes**
Counselor **Attitudes**
Death **Attitudes**
Disabled **(Attitudes** Toward)
Drinking Attitudes *USE Alcohol Drinking Attitudes*
Drug Usage **Attitudes**
Eating **Attitudes**
Employee **Attitudes**
Employer **Attitudes**
Environmental **Attitudes**
Family Planning **Attitudes**
Gender Role Attitudes *USE Sex Role Attitudes*
Health Personnel **Attitudes**
Health **Attitudes**
Homosexuality **(Attitudes** Toward)
Job Applicant **Attitudes**
Lower Class **Attitudes**
Marriage **Attitudes**
Mental Illness **(Attitudes** Toward)
Mental Retardation **(Attitudes** Toward)
Middle Class **Attitudes**
Obesity **(Attitudes** Toward)
Occupational **Attitudes**
Parental **Attitudes**
Patient Attitudes *USE Client Attitudes*
Physical Disabilities **(Attitudes** Toward)
Physical Illness **(Attitudes** Toward)
Political **Attitudes**
Psychologist **Attitudes**
Psychotherapist **Attitudes**
Public Attitudes *USE Public Opinion*
Race Attitudes *USE Racial and Ethnic Attitudes*
Racial and Ethnic **Attitudes**
Sensory Disabilities **(Attitudes** Toward)
Sex Role **Attitudes**
Sexual **Attitudes**
Social Class Attitudes
    USE Socioeconomic Class Attitudes
Socioeconomic Class **Attitudes**
Stereotyped **Attitudes**
Student **Attitudes**
Teacher **Attitudes**
Therapist **Attitudes**
Upper Class **Attitudes**
Work **(Attitudes** Toward)
Attorneys
Interpersonal **Attraction**
Physical **Attractiveness**
Attribution
Experimental **Attrition**
Student **Attrition**
Atypical Paranoid Disorder
    USE Paranoia (Psychosis)
Atypical Somatoform Disorder
    USE Body Dysmorphic Disorder
Audiences
Audiogenic Seizures
Audiology
Audiometers
Audiometry
Bekesy Audiometry *USE Audiometry*
Bone Conduction **Audiometry**
Audiotapes
Audiovisual Communications Media
Audiovisual Instruction
Educational **Audiovisual** Aids
Audition *USE Auditory Perception*
Auditory Acuity
Auditory Cortex
Auditory Discrimination
Auditory Displays
Auditory Evoked Potentials

Auditory Feedback
Auditory Hallucinations
Auditory Localization
Auditory Masking
Auditory Nerve *USE Acoustic Nerve*
Auditory Neurons
Auditory Perception
Auditory Stimulation
Auditory Thresholds
Delayed **Auditory** Feedback
Wepman **Auditory** Discrimination Test
Augmentative Communication
Aura
Intra Aural Muscle Reflex *USE Acoustic Reflex*
Aurally Handicapped
    USE Hearing Disorders
Heart **Auricles**
Auricular Fibrillation
    USE Fibrillation (Heart)
Authoritarianism
Authoritarianism Rebellion Scale
    USE Nonprojective Personality
    Measures
Parental Authoritarianism
    USE Parental Permissiveness
Authority
Authors *USE Writers*
Autism
Early Infantile **Autism**
Autistic Children
Autistic Psychopathy
    USE Aspergers Syndrome
Autistic Thinking
Autobiographical Memory
Autobiography
Autoeroticism
Autogenic Training
Autohypnosis
Autoimmune Disorders
    USE Immunologic Disorders
Autokinetic Illusion
Automated Information Coding
Automated Information Processing
Automated Information Retrieval
Automated Information Storage
Automated Speech Recognition
Automatic Speaker Recognition
    USE Automated Speech Recognition
Automation
Automatism
Automobile Accidents
    USE Motor Traffic Accidents
Automobile Safety *USE Highway Safety*
Automobiles
Autonomic Ganglia
Autonomic Nervous System
Autonomic Nervous System Disorders
Postganglionic Autonomic Fibers *USE Autonomic Ganglia*
Preganglionic Autonomic Fibers *USE Autonomic Ganglia*
Autonomy (Government)
Autopsy
Psychological **Autopsy**
Autoregulation *USE Homeostasis*
Autoshaping
Autosome Disorders
Autosomes
Autotomy *USE Self Mutilation*
Gradepoint Average *USE Academic Achievement*
Aversion
Aversion Conditioning
Aversion Therapy
Odor Aversion Conditioning
    USE Aversion Conditioning
Taste Aversion Conditioning
    USE Aversion Conditioning

Aversive Stimulation
Aviation
Aviation Personnel
    USE Aerospace Personnel
Aviation Safety
Aviators *USE Aircraft Pilots*
Avoidance
Avoidance Conditioning
Active Avoidance *USE Avoidance Conditioning*
Passive Avoidance *USE Avoidance Conditioning*
Avoidant Personality
Awareness
Body **Awareness**
Axons
Azidothymidine *USE Zidovudine*
AZT *USE Zidovudine*
Type B Personality
    USE Coronary Prone Behavior
White Betz A B Scale *USE Nonprojective Personality*
    Measures
Babbling *USE Infant Vocalization*
Bush Babies *USE Lemurs*
Test Tube Babies *USE Reproductive Technology*
Babinski Reflex
Baboons
Babysitting *USE Child Care*
Back (Anatomy)
Back Pain
Educational **Background**
Family **Background**
Parent Educational **Background**
Backward Masking *USE Masking*
Baclofen
Bacteria *USE Microorganisms*
Bacterial Disorders
Bacterial Meningitis
Baldness *USE Alopecia*
Ballet *USE Dance*
Head **Banging**
Bannister Repertory Grid
Baptists *USE Protestants*
Barbital
Barbiturate Poisoning
Barbiturates
Bargaining
Barium
Barometric Pressure
    USE Atmospheric Conditions
Baroreceptors
Epstein **Barr** Viral Disorder
Barrett Lennard Relationship Inventory
Blood Brain **Barrier**
Barron Welsh Art Scale
Basal Ganglia
Basal Metabolism
Basal Readers *USE Reading Materials*
Basal Skin Resistance
Nucleus **Basalis** Magnocellularis
Baseball
Curriculum **Based** Assessment
Knowledge Based Systems *USE Expert Systems*
Basic Skills Testing
    USE Minimum Competency Tests
Iowa Tests of **Basic** Skills
Basketball
Bass (Fish)
Bats
Battered Child Syndrome
Battered Females
General Aptitude Test **Battery**
Halstead Reitan Neuropsychological **Battery**
Kaufman Assessment **Battery** for Children
Luria Nebraska Neuropsychological **Battery**
Woodcock Johnson Psychoed **Battery**
Bayes Theorem *USE Statistical Probability*

Bayley Scales of Infant Development
Heart Beat *USE Heart Rate*
Beavers
Beck Depression Inventory
Bedwetting *USE Urinary Incontinence*
Beer
Bees
Beetles
Behavior
Behavior Analysis
Behavior Change
Behavior Contracting
Behavior Disorders
Behavior Modification
Behavior Problems
Behavior Therapy
Adaptive **Behavior**
Adjunctive **Behavior**
Aggressive **Behavior**
Agonistic Behavior *USE Aggressive Behavior*
Animal Aggressive **Behavior**
Animal Courtship **Behavior**
Animal Defensive **Behavior**
Animal Drinking **Behavior**
Animal Escape **Behavior**
Animal Exploratory **Behavior**
Animal Feeding **Behavior**
Animal Foraging **Behavior**
Animal Grooming **Behavior**
Animal Hoarding **Behavior**
Animal Innate Behavior *USE Instinctive Behavior*
Animal Instinctive Behavior *USE Instinctive Behavior*
Animal Licking Behavior *USE Licking*
Animal Maternal **Behavior**
Animal Mating **Behavior**
Animal Nocturnal **Behavior**
Animal Open Field **Behavior**
Animal Parental **Behavior**
Animal Paternal **Behavior**
Animal Predatory **Behavior**
Animal Sexual **Behavior**
Animal Social **Behavior**
Animal Behavior *USE Animal Ethology*
Antisocial **Behavior**
Assistance (Social **Behavior**)
Attachment **Behavior**
Attack **Behavior**
Charitable **Behavior**
Child **Behavior** Checklist
Childhood Play **Behavior**
Choice **Behavior**
Classroom **Behavior**
Classroom **Behavior** Modification
Cognitive Behavior Therapy *USE Cognitive Therapy*
Collective **Behavior**
Conservation (Ecological **Behavior**)
Consumer **Behavior**
Coping **Behavior**
Coronary Prone **Behavior**
Deviant Behavior *USE Antisocial Behavior*
Disruptive Behavior *USE Behavior Problems*
Drinking **Behavior**
Driving **Behavior**
Exploratory **Behavior**
Fundamental Interpersonal
Relation Orientation **Behavior** Ques
Health Care Seeking **Behavior**
Health **Behavior**
Help Seeking **Behavior**
Helping Behavior *USE Assistance (Social Behavior)*
Illness **Behavior**
Instinctive **Behavior**
Migratory **Behavior** (Animal)
Modeling Behavior *USE Imitation (Learning)*
Organizational **Behavior**

293

Planned **Behavior**
Prosocial **Behavior**
Psychosexual **Behavior**
Rotational **Behavior**
Runaway **Behavior**
Self Defeating **Behavior**
Self Destructive **Behavior**
Sexual Behavior *USE Psychosexual Behavior*
Sharing (Social **Behavior)**
Social **Behavior**
Stereotyped **Behavior**
Treatment Seeking Behavior
     USE Health Care Seeking Behavior
Trust (Social **Behavior)**
Voting **Behavior**
Wandering **Behavior**
Behavioral Assessment
Behavioral Contrast
Behavioral Ecology
Behavioral Genetics
Behavioral Health
  USE Health Care Psychology
Behavioral Medicine
  USE Health Care Psychology
Behavioral Sciences
Behaviorism
Well **Being**
Bekesy Audiometry *USE Audiometry*
Irrational **Beliefs**
Religious **Beliefs**
Wechsler **Bellevue** Intelligence Scale
Safety **Belts**
Seat Belts *USE Safety Belts*
Bem Sex Role Inventory
Bemegride
Benactyzine
Benadryl *USE Diphenhydramine*
Bender Gestalt Test
Employee Leave **Benefits**
Employee **Benefits**
Vacation Benefits *USE Employee Leave Benefits*
Benign Neoplasms
Benton Revised Visual Retention Test
Benzedrine *USE Amphetamine*
Benzodiazepine Agonists
Benzodiazepine Antagonists
Benzodiazepines
Bereavement *USE Grief*
Beta Blockers
  USE Adrenergic Blocking Drugs
Between Groups Design
White Betz A B Scale
  USE Nonprojective Personality
   Measures
Beverages (Nonalcoholic)
Alcoholic **Beverages**
Cultural Test **Bias**
Experimenter **Bias**
Item Bias *USE Test Bias*
Response **Bias**
Test **Bias**
Biased Sampling
Bible
Bibliotherapy
Bicuculline
Spina **Bifida**
Big Five Personality Model
  USE Five Factor Personality Model
Bile
Bilingual Education
Bilingualism
Double **Bind** Interaction
Receptor **Binding**
Stanford **Binet** Intelligence Scale
Binge Eating

Binocular Vision
Binomial Distribution
Bioavailability
Biochemical Markers
  USE Biological Markers
Biochemistry
Bioequivalence *USE Bioavailability*
Biofeedback
Biofeedback Training
Biographical Data
Biographical Inventories
Biography
Biological Family
Biological Markers
Biological Psychiatry
Biological Rhythms
Biological Symbiosis
Animal **Biological** Rhythms
Human **Biological** Rhythms
Biology
Cells **(Biology)**
Hybrids **(Biology)**
Biopsy
Biopsychosocial Approach
Biopsychosocial Model
  USE Biopsychosocial Approach
Biosynthesis
Bipolar Affective Disorder
  USE Bipolar Disorder
Bipolar Disorder
Bipolar Mood Disorder
  USE Bipolar Disorder
Biracial Children *USE Interracial Offspring*
Birds
Birth
Birth Control
Birth Control Attitudes
  USE Family Planning Attitudes
Birth Injuries
Birth Order
Birth Parents *USE Biological Family*
Birth Rate
Birth Rites
Birth Trauma
Birth Weight
Diaphragms **(Birth** Control)
Home Birth *USE Midwifery*
Low Birth Weight *USE Birth Weight*
Premature **Birth**
Multiple **Births**
Point **Biserial** Correlation
Bisexuality
Nail **Biting**
Bitterness *USE Taste Perception*
Black Power Movement
Blackbirds
Blacks
Blacky Pictures Test
  USE Projective Personality Measures
Bladder
Blame
Rotter Incomplete Sentences **Blank**
Strong Vocational Interest **Blank**
Blind
Deaf **Blind**
Color **Blindness**
Hysterical Blindness
  USE Hysterical Vision Disturbances
Mind Blindness *USE Theory of Mind*
Word Blindness *USE Alexia*
Blink Reflex *USE Eyeblink Reflex*
Kohs **Block** Design Test
Beta Blockers *USE Adrenergic Blocking Drugs*
Calcium Channel Blockers *USE Channel Blockers*
Channel **Blockers**

Adrenergic **Blocking** Drugs
Cholinergic **Blocking** Drugs
Ganglion **Blocking** Drugs
Neuromuscular Blocking Drugs
      USE Muscle Relaxing Drugs
Blood
Blood Alcohol Concentration
Blood and Lymphatic Disorders
Blood Brain Barrier
Blood Cells
Blood Circulation
Blood Coagulation
Blood Disorders
      USE Blood and Lymphatic Disorders
Blood Donation *USE Tissue Donation*
Blood Flow
Blood Glucose *USE Blood Sugar*
Blood Groups
Blood Plasma
Blood Platelets
Blood Pressure
Blood Pressure Disorders
Blood Proteins
Blood Serum
Blood Sugar
Blood Transfusion
Blood Vessels
Blood Volume
Cerebral **Blood** Flow
Red Blood Cells *USE Erythrocytes*
White Blood Cells *USE Leucocytes*
Blue Collar Workers
College Entrance Examination **Board** Scholastic Aptitude Test
State Board Examinations
      USE Professional Examinations
Boarding Schools
Boards of Education
Dementia with Lewy **Bodies**
Geniculate **Bodies** (Thalamus)
Body Art *USE Cosmetic Techniques*
Body Awareness
Body Dysmorphic Disorder
Body Fluids
Body Height
Body Image
Body Image Disturbances
Body Language
Body Rocking
Body Rotation *USE Rotational Behavior*
Body Size
Body Sway Testing
Body Temperature
Body Types *USE Somatotypes*
Body Weight
Amygdaloid **Body**
Lewy Body Disease
      USE Dementia with Lewy Bodies
Mind Body *USE Dualism*
Out of **Body** Experiences
Pineal **Body**
Thermoregulation **(Body)**
Tissues **(Body)**
Bombesin
Bone Conduction Audiometry
Bone Disorders
Bone Marrow
Bones
Bonobos
Bonuses
Books
Borderline Mental Retardation
Borderline Personality
Borderline States
Boredom
Botany

Bottle Feeding
Outward Bound *USE Wilderness Experience*
Upward **Bound**
Boundaries (Psychological)
Sexual Boundary Violations
      USE Professional Client Sexual Relations
Bourgeois *USE Middle Class*
Bowel Disorders *USE Colon Disorders*
Irritable **Bowel** Syndrome
Shuttle Box Grids *USE Shuttle Boxes*
Shuttle Box Hurdles *USE Shuttle Boxes*
Shuttle **Boxes**
Skinner **Boxes**
Boys *USE Human Males*
Brachial Plexus *USE Spinal Nerves*
Bradycardia
Bradykinesia
Braille
Braille Instruction
Brain
Brain Ablation *USE Brain Lesions*
Brain Concussion
Brain Damage
Brain Disorders
Brain Lesions
Brain Mapping *USE Stereotaxic Atlas*
Brain Maps *USE Stereotaxic Atlas*
Brain Metabolism *USE Neurochemistry*
Brain Neoplasms
Brain Self Stimulation
Brain Size
Brain Stem
Brain Stimulation
Brain Weight
Blood **Brain** Barrier
Chemical **Brain** Stimulation
Decortication **(Brain)**
Electrical **Brain** Stimulation
Left **Brain**
Minimal **Brain** Disorders
Organic **Brain** Syndromes
Right **Brain**
Split Brain *USE Commissurotomy*
Traumatic **Brain** Injury
Brainstorming
Brainwashing
Brand Names
Brand Preferences
Bravery *USE Courage*
Nervous Breakdown *USE Mental Disorders*
Psychotherapeutic **Breakthrough**
Breast
Breast Cancer Screening
      USE Cancer Screening
Breast Examination
      USE Self Examination (Medical)
Breast Feeding
Breast Neoplasms
Breathing *USE Respiration*
Animal **Breeding**
Selective **Breeding**
Brief Psychotherapy
Brief Reactive Psychosis
      USE Acute Psychosis
Myers **Briggs** Type Indicator
Bright Light Therapy *USE Phototherapy*
Brightness Constancy
Brightness Contrast
Brightness Perception
Watson (John **Broadus)**
Lithium Bromide *USE Bromides*
Bromides
Bromocriptine
Bronchi

Bronchial Disorders
Brothers
Spearman **Brown** Test
Bruxism
Buddhism
Zen **Buddhism**
Buddhists
Budgerigars
Budgets
Taste **Buds**
Bufotenine
Nest **Building**
Religious **Buildings**
Olfactory **Bulb**
Bulimia
Bulls *USE Cattle*
Medial Forebrain **Bundle**
Bupropion
Caregiver **Burden**
Government Bureaucracy *USE Government*
Burnout *USE Occupational Stress*
Burns
Skinner **(Burrhus** Frederic)
Buses *USE Motor Vehicles*
Bush Babies *USE Lemurs*
Business
Business and Industrial Personnel
Business Education
Business Management
Business Organizations
Business Students
Businessmen
    USE Business and Industrial Personnel
Buspirone
Butterflies
Butyrylperazine
    USE Phenothiazine Derivatives
Buying *USE Consumer Behavior*
Cadres *USE Social Groups*
Caffeine
Cage Apparatus
Calcium
Calcium Channel Blockers
    USE Channel Blockers
Calcium Ions
Calculators *USE Digital Computers*
Calculus *USE Mathematics*
California F Scale
California Psychological Inventory
California Test of Mental Maturity
California Test of Personality
Corpus **Callosum**
Animal Distress **Calls**
Calories
Cameras
Political **Campaigns**
Camping
Concentration **Camps**
Recreational Day Camps *USE Summer Camps (Recreation)*
Summer **Camps** (Recreation)
Therapeutic **Camps**
Campuses
Ear Canal *USE External Ear*
Semicircular **Canals**
Canaries
Cancer Screening
Breast Cancer Screening *USE Cancer Screening*
Prostate Cancer Screening *USE Cancer Screening*
Skin Cancer Screening *USE Cancer Screening*
Terminal **Cancer**
Cancers *USE Neoplasms*
Political **Candidates**
Canids
Cannabinoids
Cannabis

Canonical Correlation
    USE Multivariate Analysis
Human Channel **Capacity**
Capgras Syndrome
Capillaries (Anatomy)
Capital Punishment
Capitalism
Capsaicin
Animal **Captivity**
Captopril
Carbachol
Carbamazepine
Carbidopa
Carbohydrate Metabolism
Carbohydrates
Carbon
Carbon Dioxide
Carbon Monoxide
Carbon Monoxide Poisoning
Lithium **Carbonate**
Carbonic Anhydrase *USE Enzymes*
Carboxyhemoglobinemia
    USE Carbon Monoxide Poisoning
Carcinogens
Carcinomas *USE Neoplasms*
Wisconsin **Card** Sorting Test
Cardiac Arrest *USE Heart Disorders*
Cardiac Disorders *USE Heart Disorders*
Cardiac Rate *USE Heart Rate*
Cardiac Surgery *USE Heart Surgery*
Cardiography
Cardiology
Cardiotonic Drugs *USE Drugs*
Cardiovascular Disorders
Cardiovascular Reactivity
Cardiovascular System
Adult Day **Care**
Ambulatory Care *USE Outpatient Treatment*
Child Day **Care**
Child Self **Care**
Child **Care**
Child **Care** Workers
Day **Care** Centers
Elder **Care**
Foster **Care**
Health **Care** Administration
Health **Care** Costs
Health **Care** Delivery
Health **Care** Policy
Health Care Professionals *USE Health Personnel*
Health **Care** Psychology
Health **Care** Seeking Behavior
Health **Care** Services
Health **Care** Utilization
Home **Care**
Home **Care** Personnel
Intensive **Care**
Long Term **Care**
Managed **Care**
Medical Care Costs *USE Health Care Costs*
Mental Health Care Costs *USE Health Care Costs*
Mental Health Care Policy *USE Health Care Policy*
Palliative **Care**
Patient Care Planning *USE Treatment Planning*
Prenatal **Care**
Primary Health **Care**
Quality of **Care**
Residential Care Attendants
    USE Attendants (Institutions)
Residential **Care** Institutions
Respite **Care**
Self **Care** Skills
Career Aspirations
    USE Occupational Aspirations
Career Change

296

Career Choice *USE Occupational Choice*
Career Counseling
    USE Occupational Guidance
Career Development
Career Education
Career Exploration *USE Career Education*
Career Goals
    USE Occupational Aspirations
Career Guidance
    USE Occupational Guidance
Career Maturity *USE Vocational Maturity*
Career Preference
    USE Occupational Preference
Career Transitions
    USE Career Development
Careers *USE Occupations*
Dual **Careers**
Nontraditional **Careers**
Caregiver Burden
Caregivers
Family Caregivers *USE Caregivers*
Jung **(Carl)**
Rogers **(Carl)**
Carotid Arteries
Carp
Cartoons (Humor)
Case History *USE Patient History*
Case Management
Case Report
Social **Casework**
Caseworkers *USE Social Workers*
Social Caseworkers *USE Social Workers*
Caste System
Castration
Castration Anxiety
Male **Castration**
Cat Learning
CAT Scan *USE Tomography*
Crying **Cat** Syndrome
Catabolism
Catabolites *USE Metabolites*
Catalepsy
Catamnesis *USE Posttreatment Followup*
Cataplexy
Cataracts
Catatonia
Catatonic Schizophrenia
Catecholamines
Categorizing
    USE Classification (Cognitive Process)
Catharsis
Catheterization
Cathexis
Cathode Ray Tubes
    USE Video Display Units
Roman **Catholicism**
Catholics
Cats
Cattell Culture Fair Intelligence Test
    USE Culture Fair Intelligence Test
Cattell Infant Intelligence Scale
    USE Infant Intelligence Scale
Cattle
Caucasians *USE Whites*
Cauda Equina *USE Spinal Nerves*
Caudate Nucleus
Causal Analysis
Cecotrophy *USE Coprophagia*
Celiac Plexus *USE Autonomic Ganglia*
Celibacy *USE Sexual Abstinence*
Cell Nucleus
Sickle **Cell** Disease
Single Cell Organisms *USE Microorganisms*
Cells (Biology)
Blood **Cells**

Connective Tissue **Cells**
Epithelial **Cells**
Ganglion **Cells** (Retina)
Nerve Cells *USE Neurons*
Purkinje **Cells**
Red Blood Cells *USE Erythrocytes*
Retinal Ganglion Cells *USE Ganglion Cells (Retina)*
White Blood Cells *USE Leucocytes*
Censorship
Client **Centered** Therapy
Person Centered Psychotherapy
    USE Client Centered Therapy
Centering
Assessment **Centers**
Community Mental Health **Centers**
Day Care **Centers**
Growth Centers *USE Human Potential Movement*
Learning **Centers** (Educational)
Rehabilitation **Centers**
Shopping **Centers**
Suicide Prevention **Centers**
Central Nervous System
Central Nervous System Disorders
Central Nervous System Drugs
    USE CNS Affecting Drugs
Central Tendency Measures
Central Vision *USE Foveal Vision*
Cerebellar Cortex *USE Cerebellum*
Cerebellar Nuclei *USE Cerebellum*
Cerebellopontile Angle *USE Cerebellum*
Cerebellum
Cerebral Aqueduct
    USE Cerebral Ventricles
Cerebral Arteriosclerosis
Cerebral Atrophy
Cerebral Blood Flow
Cerebral Cortex
Cerebral Dominance
Cerebral Hemorrhage
Cerebral Ischemia
Cerebral Lesions *USE Brain Lesions*
Cerebral Palsy
Cerebral Vascular Disorders
    USE Cerebrovascular Disorders
Cerebral Ventricles
Trigonum Cerebrale *USE Fornix*
Cerebrospinal Fluid
Cerebrovascular Accidents
Cerebrovascular Disorders
Certification Examinations
    USE Professional Examinations
Professional **Certification**
Certified Public Accountants
    USE Accountants
Locus **Ceruleus**
Cervical Plexus *USE Spinal Nerves*
Cervical Sprain Syndrome *USE Whiplash*
Cervix
Smoking **Cessation**
Markov **Chains**
Chance (Fortune)
Attitude **Change**
Behavior **Change**
Career **Change**
Culture **Change**
Job Change *USE Career Change*
Life Change *USE Life Experiences*
Opinion Change *USE Attitude Change*
Organizational **Change**
Personality **Change**
Sex **Change**
Social **Change**
Stimulus **Change**
Lifestyle **Changes**
Channel Blockers

Calcium Channel Blockers *USE Channel Blockers*
Human **Channel** Capacity
Chaos Theory
Chaplains
Character *USE Personality*
Character Development
    USE Personality Development
Character Disorders
    USE Personality Disorders
Character Formation
    USE Personality Development
Client **Characteristics**
Counselor **Characteristics**
Demographic **Characteristics**
Employee **Characteristics**
Job **Characteristics**
Organizational **Characteristics**
Parental **Characteristics**
Patient Characteristics *USE Client Characteristics*
Population Characteristics
    USE Demographic Characteristics
Speech **Characteristics**
Student **Characteristics**
Teacher **Characteristics**
Therapist **Characteristics**
Charisma
Charitable Behavior
Cri du Chat Syndrome *USE Crying Cat Syndrome*
Cheating
Gough Adjective **Check** List
Learys Interpersonal **Check** List
Mooney Problem **Check** List
Child Behavior **Checklist**
Symptom **Checklists**
Chemical Brain Stimulation
Chemical Elements
Chemicals
Chemistry
Chemoreceptors
Chemotherapy *USE Drug Therapy*
Chess
Chest *USE Thorax*
Chewing Tobacco
    USE Smokeless Tobacco
Chi Square Test
Optic **Chiasm**
Chicanos *USE Mexican Americans*
Chickens
Child Abuse
Child Abuse Reporting
Child Advocacy *USE Advocacy*
Child Attitudes
Child Behavior Checklist
Child Care
Child Care Workers
Child Custody
Child Day Care
Child Discipline
Child Guidance Clinics
Child Molestation *USE Pedophilia*
Child Neglect
Child Psychiatric Clinics
    USE Child Guidance Clinics
Child Psychiatry
Child Psychology
Child Psychotherapy
Child Self Care
Child Support
Child Visitation
Child Welfare
Adoption **(Child)**
Battered **Child** Syndrome
Father **Child** Communication
Father **Child** Relations
Mother **Child** Communication

Mother **Child** Relations
Parent **Child** Communication
Parent **Child** Relations
Childbirth *USE Birth*
Childbirth Training
Labor **(Childbirth)**
Natural **Childbirth**
Childhood Development
Childhood Memories *USE Early Memories*
Childhood Neurosis
Childhood Play Behavior
Childhood Play Development
Childhood Psychosis
Childhood Schizophrenia
Early **Childhood** Development
Childlessness
Childrearing Attitudes
Childrearing Practices
Adopted **Children**
Adult Children *USE Adult Offspring*
Autistic **Children**
Biracial Children *USE Interracial Offspring*
Foster **Children**
Grown Children *USE Adult Offspring*
Illegitimate **Children**
Kaufman Assessment Battery for **Children**
Latchkey Children *USE Child Self Care*
Only **Children**
Wechsler Intelligence Scale for **Children**
Childrens Apperception Test
Childrens Manifest Anxiety Scale
Childrens Personality Questionnaire
Childrens Recreational Games
Chimpanzees
Pygmy Chimpanzees *USE Bonobos*
Chinchillas
Chinese Cultural Groups
Chiroptera *USE Bats*
Chloral Hydrate
Chloralose *USE Hypnotic Drugs*
Chlordiazepoxide
Chloride Ions
Choline Chloride *USE Choline*
Chlorimipramine
Chlorisondamine *USE Amines*
Chloroform
Chlorophenylpiperazine *USE Piperazines*
Chlorpromazine
Chlorprothixene
Choice Behavior
Choice Shift
Career Choice *USE Occupational Choice*
Forced **Choice** (Testing Method)
Multiple **Choice** (Testing Method)
Occupational **Choice**
Vocational Choice *USE Occupational Choice*
Cholecystokinin
Cholesterol
Choline
Choline Chloride *USE Choline*
Cholinergic Blocking Drugs
Cholinergic Drugs
Cholinergic Nerves
Cholinesterase
Cholinesterase Inhibitors
Cholinolytic Drugs
    USE Cholinergic Blocking Drugs
Cholinomimetic Drugs
Chorda Tympani Nerve *USE Facial Nerve*
Chorea
Huntingtons Chorea *USE Huntingtons Disease*
Choroid *USE Eye (Anatomy)*
Choroid Plexus *USE Cerebral Ventricles*
Christianity
Christians

Chromaticity
Chromosome Disorders
Deletion **(Chromosome)**
Sex **Chromosome** Disorders
Translocation **(Chromosome)**
Chromosomes
Sex **Chromosomes**
Chronic Alcoholic Intoxication
Chronic Fatigue Syndrome
Chronic Illness
Chronic Mental Illness
Chronic Pain
Chronic Psychosis
Chronic Schizophrenia *USE Schizophrenia*
Chronicity (Disorders)
Churches *USE Religious Buildings*
Cichlids
Cigarette Smoking *USE Tobacco Smoking*
Cimetidine
Gyrus **Cinguli**
Animal **Circadian** Rhythms
Quality Circles *USE Participative Management*
Closed **Circuit** Television
Blood **Circulation**
Circulatory Disorders
USE Cardiovascular Disorders
Circumcision
Cirrhosis (Liver)
Citalopram
Cities *USE Urban Environments*
Citizenship
Inner City *USE Urban Environments*
Civil Law
Civil Rights
Civil Rights Movement
Civil Servants *USE Government Personnel*
Volunteer **Civilian** Personnel
Clairvoyance
Class Attitudes
USE Socioeconomic Class Attitudes
Lower **Class**
Lower **Class** Attitudes
Middle **Class**
Middle **Class** Attitudes
Social **Class**
Social Class Attitudes
USE Socioeconomic Class Attitudes
Socioeconomic **Class** Attitudes
Upper **Class**
Upper **Class** Attitudes
Form **Classes** (Language)
Classical Conditioning
Classification (Cognitive Process)
Classification Systems *USE Taxonomies*
Army General **Classification** Test
International **Classification** of Diseases
Classmates
Classroom Behavior
Classroom Behavior Modification
Classroom Discipline
Classroom Environment
Classroom Instruction *USE Teaching*
Classroom Teachers *USE Teachers*
Open **Classroom** Method
Classrooms
Claustrophobia
Cleft Palate
Clergy
Clerical Personnel
Clerical Secretarial Skills
Client Abuse *USE Patient Abuse*
Client Attitudes
Client Centered Therapy
Client Characteristics

Client Compliance
USE Treatment Compliance
Client Counselor Interaction
USE Psychotherapeutic Processes
Client Dropouts *USE Treatment Dropouts*
Client Education
Client Participation
Client Records
Client Rights
Client Satisfaction
Client Transfer
Client Treatment Matching
Client Violence *USE Patient Violence*
Counselor Client Interaction
USE Psychotherapeutic Processes
Professional **Client** Sexual Relations
Treatment Client Matching
USE Client Treatment Matching
Clients
Climacteric Depression
USE Involutional Depression
Climacteric Paranoia
USE Involutional Paranoid Psychosis
Organizational **Climate**
Clinical Judgment (Not Diagnosis)
Clinical Markers *USE Biological Markers*
Clinical Methods Training
Clinical Psychologists
Clinical Psychology
Clinical Psychology Graduate Training
Clinical Psychology Internship
Clinical Supervision
USE Professional Supervision
Millon **Clinical** Multiaxial Inventory
Structured **Clinical** Interview
Clinicians
Clinics
Child Guidance **Clinics**
Child Psychiatric Clinics *USE Child Guidance Clinics*
Outpatient Psychiatric Clinics *USE Psychiatric Clinics*
Psychiatric **Clinics**
Walk In **Clinics**
Cliques *USE Social Groups*
Clomipramine *USE Chlorimipramine*
Clonazepam
Clonidine
Closed Circuit Television
Closed Head Injuries *USE Head Injuries*
Closedmindedness *USE Openmindedness*
Perceptual **Closure**
Clothing
Clozapine
Cloze Testing
School **Club** Membership
Clubs (Social Organizations)
Therapeutic Social **Clubs**
Cluster Analysis
Clustering *USE Cluster Analysis*
CNS Affecting Drugs
CNS Depressant Drug Antagonists
USE Analeptic Drugs
CNS Depressant Drugs
CNS Stimulating Drugs
Stimulants of CNS *USE CNS Stimulating Drugs*
Coaches
Test **Coaching**
Blood **Coagulation**
Coalition Formation
Coast Guard Personnel
Cobalt
Cocaine
Cochlea
Cochlear Implants
Cochran Q Test
Cockroaches
Code Switching

Codeine
Codeine Sulfate *USE Codeine*
Codependency
Automated Information **Coding**
Coeds *USE College Students*
Coeducation
Pearson Product Moment Correlation Coefficient *USE Statistical Correlation*
Phi **Coefficient**
Coercion
Coffee *USE Beverages (Nonalcoholic)*
Cognition
Cognition Enhancing Drugs
USE Nootropic Drugs
Need for **Cognition**
Social **Cognition**
Transposition **(Cognition)**
Cognitions
Cognitive Ability
Cognitive Assessment
Cognitive Behavior Therapy
USE Cognitive Therapy
Cognitive Complexity
Cognitive Contiguity
Cognitive Development
Cognitive Discrimination
Cognitive Dissonance
Cognitive Functioning *USE Cognitive Ability*
Cognitive Generalization
Cognitive Hypothesis Testing
Cognitive Load
USE Human Channel Capacity
Cognitive Maps
Cognitive Mediation
Cognitive Processes
Cognitive Processing Speed
Cognitive Psychology
Cognitive Rehabilitation
Cognitive Restructuring
Cognitive Style
Cognitive Techniques
Cognitive Therapy
Classification **(Cognitive** Process)
Rumination **(Cognitive** Process)
Cohabitation
Group **Cohesion**
Cohort Analysis
Coitus *USE Sexual Intercourse (Human)*
Cold Effects
Colitis
Ulcerative **Colitis**
Collaboration *USE Cooperation*
Blue **Collar** Workers
White **Collar** Workers
Data **Collection**
Collective Behavior
Collective Unconscious
College Academic Achievement
College Athletes
College Degrees
USE Educational Degrees
College Dropouts
College Education
USE Undergraduate Education
College Entrance Examination Board
Scholastic Aptitude Test
College Environment
College Graduates
College Major
USE Academic Specialization
College Students
College Teachers
Community **College** Students
Junior **College** Students

School and College Ability Test
USE Aptitude Measures
Colleges
Community **Colleges**
Junior Colleges *USE Colleges*
Inferior **Colliculus**
Superior **Colliculus**
Colon Disorders
Color
Color Blindness
Color Constancy
Color Contrast
Color Perception
Color Pyramid Test
USE Projective Personality Measures
Color Saturation
Achromatic **Color**
Eye **Color**
Stroop **Color** Word Test
Animal **Coloration**
Colostomy
Raven **Coloured** Progressive Matrices
Columbia Mental Maturity Scale
Spinal **Column**
Coma
Combat Experience
Physical **Comfort**
Commerce *USE Business*
Commercials *USE Television Advertising*
Commissioned Officers
Hippocampal Commissure *USE Fornix*
Commissurotomy
Commitment
Commitment (Psychiatric)
Organizational **Commitment**
Outpatient **Commitment**
Communes
Communicable Diseases
USE Infectious Disorders
Communication
Communication Apprehension
USE Speech Anxiety
Communication Disorders
Communication Skills
Communication Skills Training
Communication Systems
Communication Theory
Animal **Communication**
Augmentative **Communication**
Cross Cultural **Communication**
Electronic **Communication**
Facilitated Communication
USE Augmentative Communication
Father Child **Communication**
Intercultural Communication
USE Cross Cultural Communication
Interethnic Communication
USE Cross Cultural Communication
Interpersonal **Communication**
Manual **Communication**
Mother Child **Communication**
Nonverbal **Communication**
Oral **Communication**
Parent Child **Communication**
Persuasive **Communication**
Privileged **Communication**
Professional Communication
USE Scientific Communication
Scientific **Communication**
Verbal **Communication**
Written **Communication**
Communications Media
Audiovisual **Communications** Media
Printed **Communications** Media

Communicative Competence
USE Communication Skills
Communism
Communities
Retirement **Communities**
Community Attitudes
Community College Students
Community Colleges
Community Development
Community Facilities
Community Mental Health
Community Mental Health Centers
Community Mental Health Services
Community Mental Health Training
Community Psychiatry
Community Psychology
Community Services
Community Welfare Services
Therapeutic **Community**
Commuting (Travel)
Comorbidity
Companies *USE Business Organizations*
Comparative Psychiatry
USE Transcultural Psychiatry
Comparative Psychology
Social **Comparison**
Interpersonal **Compatibility**
Compensation (Defense Mechanism)
Workmens **Compensation** Insurance
Compensatory Education
Competence
Communicative Competence *USE Communication Skills*
Interpersonal Competence *USE Social Skills*
Professional **Competence**
Competency to Stand Trial
Minimum **Competency** Tests
Competition
Health **Complaints**
Complementary Medicine
USE Alternative Medicine
Franck Drawing **Completion** Test
Sentence **Completion** Tests
AIDS Dementia **Complex**
Electra **Complex**
Oedipal **Complex**
Cognitive **Complexity**
Stimulus **Complexity**
Task **Complexity**
Compliance
Client Compliance *USE Treatment Compliance*
Medical Regimen Compliance *USE Treatment Compliance*
Treatment **Compliance**
Obstetrical **Complications**
Postsurgical **Complications**
Surgical Complications
USE Postsurgical Complications
Comprehension
Comprehension Tests
Listening **Comprehension**
Number **Comprehension**
Reading **Comprehension**
Sentence **Comprehension**
Verbal **Comprehension**
Compressed Speech
Compulsions
Compulsive Gambling
USE Pathological Gambling
Compulsive Neurosis
USE Obsessive Compulsive Disorder
Compulsive Personality Disorder
*USE Obsessive Compulsive
Personality*
Compulsive Repetition
Obsessive **Compulsive** Disorder

Obsessive Compulsive Neurosis
USE Obsessive Compulsive Disorder
Obsessive **Compulsive** Personality
Sexual Compulsivity *USE Sexual Addiction*
Computer Anxiety
Computer Applications
Computer Assisted Design
Computer Assisted Diagnosis
Computer Assisted Instruction
Computer Assisted Testing
Computer Attitudes
Computer Conferencing
USE Teleconferencing
Computer Games
Computer Literacy
Computer Peripheral Devices
Computer Programming
Computer Programming Languages
Computer Programs
USE Computer Software
Computer Searching
Computer Simulation
Computer Software
Computer Training
Human **Computer** Interaction
Computerized Databases *USE Databases*
Computers
Analog **Computers**
Digital **Computers**
Personal Computers *USE Microcomputers*
Concentration
Concentration Camps
Blood Alcohol **Concentration**
Concept Formation
Concept Learning *USE Concept Formation*
Concept Validity *USE Statistical Validity*
Academic Self **Concept**
Conservation **(Concept)**
Self **Concept**
Temporal Spatial Concept Scale *USE Intelligence Measures*
Tennessee Self **Concept** Scale
Concepts
God **Concepts**
Mathematics **(Concepts)**
Conceptual Imagery
Conceptual Tempo
Conceptualization *USE Concept Formation*
Concurrent Reinforcement Schedules
Concurrent Validity *USE Statistical Validity*
Brain **Concussion**
Conditioned Emotional Responses
Conditioned Inhibition
USE Conditioned Suppression
Conditioned Place Preference
USE Place Conditioning
Conditioned Reflex
USE Conditioned Responses
Conditioned Responses
Conditioned Stimulus
Conditioned Suppression
Conditioning
Aversion **Conditioning**
Avoidance **Conditioning**
Classical **Conditioning**
Escape **Conditioning**
Eyelid **Conditioning**
Fading **(Conditioning)**
Higher Order **Conditioning**
Instrumental Conditioning *USE Operant Conditioning*
Odor Aversion Conditioning *USE Aversion Conditioning*
Operant **Conditioning**
Pavlovian Conditioning *USE Classical Conditioning*
Place **Conditioning**
Respondent Conditioning *USE Classical Conditioning*

Second Order Conditioning
    USE Higher Order Conditioning
Taste Aversion Conditioning *USE Aversion Conditioning*
Verbal Conditioning *USE Verbal Learning*
Atmospheric **Conditions**
Mental Disorders due to
General Medical **Conditions**
Working **Conditions**
Condoms
Conduct Disorder
Bone **Conduction** Audiometry
Skin Conduction *USE Skin Resistance*
Cones (Eye)
Confabulation
Computer Conferencing *USE Teleconferencing*
Confession (Religion)
Confidence Limits (Statistics)
Self **Confidence**
Confidentiality of Information
    USE Privileged Communication
Confirmatory Factor Analysis
    USE Factor Analysis
Conflict
Conflict Resolution
Marital **Conflict**
Role **Conflicts**
Conformity (Personality)
Mental **Confusion**
Congenital Disorders
Drug Induced **Congenital** Disorders
Congenitally Handicapped
    USE Congenital Disorders
Self **Congruence**
Conjoint Measurement
Conjoint Therapy
Connectionism
Connective Tissue Cells
Connective Tissues
Connotations
Consanguineous Marriage
Conscience
Conscientiousness
Conscious (Personality Factor)
Consciousness Disturbances
Consciousness Raising Groups
Consciousness States
Self Consciousness *USE Self Perception*
Informed **Consent**
Conservation (Concept)
Conservation (Ecological Behavior)
Conservatism
Political **Conservatism**
Wilson Patterson **Conservatism** Scale
Conservatorship *USE Guardianship*
Consistency (Measurement)
Internal Consistency *USE Test Reliability*
Response Consistency *USE Response Variability*
Consonants
Brightness **Constancy**
Color **Constancy**
Perceptual **Constancy**
Size **Constancy**
Constant Time Delay
Constipation
Construct Validity *USE Statistical Validity*
Personal Construct Theory *USE Personality Theory*
Test **Construction**
Constructionism *USE Constructivism*
Constructivism
Consultation Liaison Psychiatry
Mental Health Consultation *USE Professional Consultation*
Professional **Consultation**
Consumer Attitudes
Consumer Behavior
Consumer Fraud *USE Fraud*

Consumer Product Design
    USE Product Design
Consumer Protection
Consumer Psychology
Consumer Research
Consumer Satisfaction
Consumer Surveys
Contact Lenses
Eye **Contact**
Physical **Contact**
Contagion
Cost **Containment**
Content Analysis
Content Analysis (Test)
Dream **Content**
Emotional **Content**
Item **Content** (Test)
Thought Content *USE Cognitions*
Contextual Associations
Cognitive **Contiguity**
Contingency Management
Contingent Negative Variation
Continuing Education
Continuous Reinforcement
    USE Reinforcement Schedules
Contour *USE Form and Shape Perception*
Contour Perception
    USE Form and Shape Perception
Contraception *USE Birth Control*
Contraceptive Devices
Oral **Contraceptives**
Behavior **Contracting**
Muscle **Contraction** Headache
Muscle **Contractions**
Behavioral **Contrast**
Brightness **Contrast**
Color **Contrast**
Successive Contrast *USE Afterimage*
Visual **Contrast**
Control Groups *USE Experiment Controls*
Air Traffic **Control**
Anger **Control**
Birth **Control**
Birth Control Attitudes
    USE Family Planning Attitudes
Diaphragms (Birth **Control)**
Emotional **Control**
Gun **Control** Laws
Health Locus of Control *USE Health Attitudes*
Impulse **Control** Disorders
Internal External Locus of **Control**
Locus of Control
    USE Internal External Locus of Control
Population Control *USE Birth Control*
Quality **Control**
Rotter Internal External Locus of **Control** Scale
Self **Control**
Social **Control**
Stimulus **Control**
Thought Control *USE Brainwashing*
Weight **Control**
Experiment **Controls**
Instrument **Controls**
Eye **Convergence**
Convergent Thinking
    USE Inductive Deductive Reasoning
Conversation
Conversion Disorder
Conversion Hysteria
    USE Conversion Disorder
Conversion Neurosis
    USE Conversion Disorder
Criminal **Conviction**
Convulsions
Cooperating Teachers

Cooperation
Cooperative Education
Cooperative Learning
Cooperative Therapy *USE Cotherapy*
Motor **Coordination**
Perceptual Motor **Coordination**
Coping Behavior
Copper
Coprophagia
Copulation
    USE Sexual Intercourse (Human)
Cranial Spinal **Cord**
Lumbar Spinal **Cord**
Spinal **Cord**
Spinal **Cord** Injuries
Vocal **Cords**
Cornea
Coronary Disorders
    USE Cardiovascular Disorders
Coronary Heart Disease
    USE Heart Disorders
Coronary Prone Behavior
Coronary Thromboses
Coronary Vessels *USE Arteries (Anatomy)*
Corporal Punishment *USE Punishment*
Corporations *USE Business Organizations*
Job **Corps**
Peace **Corps**
Corpus Callosum
Corpus Striatum *USE Basal Ganglia*
Correctional Institutions
Corrective Lenses *USE Optical Aids*
Personality **Correlates**
Physiological **Correlates**
Psychological Correlates *USE Psychodynamics*
Canonical Correlation *USE Multivariate Analysis*
Pearson Product Moment Correlation Coefficient
    USE Statistical Correlation
Point Biserial **Correlation**
Rank Difference **Correlation**
Rank Order **Correlation**
Statistical **Correlation**
Tetrachoric **Correlation**
Adrenal **Cortex** Hormones
Adrenal Cortex Steroids *USE Corticosteroids*
Auditory **Cortex**
Cerebellar Cortex *USE Cerebellum*
Cerebral **Cortex**
Motor **Cortex**
Prefrontal **Cortex**
Somatosensory **Cortex**
Striate Cortex *USE Visual Cortex*
Visual **Cortex**
Organ of Corti *USE Cochlea*
Cortical Atrophy *USE Cerebral Atrophy*
Cortical Evoked Potentials
Corticoids *USE Corticosteroids*
Corticosteroids
Corticosterone
Corticotropin
Corticotropin Releasing Factor
Cortisol *USE Hydrocortisone*
Cortisone
Cosmetic Techniques
Cost Containment
Cost Effectiveness
    USE Costs and Cost Analysis
Costs and **Cost** Analysis
Response **Cost**
Costs and Cost Analysis
Health Care **Costs**
Medical Care Costs *USE Health Care Costs*
Mental Health Care Costs *USE Health Care Costs*
Cotherapy
Counselees *USE Clients*

Counseling
Counseling Psychologists
Counseling Psychology
Career Counseling *USE Occupational Guidance*
Educational **Counseling**
Family Counseling *USE Family Therapy*
Genetic **Counseling**
Group **Counseling**
Guidance Counseling *USE School Counseling*
Individual Counseling *USE Individual Psychotherapy*
Marriage **Counseling**
Pastoral **Counseling**
Peer **Counseling**
Premarital **Counseling**
Psychotherapeutic **Counseling**
Rehabilitation **Counseling**
School **Counseling**
Vocational Counseling *USE Occupational Guidance*
Counselor Attitudes
Counselor Characteristics
Counselor Client Interaction
    USE Psychotherapeutic Processes
Counselor Education
Counselor Effectiveness
    USE Counselor Characteristics
Counselor Personality
    USE Counselor Characteristics
Counselor Role
Counselor Trainees
Client Counselor Interaction
    USE Psychotherapeutic Processes
Counselors
Rehabilitation **Counselors**
School **Counselors**
Vocational **Counselors**
Over The Counter Drugs *USE Nonprescription Drugs*
Counterconditioning
Countertransference
Countries
Developed **Countries**
Developing **Countries**
Third World Countries *USE Developing Countries*
Underdeveloped Countries *USE Developing Countries*
County Agricultural Agents
    USE Agricultural Extension Workers
Couples
Couples Therapy
Married Couples *USE Spouses*
Courage
Course Evaluation
Course Objectives
    USE Educational Objectives
Course of Illness *USE Disease Course*
Disease **Course**
Disorder Course *USE Disease Course*
Court Ordered Treatment
    USE Court Referrals
Court Referrals
Juvenile Court *USE Adjudication*
Courts *USE Adjudication*
Animal **Courtship** Behavior
Animal **Courtship** Displays
Human **Courtship**
Cousins
Analysis of **Covariance**
Covert Sensitization
Least Preferred **Coworker** Scale
Cows *USE Cattle*
Coyotes *USE Canids*
Crabs
Crafts
Muscle Cramps *USE Muscular Disorders*
Cranial Nerves
Cranial Spinal Cord
Craving

Crayfish
Creative Arts Therapy
Creative Writing
Creativity
Creativity Measurement
Credibility
Creutzfeldt Jakob Syndrome
Aircraft Crew *USE Aerospace Personnel*
Cri du Chat Syndrome
    USE Crying Cat Syndrome
Crib Death *USE Sudden Infant Death*
Crime
Crime Prevention
Crime Victims
Criminal Conviction
Criminal Interrogation
    USE Legal Interrogation
Criminal Justice
Criminal Law
Criminal Responsibility
Criminally Insane
    USE Mentally Ill Offenders
Criminals
Female **Criminals**
Male **Criminals**
Criminology
Crises
Family **Crises**
Organizational **Crises**
Crisis Intervention
Crisis Intervention Services
Identity **Crisis**
Assessment Criteria *USE Evaluation Criteria*
Evaluation **Criteria**
Research Diagnostic **Criteria**
Student Admission **Criteria**
Criterion Referenced Tests
Critical Flicker Fusion Threshold
Critical Period
Critical Scores *USE Cutting Scores*
Criticism
Crocodilians
Cross Cultural Communication
Cross Cultural Differences
Cross Cultural Psychology
Cross Cultural Treatment
Cross Disciplinary Research
    USE Interdisciplinary Research
Crossed Eyes *USE Strabismus*
Crowding
Marlowe **Crowne** Social Desirability Scale
CRT *USE Video Display Units*
Cruelty
Crustacea
Crying
Crying Cat Syndrome
Cuban Americans *USE Hispanics*
Cued Recall
Cues
Cultism
Cultural Assimilation
Cultural Deprivation
Cultural Differences
    USE Cross Cultural Differences
Cultural Factors *USE Sociocultural Factors*
Cultural Familial Mental Retardation
    USE Psychosocial Mental Retardation
Cultural Pluralism *USE Multiculturalism*
Cultural Psychiatry
    USE Transcultural Psychiatry
Cultural Sensitivity
Cultural Test Bias
Chinese **Cultural** Groups
Cross **Cultural** Communication
Cross **Cultural** Differences

Cross **Cultural** Psychology
Cross **Cultural** Treatment
Japanese **Cultural** Groups
Korean **Cultural** Groups
Vietnamese **Cultural** Groups
Culturally Disadvantaged
    USE Cultural Deprivation
Culture (Anthropological)
Culture Change
Culture Fair Intelligence Test
Culture Shock
Cattell Culture Fair Intelligence Test
    USE Culture Fair Intelligence Test
Curare
Curiosity
Curricular Field Experience
Curriculum
Curriculum Based Assessment
Curriculum Development
Cursive Writing
Cushings Syndrome
Child **Custody**
Joint **Custody**
Customer Satisfaction
    USE Consumer Satisfaction
Cutaneous Receptive Fields
Cutaneous Sense
Cutting Scores
Cybernetics
Lunar Synodic **Cycle**
Menstrual **Cycle**
Sleep Wake **Cycle**
Work Rest **Cycles**
Cyclic Adenosine Monophosphate
Cycloheximide
Cyclothymic Disorder
    USE Cyclothymic Personality
Cyclothymic Personality
Cynicism
Cysteine
Cystic Fibrosis
Cytochrome Oxidase
Cytology
Cytoplasm
Daily Activities
Activities of **Daily** Living
Brain **Damage**
Dance
Dance Therapy
Dangerousness
Dark Adaptation
Darwinism
Data Collection
Data Pooling *USE Meta Analysis*
Data Processing
Biographical **Data**
Statistical **Data**
Databases
Computerized Databases *USE Databases*
Online Databases *USE Databases*
Date Rape *USE Acquaintance Rape*
Social **Dating**
Daughters
Day Care Centers
Day Hospital *USE Partial Hospitalization*
Adult **Day** Care
Child **Day** Care
Recreational Day Camps
    USE Summer Camps (Recreation)
Daydreaming
DDT (Insecticide)
Deaf
Deaf Blind
Word Deafness *USE Aphasia*
Deanol *USE Antidepressant Drugs*

Death and Dying
Death Anxiety
Death Attitudes
Death Education
Death Instinct
Death Penalty *USE Capital Punishment*
Death Rate *USE Mortality Rate*
Death Rites
Crib Death *USE Sudden Infant Death*
Near **Death** Experiences
Sudden Infant **Death**
Debates
Political Debates *USE Debates*
Presidential Debates *USE Debates*
Debriefing (Experimental)
Decarboxylase Inhibitors
Decarboxylases
Memory **Decay**
Decentralization
Deception
Decerebration
Decision Making
Decision Support Systems
Group **Decision** Making
Lexical **Decision**
Management **Decision** Making
Legal **Decisions**
Declarative Knowledge
Decoding *USE Human Information Storage*
Decompression Effects
Decortication (Brain)
Deductive Reasoning
USE Inductive Deductive Reasoning
Inductive **Deductive** Reasoning
Deer
Self **Defeating** Behavior
Defecation
Defendants
Defense Mechanisms
Compensation **(Defense** Mechanism)
Displacement **(Defense** Mechanism)
Fantasy **(Defense** Mechanism)
Identification **(Defense** Mechanism)
Insanity **Defense**
Isolation **(Defense** Mechanism)
Personal Defense *USE Self Defense*
Projection **(Defense** Mechanism)
Regression **(Defense** Mechanism)
Repression **(Defense** Mechanism)
Self **Defense**
Suppression **(Defense** Mechanism)
Withdrawal **(Defense** Mechanism)
Animal **Defensive** Behavior
Defensiveness
Oppositional **Defiant** Disorder
Nutritional **Deficiencies**
Acquired Immune **Deficiency** Syndrome
Mental Deficiency *USE Mental Retardation*
Protein **Deficiency** Disorders
Vitamin **Deficiency** Disorders
Attention **Deficit** Disorder
Attention **Deficit** Disorder with Hyperactivity
Deformity *USE Physical Disfigurement*
College Degrees *USE Educational Degrees*
Educational **Degrees**
Graduate Degrees *USE Educational Degrees*
Undergraduate Degrees *USE Educational Degrees*
Dehydration
Lactate **Dehydrogenase**
Dehydrogenases
Alcohol **Dehydrogenases**
Deinstitutionalization
Deja Vu *USE Consciousness States*
Delay of Gratification
Constant Time **Delay**

Language **Delay**
Reinforcement **Delay**
Delayed Alternation
Delayed Auditory Feedback
Delayed Development
Delayed Feedback
Delayed Parenthood
Delayed Reinforcement
USE Reinforcement Delay
Delayed Speech
USE Retarded Speech Development
Deletion (Chromosome)
Female **Delinquency**
Juvenile **Delinquency**
Male **Delinquency**
Sexual Delinquency *USE Promiscuity*
Delirium
Delirium Tremens
Health Care **Delivery**
Delta Rhythm
Delusions
Dementia
Dementia of Alzheimers Type
USE Alzheimers Disease
Dementia Paralytica *USE General Paresis*
Dementia Praecox *USE Schizophrenia*
Dementia with Lewy Bodies
AIDS **Dementia** Complex
Multi Infarct **Dementia**
Presenile **Dementia**
Senile **Dementia**
Vascular **Dementia**
Democracy
Democratic Party *USE Political Parties*
Demographic Characteristics
Demonic Possession
USE Spirit Possession
Social **Demonstrations**
Dendrites
Denial
Population Density *USE Social Density*
Social **Density**
Dental Education
Dental Students
Dental Surgery
Dental Treatment
Dentist Patient Interaction
USE Therapeutic Processes
Dentistry
Dentists
Deoxycorticosterone
Deoxyglucose
Deoxyribonucleic Acid
Field **Dependence**
Dependency (Personality)
Drug **Dependency**
Dependent Personality
Dependent Variables
State **Dependent** Learning
Depersonalization
CNS Depressant Drug Antagonists
USE Analeptic Drugs
CNS **Depressant** Drugs
Appetite **Depressing** Drugs
Depression (Emotion)
Agitated Depression *USE Major Depression*
Anaclitic **Depression**
Beck **Depression** Inventory
Climacteric Depression *USE Involutional Depression*
Endogenous **Depression**
Involutional **Depression**
Major **Depression**
Manic Depression *USE Bipolar Disorder*
Postpartum **Depression**
Reactive **Depression**

Recurrent **Depression**
Spreading **Depression**
Treatment Resistant **Depression**
Tricyclic Resistant Depression
    USE Treatment Resistant Depression
Unipolar Depression *USE Major Depression*
Winter Depression
    USE Seasonal Affective Disorder
Zungs Self Rating **Depression** Scale
Manic Depressive Psychosis
    USE Bipolar Disorder
Neurotic Depressive Reaction
    USE Major Depression
Psychotic Depressive Reaction
    USE Major Depression
Deprivation
Animal Maternal **Deprivation**
Cultural **Deprivation**
Food **Deprivation**
REM Dream **Deprivation**
Sensory **Deprivation**
Sleep **Deprivation**
Social **Deprivation**
Stimulus **Deprivation**
Water **Deprivation**
Depth Perception
Depth Psychology
Ergot **Derivatives**
Opium Derivatives *USE Opiates*
Phenothiazine **Derivatives**
Dermatitis
Dermatomes
    USE Cutaneous Receptive Fields
Desegregation *USE Social Integration*
Eye Movement **Desensitization** Therapy
Systematic **Desensitization** Therapy
Desertion *USE Abandonment*
Between Groups **Design**
Computer Assisted **Design**
Consumer Product Design *USE Product Design*
Environmental Design *USE Environmental Planning*
Experimental **Design**
Human Machine Systems **Design**
Interior **Design**
Kohs Block **Design** Test
Man Machine Systems Design
    USE Human Machine Systems Design
Product **Design**
Research Design *USE Experimental Design*
Within Subjects Design *USE Repeated Measures*
Memory for **Designs** Test
Desipramine
Edwards Social **Desirability** Scale
Marlowe Crowne Social **Desirability** Scale
Social **Desirability**
Hypoactive Sexual Desire Disorder
    USE Inhibited Sexual Desire
Inhibited Sexual **Desire**
Desires *USE Motivation*
Self **Destructive** Behavior
Anatomically **Detailed** Dolls
Signal **Detection** (Perception)
Legal **Detention**
Self **Determination**
Threshold **Determination**
Verdict Determination *USE Adjudication*
Determinism
Detoxification
Kupfer Detre Self Rating Scale
    USE Nonprojective Personality
    Measures
Folie A **Deux**
Developed Countries
Developing Countries
Development

Adolescent **Development**
Adult **Development**
Animal **Development**
Bayley Scales of Infant **Development**
Career **Development**
Character Development *USE Personality Development*
Childhood Play **Development**
Childhood **Development**
Cognitive **Development**
Community **Development**
Curriculum **Development**
Delayed **Development**
Early Childhood **Development**
Ego **Development**
Emotional **Development**
Group **Development**
Human **Development**
Infant **Development**
Intellectual **Development**
Language **Development**
Management Development *USE Career Development*
Moral **Development**
Motor **Development**
Neonatal **Development**
Neural **Development**
Organizational **Development**
Perceptual Motor **Development**
Perceptual **Development**
Personality **Development**
Personnel Development *USE Personnel Training*
Physical **Development**
Precocious **Development**
Prenatal **Development**
Professional **Development**
Program **Development**
Psychological Development *USE Psychogenesis*
Psychomotor **Development**
Psychosexual **Development**
Psychosocial **Development**
Reading **Development**
Retarded Speech **Development**
Rural Development
    USE Community Development
Sensorimotor Development
    USE Perceptual Motor Development
Sexual **Development**
Social Development
    USE Psychosocial Development
Speech **Development**
Urban Development
    USE Community Development
Developmental Age Groups
Developmental Differences
    USE Age Differences
Developmental Disabilities
Developmental Measures
Developmental Psychology
Developmental Stages
Frostig **Developmental** Test of Visual Perception
Pervasive **Developmental** Disorders
Prenatal **Developmental** Stages
Sex Linked **Developmental** Differences
Deviant Behavior *USE Antisocial Behavior*
Deviation IQ *USE Standard Scores*
Standard **Deviation**
Sexual Deviations *USE Paraphilias*
Computer Peripheral **Devices**
Contraceptive **Devices**
Intrauterine **Devices**
Medical Therapeutic **Devices**
Safety **Devices**
Dexamethasone
Dexamethasone Suppression Test
Dexamphetamine *USE Dextroamphetamine*
Dexedrine *USE Dextroamphetamine*

Physical **Dexterity**
Dextroamphetamine
Diabetes
Diabetes Insipidus
Diabetes Mellitus
Diacetylmorphine *USE Heroin*
Diagnosis
Diagnosis Related Groups
Clinical Judgment (Not **Diagnosis)**
Computer Assisted **Diagnosis**
Differential **Diagnosis**
Dual **Diagnosis**
Educational **Diagnosis**
Medical **Diagnosis**
Prenatal **Diagnosis**
X Ray Diagnosis *USE Roentgenography*
Diagnostic and Statistical Manual
Diagnostic Interview Schedule
Research **Diagnostic** Criteria
Dialect
Dialectics
Dialysis
Diaphragm (Anatomy)
Diaphragms (Birth Control)
Diarrhea
Diastolic Pressure
Diazepam
Dichoptic Stimulation
Dichotic Stimulation
Dieldrin *USE Insecticides*
Diencephalon
Dietary Restraint
Dietary Supplements
Lysergic Acid **Diethylamide**
Diets
Rank **Difference** Correlation
Age **Differences**
Animal Sex **Differences**
Animal Strain **Differences**
Cross Cultural **Differences**
Cultural Differences *USE Cross Cultural Differences*
Developmental Differences *USE Age Differences*
Ethnic Differences
USE Racial and Ethnic Differences
Gender Differences *USE Human Sex Differences*
Geographical Differences *USE Regional Differences*
Human Sex **Differences**
Individual **Differences**
Racial and Ethnic **Differences**
Racial Differences
USE Racial and Ethnic Differences
Regional **Differences**
Sex Linked Developmental **Differences**
Species **Differences**
Differential Aptitude Tests
Differential Diagnosis
Differential Limen *USE Thresholds*
Differential Personality Inventory
USE Nonprojective Personality
Measures
Differential Reinforcement
Semantic **Differential**
Sex Differentiation Disorders
USE Genital Disorders
Difficulty Level (Test)
Task Difficulty *USE Task Complexity*
Test Difficulty *USE Difficulty Level (Test)*
Digestion
Digestive System
Digestive System Disorders
Digit Span Testing
Digital Computers
Dihydroergotamine
Dihydroxyphenylacetic Acid
Dihydroxytryptamine

Dilantin *USE Diphenylhydantoin*
Pupil **Dilation**
Prisoners **Dilemma** Game
Carbon **Dioxide**
Diphenhydramine
Diphenylhydantoin
Diphenylhydantoin Sodium
USE Diphenylhydantoin
Diptera
Directed Discussion Method
Directed Reverie Therapy
USE Guided Imagery
Self Directed Learning
USE Individualized Instruction
Direction Perception
Advance **Directives**
Disabilities *USE Disorders*
Developmental **Disabilities**
Learning **Disabilities**
Multiple **Disabilities**
Physical **Disabilities** (Attitudes Toward)
Reading **Disabilities**
Sensory **Disabilities** (Attitudes Toward)
Disability Discrimination
Disability Evaluation
Disability Laws
Disability Management
Disabled (Attitudes Toward)
Disabled Personnel
Disadvantaged
Culturally Disadvantaged *USE Cultural Deprivation*
Economically Disadvantaged *USE Disadvantaged*
Socially Disadvantaged *USE Disadvantaged*
Disappointment
Disasters
Natural **Disasters**
Discharge Planning
Facility **Discharge**
Hospital **Discharge**
Psychiatric Hospital **Discharge**
Cross Disciplinary Research
USE Interdisciplinary Research
Child **Discipline**
Classroom **Discipline**
Self **Disclosure**
Discourse Analysis
Discovery Teaching Method
Discrimination
Discrimination Learning
Age **Discrimination**
Auditory **Discrimination**
Cognitive **Discrimination**
Disability **Discrimination**
Distance Discrimination *USE Distance Perception*
Drug **Discrimination**
Employment **Discrimination**
Ethnic Discrimination
USE Race and Ethnic Discrimination
Figure Ground **Discrimination**
Job Discrimination
USE Employment Discrimination
Loudness **Discrimination**
Minority Group Discrimination
USE Race and Ethnic Discrimination
Odor **Discrimination**
Pattern **Discrimination**
Perceptual **Discrimination**
Pitch **Discrimination**
Race and Ethnic **Discrimination**
Racial Discrimination
USE Race and Ethnic Discrimination
Sex **Discrimination**
Size **Discrimination**
Social **Discrimination**
Spatial Discrimination *USE Spatial Perception*

Stimulus **Discrimination**
Tactual Discrimination *USE Tactual Perception*
Taste Discrimination *USE Taste Perception*
Visual **Discrimination**
Wepman Auditory **Discrimination** Test
Discriminative Learning
    USE Discrimination Learning
Discriminative Stimulus
    USE Conditioned Stimulus
Directed **Discussion** Method
Group **Discussion**
Nondirected **Discussion** Method
Disease Course
Disease Outbreaks *USE Epidemics*
Addisons **Disease**
Alzheimers **Disease**
Coronary Heart Disease *USE Heart Disorders*
Duchennes Disease *USE Muscular Disorders*
Huntingtons **Disease**
Lewy Body Disease *USE Dementia with Lewy Bodies*
Menieres **Disease**
Parkinsons **Disease**
Picks **Disease**
Raynauds Disease *USE Cardiovascular Disorders*
Sickle Cell **Disease**
Tay Sachs Disease *USE Amaurotic Familial Idiocy*
Communicable Diseases *USE Infectious Disorders*
International Classification of **Diseases**
Kidney **Diseases**
Renal Diseases *USE Kidney Diseases*
Sexually Transmitted Diseases *USE Venereal Diseases*
Venereal **Diseases**
Physical **Disfigurement**
Disgust
Dishonesty
Dislike *USE Aversion*
Disorder Course *USE Disease Course*
Acute Paranoid Disorder *USE Paranoia (Psychosis)*
Attention Deficit **Disorder**
Attention Deficit **Disorder** with Hyperactivity
Atypical Paranoid Disorder *USE Paranoia (Psychosis)*
Atypical Somatoform Disorder *USE Body Dysmorphic Disorder*
Bipolar Affective Disorder *USE Bipolar Disorder*
Bipolar Mood Disorder *USE Bipolar Disorder*
Bipolar **Disorder**
Body Dysmorphic **Disorder**
Compulsive Personality Disorder *USE Obsessive Compulsive Personality*
Conduct **Disorder**
Conversion **Disorder**
Cyclothymic Disorder *USE Cyclothymic Personality*
Dissociative Identity **Disorder**
Dysthymic **Disorder**
Epstein Barr Viral **Disorder**
Explosive **Disorder**
Gender Identity **Disorder**
Generalized Anxiety Disorder *USE Anxiety Disorders*
Gilles de la Tourette **Disorder**
Histrionic Personality **Disorder**
Hypoactive Sexual Desire Disorder *USE Inhibited Sexual Desire*
Intermittent Explosive Disorder *USE Explosive Disorder*
Obsessive Compulsive **Disorder**
Oppositional Defiant **Disorder**
Pain Disorder *USE Somatoform Pain Disorder*
Panic **Disorder**
Paranoid Personality Disorder *USE Paranoid Personality*
Paranoid Disorder *USE Paranoia (Psychosis)*
Posttraumatic Stress **Disorder**
Reactive Attachment Disorder *USE Attachment Disorders*
Schizoaffective **Disorder**
Schizophreniform **Disorder**
Seasonal Affective **Disorder**
Shared Paranoid Disorder *USE Folie A Deux*
Somatization **Disorder**
Somatoform Pain **Disorder**
Disorders

Adjustment **Disorders**
Adrenal Gland **Disorders**
Adventitious **Disorders**
Affective **Disorders**
Allergic Skin **Disorders**
Allergic **Disorders**
Anxiety **Disorders**
Appetite Disorders *USE Eating Disorders*
Articulation **Disorders**
Attachment **Disorders**
Autoimmune Disorders *USE Immunologic Disorders*
Autonomic Nervous System **Disorders**
Autosome **Disorders**
Bacterial **Disorders**
Behavior **Disorders**
Blood and Lymphatic **Disorders**
Blood Pressure **Disorders**
Blood Disorders
    USE Blood and Lymphatic Disorders
Bone **Disorders**
Bowel Disorders *USE Colon Disorders*
Brain **Disorders**
Bronchial **Disorders**
Cardiac Disorders *USE Heart Disorders*
Cardiovascular **Disorders**
Central Nervous System **Disorders**
Cerebral Vascular Disorders *USE Cerebrovascular Disorders*
Cerebrovascular **Disorders**
Character Disorders *USE Personality Disorders*
Chromosome **Disorders**
Chronicity **(Disorders)**
Circulatory Disorders *USE Cardiovascular Disorders*
Colon **Disorders**
Communication **Disorders**
Congenital **Disorders**
Coronary Disorders *USE Cardiovascular Disorders*
Digestive System **Disorders**
Dissociative **Disorders**
Drug Induced Congenital **Disorders**
Ear **Disorders**
Eating **Disorders**
Endocrine Sexual **Disorders**
Endocrine **Disorders**
Ethnic Disorders *USE Ethnospecific Disorders*
Ethnospecific **Disorders**
Eye **Disorders**
Factitious **Disorders**
Gastrointestinal **Disorders**
Genetic **Disorders**
Genital **Disorders**
Gynecological **Disorders**
Hearing **Disorders**
Heart **Disorders**
Hematologic Disorders
    USE Blood and Lymphatic Disorders
Hepatic Disorders *USE Liver Disorders*
Hereditary Disorders *USE Genetic Disorders*
Hypophysis Disorders *USE Pituitary Disorders*
Immunologic **Disorders**
Impulse Control **Disorders**
Infectious **Disorders**
Joint **Disorders**
Karyotype Disorders *USE Chromosome Disorders*
Labyrinth **Disorders**
Language **Disorders**
Laryngeal **Disorders**
Learning **Disorders**
Lipid Metabolism **Disorders**
Liver **Disorders**
Lung **Disorders**
Lymphatic Disorders
    USE Blood and Lymphatic Disorders
Male Genital **Disorders**
Memory **Disorders**
Menstrual **Disorders**

Mental **Disorders**
Mental **Disorders** due to General Medical
    Conditions
Metabolism **Disorders**
Minimal Brain **Disorders**
Mood Disorders *USE Affective Disorders*
Motor Disorders *USE Nervous System Disorders*
Movement **Disorders**
Muscular **Disorders**
Musculoskeletal **Disorders**
Neonatal **Disorders**
Nervous System **Disorders**
Neurological Disorders *USE Nervous System Disorders*
Neuromuscular **Disorders**
Onset **(Disorders)**
Ovary Disorders *USE Endocrine Sexual Disorders*
Parasitic **Disorders**
Parathyroid **Disorders**
Peripheral Nerve **Disorders**
Personality **Disorders**
Pervasive Developmental **Disorders**
Pharyngeal **Disorders**
Physical **Disorders**
Pituitary **Disorders**
Protein Deficiency **Disorders**
Psychiatric Disorders *USE Mental Disorders*
Psychophysiologic Disorders *USE Somatoform Disorders*
Psychosomatic Disorders *USE Somatoform Disorders*
Pulmonary Disorders *USE Lung Disorders*
Recovery **(Disorders)**
Relapse **(Disorders)**
Remission **(Disorders)**
Respiratory Tract **Disorders**
Scalp Disorders *USE Skin Disorders*
Sense Organ **Disorders**
Sensory System **Disorders**
Severity **(Disorders)**
Sex Chromosome **Disorders**
Sex Differentiation Disorders *USE Genital Disorders*
Sex Linked Hereditary **Disorders**
Skeletomuscular Disorders *USE Musculoskeletal Disorders*
Skin **Disorders**
Sleep **Disorders**
Somatoform **Disorders**
Somatosensory **Disorders**
Speech **Disorders**
Susceptibility **(Disorders)**
Taste **Disorders**
Testes Disorders *USE Endocrine Sexual Disorders*
Thyroid **Disorders**
Toxic **Disorders**
Treatment Resistant **Disorders**
Urinary Function **Disorders**
Urogenital **Disorders**
Vascular Disorders *USE Cardiovascular Disorders*
Viral **Disorders**
Vision **Disorders**
Vitamin Deficiency **Disorders**
Voice Disorders *USE Dysphonia*
Schizophrenia **(Disorganized** Type)
Place **Disorientation**
Time **Disorientation**
Displacement (Defense Mechanism)
Video Display Terminals *USE Video Display Units*
Video **Display** Units
Displays
Animal Courtship **Displays**
Auditory **Displays**
Graphical **Displays**
Tactual **Displays**
Visual **Displays**
Disposition *USE Personality*
Disruptive Behavior
    USE Behavior Problems
Dissatisfaction

Dissociation
Drug Dissociation
    USE State Dependent Learning
Dissociative Disorders
Dissociative Identity Disorder
Dissociative Neurosis
    USE Dissociative Disorders
Dissociative Patterns
    USE Dissociative Disorders
Cognitive **Dissonance**
Distance Discrimination
    USE Distance Perception
Distance Perception
Apparent **Distance**
Interpersonal Distance *USE Personal Space*
Perceptual **Distortion**
Spatial **Distortion**
Distractibility
Distraction
Distress
Animal **Distress** Calls
Respiratory **Distress**
Distributed Practice
Binomial **Distribution**
Drug **Distribution**
Frequency **Distribution**
Gaussian Distribution *USE Normal Distribution*
Normal **Distribution**
Poisson Distribution *USE Skewed Distribution*
Skewed **Distribution**
Distributive Justice *USE Justice*
Distrust *USE Suspicion*
Affective Disturbances *USE Affective Disorders*
Body Image **Disturbances**
Consciousness **Disturbances**
Fantasies (Thought **Disturbances)**
Hysterical Vision **Disturbances**
Judgment **Disturbances**
Perceptual **Disturbances**
Sexual Function **Disturbances**
Thought **Disturbances**
Emotionally **Disturbed**
Disulfiram
Diuresis
Diuretics
Diurnal Variations
    USE Human Biological Rhythms
Divergent Thinking
Divided Attention
Division of Labor
Animal **Division** of Labor
Divorce
Divorced Persons
Dizygotic Twins *USE Heterozygotic Twins*
Dizziness *USE Vertigo*
Doctors *USE Physicians*
Dogmatism
Rokeach **Dogmatism** Scale
Dogs
Seeing Eye Dogs *USE Mobility Aids*
Doll Play
Anatomically Detailed **Dolls**
Tic Doloureux *USE Trigeminal Neuralgia*
Dolphins
Domestic Service Personnel
Domestic Violence *USE Family Violence*
Animal **Domestication**
Dominance
Dominance Hierarchy
Animal **Dominance**
Cerebral **Dominance**
Eye Dominance *USE Ocular Dominance*
Genetic **Dominance**
Lateral **Dominance**
Ocular **Dominance**

Domination *USE Authoritarianism*
Blood Donation *USE Tissue Donation*
Organ Donation *USE Tissue Donation*
Sperm Donation *USE Tissue Donation*
Tissue **Donation**
DOPA
L Dopa *USE Levodopa*
DOPAC *USE Dihydroxyphenylacetic Acid*
Dopamine
Dopamine Agonists
Dopamine Antagonists
Dopamine Metabolites
Dormitories
Dorsal Horns
Dorsal Roots
Drug **Dosages**
Double Bind Interaction
Doubt
Doves
Downs Syndrome
Doxepin
Draftees
Drama
Draw A Man Test
    USE Human Figures Drawing
Goodenough Harris **Draw** A Person Test
Drawing
Franck **Drawing** Completion Test
Human Figures **Drawing**
Dream Analysis
Dream Content
Dream Interpretation *USE Dream Analysis*
Dream Recall
REM **Dream** Deprivation
Dreaming
Lucid **Dreaming**
Rapid Eye Movement Dreams *USE REM Dreams*
REM **Dreams**
DRGs *USE Diagnosis Related Groups*
Drinking Attitudes
    USE Alcohol Drinking Attitudes
Drinking Behavior
Alcohol **Drinking** Attitudes
Alcohol **Drinking** Patterns
Animal **Drinking** Behavior
Problem Drinking *USE Alcohol Abuse*
Social **Drinking**
Drive *USE Motivation*
Sex **Drive**
Driver Education
Driver Safety *USE Highway Safety*
Drivers
Driving Behavior
Driving Under The Influence
Drunk Driving *USE Driving Under The Influence*
Dropouts
Client Dropouts *USE Treatment Dropouts*
College **Dropouts**
Patient Dropouts *USE Treatment Dropouts*
Potential **Dropouts**
Research Dropouts *USE Experimental Attrition*
School **Dropouts**
Treatment **Dropouts**
Drosophila
Drowsiness *USE Sleep Onset*
Drug Abstinence
Drug Abuse
Drug Abuse Liability
Drug Abuse Prevention
Drug Addiction
Drug Administration Methods
Drug Adverse Reactions
    USE Side Effects (Drug)
Drug Allergies
Drug Dependency

Drug Discrimination
Drug Dissociation
    USE State Dependent Learning
Drug Distribution
Drug Dosages
Drug Education
Drug Effects *USE Drugs*
Drug Induced Congenital Disorders
Drug Induced Hallucinations
Drug Interactions
Drug Laws
Drug Legalization
Drug Overdoses
Drug Potentiation *USE Drug Interactions*
Drug Rehabilitation
Drug Sensitivity
Drug Synergism *USE Drug Interactions*
Drug Testing *USE Drug Usage Screening*
Drug Therapy
Drug Tolerance
Drug Usage
Drug Usage Attitudes
Drug Usage Screening
Drug Withdrawal
Drug Withdrawal Effects
    USE Drug Withdrawal
CNS Depressant Drug Antagonists *USE Analeptic Drugs*
Intravenous **Drug** Usage
IV Drug Usage *USE Intravenous Drug Usage*
Side Effects **(Drug)**
Drugs
Adrenergic Blocking **Drugs**
Adrenergic **Drugs**
Adrenolytic Drugs *USE Adrenergic Drugs*
Analeptic **Drugs**
Analgesic **Drugs**
Anesthetic **Drugs**
Anorexigenic Drugs *USE Appetite Depressing Drugs*
Anti Inflammatory **Drugs**
Antiadrenergic Drugs *USE Sympatholytic Drugs*
Antianxiety Drugs *USE Tranquilizing Drugs*
Anticholinergic Drugs *USE Cholinergic Blocking Drugs*
Anticholinesterase Drugs *USE Cholinesterase Inhibitors*
Anticoagulant **Drugs**
Anticonvulsive **Drugs**
Antidepressant **Drugs**
Antiemetic **Drugs**
Antiepileptic Drugs *USE Anticonvulsive Drugs*
Antihistaminic **Drugs**
Antihypertensive **Drugs**
Antinauseant Drugs *USE Antiemetic Drugs*
Antineoplastic **Drugs**
Antiparkinsonian Drugs *USE Antitremor Drugs*
Antipsychotic Drugs *USE Neuroleptic Drugs*
Antipyretic Drugs *USE Anti Inflammatory Drugs*
Antischizophrenic Drugs *USE Neuroleptic Drugs*
Antispasmodic **Drugs**
Antitremor **Drugs**
Antitubercular **Drugs**
Antiviral **Drugs**
Anxiety Reducing Drugs *USE Tranquilizing Drugs*
Anxiolytic Drugs *USE Tranquilizing Drugs*
Appetite Depressing **Drugs**
Ataractic Drugs *USE Tranquilizing Drugs*
Ataraxic Drugs *USE Tranquilizing Drugs*
Cardiotonic Drugs *USE Drugs*
Central Nervous System Drugs *USE CNS Affecting Drugs*
Cholinergic Blocking **Drugs**
Cholinergic **Drugs**
Cholinolytic Drugs *USE Cholinergic Blocking Drugs*
Cholinomimetic **Drugs**
CNS Affecting **Drugs**
CNS Depressant **Drugs**
CNS Stimulating **Drugs**
Cognition Enhancing Drugs *USE Nootropic Drugs*

310

Emetic **Drugs**
Ganglion Blocking **Drugs**
Hallucinogenic **Drugs**
Heart Rate Affecting **Drugs**
Hypnotic **Drugs**
Memory Enhancing Drugs *USE Nootropic Drugs*
Muscarinic Drugs *USE Cholinergic Drugs*
Muscle Relaxing **Drugs**
Narcoanalytic Drugs *USE Drugs*
Narcotic **Drugs**
Neuroleptic **Drugs**
Neuromuscular Blocking Drugs *USE Muscle Relaxing Drugs*
Nonprescription **Drugs**
Nootropic **Drugs**
Over The Counter Drugs *USE Nonprescription Drugs*
Pain Relieving Drugs *USE Analgesic Drugs*
Parasympatholytic Drugs *USE Cholinergic Blocking Drugs*
Parasympathomimetic Drugs *USE Cholinomimetic Drugs*
Prescribing **(Drugs)**
Prescription **Drugs**
Psychedelic **Drugs**
Psychoactive Drugs *USE Drugs*
Psychotomimetic **Drugs**
Psychotropic Drugs *USE Drugs*
Respiration Stimulating **Drugs**
Sleep Inducing Drugs *USE Hypnotic Drugs*
Sympatholytic **Drugs**
Sympathomimetic **Drugs**
Thymoleptic Drugs *USE Tranquilizing Drugs*
Tranquilizing **Drugs**
Tricyclic Antidepressant **Drugs**
Vasoconstrictor **Drugs**
Vasodilator **Drugs**
Vasopressor Drugs *USE Vasoconstrictor Drugs*
Vomit Inducing Drugs *USE Emetic Drugs*
Drunk Driving
USE Driving Under The Influence
Drunkenness *USE Alcohol Intoxication*
DSM
USE Diagnostic and Statistical Manual
Dual Careers
Dual Diagnosis
Dualism
Duchennes Disease
USE Muscular Disorders
Ducks
Mental Disorders **due** to General Medical Conditions
Duodenum *USE Intestines*
Response **Duration**
Stimulus **Duration**
Treatment **Duration**
Duty to Warn
Pituitary Dwarfism *USE Hypopituitarism*
Dyads
Dying *USE Death and Dying*
Dying Patients *USE Terminally Ill Patients*
Death and **Dying**
Group **Dynamics**
Intergroup **Dynamics**
Dynorphins
Dysarthria
Dyscalculia *USE Acalculia*
Dysfunctional Family
Dyskinesia
Tardive **Dyskinesia**
Dyslexia
Dysmenorrhea
Dysmetria *USE Ataxia*
Body **Dysmorphic** Disorder
Dysmorphophobia
USE Body Dysmorphic Disorder
Dyspareunia
Dysphasia
Dysphonia
Dysphoria *USE Major Depression*

Postnatal Dysphoria *USE Postpartum Depression*
Dyspnea
Dyspraxia *USE Movement Disorders*
Dysthymia *USE Dysthymic Disorder*
Dysthymic Disorder
Dystonia *USE Muscular Disorders*
Muscular **Dystrophy**
Eagerness *USE Enthusiasm*
Ear (Anatomy)
Ear Canal *USE External Ear*
Ear Disorders
Ear Ossicles *USE Middle Ear*
External **Ear**
Inner Ear *USE Labyrinth (Anatomy)*
Middle **Ear**
Early Childhood Development
Early Experience
Early Infantile Autism
Early Intervention
Early Memories
Earthworms
Eating *USE Ingestion*
Eating Attitudes
Eating Disorders
Eating Patterns *USE Feeding Practices*
Binge **Eating**
Rumination **(Eating)**
Retinal **Eccentricity**
Echinodermata
Echoencephalography
Echolalia
Echolocation
Eclectic Psychology
USE Theoretical Orientation
Eclectic Psychotherapy
Ecological Factors
Ecological Psychology
Conservation **(Ecological** Behavior)
Ecology
Behavioral **Ecology**
Income **(Economic)**
Political **Economic** Systems
Economically Disadvantaged
USE Disadvantaged
Economics
Home **Economics**
Economy
Token **Economy** Programs
ECS Therapy
USE Electroconvulsive Shock Therapy
Eczema
Educable Mentally Retarded
USE Mild Mental Retardation
Education
Education Students
Accreditation **(Education** Personnel)
Adult **Education**
Affective **Education**
Alcohol Education *USE Drug Education*
Art **Education**
Bilingual **Education**
Boards of **Education**
Business **Education**
Career **Education**
Client **Education**
College Education *USE Undergraduate Education*
Compensatory **Education**
Continuing **Education**
Cooperative **Education**
Counselor **Education**
Death **Education**
Dental **Education**
Driver **Education**
Drug **Education**
Elementary **Education**

311

Environmental **Education**
Equal **Education**
Family Life **Education**
Foreign Language **Education**
Graduate Psychology **Education**
Graduate **Education**
Health **Education**
Higher **Education**
Humanistic Education *USE Affective Education*
Industrial Arts Education *USE Vocational Education*
Inservice Teacher **Education**
Language Arts **Education**
Marriage and Family Education *USE Family Life Education*
Mathematics **Education**
Medical **Education**
Middle School **Education**
Multicultural **Education**
Music **Education**
Nontraditional **Education**
Nursing **Education**
Paraprofessional **Education**
Parochial School Education *USE Private School Education*
Patient Education *USE Client Education*
Physical **Education**
Preschool **Education**
Private School **Education**
Psychology **Education**
Public School **Education**
Quality of Education *USE Educational Quality*
Reading **Education**
Rehabilitation **Education**
Religious **Education**
Remedial **Education**
Science **Education**
Second Language Education
   USE Foreign Language Education
Secondary **Education**
Sex **Education**
Social Studies **Education**
Social Work **Education**
Special **Education**
Special **Education** Students
Special **Education** Teachers
Teacher **Education**
Technical Education Teachers
   USE Vocational Education Teachers
Theories of **Education**
Undergraduate **Education**
Vocational **Education**
Vocational **Education** Teachers
Educational Administration
Educational Administrators
   USE School Administrators
Educational Aspirations
Educational Attainment Level
Educational Audiovisual Aids
Educational Background
Educational Counseling
Educational Degrees
Educational Diagnosis
Educational Environment
   USE School Environment
Educational Field Trips
Educational Financial Assistance
Educational Guidance
   USE Educational Counseling
Educational Incentives
Educational Inequality
   USE Equal Education
Educational Laboratories
Educational Measurement
Educational Objectives
Educational Personnel
Educational Placement
Educational Process *USE Education*

Educational Program Accreditation
Educational Program Evaluation
Educational Program Planning
Educational Programs
Educational Psychologists
Educational Psychology
Educational Quality
Educational Reform
Educational Supervision
   USE Professional Supervision
Educational Television
Educational Theory
   USE Theories of Education
Educational Therapy
Educational Toys
Grading **(Educational)**
Learning Centers **(Educational)**
Mainstreaming **(Educational)**
Motion Pictures **(Educational)**
Parent **Educational** Background
Edwards Personal Preference Schedule
Edwards Personality Inventory
Edwards Social Desirability Scale
Effect Size (Statistical)
Generation **Effect** (Learning)
Halo **Effect**
Isolation **Effect**
Primacy **Effect**
Pygmalion Effect *USE Self Fulfilling Prophecies*
Recency **Effect**
Serial Position **Effect**
Stroop **Effect**
Cost Effectiveness *USE Costs and Cost Analysis*
Counselor Effectiveness
   USE Counselor Characteristics
Organizational **Effectiveness**
Parent Effectiveness Training *USE Parent Training*
Teacher Effectiveness *USE Teacher Characteristics*
Teacher **Effectiveness** Evaluation
Therapist Effectiveness
   USE Therapist Characteristics
Treatment **Effectiveness** Evaluation
Acceleration **Effects**
Altitude **Effects**
Cold **Effects**
Decompression **Effects**
Drug Withdrawal Effects *USE Drug Withdrawal*
Drug Effects *USE Drugs*
Environmental **Effects**
Gravitational **Effects**
Heat **Effects**
Iatrogenic Effects *USE Side Effects (Treatment)*
Noise **Effects**
Practice Effects *USE Practice*
Side **Effects** (Drug)
Side **Effects** (Treatment)
Temperature **Effects**
Underwater **Effects**
Efferent Pathways
Efficacy Expectations *USE Self Efficacy*
Self **Efficacy**
Employee **Efficiency**
Effort *USE Energy Expenditure*
Egalitarianism
Ego
Ego Development
Ego Identity
Egocentrism
Egotism
Eidetic Imagery
Ejaculation *USE Male Orgasm*
Premature **Ejaculation**
Elavil *USE Amitriptyline*
Elbow (Anatomy)
Elder Abuse

Elder Care
Elected Government Officials
    USE Government Personnel
Political **Elections**
Elective Abortion *USE Induced Abortion*
Elective Mutism
Electra Complex
Electric Fishes
Electrical Activity
Electrical Brain Stimulation
Electrical Injuries
Electrical Stimulation
Skin **Electrical** Properties
Electro Oculography
Electrocardiography
Electroconvulsive Shock
Electroconvulsive Shock Therapy
Electrodermal Response
    USE Galvanic Skin Response
Electrodes
Electroencephalography
Electrolytes
Electromyography
Electronic Communication
Electronystagmography
Electrophysiology
Electroplethysmography
Electroretinography
Electroshock Therapy
    USE Electroconvulsive Shock Therapy
Electrosleep Treatment
Elementarism *USE Reductionism*
Elementary Education
Elementary School Students
Elementary School Teachers
Elementary Schools
Chemical **Elements**
Metallic **Elements**
Nonmetallic Elements *USE Chemical Elements*
Elephants
Ellis (Albert)
Embarrassment
Embedded Figures Testing
Embolisms
Embryo
EMDR *USE Eye Movement Desensitization*
    Therapy
Emergency Services
Emetic Drugs
Nocturnal **Emission**
Positron Emission Tomography *USE Tomography*
Depression **(Emotion)**
Expressed **Emotion**
Emotional Abuse
Emotional Adjustment
Emotional Content
Emotional Control
Emotional Development
Emotional Expressiveness
    USE Emotionality (Personality)
Emotional Immaturity
Emotional Inferiority
Emotional Insecurity
    USE Emotional Security
Emotional Instability
Emotional Maladjustment
    USE Emotional Adjustment
Emotional Maturity
Emotional Needs
    USE Psychological Needs
Emotional Responses
Emotional Restraint *USE Emotional Control*
Emotional Security
Emotional Stability
Emotional States

Emotional Superiority
Emotional Trauma
Conditioned **Emotional** Responses
Emotionality (Personality)
Animal **Emotionality**
Emotionally Disturbed
Emotions
Rational **Emotive** Therapy
Empathy
Pulmonary **Emphysema**
Empirical Methods
Employability
Employee Absenteeism
Employee Assistance Programs
Employee Attitudes
Employee Benefits
Employee Characteristics
Employee Efficiency
Employee Health Insurance
Employee Interaction
Employee Leave Benefits
Employee Motivation
Employee Pension Plans
Employee Productivity
Employee Selection
    USE Personnel Selection
Employee Skills
Employee Supervisor Interaction
    USE Supervisor Employee Interaction
Employee Termination
    USE Personnel Termination
Employee Turnover
Manager Employee Interaction
    USE Supervisor Employee Interaction
Supervisor **Employee** Interaction
Employees *USE Personnel*
Employer Attitudes
Employment *USE Employment Status*
Employment Discrimination
Employment History
Employment Interviews
    USE Job Applicant Interviews
Employment Processes
    USE Personnel Recruitment
Employment Status
Employment Tests
Self **Employment**
Supported **Employment**
Empowerment
Empty Nest
Enabling
Enactments
Encephalitis
Encephalography
Air Encephalography
    USE Pneumoencephalography
Encephalomyelitis
Encephalopathies
Toxic **Encephalopathies**
Encoding *USE Human Information Storage*
Encopresis *USE Fecal Incontinence*
Encounter Group Therapy
Encouragement
Nerve **Endings**
Endocrine Disorders
Endocrine Gland Secretion
Endocrine Gland Surgery
Endocrine Glands
Endocrine Neoplasms
Endocrine Sexual Disorders
Endocrine System
Endocrinology
Endogamous Marriage
Endogenous Depression
Endogenous Opiates

313

Endorphins
Endurance
Physical Endurance
Psychological Endurance
Energy Expenditure
Law Enforcement
Law Enforcement Personnel
Engineering Psychology
Genetic Engineering
Human Factors Engineering
Engineers
English as Second Language
Limited English Proficiency
    USE Language Proficiency
Nonstandard English
Fertility Enhancement
Cognition Enhancing Drugs USE Nootropic Drugs
Memory Enhancing Drugs USE Nootropic Drugs
Enjoyment USE Pleasure
Enkephalins
Enlisted Military Personnel
Military Enlistment
Job Enrichment
School Enrollment
Enteropeptidase USE Kinases
Motion Pictures (Entertainment)
Enthusiasm
Entrance Examinations
College Entrance Examination Board Scholastic
    Aptitude Test
Entrapment Games
Entrepreneurship
Enuresis USE Urinary Incontinence
Environment
Academic Environment
Classroom Environment
College Environment
Educational Environment USE School Environment
Experimental Environment USE Research Setting
Facility Environment
Home Environment
Hospital Environment
Office Environment USE Working Conditions
Person Environment Fit
School Environment
Therapeutic Environment
Treatment Environment USE Therapeutic Environment
Zoo Environment USE Animal Captivity
Environmental Adaptation
Environmental Attitudes
Environmental Design
    USE Environmental Planning
Environmental Education
Environmental Effects
Environmental Planning
Environmental Psychology
Environmental Stress
Environmental Therapy
    USE Milieu Therapy
Restricted Environmental Stimulation
    USE Stimulus Deprivation
Animal Environments
Factory Environments USE Working Conditions
Female Only Environments
    USE Single Sex Environments
Male Only Environments
    USE Single Sex Environments
Rural Environments
Same Sex Environments
    USE Single Sex Environments
Single Sex Environments
Social Environments
Suburban Environments
Urban Environments
Work Environments USE Working Conditions

Envy USE Jealousy
Penis Envy
Enzyme Inhibitors
Enzymes
Ependyma USE Cerebral Ventricles
Ephedrine
Epidemics
Epidemiology
Epilepsy
Experimental Epilepsy
Grand Mal Epilepsy
Petit Mal Epilepsy
Epileptic Seizures
Epinephrine
Episcopalians USE Protestants
Acute Psychotic Episode USE Acute Psychosis
Episodic Memory
Epistemology
Epithelial Cells
Epithelium USE Skin (Anatomy)
Epstein Barr Viral Disorder
Equal Education
Social Equality
Score Equating
Test Equating USE Score Equating
Structural Equation Modeling
Equilibrium
Equimax Rotation
Cauda Equina USE Spinal Nerves
Equipment USE Apparatus
Equity (Payment)
Equity (Social)
High School Equivalency USE Adult Education
Erection (Penis)
Ergonomics
    USE Human Factors Engineering
Ergot Derivatives
Erikson (Erik)
Erikson (Erik)
Eroticism
Erotomania
Error Analysis
Error of Measurement
Error Variance USE Error of Measurement
Standard Error of Measurement
    USE Error of Measurement
Trial and Error Learning
Errors
Prediction Errors
Refraction Errors
Type I Errors
Type II Errors
Erythroblastosis Fetalis
    USE Rh Incompatibility
Erythrocytes
Escape USE Avoidance
Escape Conditioning
Animal Escape Behavior
Eserine USE Physostigmine
Eskimos USE Inuit
ESL USE English as Second Language
Esophagus
Essay Testing
Essential Hypertension
Self Esteem
Esterases
Estimation
Magnitude Estimation
Parameter Estimation USE Statistical Estimation
Statistical Estimation
Time Estimation
Estradiol
Estrogen Antagonists USE Antiestrogens
Estrogen Replacement Therapy
    USE Hormone Therapy

314

Estrogens

Estrone

Estrus

Ethanal *USE Acetaldehyde*

Ethanol

Ether (Anesthetic)

Work Ethic *USE Work (Attitudes Toward)*

Ethics

Experimental **Ethics**

Professional **Ethics**

Ethnic Differences
   USE Racial and Ethnic Differences

Ethnic Discrimination
   USE Race and Ethnic Discrimination

Ethnic Disorders
   USE Ethnospecific Disorders

Ethnic Groups
   USE Racial and Ethnic Groups

Ethnic Identity

Ethnic Sensitivity *USE Cultural Sensitivity*

Ethnic Values

Race and **Ethnic** Discrimination

Racial and **Ethnic** Attitudes

Racial and **Ethnic** Differences

Racial and **Ethnic** Groups

Racial and **Ethnic** Relations

Ethnocentrism

Ethnography

Ethnolinguistics

Ethnology

Ethnospecific Disorders

Animal **Ethology**

Ethyl Alcohol *USE Ethanol*

Ethylaldehyde *USE Acetaldehyde*

Etiology

Etymology

Eugenics

Euphoria

Eustachian Tube *USE Middle Ear*

Euthanasia

Evaluation

Evaluation Criteria

Course **Evaluation**

Disability **Evaluation**

Educational Program **Evaluation**

Forensic **Evaluation**

Mental Health Program **Evaluation**

Peer **Evaluation**

Personnel **Evaluation**

Program **Evaluation**

Psychiatric **Evaluation**

Self **Evaluation**

Teacher Effectiveness **Evaluation**

Treatment Effectiveness **Evaluation**

Vocational **Evaluation**

Evangelists

Anniversary **Events**

Experiences **(Events)**

Legal **Evidence**

Evoked Potentials

Auditory **Evoked** Potentials

Cortical **Evoked** Potentials

Motor Evoked Potentials
   USE Somatosensory Evoked Potentials

Olfactory **Evoked** Potentials

Somatosensory **Evoked** Potentials

Visual **Evoked** Potentials

Theory of **Evolution**

Breast Examination
   USE Self Examination (Medical)

College Entrance **Examination** Board Scholastic Aptitude
   Test

Eye Examination
   USE Ophthalmologic Examination

Graduate Record **Examination**

Mini Mental State **Examination**

Ophthalmologic **Examination**

Physical **Examination**

Self **Examination** (Medical)

Certification Examinations
   USE Professional Examinations

Entrance **Examinations**

Licensure Examinations
   USE Professional Examinations

Professional **Examinations**

State Board Examinations
   USE Professional Examinations

Information Exchange *USE Communication*

Needle **Exchange** Programs

Excretion

Executive Functioning
   USE Cognitive Ability

Executives *USE Top Level Managers*

Exercise

Aerobic **Exercise**

Physical Exercise *USE Exercise*

Exhaustion *USE Fatigue*

Exhibitionism

Existential Therapy

Existentialism

Exogamous Marriage

Life **Expectancy**

Expectant Fathers

Expectant Mothers

Expectant Parents

Expectations

Efficacy Expectations *USE Self Efficacy*

Experimenter **Expectations**

Parental **Expectations**

Role **Expectations**

Teacher **Expectations**

Energy **Expenditure**

Experience Level

Combat **Experience**

Curricular Field **Experience**

Early **Experience**

Job **Experience** Level

Openness to **Experience**

Therapist Experience *USE Therapist Characteristics*

Wilderness **Experience**

Experiences (Events)

Life **Experiences**

Near Death **Experiences**

Out of Body **Experiences**

Psychedelic **Experiences**

Religious **Experiences**

Vicarious **Experiences**

Experiential Learning

Experiential Psychotherapy

Experiment Controls

Experiment Volunteers

Experimental Apparatus *USE Apparatus*

Experimental Attrition

Experimental Design

Experimental Environment
   USE Research Setting

Experimental Epilepsy

Experimental Ethics

Experimental Instructions

Experimental Laboratories

Experimental Methods

Experimental Neurosis

Experimental Psychologists

Experimental Psychology

Experimental Psychosis

Experimental Replication

Experimental Subjects

Debriefing **(Experimental)**

Sampling **(Experimental)**

Experimentation

Experimenter Bias
Experimenter Expectations
Experimenters
Expert Systems
Expert Testimony
Expertise *USE Experience Level*
Explicit Memory
Career Exploration *USE Career Education*
Exploratory Behavior
Animal **Exploratory** Behavior
Explosive Disorder
Explosive Personality
    USE Explosive Disorder
Intermittent Explosive Disorder *USE Explosive Disorder*
Exposure Therapy
Fetal Exposure *USE Prenatal Exposure*
Occupational **Exposure**
Prenatal **Exposure**
Expressed Emotion
Facial **Expressions**
Expressive Psychotherapy
Emotional Expressiveness
    USE Emotionality (Personality)
School **Expulsion**
Extended Family
Agricultural **Extension** Workers
External Ear
External Rewards
Internal **External** Locus of Control
Rotter Internal **External** Locus of Control Scale
Externalization
Extinction (Learning)
Thyroid Extract *USE Thyroid Hormones*
Extracurricular Activities
Extradimensional Shift Learning
    USE Nonreversal Shift Learning
Extramarital Intercourse
Extrapyramidal Symptoms
Extrapyramidal Tracts
Extrasensory Perception
Extraversion
Extrinsic Motivation
Extrinsic Rewards *USE External Rewards*
Eye (Anatomy)
Eye Accommodation
    USE Ocular Accommodation
Eye Color
Eye Contact
Eye Convergence
Eye Disorders
Eye Dominance *USE Ocular Dominance*
Eye Examination
    USE Ophthalmologic Examination
Eye Fixation
Eye Movement Desensitization Therapy
Eye Movements
Cones **(Eye)**
Iris **(Eye)**
Lens **(Eye)**
Nonrapid Eye Movement Sleep *USE NREM Sleep*
Pupil **(Eye)**
Rapid **Eye** Movement
Rapid Eye Movement Dreams *USE REM Dreams*
Rapid Eye Movement Sleep *USE REM Sleep*
Rods **(Eye)**
Saccadic Eye Movements *USE Eye Movements*
Seeing Eye Dogs *USE Mobility Aids*
Eyeblink Reflex
Eyelid Conditioning
Crossed Eyes *USE Strabismus*
Eyewitnesses *USE Witnesses*
Eysenck Personality Inventory
F Test
California **F** Scale
Face (Anatomy)

Face Perception
Face Recognition *USE Face Perception*
Lips **(Face)**
Facial Expressions
Facial Features
Facial Muscles
Facial Nerve
Facilitated Communication
    USE Augmentative Communication
Social **Facilitation**
Community **Facilities**
Maximum Security **Facilities**
School **Facilities**
Treatment **Facilities**
Facility Admission
Facility Discharge
Facility Environment
Facility Readmission
    USE Facility Admission
Factitious Disorders
Factor Analysis
Factor Structure
ACTH Releasing Factor *USE Corticotropin Releasing Factor*
Confirmatory Factor Analysis *USE Factor Analysis*
Conscious (Personality **Factor)**
Corticotropin Releasing **Factor**
Five **Factor** Personality Model
Nerve Growth **Factor**
Unconscious (Personality **Factor)**
Factorial Validity *USE Statistical Validity*
Cultural Factors *USE Sociocultural Factors*
Ecological **Factors**
Human **Factors** Engineering
Personality Factors *USE Personality Traits*
Psychoanalytic Personality **Factors**
Psychosocial **Factors**
Risk **Factors**
Sixteen Personality **Factors** Questionnaire
Sociocultural **Factors**
Thermal Factors *USE Temperature Effects*
Factory Environments
    USE Working Conditions
Factual Knowledge
    USE Declarative Knowledge
Faculty *USE Educational Personnel*
Fading (Conditioning)
Fads and Fashions
Failure
Failure to Thrive
Academic **Failure**
Fainting *USE Syncope*
Cattell Culture Fair Intelligence Test
    USE Culture Fair Intelligence Test
Culture **Fair** Intelligence Test
Fairbairnian Theory *USE Object Relations*
Fairy Tales *USE Folklore*
Faith Healing
Faking
False Memory
False Pregnancy *USE Pseudocyesis*
True False Tests
    USE Forced Choice (Testing Method)
Fame
Amaurotic **Familial** Idiocy
Cultural Familial Mental Retardation
    USE Psychosocial Mental Retardation
Familiarity
Family
Family Background
Family Caregivers *USE Caregivers*
Family Counseling *USE Family Therapy*
Family Crises
Family Life Education
Family Life *USE Family Relations*
Family Medicine

Family Members
Family of Origin
Family Physicians
Family Planning
Family Planning Attitudes
Family Relations
Family Resemblance
Family Size
Family Socioeconomic Level
Family Structure
Family Therapy
Family Violence
Family Work Relationship
Biological **Family**
Dysfunctional **Family**
Extended **Family**
Interethnic **Family**
Interracial **Family**
Job Family Relationship
    USE Family Work Relationship
Marriage and Family Education
    USE Family Life Education
Natural Family *USE Biological Family*
Nuclear **Family**
Schizophrenogenic **Family**
Work Family Relationship
    USE Family Work Relationship
Fantasies (Thought Disturbances)
Fantasy
Fantasy (Defense Mechanism)
Guided Fantasy *USE Guided Imagery*
Sexual **Fantasy**
Migrant **Farm** Workers
Farmers *USE Agricultural Workers*
Fascism
Fads and **Fashions**
Fat Metabolism *USE Lipid Metabolism*
Fatalism
Father Absence
Father Child Communication
Father Child Relations
Fathers
Adolescent **Fathers**
Expectant **Fathers**
Single **Fathers**
Teenage Fathers *USE Adolescent Fathers*
Fatigue
Chronic **Fatigue** Syndrome
Fatty Acids
Fear
Fear of Public Speaking
    USE Speech Anxiety
Fear of Strangers *USE Stranger Reactions*
Fear of Success
Fear Survey Schedule
Facial **Features**
Fecal Incontinence
School Federal Aid
    USE Educational Financial Assistance
Fee for Service
Feedback
Auditory **Feedback**
Delayed Auditory **Feedback**
Delayed **Feedback**
Sensory **Feedback**
Visual **Feedback**
Feeding Practices
Animal **Feeding** Behavior
Bottle **Feeding**
Breast **Feeding**
Anesthesia **(Feeling)**
Feelings *USE Emotions*
Professional **Fees**
Feet (Anatomy)
Felids

Felonies *USE Crime*
Female Animals
Female Criminals
Female Delinquency
Female Genital Mutilation
    USE Circumcision
Female Genitalia
Female Only Environments
    USE Single Sex Environments
Female Orgasm
Male **Female** Relations
Battered **Females**
Human **Females**
Femininity
Feminism
Feminist Therapy
Testicular **Feminization** Syndrome
Femoral Nerve *USE Spinal Nerves*
Fenfluramine
Fentanyl
Fertility
Fertility Enhancement
Fertilization
In Vitro Fertilization *USE Reproductive Technology*
Fetal Alcohol Syndrome
Fetal Exposure *USE Prenatal Exposure*
Erythroblastosis Fetalis *USE Rh Incompatibility*
Fetishism
Sexual Fetishism *USE Fetishism*
Fetus
Fever *USE Hyperthermia*
Hay **Fever**
Rheumatic **Fever**
Postganglionic Autonomic Fibers *USE Autonomic Ganglia*
Preganglionic Autonomic Fibers *USE Autonomic Ganglia*
Fibrillation (Heart)
Atrial Fibrillation *USE Fibrillation (Heart)*
Auricular Fibrillation *USE Fibrillation (Heart)*
Ventricular Fibrillation *USE Fibrillation (Heart)*
Fibromyalgia Syndrome
    USE Muscular Disorders
Cystic **Fibrosis**
Fiction *USE Literature*
Marital Fidelity *USE Monogamy*
Field Dependence
Field Instruction
    USE Curricular Field Experience
Animal Open **Field** Behavior
Curricular **Field** Experience
Educational **Field** Trips
Visual **Field**
Cutaneous Receptive **Fields**
Receptive **Fields**
Visual Receptive **Fields**
Fire **Fighters**
Fighting *USE Aggressive Behavior*
Figurative Language
Figure Ground Discrimination
Welsh **Figure** Preference Test
Figures of Speech
    USE Figurative Language
Embedded **Figures** Testing
Hidden **Figures** Test
Human **Figures** Drawing
Perceptual Fill *USE Perceptual Closure*
Film Strips
Filtered Noise
Filtered Speech
Educational **Financial** Assistance
School Financial Assistance
    USE Educational Financial Assistance
Fine Motor Skill Learning
Finger Tapping
Fingers (Anatomy)
Fingerspelling

Fire Fighters
Fire Prevention
Firearms *USE Weapons*
Firesetting *USE Arson*
FIRO-B *USE Fundamental Interpersonal*
Relation Orientation Behavior Ques
Bass **(Fish)**
Fishes
Electric **Fishes**
Goodness of **Fit**
Person Environment **Fit**
Physical **Fitness**
Five Factor Personality Model
Big Five Personality Model
USE Five Factor Personality Model
Eye **Fixation**
Ocular Fixation *USE Eye Fixation*
Visual Fixation *USE Eye Fixation*
Fixed Interval Reinforcement
Fixed Ratio Reinforcement
Flashbacks *USE Hallucinations*
Flexion Reflex
Flextime *USE Work Scheduling*
Flicker Fusion Frequency
USE Critical Flicker Fusion Threshold
Critical **Flicker** Fusion Threshold
Flies *USE Diptera*
Flight Attendants
USE Aerospace Personnel
Flight Instrumentation
Flight Simulation
Flooding Therapy *USE Implosive Therapy*
Blood **Flow**
Cerebral Blood **Flow**
Fluency *USE Verbal Fluency*
Verbal **Fluency**
Fluid Intake
Amniotic **Fluid**
Cerebrospinal **Fluid**
Spinal Fluid *USE Cerebrospinal Fluid*
Body **Fluids**
Fluoxetine
Fluphenazine
Flurazepam
Fluvoxamine
Fruit Fly *USE Drosophila*
Folic Acid
Folie A Deux
Folk Medicine
Folk Psychology
Folklore
Folktales *USE Folklore*
Follicle Stimulating Hormone
Project **Follow** Through
Followup Studies
Posttreatment **Followup**
Food
Food Additives
Food Allergies
Food Deprivation
Food Intake
Food Preferences
Football
Animal **Foraging** Behavior
Air **Force** Personnel
Forced Choice (Testing Method)
Forebrain
Medial **Forebrain** Bundle
Foreign Language Education
Foreign Language Learning
Foreign Language Translation
Foreign Languages
Foreign Nationals
Foreign Organizations
Foreign Policy Making

Foreign Students
Foreign Study
Foreign Workers
Industrial **Foremen**
Forensic Evaluation
Forensic Psychiatry
Forensic Psychology
Forgetting
Forgiveness
Form and Shape Perception
Form Classes (Language)
Form Perception
USE Form and Shape Perception
Attitude **Formation**
Character Formation *USE Personality Development*
Coalition **Formation**
Concept **Formation**
Impression **Formation**
Reaction **Formation**
Reticular **Formation**
Test **Forms**
Theory **Formulation**
Fornix
FORTRAN *USE Computer Programming*
Languages
Chance **(Fortune)**
Forward Masking *USE Masking*
Foster Care
Foster Children
Foster Homes *USE Foster Care*
Foster Parents
Fovea
Foveal Vision
Fowl *USE Birds*
Foxes
Fragile X Syndrome
Fragmentation (Schizophrenia)
Frail *USE Health Impairments*
Rod and **Frame** Test
Franck Drawing Completion Test
Frankness *USE Honesty*
Fraternal Twins *USE Heterozygotic Twins*
Fraternity Membership
Fraud
Consumer Fraud *USE Fraud*
Skinner (Burrhus **Frederic)**
Free Association
Free Recall
Free Will *USE Volition*
Freedom
Frequency Distribution
Flicker Fusion Frequency
USE Critical Flicker Fusion Threshold
Pitch **(Frequency)**
Response **Frequency**
Spatial **Frequency**
Stimulus **Frequency**
Temporal **Frequency**
Word **Frequency**
Freud (Sigmund)
Freudian Psychoanalytic School
Friendship
Frigidity
Frogs
Frontal Lobe
Frostig Developmental Test of Visual
Perception
Fruit Fly *USE Drosophila*
Frustration
Rosenzweig Picture **Frustration** Study
Fugue Reaction
Self **Fulfilling** Prophecies
Fulfillment *USE Satisfaction*
Sexual **Function** Disturbances
Urinary **Function** Disorders

Functional Analysis
Functional Knowledge
    USE Procedural Knowledge
Functional Status *USE Ability Level*
Functionalism
Cognitive Functioning *USE Cognitive Ability*
Executive Functioning *USE Cognitive Ability*
Intellectual Functioning *USE Cognitive Ability*
Level of Functioning *USE Ability Level*
Fundamental Interpersonal Relation
    Orientation Behavior Ques
Fundamentalism
Funding
Funerals *USE Death Rites*
Furniture
Critical Flicker **Fusion** Threshold
Flicker Fusion Frequency
    USE Critical Flicker Fusion Threshold
Future
Fuzzy Set Theory
GABA Agonists
    USE Gamma Aminobutyric Acid
        Agonists
GABA Antagonists
    USE Gamma Aminobutyric Acid
        Antagonists
Galanin *USE Peptides*
Galanthamine
Galvanic Skin Response
Gamblers Anonymous
    USE Twelve Step Programs
Gambling
Compulsive Gambling *USE Pathological Gambling*
Pathological **Gambling**
Game Theory
Prisoners Dilemma **Game**
Games
Childrens Recreational **Games**
Computer **Games**
Entrapment **Games**
Non Zero Sum **Games**
Simulation **Games**
Video Games *USE Computer Games*
Gamma Aminobutyric Acid
Gamma Aminobutyric Acid Agonists
Gamma Aminobutyric Acid Antagonists
Gamma Globulin
Ganglia
Autonomic **Ganglia**
Basal **Ganglia**
Spinal **Ganglia**
Ganglion Blocking Drugs
Ganglion Cells (Retina)
Retinal Ganglion Cells
    USE Ganglion Cells (Retina)
Stellate Ganglion *USE Autonomic Ganglia*
Juvenile **Gangs**
Ganser Syndrome
    USE Factitious Disorders
Generation **Gap**
Gastrointestinal Disorders
Gastrointestinal System
Gastrointestinal Ulcers
Gastropods *USE Mollusca*
Gates MacGinitie Reading Tests
Gates Reading Readiness Tests
    USE Gates MacGinitie Reading Tests
Gates Reading Test
    USE Gates MacGinitie Reading Tests
Sensory **Gating**
Gaussian Distribution
    USE Normal Distribution
Gay Liberation Movement
    USE Homosexual Liberation Movement
Gay Males *USE Male Homosexuality*

Gay Parents *USE Homosexual Parents*
Gazing *USE Eye Fixation*
Geese
Gender Differences
    USE Human Sex Differences
Gender Identity
Gender Identity Disorder
Gender Role Attitudes
    USE Sex Role Attitudes
Gender Roles *USE Sex Roles*
General Anesthetics
General Aptitude Test Battery
General Health Questionnaire
General Paresis
General Practitioners
Army **General** Classification Test
Medical Treatment **(General)**
Mental Disorders due to **General** Medical Conditions
Generalization (Learning)
Cognitive **Generalization**
Response **Generalization**
Semantic **Generalization**
Stimulus **Generalization**
Generalized Anxiety Disorder
    USE Anxiety Disorders
Generation Effect (Learning)
Generation Gap
Transformational **Generative** Grammar
Generativity
Generators (Apparatus)
Genes
Genetic Counseling
Genetic Disorders
Genetic Dominance
Genetic Engineering
Genetic Linkage
Genetic Recessiveness
Genetics
Behavioral **Genetics**
Population **Genetics**
Geniculate Bodies (Thalamus)
Genital Disorders
Genital Herpes *USE Herpes Genitalis*
Female Genital Mutilation *USE Circumcision*
Male **Genital** Disorders
Female **Genitalia**
Male **Genitalia**
Herpes **Genitalis**
Geniuses *USE Gifted*
Genocide
Genotypes
Genuineness *USE Sincerity*
Geographic Regions *USE Geography*
Geographical Differences
    USE Regional Differences
Geographical Mobility
Geography
Physical Geography *USE Geography*
Geomagnetism *USE Magnetism*
Geometry *USE Mathematics*
Gerbils
Geriatric Assessment
Geriatric Patients
Geriatric Psychiatry
Geriatric Psychotherapy
Geriatrics
German Measles *USE Rubella*
Gerontology
Gestalt Psychology
Gestalt Therapy
Bender **Gestalt** Test
Gestation *USE Pregnancy*
Gestures
Ghettoes
Urban Ghettoes *USE Ghettoes*

Gifted
Intellectually Gifted *USE Gifted*
Gilles de la Tourette Disorder
Gipsies *USE Gypsies*
Girls *USE Human Females*
Adrenal **Gland** Disorders
Adrenal **Gland** Secretion
Endocrine **Gland** Secretion
Endocrine **Gland** Surgery
Pituitary **Gland**
Pituitary Gland Surgery *USE Hypophysectomy*
Secretion **(Gland)**
Thyroid **Gland**
Glands
Adrenal **Glands**
Endocrine **Glands**
Mammary **Glands**
Parathyroid **Glands**
Salivary **Glands**
Glaucoma
Global Amnesia
Gamma **Globulin**
Globulins
Globus Pallidus
Glossolalia
Glossopharyngeal Nerve
    USE Cranial Nerves
Glucagon
Glucocorticoids
Glucose
Glucose Metabolism
Blood Glucose *USE Blood Sugar*
Glue Sniffing
Glutamic Acid
Glutamine
Glutethimide
Glycine
Glycogen
Glycoproteins *USE Globulins*
Goal Setting
Goals
Career Goals *USE Occupational Aspirations*
Organizational Goals *USE Organizational Objectives*
Goats
God Concepts
Goiters
Goldfish
Goldstein Scheerer Object Sort Test
Gonadotropic Hormones
Gonadotropin
    USE Gonadotropic Hormones
Gonads
Gonorrhea
Goodenough Harris Draw A Person Test
Goodness of Fit
Gorillas
Gossip
Gough Adjective Check List
Government
Government Agencies
Government Bureaucracy
    USE Government
Government Personnel
Government Policy Making
Government Programs
Autonomy **(Government)**
Elected Government Officials
    USE Government Personnel
Law **(Government)**
Welfare Services **(Government)**
Grade Level
Academic Grade Level *USE Grade Level*
Gradepoint Average
    USE Academic Achievement
Grading (Educational)

Graduate Degrees
    USE Educational Degrees
Graduate Education
Graduate Psychology Education
Graduate Record Examination
Graduate Schools
Graduate Students
Clinical Psychology **Graduate** Training
College **Graduates**
High School **Graduates**
School **Graduation**
Grammar
Grammar Schools
    USE Elementary Schools
Transformational Generative **Grammar**
Grand Mal Epilepsy
Grandchildren
Grandiosity
Grandparents
Great Grandparents *USE Ancestors*
Graphical Displays
Graphology *USE Handwriting*
Grasping
Grasshoppers
Delay of **Gratification**
Myasthenia **Gravis**
Gravitational Effects
Periaqueductal **Gray**
Great Grandparents *USE Ancestors*
Gregariousness
Bannister Repertory **Grid**
Shuttle Box Grids *USE Shuttle Boxes*
Grief
Grimaces
Nocturnal Teeth **Grinding**
Teeth Grinding *USE Bruxism*
Animal **Grooming** Behavior
Gross Motor Skill Learning
Ground Transportation
Figure **Ground** Discrimination
Group Cohesion
Group Counseling
Group Decision Making
Group Development
Group Discussion
Group Dynamics
Group Health Plans
    *USE Health Maintenance
        Organizations*
Group Homes
Group Instruction
Group Participation
Group Performance
Group Problem Solving
Group Psychotherapy
Group Size
Group Structure
Group Testing
Group Therapy *USE Group Psychotherapy*
Encounter **Group** Therapy
Marathon **Group** Therapy
Minority Group Discrimination
    USE Race and Ethnic Discrimination
Ability **Grouping**
Between **Groups** Design
Blood **Groups**
Chinese Cultural **Groups**
Consciousness Raising **Groups**
Control Groups *USE Experiment Controls*
Developmental Age **Groups**
Diagnosis Related **Groups**
Ethnic Groups *USE Racial and Ethnic Groups*
Japanese Cultural **Groups**
Korean Cultural **Groups**
Minority **Groups**

320

Racial and Ethnic **Groups**
Reference **Groups**
Religious **Groups**
Social **Groups**
Support **Groups**
T Groups *USE Human Relations Training*
Vietnamese Cultural **Groups**
Grown Children *USE Adult Offspring*
Growth *USE Development*
Growth Centers
USE Human Potential Movement
Growth Hormone Inhibitor
USE Somatostatin
Growth Hormone *USE Somatotropin*
Nerve **Growth** Factor
Personal Growth Techniques
USE Human Potential Movement
Physical Growth *USE Physical Development*
Guanethidine
Guanosine
Coast **Guard** Personnel
Guardianship
National **Guardsmen**
Guessing
Guest Workers *USE Foreign Workers*
Guidance Counseling
USE School Counseling
Career Guidance *USE Occupational Guidance*
Child **Guidance** Clinics
Educational Guidance *USE Educational Counseling*
Occupational **Guidance**
School Guidance *USE School Counseling*
Vocational Guidance *USE Occupational Guidance*
Guided Fantasy *USE Guided Imagery*
Guided Imagery
Treatment **Guidelines**
Guilford Zimmerman Temperament Survey
Guilt
Guinea Pigs
Gulls *USE Sea Gulls*
Sea **Gulls**
Gun Control Laws
Gustatory Perception
USE Taste Perception
Gymnastic Therapy
USE Recreation Therapy
Gynecological Disorders
Gynecologists
Gynecology
Gypsies
Gyrus Cinguli
Habilitation
Habitat Selection *USE Territoriality*
Habits
Study **Habits**
Habituation
Hair
Hair Loss *USE Alopecia*
Hair Pulling
Halcion *USE Triazolam*
Halfway Houses
Residence Halls *USE Dormitories*
Hallucinations
Auditory **Hallucinations**
Drug Induced **Hallucinations**
Hypnagogic **Hallucinations**
Visual **Hallucinations**
Hallucinogenic Drugs
Hallucinosis
Alcoholic **Hallucinosis**
Halo Effect
Haloperidol
Halstead Reitan Neuropsychological
Battery
Hamsters

Hand (Anatomy)
Handedness
Adventitiously Handicapped *USE Adventitious Disorders*
Aurally Handicapped *USE Hearing Disorders*
Congenitally Handicapped *USE Congenital Disorders*
Multiply Handicapped *USE Multiple Disabilities*
Orthopedically Handicapped *USE Physical Disorders*
Physically Handicapped *USE Physical Disorders*
Sensorially Handicapped
USE Sensory System Disorders
Speech Handicapped *USE Speech Disorders*
Visually Handicapped *USE Vision Disorders*
Self **Handicapping** Strategy
Handicaps *USE Disorders*
Handicrafts *USE Crafts*
Handwriting
Handwriting Legibility
Printing **(Handwriting)**
Happiness
Haptic Perception *USE Cutaneous Sense*
Harassment
Sexual **Harassment**
Hardiness
Maslow (Abraham **Harold)**
Goodenough **Harris** Draw A Person Test
Hashish
Hate
Hawaii Natives
Native Hawaiians *USE Hawaii Natives*
Hay Fever
Hazardous Materials
Hazards
Head (Anatomy)
Head Banging
Head Injuries
Head Start *USE Project Head Start*
Closed Head Injuries *USE Head Injuries*
Project **Head** Start
Headache
Migraine **Headache**
Muscle Contraction **Headache**
Tension Headache
USE Muscle Contraction Headache
Faith **Healing**
Psychic Healing *USE Faith Healing*
Health
Health Attitudes
Health Behavior
Health Care Administration
Health Care Costs
Health Care Delivery
Health Care Policy
Health Care Professionals
USE Health Personnel
Health Care Psychology
Health Care Seeking Behavior
Health Care Services
Health Care Utilization
Health Complaints
Health Education
Health Impairments
Health Insurance
Health Knowledge
Health Locus of Control
USE Health Attitudes
Health Maintenance Organizations
Health Personnel
Health Personnel Attitudes
Health Promotion
Health Psychology
USE Health Care Psychology
Health Screening
Health Service Needs
Health Service Utilization
USE Health Care Utilization

Behavioral Health *USE Health Care Psychology*
Community Mental **Health**
Community Mental **Health** Centers
Community Mental **Health** Services
Community Mental **Health** Training
Employee **Health** Insurance
General **Health** Questionnaire
Group Health Plans *USE Health Maintenance Organizations*
Holistic **Health**
Home Health Aides *USE Home Care Personnel*
Mental **Health**
Mental Health Care Costs *USE Health Care Costs*
Mental Health Care Policy *USE Health Care Policy*
Mental Health Consultation *USE Professional Consultation*
Mental **Health** Inservice Training
Mental **Health** Personnel
Mental **Health** Personnel Supply
Mental **Health** Program Evaluation
Mental **Health** Programs
Mental Health Service Needs *USE Health Service Needs*
Mental **Health** Services
Primary Mental **Health** Prevention
Primary **Health** Care
Public **Health**
Public **Health** Service Nurses
Public **Health** Services
Wholistic Health *USE Holistic Health*
Hearing Acuity *USE Auditory Acuity*
Hearing Aids
Hearing Disorders
Hearing Measures *USE Speech and Hearing Measures*
Partially **Hearing** Impaired
Sensorineural Hearing Loss *USE Hearing Disorders*
Speech and **Hearing** Measures
Heart
Heart Attacks *USE Heart Disorders*
Heart Auricles
Heart Beat *USE Heart Rate*
Heart Disorders
Heart Rate
Heart Rate Affecting Drugs
Heart Surgery
Heart Transplants *USE Organ Transplantation*
Heart Valves
Heart Ventricles
Arrhythmias **(Heart)**
Coronary Heart Disease *USE Heart Disorders*
Fibrillation **(Heart)**
Rapid Heart Rate *USE Tachycardia*
Heartbeat *USE Heart Rate*
Heat Effects
Hebephrenic Schizophrenia *USE Schizophrenia (Disorganized Type)*
Hedonism
Body **Height**
Helicopters
Helium
Help Seeking Behavior
Self **Help** Techniques
Helping Behavior *USE Assistance (Social Behavior)*
Helplessness
Learned **Helplessness**
Hematologic Disorders *USE Blood and Lymphatic Disorders*
Hematoma
Hemianopia
Hemiopia *USE Hemianopia*
Hemiplegia

Hemispherectomy
Hemispheric Specialization *USE Lateral Dominance*
Hemodialysis
Hemoglobin
Hemophilia
Hemorrhage
Cerebral **Hemorrhage**
Henmon Nelson Tests of Mental Ability *USE Intelligence Measures*
Heparin
Hepatic Disorders *USE Liver Disorders*
Hepatitis
Toxic **Hepatitis**
Medicinal **Herbs** and Plants
Hereditary Disorders *USE Genetic Disorders*
Sex Linked **Hereditary** Disorders
Heredity *USE Genetics*
Hermaphroditism
Hermeneutics
Heroin
Heroin Addiction
Herpes Genitalis
Herpes Simplex
Genital Herpes *USE Herpes Genitalis*
Heterogeneity of Variance *USE Variance Homogeneity*
Heterosexism *USE Homosexuality (Attitudes Toward)*
Heterosexual Interaction *USE Male Female Relations*
Heterosexuality
Heterozygotic Twins
Heuristic Modeling
Hexamethonium
Hexobarbital
Hibernation
Hidden Figures Test
Dominance **Hierarchy**
High Risk Populations *USE At Risk Populations*
High School Equivalency *USE Adult Education*
High School Graduates
High School Personality Questionnaire
High School Students
High School Teachers
High Schools
Junior **High** School Students
Junior **High** School Teachers
Junior **High** Schools
Higher Education
Higher Order Conditioning
Highway Safety
Hindbrain
Hinduism
Hindus
Hippies *USE Subculture (Anthropological)*
Hippocampal Commissure *USE Fornix*
Hippocampus
Hips
Hiring *USE Personnel Selection*
Hispanics
Histamine
Histidine
Histology
History
History of Psychology
Case History *USE Patient History*
Employment **History**
Medical History *USE Patient History*
Patient **History**
Psychiatric History *USE Patient History*
Histrionic Personality Disorder

HIV *USE Human Immunodeficiency Virus*
HIV Testing
HMO *USE Health Maintenance*
Organizations
Animal **Hoarding** Behavior
Hobbies
Hoffmanns Reflex
Holidays
Holistic Health
Holocaust
Holocaust Survivors
Holtzman Inkblot Technique
Homatropine *USE Alkaloids*
Home Accidents
Home Birth *USE Midwifery*
Home Care
Home Care Personnel
Home Economics
Home Environment
Home Health Aides
USE Home Care Personnel
Home Reared Mentally Retarded
Home Schooling
Home Visiting Programs
Return to Home *USE Empty Nest*
Homebound
Homeless
Homeless Mentally Ill
Mentally Ill Homeless *USE Homeless Mentally Ill*
Homemaking *USE Household Management*
Homeopathic Medicine
USE Alternative Medicine
Homeostasis
Foster Homes *USE Foster Care*
Group **Homes**
Nursing **Homes**
Homesickness
Homework
Homicide
Animal **Homing**
Variance **Homogeneity**
Homographs
Homonyms
Homophobia
USE Homosexuality (Attitudes Toward)
Homosexual Liberation Movement
Homosexual Parents
Homosexuality
Homosexuality (Attitudes Toward)
Male **Homosexuality**
Homovanillic Acid
Honesty
Hope
Hopelessness
Hormone Therapy
Follicle Stimulating **Hormone**
Growth Hormone *USE Somatotropin*
Growth Hormone Inhibitor *USE Somatostatin*
Luteinizing **Hormone**
Melanocyte Stimulating **Hormone**
Parathyroid **Hormone**
Thyroid Stimulating Hormone *USE Thyrotropin*
Thyrotropic Hormone *USE Thyrotropin*
Hormones
Adrenal Cortex **Hormones**
Adrenal Medulla **Hormones**
Gonadotropic **Hormones**
Pituitary **Hormones**
Progestational **Hormones**
Sex **Hormones**
Thyroid **Hormones**
Dorsal **Horns**
Horses
Hospice
Hospital Accreditation

Hospital Addiction Syndrome
USE Munchausen Syndrome
Hospital Administration
Hospital Admission
Hospital Attendants
USE Attendants (Institutions)
Hospital Discharge
Hospital Environment
Hospital Programs
Hospital Psychiatric Units
USE Psychiatric Units
Hospital Staff *USE Medical Personnel*
Day Hospital *USE Partial Hospitalization*
Psychiatric **Hospital** Admission
Psychiatric **Hospital** Discharge
Psychiatric **Hospital** Programs
Psychiatric **Hospital** Readmission
Psychiatric **Hospital** Staff
Hospitalization
Partial **Hospitalization**
Psychiatric **Hospitalization**
Hospitalized Patients
Hospitals
Mental Hospitals *USE Psychiatric Hospitals*
Psychiatric **Hospitals**
State Hospitals *USE Psychiatric Hospitals*
Hostages
Hostility
Hot Line Services
Telephone Hot Lines *USE Hot Line Services*
Household Management
Household Structure
USE Living Arrangements
Halfway **Houses**
Housewives
Housework *USE Household Management*
Housing
Hue
Human Animal Interaction
USE Interspecies Interaction
Human Biological Rhythms
Human Channel Capacity
Human Computer Interaction
Human Courtship
Human Development
Human Factors Engineering
Human Females
Human Figures Drawing
Human Immunodeficiency Virus
Human Information Processes
USE Cognitive Processes
Human Information Storage
Human Machine Systems
Human Machine Systems Design
Human Males
Human Mate Selection
Human Migration
Human Nature
Human Potential Movement
Human Relations Training
Human Resources
USE Personnel Management
Human Rights
Human Sex Differences
Animal Human Interaction
USE Interspecies Interaction
Sexual Intercourse **(Human)**
Humanism
Humanistic Education
USE Affective Education
Humanistic Psychology
Surrogate Parents **(Humans)**
Humor
Cartoons **(Humor)**
Hunger

Huntingtons Chorea
    USE Huntingtons Disease
Huntingtons Disease
Shuttle Box **Hurdles** *USE Shuttle Boxes*
Husbands
Hybrids (Biology)
Hydralazine
Chloral **Hydrate**
Arecoline **Hydrobromide** *USE Arecoline*
Scopolamine **Hydrobromide** *USE Scopolamine*
Hydrocephaly
Apomorphine **Hydrochloride** *USE Apomorphine*
Hydrocortisone
Hydrogen
Hydroxydopamine (6-)
Hydroxyindoleacetic Acid (5-)
Hydroxylamine
Hydroxylase Inhibitors
Hydroxylases
Hydroxytryptophan (5-)
Hydroxyzine
Hygiene
Hyoscine *USE Scopolamine*
Hyperactivity *USE Hyperkinesis*
Attention Deficit Disorder with **Hyperactivity**
Hyperalgesia
    USE Somatosensory Disorders
Hypercholesterolemia
    USE Metabolism Disorders
Hyperesthesia
    USE Somatosensory Disorders
Hyperglycemia
Hyperkinesis
Hypermedia
Hyperparathyroidism
    USE Parathyroid Disorders
Hyperphagia
Hypersexuality
Hypersomnia
Hypertension
Essential **Hypertension**
Hypertext
Hyperthermia
Hyperthyroidism
Hyperventilation
Hypesthesia
    USE Somatosensory Disorders
Hypnagogic Hallucinations
Hypnoanalysis *USE Hypnotherapy*
Hypnosis
Self Hypnosis *USE Autohypnosis*
Hypnotherapists
Hypnotherapy
Hypnotic Drugs
Hypnotic Susceptibility
Age Regression **(Hypnotic)**
Hypnotists
Hypoactive Sexual Desire Disorder
    USE Inhibited Sexual Desire
Hypochondriasis
Hypogastric Plexus
    USE Autonomic Ganglia
Hypoglossal Nerve *USE Cranial Nerves*
Hypoglycemia
Hypogonadism
Hypokinesia *USE Bradykinesia*
Hypomania
Hyponatremia
Hypoparathyroidism
    USE Parathyroid Disorders
Hypothalamo **Hypophyseal** System
Hypophysectomy
Hypophysis Disorders
    USE Pituitary Disorders
Hypopituitarism

Hypotension
Hypothalamo Hypophyseal System
Hypothalamo Pituitary Adrenal System
Hypothalamus
Hypothalamus Lesions
Hypothermia
Hypothesis Testing
Cognitive **Hypothesis** Testing
Null **Hypothesis** Testing
Hypothyroidism
Hypoxia *USE Anoxia*
Hysterectomy
Hysteria
Conversion Hysteria *USE Conversion Disorder*
Mass **Hysteria**
Hysterical Blindness
    USE Hysterical Vision Disturbances
Hysterical Paralysis
Hysterical Personality
    USE Histrionic Personality Disorder
Hysterical Vision Disturbances
Iatrogenic Effects
    USE Side Effects (Treatment)
Ibotenic Acid
ICD *USE International Classification of
    Diseases*
Iconic Memory
Id
Ideal Self *USE Self Concept*
Idealism
Ideation
Suicidal **Ideation**
Identical Twins *USE Monozygotic Twins*
Identification (Defense Mechanism)
Projective **Identification**
Identity Crisis
Dissociative **Identity** Disorder
Ego **Identity**
Ethnic **Identity**
Gender **Identity**
Gender **Identity** Disorder
Professional **Identity**
Social **Identity**
Amaurotic Familial **Idiocy**
Idiot Savants *USE Savants*
Ileum *USE Intestines*
Homeless Mentally **Ill**
Mentally Ill Homeless *USE Homeless Mentally Ill*
Mentally **Ill** Offenders
Terminally **Ill** Patients
Illegitimate Children
Illinois Test of Psycholinguistic Abilities
Illiteracy *USE Literacy*
Illness Behavior
Chronic Mental **Illness**
Chronic **Illness**
Course of Illness *USE Disease Course*
Mental **Illness** (Attitudes Toward)
Mental Illness *USE Mental Disorders*
Persistent Mental Illness *USE Chronic Mental Illness*
Physical **Illness** (Attitudes Toward)
Physical Illness *USE Physical Disorders*
Work Related **Illnesses**
Illumination
Illumination Therapy *USE Phototherapy*
Autokinetic **Illusion**
Mueller Lyer **Illusion**
Illusions (Perception)
Optical Illusions *USE Illusions (Perception)*
Body **Image**
Body **Image** Disturbances
Mirror **Image**
Retinal **Image**
Self Image *USE Self Concept*
Imagery

Conceptual **Imagery**
Eidetic **Imagery**
Guided **Imagery**
Spatial **Imagery**
Onomatopoeia and Images Test
    USE Projective Personality Measures
Imagination
Imaginativeness
    USE Openness to Experience
Magnetic Resonance **Imaging**
Imipramine
Imitation (Learning)
Emotional **Immaturity**
Immersion Programs
    USE Foreign Language Education
Immigrants *USE Immigration*
Immigration
Social Immobility *USE Social Mobility*
Tonic **Immobility**
Acquired **Immune** Deficiency Syndrome
Immunization
Human **Immunodeficiency** Virus
Immunogens *USE Antigens*
Immunoglobulins
Immunologic Disorders
Immunology
Immunopathology *USE Immunology*
Immunoreactivity
Impaired Professionals
Partially Hearing **Impaired**
Olfactory Impairment *USE Anosmia*
Health **Impairments**
Cochlear **Implants**
Implosive Therapy
Impotence
Impression Formation
Impression Management
Imprinting
Impulse Control Disorders
Impulsiveness
Inadequate Personality
Incarceration
Incentives
Educational **Incentives**
Monetary **Incentives**
Incest
Incidental Learning
Income (Economic)
Income Level
Lower **Income** Level
Middle **Income** Level
Upper **Income** Level
Rh **Incompatibility**
Incomplete Man Test
Rotter **Incomplete** Sentences Blank
Fecal **Incontinence**
Urinary **Incontinence**
Incubators (Apparatus)
Independence (Personality)
Independent Living Programs
Independent Living *USE Self Care Skills*
Independent Study
    USE Individualized Instruction
Independent Variables
American **Indians**
Myers Briggs Type **Indicator**
Indifference *USE Apathy*
Indigenous Populations
Individual Counseling
    USE Individual Psychotherapy
Individual Differences
Individual Problem Solving
    USE Problem Solving
Individual Psychology
Individual Psychotherapy

Individual Testing
Individual Therapy
    USE Individual Psychotherapy
Individualism *USE Individuality*
Individuality
Individualized Instruction
Separation **Individuation**
Induced Abortion
Drug **Induced** Congenital Disorders
Drug **Induced** Hallucinations
Sleep Inducing Drugs *USE Hypnotic Drugs*
Vomit Inducing Drugs *USE Emetic Drugs*
Inductive Deductive Reasoning
Industrial Accidents
Industrial Arts Education
    USE Vocational Education
Industrial Foremen
Industrial Personnel
    USE Business and Industrial Personnel
Industrial Psychologists
Industrial Psychology
Industrial Safety *USE Occupational Safety*
Business and **Industrial** Personnel
Skilled **Industrial** Workers
Unskilled **Industrial** Workers
Industrialization
Industry *USE Business*
Educational Inequality *USE Equal Education*
Infant Development
Infant Intelligence Scale
Infant Vocalization
Bayley Scales of **Infant** Development
Cattell Infant Intelligence Scale
    USE Infant Intelligence Scale
Sudden **Infant** Death
Infanticide
Infantile Neurosis *USE Childhood Neurosis*
Infantile Paralysis *USE Poliomyelitis*
Infantile Psychosis
    USE Childhood Psychosis
Early **Infantile** Autism
Symbiotic **Infantile** Psychosis
Infantilism
Infants (Animal)
Multi **Infarct** Dementia
Myocardial **Infarctions**
Infections *USE Infectious Disorders*
Infectious Disorders
Inference
Inferior Colliculus
Emotional **Inferiority**
Infertility
Infirmaries *USE Hospitals*
Anti **Inflammatory** Drugs
Inflection
Self **Inflicted** Wounds
Driving Under The **Influence**
Parental Influence *USE Parent Child Relations*
Interpersonal **Influences**
Social **Influences**
Influenza
Informants
Information
Information Exchange *USE Communication*
Information Processing Speed
    USE Cognitive Processing Speed
Information Seeking
Information Services
Information Specialists
Information Systems
Information Theory
Automated **Information** Coding
Automated **Information** Processing
Automated **Information** Retrieval
Automated **Information** Storage

Confidentiality of Information *USE Privileged Communication*
Human Information Processes
    USE Cognitive Processes
Human **Information** Storage
Management Information Systems
    USE Information Systems
Informed Consent
Ingestion
Ingratiation *USE Impression Management*
Ingroup Outgroup
Outgroup Ingroup *USE Ingroup Outgroup*
Inhalant Abuse
Inhibited Sexual Desire
Inhibition (Personality)
Conditioned Inhibition *USE Conditioned Suppression*
Latent **Inhibition**
Prepulse **Inhibition**
Proactive **Inhibition**
Reciprocal **Inhibition** Therapy
Retroactive **Inhibition**
Growth Hormone Inhibitor *USE Somatostatin*
Amine Oxidase **Inhibitors**
Cholinesterase **Inhibitors**
Decarboxylase **Inhibitors**
Enzyme **Inhibitors**
Hydroxylase **Inhibitors**
Monoamine Oxidase **Inhibitors**
Serotonin Reuptake **Inhibitors**
Initial Teaching Alphabet
Initiation Rites
Initiative
Injections
Intramuscular **Injections**
Intraperitoneal **Injections**
Intravenous **Injections**
Subcutaneous **Injections**
Injuries
Birth **Injuries**
Closed Head Injuries *USE Head Injuries*
Electrical **Injuries**
Head **Injuries**
Spinal Cord **Injuries**
Traumatic Brain **Injury**
Holtzman **Inkblot** Technique
Inlaws
Animal Innate Behavior *USE Instinctive Behavior*
Inner City *USE Urban Environments*
Inner Ear *USE Labyrinth (Anatomy)*
Inner Speech *USE Self Talk*
Kirton Adaption **Innovation** Inventory
Innovativeness *USE Creativity*
Inquisitiveness *USE Curiosity*
Criminally Insane *USE Mentally Ill Offenders*
Insanity *USE Mental Disorders*
Insanity Defense
DDT **(Insecticide)**
Insecticides
Insects
Emotional Insecurity *USE Emotional Security*
Artificial Insemination *USE Reproductive Technology*
Inservice Teacher Education
Inservice Training
Mental Health **Inservice** Training
Insight
Insight (Psychotherapeutic Process)
Insight Therapy
Diabetes **Insipidus**
Insomnia
Emotional **Instability**
Death **Instinct**
Survival Instinct *USE Self Preservation*
Instinctive Behavior
Animal Instinctive Behavior
    USE Instinctive Behavior
Institution Visitation

Institutional Release
Institutional Schools
Institutionalization
Institutionalized Mentally Retarded
Attendants **(Institutions)**
Correctional **Institutions**
Residential Care **Institutions**
Instruction *USE Teaching*
Audiovisual **Instruction**
Braille **Instruction**
Classroom Instruction *USE Teaching*
Computer Assisted **Instruction**
Field Instruction *USE Curricular Field Experience*
Group **Instruction**
Individualized **Instruction**
Programmed **Instruction**
Self Instruction *USE Individualized Instruction*
Televised **Instruction**
Videotape **Instruction**
Instructional Media
Instructional Objectives
    USE Educational Objectives
Self **Instructional** Training
Experimental **Instructions**
Instructors *USE Teachers*
Instrument Controls
Parent Attitude Research **Instrument**
Instrumental Conditioning
    USE Operant Conditioning
Instrumental Learning
    USE Operant Conditioning
Instrumentality
Flight **Instrumentation**
Musical **Instruments**
Insulin
Insulin Shock Therapy
Insurance
Insurance Agents *USE Sales Personnel*
Employee Health **Insurance**
Health **Insurance**
Life **Insurance**
Workmens Compensation **Insurance**
Intake Interview
Fluid **Intake**
Food **Intake**
Water **Intake**
Integrated Services
Intersensory Integration *USE Sensory Integration*
Racial Integration *USE Social Integration*
School **Integration**
Sensory **Integration**
Social **Integration**
Integrity
Intellectual Development
Intellectual Functioning
    USE Cognitive Ability
Intellectualism
Intellectualization
Intellectually Gifted *USE Gifted*
Intelligence
Intelligence Age *USE Mental Age*
Intelligence Measures
Intelligence Quotient
Artificial **Intelligence**
Cattell Culture Fair Intelligence Test
    USE Culture Fair Intelligence Test
Cattell Infant Intelligence Scale
    USE Infant Intelligence Scale
Culture Fair **Intelligence** Test
Infant **Intelligence** Scale
Leiter Adult Intelligence Scale
    USE Intelligence Measures
Lorge Thorndike **Intelligence** Test
Slosson **Intelligence** Test
Stanford Binet **Intelligence** Scale

Wechsler Adult **Intelligence** Scale
Wechsler Bellevue **Intelligence** Scale
Wechsler **Intelligence** Scale for Children
Signal Intensity *USE Stimulus Intensity*
Stimulus **Intensity**
Intensive Care
Intention
Intentional Learning
Interaction Analysis (Statistics)
Interaction Variance
Animal Human Interaction *USE Interspecies Interaction*
Client Counselor Interaction
　　USE Psychotherapeutic Processes
Counselor Client Interaction
　　USE Psychotherapeutic Processes
Dentist Patient Interaction *USE Therapeutic Processes*
Double Bind **Interaction**
Employee Supervisor Interaction
　　USE Supervisor Employee Interaction
Employee **Interaction**
Heterosexual Interaction *USE Male Female Relations*
Human Animal Interaction *USE Interspecies Interaction*
Human Computer **Interaction**
Interhemispheric **Interaction**
Interpersonal **Interaction**
Interspecies **Interaction**
Manager Employee Interaction
　　USE Supervisor Employee Interaction
Nurse Patient Interaction *USE Therapeutic Processes*
Patient Therapist Interaction
　　USE Psychotherapeutic Processes
Physician Patient Interaction *USE Therapeutic Processes*
Social **Interaction**
Supervisor Employee **Interaction**
Teacher Student **Interaction**
Therapist Patient Interaction
　　USE Psychotherapeutic Processes
Symbolic **Interactionism**
Drug **Interactions**
Interagency Services
　　USE Integrated Services
Extramarital **Intercourse**
Premarital **Intercourse**
Sexual **Intercourse** (Human)
Intercultural Communication
　　USE Cross Cultural Communication
Interdisciplinary Research
Interdisciplinary Treatment Approach
Interest Inventories
Interest Patterns *USE Interests*
Kuder Occupational **Interest** Survey
Occupational **Interest** Measures
Opinion Attitude and Interest Survey *USE Attitude Measures*
Strong Vocational **Interest** Blank
Interests
Occupational **Interests**
Vocational Interests *USE Occupational Interests*
Interethnic Communication
　　USE Cross Cultural Communication
Interethnic Family
Interethnic Marriage
　　USE Exogamous Marriage
Interfaith Marriage
Interference (Learning)
Interferons
Intergenerational Relations
Intergenerational Transmission
　　USE Transgenerational Patterns
Intergroup Dynamics
Interhemispheric Interaction
Interhemispheric Transfer
　　USE Interhemispheric Interaction
Interior Design
Interleukins
Intermarriage *USE Exogamous Marriage*

Intermediate School Students
Intermittent Explosive Disorder
　　USE Explosive Disorder
Intermittent Reinforcement
　　USE Reinforcement Schedules
Internal Consistency *USE Test Reliability*
Internal External Locus of Control
Internal Rewards
Rotter **Internal** External Locus of Control Scale
Internalization
International Classification of Diseases
International Organizations
International Relations
Internet
Internists
Clinical Psychology **Internship**
Medical **Internship**
Teaching Internship *USE Student Teaching*
Interobserver Reliability
　　USE Interrater Reliability
Interocular Transfer
Interpersonal Attraction
Interpersonal Communication
Interpersonal Compatibility
Interpersonal Competence
　　USE Social Skills
Interpersonal Distance
　　USE Personal Space
Interpersonal Influences
Interpersonal Interaction
Interpersonal Perception
　　USE Social Perception
Interpersonal Psychotherapy
Interpersonal Relationship Satisfaction
　　USE Relationship Satisfaction
Fundamental **Interpersonal** Relation Orientation
　　Behavior Ques
Learys **Interpersonal** Check List
Listening **(Interpersonal)**
Dream Interpretation *USE Dream Analysis*
Psychoanalytic **Interpretation**
Psychological Interpretation
　　USE Theoretical Interpretation
Test **Interpretation**
Theoretical **Interpretation**
Interracial Adoption
Interracial Family
Interracial Marriage
Interracial Offspring
Interrater Reliability
Interresponse Time
Criminal Interrogation *USE Legal Interrogation*
Legal **Interrogation**
Police Interrogation *USE Legal Interrogation*
Intersensory Integration
　　USE Sensory Integration
Intersensory Processes
Intersexuality *USE Hermaphroditism*
Interspecies Interaction
Interstimulus Interval
Intertrial Interval
Interval Reinforcement
　　USE Fixed Interval Reinforcement
Interval Reinforcement
　　USE Variable Interval Reinforcement
Fixed **Interval** Reinforcement
Interstimulus **Interval**
Intertrial **Interval**
Variable **Interval** Reinforcement
Stimulus **Intervals**
Crisis **Intervention**
Crisis **Intervention** Services
Early **Intervention**
Interview Schedules
Diagnostic **Interview** Schedule

Intake **Interview**
Psychodiagnostic **Interview**
Structured Clinical **Interview**
Interviewers
Interviewing
Interviews
Employment **Interviews** *USE Job Applicant Interviews*
Job Applicant **Interviews**
Intestines
Intimacy
Intoxication *USE Toxic Disorders*
Acute Alcoholic **Intoxication**
Alcohol **Intoxication**
Chronic Alcoholic **Intoxication**
Intra Aural Muscle Reflex
  USE Acoustic Reflex
Intracranial Self Stimulation
  USE Brain Self Stimulation
Intramuscular Injections
Intraperitoneal Injections
Intrauterine Devices
Intravenous Drug Usage
Intravenous Injections
Intrinsic Motivation
Intrinsic Rewards *USE Internal Rewards*
Introjection
Introspection
Introversion
Intuition
Inuit
Inventories
Biographical **Inventories**
Interest **Inventories**
Barrett Lennard Relationship **Inventory**
Beck Depression **Inventory**
Bem Sex Role **Inventory**
California Psychological **Inventory**
Differential Personality **Inventory** *USE Nonprojective Personality*
  Measures
Edwards Personality **Inventory**
Eysenck Personality **Inventory**
Kirton Adaption Innovation **Inventory**
Maudsley Personality **Inventory**
Millon Clinical Multiaxial **Inventory**
Minnesota Multiphasic Personality **Inventory**
Minnesota Teacher Attitude Inventory *USE Attitude Measures*
NEO Personality **Inventory**
Omnibus Personality **Inventory**
Personal Orientation **Inventory**
Psychological Screening **Inventory**
State Trait Anxiety **Inventory**
Invertebrates
Investigation *USE Experimentation*
Maternal Investment *USE Parental Investment*
Parental **Investment**
Paternal Investment *USE Parental Investment*
Involuntary Treatment
Involutional Depression
Involutional Paranoid Psychosis
Involvement
Job **Involvement**
Political Involvement *USE Political Participation*
Ions *USE Electrolytes*
Calcium **Ions**
Chloride **Ions**
Magnesium **Ions**
Potassium **Ions**
Sodium **Ions**
Iowa Tests of Basic Skills
Iproniazid
Deviation IQ *USE Standard Scores*
Iris (Eye)
Iron
Irradiation *USE Radiation*
Laser **Irradiation**

Irrational Beliefs
Irritability
Irritable Bowel Syndrome
Ischemia
Cerebral **Ischemia**
Islam
Pacific **Islanders**
Isocarboxazid
Isoenzymes *USE Isozymes*
Isolation (Defense Mechanism)
Isolation Effect
Social **Isolation**
Isoniazid
Isoproterenol
Isozymes
Political **Issues**
Social **Issues**
Itching *USE Pruritus*
Item Analysis (Statistical)
Item Analysis (Test)
Item Bias *USE Test Bias*
Item Content (Test)
Item Response Theory
Test **Items**
IV Drug Usage
  USE Intravenous Drug Usage
Pavlov **(Ivan)**
Jails *USE Prisons*
Creutzfeldt **Jakob** Syndrome
James (William)
Japanese Americans
Japanese Cultural Groups
Jaundice
Jaw
Jealousy
Piaget **(Jean)**
Jews
Job Analysis
Job Applicant Attitudes
Job Applicant Interviews
Job Applicant Screening
Job Applicants
Job Change *USE Career Change*
Job Characteristics
Job Corps
Job Discrimination
  USE Employment Discrimination
Job Enrichment
Job Experience Level
Job Family Relationship
  USE Family Work Relationship
Job Involvement
Job Knowledge
Job Mobility *USE Occupational Mobility*
Job Performance
Job Promotion *USE Personnel Promotion*
Job Reentry *USE Reemployment*
Job Satisfaction
Job Search
Job Security
Job Selection *USE Occupational Choice*
Job Status *USE Occupational Status*
Job Training *USE Personnel Training*
On the **Job** Training
Jobs *USE Occupations*
Watson **(John** Broadus)
Woodcock **Johnson** Psychoeducational Battery
Joint Custody
Joint Disorders
Temporomandibular Joint Syndrome
  USE Musculoskeletal Disorders
Joints (Anatomy)
Jokes
Journalists
Joy *USE Happiness*

Judaism
Judges
Judgment
Judgment Disturbances
Clinical **Judgment** (Not Diagnosis)
Probability **Judgment**
Judo
Jumping
Jung (Carl)
Jungian Psychology
Jungian Psychotherapy
    USE Analytical Psychotherapy
Junior College Students
Junior Colleges *USE Colleges*
Junior High School Students
Junior High School Teachers
Junior High Schools
Juries
Jury Selection
Justice
Criminal **Justice**
Distributive Justice *USE Justice*
Juvenile Court *USE Adjudication*
Juvenile Delinquency
Juvenile Gangs
Kainic Acid
Kangaroos
Karate *USE Martial Arts*
Karyotype Disorders
    USE Chromosome Disorders
Kaufman Assessment Battery for Children
Ketamine
Keyboards
Keypunch Operators
    USE Clerical Personnel
Kibbutz
Kidnapping
Kidney Diseases
Kidney Transplants
    USE Organ Transplantation
Kidneys
Mercy Killing *USE Euthanasia*
Mouse Killing *USE Muricide*
Kinases
Kindergarten Students
Vane Kindergarten Test
    USE Intelligence Measures
Kindergartens
Kindling
Kinesics *USE Body Language*
Kinesthetic Perception
Kinship
Kinship Recognition
Kinship Structure
Kirton Adaption Innovation Inventory
Kleine Levin Syndrome
Kleptomania
Klinefelters Syndrome
Knee
Knowledge Based Systems
    USE Expert Systems
Knowledge Level
Knowledge of Results
Declarative **Knowledge**
Factual Knowledge *USE Declarative Knowledge*
Functional Knowledge *USE Procedural Knowledge*
Health **Knowledge**
Job **Knowledge**
Practical Knowledge *USE Procedural Knowledge*
Procedural **Knowledge**
Kohlberg (Lawrence)
Kohs Block Design Test
Kolmogorov Smirnov Test
Korean Cultural Groups
Koro

Korsakoffs Psychosis
Kuder Occupational Interest Survey
Kuder Preference Record
Kupfer Detre Self Rating Scale
    USE Nonprojective Personality
    Measures
Kwashiorkor
L Dopa *USE Levodopa*
Labeling
Warning **Labels**
Labor (Childbirth)
Labor Management Relations
Labor Relations
    USE Labor Management Relations
Labor Union Members
Labor Unions
Animal Division of **Labor**
Division of **Labor**
Educational **Laboratories**
Experimental **Laboratories**
Language **Laboratories**
Labyrinth (Anatomy)
Labyrinth Disorders
Lactate Dehydrogenase
Sodium Lactate *USE Lactic Acid*
Lactation
Lactic Acid
Response Lag *USE Reaction Time*
Landscapes *USE Topography*
Language
Language Alternation *USE Code Switching*
Language Arts Education
Language Delay
Language Development
Language Disorders
Language Laboratories
Language Proficiency
Body **Language**
English as Second **Language**
Figurative **Language**
Foreign **Language** Education
Foreign **Language** Learning
Foreign **Language** Translation
Form Classes **(Language)**
Modern **Language** Aptitude Test
Morphology **(Language)**
Second Language Education
    USE Foreign Language Education
Sign **Language**
Written **Language**
Computer Programming **Languages**
Foreign **Languages**
Larvae
Laryngeal Disorders
Larynx
Laser Irradiation
Latchkey Children *USE Child Self Care*
Response **Latency**
Latent Inhibition
Latent Learning
Latent Trait Theory
    USE Item Response Theory
Lateral Dominance
Latinos/Latinas *USE Hispanics*
Laughter
Law (Government)
Law Enforcement
Law Enforcement Personnel
Law Students
Civil **Law**
Criminal **Law**
Kohlberg **(Lawrence)**
Laws
Abortion **Laws**
Disability **Laws**

329

Drug **Laws**
Gun Control **Laws**
Marihuana **Laws**
Lawyers *USE Attorneys*
Lay Religious Personnel
Lead (Metal)
Lead Poisoning
Leadership
Leadership Qualities
Leadership Style
Learned Helplessness
Slow Learners
    USE Borderline Mental Retardation
Learning
Learning Ability
Learning Centers (Educational)
Learning Disabilities
Learning Disorders
Learning Rate
Learning Schedules
Learning Strategies
Learning Style *USE Cognitive Style*
Learning Theory
Adult **Learning**
Cat **Learning**
Concept Learning *USE Concept Formation*
Cooperative **Learning**
Discrimination **Learning**
Discriminative Learning *USE Discrimination Learning*
Experiential **Learning**
Extinction **(Learning)**
Extradimensional Shift Learning *USE Nonreversal Shift Learning*
Fine Motor Skill **Learning**
Foreign Language **Learning**
Generalization **(Learning)**
Generation Effect **(Learning)**
Gross Motor Skill **Learning**
Imitation **(Learning)**
Incidental **Learning**
Instrumental Learning *USE Operant Conditioning*
Intentional **Learning**
Interference **(Learning)**
Latent **Learning**
Mastery **Learning**
Maze **Learning**
Mnemonic **Learning**
Motor Skill Learning *USE Perceptual Motor Learning*
Nonreversal Shift **Learning**
Nonsense Syllable **Learning**
Nonverbal **Learning**
Observational **Learning**
Paired Associate **Learning**
Perceptual Motor **Learning**
Probability **Learning**
Rat **Learning**
Recall **(Learning)**
Recognition **(Learning)**
Reconstruction **(Learning)**
Reversal Shift **Learning**
Rote **Learning**
Rule Learning *USE Cognitive Hypothesis Testing*
School **Learning**
Self Directed Learning *USE Individualized Instruction*
Sequential **Learning**
Serial Anticipation **(Learning)**
Serial **Learning**
Skill **Learning**
Social **Learning**
Spatial **Learning**
Spontaneous Recovery **(Learning)**
State Dependent **Learning**
Transfer **(Learning)**
Trial and Error **Learning**
Verbal **Learning**
Learys Interpersonal Check List

Least Preferred Coworker Scale
Least Squares
Annual Leave *USE Employee Leave Benefits*
Employee **Leave** Benefits
Sick Leave *USE Employee Leave Benefits*
School **Leavers**
Lecithin
Lecture Method
Left Brain
Leg (Anatomy)
Legal Arrest
Legal Decisions
Legal Detention
Legal Evidence
Legal Interrogation
Legal Personnel
Legal Processes
Legal Psychology
    USE Forensic Psychology
Legal Testimony
Drug **Legalization**
Marihuana **Legalization**
Legibility
Handwriting **Legibility**
Legislative Processes
Leisure Time
Leiter Adult Intelligence Scale
    USE Intelligence Measures
Lemniscal System
Lemurs
Length of Stay *USE Treatment Duration*
Work Week **Length**
Barrett **Lennard** Relationship Inventory
Lens (Eye)
Contact **Lenses**
Corrective Lenses *USE Optical Aids*
Lesbian Parents *USE Homosexual Parents*
Lesbianism
Lesions
Brain **Lesions**
Cerebral Lesions *USE Brain Lesions*
Hypothalamus **Lesions**
Neural **Lesions**
Subcortical Lesions *USE Brain Lesions*
Lesson Plans
Letters (Alphabet)
Leucine
Leucocytes
Leukemias
Leukocytes *USE Leucocytes*
Leukotomy *USE Psychosurgery*
Vygotsky **(Lev)**
Level of Functioning *USE Ability Level*
Ability **Level**
Academic Grade Level *USE Grade Level*
Activity **Level**
Aspiration **Level**
Difficulty **Level** (Test)
Educational Attainment **Level**
Experience **Level**
Family Socioeconomic **Level**
Grade **Level**
Income **Level**
Job Experience **Level**
Knowledge **Level**
Lower Income **Level**
Middle Income **Level**
Middle **Level** Managers
Sound Pressure Level *USE Loudness*
Top **Level** Managers
Upper Income **Level**
Noise **Levels** (Work Areas)
Kleine **Levin** Syndrome
Levodopa

Lewy Body Disease
  USE Dementia with Lewy Bodies
Dementia with **Lewy** Bodies
Lexical Access
Lexical Decision
Drug Abuse **Liability**
Professional **Liability**
Consultation **Liaison** Psychiatry
Liberalism
Political **Liberalism**
Gay Liberation Movement
  USE Homosexual Liberation Movement
Homosexual **Liberation** Movement
Womens **Liberation** Movement
Libido
Librarians
Libraries
School **Libraries**
Librium *USE Chlordiazepoxide*
Professional **Licensing**
Licensure Examinations
  USE Professional Examinations
Licking
Animal Licking Behavior *USE Licking*
Lidocaine
Life Change *USE Life Experiences*
Life Expectancy
Life Experiences
Life Insurance
Life Review
Life Satisfaction
Life Span *USE Life Expectancy*
Life Sustaining Treatment
Family Life *USE Family Relations*
Family **Life** Education
Philosophy of Life *USE World View*
Quality of Work **Life**
Quality of **Life**
Lifesaving *USE Artificial Respiration*
Lifestyle
Lifestyle Changes
Tubal **Ligation**
Light *USE Illumination*
Light Adaptation
Light Refraction
Bright Light Therapy *USE Phototherapy*
Likability
Maximum **Likelihood**
Likert Scales
Liking *USE Affection*
Limbic System
Artificial Limbs *USE Prostheses*
Phantom **Limbs**
Limen *USE Thresholds*
Differential Limen *USE Thresholds*
Limited English Proficiency
  USE Language Proficiency
Time Limited Psychotherapy
  USE Brief Psychotherapy
Confidence **Limits** (Statistics)
Allport Vernon **Lindzey** Study Values
  USE Attitude Measures
Hot **Line** Services
Linear Perspective
Linear Regression
Telephone Hot Lines *USE Hot Line Services*
Linguistics
Linkage Analysis *USE Genetic Linkage*
Genetic **Linkage**
Sex **Linked** Developmental Differences
Sex **Linked** Hereditary Disorders
Lions *USE Felids*
Lipid Metabolism
Lipid Metabolism Disorders
Lipids

Lipoproteins
Lipreading
Lips (Face)
Liquor
Gough Adjective Check **List**
Learys Interpersonal Check **List**
Mooney Problem Check **List**
Listening (Interpersonal)
Listening *USE Auditory Perception*
Listening Comprehension
Literacy
Literacy Programs
Computer **Literacy**
Literature
Literature Review
Religious **Literature**
Lithium
Lithium Bromide *USE Bromides*
Lithium Carbonate
Litter Size
Liver
Liver Disorders
Cirrhosis **(Liver)**
Living Alone
Living Arrangements
Living Wills *USE Advance Directives*
Activities of Daily **Living**
Independent Living *USE Self Care Skills*
Independent **Living** Programs
Lizards
Cognitive Load *USE Human Channel Capacity*
Mental Load *USE Human Channel Capacity*
Work **Load**
Frontal **Lobe**
Occipital **Lobe**
Optic **Lobe**
Parietal **Lobe**
Temporal **Lobe**
Lobectomy *USE Psychosurgery*
Lobotomy *USE Psychosurgery*
Local Anesthetics
Auditory **Localization**
Perceptual **Localization**
Sound Localization *USE Auditory Localization*
Animal **Locomotion**
Locus Ceruleus
Locus of Control
  USE Internal External Locus of Control
Health Locus of Control *USE Health Attitudes*
Internal External **Locus** of Control
Rotter Internal External **Locus** of Control Scale
Logic (Philosophy)
Logical Thinking
Logistic Models
  USE Item Response Theory
Logotherapy
Loneliness
Long Term Care
Long Term Memory
Long Term Potentiation
  USE Postactivation Potentials
Longevity *USE Life Expectancy*
Longitudinal Studies
Loosening of Associations
  USE Fragmentation (Schizophrenia)
Lorazepam
Lorge Thorndike Intelligence Test
Hair Loss *USE Alopecia*
Sensorineural Hearing Loss *USE Hearing Disorders*
Loudness
Loudness Discrimination
Loudness Perception
Love
Low Birth Weight *USE Birth Weight*
Lowenfeld Mosaic Test

Lower Class
Lower Class Attitudes
Lower Income Level
Loxapine
Loyalty
Lucid Dreaming
Luck *USE Chance (Fortune)*
Lumbar Spinal Cord
Lumbrosacral Plexus *USE Spinal Nerves*
Luminance
Luminance Threshold
    USE Brightness Perception
Luminance Threshold
    USE Visual Thresholds
Lunar Synodic Cycle
Lung
Lung Disorders
Lupus
Luria Nebraska Neuropsychological Battery
Luteinizing Hormone
Lutherans *USE Protestants*
Mueller **Lyer** Illusion
Lying *USE Deception*
Lymphatic Disorders
    USE Blood and Lymphatic Disorders
Blood and **Lymphatic** Disorders
Lymphocytes
Lysergic Acid Diethylamide
Gates **MacGinitie** Reading Tests
Machiavellianism
Human **Machine** Systems
Human **Machine** Systems Design
Man Machine Systems Design
    USE Human Machine Systems Design
Man Machine Systems
    USE Human Machine Systems
Teaching **Machines**
Magazines
Magical Thinking
Magnesium
Magnesium Ions
Magnet Schools
    USE Nontraditional Education
Magnetic Resonance Imaging
Magnetism
Magnetoencephalography
Magnitude Estimation
Nucleus Basalis **Magnocellularis**
Maids *USE Domestic Service Personnel*
Mail Surveys
Mainstreaming
Mainstreaming (Educational)
Maintenance Therapy
Health **Maintenance** Organizations
Methadone **Maintenance**
Major Depression
Major Tranquilizers *USE Neuroleptic Drugs*
College Major *USE Academic Specialization*
Decision **Making**
Foreign Policy **Making**
Government Policy **Making**
Group Decision **Making**
Management Decision **Making**
Organizational Policy Making *USE Policy Making*
Policy **Making**
Grand **Mal** Epilepsy
Petit **Mal** Epilepsy
Emotional Maladjustment *USE Emotional Adjustment*
Social Maladjustment *USE Social Adjustment*
Malaria
Male Animals
Male Castration
Male Criminals
Male Delinquency
Male Female Relations

Male Genital Disorders
Male Genitalia
Male Homosexuality
Male Only Environments
    USE Single Sex Environments
Male Orgasm
Gay Males *USE Male Homosexuality*
Human **Males**
Malignant Neoplasms *USE Neoplasms*
Neuroleptic **Malignant** Syndrome
Malingering
Malnutrition *USE Nutritional Deficiencies*
Malpractice *USE Professional Liability*
Mammals
Mammary Glands
Mammary Neoplasms
    USE Breast Neoplasms
Mammography
Man Machine Systems Design
    USE Human Machine Systems Design
Man Machine Systems
    USE Human Machine Systems
Draw A Man Test *USE Human Figures Drawing*
Incomplete **Man** Test
Managed Care
Management
Management Decision Making
Management Development
    USE Career Development
Management Information Systems
    USE Information Systems
Management Methods
Management Personnel
Management Planning
Management Training
Anxiety **Management**
Business **Management**
Case **Management**
Contingency **Management**
Disability **Management**
Household **Management**
Impression **Management**
Labor **Management** Relations
Pain **Management**
Participative **Management**
Personnel **Management**
Risk **Management**
Self **Management**
Stress **Management**
Time **Management**
Manager Employee Interaction
    USE Supervisor Employee Interaction
Middle Level **Managers**
Top Level **Managers**
Self **Managing** Work Teams
Mandibula *USE Jaw*
Mania
Manic Depression *USE Bipolar Disorder*
Manic Depressive Psychosis
    USE Bipolar Disorder
Childrens **Manifest** Anxiety Scale
Taylor **Manifest** Anxiety Scale
Mann Whitney U Test
Mannerisms *USE Habits*
Manpower *USE Personnel Supply*
Mantis
Praying Mantis *USE Mantis*
Manual Communication
Diagnostic and Statistical **Manual**
Manufacturing *USE Business*
Maori *USE Indigenous Populations*
Brain Mapping *USE Stereotaxic Atlas*
Maprotiline
Brain Maps *USE Stereotaxic Atlas*
Cognitive **Maps**

Tactual Maps *USE Mobility Aids*
Marathon Group Therapy
Marihuana
Marihuana Laws
Marihuana Legalization
Marihuana Usage
Marijuana *USE Marihuana*
Marine Personnel
Marital Adjustment *USE Marital Relations*
Marital Conflict
Marital Fidelity *USE Monogamy*
Marital Relations
Marital Satisfaction
Marital Separation
Marital Status
Marital Therapy *USE Marriage Counseling*
Biochemical Markers *USE Biological Markers*
Biological **Markers**
Clinical Markers *USE Biological Markers*
Marketing
Animal Scent **Marking**
Markov Chains
Marlowe Crowne Social Desirability Scale
Marriage
Marriage and Family Education
USE Family Life Education
Marriage Attitudes
Marriage Counseling
Marriage Rites
Marriage Therapy
USE Marriage Counseling
Consanguineous **Marriage**
Endogamous **Marriage**
Exogamous **Marriage**
Interethnic Marriage *USE Exogamous Marriage*
Interfaith **Marriage**
Interracial **Marriage**
Miscegenous Marriage *USE Interracial Marriage*
Married Couples *USE Spouses*
Never **Married**
Bone **Marrow**
Marsupials
Martial Arts
Marxism *USE Communism*
Masculinity
Masking
Auditory **Masking**
Backward Masking *USE Masking*
Forward Masking *USE Masking*
Visual **Masking**
Maslow (Abraham Harold)
Masochism
Sexual **Masochism**
Masochistic Personality
Mass Hysteria
Mass Media
Massage
Massed Practice
Mastectomy
Mastery Learning
Mastery Tests
USE Criterion Referenced Tests
Masticatory Muscles
Masturbation
Matching Test *USE Matching to Sample*
Matching to Sample
Client Treatment **Matching**
Patient Treatment Matching *USE Client Treatment Matching*
Treatment Client Matching *USE Client Treatment Matching*
Mate Selection *USE Animal Mate Selection*
Mate Selection
USE Human Mate Selection
Mate Swapping
USE Extramarital Intercourse
Animal **Mate** Selection

Human **Mate** Selection
Materialism
Hazardous **Materials**
Reading **Materials**
X Rated Materials *USE Pornography*
Maternal Investment
USE Parental Investment
Animal **Maternal** Behavior
Animal **Maternal** Deprivation
Mathematical Ability
Mathematical Modeling
Mathematical Psychology
Mathematicians
Mathematics
Mathematics (Concepts)
Mathematics Achievement
Mathematics Anxiety
Mathematics Education
Animal **Mating** Behavior
Assortative **Mating**
Assortive Mating *USE Assortative Mating*
Matriarchy
Raven Coloured Progressive **Matrices**
Raven Progressive **Matrices**
Matriculation *USE School Enrollment*
Maturation *USE Human Development*
California Test of Mental **Maturity**
Career Maturity *USE Vocational Maturity*
Columbia Mental **Maturity** Scale
Emotional **Maturity**
Physical **Maturity**
Vineland Social **Maturity** Scale
Vocational **Maturity**
Maudsley Personality Inventory
Maxilla *USE Jaw*
Maximum Likelihood
Maximum Security Facilities
Maze Learning
Maze Pathways
Porteus **Maze** Test
Mazes
T **Mazes**
MCPP *USE Piperazines*
MDMA
USE Methylenedioxymethamphetamine
Mealtimes *USE Feeding Practices*
Mean
Meaning
Nonverbal **Meaning**
Verbal **Meaning**
Word **Meaning**
Meaningfulness
Measles
German Measles *USE Rubella*
Measurement
Attitude **Measurement**
Conjoint **Measurement**
Consistency **(Measurement)**
Creativity **Measurement**
Educational **Measurement**
Error of **Measurement**
Pain **Measurement**
Predictability **(Measurement)**
Profiles **(Measurement)**
Psychophysical **Measurement**
Standard Error of Measurement *USE Error of Measurement*
Statistical **Measurement**
Variability **Measurement**
Achievement **Measures**
Aptitude **Measures**
Attitude **Measures**
Central Tendency **Measures**
Developmental **Measures**
Hearing Measures
USE Speech and Hearing Measures

Intelligence **Measures**
Nonprojective Personality **Measures**
Occupational Interest **Measures**
Perceptual Motor Measures *USE Sensorimotor Measures*
Perceptual **Measures**
Personality **Measures**
Preference **Measures**
Projective Personality **Measures**
Reading **Measures**
Repeated **Measures**
Retention **Measures**
Sensorimotor **Measures**
Speech and Hearing **Measures**
Speech Measures
      USE Speech and Hearing Measures
Mecamylamine
Mechanical Aptitude
Speech Processing **(Mechanical)**
Compensation (Defense **Mechanism)**
Displacement (Defense **Mechanism)**
Fantasy (Defense **Mechanism)**
Identification (Defense **Mechanism)**
Isolation (Defense **Mechanism)**
Projection (Defense **Mechanism)**
Regression (Defense **Mechanism)**
Repression (Defense **Mechanism)**
Suppression (Defense **Mechanism)**
Withdrawal (Defense **Mechanism)**
Defense **Mechanisms**
Mechanoreceptors
Audiovisual Communications **Media**
Communications **Media**
Instructional **Media**
Mass **Media**
News **Media**
Printed Communications **Media**
Telecommunications **Media**
Medial Forebrain Bundle
Median
Median Nerve *USE Spinal Nerves*
Mediated Responses
Mediation
Cognitive **Mediation**
Medicaid
Medical Care Costs
      USE Health Care Costs
Medical Diagnosis
Medical Education
Medical History *USE Patient History*
Medical Internship
Medical Model
Medical Patients
Medical Personnel
Medical Personnel Supply
Medical Psychology
Medical Records
Medical Regimen Compliance
      USE Treatment Compliance
Medical Residency
Medical Sciences
Medical Students
Medical Therapeutic Devices
Medical Treatment (General)
Mental Disorders due to General **Medical** Conditions
Military **Medical** Personnel
Self Examination **(Medical)**
Medicare
Medication *USE Drug Therapy*
Self **Medication**
Medicinal Herbs and Plants
Alternative **Medicine**
Behavioral Medicine *USE Health Care Psychology*
Complementary Medicine *USE Alternative Medicine*
Family **Medicine**

Folk **Medicine**
Homeopathic Medicine *USE Alternative Medicine*
Preventive **Medicine**
Psychosomatic **Medicine**
Veterinary **Medicine**
Medics *USE Paramedical Personnel*
Meditation
Medulla Oblongata
Adrenal **Medulla** Hormones
Melancholia *USE Major Depression*
Melancholy *USE Sadness*
Melanin
Melanocyte Stimulating Hormone
Melanotropin
      USE Melanocyte Stimulating Hormone
Melatonin
Mellaril *USE Thioridazine*
Diabetes **Mellitus**
Family **Members**
Labor Union **Members**
Fraternity **Membership**
School Club **Membership**
Sorority **Membership**
Nictitating **Membrane**
Tympanic Membrane *USE Middle Ear*
Membranes
Childhood Memories *USE Early Memories*
Early **Memories**
Memory
Memory Decay
Memory Disorders
Memory Enhancing Drugs
      USE Nootropic Drugs
Memory for Designs Test
Memory Trace
Memory Training
Autobiographical **Memory**
Episodic **Memory**
Explicit **Memory**
False **Memory**
Iconic **Memory**
Long Term **Memory**
Photographic Memory *USE Eidetic Imagery*
Repressed **Memory**
Semantic **Memory**
Short Term **Memory**
Spatial **Memory**
Verbal **Memory**
Visual Spatial Memory *USE Visuospatial Memory*
Visual **Memory**
Visuospatial **Memory**
Wechsler **Memory** Scale
Working Memory *USE Short Term Memory*
Men *USE Human Males*
Menarche
Menieres Disease
Meninges
Meningitis
Bacterial **Meningitis**
Meningomyelocele *USE Spina Bifida*
Menopause
Menstrual Cycle
Menstrual Disorders
Menstruation
Mental Age
Mental Confusion
Mental Deficiency *USE Mental Retardation*
Mental Disorders
Mental Disorders due to General Medical Conditions
Mental Health
Mental Health Care Costs
      USE Health Care Costs
Mental Health Care Policy
      USE Health Care Policy

Mental Health Consultation
    USE Professional Consultation
Mental Health Inservice Training
Mental Health Personnel
Mental Health Personnel Supply
Mental Health Program Evaluation
Mental Health Programs
Mental Health Service Needs
    USE Health Service Needs
Mental Health Services
Mental Hospitals *USE Psychiatric Hospitals*
Mental Illness (Attitudes Toward)
Mental Illness *USE Mental Disorders*
Mental Load
    USE Human Channel Capacity
Mental Retardation
Mental Retardation (Attitudes Toward)
Mental Rotation
Borderline **Mental** Retardation
California Test of **Mental** Maturity
Chronic **Mental** Illness
Columbia **Mental** Maturity Scale
Community **Mental** Health
Community **Mental** Health Centers
Community **Mental** Health Services
Community **Mental** Health Training
Cultural Familial Mental Retardation
    USE Psychosocial Mental Retardation
Henmon Nelson Tests of Mental Ability *USE Intelligence Measures*
Mild **Mental** Retardation
Mini **Mental** State Examination
Moderate **Mental** Retardation
Persistent Mental Illness *USE Chronic Mental Illness*
Primary **Mental** Health Prevention
Profound **Mental** Retardation
Psychosocial **Mental** Retardation
Severe **Mental** Retardation
Mentally Ill Homeless
    USE Homeless Mentally Ill
Mentally Ill Offenders
Educable Mentally Retarded
    USE Mild Mental Retardation
Home Reared **Mentally** Retarded
Homeless **Mentally** Ill
Institutionalized **Mentally** Retarded
Trainable Mentally Retarded
    USE Moderate Mental Retardation
Mentor
Meperidine
Mephenesin *USE Muscle Relaxing Drugs*
Meprobamate
Mercury (Metal)
Mercury Poisoning
Mercy Killing *USE Euthanasia*
Organizational **Merger**
Mescaline
Mesencephalon
Mesoridazine
Messages
Meta Analysis
Metabolic Rates
Metabolism
Metabolism Disorders
Basal **Metabolism**
Brain Metabolism *USE Neurochemistry*
Carbohydrate **Metabolism**
Fat Metabolism *USE Lipid Metabolism*
Glucose **Metabolism**
Lipid **Metabolism**
Lipid **Metabolism** Disorders
Protein **Metabolism**
Metabolites
Dopamine **Metabolites**
Norepinephrine **Metabolites**
Serotonin **Metabolites**

Metacognition
Lead **(Metal)**
Mercury **(Metal)**
Metalinguistics
Metallic Elements
Metals
Metamemory *USE Metacognition*
Metaphor
Metaphysics
Metapsychology
Volt Meters *USE Apparatus*
Methadone
Methadone Maintenance
Methamphetamine
Methanol
Methaqualone
Methedrine *USE Methamphetamine*
Methionine
Directed Discussion **Method**
Discovery Teaching **Method**
Forced Choice (Testing **Method)**
Lecture **Method**
Montessori **Method**
Multiple Choice (Testing **Method)**
Nondirected Discussion **Method**
Open Classroom **Method**
Rhythm **Method**
Team Teaching **Method**
Methodists *USE Protestants*
Methodology
Clinical **Methods** Training
Drug Administration **Methods**
Empirical **Methods**
Experimental **Methods**
Management **Methods**
Observation **Methods**
Physical Treatment **Methods**
Psychotherapeutic Methods
    USE Psychotherapeutic Techniques
Research Methods *USE Methodology*
Scientific Methods *USE Experimental Methods*
Stimulus Presentation **Methods**
Teaching **Methods**
Testing **Methods**
Methohexital
Methoxamine
Methoxyhydroxyphenylglycol (3,4)
Methyl Alcohol *USE Methanol*
Methylatropine *USE Atropine*
Methyldiphenylhydramine
    USE Orphenadrine
Methyldopa
Methylenedioxymethamphetamine
Methylmorphine *USE Codeine*
Alpha **Methylparatyrosine**
Methylphenidate
Methylphenyltetrahydropyridine
Alpha Methyltyrosine
    USE Alpha Methylparatyrosine
Methysergide *USE Serotonin Antagonists*
Metrazole *USE Pentylenetetrazol*
Metronomes
Metropolitan Readiness Tests
Mexican Americans
MHPG
    USE Methoxyhydroxyphenylglycol (3,4)
Mianserin
Mice
Microcephaly
Microcomputers
Microcounseling
Microorganisms
Microscopes
Micturition *USE Urination*
Midazolam

335

Midbrain *USE Mesencephalon*
Middle Class
Middle Class Attitudes
Middle Ear
Middle Income Level
Middle Level Managers
Middle School Education
Middle School Students
Midwifery
Migraine Headache
Migrant Farm Workers
Human **Migration**
Migratory Behavior (Animal)
Mild Mental Retardation
Milieu Therapy
Militancy
Military Enlistment
Military Medical Personnel
Military Officers
    USE Commissioned Officers
Military Personnel
Military Psychologists
Military Psychology
Military Recruitment
Military Schools
Military Training
Military Veterans
Enlisted **Military** Personnel
Volunteer **Military** Personnel
Miller Analogies Test
Millon Clinical Multiaxial Inventory
Mind
Mind Blindness *USE Theory of Mind*
Mind Body *USE Dualism*
Theory of **Mind**
Mini Mental State Examination
Minimal Brain Disorders
Minimum Competency Tests
Ministers (Religion)
Minks
Minnesota Multiphasic Personality
    Inventory
Minnesota Teacher Attitude Inventory
    USE Attitude Measures
Minor Tranquilizers
Minority Group Discrimination
    USE Race and Ethnic Discrimination
Minority Groups
Mirror Image
Mirroring
Misanthropy
Misarticulation *USE Articulation Disorders*
Misbehavior *USE Behavior Problems*
Miscarriage *USE Spontaneous Abortion*
Miscegenous Marriage
    USE Interracial Marriage
Misconduct *USE Behavior Problems*
Misdemeanors *USE Crime*
Misdiagnosis
Misogyny *USE Misanthropy*
Missionaries
Mistakes *USE Errors*
MMPI
    USE Minnesota Multiphasic Personality
    Inventory
Mnemonic Learning
Mobility Aids
Geographical **Mobility**
Job Mobility *USE Occupational Mobility*
Occupational **Mobility**
Physical **Mobility**
Social **Mobility**
Upward Mobility *USE Social Mobility*
Vocational Mobility *USE Occupational Mobility*
Moclobemide

Big Five Personality Model *USE Five Factor Personality Model*
Biopsychosocial Model *USE Biopsychosocial Approach*
Five Factor Personality **Model**
Medical **Model**
Rasch Model *USE Item Response Theory*
Modeling *USE Simulation*
Modeling Behavior
    USE Imitation (Learning)
Heuristic **Modeling**
Mathematical **Modeling**
Stochastic **Modeling**
Structural Equation **Modeling**
Models
Animal **Models**
Logistic Models *USE Item Response Theory*
Role **Models**
Moderate Mental Retardation
Modern Language Aptitude Test
Behavior **Modification**
Classroom Behavior **Modification**
Child Molestation *USE Pedophilia*
Molindone
Mollusca
Pearson Product Moment Correlation Coefficient
    USE Statistical Correlation
Monetary Incentives
Monetary Rewards
Money
Mongolism *USE Downs Syndrome*
Monitoring
Self **Monitoring**
Self **Monitoring** (Personality)
Monkeys
Monoamine Oxidase Inhibitors
Monoamine Oxidases
Monocular Vision
Monogamy
Monolingualism
Cyclic Adenosine **Monophosphate**
Monotony
Carbon **Monoxide**
Carbon **Monoxide** Poisoning
Monozygotic Twins
Montessori Method
Mood Disorders *USE Affective Disorders*
Bipolar Mood Disorder *USE Bipolar Disorder*
Moodiness
Moods *USE Emotional States*
Mooney Problem Check List
Moral Development
Morale
Morality
Morals *USE Morality*
Mores *USE Values*
Morita Therapy
Morphemes
Morphine
Morphology
Morphology (Language)
Mortality *USE Death and Dying*
Mortality Rate
Lowenfeld **Mosaic** Test
Mosaicism *USE Chromosome Disorders*
Moslems *USE Muslims*
Mother Absence
Mother Child Communication
Mother Child Relations
Mothers
Adolescent **Mothers**
Expectant **Mothers**
Schizophrenogenic **Mothers**
Single **Mothers**
Teenage Mothers *USE Adolescent Mothers*
Unwed **Mothers**
Moths

Motion Parallax
Motion Perception
Motion Pictures
Motion Pictures (Educational)
Motion Pictures (Entertainment)
Motion Sickness
Motivation
Motivation Training
Academic Achievement Motivation
Achievement Motivation
Affiliation Motivation
Animal Motivation
Employee Motivation
Extrinsic Motivation
Intrinsic Motivation
Motor Coordination
Motor Cortex
Motor Development
Motor Disorders
    USE Nervous System Disorders
Motor Evoked Potentials
    USE Somatosensory Evoked Potentials
Motor Neurons
Motor Pathways USE Efferent Pathways
Motor Performance
Motor Processes
Motor Skill Learning
    USE Perceptual Motor Learning
Motor Skills
Motor Traffic Accidents
Motor Vehicles
Fine Motor Skill Learning
Gross Motor Skill Learning
Perceptual Motor Coordination
Perceptual Motor Development
Perceptual Motor Learning
Perceptual Motor Measures
    USE Sensorimotor Measures
Perceptual Motor Processes
Purdue Perceptual Motor Survey
Motorcycles USE Motor Vehicles
Mourning USE Grief
Mouse Killing USE Muricide
Mouth (Anatomy)
Movement Disorders
Movement Perception
    USE Motion Perception
Movement Therapy
Apparent Movement
Black Power Movement
Civil Rights Movement
Eye Movement Desensitization Therapy
Gay Liberation Movement
    USE Homosexual Liberation Movement
Homosexual Liberation Movement
Human Potential Movement
Nonrapid Eye Movement Sleep USE NREM Sleep
Rapid Eye Movement
Rapid Eye Movement Dreams USE REM Dreams
Rapid Eye Movement Sleep USE REM Sleep
Stroboscopic Movement USE Apparent Movement
Womens Liberation Movement
Activist Movements
Eye Movements
Radical Movements
Saccadic Eye Movements USE Eye Movements
Social Movements
Vergence Movements USE Eye Convergence
Movies
    USE Motion Pictures (Entertainment)
MPTP USE Methylphenyltetrahydropyridine
MRI USE Magnetic Resonance Imaging
Nasal Mucosa
Olfactory Mucosa
Mucus

Mueller Lyer Illusion
Multi Infarct Dementia
Millon Clinical Multiaxial Inventory
Multicultural Education
Multiculturalism
Multidimensional Scaling
Multidisciplinary Research
    USE Interdisciplinary Research
Multidisciplinary Treatment Approach
    USE Interdisciplinary Treatment
        Approach
Multidrug Abuse USE Polydrug Abuse
Multilingualism
Multimodal Treatment Approach
Minnesota Multiphasic Personality Inventory
Multiple Births
Multiple Choice (Testing Method)
Multiple Disabilities
Multiple Personality
    USE Dissociative Identity Disorder
Multiple Regression
Multiple Sclerosis
Multiple Therapy USE Cotherapy
Multiply Handicapped
    USE Multiple Disabilities
Multivariate Analysis
Munchausen Syndrome
Munchausen Syndrome by Proxy
Murder USE Homicide
Muricide
Muscarinic Drugs USE Cholinergic Drugs
Muscimol
Muscle Contraction Headache
Muscle Contractions
Muscle Cramps USE Muscular Disorders
Muscle Relaxation
Muscle Relaxation Therapy
    USE Relaxation Therapy
Muscle Relaxing Drugs
Muscle Spasms
Muscle Tone
Intra Aural Muscle Reflex USE Acoustic Reflex
Muscles
Facial Muscles
Masticatory Muscles
Oculomotor Muscles
Muscular Atrophy
Muscular Disorders
Muscular Dystrophy
Musculocutaneous Nerve
    USE Spinal Nerves
Musculoskeletal Disorders
Musculoskeletal System
Music
Music Education
Music Perception
Music Therapy
Rock Music
Musical Ability
Musical Instruments
Musicians
Muslims
Mutations
Female Genital Mutilation USE Circumcision
Self Mutilation
Mutism
Elective Mutism
Selective Mutism USE Elective Mutism
Mutual Storytelling Technique
Myasthenia
Myasthenia Gravis
Myelin Sheath
Myelitis
Myelomeningocele USE Spina Bifida
Myenteric Plexus USE Autonomic Ganglia

Myers Briggs Type Indicator
Myocardial Infarctions
Myocardium
Myoclonia
Myofascial Pain
Myopia
Myotonia
Mysticism
Myths
Myxedema *USE Hypothyroidism*
N-Methyl-D-Aspartate
Nabilone *USE Cannabinoids*
NAch *USE Achievement Motivation*
Nail Biting
Nalorphine
Naloxone
Naltrexone
Names
Brand **Names**
Naming
Napping
Narcissism
Narcissistic Personality
Narcoanalysis
Narcoanalytic Drugs *USE Drugs*
Narcolepsy
Narcosis
Narcotic Agonists
Narcotic Antagonists
Narcotic Drugs
Narcotics Anonymous
　　　USE Twelve Step Programs
Narratives
Nasal Mucosa
National Guardsmen
Nationalism
Foreign **Nationals**
Native Alaskans *USE Alaska Natives*
Native Americans *USE American Indians*
Native Hawaiians *USE Hawaii Natives*
Natives *USE Indigenous Populations*
Alaska **Natives**
Hawaii **Natives**
Natural Childbirth
Natural Disasters
Natural Family *USE Biological Family*
Natural Selection
Naturalistic Observation
　　　USE Observation Methods
Nature Nurture
Human **Nature**
Nausea
Animal Navigation
　　　USE Migratory Behavior (Animal)
Navy Personnel
Nazism *USE Fascism*
Near Death Experiences
Nearsightedness *USE Myopia*
Luria **Nebraska** Neuropsychological Battery
Neck (Anatomy)
Need Achievement
　　　USE Achievement Motivation
Need for Affiliation
　　　USE Affiliation Motivation
Need for Approval
Need for Cognition
Need Satisfaction
Needle Exchange Programs
Needle Sharing
Needs
Needs Assessment
Emotional Needs *USE Psychological Needs*
Health Service **Needs**
Mental Health Service Needs *USE Health Service Needs*
Psychological **Needs**

Special **Needs**
Negative and Positive Symptoms
　　　USE Positive and Negative Symptoms
Negative Reinforcement
Negative Therapeutic Reaction
Negative Transfer
Contingent **Negative** Variation
Positive and **Negative** Symptoms
Negativism
Child **Neglect**
Perceptual Neglect *USE Sensory Neglect*
Sensory **Neglect**
Spatial Neglect *USE Sensory Neglect*
Visual Neglect *USE Sensory Neglect*
Negotiation
Negroes *USE Blacks*
Neighborhoods
Henmon Nelson Tests of Mental Ability
　　　USE Intelligence Measures
Nembutal *USE Pentobarbital*
NEO Personality Inventory
NeoFreudian School
　　　USE Neopsychoanalytic School
Neologisms
Neonatal Development
Neonatal Disorders
Neonatal Period
Neonaticide *USE Infanticide*
Neophobia
Neoplasms
Benign **Neoplasms**
Brain **Neoplasms**
Breast **Neoplasms**
Endocrine **Neoplasms**
Malignant Neoplasms *USE Neoplasms*
Mammary Neoplasms *USE Breast Neoplasms*
Nervous System **Neoplasms**
Neopsychoanalytic School
Neostigmine
Nerve Cells *USE Neurons*
Nerve Endings
Nerve Growth Factor
Nerve Tissues
Abducens **Nerve**
Accessory Nerve *USE Cranial Nerves*
Acoustic **Nerve**
Auditory Nerve *USE Acoustic Nerve*
Chorda Tympani Nerve *USE Facial Nerve*
Facial **Nerve**
Femoral Nerve *USE Spinal Nerves*
Glossopharyngeal Nerve *USE Cranial Nerves*
Hypoglossal Nerve *USE Cranial Nerves*
Median Nerve *USE Spinal Nerves*
Musculocutaneous Nerve *USE Spinal Nerves*
Obturator Nerve *USE Spinal Nerves*
Oculomotor Nerve *USE Cranial Nerves*
Olfactory **Nerve**
Optic **Nerve**
Peripheral **Nerve** Disorders
Phrenic Nerve *USE Spinal Nerves*
Radial Nerve *USE Spinal Nerves*
Sciatic Nerve *USE Spinal Nerves*
Trigeminal **Nerve**
Trochlear Nerve *USE Cranial Nerves*
Ulnar Nerve *USE Spinal Nerves*
Vagus **Nerve**
Adrenergic **Nerves**
Cholinergic **Nerves**
Cranial **Nerves**
Spinal **Nerves**
Thoracic Nerves *USE Spinal Nerves*
Anorexia **Nervosa**
Nervous Breakdown *USE Mental Disorders*
Nervous System
Nervous System Disorders

Nervous System Neoplasms
Nervous System Plasticity
USE Neural Plasticity
Autonomic **Nervous** System
Autonomic **Nervous** System Disorders
Central **Nervous** System
Central **Nervous** System Disorders
Central Nervous System Drugs
USE CNS Affecting Drugs
Parasympathetic **Nervous** System
Peripheral **Nervous** System
Sclerosis **(Nervous** System)
Sympathetic **Nervous** System
Nervousness
Nest Building
Empty **Nest**
Neural **Networks**
Social Support **Networks**
Social **Networks**
Neural Analyzers
Neural Development
Neural Lesions
Neural Networks
Neural Pathways
Neural Plasticity
Neural Receptors
Neural Regeneration
USE Neural Development
Neural Transplantation
Neuralgia
Trigeminal **Neuralgia**
Neurasthenic Neurosis
Neuroanatomy
Neurobiology
Neurochemistry
Neurodermatitis
Neuroendocrinology
Neuroinfections *USE Infectious Disorders*
Neuroinfections
USE Nervous System Disorders
Neurokinins
Neuroleptic Drugs
Neuroleptic Malignant Syndrome
Neurolinguistic Programming
Neurolinguistics
Neurological Disorders
USE Nervous System Disorders
Neurologists
Neurology
Neuromuscular Blocking Drugs
USE Muscle Relaxing Drugs
Neuromuscular Disorders
Neurons
Auditory **Neurons**
Motor **Neurons**
Sensory **Neurons**
Neuropathologists *USE Neurologists*
Neuropathology
Neuropathy
USE Nervous System Disorders
Neuropeptides *USE Peptides*
Neurophysiology
Neuropsychiatrists *USE Psychiatrists*
Neuropsychiatry
Neuropsychological Assessment
Neuropsychological Rehabilitation
Halstead Reitan **Neuropsychological** Battery
Luria Nebraska **Neuropsychological** Battery
Neuropsychology
Neurosciences
Neurosis
Anxiety Neurosis *USE Anxiety Disorders*
Childhood **Neurosis**
Compulsive Neurosis
USE Obsessive Compulsive Disorder

Conversion Neurosis *USE Conversion Disorder*
Dissociative Neurosis *USE Dissociative Disorders*
Experimental **Neurosis**
Infantile Neurosis *USE Childhood Neurosis*
Neurasthenic **Neurosis**
Obsessive Compulsive Neurosis
USE Obsessive Compulsive Disorder
Obsessive Neurosis
USE Obsessive Compulsive Disorder
Occupational **Neurosis**
Phobic Neurosis *USE Phobias*
Traumatic **Neurosis**
Neurosurgeons *USE Surgeons*
Neurosurgery
Neurosyphilis
Neurotensin
Neurotic Depressive Reaction
USE Major Depression
Neuroticism
Neurotoxins
Neurotransmitters
Psychotherapeutic **Neutrality**
Never Married
News Media
Professional Newsletters *USE Scientific Communication*
Newspapers
Niacin *USE Nicotinic Acid*
Niacinamide *USE Nicotinamide*
Nialamide
Nicotinamide
Nicotine
Nicotine Withdrawal
Nicotinic Acid
Nicotinic Acid Amide *USE Nicotinamide*
Nictitating Membrane
Night Terrors *USE Sleep Disorders*
Nightmares
Substantia **Nigra**
Nihilism
Nitrazepam
Nitrogen
NMDA *USE N-Methyl-D-Aspartate*
Nociception *USE Pain Perception*
Nociceptors
Nocturnal Emission
Nocturnal Teeth Grinding
Animal **Nocturnal** Behavior
Noise Effects
Noise Levels (Work Areas)
Filtered **Noise**
White **Noise**
Nomifensine
Non Zero Sum Games
Beverages **(Nonalcoholic)**
Noncommissioned Officers
Nonconformity (Personality)
Noncontingent Reinforcement
Nondirected Discussion Method
Nondirective Therapy
USE Client Centered Therapy
Nongraded Schools
Primates **(Nonhuman)**
Nonlinear Regression
Nonmetallic Elements
USE Chemical Elements
Nonparametric Statistical Tests
Nonprescription Drugs
Nonprofessional Personnel
Nonprofit Organizations
Nonprojective Personality Measures
Nonrapid Eye Movement Sleep
USE NREM Sleep
Rites **(Nonreligious)**
NonREM Sleep *USE NREM Sleep*
Nonreversal Shift Learning

339

Nonsense Syllable Learning
Nonstandard English
Nontraditional Careers
Nontraditional Education
Nonverbal Ability
Nonverbal Communication
Nonverbal Learning
Nonverbal Meaning
Nonverbal Reinforcement
Nonviolence
Nootropic Drugs
Noradrenaline *USE Norepinephrine*
Norepinephrine
Norepinephrine Metabolites
Normal Distribution
Test Normalization *USE Test Standardization*
Social **Norms**
Statistical **Norms**
Test **Norms**
Nortriptyline
Norway Rats
Nose
Note Taking
Nouns
Novel Stimuli *USE Stimulus Novelty*
Novelty Seeking *USE Sensation Seeking*
Stimulus **Novelty**
Novocaine *USE Procaine*
NREM Sleep
Nuclear Family
Nuclear Technology
Nuclear War
Cerebellar Nuclei *USE Cerebellum*
Raphe **Nuclei**
Septal **Nuclei**
Thalamic **Nuclei**
Nucleic Acids
Nucleotides
Nucleus Accumbens
Nucleus Basalis Magnocellularis
Caudate **Nucleus**
Cell **Nucleus**
Red Nucleus *USE Mesencephalon*
Nudity
Null Hypothesis Testing
Number Comprehension
Number Systems
Numbers (Numerals)
Numbers **(Numerals)**
Numerical Ability *USE Mathematical Ability*
Numerosity Perception
Nuns
Nurse Patient Interaction
    USE Therapeutic Processes
Nursery School Students
Nursery Schools
Nurses
Psychiatric **Nurses**
Public Health Service **Nurses**
School **Nurses**
Nursing
Nursing Education
Nursing Homes
Nursing Students
Nurturance
Nature **Nurture**
Nutrition
Nutritional Deficiencies
Nutritional Supplements
    USE Dietary Supplements
Nymphomania *USE Hypersexuality*
Nystagmus
Optokinetic Nystagmus *USE Nystagmus*
Vestibular Nystagmus *USE Nystagmus*
Obedience

Obesity
Obesity (Attitudes Toward)
Object Permanence
Object Recognition
Object Relations
Goldstein Scheerer **Object** Sort Test
Objective Referenced Tests
    USE Criterion Referenced Tests
Objectives *USE Goals*
Course Objectives *USE Educational Objectives*
Educational **Objectives**
Instructional Objectives *USE Educational Objectives*
Organizational **Objectives**
Objectivity
Transitional **Objects**
Oblique Rotation
Medulla **Oblongata**
Obscenity
Observation Methods
Naturalistic Observation *USE Observation Methods*
Self Observation *USE Self Monitoring*
Observational Learning
Observers
Obsessions
Obsessive Compulsive Disorder
Obsessive Compulsive Neurosis
    USE Obsessive Compulsive Disorder
Obsessive Compulsive Personality
Obsessive Neurosis
    USE Obsessive Compulsive Disorder
Obstetrical Complications
Obstetricians
Obstetrics
Obturator Nerve *USE Spinal Nerves*
Occipital Lobe
Occultism
Parental **Occupation**
Occupational Adjustment
Occupational Aspirations
Occupational Attitudes
Occupational Choice
Occupational Exposure
Occupational Guidance
Occupational Interest Measures
Occupational Interests
Occupational Mobility
Occupational Neurosis
Occupational Preference
Occupational Safety
Occupational Status
Occupational Stress
Occupational Success
Occupational Success Prediction
Occupational Tenure
Occupational Therapists
Occupational Therapy
Kuder **Occupational** Interest Survey
Occupations
Religious Occupations *USE Religious Personnel*
Octopus
Ocular Accommodation
Ocular Dominance
Ocular Fixation *USE Eye Fixation*
Electro **Oculography**
Oculomotor Muscles
Oculomotor Nerve *USE Cranial Nerves*
Oculomotor Response
    USE Eye Movements
Odor Aversion Conditioning
    USE Aversion Conditioning
Odor Discrimination
Oedipal Complex
Mentally Ill **Offenders**
Sex **Offenses**

340

Office Environment
USE Working Conditions
Commissioned **Officers**
Military Officers *USE Commissioned Officers*
Noncommissioned **Officers**
Parole **Officers**
Probation **Officers**
Elected Government Officials *USE Government Personnel*
Stimulus **Offset**
Offspring
Adult **Offspring**
Interracial **Offspring**
Olfactory Bulb
Olfactory Evoked Potentials
Olfactory Impairment *USE Anosmia*
Olfactory Mucosa
Olfactory Nerve
Olfactory Perception
Olfactory Stimulation
Olfactory Thresholds
Oligophrenia *USE Mental Retardation*
Omission Training
Omnibus Personality Inventory
Omnipotence
Online Databases *USE Databases*
Online Searching
USE Computer Searching
Only Children
Female Only Environments
USE Single Sex Environments
Male Only Environments
USE Single Sex Environments
Onomatopoeia and Images Test
USE Projective Personality Measures
Onset (Disorders)
Sleep **Onset**
Stimulus **Onset**
Ontogeny *USE Development*
Open Classroom Method
Open Universities
USE Nontraditional Education
Animal **Open** Field Behavior
Openmindedness
Openness to Experience
Operant Conditioning
Keypunch Operators *USE Clerical Personnel*
Ophidiophobia
Ophthalmologic Examination
Ophthalmology
Opiate Agonists *USE Narcotic Agonists*
Opiate Antagonists
USE Narcotic Antagonists
Opiates
Endogenous **Opiates**
Opinion Attitude and Interest Survey
USE Attitude Measures
Opinion Change *USE Attitude Change*
Opinion Questionnaires
USE Attitude Measures
Opinion Surveys *USE Attitude Measures*
Public **Opinion**
Opinions *USE Attitudes*
Opioid Antagonists
USE Narcotic Antagonists
Opioids *USE Opiates*
Opium Alkaloids *USE Alkaloids*
Opium Alkaloids *USE Opiates*
Opium Derivatives *USE Opiates*
Opossums
Oppositional Defiant Disorder
Optic Chiasm
Optic Lobe
Optic Nerve
Optic Tract
Optical Aids
Optical Illusions *USE Illusions (Perception)*

Optimism
Optokinetic Nystagmus *USE Nystagmus*
Optometrists
Optometry
Oral Communication
Oral Contraceptives
Oral Reading
Birth **Order**
Higher **Order** Conditioning
Pecking Order *USE Animal Dominance*
Rank **Order** Correlation
Second Order Conditioning
USE Higher Order Conditioning
Court Ordered Treatment *USE Court Referrals*
Organ Donation *USE Tissue Donation*
Organ of Corti *USE Cochlea*
Organ Transplantation
Sense **Organ** Disorders
Organic Brain Syndromes
Organic Therapies
USE Physical Treatment Methods
Single Cell Organisms *USE Microorganisms*
School Organization
USE Educational Administration
Spatial **Organization**
Organizational Behavior
Organizational Change
Organizational Characteristics
Organizational Climate
Organizational Commitment
Organizational Crises
Organizational Development
Organizational Effectiveness
Organizational Goals
USE Organizational Objectives
Organizational Merger
Organizational Objectives
Organizational Performance
USE Organizational Effectiveness
Organizational Policy Making
USE Policy Making
Organizational Psychology
USE Industrial Psychology
Organizational Structure
Organizations
Business **Organizations**
Clubs (Social **Organizations)**
Foreign **Organizations**
Health Maintenance **Organizations**
International **Organizations**
Nonprofit **Organizations**
Professional **Organizations**
Religious **Organizations**
Advance **Organizers**
Sense **Organs**
Orgasm
Female **Orgasm**
Male **Orgasm**
Orientals *USE Asians*
Fundamental Interpersonal Relation **Orientation** Behavior Ques
Perceptual **Orientation**
Personal **Orientation** Inventory
Professional Orientation *USE Theoretical Orientation*
Sexual **Orientation**
Spatial **Orientation** (Perception)
Theoretical **Orientation**
Orienting Reflex
Orienting Responses
Family of **Origin**
Originality *USE Creativity*
Word Origins *USE Etymology*
Orphanages
Orphans
Orphenadrine
Orthogonal Rotation

Orthography
Orthopedically Handicapped
    USE Physical Disorders
Orthopsychiatry
Oscilloscopes
Ear Ossicles *USE Middle Ear*
Osteoporosis
Significant **Others**
Otosclerosis *USE Ear Disorders*
Out of Body Experiences
Acting **Out**
Time **Out**
Disease Outbreaks *USE Epidemics*
Psychotherapeutic **Outcomes**
Therapeutic Outcomes *USE Treatment Outcomes*
Treatment **Outcomes**
Outgroup Ingroup *USE Ingroup Outgroup*
Ingroup **Outgroup**
Outpatient Commitment
Outpatient Psychiatric Clinics
    USE Psychiatric Clinics
Outpatient Treatment
Outpatients
Outreach Programs
Outward Bound
    USE Wilderness Experience
Ovariectomy
Ovaries
Ovary Disorders
    USE Endocrine Sexual Disorders
Over The Counter Drugs
    USE Nonprescription Drugs
Academic **Overachievement**
Overcorrection
Drug **Overdoses**
Overlearning
Overpopulation
Structured Overview *USE Advance Organizers*
Overweight *USE Obesity*
Ovulation
Owls
Ownership
Oxazepam
Amine **Oxidase** Inhibitors
Cytochrome **Oxidase**
Monoamine **Oxidase** Inhibitors
Oxidases
Monoamine **Oxidases**
Oxidopamine *USE Hydroxydopamine (6-)*
Oxilapine *USE Loxapine*
Oxygen
Oxygenation
Oxytocin
Artificial **Pacemakers**
Pacific Islanders
Pacifism
Pain
Pain Disorder
    USE Somatoform Pain Disorder
Pain Management
Pain Measurement
Pain Perception
Pain Receptors *USE Nociceptors*
Pain Relieving Drugs *USE Analgesic Drugs*
Pain Thresholds
Back **Pain**
Chronic **Pain**
Myofascial **Pain**
Psychogenic Pain *USE Somatoform Pain Disorder*
Somatoform **Pain** Disorder
Painting (Art)
Paired Associate Learning
Cleft **Palate**
Palestinians *USE Arabs*
Palliative Care

Globus **Pallidus**
Palm (Anatomy)
Palsy *USE Paralysis*
Cerebral **Palsy**
Progressive Supranuclear **Palsy**
Pancreas
Pancreozymin *USE Cholecystokinin*
Panic
Panic Disorder
Pantherine *USE Muscimol*
Papaverine
Parachlorophenylalanine
Paradigmatic Techniques
    USE Paradoxical Techniques
Paradoxical Sleep *USE REM Sleep*
Paradoxical Techniques
Paragraphs
Paraldehyde *USE Anticonvulsive Drugs*
Paralegal Personnel *USE Legal Personnel*
Motion **Parallax**
Paralysis
Paralysis Agitans *USE Parkinsons Disease*
Hysterical **Paralysis**
Infantile Paralysis *USE Poliomyelitis*
Dementia Paralytica *USE General Paresis*
Paramedical Personnel
Paramedical Sciences
Parameter Estimation
    USE Statistical Estimation
Response **Parameters**
Statistical Sample **Parameters**
Stimulus **Parameters**
Parametric Statistical Tests
Paranoia
Paranoia (Psychosis)
Climacteric Paranoia
    USE Involutional Paranoid Psychosis
Paranoid Disorder
    USE Paranoia (Psychosis)
Paranoid Personality
Paranoid Personality Disorder
    USE Paranoid Personality
Paranoid Schizophrenia
Acute Paranoid Disorder
    USE Paranoia (Psychosis)
Atypical Paranoid Disorder
    USE Paranoia (Psychosis)
Involutional **Paranoid** Psychosis
Shared Paranoid Disorder *USE Folie A Deux*
Paraphilias
Paraplegia
Paraprofessional Education
Paraprofessional Personnel
Parapsychological Phenomena
Parapsychology
Parasitic Disorders
Parasitism *USE Biological Symbiosis*
Parasuicide *USE Attempted Suicide*
Parasympathetic Nervous System
Parasympatholytic Drugs
    USE Cholinergic Blocking Drugs
Parasympathomimetic Drugs
    USE Cholinomimetic Drugs
Parathion
Parathyroid Disorders
Parathyroid Glands
Parathyroid Hormone
Parent Attitude Research Instrument
Parent Child Communication
Parent Child Relations
Parent Educational Background
Parent Effectiveness Training
    USE Parent Training
Parent School Relationship
Parent Training

Parental Absence
Parental Attitudes
Parental Authoritarianism
    USE Parental Permissiveness
Parental Characteristics
Parental Expectations
Parental Influence
    USE Parent Child Relations
Parental Investment
Parental Occupation
Parental Permissiveness
Parental Role
Animal **Parental** Behavior
Parenthood Status
Delayed **Parenthood**
Parenting Skills
Parents
Adoptive **Parents**
Birth Parents _USE Biological Family_
Expectant **Parents**
Foster **Parents**
Gay Parents _USE Homosexual Parents_
Homosexual **Parents**
Lesbian Parents _USE Homosexual Parents_
Single **Parents**
Surrogate **Parents** (Humans)
General **Paresis**
Paresthesia _USE Somatosensory Disorders_
Pargyline
Parietal Lobe
Parkinsonism
Parkinsons Disease
Parochial School Education
    USE Private School Education
Parole
Parole Officers
Parolees _USE Parole_
Paroxetine
Paroxysmal Sleep _USE Narcolepsy_
Partial Hospitalization
Partial Reinforcement
    USE Reinforcement Schedules
Partially Hearing Impaired
Partially Sighted
Participation
Athletic **Participation**
Client **Participation**
Group **Participation**
Patient Participation _USE Client Participation_
Political **Participation**
Participative Management
Political **Parties**
Partner Abuse
Parturition _USE Birth_
Democratic Party _USE Political Parties_
Republican Party _USE Political Parties_
Rites of **Passage**
Passive Aggressive Personality
Passive Avoidance
    USE Avoidance Conditioning
Passiveness
Pastoral Counseling
Pastors _USE Ministers (Religion)_
Paternal Investment
    USE Parental Investment
Animal **Paternal** Behavior
Path Analysis
Pathogenesis _USE Etiology_
Pathological Gambling
Pathologists
Pathology
Afferent **Pathways**
Efferent **Pathways**
Maze **Pathways**
Motor Pathways _USE Efferent Pathways_

Neural **Pathways**
Sensory Pathways _USE Afferent Pathways_
Patient Abuse
Patient Attitudes _USE Client Attitudes_
Patient Care Planning
    USE Treatment Planning
Patient Characteristics
    USE Client Characteristics
Patient Dropouts _USE Treatment Dropouts_
Patient Education _USE Client Education_
Patient History
Patient Participation
    USE Client Participation
Patient Records _USE Client Records_
Patient Rights _USE Client Rights_
Patient Satisfaction _USE Client Satisfaction_
Patient Seclusion
Patient Selection
Patient Therapist Interaction
    USE Psychotherapeutic Processes
Patient Therapist Sexual Relations
    USE Professional Client Sexual
        Relations
Patient Transfer _USE Client Transfer_
Patient Treatment Matching
    USE Client Treatment Matching
Patient Violence
Dentist Patient Interaction
    USE Therapeutic Processes
Nurse Patient Interaction
    USE Therapeutic Processes
Physician Patient Interaction
    USE Therapeutic Processes
Therapist Patient Interaction
    USE Psychotherapeutic Processes
Therapist Patient Sexual Relations
    USE Professional Client Sexual
        Relations
Patients
Dying Patients _USE Terminally Ill Patients_
Geriatric **Patients**
Hospitalized **Patients**
Medical **Patients**
Psychiatric **Patients**
Surgical **Patients**
Terminally Ill **Patients**
Patriarchy
Pattern Discrimination
Stimulus Pattern _USE Stimulus Variability_
Alcohol Drinking **Patterns**
Dissociative Patterns _USE Dissociative Disorders_
Eating Patterns _USE Feeding Practices_
Interest Patterns _USE Interests_
Transgenerational **Patterns**
Wilson **Patterson** Conservatism Scale
Speech **Pauses**
Pavlov (Ivan)
Pavlovian Conditioning
    USE Classical Conditioning
Pay _USE Salaries_
Equity **(Payment)**
PCP _USE Phencyclidine_
Peabody Picture Vocabulary Test
Peace
Peace Corps
Pearson Product Moment Correlation
    Coefficient _USE Statistical Correlation_
Pecking Order _USE Animal Dominance_
Angina **Pectoris**
Pederasty _USE Pedophilia_
Pedestrian Accidents
Pedestrians
Pediatricians
Pediatrics
Pedophilia
Peer Counseling

Peer Evaluation
Peer Pressure
Peer Relations
Peer Review *USE Peer Evaluation*
Peer Tutoring
Peers
Pellagra
Pemoline
Death Penalty *USE Capital Punishment*
Penguins
Penicillins
Penis
Penis Envy
Erection **(Penis)**
Penitentiaries *USE Prisons*
Penology
Employee **Pension** Plans
Pentazocine
Pentobarbital
Sodium Pentobarbital *USE Pentobarbital*
Pentothal *USE Thiopental*
Pentylenetetrazol
Pentylenetetrazole *USE Pentylenetetrazol*
Peptic Ulcers *USE Gastrointestinal Ulcers*
Peptides
Perception
Auditory **Perception**
Brightness **Perception**
Color **Perception**
Contour Perception
    USE Form and Shape Perception
Depth **Perception**
Direction **Perception**
Distance **Perception**
Extrasensory **Perception**
Face **Perception**
Form and Shape **Perception**
Form Perception
    USE Form and Shape Perception
Frostig Developmental Test of Visual **Perception**
Gustatory Perception *USE Taste Perception*
Haptic Perception *USE Cutaneous Sense*
Illusions **(Perception)**
Interpersonal Perception *USE Social Perception*
Kinesthetic **Perception**
Loudness **Perception**
Motion **Perception**
Movement Perception *USE Motion Perception*
Music **Perception**
Numerosity **Perception**
Olfactory **Perception**
Pain **Perception**
Pitch **Perception**
Risk **Perception**
Role **Perception**
Self **Perception**
Shape Perception
    USE Form and Shape Perception
Signal Detection **(Perception)**
Smell Perception *USE Olfactory Perception*
Social **Perception**
Somesthetic **Perception**
Spatial Orientation **(Perception)**
Spatial **Perception**
Speech **Perception**
Subliminal **Perception**
Tactual **Perception**
Taste **Perception**
Temperature **Perception**
Texture **Perception**
Time **Perception**
Visual **Perception**
Weight **Perception**
Perceptiveness (Personality)
Perceptual Aftereffect

Perceptual Closure
Perceptual Constancy
Perceptual Development
Perceptual Discrimination
Perceptual Distortion
Perceptual Disturbances
Perceptual Fill *USE Perceptual Closure*
Perceptual Localization
Perceptual Measures
Perceptual Motor Coordination
Perceptual Motor Development
Perceptual Motor Learning
Perceptual Motor Measures
    USE Sensorimotor Measures
Perceptual Motor Processes
Perceptual Neglect *USE Sensory Neglect*
Perceptual Orientation
Perceptual Stimulation
Perceptual Style
Purdue **Perceptual** Motor Survey
Perfectionism
Performance
Performance Anxiety
Performance Tests
Athletic **Performance**
Group **Performance**
Job **Performance**
Motor **Performance**
Organizational Performance
    USE Organizational Effectiveness
Sport Performance *USE Athletic Performance*
Performing Arts *USE Arts*
Periaqueductal Gray
Perinatal Period
Critical **Period**
Neonatal **Period**
Perinatal **Period**
Postnatal **Period**
Peripheral Nerve Disorders
Peripheral Nervous System
Peripheral Vision
Computer **Peripheral** Devices
Object **Permanence**
Parental **Permissiveness**
Perpetrators
Perphenazine
Persecution
Perseverance *USE Persistence*
Perseveration
Persistence
Persistent Mental Illness
    USE Chronic Mental Illness
Person Centered Psychotherapy
    USE Client Centered Therapy
Person Environment Fit
Goodenough Harris Draw A **Person** Test
Personal Adjustment
    USE Emotional Adjustment
Personal Computers *USE Microcomputers*
Personal Construct Theory
    USE Personality Theory
Personal Defense *USE Self Defense*
Personal Growth Techniques
    USE Human Potential Movement
Personal Orientation Inventory
Personal Space
Personal Therapy
Personal Values
Edwards **Personal** Preference Schedule
Personality
Personality Assessment
    USE Personality Measures
Personality Change
Personality Correlates
Personality Development

Personality Disorders
Personality Factors *USE Personality Traits*
Personality Measures
Personality Processes
Personality Tests
    USE Personality Measures
Personality Theory
Personality Traits
Adaptability **(Personality)**
Anankastic Personality *USE Obsessive Compulsive*
    Personality
Antisocial **Personality**
Asthenic Personality *USE Personality Disorders*
Avoidant **Personality**
Big Five Personality Model
    USE Five Factor Personality Model
Borderline **Personality**
California Test of **Personality**
Childrens **Personality** Questionnaire
Compulsive Personality Disorder
    USE Obsessive Compulsive
    Personality
Conformity **(Personality)**
Conscious **(Personality** Factor)
Counselor Personality *USE Counselor Characteristics*
Cyclothymic **Personality**
Dependency **(Personality)**
Dependent **Personality**
Differential Personality Inventory
    USE Nonprojective Personality
    Measures
Edwards **Personality** Inventory
Emotionality **(Personality)**
Explosive Personality *USE Explosive Disorder*
Eysenck **Personality** Inventory
Five Factor **Personality** Model
High School **Personality** Questionnaire
Histrionic **Personality** Disorder
Hysterical Personality
    USE Histrionic Personality Disorder
Inadequate **Personality**
Independence **(Personality)**
Inhibition **(Personality)**
Masochistic **Personality**
Maudsley **Personality** Inventory
Minnesota Multiphasic **Personality** Inventory
Multiple Personality
    USE Dissociative Identity Disorder
Narcissistic **Personality**
NEO **Personality** Inventory
Nonconformity **(Personality)**
Nonprojective **Personality** Measures
Obsessive Compulsive **Personality**
Omnibus **Personality** Inventory
Paranoid **Personality**
Paranoid Personality Disorder
    USE Paranoid Personality
Passive Aggressive **Personality**
Perceptiveness **(Personality)**
Projective **Personality** Measures
Psychoanalytic **Personality** Factors
Rigidity **(Personality)**
Sadomasochistic **Personality**
Schizoid **Personality**
Schizotypal **Personality**
Self Monitoring **(Personality)**
Sensitivity **(Personality)**
Sixteen **Personality** Factors Questionnaire
Split Personality
    USE Dissociative Identity Disorder
Teacher **Personality**
Therapist Personality *USE Therapist Characteristics*
Type A Personality *USE Coronary Prone Behavior*
Type B Personality *USE Coronary Prone Behavior*
Unconscious **(Personality** Factor)

Personnel
Personnel Development
    USE Personnel Training
Personnel Evaluation
Personnel Management
Personnel Placement
Personnel Promotion
Personnel Recruitment
Personnel Selection
Personnel Supply
Personnel Termination
Personnel Training
Personnel Turnover
    USE Employee Turnover
Accreditation (Education **Personnel)**
Aerospace **Personnel**
Air Force **Personnel**
Army **Personnel**
Aviation Personnel *USE Aerospace Personnel*
Business and Industrial **Personnel**
Clerical **Personnel**
Coast Guard **Personnel**
Disabled **Personnel**
Domestic Service **Personnel**
Educational **Personnel**
Enlisted Military **Personnel**
Government **Personnel**
Health **Personnel**
Health **Personnel** Attitudes
Home Care **Personnel**
Industrial Personnel
    USE Business and Industrial Personnel
Law Enforcement **Personnel**
Lay Religious **Personnel**
Legal **Personnel**
Management **Personnel**
Marine **Personnel**
Medical **Personnel**
Medical **Personnel** Supply
Mental Health **Personnel**
Mental Health **Personnel** Supply
Military Medical **Personnel**
Military **Personnel**
Navy **Personnel**
Nonprofessional **Personnel**
Paralegal Personnel *USE Legal Personnel*
Paramedical **Personnel**
Paraprofessional **Personnel**
Police **Personnel**
Prison **Personnel**
Professional **Personnel**
Religious **Personnel**
Sales **Personnel**
Secretarial **Personnel**
Service **Personnel**
Student **Personnel** Services
Technical Service **Personnel**
Technical **Personnel**
Volunteer Civilian **Personnel**
Volunteer Military **Personnel**
Volunteer **Personnel**
Divorced **Persons**
Single **Persons**
Perspective Taking *USE Role Taking*
Linear **Perspective**
Time **Perspective**
Visual Perspective *USE Linear Perspective*
Perspiration *USE Sweat*
Persuasion Therapy
Persuasive Communication
Pervasive Developmental Disorders
Pessimism
Pesticides *USE Insecticides*
Pet Therapy *USE Animal Assisted Therapy*
Petit Mal Epilepsy

Pets
Peyote
Phantom Limbs
Pharmacists
Pharmacology
Pharmacotherapy *USE Drug Therapy*
Pharyngeal Disorders
Pharynx
Phenaglycodol *USE Sedatives*
Phencyclidine
Phenelzine
Phenethylamines
Pheniprazine
Phenmetrazine
Phenobarbital
Parapsychological **Phenomena**
Phenomenology
Phenothiazine Derivatives
Phenotypes
Phenoxybenzamine
Phenylalanine
Phenylethylamines *USE Phenethylamines*
Phenylketonuria
Phenytoin *USE Diphenylhydantoin*
Pheromones
Phi Coefficient
Philosophies
Philosophy of Life *USE World View*
Logic **(Philosophy)**
Positivism **(Philosophy)**
Realism **(Philosophy)**
School **Phobia**
Snake **Phobia** *USE Ophidiophobia*
Social **Phobia**
Spider **Phobia** *USE Phobias*
Phobias
Phobic Neurosis *USE Phobias*
Phonemes
Words **(Phonetic** Units)
Phonetics
Phonics
Phonology
Phosphatases
Phosphatides
Phospholipids *USE Phosphatides*
Phosphorus
Phosphorylases
Photic Threshold *USE Illumination*
Photic Threshold *USE Visual Thresholds*
Photographic Art
Photographic Memory
   USE Eidetic Imagery
Photographs
Photopic Stimulation
Photoreceptors
Phototherapy
Phrases
Phrenic Nerve *USE Spinal Nerves*
Phylogenesis
Physical Abuse
Physical Agility
Physical Appearance
Physical Attractiveness
Physical Comfort
Physical Contact
Physical Development
Physical Dexterity
Physical Disabilities (Attitudes Toward)
Physical Disfigurement
Physical Disorders
Physical Education
Physical Endurance
Physical Examination
Physical Exercise *USE Exercise*
Physical Fitness

Physical Geography *USE Geography*
Physical Growth
   USE Physical Development
Physical Illness (Attitudes Toward)
Physical Illness *USE Physical Disorders*
Physical Maturity
Physical Mobility
Physical Restraint
Physical Strength
Physical Therapists
Physical Therapy
Physical Trauma *USE Injuries*
Physical Treatment Methods
Physically Handicapped
   USE Physical Disorders
Physician Patient Interaction
   USE Therapeutic Processes
Physicians
Family **Physicians**
Physicists
Physics
Physiological Aging
Physiological Arousal
Physiological Correlates
Physiological Psychology
Physiological Stress
Absorption **(Physiological)**
Physiology
Physiotherapy *USE Physical Therapy*
Physique
Physostigmine
Piaget (Jean)
Piagetian Tasks
Piano *USE Musical Instruments*
Pica
Picketing *USE Social Demonstrations*
Picks Disease
Picrotoxin
Pictorial Stimuli
Peabody **Picture** Vocabulary Test
Rosenzweig **Picture** Frustration Study
Blacky Pictures Test
   USE Projective Personality Measures
Motion **Pictures**
Motion **Pictures** (Educational)
Motion **Pictures** (Entertainment)
Piercings *USE Cosmetic Techniques*
Pigeons
Pigments
Pigs
Guinea **Pigs**
Pilocarpine
Aircraft **Pilots**
Pimozide
Pineal Body
Pinealectomy
Piperazines
Pipradrol
Piracetam
Pitch (Frequency)
Pitch Discrimination
Pitch Perception
Speech **Pitch**
Pituitary Disorders
Pituitary Dwarfism *USE Hypopituitarism*
Pituitary Gland
Pituitary Gland Surgery
   USE Hypophysectomy
Pituitary Hormones
Hypothalamo **Pituitary** Adrenal System
Place Conditioning
Place Disorientation
Conditioned Place Preference *USE Place Conditioning*
Placebo
Educational **Placement**

Personnel **Placement**
Placenta
Planarians
Planned Behavior
Discharge **Planning**
Educational Program **Planning**
Environmental **Planning**
Family **Planning**
Family **Planning** Attitudes
Management **Planning**
Patient Care Planning *USE Treatment Planning*
Program Planning *USE Program Development*
Treatment **Planning**
Urban **Planning**
Employee Pension **Plans**
Group Health Plans *USE Health Maintenance Organizations*
Lesson **Plans**
Medicinal Herbs and **Plants**
Blood **Plasma**
Plastic Surgery
Nervous System Plasticity *USE Neural Plasticity*
Neural **Plasticity**
Blood **Platelets**
Play *USE Recreation*
Play Therapy
Animal **Play**
Childhood **Play** Behavior
Childhood **Play** Development
Doll **Play**
Playgrounds
Role **Playing**
Stage Plays *USE Theatre*
Pleasure
Plethysmography
Brachial Plexus *USE Spinal Nerves*
Celiac Plexus *USE Autonomic Ganglia*
Cervical Plexus *USE Spinal Nerves*
Choroid Plexus *USE Cerebral Ventricles*
Hypogastric Plexus *USE Autonomic Ganglia*
Lumbrosacral Plexus *USE Spinal Nerves*
Myenteric Plexus *USE Autonomic Ganglia*
Submucous Plexus *USE Autonomic Ganglia*
Cultural Pluralism *USE Multiculturalism*
PMS *USE Premenstrual Tension*
Pneumoencephalography
Pneumonia
Poetry
Poetry Therapy
Point Biserial Correlation
Poisoning *USE Toxic Disorders*
Barbiturate **Poisoning**
Carbon Monoxide **Poisoning**
Lead **Poisoning**
Mercury **Poisoning**
Poisons
Poisson Distribution *USE Skewed Distribution*
Police Interrogation *USE Legal Interrogation*
Police Personnel
Policy Making
Foreign **Policy** Making
Government **Policy** Making
Health Care **Policy**
Mental Health Care Policy *USE Health Care Policy*
Organizational Policy Making *USE Policy Making*
Public Policy *USE Government Policy Making*
Poliomyelitis
Political Assassination
Political Attitudes
Political Campaigns
Political Candidates
Political Conservatism
Political Debates *USE Debates*

Political Economic Systems
Political Elections
Political Involvement *USE Political Participation*
Political Issues
Political Liberalism
Political Participation
Political Parties
Political Processes
Political Psychology
Political Radicalism
Political Refugees *USE Refugees*
Political Revolution
Political Socialization
Politicians
Politics
Pollution
Polydipsia
Polydrug Abuse
Polygamy
Polygraphs
Polyphagia *USE Hyperphagia*
Pons
Data Pooling *USE Meta Analysis*
Popularity
Population
Population (Statistics)
Population Characteristics *USE Demographic Characteristics*
Population Control *USE Birth Control*
Population Density *USE Social Density*
Population Genetics
Population Shifts *USE Human Migration*
Aboriginal Populations *USE Indigenous Populations*
At Risk **Populations**
High Risk Populations *USE At Risk Populations*
Indigenous **Populations**
Risk Populations *USE At Risk Populations*
Pornography
Porphyria
Porpoises
Porteus Maze Test
Serial **Position** Effect
Positive and Negative Symptoms
Positive Reinforcement
Positive Transfer
Negative and Positive Symptoms *USE Positive and Negative Symptoms*
Positivism
Positivism (Philosophy)
Positron Emission Tomography *USE Tomography*
Possession *USE Ownership*
Demonic Possession *USE Spirit Possession*
Spirit **Possession**
Postactivation Potentials
Postganglionic Autonomic Fibers *USE Autonomic Ganglia*
Postgraduate Students
Postgraduate Training
Posthypnotic Suggestions
Postmodernism
Postnatal Dysphoria *USE Postpartum Depression*
Postnatal Period
Postpartum Depression
Postpartum Psychosis *USE Postpartum Depression*
Postsurgical Complications
Posttesting
Posttraumatic Stress Disorder
Posttreatment Followup
Posture
Threat **Postures**
Potassium

Potassium Ions
Potential Dropouts
Achievement **Potential**
Human **Potential** Movement
Readiness Potential
    USE Contingent Negative Variation
Skin **Potential**
Auditory Evoked **Potentials**
Cortical Evoked **Potentials**
Evoked **Potentials**
Motor Evoked Potentials
    USE Somatosensory Evoked Potentials
Olfactory Evoked **Potentials**
Postactivation **Potentials**
Somatosensory Evoked **Potentials**
Visual Evoked **Potentials**
Drug Potentiation *USE Drug Interactions*
Long Term Potentiation *USE Postactivation Potentials*
Short Term Potentiation *USE Postactivation Potentials*
Poverty
Poverty Areas
Power
Abuse of **Power**
Black **Power** Movement
Statistical **Power**
Practical Knowledge
    USE Procedural Knowledge
Practice
Practice Effects *USE Practice*
Distributed **Practice**
Massed **Practice**
Private **Practice**
Childrearing **Practices**
Feeding **Practices**
Religious **Practices**
Practicum Supervision
General **Practitioners**
Prader Willi Syndrome
Dementia Praecox *USE Schizophrenia*
Pragmatics
Pragmatism
Praise
Prayer
Praying Mantis *USE Mantis*
Precocious Development
Precognition
Preconditioning
Sensory Preconditioning *USE Preconditioning*
Serotonin **Precursors**
Animal **Predatory** Behavior
Predelinquent Youth
Predictability (Measurement)
Prediction
Prediction Errors
Academic Achievement **Prediction**
Occupational Success **Prediction**
Predictive Validity *USE Statistical Validity*
Predisposition
Prednisolone
Preference Measures
Career Preference *USE Occupational Preference*
Conditioned Place Preference *USE Place Conditioning*
Edwards Personal **Preference** Schedule
Kuder **Preference** Record
Occupational **Preference**
Vocational Preference *USE Occupational Preference*
Welsh Figure **Preference** Test
Preferences
Aesthetic **Preferences**
Brand **Preferences**
Food **Preferences**
Preferred Rewards
Least **Preferred** Coworker Scale
Prefrontal Cortex

Preganglionic Autonomic Fibers
    USE Autonomic Ganglia
Pregnancy
Adolescent **Pregnancy**
False Pregnancy *USE Pseudocyesis*
Teenage Pregnancy *USE Adolescent Pregnancy*
Prejudice
Religious **Prejudices**
Preliminary Scholastic Aptitude Test
    USE College Entrance Examination
        Board Scholastic Aptitude Test
Premarital Counseling
Premarital Intercourse
Premature Birth
Premature Ejaculation
Premenstrual Syndrome
    USE Premenstrual Tension
Premenstrual Tension
Premorbidity
Prenatal Care
Prenatal Development
Prenatal Developmental Stages
Prenatal Diagnosis
Prenatal Exposure
Preoptic Area
Prepulse Inhibition
Presbyterians *USE Protestants*
Preschool Education
Preschool Students
Preschool Teachers
Wechsler **Preschool** Primary Scale
Prescribing (Drugs)
Prescription Drugs
Symptom Prescription *USE Paradoxical Techniques*
Presenile Dementia
Stereoscopic **Presentation**
Stimulus **Presentation** Methods
Tachistoscopic **Presentation**
Self **Preservation**
Preservice Teachers
Presidential Debates *USE Debates*
Pressoreceptors *USE Baroreceptors*
Pressure Sensation
Barometric Pressure *USE Atmospheric Conditions*
Blood **Pressure**
Blood **Pressure** Disorders
Diastolic **Pressure**
Peer **Pressure**
Sound Pressure Level *USE Loudness*
Systolic **Pressure**
Pretesting
Prevention
Accident **Prevention**
AIDS **Prevention**
Crime **Prevention**
Drug Abuse **Prevention**
Fire **Prevention**
Primary Mental Health **Prevention**
Relapse **Prevention**
Substance Abuse Prevention *USE Drug Abuse Prevention*
Suicide **Prevention**
Suicide **Prevention** Centers
Preventive Medicine
Price *USE Costs and Cost Analysis*
Pride
Priests
Primacy Effect
Primal Therapy
Primary Health Care
Primary Mental Health Prevention
Primary Reinforcement
Primary School Students
Primary Schools *USE Elementary Schools*
Wechsler Preschool **Primary** Scale
Primates (Nonhuman)

Primidone
Priming
Semantic **Priming**
Primipara
School **Principals**
Printed Communications Media
Printing (Handwriting)
Prismatic Stimulation
Prison Personnel
Prisoners
Prisoners Dilemma Game
Prisoners of War
Prisons
Privacy
Private Practice
Private School Education
Private Sector
Privileged Communication
Proactive Inhibition
Probability
Probability Judgment
Probability Learning
Response **Probability**
Statistical **Probability**
Probation
Probation Officers
Probenecid
Problem Drinking *USE Alcohol Abuse*
Problem Solving
Anagram **Problem** Solving
Group **Problem** Solving
Individual Problem Solving *USE Problem Solving*
Mooney **Problem** Check List
Behavior **Problems**
Social Problems *USE Social Issues*
Procaine
Procedural Knowledge
Process Psychosis
Process Schizophrenia
        USE Process Psychosis
Process Schizophrenia *USE Schizophrenia*
Classification (Cognitive **Process)**
Educational Process *USE Education*
Insight (Psychotherapeutic **Process)**
Rumination (Cognitive **Process)**
Associative **Processes**
Cognitive **Processes**
Employment Processes *USE Personnel Recruitment*
Human Information Processes *USE Cognitive Processes*
Intersensory **Processes**
Legal **Processes**
Legislative **Processes**
Motor **Processes**
Perceptual Motor **Processes**
Personality **Processes**
Political **Processes**
Psychomotor Processes
        USE Perceptual Motor Processes
Psychotherapeutic **Processes**
Sensorimotor Processes
        USE Perceptual Motor Processes
Social **Processes**
Therapeutic **Processes**
Automated Information **Processing**
Cognitive **Processing** Speed
Data **Processing**
Information Processing Speed
        USE Cognitive Processing Speed
Speech **Processing** (Mechanical)
Word **Processing**
Prochlorperazine
Procrastination
Product Design
Consumer Product Design *USE Product Design*

Pearson Product Moment Correlation Coefficient
        USE Statistical Correlation
Employee **Productivity**
Profanity
Professional Certification
Professional Client Sexual Relations
Professional Communication
        USE Scientific Communication
Professional Competence
Professional Consultation
Professional Development
Professional Ethics
Professional Examinations
Professional Fees
Professional Identity
Professional Liability
Professional Licensing
Professional Newsletters
        USE Scientific Communication
Professional Organizations
Professional Orientation
        USE Theoretical Orientation
Professional Personnel
Professional Referral
Professional Specialization
Professional Standards
Professional Supervision
Health Care Professionals *USE Health Personnel*
Impaired **Professionals**
Professors *USE College Teachers*
Language **Proficiency**
Limited English Proficiency *USE Language Proficiency*
Profiles (Measurement)
Profound Mental Retardation
Progestational Hormones
Progesterone
Progestins *USE Progestational Hormones*
Prognosis
Program Development
Program Evaluation
Program Planning
        USE Program Development
Educational **Program** Accreditation
Educational **Program** Evaluation
Educational **Program** Planning
Mental Health **Program** Evaluation
Programmed Instruction
Programmed Textbooks
Computer **Programming**
Computer **Programming** Languages
Neurolinguistic **Programming**
Computer Programs *USE Computer Software*
Educational **Programs**
Employee Assistance **Programs**
Government **Programs**
Home Visiting **Programs**
Hospital **Programs**
Immersion Programs
        USE Foreign Language Education
Independent Living **Programs**
Literacy **Programs**
Mental Health **Programs**
Needle Exchange **Programs**
Outreach **Programs**
Psychiatric Hospital **Programs**
Social **Programs**
Token Economy **Programs**
Twelve Step **Programs**
Work Study Programs *USE Educational Programs*
Progressive Relaxation Therapy
Progressive Supranuclear Palsy
Raven Coloured **Progressive** Matrices
Raven **Progressive** Matrices
Project Follow Through
Project Head Start

349

Projection (Defense Mechanism)
Projective Identification
Projective Personality Measures
Projective Techniques
Projective Testing Technique
Projective Tests *USE Projective Techniques*
Prolactin
Proline
Prolixin *USE Fluphenazine*
Promazine
Promethazine
Promiscuity
Health **Promotion**
Job Promotion *USE Personnel Promotion*
Personnel **Promotion**
Prompting
Coronary **Prone** Behavior
Accident **Proneness**
Pronouns
Pronunciation
Proofreading
Propaganda
Skin Electrical **Properties**
Property *USE Ownership*
Self Fulfilling **Prophecies**
Propranolol
Proprioceptors
Prose
Prosencephalon *USE Forebrain*
Proserine *USE Neostigmine*
Prosocial Behavior
Prosody
Prosopagnosia
Prospective Studies
Prostaglandins
Prostate
Prostate Cancer Screening
USE Cancer Screening
Prostheses
Prostitution
Consumer **Protection**
Protective Services
Protein Deficiency Disorders
Protein Metabolism
Protein Sensitization
USE Anaphylactic Shock
Proteinases
Proteins
Blood **Proteins**
Student Protest *USE Student Activism*
Protestantism
Protestants
Protozoa
Munchausen Syndrome by **Proxy**
Prozac *USE Fluoxetine*
Pruritus
Pseudocyesis
Pseudodementia
Pseudohermaphroditism
USE Hermaphroditism
Pseudomemory *USE False Memory*
Pseudopregnancy *USE Pseudocyesis*
Pseudopsychopathic Schizophrenia
USE Schizophrenia
Psilocybin
Psychedelic Drugs
Psychedelic Experiences
Psychiatric Aides
Psychiatric Clinics
Psychiatric Disorders
USE Mental Disorders
Psychiatric Evaluation
Psychiatric History *USE Patient History*
Psychiatric Hospital Admission
Psychiatric Hospital Discharge

Psychiatric Hospital Programs
Psychiatric Hospital Readmission
Psychiatric Hospital Staff
Psychiatric Hospitalization
Psychiatric Hospitals
Psychiatric Nurses
Psychiatric Patients
Psychiatric Report
USE Psychological Report
Psychiatric Residency
USE Medical Residency
Psychiatric Residency
USE Psychiatric Training
Psychiatric Social Workers
Psychiatric Symptoms
Psychiatric Training
Psychiatric Units
Child Psychiatric Clinics
USE Child Guidance Clinics
Commitment **(Psychiatric)**
Hospital Psychiatric Units *USE Psychiatric Units*
Outpatient Psychiatric Clinics *USE Psychiatric Clinics*
Psychiatrists
Psychiatry
Adolescent **Psychiatry**
Biological **Psychiatry**
Child **Psychiatry**
Community **Psychiatry**
Comparative Psychiatry *USE Transcultural Psychiatry*
Consultation Liaison **Psychiatry**
Cultural Psychiatry *USE Transcultural Psychiatry*
Forensic **Psychiatry**
Geriatric **Psychiatry**
Social **Psychiatry**
Transcultural **Psychiatry**
Psychic Healing *USE Faith Healing*
Psychoactive Drugs *USE Drugs*
Psychoanalysis
Psychoanalysts
Psychoanalytic Interpretation
Psychoanalytic Personality Factors
Psychoanalytic Theory
Psychoanalytic Therapy
USE Psychoanalysis
Psychoanalytic Training
Freudian **Psychoanalytic** School
Psychobiology
Psychodiagnosis
Psychodiagnostic Interview
Psychodiagnostic Typologies
Psychodrama
Psychodynamics
Psychoeducation
Woodcock Johnson **Psychoeducational** Battery
Psychogalvanic Reflex
USE Galvanic Skin Response
Psychogenesis
Psychogenic Pain
USE Somatoform Pain Disorder
Psychohistory
Psychoimmunology
USE Psychoneuroimmunology
Psychokinesis
Illinois Test of **Psycholinguistic** Abilities
Psycholinguistics
Psychological Abuse
USE Emotional Abuse
Psychological Adjustment
USE Emotional Adjustment
Psychological Assessment
Psychological Autopsy
Psychological Correlates
USE Psychodynamics
Psychological Development
USE Psychogenesis

Psychological Endurance
Psychological Interpretation
    USE Theoretical Interpretation
Psychological Needs
Psychological Reactance
Psychological Report
Psychological Screening Inventory
Psychological Stress
Psychological Terminology
Psychological Testing *USE Psychometrics*
Psychological Theories
Boundaries **(Psychological)**
California **Psychological** Inventory
Psychologist Attitudes
Psychologists
Clinical **Psychologists**
Counseling **Psychologists**
Educational **Psychologists**
Experimental **Psychologists**
Industrial **Psychologists**
Military **Psychologists**
School **Psychologists**
Social **Psychologists**
Psychology
Psychology Education
Adolescent **Psychology**
Analytic Psychology *USE Jungian Psychology*
Applied **Psychology**
Child **Psychology**
Clinical **Psychology**
Clinical **Psychology** Graduate Training
Clinical **Psychology** Internship
Cognitive **Psychology**
Community **Psychology**
Comparative **Psychology**
Consumer **Psychology**
Counseling **Psychology**
Cross Cultural **Psychology**
Depth **Psychology**
Developmental **Psychology**
Eclectic Psychology *USE Theoretical Orientation*
Ecological **Psychology**
Educational **Psychology**
Engineering **Psychology**
Environmental **Psychology**
Experimental **Psychology**
Folk **Psychology**
Forensic **Psychology**
Gestalt **Psychology**
Graduate **Psychology** Education
Health Care **Psychology**
Health Psychology *USE Health Care Psychology*
History of **Psychology**
Humanistic **Psychology**
Individual **Psychology**
Industrial **Psychology**
Jungian **Psychology**
Legal Psychology *USE Forensic Psychology*
Mathematical **Psychology**
Medical **Psychology**
Military **Psychology**
Organizational Psychology *USE Industrial Psychology*
Physiological **Psychology**
Political **Psychology**
School **Psychology**
Self **Psychology**
Social **Psychology**
Sport **Psychology**
Transpersonal **Psychology**
Psychometrics
Psychomotor Development
Psychomotor Processes
    USE Perceptual Motor Processes
Psychoneuroimmunology
Psychoneurosis *USE Neurosis*

Psychopath *USE Antisocial Personality*
Psychopathology
Psychopathy *USE Antisocial Personality*
Autistic Psychopathy *USE Aspergers Syndrome*
Psychopharmacology
Psychophysical Measurement
Psychophysics
Psychophysiologic Disorders
    USE Somatoform Disorders
Psychophysiology
Toxic **Psychoses**
Psychosexual Behavior
Psychosexual Development
Psychosis
Acute **Psychosis**
Affective **Psychosis**
Alcoholic **Psychosis**
Brief Reactive Psychosis *USE Acute Psychosis*
Childhood **Psychosis**
Chronic **Psychosis**
Experimental **Psychosis**
Infantile Psychosis *USE Childhood Psychosis*
Involutional Paranoid **Psychosis**
Korsakoffs **Psychosis**
Manic Depressive Psychosis *USE Bipolar Disorder*
Paranoia **(Psychosis)**
Postpartum Psychosis *USE Postpartum Depression*
Process **Psychosis**
Reactive **Psychosis**
Senile **Psychosis**
Symbiotic Infantile **Psychosis**
Traumatic Psychosis *USE Reactive Psychosis*
Psychosocial Development
Psychosocial Factors
Psychosocial Mental Retardation
Psychosocial Readjustment
Psychosocial Rehabilitation
Psychosocial Resocialization
    USE Psychosocial Readjustment
Psychosomatic Disorders
    USE Somatoform Disorders
Psychosomatic Medicine
Psychosurgery
Psychotherapeutic Breakthrough
Psychotherapeutic Counseling
Psychotherapeutic Methods
    USE Psychotherapeutic Techniques
Psychotherapeutic Neutrality
Psychotherapeutic Outcomes
Psychotherapeutic Processes
Psychotherapeutic Resistance
Psychotherapeutic Techniques
Psychotherapeutic Transference
Insight **(Psychotherapeutic** Process)
Psychotherapist Attitudes
Psychotherapist Trainees
    USE Therapist Trainees
Psychotherapists
Psychotherapy
Psychotherapy Training
Adlerian **Psychotherapy**
Adolescent **Psychotherapy**
Analytical **Psychotherapy**
Brief **Psychotherapy**
Child **Psychotherapy**
Eclectic **Psychotherapy**
Experiential **Psychotherapy**
Expressive **Psychotherapy**
Geriatric **Psychotherapy**
Group **Psychotherapy**
Individual **Psychotherapy**
Interpersonal **Psychotherapy**
Jungian Psychotherapy
    USE Analytical Psychotherapy

Person Centered Psychotherapy
    USE Client Centered Therapy
Reconstructive Psychotherapy *USE Psychotherapy*
Short Term Psychotherapy *USE Brief Psychotherapy*
Supportive **Psychotherapy**
Time Limited Psychotherapy *USE Brief Psychotherapy*
    Psychotic Depressive Reaction
    USE Major Depression
    Psychotic Symptoms
    USE Psychiatric Symptoms
Acute Psychotic Episode *USE Acute Psychosis*
    Psychoticism
    Psychotomimetic Drugs
    Psychotropic Drugs *USE Drugs*
    PTA *USE Parent School Relationship*
    Puberty
    Pubescence *USE Sexual Development*
    Public Attitudes *USE Public Opinion*
    Public Health
    Public Health Service Nurses
    Public Health Services
    Public Opinion
    Public Policy
    USE Government Policy Making
    Public Relations
    Public School Education
    Public Sector
    Public Speaking
    Public Transportation
    Public Welfare Services
    USE Community Welfare Services
Certified Public Accountants *USE Accountants*
Fear of Public Speaking *USE Speech Anxiety*
    Puerto Rican Americans *USE Hispanics*
Hair **Pulling**
    Pulmonary Disorders *USE Lung Disorders*
    Pulmonary Emphysema
    Pulmonary Tuberculosis
Arterial **Pulse**
    Punishment
Capital **Punishment**
Corporal Punishment *USE Punishment*
    Pupil (Eye)
    Pupil Dilation
    Purdue Perceptual Motor Survey
    Purkinje Cells
    Puromycin
Rotary **Pursuit**
    Putamen
    Pygmalion Effect
    USE Self Fulfilling Prophecies
    Pygmy Chimpanzees *USE Bonobos*
Color Pyramid Test
    USE Projective Personality Measures
    Pyramidal Tracts
    Pyramidotomy
    Pyromania
    Q Sort Testing Technique
    Q Test *USE Cochran Q Test*
Cochran **Q** Test
    Quaalude *USE Methaqualone*
    Quadriplegia
    Quails
Leadership **Qualities**
    Quality Circles
    USE Participative Management
    Quality Control
    Quality of Care
    Quality of Education
    USE Educational Quality
    Quality of Life
    Quality of Services
    Quality of Work Life
Educational **Quality**
Service Quality *USE Quality of Services*
    Quartimax Rotation

Fund Interper Rela Orientat Beh **Ques**
    Questioning
Childrens Personality **Questionnaire**
General Health **Questionnaire**
High School Personality **Questionnaire**
Sixteen Personality Factors **Questionnaire**
    Questionnaires
Opinion Questionnaires *USE Attitude Measures*
    Quinidine *USE Alkaloids*
    Quinine
    Quinpirole
Intelligence **Quotient**
    Rabbis
    Rabbits
    Race (Anthropological)
    Race and Ethnic Discrimination
    Race Attitudes
    USE Racial and Ethnic Attitudes
    Race Relations
    USE Racial and Ethnic Relations
    Racial and Ethnic Attitudes
    Racial and Ethnic Differences
    Racial and Ethnic Groups
    Racial and Ethnic Relations
    Racial Differences
    USE Racial and Ethnic Differences
    Racial Discrimination
    USE Race and Ethnic Discrimination
    Racial Integration *USE Social Integration*
    Racism
    Radial Nerve *USE Spinal Nerves*
    Radiation
    Radiation Therapy
    Radical Movements
Political **Radicalism**
    Radio
    Radiography *USE Roentgenography*
    Radiology
    Rage *USE Anger*
    Railroad Trains
Consciousness **Raising** Groups
    Random Sampling
Wide **Range** Achievement Test
    Rank Difference Correlation
    Rank Order Correlation
Sign Rank Test *USE Wilcoxon Sign Rank Test*
Wilcoxon Sign **Rank** Test
    Rape
Acquaintance **Rape**
Date Rape *USE Acquaintance Rape*
    Raphe Nuclei
    Rapid Eye Movement
    Rapid Eye Movement Dreams
    USE REM Dreams
    Rapid Eye Movement Sleep
    USE REM Sleep
    Rapid Heart Rate *USE Tachycardia*
    Rapport *USE Interpersonal Interaction*
    Rasch Model *USE Item Response Theory*
    Rat Learning
Birth **Rate**
Cardiac Rate *USE Heart Rate*
Death Rate *USE Mortality Rate*
Heart **Rate**
Heart **Rate** Affecting Drugs
Learning **Rate**
Mortality **Rate**
Rapid Heart Rate *USE Tachycardia*
Response Rate *USE Response Frequency*
Speech **Rate**
X Rated Materials *USE Pornography*
Metabolic **Rates**
    Rating
    Rating Scales

Kupfer Detre Self Rating Scale
USE *Nonprojective Personality*
Measures
Zungs Self **Rating** Depression Scale
Ratio Reinforcement
USE *Fixed Ratio Reinforcement*
Ratio Reinforcement
USE *Variable Ratio Reinforcement*
Fixed **Ratio** Reinforcement
Variable **Ratio** Reinforcement
Ratiocination USE *Logical Thinking*
Rational Emotive Therapy
Rationalization
Rats
Albino Rats USE *Rats*
Norway **Rats**
White Rats USE *Rats*
Rauwolfia USE *Alkaloids*
Raven Coloured Progressive Matrices
Raven Progressive Matrices
Cathode Ray Tubes USE *Video Display Units*
X Ray Diagnosis USE *Roentgenography*
X Ray Therapy USE *Radiation Therapy*
Raynauds Disease
USE *Cardiovascular Disorders*
RDC USE *Research Diagnostic Criteria*
Reactance USE *Psychological Reactance*
Psychological **Reactance**
Reaction Formation
Reaction Time
Fugue **Reaction**
Negative Therapeutic **Reaction**
Neurotic Depressive Reaction USE *Major Depression*
Psychotic Depressive Reaction USE *Major Depression*
Anniversary Reactions USE *Anniversary Events*
Drug Adverse Reactions USE *Side Effects (Drug)*
Separation **Reactions**
Stranger **Reactions**
Stress **Reactions**
Reactive Attachment Disorder
USE *Attachment Disorders*
Reactive Depression
Reactive Psychosis
Reactive Schizophrenia
USE *Reactive Psychosis*
Reactive Schizophrenia
USE *Schizophrenia*
Brief Reactive Psychosis USE *Acute Psychosis*
Cardiovascular **Reactivity**
Readability
Readaptation USE *Adaptation*
Basal Readers USE *Reading Materials*
Readiness Potential
USE *Contingent Negative Variation*
Gates Reading Readiness Tests
USE *Gates MacGinitie Reading Tests*
Metropolitan **Readiness** Tests
Reading **Readiness**
School **Readiness**
Reading
Reading Ability
Reading Achievement
Reading Aloud USE *Oral Reading*
Reading Comprehension
Reading Development
Reading Disabilities
Reading Education
Reading Materials
Reading Measures
Reading Readiness
Reading Skills
Reading Speed
Gates MacGinitie **Reading** Tests
Gates Reading Readiness Tests
USE *Gates MacGinitie Reading Tests*

Gates Reading Test
USE *Gates MacGinitie Reading Tests*
Oral **Reading**
Remedial **Reading**
Silent **Reading**
Psychosocial **Readjustment**
Facility Readmission USE *Facility Admission*
Psychiatric Hospital **Readmission**
Realism (Philosophy)
Reality
Reality Testing
Reality Therapy
Virtual **Reality**
Self Realization USE *Self Actualization*
Home **Reared** Mentally Retarded
Animal **Rearing**
Reasoning
Deductive Reasoning
USE *Inductive Deductive Reasoning*
Inductive Deductive **Reasoning**
Syllogistic Reasoning
USE *Inductive Deductive Reasoning*
Sexual Reassignment USE *Sex Change*
Authoritarianism Rebellion Scale
USE *Nonprojective Personality*
Measures
Recall (Learning)
Cued **Recall**
Dream **Recall**
Free **Recall**
Serial **Recall**
Recency Effect
Receptive Fields
Cutaneous **Receptive** Fields
Visual **Receptive** Fields
Animal Sexual **Receptivity**
Receptor Binding
Neural **Receptors**
Pain Receptors USE *Nociceptors*
Genetic **Recessiveness**
Recidivism
Reciprocal Inhibition Therapy
Reciprocity
Recognition (Learning)
Automated Speech **Recognition**
Automatic Speaker Recognition
USE *Automated Speech Recognition*
Face Recognition USE *Face Perception*
Kinship **Recognition**
Object **Recognition**
Sex **Recognition**
Species **Recognition**
Word **Recognition**
Reconstruction (Learning)
Reconstructive Psychotherapy
USE *Psychotherapy*
Graduate **Record** Examination
Kuder Preference **Record**
Tape **Recorders**
Videotape **Recorders**
Academic Records USE *Student Records*
Client **Records**
Medical **Records**
Patient Records USE *Client Records*
Student **Records**
Recovery (Disorders)
Spontaneous **Recovery** (Learning)
Recreation
Recreation Areas
Recreation Therapy
Summer Camps **(Recreation)**
Recreational Day Camps
USE *Summer Camps (Recreation)*
Childrens **Recreational** Games
Military **Recruitment**

Personnel **Recruitment**
Teacher **Recruitment**
Recurrent Depression
Red Blood Cells *USE Erythrocytes*
Red Nucleus *USE Mesencephalon*
Anxiety Reducing Drugs *USE Tranquilizing Drugs*
Reductionism
Reemployment
Reenactments *USE Enactments*
Reentry Students
Job Reentry *USE Reemployment*
Reference Groups
Self **Reference**
Criterion **Referenced** Tests
Objective Referenced Tests
USE Criterion Referenced Tests
Professional **Referral**
Self **Referral**
Court **Referrals**
Reflectiveness
Achilles Tendon **Reflex**
Acoustic **Reflex**
Babinski **Reflex**
Blink Reflex *USE Eyeblink Reflex*
Conditioned Reflex *USE Conditioned Responses*
Eyeblink **Reflex**
Flexion **Reflex**
Hoffmanns **Reflex**
Intra Aural Muscle Reflex *USE Acoustic Reflex*
Orienting **Reflex**
Psychogalvanic Reflex *USE Galvanic Skin Response*
Stapedius Reflex *USE Acoustic Reflex*
Startle **Reflex**
Unconditioned Reflex *USE Reflexes*
Reflexes
Educational **Reform**
Reformatories
Refraction Errors
Light **Refraction**
Reframing *USE Paradoxical Techniques*
Refugees
Political Refugees *USE Refugees*
School **Refusal**
Treatment **Refusal**
Neural Regeneration *USE Neural Development*
Medical Regimen Compliance
USE Treatment Compliance
Regional Differences
Geographic Regions *USE Geography*
Regression (Defense Mechanism)
Regression Analysis
USE Statistical Regression
Regression Artifact
USE Statistical Regression
Age **Regression** (Hypnotic)
Linear **Regression**
Multiple **Regression**
Nonlinear **Regression**
Statistical **Regression**
Regurgitation *USE Vomiting*
Rehabilitation
Rehabilitation Centers
Rehabilitation Counseling
Rehabilitation Counselors
Rehabilitation Education
Alcohol **Rehabilitation**
Cognitive **Rehabilitation**
Drug **Rehabilitation**
Neuropsychological **Rehabilitation**
Psychosocial **Rehabilitation**
Vocational **Rehabilitation**
Rehearsal *USE Practice*
Reinforcement
Reinforcement Amounts
Reinforcement Delay

Reinforcement Schedules
Concurrent **Reinforcement** Schedules
Continuous Reinforcement
USE Reinforcement Schedules
Delayed Reinforcement *USE Reinforcement Delay*
Differential **Reinforcement**
Fixed Interval **Reinforcement**
Fixed Ratio **Reinforcement**
Intermittent Reinforcement
USE Reinforcement Schedules
Interval Reinforcement
USE Fixed Interval Reinforcement
Interval Reinforcement
USE Variable Interval Reinforcement
Negative **Reinforcement**
Noncontingent **Reinforcement**
Nonverbal **Reinforcement**
Partial Reinforcement
USE Reinforcement Schedules
Positive **Reinforcement**
Primary **Reinforcement**
Ratio Reinforcement
USE Fixed Ratio Reinforcement
Ratio Reinforcement
USE Variable Ratio Reinforcement
Secondary **Reinforcement**
Self **Reinforcement**
Social **Reinforcement**
Token Reinforcement
USE Secondary Reinforcement
Variable Interval **Reinforcement**
Variable Ratio **Reinforcement**
Verbal **Reinforcement**
Vicarious Reinforcement *USE Vicarious Experiences*
Reinnervation *USE Neural Development*
Halstead **Reitan** Neuropsychological Battery
Social Rejection *USE Social Acceptance*
Relapse (Disorders)
Relapse Prevention
Diagnosis **Related** Groups
Work **Related** Illnesses
Fundamental Interpersonal **Relation** Orientation Behavior Ques
Family **Relations**
Father Child **Relations**
Human **Relations** Training
Intergenerational **Relations**
International **Relations**
Labor Management **Relations**
Labor Relations
USE Labor Management Relations
Male Female **Relations**
Marital **Relations**
Mother Child **Relations**
Object **Relations**
Parent Child **Relations**
Patient Therapist Sexual Relations *USE Professional Client Sexual Relations*
Peer **Relations**
Professional Client Sexual **Relations**
Public **Relations**
Race Relations *USE Racial and Ethnic Relations*
Racial and Ethnic **Relations**
Sibling **Relations**
Therapist Patient Sexual Relations *USE Professional Client Sexual Relations*
Relationship Satisfaction
Relationship Termination
Relationship Therapy
Barrett Lennard **Relationship** Inventory
Family Work **Relationship**
Interpersonal Relationship Satisfaction
USE Relationship Satisfaction
Job Family Relationship *USE Family Work Relationship*
Parent School **Relationship**
Work Family Relationship *USE Family Work Relationship*

Relativism
Relaxation
Relaxation Therapy
Muscle Relaxation
Muscle Relaxation Therapy
    USE Relaxation Therapy
Progressive Relaxation Therapy
Muscle Relaxing Drugs
Relearning
Institutional Release
ACTH Releasing Factor
    USE Corticotropin Releasing Factor
Corticotropin Releasing Factor
Interobserver Reliability USE Interrater Reliability
Interrater Reliability
Statistical Reliability
Test Reliability
Pain Relieving Drugs USE Analgesic Drugs
Religion
Confession (Religion)
Ministers (Religion)
Religiosity
Religious Affiliation
Religious Beliefs
Religious Buildings
Religious Education
Religious Experiences
Religious Groups
Religious Literature
Religious Occupations
    USE Religious Personnel
Religious Organizations
Religious Personnel
Religious Practices
Religious Prejudices
Lay Religious Personnel
REM USE Rapid Eye Movement
REM Dream Deprivation
REM Dreams
REM Sleep
Remarriage
Remedial Education
Remedial Reading
Remembering USE Retention
Reminiscence
Remission (Disorders)
Spontaneous Remission
Symptom Remission
Remote Associates Test
Renal Diseases USE Kidney Diseases
Renal Transplantation
    USE Organ Transplantation
Repairmen
    USE Technical Service Personnel
Repeated Measures
Bannister Repertory Grid
Compulsive Repetition
Estrogen Replacement Therapy
    USE Hormone Therapy
Experimental Replication
Case Report
Psychiatric Report USE Psychological Report
Psychological Report
Self Report
Abuse Reporting
Child Abuse Reporting
Repressed Memory
Repression (Defense Mechanism)
Repression Sensitization
Repression Sensitization Scale
Sensitization Repression USE Repression Sensitization
Sexual Reproduction
Reproductive Technology
Reptiles
Republican Party USE Political Parties

Reputation
Research USE Experimentation
Research Design
    USE Experimental Design
Research Diagnostic Criteria
Research Dropouts
    USE Experimental Attrition
Research Methods USE Methodology
Research Setting
Research Subjects
    USE Experimental Subjects
Consumer Research
Cross Disciplinary Research USE Interdisciplinary Research
Interdisciplinary Research
Multidisciplinary Research USE Interdisciplinary Research
Parent Attitude Research Instrument
Family Resemblance
Resentment USE Hostility
Reserpine
Residence Halls USE Dormitories
Medical Residency
Psychiatric Residency USE Medical Residency
Psychiatric Residency USE Psychiatric Training
Residential Care Attendants
    USE Attendants (Institutions)
Residential Care Institutions
Resistance
Basal Skin Resistance
Psychotherapeutic Resistance
Skin Resistance
Treatment Resistant Depression
Treatment Resistant Disorders
Tricyclic Resistant Depression
    USE Treatment Resistant Depression
Psychosocial Resocialization
    USE Psychosocial Readjustment
Conflict Resolution
Resonance USE Vibration
Magnetic Resonance Imaging
Resource Allocation
Resource Teachers
Allocation of Resources USE Resource Allocation
Human Resources USE Personnel Management
Self Respect USE Self Esteem
Respiration
Respiration Stimulating Drugs
Artificial Respiration
Respiratory Distress
Respiratory System
Respiratory Tract Disorders
Respite Care
Respondent Conditioning
    USE Classical Conditioning
Response Amplitude
Response Bias
Response Consistency
    USE Response Variability
Response Cost
Response Duration
Response Frequency
Response Generalization
Response Lag USE Reaction Time
Response Latency
Response Parameters
Response Probability
Response Rate USE Response Frequency
Response Set
Response Speed USE Reaction Time
Response Time USE Reaction Time
Response Variability
Electrodermal Response USE Galvanic Skin Response
Galvanic Skin Response
Item Response Theory
Oculomotor Response USE Eye Movements
Responses

355

Alarm **Responses**
Conditioned Emotional **Responses**
Conditioned **Responses**
Emotional **Responses**
Mediated **Responses**
Orienting **Responses**
Unconditioned **Responses**
Responsibility
Criminal **Responsibility**
Work **Rest** Cycles
Restlessness
Dietary **Restraint**
Emotional Restraint *USE Emotional Control*
Physical **Restraint**
Restricted Environmental Stimulation
  USE Stimulus Deprivation
Cognitive **Restructuring**
Knowledge of **Results**
Retail Stores *USE Retailing*
Retailing
Retaliation
Borderline Mental **Retardation**
Cultural Familial Mental Retardation
  USE Psychosocial Mental Retardation
Mental **Retardation**
Mental **Retardation** (Attitudes Toward)
Mild Mental **Retardation**
Moderate Mental **Retardation**
Profound Mental **Retardation**
Psychosocial Mental **Retardation**
Severe Mental **Retardation**
Retarded Speech Development
Educable Mentally Retarded *USE Mild Mental Retardation*
Home Reared Mentally **Retarded**
Institutionalized Mentally **Retarded**
Trainable Mentally Retarded
  USE Moderate Mental Retardation
Retention
Retention Measures
Benton Revised Visual **Retention** Test
School **Retention**
Reticular Formation
Retina
Ganglion Cells **(Retina)**
Retinal Eccentricity
Retinal Ganglion Cells
  USE Ganglion Cells (Retina)
Retinal Image
Retinal Vessels *USE Arteries (Anatomy)*
Retirement
Retirement Communities
Automated Information **Retrieval**
Retroactive Inhibition
Retrospective Studies
Rett Syndrome
Return to Home *USE Empty Nest*
Return to Work *USE Reemployment*
Serotonin **Reuptake** Inhibitors
Revenge *USE Retaliation*
Directed Reverie Therapy *USE Guided Imagery*
Reversal Shift Learning
Life **Review**
Literature **Review**
Peer Review *USE Peer Evaluation*
Benton **Revised** Visual Retention Test
Political **Revolution**
Reward Allocation
Rewards
External **Rewards**
Extrinsic Rewards *USE External Rewards*
Internal **Rewards**
Intrinsic Rewards *USE Internal Rewards*
Monetary **Rewards**
Preferred **Rewards**
Rh Incompatibility

Rheoencephalography
Rhetoric
Rheumatic Fever
Rheumatism *USE Arthritis*
Rheumatoid Arthritis
Spearman Rho *USE Rank Difference Correlation*
Rhodopsin
Rhombencephalon *USE Hindbrain*
Rhythm
Rhythm Method
Alpha **Rhythm**
Delta **Rhythm**
Speech **Rhythm**
Theta **Rhythm**
Animal Biological **Rhythms**
Animal Circadian **Rhythms**
Biological **Rhythms**
Human Biological **Rhythms**
Ribonucleic Acid
Puerto Rican Americans *USE Hispanics*
Right Brain
Right to Treatment
Civil **Rights**
Civil **Rights** Movement
Client **Rights**
Human **Rights**
Patient Rights *USE Client Rights*
Visitation Rights *USE Child Visitation*
Rigidity (Personality)
Riots
Risk Analysis
Risk Factors
Risk Management
Risk Perception
Risk Populations *USE At Risk Populations*
Risk Taking
At **Risk** Populations
High Risk Populations *USE At Risk Populations*
Sexual **Risk** Taking
Risky Shift *USE Choice Shift*
Risperidone
Ritalin *USE Methylphenidate*
Ritanserin
Rites (Nonreligious)
Rites of Passage
Birth **Rites**
Death **Rites**
Initiation **Rites**
Marriage **Rites**
Rivalry
Robbery *USE Theft*
Robins
Robotics
Rock Music
Body **Rocking**
Rod and Frame Test
Rodents
Rods (Eye)
Roentgenography
Rogerian Therapy
  USE Client Centered Therapy
Rogers (Carl)
Rokeach Dogmatism Scale
Role Conflicts
Role Expectations
Role Models
Role Perception
Role Playing
Role Satisfaction
Role Strain *USE Role Conflicts*
Role Taking
Bem Sex **Role** Inventory
Counselor **Role**
Gender Role Attitudes *USE Sex Role Attitudes*
Parental **Role**

356

Sex **Role** Attitudes
Therapist **Role**
Roles
Gender Roles *USE Sex Roles*
Sex **Roles**
Roman Catholicism
Romance
Roommates
Dorsal **Roots**
Ventral **Roots**
Rorschach Test
Rosenzweig Picture Frustration Study
Rotary Pursuit
Body Rotation *USE Rotational Behavior*
Equimax **Rotation**
Mental **Rotation**
Oblique **Rotation**
Orthogonal **Rotation**
Quartimax **Rotation**
Statistical **Rotation**
Varimax **Rotation**
Rotational Behavior
ROTC Students
Rote Learning
Rotter Incomplete Sentences Blank
Rotter Internal External Locus of Control
Scale
Rubella
Rule Learning
USE Cognitive Hypothesis Testing
Rumination (Cognitive Process)
Rumination (Eating)
Rumors *USE Gossip*
Runaway Behavior
Running
Rural Development
USE Community Development
Rural Environments
Saccadic Eye Movements
USE Eye Movements
Saccharin
Tay Sachs Disease
USE Amaurotic Familial Idiocy
SAD *USE Seasonal Affective Disorder*
Sadism
Sexual **Sadism**
Sadness
Sadomasochism
Sadomasochistic Personality
Safety
Safety Belts
Safety Devices
Safety Warnings *USE Warnings*
Automobile Safety *USE Highway Safety*
Aviation **Safety**
Driver Safety *USE Highway Safety*
Highway **Safety**
Industrial Safety *USE Occupational Safety*
Occupational **Safety**
Water **Safety**
Salamanders
Salaries
Sales Personnel
Stimulus **Salience**
Saliva
Salivary Glands
Salivation
Salmon
Saltiness *USE Taste Perception*
Same Sex Environments
USE Single Sex Environments
Sample Size
Matching to **Sample**
Statistical **Sample** Parameters
Statistical **Samples**

Sampling (Experimental)
Biased **Sampling**
Random **Sampling**
Sanatoriums
Sarcomas *USE Neoplasms*
SAT *USE College Entrance Examination
Board Scholastic Aptitude Test*
Satiation
Satisfaction
Client **Satisfaction**
Consumer **Satisfaction**
Customer Satisfaction *USE Consumer Satisfaction*
Interpersonal Relationship Satisfaction *USE Relationship Satisfaction*
Job **Satisfaction**
Life **Satisfaction**
Marital **Satisfaction**
Need **Satisfaction**
Patient Satisfaction *USE Client Satisfaction*
Relationship **Satisfaction**
Role **Satisfaction**
Sexual **Satisfaction**
Work Satisfaction *USE Job Satisfaction*
Color **Saturation**
Savants
Idiot Savants *USE Savants*
Authoritarianism Rebellion Scale *USE Nonprojective Personality
Measures*
Barron Welsh Art **Scale**
California F **Scale**
Cattell Infant Intelligence Scale *USE Infant Intelligence Scale*
Childrens Manifest Anxiety **Scale**
Columbia Mental Maturity **Scale**
Edwards Social Desirability **Scale**
Infant Intelligence **Scale**
Kupfer Detre Self Rating Scale *USE Nonprojective Personality
Measures*
Least Preferred Coworker **Scale**
Leiter Adult Intelligence Scale *USE Intelligence Measures*
Marlowe Crowne Social Desirability **Scale**
Repression Sensitization **Scale**
Rokeach Dogmatism **Scale**
Rotter Internal External
Locus of Control **Scale**
Sensation Seeking **Scale**
Stanford Binet Intelligence **Scale**
Taylor Manifest Anxiety **Scale**
Temporal Spatial Concept Scale *USE Intelligence Measures*
Tennessee Self Concept **Scale**
Vineland Social Maturity **Scale**
Wechsler Adult Intelligence **Scale**
Wechsler Bellevue Intelligence **Scale**
Wechsler Intelligence **Scale** for Children
Wechsler Memory **Scale**
Wechsler Preschool Primary **Scale**
White Betz A B Scale *USE Nonprojective Personality
Measures*
Wilson Patterson Conservatism **Scale**
Zungs Self Rating Depression **Scale**
Bayley **Scales** of Infant Development
Likert **Scales**
Rating **Scales**
Scaling (Testing)
Multidimensional **Scaling**
Scalp (Anatomy)
Scalp Disorders *USE Skin Disorders*
CAT Scan *USE Tomography*
Animal **Scent** Marking
Diagnostic Interview **Schedule**
Edwards Personal Preference **Schedule**
Fear Survey **Schedule**
Concurrent Reinforcement **Schedules**
Interview **Schedules**
Learning **Schedules**
Reinforcement **Schedules**
Work **Scheduling**

Goldstein **Scheerer** Object Sort Test
Schema
Schizoaffective Disorder
Schizoid Personality
Schizophrenia
Schizophrenia (Disorganized Type)
Acute **Schizophrenia**
Catatonic **Schizophrenia**
Childhood **Schizophrenia**
Chronic Schizophrenia *USE Schizophrenia*
Fragmentation **(Schizophrenia)**
Hebephrenic Schizophrenia
USE Schizophrenia (Disorganized Type)
Paranoid **Schizophrenia**
Process Schizophrenia *USE Process Psychosis*
Process Schizophrenia *USE Schizophrenia*
Pseudopsychopathic Schizophrenia *USE Schizophrenia*
Reactive Schizophrenia *USE Reactive Psychosis*
Reactive Schizophrenia *USE Schizophrenia*
Simple Schizophrenia *USE Schizophrenia*
Undifferentiated **Schizophrenia**
Schizophreniform Disorder
Schizophrenogenic Family
Schizophrenogenic Mothers
Schizotypal Personality
Scholarships
USE Educational Financial Assistance
Scholastic Achievement
USE Academic Achievement
Scholastic Aptitude Test
USE College Entrance Examination Board Scholastic Aptitude Test
Scholastic Aptitude
USE Academic Aptitude
College Entrance Examination Board **Scholastic** Aptitude Test
Preliminary Scholastic Aptitude Test
USE College Entrance Examination Board Scholastic Aptitude Test
School Accreditation
USE Educational Program Accreditation
School Achievement
USE Academic Achievement
School Adjustment
School Administration
USE Educational Administration
School Administrators
School and College Ability Test
USE Aptitude Measures
School Attendance
School Club Membership
School Counseling
School Counselors
School Dropouts
School Enrollment
School Environment
School Expulsion
School Facilities
School Federal Aid
USE Educational Financial Assistance
School Financial Assistance
USE Educational Financial Assistance
School Graduation
School Guidance *USE School Counseling*
School Integration
School Learning
School Leavers
School Libraries
School Nurses
School Organization
USE Educational Administration
School Phobia
School Principals
School Psychologists

School Psychology
School Readiness
School Refusal
School Retention
School Superintendents
School Suspension
School to Work Transition
School Transition
School Truancy
Elementary **School** Students
Elementary **School** Teachers
Freudian Psychoanalytic **School**
High School Equivalency *USE Adult Education*
High **School** Graduates
High **School** Personality Questionnaire
High **School** Students
High **School** Teachers
Intermediate **School** Students
Junior High **School** Students
Junior High **School** Teachers
Middle **School** Education
Middle **School** Students
NeoFreudian School *USE Neopsychoanalytic School*
Neopsychoanalytic **School**
Nursery **School** Students
Parent **School** Relationship
Parochial School Education
USE Private School Education
Primary **School** Students
Private **School** Education
Public **School** Education
Vocational **School** Students
Home **Schooling**
Schools
Alternative Schools *USE Nontraditional Education*
Boarding **Schools**
Elementary **Schools**
Graduate **Schools**
Grammar Schools *USE Elementary Schools*
High **Schools**
Institutional **Schools**
Junior High **Schools**
Magnet Schools *USE Nontraditional Education*
Military **Schools**
Nongraded **Schools**
Nursery **Schools**
Primary Schools *USE Elementary Schools*
Technical **Schools**
Vocational Schools *USE Technical Schools*
Sciatic Nerve *USE Spinal Nerves*
SCID *USE Structured Clinical Interview*
Science Achievement
Science Education
Sciences
Behavioral **Sciences**
Medical **Sciences**
Paramedical **Sciences**
Social **Sciences**
Scientific Communication
Scientific Methods
USE Experimental Methods
Scientists
Sclera *USE Eye (Anatomy)*
Sclerosis (Nervous System)
Multiple **Sclerosis**
Scopolamine
Scopolamine Hydrobromide
USE Scopolamine
Score Equating
Critical Scores *USE Cutting Scores*
Cutting **Scores**
Standard **Scores**
Test **Scores**
Z Scores *USE Standard Scores*
Scoring (Testing)

Scotopic Stimulation
Scratching
Screening
Screening Tests
Breast Cancer Screening *USE Cancer Screening*
Cancer Screening
Drug Usage Screening
Health Screening
Job Applicant Screening
Prostate Cancer Screening *USE Cancer Screening*
Psychological Screening Inventory
Skin Cancer Screening *USE Cancer Screening*
Scripts *USE Schema*
Sculpturing
Sea Gulls
Seals (Animal)
Job Search
Visual Search
Computer Searching
Online Searching *USE Computer Searching*
Seasonal Affective Disorder
Seasonal Variations
Seat Belts *USE Safety Belts*
Patient Seclusion
Secobarbital
Seconal *USE Secobarbital*
Second Language Education
USE Foreign Language Education
Second Order Conditioning
USE Higher Order Conditioning
English as Second Language
Secondary Education
Secondary Reinforcement
Secrecy
Secretarial Personnel
Secretarial Skills
USE Clerical Secretarial Skills
Clerical Secretarial Skills
Secretion (Gland)
Adrenal Gland Secretion
Endocrine Gland Secretion
Private Sector
Public Sector
Emotional Security
Job Security
Maximum Security Facilities
Social Security
Sedatives
Seduction
Seeing Eye Dogs *USE Mobility Aids*
Health Care Seeking Behavior
Help Seeking Behavior
Information Seeking
Novelty Seeking *USE Sensation Seeking*
Sensation Seeking
Sensation Seeking Scale
Treatment Seeking Behavior
USE Health Care Seeking Behavior
Seizures *USE Convulsions*
Audiogenic Seizures
Epileptic Seizures
Selection Tests
Animal Mate Selection
Employee Selection *USE Personnel Selection*
Habitat Selection *USE Territoriality*
Human Mate Selection
Job Selection *USE Occupational Choice*
Jury Selection
Mate Selection *USE Animal Mate Selection*
Mate Selection *USE Human Mate Selection*
Natural Selection
Patient Selection
Personnel Selection
Therapist Selection
Toy Selection

Selective Attention
Selective Breeding
Selective Mutism *USE Elective Mutism*
Self Acceptance *USE Self Perception*
Self Actualization
Self Analysis
Self Assessment *USE Self Evaluation*
Self Care Skills
Self Concept
Self Confidence
Self Congruence
Self Consciousness *USE Self Perception*
Self Control
Self Defeating Behavior
Self Defense
Self Destructive Behavior
Self Determination
Self Directed Learning
USE Individualized Instruction
Self Disclosure
Self Efficacy
Self Employment
Self Esteem
Self Evaluation
Self Examination (Medical)
Self Fulfilling Prophecies
Self Handicapping Strategy
Self Help Techniques
Self Hypnosis *USE Autohypnosis*
Self Image *USE Self Concept*
Self Inflicted Wounds
Self Instruction
USE Individualized Instruction
Self Instructional Training
Self Management
Self Managing Work Teams
Self Medication
Self Monitoring
Self Monitoring (Personality)
Self Mutilation
Self Observation *USE Self Monitoring*
Self Perception
Self Preservation
Self Psychology
Self Realization *USE Self Actualization*
Self Reference
Self Referral
Self Reinforcement
Self Report
Self Respect *USE Self Esteem*
Self Stimulation
Self Talk
Academic Self Concept
Brain Self Stimulation
Child Self Care
Ideal Self *USE Self Concept*
Intracranial Self Stimulation *USE Brain Self Stimulation*
Kupfer Detre Self Rating Scale
USE Nonprojective Personality Measures
Tennessee Self Concept Scale
Zungs Self Rating Depression Scale
Selfishness
Semantic Differential
Semantic Generalization
Semantic Memory
Semantic Priming
Semantics
Semicircular Canals
Seminarians
Seminaries
Semiotics
Senile Dementia
Senile Psychosis
Sensation *USE Perception*

359

Sensation Seeking
Sensation Seeking Scale
Pressure **Sensation**
Sense Organ Disorders
Sense Organs
Cutaneous **Sense**
Vomeronasal **Sense**
Sensitivity (Personality)
Sensitivity Training
Cultural **Sensitivity**
Drug **Sensitivity**
Ethnic Sensitivity *USE Cultural Sensitivity*
Spectral Sensitivity *USE Color Perception*
Sensitization Repression
        USE Repression Sensitization
Covert **Sensitization**
Protein Sensitization *USE Anaphylactic Shock*
Repression **Sensitization**
Repression **Sensitization** Scale
Sensorially Handicapped
        USE Sensory System Disorders
Sensorimotor Development
        USE Perceptual Motor Development
Sensorimotor Measures
Sensorimotor Processes
        USE Perceptual Motor Processes
Sensorineural Hearing Loss
        USE Hearing Disorders
Sensory Adaptation
Sensory Deprivation
Sensory Disabilities (Attitudes Toward)
Sensory Feedback
Sensory Gating
Sensory Integration
Sensory Neglect
Sensory Neurons
Sensory Pathways *USE Afferent Pathways*
Sensory Preconditioning
        USE Preconditioning
Sensory System Disorders
Sentence Completion Tests
Sentence Comprehension
Sentence Structure
Sentences
Rotter Incomplete **Sentences** Blank
Sentencing *USE Adjudication*
Separation Anxiety
Separation Individuation
Separation Reactions
Marital **Separation**
Septal Nuclei
Septum *USE Septal Nuclei*
Sequential Learning
Serial Anticipation (Learning)
Serial Learning
Serial Position Effect
Serial Recall
Time **Series**
Seriousness
Serotonin
Serotonin Agonists
Serotonin Antagonists
Serotonin Metabolites
Serotonin Precursors
Serotonin Reuptake Inhibitors
Serpasil *USE Reserpine*
Sertraline
Serum Albumin
Blood **Serum**
Civil Servants *USE Government Personnel*
Service Personnel
Service Quality *USE Quality of Services*
Domestic **Service** Personnel
Fee for **Service**
Health **Service** Needs

Health Service Utilization
        USE Health Care Utilization
Mental Health Service Needs *USE Health Service Needs*
Public Health **Service** Nurses
Technical **Service** Personnel
Volunteers in **Service** to America
Servicemen *USE Military Personnel*
Community Mental Health **Services**
Community Welfare **Services**
Community **Services**
Crisis Intervention **Services**
Emergency **Services**
Health Care **Services**
Hot Line **Services**
Information **Services**
Integrated **Services**
Interagency Services *USE Integrated Services*
Mental Health **Services**
Protective **Services**
Public Health **Services**
Public Welfare Services *USE Community Welfare Services*
Quality of **Services**
Social **Services**
Student Personnel **Services**
Welfare **Services** (Government)
Fuzzy **Set** Theory
Response **Set**
Goal **Setting**
Research **Setting**
Severe Mental Retardation
Severity (Disorders)
Sex
Sex Change
Sex Chromosome Disorders
Sex Chromosomes
Sex Differentiation Disorders
        USE Genital Disorders
Sex Discrimination
Sex Drive
Sex Education
Sex Hormones
Sex Linked Developmental Differences
Sex Linked Hereditary Disorders
Sex Offenses
Sex Recognition
Sex Role Attitudes
Sex Roles
Sex Therapy
Animal **Sex** Differences
Bem **Sex** Role Inventory
Human **Sex** Differences
Same Sex Environments
        USE Single Sex Environments
Single **Sex** Environments
Sterilization **(Sex)**
Sexism
Sexual Abstinence
Sexual Abuse
Sexual Addiction
Sexual Arousal
Sexual Attitudes
Sexual Behavior
        USE Psychosexual Behavior
Sexual Boundary Violations
        *USE Professional Client Sexual
                Relations*
Sexual Compulsivity *USE Sexual Addiction*
Sexual Delinquency *USE Promiscuity*
Sexual Development
Sexual Deviations *USE Paraphilias*
Sexual Fantasy
Sexual Fetishism *USE Fetishism*
Sexual Function Disturbances
Sexual Harassment
Sexual Intercourse (Human)

Sexual Masochism
Sexual Orientation
Sexual Reassignment *USE Sex Change*
Sexual Reproduction
Sexual Risk Taking
Sexual Sadism
Sexual Satisfaction
Animal Sexual Behavior
Animal Sexual Receptivity
Endocrine Sexual Disorders
Hypoactive Sexual Desire Disorder
    USE Inhibited Sexual Desire
Inhibited Sexual Desire
Patient Therapist Sexual Relations
    USE Professional Client Sexual
      Relations
Professional Client Sexual Relations
Therapist Patient Sexual Relations
    USE Professional Client Sexual
      Relations
Sexuality
Sexually Transmitted Diseases
    USE Venereal Diseases
Shamanism
Shame
Shape Perception
    USE Form and Shape Perception
Form and Shape Perception
Shared Paranoid Disorder
    USE Folie A Deux
Sharing (Social Behavior)
Needle Sharing
Myelin Sheath
Sheep
Sheltered Workshops
Shelters
Choice Shift
Extradimensional Shift Learning
    USE Nonreversal Shift Learning
Nonreversal Shift Learning
Reversal Shift Learning
Risky Shift *USE Choice Shift*
Population Shifts *USE Human Migration*
Workday Shifts
Shock
Shock Therapy
Shock Units
Anaphylactic Shock
Culture Shock
Electroconvulsive Shock
Electroconvulsive Shock Therapy
Insulin Shock Therapy
Shoplifting
Shopping
Shopping Centers
Short Term Memory
Short Term Potentiation
    USE Postactivation Potentials
Short Term Psychotherapy
    USE Brief Psychotherapy
Shoulder (Anatomy)
Shuttle Box Grids *USE Shuttle Boxes*
Shuttle Box Hurdles *USE Shuttle Boxes*
Shuttle Boxes
Shyness *USE Timidity*
Siamese Twins
Sibling Relations
Siblings
Sick Leave *USE Employee Leave Benefits*
Sickle Cell Disease
Motion Sickness
Side Effects (Drug)
Side Effects (Treatment)
Sight Vocabulary
Partially Sighted

Freud (Sigmund)
Sign Language
Sign Rank Test
    USE Wilcoxon Sign Rank Test
Sign Test
Wilcoxon Sign Rank Test
Signal Detection (Perception)
Signal Intensity *USE Stimulus Intensity*
Statistical Significance
Significant Others
Warning Signs *USE Warnings*
Silent Reading
Attitude Similarity
Stimulus Similarity
Simile *USE Figurative Language*
Simple Schizophrenia *USE Schizophrenia*
Herpes Simplex
Simulation
Simulation Games
Computer Simulation
Flight Simulation
Simulators *USE Simulation*
Sin
Sincerity
Singing
Single Cell Organisms
    USE Microorganisms
Single Fathers
Single Mothers
Single Parents
Single Persons
Single Sex Environments
Sisters
Sixteen Personality Factors Questionnaire
Size
Size Constancy
Size Discrimination
Apparent Size
Body Size
Brain Size
Effect Size (Statistical)
Family Size
Group Size
Litter Size
Sample Size
Skeletomuscular Disorders
    USE Musculoskeletal Disorders
Skewed Distribution
Skill Learning
Fine Motor Skill Learning
Gross Motor Skill Learning
Motor Skill Learning
    USE Perceptual Motor Learning
Skilled Industrial Workers
Skills *USE Ability*
Basic Skills Testing
    USE Minimum Competency Tests
Clerical Secretarial Skills
Communication Skills
Communication Skills Training
Employee Skills
Iowa Tests of Basic Skills
Motor Skills
Parenting Skills
Reading Skills
Secretarial Skills *USE Clerical Secretarial Skills*
Self Care Skills
Social Skills
Social Skills Training
Study Skills *USE Study Habits*
Writing Skills
Skin (Anatomy)
Skin Cancer Screening
    USE Cancer Screening
Skin Conduction *USE Skin Resistance*

Skin Disorders
Skin Electrical Properties
Skin Potential
Skin Resistance
Skin Temperature
Allergic **Skin** Disorders
Basal **Skin** Resistance
Galvanic **Skin** Response
Skinner (Burrhus Frederic)
Skinner Boxes
Skull
Slang
Sleep
Sleep Apnea
Sleep Deprivation
Sleep Disorders
Sleep Inducing Drugs *USE Hypnotic Drugs*
Sleep Onset
Sleep Talking
Sleep Treatment
Sleep Wake Cycle
Nonrapid Eye Movement Sleep *USE NREM Sleep*
NonREM Sleep *USE NREM Sleep*
NREM **Sleep**
Paradoxical Sleep *USE REM Sleep*
Paroxysmal Sleep *USE Narcolepsy*
Rapid Eye Movement Sleep *USE REM Sleep*
REM **Sleep**
Slow Wave Sleep *USE NREM Sleep*
Sleeplessness *USE Insomnia*
Sleepwalking
Slosson Intelligence Test
Slow Learners
    USE Borderline Mental Retardation
Slow Wave Sleep *USE NREM Sleep*
Slums *USE Poverty Areas*
Smell Perception *USE Olfactory Perception*
Smiles
Kolmogorov **Smirnov** Test
Smokeless Tobacco
Smoking Cessation
Cigarette Smoking *USE Tobacco Smoking*
Tobacco **Smoking**
Snails
Snake Phobia *USE Ophidiophobia*
Snakes
Glue **Sniffing**
Snuff *USE Smokeless Tobacco*
Sobriety
Soccer
Sociability
Social Acceptance
Social Adaptation *USE Social Adjustment*
Social Adjustment
Social Anxiety
Social Approval
Social Behavior
Social Casework
Social Caseworkers *USE Social Workers*
Social Change
Social Class
Social Class Attitudes
    USE Socioeconomic Class Attitudes
Social Cognition
Social Comparison
Social Control
Social Dating
Social Demonstrations
Social Density
Social Deprivation
Social Desirability
Social Development
    USE Psychosocial Development
Social Discrimination
Social Drinking

Social Environments
Social Equality
Social Facilitation
Social Groups
Social Identity
Social Immobility *USE Social Mobility*
Social Influences
Social Integration
Social Interaction
Social Isolation
Social Issues
Social Learning
Social Maladjustment
    USE Social Adjustment
Social Mobility
Social Movements
Social Networks
Social Norms
Social Perception
Social Phobia
Social Problems *USE Social Issues*
Social Processes
Social Programs
Social Psychiatry
Social Psychologists
Social Psychology
Social Reinforcement
Social Rejection *USE Social Acceptance*
Social Sciences
Social Security
Social Services
Social Skills
Social Skills Training
Social Stigma *USE Stigma*
Social Stress
Social Structure
Social Studies Education
Social Support Networks
Social Values
Social Work Education
Social Work *USE Social Casework*
Social Workers
Animal **Social** Behavior
Assistance **(Social** Behavior)
Clubs **(Social** Organizations)
Edwards **Social** Desirability Scale
Equity **(Social)**
Marlowe Crowne **Social** Desirability Scale
Psychiatric **Social** Workers
Sharing **(Social** Behavior)
Therapeutic **Social** Clubs
Trust **(Social** Behavior)
Vineland **Social** Maturity Scale
Socialism
Socialization
Political **Socialization**
Socially Disadvantaged
    USE Disadvantaged
Society
Sociobiology
Sociocultural Factors
Socioeconomic Class Attitudes
Socioeconomic Status
Family **Socioeconomic** Level
Socioenvironmental Therapy
    USE Milieu Therapy
Sociograms
Sociolinguistics
Sociologists
Sociology
Sociometric Tests
Sociometry
Sociopath *USE Antisocial Personality*
Sociopathology *USE Antisocial Behavior*
Sociotherapy

ROTATED ALPHABETICAL TERMS SECTION

Sodium
Sodium Ions
Sodium Lactate *USE Lactic Acid*
Sodium Pentobarbital *USE Pentobarbital*
Amobarbital Sodium *USE Amobarbital*
Diphenylhydantoin Sodium *USE Diphenylhydantoin*
Computer **Software**
Solvent Abuse *USE Inhalant Abuse*
Solvents
Anagram Problem **Solving**
Group Problem **Solving**
Individual Problem Solving *USE Problem Solving*
Problem **Solving**
Somatization
Somatization Disorder
Somatoform Disorders
Somatoform Pain Disorder
Atypical Somatoform Disorder
    USE Body Dysmorphic Disorder
Somatosensory Cortex
Somatosensory Disorders
Somatosensory Evoked Potentials
Somatostatin
Somatotropin
Somatotypes
Somesthetic Perception
Somesthetic Stimulation
Somnambulism *USE Sleepwalking*
Sonar
Songs *USE Music*
Sons
Sorority Membership
Goldstein Scheerer Object **Sort** Test
Q **Sort** Testing Technique
Wisconsin Card **Sorting** Test
Sound *USE Auditory Stimulation*
Sound Localization
    USE Auditory Localization
Sound Pressure Level *USE Loudness*
Sound Waves *USE Acoustics*
Sourness *USE Taste Perception*
Personal **Space**
Working **Space**
Spacecraft
Spaceflight
Attention **Span**
Digit **Span** Testing
Life Span *USE Life Expectancy*
Spanish Americans *USE Hispanics*
Spasms
Muscle **Spasms**
Spatial Ability
Spatial Discrimination
    USE Spatial Perception
Spatial Distortion
Spatial Frequency
Spatial Imagery
Spatial Learning
Spatial Memory
Spatial Neglect *USE Sensory Neglect*
Spatial Organization
Spatial Orientation (Perception)
Spatial Perception
Temporal Spatial Concept Scale
    USE Intelligence Measures
Visual Spatial Ability *USE Visuospatial Ability*
Visual Spatial Memory *USE Visuospatial Memory*
Automatic Speaker Recognition
    USE Automated Speech Recognition
Fear of Public Speaking *USE Speech Anxiety*
Public **Speaking**
Spearman Brown Test
Spearman Rho
    USE Rank Difference Correlation
Special Education

Special Education Students
Special Education Teachers
Special Needs
Information **Specialists**
Academic **Specialization**
Hemispheric Specialization *USE Lateral Dominance*
Professional **Specialization**
Species Differences
Species Recognition
Sports **Spectators**
Spectral Sensitivity *USE Color Perception*
Speech *USE Oral Communication*
Speech and Hearing Measures
Speech Anxiety
Speech Characteristics
Speech Development
Speech Disorders
Speech Handicapped
    USE Speech Disorders
Speech Measures
    USE Speech and Hearing Measures
Speech Pauses
Speech Perception
Speech Pitch
Speech Processing (Mechanical)
Speech Rate
Speech Rhythm
Speech Therapists
Speech Therapy
Accelerated Speech *USE Speech Rate*
Articulation **(Speech)**
Automated **Speech** Recognition
Compressed **Speech**
Delayed Speech
    USE Retarded Speech Development
Figures of Speech *USE Figurative Language*
Filtered **Speech**
Inner Speech *USE Self Talk*
Retarded **Speech** Development
Synthetic **Speech**
Speechreading *USE Lipreading*
Speed *USE Velocity*
Cognitive Processing **Speed**
Information Processing Speed *USE Cognitive Processing Speed*
Reading **Speed**
Response Speed *USE Reaction Time*
Spelling
Sperm
Sperm Donation *USE Tissue Donation*
Spider Phobia *USE Phobias*
Spiders *USE Arachnida*
Spina Bifida
Spinal Column
Spinal Cord
Spinal Cord Injuries
Spinal Fluid *USE Cerebrospinal Fluid*
Spinal Ganglia
Spinal Nerves
Cranial **Spinal** Cord
Lumbar **Spinal** Cord
Spinothalamic Tracts
Spiperone *USE Spiroperidol*
Spirit Possession
Spirituality
Spiroperidol
Spleen
Split Brain *USE Commissurotomy*
Split Personality
    USE Dissociative Identity Disorder
Spontaneous Abortion
Spontaneous Alternation
Spontaneous Recovery (Learning)
Spontaneous Remission
Sport Performance
    USE Athletic Performance

363

Sport Psychology
Sport Training *USE Athletic Training*
Sports
Sports Spectators
Spouse Abuse *USE Partner Abuse*
Spouses
Cervical Sprain Syndrome *USE Whiplash*
Spreading Depression
Chi **Square** Test
Least **Squares**
Squirrels
Emotional **Stability**
Hospital Staff *USE Medical Personnel*
Psychiatric Hospital **Staff**
Stage Plays *USE Theatre*
Developmental **Stages**
Prenatal Developmental **Stages**
Stalking
Stammering *USE Stuttering*
Competency to **Stand** Trial
Standard Deviation
Standard Error of Measurement
   USE Error of Measurement
Standard Scores
Test **Standardization**
Standardized Tests
Professional **Standards**
Stanford Achievement Test
Stanford Binet Intelligence Scale
Stanines *USE Standard Scores*
Stapedius Reflex *USE Acoustic Reflex*
Starfish *USE Echinodermata*
Head Start *USE Project Head Start*
Project Head **Start**
Startle Reflex
Starvation
State Board Examinations
   USE Professional Examinations
State Dependent Learning
State Hospitals *USE Psychiatric Hospitals*
State Trait Anxiety Inventory
Mini Mental **State** Examination
Borderline **States**
Consciousness **States**
Emotional **States**
Statistical Analysis
Statistical Correlation
Statistical Data
Statistical Estimation
Statistical Measurement
Statistical Norms
Statistical Power
Statistical Probability
Statistical Regression
Statistical Reliability
Statistical Rotation
Statistical Sample Parameters
Statistical Samples
Statistical Significance
Statistical Tables
Statistical Tests
Statistical Validity
Statistical Variables
Statistical Weighting
Diagnostic and **Statistical** Manual
Effect Size **(Statistical)**
Item Analysis **(Statistical)**
Nonparametric **Statistical** Tests
Parametric **Statistical** Tests
Statistics
Confidence Limits **(Statistics)**
Interaction Analysis **(Statistics)**
Population **(Statistics)**
Status
Employment **Status**

Functional Status *USE Ability Level*
Job Status *USE Occupational Status*
Marital **Status**
Occupational **Status**
Parenthood **Status**
Socioeconomic **Status**
Length of Stay *USE Treatment Duration*
Stealing *USE Theft*
Stelazine *USE Trifluoperazine*
Stellate Ganglion *USE Autonomic Ganglia*
Brain **Stem**
Twelve **Step** Programs
Stepchildren
Stepfamily
Stepparents
Stereopsis *USE Stereoscopic Vision*
Stereoscopic Presentation
Stereoscopic Vision
Stereotaxic Atlas
Stereotaxic Techniques
Stereotyped Attitudes
Stereotyped Behavior
Stereotyping *USE Stereotyped Attitudes*
Sterility
Sterilization (Sex)
Steroids
Adrenal Cortex Steroids *USE Corticosteroids*
Sticklebacks
Stigma
Social Stigma *USE Stigma*
Stimulants of CNS
   USE CNS Stimulating Drugs
CNS **Stimulating** Drugs
Follicle **Stimulating** Hormone
Melanocyte **Stimulating** Hormone
Respiration **Stimulating** Drugs
Thyroid Stimulating Hormone *USE Thyrotropin*
Stimulation
Afferent **Stimulation**
Auditory **Stimulation**
Aversive **Stimulation**
Brain Self **Stimulation**
Brain **Stimulation**
Chemical Brain **Stimulation**
Dichoptic **Stimulation**
Dichotic **Stimulation**
Electrical Brain **Stimulation**
Electrical **Stimulation**
Intracranial Self Stimulation *USE Brain Self Stimulation*
Olfactory **Stimulation**
Perceptual **Stimulation**
Photopic **Stimulation**
Prismatic **Stimulation**
Restricted Environmental Stimulation *USE Stimulus Deprivation*
Scotopic **Stimulation**
Self **Stimulation**
Somesthetic **Stimulation**
Subliminal **Stimulation**
Tactual **Stimulation**
Taste **Stimulation**
Vestibular Stimulation *USE Somesthetic Stimulation*
Visual **Stimulation**
Stimulators (Apparatus)
Acoustic Stimuli *USE Auditory Stimulation*
Novel Stimuli *USE Stimulus Novelty*
Pictorial **Stimuli**
Verbal **Stimuli**
Stimulus Ambiguity
Stimulus Attenuation
Stimulus Change
Stimulus Complexity
Stimulus Control
Stimulus Deprivation
Stimulus Discrimination
Stimulus Duration

Stimulus Frequency
Stimulus Generalization
Stimulus Intensity
Stimulus Intervals
Stimulus Novelty
Stimulus Offset
Stimulus Onset
Stimulus Parameters
Stimulus Pattern *USE Stimulus Variability*
Stimulus Presentation Methods
Stimulus Salience
Stimulus Similarity
Stimulus Variability
Conditioned **Stimulus**
Discriminative Stimulus *USE Conditioned Stimulus*
Unconditioned **Stimulus**
Stipends
　　USE Educational Financial Assistance
Stochastic Modeling
Stomach
Automated Information **Storage**
Human Information **Storage**
Retail Stores *USE Retailing*
Storytelling
Storytelling Technique
　　USE Mutual Storytelling Technique
Mutual **Storytelling** Technique
Strabismus
Animal **Strain** Differences
Role Strain *USE Role Conflicts*
Stranger Reactions
Fear of Strangers *USE Stranger Reactions*
Strategies
Learning **Strategies**
Self Handicapping **Strategy**
Physical **Strength**
Stress
Stress Management
Stress Reactions
Environmental **Stress**
Occupational **Stress**
Physiological **Stress**
Posttraumatic **Stress** Disorder
Psychological **Stress**
Social **Stress**
Striate Cortex *USE Visual Cortex*
Corpus Striatum *USE Basal Ganglia*
Strikes
Film **Strips**
Stroboscopic Movement
　　USE Apparent Movement
Strong Vocational Interest Blank
Stroop Color Word Test
Stroop Effect
Structural Equation Modeling
Structuralism
Factor **Structure**
Family **Structure**
Group **Structure**
Household Structure *USE Living Arrangements*
Kinship **Structure**
Organizational **Structure**
Sentence **Structure**
Social **Structure**
Text **Structure**
Structured Clinical Interview
Structured Overview
　　USE Advance Organizers
Strychnine
Student Activism
Student Adjustment
　　USE School Adjustment
Student Admission Criteria
Student Attitudes
Student Attrition

Student Characteristics
Student Personnel Services
Student Protest *USE Student Activism*
Student Records
Student Teachers
Student Teaching
Teacher **Student** Interaction
Students
Students T Test *USE T Test*
Business **Students**
College **Students**
Community College **Students**
Dental **Students**
Education **Students**
Elementary School **Students**
Foreign **Students**
Graduate **Students**
High School **Students**
Intermediate School **Students**
Junior College **Students**
Junior High School **Students**
Kindergarten **Students**
Law **Students**
Medical **Students**
Middle School **Students**
Nursery School **Students**
Nursing **Students**
Postgraduate **Students**
Preschool **Students**
Primary School **Students**
Reentry **Students**
ROTC **Students**
Special Education **Students**
Transfer **Students**
Vocational School **Students**
Followup **Studies**
Longitudinal **Studies**
Prospective **Studies**
Retrospective **Studies**
Social **Studies** Education
Study Habits
Study Skills *USE Study Habits*
Allport Vernon Lindzey Study Values *USE Attitude Measures*
Foreign **Study**
Independent Study *USE Individualized Instruction*
Rosenzweig Picture Frustration **Study**
Work Study Programs
　　USE Educational Programs
Stuttering
Cognitive **Style**
Leadership **Style**
Learning Style *USE Cognitive Style*
Perceptual **Style**
Subconscious
Subcortical Lesions *USE Brain Lesions*
Subculture (Anthropological)
Subcutaneous Injections
Subjectivity
Experimental **Subjects**
Research Subjects *USE Experimental Subjects*
Within Subjects Design *USE Repeated Measures*
Sublimation
Subliminal Perception
Subliminal Stimulation
Submarines
Submissiveness *USE Obedience*
Submucous Plexus
　　USE Autonomic Ganglia
Substance Abuse Prevention
　　USE Drug Abuse Prevention
Substance Abuse *USE Drug Abuse*
Substance P
Substantia Nigra
Subtests
Suburban Environments

Subvocalization
Success *USE Achievement*
Fear of **Success**
Occupational **Success**
Occupational **Success** Prediction
Successive Contrast *USE Afterimage*
Succinylcholine
Sucking
Sudden Infant Death
Suffering
Suffocation *USE Anoxia*
Blood **Sugar**
Sugars
Suggestibility
Posthypnotic **Suggestions**
Suicidal Ideation
Suicide
Suicide Prevention
Suicide Prevention Centers
Assisted **Suicide**
Attempted **Suicide**
Amphetamine Sulfate *USE Amphetamine*
Codeine Sulfate *USE Codeine*
Sulpiride
Non Zero **Sum** Games
Summer Camps (Recreation)
Superego
School **Superintendents**
Superior Colliculus
Emotional **Superiority**
Superstitions
Supervising Teachers
    USE Cooperating Teachers
Clinical Supervision *USE Professional Supervision*
Educational Supervision *USE Professional Supervision*
Practicum **Supervision**
Professional **Supervision**
Supervisor Employee Interaction
Employee Supervisor Interaction
    USE Supervisor Employee Interaction
Supervisors *USE Management Personnel*
Dietary **Supplements**
Nutritional Supplements *USE Dietary Supplements*
Medical Personnel **Supply**
Mental Health Personnel **Supply**
Personnel **Supply**
Support Groups
Child **Support**
Decision **Support** Systems
Social **Support** Networks
Supported Employment
Supportive Psychotherapy
Suppression (Defense Mechanism)
Conditioned **Suppression**
Dexamethasone **Suppression** Test
Progressive **Supranuclear** Palsy
Surgeons
Surgery
Cardiac Surgery *USE Heart Surgery*
Dental **Surgery**
Endocrine Gland **Surgery**
Heart **Surgery**
Pituitary Gland Surgery *USE Hypophysectomy*
Plastic **Surgery**
Surgical Complications
    USE Postsurgical Complications
Surgical Patients
Surrogate Parents (Humans)
Fear **Survey** Schedule
Guilford Zimmerman Temperament **Survey**
Kuder Occupational Interest **Survey**
Opinion Attitude and Interest Survey *USE Attitude Measures*
Purdue Perceptual Motor **Survey**
Surveys
Consumer **Surveys**

Mail **Surveys**
Opinion Surveys *USE Attitude Measures*
Telephone **Surveys**
Survival Instinct *USE Self Preservation*
Survivors
Holocaust **Survivors**
Susceptibility (Disorders)
Hypnotic **Susceptibility**
School **Suspension**
Suspicion
Sustained Attention
Life **Sustaining** Treatment
Swallowing
Mate Swapping *USE Extramarital Intercourse*
Body **Sway** Testing
Sweat
Sweating
Sweetness *USE Taste Perception*
Swimming
Code **Switching**
Nonsense **Syllable** Learning
Syllables
Syllogistic Reasoning
    USE Inductive Deductive Reasoning
Biological **Symbiosis**
Symbiotic Infantile Psychosis
Symbolic Interactionism
Symbolism
Sympathectomy
Sympathetic Nervous System
Sympatholytic Drugs
Sympathomimetic Amines
Sympathomimetic Drugs
Sympathy
Symptom Checklists
Symptom Prescription
    USE Paradoxical Techniques
Symptom Remission
Symptoms
Extrapyramidal **Symptoms**
Negative and Positive Symptoms
    USE Positive and Negative Symptoms
Positive and Negative **Symptoms**
Psychiatric **Symptoms**
Psychotic Symptoms *USE Psychiatric Symptoms*
Synapses
Syncope
Acquired Immune Deficiency **Syndrome**
Aspergers **Syndrome**
Battered Child **Syndrome**
Capgras **Syndrome**
Cervical Sprain Syndrome *USE Whiplash*
Chronic Fatigue **Syndrome**
Creutzfeldt Jakob **Syndrome**
Cri du Chat Syndrome *USE Crying Cat Syndrome*
Crying Cat **Syndrome**
Cushings **Syndrome**
Downs **Syndrome**
Fetal Alcohol **Syndrome**
Fibromyalgia Syndrome *USE Muscular Disorders*
Fragile X **Syndrome**
Ganser Syndrome *USE Factitious Disorders*
Hospital Addiction Syndrome *USE Munchausen Syndrome*
Irritable Bowel **Syndrome**
Kleine Levin **Syndrome**
Klinefelters **Syndrome**
Munchausen **Syndrome**
Munchausen **Syndrome** by Proxy
Neuroleptic Malignant **Syndrome**
Prader Willi **Syndrome**
Premenstrual Syndrome *USE Premenstrual Tension*
Rett **Syndrome**
Temporomandibular Joint Syndrome *USE Musculoskeletal Disorders*
Testicular Feminization **Syndrome**

Tourette Syndrome
    USE Gilles de la Tourette Disorder
Turners **Syndrome**
Wernickes **Syndrome**
Syndromes
Organic Brain **Syndromes**
Drug Synergism *USE Drug Interactions*
Lunar **Synodic** Cycle
Synonyms
Syntax
Synthetic Speech
Syphilis
Autonomic Nervous **System**
Autonomic Nervous **System** Disorders
Cardiovascular **System**
Caste **System**
Central Nervous **System**
Central Nervous **System** Disorders
Central Nervous System Drugs *USE CNS Affecting Drugs*
Digestive **System**
Digestive **System** Disorders
Endocrine **System**
Gastrointestinal **System**
Hypothalamo Hypophyseal **System**
Hypothalamo Pituitary Adrenal **System**
Lemniscal **System**
Limbic **System**
Musculoskeletal **System**
Nervous **System**
Nervous **System** Disorders
Nervous **System** Neoplasms
Nervous System Plasticity *USE Neural Plasticity*
Parasympathetic Nervous **System**
Peripheral Nervous **System**
Respiratory **System**
Sclerosis (Nervous **System)**
Sensory **System** Disorders
Sympathetic Nervous **System**
Urogenital **System**
Systematic Desensitization Therapy
Systems
Systems Analysis
Systems Theory
Anatomical **Systems**
Classification Systems *USE Taxonomies*
Communication **Systems**
Decision Support **Systems**
Expert **Systems**
Human Machine **Systems**
Human Machine **Systems** Design
Information **Systems**
Knowledge Based Systems *USE Expert Systems*
Man Machine Systems *USE Human Machine Systems*
Man Machine Systems Design
    USE Human Machine Systems Design
Management Information Systems *USE Information Systems*
Number **Systems**
Political Economic **Systems**
Telephone **Systems**
Systolic Pressure
Szondi Test
T Groups *USE Human Relations Training*
T Mazes
T Test
Students T Test *USE T Test*
Statistical **Tables**
Taboos
Tachistoscopes
Tachistoscopic Presentation
Tachycardia
Tactual Discrimination
    USE Tactual Perception
Tactual Displays
Tactual Maps *USE Mobility Aids*
Tactual Perception

Tactual Stimulation
Tailored Testing *USE Adaptive Testing*
Note **Taking**
Perspective Taking *USE Role Taking*
Risk **Taking**
Role **Taking**
Sexual Risk **Taking**
Test **Taking**
Talent *USE Ability*
Talented *USE Gifted*
Fairy Tales *USE Folklore*
Self **Talk**
Sleep **Talking**
Tantrums
Tape Recorders
Finger **Tapping**
Tardive Dyskinesia
Task Analysis
Task Complexity
Task Difficulty *USE Task Complexity*
Time On **Task**
Piagetian **Tasks**
Taste Aversion Conditioning
    USE Aversion Conditioning
Taste Buds
Taste Discrimination *USE Taste Perception*
Taste Disorders
Taste Perception
Taste Stimulation
Tattoos *USE Cosmetic Techniques*
Taurine
Taxation
Taxonomies
Tay Sachs Disease
    USE Amaurotic Familial Idiocy
Taylor Manifest Anxiety Scale
Tea *USE Beverages (Nonalcoholic)*
Teacher Accreditation
    USE Accreditation (Education Personnel)
Teacher Aides
Teacher Attitudes
Teacher Characteristics
Teacher Education
Teacher Effectiveness Evaluation
Teacher Effectiveness
    USE Teacher Characteristics
Teacher Expectations
Teacher Personality
Teacher Recruitment
Teacher Student Interaction
Teacher Tenure
Teacher Training *USE Teacher Education*
Inservice **Teacher** Education
Minnesota Teacher Attitude Inventory
    USE Attitude Measures
Teachers
Classroom Teachers *USE Teachers*
College **Teachers**
Cooperating **Teachers**
Elementary School **Teachers**
High School **Teachers**
Junior High School **Teachers**
Preschool **Teachers**
Preservice **Teachers**
Resource **Teachers**
Special Education **Teachers**
Student **Teachers**
Supervising Teachers *USE Cooperating Teachers*
Technical Education Teachers
    USE Vocational Education Teachers
Vocational Education **Teachers**
Teaching
Teaching Internship *USE Student Teaching*
Teaching Machines

Teaching Methods
Discovery **Teaching** Method
Initial **Teaching** Alphabet
Student **Teaching**
Team **Teaching** Method
Team Teaching Method
Teams
Self Managing Work **Teams**
Work **Teams**
Technical Education Teachers
    USE Vocational Education Teachers
Technical Personnel
Technical Schools
Technical Service Personnel
Holtzman Inkblot **Technique**
Mutual Storytelling **Technique**
Projective Testing **Technique**
Q Sort Testing **Technique**
Storytelling Technique
    USE Mutual Storytelling Technique
Cognitive **Techniques**
Cosmetic **Techniques**
Paradigmatic Techniques *USE Paradoxical Techniques*
Paradoxical **Techniques**
Personal Growth Techniques
    USE Human Potential Movement
Projective **Techniques**
Psychotherapeutic **Techniques**
Self Help **Techniques**
Stereotaxic **Techniques**
Technology
Nuclear **Technology**
Reproductive **Technology**
Teenage Fathers *USE Adolescent Fathers*
Teenage Mothers *USE Adolescent Mothers*
Teenage Pregnancy
    USE Adolescent Pregnancy
Teeth (Anatomy)
Teeth Grinding *USE Bruxism*
Nocturnal **Teeth** Grinding
Ventral Tegmental Area *USE Tegmentum*
Tegmentum
Telecommunications Media
Teleconferencing
Telekinesis *USE Psychokinesis*
Telemetry
Telencephalon
Telepathy
Telephone Hot Lines
    USE Hot Line Services
Telephone Surveys
Telephone Systems
Televised Instruction
Television
Television Advertising
Television Viewing
Closed Circuit **Television**
Educational **Television**
Temperament *USE Personality*
Guilford Zimmerman **Temperament** Survey
Temperature Effects
Temperature Perception
Body **Temperature**
Skin **Temperature**
Tempo
Conceptual **Tempo**
Temporal Frequency
Temporal Lobe
Temporal Spatial Concept Scale
    USE Intelligence Measures
Temporomandibular Joint Syndrome
    USE Musculoskeletal Disorders
Temptation
Central **Tendency** Measures
Achilles **Tendon** Reflex

Tendons
Tennessee Self Concept Scale
Tennis
Tension Headache
    USE Muscle Contraction Headache
Premenstrual **Tension**
Occupational **Tenure**
Teacher **Tenure**
Teratogens
Long **Term** Care
Long **Term** Memory
Long Term Potentiation
    USE Postactivation Potentials
Short **Term** Memory
Short Term Potentiation
    USE Postactivation Potentials
Short Term Psychotherapy
    USE Brief Psychotherapy
Terminal Cancer
Terminally Ill Patients
Video Display Terminals *USE Video Display Units*
Employee Termination *USE Personnel Termination*
Personnel **Termination**
Relationship **Termination**
Treatment **Termination**
Terminology
Psychological **Terminology**
Territoriality
Terrorism
Night Terrors *USE Sleep Disorders*
Test Administration
Test Anxiety
Test Bias
Test Coaching
Test Construction
Test Difficulty *USE Difficulty Level (Test)*
Test Equating *USE Score Equating*
Test Forms
Test Interpretation
Test Items
Test Normalization
    USE Test Standardization
Test Norms
Test Reliability
Test Scores
Test Standardization
Test Taking
Test Tube Babies
    USE Reproductive Technology
Test Validity
Army General Classification **Test**
Bender Gestalt **Test**
Benton Revised Visual Retention **Test**
Blacky Pictures Test *USE Projective Personality Measures*
California **Test** of Mental Maturity
California **Test** of Personality
Cattell Culture Fair Intelligence Test *USE Culture Fair Intelligence Test*
Chi Square **Test**
Childrens Apperception **Test**
Cochran Q **Test**
Col Ent Exam Bd Scholastic Apt **Test**
Color Pyramid Test *USE Projective Personality Measures*
Content Analysis **(Test)**
Cultural **Test** Bias
Culture Fair Intelligence **Test**
Dexamethasone Suppression **Test**
Difficulty Level **(Test)**
Draw A Man Test *USE Human Figures Drawing*
F **Test**
Franck Drawing Completion **Test**
Frostig Developmental **Test** of Visual Perception
Gates Reading Test *USE Gates MacGinitie Reading Tests*
General Aptitude **Test** Battery
Goldstein Scheerer Object Sort **Test**
Goodenough Harris Draw A Person **Test**

Hidden Figures **Test**
Illinois **Test** of Psycholinguistic Abilities
Incomplete Man **Test**
Item Analysis **(Test)**
Item Content **(Test)**
Kohs Block Design **Test**
Kolmogorov Smirnov **Test**
Lorge Thorndike Intelligence **Test**
Lowenfeld Mosaic **Test**
Mann Whitney U **Test**
Matching Test *USE Matching to Sample*
Memory for Designs **Test**
Miller Analogies **Test**
Modern Language Aptitude **Test**
Onomatopoeia and Images Test *USE Projective Personality Measures*
Peabody Picture Vocabulary **Test**
Porteus Maze **Test**
Preliminary Scholastic Aptitude Test *USE College Entrance Examination Board Scholastic Aptitude Test*
Q Test *USE Cochran Q Test*
Remote Associates **Test**
Rod and Frame **Test**
Rorschach **Test**
Scholastic Aptitude Test *USE College Entrance Examination Board Scholastic Aptitude Test*
School and College Ability Test *USE Aptitude Measures*
Sign Rank Test *USE Wilcoxon Sign Rank Test*
Sign **Test**
Slosson Intelligence **Test**
Spearman Brown **Test**
Stanford Achievement **Test**
Stroop Color Word **Test**
Students T Test *USE T Test*
Szondi **Test**
T **Test**
Thematic Apperception **Test**
Vane Kindergarten Test *USE Intelligence Measures*
Welsh Figure Preference **Test**
Wepman Auditory Discrimination **Test**
Wide Range Achievement **Test**
Wilcoxon Sign Rank **Test**
Wisconsin Card Sorting **Test**
Zulliger Z **Test**
Testes
Testes Disorders
USE Endocrine Sexual Disorders
Testicular Feminization Syndrome
Expert **Testimony**
Legal **Testimony**
Testing
Testing Methods
Adaptive **Testing**
AIDS Testing *USE HIV Testing*
Basic Skills Testing *USE Minimum Competency Tests*
Body Sway **Testing**
Cloze **Testing**
Cognitive Hypothesis **Testing**
Computer Assisted **Testing**
Digit Span **Testing**
Drug Testing *USE Drug Usage Screening*
Embedded Figures **Testing**
Essay **Testing**
Forced Choice **(Testing** Method)
Group **Testing**
HIV **Testing**
Hypothesis **Testing**
Individual **Testing**
Multiple Choice **(Testing** Method)
Null Hypothesis **Testing**
Projective Testing Technique
Psychological Testing *USE Psychometrics*
Q Sort **Testing** Technique
Reality **Testing**
Scaling **(Testing)**
Scoring **(Testing)**

Tailored Testing *USE Adaptive Testing*
Testosterone
Tests *USE Measurement*
Ability Tests *USE Aptitude Measures*
Comprehension **Tests**
Criterion Referenced **Tests**
Differential Aptitude **Tests**
Employment **Tests**
Gates MacGinitie Reading **Tests**
Gates Reading Readiness Tests *USE Gates MacGinitie Reading Tests*
Henmon Nelson Tests of Mental Ability
USE Intelligence Measures
Iowa **Tests** of Basic Skills
Mastery Tests *USE Criterion Referenced Tests*
Metropolitan Readiness **Tests**
Minimum Competency **Tests**
Nonparametric Statistical **Tests**
Objective Referenced Tests *USE Criterion Referenced Tests*
Parametric Statistical **Tests**
Performance **Tests**
Personality Tests *USE Personality Measures*
Projective Tests *USE Projective Techniques*
Screening **Tests**
Selection **Tests**
Sentence Completion **Tests**
Sociometric **Tests**
Standardized **Tests**
Statistical **Tests**
True False Tests *USE Forced Choice (Testing Method)*
Verbal **Tests**
Testwiseness
Tetrabenazine
Tetrachoric Correlation
Tetrahydrocannabinol
Text Structure
Textbooks
Programmed **Textbooks**
Texture Perception
Thalamic Nuclei
Thalamotomy
Thalamus
Geniculate Bodies **(Thalamus)**
Thalidomide
Thanatology *USE Death Education*
Thanatos *USE Death Instinct*
Theatre
Theft
Thematic Apperception Test
Theology *USE Religion*
Theophylline
Bayes Theorem *USE Statistical Probability*
Theoretical Interpretation
Theoretical Orientation
Theories
Theories of Education
Psychological **Theories**
Theory Formulation
Theory of Evolution
Theory of Mind
Theory Verification
Chaos **Theory**
Communication **Theory**
Educational Theory *USE Theories of Education*
Fairbairnian Theory *USE Object Relations*
Fuzzy Set **Theory**
Game **Theory**
Information **Theory**
Item Response **Theory**
Latent Trait Theory *USE Item Response Theory*
Learning **Theory**
Personal Construct Theory *USE Personality Theory*
Personality **Theory**
Psychoanalytic **Theory**
Systems **Theory**
Winnicottian Theory *USE Object Relations*

Therapeutic Abortion
    USE Induced Abortion
Therapeutic Alliance
Therapeutic Camps
Therapeutic Community
Therapeutic Environment
Therapeutic Outcomes
    USE Treatment Outcomes
Therapeutic Processes
Therapeutic Social Clubs
Medical **Therapeutic** Devices
Negative **Therapeutic** Reaction
Organic Therapies
    USE Physical Treatment Methods
Therapist Attitudes
Therapist Characteristics
Therapist Effectiveness
    USE Therapist Characteristics
Therapist Experience
    USE Therapist Characteristics
Therapist Patient Interaction
    USE Psychotherapeutic Processes
Therapist Patient Sexual Relations
    USE Professional Client Sexual
      Relations
Therapist Personality
    USE Therapist Characteristics
Therapist Role
Therapist Selection
Therapist Trainees
Patient Therapist Interaction
    USE Psychotherapeutic Processes
Patient Therapist Sexual Relations
    USE Professional Client Sexual
      Relations
Therapists
Occupational **Therapists**
Physical **Therapists**
Speech **Therapists**
Therapy *USE Treatment*
Activity Therapy *USE Recreation Therapy*
Animal Assisted **Therapy**
Art **Therapy**
Aversion **Therapy**
Behavior **Therapy**
Bright Light Therapy *USE Phototherapy*
Client Centered **Therapy**
Cognitive Behavior Therapy *USE Cognitive Therapy*
Cognitive **Therapy**
Conjoint **Therapy**
Cooperative Therapy *USE Cotherapy*
Couples **Therapy**
Creative Arts **Therapy**
Dance **Therapy**
Directed Reverie Therapy *USE Guided Imagery*
Drug **Therapy**
ECS Therapy
    USE Electroconvulsive Shock Therapy
Educational **Therapy**
Electroconvulsive Shock **Therapy**
Electroshock Therapy
    USE Electroconvulsive Shock Therapy
Encounter Group **Therapy**
Environmental Therapy *USE Milieu Therapy*
Estrogen Replacement Therapy *USE Hormone Therapy*
Existential **Therapy**
Exposure **Therapy**
Eye Movement Desensitization **Therapy**
Family **Therapy**
Feminist **Therapy**
Flooding Therapy *USE Implosive Therapy*
Gestalt **Therapy**
Group Therapy *USE Group Psychotherapy*
Gymnastic Therapy *USE Recreation Therapy*
Hormone **Therapy**

Illumination Therapy *USE Phototherapy*
Implosive **Therapy**
Individual Therapy *USE Individual Psychotherapy*
Insight **Therapy**
Insulin Shock **Therapy**
Maintenance **Therapy**
Marathon Group **Therapy**
Marital Therapy *USE Marriage Counseling*
Marriage Therapy *USE Marriage Counseling*
Milieu **Therapy**
Morita **Therapy**
Movement **Therapy**
Multiple Therapy *USE Cotherapy*
Muscle Relaxation Therapy *USE Relaxation Therapy*
Music **Therapy**
Nondirective Therapy *USE Client Centered Therapy*
Occupational **Therapy**
Personal **Therapy**
Persuasion **Therapy**
Pet Therapy *USE Animal Assisted Therapy*
Physical **Therapy**
Play **Therapy**
Poetry **Therapy**
Primal **Therapy**
Progressive Relaxation **Therapy**
Psychoanalytic Therapy *USE Psychoanalysis*
Radiation **Therapy**
Rational Emotive **Therapy**
Reality **Therapy**
Reciprocal Inhibition **Therapy**
Recreation **Therapy**
Relationship **Therapy**
Relaxation **Therapy**
Rogerian Therapy *USE Client Centered Therapy*
Sex **Therapy**
Shock **Therapy**
Socioenvironmental Therapy *USE Milieu Therapy*
Speech **Therapy**
Systematic Desensitization **Therapy**
Triadic Therapy *USE Conjoint Therapy*
Vitamin **Therapy**
X Ray Therapy *USE Radiation Therapy*
Thermal Acclimatization
Thermal Factors *USE Temperature Effects*
Thermoreceptors
Thermoregulation (Body)
Theta Rhythm
Thigh
Thinking
Autistic **Thinking**
Convergent Thinking
    USE Inductive Deductive Reasoning
Divergent **Thinking**
Logical **Thinking**
Magical **Thinking**
Thiopental
Thioridazine
Thiothixene
Third World Countries
    USE Developing Countries
Thirst
Thoracic Nerves *USE Spinal Nerves*
Thorax
Thorazine *USE Chlorpromazine*
Lorge **Thorndike** Intelligence Test
Thought Content *USE Cognitions*
Thought Control *USE Brainwashing*
Thought Disturbances
Fantasies **(Thought** Disturbances)
Threat
Threat Postures
Threshold Determination
Critical Flicker Fusion **Threshold**
Luminance Threshold *USE Brightness Perception*
Luminance Threshold *USE Visual Thresholds*

Photic Threshold *USE Illumination*
Photic Threshold *USE Visual Thresholds*
Thresholds
Auditory **Thresholds**
Olfactory **Thresholds**
Pain **Thresholds**
Vibrotactile **Thresholds**
Visual **Thresholds**
Failure to **Thrive**
Thromboses
Coronary **Thromboses**
Project Follow **Through**
Thumb
Thumbsucking
Thymoleptic Drugs
    USE Tranquilizing Drugs
Thyroid Disorders
Thyroid Extract *USE Thyroid Hormones*
Thyroid Gland
Thyroid Hormones
Thyroid Stimulating Hormone
    USE Thyrotropin
Thyroidectomy
Thyrotoxicosis
Thyrotropic Hormone *USE Thyrotropin*
Thyrotropin
Thyroxine
Tic Douloureux *USE Trigeminal Neuralgia*
Tics
Tigers *USE Felids*
Time
Time Disorientation
Time Estimation
Time Limited Psychotherapy
    USE Brief Psychotherapy
Time Management
Time On Task
Time Out
Time Perception
Time Perspective
Time Series
Constant **Time** Delay
Interresponse **Time**
Leisure **Time**
Reaction **Time**
Response Time *USE Reaction Time*
Timers (Apparatus)
Timidity
Tinnitus
Tiredness *USE Fatigue*
Tissue Donation
Connective **Tissue** Cells
Tissues (Body)
Connective **Tissues**
Nerve **Tissues**
Toads
Tobacco Smoking
Chewing Tobacco *USE Smokeless Tobacco*
Smokeless **Tobacco**
Tofranil *USE Imipramine*
Toilet Training
Token Economy Programs
Token Reinforcement
    USE Secondary Reinforcement
Tolerance
Tolerance for Ambiguity
Drug **Tolerance**
Toluene
Tomography
Positron Emission Tomography *USE Tomography*
Muscle **Tone**
Tongue
Tonic Immobility
Tool Use
Animal Tool Use *USE Tool Use*

Top Level Managers
Topography
Torticollis
Tortoises *USE Turtles*
Torture
Totalitarianism
Touch *USE Tactual Perception*
Touching *USE Physical Contact*
Tourette Syndrome
    USE Gilles de la Tourette Disorder
Gilles de la **Tourette** Disorder
Aged (Attitudes **Toward)**
Aging (Attitudes **Toward)**
AIDS (Attitudes **Toward)**
Disabled (Attitudes **Toward)**
Homosexuality (Attitudes **Toward)**
Mental Illness (Attitudes **Toward)**
Mental Retardation (Attitudes **Toward)**
Obesity (Attitudes **Toward)**
Physical Disabilities (Attitudes **Toward)**
Physical Illness (Attitudes **Toward)**
Sensory Disabilities (Attitudes **Toward)**
Work (Attitudes **Toward)**
Towns
Toxic Disorders
Toxic Encephalopathies
Toxic Hepatitis
Toxic Psychoses
Toxic Waste *USE Hazardous Materials*
Toxicity
Toxicomania
Toxins *USE Poisons*
Toy Selection
Toys
Educational **Toys**
Memory **Trace**
Trachea
Tracking
Visual **Tracking**
Optic **Tract**
Respiratory **Tract** Disorders
Tractotomy
Extrapyramidal **Tracts**
Pyramidal **Tracts**
Spinothalamic **Tracts**
Traditionalism *USE Conservatism*
Air **Traffic** Accidents
Air **Traffic** Control
Motor **Traffic** Accidents
Trainable Mentally Retarded
    USE Moderate Mental Retardation
Counselor **Trainees**
Psychotherapist Trainees *USE Therapist Trainees*
Therapist **Trainees**
Training *USE Education*
Assertiveness **Training**
Athletic **Training**
Autogenic **Training**
Biofeedback **Training**
Childbirth **Training**
Clinical Methods **Training**
Clinical Psychology Graduate **Training**
Communication Skills **Training**
Community Mental Health **Training**
Computer **Training**
Human Relations **Training**
Inservice **Training**
Job Training *USE Personnel Training*
Management **Training**
Memory **Training**
Mental Health Inservice **Training**
Military **Training**
Motivation **Training**
Omission **Training**
On the Job **Training**

Parent Effectiveness Training *USE Parent Training*
Parent **Training**
Personnel **Training**
Postgraduate **Training**
Psychiatric **Training**
Psychoanalytic **Training**
Psychotherapy **Training**
Self Instructional **Training**
Sensitivity **Training**
Social Skills **Training**
Sport Training *USE Athletic Training*
Teacher Training *USE Teacher Education*
Toilet **Training**
Work Adjustment **Training**
Railroad **Trains**
Latent Trait Theory *USE Item Response Theory*
State **Trait** Anxiety Inventory
Personality **Traits**
Major Tranquilizers *USE Neuroleptic Drugs*
Minor **Tranquilizers**
Tranquilizing Drugs
Transactional Analysis
Transaminases
Transcultural Psychiatry
Transducers
Transfer (Learning)
Transfer Students
Client **Transfer**
Interhemispheric Transfer *USE Interhemispheric Interaction*
Interocular **Transfer**
Negative **Transfer**
Patient Transfer *USE Client Transfer*
Positive **Transfer**
Transferases
Psychotherapeutic **Transference**
Transformational Generative Grammar
Blood **Transfusion**
Transgendered *USE Transsexualism*
Transgenerational Patterns
School to Work **Transition**
School **Transition**
Transitional Objects
Career Transitions *USE Career Development*
Foreign Language **Translation**
Translocation (Chromosome)
Intergenerational Transmission
    USE Transgenerational Patterns
Sexually Transmitted Diseases
    USE Venereal Diseases
Transpersonal Psychology
Neural **Transplantation**
Organ **Transplantation**
Renal Transplantation *USE Organ Transplantation*
Heart Transplants *USE Organ Transplantation*
Kidney Transplants *USE Organ Transplantation*
Transportation
Transportation Accidents
Air **Transportation**
Ground **Transportation**
Public **Transportation**
Water **Transportation**
Transposition (Cognition)
Transracial Adoption
    USE Interracial Adoption
Transsexualism
Transvestism
Tranylcypromine
Birth **Trauma**
Emotional **Trauma**
Physical Trauma *USE Injuries*
Traumatic Brain Injury
Traumatic Neurosis
Traumatic Psychosis
    USE Reactive Psychosis
Commuting **(Travel)**

Traveling
Trazodone
Treatment
Treatment Client Matching
    USE Client Treatment Matching
Treatment Compliance
Treatment Dropouts
Treatment Duration
Treatment Effectiveness Evaluation
Treatment Environment
    USE Therapeutic Environment
Treatment Facilities
Treatment Guidelines
Treatment Outcomes
Treatment Planning
Treatment Refusal
Treatment Resistant Depression
Treatment Resistant Disorders
Treatment Seeking Behavior
    USE Health Care Seeking Behavior
Treatment Termination
Treatment Withholding
Client **Treatment** Matching
Court Ordered Treatment *USE Court Referrals*
Cross Cultural **Treatment**
Dental **Treatment**
Electrosleep **Treatment**
Interdisciplinary **Treatment** Approach
Involuntary **Treatment**
Life Sustaining **Treatment**
Medical **Treatment** (General)
Multidisciplinary Treatment Approach
    USE Interdisciplinary Treatment
    Approach
Multimodal **Treatment** Approach
Outpatient **Treatment**
Patient Treatment Matching
    USE Client Treatment Matching
Physical **Treatment** Methods
Right to **Treatment**
Side Effects **(Treatment)**
Sleep **Treatment**
Delirium **Tremens**
Tremor
Trends
Triadic Therapy *USE Conjoint Therapy*
Trial and Error Learning
Competency to Stand **Trial**
Triazolam
Tribes
Trichotillomania *USE Hair Pulling*
Tricyclic Antidepressant Drugs
Tricyclic Resistant Depression
    USE Treatment Resistant Depression
Trifluoperazine
Triflupromazine
    USE Phenothiazine Derivatives
Trigeminal Nerve
Trigeminal Neuralgia
Trigonum Cerebrale *USE Fornix*
Trihexyphenidyl
Triiodothyronine
Triplets
Educational Field **Trips**
Trisomy
Trisomy 21
Trochlear Nerve *USE Cranial Nerves*
Truancy
School **Truancy**
Trucks *USE Motor Vehicles*
True False Tests
    USE Forced Choice (Testing Method)
Trust (Social Behavior)
Tryptamine
Tryptophan

Tubal Ligation
Eustachian Tube *USE Middle Ear*
Test Tube Babies *USE Reproductive Technology*
Tuberculosis
Pulmonary **Tuberculosis**
Cathode Ray Tubes *USE Video Display Units*
Tubocurarine
Tumors *USE Neoplasms*
Tunnel Vision
Turners Syndrome
Turnover *USE Employee Turnover*
Employee **Turnover**
Personnel Turnover *USE Employee Turnover*
Turtles
Tutoring
Peer **Tutoring**
Tutors *USE Teachers*
Twelve Step Programs
Twins
Dizygotic Twins *USE Heterozygotic Twins*
Fraternal Twins *USE Heterozygotic Twins*
Heterozygotic **Twins**
Identical Twins *USE Monozygotic Twins*
Monozygotic **Twins**
Siamese **Twins**
Chorda Tympani Nerve *USE Facial Nerve*
Tympanic Membrane *USE Middle Ear*
Type A Personality
    USE Coronary Prone Behavior
Type B Personality
    USE Coronary Prone Behavior
Type I Errors
Type II Errors
Dementia of Alzheimers Type *USE Alzheimers Disease*
Myers Briggs **Type** Indicator
Schizophrenia (Disorganized **Type)**
Body Types *USE Somatotypes*
Typing
Typists *USE Clerical Personnel*
Psychodiagnostic **Typologies**
Tyramine
Tyrosine
Mann Whitney **U** Test
Ulcerative Colitis
Gastrointestinal **Ulcers**
Peptic Ulcers *USE Gastrointestinal Ulcers*
Ulnar Nerve *USE Spinal Nerves*
Ultrasound
Uncertainty
Unconditioned Reflex *USE Reflexes*
Unconditioned Responses
Unconditioned Stimulus
Unconscious (Personality Factor)
Collective **Unconscious**
Driving **Under** The Influence
Academic **Underachievement**
Underdeveloped Countries
    USE Developing Countries
Undergraduate Degrees
    USE Educational Degrees
Undergraduate Education
Undergraduates *USE College Students*
Underprivileged *USE Disadvantaged*
Understanding *USE Comprehension*
Underwater Effects
Underweight
Undifferentiated Schizophrenia
Unemployment
Labor **Union** Members
Labor **Unions**
Unipolar Depression
    USE Major Depression
Hospital Psychiatric Units *USE Psychiatric Units*
Psychiatric **Units**
Shock **Units**

Video Display **Units**
Words (Phonetic **Units)**
Universities *USE Colleges*
Open Universities *USE Nontraditional Education*
Unskilled Industrial Workers
Unwed Mothers
Upper Class
Upper Class Attitudes
Upper Income Level
Upward Bound
Upward Mobility *USE Social Mobility*
Urban Development
    USE Community Development
Urban Environments
Urban Ghettoes *USE Ghettoes*
Urban Planning
Urbanization
Uric Acid
Urinalysis
Urinary Function Disorders
Urinary Incontinence
Urination
Urine
Urogenital Disorders
Urogenital System
Drug **Usage**
Drug **Usage** Attitudes
Drug **Usage** Screening
Intravenous Drug **Usage**
IV Drug Usage *USE Intravenous Drug Usage*
Marihuana **Usage**
Animal Tool Use *USE Tool Use*
Tool **Use**
Uterus
Health Care **Utilization**
Health Service Utilization *USE Health Care Utilization*
Vacation Benefits
    USE Employee Leave Benefits
Vacationing
Vaccination *USE Immunization*
Vagina
Vaginismus
Vagotomy
Vagus Nerve
Concept Validity *USE Statistical Validity*
Concurrent Validity *USE Statistical Validity*
Construct Validity *USE Statistical Validity*
Factorial Validity *USE Statistical Validity*
Predictive Validity *USE Statistical Validity*
Statistical **Validity**
Test **Validity**
Valium *USE Diazepam*
Valproic Acid
Values
Allport Vernon Lindzey Study Values *USE Attitude Measures*
Ethnic **Values**
Personal **Values**
Social **Values**
Heart **Valves**
Vandalism
Vane Kindergarten Test
    USE Intelligence Measures
Variability Measurement
Response **Variability**
Stimulus **Variability**
Variable Interval Reinforcement
Variable Ratio Reinforcement
Dependent **Variables**
Independent **Variables**
Statistical **Variables**
Variance Homogeneity
Analysis of **Variance**
Error Variance *USE Error of Measurement*
Heterogeneity of Variance *USE Variance Homogeneity*
Interaction **Variance**

Contingent Negative **Variation**
Diurnal Variations *USE Human Biological Rhythms*
Seasonal **Variations**
Varimax Rotation
Vascular Dementia
Vascular Disorders
  USE Cardiovascular Disorders
Cerebral Vascular Disorders
  USE Cerebrovascular Disorders
Vasectomy
Vasoconstriction
Vasoconstrictor Drugs
Vasodilation
Vasodilator Drugs
Vasopressin
Vasopressor Drugs
  USE Vasoconstrictor Drugs
Motor **Vehicles**
Veins (Anatomy)
Velocity
Venereal Diseases
Ventral Roots
Ventral Tegmental Area *USE Tegmentum*
Cerebral **Ventricles**
Heart **Ventricles**
Ventricular Fibrillation
  USE Fibrillation (Heart)
Verapamil
Verbal Ability
Verbal Communication
Verbal Comprehension
Verbal Conditioning *USE Verbal Learning*
Verbal Fluency
Verbal Learning
Verbal Meaning
Verbal Memory
Verbal Reinforcement
Verbal Stimuli
Verbal Tests
Verbalization *USE Oral Communication*
Verbs
Verdict Determination *USE Adjudication*
Vergence Movements
  USE Eye Convergence
Theory **Verification**
Vernier Acuity *USE Visual Acuity*
Allport Vernon Lindzey Study Values
  USE Attitude Measures
Vertebrates
Vertigo
Blood **Vessels**
Coronary Vessels *USE Arteries (Anatomy)*
Retinal Vessels *USE Arteries (Anatomy)*
Vestibular Apparatus
Vestibular Nystagmus *USE Nystagmus*
Vestibular Stimulation
  USE Somesthetic Stimulation
Military **Veterans**
Veterinary Medicine
Vibration
Vibrators (Apparatus)
Vibrotactile Thresholds
Vicarious Experiences
Vicarious Reinforcement
  USE Vicarious Experiences
Victimization
Crime **Victims**
Video Display Terminals
  USE Video Display Units
Video Display Units
Video Games *USE Computer Games*
Videotape Instruction
Videotape Recorders
Videotapes
Vietnamese Cultural Groups

World **View**
Television **Viewing**
Vigilance
Vineland Social Maturity Scale
Sexual Boundary Violations *USE Professional Client Sexual*
  Relations
Violence
Client Violence *USE Patient Violence*
Domestic Violence *USE Family Violence*
Family **Violence**
Patient **Violence**
Viral Disorders
Epstein Barr **Viral** Disorder
Virginity
Virtual Reality
Human Immunodeficiency **Virus**
Vision
Vision Disorders
Binocular **Vision**
Central Vision *USE Foveal Vision*
Foveal **Vision**
Hysterical **Vision** Disturbances
Monocular **Vision**
Peripheral **Vision**
Stereoscopic **Vision**
Tunnel **Vision**
Visitation Rights *USE Child Visitation*
Child **Visitation**
Institution **Visitation**
Home **Visiting** Programs
VISTA Volunteers
  USE Volunteers in Service to America
Visual Acuity
Visual Contrast
Visual Cortex
Visual Discrimination
Visual Displays
Visual Evoked Potentials
Visual Feedback
Visual Field
Visual Fixation *USE Eye Fixation*
Visual Hallucinations
Visual Masking
Visual Memory
Visual Neglect *USE Sensory Neglect*
Visual Perception
Visual Perspective *USE Linear Perspective*
Visual Receptive Fields
Visual Search
Visual Spatial Ability
  USE Visuospatial Ability
Visual Spatial Memory
  USE Visuospatial Memory
Visual Stimulation
Visual Thresholds
Visual Tracking
Benton Revised **Visual** Retention Test
Frostig Developmental Test of **Visual** Perception
Visualization *USE Imagery*
Visually Handicapped
  USE Vision Disorders
Visuospatial Ability
Visuospatial Memory
Vitamin C *USE Ascorbic Acid*
Vitamin Deficiency Disorders
Vitamin Therapy
Vitamins
In Vitro Fertilization
  USE Reproductive Technology
Vocabulary
Peabody Picture **Vocabulary** Test
Sight **Vocabulary**
Vocal Cords
Vocalization
Infant **Vocalization**

Animal **Vocalizations**
Vocational Adjustment
    USE Occupational Adjustment
Vocational Aspirations
    USE Occupational Aspirations
Vocational Choice
    USE Occupational Choice
Vocational Counseling
    USE Occupational Guidance
Vocational Counselors
Vocational Education
Vocational Education Teachers
Vocational Evaluation
Vocational Guidance
    USE Occupational Guidance
Vocational Interests
    USE Occupational Interests
Vocational Maturity
Vocational Mobility
    USE Occupational Mobility
Vocational Preference
    USE Occupational Preference
Vocational Rehabilitation
Vocational School Students
Vocational Schools *USE Technical Schools*
Strong **Vocational** Interest Blank
Vocations *USE Occupations*
Voice
Voice Disorders *USE Dysphonia*
Voles *USE Rodents*
Volition
Volt Meters *USE Apparatus*
Blood **Volume**
Volunteer Civilian Personnel
Volunteer Military Personnel
Volunteer Personnel
Volunteers in Service to America
Experiment **Volunteers**
VISTA Volunteers
    USE Volunteers in Service to America
Vomeronasal Sense
Vomit Inducing Drugs *USE Emetic Drugs*
Vomiting
Voting Behavior
Vowels
Voyeurism
Deja Vu *USE Consciousness States*
Vygotsky (Lev)
Wages *USE Salaries*
Sleep **Wake** Cycle
Wakefulness
Walk In Clinics
Walking
Abdominal **Wall**
Wandering Behavior
War
Nuclear **War**
Prisoners of **War**
Duty to **Warn**
Warning Labels
Warning Signs *USE Warnings*
Warnings
Safety Warnings *USE Warnings*
Wasps
Toxic Waste *USE Hazardous Materials*
Water Deprivation
Water Intake
Water Safety
Water Transportation
Watson (John Broadus)
Slow Wave Sleep *USE NREM Sleep*
Sound Waves *USE Acoustics*
Weaning
Weapons
Weather *USE Atmospheric Conditions*

Wechsler Adult Intelligence Scale
Wechsler Bellevue Intelligence Scale
Wechsler Intelligence Scale for Children
Wechsler Memory Scale
Wechsler Preschool Primary Scale
Work **Week** Length
Weight Control
Weight Perception
Birth **Weight**
Body **Weight**
Brain **Weight**
Low Birth Weight *USE Birth Weight*
Statistical **Weighting**
Weightlessness
Weightlifting
Welfare Services (Government)
Animal **Welfare**
Child **Welfare**
Community **Welfare** Services
Public Welfare Services
    USE Community Welfare Services
Well Being
Wellness *USE Health*
Welsh Figure Preference Test
Barron **Welsh** Art Scale
Wepman Auditory Discrimination Test
Wernickes Syndrome
Whales
Wheelchairs *USE Mobility Aids*
Whiplash
Whistleblowing *USE Informants*
White Betz A B Scale
    USE Nonprojective Personality
       Measures
White Blood Cells *USE Leucocytes*
White Collar Workers
White Noise
White Rats *USE Rats*
Whites
Mann **Whitney** U Test
Wholistic Health *USE Holistic Health*
Wide Range Achievement Test
Widowers
Widows
Wilcoxon Sign Rank Test
Wilderness Experience
Free Will *USE Volition*
Prader **Willi** Syndrome
James **(William)**
Willpower *USE Self Control*
Living Wills *USE Advance Directives*
Wilson Patterson Conservatism Scale
Wine
Winnicottian Theory *USE Object Relations*
Winter Depression
    USE Seasonal Affective Disorder
Wisconsin Card Sorting Test
Wisdom
Witchcraft
Attention Deficit Disorder **with** Hyperactivity
Dementia **with** Lewy Bodies
Withdrawal (Defense Mechanism)
Alcohol **Withdrawal**
Drug **Withdrawal**
Drug Withdrawal Effects *USE Drug Withdrawal*
Nicotine **Withdrawal**
Treatment **Withholding**
Within Subjects Design
    USE Repeated Measures
Witnesses
Wives
Wolves
Women *USE Human Females*
Working **Women**
Womens Liberation Movement

Woodcock Johnson Psychoeducational
Battery
Word Associations
Word Blindness *USE Alexia*
Word Deafness *USE Aphasia*
Word Frequency
Word Meaning
Word Origins *USE Etymology*
Word Processing
Word Recognition
Stroop Color **Word** Test
Words (Phonetic Units)
Work (Attitudes Toward)
Work Adjustment Training
Work Environments
USE Working Conditions
Work Ethic *USE Work (Attitudes Toward)*
Work Family Relationship
USE Family Work Relationship
Work Load
Work Related Illnesses
Work Rest Cycles
Work Satisfaction *USE Job Satisfaction*
Work Scheduling
Work Study Programs
USE Educational Programs
Work Teams
Work Week Length
Family **Work** Relationship
Noise Levels **(Work** Areas)
Quality of **Work** Life
Return to Work *USE Reemployment*
School to **Work** Transition
Self Managing **Work** Teams
Social Work *USE Social Casework*
Social **Work** Education
Workday Shifts
Workers *USE Personnel*
Agricultural Extension **Workers**
Agricultural **Workers**
Blue Collar **Workers**
Child Care **Workers**
Foreign **Workers**
Guest Workers *USE Foreign Workers*
Migrant Farm **Workers**
Psychiatric Social **Workers**
Skilled Industrial **Workers**
Social **Workers**

Unskilled Industrial **Workers**
White Collar **Workers**
Working Alliance *USE Therapeutic Alliance*
Working Conditions
Working Memory *USE Short Term Memory*
Working Space
Working Women
Workmens Compensation Insurance
Sheltered **Workshops**
World View
Third World Countries
USE Developing Countries
Worms
Worry *USE Anxiety*
Worship *USE Religious Practices*
Wounds
Self Inflicted **Wounds**
Wrist
Writers
Writing Skills
Creative **Writing**
Cursive **Writing**
Written Communication
Written Language
Wryneck *USE Torticollis*
X Rated Materials *USE Pornography*
X Ray Diagnosis *USE Roentgenography*
X Ray Therapy *USE Radiation Therapy*
Fragile **X** Syndrome
Xenophobia *USE Stranger Reactions*
Xylocaine *USE Lidocaine*
Yawning
Yoga
Yohimbine
Predelinquent **Youth**
Z Scores *USE Standard Scores*
Zulliger **Z** Test
Zen Buddhism
Non **Zero** Sum Games
Zidovudine
Zimeldine
Guilford **Zimmerman** Temperament Survey
Zinc
Zoo Environment *USE Animal Captivity*
Zoology
Zulliger Z Test
Zungs Self Rating Depression Scale

TERM CLUSTERS SECTION

Term Cluster/Subcluster Subject Areas

Computers Cluster
- Computer Applications
- Computer Automation
- Computers & Communication
- Computers & Media
- Education & Training
- Equipment
- Human Machine Systems & Engineering
- Information

Disorders Cluster
- Antisocial Behavior & Behavior Disorders
- Diagnosis
- Disorder Characteristics
- Learning Disorders & Mental Retardation
- Physical & Psychosomatic Disorders
- Psychological Disorders
- Speech & Language Disorders
- Symptomatology

Educational Cluster
- Academic Learning & Achievement
- Curricula
- Educational Personnel & Administration
- Educational Testing & Counseling
- Schools & Institutions
- Special Education
- Student Characteristics & Academic Environment
- Student Populations
- Teaching & Teaching Methods

Legal Cluster
- Adjudication
- Criminal Groups
- Criminal Offenses
- Criminal Rehabilitation
- Laws
- Legal Issues
- Legal Personnel
- Legal Processes

Neuropsychology & Neurology Cluster
- Assessment & Diagnosis
- Electrophysiology
- Neuroanatomy
- Neurological Disorders
- Neurological Intervention
- Neurosciences
- Neurotransmitters & Neuroregulators

Occupational & Employment Cluster
- Career Areas
- Employee, Occupational & Job Characteristics
- Occupational Groups
- Organizations & Organizational Behavior
- Personnel Management & Professional Personnel Issues

Statistical Cluster
- Design, Analysis & Interpretation
- Statistical Reliability & Validity
- Statistical Theory & Experimental

Tests & Testing Cluster
- Academic Achievement & Aptitude Measures
- Attitude & Interest Measures
- Developmental Measures
- Intelligence Measures
- Neuropsychological Measures
- Nonprojective Personality Measures
- Perceptual Measures
- Projective Personality Measures
- Testing
- Testing Methods

Treatment Cluster
- Alternative Therapies
- Behavior Modification & Therapy
- Counseling
- Hospitalization & Institutionalization
- Medical & Physical Treatment
- Psychotherapy
- Rehabilitation
- Treatment (General)
- Treatment Facilities

COMPUTERS CLUSTER

- Computer Applications
- Computer Automation
- Computers & Communication
- Computers & Media
- Education & Training
- Equipment
- Human Machine Systems & Engineering
- Information

Computer Applications

Algorithms
Artificial Intelligence
Audiovisual Communications Media
Automated Information Coding
Automated Information Processing
Automated Information Retrieval
Automated Information Storage
Automated Speech Recognition
Computer Applications
Computer Assisted Design
Computer Assisted Diagnosis
Computer Assisted Instruction
Computer Assisted Testing
Computer Games
Computer Programming
Computer Programming Languages
Computer Searching
Computer Simulation
Computer Software
Cybernetics
Data Processing
Databases
Decision Support Systems
Electronic Communication
Error Analysis
Expert Systems
Hypermedia
Hypertext
Information Systems
Internet
Neural Networks
Word Processing

Computer Automation

Artificial Intelligence
Automated Information Coding
Automated Information Processing
Automated Information Retrieval
Automated Information Storage
Automated Speech Recognition
Automation
Computer Assisted Design
Computer Assisted Diagnosis
Computer Assisted Instruction
Computer Assisted Testing

Cybernetics
Decision Support Systems
Human Machine Systems
Neural Networks
Robotics

Computers & Communication

Audiovisual Communications Media
Communication Systems
Communication Theory
Communications Media
Electronic Communication
Hot Line Services
Hypermedia
Hypertext
Internet
Mass Media
Scientific Communication
Telecommunications Media
Television Advertising

Computers & Media

Audiovisual Communications Media
Communications Media
Computer Software
Databases
Electronic Communication
Hot Line Services
Hypermedia
Hypertext
Information Services
Information Systems
Internet
Mass Media
News Media
Telecommunications Media
Televised Instruction

Education & Training

Computer Assisted Instruction
Computer Assisted Testing
Computer Literacy
Computer Training
Educational Television
Teaching Machines
Televised Instruction

Equipment

Analog Computers
Apparatus
Computer Peripheral Devices
Digital Computers
Human Computer Interaction
Keyboards
Microcomputers
Robotics
Video Display Units
Visual Displays

Human Machine Systems & Engineering

Automated Speech Recognition
Computer Peripheral Devices
Decision Support Systems
Human Computer Interaction
Human Factors Engineering
Human Machine Systems
Human Machine Systems Design
Instrument Controls
Person Environment Fit
Teaching Machines
Virtual Reality

Information

Automated Information Coding
Automated Information Processing
Automated Information Retrieval
Automated Information Storage
Communication Theory
Communications Media
Computer Searching
Data Collection
Data Processing
Databases
Expert Systems
Hot Line Services
Hypermedia
Hypertext
Information
Information Seeking
Information Services
Information Specialists
Information Systems
Information Theory
Internet
Mass Media
Telecommunications Media

DISORDERS CLUSTER

- Antisocial Behavior & Behavior Disorders
- Diagnosis
- Disorder Characteristics
- Learning Disorders & Mental Retardation
- Physical & Psychosomatic Disorders
- Psychological Disorders
- Speech & Language Disorders
- Symptomatology

Antisocial Behavior & Behavior Disorders

Abuse of Power
Acquaintance Rape
Acute Alcoholic Intoxication

Consult Relationship Section for more information

Antisocial Behavior & Behavior Disorders — (cont'd)

Addiction
Alcohol Abuse
Alcoholism
Antisocial Behavior
Antisocial Personality
Arson
Attachment Disorders
Attempted Suicide
Attention Deficit Disorder
Attention Deficit Disorder with Hyperactivity
Battered Child Syndrome
Battered Females
Behavior Disorders
Behavior Problems
Child Abuse
Child Neglect
Chronic Alcoholic Intoxication
Conduct Disorder
Crime
Criminals
Cruelty
Driving Under the Influence
Drug Abuse
Drug Addiction
Drug Dependency
Drug Distribution
Elder Abuse
Emotional Abuse
Erotomania
Exhibitionism
Family Violence
Female Criminals
Female Delinquency
Fetishism
Genocide
Glue Sniffing
Harassment
Heroin Addiction
Homicide
Impulse Control Disorders
Incest
Infanticide
Inhalant Abuse
Intravenous Drug Usage
Juvenile Delinquency
Juvenile Gangs
Kidnapping
Kleptomania
Male Criminals
Male Delinquency
Masochism
Mentally Ill Offenders
Oppositional Defiant Disorder
Paraphilias
Partner Abuse

Pathological Gambling
Patient Abuse
Patient Violence
Pedophilia
Perpetrators
Persecution
Physical Abuse
Polydrug Abuse
Pyromania
Rape
Recidivism
Runaway Behavior
Sadism
Sadomasochism
Sadomasochistic Personality
School Truancy
Self Destructive Behavior
Self Mutilation
Sex Offenses
Sexual Abuse
Sexual Addiction
Sexual Harassment
Sexual Masochism
Sexual Sadism
Shoplifting
Stalking
Suicidal Ideation
Suicide
Tantrums
Terrorism
Theft
Torture
Transvestism
Truancy
Vandalism
Victimization
Violence
Voyeurism

Diagnosis

Anatomically Detailed Dolls
Angiography
Biological Markers
Biopsy
Cancer Screening
Cardiography
Clinical Judgment (Not Diagnosis)
Cognitive Assessment
Computer Assisted Diagnosis
Dexamethasone Suppression Test
Diagnosis
Diagnosis Related Groups
Diagnostic and Statistical Manual
Diagnostic Interview Schedule
Differential Diagnosis
Drug Usage Screening
Dual Diagnosis
Echoencephalography

Electro Oculography
Electrocardiography
Electroencephalography
Electromyography
Electronystagmography
Electroplethysmography
Electroretinography
Encephalography
General Health Questionnaire
Geriatric Assessment
Health Screening
HIV Testing
Intake Interview
International Classification of Diseases
Magnetic Resonance Imaging
Mammography
Medical Diagnosis
Medical Model
Misdiagnosis
Needs Assessment
Neuropsychological Assessment
Ophthalmologic Examination
Pain Measurement
Physical Examination
Plethysmography
Pneumoencephalography
Prenatal Diagnosis
Psychiatric Evaluation
Psychodiagnosis
Psychodiagnostic Interview
Psychodiagnostic Typologies
Psychological Assessment
Research Diagnostic Criteria
Rheoencephalography
Roentgenography
Screening
Structured Clinical Interview
Symptom Checklists
Tomography
Urinalysis

Disorder Characteristics

At Risk Populations
Chronicity (Disorders)
Client Attitudes
Client Characteristics
Comorbidity
Diagnosis
Disease Course
Dual Diagnosis
Epidemics
Epidemiology
Etiology
Health Complaints
Illness Behavior
Mortality Rate
Onset (Disorders)
Patient History

Consult Relationship Section for more information

Disorder Characteristics — (cont'd)

Positive and Negative Symptoms
Predisposition
Premorbidity
Prognosis
Psychiatric Symptoms
Recovery (Disorders)
Relapse (Disorders)
Remission (Disorders)
Risk Factors
Seasonal Variations
Severity (Disorders)
Spontaneous Remission
Susceptibility (Disorders)
Symptom Remission
Symptoms
Treatment Resistant Disorders

Learning Disorders & Mental Retardation

Acalculia
Agnosia
Agraphia
Alexia
Amaurotic Familial Idiocy
Anencephaly
Attention Deficit Disorder
Attention Deficit Disorder with Hyperactivity
Autism
Borderline Mental Retardation
Crying Cat Syndrome
Downs Syndrome
Dyslexia
Dysphasia
Home Reared Mentally Retarded
Hyperkinesis
Institutionalized Mentally Retarded
Learning Disabilities
Learning Disorders
Mental Retardation
Mental Retardation (Attitudes Toward)
Microcephaly
Mild Mental Retardation
Moderate Mental Retardation
Profound Mental Retardation
Psychosocial Mental Retardation
Reading Disabilities
Rett Syndrome
Savants
Severe Mental Retardation

Trisomy
Trisomy 21

Physical & Psychosomatic Disorders

Acalculia
Acquired Immune Deficiency Syndrome
Addisons Disease
Adrenal Gland Disorders
Adventitious Disorders
Agnosia
Agraphia
AIDS (Attitudes Toward)
AIDS Dementia Complex
Albinism
Allergic Disorders
Allergic Skin Disorders
Alopecia
Alzheimers Disease
Amaurotic Familial Idiocy
Amblyopia
Amenorrhea
Amnesia
Anaphylactic Shock
Anemia
Anencephaly
Aneurysms
Angina Pectoris
Anorexia Nervosa
Anosmia
Anosognosia
Aphagia
Aphasia
Apnea
Apraxia
Arrhythmias (Heart)
Arteriosclerosis
Arthritis
Asthenia
Asthma
Ataxia
Atherosclerosis
Athetosis
Audiogenic Seizures
Autonomic Nervous System Disorders
Autosome Disorders
Back Pain
Bacterial Disorders
Bacterial Meningitis
Barbiturate Poisoning
Benign Neoplasms
Birth Injuries
Blind
Blood and Lymphatic Disorders
Blood Pressure Disorders
Body Dysmorphic Disorder
Bone Disorders
Bradycardia

Bradykinesia
Brain Concussion
Brain Damage
Brain Disorders
Brain Neoplasms
Breast Neoplasms
Bronchial Disorders
Bruxism
Bulimia
Burns
Carbon Monoxide Poisoning
Cardiovascular Disorders
Catabolism
Catalepsy
Cataplexy
Cataracts
Central Nervous System Disorders
Cerebral Arteriosclerosis
Cerebral Hemorrhage
Cerebral Ischemia
Cerebral Palsy
Cerebrovascular Accidents
Cerebrovascular Disorders
Chorea
Chromosome Disorders
Chronic Fatigue Syndrome
Chronic Illness
Chronic Pain
Cirrhosis (Liver)
Cleft Palate
Colitis
Colon Disorders
Color Blindness
Congenital Disorders
Constipation
Conversion Disorder
Convulsions
Coronary Prone Behavior
Coronary Thromboses
Creutzfeldt Jakob Syndrome
Crying Cat Syndrome
Cushings Syndrome
Cystic Fibrosis
Deaf
Deaf Blind
Delirium Tremens
Dementia
Dementia with Lewy Bodies
Dermatitis
Developmental Disabilities
Diabetes
Diabetes Insipidus
Diabetes Mellitus
Diarrhea
Digestive System Disorders
Disabled (Attitudes Toward)
Disorders
Downs Syndrome
Drug Allergies

Consult Relationship Section for more information

Physical & Psychosomatic Disorders — (cont'd)

Drug Induced Congenital Disorders
Drug Induced Hallucinations
Dysarthria
Dyskinesia
Dysmenorrhea
Dyspareunia
Dysphasia
Dyspnea
Ear Disorders
Eating Disorders
Eczema
Electrical Injuries
Embolisms
Encephalitis
Encephalomyelitis
Encephalopathies
Endocrine Disorders
Endocrine Neoplasms
Endocrine Sexual Disorders
Epilepsy
Epileptic Seizures
Epstein Barr Viral Disorder
Essential Hypertension
Ethnospecific Disorders
Eye Disorders
Failure to Thrive
Fecal Incontinence
Fetal Alcohol Syndrome
Fibrillation (Heart)
Food Allergies
Fragile X Syndrome
Frigidity
Gastrointestinal Disorders
Gastrointestinal Ulcers
General Paresis
Genetic Disorders
Genital Disorders
Gilles de la Tourette Disorder
Glaucoma
Global Amnesia
Goiters
Gonorrhea
Grand Mal Epilepsy
Gynecological Disorders
Hay Fever
Head Injuries
Headache
Health Impairments
Hearing Disorders
Heart Disorders
Hematoma
Hemianopia
Hemiplegia
Hemophilia
Hemorrhage
Hepatitis

Hermaphroditism
Herpes Genitalis
Herpes Simplex
Human Immunodeficiency Virus
Huntingtons Disease
Hydrocephaly
Hyperglycemia
Hyperkinesis
Hyperphagia
Hypersexuality
Hypersomnia
Hypertension
Hyperthyroidism
Hypochondriasis
Hypoglycemia
Hypogonadism
Hyponatremia
Hypopituitarism
Hypotension
Hypothyroidism
Hysterical Paralysis
Hysterical Vision Disturbances
Immunologic Disorders
Impotence
Infectious Disorders
Infertility
Influenza
Injuries
Insomnia
Irritable Bowel Syndrome
Ischemia
Jaundice
Joint Disorders
Kidney Diseases
Kleine Levin Syndrome
Klinefelters Syndrome
Korsakoffs Psychosis
Kwashiorkor
Labyrinth Disorders
Laryngeal Disorders
Lead Poisoning
Leukemias
Lipid Metabolism Disorders
Liver Disorders
Lung Disorders
Lupus
Malaria
Male Genital Disorders
Measles
Memory Disorders
Menieres Disease
Meningitis
Menstrual Disorders
Mercury Poisoning
Metabolism Disorders
Microcephaly
Migraine Headache
Minimal Brain Disorders
Motion Sickness

Movement Disorders
Multi Infarct Dementia
Multiple Disabilities
Multiple Sclerosis
Munchausen Syndrome
Munchausen Syndrome by Proxy
Muscle Contraction Headache
Muscle Spasms
Muscular Atrophy
Muscular Disorders
Muscular Dystrophy
Musculoskeletal Disorders
Myasthenia
Myasthenia Gravis
Myelitis
Myocardial Infarctions
Myoclonia
Myofascial Pain
Myopia
Myotonia
Narcolepsy
Narcosis
Neonatal Disorders
Neoplasms
Nervous System Disorders
Nervous System Neoplasms
Neuralgia
Neurasthenic Neurosis
Neurodermatitis
Neuroleptic Malignant Syndrome
Neuromuscular Disorders
Neurosyphilis
Nocturnal Teeth Grinding
Nutritional Deficiencies
Nystagmus
Obesity
Obesity (Attitudes Toward)
Obstetrical Complications
Organic Brain Syndromes
Osteoporosis
Pain
Paralysis
Paraplegia
Parasitic Disorders
Parathyroid Disorders
Parkinsonism
Parkinsons Disease
Partially Hearing Impaired
Partially Sighted
Pellagra
Perceptual Disturbances
Peripheral Nerve Disorders
Petit Mal Epilepsy
Phantom Limbs
Pharyngeal Disorders
Phenylketonuria
Physical Disabilities (Attitudes Toward)
Physical Disfigurement
Physical Disorders

Consult Relationship Section for more information

Physical & Psychosomatic Disorders — (cont'd)

Physical Illness (Attitudes Toward)
Pica
Picks Disease
Pituitary Disorders
Pneumonia
Poliomyelitis
Porphyria
Prader Willi Syndrome
Premature Ejaculation
Premenstrual Tension
Presenile Dementia
Progressive Supranuclear Palsy
Prosopagnosia
Protein Deficiency Disorders
Pruritus
Pseudocyesis
Pseudodementia
Pulmonary Emphysema
Pulmonary Tuberculosis
Quadriplegia
Refraction Errors
Respiratory Distress
Respiratory Tract Disorders
Rett Syndrome
Rheumatic Fever
Rheumatoid Arthritis
Rubella
Sclerosis (Nervous System)
Self Inflicted Wounds
Senile Dementia
Senile Psychosis
Sense Organ Disorders
Sensory Disabilities (Attitudes Toward)
Sensory System Disorders
Sex Chromosome Disorders
Sex Linked Hereditary Disorders
Sexual Function Disturbances
Sickle Cell Disease
Skin Disorders
Sleep Apnea
Sleep Disorders
Somatization
Somatoform Disorders
Somatoform Pain Disorder
Somatosensory Disorders
Spasms
Spina Bifida
Spinal Cord Injuries
Sterility
Strabismus
Sudden Infant Death
Syncope
Syndromes
Syphilis
Tachycardia
Tardive Dyskinesia

Taste Disorders
Terminal Cancer
Terminally Ill Patients
Testicular Feminization Syndrome
Thromboses
Thyroid Disorders
Thyrotoxicosis
Tics
Tinnitus
Torticollis
Toxic Disorders
Toxic Encephalopathies
Toxic Hepatitis
Toxic Psychoses
Toxicomania
Traumatic Brain Injury
Tremor
Trigeminal Neuralgia
Trisomy 21
Tuberculosis
Tunnel Vision
Turners Syndrome
Ulcerative Colitis
Urinary Function Disorders
Urinary Incontinence
Urogenital Disorders
Vaginismus
Vascular Dementia
Venereal Diseases
Viral Disorders
Vision Disorders
Vitamin Deficiency Disorders
Vomiting
Wernickes Syndrome
Whiplash
Work Related Illnesses
Wounds

Psychological Disorders

Acrophobia
Acute Psychosis
Acute Schizophrenia
Adjustment Disorders
Affective Disorders
Affective Psychosis
Agoraphobia
AIDS Dementia Complex
Alcoholic Hallucinosis
Alcoholic Psychosis
Alexithymia
Alzheimers Disease
Amnesia
Anaclitic Depression
Anorexia Nervosa
Antisocial Personality
Anxiety Disorders
Aspergers Syndrome
Auditory Hallucinations

Autism
Autistic Children
Avoidant Personality
Bipolar Disorder
Body Dysmorphic Disorder
Body Image Disturbances
Borderline Personality
Borderline States
Bulimia
Capgras Syndrome
Castration Anxiety
Catatonic Schizophrenia
Childhood Neurosis
Childhood Psychosis
Childhood Schizophrenia
Chronic Mental Illness
Chronic Psychosis
Claustrophobia
Compulsive Repetition
Confabulation
Consciousness Disturbances
Coprophagia
Creutzfeldt Jakob Syndrome
Cyclothymic Personality
Death Anxiety
Delirium Tremens
Delusions
Dementia
Dementia with Lewy Bodies
Dependent Personality
Depersonalization
Depression (Emotion)
Dissociative Disorders
Dissociative Identity Disorder
Dysfunctional Family
Dysthymic Disorder
Early Infantile Autism
Eating Disorders
Elective Mutism
Electra Complex
Emotionally Disturbed
Endogenous Depression
Erotomania
Explosive Disorder
Factitious Disorders
Fantasies (Thought Disturbances)
Fetal Alcohol Syndrome
Folie A Deux
Fragmentation (Schizophrenia)
Fugue Reaction
Gender Identity Disorder
Global Amnesia
Hallucinations
Hallucinosis
Histrionic Personality Disorder
Homeless Mentally Ill
Hypnagogic Hallucinations
Hypomania
Hysteria

Consult Relationship Section for more information

Psychological Disorders — (cont'd)

Impulse Control Disorders
Inadequate Personality
Infantilism
Inhibited Sexual Desire
Involutional Depression
Involutional Paranoid Psychosis
Judgment Disturbances
Koro
Korsakoffs Psychosis
Magical Thinking
Major Depression
Malingering
Mania
Masochistic Personality
Mass Hysteria
Memory Disorders
Mental Disorders
Mental Disorders due to General Medical Conditions
Mental Illness (Attitudes Toward)
Mentally Ill Offenders
Multi Infarct Dementia
Munchausen Syndrome
Munchausen Syndrome by Proxy
Narcissistic Personality
Neurosis
Obsessive Compulsive Disorder
Obsessive Compulsive Personality
Occupational Neurosis
Oedipal Complex
Ophidiophobia
Organic Brain Syndromes
Panic Disorder
Paranoia (Psychosis)
Paranoid Personality
Paranoid Schizophrenia
Paraphilias
Passive Aggressive Personality
Personality Disorders
Pervasive Developmental Disorders
Phobias
Pica
Picks Disease
Postpartum Depression
Posttraumatic Stress Disorder
Presenile Dementia
Process Psychosis
Pseudodementia
Psychosis
Reactive Depression
Reactive Psychosis
Recurrent Depression
Sadomasochistic Personality
Schizoaffective Disorder
Schizoid Personality
Schizophrenia

Schizophrenia (Disorganized Type)
Schizophreniform Disorder
Schizophrenogenic Family
Schizophrenogenic Mothers
Schizotypal Personality
School Phobia
Seasonal Affective Disorder
Self Defeating Behavior
Self Destructive Behavior
Self Mutilation
Senile Dementia
Senile Psychosis
Separation Anxiety
Sexual Addiction
Social Anxiety
Social Phobia
Speech Anxiety
Stress Reactions
Symbiotic Infantile Psychosis
Syndromes
Thought Disturbances
Toxic Psychoses
Traumatic Neurosis
Treatment Resistant Depression
Undifferentiated Schizophrenia
Vascular Dementia
Visual Hallucinations
Work Related Illnesses

Speech & Language Disorders

Acalculia
Agnosia
Agraphia
Alexia
Anosognosia
Aphasia
Articulation Disorders
Communication Disorders
Dysarthria
Dyslexia
Dysphasia
Dysphonia
Echolalia
Elective Mutism
Glossolalia
Language Delay
Language Disorders
Mutism
Prosopagnosia
Reading Disabilities
Retarded Speech Development
Speech Disorders
Stuttering

Symptomatology

Acting Out
Agitation
Akathisia

Amnesia
Anhedonia
Anoxia
Anxiety
Aphagia
Apnea
Apraxia
Asthenia
Ataxia
Automatism
Back Pain
Behavior Change
Binge Eating
Body Rocking
Bruxism
Catalepsy
Catatonia
Chronic Pain
Coma
Constipation
Convulsions
Craving
Delirium
Depersonalization
Diarrhea
Dissociation
Distractibility
Drug Withdrawal
Dyskinesia
Dyspnea
Extrapyramidal Symptoms
Fatigue
Fecal Incontinence
Hair Pulling
Head Banging
Headache
Health Complaints
Hematoma
Hemorrhage
Hyperglycemia
Hypersomnia
Hypertension
Hyperthermia
Hyperventilation
Hypoglycemia
Hyponatremia
Hypotension
Hypothermia
Insomnia
Mental Confusion
Muscle Spasms
Nail Biting
Nausea
Nicotine Withdrawal
Nocturnal Teeth Grinding
Pain
Parkinsonism
Personality Change
Physiological Correlates

Consult Relationship Section for more information

Symptomatology — (cont'd)

Place Disorientation
Positive and Negative Symptoms
Pruritus
Psychiatric Symptoms
Respiratory Distress
Restlessness
Scratching
Self Destructive Behavior
Shock
Somatization
Spasms
Symptom Checklists
Symptom Remission
Symptoms
Syncope
Tics
Time Disorientation
Tremor
Urinary Incontinence
Vertigo
Vomiting
Wandering Behavior

EDUCATIONAL CLUSTER

- Academic Learning & Achievement
- Curricula
- Educational Personnel & Administration
- Educational Testing & Counseling
- Schools & Institutions
- Special Education
- Student Characteristics & Academic Environment
- Student Populations
- Teaching & Teaching Methods

Academic Learning & Achievement

Academic Achievement
Academic Achievement Motivation
Academic Achievement Prediction
Academic Aptitude
Academic Failure
Academic Overachievement
Academic Self Concept
Academic Specialization
Academic Underachievement
Adult Learning
College Academic Achievement
Cooperative Learning
Discrimination Learning
Educational Attainment Level
Experiential Learning
Foreign Language Learning
Generalization (Learning)

Grade Level
Incidental Learning
Intentional Learning
Interference (Learning)
Latent Learning
Learning
Learning Ability
Learning Rate
Learning Schedules
Learning Strategies
Learning Theory
Literacy
Mastery Learning
Mathematics Achievement
Metacognition
Mnemonic Learning
Nonsense Syllable Learning
Nonverbal Learning
Note Taking
Observational Learning
Overlearning
Paired Associate Learning
Perceptual Motor Learning
Probability Learning
Reading Achievement
Reading Readiness
Reading Skills
Reading Speed
Recall (Learning)
Recognition (Learning)
Reconstruction (Learning)
Relearning
Retention
Rote Learning
School Graduation
School Learning
School Retention
Science Achievement
Sequential Learning
Serial Anticipation (Learning)
Serial Learning
Skill Learning
Social Learning
Spatial Learning
State Dependent Learning
Time On Task
Transfer (Learning)
Trial and Error Learning
Verbal Learning
Writing Skills

Curricula

Adult Education
Affective Education
Apprenticeship
Art Education
Bilingual Education
Braille Instruction

Business Education
Career Education
Clinical Methods Training
Clinical Psychology Graduate Training
Clinical Psychology Internship
Community Mental Health Training
Compensatory Education
Computer Training
Continuing Education
Cooperative Education
Counselor Education
Curriculum
Curriculum Development
Death Education
Dental Education
Driver Education
Drug Education
Education
Educational Program Accreditation
Educational Program Planning
Educational Programs
Elementary Education
English as Second Language
Environmental Education
Equal Education
Extracurricular Activities
Family Life Education
Foreign Language Education
Foreign Study
Graduate Education
Graduate Psychology Education
Health Education
Higher Education
Home Economics
Home Schooling
Inservice Teacher Education
Inservice Training
Language Arts Education
Literacy Programs
Management Training
Mathematics Education
Medical Education
Medical Internship
Medical Residency
Mental Health Inservice Training
Middle School Education
Military Training
Multicultural Education
Music Education
Nontraditional Education
Nursing Education
On the Job Training
Paraprofessional Education
Parent Training
Personnel Training
Phonics
Physical Education
Postgraduate Training
Preschool Education

Consult Relationship Section for more information

Curricula — (cont'd)

Private School Education
Project Follow Through
Project Head Start
Psychiatric Training
Psychoanalytic Training
Psychology Education
Psychotherapy Training
Public School Education
Reading Education
Rehabilitation Education
Religious Education
Remedial Education
Remedial Reading
Science Education
Secondary Education
Sex Education
Social Studies Education
Social Work Education
Special Education
Spelling
Sports
Student Teaching
Teacher Education
Undergraduate Education
Upward Bound
Vocational Education

Educational Personnel & Administration

Accreditation (Education Personnel)
Boards of Education
Budgets
College Teachers
Cooperating Teachers
Educational Administration
Educational Personnel
Educational Program Accreditation
Educational Psychologists
Educational Quality
Educational Reform
Elementary School Teachers
High School Teachers
Junior High School Teachers
Librarians
Parent School Relationship
Preschool Teachers
Preservice Teachers
Resource Teachers
School Administrators
School Counselors
School Nurses
School Principals
School Psychologists
School Superintendents
Special Education Teachers
Speech Therapists
Student Teachers

Teacher Aides
Teacher Attitudes
Teacher Characteristics
Teacher Education
Teacher Effectiveness Evaluation
Teacher Expectations
Teacher Personality
Teacher Recruitment
Teacher Student Interaction
Teacher Tenure
Teachers
Vocational Counselors
Vocational Education Teachers

Educational Testing & Counseling

Achievement Measures
Adaptive Testing
Aptitude Measures
College Entrance Examination Board
Scholastic Aptitude Test
Computer Assisted Testing
Course Evaluation
Criterion Referenced Tests
Cultural Test Bias
Curriculum Based Assessment
Educational Counseling
Educational Diagnosis
Educational Financial Assistance
Educational Measurement
Educational Placement
Educational Program Evaluation
Educational Psychology
Educational Therapy
Entrance Examinations
Essay Testing
Grading (Educational)
Graduate Record Examination
Group Testing
Minimum Competency Tests
Posttesting
School Counseling
School Psychology
Student Admission Criteria
Student Personnel Services
Student Records
Teacher Effectiveness Evaluation
Test Coaching
Test Taking
Testing
Testing Methods
Testwiseness
Woodcock Johnson Psychoeducational Battery

Schools & Institutions

Boarding Schools
Campuses
Classrooms

Colleges
Community Colleges
Dormitories
Educational Laboratories
Elementary Schools
Graduate Schools
High Schools
Institutional Schools
Junior High Schools
Kindergartens
Learning Centers (Educational)
Military Schools
Nongraded Schools
Nursery Schools
School Facilities
School Libraries
Schools
Seminaries
Technical Schools

Special Education

Acalculia
Agnosia
Agraphia
Alexia
Amaurotic Familial Idiocy
Anencephaly
Aphasia
Apraxia
Articulation Disorders
Aspergers Syndrome
Ataxia
Attention Deficit Disorder
Attention Deficit Disorder with Hyperactivity
Augmentative Communication
Autism
Autistic Children
Behavior Disorders
Behavior Modification
Behavior Problems
Blind
Borderline Mental Retardation
Braille Instruction
Classroom Behavior Modification
Cleft Palate
Communication Disorders
Communication Skills Training
Compensatory Education
Crying Cat Syndrome
Deaf
Deaf Blind
Delayed Development
Developmental Disabilities
Downs Syndrome
Dysarthria
Dyskinesia
Dyslexia

Consult Relationship Section for more information

Special Education — (cont'd)

Dysphasia
Dysphonia
Ear Disorders
Early Infantile Autism
Early Intervention
Echolalia
Educational Placement
Educational Therapy
Emotionally Disturbed
Gifted
Hearing Disorders
Home Reared Mentally Retarded
Hyperkinesis
Institutionalized Mentally Retarded
Language Delay
Language Disorders
Learning Disabilities
Learning Disorders
Literacy Programs
Mainstreaming
Mainstreaming (Educational)
Memory Disorders
Mental Retardation
Microcephaly
Mild Mental Retardation
Minimal Brain Disorders
Moderate Mental Retardation
Mutism
Partially Hearing Impaired
Perceptual Disturbances
Pervasive Developmental Disorders
Profound Mental Retardation
Psychosocial Mental Retardation
Reading Disabilities
Remedial Education
Remedial Reading
Retarded Speech Development
Rett Syndrome
Savants
Severe Mental Retardation
Social Skills Training
Special Education
Special Education Students
Special Needs
Speech Disorders
Speech Therapy
Stuttering
Vision Disorders

Student Characteristics & Academic Environment

Ability Level
Academic Achievement
Academic Achievement Motivation
Academic Aptitude
Academic Environment
Academic Failure

Academic Overachievement
Academic Self Concept
Academic Specialization
Academic Underachievement
Artistic Ability
Athletic Participation
Classroom Behavior
Classroom Environment
Classrooms
Coeducation
Cognitive Ability
College Academic Achievement
College Environment
Computer Anxiety
Computer Literacy
Declarative Knowledge
Educational Aspirations
Educational Attainment Level
Educational Background
Educational Degrees
Educational Incentives
Educational Objectives
Fraternity Membership
Grade Level
Learning Ability
Literacy
Mathematical Ability
Mathematics Anxiety
Musical Ability
Nonverbal Ability
Performance Anxiety
Procedural Knowledge
Reading Ability
Reading Comprehension
Reading Skills
School Adjustment
School Attendance
School Club Membership
School Enrollment
School Environment
School Expulsion
School Graduation
School Integration
School Phobia
School Readiness
School Refusal
School Retention
School Suspension
School to Work Transition
School Transition
School Truancy
Sorority Membership
Special Needs
Speech Anxiety
Student Activism
Student Attitudes
Student Attrition
Student Characteristics
Student Records

Study Habits
Teacher Student Interaction
Test Anxiety
Truancy
Verbal Ability
Writing Skills

Student Populations

Business Students
Classmates
College Athletes
College Dropouts
College Graduates
College Students
Community College Students
Counselor Trainees
Dental Students
Dropouts
Education Students
Elementary School Students
Foreign Students
Gifted
Graduate Students
High School Graduates
High School Students
Intermediate School Students
Junior College Students
Junior High School Students
Kindergarten Students
Law Students
Medical Students
Middle School Students
Nursery School Students
Nursing Students
Postgraduate Students
Potential Dropouts
Preschool Students
Preservice Teachers
Primary School Students
Reentry Students
ROTC Students
School Dropouts
School Leavers
Seminarians
Special Education Students
Student Teachers
Students
Therapist Trainees
Transfer Students
Vocational School Students

Teaching & Teaching Methods

Ability Grouping
Advance Organizers
Apprenticeship
Audiovisual Instruction
Braille Instruction
Classroom Behavior Modification

Consult Relationship Section for more information

Teaching & Teaching Methods — (cont'd)

Classroom Discipline
Computer Assisted Instruction
Constant Time Delay
Cooperative Learning
Curricular Field Experience
Directed Discussion Method
Discovery Teaching Method
Education
Educational Audiovisual Aids
Educational Field Trips
Educational Incentives
Educational Laboratories
Educational Objectives
Educational Programs
Educational Television
Educational Toys
Experiential Learning
Feedback
Film Strips
Group Discussion
Group Instruction
Home Schooling
Homework
Individualized Instruction
Initial Teaching Alphabet
Instructional Media
Language Laboratories
Learning Strategies
Lecture Method
Lesson Plans
Montessori Method
Motion Pictures (Educational)
Nondirected Discussion Method
On the Job Training
Open Classroom Method
Peer Tutoring
Programmed Instruction
Programmed Textbooks
Prompting
Psychoeducation
Reading Materials
Remedial Reading
School Learning
Self Instructional Training
Sight Vocabulary
Silent Reading
Student Teaching
Teaching
Teaching Machines
Teaching Methods
Team Teaching Method
Televised Instruction
Textbooks
Theories of Education
Tutoring
Videotape Instruction

LEGAL CLUSTER

- Adjudication
- Criminal Groups
- Criminal Offenses
- Criminal Rehabilitation
- Laws
- Legal Issues
- Legal Personnel
- Legal Processes

Adjudication

Adjudication
Capital Punishment
Commitment (Psychiatric)
Competency to Stand Trial
Court Referrals
Crime
Crime Victims
Criminal Conviction
Criminal Justice
Criminal Responsibility
Defendants
Expert Testimony
Forensic Evaluation
Informants
Informed Consent
Insanity Defense
Juries
Jury Selection
Justice
Law Enforcement
Legal Arrest
Legal Decisions
Legal Detention
Legal Evidence
Legal Interrogation
Legal Processes
Legal Testimony
Parole
Perpetrators
Polygraphs
Probation
Protective Services
Witnesses

Criminal Groups

Criminals
Defendants
Female Criminals
Female Delinquency
Juvenile Delinquency
Juvenile Gangs
Male Criminals
Male Delinquency
Mentally Ill Offenders
Perpetrators

Predelinquent Youth
Prisoners

Criminal Offenses

Abandonment
Acquaintance Rape
Age Discrimination
Arson
Assisted Suicide
Battered Child Syndrome
Battered Females
Child Abuse
Child Neglect
Crime
Disability Discrimination
Driving Under The Influence
Drug Distribution
Elder Abuse
Employment Discrimination
Family Violence
Fraud
Gambling
Genocide
Harassment
Homicide
Incest
Infanticide
Kidnapping
Kleptomania
Partner Abuse
Pathological Gambling
Patient Abuse
Pedophilia
Persecution
Physical Abuse
Political Assassination
Pornography
Prostitution
Race and Ethnic Discrimination
Rape
Runaway Behavior
Sex Discrimination
Sex Offenses
Sexual Abuse
Sexual Harassment
Shoplifting
Social Discrimination
Stalking
Terrorism
Theft
Torture
Vandalism
Victimization

Criminal Rehabilitation

Correctional Institutions
Criminology
Forensic Psychiatry

Consult Relationship Section for more information

Criminal Rehabilitation — (cont'd)

Forensic Psychology
Incarceration
Institutional Release
Institutional Schools
Institutionalization
Maximum Security Facilities
Parole
Penology
Prisons
Probation
Recidivism
Reformatories

Laws

Abortion Laws
Abuse Reporting
Affirmative Action
Child Abuse Reporting
Civil Law
Criminal Law
Disability Laws
Drug Laws
Equal Education
Government Policy Making
Gun Control Laws
Health Care Policy
Law (Government)
Laws
Legal Decisions
Legislative Processes
Marihuana Laws
Medicare
Social Security
Taxation

Legal Issues

Affirmative Action
Age Discrimination
Assisted Suicide
Capital Punishment
Censorship
Child Care
Child Welfare
Civil Rights
Crime Prevention
Criminal Justice
Criminal Responsibility
Dangerousness
Disability Discrimination
Drug Legalization
Drug Usage Screening
Duty to Warn
Employment Discrimination
Equal Education
Eugenics
Euthanasia

HIV Testing
Human Rights
Informed Consent
Life Sustaining Treatment
Marihuana Legalization
Morality
Political Revolution
Privileged Communication
Professional Client Sexual Relations
Professional Liability
Race and Ethnic Discrimination
Refugees
Right to Treatment
Riots
Safety Belts
Safety Devices
School Integration
School Truancy
Self Defense
Sex Discrimination
Social Discrimination
Social Equality
Social Integration
Surrogate Parents (Humans)
Treatment Withholding
Victimization
Warning Labels

Legal Personnel

Attorneys
Judges
Juries
Law Enforcement Personnel
Law Students
Legal Personnel
Parole Officers
Police Personnel
Prison Personnel
Probation Officers

Legal Processes

Abuse Reporting
Adoption (Child)
Advance Directives
Advocacy
Autopsy
Censorship
Child Abuse Reporting
Child Custody
Child Support
Child Visitation
Child Welfare
Citizenship
Civil Rights
Client Rights
Commitment (Psychiatric)
Conflict Resolution
Consumer Protection

Court Referrals
Crime Prevention
Criminology
Divorce
Drug Legalization
Forensic Evaluation
Forensic Psychiatry
Forensic Psychology
Foster Care
Guardianship
Immigration
Interracial Adoption
Involuntary Treatment
Joint Custody
Labor Management Relations
Labor Union Members
Labor Unions
Legal Processes
Marihuana Legalization
Marital Separation
Mediation
Organizational Merger
Outpatient Commitment
Professional Licensing
Protective Services
Psychiatric Evaluation
School Integration
Social Integration
Strikes

NEUROPSYCHOLOGY & NEUROLOGY CLUSTER

- Assessment & Diagnosis
- Electrophysiology
- Neuroanatomy
- Neurological Disorders
- Neurological Intervention
- Neurosciences
- Neurotransmitters & Neuroregulators

Assessment & Diagnosis

Bender Gestalt Test
Echoencephalography
Electroencephalography
Halstead Reitan Neuropsychological Battery
Luria Nebraska Neuropsychological Battery
Magnetic Resonance Imaging
Magnetoencephalography
Memory for Designs Test
Mini Mental State Examination
Neuropsychological Assessment
Pneumoencephalography
Rheoencephalography

Consult Relationship Section for more information

Assessment & Diagnosis — (cont'd)

Wechsler Memory Scale
Wisconsin Card Sorting Test

Electrophysiology

Alpha Rhythm
Auditory Evoked Potentials
Basal Skin Resistance
Contingent Negative Variation
Cortical Evoked Potentials
Delta Rhythm
Electrical Activity
Electrical Brain Stimulation
Electroencephalography
Electrophysiology
Evoked Potentials
Galvanic Skin Response
Kindling
Magnetoencephalography
Olfactory Evoked Potentials
Postactivation Potentials
Skin Electrical Properties
Skin Potential
Skin Resistance
Somatosensory Evoked Potentials
Theta Rhythm
Visual Evoked Potentials

Neuroanatomy

Abducens Nerve
Acoustic Nerve
Adrenergic Nerves
Afferent Pathways
Amygdaloid Body
Auditory Cortex
Auditory Neurons
Autonomic Ganglia
Autonomic Nervous System
Axons
Baroreceptors
Basal Ganglia
Blood Brain Barrier
Brain
Brain Size
Brain Stem
Brain Weight
Caudate Nucleus
Central Nervous System
Cerebellum
Cerebral Blood Flow
Cerebral Cortex
Cerebral Dominance
Cerebral Ventricles
Cerebrospinal Fluid
Chemoreceptors
Cholinergic Nerves

Cones (Eye)
Corpus Callosum
Cranial Spinal Cord
Cutaneous Receptive Fields
Cutaneous Sense
Dendrites
Diencephalon
Dorsal Horns
Dorsal Roots
Efferent Pathways
Extrapyramidal Tracts
Facial Nerve
Forebrain
Fornix
Fovea
Frontal Lobe
Ganglia
Ganglion Cells (Retina)
Geniculate Bodies (Thalamus)
Globus Pallidus
Gyrus Cinguli
Hindbrain
Hippocampus
Hypothalamo Hypophyseal System
Hypothalamo Pituitary Adrenal System
Hypothalamus
Inferior Colliculus
Interhemispheric Interaction
Lateral Dominance
Left Brain
Lemniscal System
Limbic System
Locus Ceruleus
Lumbar Spinal Cord
Mechanoreceptors
Medial Forebrain Bundle
Medulla Oblongata
Meninges
Mesencephalon
Motor Cortex
Motor Neurons
Myelin Sheath
Nerve Endings
Nerve Growth Factor
Nerve Tissues
Nervous System
Neural Analyzers
Neural Development
Neural Pathways
Neural Plasticity
Neural Receptors
Neurons
Nociceptors
Nucleus Basalis Magnocellularis
Occipital Lobe
Ocular Dominance
Olfactory Bulb
Olfactory Nerve
Optic Chiasm

Optic Lobe
Optic Nerve
Optic Tract
Parasympathetic Nervous System
Parietal Lobe
Periaqueductal Gray
Peripheral Nervous System
Photoreceptors
Pons
Preoptic Area
Proprioceptors
Purkinje Cells
Putamen
Pyramidal Tracts
Raphe Nuclei
Receptive Fields
Receptor Binding
Reticular Formation
Retina
Right Brain
Rods (Eye)
Sense Organs
Sensory Neurons
Septal Nuclei
Somatosensory Cortex
Spinal Column
Spinal Cord
Spinal Ganglia
Spinothalamic Tracts
Substantia Nigra
Sympathetic Nervous System
Tegmentum
Telencephalon
Thalamic Nuclei
Thalamus
Trigeminal Nerve
Vagus Nerve
Ventral Roots
Visual Cortex

Neurological Disorders

Acalculia
Agnosia
Agraphia
AIDS Dementia Complex
Alcoholic Hallucinosis
Alcoholic Psychosis
Alexia
Alzheimers Disease
Anencephaly
Anosognosia
Anoxia
Aphasia
Apraxia
Ataxia
Athetosis
Audiogenic Seizures
Autonomic Nervous System Disorders

Consult Relationship Section for more information

Neurological Disorders — (cont'd)

Back Pain
Bacterial Meningitis
Bradykinesia
Brain Concussion
Brain Damage
Brain Disorders
Brain Neoplasms
Catalepsy
Cataplexy
Central Nervous System Disorders
Cerebral Arteriosclerosis
Cerebral Atrophy
Cerebral Hemorrhage
Cerebral Ischemia
Cerebral Palsy
Cerebrovascular Accidents
Cerebrovascular Disorders
Chorea
Chronic Pain
Coma
Convulsions
Creutzfeldt Jakob Syndrome
Delirium Tremens
Dementia
Dementia with Lewy Bodies
Dysarthria
Dyskinesia
Dyslexia
Dysphasia
Dysphonia
Encephalitis
Encephalomyelitis
Encephalopathies
Epilepsy
Epileptic Seizures
Extrapyramidal Symptoms
General Paresis
Gilles de la Tourette Disorder
Global Amnesia
Grand Mal Epilepsy
Head Injuries
Headache
Hemianopia
Hemiplegia
Huntingtons Disease
Hydrocephaly
Hyperkinesis
Korsakoffs Psychosis
Memory Disorders
Meningitis
Microcephaly
Migraine Headache
Minimal Brain Disorders
Movement Disorders
Multi Infarct Dementia
Multiple Sclerosis
Muscle Contraction Headache

Muscular Dystrophy
Myasthenia Gravis
Myelitis
Myoclonia
Myofascial Pain
Narcolepsy
Nervous System Disorders
Nervous System Neoplasms
Neuralgia
Neuroleptic Malignant Syndrome
Neuromuscular Disorders
Neuropathology
Neurosyphilis
Organic Brain Syndromes
Pain
Paralysis
Paraplegia
Parkinsons Disease
Peripheral Nerve Disorders
Petit Mal Epilepsy
Picks Disease
Poliomyelitis
Presenile Dementia
Progressive Supranuclear Palsy
Prosopagnosia
Quadriplegia
Sclerosis (Nervous System)
Senile Dementia
Senile Psychosis
Spasms
Spinal Cord Injuries
Tardive Dyskinesia
Tics
Torticollis
Toxic Encephalopathies
Traumatic Brain Injury
Tremor
Trigeminal Neuralgia
Vascular Dementia
Wernickes Syndrome

Neurological Intervention

Afferent Stimulation
Brain Lesions
Brain Self Stimulation
Brain Stimulation
Chemical Brain Stimulation
Commissurotomy
Decerebration
Decortication (Brain)
Electrical Brain Stimulation
Hemispherectomy
Hypothalamus Lesions
Kindling
Neural Lesions
Neural Transplantation
Neurosurgery
Psychosurgery

Pyramidotomy
Stereotaxic Techniques
Sympathectomy
Thalamotomy
Tractotomy
Vagotomy

Neurosciences

Neural Networks
Neuroanatomy
Neurobiology
Neurochemistry
Neuroendocrinology
Neurolinguistics
Neurology
Neuropathology
Neurophysiology
Neuropsychiatry
Neuropsychology
Neurosciences
Neurosurgery
Psychoneuroimmunology
Psychopharmacology
Psychosurgery

Neurotransmitters & Neuroregulators

Acetylcholine
Acetylcholinesterase
Adenosine
Alanines
Amino Acids
Angiotensin
Aspartic Acid
Bombesin
Catecholamines
Cholecystokinin
Choline
Cholinesterase
Dihydroxyphenylacetic Acid
Dihydroxytryptamine
Dopamine
Dopamine Metabolites
Dynorphins
Endogenous Opiates
Endorphins
Enkephalins
Epinephrine
Gamma Aminobutyric Acid
Glutamic Acid
Glycine
Histamine
Homovanillic Acid
Hydroxydopamine (6-)
Hydroxyindoleacetic Acid (5-)
Ibotenic Acid
Kainic Acid
Melanocyte Stimulating Hormone

Consult Relationship Section for more information

391

Neurotransmitters & Neuroregulators — (cont'd)

Methoxyhydroxyphenylglycol (3,4)
Monoamine Oxidases
Neurokinins
Neurotensin
Neurotoxins
Neurotransmitters
Norepinephrine
Norepinephrine Metabolites
Oxytocin
Peptides
Phenethylamines
Serotonin
Serotonin Metabolites
Somatostatin
Substance P
Taurine
Tryptamine
Tyramine

OCCUPATIONAL & EMPLOYMENT CLUSTER

- Career Areas
- Employee, Occupational & Job Characteristics
- Occupational Groups
- Organizations & Organizational Behavior
- Personnel Management & Professional Personnel Issues

Career Areas

Advertising
Air Traffic Control
Behavioral Sciences
Business
Business Management
Child Care
Child Day Care
Community Psychology
Computer Programming
Consultation Liaison Psychiatry
Counseling
Cross Cultural Psychology
Data Processing
Education
Educational Administration
Educational Psychology
Entrepreneurship
Experimental Psychology
Family Therapy
Forensic Psychiatry
Forensic Psychology
Geriatric Psychiatry
Gynecology
Health Care Administration

Health Promotion
Human Factors Engineering
Hypnotherapy
Industrial Psychology
Job Corps
Law Enforcement
Marketing
Marriage Counseling
News Media
Nontraditional Careers
Nursing
Obstetrics
Occupational Therapy
Optometry
Paramedical Sciences
Pathology
Peace Corps
Pediatrics
Physical Therapy
Politics
Product Design
Psychiatry
Psychology
Psychotherapy
Public Relations
Rehabilitation
Rehabilitation Counseling
Retailing
School Psychology
Sciences
Self Employment
Social Casework
Social Psychology
Speech Therapy
Sports
Surgery
Teaching
Veterinary Medicine
Vocational Rehabilitation
Zoology

Employee, Occupational & Job Characteristics

Bonuses
Career Change
Clerical Secretarial Skills
Disabled Personnel
Division of Labor
Dual Careers
Employability
Employee Absenteeism
Employee Attitudes
Employee Benefits
Employee Characteristics
Employee Efficiency
Employee Health Insurance
Employee Interaction
Employee Leave Benefits

Employee Motivation
Employee Pension Plans
Employee Productivity
Employee Skills
Employee Turnover
Employment History
Employment Status
Family Work Relationship
Health Personnel Attitudes
Impaired Professionals
Income Level
Industrial Accidents
Job Applicant Attitudes
Job Characteristics
Job Enrichment
Job Experience Level
Job Involvement
Job Knowledge
Job Performance
Job Satisfaction
Job Search
Job Security
Labor Union Members
Leadership Qualities
Mentor
Noise Levels (Work Areas)
Occupational Adjustment
Occupational Aspirations
Occupational Attitudes
Occupational Choice
Occupational Exposure
Occupational Interests
Occupational Mobility
Occupational Neurosis
Occupational Preference
Occupational Safety
Occupational Status
Occupational Stress
Occupational Success
Occupational Tenure
Organizational Characteristics
Organizational Climate
Organizational Commitment
Private Practice
Professional Competence
Professional Identity
Professional Specialization
Quality of Work Life
Reemployment
Retirement
Salaries
School to Work Transition
Supervisor Employee Interaction
Typing
Unemployment
Vocational Maturity
Work (Attitudes Toward)
Work Adjustment Training
Work Load

Consult Relationship Section for more information

Employee, Occupational & Job Characteristics — (cont'd)

Work Related Illnesses
Work Rest Cycles
Work Scheduling
Work Week Length
Workday Shifts
Working Conditions
Working Space
Working Women

Occupational Groups

Accountants
Aerospace Personnel
Agricultural Extension Workers
Agricultural Workers
Air Force Personnel
Aircraft Pilots
Anthropologists
Apprenticeship
Architects
Army Personnel
Artists
Astronauts
Athletes
Attendants (Institutions)
Attorneys
Blue Collar Workers
Business and Industrial Personnel
Chaplains
Child Care Workers
Clergy
Clerical Personnel
Clinical Psychologists
Clinicians
Coaches
Coast Guard Personnel
College Teachers
Commissioned Officers
Cooperating Teachers
Counseling Psychologists
Counselor Trainees
Counselors
Dentists
Disabled Personnel
Domestic Service Personnel
Draftees
Educational Personnel
Educational Psychologists
Elementary School Teachers
Engineers
Enlisted Military Personnel
Evangelists
Experimental Psychologists
Family Physicians
Fire Fighters
Foreign Workers
General Practitioners

Government Personnel
Gynecologists
Health Personnel
High School Teachers
Home Care Personnel
Hypnotherapists
Hypnotists
Industrial Foremen
Industrial Psychologists
Information Specialists
Internists
Interviewers
Job Applicants
Journalists
Judges
Junior High School Teachers
Labor Union Members
Law Enforcement Personnel
Lay Religious Personnel
Legal Personnel
Librarians
Management Personnel
Marine Personnel
Mathematicians
Medical Personnel
Mental Health Personnel
Mentor
Middle Level Managers
Migrant Farm Workers
Military Medical Personnel
Military Personnel
Military Psychologists
Ministers (Religion)
Missionaries
Musicians
National Guardsmen
Navy Personnel
Neurologists
Noncommissioned Officers
Nonprofessional Personnel
Nuns
Nurses
Obstetricians
Occupational Therapists
Occupations
Optometrists
Paramedical Personnel
Paraprofessional Personnel
Parole Officers
Pathologists
Pediatricians
Personnel
Pharmacists
Physical Therapists
Physicians
Physicists
Police Personnel
Politicians
Preschool Teachers

Preservice Teachers
Priests
Prison Personnel
Probation Officers
Professional Personnel
Psychiatric Aides
Psychiatric Hospital Staff
Psychiatric Nurses
Psychiatric Social Workers
Psychiatrists
Psychoanalysts
Psychologists
Psychotherapists
Public Health Service Nurses
Rabbis
Rehabilitation Counselors
Religious Personnel
Resource Teachers
Sales Personnel
School Administrators
School Counselors
School Nurses
School Principals
School Psychologists
School Superintendents
Scientists
Secretarial Personnel
Seminarians
Service Personnel
Skilled Industrial Workers
Social Psychologists
Social Workers
Sociologists
Special Education Teachers
Speech Therapists
Student Teachers
Surgeons
Teacher Aides
Teachers
Technical Personnel
Technical Service Personnel
Therapist Trainees
Therapists
Top Level Managers
Unskilled Industrial Workers
Vocational Counselors
Vocational Education Teachers
Volunteer Civilian Personnel
Volunteer Military Personnel
Volunteer Personnel
Volunteers in Service to America
White Collar Workers
Working Women
Writers

Organizations & Organizational Behavior

Business Organizations

Consult Relationship Section for more information

393

Organizations & Organizational Behavior — (cont'd)

Decentralization
Division of Labor
Entrepreneurship
Foreign Organizations
Government Agencies
Government Policy Making
Health Care Policy
Health Maintenance Organizations
International Organizations
Labor Unions
Nonprofit Organizations
Organizational Behavior
Organizational Change
Organizational Characteristics
Organizational Climate
Organizational Commitment
Organizational Crises
Organizational Development
Organizational Effectiveness
Organizational Merger
Organizational Objectives
Organizational Structure
Organizations
Policy Making
Professional Organizations
Religious Organizations
Self Managing Work Teams
Teams
Work Teams

Personnel Management & Professional Personnel Issues

Affirmative Action
Age Discrimination
Assessment Centers
Bonuses
Budgets
Career Development
Career Education
Conflict Resolution
Disability Discrimination
Disability Evaluation
Disability Management
Employee Assistance Programs
Employee Attitudes
Employee Benefits
Employee Health Insurance
Employee Leave Benefits
Employee Pension Plans
Employee Turnover
Employer Attitudes
Employment Discrimination
Employment Tests
Entrepreneurship
Inservice Training
Job Analysis

Job Applicant Interviews
Job Applicant Screening
Job Enrichment
Job Search
Labor Management Relations
Leadership
Leadership Qualities
Leadership Style
Management
Management Decision Making
Management Methods
Management Personnel
Management Planning
Management Training
Mediation
Medical Personnel Supply
Mental Health Inservice Training
Mental Health Personnel Supply
Middle Level Managers
Military Recruitment
Military Training
Negotiation
Occupational Guidance
Occupational Success Prediction
On the Job Training
Participative Management
Personnel Evaluation
Personnel Management
Personnel Placement
Personnel Promotion
Personnel Recruitment
Personnel Selection
Personnel Supply
Personnel Termination
Personnel Training
Policy Making
Private Practice
Professional Certification
Professional Consultation
Professional Development
Professional Ethics
Professional Examinations
Professional Fees
Professional Identity
Professional Liability
Professional Licensing
Professional Referral
Professional Specialization
Professional Standards
Professional Supervision
Quality Control
Race and Ethnic Discrimination
Reemployment
Retirement
Salaries
Sex Discrimination
Sexual Harassment
Social Security
Stress Management

Strikes
Supervisor Employee Interaction
Supported Employment
Teacher Recruitment
Top Level Managers
Unemployment
Vocational Evaluation
Workmens Compensation Insurance

STATISTICAL CLUSTER

- Design, Analysis & Interpretation
- Statistical Reliability & Validity
- Statistical Theory & Experimentation

Design, Analysis & Interpretation

Algorithms
Analysis of Covariance
Analysis of Variance
Between Groups Design
Causal Analysis
Central Tendency Measures
Chi Square Test
Cluster Analysis
Cochran Q Test
Cohort Analysis
Content Analysis
Content Analysis (Test)
Equimax Rotation
Error Analysis
Error of Measurement
Evaluation Criteria
Experimental Design
F Test
Factor Analysis
Factor Structure
Fuzzy Set Theory
Goodness of Fit
Heuristic Modeling
Interaction Analysis (Statistics)
Interaction Variance
Item Analysis (Statistical)
Item Analysis (Test)
Item Response Theory
Kolmogorov Smirnov Test
Least Squares
Linear Regression
Mann Whitney U Test
Markov Chains
Mathematical Modeling
Maximum Likelihood
Mean
Median
Meta Analysis
Multidimensional Scaling
Multiple Regression
Multivariate Analysis

Consult Relationship Section for more information

Design, Analysis & Interpretation — (cont'd)

Nonlinear Regression
Nonparametric Statistical Tests
Oblique Rotation
Orthogonal Rotation
Parametric Statistical Tests
Path Analysis
Phi Coefficient
Point Biserial Correlation
Probability
Q Sort Testing Technique
Quartimax Rotation
Rank Difference Correlation
Rank Order Correlation
Repeated Measures
Scaling (Testing)
Score Equating
Scoring (Testing)
Sign Test
Spearman Brown Test
Standard Deviation
Standard Scores
Statistical Analysis
Statistical Correlation
Statistical Data
Statistical Estimation
Statistical Measurement
Statistical Norms
Statistical Probability
Statistical Regression
Statistical Reliability
Statistical Rotation
Statistical Significance
Statistical Tables
Statistical Tests
Statistical Validity
Statistical Variables
Statistical Weighting
Stochastic Modeling
Structural Equation Modeling
T Test
Tetrachoric Correlation
Time Series
Variability Measurement
Variance Homogeneity
Varimax Rotation
Wilcoxon Sign Rank Test
Zulliger Z Test

Statistical Reliability & Validity

Content Analysis
Content Analysis (Test)
Error Analysis
Error of Measurement
Interrater Reliability
Item Analysis (Statistical)

Item Content (Test)
Statistical Power
Statistical Reliability
Statistical Validity
Test Reliability
Test Validity

Statistical Theory & Experimentation

Biased Sampling
Binomial Distribution
Chaos Theory
Confidence Limits (Statistics)
Conjoint Measurement
Consistency (Measurement)
Cutting Scores
Data Collection
Data Processing
Dependent Variables
Double Bind Interaction
Effect Size (Statistical)
Empirical Methods
Experiment Controls
Experimental Design
Experimental Replication
Experimental Subjects
Experimentation
Experimenter Bias
Followup Studies
Frequency Distribution
Fuzzy Set Theory
Halo Effect
Independent Variables
Knowledge of Results
Longitudinal Studies
Maximum Likelihood
Methodology
Normal Distribution
Null Hypothesis Testing
Population (Statistics)
Prediction Errors
Prospective Studies
Random Sampling
Research Setting
Retrospective Studies
Sample Size
Sampling (Experimental)
Skewed Distribution
Statistical Data
Statistical Sample Parameters
Statistical Samples
Statistical Significance
Statistical Tables
Statistical Variables
Statistics
Type I Errors
Type II Errors

TESTS & TESTING CLUSTER

- Academic Achievement & Aptitude Measures
- Attitude & Interest Measures
- Developmental Measures
- Intelligence Measures
- Neuropsychological Measures
- Nonprojective Personality Measures
- Perceptual Measures
- Projective Personality Measures
- Testing
- Testing Methods

Academic Achievement & Aptitude Measures

Achievement Measures
Aptitude Measures
Army General Classification Test
College Entrance Examination Board
Scholastic Aptitude Test
Comprehension Tests
Curriculum Based Assessment
Differential Aptitude Tests
Educational Measurement
Entrance Examinations
Gates MacGinitie Reading Tests
General Aptitude Test Battery
Graduate Record Examination
Iowa Tests of Basic Skills
Metropolitan Readiness Tests
Minimum Competency Tests
Modern Language Aptitude Test
Professional Examinations
Reading Measures
Retention Measures
Stanford Achievement Test
Verbal Tests
Wide Range Achievement Test
Woodcock Johnson Psychoeducational Battery

Attitude & Interest Measures

Attitude Measurement
Attitude Measures
Consumer Surveys
Interest Inventories
Kuder Occupational Interest Survey
Kuder Preference Record
Least Preferred Coworker Scale
Occupational Interest Measures
Parent Attitude Research Instrument
Preference Measures
Strong Vocational Interest Blank
Wilson Patterson Conservatism Scale

Consult Relationship Section for more information

Developmental Measures

Bayley Scales of Infant Development
Cattell Infant Intelligence Scale
Developmental Measures

Intelligence Measures

Benton Revised Visual Retention Test
California Test of Mental Maturity
Cattell Infant Intelligence Scale
Cognitive Assessment
Columbia Mental Maturity Scale
Creativity Measurement
Culture Fair Intelligence Test
Frostig Developmental Test of Visual Perception
Goodenough Harris Draw A Person Test
Hidden Figures Test
Illinois Test of Psycholinguistic Abilities
Infant Intelligence Scale
Intelligence Measures
Kaufman Assessment Battery for Children
Kohs Block Design Test
Lorge Thorndike Intelligence Test
Lowenfeld Mosaic Test
Miller Analogies Test
Peabody Picture Vocabulary Test
Porteus Maze Test
Raven Coloured Progressive Matrices
Raven Progressive Matrices
Remote Associates Test
Slosson Intelligence Test
Stanford Binet Intelligence Scale
Verbal Tests
Wechsler Adult Intelligence Scale
Wechsler Bellevue Intelligence Scale
Wechsler Intelligence Scale for Children
Wechsler Memory Scale
Wechsler Preschool Primary Scale

Neuropsychological Measures

Bender Gestalt Test
Benton Revised Visual Retention Test
Body Sway Testing
Halstead Reitan Neuropsychological Battery
Luria Nebraska Neuropsychological Battery
Memory for Designs Test
Mini Mental State Examination
Neuropsychological Assessment
Wechsler Memory Scale
Wisconsin Card Sorting Test

Nonprojective Personality Measures

Bannister Repertory Grid

Barrett Lennard Relationship Inventory
Barron Welsh Art Scale
Beck Depression Inventory
Bem Sex Role Inventory
California F Scale
California Psychological Inventory
California Test of Personality
Child Behavior Checklist
Childrens Manifest Anxiety Scale
Childrens Personality Questionnaire
Edwards Personal Preference Schedule
Edwards Personality Inventory
Edwards Social Desirability Scale
Embedded Figures Testing
Eysenck Personality Inventory
Fear Survey Schedule
Fundamental Interpersonal Relation Orientation Behavior Ques
General Health Questionnaire
Goldstein Scheerer Object Sort Test
Gough Adjective Check List
Guilford Zimmerman Temperament Survey
High School Personality Questionnaire
Kirton Adaption Innovation Inventory
Learys Interpersonal Check List
Marlowe Crowne Social Desirability Scale
Maudsley Personality Inventory
Memory for Designs Test
Millon Clinical Multiaxial Inventory
Minnesota Multiphasic Personality Inventory
Mooney Problem Check List
Myers Briggs Type Indicator
NEO Personality Inventory
Nonprojective Personality Measures
Omnibus Personality Inventory
Personal Orientation Inventory
Personality Measures
Psychological Screening Inventory
Repression Sensitization Scale
Rod and Frame Test
Rokeach Dogmatism Scale
Rotter Internal External Locus of Control Scale
Sensation Seeking Scale
Sixteen Personality Factors Questionnaire
State Trait Anxiety Inventory
Taylor Manifest Anxiety Scale
Tennessee Self Concept Scale
Vineland Social Maturity Scale
Welsh Figure Preference Test
Zungs Self Rating Depression Scale

Perceptual Measures

Audiometry

Bone Conduction Audiometry
Pain Measurement
Perceptual Measures
Psychophysical Measurement
Purdue Perceptual Motor Survey
Rod and Frame Test
Sensorimotor Measures
Speech and Hearing Measures
Stroop Color Word Test
Wepman Auditory Discrimination Test

Projective Personality Measures

Bender Gestalt Test
Childrens Apperception Test
Franck Drawing Completion Test
Holtzman Inkblot Technique
Human Figures Drawing
Incomplete Man Test
Personality Measures
Projective Personality Measures
Projective Techniques
Projective Testing Technique
Rorschach Test
Rosenzweig Picture Frustration Study
Rotter Incomplete Sentences Blank
Sentence Completion Tests
Szondi Test
Thematic Apperception Test
Zulliger Z Test

Testing

Consistency (Measurement)
Content Analysis (Test)
Cultural Test Bias
Cutting Scores
Difficulty Level (Test)
Employment Tests
Evaluation Criteria
Factor Analysis
Factor Structure
Foreign Language Translation
Interview Schedules
Inventories
Item Analysis (Test)
Item Content (Test)
Item Response Theory
Measurement
Performance Tests
Piagetian Tasks
Profiles (Measurement)
Psychometrics
Rating Scales
Score Equating
Scoring (Testing)
Screening Tests
Selection Tests
Semantic Differential
Sociometric Tests

Consult Relationship Section for more information

Testing — (cont'd)

Sociometry
Standard Scores
Standardized Tests
Statistical Validity
Statistical Weighting
Subtests
Test Administration
Test Anxiety
Test Bias
Test Construction
Test Forms
Test Interpretation
Test Items
Test Norms
Test Reliability
Test Scores
Test Standardization
Test Taking
Testing
Testwiseness

Testing Methods

Adaptive Testing
Behavioral Assessment
Biographical Inventories
Body Sway Testing
Cloze Testing
Cognitive Assessment
Computer Assisted Testing
Consumer Surveys
Criterion Referenced Tests
Digit Span Testing
Essay Testing
Forced Choice (Testing Method)
Group Testing
Individual Testing
Interview Schedules
Inventories
Likert Scales
Mail Surveys
Matching to Sample
Multidimensional Scaling
Multiple Choice (Testing Method)
Neuropsychological Assessment
Performance Tests
Posttesting
Pretesting
Psychological Assessment
Q Sort Testing Technique
Questionnaires
Rating Scales
Scaling (Testing)
Screening
Screening Tests
Standardized Tests
Surveys
Symptom Checklists

Telephone Surveys
Testing Methods
Verbal Tests

TREATMENT CLUSTER

- Alternative Therapies
- Behavior Modification & Therapy
- Counseling
- Hospitalization & Institutionalization
- Medical & Physical Treatment
- Psychotherapy
- Rehabilitation
- Treatment (General)
- Treatment Facilities

Alternative Therapies

Acupuncture
Aerobic Exercise
Alternative Medicine
Animal Assisted Therapy
Art Therapy
Autohypnosis
Biofeedback Training
Communication Skills Training
Consciousness Raising Groups
Creative Arts Therapy
Dance Therapy
Dietary Supplements
Encounter Group Therapy
Eye Movement Desensitization Therapy
Faith Healing
Folk Medicine
Guided Imagery
Holistic Health
Human Relations Training
Hypnosis
Hypnotherapy
Imagery
Massage
Medicinal Herbs and Plants
Meditation
Milieu Therapy
Morita Therapy
Motivation Training
Movement Therapy
Music Therapy
Narcoanalysis
Pain Management
Phototherapy
Poetry Therapy
Recreation Therapy
Relaxation Therapy
Role Playing
Self Medication
Sensitivity Training
Sex Therapy

Sleep Treatment
Social Skills Training
Sociotherapy
Stress Management
Support Groups
Therapeutic Camps
Therapeutic Social Clubs
Wilderness Experience

Behavior Modification & Therapy

Anger Control
Anxiety Management
Assertiveness Training
Aversion Therapy
Behavior Contracting
Behavior Modification
Behavior Therapy
Biofeedback Training
Cognitive Restructuring
Cognitive Techniques
Cognitive Therapy
Conditioning
Contingency Management
Counterconditioning
Covert Sensitization
Differential Reinforcement
Exposure Therapy
Fading (Conditioning)
Functional Analysis
Implosive Therapy
Omission Training
Operant Conditioning
Overcorrection
Paradoxical Techniques
Progressive Relaxation Therapy
Reciprocal Inhibition Therapy
Relaxation Therapy
Response Cost
Self Help Techniques
Self Management
Self Monitoring
Stress Management
Systematic Desensitization Therapy
Time Out
Token Economy Programs

Counseling

AIDS Prevention
Counseling
Counseling Psychology
Couples Therapy
Crisis Intervention
Crisis Intervention Services
Drug Abuse Prevention
Family Planning
Feminist Therapy
Genetic Counseling
Group Counseling

Consult Relationship Section for more information

Counseling — (cont'd)

Health Promotion
Hot Line Services
Marriage Counseling
Microcounseling
Pastoral Counseling
Peer Counseling
Premarital Counseling
Psychotherapeutic Counseling
Rehabilitation Counseling
Social Casework
Suicide Prevention
Suicide Prevention Centers

Hospitalization & Institutionalization

Aftercare
Client Transfer
Commitment (Psychiatric)
Deinstitutionalization
Discharge Planning
Emergency Services
Facility Admission
Facility Discharge
Hospice
Hospital Admission
Hospital Discharge
Hospital Environment
Hospital Programs
Hospitalization
Hospitalized Patients
Hospitals
Institution Visitation
Institutional Release
Institutionalization
Intensive Care
Outpatient Commitment
Outpatient Treatment
Outpatients
Partial Hospitalization
Patient Seclusion
Psychiatric Hospital Admission
Psychiatric Hospital Discharge
Psychiatric Hospital Programs
Psychiatric Hospital Readmission
Psychiatric Hospitalization
Psychiatric Units
Sanatoriums
Therapeutic Community

Medical & Physical Treatment

Acupuncture
Adolescent Psychiatry
Adrenalectomy
Amputation
Artificial Pacemakers
Artificial Respiration

Biological Psychiatry
Biopsy
Blood Transfusion
Castration
Catheterization
Child Psychiatry
Circumcision
Cochlear Implants
Colostomy
Commissurotomy
Community Psychiatry
Dental Surgery
Dental Treatment
Dialysis
Drug Therapy
Electroconvulsive Shock Therapy
Electrosleep Treatment
Endocrine Gland Surgery
Family Medicine
Fertility Enhancement
Geriatric Psychiatry
Health Care Services
Health Maintenance Organizations
Heart Surgery
Hemispherectomy
Hemodialysis
Hormone Therapy
Hypophysectomy
Hysterectomy
Immunization
Induced Abortion
Insulin Shock Therapy
Intensive Care
Laser Irradiation
Male Castration
Massage
Mastectomy
Medical Therapeutic Devices
Medical Treatment (General)
Mobility Aids
Movement Therapy
Narcoanalysis
Neural Transplantation
Neurosurgery
Organ Transplantation
Orthopsychiatry
Ovariectomy
Pain Management
Phototherapy
Physical Therapy
Physical Treatment Methods
Pinealectomy
Plastic Surgery
Postsurgical Complications
Prenatal Care
Prescribing (Drugs)
Prescription Drugs
Preventive Medicine
Primary Health Care

Prostheses
Psychiatric Patients
Psychiatry
Psychosomatic Medicine
Psychosurgery
Public Health Services
Pyramidotomy
Radiation Therapy
Self Medication
Sex Change
Shock Therapy
Sleep Treatment
Stereotaxic Techniques
Surgery
Surgical Patients
Sympathectomy
Thalamotomy
Thyroidectomy
Tractotomy
Tubal Ligation
Vagotomy
Vasectomy
Vitamin Therapy

Psychotherapy

Adlerian Psychotherapy
Adolescent Psychotherapy
Age Regression (Hypnotic)
Analytical Psychotherapy
Autogenic Training
Bibliotherapy
Brief Psychotherapy
Centering
Child Psychotherapy
Client Centered Therapy
Cognitive Restructuring
Cognitive Techniques
Cognitive Therapy
Conjoint Therapy
Consultation Liaison Psychiatry
Cotherapy
Countertransference
Couples Therapy
Crisis Intervention
Dream Analysis
Eclectic Psychotherapy
Enactments
Encounter Group Therapy
Existential Therapy
Experiential Psychotherapy
Expressive Psychotherapy
Family Therapy
Feminist Therapy
Free Association
Geriatric Psychotherapy
Gestalt Therapy
Group Psychotherapy
Guided Imagery

Consult Relationship Section for more information

Psychotherapy — (cont'd)

Hypnotherapy
Individual Psychotherapy
Insight (Psychotherapeutic Process)
Insight Therapy
Interpersonal Psychotherapy
Logotherapy
Marathon Group Therapy
Marriage Counseling
Mirroring
Morita Therapy
Mutual Storytelling Technique
Negative Therapeutic Reaction
Paradoxical Techniques
Personal Therapy
Persuasion Therapy
Play Therapy
Primal Therapy
Psychoanalysis
Psychodrama
Psychotherapeutic Breakthrough
Psychotherapeutic Counseling
Psychotherapeutic Neutrality
Psychotherapeutic Outcomes
Psychotherapeutic Processes
Psychotherapeutic Resistance
Psychotherapeutic Techniques
Psychotherapeutic Transference
Psychotherapy
Rational Emotive Therapy
Reality Therapy
Relationship Therapy
Self Analysis
Supportive Psychotherapy
Therapeutic Alliance
Therapeutic Community
Therapist Selection
Transactional Analysis

Rehabilitation

Activities of Daily Living
Adaptive Behavior
Aftercare
Alcohol Rehabilitation
Alcoholics Anonymous
Augmentative Communication
Cochlear Implants
Cognitive Rehabilitation
Detoxification
Disability Management
Drug Rehabilitation
Habilitation
Halfway Houses
Independent Living Programs
Mainstreaming
Memory Training
Methadone Maintenance

Needle Exchange Programs
Neuropsychological Rehabilitation
Occupational Therapy
Physical Therapy
Prostheses
Psychosocial Rehabilitation
Rehabilitation
Rehabilitation Centers
Rehabilitation Counseling
Self Care Skills
Sheltered Workshops
Smoking Cessation
Speech Therapy
Support Groups
Therapeutic Community
Therapeutic Social Clubs
Twelve Step Programs
Vocational Evaluation
Vocational Rehabilitation
Wilderness Experience
Work Adjustment Training

Treatment (General)

Adolescent Psychiatry
Adult Day Care
Advance Directives
AIDS Prevention
Assisted Suicide
Biological Psychiatry
Biopsychosocial Approach
Caregiver Burden
Caregivers
Case Management
Child Psychiatry
Child Psychology
Childbirth Training
Client Education
Client Participation
Client Records
Client Rights
Client Transfer
Client Treatment Matching
Clinical Psychology
Community Psychiatry
Cross Cultural Treatment
Discharge Planning
Drug Abuse Prevention
Drug Education
Early Intervention
Elder Care
Euthanasia
Fee for Service
Geriatric Patients
Geriatric Psychiatry
Health Care Costs
Health Care Delivery
Health Care Policy
Health Care Psychology

Health Care Seeking Behavior
Health Care Services
Health Care Utilization
Health Education
Health Insurance
Health Promotion
Health Service Needs
Help Seeking Behavior
Holistic Health
Home Visiting Programs
Hospice
Informed Consent
Integrated Services
Interdisciplinary Treatment Approach
Involuntary Treatment
Life Sustaining Treatment
Long Term Care
Maintenance Therapy
Managed Care
Medicaid
Medical Patients
Medical Psychology
Medical Records
Medical Treatment (General)
Medicare
Multimodal Treatment Approach
Nonprescription Drugs
Optical Aids
Orthopsychiatry
Outreach Programs
Palliative Care
Patient Abuse
Patient History
Patient Selection
Patients
Physical Examination
Posttreatment Followup
Prescribing (Drugs)
Prescription Drugs
Primary Mental Health Prevention
Private Practice
Psychiatric Patients
Psychiatry
Psychoeducation
Quality of Care
Quality of Services
Relapse Prevention
Respite Care
Right to Treatment
Self Examination (Medical)
Self Medication
Self Referral
Sex Education
Side Effects (Treatment)
Social Psychiatry
Social Services
Surgical Patients
Therapeutic Alliance
Therapeutic Processes

Consult Relationship Section for more information

Treatment (General) — (cont'd)

Treatment
Treatment Compliance
Treatment Dropouts
Treatment Duration
Treatment Effectiveness Evaluation
Treatment Guidelines
Treatment Outcomes
Treatment Planning
Treatment Refusal
Treatment Termination
Treatment Withholding

Treatment Facilities

Adult Day Care
Child Guidance Clinics
Clinics
Community Facilities
Community Mental Health Centers
Community Mental Health Services
Day Care Centers
Facility Environment
Group Homes
Halfway Houses
Health Care Services
Health Maintenance Organizations
Home Care
Hospital Environment
Hospitals
Institutional Schools
Intensive Care
Maximum Security Facilities
Mental Health Programs
Mental Health Services
Nursing Homes
Orphanages
Psychiatric Clinics
Psychiatric Hospitals
Psychiatric Units
Public Health Services
Rehabilitation Centers
Residential Care Institutions
Sanatoriums
Shelters
Social Services
Suicide Prevention Centers
Therapeutic Camps
Therapeutic Community
Therapeutic Environment
Treatment Facilities
Walk In Clinics

Consult Relationship Section for more information

WITHDRAWAL